I0729529

HiROShiGE
&
Eisen

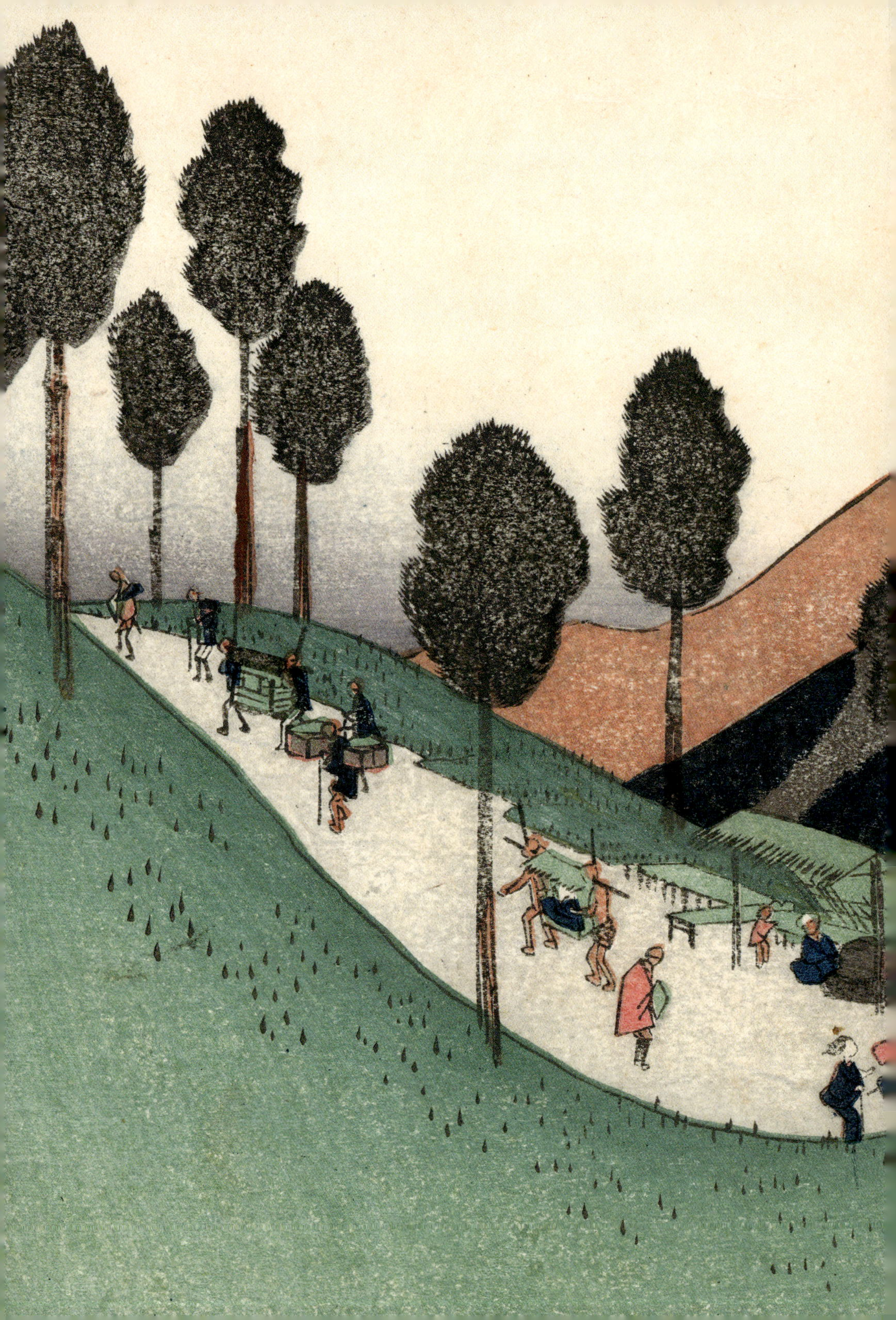

ANDREAS MARKS (ED.)
RHIANNON PAGET

HiROShiGe
& EiSEN

The Sixty-Nine Stations along the Kisokaidō
Die neunundsechzig Stationen des Kisokaidō
Les soixante-neuf stations de la route Kisokaidō

The series used for printing belongs to the
COLLECTION OF GEORGES LESKOWICZ

Directed and produced by
BENEDIKT TASCHEN

TASCHEN

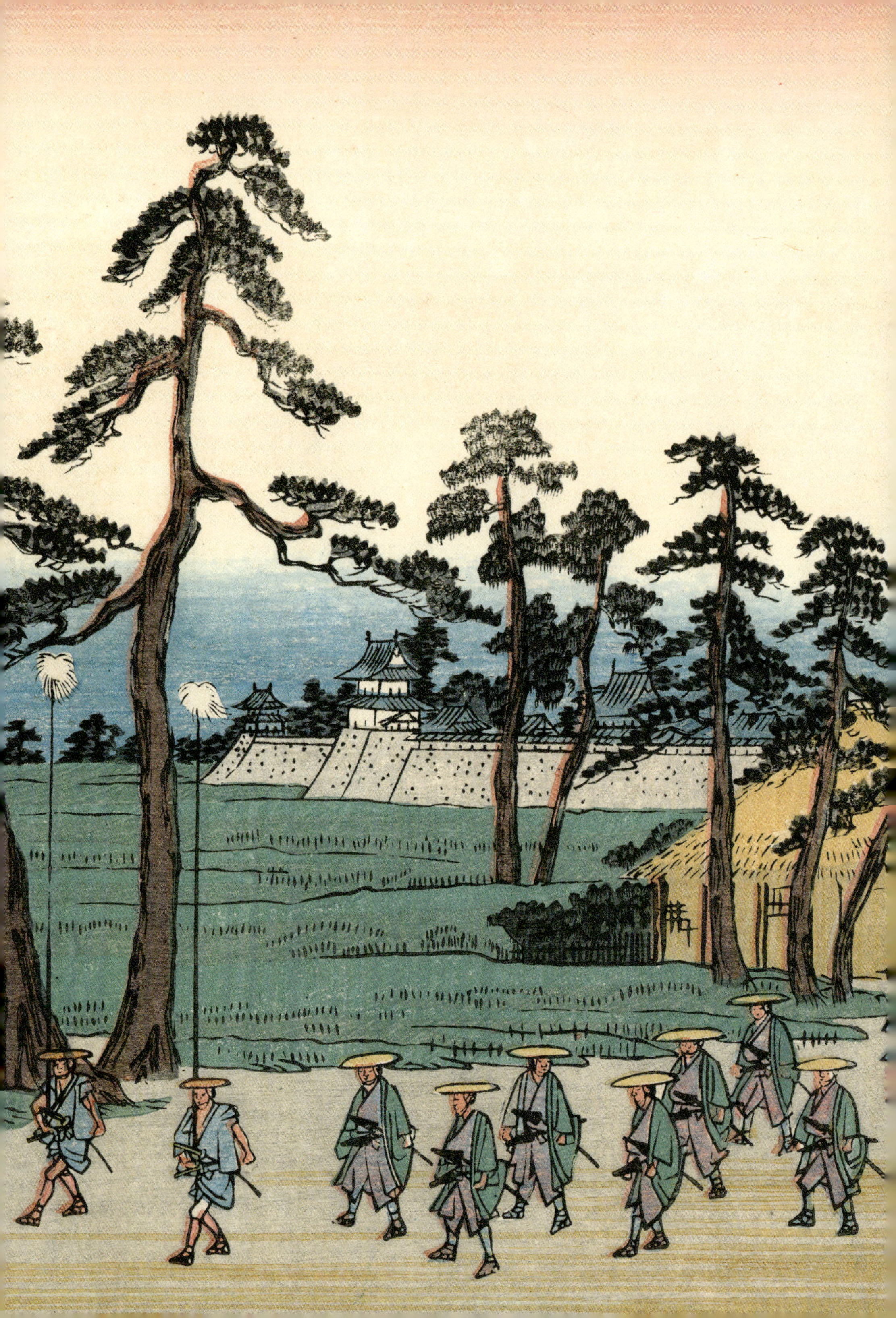

Contents

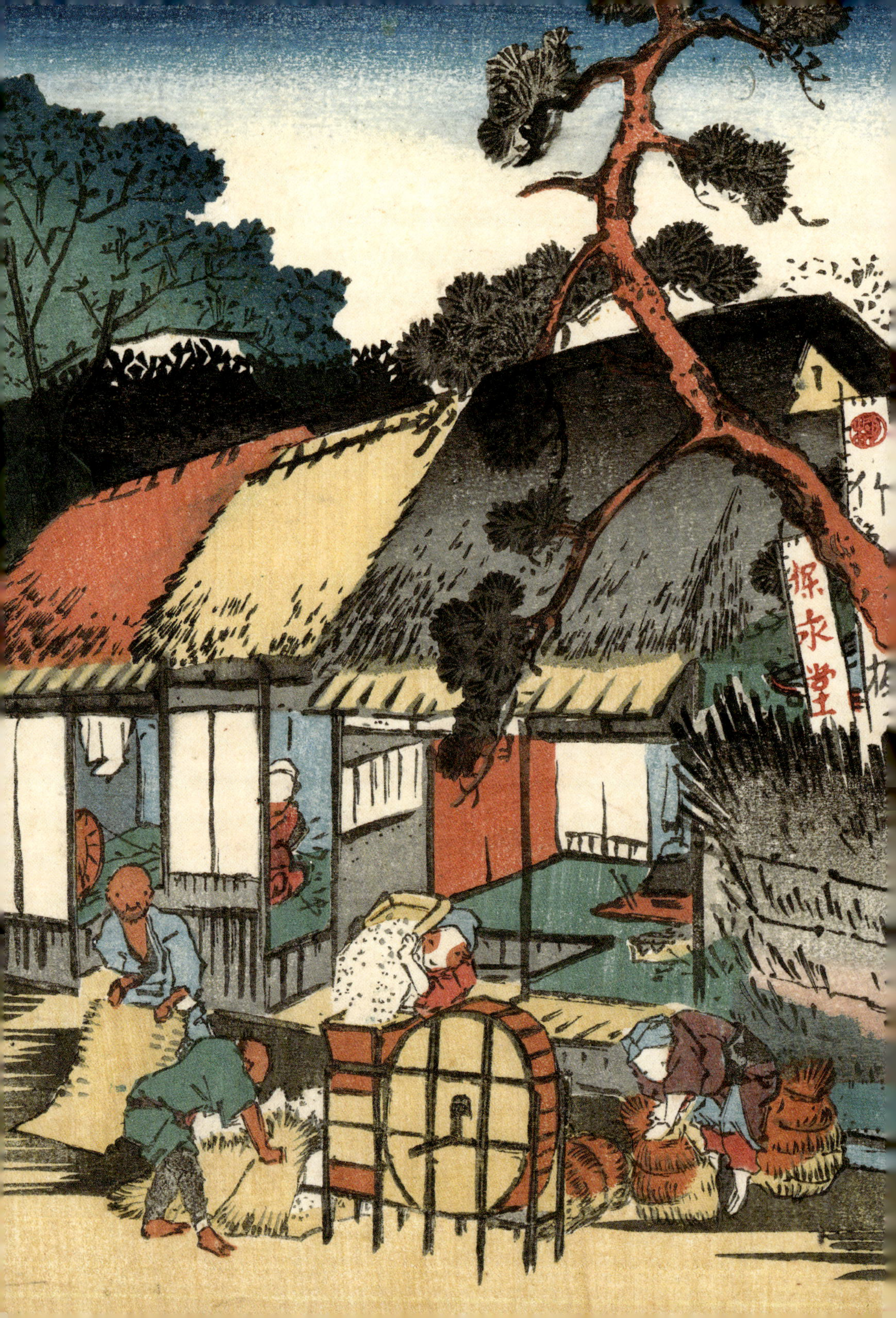
保永堂

Andreas Marks

From Edo to Kyoto

Embarking on a Journey of Adventure

Travel in Japan

When the shogun Tokugawa Ieyasu (1543–1616) united Japan in the early 1600s and began to establish a centralised government from the city of Edo, today's Tokyo, it was clear to him that he could only stay in power if he was able to maintain authority over the remote areas of his country. To control the many local feudal lords (*daimyō*), an alternating system of residence was put in place that forced them to maintain two households, one in their own domain and one in Edo. Their presence in the capital was demanded on a regular basis and if a lord was absent, his wife and family were required to live there instead, essentially as hostages. Inspired by the impressive system of roads that was maintained in China, Ieyasu ordered the enlargement and imposition of a network of highways, the basis for which had already been established hundreds of years earlier. Even though China was much larger than Japan, messages in China could be delivered to remote areas in an astoundingly short time by means of a well-organised relay system of couriers on horseback using pre-established routes.

To ensure Ieyasu's reach into the remote parts of his realm, a network of five main roads emanated from the Nihonbashi Bridge, the centre of Edo and the heart of Japan (pp. 49, 50–51). Checkpoints manned by armed guards were installed at intervals along these roads to ensure that no large, hostile force could approach Edo without detection, or equally that no lord's family could flee the capital undetected. Of these major roads, the Nakasendō, also called Kisokaidō, went from Edo's Nihonbashi Bridge inland through the mountains for almost 136 *ri*, around 534 kilometres (332 miles), to Kyoto's Sanjō Ōhashi Bridge (p. 13; see the map on pp. 96–97). Japan's most sacred mountain, Mount Fuji (p. 16), is only visible from the Kisokaidō road while it runs relatively close to Edo; however, travellers would have frequently glimpsed the active volcano Mount Asama, which erupted with devastating effect in 1783 with the result that many people avoided the Kisokaidō. The Kisokaidō passed through six provinces: Musashi, Kōzuke, Shinano, Mino, Ōmi and Yamashiro, equivalent to today's prefectures of Saitama, Gunma, Nagano, Gifu and Shiga. Hackberry trees (*enoki*) were planted in rows along sections of the road and a system of

69 post stations was established, with horses and porters to serve transportation needs as well as inns providing food and lodging for travellers.

In 1874 and again in 1875, the German geographer Johannes Justus Rein (1835–1918) travelled the Kisokaidō and came to the conclusion that "whoever would like to enjoy beautiful Japanese mountain views should choose the Nakasendō because there is hardly a road anywhere else in Japan that offers so many diverse scenic attractions" (pp. 19, 82).[1] Rein was evidently not alone in his favourable opinion of the Kisokaidō, as already by mid-1835 the road had become a motif in a series of woodblock prints designed by the popular artists Eisen (1790–1848) and Hiroshige (1797–1858). By early 1838, printing of the 71 designs – 24 by Eisen and 47 by Hiroshige – had finished and the series became known by the title *The Sixty-Nine Stations along the Kisokaidō (Kisokaidō rokujūkyū tsugi no uchi).*[2]

Another of these five main roads was the Tōkaidō or Eastern Sea Route, named after its passage along the coast; it too went as far as Kyoto, the ancient capital and seat of the emperor, and was 126 *ri* long, or about 495 kilometres (308 miles). Right after the Nihonbashi Bridge, the two roads Kisokaidō and Tōkaidō separated and did not meet again until Kusatsu, some 26 kilometres (16 miles) from Kyoto. The Tōkaidō was the shortest and quickest connection between these two major cities during the Edo period (1603–1868) but that was not the only reason for its popularity. For a substantial part of the journey, travellers were able to catch a glimpse of the imposing volcano Mount Fuji (p. 17). A branch of this road also led to the Ise Grand Shrine, a highly popular destination for pilgrims.

The Kisokaidō was considered a more difficult route than the Tōkaidō. As can be seen by the fact that 146 *daimyō* regularly travelled along the Tōkaidō compared with 30 along the Kisokaidō. Furthermore, there are very few travel accounts, especially by foreigners. There were nine mountain passes on the Kisokaidō, six at a height of about 1,000 metres.[3] Steep passes were especially difficult to cross in winter so the government had eight stretches of road paved to facilitate passage (pp. 24–25, 30, 31).[4] Because there was no easy access to the sea, there was a general lack of fresh fish, though other food choices varied greatly compared with those along the Tōkaidō. But there were fewer time-consuming river crossings on the Kisokaidō and transport rates as a result were one-third less expensive.[5] Travellers tended to use the Kisokaidō for one leg of their trip as that allowed them to enjoy different scenery and discover other experiences; taking into account that the journey itself was as important to a traveller as the destination, this contrasts with modern times, where the journey is, unfortunately, considered by many to be an unavoidable nuisance in the way of reaching the desired destination.

Four of the towns the Kisokaidō went through had castles: Takasaki (plate 14), Annaka (plate 16), Iwamurata (plate 23) and Kanō (plate 54). In 1843, with a population of 14,892, Ōtsu was the largest post-station town along the Kisokaidō (as well as on the Tōkaidō) while Unuma, with only 246 inhabitants,

<table>
<tr><td>

P. 2
Ashida (detail from plate 27)

P. 4
Kanō (detail from plate 54)

P. 6
Ageo (detail from plate 6)

</td><td>

Utagawa Kunisada, *Memorial Portrait of Utagawa Hiroshige / Gedächtnisbild von Utagawa Hiroshige / Portrait posthume d'Utagawa Hiroshige*, 1858.
Published by Sakanaya Eikichi; carved by Yokogawa Takejirō. Colour woodblock print, *ōban*.
Minneapolis Institute of Art, Gift of Louis W. Hill, Jr.,
P.75.51.631

</td></tr>
</table>

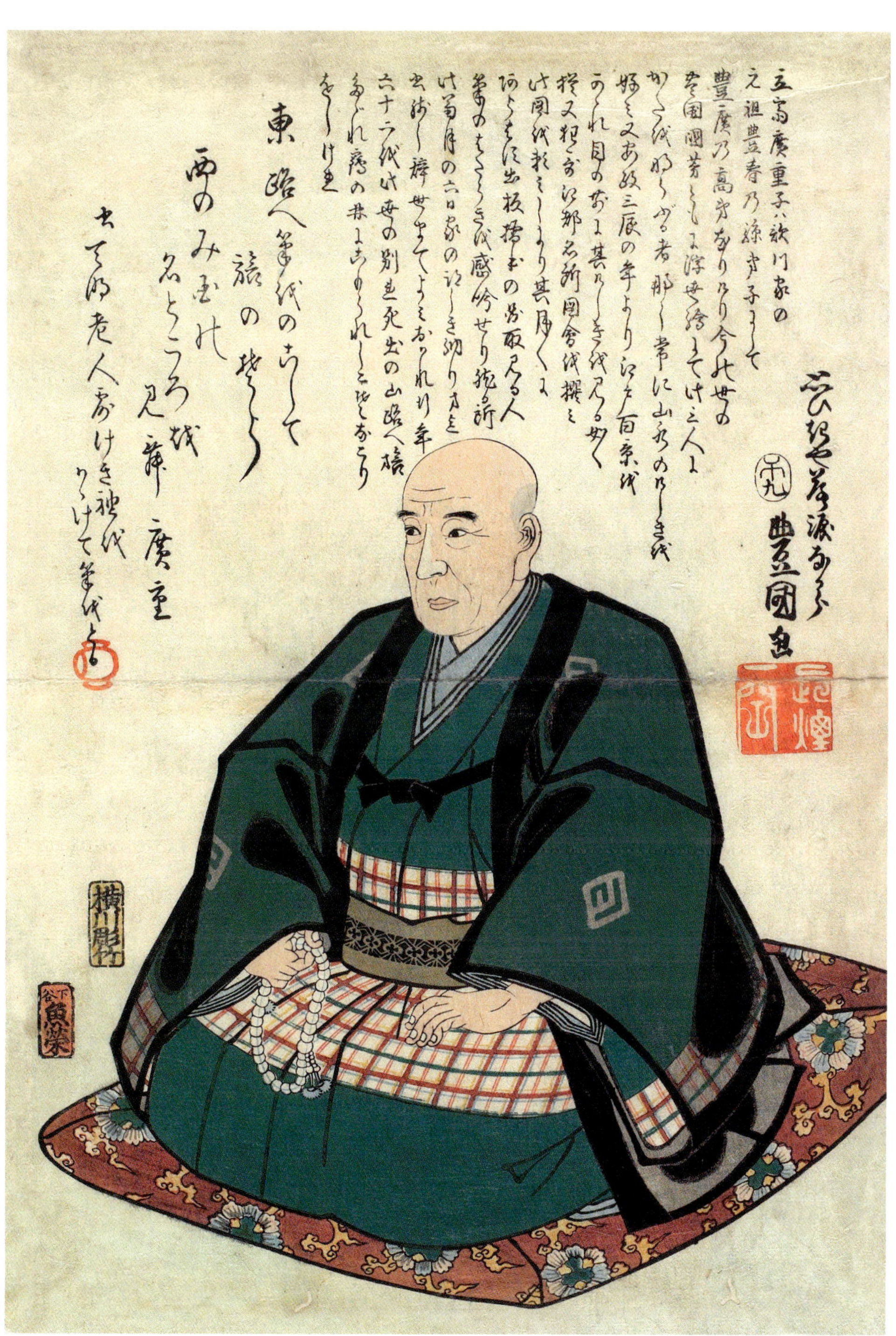

元祖豊廣豊國門人歌川家の
豊國國芳乃高弟なり今此世の
空けて人と浮世絵を常に山水の図をよくし
好ミよく数度の�) 江戸百景代
名所圖会代撰を
板摺本の労取ぬる人
其月の六日家の路へ橋
二十二代其他別画死出の山路へ橋
あ々れ病の

東都筆代のうして
西のみ玉れ
旅の
名ところ城
見華廣重

嵩光老人寿けき神代
つゝけて筆代る

豊原國周画

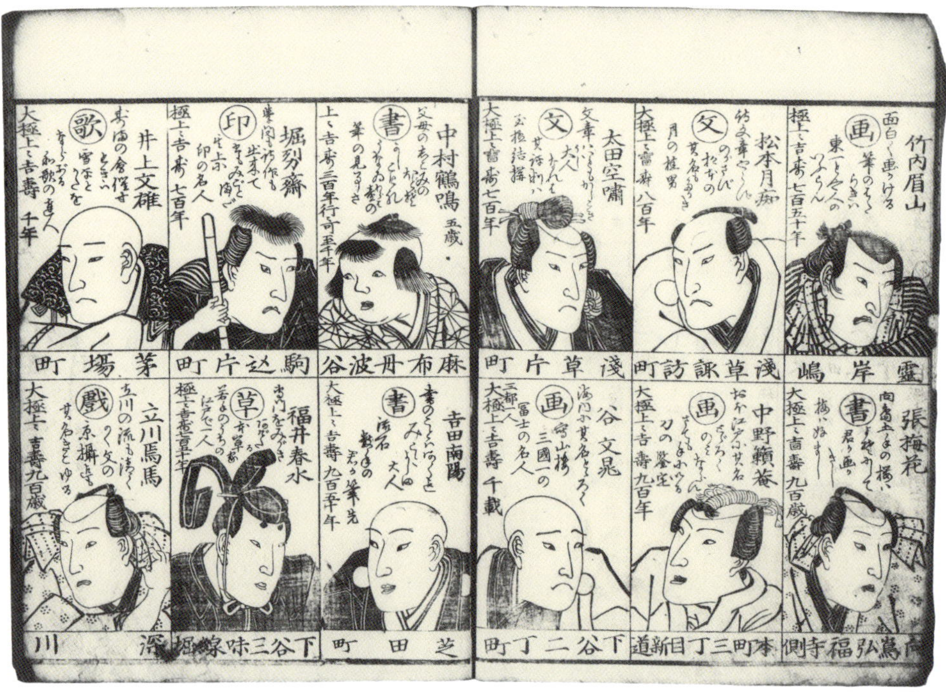

was the smallest.[6] There were three types of inns available in most towns but travellers could not stay just anywhere they desired. Luxurious inns, called *honjin*, were reserved for the *daimyō* and other high-ranking officials, whereas lower officials and the like stayed in *waki-honjin*, and ordinary travellers lodged in *hatagoya*. Only a few towns were without any *honjin*, although some had as many as eight. *Hatagoya*, however, were available in every post-station town along the Kisokaidō, ranging from as few as three in Yawata (plate 25) to 80 in Fukaya (plate 10), with the average being 28 *hatagoya*.[7]

A travel permit was needed in order to pass through the checkpoints (*sekisho*) that were set up on all five major roads to control the supply of weapons into Edo, and to prevent the departure of *daimyō* family members out of the city (*iri-deppō ni de-onna*). The Kisokaidō had two checkpoints: Usui, near Sakamoto (plate 18), and Fukushima (plate 38). Every pilgrim, merchant, courier, craftsman, sightseer etc. was stopped, so too the entourage of a *daimyō*. The size of a *daimyō*'s entourage was fixed, based

Portrait of Takenouchi Magohachi in the top right corner / Porträt von Takenouchi Magohachi in der Ecke rechts oben / Portrait de Takenouchi Magohachi dans l'angle en haut à droite.
From: *Evaluation of Well-Known Contemporary Edo Literati (Genzon raimei Edo bunjin jumyō zuke)*, vol. 1, 1849. Published by Toyoshimaya Bunjiemon. Woodblock-printed book. Gifu University Library

Portrait of Eisen / Porträt von Eisen / Portrait d'Eisen.
From: *Evaluation of Well-Known Contemporary Edo Literati (Genzon raimei Edo bunjin jumyō zuke)*, vol. 1, 1849. Published by Toyoshimaya Bunjiemon. Woodblock-printed book. Gifu University Library

on the quantity of rice produced in his domain. Consisting of banner men, foot soldiers, porters and servants, they ranged from 50 to over 400 men.

Travellers usually made their journey on foot and the walking time varied greatly depending on the terrain, the age and health of the walker, the load being carried etc. The average person needed at least two weeks for the whole journey. Higher-ranking or wealthier travellers rode on horseback or were carried in a sedan, depending on their status. The basic sedans were carried by one man in the front and one in the back. Because they damaged the roads, carts with wheels were banned and those who could afford it hired porters with pack horses to transport their goods.

The Kisokaidō in Japanese Woodblock Prints

The Kisokaidō was a rare motif in Japanese art, in contrast to the Tōkaidō. The National Diet Library, in Tokyo, has in its collection a 19-metre-long (62 feet), painted hand-scroll from 1668 showing a topographical map that incorporates both roads.[8] The so-called *Panorama Map of the Nakasendō* (*Nakasendō bunken nobe ezu*) in the collection of the Tokyo National Museum, dating from 1806, is a hand-coloured map that shows the road from Itabashi (plate 2) to Moriyama (plate 68) in ten hand-scrolls (p. 39). Both maps were created for official administrative purposes, rather than for the general public or for connoisseurs.

Outside the government administration, it was wood-block-printed books in monochrome that offered a general audience information on the Kisokaidō. A few illustrations appear in the travel diary *An Account of the Kiso Road* (*Kisoji no ki*) by Kaibara Ekiken (1630–1714) from 1713 (p. 43). Sōyō's (dates unknown) *Illustrated Guide to the Kiso-Road* (*Kisoji anken ezu*) from 1756 is the opposite: a small handbook without commentary but instead showing the entire road over 73 pages in simple drawings, followed by a table of distances and transportation fees (p. 42). The most widely available publication was Akisato Ritō's (active 1780–1814) *Views of Famous Sights along the Kiso Road* (*Kisoji meisho zue*) from 1805, which was issued in six volumes combining informative text with detailed illustrations by Nishimura Chūwa (dates unknown).

Jippensha Ikku's (1766–1831) comic novel *Strolling along the Tōkaidō* (*Tōkaidōchū hizakurige*), published from 1802 to 1809, successfully brought travel into more general focus and was likely the catalyst for Katsushika Hokusai (1760–1849) to design the first colour prints related to the Tōkaidō in the early 1800s, which were

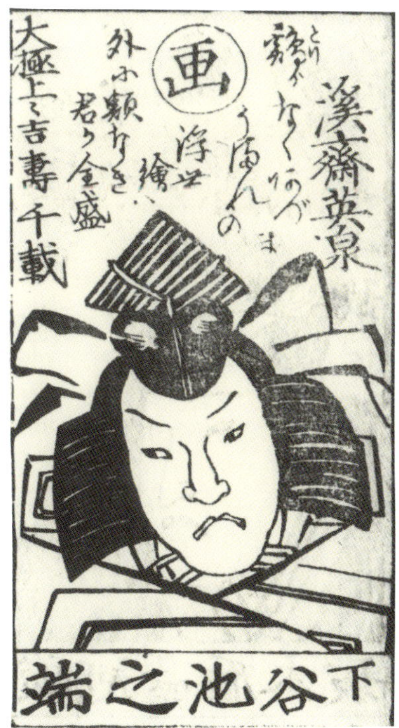

followed by others within a few years (pp. 44, 45).[9] Volumes three to eight of Ikku's sequel to *Strolling along the Tōkaidō*, published between 1812 and 1816, let the protagonists Kitahachi and Yajirōbei travel along the Kisokaidō, where they once again have humorous adventures. However, this did not lead to a wave of prints at this time with the Kisokaidō as subject matter.

In 1818, capitalising on the general interest in travel, Hokusai began to create bird's-eye-view maps of the entire topography of a route in single, impressive compositions. The first showed the Tōkaidō, published by Kadomaruya Jinsuke, who then teamed up with two other publishers a few months later and together they issued Hokusai's bird's-eye-view map of the Kisokaidō which was also the first Kisokaidō print (pp. 50–51).[10]

The Kisokaidō Series and its Artists

The large market for landscape prints as souvenirs for travellers, which also catered for those who could not undertake such journeys, grew significantly in the 1830s, particularly in relation to Mount Fuji and variations on the theme of the *Eight Views of Lake Biwa*. The little-known Hiroshige (p. 9) achieved considerable success in 1832 when the first prints of his series *The Fifty-Three Stations along the Tōkaidō* (*Tōkaidō gojūsan tsugi no uchi*), commonly called "Hōeidō Tōkaidō", were published by Takenouchi Magohachi's (1781–1854) recently founded firm Hōeidō (p. 10).

Hiroshige was born Andō Tokutarō in the Yayosugashi district of Edo in 1797, the son of a fire warden. The death of both his parents in his 13th year obliged him to take over his father's position. Hiroshige, however, had other plans for his future, and in 1810 or 1811, after applying unsuccessfully to enter the studio of the Utagawa school artist Toyokuni (1769–1825), he became a student of Toyohiro (1773–1828), another follower of the Utagawa school. In 1812, he began using the name Hiroshige. The first recognised works by him are illustrations for a three-volume anthology of humorous poems published in 1818, and several prints of actors. In 1823, he relinquished his post as fire warden in order to devote himself to his artistic career. Over the following decade he designed a number of series of beauties and warrior subjects.

The first of Hiroshige's landscape designs, for which he became famous, appeared in the early 1830s. The foremost of these was *The Fifty-Three Stations along the Tōkaidō*, published by Hōeidō in around 1832–33, which was one of 20 series depicting this road (p. 70). As well as the Tōkaidō, his landscape designs, sometimes produced in collaboration with other artists, include series of views of Ōmi Province, the Tama River, famous places in Kyoto and Osaka, and around 20 of his home town of Edo, culminating with his masterpiece, *One Hundred Famous Views of Edo* (*Meisho Edo hyakkei*, 1856–58; p. 71). Together these amount to thousands of unique designs.

Hiroshige also excelled at *kachōga*, pictures of birds and flowers, and created hundreds of designs in this genre. His total output of prints comes to more than 4,500 designs, as well as illustrations to almost 150 books, together with hundreds of paintings, including 200 commissioned by the lords of the Oda clan in Tendō Province.

The success of Hiroshige's designs was multifarious. He was highly skilled at adapting imagery by other artists and illustrators into the single-sheet, colour-woodblock print medium, but his striking

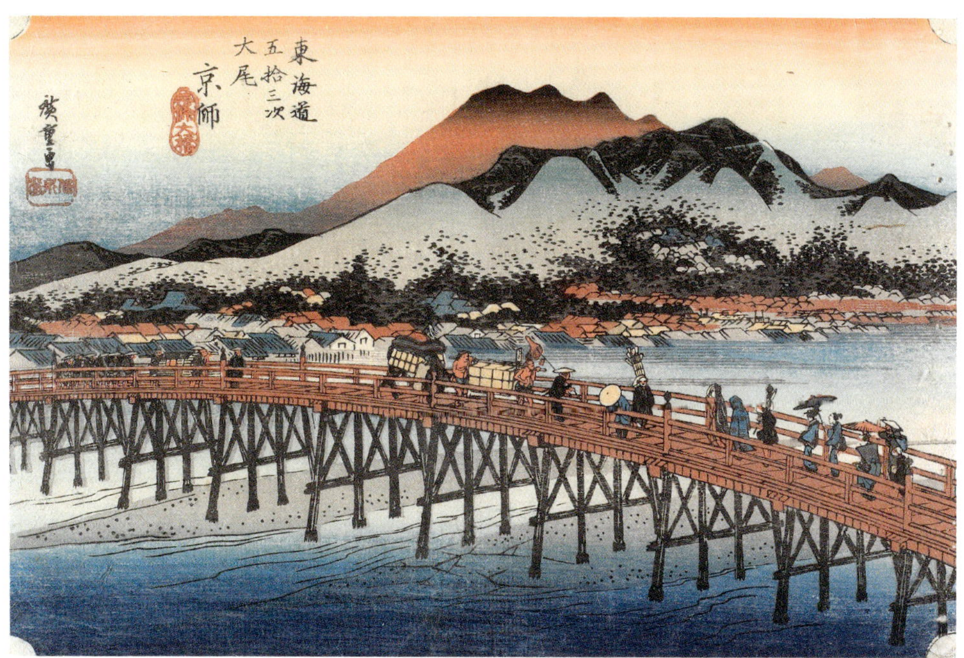

compositions, which employ bold framing devices and single-point perspective, occasionally to dramatic effect, demonstrate an acute and imaginative approach to design. Like his teacher Toyohiro, Hiroshige was adept at integrating figures, depicted with sensitivity and sometimes gentle humour, into landscape settings imbued with quiet lyricism.

In the Hōeidō Tōkaidō series Hiroshige emphasised the scenic aspect of the road by using an innovative style, and presented in the *ōban* format (c. 27 × 39 cm / 10½ × 15½ in.), at that time an unusually large format for landscape subjects.[11] While Hiroshige's interpretations for the first prints in this series might have been based on personal travel experiences, soon more and more views were clearly originating from monochrome illustrations by other artists that had been published in various travel guidebooks.[12] Inspired by their success, he and Takenouchi ironed out plans for other landscape themes and publicised them in a new advertising sheet that was inserted into bound albums of complete Tōkaidō sets sold from the first month of 1834. Amongst these is the first Kisokaidō series, which was announced as a *Series of True Views along the Kiso in Landscape and Genre Pictures (Kiso dōchū shinkei tsuzuki sansui jinbutsu-e).*

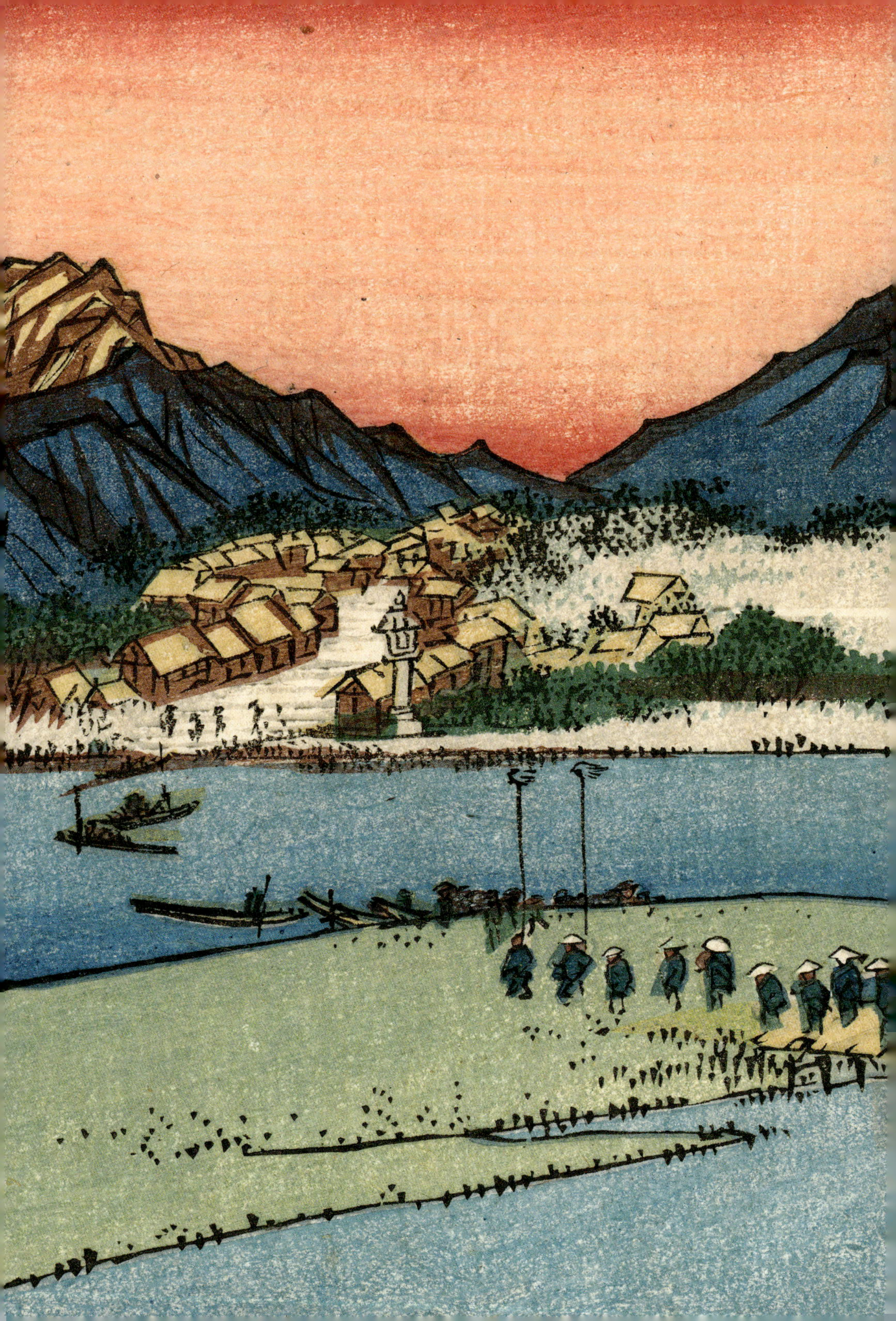

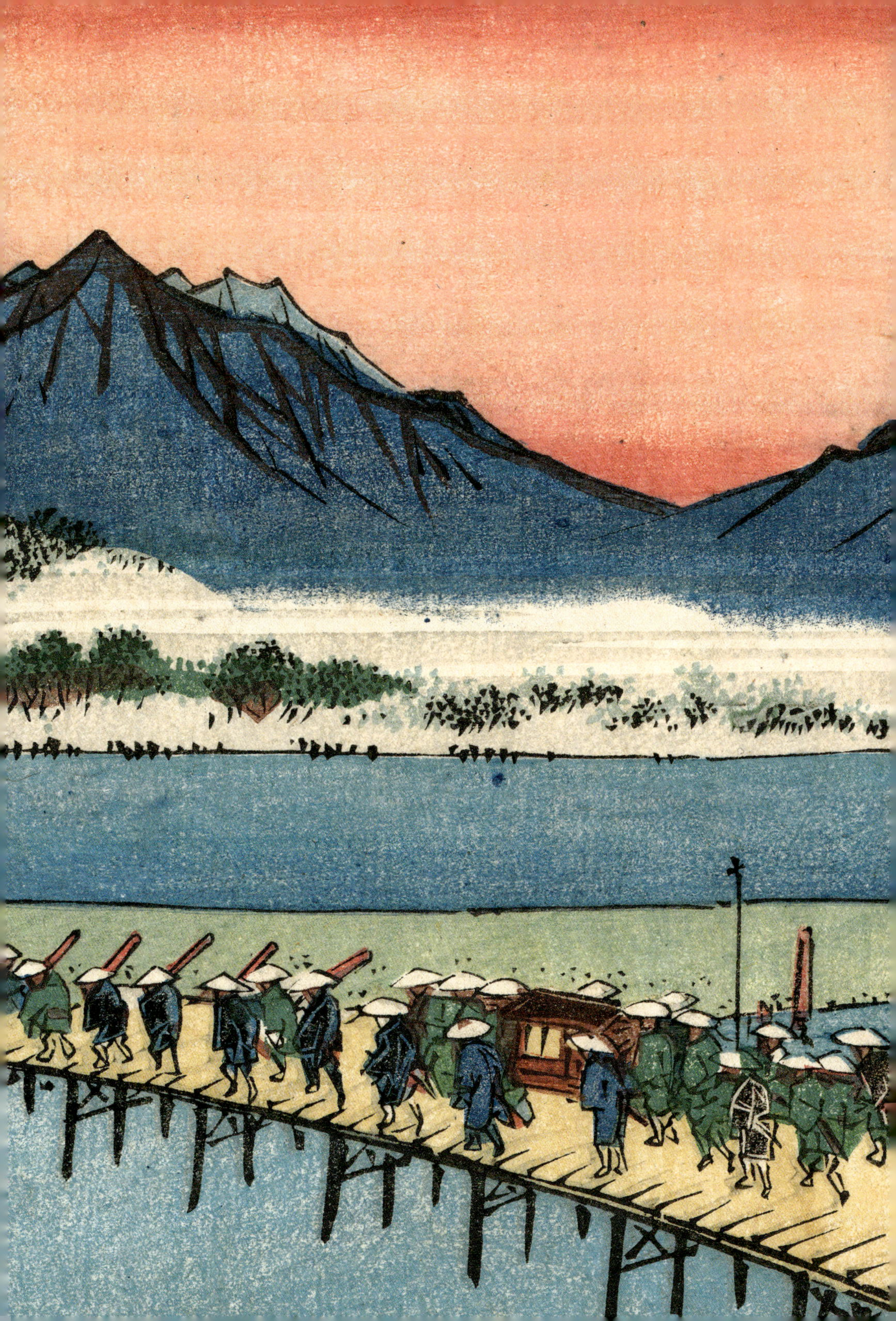

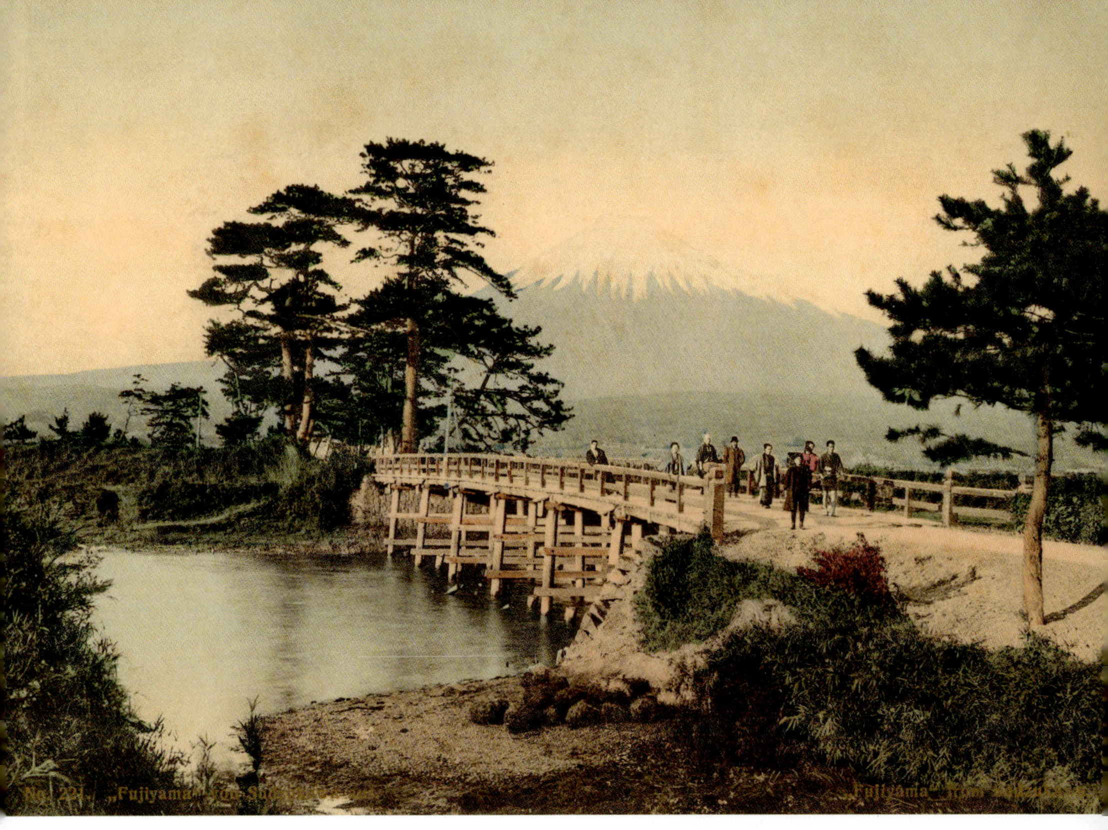

Like Hiroshige, Eisen was born into a samurai family in Edo, the son of the renowned calligrapher Ikeda Masahei Shigeharu (pp. 11, 90). Eisen was born Ikeda Yoshinobu and while still young studied painting under the Kano-school artist Hakkeisai (fl. early 19th century). Later, he boarded with the son of the print designer Kikugawa Eizan (1787–1867), and although he later identified himself as a student of Eizan, the extent and details of this relationship are unclear. Eisen did not become an affiliate of an *ukiyo-e* school like Utagawa or Torii, but signed many of his works using the artistic name Keisai.

His earliest published design is probably an illustration of a beautiful woman in a book from 1811 and he continued to make a name for himself as a print designer and painter of women (p. 74).[13] Eisen designed around 1,900 prints and created illustrations for almost 400 books across a range of genres and subjects. His speciality, however, was images of beautiful women, or *bijinga*. Following Eizan, Eisen initially modelled his beauties on those of Kitagawa Utamaro (1753–1806), but gradually developed

Fuji seen from Suzukawa / Der Fuji, von Suzukawa aus gesehen / Le Fuji vu de Suzukawa, c. 1895. Photochrom, hand-coloured. Paris, Marc Walter Collection

Fuji seen from Taganoura (near the station Ejiri on the Tōkaidō) / Der Fuji, gesehen von Taganoura (nahe der Station Ejiri am Tōkaidō) / Le Fuji vu de Taganoura (près de la station Ejiri sur la Tōkaidō), c. 1895. Photochrom, hand-coloured. Paris, Marc Walter Collection

his own hard-edged, overtly sensuous style that dominated the market. Like many of his peers, Eisen also designed explicit erotic imagery, known as *shunga*.

Eisen also engaged in a range of pursuits other than designing prints. He sold cosmetic face powder and managed a brothel in Nezu under the name Wakatakeya Satosuke. He learned to write kabuki plays under the tutelage of Namiki Gohei II (1768–1819), which were published under the name Chiyoda Saiichi. A prolific writer, he penned light fiction as Ippitsuan Kakō, and essays as Mumeiō and Kaedegawa Shiin. One of his best-known works of literature is *Essays of a Nameless Old Man* (*Mumeiō zuihitsu*, 1833), a revision of *Ukiyo-e Miscellany* (*Ukiyo-e ruikō*), a collection of biographies of print designers first compiled by Ōta Nanpo (1749–1823) in 1789. Eisen's addition to Nanpo's compilation makes reference to his lifestyle of heavy drinking and carousing in the pleasure quarters of Edo.

Takenouchi Magohachi was born in 1781 in Edo's Kyōbashi district as the second son of the pawn-broker Magoshichi (p. 10). Between 1832 and 1837 (Tenpō 3–8) at least he illustrated *kyōka* poetry books under the name Bizan. With the Hōeidō firm he presumably began, also in 1832, to publish the first designs of Hiroshige's earliest Tōkaidō series. By 1833 Takenouchi started to issue prints of kabuki actors and beautiful women by Kunisada (1786–1865) as well as warriors by Kuniyoshi (1797–1861). In 1834, he began to publish illustrated fiction books, amongst them *The Legend of Mikuni Tarō's Return* (*Mikuni Tarō sairai den*) with illustrations by Utagawa Kuniyoshi, Utagawa Kuninao (1793–1854) and Takenouchi himself. This three-volume work was published in the first month of 1835 and in the back of two of the volumes there are identical advertisement sheets (p. 28) again listing Hiroshige as the artist

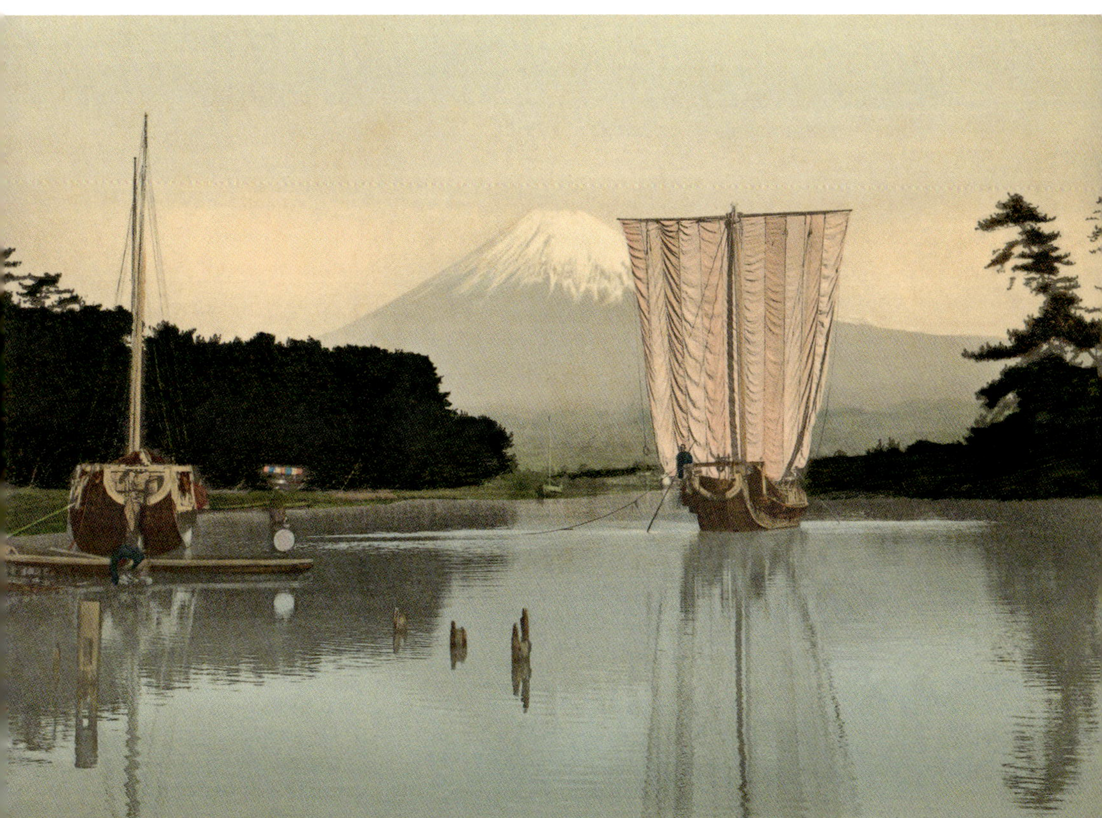

of a new Kisokaidō series which at this time was referred to as *Picture Series of Sceneries along the Kiso* (*Kiso dōchū fūkei tsuzuki-e*).[14]

Both the 1834 and 1835 announcements were released prior to publication of the first designs in this series and merely reflect the intentions of the Takenouchi-Hiroshige collaboration; however, the reality proved to be quite different. Instead of Hiroshige, it was Eisen who began designing this series for Takenouchi in 1835. Eisen did not belong to the powerful Utagawa school of print artists as Hiroshige did, and Takenouchi must have consciously chosen Eisen over other, popular Utagawa-school artists he had already worked with, like Kunisada and Kuniyoshi, maybe because these two had limited interest in landscape prints. In the previous decades, Eisen had already designed several landscapes for a number of publishers, however, without very much success, apart from a series of perspective landscapes of famous places in Edo, each surrounded by a thick, black frame decorated with white writing in Dutch, which were issued in the early 1830s.[15] Eisen had also designed a Tōkaidō series in the mid-1820s, but that focused on beautiful women, and the landscapes were confined to small inset cartouches placed next to the figures (p. 77).[16]

This first Kisokaidō series begins with the Nihonbashi Bridge in Edo, and Eisen integrated into his design a reference to the zodiac calendar sign for the year Tenpō six (roughly corresponding to 1835): the character for the sheep (*hitsuji*) inscribed on an open umbrella in the centre of the picture.[17] The first designs are therefore believed to have been published during that year, but why Eisen was the designer and not Hiroshige can only be speculated on. Maybe because Takenouchi did not want to wait any longer and Hiroshige was travelling and not available; in the fifth month, for example, Hiroshige left Edo for several weeks and went to Senkokuji Temple in nearby Kanagawa to paint. In any case, Hiroshige seems not to have had an issue with Eisen's participation as he joined the project later.

In the advertisement sheet inside a book Takenouchi published in the first month of 1836 Eisen is now proclaimed as the designer; that prints had already been issued is suggested by the way this series is described: *Series of Large Brocade Prints of the Kiso Road* (*Kisoji tsuzuki ōnishiki-e*).[18] The advertisement in a second book from the same year lists Eisen again as the designer and points out that the prints are in horizontal and not vertical format: *Series of Horizontal Pictures along the Kiso* (*Kiso dōchū tsuzuki yoko-e*).[19]

Of the 71 prints that were ultimately produced, Eisen, however, designed only 24. All the prints are numbered, starting with Edo's Nihonbashi as number one, which is also titled *First of the Kisokaidō Series* (*Kisokaidō tsuzuki no ichi*). The first 11 prints in the set are by Eisen. In the subsequent prints there is no consistency, and Eisen seems to have had the freedom to choose which following 11 stations he worked on. Two more unsigned prints are also attributed to Eisen. The 22 signed designs could have been printed by late 1836, by which time Eisen was finished with this project. He instead returned to the Tōkaidō and created a series of designs of beautiful women, each placed on a cloud band in front of a landscape that covers the upper third of a print's background.[20]

From the lack of any explicit reference to the 69 stations in the advertisements or in Eisen's print titles it can be concluded that neither in the original planning by Takenouchi and Hiroshige nor during this first phase with Eisen was there any intention to produce a full series with one print per station. The Kisokaidō was too risky for the publishers from an economic point of view because it was not popular

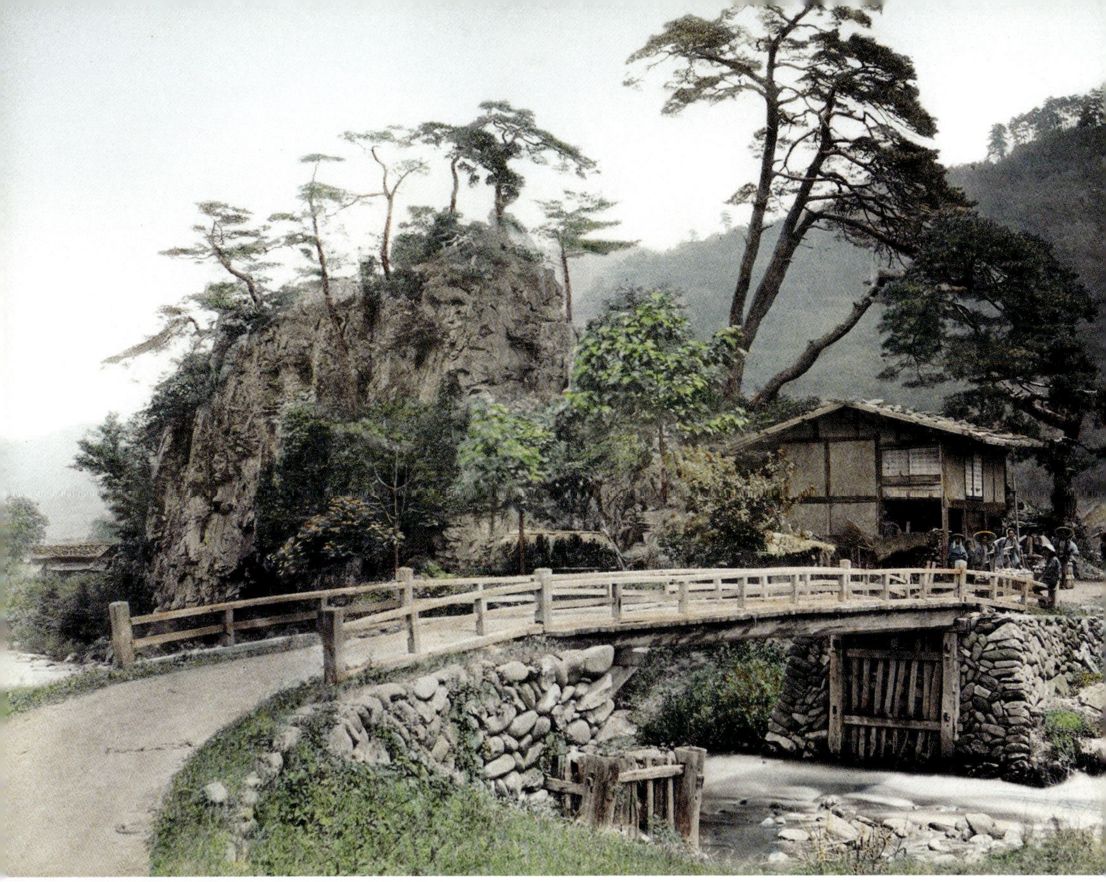

enough to commit to investing in 71 prints. This interpretation is supported by the fact that there are no other Kisokaidō landscape series in the history of *ukiyo-e*; the Kisokaidō would only occur twice again as the motif for a series, both produced in 1852/53 at the historical climax of *ukiyo-e*. These two series of 72 prints each, by Kuniyoshi and Kunisada respectively, use the Kisokaidō only as a serial device and in reality present legends and kabuki plays, with both of them featuring almost always generic landscape elements that are unrelated to the named post-station towns and could be anywhere in rural Japan (pp. 53, 56, 59).[21] This is actually also true for most of Eisen's designs. He clearly depended on other imagery for inspiration, as seen in his first three designs, Nihonbashi, Itabashi and Warabi, which remind the viewer of Nihonbashi, Shinagawa and Kawasaki, the first three prints of Hiroshige's Tōkaidō series. The other prints by Eisen show no distinct landscape features that could be connected to a specific geographic location but are based on an illustration in the aforementioned multi-volume work *Kisoji meisho zue* (pp. 23, 30, 49).[22]

Kusakabe Kinbei, *The Ochiai Bridge on the Kisokaidō Route, near Wada / Die Ochiai-Brücke auf dem Kisokaidō, nahe Wada / Le pont Ochiai sur la route Kisokaidō, près de Wada*, c. 1880. Albumen print, hand-coloured. Pump Park Collection

PP. 20/21
Kōnosu (detail from plate 8)

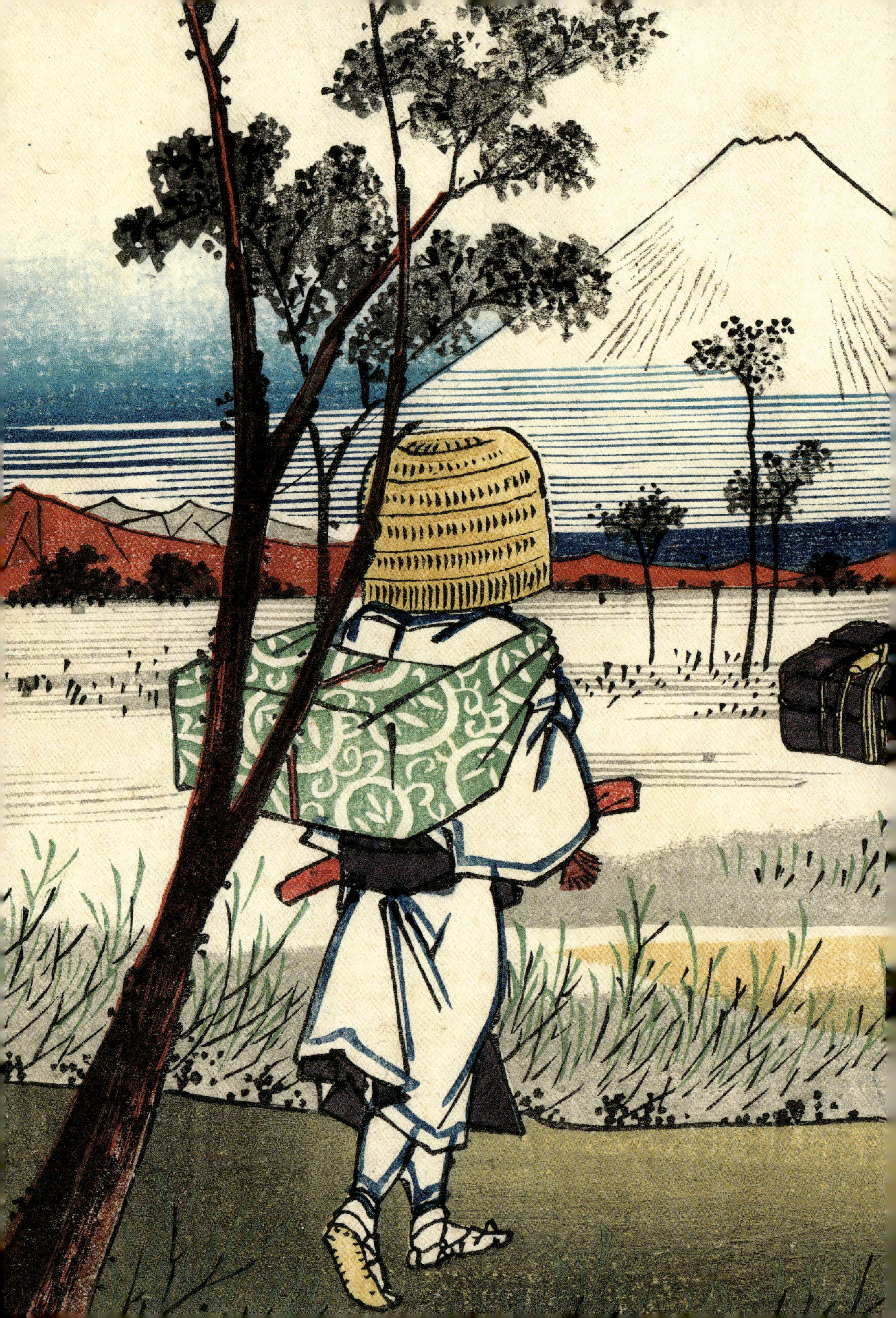

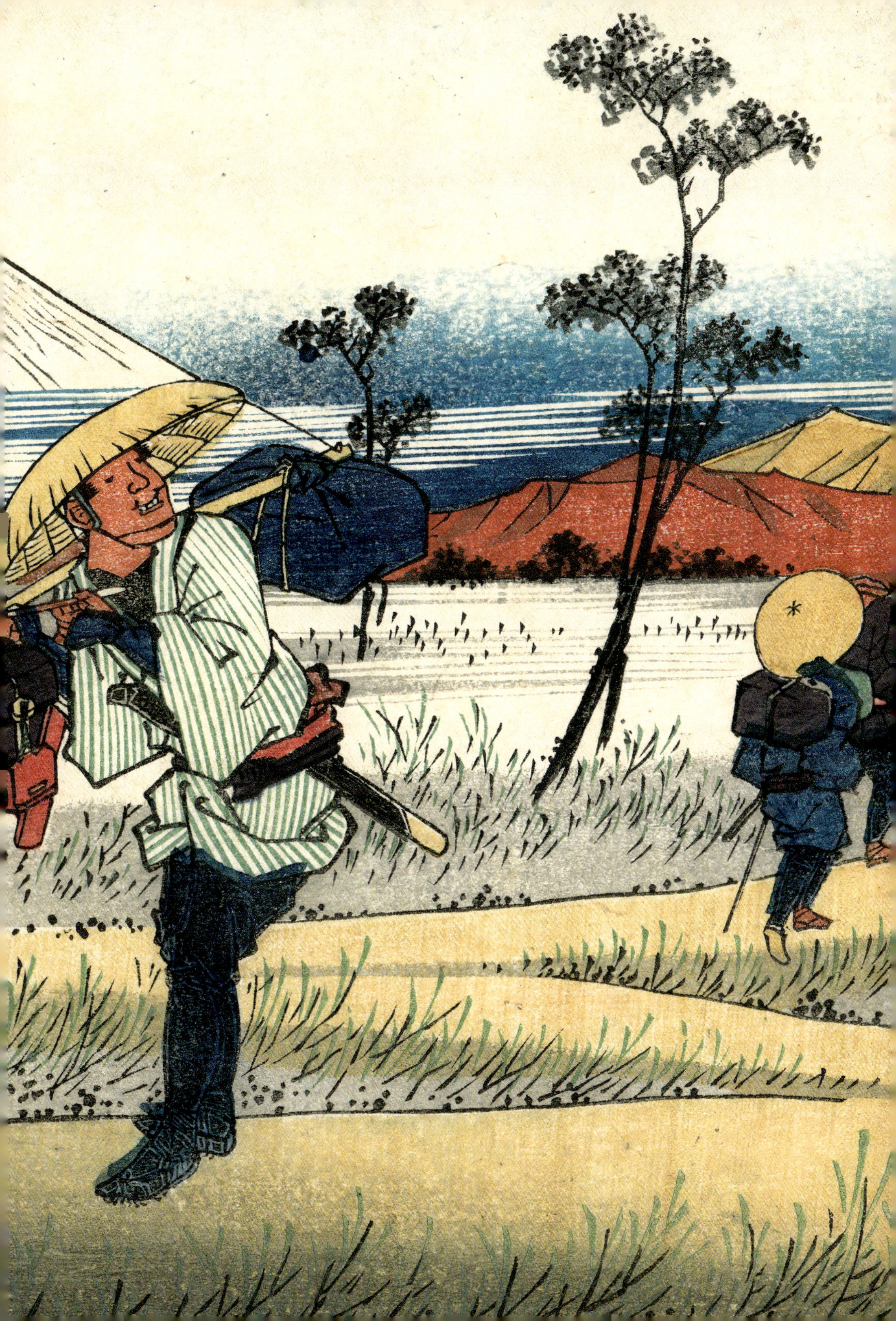

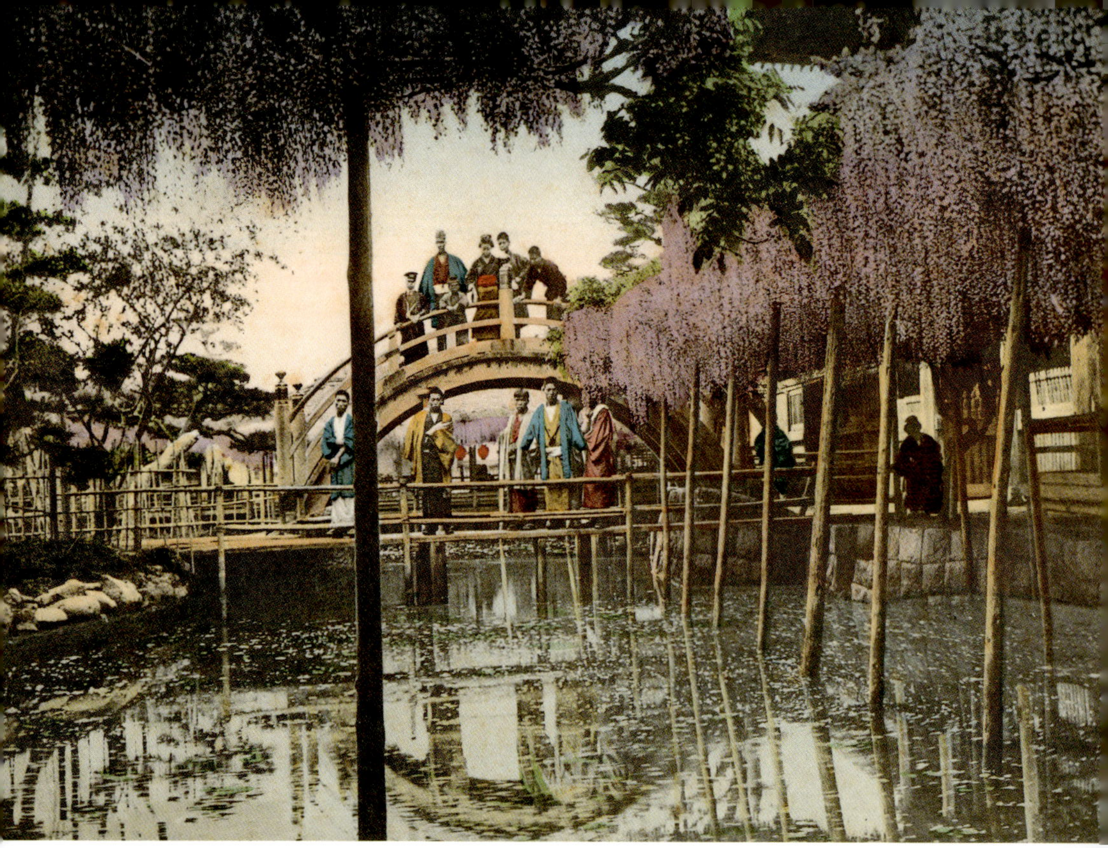

Consequently, Takenouchi's Kisokaidō project came to a halt and it seems that at this time Takenouchi himself had begun to lose interest in the publishing business in general. Some historians believe that the small and relatively young publishing firm of Takenouchi ran into financial difficulties after taking on this Kisokaidō series and therefore he had to enter into partnership with another publisher, Iseya Rihei. However, unlike the case of the Tōkaidō series a few years earlier where Takenouchi had joined forces with the well-established publishing house of Tsuruya Kiemon, Iseya Rihei actually took over the Kisokaidō project and ultimately published almost two-thirds of the prints without Takenouchi's involvement. The so-called Tenpō famine in the second half of the 1830s had little impact on Edo but might have disrupted the print market as there were fewer travellers from the affected provinces and therefore fewer sales of souvenirs, including landscape prints. However, sales of Hiroshige's Tōkaidō series as well as Eisen's Kisokaidō prints must have been phenomenal, judging by the many extant variations of each design which indicate that the printing blocks were run to their limit and some even replaced with new

Drum Bridge in Edo / Trommelbrücke in Edo / Pont tambour à Edo, c. 1898. Photochrom, hand-coloured. Paris, Marc Walter Collection

Nishimura Chūwa, *Lake Suwa / Der Suwa-See / Le lac Suwa*. From: Akisato Ritō, *Views of Famous Sights along the Kiso Road* (*Kisoji meisho zue*), vol. 5, 1805. Woodblock-printed book. Munich, Bayerische Staatsbibliothek

ones. It seems likely therefore that Takenouchi consciously retired from the publishing business, considering that it was not his only source of income but one that he, as a hobby writer and painter himself, had taken up out of pleasure late in life, when he was in his early 50s. The last safely datable works are from the spring of 1837 when Takenouchi published a few actor prints by Kunisada and one more book by himself. He died in 1854.

Presumably in late 1836 or early 1837, the well-established Iseya Rihei firm of Kinjudō, which had been active since the 1790s, took over Takenouchi's Kisokaidō project and invested in it heavily: Iseya bought the blocks for Eisen's prints and hired Hiroshige to furnish new designs that would complete the set. Iseya Rihei had considerable experience in landscape prints and had also published two Tōkaidō-genre series by Hokusai in the early 1800s. He had published only a handful of beauty prints by Eisen in the 1820s and usually worked with Utagawa-school artists like Toyokuni, Kuniyasu (1794–1832), Kuniyoshi and especially Kunisada, but he had not yet worked with Hiroshige. Takenouchi might have recommended that Iseya turn to Hiroshige or maybe he was recommended by Kunisada, Iseya's foremost designer in the 1830s, who is believed to have been a friend of Hiroshige. In any case, the new team embarked on the challenge to complete a full set, as the new title for all the Hiroshige prints indicates: *The Sixty-Nine Stations along the Kisokaidō* (*Kisokaidō rokujūkyū tsugi no uchi*).

Four of the prints by Hiroshige – Takasaki, Karuizawa, Fukushima and Toriimoto (plates 14, 19, 38, 64) – bear publisher marks by both Takenouchi and Iseya and might therefore have been issued first.

These are followed by two unsigned prints, Itahana and Sakamoto (plates 15, 18), which are believed to be designs by Eisen that Takenouchi had received but, for whatever reason, decided not to publish. Of these two unsigned Eisen designs, Itahana was printed first, as some impressions carry a hand-applied publisher's seal of Takenouchi in the left margin, which also seems to be Takenouchi's last contribution to this project. Sakamoto was produced by Iseya alone, as were the 22 designs by Hiroshige that followed in 1837 until there is yet another caesura: Hiroshige left Edo and actually travelled along the Kisokaidō.

Almost all of the Kisokaidō prints relating to the last part of the journey from Ochiai (plate 45) to Kyoto are based on sketches Hiroshige made while actually travelling along this road

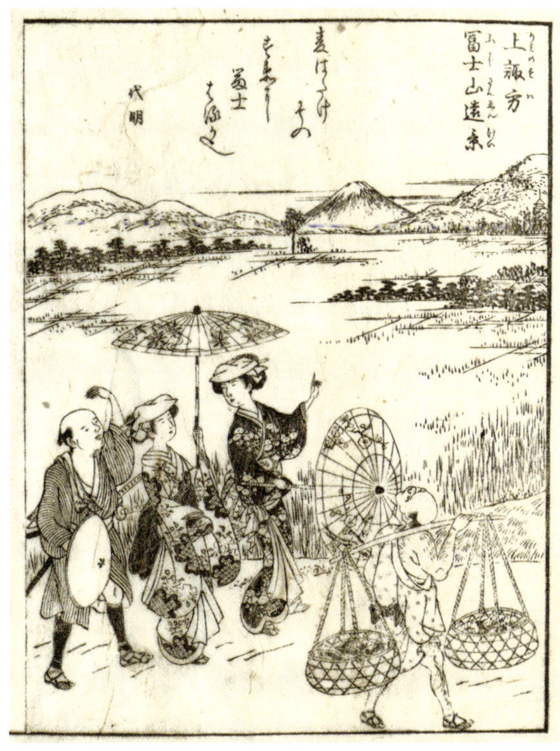

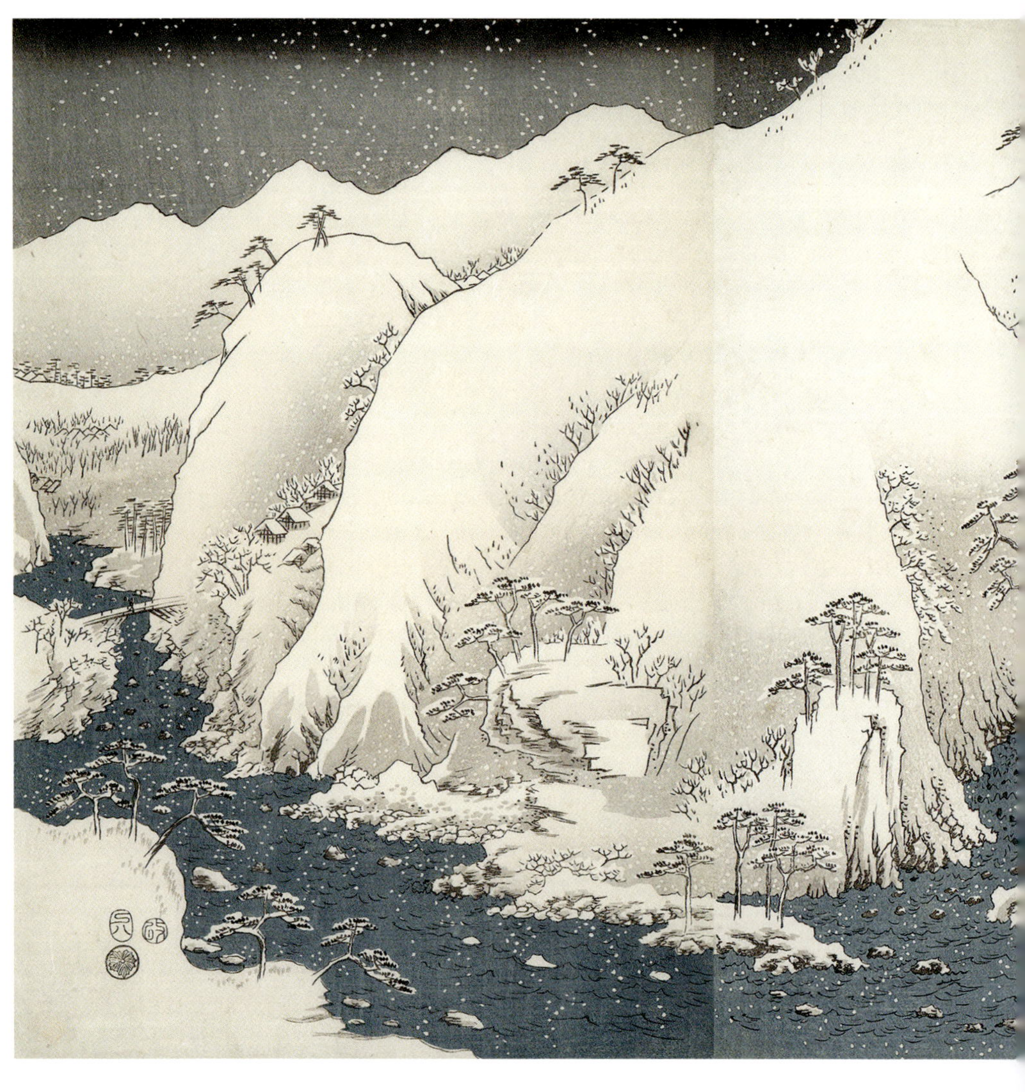

Utagawa Hiroshige, *Mountain River on the
Kiso Road / Gebirgsfluss an der Kiso-Straße /
Montagnes et rivières sur la route de Kiso*, 1857.
Published by Okazawaya Taheiji. Colour woodblock print,
ōban triptych, 37.1 × 76.5 cm / 14 ⅝ × 30 ⅛ in.
London, The British Museum

PP. 26/27
Itahana (detail from plate 15)

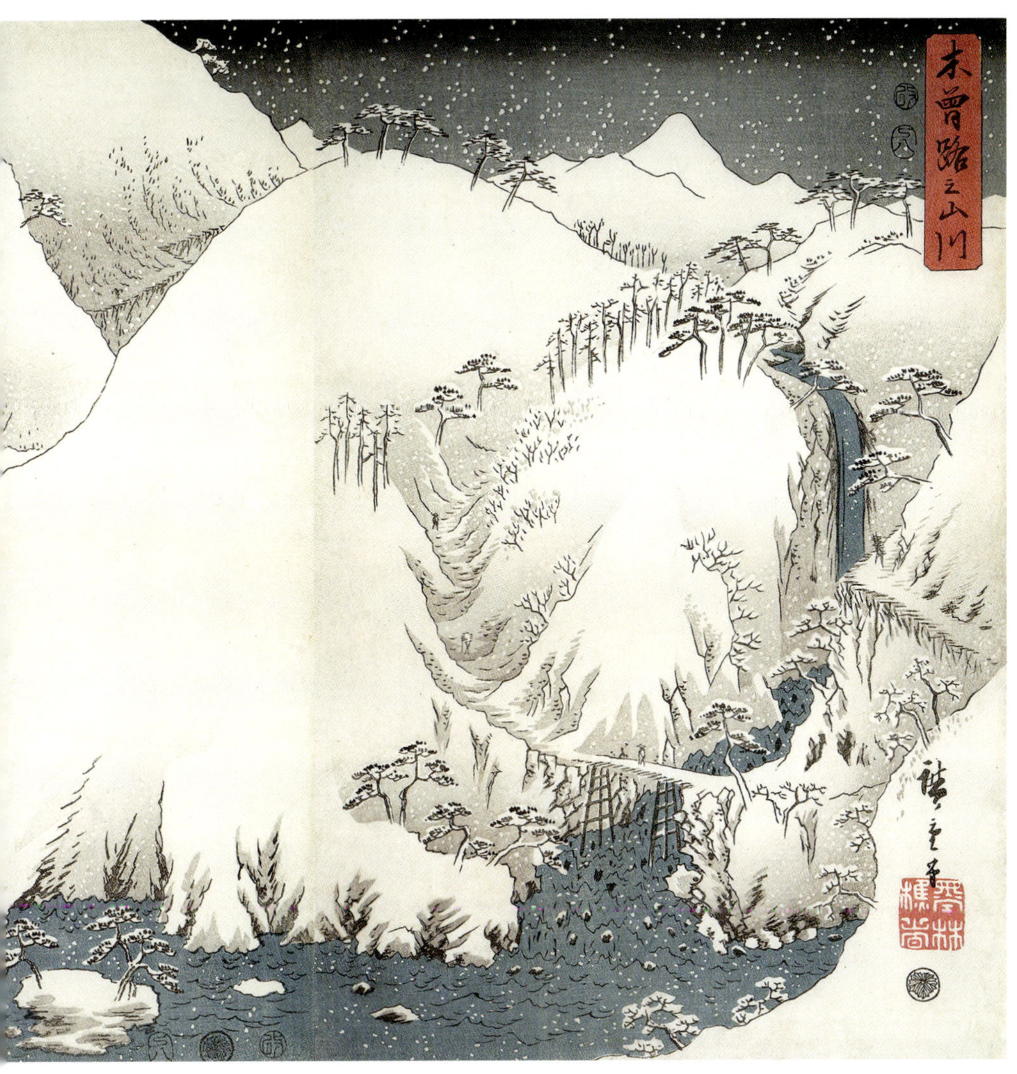

(see pp. 444 ff.). Sixteen prints closely follow his sketches, which have survived in two books, today in the collection of the British Museum in London.[23] Five more designs of stations after Ochiai must also have been produced once Hiroshige had returned to Edo because his signature in all these 21 prints differs from the previous prints.[24] To model the Kisokaidō series on actual sketches follows the original idea of Takenouchi and Hiroshige, as can be seen in the first announcement from 1834 which used the expression *shinkei*, literally true views, indicating that the scenes depicted are taken from nature (p. 56, see detail on pp. 54–55); however, that proposition was not fulfilled until 1837.

While the series has a print for its starting point, Nihonbashi, there is surprisingly no print for Kyoto. Hiroshige designed a few series with Kyoto landscapes and it seems strange that he travelled all the way

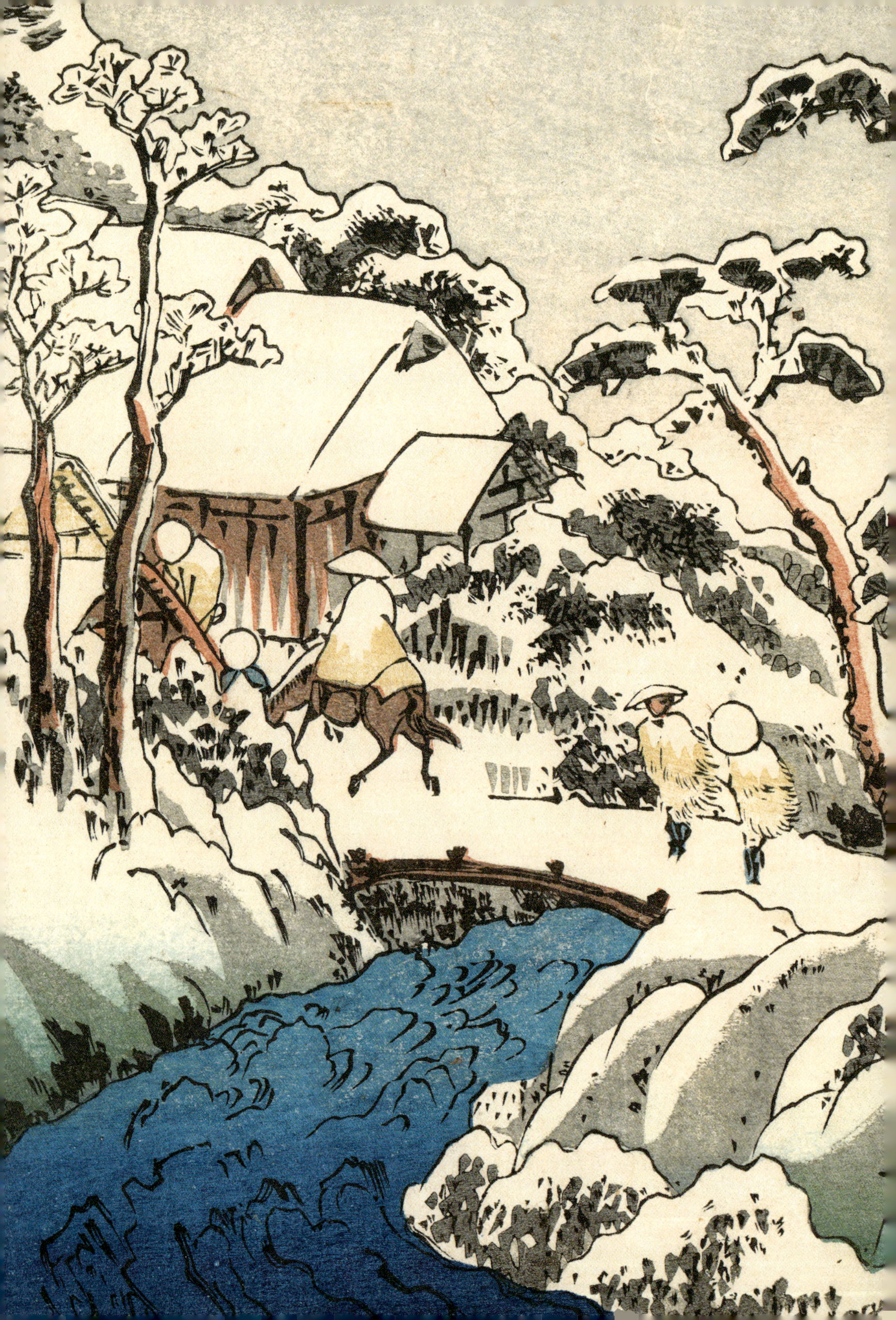

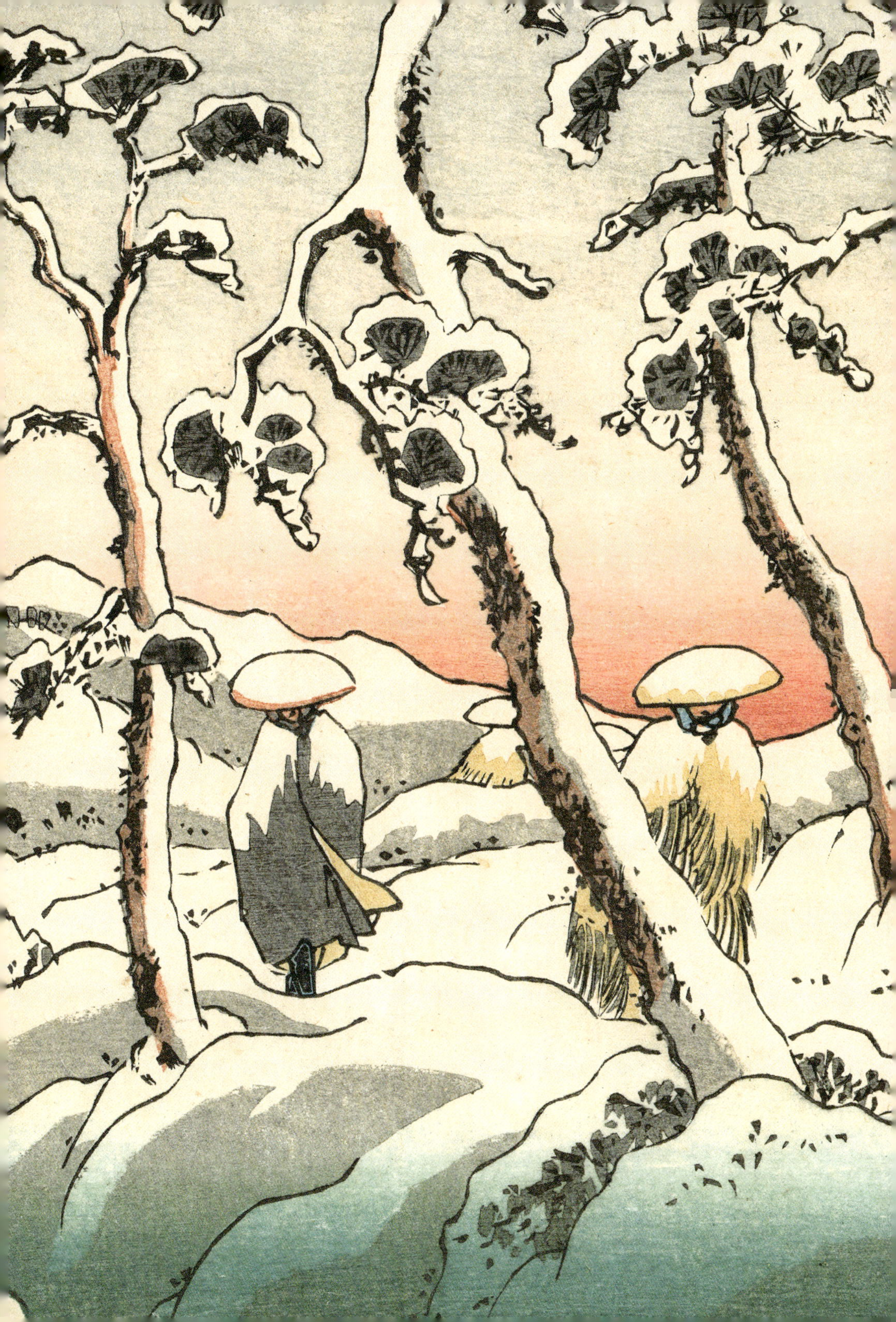

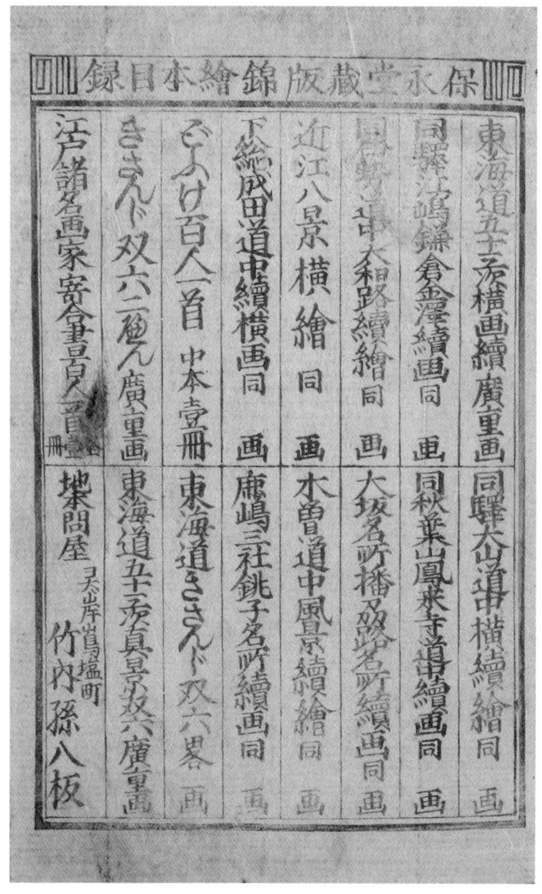

along the road but then did not provide a design for this immensely important city. Another anomaly is that two designs exist for one of the stations, Nakatsugawa. The first (here counted as plate 46a) is very rare and only one version exists, without any colour variations, indicating that the blocks were significantly damaged before they could have been reprinted. This must have happened relatively soon after the first print run was started because of the few remaining impressions. When Hiroshige returned from his journey he created a significantly different second version based on his sketches (plate 46b).

Art historians used to believe that it took until 1842 to print all the sheets in the series, even though a production time of seven years is highly unlikely given the fast-paced print market with its thirst for ever newer designs.[25] Recent research claims that the end date must be revised to 1838 because of an impression of the last design, Ōtsu (plate 70), assumed to have been produced within the last batch of Hiroshige's designs, which has this date inscribed on the back along with the name of the collector (see the summary table in the appendix on p. 505).[26] However, this still only indicates an end date for the first edition but no information whatsoever exists about when exactly sheets were reprinted, which must have happened quite often for some designs, given the many different variations that exist.

During the course of history, the Japanese government changed the censorship rules for prints several times. At the time when this series was created it was the so-called *kiwame* censor seal that had to be obtained for each design before it could go to print. This seal did not itself carry any precise information about the approval date. The *kiwame* seal was usually applied to the margin of a print and as collectors tended to trim their prints right to the margin some impressions are lacking the mark of this seal today.

Once a design was approved for publication, it did not have to be resubmitted for approval when a publisher, the owner of the blocks, later decided to reprint, even after censorship regulations changed, as was the case in the early 1840s. Reprints can thus only be determined by the changes that are visible when comparing several impressions and by the quality of the printing, which depends on the condition of the blocks. Colours that align perfectly prove there is little wear and tear to the blocks, thereby indicating an early impression. As some of the designs in this series were very popular, there are vast quality differences between the impressions. In general, publishers ordered batches of 200 impressions and a publisher had to sell around 600 in order to break even when taking into consideration the fee to the artist for the design, the fee to the carver for the blocks and his labour, and the fee to the printer for the paper and pigments, as well as his labour, which could include special printing features such as colour gradation (*bokashi*), if ordered.[27]

Iseya Rihei remained very active as a publisher until the early 1840s when a dramatic change occurred in the print world and the government attempted to exert greater control over it through the so-called Tenpō Reforms, new sumptuary laws that included severe restrictions on designers and craftsmen and therefore drove some publishers into financial crises. Iseya seems to have stopped publishing new prints in the mid-1840s but was still listed as a member of the New Faction of the Picture Book and Print Publishers Guild in 1851.[28] Presumably in the second half of the 1830s, while he was producing Hiroshige's new designs, Iseya reprinted Eisen's designs and in some cases made changes to the blocks by removing Takenouchi's seal and/or name, which he sometimes replaced with his own, for example, in the case of Nihonbashi. As the print artists received lump sums for their designs when they delivered them to the publisher, Iseya could make later changes as he pleased and also removed Eisen's signature, probably because Hiroshige had by now established himself as the shining star of landscape design. Iseya might also have speculated that he would be able to increase sales if he pretended that Hiroshige had designed every print in the series.[29]

At some point, perhaps in the mid-1840s when Iseya stopped publishing new prints, he sold the Kisokaidō blocks to the Kinkyōdō publisher Yamadaya Shōbei (dates unknown). The latter was very successful with the publication of illustrated novelettes beginning in 1846 and his heir, Shōjirō (dates unknown), took over in late 1851 and continued with this formula until around 1866. Probably in the early 1850s, Yamadaya reprinted the so-called *Gyōsho Tōkaidō* (*Informal Script Tōkaidō*) series by Hiroshige which was initially published around 1841–42 (p. 81). When exactly Yamadaya reprinted the Kisokaidō series is unclear but he modified most of the blocks by removing old publisher seals, a simpler method than the more costly way of replacing the seals with his own. In only two instances, the designs for Nihonbashi and Ōta (plates 1, 52), did he use his own seal. As the blocks had now been reprinted multiple times there is significant wear and tear visible in the Yamadaya impressions, which are in a very poor condition (p. 83).[30]

In modern times, a few Japanese businesses have specialised in producing reproductions of old, popular designs, amongst them this Kisokaidō series. To maintain an authentic appearance they are printed using traditional methods from woodblocks, however, not from the original blocks but from newly carved ones. The publisher Watanabe Shōzaburō, for example, offered reproduction prints of the entire Kisokaidō series in his 1935 catalogue which he sold for 35 Sen each, 20 Yen for the full set. Some

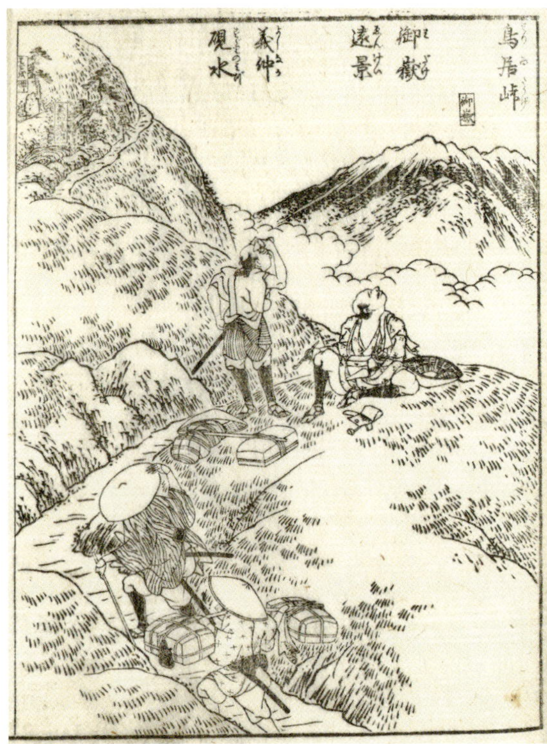

of these reproduction prints were bound into albums; one seller even added a new, woodblock-printed table of contents (*mokuroku*).[31]

The value of a print from the Kisokaidō series today depends on many different factors, the first being the design itself, with some being more desirable than others. Eisen's Kutsukake (plate 20), for example, was identified by Basil Stewart in 1922 and Edward Strange in 1925 as one of the series' best contributions.[32] So was Hiroshige's Nagakubo (plate 28), which Stewart referred to as "perhaps the masterpiece of the series".[33] Ōi (plate 47) was equally admired by Stewart and Strange, the latter also citing the famous print collector John S. Happer (1863–1936), who said about Ōi that "there is no finer representation of falling snow in any of [Hiroshige's] other series."[34]

The quality of the impression and its condition are decisive factors in the appraisal of a print. If a design sold well, a publisher continued to reprint it, possibly making colour changes in some areas, which is the reason why several designs of the Kisokaidō series exist in six versions. The larger the print-run, the worse the impressions became due to the wear of the blocks. Impressions from the earliest edition show the more precise registration; however, these are not necessarily the "finest" editions that contain the *de luxe* printing features – in the case of Kisokaidō prints, this translates as colour gradations or *bokashi*. The impressions presented on the following pages are from a private collection which is without doubt the finest set in the world, composed almost entirely of exceptional impressions from the earliest and/or finest edition of each design.

NISHIMURA CHŪWA, *Yabuhara Station, Torii Pass / Die Station Yabuhara, Torii Pass / La station Yabuhara, col de Torii*. From: Akisato Ritō, *Views of Famous Sights along the Kiso Road (Kisoji meisho zue)*, vol. 5, 1805. Woodblock-printed book. Munich, Bayerische Staatsbibliothek

KUSAKABE KINBEI, *Mount Myōgi in Gunma / Der Myōgi in Gunma / Le mont Myōgi à Gunma*, c. 1880. Albumen print, hand-coloured. Kjeld Duits Collection

PP. 32/33
Yabuhara (detail from plate 36)

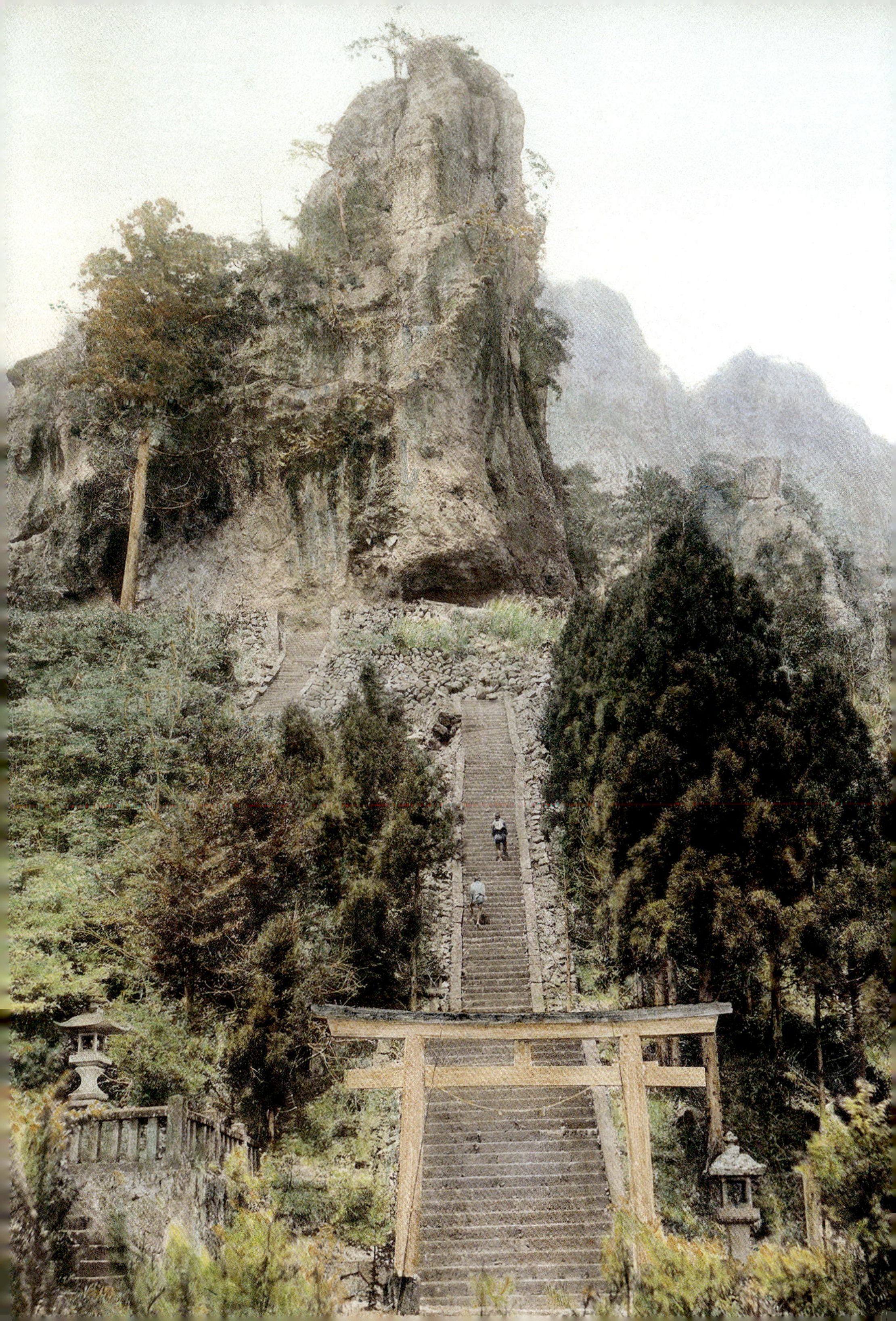

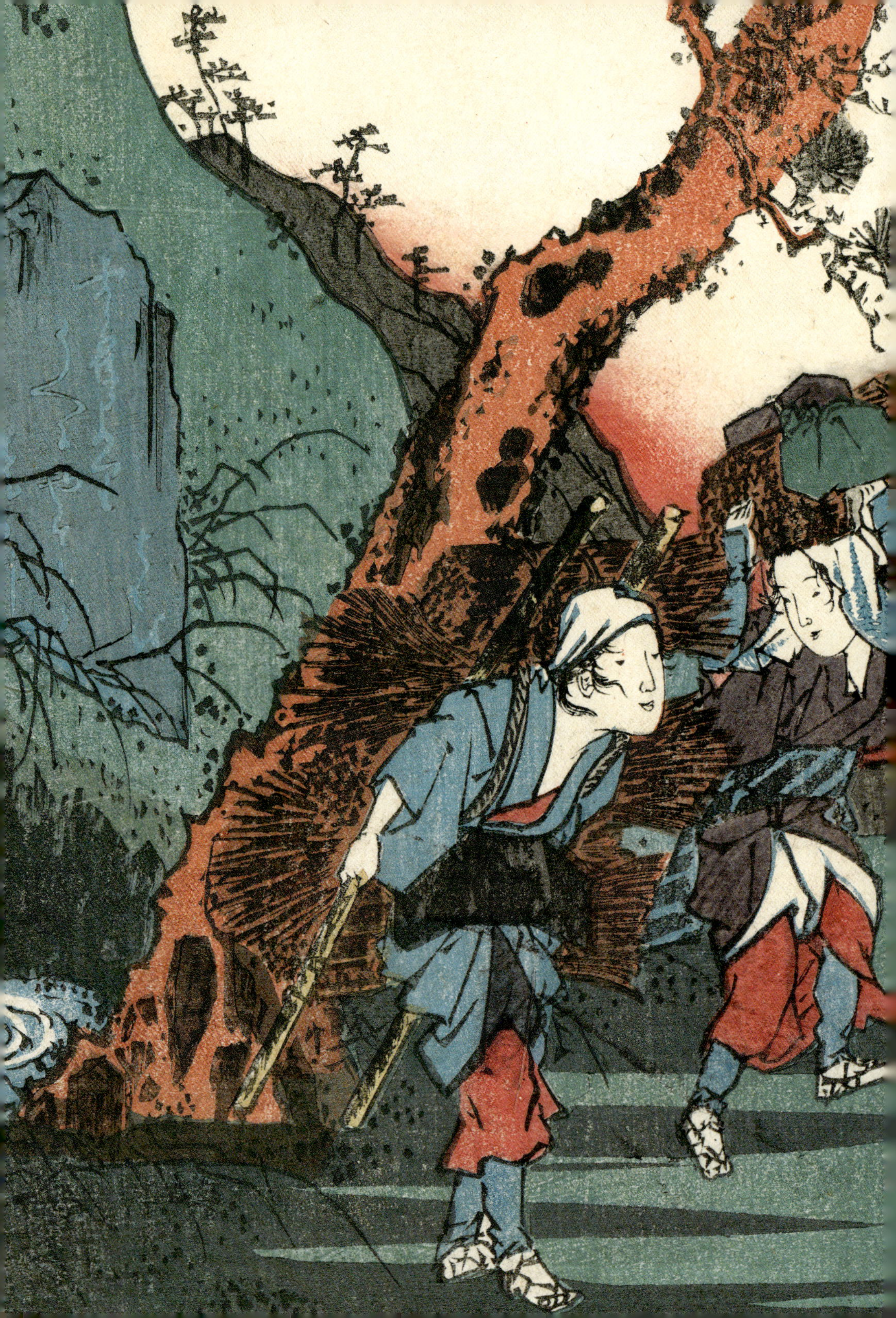

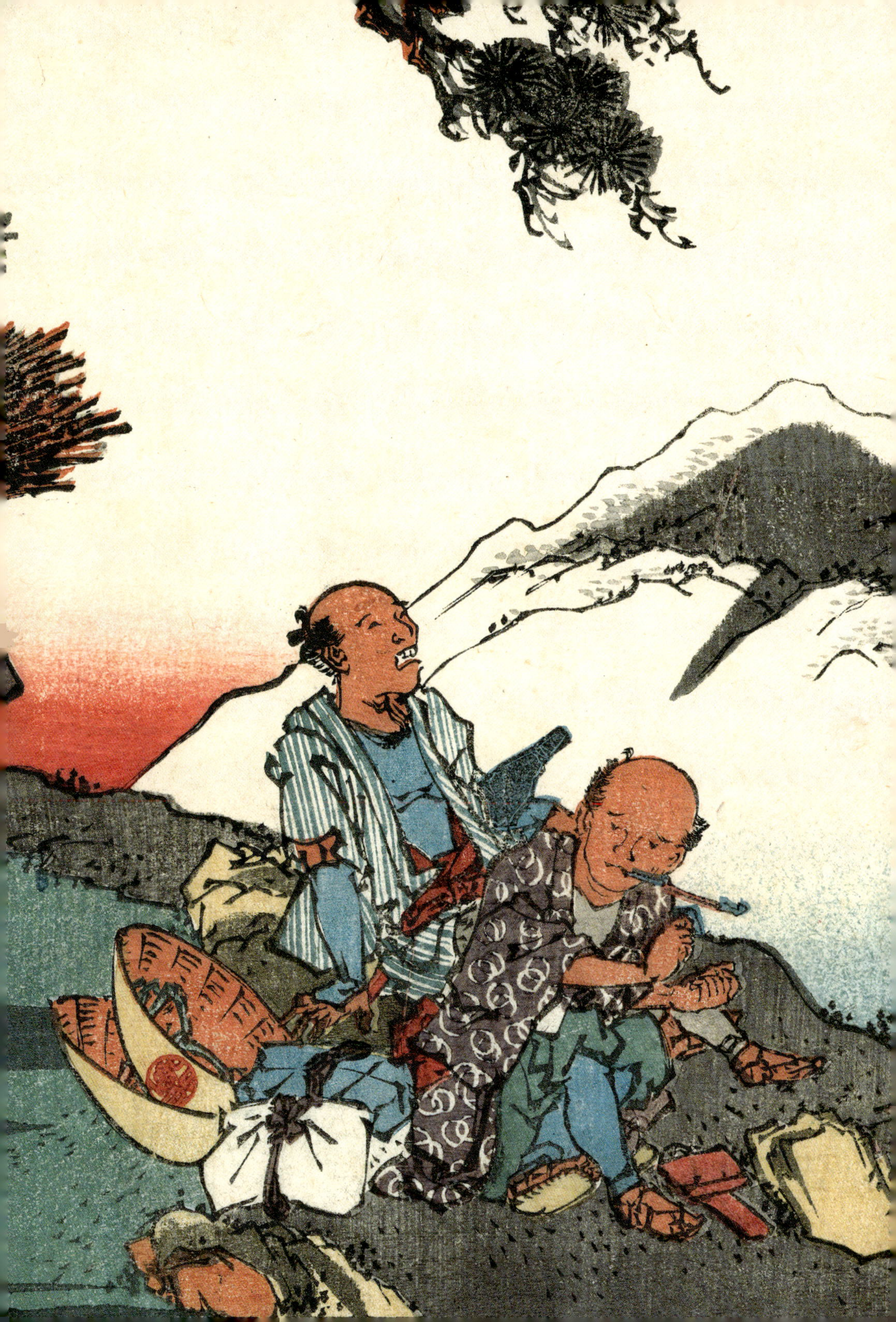

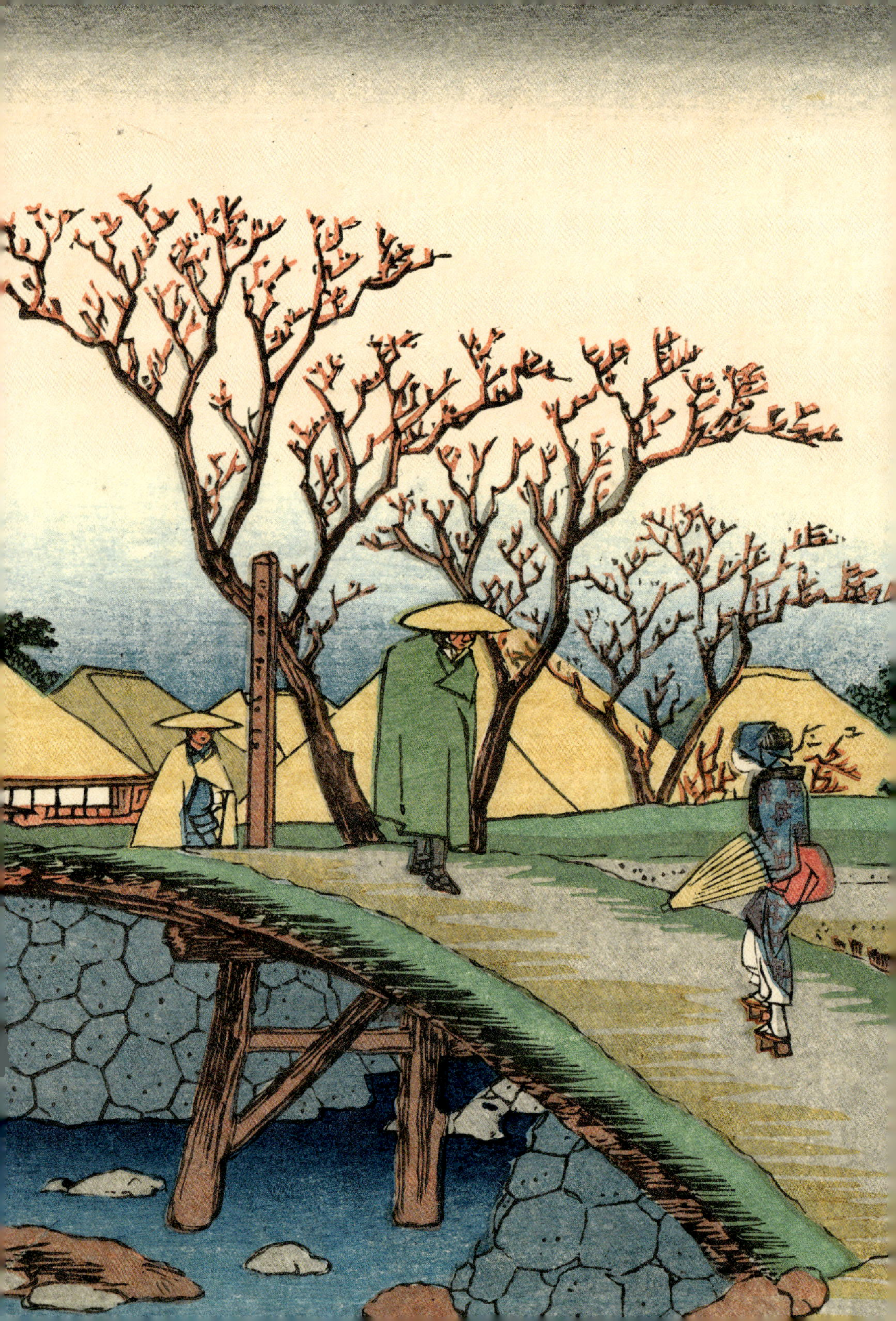

Andreas Marks

Von Edo nach Kyoto

Ein Reiseabenteuer

Reisen in Japan

Als der Shogun Tokugawa Ieyasu (1543–1616) im frühen 17 Jahrhundert Japan einte und in Edo, dem heutigen Tokio, eine Zentralregierung zu errichten begann, war ihm bewusst, dass er nur an der Macht bleiben konnte, wenn es ihm gelänge, seinen Einfluss über die entlegenen Gebiete des Landes aufrechtzuerhalten. Um die vielen lokalen Lehensfürsten (*daimyō*) zu kontrollieren, wurde ein System der wechselnden Residenzen eingeführt, das die Fürsten zwang, zwei Wohnsitze zu unterhalten, einen in ihrem Herrschaftsbereich und einen in Edo. Ihre regelmäßige Anwesenheit in der Hauptstadt wurde zur Pflicht, und in Zeiten ihrer Abwesenheit hatten ihre Ehefrauen und Kinder gleichsam als Geiseln in Edo zu bleiben. Unter dem Eindruck des stattlichen Straßennetzes, das in China unterhalten wurde, befahl Ieyasu die Erneuerung und Erweiterung eines Systems von Landstraßen, dessen Basis bereits Jahrhunderte zuvor gelegt worden war. Obwohl China wesentlich größer war als Japan, konnten dort Botschaften über ein gut organisiertes Staffelsystem von berittenen Kurieren, die sich auf vorgegebenen Routen bewegten, in erstaunlich kurzer Zeit auch in abgeschiedene Regionen überbracht werden.

Um den Zugriff Ieyasus auf die entlegenen Teile seines Reiches zu sichern, wurde ein Netzwerk von fünf Hauptstraßen geschaffen, die ihren Ausgang von der Nihonbashi nahmen, der Brücke, die das Zentrum Edos und das Herz Japans bildete (S. 49, 50–51). Entlang dieser Straßen wurden in Abständen bewaffnete Kontrollposten errichtet, die sicherstellten, dass keine größere feindliche Macht sich Edo unentdeckt nähern und umgekehrt keine Fürstenfamilie unbemerkt aus der Hauptstadt fliehen konnte. Eine dieser Hauptstraßen, Nakasendō oder Kisokaidō genannt, führte von der Brücke Nihonbashi in Edo landeinwärts durch die Berge über fast 136 *ri*, etwa 534 Kilometer, bis zur Brücke Sanjō Ōhashi in Kyoto (S. 13; siehe Übersichtskarte auf S. 96–97). Japans heiligster Berg, der Fuji (S. 16), ist vom Kisokaidō aus nur in der näheren Umgebung von Edo zu sehen; häufiger sahen Reisende den aktiven Vulkan Asama, dessen verheerender Ausbruch im Jahr 1783 dazu führte, dass viele Menschen den Kisokaidō mieden. Er verlief durch sechs Provinzen: Musashi, Kōzuke, Shinano, Mino, Ōmi und Yamashiro, was den heutigen

Präfekturen Saitama, Gunma, Nagano, Gifu und Shiga entspricht. In Reihen angepflanzte Zürgelbäume *(enoki)* säumten ganze Straßenabschnitte, und entlang der Strecke wurde ein System von 69 Poststationen errichtet, an denen zu Transportzwecken Pferde und Lastenträger bereitstanden, während Gasthäuser den Reisenden Verpflegung und Unterkunft boten.

In den Jahren 1874 und 1875 bereiste der deutsche Geograf Johannes Justus Rein (1835–1918) zweimal den Kisokaidō und kam zu dem Schluss: „Wer sich an schönen japanischen Gebirgslandschaften erfreuen will, der mag den Nakasendō wählen, denn kaum findet er in ganz Japan eine Strasse, welche ihm ein so reiches Maass [sic] der verschiedensten Naturschönheiten bietet" (S. 19, 82).[1] Rein war mit seiner Begeisterung für den Kisokaidō offensichtlich nicht allein, denn schon im Sommer 1835 war die Straße erstmals zum Motiv einer Serie von Farbholzschnitten geworden, geschaffen von den beliebten Künstlern Eisen (1790–1848) und Hiroshige (1797–1858). Anfang 1838 war der Druck der 71 Entwürfe – 24 von Eisen und 47 von Hiroshige – abgeschlossen, und die Serie wurde unter dem Titel *Die neunundsechzig Stationen des Kisokaidō (Kisokaidō rokujūkyū tsugi no uchi)* bekannt.[2]

Eine andere jener fünf Hauptstraßen war der Tōkaidō, der nach seinem küstennahen Verlauf Ostmeerstraße genannt wurde; er endete nach 126 *ri* oder rund 495 Kilometern ebenfalls in Kyoto, der alten Hauptstadt und dem Sitz des Kaisers. Gleich hinter der Nihonbashi teilten sich der Kisokaidō und der Tōkaidō und trafen erst in Kusatsu, etwa 26 Kilometer vor Kyoto, wieder zusammen. In der Edo-Zeit (1603–1868) bildete der Tōkaidō die kürzeste und schnellste Verbindung zwischen den beiden Großstädten, was jedoch nicht der einzige Grund für seine Beliebtheit war. Ein beträchtlicher Teil der Strecke bot den Reisenden imposante Ausblicke auf den Vulkan Fuji (S. 17). Darüber hinaus führte eine Abzweigung des Tōkaidō zum Großschrein von Ise, einem sehr populären Pilgerziel.

Der Kisokaidō galt gegenüber dem Tōkaidō als der beschwerlichere Weg, wie sich am Beispiel der *daimyō* zeigt, von denen 146 den Tōkaidō und nur 30 den Kisokaidō als Reiseroute wählten. Außerdem sind vom Kisokaidō, insbesondere von Ausländern, nur wenige Reiseberichte überliefert. Von den insgesamt neun Gebirgspässen des Kisokaidō lagen sechs auf rund 1000 Metern Meereshöhe.[3] Weil steile Pässe besonders im Winter schwer zu überwinden waren, ließ die Regierung acht Streckenabschnitte pflastern, um die Überquerung zu erleichtern (S. 24–25, 30, 31).[4] Weil zudem der Zugang zum Meer erschwert war, unterschied sich der Kisokaidō in der Verpflegungsauswahl erheblich vom Tōkaidō, und frischer Fisch war hier generell Mangelware. Andererseits gab es weniger zeitraubende Flussquerungen als auf dem Tōkaidō, was die Transportkosten um ein Drittel senkte.[5] Reisende neigten dazu, zumindest eine Etappe ihrer Reise auf dem Kisokaidō zurückzulegen, weil sie auf diese Weise unterschiedliche Landschaften genießen und andere Erfahrungen machen konnten; dass ihnen die Reise selbst genauso wichtig war wie das Reiseziel, unterscheidet ihre Zeit von der heutigen, in der viele Menschen die Anreise leider als Ärgernis ansehen, das sie auf sich nehmen müssen, um am ersehnten Ort anzukommen.

Vier der Städte, durch die der Kisokaidō verlief, wurden von Burgen überragt: Takasaki (Tafel 14), Annaka (Tafel 16), Iwamurata (Tafel 23) und Kanō (Tafel 54). Mit 14 892 Einwohnern war Ōtsu 1843

P. 34
Akasaka (detail from plate 57)

Day labourer / Tagelöhner / Travailleur journalier,
c. 1895. Photochrom, hand-coloured.
Paris, Marc Walter Collection

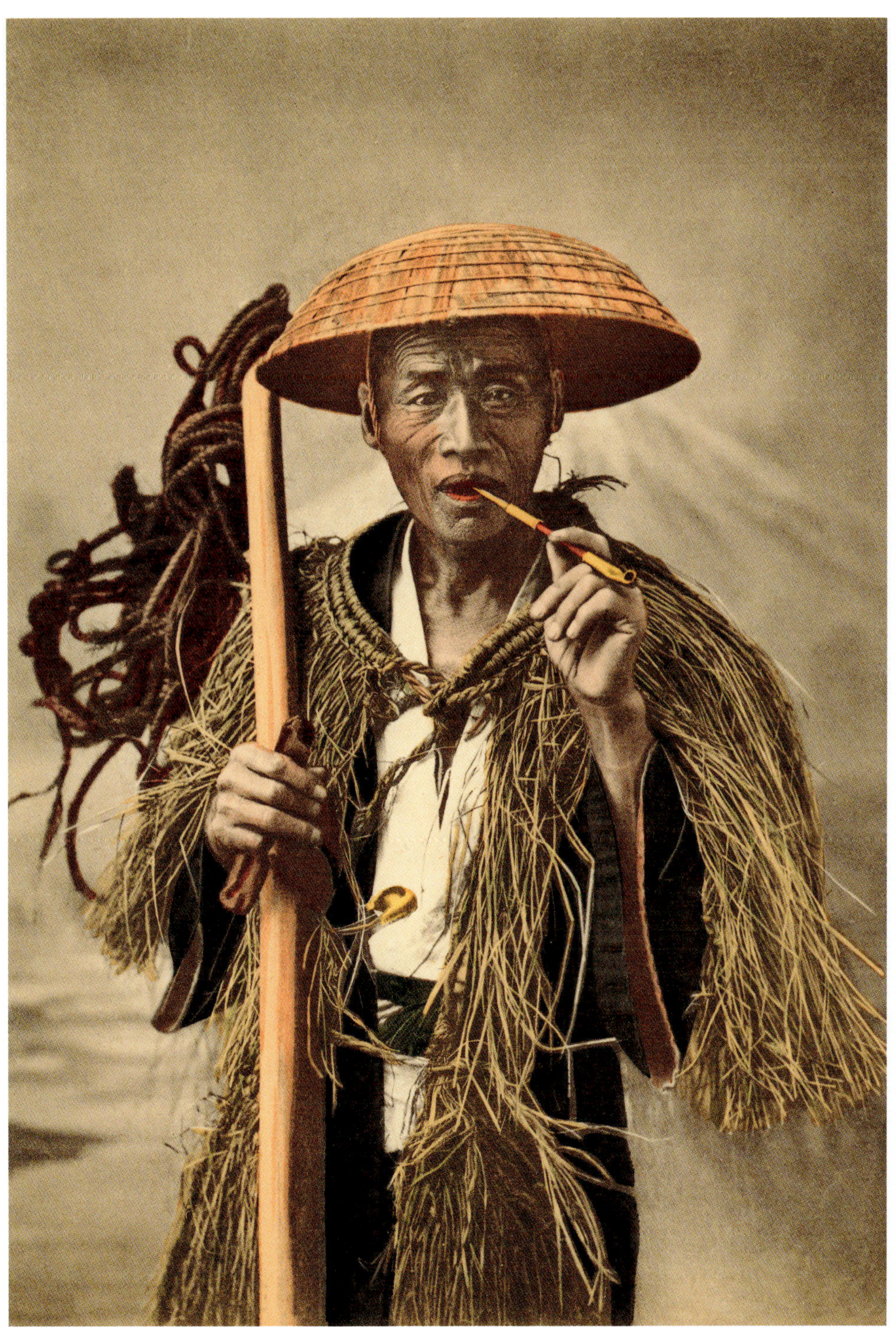

die größte Poststation des Kisokaidō (wie auch des Tōkaidō) und Unuma mit nur 246 Einwohnern die kleinste.[6] In den meisten Ortschaften gab es drei Arten von Gasthäusern, doch frei wählen konnten die Reisenden ihre Unterkunft nicht. Luxusherbergen, *honjin* genannt, waren den *daimyō* und anderen hochrangigen Amtsträgern vorbehalten, während kleinere Beamte und vergleichbare Personen in *waki-honjin* logierten und gewöhnliche Reisende in *hatagoya* abstiegen. Nur wenige Gemeinden besaßen gar kein *honjin*, andere bis zu acht. *Hatagoya* dagegen waren in jeder Ortschaft mit Poststation am Kisokaidō verfügbar, von dreien in Yawata (Tafel 25) bis zu 80 in Fukaya (Tafel 10), bei einem Durchschnitt von 28.[7]

Eine Reiseerlaubnis war erforderlich, um die Kontrollstellen *(sekisho)* zu passieren, die an allen fünf Hauptstraßen eingerichtet waren, um die Waffenlieferungen nach Edo zu überwachen und Familienmitglieder der *daimyō* am Verlassen der Stadt zu hindern *(iri-deppō ni de-onna)*. Der Kisokaidō hatte zwei Kontrollstellen: Usui bei Sakamoto (Tafel 18) und Fukushima (Tafel 38). Jeder Pilger, Händler, Kurier, Handwerker, Tourist und sonstige Reisende wurde angehalten, ebenso wie das Gefolge eines jeden *daimyō*. Die Größe eines *daimyō*-Zuges hing von der Reismenge ab, die im Lehen des Fürsten produziert wurde, und konnte mit Bannerträgern, Fußsoldaten, Lastenträgern und Dienern zwischen 50 und mehr als 400 Mann betragen.

Die Reisenden waren in der Regel zu Fuß unterwegs. Je nach Beschaffenheit des Geländes, Alter und Gesundheitszustand des Wanderers, mitgeführtem Gepäck und anderen Faktoren variierte die Reisezeit teils erheblich. Der durchschnittliche Reisende benötigte für die gesamte Wegstrecke mindestens zwei Wochen. Wer höheren Ranges oder wohlhabend genug war, reiste entsprechend seinem gesellschaftlichem Status zu Pferd oder in der Sänfte. Einfache Sänften wurden von einem Mann vorn und einem Mann hinten getragen. Räderkarren waren verboten, weil sie die Straßen beschädigten; wer es sich aber leisten konnte, engagierte für den Transport seiner Güter Träger mit Packpferden.

Der Kisokaidō im japanischen Holzschnitt

Im Gegensatz zum Tōkaidō war der Kisokaidō in der japanischen Kunst ein sehr seltenes Motiv. Eine 19 Meter lange gemalte Bildrolle aus dem Jahr 1668, die sich in der Sammlung der Staatlichen Parlamentsbibliothek in Tokio befindet, berücksichtigt auf einer topografischen Karte beide Straßen.[8] Bei der sog. *Panoramakarte des Nakasendō (Nakasendō bunken nobe ezu)* in der Sammlung des Nationalmuseums Tokio handelt es sich um eine handkolorierte Landkarte von 1806, die den Kisokaidō von Itabashi (Tafel 2) bis Moriyama (Tafel 68) in zehn Bildrollen zeigt (S. 39). Beide Karten wurden weder für die Allgemeinheit noch als Kunstwerke für Liebhaber geschaffen, sondern dienten den Behörden zu Verwaltungszwecken.

Außerhalb der Regierungsbehörden brachten einfarbige Holzschnittbücher einem allgemeinen Publikum den Kisokaidō näher. Das 1713 erschienene Reisetagebuch *Bericht über die Kiso-Straße (Kisoji no ki)* von Kaibara Ekiken (1630–1714) enthält nur eine Handvoll Abbildungen (S. 43). Der *Illustrierte Wegweiser für die Kiso-Straße (Kisoji anken ezu)* von Sōyō (Lebensdaten unbekannt) aus dem Jahr 1756 ist das genaue Gegenteil: ein kleines Handbuch ohne jeden erzählenden Text, aber

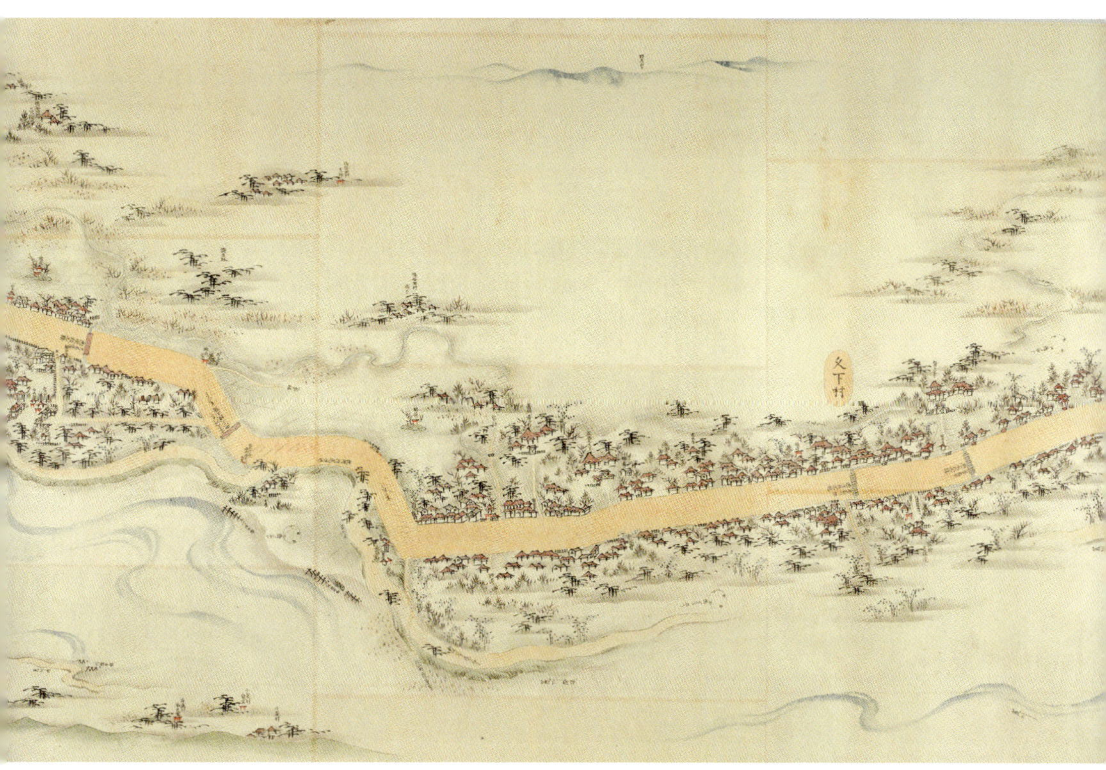

mit 73 Abbildungsseiten, die in einfachen Zeichnungen die gesamte Route zeigen, gefolgt von einer Tabelle der Entfernungen und Transportentgelte (S. 42). Die am weitesten verbreitete Publikation waren die *Ansichten berühmter Stätten an der Kiso-Straße (Kisoji meisho zue)* von Akisato Ritō (aktiv 1780–1814). Sie erschien 1805 in sechs Bänden und kombinierte informative Texte mit detaillierten Illustrationen von Nishimura Chūwa (Lebensdaten unbekannt).

Mit dem 1802 bis 1809 veröffentlichten komischen Roman *Spaziergänge auf dem Tōkaidō (Tōkaidōchū hizakurige)* von Jippensha Ikku (1766–1831) gelang es, das Interesse einer noch breiteren Öffentlichkeit am Reisen zu wecken. Das Werk war vermutlich der Anlass für Katsushika Hokusai (1760–1849), im frühen 19. Jahrhundert die ersten Farbdrucke zum Tōkaidō zu entwerfen, denen innerhalb weniger Jahre weitere folgten (S. 44, 45).[9] In den Fortsetzungsbänden drei bis acht der *Spaziergänge*, die zwischen 1812 und 1816 auf den Markt kamen, bereisen Ikkus Hauptfiguren Kitahachi

The Stations Kumagaya, Fukaya, Honjō, Shinmachi and Kuragano / Die Stationen Kumagaya, Fukaya, Honjō, Shinmachi und Kuragano / Les stations Kumagaya, Fukaya, Honjō, Shinmachi et Kuragano, 1806. Detail from the *Panorama Map of the Nakasendō (Nakasendō bunken nobe ezu).* Ink and colour on paper. Tokyo, National Museum

PP. 40/41
Kumagaya (detail from plate 9)

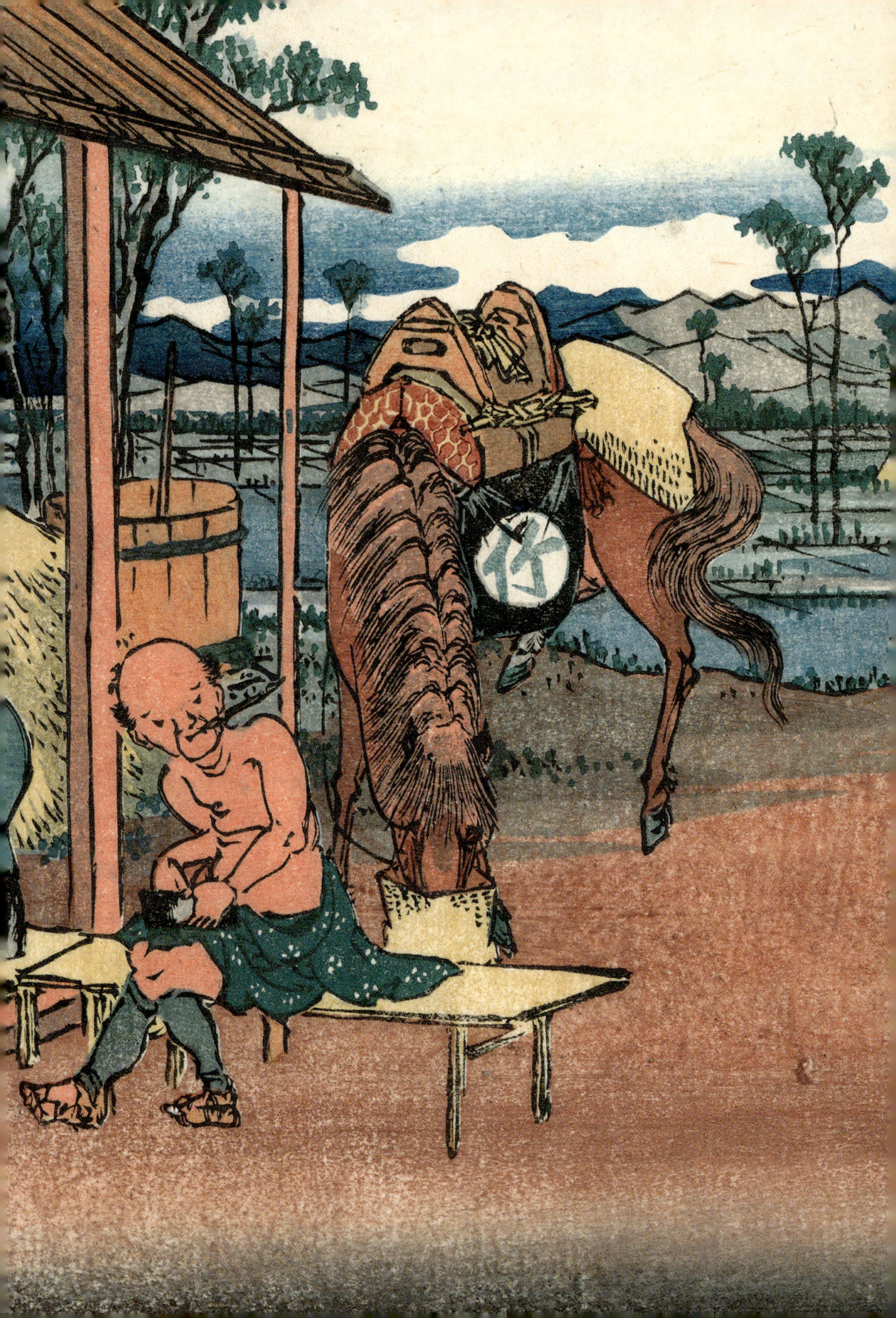

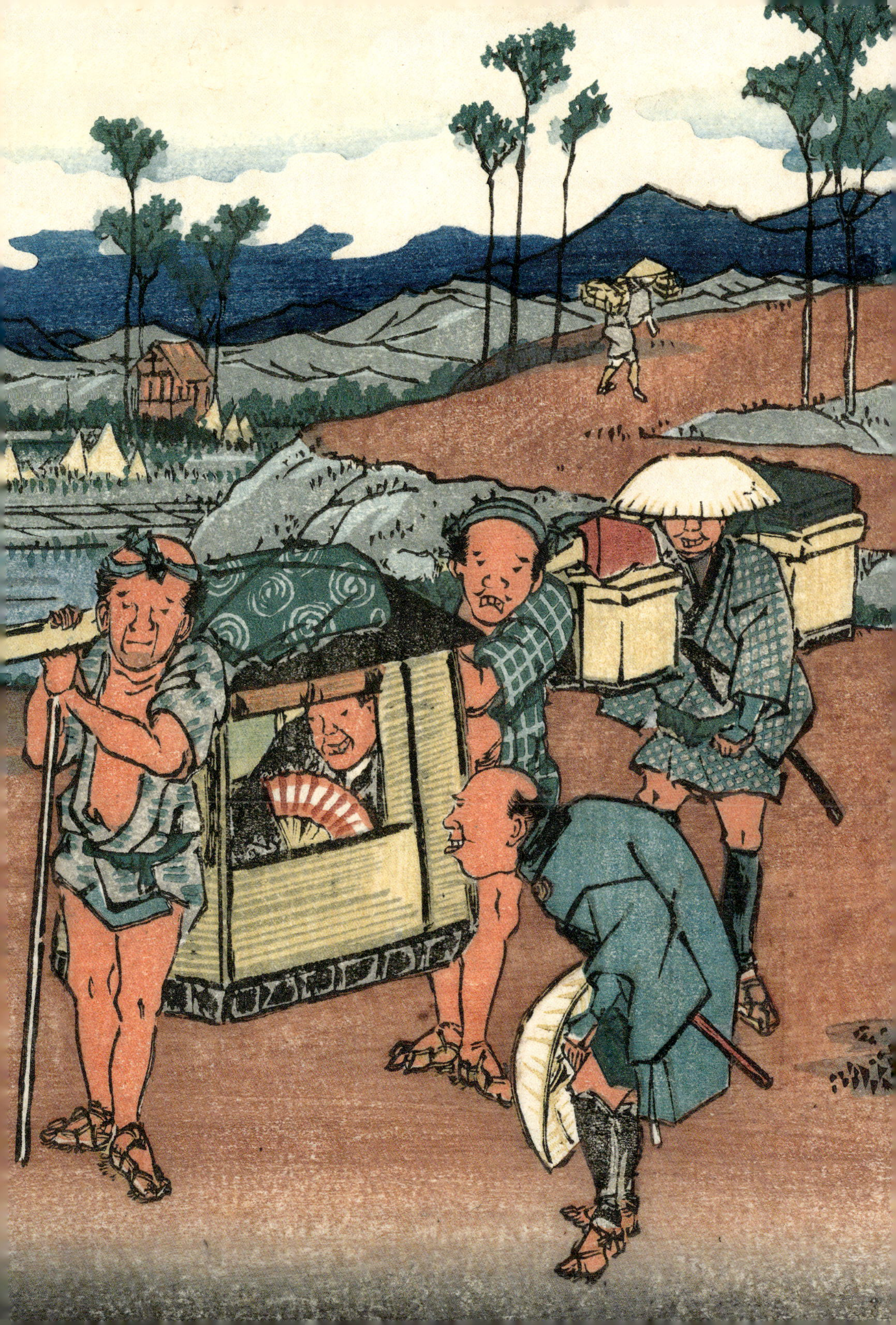

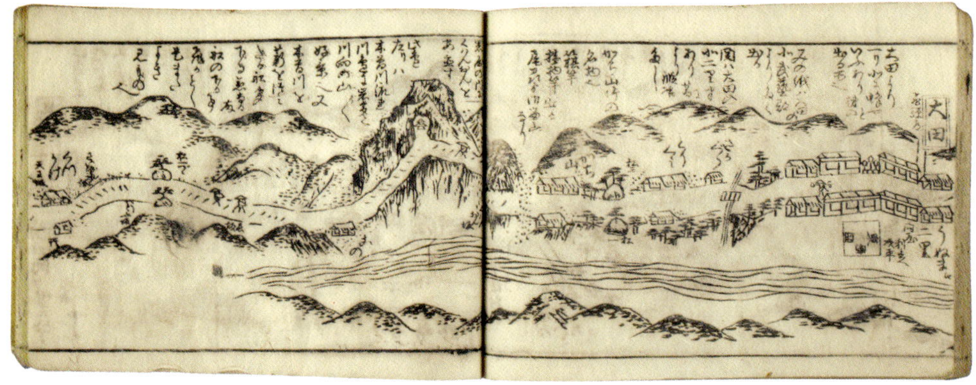

und Yajirōbei den Kisokaidō und erleben auch dort wieder lustige Abenteuer. Eine Welle von Drucken mit dem Kisokaidō als Thema lösten ihre Geschichten zu dieser Zeit jedoch nicht aus.

1818 nutzte Hokusai das allgemeine Interesse am Reisen und begann topografische Karten ganzer Reiserouten aus der Vogelperspektive in beeindruckenden Einzelblattkompositionen zu gestalten. Das erste dieser Werke zeigte den Tōkaidō und wurde von Kadomaruya Jinsuke herausgegeben, der sich einige Monate später mit zwei weiteren Verlegern zusammentat und mit ihnen gemeinsam die Karte des Kisokaidō aus der Vogelschau publizierte, der zugleich der erste Kisokaidō-Druck war (S. 50–51).[10]

Die Kisokaidō-Serie und ihre Künstler

Der Markt für Landschaftsdrucke erlebte in den 1830er Jahren eine beträchtliche Ausweitung. Er bediente nicht nur Reisende, die ein Andenken suchten, sondern auch Kunden, die selbst nicht reisen konnten; vor allem Darstellungen des Fuji und Variationen des Themas der *Acht Ansichten des Biwa-Sees* waren gefragt. Der damals noch kaum bekannte Hiroshige (S. 9) erzielte einen beachtlichen Erfolg, als 1832 die ersten Blätter seiner Serie *Die dreiundfünfzig Stationen des Tōkaidō (Tōkaidō gojūsan tsugi no uchi)*, gemeinhin als „Hōeidō-Tōkaidō" bezeichnet, von Takenouchi Magohachis (1781–1854) kurz zuvor gegründetem Verlag Hōeidō veröffentlicht wurden (S. 10).

Hiroshige wurde 1797 unter dem Namen Andō Tokutarō im Edoer Stadtteil Yayosugashi als Sohn eines Feuerwehroffiziers geboren. Als er im Alter von zwölf Jahren Vollwaise wurde, war er verpflichtet, den väterlichen Posten zu übernehmen. Hiroshige aber hatte andere Zukunftspläne und ging 1810 oder 1811, nachdem er sich erfolglos um die Aufnahme ins Atelier des Künstlers Toyokuni (1769–1825) aus

Ōta. From: Sōyō, *Illustrated Guide to the Kiso-Road (Kisoji anken ezu)*, 1756. Woodblock-printed book. Tokyo, Waseda University Library

View of Lake Suwa / Ansicht des Suwa-Sees / Vue du lac Suwa. From: Kaibara Ekiken, *An Account of the Kiso Road (Kisoji no ki)*, vol. II, 1713. Published by Ibaraki Tazaemon. Woodblock-printed book. Tokyo, National Diet Library

der Utagawa-Schule beworben hatte, bei Toyohiro (1773–1828) in die Lehre, der ebenfalls Anhänger der Utagawa-Schule war.

1812 begann er den Namen Hiroshige zu verwenden. Die ersten anerkannten Werke aus seiner Hand sind Illustrationen für eine 1818 erschienene dreibändige Anthologie von komischen Gedichten sowie mehrere Holzschnitte mit Darstellungen von Schauspielern. 1823 gab er sein Amt bei der Feuerwehr weiter, um sich ganz seiner künstlerischen Laufbahn zu widmen. In den folgenden zehn Jahren entwarf er zahlreiche Serien, in denen er Krieger oder schöne Frauen wiedergab.

Die ersten Landschaftsentwürfe, mit denen Hiroshige Berühmtheit erlangte, erschienen Anfang der 1830er Jahre, darunter an erster Stelle die Serie *Die dreiundfünfzig Stationen des Tōkaidō (Tōkaidō gojūsan tsugi no uchi)*. Der um 1832/33 von Hōeidō verlegte Bilderzyklus war einer von 20, die diese Überlandstraße darstellten (S. 70). Neben dem Tōkaidō umfassten Hiroshiges Landschaften, die bisweilen in Zusammenarbeit mit anderen Künstlern entstanden, Serien mit Ansichten der Provinz Ōmi, des Flusses Tama, berühmter Stätten in Kyoto und Osaka sowie rund 20 Bildfolgen mit Motiven seiner Heimatstadt Edo, die von seinem Meisterwerk *Einhundert berühmte Ansichten von Edo* (*Meisho Edo hyakkei*, 1856–1858; S. 71) gekrönt wurden. Insgesamt kamen auf diese Weise Tausende von einzigartigen Entwürfen zusammen.

Hiroshige tat sich auch mit *kachōga*, Bildern von Vögeln und Blumen, hervor und schuf Hunderte von Blättern dieses Genres. Seine gesamte Holzschnittproduktion beläuft sich auf mehr als 4500 Druckvorlagen sowie Illustrationen für fast 150 Bücher. Hinzu kommen mehrere hundert Gemälde, darunter 200 Auftragsarbeiten für die Fürsten des Oda-Clans in der Provinz Tendō.

Der Erfolg seiner Entwürfe hatte viele Facetten. Hiroshige besaß große Übung darin, die Bildsprache anderer Künstler und Illustratoren auf den Einzelblattdruck im Farbholzschnitt zu übertragen. Darüber hinaus zeugen seine eindrucksvollen Kompositionen, die mit ihren kühnen Rahmungen und

der Zentralperspektive bisweilen einen dramatischen Effekt erzielen, von einem ebenso scharfsinnigen wie fantasievollen Gestaltungskonzept. Wie sein Lehrmeister Toyohiro vermochte Hiroshige die Figuren, die er mit Feingefühl und gelegentlich einem Schuss sanften Humors darstellte, geschickt in die lyrische Stille seiner Landschaftssituationen einzubinden.

Im Hōeidō-Tōkaidō-Zyklus betonte Hiroshige

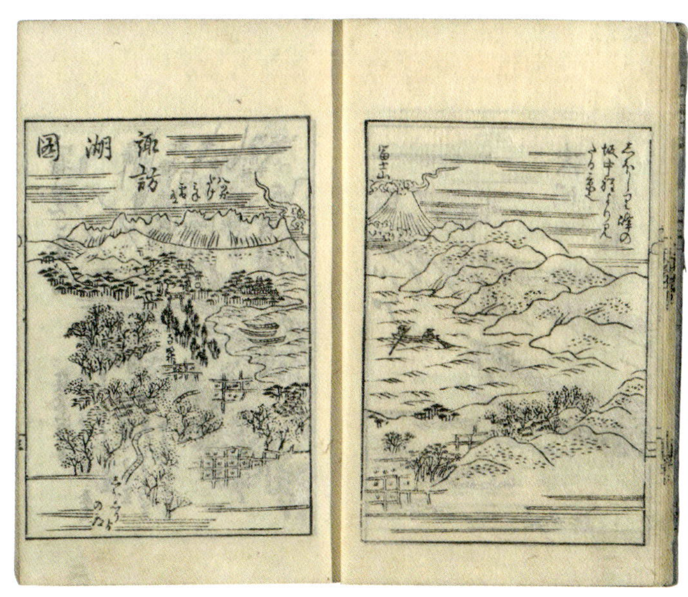

den malerischen Aspekt der Straße, indem er einen neuartigen Stil verwendete und diesen im *ōban*-Format präsentierte (ca. 27 × 39 cm), einem seinerzeit ungewöhnlich großen Format für Landschaftsmotive.[11] Könnten Hiroshiges Interpretationen für die ersten Blätter der Serie noch auf eigenen Reiseerfahrungen beruht haben, so entsprangen bald mehr und mehr Ansichten eindeutig den Schwarz-Weiß-Abbildungen anderer Künstler, die in diversen Reisehandbüchern publiziert worden waren.[12] Von ihrem eigenen Erfolg beflügelt, schmiedeten Hiroshige und Takenouchi Pläne für weitere Landschaftsthemen und machten sie auf neuen Werbezetteln publik, die sie in gebundene, vom ersten Monat des Jahres 1834 an verkaufte Alben der vollständigen Tōkaidō-Serie einlegten. So warben sie unter anderem für die erste Kisokaidō-Serie, die als eine *Folge wahrhaftiger Ansichten des Kiso in Landschafts- und Genrebildern (Kiso dōchū shinkei tsuzuki sansui jinbutsu-e)* angekündigt wurde.

Wie Hiroshige entstammte auch Eisen (S. 11, 90) einer in Edo ansässigen Samurai-Familie. Sein Vater war der berühmte Kalligraf Ikeda Masahei Shigeharu. In jungen Jahren studierte der als Ikeda Yoshinobu zur Welt gekommene Eisen Malerei bei Hakkeisai, einem Künstler der Kano-Schule, der Anfang des 19. Jahrhunderts aktiv war. Später lebte er bei dem Sohn des Holzschnittmeisters Kikugawa Eizan (1787–1867), und auch wenn er sich später als Schüler Eizans ausgab, sind das Ausmaß und die Details dieser Verbindung unklar. Eisen schloss sich keiner Schule des *ukiyo-e* wie Utagawa oder Torii an und signierte viele seiner Werke mit dem Künstlernamen Keisai.

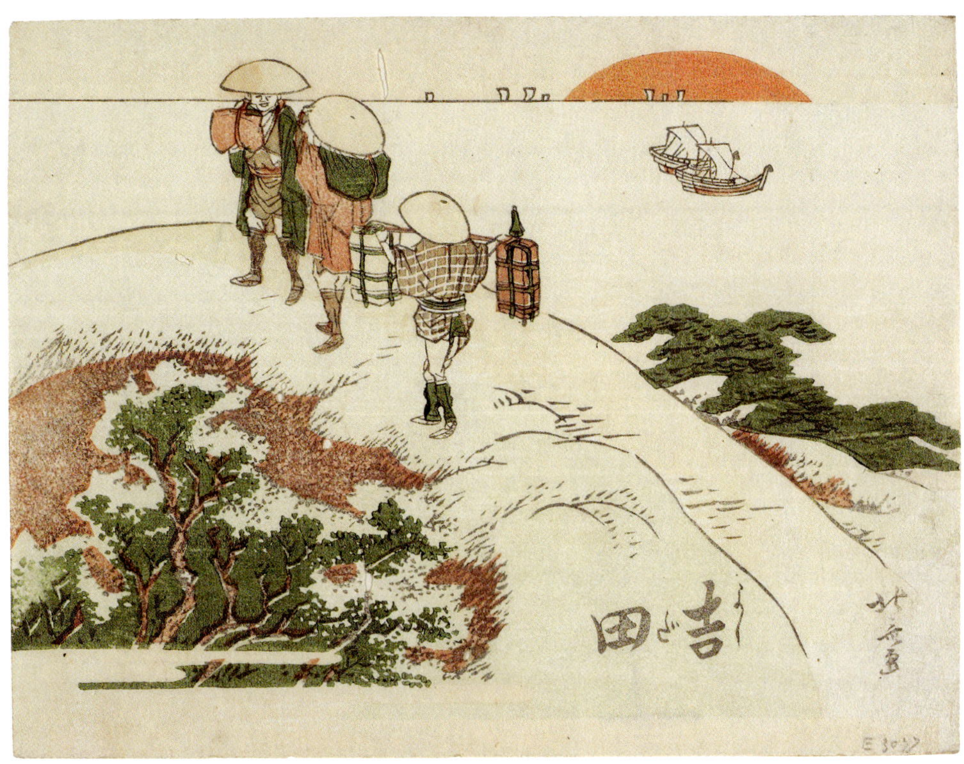

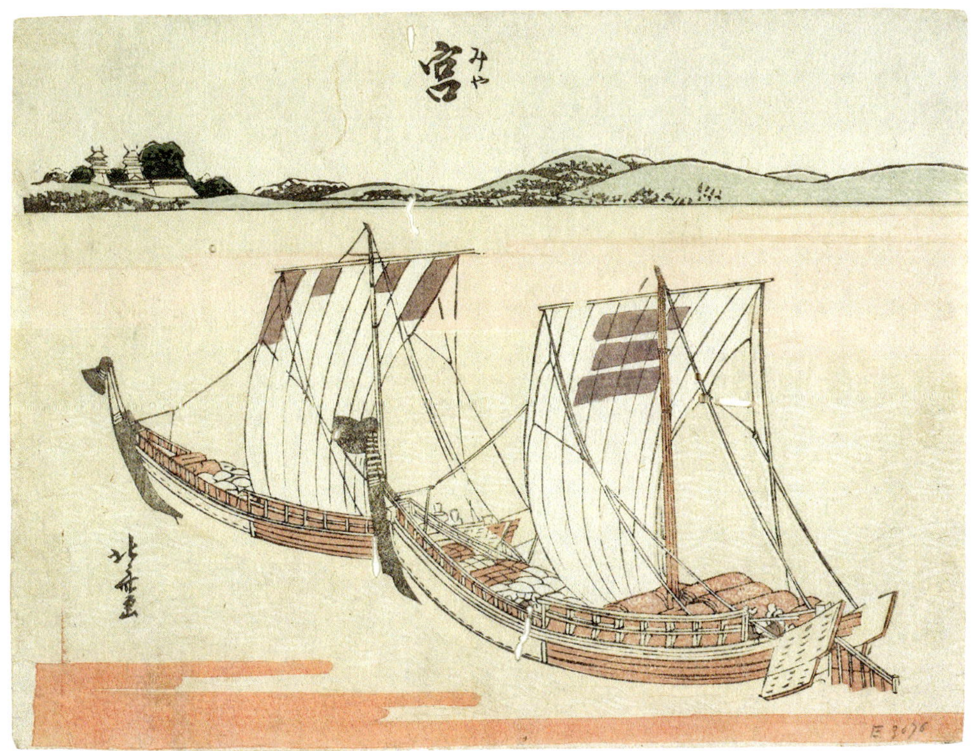

Eisen entwarf rund 1900 Holzdrucke und schuf Illustrationen für annähernd 400 Bücher aller Genres und Themen. Seine Spezialität aber waren *bijinga*, Darstellungen schöner Frauen (S. 74). Das erste von ihm veröffentlichte Werk ist wahrscheinlich eine Schönheit, die in einem 1811 erschienenen Buch gezeigt wird.[13] In Anlehnung an Eizan gestaltete auch Eisen seine Schönheiten anfangs nach Vorbildern von Kitagawa Utamaro (1753–1806), bevor er allmählich seinen eigenen kantigen und unverhohlen sinnlichen Stil entwickelte, der schließlich den Markt beherrschte. Wie viele seiner Mitstreiter entwarf Eisen auch erotische Bilder, die als *shunga* bekannt waren.

Neben seiner Tätigkeit als Holzschnittkünstler ging Eisen vielen anderen Beschäftigungen nach. Er verkaufte kosmetischen Gesichtspuder, leitete unter dem Namen Wakatakeya Satosuke ein Bordell in Nezu und erwies sich als produktiver Schriftsteller. Unter Anleitung von Namiki Gohei II. (1768–1819) lernte er, Stücke für das Kabuki-Theater zu schreiben, die unter dem Pseudonym Chiyoda Saiichi veröffentlicht wurden. Als Ippitsuan Kakō verfasste er Unterhaltungsliteratur, seine Essays erschienen unter den Namen Mumeiō und Kaedegawa Shiin. Eines seiner bekanntesten literarischen Werke, *Essays eines*

Katsushika Hokusai, *Yoshida*. From an untitled Tōkaidō series known as *Yoko koban Tōkaidō*, c. 1802. Colour woodblock print, *yotsugiriban*. Minneapolis Institute of Art, X2003.1.7

Katsushika Hokusai, *Miya*. From an untitled Tōkaidō series known as *Yoko koban Tōkaidō*, c. 1802. Colour woodblock print, *yotsugiriban*. Minneapolis Institute of Art, X2003.1.10

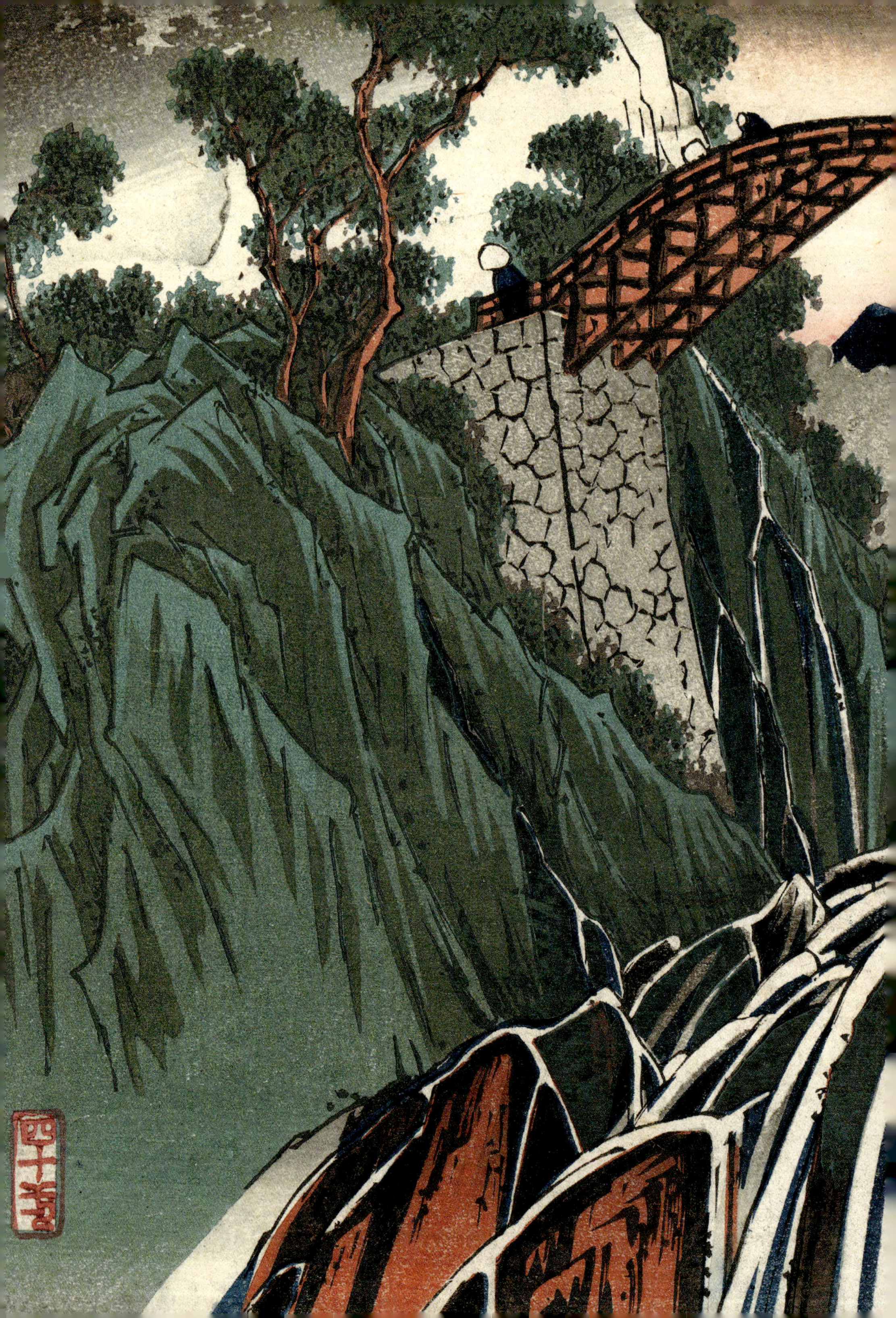

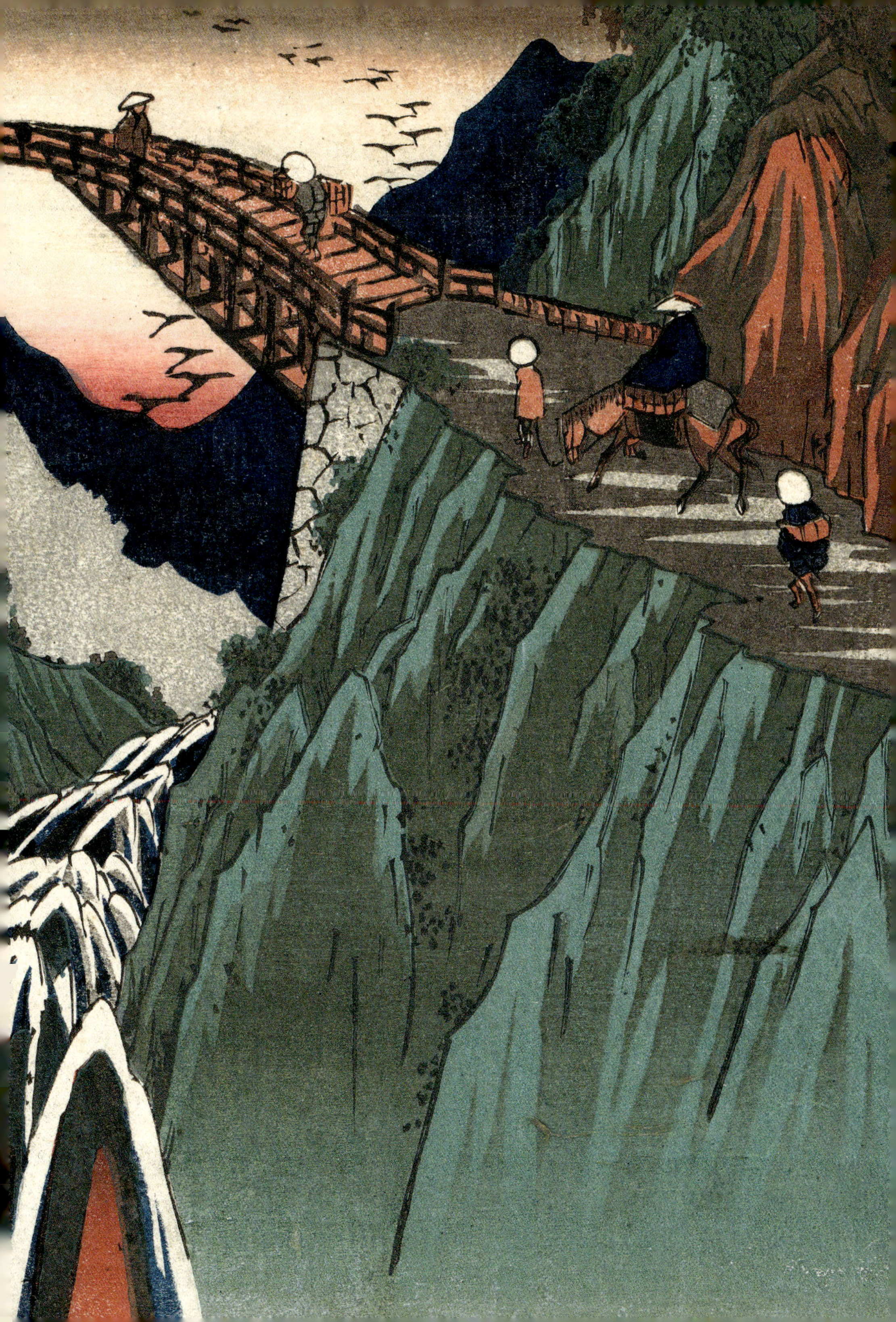

namenlosen Alten (Mumeiō zuihitsu, 1833), ist die Überarbeitung einer erstmals 1789 von Ōta Nanpo (1749–1823) zusammengestellten Sammlung von Holzschnittkünstlerbiografien namens *Ukiyo-e-Miszellen (Ukiyo-e ruikō)*. Eisens Ergänzung zu Nanpos Sammelwerk nimmt Bezug auf seine eigene Lebensweise als starker Trinker und auf seine Zechgelage in den Freudenvierteln von Edo.

Takenouchi Magohachi wurde 1781 im Edoer Stadtbezirk Kyōbashi als zweiter Sohn des Pfandleihers Magoshichi geboren (S. 10). Zwischen 1832 und 1837 (Tenpō 3–8), wenn nicht länger, illustrierte er unter dem Namen Bizan *kyōka*-Gedichtbände. Vermutlich begann er ebenfalls 1832 mit dem Hōeidō-Verlag die ersten Blätter der frühesten Tōkaidō-Serie Hiroshiges herauszugeben. 1833 brachte Takenouchi erstmals Drucke von Kabuki-Schauspielern und schönen Frauen nach Vorlagen von Kunisada (1786–1865) sowie gedruckte Kriegerdarstellungen von Utagawa Kuniyoshi (1797–1861) auf den Markt. 1834 begann er illustrierte Erzählungen zu verlegen, darunter *Die Legende von Mikuni Tarōs Rückkehr (Mikuni Tarō sairai den)* mit Illustrationen von Kuniyoshi, Utagawa Kuninao (1793–1854) und ihm selbst. Zwei Bände dieses dreibändigen Werks, das im ersten Monat des Jahres 1835 erschien, enthielten im hinteren Teil identische Werbezettel (S. 28), die wiederum Hiroshige als Künstler eines neuen, diesmal als *Bildfolge von Landschaften am Kiso (Kiso dōchū fūkei tsuzuki-e)* bezeichneten Kisokaidō-Zyklus aufführten.[14]

Die Ankündigungen von 1834 und 1835 wurden noch vor dem Erscheinen der ersten Blätter dieser Serie veröffentlicht und spiegeln lediglich die Ziele der Zusammenarbeit zwischen Takenouchi und Hiroshige wider. Die Wirklichkeit aber sollte ganz anders aussehen. Anstelle von Hiroshige war es Eisen, der 1835 begann, für Takenouchi an der Serie zu arbeiten. Anders als Hiroshige gehörte Eisen nicht der einflussreichen Utagawa-Schule von Holzschnittkünstlern an. Takenouchi muss ihn daher ganz bewusst so beliebten Utagawa-Künstlern wie Kunisada und Kuniyoshi, mit denen er schon früher zusammengearbeitet hatte, vorgezogen haben – womöglich, weil diese beiden sich nur bedingt für Landschaftsdrucke interessierten. In den Jahrzehnten zuvor hatte Eisen bereits etliche Landschaften für eine Reihe von Verlegern ausgeführt, allerdings ohne großen Erfolg, wenn man von einer Serie perspektivischer Ansichten berühmter Stätten in Edo absieht. Diese waren Anfang der 1830er Jahre erschienen und wiesen jeweils einen breiten schwarzen Rahmen auf, der mit weißer Schrift in niederländischer Sprache verziert war.[15] Mitte der 1820er Jahre hatte Eisen auch eine Tōkaidō-Serie entworfen, die sich jedoch auf schöne Frauen konzentrierte, während die Landschaften auf kleine, neben den Figurendarstellungen eingefügte Kartuschen begrenzt waren (S. 77).[16]

Die erste Kisokaidō-Serie beginnt mit der Brücke Nihonbashi in Edo. In seine Zeichnung fügte Eisen einen Verweis auf das Tierkreiszeichen für das Jahr Tenpō 6 (gleichgesetzt mit 1835) ein: Das Zeichen für Schaf *(hitsuji)* prangt auf einem aufgespannten Schirm in der Bildmitte.[17] Man nimmt daher an, dass die ersten Blätter der Serie in diesem Jahr veröffentlicht wurden; warum jedoch Eisen und nicht Hiroshige sie ausführte, darüber lässt sich nur spekulieren. Vielleicht wollte Takenouchi nicht länger warten, während Hiroshige auf Reisen und nicht verfügbar war; im fünften Monat des Jahres z. B. verließ der Künstler Edo für mehrere Wochen, um am Senkokuji-Tempel im nahe gelegenen Kanagawa zu malen. Hiroshige scheint keine Einwände gegen Eisens Beteiligung an dem Projekt gehabt zu haben, als er selbst später dazustieß. In der Werbebeilage eines Buches, das Takenouchi im ersten Monat des Jahres 1836 herausgab, wird Eisen schließlich als Künstler genannt; dass bereits Drucke veröffentlicht wurden, legt

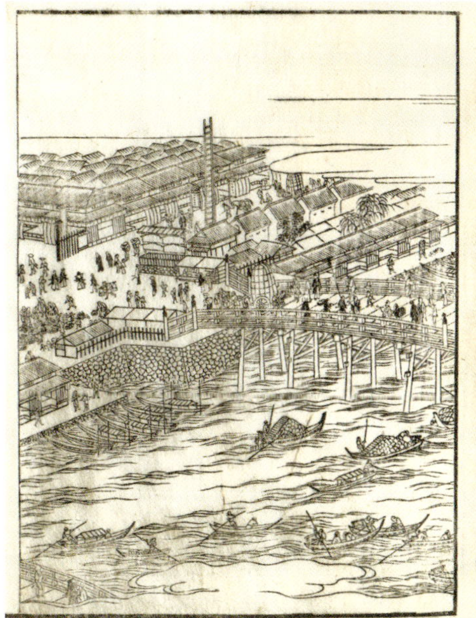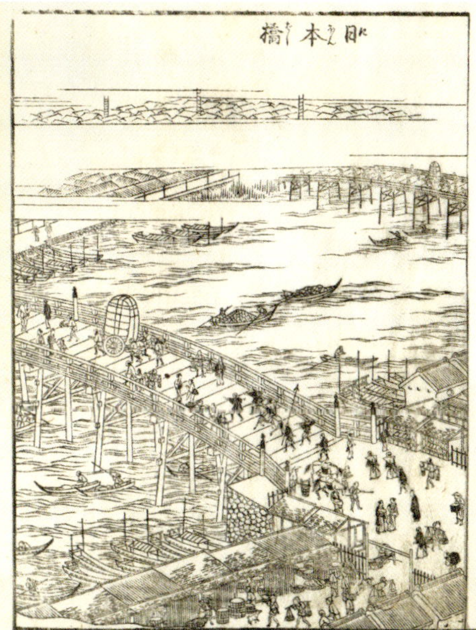

die Art nahe, wie die Serie beschrieben wird: als *Folge großformatiger Brokatdrucke der Kiso-Straße (Kisoji tsuzuki ōnishiki-e)*.[18] Die Werbung in einem zweiten Buch von 1836 verzeichnet Eisen erneut als Künstler und weist mit dem Titel *Folge von Darstellungen des Kiso im Querformat (Kiso dōchū tsuzuki yoko-e)* darauf hin, dass die Serie nicht aus Hochformaten, sondern aus querformatigen Holzschnitten besteht.[19]

Von den 71 Blättern, die am Ende gedruckt wurden, gingen allerdings nur 24 auf Eisens Entwürfe zurück. Alle Drucke sind nummeriert, beginnend mit der Nihonbashi als Blatt Nummer eins, das auch den Titel *Erstes Blatt des Kisokaidō in Fortsetzungen (Kisokaidō tsuzuki no ichi)* trägt. Hatte Eisen die ersten elf Blätter noch chronologisch ausgeführt, so scheint er die anschließend von ihm dargestellten Stationen frei gewählt zu haben. Takenouchi gab daraufhin elf weitere Blätter von Eisen heraus; ferner werden zwei unsignierte Drucke dem Künstler zugeschrieben. Die 22 signierten Entwürfe dürften bis Ende 1836 in gedruckter Form vorgelegen haben. Um diese Zeit endete Eisens Beteiligung an dem Projekt. Er wandte sich stattdessen wieder dem Tōkaidō zu und schuf eine Serie von Darstellungen schöner Frauen. Dabei platzierte er jede von ihnen auf einem Wolkenband vor einer Landschaft, die das obere Drittel des Bildhintergrunds einnimmt.[20]

PP. 46/47
Nojiri (detail from plate 41)

Nishimura Chūwa, *The Nihonbashi Bridge /*
Die Nihonbashi-Brücke / Le pont Nihonbashi.
From: Akisatō Ritō, *Views of Famous Sights along the*
Kiso Road (Kisoji meisho zue), vol. 5, 1805. Woodblock-
printed book. Munich, Bayerische Staatsbibliothek

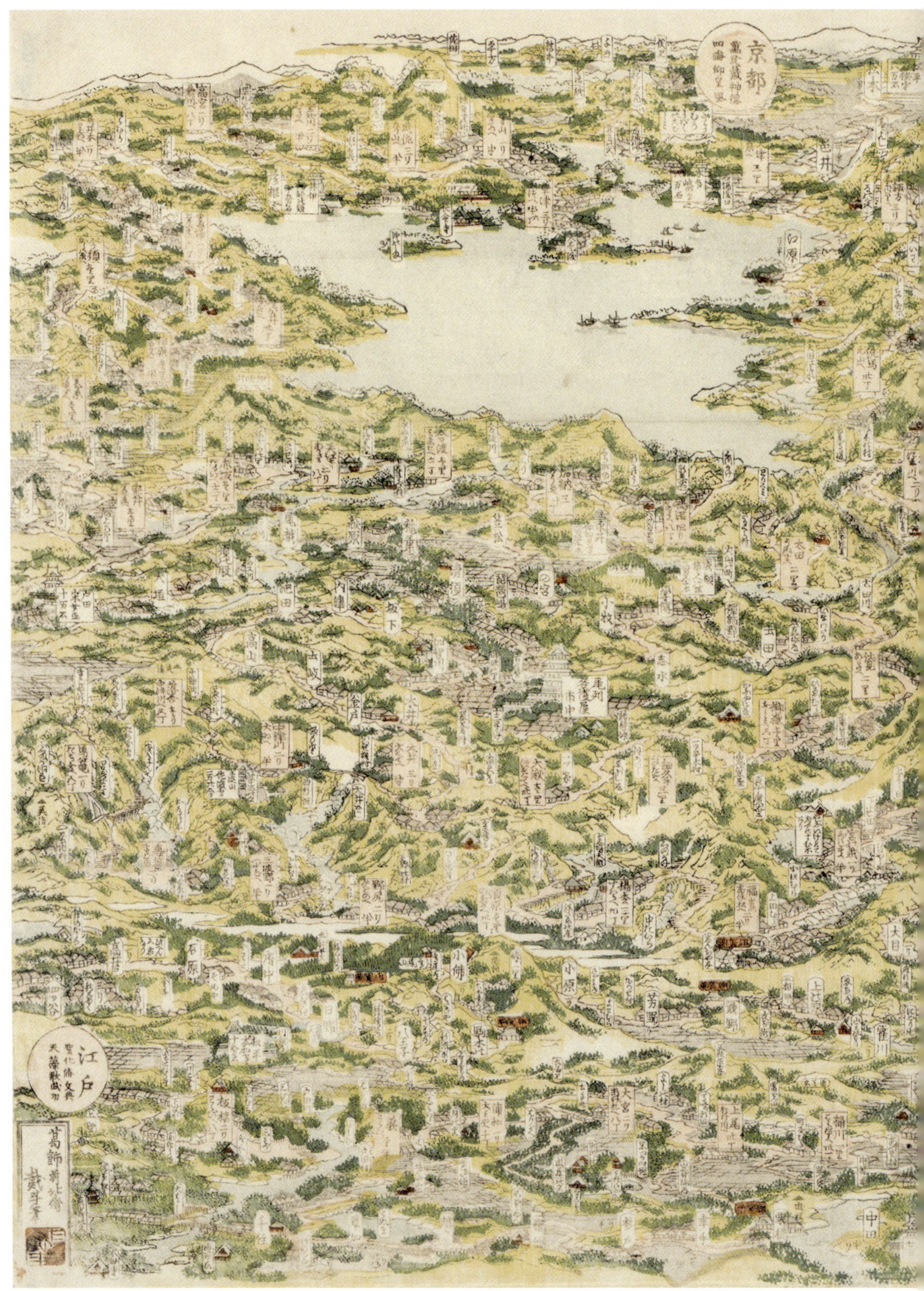

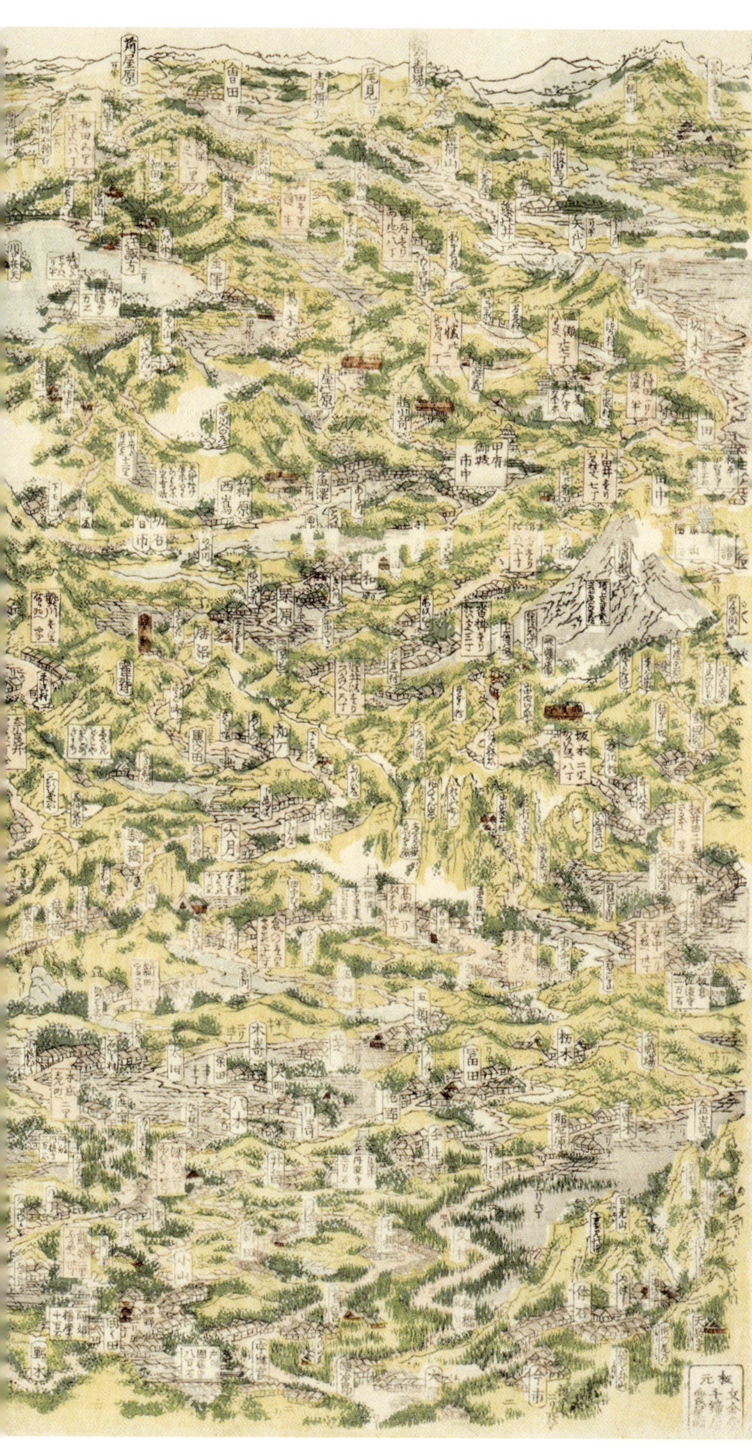

KATSUSHIKA HOKUSAI, *Pictorial Map of Central Japan: Famous Sights along the Kiso Road / Bildkarte Zentraljapans: Berühmte Stätten der Kiso-Straße / Carte illustrée du Japon central: Vues célèbres le long de la route Kiso*, 1819. Publishers: Kadomaruya Jinsuke, Suharaya Mohei and Kawachiya Tasuke. Colour woodblock print, 43 × 54 cm / 16 ⅞ × 21 ¼ in. San Diego Museum of Art, 1985.19

Das Fehlen jedes expliziten Hinweises auf die 69 Kisokaidō-Stationen in der Werbung oder in Eisens Bildtiteln lässt den Schluss zu, dass weder in der ursprünglichen Planung von Takenouchi und Hiroshige noch während der ersten Projektphase mit Eisen als Künstler die Absicht bestand, einen vollständigen Zyklus mit je einem Motiv pro Station zu produzieren. In wirtschaftlicher Hinsicht war dies für den Verleger mit einem zu hohen Risiko verbunden, denn der Kisokaidō war nicht populär genug, um sich vorab auf Investitionen in 71 Drucke festzulegen. Gestützt wird diese These durch die Tatsache, dass es in der Geschichte des *ukiyo-e* keine weiteren Kisokaidō-Serien gibt. Nur zweimal noch sollte der Kisokaidō als Serienmotiv in Erscheinung treten; beide Druckfolgen entstanden 1852/53 auf dem historischen Höhepunkt des *ukiyo-e*. Die jeweils 72 Blätter umfassenden Serien nach Vorlagen von Kuniyoshi bzw. Kunisada nutzen den Kisokaidō jedoch lediglich als Klammer: In Wirklichkeit dienen sie der Präsentation von Legenden und Kabuki-Theaterstücken und zeigen nahezu ausschließlich allgemeine Landschaftselemente, die keinerlei Bezug zu den benannten Orten mit Poststationen aufweisen und überall im ländlichen Japan angesiedelt sein könnten (S. 53, 56, 59).[21] Genau genommen trifft dies auch auf die meisten Entwürfe Eisens zu. Dass er sich offensichtlich von anderen Bildwelten inspirieren ließ, beweisen seine ersten drei Kisokaidō-Entwürfe Nihonbashi, Itabashi und Warabi. Sie erinnern den Betrachter an Nihonbashi, Shinagawa und Kawasaki, die ersten drei Blätter der Tōkaidō-Serie von Hiroshige. Die übrigen Eisen-Drucke enthalten keine spezifischen Landschaftsmerkmale, die mit bestimmten geografischen Orten verknüpft werden könnten, sondern basieren auf Illustrationen aus dem oben erwähnten Werk *Kisoji meisho zue* (S. 23, 30, 49).[22]

Takenouchis Kisokaidō-Projekt kam also zum Stillstand, und anscheinend begann er zu dieser Zeit auch generell das Interesse am Verlegen zu verlieren. Manche Historiker meinen, dass der kleine und relativ junge Verlag Takenouchis in finanzielle Schwierigkeiten geriet, nachdem er den Kisokaidō-Zyklus ins Programm genommen hatte, und dass er deshalb eine Partnerschaft mit dem Verlagshaus Iseya Rihei eingehen musste. Doch anders als im Fall der Tōkaidō-Serie einige Jahre zuvor, als es zu einer echten Zusammenarbeit Takenouchis mit dem etablierten Verlag Tsuruya Kiemon gekommen war, übernahm Iseya Rihei praktisch das gesamte Kisokaidō-Projekt und publizierte letzten Endes fast zwei Drittel der Drucke ohne Takenouchis Beteiligung. Der sog. Tenpō-Hunger in der zweiten Hälfte der 1830er Jahre wirkte sich auf Edo zwar kaum aus, er könnte aber den Markt für Drucke negativ beeinflusst haben, da weniger Reisende aus den von der Hungersnot betroffenen Provinzen kamen und folglich weniger Landschaftsdrucke und andere Souvenirs verkauft wurden. Nach den vielen erhaltenen Varianten zu urteilen, die darauf hindeuten, dass die Druckstöcke bis zur völligen Abnutzung verwendet und bisweilen sogar durch neue ersetzt wurden, muss der Absatz von Hiroshiges Tōkaidō-Serie und Eisens Kisokaidō-Drucken gleichwohl phänomenal gewesen sein. Es liegt daher nahe, dass Takenouchis Rückzug aus dem Verlagsgeschäft auf einer bewussten Entscheidung beruhte, zumal er sich den Verlag als Hobbyschriftsteller und -maler erst mit Anfang 50 aus purem Vergnügen zugelegt hatte und dieser nicht seine einzige, sondern eine zusätzliche Einnahmequelle war. Die letzten mit Sicherheit datierbaren Werke aus dem Verlag stammen aus dem Frühjahr 1837, als Takenouchi einige Schauspielerdrucke und ein weiteres seiner selbst verfassten Bücher veröffentlichte. Er starb 1854.

Vermutlich Ende 1836 oder Anfang 1837 übernahm der alteingesessene Verlag Iseya Rihei, der offiziell als Kinjudō firmierte und seit 1790 tätig war, die Kisokaidō-Serie von Takenouchi und investierte

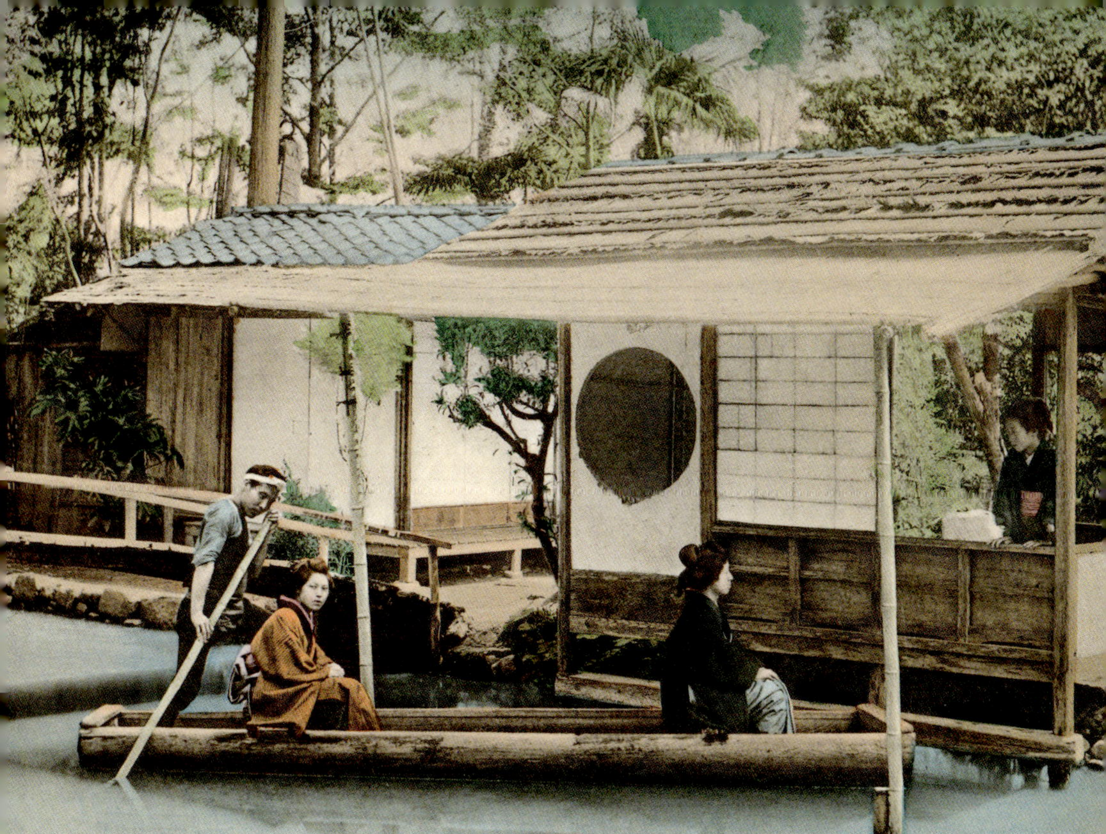

kräftig in das Projekt: Iseya erwarb die Druckstöcke der Eisen-Entwürfe und beauftragte Hiroshige, die Serie mit neuen Entwürfen zu vervollständigen. Iseya Rihei verfügte über große Erfahrung im Druck von Landschaften und hatte Anfang des 19. Jahrhunderts überdies zwei Tōkaidō-Genreserien von Hokusai herausgegeben. Von Eisen waren bei Iseya in den 1820er Jahren nur einige „Schönheiten"-Drucke erschienen, und wenngleich der Verlag sonst mit Künstlern der Utagawa-Schule wie Toyokuni, Kuniyasu (1794–1832), Kuniyoshi und vor allem Kunisada kooperierte, hatte er noch nie mit Hiroshige gearbeitet. Die Empfehlung, sich an Hiroshige zu wenden, könnte von Takenouchi oder Kunisada gekommen sein, Iseyas führendem Künstler der 1830er Jahre, der mit Hiroshige befreundet gewesen sein soll. In jedem Fall verriet der neue Serientitel für alle von Hiroshige entworfenen Blätter, dass das neu gebildete Produktionsteam das Ziel hatte, eine lückenlose Bildfolge vorzulegen: *Die neunundsechzig Stationen des Kisokaidō (Kisokaidō rokujūkyū tsugi no uchi)*.

Vier der Drucke nach Hiroshiges Entwürfen – Takasaki, Karuizawa, Fukushima und Toriimoto (Tafeln 14, 19, 38, 64) – tragen Verlagszeichen sowohl von Takenouchi als auch von Iseya und wurden daher womöglich zuerst publiziert. Auf sie folgen zwei unsignierte Drucke, Itahana und Sakamoto

Two girls in a canoe / Zwei Mädchen im Kanu /
Deux filles dans un canoë, c. 1895. Photochrom,
hand-coloured. Paris, Marc Walter Collection

PP. 54/55
Okegawa (detail from plate 7)

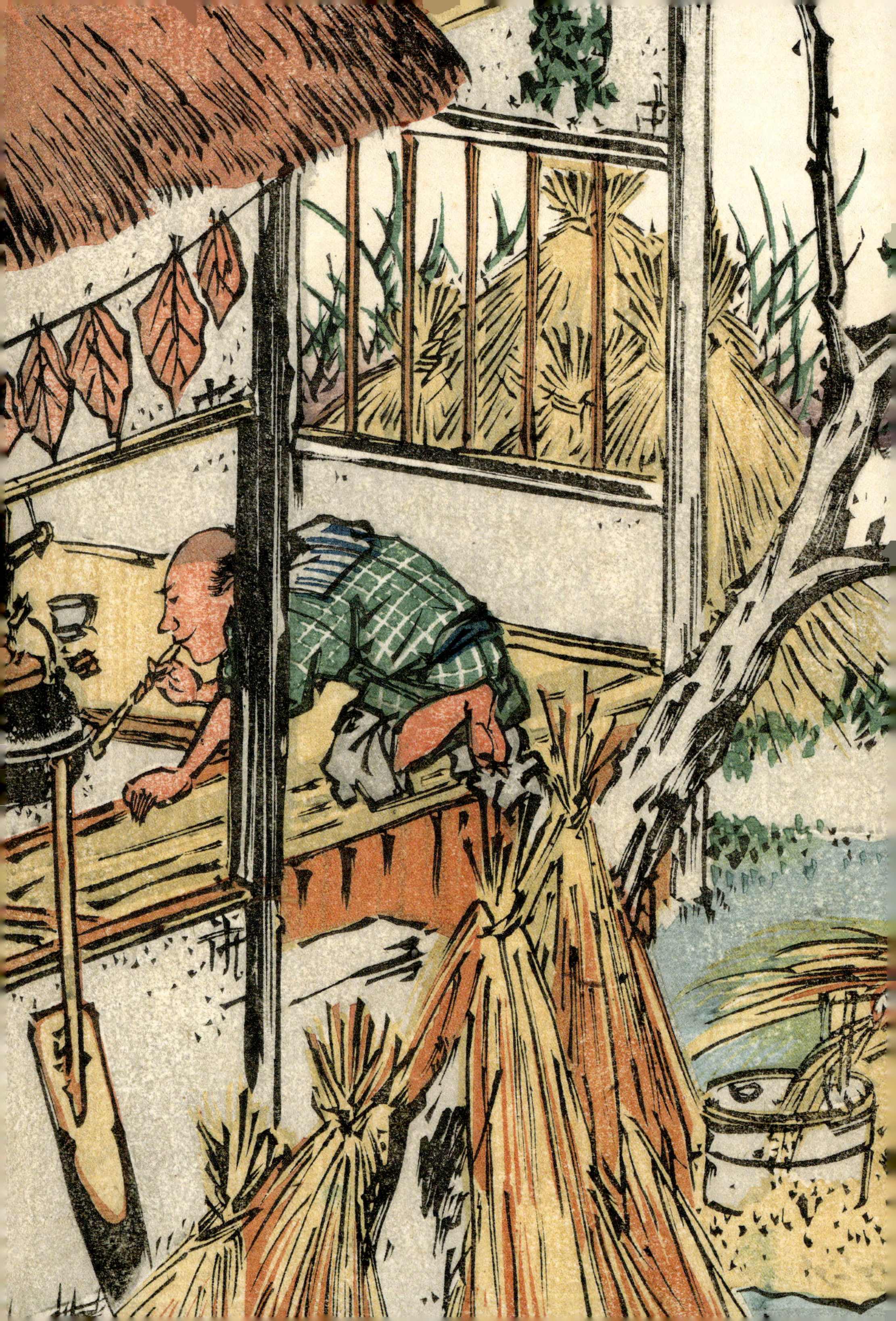

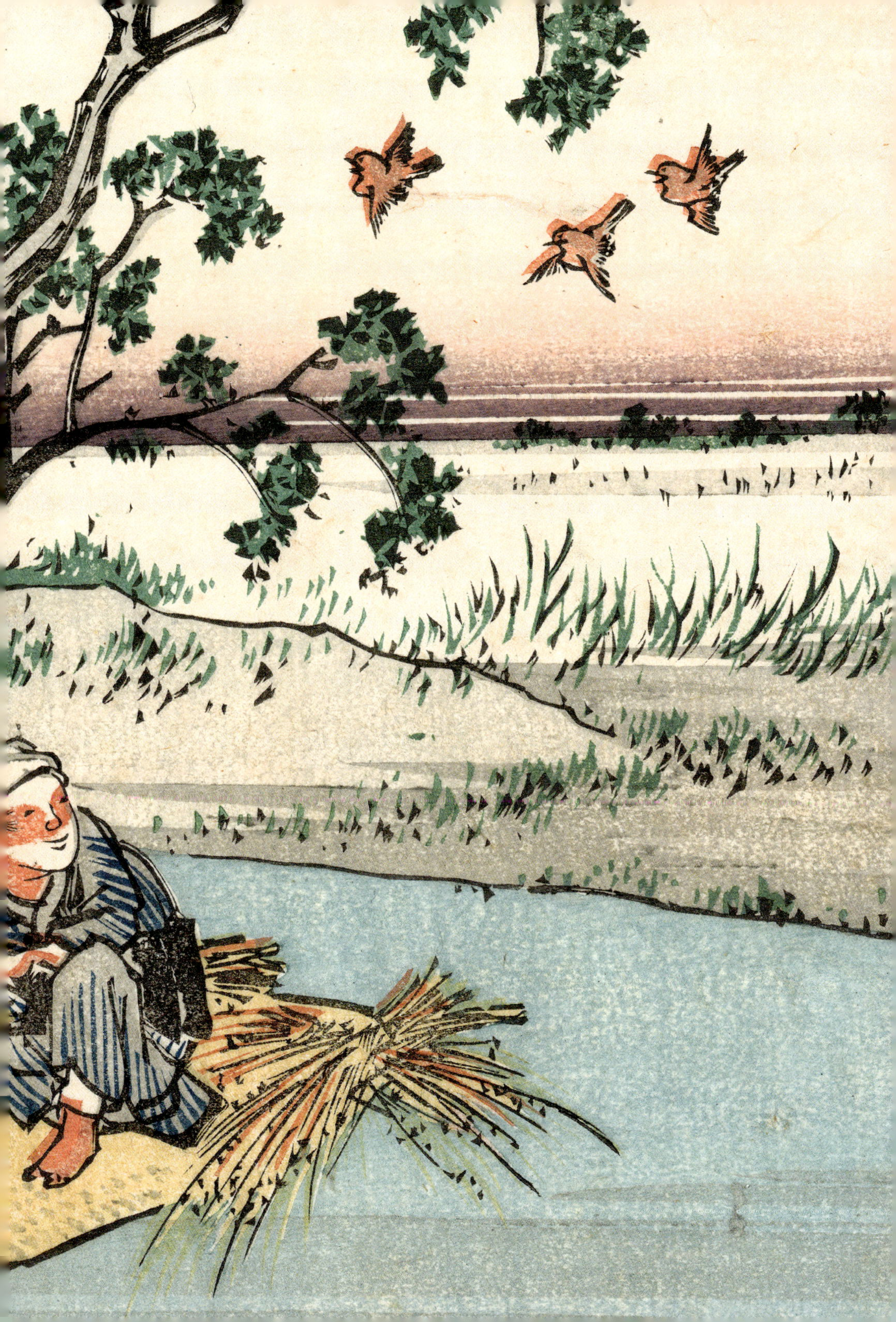

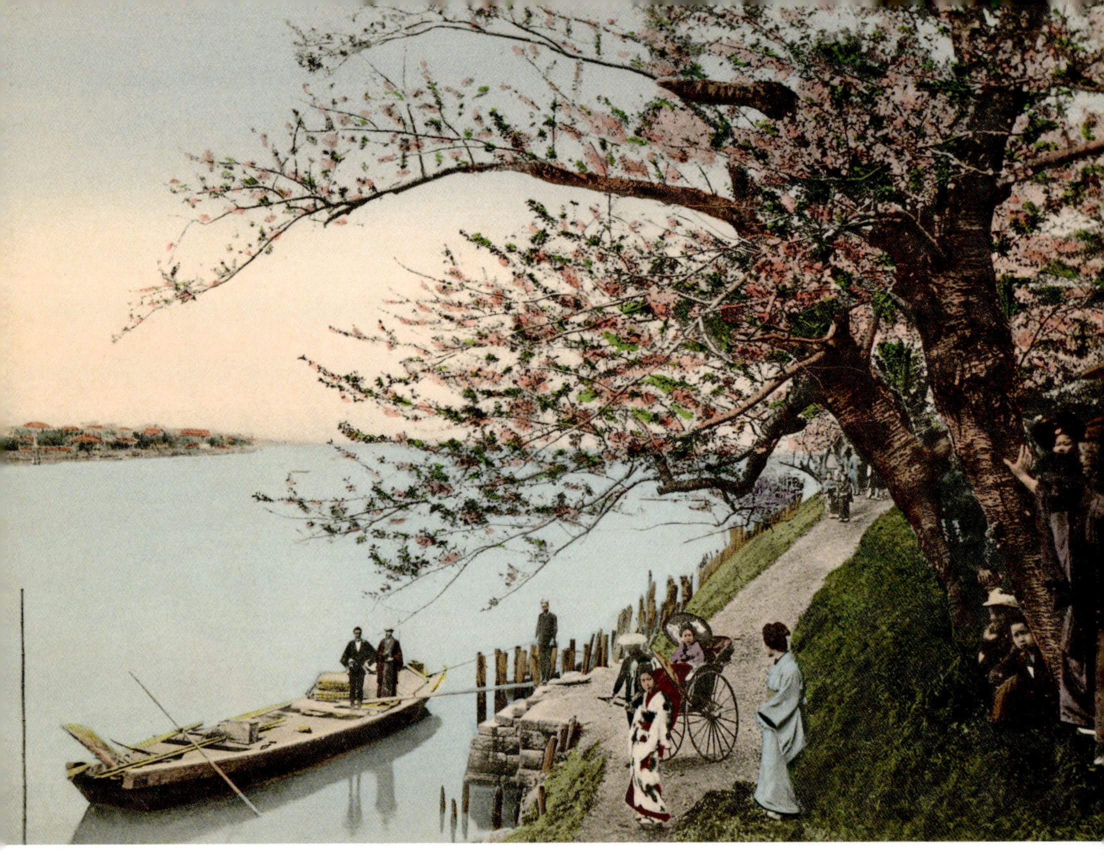

(Tafeln 15, 18), von denen man annimmt, dass Takenouchi die Entwürfe dazu von Eisen erhalten, aber aus unbekannten Gründen bis dahin nicht veröffentlicht hatte. Von diesen unsignierten Eisen-Entwürfen ging zunächst Itahana in Druck: Das handgestempelte Verlegersiegel Takenouchis, das einige Itahana-Abzüge am linken Rand aufweisen, scheint zugleich Takenouchis letzter Beitrag zu dem Projekt gewesen zu sein. Sakamoto wurde von Iseya allein produziert, ebenso wie die 22 Entwürfe von Hiroshige, die 1837 folgten, bevor eine abermalige Zäsur eintrat: Hiroshige verließ Edo und bereiste tatsächlich den Kisokaidō.

Nahezu alle Kisokaidō-Drucke, die den letzten Teil der Reise von Ochiai (Tafel 45) nach Kyoto betreffen, beruhen auf Skizzen, die Hiroshige während seiner Reise auf dieser Route anfertigte (siehe S. 444 ff.). 16 Blätter lehnen sich eng an seine Skizzen an, die in zwei Büchern erhalten sind und sich heute in der Sammlung des British Museum in London befinden.[23] Fünf weitere Entwürfe von Stationen, die hinter Ochiai liegen, müssen ebenfalls gedruckt worden sein, nachdem Hiroshige wieder in Edo war, denn in allen 21 Fällen unterscheidet sich seine Signatur von der auf den vorangegangenen Drucken.[24] Den Kisokaidō-Zyklus tatsächlich nach Skizzen zu gestalten, entsprach der Ursprungsidee,

Cherry blossoms beside the river / Blühender Kirschbaum am Fluss / Cerisier en fleurs au bord de la rivière, c. 1895. Photochrom, hand-coloured. Paris, Marc Walter Collection

die Takenouchi und Hiroshige in der ersten Ankündigung von 1834 mit dem Begriff *shinkei* (wörtlich: wahrhaftige Ansichten) zum Ausdruck gebracht hatten: Die dargestellten Szenen sollten nach der Natur gezeichnet sein (S. 56, vgl. Detail S. 54–55), auch wenn diesem Anspruch bis 1837 nicht Genüge getan wurde.

Während für den Anfangspunkt der Serie, die Nihonbashi, ein eigenes Blatt existiert, fehlt überraschenderweise ein Blatt für Kyoto. Da Hiroshige mehrere Bildfolgen von Kyotoer Landschaften entwarf, erscheint es merkwürdig, dass er den weiten Weg in die Kaiserstadt zurücklegte, ohne am Ende einen Entwurf für diesen ungemein bedeutenden Ort zu liefern. Absonderlich ist ferner, dass für die Station Nakatsugawa zwei Entwürfe vorliegen. Der erste (hier gezählt als Tafel 46a) ist sehr selten und existiert nur in einer einzigen Version ohne jegliche Farbvariationen, was darauf hindeutet, dass die Druckstöcke erheblich beschädigt wurden, bevor ein Nachdruck möglich gewesen wäre. Angesichts der wenigen erhaltenen Abzüge muss dieser Schaden relativ bald nach Druckbeginn der ersten Auflage entstanden sein, und als Hiroshige von seiner Reise zurückkehrte, schuf er eine deutlich abweichende zweite Version (Tafel 46b), für die er auf seine Skizzen zurückgriff.

Obwohl eine Produktionsdauer von sieben Jahren angesichts des schnelllebigen Druckmarktes mit seinem Durst nach immer neuen Entwürfen mehr als unwahrscheinlich ist, waren Kunsthistoriker lange der Ansicht, dass die letzten Blätter dieser Serie erst 1842 in Druck gingen.[25] Jüngere Forschungen gehen davon aus, dass das Enddatum des Drucks auf 1838 korrigiert werden muss (siehe Übersichtstabelle im Anhang, S. 507). Dieses Datum findet sich nämlich neben dem Namen des Sammlers auf der Rückseite eines Abzugs des letzten Blatts, Ōtsu (Tafel 70), das vermutlich mit dem letzten Stoß der Hiroshige-Entwürfe gedruckt wurde.[26] Gleichwohl ist damit nur für die erste Auflage ein Enddatum markiert, während keinerlei Informationen zu der Frage vorliegen, wann genau welche Blätter nachgedruckt wurden – was angesichts der zahlreichen Varianten, die von manchen Entwürfen existieren, recht häufig vorgekommen sein muss.

Im Verlauf der Geschichte änderte die japanische Regierung mehrfach die Zensurvorschriften für Drucke. Zu der Zeit, als die Kisokaidō-Serie geschaffen wurde, musste jeder Entwurf den Zensurstempel *kiwame* erhalten, bevor er in Druck gehen konnte. Der *kiwame*-Stempel selbst enthielt keine genauen Angaben zum Datum der Druckgenehmigung. Weil er üblicherweise am Rand eines Drucks angebracht wurde und Sammler dazu neigten, ihre Drucke bis direkt an den Rand zu beschneiden, fehlt er heute auf manchen Abzügen. Sobald die Veröffentlichung einmal genehmigt worden war, musste ein Druck nicht erneut zur Prüfung vorgelegt werden, wenn ein Verleger als Eigentümer der Druckstöcke sich später zum Nachdruck entschied. Dies galt selbst dann, wenn sich die Zensurbestimmungen änderten, wie es Anfang der 1840er Jahre der Fall war. Dementsprechend sind Nachdrucke lediglich anhand der Veränderungen, die beim Vergleich mehrerer Abzüge sichtbar werden, und anhand der vom Zustand der Druckstöcke abhängigen Druckqualität zu bestimmen. Perfekt aufeinander abgestimmte Farben deuten auf geringe Abnutzung und damit auf einen frühen Abzug hin. Weil einige Motive dieser Serie sehr beliebt waren, bestehen zwischen den Abzügen immense Qualitätsunterschiede. Im Allgemeinen gab ein Verleger jeweils 200 Abzüge auf einmal in Auftrag und musste insgesamt rund 600 verkaufen, um die Gewinnzone zu erreichen – nach Abzug der Honorare, die der Künstler für seinen Entwurf, der Holzschneider für die Druckstöcke und für seine Arbeit und schließlich der Drucker für Papier, Farbe und für seine Tätigkeit erhielt, die auf Bestellung auch spezielle Druckverfahren wie das der Farbabstufung *(bokashi)* umfassen konnte.[27]

Iseya Rihei war verlegerisch sehr aktiv, bis in den frühen 1840er Jahren ein dramatischer Wandel das Druckwesen erfasste: Um es schärfer zu kontrollieren, erließ die Regierung die sog. Tenpō-Reformen, neue Luxusgesetze, die unter anderem Entwerfern und Handwerkern strenge Einschränkungen auferlegten und so einige Verlage in eine finanzielle Krise stürzten. Mitte der 1840er Jahre scheint Iseya die Veröffentlichung neuer Drucke eingestellt zu haben, er ist jedoch noch 1851 als Mitglied der Neuen Fraktion in der Gilde der Bildbuch- und Holzschnittverleger gelistet.[28] Wahrscheinlich in der zweiten Hälfte der 1830er Jahre, als er gerade die neuen Hiroshige-Entwürfe druckte, legte Iseya Rihei auch Eisens Blätter neu auf und nahm in manchen Fällen Veränderungen an den Druckstöcken vor, indem er Takenouchis Siegel und/oder Namen entfernte und bisweilen, wie etwa beim Nihonbashi-Motiv, durch seine eigenen Zeichen ersetzte. Da die Holzschnittkünstler pauschal für ihre Arbeit abgegolten wurden, wenn sie ihre Entwürfe beim Verlag ablieferten, konnte Iseya diese später nach Belieben verändern und entfernte auch Eisens Signatur – vermutlich, weil Hiroshiges Stern unter den Gestaltern von Landschaften inzwischen heller strahlte als alle anderen. Iseya könnte auch darauf spekuliert haben, höhere Verkaufszahlen zu erreichen, wenn er vorgab, sämtliche Vorlagen für die Serie gingen auf Hiroshige zurück.[29]

Irgendwann, vielleicht Mitte der 1840er Jahre, als er die Herausgabe neuer Drucke einstellte, verkaufte Iseya die Druckstöcke der Kisokaidō-Serie an Yamadaya Shōbei (Lebensdaten unbekannt) und dessen Verlag Kinkyōdō. Yamadaya Shōbei feierte ab 1846 große Erfolge mit der Publikation illustrierter Kurzromane; sein Erbe Shōjirō (Lebensdaten unbekannt), der 1851 den Verlag übernahm, führte dessen Erfolgsrezept bis etwa 1866 fort. Yamadaya legte den sog. *Gyōsho Tōkaidō (Kursivschrift-Tōkaidō)*, Hiroshiges ursprünglich um 1841/42 erschienene Tōkaidō-Serie, neu auf (S. 81). Wann genau er auch die Kisokaidō-Serie nachdruckte, ist unklar, doch modifizierte er die meisten Druckstöcke, indem er alte Verlegersiegel entfernte, was einfacher und preiswerter war, als sie durch eigene zu ersetzen. Nur für zwei Blätter, Nihonbashi und Ōta (Tafeln 1, 52), verwendete er sein eigenes Siegel. Dass die Druckstöcke mittlerweile für mehrere Neuauflagen zum Einsatz gekommen und entsprechend abgenutzt waren, ist am besonders schlechten Zustand der Yamadaya-Abzüge deutlich zu erkennen (S. 83).[30]

In jüngerer Zeit haben sich einige japanische Unternehmen darauf spezialisiert, Reproduktionen beliebter alter Holzschnitte herzustellen, darunter auch die Motive dieser Kisokaidō-Serie. Um ein authentisches Erscheinungsbild zu wahren, nutzen sie Holzstöcke und traditionelle Druckverfahren, sie verwenden dabei jedoch keine Originaldruckstöcke, sondern neu geschnittene Platten. Der Verleger Watanabe Shōzaburō z. B. bot in seinem Katalog für das Jahr 1935 Reproduktionen des gesamten Kisokaidō-Zyklus zum Preis von 35 Sen pro Stück und 20 Yen für den vollständigen Satz an. Manche dieser Nachdrucke wurden zu Alben gebunden; ein Anbieter fügte sogar ein im Holztafeldruck erstelltes neues Inhaltsverzeichnis *(mokuroku)* hinzu.[31]

Der Wert eines Holzschnitts aus der Kisokaidō-Serie hängt heute von vielen Faktoren ab, allen voran vom Motiv selbst, da manche unter ihnen gefragter sind als andere. Eisens Kutsukake (Tafel 20) beispielsweise wurde 1922 von Basil Stewart und 1925 von Edward Strange als eines der besten Blätter der Serie bezeichnet.[32] Das gilt auch für Hiroshiges Nagakubo (Tafel 28), in dem Stewart „vielleicht das Meisterstück der Serie"[33] erkannte. Ōi (Tafel 47) wurde von Stewart und Strange gleichermaßen bewundert,

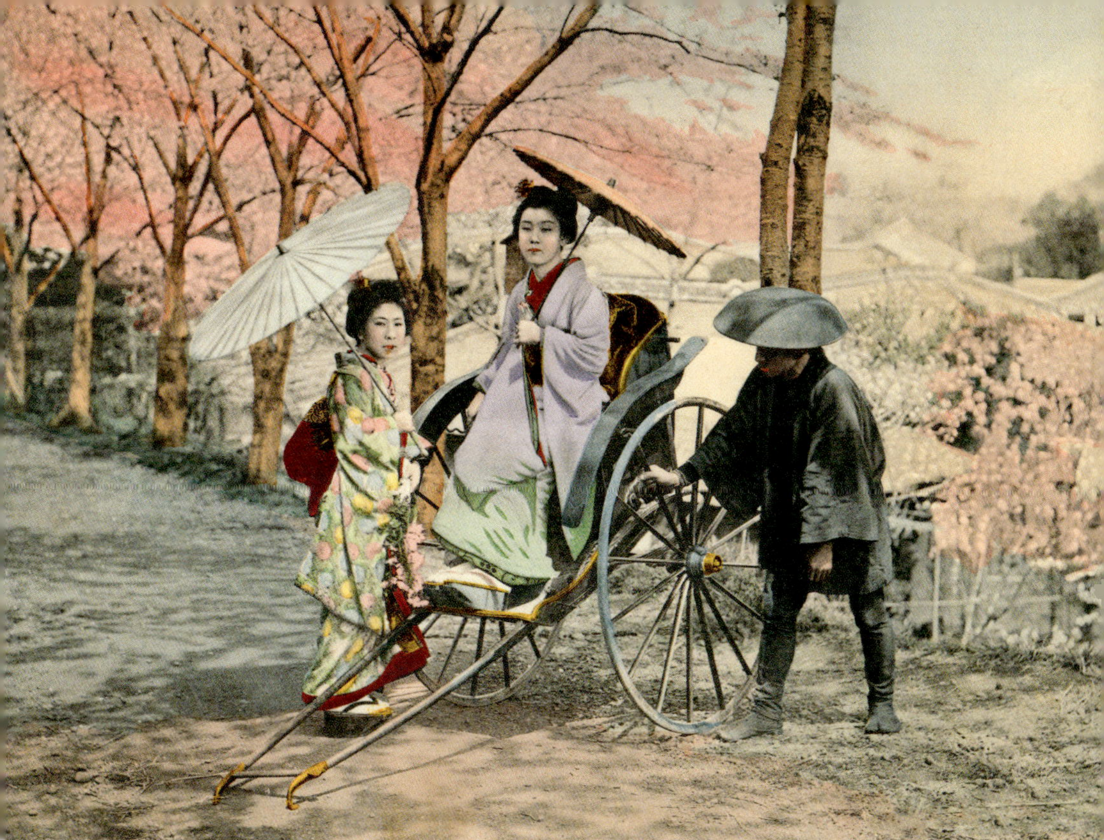

wobei Strange auch den berühmten Holzschnittsammler John S. Happer (1863–1936) zitierte, der über Ōi
äußerte: „In keiner anderen Serie [Hiroshiges] gibt es eine schönere Darstellung von fallendem Schnee."[34]

Die Qualität und der Zustand des Abzugs sind entscheidende Kriterien für die Beurteilung eines
Drucks. Verkaufte sich ein Entwurf gut, druckte der Verleger ihn immer wieder nach und veränderte
in manchen Bereichen möglicherweise die Farben. Das ist auch der Grund dafür, dass einige Motive
der Kisokaidō-Serie in sechs verschiedenen Versionen existieren. Mit steigender Auflage nutzten die
Druckstöcke ab und lieferten immer schlechtere Qualität. Die Abzüge der Erstauflage sind präziser in
der Wiedergabe, stellen aber nicht unbedingt die „schönsten" Fassungen dar, da ihnen die Eigenschaften
von Prachtdrucken fehlen – im Fall der Kisokaidō-Drucke die Farbabstufungen oder *bokashi*. Die auf
den folgenden Seiten präsentierten Holzschnitte stammen aus einer Privatsammlung, die ohne jeden
Zweifel den erlesensten Kisokaidō-Satz der Welt bildet. Er besticht nahezu durchgängig durch außerge-
wöhnliche Abzüge aus der frühesten und/oder schönsten Auflage jedes einzelnen Motivs.

Girls taking a rickshaw / Mädchen in einer Rikscha /
Filles prenant un pousse-pousse, c. 1895.
Photochrom, hand-coloured. Paris, Marc Walter Collection

PP. 60/61
Moriyama (detail from plate 68)

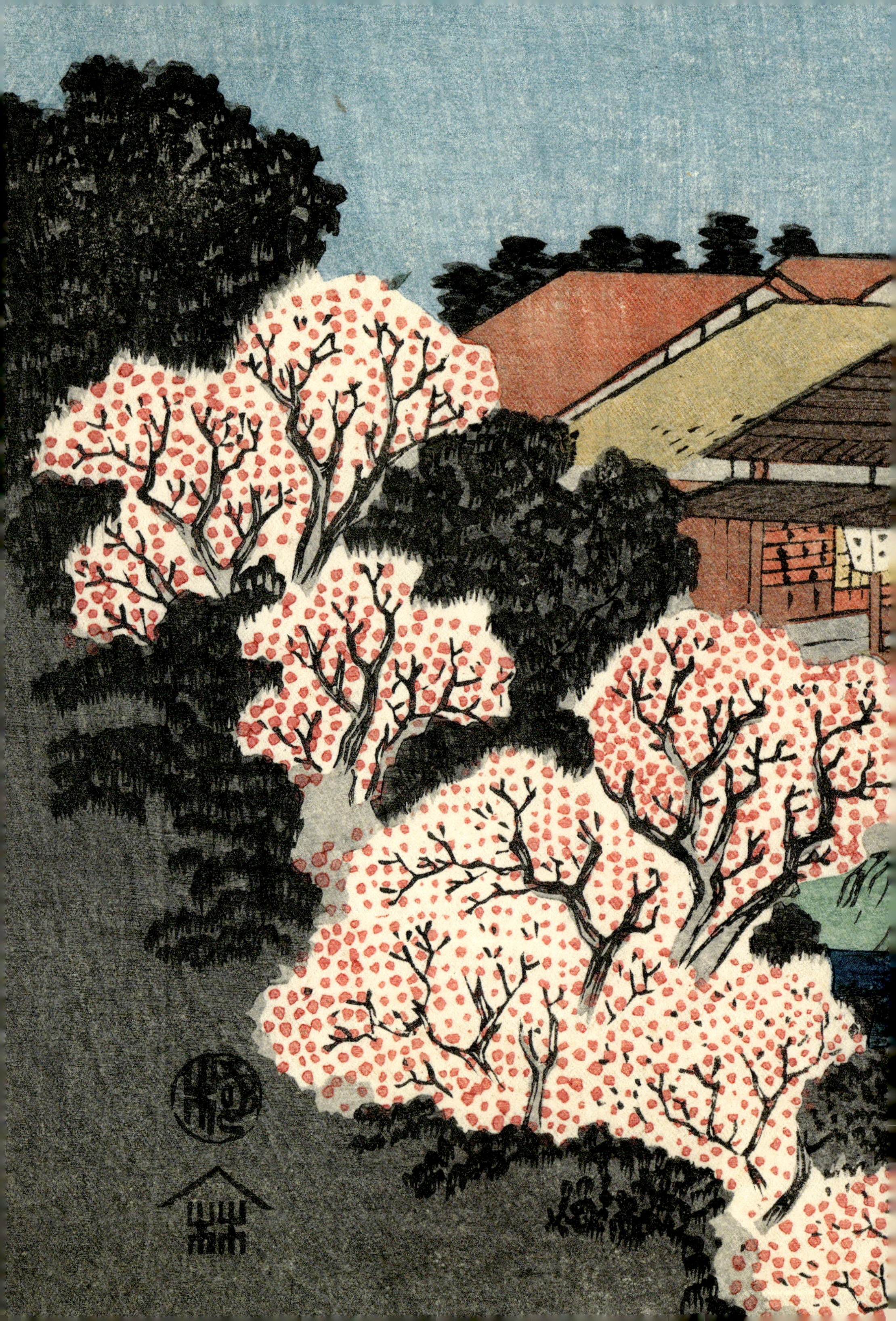

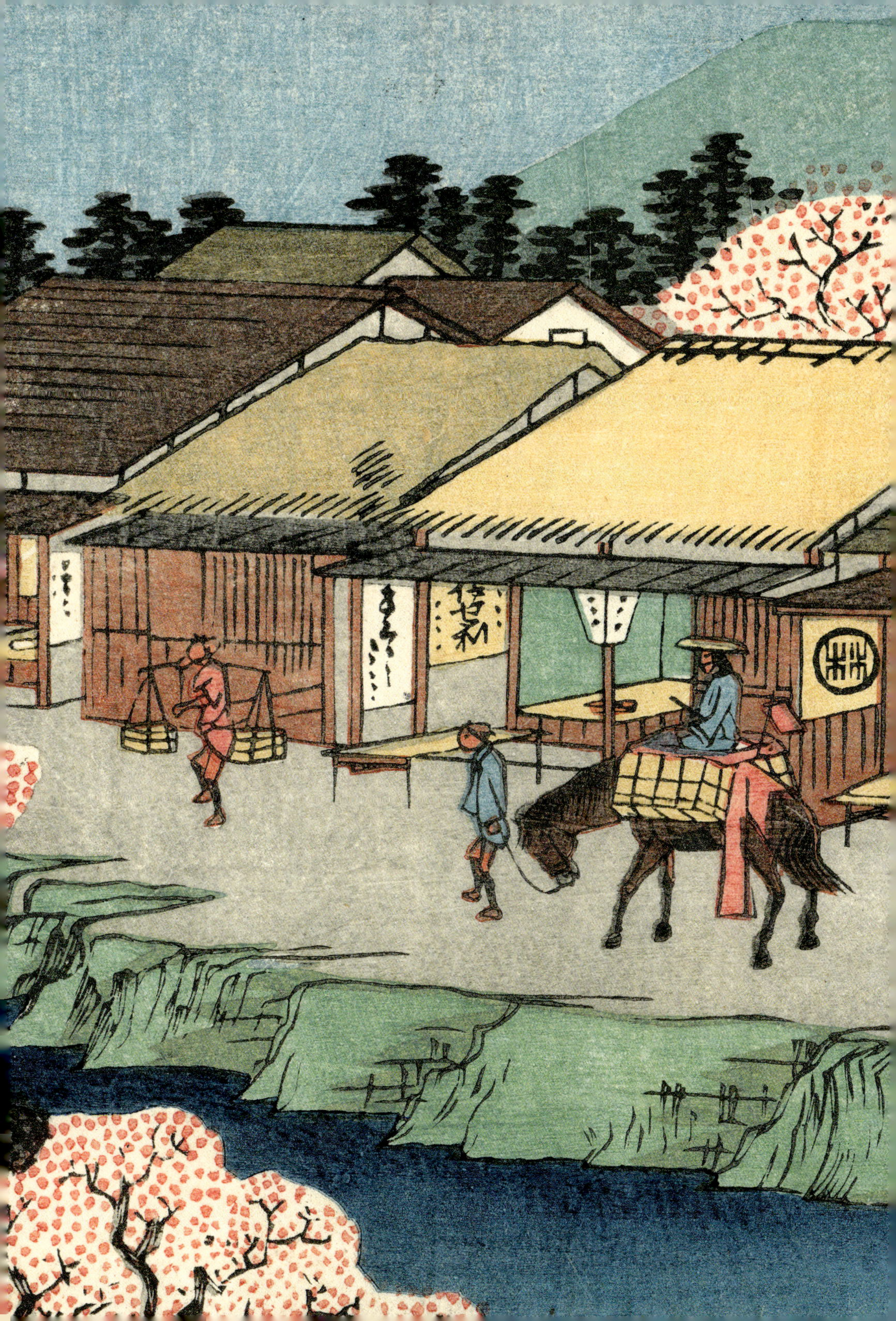

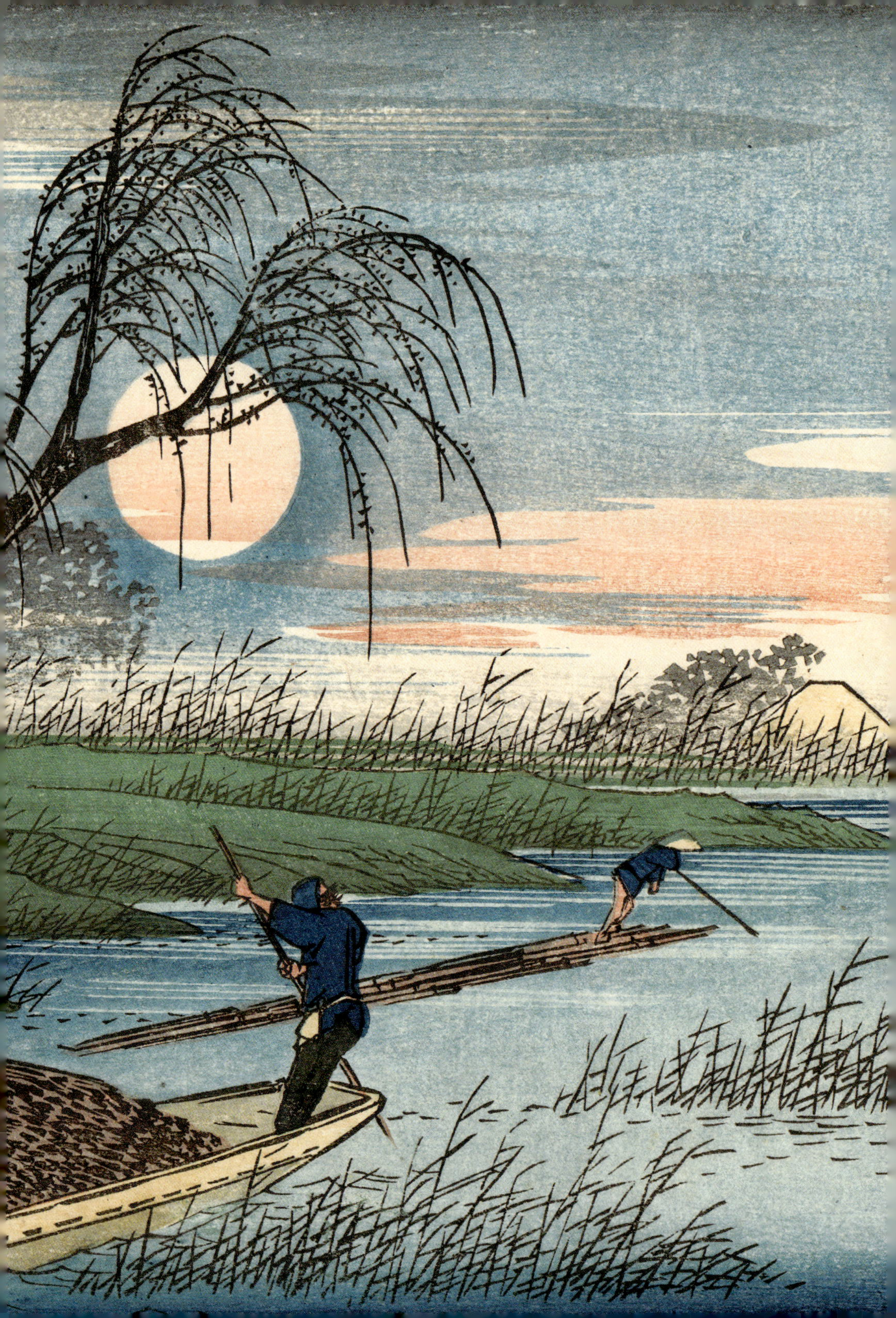

Andreas Marks

D'Edo à Kyoto

Un voyage épique

Les déplacements au Japon

Lorsque le shogun Tokugawa Ieyasu (1543–1616) unifie le Japon au début du XVIIe siècle et crée un gouvernement centralisé dans la ville d'Edo, aujourd'hui Tokyo, il lui semble évident qu'il ne pourra conserver le pouvoir que s'il est capable d'asseoir son autorité sur les régions éloignées du pays. Afin de contrôler les nombreux seigneurs féodaux (*daïmio*), un nouveau système de résidence est mis en place, qui les contraint à entretenir deux foyers, l'un dans leur domaine, l'autre à Edo. Leur présence régulière dans la capitale est exigée et, si un seigneur est absent, son épouse et sa famille sont tenues d'y résider. Inspiré par l'impressionnant maillage routier en vigueur en Chine, Ieyasu ordonne l'extension et l'imposition d'un réseau de grandes routes, dont il existe une trame depuis plusieurs siècles. Alors que la Chine est beaucoup plus vaste que le Japon, la diffusion de messages dans des contrées retirées peut s'y faire en un temps court grâce à un système très efficace de relais de messagers à cheval, selon des parcours préétablis.

Afin d'atteindre les régions éloignées de son royaume, Ieyasu crée un réseau de cinq routes partant du pont Nihonbashi, centre d'Edo et cœur du Japon (pp. 49, 50–51). Des postes de contrôle surveillés par des hommes armés sont installés le long de ces routes pour prémunir Edo de l'approche de forces hostiles ou pour empêcher la fuite de la famille d'un seigneur habitant dans la capitale. Parmi ces routes principales, la Nakasendō, également connue sous le nom de Kisokaidō, part du pont Nihonbashi vers l'intérieur du pays, traverse les montagnes sur une distance de 136 *ri* (environ 534 kilomètres) et rallie le pont Sanjō Ōhashi à Kyoto (p. 13 ; voir la carte sur la p. 96–97). Le mont Fuji (p. 16), montagne la plus sacrée du Japon, n'est visible de la Kisokaidō qu'à une distance proche d'Edo ; cependant, les voyageurs peuvent apercevoir le volcan actif du mont Asama, qui connaîtra une éruption dévastatrice en 1783 et incitera beaucoup de gens à éviter cette route. La Kisokaidō traverse six provinces : Musashi, Kōzuke, Shinano, Mino, Ōmi et Yamashiro, qui correspondent aux préfectures actuelles de Saitama, Gunma, Nagano, Gifu et Shiga. Des micocouliers (*enoki*) sont plantés le long de certaines sections de la route et un système de

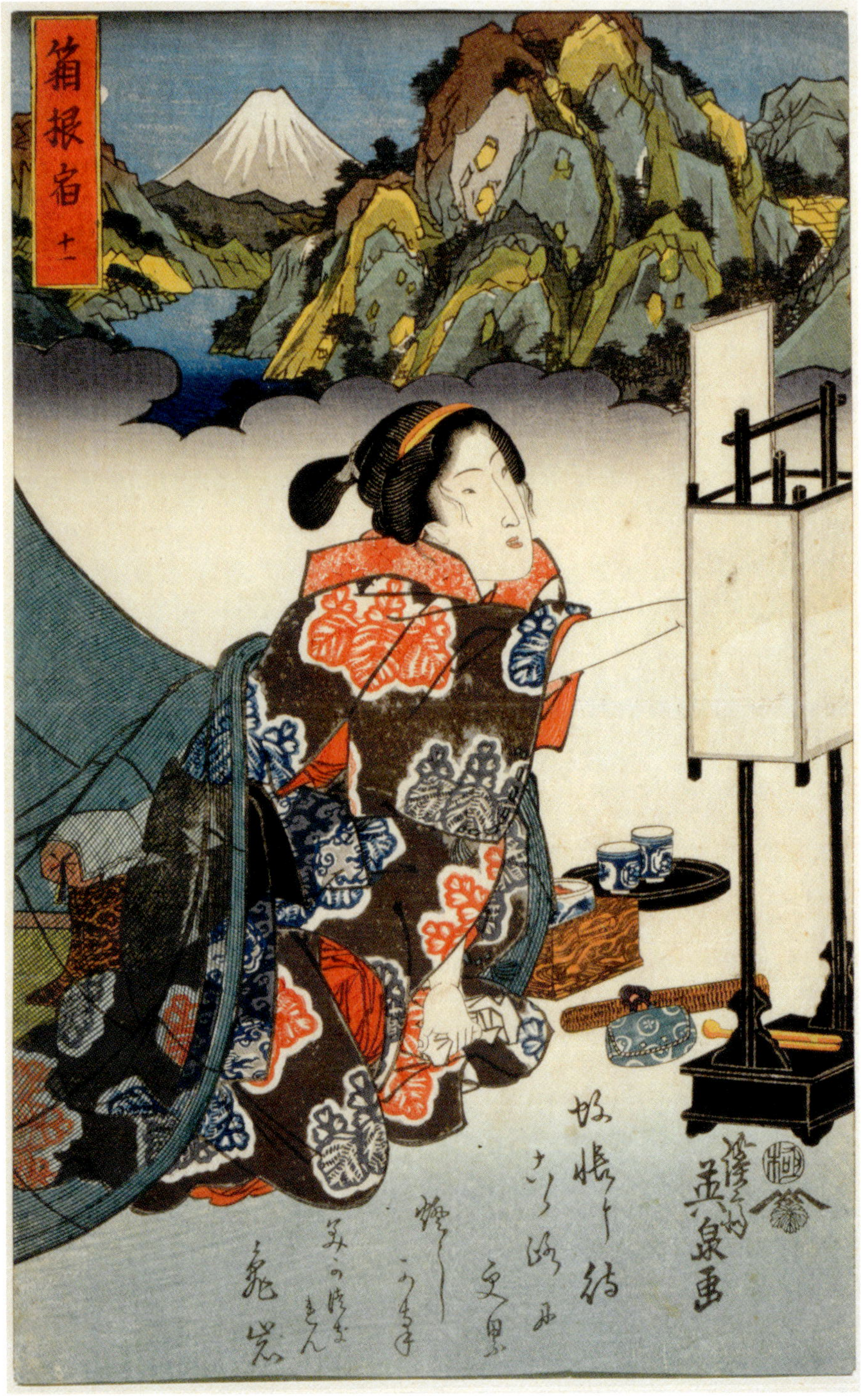

箱根宿 十一

soixante-neuf relais de poste est créé, avec chevaux et porteurs, afin d'assurer les besoins en transport, ainsi que des auberges proposant gîte et couvert aux voyageurs.

En 1874, puis en 1875, le géographe allemand Johannes Justus Rein (1835–1918) emprunte la Kisokaidō et en conclut que « quiconque souhaite jouir de splendides points de vue sur les montagnes japonaises choisira la Nakasendō, car il n'existe guère d'autres routes au Japon qui offrent autant de paysages aussi divers et magnifiques[1] » (pp. 19, 82). Rein n'est pas le seul à avoir une opinion favorable de la Kisokaidō ; au milieu de 1835, la route est déjà le sujet d'une série de xylographies, réalisée par les célèbres artistes Eisen (1790–1848) et Hiroshige (1797–1858). Au début de 1838, l'impression de soixante et onze dessins – vingt-quatre d'Eisen et quarante-sept d'Hiroshige – est achevée et cette série devient alors connue sous le titre *Les soixante-neuf stations de la route Kisokaidō* (*Kisokaidō rokujūkyū tsugi no uchi*)[2].

Les cinq grandes routes comptent également la Tōkaidō, ou route maritime orientale, ainsi nommée parce qu'elle longe la côte ; elle aussi rallie Kyoto, ancienne capitale et siège de l'empereur, sur une distance de 126 *ri* (environ 495 kilomètres). Juste après le pont Nihonbashi, les deux routes de la Kisokaidō et de la Tōkaidō se séparent, pour ne se rejoindre qu'à Kusatsu, à quelque vingt-six kilomètres de Kyoto. Au cours de l'ère Edo (1603–1868), la Tōkaidō est la route la plus courte entre Edo et Kyoto. Sur une grande partie du parcours, les voyageurs peuvent apercevoir l'imposant volcan du mont Fuji (p. 17). Par une bifurcation de cette route, on peut se rendre au grand sanctuaire d'Ise, destination prisée des pèlerins.

La Kisokaidō était considérée comme une route plus difficile que la Tōkaidō, comme en témoignent les déplacements des *daïmio*, dont cent quarante-six empruntent la Tōkaidō contre trente pour la Kisokaidō. Il y a neuf cols sur la Kisokaidō, dont six à une altitude de mille mètres[3]. Les récits de voyage par cette route sont rares, notamment de la part d'étrangers. Les cols escarpés sont si difficiles à franchir en hiver que le gouvernement fait paver huit sections de route pour faciliter le passage (pp. 24–25, 30, 31)[4]. L'accès à la mer étant peu aisé, les possibilités de se restaurer diffèrent sur la Kisokaidō par rapport à la Tōkaidō, le poisson frais faisant particulièrement défaut. En revanche, cette route compte moins de fastidieux passages de rivières que la Tōkaidō : les tarifs de transport s'en trouvent inférieurs d'un tiers[5]. Les voyageurs ont tendance à emprunter la Kisokaidō pour leur déplacement, car il leur permet de profiter des paysages ; et l'on note ici un net contraste avec l'époque moderne, où le voyage est considéré par beaucoup comme un mal nécessaire pour atteindre la destination souhaitée.

Quatre des villes desservies par la Kisokaidō possèdent des châteaux : Takasaki (planche 14), Annaka (planche 16), Iwamurata (planche 23) et Kanō (planche 54). En 1843, Ōtsu (planche 70), avec 14 892 habitants, est la plus grande ville dotée d'un relais de poste sur cette route (de même que sur la Tōkaidō), tandis qu'Unuma (planche 53) est la plus petite, avec 246 habitants seulement[6]. Il existe trois sortes d'auberges dans la plupart des villes. Les établissements luxueux, appelés *honjin*, sont réservés aux

P. 62
Seba (detail from plate 32)

PP. 66/67
Nihonbashi (detail from plate 1)

KEISAI EISEN, *Woman at the Hakone Station / Frau an der Station Hakone / Une femme à la station de Hakone*, c. 1837. From an untitled series of beauties juxtaposed to Tōkaidō stations. Published by Tsutaya Kichizō. Colour woodblock print, *ōban*, 37.8 × 26 cm / 14 ⅝ × 10 ¼ in. Washington, Library of Congress, FP 2-JPD, no. 2336

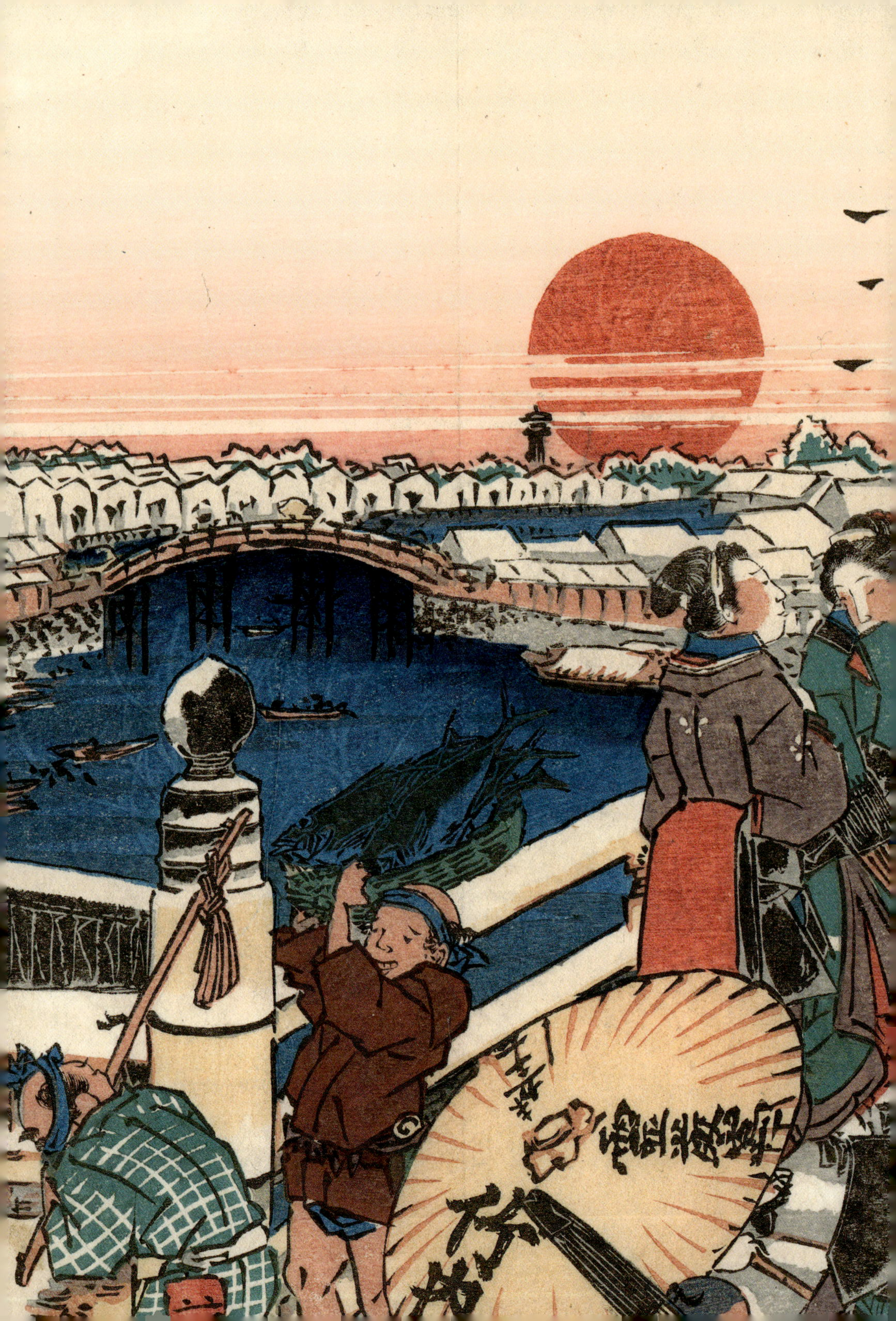

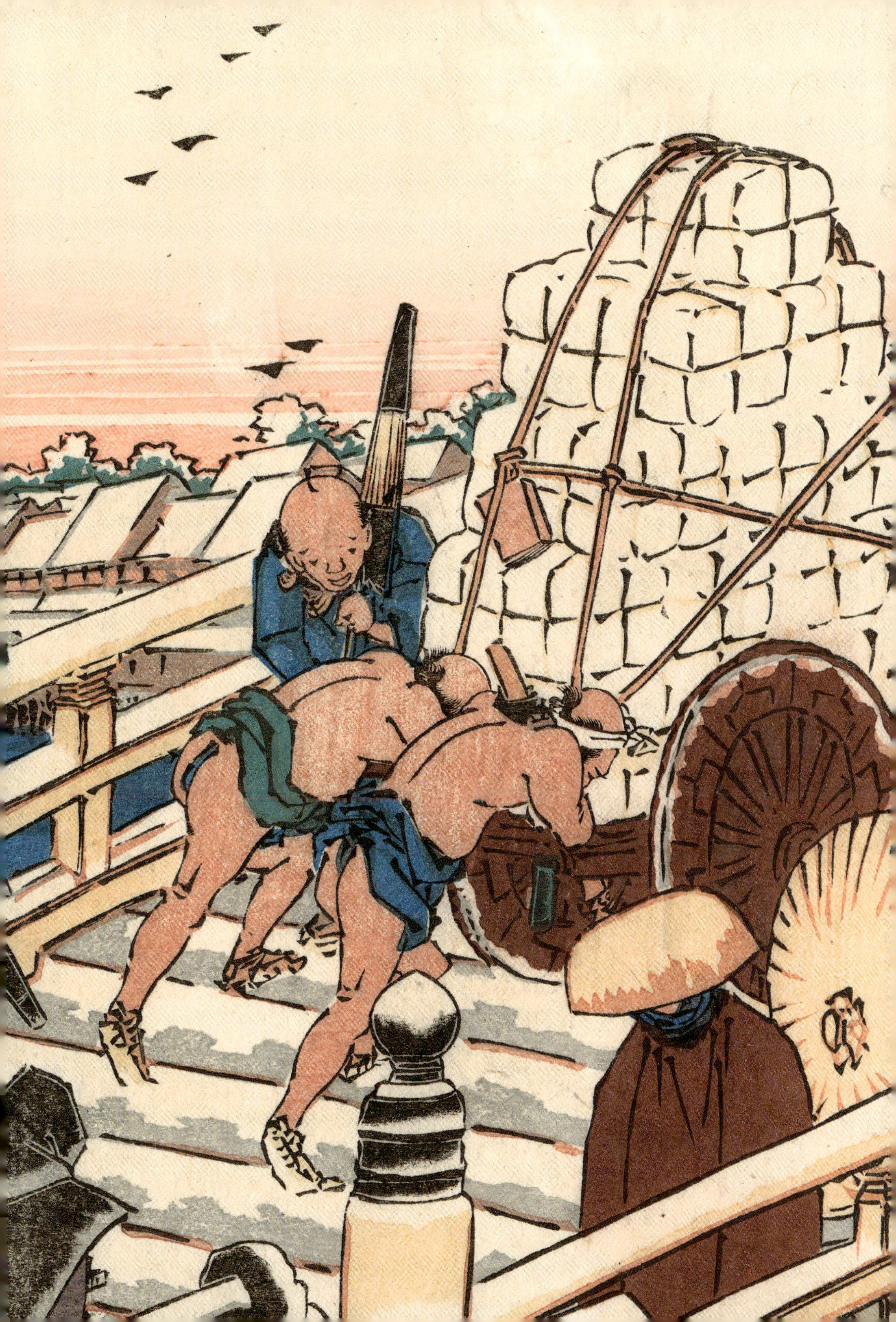

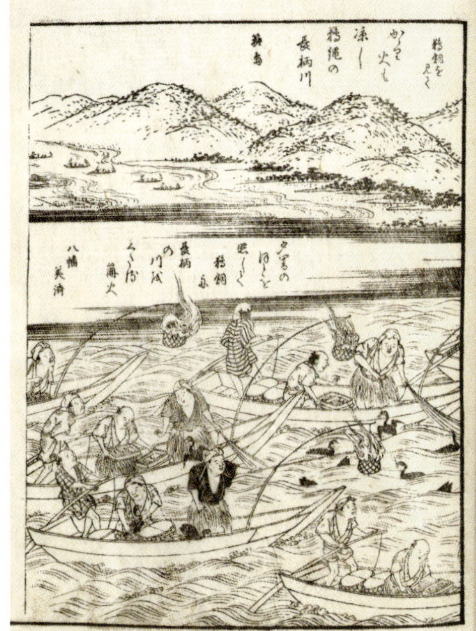
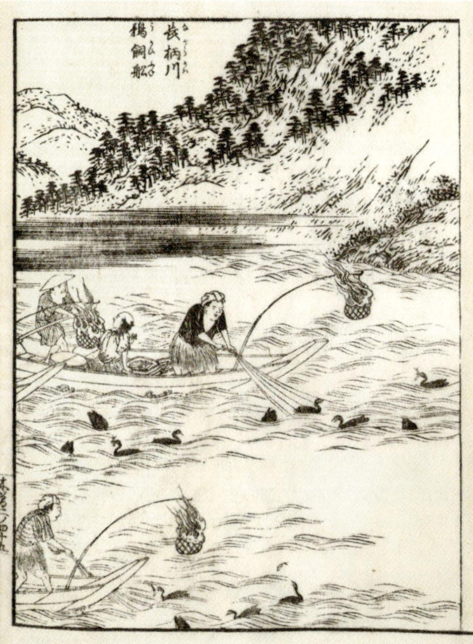

daïmio et à d'autres fonctionnaires de haut rang, tandis que ceux de moindre rang descendent dans les *waki-honjin* et que les voyageurs ordinaires passent la nuit dans des *hatagoya*. Peu de villes manquent de *honjin* ; certaines en comptent jusqu'à huit. Et l'on trouve des *hatagoya* dans tous les relais de poste de la Kisokaidō : trois seulement à Yawata (planche 25) et jusqu'à quatre-vingts à Fukaya (planche 10), la moyenne se situant à vingt-huit[7].

Un permis de voyage est nécessaire pour franchir les postes de contrôles (*sekisho*) établis sur les cinq grandes voies de communication, afin de contrôler l'approvisionnement d'Edo en armes et d'empêcher les familles de *daïmio* de quitter la ville (*iri-deppō ni de-onna*). Deux postes de contrôle se trouvent sur la Kisokaidō : Usui, près de Sakamoto (planche 18), et Fukushima (planche 38). Tout pèlerin, marchand, messager, artisan ou touriste y est contrôlé, de même que l'entourage d'un *daïmio*. La taille d'un entourage est fixée en fonction de la quantité de riz produite par le domaine du *daïmio*. Composé de porte-étendards, de fantassins, de porteurs et de domestiques, un entourage compte de cinquante à plus de quatre cents hommes. Généralement, les voyageurs se déplacent à pied et leur temps de trajet varie selon le terrain, l'âge et la santé du marcheur, la charge portée, etc. Il faut deux semaines pour qu'un

Nishimura Chūwa, *Cormorant Fishing Boats on the Nagara River / Kormoran-Fischerboote auf dem Nagara-Fluss / Bateaux de pêche au cormoran sur la rivière Nagara*. From: Akisato Ritō, *Views of Famous Sights along the Kiso Road (Kisoji meisho zue)*, vol. 3, 1805. Woodblock printed book. Munich, Bayerische Staatsbibliothek

Utagawa Hiroshige, *Nihonbashi*, c. 1850/51. From the series: *Tōkaidō-Fifty-Three Stations*. Published by Maruya Seijirō. Colour woodblock print, *ōban*, 25.5 × 38.2 cm / 10 × 15 in. Minneapolis Institute of Art, Gift of Louis W. Hill, Jr., 81.133.111

marcheur effectue le trajet complet. Les voyageurs de haut rang ou fortunés se déplacent, selon leur statut social, à cheval ou en chaise à porteurs (l'un à l'avant, l'autre à l'arrière). Ceux qui en ont les moyens engagent des porteurs, accompagnés de chevaux de bât transportant leurs marchandises.

La Kisokaidō dans les gravures sur bois japonaises

Contrairement à la Tōkaidō, la Kisokaidō a été rarement traitée dans l'art japonais. La bibliothèque du Parlement japonais à Tokyo possède un rouleau peint à la main d'une longueur de dix-neuf mètres, datant de 1668, sur lequel figure une carte topographique comprenant les deux routes[8]. Conservée au Musée national de Tokyo, la *Carte panoramique de la Nakasendō* (*Nakasendō bunken nobe ezu*, 1806) illustre la route depuis Itabashi (planche 2) jusqu'à Moriyama (planche 68) sur dix rouleaux faits main (p. 39). Ces deux cartes n'ont pas été réalisées pour le grand public ou les amateurs d'art, mais ont joué un rôle officiel à des fins administratives.

Hors de la sphère administrative, ce sont les livres de gravures sur bois monochromes qui renseignent le grand public sur la Kisokaidō. Le *Récit de la route Kiso* (*Kisoji no ki*, 1713), journal de voyage de Kaibara Ekiken (1630–1714), contient quelques illustrations (p. 43). Le *Guide illustré de la route Kiso* (*Kisoji anken ezu*, 1756) de Sōyō (dates inconnues) est un petit manuel sans commentaire révélant le parcours intégral de la route sur 73 pages de simples dessins, suivis d'un tableau des distances et des frais de transport (p. 42). La *Collection de vues de paysages célèbres sur la route Kiso* (*Kisoji meisho zue*, 1805), dues à Akisato Ritō (en activité à partir de 1780–1814), constituent la publication la plus

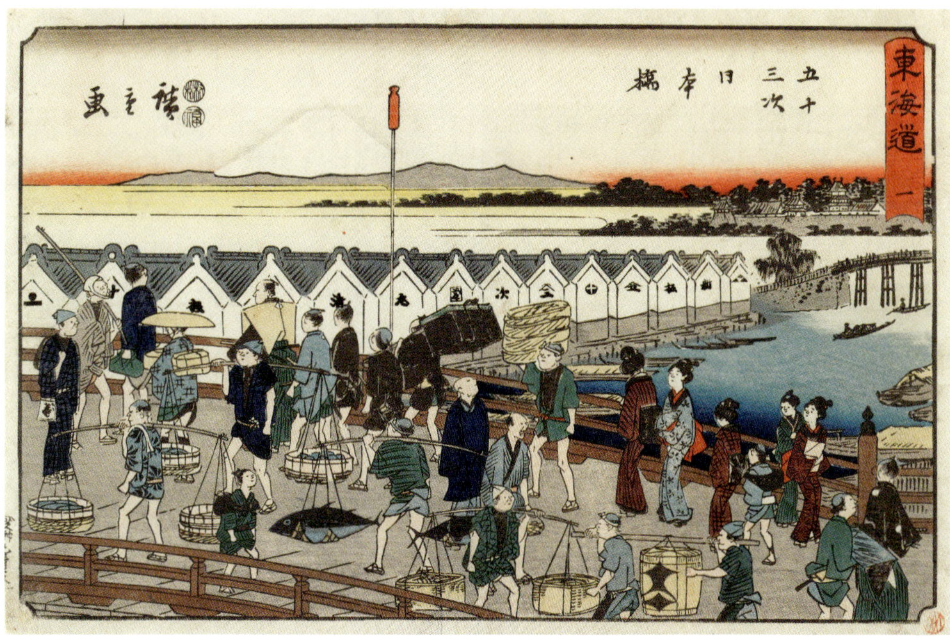

répandue et réunissent six volumes associant des textes informatifs et des illustrations détaillées de Nishimura Chūwa (dates inconnues).

Roman humoristique de Jippensha Ikku (1766–1831) publié de 1802 à 1809, *Promenade sur la Tōkaidō (Tōkaidōchū hizakurige)* a mis en lumière le thème du voyage et probablement incité Katsushika Hokusai (1760–1849) à réaliser, au début du XIXe siècle, les premières estampes en couleur ayant pour thème la Tōkaidō, auxquelles s'ajouteront d'autres gravures au cours des années suivantes (pp. 44, 45)[9]. Dans les volumes trois à huit de la suite à la *Promenade sur la Tōkaidō* d'Ikku, publiés de 1812 à 1816, Kitahachi et Yajirōbei, les personnages de l'histoire, parcourent la Kisokaidō où ils connaissent à nouveau des aventures comiques. Mais ces divers récits ne déclenchent pas, à cette époque, une vague de gravures ayant pour sujet la Kisokaidō.

En 1818, tirant profit de l'intérêt du public pour le voyage, Hokusai réalise des cartes en vue aérienne de toute la topographie d'une route grâce à d'impressionnantes compositions individuelles. La première montre la Tōkaidō ; elle est publiée par Kadomaruya Jinsuke qui, quelques mois plus tard, s'associe à deux autres éditeurs. Ensemble, ils font paraître une carte aérienne de la Kisokaidō par Hokusai ; c'est aussi la première estampe dépeignant cette route (pp. 50–51)[10].

La série de la Kisokaidō et ses artistes

Dans les années 1830, le marché déjà important des estampes de paysages, vendues comme souvenirs aux voyageurs ainsi qu'à ceux qui ne peuvent effectuer ce genre de voyage, connaît une nouvelle expansion,

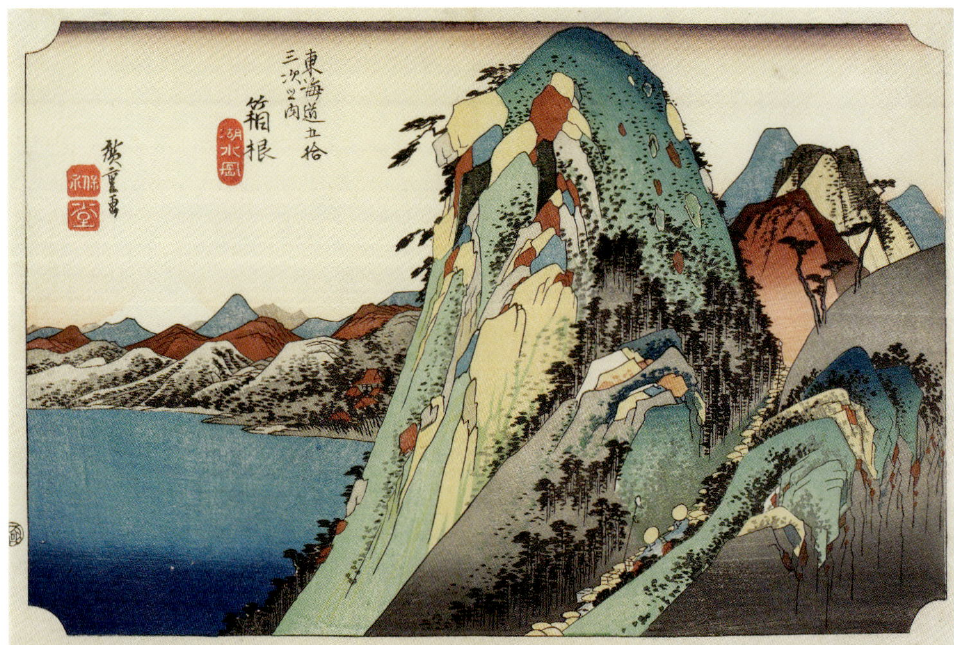

surtout en ce qui concerne le mont Fuji
et les variations sur le thème des *Huit
vues du lac Biwa*. Utagawa Hiroshige
(p. 9), alors peu connu, rencontre un
succès considérable en 1832 avec la
publication des premières gravures de
sa série des *Cinquante-trois stations
sur la route Tōkaidō* (*Tōkaidō gojūsan
tsugi no uchi*), couramment connue
sous le titre « Hōeidō Tōkaidō », éditée
par Hōeidō, nouvelle maison d'édition
fondée par Takenouchi Magohachi
(1781–1854 ; p. 10).

    Fils de pompier, Hiroshige est né
sous le nom de Andō Tokutarō à Edo,
dans le quartier de Yayosugashi, en
1797. Ayant perdu ses deux parents à
l'âge de treize ans, il est contraint de
reprendre la charge de pompier de son
père. Il envisage pourtant un autre ave-
nir et, n'ayant pas réussi à entrer dans
l'atelier d'Utagawa Toyokuni (1769–
1825), il devient étudiant de Toyohiro
(1773–1828) en 1810 ou 1811.

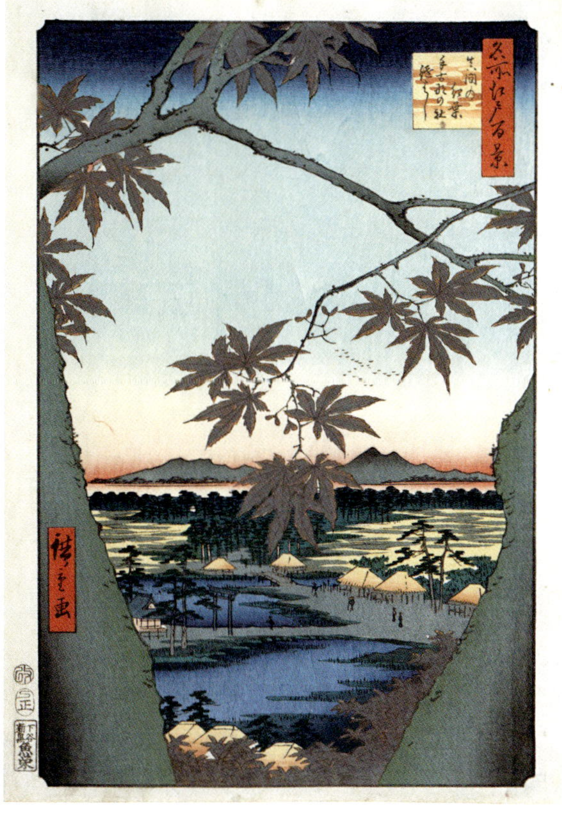

    C'est en 1812 qu'il prend le nom d'Hiroshige. Ses premières œuvres reconnues sont les illustra-
tions d'une anthologie de poèmes humoristiques en trois volumes, publiée en 1818, ainsi que plusieurs
estampes d'acteurs. En 1823, il renonce à sa charge de pompier afin de se consacrer à sa carrière artis-
tique. Au cours de la décennie suivante, il réalise plusieurs séries d'estampes de jolies femmes et de
sujets guerriers.

    Les premiers paysages ayant valu la notoriété à Hiroshige ont été édités au début des années 1830.
La série la plus importante est *Les cinquante-trois stations de la Tōkaidō* (*Tōkaidō gojūsan tsugi no*

UTAGAWA HIROSHIGE, *Hakone. View of the Lake /
Hakone. Ansicht des Sees / Hakone. Vue du lac*,
c. 1832–33. From the series: *The Fifty-Three Stations
along the Tōkaidō*. Published by Takenouchi Magohachi.
Colour woodblock print, *ōban*. Minneapolis Institute
of Art, Bequest of Richard P. Gale, 74.1.262

PP. 72/73
Kuragano (detail from plate 13)

UTAGAWA HIROSHIGE, *Maple Trees at Mama, Tekona
Shrine and Linked Bridge / Ahornbäume in Mama und
der Tekona-Schrein mit Verbindungsbrücke / Érables
à Mama, près du sanctuaire de Tekona, et le pont
Tsugihashi*, 1857. From the series: *One Hundred Famous
Views of Edo*. Published by Sakanaya Eikichi.
Colour woodblock print, *ōban*. Minncapolis Institute
of Art, Gift of Louis W. Hill, Jr., 96.146.193

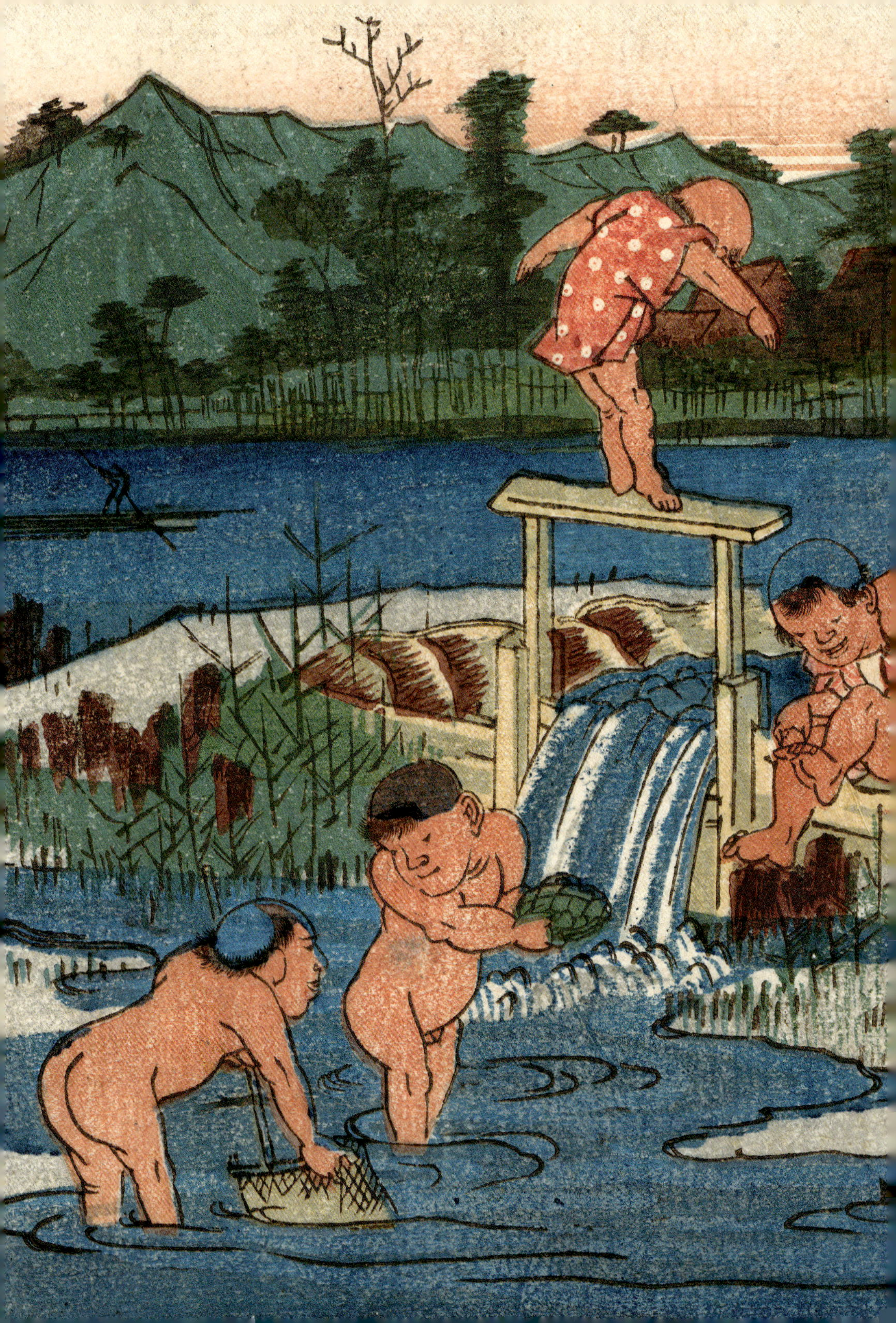

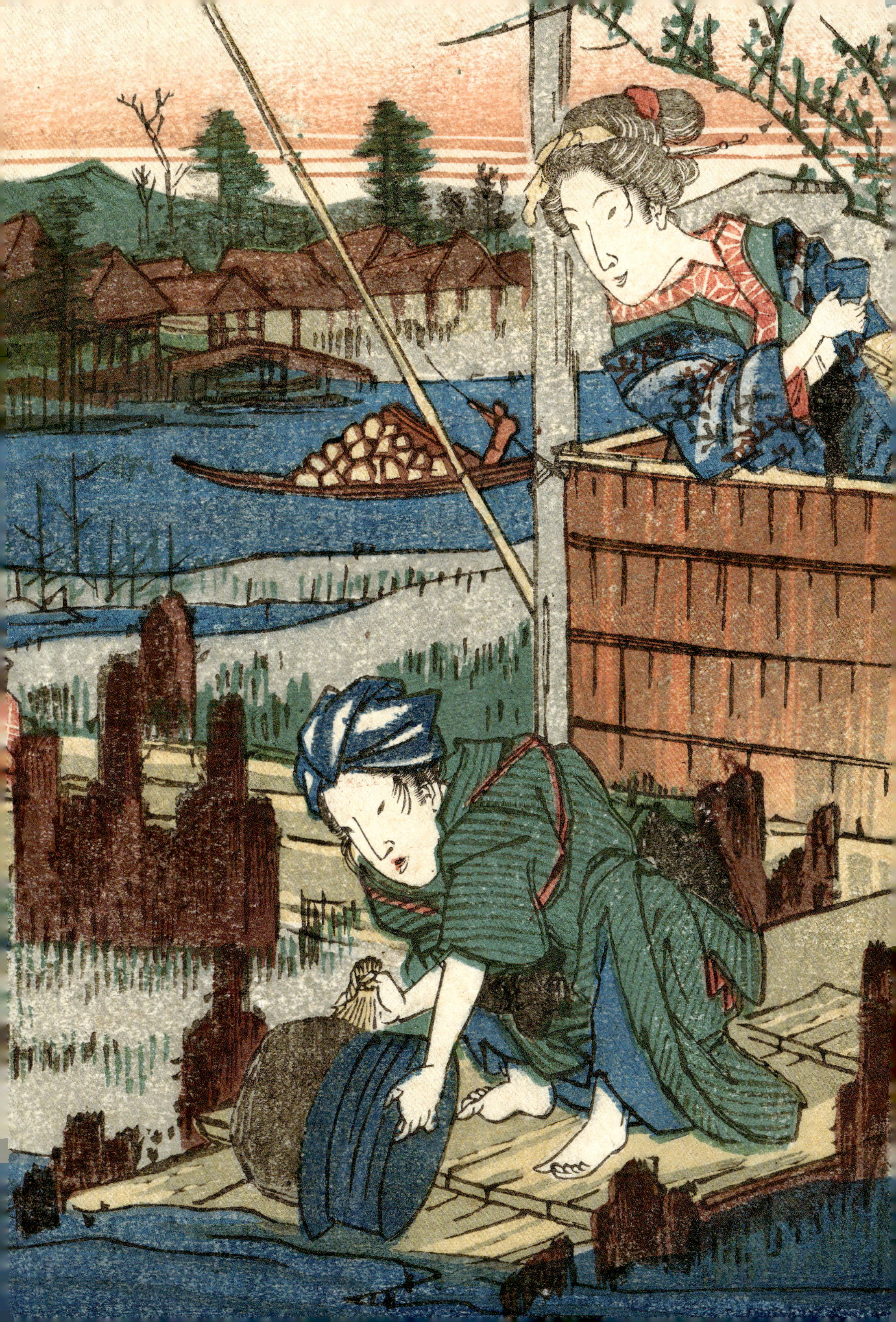

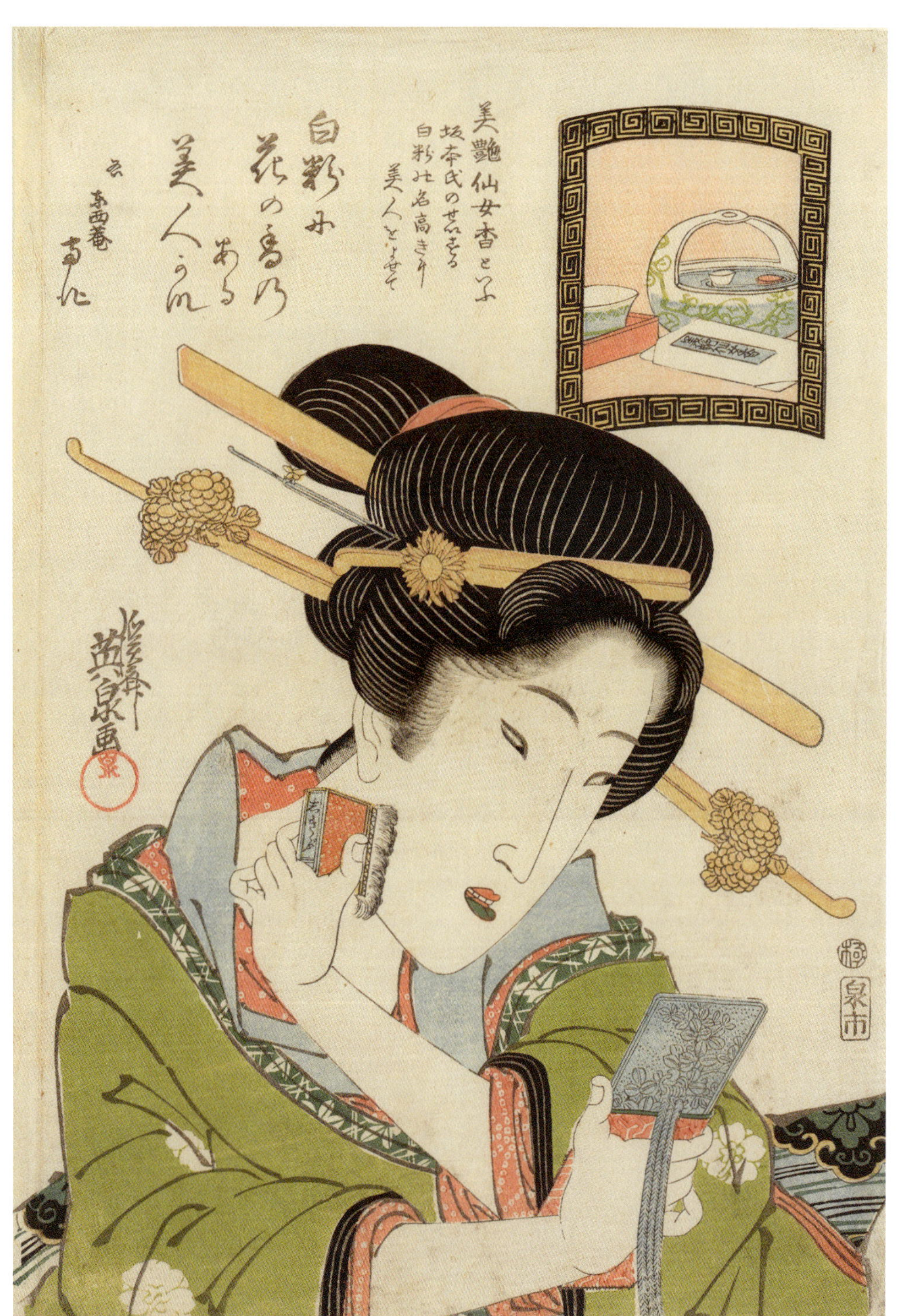
美艶 仙女香と子
坂本氏のせんをる
白粉み名高きり
美人をよせて

白粉み
花の色乃
ある
美人うれ

云
東西菴
るん

uchi), publiée vers 1832–1833 par Hōeidō, l'une des vingt séries illustrant cette route (p. 70). En plus de la Tōkaidō, ses dessins de paysages, parfois réalisés en collaboration avec d'autres artistes, comprennent des séries de vues de la province d'Ōmi, du fleuve Tama, de lieux célèbres de Kyoto et d'Osaka, ainsi qu'une vingtaine d'illustrations de sa ville natale, Edo, dont son chef-d'œuvre, *Cent Vues célèbres d'Edo*, (*Meisho Edo hyakkei* 1856–1858 ; p. 71). Ces estampes représentent des milliers d'illustrations exceptionnelles.

Hiroshige était aussi passé maître dans l'art des *kachōga*, images d'oiseaux et de fleurs qu'il réalisa par centaines. Le nombre total de ses estampes dépasse les 4500, sans compter les illustrations de quelque 150 ouvrages, des centaines de peintures, dont 200 que lui avaient commandées les seigneurs du clan Oda, dans la province de Tendō. Le succès des illustrations d'Hiroshige est de plusieurs ordres. Celui-ci excellait dans l'adaptation d'images créées par d'autres artistes et illustrateurs au format de la gravure sur bois en couleur à feuille unique, mais ses compositions saisissantes, grâce à des cadrages hardis et à la perspective à point de fuite unique, suscitant un effet spectaculaire, dénotent une approche novatrice du dessin. Comme son maître Toyohiro, Hiroshige avait un talent unique pour incorporer des figures, représentées avec sensibilité et même un humour tendre, dans des paysages empreints d'un lyrisme tranquille.

Dans la série « Hōeidō Tōkaidō », Hiroshige souligne la splendeur des paysages traversés par la route avec un style innovateur et en adoptant le format *ōban* (environ 27 × 39 cm), aux dimensions inhabituellement grandes pour les sujets paysagers à cette époque[11]. Alors que les premières estampes de cette série s'inspirent peut-être des voyages personnels d'Hiroshige, bientôt, de plus en plus de vues trouvent leur origine dans les illustrations monochromes d'autres artistes, publiées dans divers guides de voyage[12]. Enthousiasmés par leur succès, Hiroshige et Takenouchi élaborent un autre projet de thèmes paysagers et l'annoncent dans une feuille publicitaire insérée dans des albums reliés de collections complètes de gravures de la Tōkaidō, vendues à compter du premier mois de 1834. Y figure la première série de la Kisokaidō, portant le titre *Série d'authentiques vues sur la route Kiso dans le style des peintures de paysages et des scènes de genre* (*Kiso dōchū shinkei tsuzuki sansui jinbutsu-e*).

Comme Hiroshige, Eisen (pp. 11, 90) est né à Edo, dans une famille de samouraïs. Son père était le célèbre calligraphe Ikeda Masahei Shigeharu. Très jeune, Eisen étudie la peinture auprès d'Hakkeisai, peintre de l'école de Kano et actif au début du XIXe siècle. Par la suite, il est en pension chez le fils du créateur d'estampes Kikugawa Eizan (1787–1867) ; il déclarera plus tard avoir étudié auprès d'Eizan, mais l'incertitude plane sur les détails de cette relation.

Eisen est l'auteur de 1900 estampes, ainsi que d'illustrations de quelque 400 ouvrages couvrant toutes sortes de genres et de sujets. Sa spécialité était les portraits de belles femmes, ou *bijinga* (p. 74). Imitant Eizan, Eisen s'est inspiré, pour ces portraits, de ceux de Kitagawa Utamaro (1753–1806), avant d'élaborer un style propre, sensuel et aux contours marqués, qui domina le marché de l'estampe. Comme

KEISAI EISEN, *Woman Putting on Face Powder / Frau beim Auftragen von Gesichtspuder / Femme se poudrant le visage*, c. 1824. From the series: *Senjokō Face Powder*. Published by Izumiya Ichibei. Woodblock print, ink and colour on paper, ōban, 36.8 × 25.7 cm / 14 ½ × 10 ¼ in. Minneapolis Institute of Art, Gift of Louis W. Hill, Jr.

nombre de ses pairs, Eisen a réalisé des images érotiques, connues sous l'appellation de *shunga*. Il vendit des cosmétiques et dirigea une maison close à Nezu sous le nom de Wakatakeya Satosuke. Sous la tutelle de Namiki Gohei II (1768–1819), il apprit à écrire des pièces kabuki publiées sous le nom de Chiyoda Saiichi. Écrivain prolifique, il est l'auteur d'œuvres légères sous le nom d'Ippitsuan Kakō, ainsi que d'essais sous les pseudonymes de Mumeiō et de Kaedegawa Shiin. Ses meilleures œuvres littéraires comptent les *Essais d'un vieillard anonyme* (*Mumeiō zuihitsu*, 1833), édition revue de l'*Anthologie de l'ukiyo-e* (*Ukiyo-e ruikō*), recueil de biographies d'artistes de l'estampe, réunies par Ōta Nanpo (1749–1823) en 1789. Les ajouts d'Eisen au recueil de Nanpo évoquent ses beuveries et ses soirées de débauche dans les quartiers des plaisirs d'Edo.

Né à Edo, dans le quartier de Kyōbashi, en 1781, Takenouchi Magohachi est le deuxième fils de Magoshichi, prêteur sur gages (p. 10). De 1832 à 1837 (Tenpō 3–8), il illustre des recueils de poésie *kyōka* sous le pseudonyme de Bizan. C'est probablement avec la maison d'édition Hōeidō qu'il publie, en 1832 également, les premiers dessins d'Hiroshige dans la série initiale de la Tōkaidō. En 1833, Takenouchi se lance dans l'édition d'estampes d'acteurs du théâtre kabuki et de belles femmes, réalisées par Kunisada (1786–1865), et de guerriers, signées Utagawa Kuniyoshi (1797–1861). En 1834, il publie des romans illustrés, parmi lesquels *La Légende du retour de Mikuni Tarō* (*Mikuni Tarō sairai den*), avec des illustrations de Kuniyoshi, d'Utagawa Kuninao (1793–1854) et de lui-même. Cet ouvrage en trois volumes paraît au cours du premier mois de 1835 ; au dos de deux des volumes figurent des annonces publicitaires identiques désignant Hiroshige comme l'auteur d'une nouvelle série de la Kisokaidō (p. 28), intitulée *Série d'images de paysages de la route Kiso* (*Kiso dōchū fūkei tsuzuki-e*)[13].

Diffusées avant la publication des premiers dessins de cette série, les annonces publicitaires de 1834 et 1835 reflètent les projets de la collaboration Takenouchi-Hiroshige ; toutefois, la réalité s'avère différente. Ce n'est pas Hiroshige, mais Eisen qui a réalisé ces premiers dessins pour Takenouchi en 1835. Eisen ne fait pas partie des auteurs d'estampes de l'école d'Utagawa, comme Hiroshige. Takenouchi doit avoir choisi Eisen plutôt que d'autres artistes de cette école avec lesquels il avait déjà collaboré, comme Kunisada et Kuniyoshi, peut-être parce que ces deux artistes s'intéressaient peu aux estampes de paysages. Au cours des décennies précédentes, Eisen avait réalisé plusieurs paysages pour différents éditeurs, mais sans succès, si ce n'est une série de vues en perspective de lieux célèbres d'Edo, chacune accompagnée d'un épais cadre noir portant des inscriptions blanches en néerlandais, série parue au début des années 1830[14]. Eisen est aussi l'auteur d'une série sur la Tōkaidō (au milieu des années 1820), mais dont les jolies femmes étaient le sujet principal, les paysages étant confinés dans des cartouches placés près des figures (p. 77)[15].

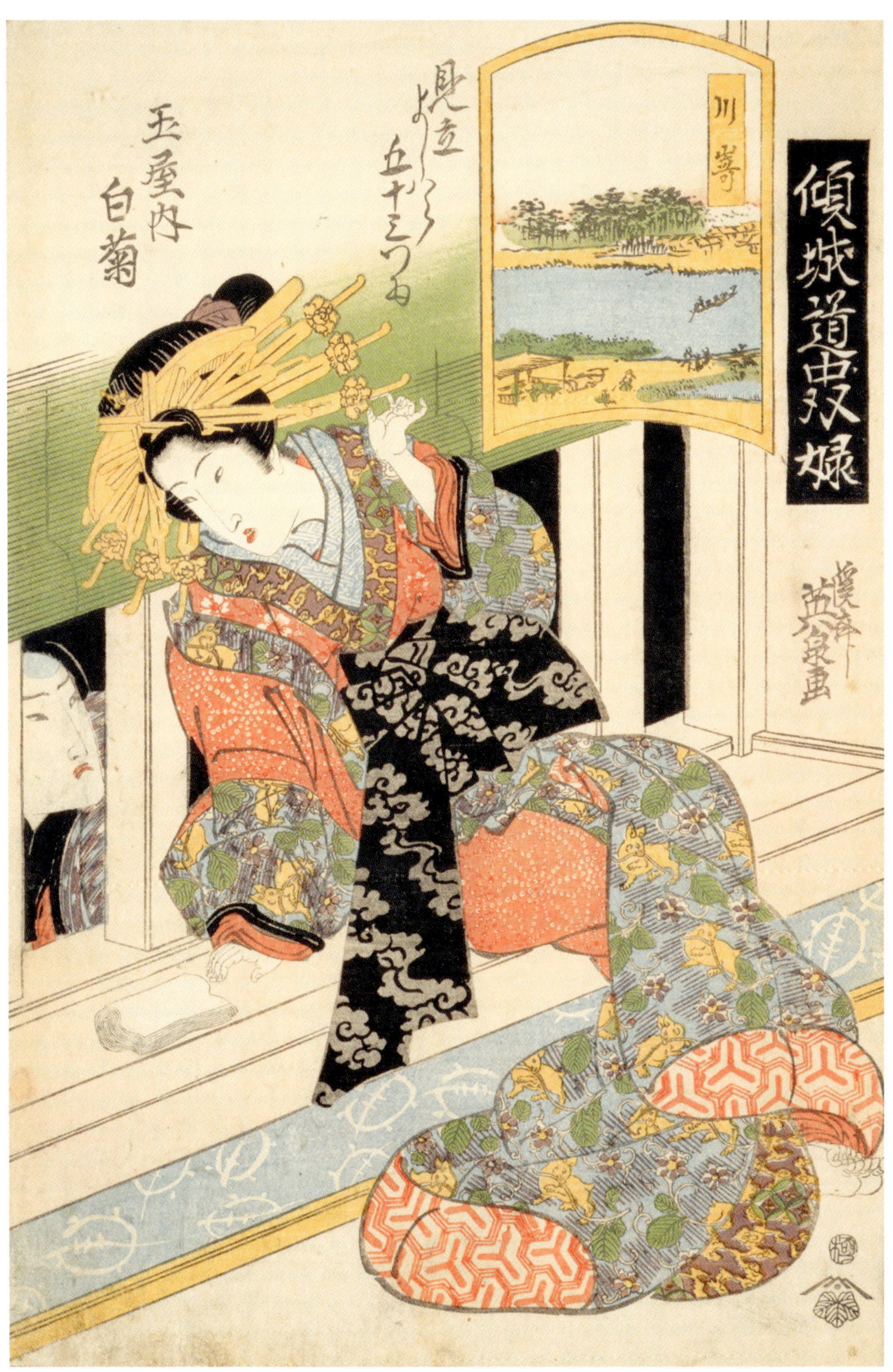
傾城道中双娯
川崎
見立
よし〳〵
五十三つぎ
玉屋内
白菊
渓斎
英泉画

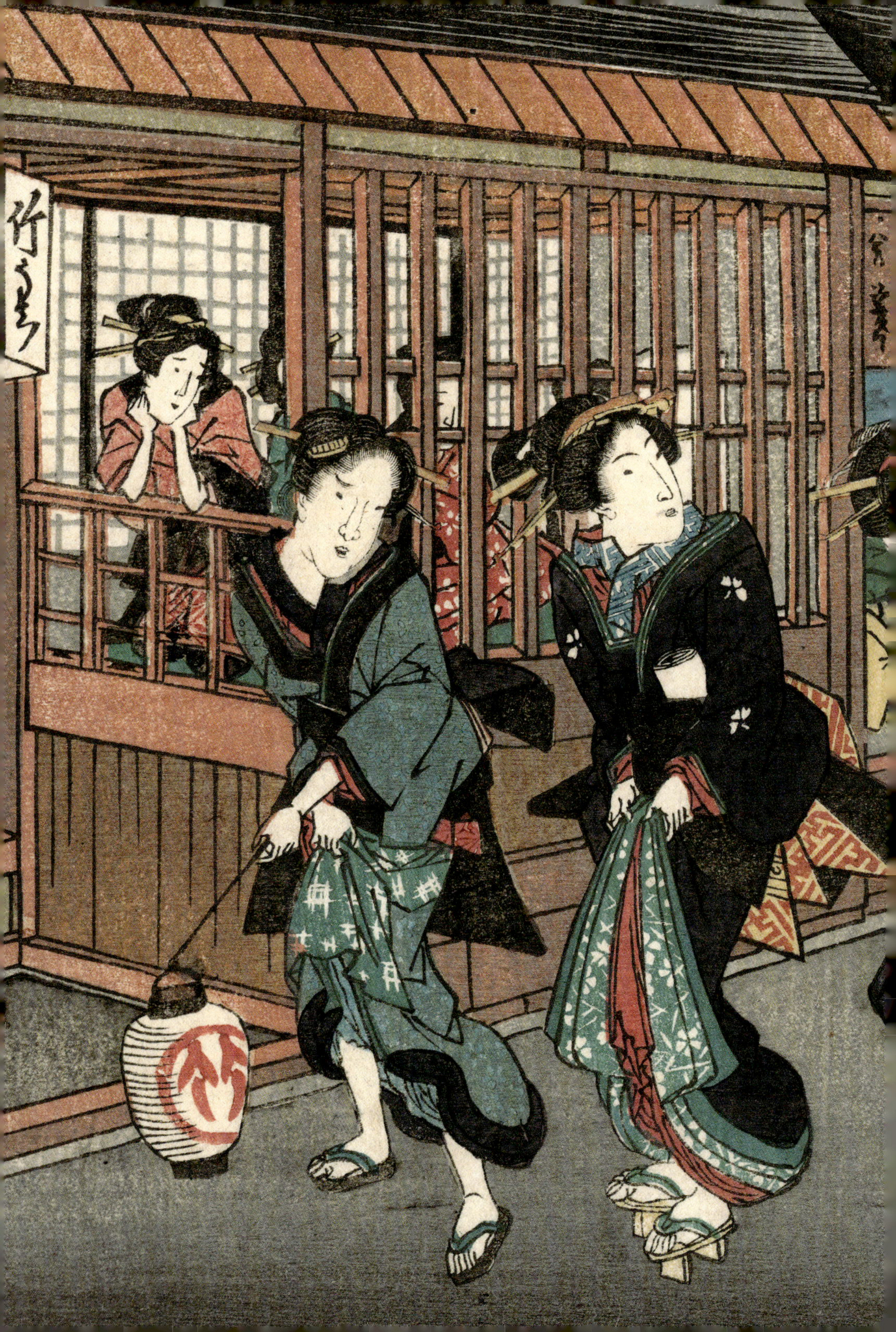

竹うち

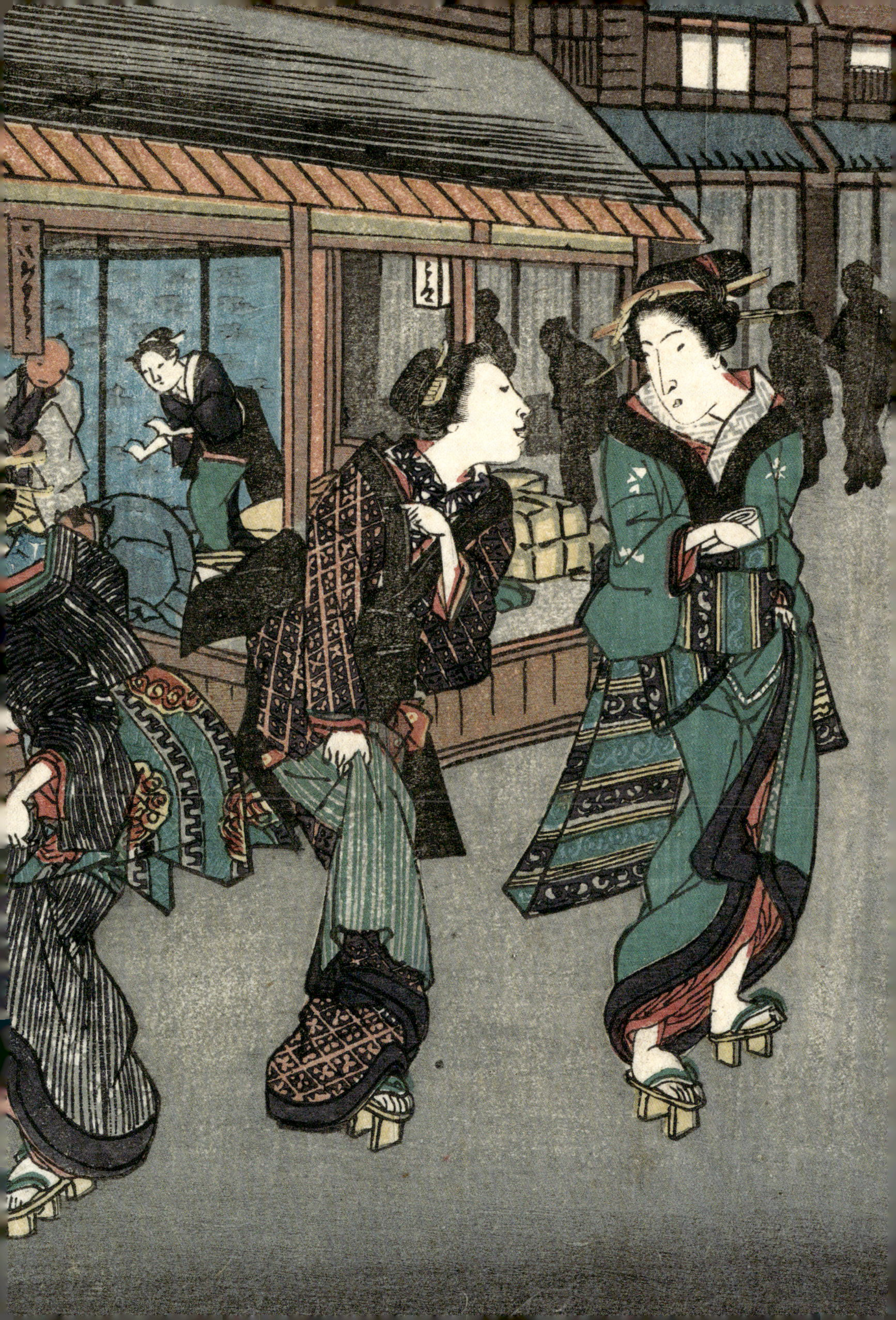

La première série de la Kisokaidō s'ouvre avec le pont Nihonbashi à Edo. Eisen a incorporé à son dessin une référence au signe zodiacal de l'an six de l'ère Tenpō (généralement associée à l'année 1835), avec le caractère du mouton (*hitsuji*) inscrit sur une ombrelle ouverte au centre de l'image[16]. On estime que ces premiers dessins ont été publiés cette année-là, mais on s'interroge encore sur les raisons qui font d'Eisen leur auteur et non Hiroshige. Il est possible que Takenouchi n'ait plus voulu attendre et qu'Hiroshige ait été en voyage ; au cours du cinquième mois, par exemple, Hiroshige a quitté Edo pendant plusieurs semaines afin d'aller peindre au temple Senkokuji, dans la préfecture voisine de Kanagawa. La participation d'Eisen ne semble pas avoir gêné Hiroshige quand ce dernier a rejoint le projet par la suite. Dans l'annonce accompagnant un livre publié par Takenouchi au cours du premier mois de 1836, Eisen apparaît comme auteur des illustrations ; le titre de la série semble attester que des gravures ont déjà été publiées : *Série de grandes estampes de brocart de la route Kiso (Kisoji tsuzuki ōnishiki-e)*[17]. L'annonce publicitaire figurant dans un deuxième ouvrage paru la même année indique qu'Eisen est l'auteur des gravures et souligne que celles-ci ont un format horizontal et non vertical : *Série d'images horizontales sur la route Kiso (Kiso dōchū tsuzuki yoko-e)*[18].

Toutefois, Eisen n'est l'auteur que de vingt-quatre des soixante et onze estampes réalisées. Elles sont toutes numérotées, la première étant la vue de Nihonbashi à Edo, également intitulée *Première vue de la série de la Kisokaidō (Kisokaidō tsuzuki no ichi)*. Les onze premières estampes sont d'Eisen, mais la cohérence s'arrête là, car l'artiste semble avoir choisi à son gré les stations qu'il voulait illustrer, et Takenouchi en a publié onze autres de lui ; deux estampes supplémentaires non signées sont attribuées

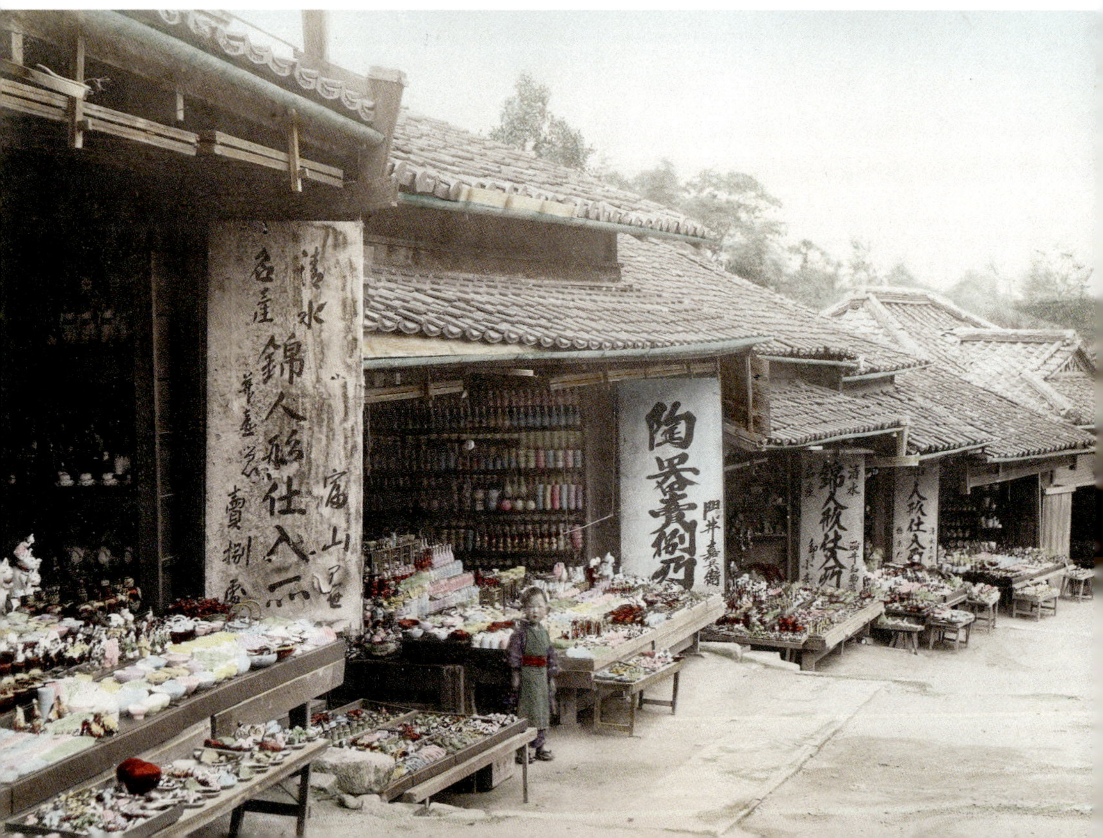

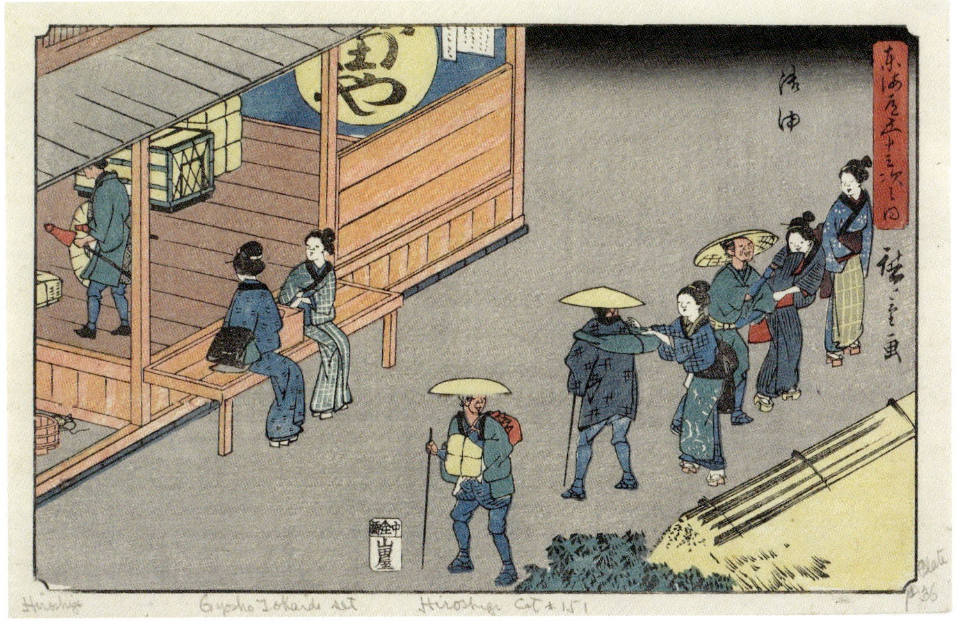

à Eisen. Les vingt-deux estampes signées ont peut-être été gravées à la fin de 1836, époque à laquelle Eisen en avait terminé avec cet ouvrage. Il s'est ensuite à nouveau consacré à la Tōkaidō et à une série de belles femmes, chacune placée sur une bande de nuages, devant un paysage occupant le tiers supérieur de l'arrière-plan d'une estampe[19].

L'absence de référence précise aux soixante-neuf stations dans les annonces publicitaires ou dans les titres des estampes d'Eisen permet de conclure qu'il n'y a eu aucune intention de produire une série complète à raison d'une estampe par station, lors des préparatifs initiaux de Takenouchi et d'Hiroshige ou au cours de la première phase avec Eisen. Du point de vue économique, la Kisokaidō était trop risquée pour les éditeurs, car cette route n'était pas assez connue pour engager un investissement sur soixante et onze estampes, ce que corrobore l'absence d'autres séries de paysages de la Kisokaidō dans l'histoire de l'*ukiyo-e* ; la Kisokaidō n'allait réapparaître qu'à deux reprises comme thème de série, en 1852–1853, à l'apogée de l'histoire de ce genre pictural. Ces deux séries de soixante-douze estampes chacune, que l'on doit respectivement à Kuniyoshi et à Kunisada, se servent de la Kisokaidō comme motif récurrent pour présenter, en réalité, des légendes et des pièces kabuki ; l'une et l'autre ne comprennent presque toujours que des éléments de paysage génériques sans lien avec les relais de poste et pourraient se situer

Tᴀᴍᴀᴍᴜʀᴀ Kōᴢᴀʙᴜʀō, *Souvenir Shops in Kyoto / Souvenirshops in Kyoto / Boutiques de souvenirs à Kyoto*, c. 1880. Albumen print, hand-coloured. Kjeld Duits Collection

Uᴛᴀɢᴀᴡᴀ Hɪʀᴏsʜɪɢᴇ, *Goyu*, early 1850s. From the series: *The Fifty-Three Stations along the Tōkaidō*. Published by Yamadaya Shōjirō. Colour woodblock print, *aiban*, 31.9 × 34.4 cm / 12 ½ × 13 ½ in. Minneapolis Institute of Art, Gift of Louis W. Hill, Jr., 81.133.224

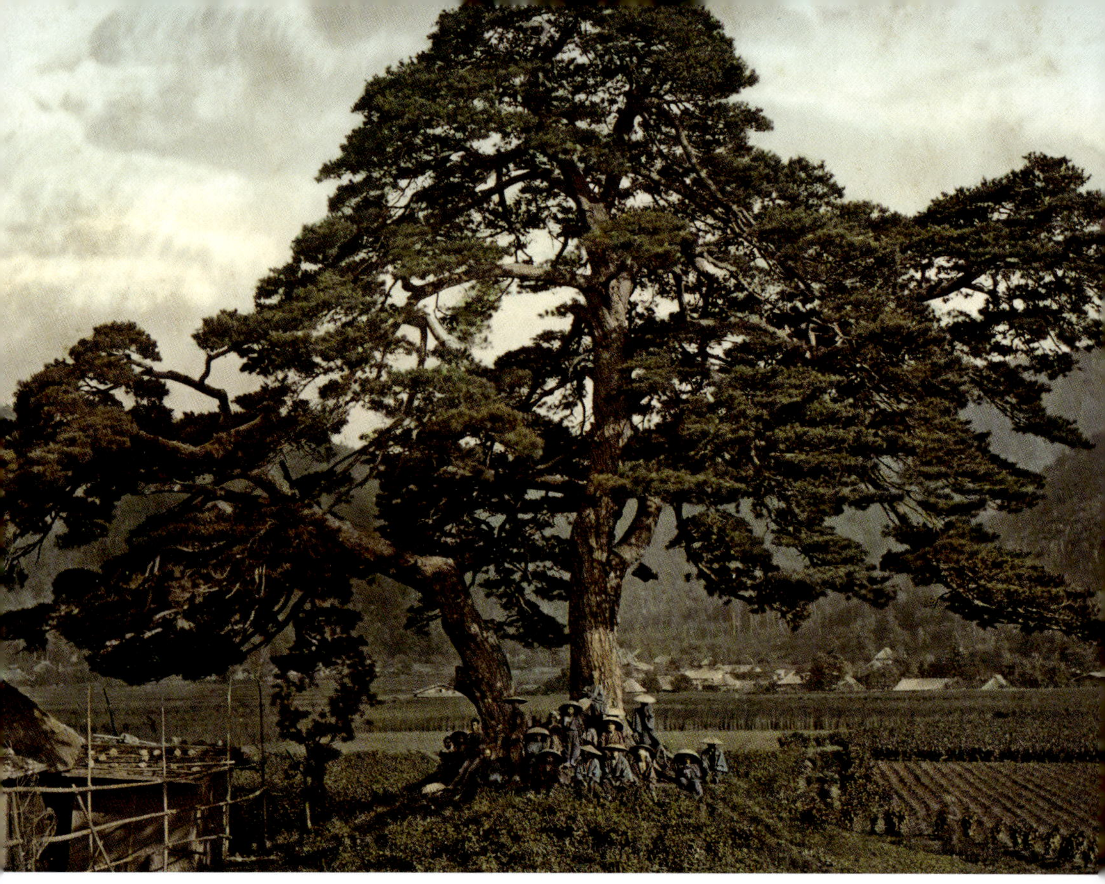

n'importe où dans le Japon rural (pp. 53, 56, 59)[20]. Il en va de même pour les dessins d'Eisen. Celui-ci s'est inspiré d'autres images, comme on peut le voir dans ses trois premiers dessins, Nihonbashi, Itabashi et Warabi, qui évoquent pour le spectateur Nihonbashi, Shinagawa et Kawasaki, les trois premières estampes destinées par Hiroshige à la série de la Tōkaidō. Les autres estampes d'Eisen ne représentent pas des éléments de paysages précis susceptibles d'être associés à un lieu géographique, mais s'inspirent d'illustrations figurant dans l'ouvrage en plusieurs volumes déjà cité, *Kisoji meisho zue* (pp. 23, 30, 49)[21].

Takenouchi a donc fini par interrompre le projet d'estampes de la Kisokaidō et il semble avoir cessé à cette époque de s'intéresser à l'édition en général. Selon certains historiens, la maison Takenouchi, modeste et relativement jeune, rencontra des difficultés après s'être lancée dans la série de la Kisokaidō,

KUSAKABE KINBEI, *Travellers Resting below a Huge Pine Tree on the Nakasendō / Reisende während der Rast unter einer großen Pinie auf dem Nakasendō / Voyageurs se reposant sous un grand pin sur la route Nakasendō*, c. 1880. Albumen print, hand-coloured. Pump Park Collection

PP. 84/85
Kutsukake (detail from plate 20)

KEISAI EISEN, *Kutsukake Station. View of Rain on the Plain of Hiratsuka / Station Kutsukake. Ansicht des Regens auf der Ebene von Hiratsuka / Station de Kutsukake. La plaine de Hiratsuka sous la pluie*, c. 1840. From the series: *The Sixty-Nine Stations along the Kisokaidō*, plate 20. Colour woodblock print, *ōban*, 31.9 × 34.4 cm / 12 ½ × 13 ½ in. Minneapolis Institute of Art, Gift of Louis W. Hill, Jr., 81.133.6

et son propriétaire dut s'associer à un autre éditeur, Iseya Rihei. Toutefois, contrairement à la série de la Tōkaidō pour laquelle, quelques années auparavant, Takenouchi s'était associé à la solide maison d'édition de Tsuruya Kiemon, Iseya Rihei reprit le projet de la Kisokaidō et finit par publier près des deux tiers des estampes sans que Takenouchi n'y participe. La grande famine de l'ère Tenpō, qui sévit dans la seconde moitié des années 1830, affecta peu Edo, mais a pu perturber le marché des estampes en raison de la chute du nombre de voyageurs en provenance des provinces touchées, ce qui provoqua une baisse des ventes de souvenirs et des gravures de paysages. Pourtant, les ventes de la série de la Tōkaidō d'Hiroshige, ainsi que celles d'estampes de la Kisokaidō par Eisen, durent être phénoménales, à en juger par les nombreuses variantes existantes de chaque dessin, preuve que les matrices furent utilisées jusqu'à usure complète et que certaines furent remplacées par des neuves. Il paraît probable que Takenouchi ait délibérément quitté le domaine de l'édition, puisque ce n'était pas sa seule source de revenus, mais un métier que l'écrivain et peintre qu'il était à ses heures avait adopté par plaisir, alors qu'il avait dépassé les cinquante ans. Les dernières œuvres de sa production qu'il est possible de dater avec certitude sont du printemps 1837, lorsque Takenouchi publia quelques portraits d'acteurs de Kunisada, ainsi qu'un autre de ses propres livres. Il est mort en 1854.

C'est vraisemblablement fin 1836 ou début 1837 que la maison d'édition Kinjudō d'Iseya Rihei, en activité depuis les années 1790, reprit le projet de la Kisokaidō de Takenouchi en y investissant d'importantes sommes d'argent, avec l'acquisition des matrices des estampes d'Eisen et l'engagement d'Hiroshige pour la réalisation de nouveaux dessins qui allaient compléter la série. Doté d'une expérience considérable en matière d'estampes de paysage, Iseya Rihei avait aussi publié, au début des années 1800, deux séries d'Hokusai sur la Tōkaidō. Iseya n'avait édité qu'un petit nombre d'estampes de jolies femmes

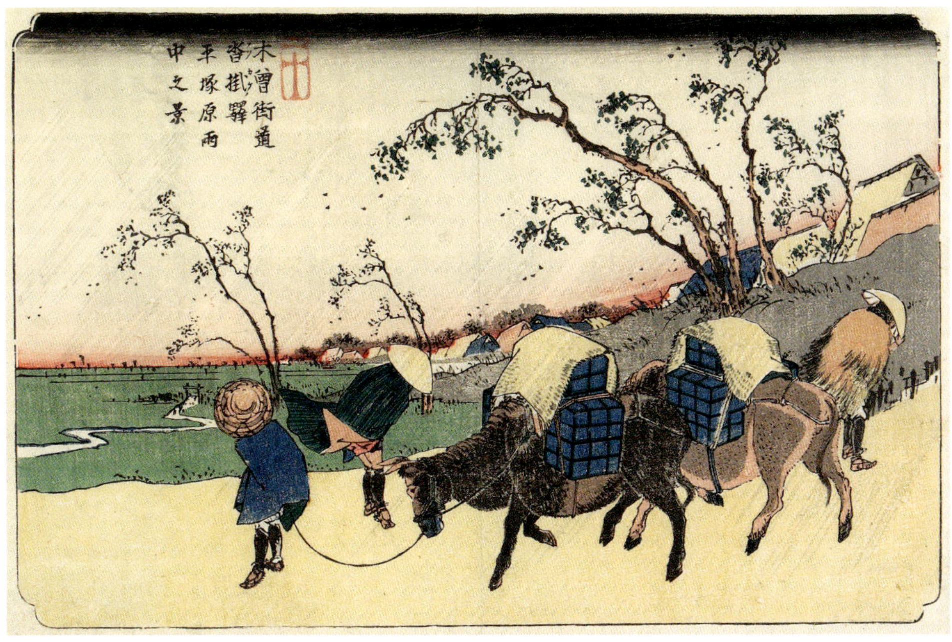

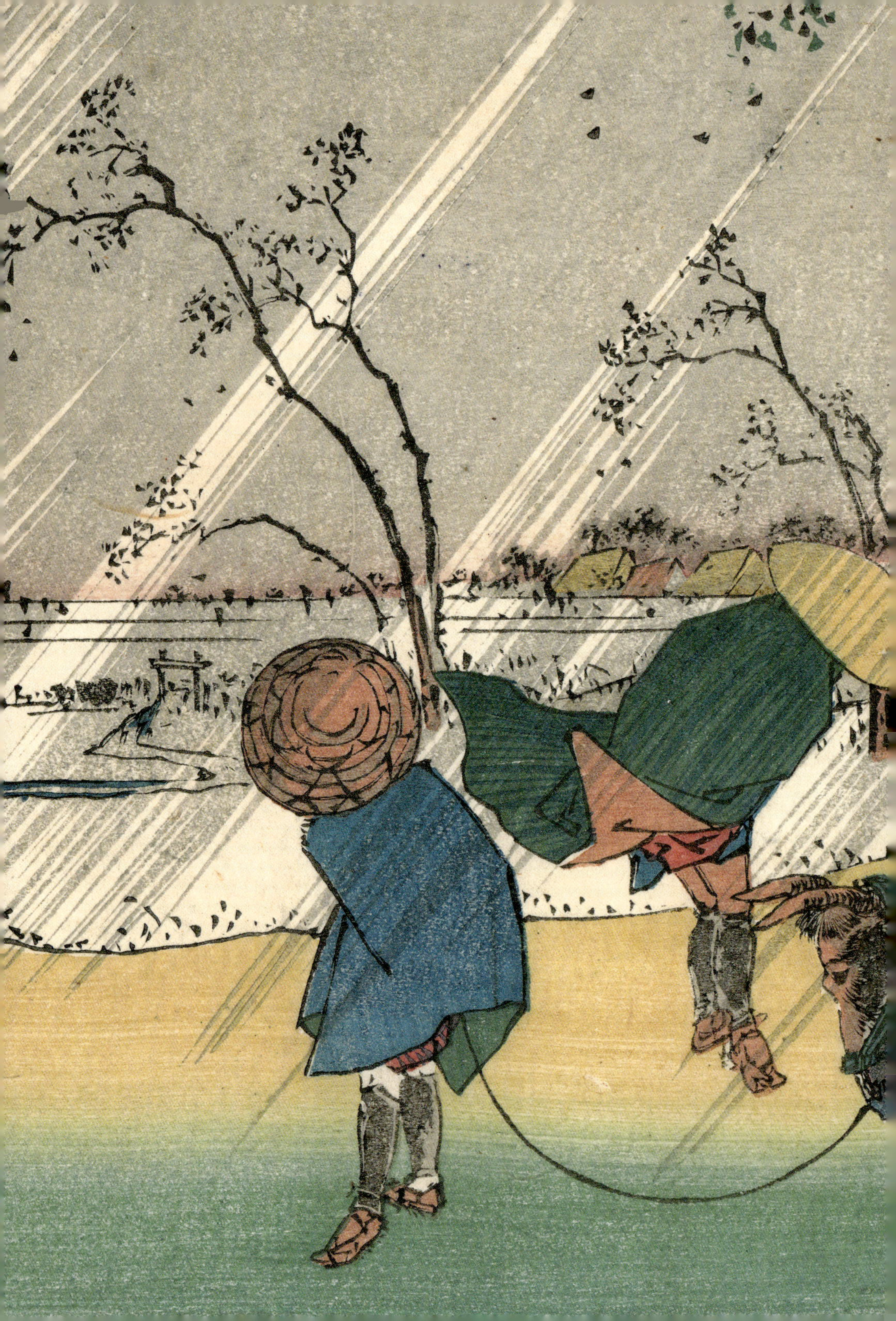

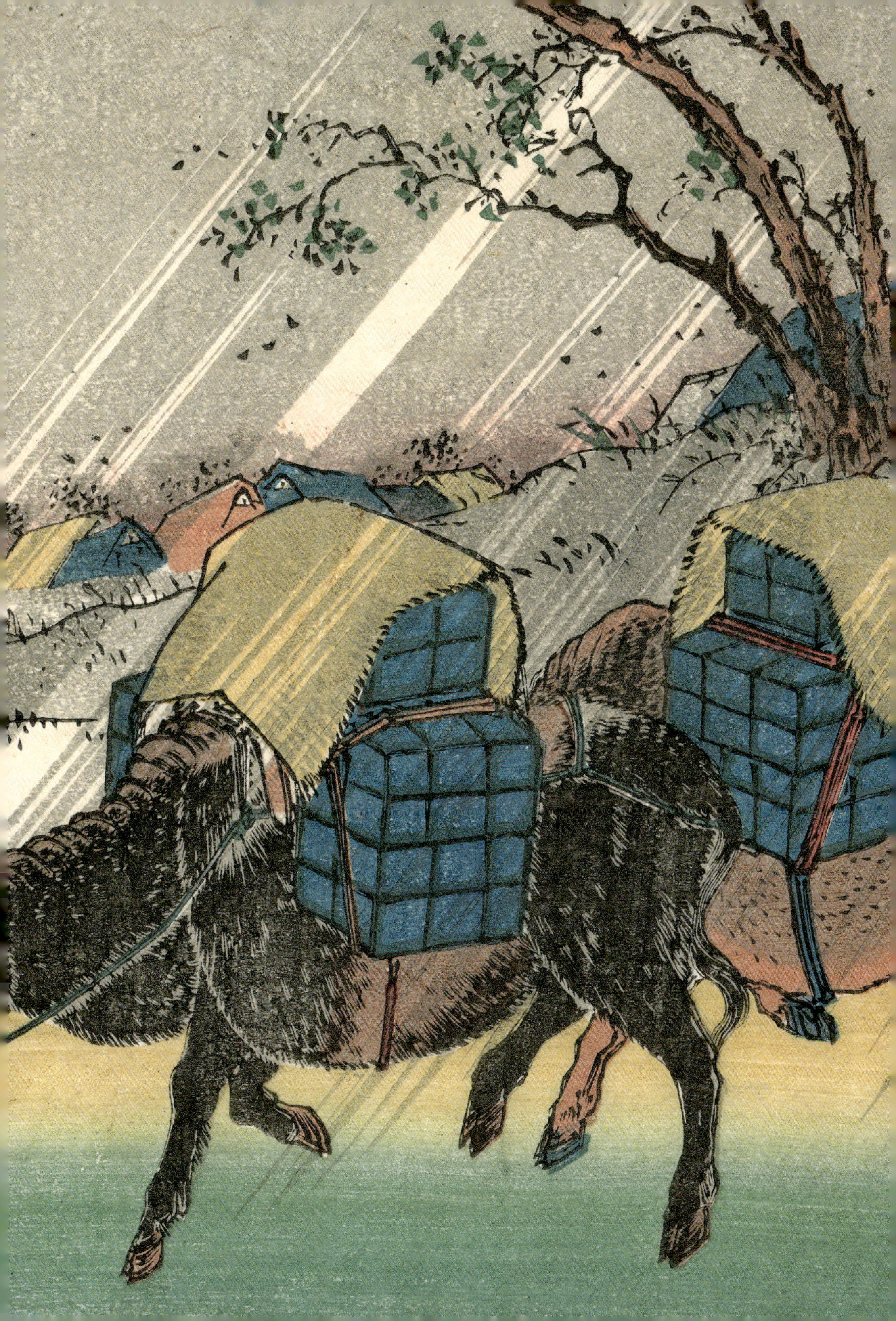

d'Eisen dans les années 1820 et travaillait habituellement avec des artistes de l'école d'Utagawa comme Toyokuni, Kuniyasu (1794–1832), Kuniyoshi et, surtout, Kunisada, mais il n'avait jamais encore collaboré avec Hiroshige. C'est peut-être Takenouchi qui a recommandé à Iseya de faire appel à ce dernier, à moins que ce ne soit Kunisada, créateur le plus important d'Iseya dans les années 1830 et qui aurait été un ami d'Hiroshige. La nouvelle équipe s'engagea à relever le défi de réaliser une série complète, comme l'indique le nouveau titre de toutes les estampes d'Hiroshige : *Les soixante-neuf stations de la route Kisokaidō* (*Kisokaidō rokujūkyū tsugi no uchi*).

Quatre des estampes d'Hiroshige – Takasaki, Karuizawa, Fukushima et Toriimoto (planches 14, 19, 38, 64) – portent les sceaux d'éditeur de Takenouchi et d'Iseya et ont peut-être été les premières publiées. Suivent deux estampes non signées, Itahana et Sakamoto (planches 15, 18), qui seraient de la main d'Eisen et que Takenouchi avaient reçues, mais que, pour une raison inconnue, celui-ci décida de ne pas éditer. De ces deux estampes, c'est Itahana qui a été tirée la première, car certains tirages portent le sceau d'éditeur de Takenouchi appliqué à la main ; ces tirages semblent constituer l'ultime contribution de ce dernier au projet. L'estampe de Sakamoto a été réalisée par Iseya seul, de même que les vingt-deux dessins produits ensuite par Hiroshige en 1837 jusqu'à une nouvelle césure, quand l'artiste a quitté Edo pour voyager sur la Kisokaidō.

Presque toutes les estampes de la Kisokaidō liées à la dernière partie du trajet, d'Ochiai (planche 45) à Kyoto, s'inspirent de croquis réalisés par Hiroshige pendant ce voyage (cf. p. 444 sq.). Seize d'entre elles reprennent ses croquis, qui figurent dans deux livres parvenus jusqu'à nous et sont aujourd'hui conservés au British Museum à Londres[22]. Cinq autres dessins de stations qui suivent celle d'Ochiai ont dû être effectués après le retour d'Hiroshige à Edo car, dans ces vingt et une estampes, sa signature

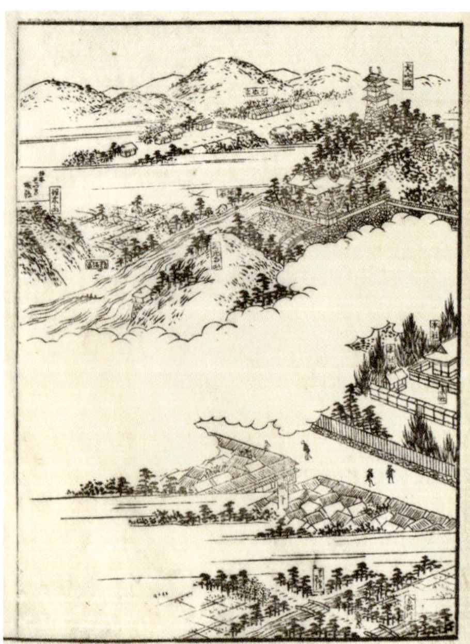
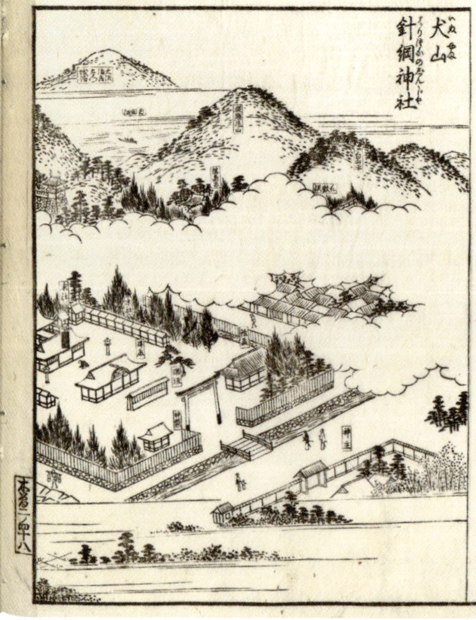

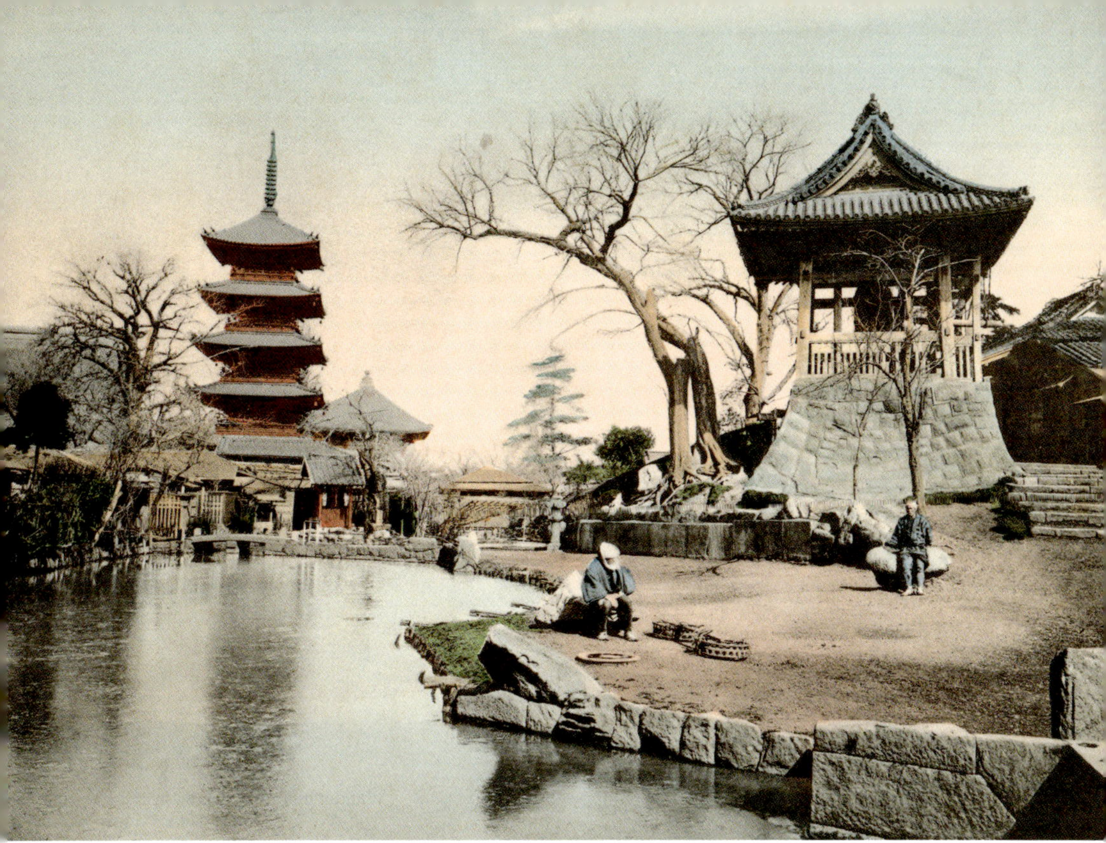

diffère de celles des estampes précédentes[23]. La réalisation de la série de la Kisokaidō à partir des croquis réels reprend l'idée originale de Takenouchi et d'Hiroshige telle qu'elle figure dans l'annonce publicitaire de 1834 où l'on trouve l'expression *shinkei*, « vues authentiques », signe que les scènes représentées ont été dessinées sur les lieux (p. 56, cf. le détail pp. 54 55), ce qui ne s'était jamais fait avant 1837.

Alors que le point de départ, Nihonbashi, est illustré par une estampe de la série, on n'en trouve aucune pour Kyoto. Hiroshige ayant dessiné quelques séries comprenant des paysages de Kyoto, il paraît étrange qu'il ait parcouru toute la route sans proposer une illustration de cette ville importante. L'existence de deux dessins de l'une des stations, Nakatsugawa, constitue une autre anomalie. La première (répertoriée ici sous le numéro 46a) est très rare, et il n'existe qu'une seule version sans variations de couleur, ce qui indique que les matrices étaient très endommagées avant la réalisation de nouveaux tirages. Cette usure a dû se produire après le début du premier tirage, à en juger par les rares épreuves qui subsistent ; à son retour, Hiroshige a réalisé une seconde version très différente (planche 46b), inspirée de ses croquis.

NISHIMURA CHŪWA, *Unuma*. From: Akisato Ritō,
*Views of Famous Sights along the Kiso Road (Kisoji
meisho zue)*, vol. 5, 1805. Woodblock-printed book.
Munich, Bayerische Staatsbibliothek

*Asakusa District in Tokyo / Das Asakusa-Viertel
in Tokio / Le quartier Asakusa à Tokyo*, c. 1895.
Photochrom, hand-coloured.
Paris, Marc Walter Collection

Les historiens ont longtemps cru que la réalisation de toutes les feuilles de cette série dura jusqu'en 1842, alors qu'une période de sept ans paraît très improbable, vu le rythme très soutenu du marché de l'estampe, avide de nouvelles illustrations[24]. Selon des recherches récentes, la date de fin de la production serait plutôt 1838, car une épreuve de la dernière estampe, Ōtsu (planche 70), considérée comme appartenant au dernier lot d'illustrations réalisées par Hiroshige, porte cette date au verso, ainsi que le nom du collectionneur (voir le tableau synoptique dans l'appendice, p. 509)[25]. En revanche, cette date ne signale que la fin de la première édition, car il n'existe aucun indice quant au moment précis où de nouvelles épreuves ont été tirées, ce qui a dû être fréquent pour certaines estampes, d'après les nombreuses variations qui les distinguent.

Au fil de l'histoire, l'État japonais a modifié plusieurs fois la réglementation de la censure régissant les estampes. À l'époque de la création de cette série, c'est le sceau du censeur *kiwame* qui devait être obtenu pour chaque illustration avant la réalisation du tirage. Ce sceau ne portait aucune information précise sur la date d'agrément. Le sceau *kiwame* était appliqué dans la marge de l'estampe, mais, comme les collectionneurs rognaient souvent leurs épreuves au bord de la marge, certaines d'entre elles sont aujourd'hui dépourvues du sceau. Lorsqu'une illustration avait été autorisée à la publication, elle ne devait plus être soumise à la censure quand un éditeur, propriétaire des matrices, décidait par la suite de réimprimer, même si les règles de la censure avaient changé entre-temps, comme au début des années 1840. On ne peut distinguer les retirages que par les changements visibles à la comparaison de plusieurs épreuves et par la qualité de l'impression, laquelle dépend de l'état des matrices. Des couleurs parfaitement alignées sont le signe d'une faible usure des matrices et donc d'un premier tirage. Certaines estampes de cette série ayant rencontré un vif succès, la qualité des épreuves varie considérablement. En général, un éditeur commandait des lots de deux cents épreuves et devait en vendre environ six cents pour amortir ses frais : honoraires de l'artiste, du graveur ayant réalisé les matrices, de l'imprimeur pour le papier, les pigments et la main-d'œuvre, celle-ci pouvant inclure des opérations de tirage spéciales comme la gradation des couleurs (*bokashi*), si elles figuraient dans la commande[26].

L'activité d'Iseya Rihei reste soutenue jusqu'au début des années 1840, époque où le monde de l'édition connaît un bouleversement quand l'État cherche à le contrôler plus strictement avec les réformes de l'ère Tenpō : ces nouvelles lois somptuaires imposent des contraintes aux dessinateurs et aux artisans et mettent certains éditeurs dans de graves difficultés financières. Iseya semble avoir cessé de publier de nouvelles estampes au milieu des années 1840, mais, en 1851, il figure encore au répertoire de la Nouvelle Faction de la Guilde des éditeurs de livres illustrés et d'estampes[27]. C'est vraisemblablement dans la seconde moitié des années 1830, alors qu'il fait imprimer les nouvelles estampes d'Hiroshige, qu'Iseya réimprime les dessins d'Eisen : dans certains cas, il modifie les matrices en supprimant le sceau et/ou le nom de Takenouchi qu'il remplace parfois par le sien, comme dans le cas de Nihonbashi. Les artistes étant payés au forfait pour leurs créations lors de la livraison à l'éditeur, Iseya peut ensuite les modifier à son gré ; il supprime également la signature d'Eisen, sans doute parce qu'Hiroshige est désormais devenu

Kusakabe Kinbei, *Yasaka Pagoda in Kyoto / Die Yasaka-Pagode in Kyoto / La pagode Yasaka à Kyoto*, c. 1890s. Albumen print, hand-coloured. Pump Park Collection

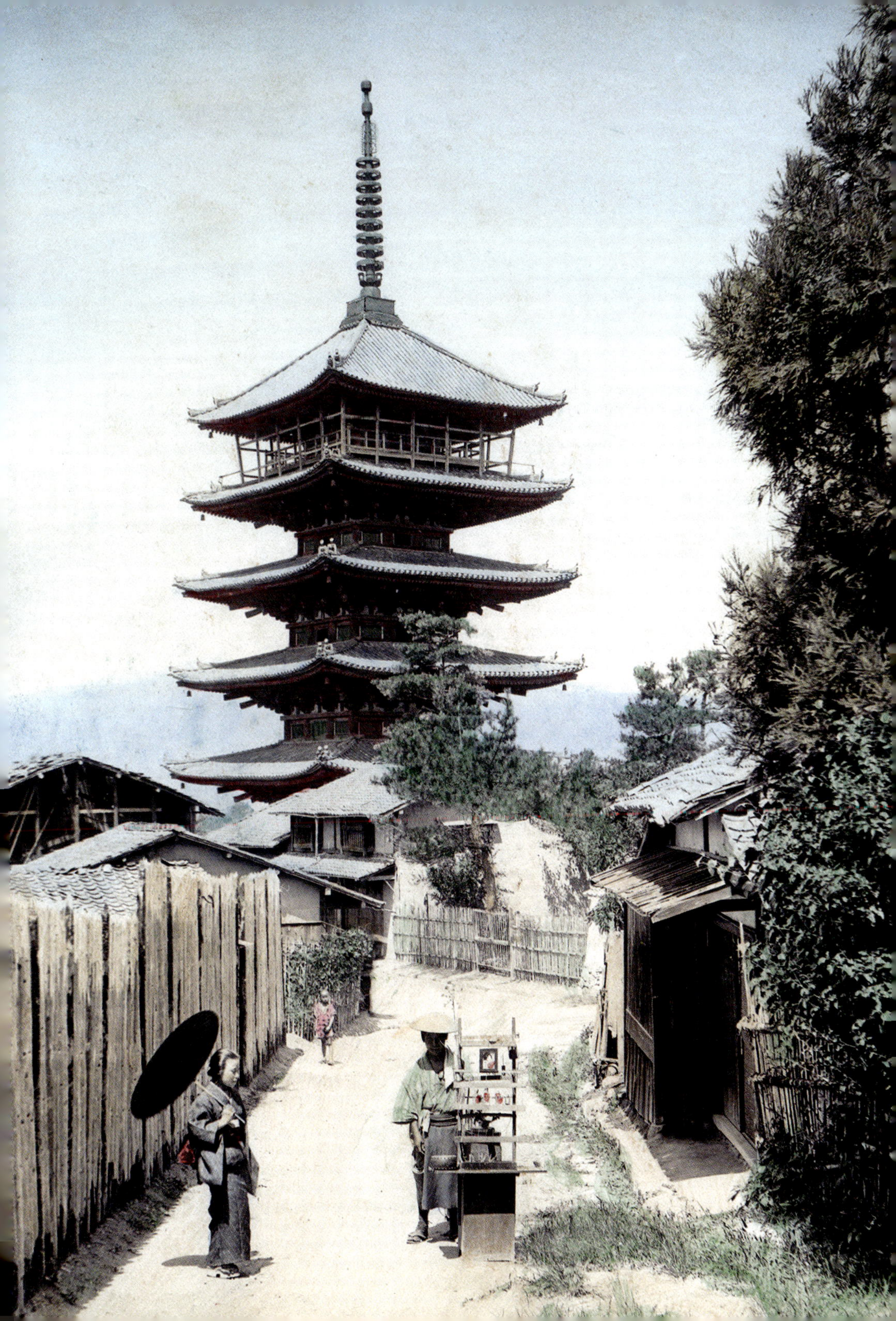

l'étoile qui brille au firmament de l'estampe de paysage. Peut-être Iseya a-t-il spéculé sur la possibilité de meilleures ventes s'il prétendait qu'Hiroshige était l'auteur de toutes les estampes de cette série[28].

C'est peut-être au milieu des années 1840, au moment où il cesse de publier de nouvelles estampes, qu'Iseya vend les matrices de la Kisokaidō à la société Kinkyōdō de l'éditeur Yamadaya Shōbei (dates inconnues). À partir de 1846, ce dernier connaît un grand succès avec la publication de romans sentimentaux illustrés ; à la fin de 1851, Shōjirō (dates inconnues), son héritier, reprend l'affaire et conserve cette formule jusqu'en 1866 environ. Au début des années 1850 probablement, Yamadaya réimprime la série *Gyōsho Tōkaidō* (*La Tōkaidō en calligraphie cursive*) d'Hiroshige, publiée pour la première fois vers 1841–1842 (p. 81). On ignore quand il a procédé à un nouveau tirage de la série de la Kisokaidō, mais il en a modifié la plupart des matrices en supprimant les anciens sceaux d'éditeur, méthode plus simple que le remplacement coûteux de ces sceaux par le sien. Il n'a apposé son propre sceau que dans deux cas : l'estampe de Nihonbashi et celle d'Ōta. Les vieilles matrices ayant été utilisées à de nombreuses reprises, leur usure est visible dans les épreuves réalisées par Yamadaya, qui sont de très mauvaise qualité (p. 83).[29]

À l'époque moderne, quelques entreprises japonaises se sont spécialisées dans la reproduction d'anciens dessins célèbres, dont les estampes de cette série de la Kisokaidō. Pour leur conserver un aspect authentique, elles ont été imprimées selon des méthodes traditionnelles à partir de matrices en bois qui n'étaient pas les matrices originales, mais des matrices nouvellement gravées. Par exemple, l'éditeur Watanabe Shōzaburō proposait des reproductions de toute la série de la Kisokaidō dans son catalogue de 1935, au prix de trente-cinq sen l'estampe et de vingt yen pour la série complète. Certaines reproductions étaient reliées en albums ; l'un des vendeurs y avait ajouté une nouvelle table des matières gravée sur bois (*mokuroku*)[30].

Aujourd'hui, la valeur d'une estampe de la série de la Kisokaidō dépend de plusieurs facteurs, le premier étant le dessin. Basil Stewart en 1922 et Edward Strange en 1925 considéraient que la station Kutsukake (planche 20) d'Eisen était l'une des meilleures de la série[31]. De même pour la Nagakubo d'Hiroshige (planche 28) qui, selon Stewart, est « peut-être le chef-d'œuvre de la série[32] ». La station Ōi (planche 47) fait aussi l'admiration de Stewart et de Strange ; ce dernier cite le célèbre collectionneur d'estampes John S. Happer (1863–1936) qui disait de cette estampe qu'« il n'existe de plus belle représentation de la neige qui tombe dans aucune autre série d'[Hiroshige][33] ».

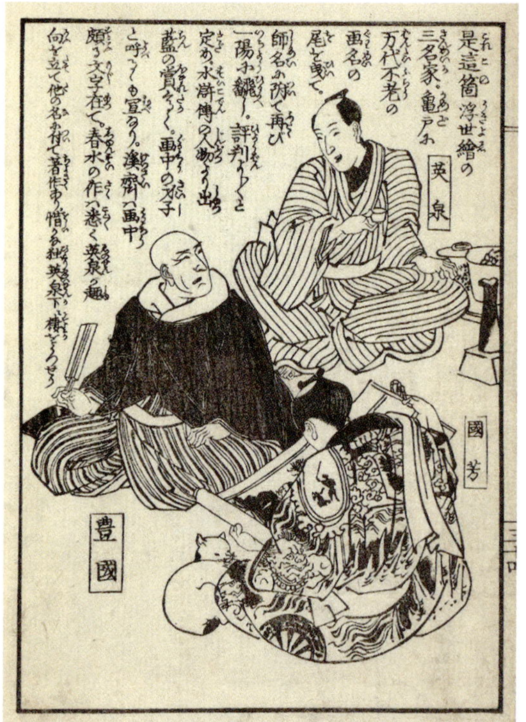

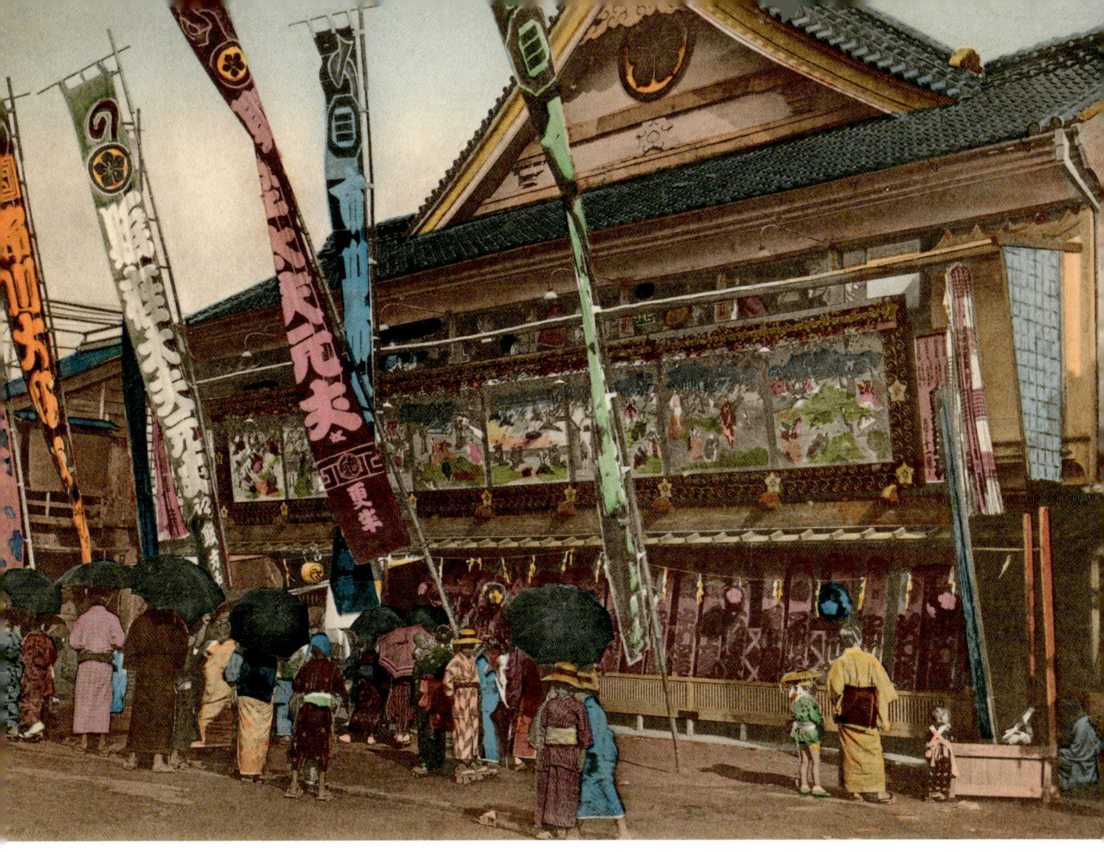

La qualité et l'état de l'impression sont des facteurs décisifs dans l'évaluation d'une estampe. Quand un dessin se vendait bien, un éditeur continuait d'en faire des tirages, en effectuant des modifications de couleur par endroits, c'est pourquoi il existe six versions de plusieurs dessins de la série de la Kisokaidō. Plus le tirage était important, plus les épreuves devenaient médiocres à cause de l'usure des matrices. C'est dans les épreuves de la toute première édition que la disposition la plus précise des couleurs est visible ; mais ce ne sont pas nécessairement les « plus belles » éditions qui comprennent les éléments d'impression les plus raffinés : dans le cas des estampes de la Kisokaidō, ceci se traduit par des gradations de couleur ou *bokashi*. Les épreuves présentées dans les pages suivantes proviennent d'une collection privée et constituent la plus belle série au monde, composée d'épreuves exceptionnelles, issues de la toute première et/ou de la plus belle édition de chaque dessin.

UTAGAWA KUNIYOSHI, *Portrait of the Artists Eisen (top), Kunisada (centre) and Kuniyoshi (bottom) / Darstellung der Künstler Eisen (oben), Kunisada (Mitte) und Kuniyoshi (unten) / Portrait des artistes Eisen (en haut), Kunisada (au centre) et Kuniyoshi (en bas)*, c. 1845. From: *Biographies of Remarkable Japanese (Nihon kijin den)*. Published by Yamazakiya Seishichi. Woodblock-printed book. Washington, Freer and Sackler Galleries, Freer Study Collection, FSC-GR-780.721.1-2

Theatre district / Theaterviertel / Le quartier des théâtres, c. 1895. Photochrom, hand-coloured. Paris, Marc Walter Collection

PP. 92/93
Mitake (detail from plate 50)

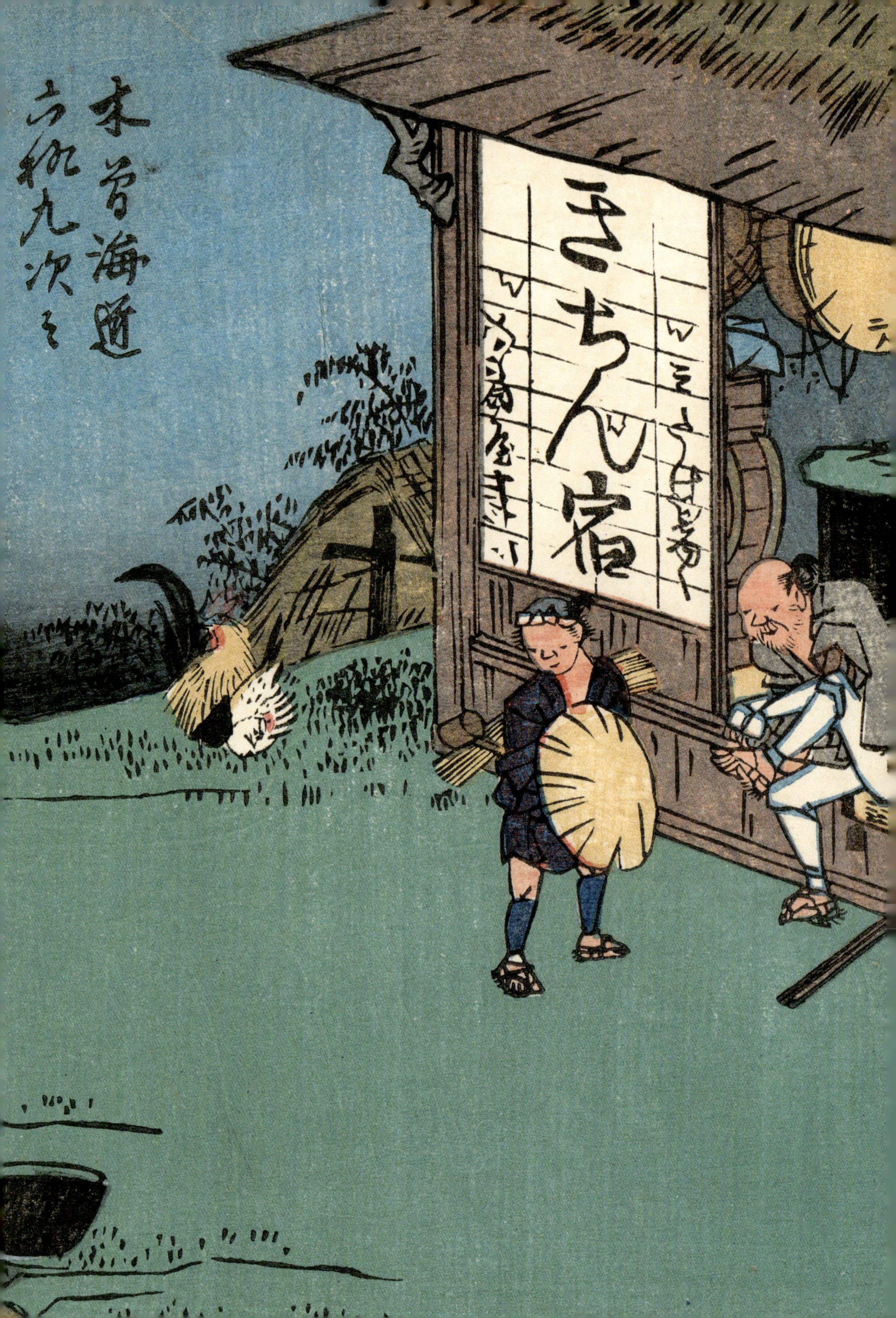

木曽海道
六拾九次之
きちん宿

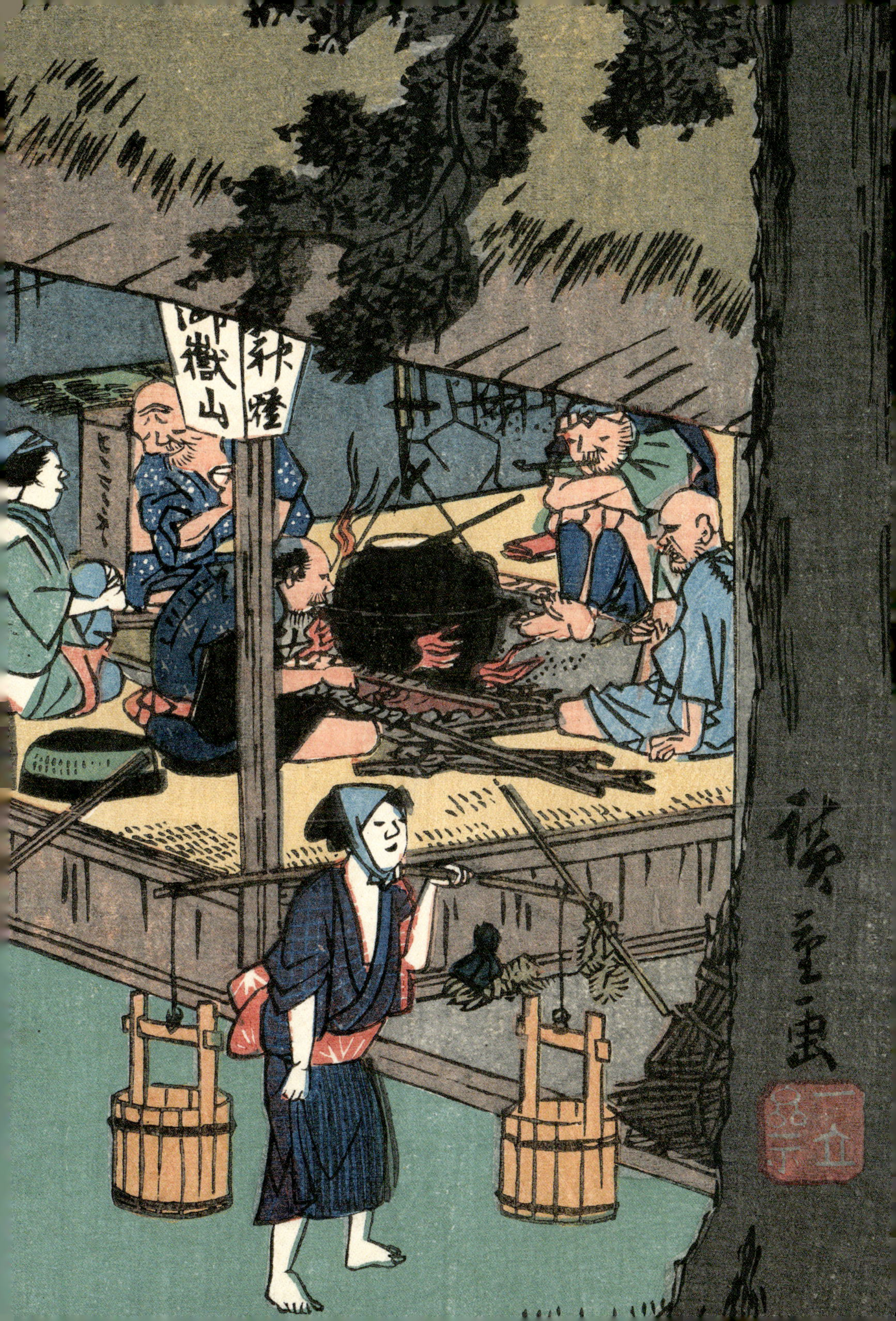
秋種
御嶽山

UTAGAWA HIROSHIGE
KEISAI EISEN

*The Sixty-Nine Stations
along the Kisokaidō*

*Die neunundsechzig Stationen
des Kisokaidō*

*Les soixante-neuf stations
de la route Kisokaidō*

Map of the Sixty-Nine Stations along
the Kisokaidō between Edo and Kyoto

Karte der neunundsechzig Stationen
des Kisokaidō zwischen Edo und Kyoto

Carte des soixante-neuf stations de
la route Kisokaidō entre Edo et Kyoto

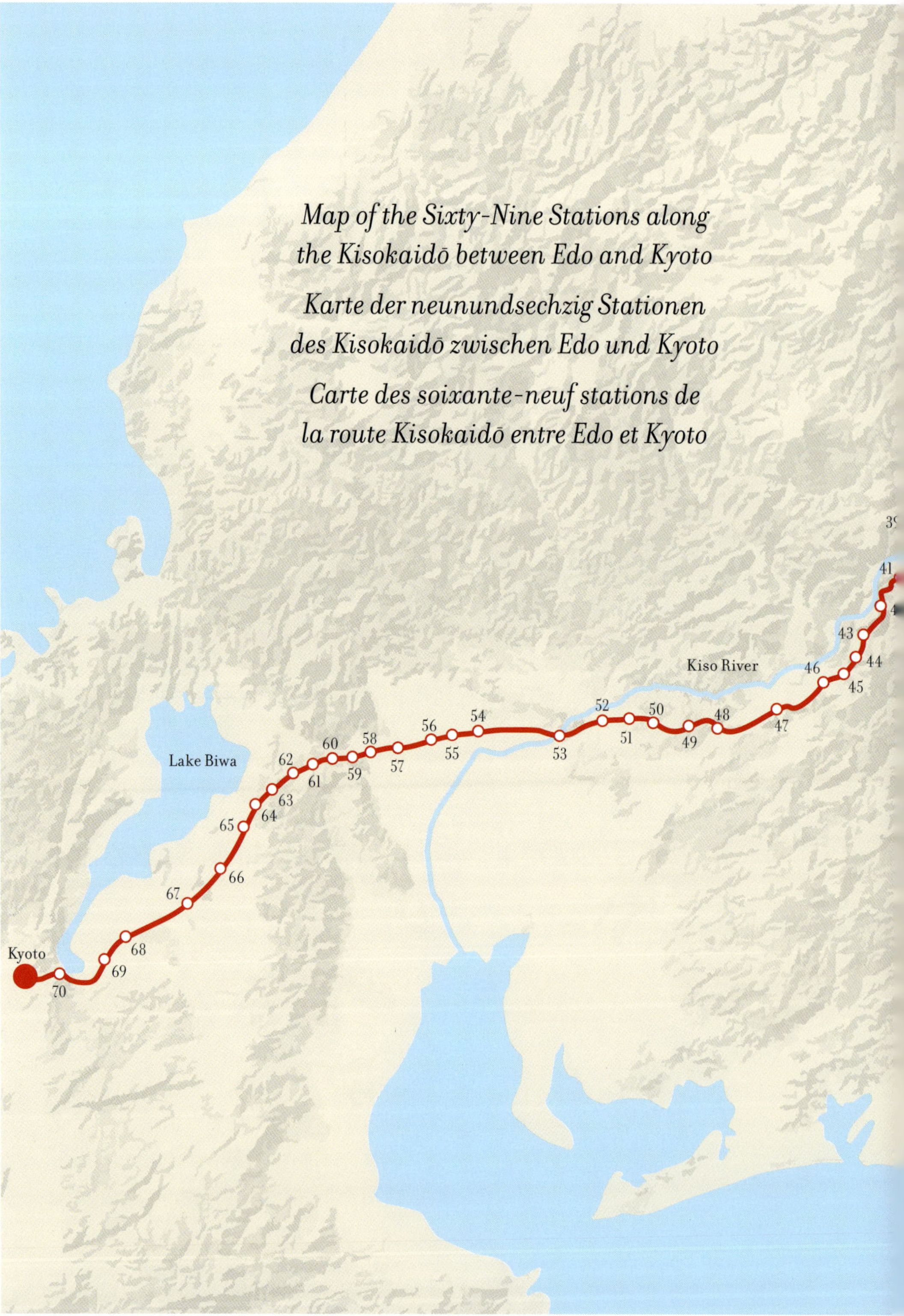

Kiso River
Lake Biwa
Kyoto

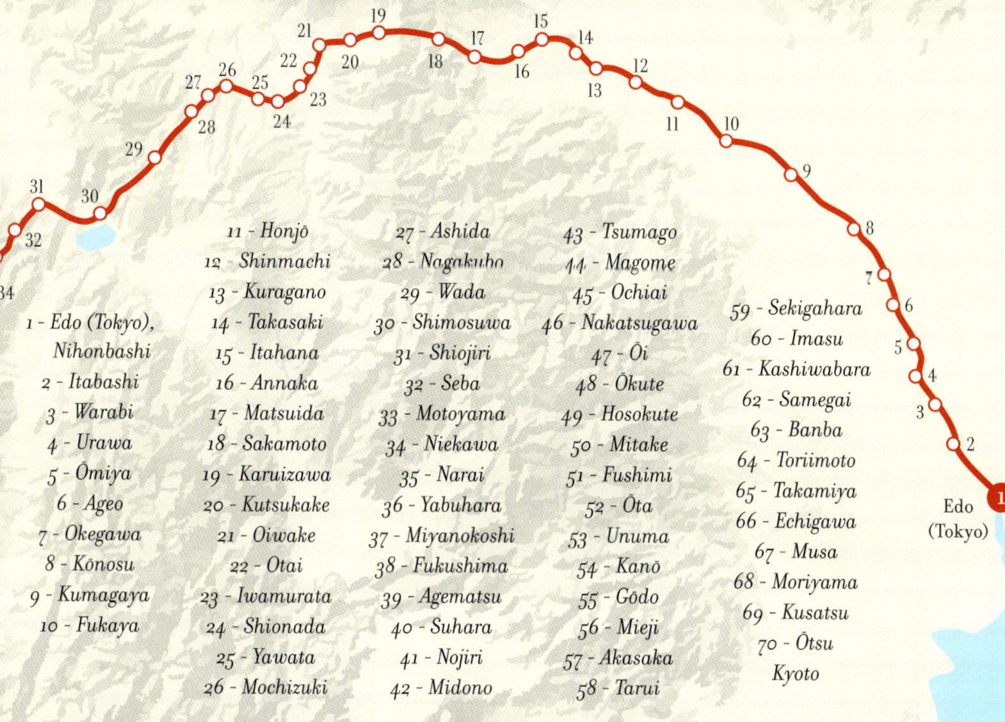
11 - Honjō
12 - Shinmachi
13 - Kuragano
14 - Takasaki
15 - Itahana
16 - Annaka
17 - Matsuida
18 - Sakamoto
19 - Karuizawa
20 - Kutsukake
21 - Oiwake
22 - Otai
23 - Iwamurata
24 - Shionada
25 - Yawata
26 - Mochizuki
27 - Ashida
28 - Nagakubo
29 - Wada
30 - Shimosuwa
31 - Shiojiri
32 - Seba
33 - Motoyama
34 - Niekawa
35 - Narai
36 - Yabuhara
37 - Miyanokoshi
38 - Fukushima
39 - Agematsu
40 - Suhara
41 - Nojiri
42 - Midono
43 - Tsumago
44 - Magome
45 - Ochiai
46 - Nakatsugawa
47 - Ōi
48 - Ōkute
49 - Hosokute
50 - Mitake
51 - Fushimi
52 - Ōta
53 - Unuma
54 - Kanō
55 - Gōdo
56 - Mieji
57 - Akasaka
58 - Tarui
59 - Sekigahara
60 - Imasu
61 - Kashiwabara
62 - Samegai
63 - Banba
64 - Toriimoto
65 - Takamiya
66 - Echigawa
67 - Musa
68 - Moriyama
69 - Kusatsu
70 - Ōtsu
Kyoto
1 - Edo (Tokyo), Nihonbashi
2 - Itabashi
3 - Warabi
4 - Urawa
5 - Ōmiya
6 - Ageo
7 - Okegawa
8 - Kōnosu
9 - Kumagaya
10 - Fukaya
Edo (Tokyo)
Mount Fuji

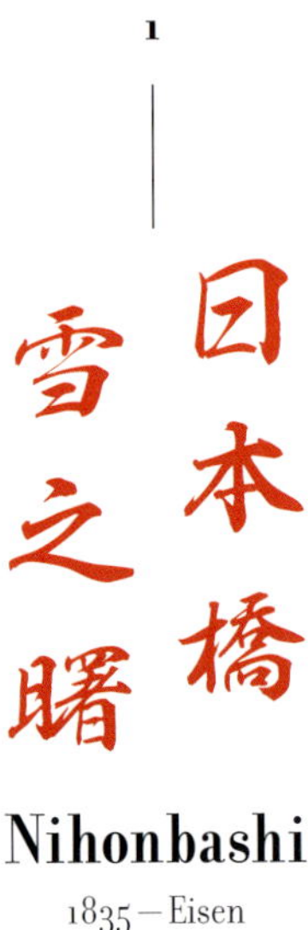

Nihonbashi

1835 — Eisen

The oldest wooden bridge over Edo's Nihonbashi River, a branch of the Sumida River, was built in 1603. The following year, this bridge was designated as the starting point of the network of five main roads that were constructed to provide access into the provinces. Based on previously built routes that were expanded and upgraded, the first road was completed in 1624, and 70 years later work finished on the fourth road, the Kisokaidō. Fires frequently destroyed parts of Edo and in 1657 the bridge burnt down completely, with the same thing happening another nine times before the Meiji period (1868–1912). The current stone bridge dates from 1911 and is the 19th structure to be built here.

Hiroshige had shown this bridge from an entirely different perspective in his first Tōkaidō series issued just a few years earlier, in about 1832. Where he chose to present only the first characters in the entourage of a lord, Eisen focused instead on ordinary people, and left almost no space as he packed the bridge with travellers, porters and merchants. Furthermore, Eisen's depiction may be the first to show the bustling hub in winter, covered in snow on a sunny morning, an idea that seems to have fallen on fruitful ground as it was then picked up by Hiroshige for at least seven different prints.

There is snow too on the roofs of the long line of warehouses alongside the river, just like the bridge, making it remarkable that Eisen included on the right two men with bare chests and legs who are pushing a two-wheeled cart, loaded high with packed goods. In the distance crows are flying, and behind a fire tower the red sun is rising through streaks of mist. The sun would be omitted in later editions of this popular design.

Die erste Holzbrücke über den Nihonbashigawa in Edo, einen Seitenarm des Sumida, wurde 1603 erbaut. Im Jahr darauf wurde sie zum Ausgangspunkt eines Netzes von fünf Hauptstraßen bestimmt, die den Zugang zu den Provinzen sicherstellen sollten und auf vorher angelegten Straßen beruhten, die erweitert und ausgebaut wurden. Die erste dieser Überlandstraßen wurde 1624 fertiggestellt, die vierte – der Kisokaidō – 70 Jahre später. In einem der Feuer, die regelmäßig Teile Edos zerstörten, brannte die Brücke 1657 vollständig nieder und ging bis zum Beginn der Meiji-Zeit (1868–1912) weitere neunmal in Flammen auf. Die heutige Steinkonstruktion aus dem Jahr 1911 ist die 19. Brücke an dieser Stelle.

Hiroshige hatte die alte Holzbrücke in seiner wenige Jahre zuvor erschienenen Tōkaidō-Serie um 1832 aus einer vollkommen anderen Perspektive gezeigt und nur die ersten Figuren im Gefolge eines Lehensfürsten oder *daimyō* abgebildet. Eisen dagegen konzentrierte sich auf die einfachen Leute und ließ kaum Platz zwischen den vielen Reisenden, Lastenträgern und Händlern, die die Brücke bevölkern. Zudem war seine Darstellung vielleicht die erste, die den geschäftigen Knotenpunkt im Winter zeigt, von Schnee bedeckt an einem sonnigen Morgen. Eisens Idee scheint auf fruchtbaren Boden gefallen zu sein, denn Hiroshige griff bei mindestens sieben verschiedenen Drucken auf sie zurück.

Auch auf den Dächern der langen Lagerhauszeile am Flussufer liegt Schnee. Umso bemerkenswerter sind die nackten Beine und Oberkörper der beiden Männer rechts, die einen zweirädrigen, mit Warenbündeln hoch beladenen Wagen die Brücke hinaufschieben. In der Ferne ziehen Krähen über den Himmel, während hinter einem Feuerwachturm zwischen Nebelschwaden der rote Sonnenball aufgeht. In späteren Auflagen dieses beliebten Motivs wurde die Sonne weggelassen.

C'est en 1603 qu'a été bâti à Edo le plus ancien pont en bois sur la rivière Nihonbashi, affluent du Sumida. L'année suivante, ce pont fut choisi comme point de départ du réseau de cinq routes principales, construites pour accéder aux provinces et aménagées sur d'anciennes voies qui furent élargies et modernisées. La première route fut achevée en 1624, mais c'est soixante-dix ans plus tard que se terminèrent les travaux de la quatrième route, la Kisokaidō. Les incendies détruisaient régulièrement des quartiers d'Edo ; en 1657, le pont brûla entièrement, événement qui se reproduisit neuf fois avant l'ère Meiji (1868–1912). L'actuel pont en pierres date de 1911 ; c'est la dix-neuvième structure construite à cet emplacement.

Hiroshige avait représenté ce pont depuis un tout autre point de vue dans sa première série de la Tōkaidō, publiée quelques années auparavant vers 1832. Là où Hiroshige choisit de ne montrer que les premiers personnages de l'entourage d'un seigneur, Eisen préfère s'intéresser aux gens ordinaires et ne laisse pratiquement aucun espace vide, en peuplant le pont de voyageurs, de porteurs et de marchands. En outre, la représentation d'Eisen est peut-être la première à dépeindre ce quartier animé en hiver, recouvert de neige par un matin ensoleillé, idée qui semble avoir trouvé un terrain fertile car Hiroshige l'a ensuite reprise dans au moins sept estampes.

La neige recouvre aussi les toits de la longue rangée d'entrepôts qui se dressent sur le bord de la rivière, de même que sur le pont ; il est donc d'autant plus remarquable qu'Eisen ait figuré à droite deux hommes torse et jambes nus, poussant une charrette à deux roues, croulant sous des marchandises empilées. Au loin volent des corbeaux et, derrière une tour de guet, le soleil rouge se lève à travers des nappes de brume. Le soleil disparaîtra d'éditions ultérieures de ce dessin très apprécié.

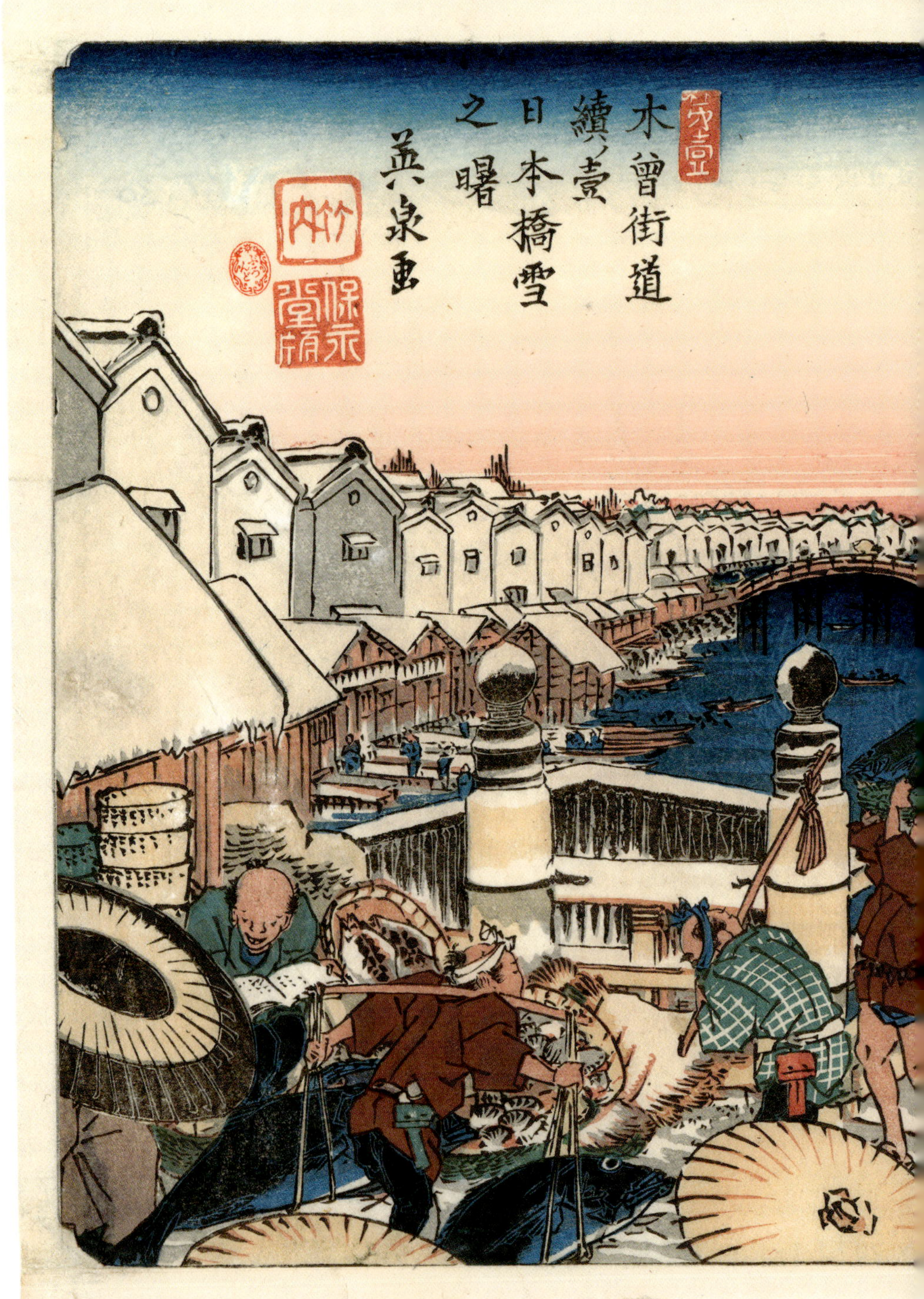

木曾街道
續ノ壹
日本橋雪
之曙
英泉画

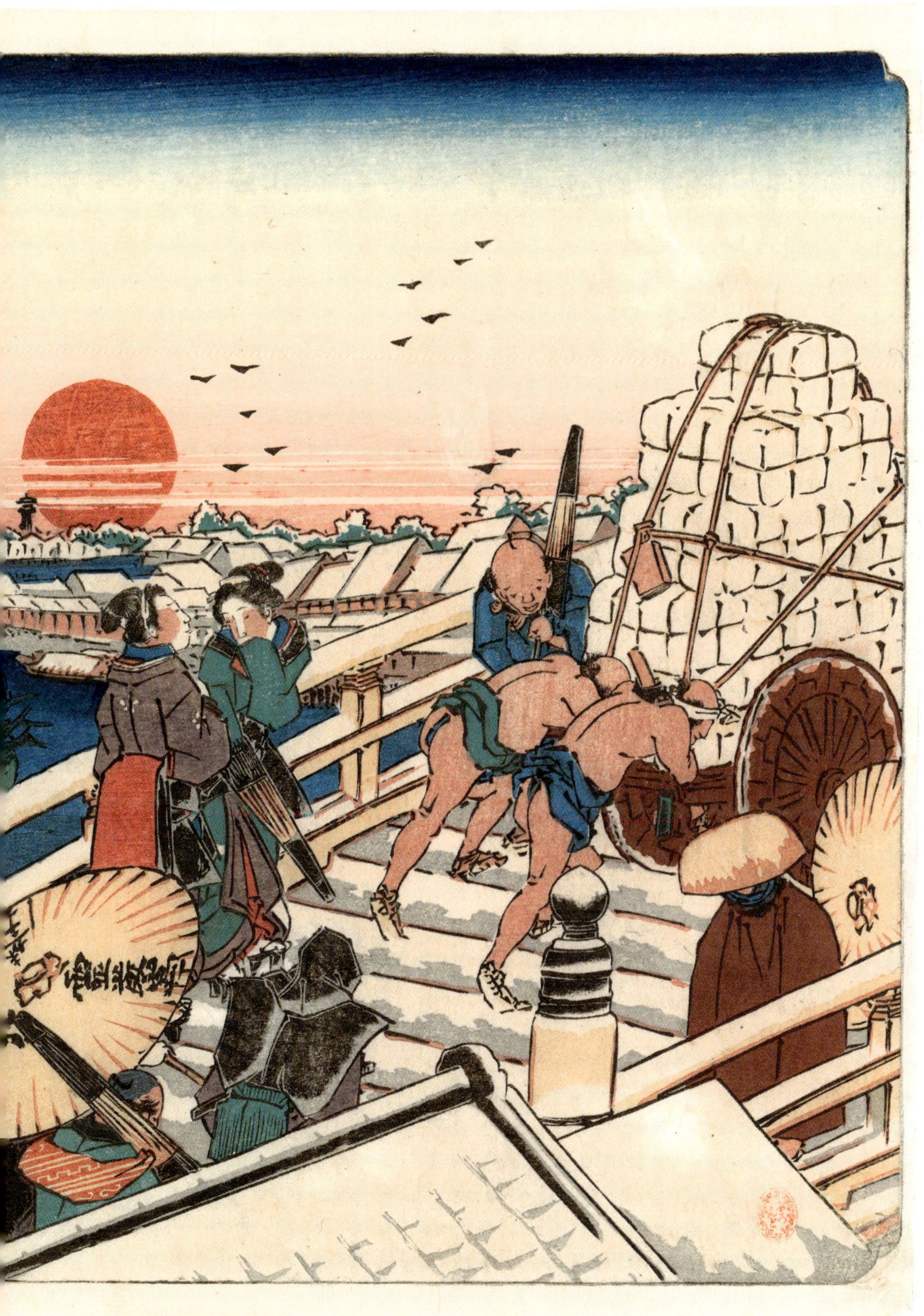

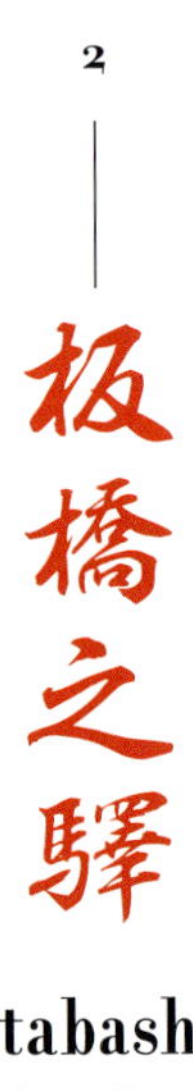

2

Itabashi

1835 – Eisen

Travellers have departed from Edo heading north-west and are reaching the first houses on the outskirts of the village of Itabashi, the first station along the Kisokaidō. Itabashi means "plank bridge" and refers to the small bridge over the Shakujii River which gave the town its name. On the far left is a wooden boundary-marker with a little bamboo fence around it, which indicates the official extent of the village land. A stone road-marker in the centre reads, on the right, "Right, road to Ōji", directing the way to Ōji with its famous shrines, and on the left, "Blue-Faced Vajra" (*Shōmen Kongō*). This was the main divinity in the popular Kōshin cult, a folk belief that sought to ensure good health and which was followed by many travellers.

A samurai and a woman with a walking-stick, both wearing straw hats and sleeved raincoats, are walking towards the village. The scabbard of the man's sword is depicted in red, setting it apart from his blue coat. Two men are seen chatting in the centre of the image, one carrying a couple of woven baskets on a pole while the other is a palanquin-bearer who seems to be offering his services. His palanquin is standing on the right outside the *tateba-chaya*, a resting-place that also offers tea. A pack-horse driver is fitting new straw horseshoes on his horse, which is available for hire. The three characters inscribed on the horse's saddle stand for the luck and good fortune the horse's owner desires.

Eisen's design is somewhat reminiscent of Hiroshige's design of Shinagawa in his first Tōkaidō series, which was produced by the same publisher a few years earlier. Hiroshige had also shown the boundary-marker and the arrival at the first post station on the route out of Edo; however, he imagined a lord's procession entering the village.

Reisende haben Edo in Richtung Nordwesten verlassen und erreichen die ersten Häuser am Dorfrand von Itabashi, der ersten Station des Kisokaidō. Itabashi bedeutet „Bohlenbrücke" und bezieht sich auf die kleine Brücke über den Shakujii, die der Ortschaft ihren Namen gab. Die hölzerne Grenzmarke am linken Rand, um die ein kleiner Bambuszaun gezogen ist, zeigt an, wie weit das Dorf offiziell reichte. Eine Steinsäule als Straßenmarkierung in der Bildmitte weist rechts mit den Worten „Rechts, Straße nach Ōji" den Weg zu den berühmten Schreinen von Ōji, während der Schriftzug links, „Blaugesichtiger Vajra" (*Shōmen Kongō*), die Hauptgottheit des Kōshin-Kults nennt, eines Volksglaubens, dem viele Reisende anhingen, weil er Gesundheit versprach.

Ein Samurai und eine Frau mit Wanderstab, beide mit langärmeligen Regenmänteln und Strohhüten bekleidet, gehen auf das Dorf zu. Die rot gefärbte Schwertscheide des Mannes hebt sich vom Blau seines Mantels ab. In der Mitte der Szene unterhalten sich zwei Männer. Der eine trägt ein Paar Flechtkörbe an einer Tragestange, der andere ist ein Sänftenträger, der anscheinend seine Dienste feilbietet. Seine Sänfte steht rechts vor dem *tateba-chaya*, einer Raststätte, die Tee ausschenkt. Ein Packpferdtreiber legt seinem Tier, das zur Miete bereitsteht, neue Hufschoner aus Stroh an. Die drei Schriftzeichen auf dem Pferdesattel stehen für das Glück und Geschick, das der Besitzer des Pferdes sich wünscht.

Eisens Entwurf erinnert in gewisser Weise an denjenigen, den Hiroshige für Shinagawa in seiner ersten, einige Jahre zuvor im selben Verlag erschienenen Tōkaidō-Serie schuf. Hiroshige hatte ebenfalls die Grenzmarke und die Ankunft an der ersten Poststation entlang der Strecke abgebildet, die aus Edo herausführte, sich dabei jedoch eine *daimyō*-Prozession vorgestellt, die ins Dorf einzog.

Des voyageurs sont partis d'Edo vers le nord-ouest et atteignent les premières maisons à la lisière du village d'Itabashi, première station de la Kisokaidō. Itabashi signifie « pont de planches » et désigne le petit pont enjambant la rivière Shakujii qui a donné son nom à la ville. À l'extrême gauche se dresse une borne de démarcation, entourée d'une toute petite clôture en bambou, qui marque la limite officielle du territoire de la commune. Au centre se trouve une borne directionnelle indiquant, sur son flanc droit, « Route d'Ōji à droite », direction à suivre pour se rendre à Ōji et y voir ses célèbres sanctuaires, et, à gauche, « Vajra au visage bleu » (*Shōmen Kongō*). Il s'agit de la principale divinité du culte *kōshin*, croyance populaire garantissant une bonne santé et observée par de nombreux voyageurs.

Coiffés de chapeaux de paille et vêtus de manteaux de pluie à manches, un samouraï et une femme s'aidant d'une canne marchent en direction du village. De couleur rouge, le fourreau de l'épée de l'homme ressort sur le bleu de son manteau. Deux hommes bavardent au centre de l'image : l'un porte deux paniers en osier sur une palanche, l'autre est un porteur de palanquin qui semble proposer ses services. Son palanquin se trouve à droite, à l'extérieur du *tateba-chaya*, lieu de halte offrant aussi du thé. Un conducteur de cheval de bât équipe son cheval de nouveaux chaussons de paille afin qu'il soit prêt à être loué. Les trois caractères inscrits sur la selle évoquent la bonne fortune souhaitée par le propriétaire du cheval.

Le dessin d'Eisen rappelle quelque peu l'illustration de Shinagawa par Hiroshige dans sa première série de la Tōkaidō, réalisée par le même éditeur quelques années auparavant. Hiroshige avait aussi représenté la borne de démarcation, ainsi que l'arrivée à la première station après avoir quitté Edo ; mais c'est l'entrée dans le village de la procession d'un seigneur qu'il avait imaginée.

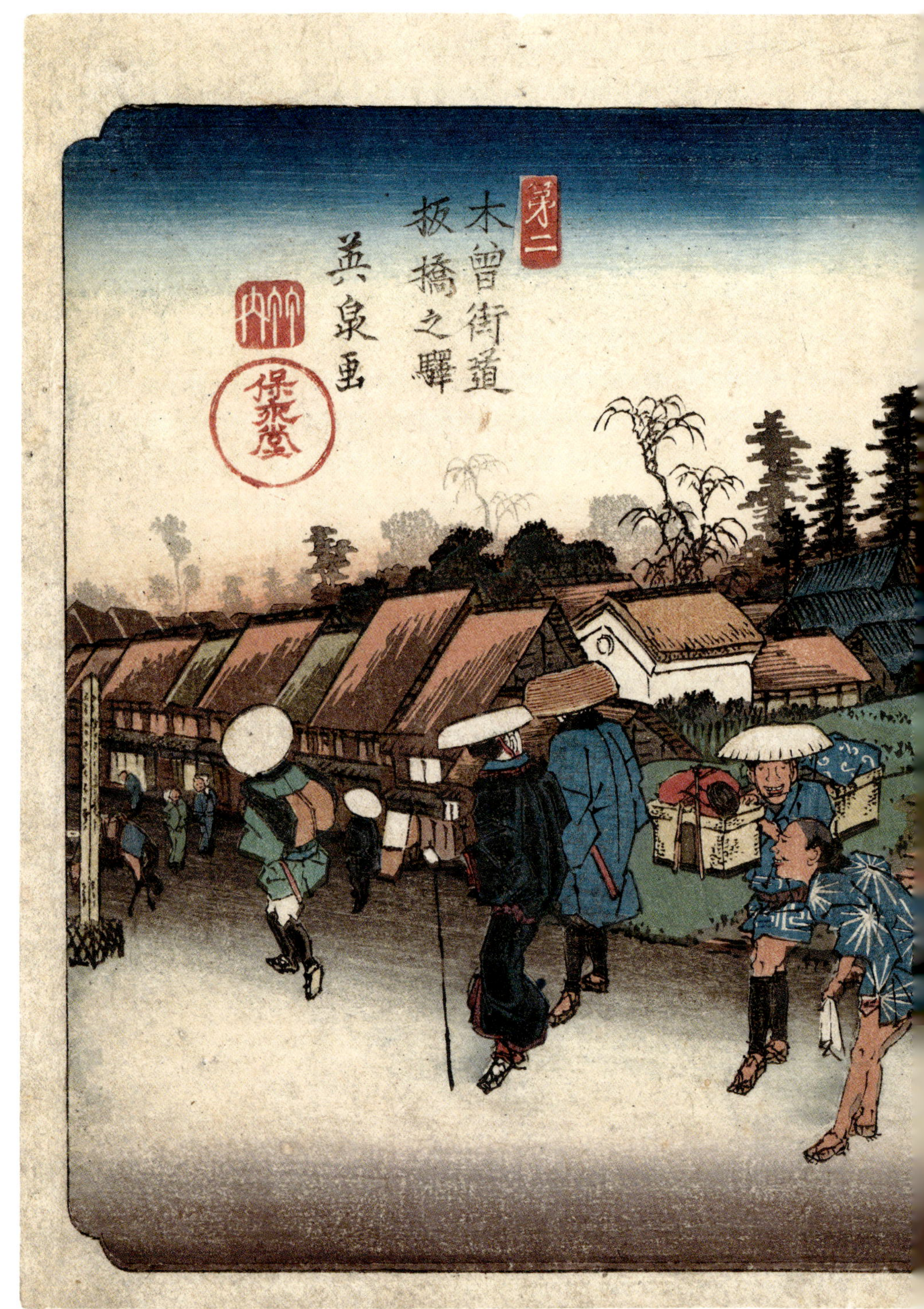
第二
木曽街道
板橋之驛
英泉畫
保永堂

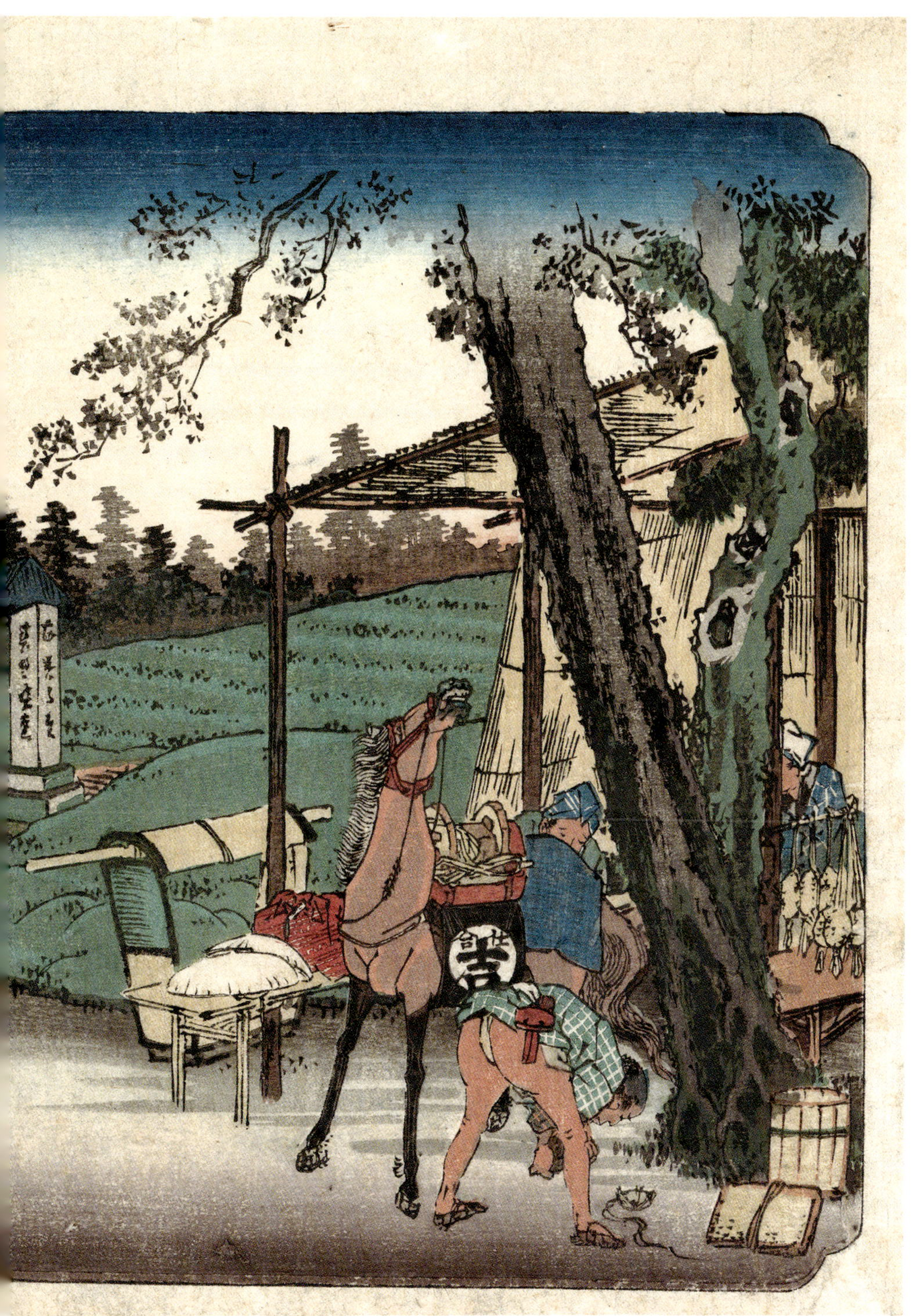

3

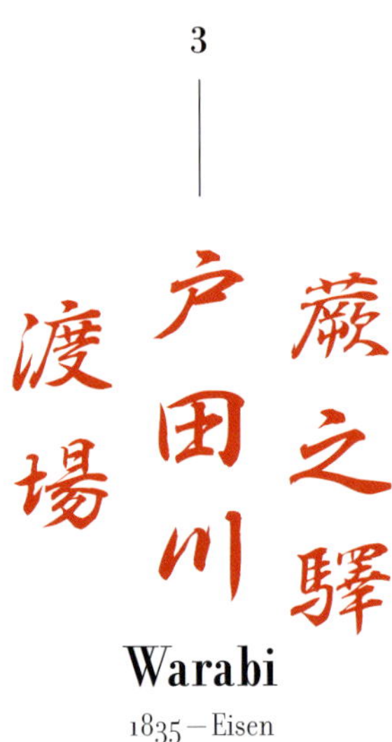

Warabi

1835 — Eisen

A ferry packed with all kinds of travellers sets out across the Toda River (today called the Ara) for the village of Warabi, some of whose thatched roofs can be seen on the far bank. In most places the Toda River was about 100 metres (c. 300 feet) wide, but during the rainy season it could burst its banks and flood an area four kilometres (2½ miles) across. Bridges were not built on the Toda until the Meiji period, and depending on the height of the river, travellers could be stranded on one side, with their travel funds dwindling to the advantage of the various businesses at the nearby stations.

The ferryman is pushing the boat firmly away from the shore with his long bamboo pole. Apart from the seven passengers, the boat also carries a hired horse and some luggage. Some of the passengers sitting on the right of the horse are *goze*, blind female beggars who sing or play the *shamisen*, a stringed instrument. Two egrets are flying over the boat, to catch up with their flock to the north. Traffic on the river seems to be slow today as there are two other boats without passengers moored on the opposite side of the river. On the left of the road is the *kawakaisho*, the meeting point where travellers gathered before setting off over a river.

Eisen's design seems to have been inspired by Hiroshige's design of Kawasaki, the third print in his first Tōkaidō series, which was produced a few years earlier by the same publisher. Instead of featuring the station town, Hiroshige also depicted a ferry crossing a river, but although he showed a man smoking, the boat was considerably less packed than in Eisen's version.

Eine mit unterschiedlichsten Passagieren besetzte Fähre bricht zur Überquerung des Toda (des heutigen Ara) ins Dorf Warabi auf, dessen erste Strohdächer am jenseitigen Ufer zu erkennen sind. An den meisten Stellen war der Toda etwa 100 Meter breit, doch während der Regenzeit konnte er über die Ufer treten und ein bis zu vier Kilometer breites Gebiet überschwemmen. Bis zur Meiji-Zeit gab es hier keine Brücken, sodass Reisende je nach Pegelstand des Flusses am einen oder anderen Ufer festsitzen konnten, während sich ihre Reisekasse zum Vorteil der Geschäftsleute in den nahe gelegenen Stationen langsam leerte.

Mit seinem langen Bambusstab stößt der Fährmann das Boot kräftig vom Ufer ab. Neben den sieben Passagieren befinden sich auch ein Mietpferd und etwas Gepäck an Bord. Einige der Passagiere, die rechts neben dem Pferd sitzen, sind *goze*, blinde Bettlerinnen, die singen oder auf der *shamisen* spielen, einem Saiteninstrument. Zwei Reiher fliegen über das Boot, um ihren nach Norden ziehenden Schwarm einzuholen. Auf dem Fluss scheint an diesem Tag wenig los zu sein, denn zwei weitere Boote liegen festgemacht und ohne Fahrgäste am anderen Ufer. Links der Straße steht der überdachte *kawakaisho*, der Treffpunkt, an dem sich Reisende vor einer Überfahrt versammelten.

Eisens Blatt scheint von Hiroshiges Entwurf für Kawasaki inspiriert zu sein, dem dritten Blatt seiner ersten Tōkaidō-Serie, die derselbe Verlag einige Jahre zuvor herausgegeben hatte. Anstelle des Stationsortes bildete auch Hiroshige eine Fähre bei einer Flussüberquerung ab. Er zeigte zwar ebenfalls einen Mann beim Rauchen, doch auf seinem Boot drängten sich deutlich weniger Menschen als in Eisens Version.

Une grande barque chargée de toutes sortes de voyageurs s'apprête à traverser la rivière Toda (aujourd'hui Ara) en direction du village de Warabi, dont on aperçoit quelques toits de chaume sur l'autre rive. Sur la majeure partie de son cours, la Toda était large d'une centaine de mètres mais, durant la saison des pluies, ses crues pouvaient inonder une surface de quatre kilomètres de large. Ce n'est qu'à partir de l'ère Meiji qu'on a commencé à construire des ponts sur la Toda ; selon le niveau des eaux, les voyageurs pouvaient se retrouver bloqués d'un côté ou de l'autre et voir l'argent alloué à leur voyage fondre au profit des différentes échoppes installées dans les stations environnantes.

Le passeur éloigne l'embarcation de la rive en s'appuyant d'un geste ferme sur sa longue perche de bambou. En plus de ses sept passagers, la barque transporte un cheval de louage et quelques bagages. Une partie des passagers assis à droite du cheval sont des *goze*, des mendiantes aveugles qui chantent ou jouent du *shamisen*, un instrument à cordes. Deux aigrettes passent au-dessus du bateau pour rejoindre leurs congénères qui s'envolent vers le nord. L'activité semble être au ralenti, car deux autres barques sans passagers sont amarrées sur l'autre rive. À gauche de la route se trouve le *kawakaisho*, l'embarcadère où se rassemblent les passagers avant de traverser une rivière.

Ce dessin d'Eisen paraît s'inspirer de l'illustration d'Hiroshige pour l'estampe de Kawasaki, la troisième de sa première série de la Tōkaidō, réalisée quelques années auparavant par le même éditeur. Au lieu de représenter la station, Hiroshige a lui aussi dessiné une barque de passeur traversant une rivière. Mais, s'il figure un homme en train de fumer, son bateau est nettement moins chargé que celui d'Eisen.

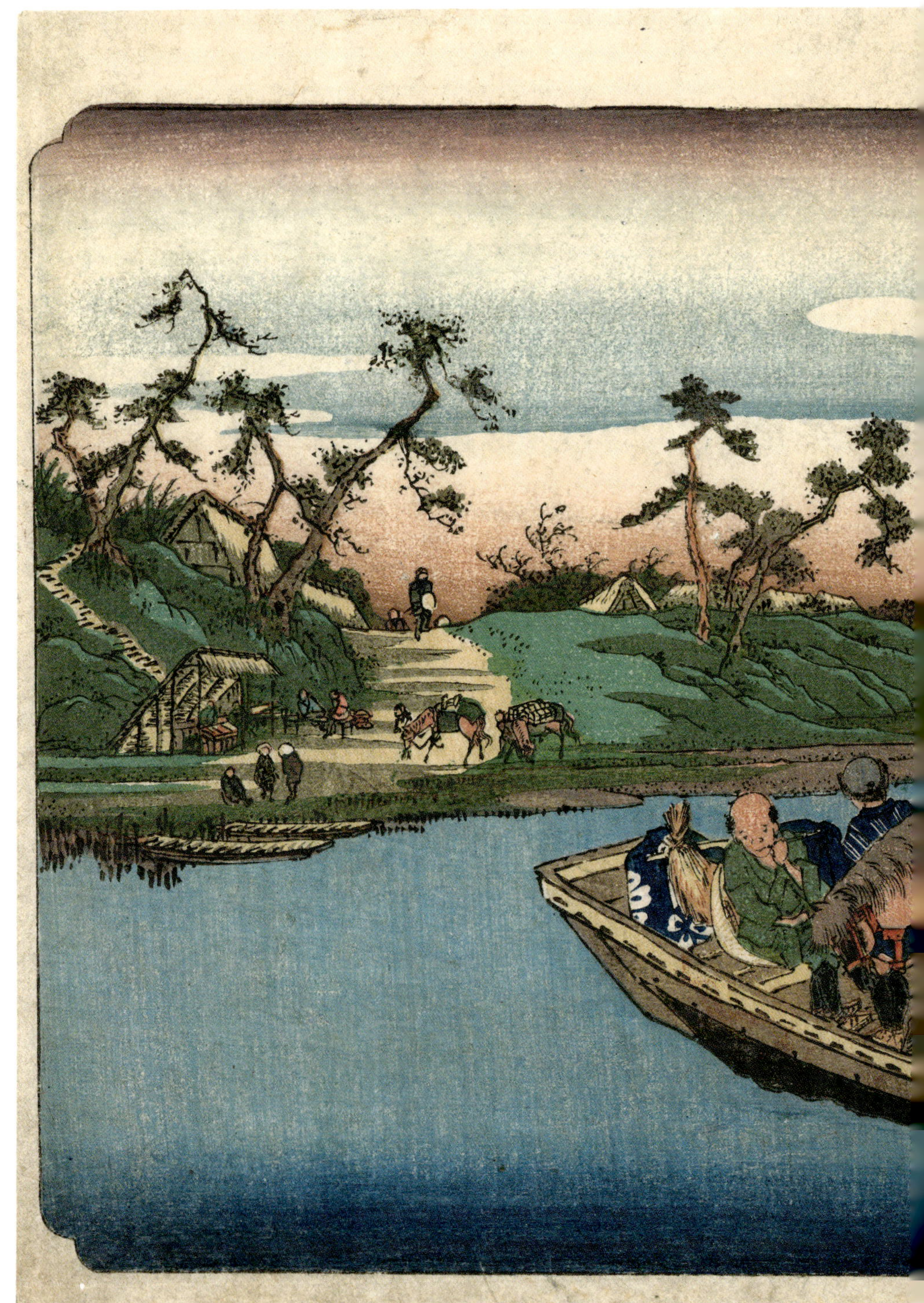

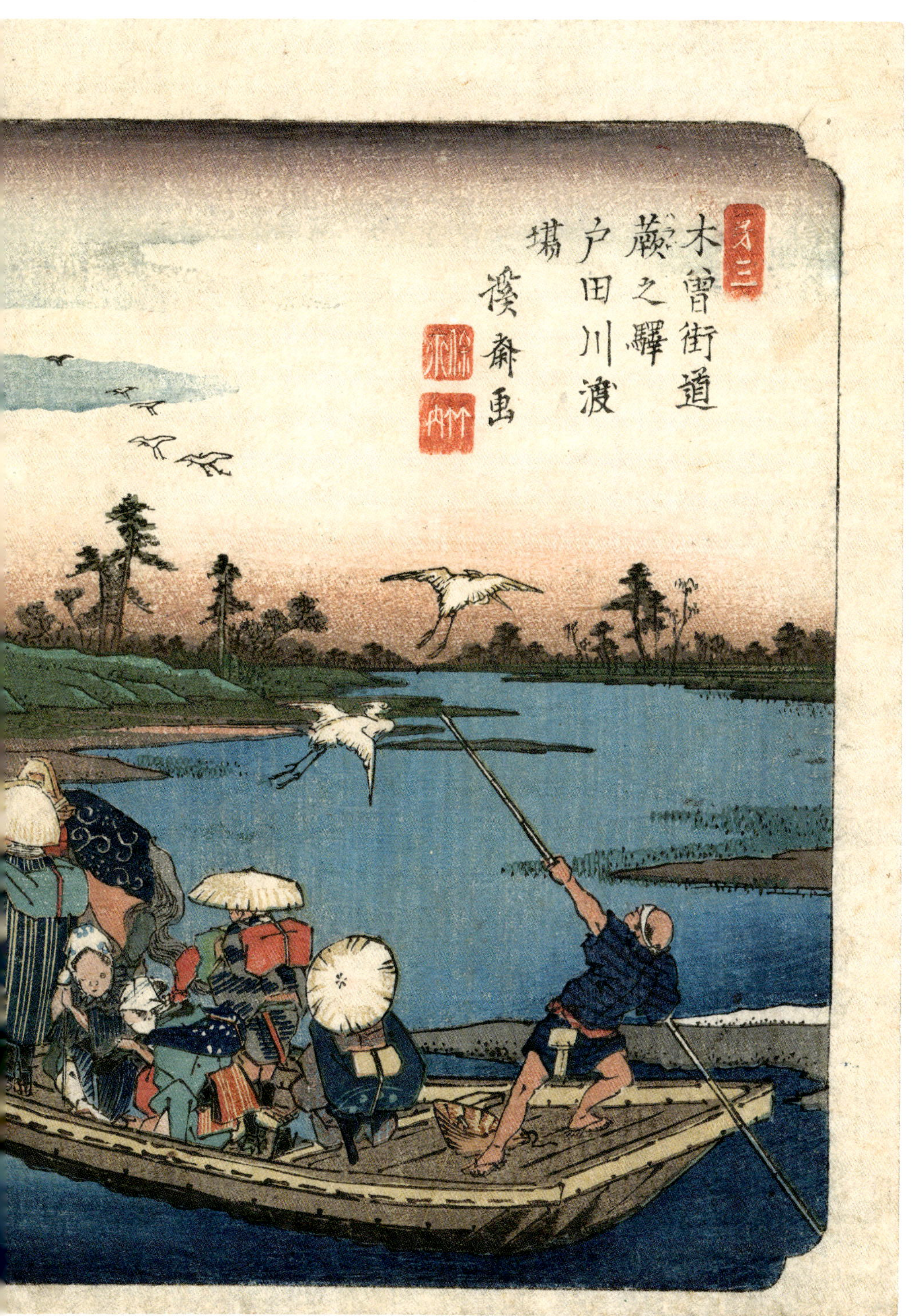

木曽街道
巌之驛
戸田川渡
場
溪齋画

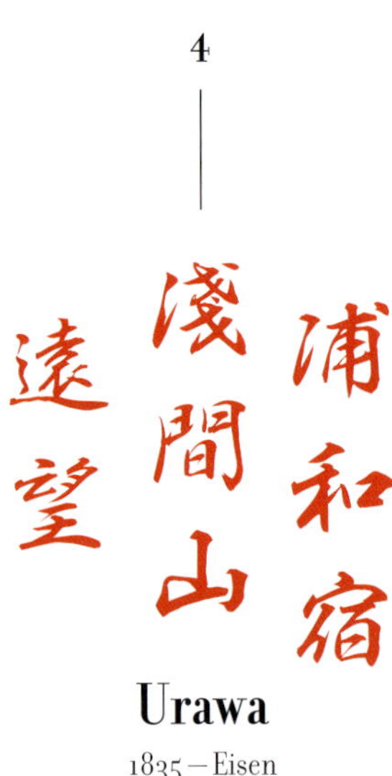

Urawa

1835 – Eisen

A pack-horse driver is leading his horse away from the village of Urawa. The pack horse appears to be carrying a heavy load with these three large bundles on its back. Prices for pack-horses were fixed and depended on the weight of the load to be carried, with a maximum of around 150 kilogrammes (40 *kan*/330 lb). Behind the horse is a young boy collecting the dung, a valuable fertiliser for the fields seen on the right. With a folding fan held open in his hand, a samurai, identifiable by his long sword in a red scabbard, is about to enter the town. He is accompanied by a porter who is walking behind him, carrying his luggage attached to either end of a pole. In the far distance the houses of Ōmiya are visible, the next station on the road.

The main focus of this scene, however, is the smoking peak of Mount Asama, rising high in the far distance. Eisen here followed accounts in the travel guidebooks *Illustrated Guide to the Kiso Road* (*Kisoji anken ezu*) and *Views of Famous Sights along the Kiso Road* (*Kisoji meisho zue*) that claimed Mount Asama was visible from Urawa on a clear summer day. Asama is an active volcano, 2,568 metres (8,425 feet) in height and some 120 kilometres (75 miles) from Urawa. The first recorded eruption dates from 685 and the most recent at the time of writing was in June 2015. No activity was reported between 1815 and 1869, and Eisen's depiction of a smoking peak is derived from the illustration in *Kisoji meisho zue* that was published in 1805, two years after an eruption of the volcano.

Ein Packpferdtreiber führt sein Pferd am Zügel aus dem Dorf Urawa. Das Tier scheint mit den drei großen Bündeln auf dem Rücken eine schwere Last zu tragen. Die Preise für Packpferde waren festgelegt
und hingen von der Traglast ab, die maximal etwa 150 Kilogramm (40 *kan*) betrug. Hinter dem Pferd
sammelt ein Junge die Pferdeäpfel auf, die einen wertvollen Dünger für die Felder abgaben, wie sie rechts
im Bild sichtbar sind. Mit geöffnetem Faltfächer in der Hand geht ein Samurai, der an der roten Scheide
seines Langschwerts zu erkennen ist, auf den Ort zu. Ihm folgt ein Lastenträger mit dem Gepäck, das an
zwei Enden einer Tragestange befestigt ist. In weiter Ferne sind die Häuser von Ōmiya zu sehen, der
nächsten Station des Kisokaidō.

Das Hauptaugenmerk der Szene aber gilt dem rauchenden Gipfel des Asama, der in weiter Ferne
aufragt. Eisen folgte hier Berichten aus den Reiseführern *Illustrierter Wegweiser für die Kiso-Straße
(Kisoji anken ezu)* und *Ansichten berühmter Stätten an der Kiso-Straße (Kisoji meisho zue)*, die
behaupteten, der Asama sei an klaren Sommertagen von Urawa aus zu sehen. Der aktive Vulkan ist
2568 Meter hoch und liegt etwa 120 Kilometer von Urawa entfernt. Der erste dokumentierte Ausbruch
ereignete sich im Jahr 685, der bisher letzte im Juni 2015. Da zwischen 1815 und 1869 keine Aktivität
gemeldet wurde, entstand Eisens Darstellung eines rauchenden Vulkans nach der Abbildung im mehr-
bändigen *Kisoji meisho zue*, das 1805, zwei Jahre nach einem Ausbruch des Asama, auf den Markt kam.

Un conducteur de cheval de bât quitte le village d'Urawa en guidant son animal qui semble porter une
lourde charge, composée de trois gros ballots. Les tarifs des chevaux de bât étaient fixés en fonction du
poids de la charge à transporter, avec un maximum d'environ 150 (40 *kan*) kilogrammes. Derrière l'animal, un jeune garçon ramasse le crottin, engrais précieux destiné aux champs, visibles à droite. Un éventail ouvert à la main, un samouraï, reconnaissable à sa longue épée rangée dans un fourreau rouge,
s'apprête à entrer dans la petite ville. Il est accompagné d'un porteur qui marche à sa suite et porte ses
bagages attachés aux extrémités d'une perche. On devine au loin les maisons d'Ōmiya, la station suivante
sur la route.

Toutefois, le sujet principal de cette scène est le sommet fumant du mont Asama qui s'élève sur
l'horizon. Ici, Eisen s'est fié aux récits de deux guides de voyage, *Guide illustré de la route Kiso (Kisoji
anken ezu)* et *Collection de vues de paysages célèbres sur la route Kiso (Kisoji meisho zue)*, selon lesquels le mont Asama était visible d'Urawa par une claire journée d'été. D'une altitude de 2568 mètres,
cette montagne est un volcan en activité, situé à environ cent vingt kilomètres d'Urawa. La première
éruption répertoriée date de l'an 685 et la plus récente, au moment de la rédaction de cette notice, a eu
lieu en juin 2015. Aucune activité n'ayant été relevée de 1815 à 1869, la représentation que donne Eisen
d'un sommet fumant s'inspire d'une illustration de *Kisoji meisho zue*, publiée en 1805, deux ans après
une éruption du volcan.

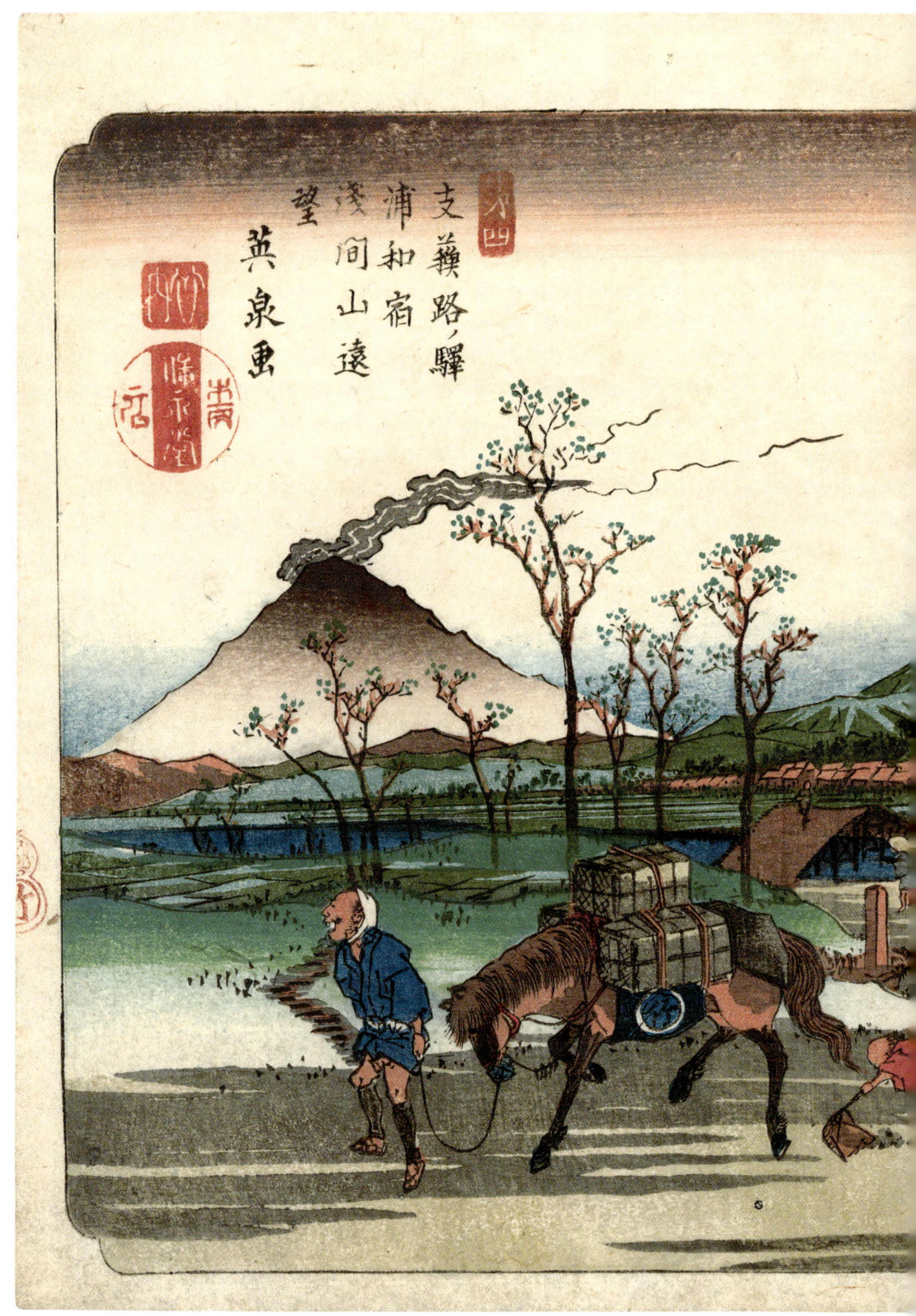

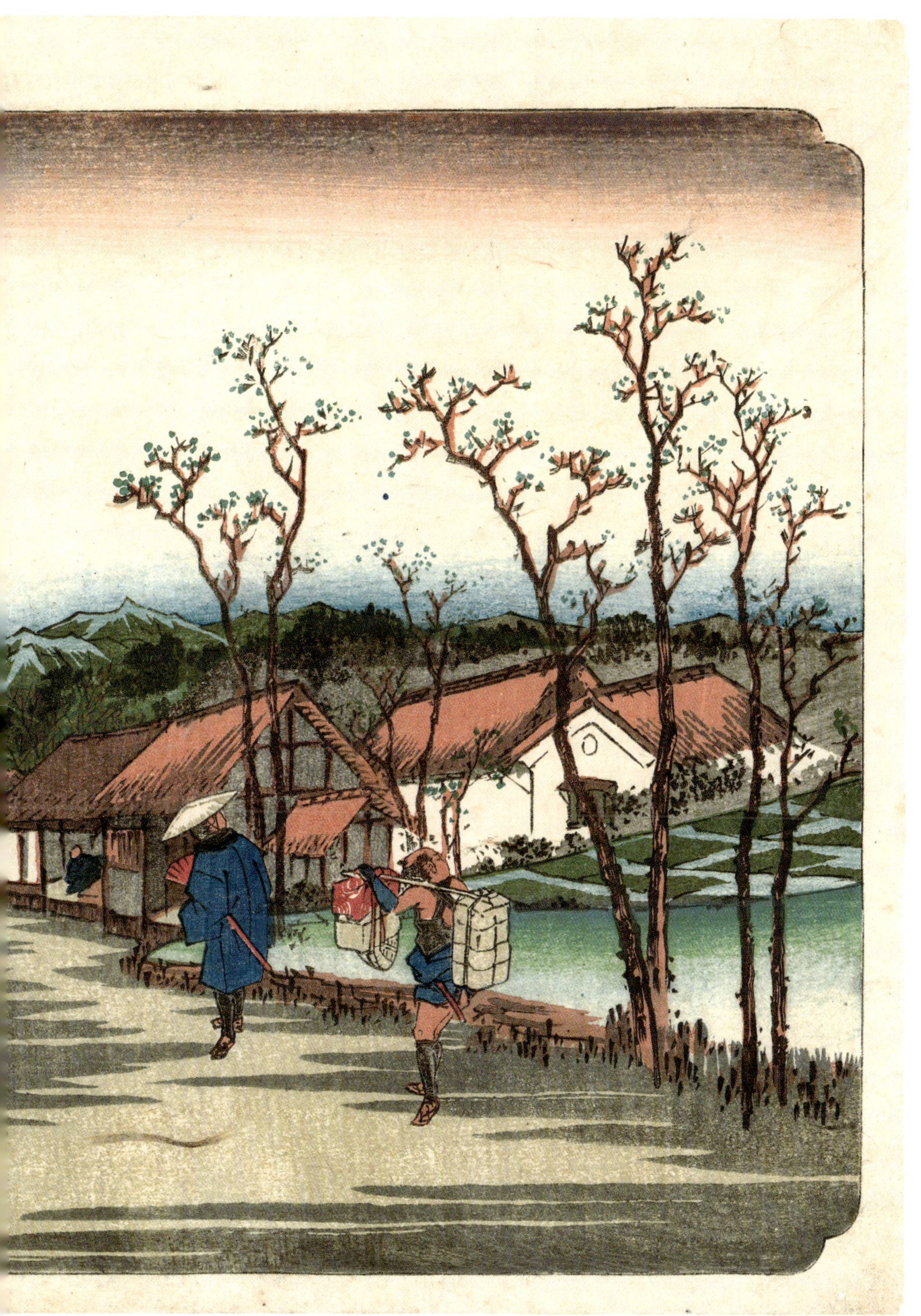

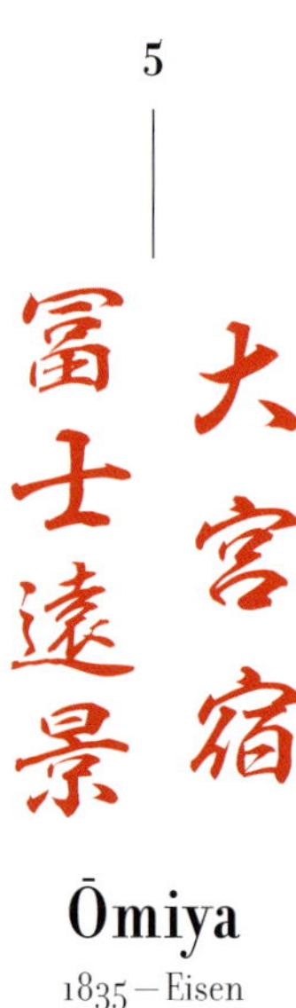

Ōmiya

1835 — Eisen

This is the first of only three prints in this series depicting Mount Fuji, the other two being Kōnosu and Shiojiri. Eisen depicted the snow-capped mountain rising between two cherry trees in blossom, indicating that it was early spring. Japan's highest peak at 3,776 metres (12,388 feet), Mount Fuji is around 100 kilometres (62 miles) from the village of Ōmiya. The view of Mount Fuji from Ōmiya also features in the fourth volume of the book *One Hundred Fuji* (*Hyaku Fuji*) from 1767, however, in the centre of that image there is a massive *torii* gate, and to its left the entrance to Hikawa Shrine, the main Shinto shrine of Musashi Province, founded in the year 473. Eisen, somewhat surprisingly, did not deem this to be of sufficient interest and included no trace of the shrine in his image.

On the left a farmer with a hoe over his shoulder and a child who is carrying a bamboo basket are walking towards their field. Behind them is a roofed stone stele that bears the inscription "Blue-Faced Vajra", referring to the main divinity of the Kōshin cult, as appeared earlier in the scene for the Itabashi station. Next to the stele are a number of haystacks, while on the right, a more affluent traveller is being carried in a palanquin by two bearers. The roofs of the station's houses are just visible over the embankment.

Dies ist das erste von nur drei Blättern in diesem Zyklus, die den Fuji zeigen. Die beiden anderen sind Kōnosu und Shiojiri. Eisen stellte den Berg mit seinem schneebedeckten Gipfel als Erhebung zwischen zwei blühenden Kirschbäumen dar und machte so den Vorfrühling kenntlich. Der mit 3776 Metern höchste Berg Japans liegt rund 100 Kilometer von Ōmiya entfernt. Der Blick von dem Dorf auf den Fuji taucht auch im vierten Band des Buches *Einhundert Fuji (Hyaku Fuji)* von 1767 auf, allerdings stehen dort ein mächtiges *torii* (Tor) und links daneben der Eingang des Hikawa-Schreins im Mittelpunkt, des im Jahr 473 gegründeten obersten Shinto-Schreins der Provinz Musashi. Es überrascht ein wenig, dass sich in Eisens Bild keine Spur dieses Schreins findet: Er schien ihm wohl nicht interessant genug.

Zur Linken gehen ein Bauer mit geschulterter Hacke und ein Kind, das eine Bambuskiepe trägt, zu ihrem Feld. Die überdachte Steinstele hinter ihnen trägt die Aufschrift „Blaugesichtiger Vajra" und verweist auf die Hauptgottheit des Kōshin-Kults, die bereits im Entwurf für die Station Itabashi eine Rolle spielte. Neben der Stele sind einige Heumieten zu sehen, während rechts im Bild ein wohlhabender Reisender von zwei Trägern in einer Sänfte transportiert wird. Die Dächer der Stationshäuser ragen nur knapp hinter dem Straßendamm hervor.

Cette image est la première de trois estampes représentant le mont Fuji dans cette série, les deux autres étant Kōnosu et Shiojiri. Eisen a figuré la montagne au sommet enneigé entre deux cerisiers en fleur, indice du début du printemps. Point culminant du Japin avec ses 3776 mètres, le mont Fuji se trouve à une centaine de kilomètres du village d'Ōmiya. La vue du mont Fuji depuis Ōmiya est aussi présente dans le quatrième volume du livre intitulé *Cent Fuji (Hyaku Fuji)*, paru en 1767 ; en revanche, au centre de cette image s'élève une monumentale porte *torii* et, à sa gauche, l'entrée d'Hikawa, principal sanctuaire shintoïste de la province de Musashi, fondé en 473. Il est un peu étonnant qu'Eisen ne l'ait pas jugé suffisamment intéressant, au point de n'en faire apparaître aucune trace dans son dessin.

À gauche, un fermier portant une houe sur l'épaule et un enfant chargé d'un panier de bambou se dirigent vers leur champ. Derrière eux se dresse une stèle de pierre, surmontée d'un petit toit, sur laquelle sont inscrits les caractères « Vajra au visage bleu », en référence à la divinité du culte *kōshin*, qui figure dans une scène précédente représentant la station d'Itabashi. Près de la stèle se trouvent quelques meules de foin, tandis qu'à droite un voyageur plus fortuné est transporté dans un palanquin par deux porteurs. Les toits des maisons de la station sont tout juste visibles au-dessus du talus.

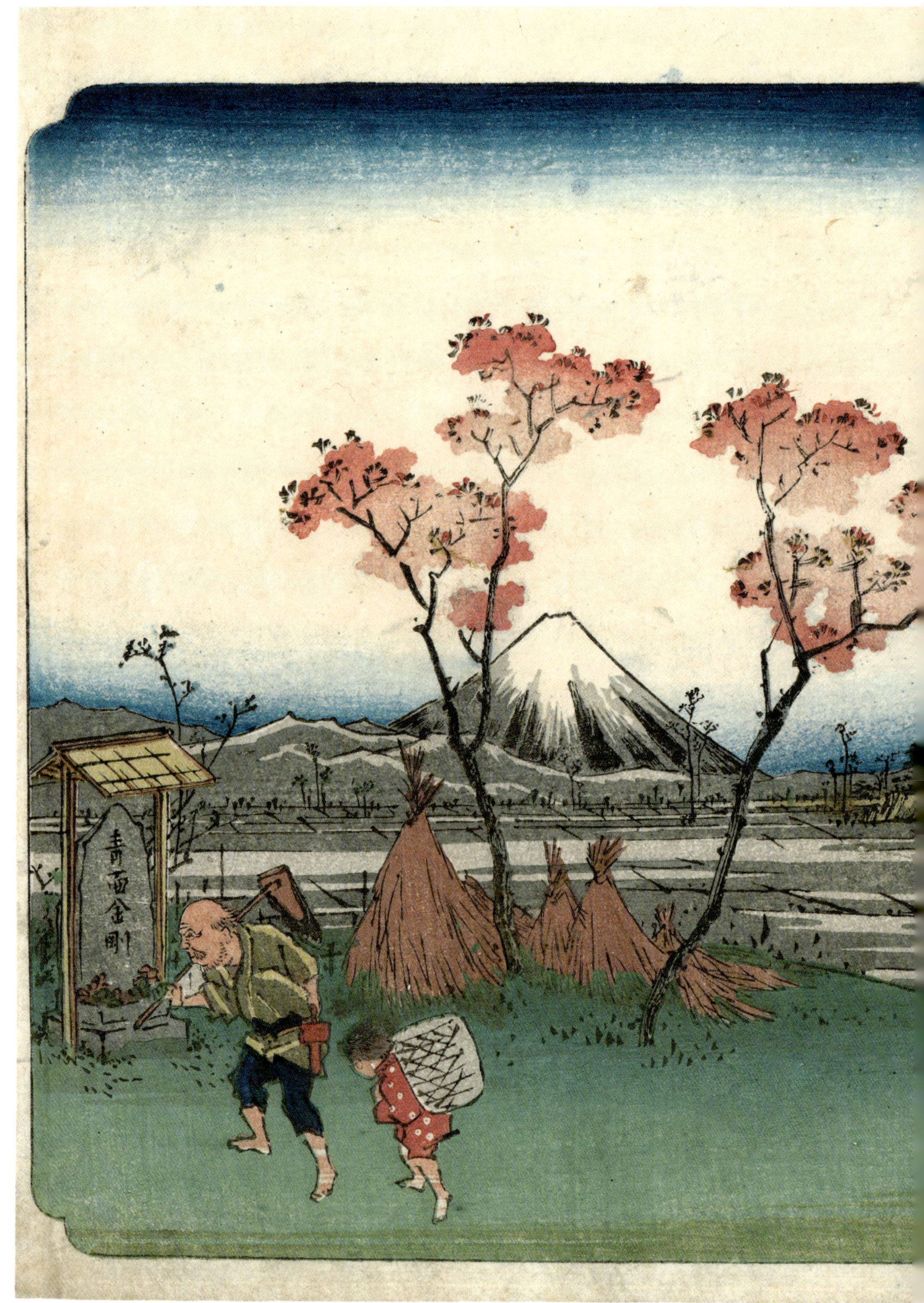

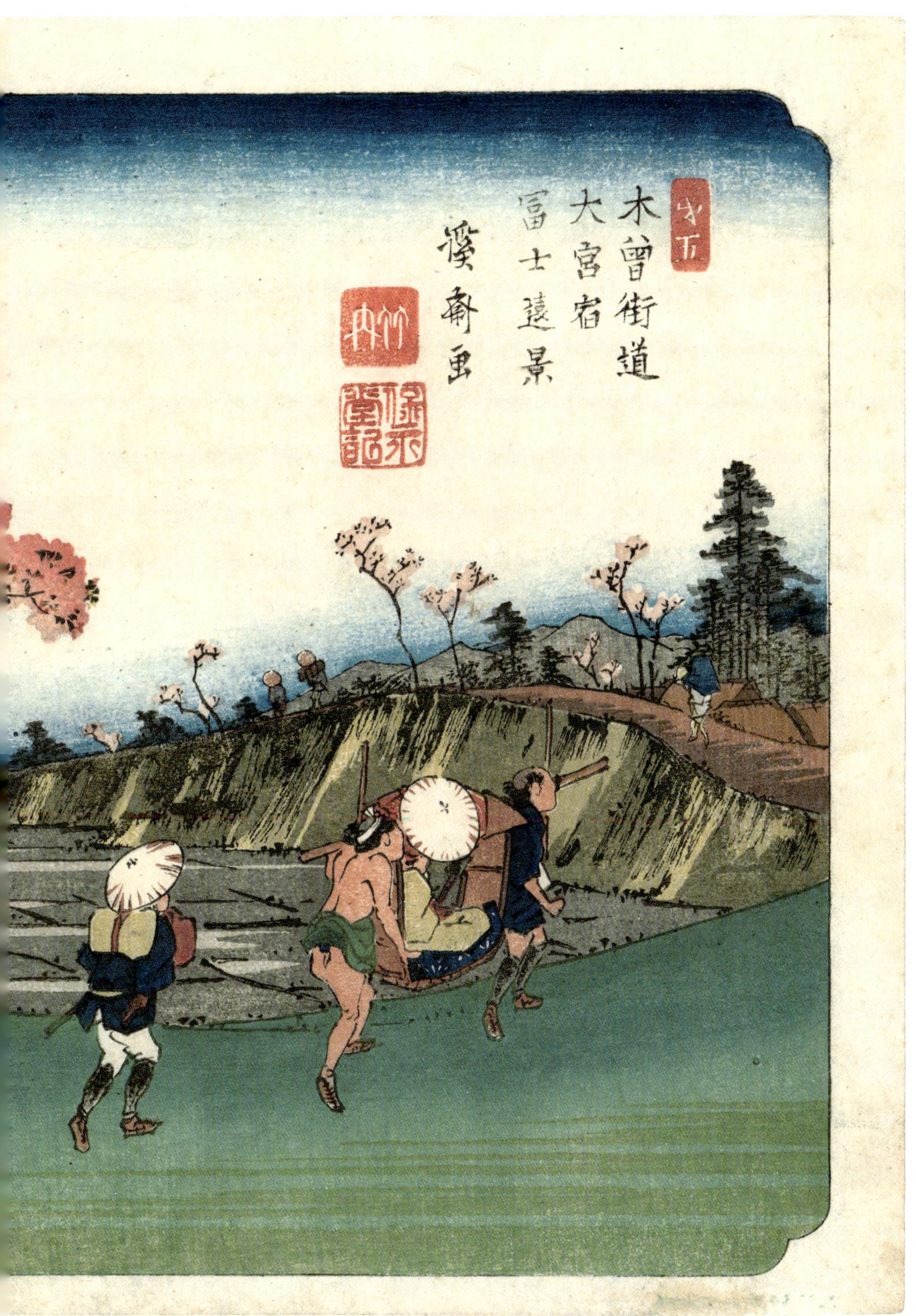

木曽街道
大宮宿
冨士遠景
溪斎画

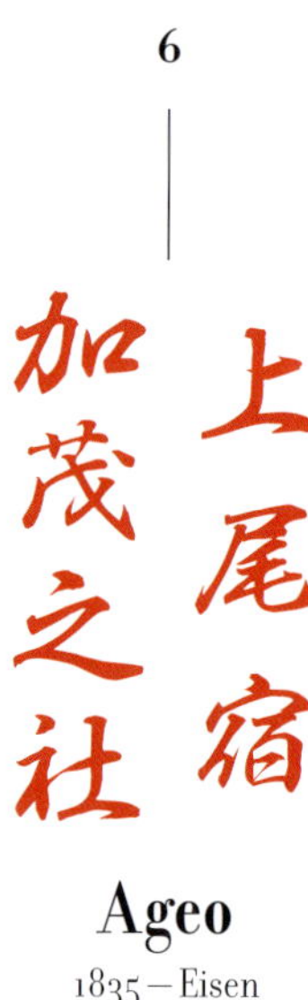

Ageo

1835 – Eisen

After leaving Ōmiya, travellers passed through the village of Kamo before reaching the next station, Ageo, after a journey of 8.7 kilometres (5.4 miles). The banners on the right identify the tiled roofs behind as being part of Kamo Daimyōjin, the Kamo Shrine, from which this village took its name. This one was a branch of the two Kamo shrines in Kyoto, Shimogamo and Kamigamo, which date from the 6th and 7th centuries respectively and are dedicated to the thunder god. The Kamo shrine depicted in this print first appeared in an official document from 1810 but may be considerably older.

In front of the houses farmers are winnowing the rice with a large rotary fan machine that originally derived from Chinese prototypes and was operated with a hand crank. The travelling samurai on the far left turn back to watch what was for them a rather unusual spectacle.

The Ageo station itself dates back to the 16th century and was already designated a post station in 1603, serving also as a dispatch centre for rice shipments. Several of its historic buildings were burnt down in a devastating fire in 1860. At close to 40 kilometres (almost 25 miles) from Edo, Ageo was a popular first-night stop for many travellers and in 1843 was able to offer 41 standard inns.

Nachdem sie Ōmiya hinter sich gelassen hatten, durchquerten Reisende das Dorf Kamo, bevor sie nach 8,7 Kilometern die nächste Station, Ageo, erreichten. Die Banner rechts kennzeichnen die Ziegeldächer dahinter als Teile des Kamo Daimyōjin oder Kamo-Schreins, dem dieses Dorf seinen Namen verdankt. Er war ein Ableger der beiden Kamo-Schreine Shimogamo und Kamigamo in Kyoto, die aus dem 6. und 7. Jahrhundert datieren und dem Donnergott gewidmet sind. Der in diesem Druck abgebildete Kamo-Schrein tauchte erstmals 1810 in einem offiziellen Dokument auf, könnte tatsächlich aber deutlich älter sein.

Vor den Häusern reinigen Bauern den Reis in einer großen Windfege, auch Putzmühle genannt, die ursprünglich auf chinesische Vorbilder zurückging und mit einer Handkurbel betrieben wurde. Die reisenden Samurai ganz links wenden sich zurück, um das für sie eher ungewöhnliche Schauspiel zu verfolgen.

Die Anfänge der Station reichen bis ins 16. Jahrhundert zurück. Bereits 1603 wurde Ageo zur Poststation bestimmt und diente zugleich als Abfertigungszentrum für Reistransporte. Mehrere ihrer historischen Gebäude fielen 1860 einem verheerenden Brand zum Opfer. Mit fast 40 Kilometern Entfernung von Edo war Ageo bei vielen Reisenden ein beliebtes erstes Übernachtungsziel, das 1843 insgesamt 41 Standardherbergen aufbieten konnte.

Une fois qu'ils ont quitté Ōmiya, les voyageurs passent par le village de Kamo avant d'atteindre la station suivante, Ageo, distante de 8,7 kilomètres. D'après les inscriptions des bannières à droite, les constructions aux toits de tuiles situées à l'arrière-plan font partie du Kamo Daimyōjin, le sanctuaire *kamo*, qui a donné son nom au village. Ce lieu appartient à l'un des deux sanctuaires *kamo* de Kyoto, Shimogamo et Kamigamo, datant respectivement des VIe et VIIe siècles et consacrés au dieu du tonnerre. Le sanctuaire *kamo* représenté dans cette estampe figure pour la première fois dans un document officiel de 1810, mais pourrait être beaucoup plus ancien.

Devant les maisons, des fermiers vannent du riz à l'aide d'un grand van rotatif, inspiré initialement de prototypes chinois et que l'on actionne avec une manivelle. Les samouraïs se trouvant à l'extrême gauche se retournent pour observer ce qui, pour eux, est un spectacle inhabituel.

Datant du XVIe siècle, la station d'Ageo fut désignée comme relais de poste dès 1603 et servait aussi de centre de distribution des cargaisons de riz. En 1860, un incendie dévastateur détruisit plusieurs de ses bâtiments historiques. Située à près de quarante kilomètres d'Edo, Ageo était, pour la première nuit, une halte très appréciée de nombreux voyageurs. En 1843, elle proposait quarante et une auberges ordinaires.

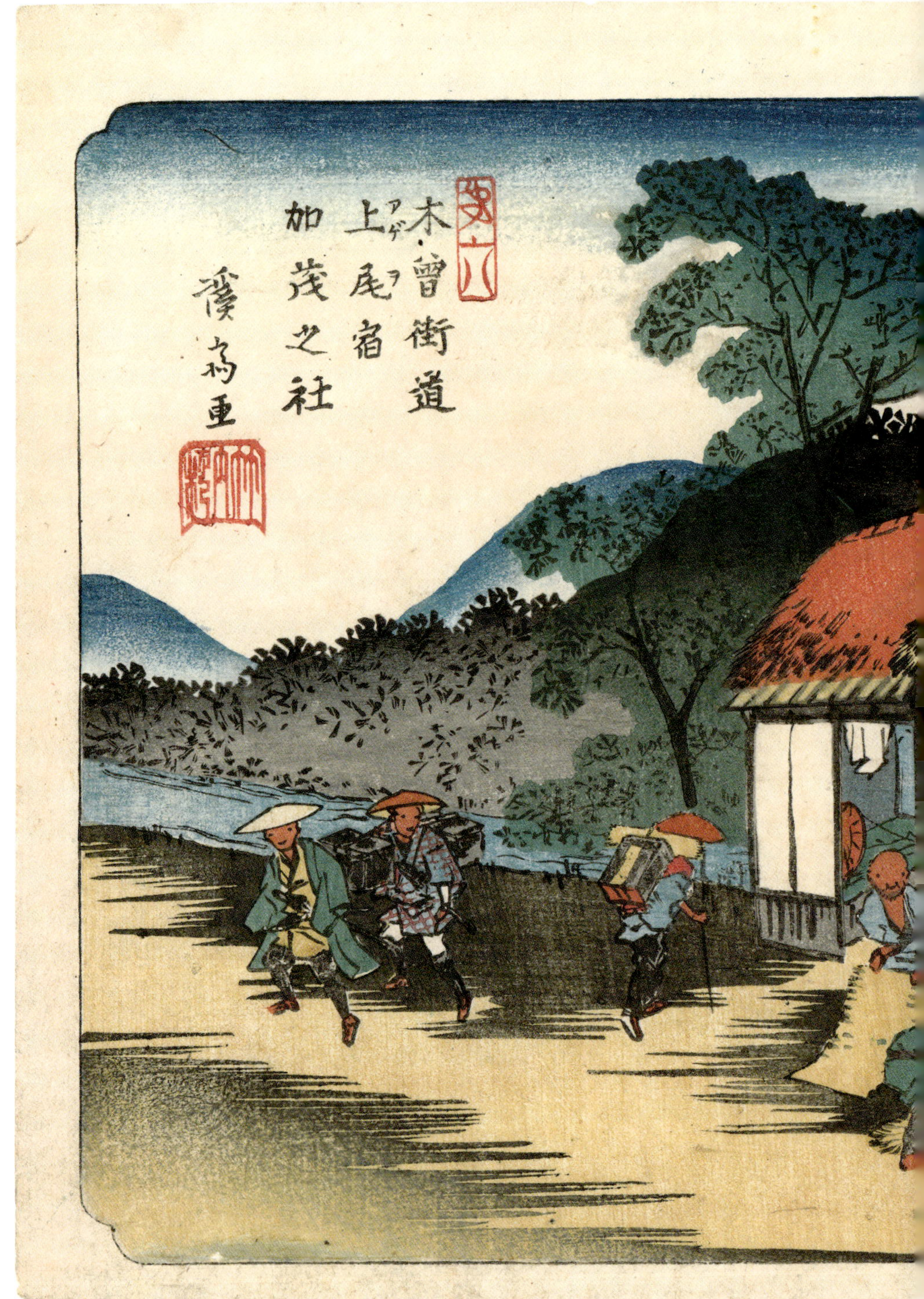

木曾街道
上尾宿
加茂之社
溪斎英重

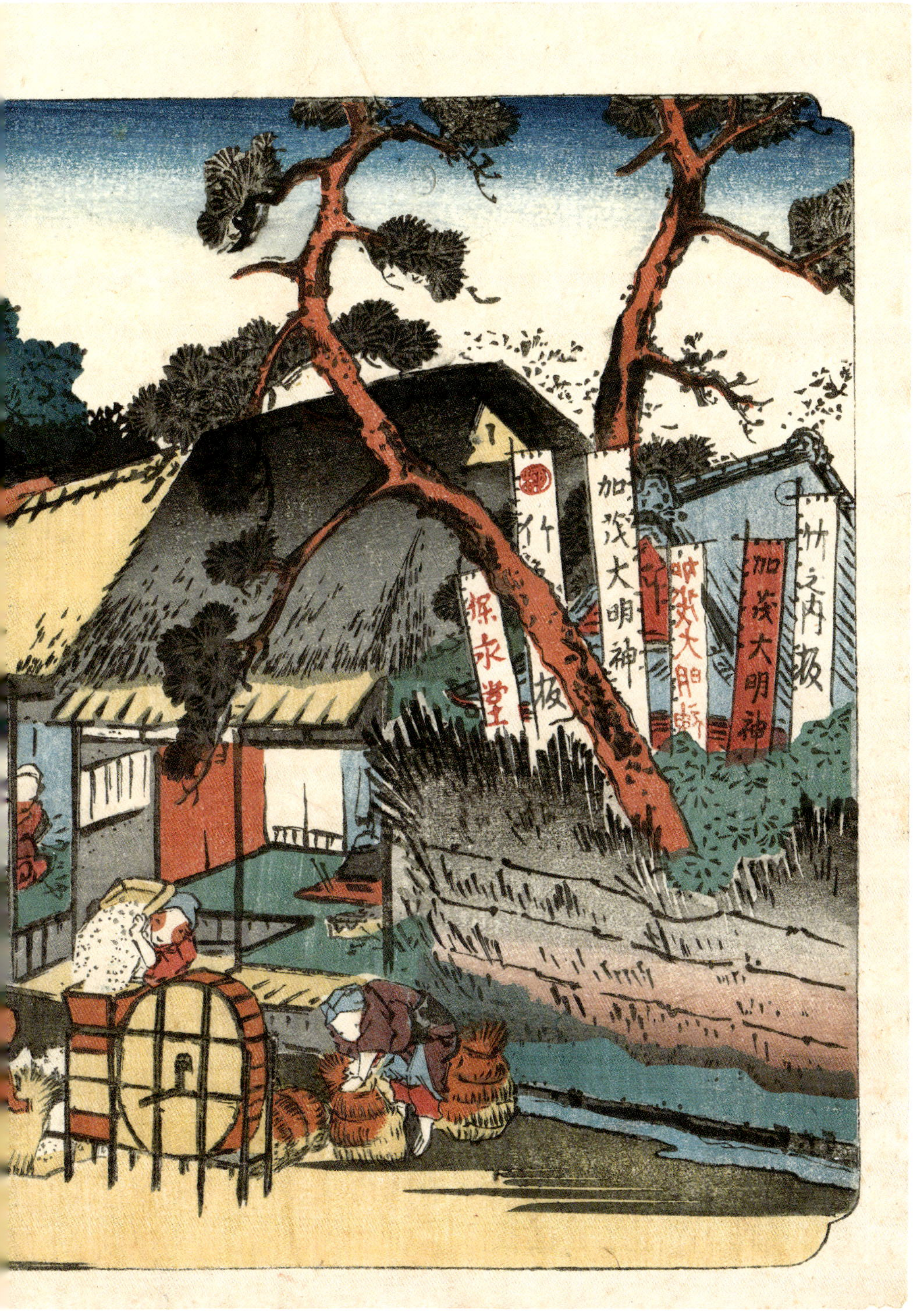

加茂大明神
加茂大明神
加茂大明神
採永堂
竹
板
竹之内坂

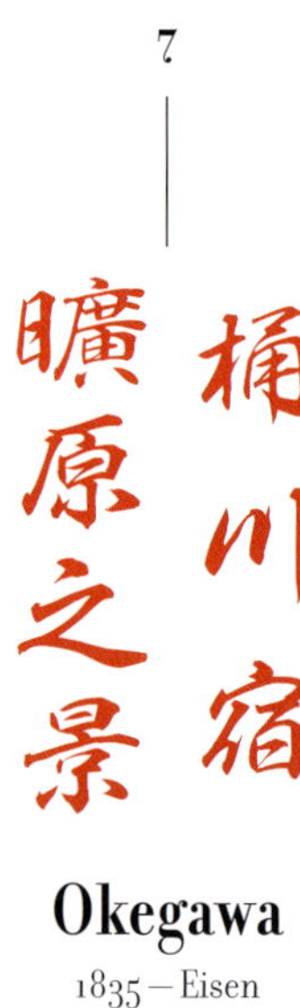

Okegawa

1835 — Eisen

Eisen's image for the station at Okegawa is rather neutral and could be just about anywhere in the flat countryside of Japan. According to the sub-title, the Kantō Plain seen in the background is the main focus. Covering 17,000 square kilometres (4.2 million acres), it is Japan's largest area of open landscape. On the far right, Eisen placed a hired horse being ridden by its owner, who has been unable to find a traveller to carry on the journey home. In the foreground, a traveller is asking a farmer woman for directions while she continues threshing barley with a small millstone. Her husband is lighting his pipe from the fire of the sunken hearth built into the house. Outside the house on the far left tobacco leaves are drying. The idyllic scene is further enhanced by swallows flying to a tree.

The Okegawa station itself is nowhere to be seen. The first time its name is mentioned is in an edict from 1352 issued by Ashikaga Takauji (1305–1358), the first shogun of the Ashikaga family. Okegawa was the centre of safflower cultivation, which was marketed nationwide as "Okegawa enji" (Okegawa Dark Red).

Eisens Bild für die Station Okegawa wirkt eher neutral und könnte fast überall im japanischen Flachland angesiedelt sein. Dem Untertitel zufolge gilt das Hauptaugenmerk der Kantō-Ebene im Hintergrund, der mit 17 000 Quadratkilometern größten offenen Landfläche Japans. Das von Eisen ganz rechts im Bild platzierte Mietpferd wird von seinem Besitzer selbst geritten, da dieser für den Heimweg niemanden finden konnte, dem er das Pferd hätte vermieten können. Im Vordergrund fragt ein Reisender eine Bäuerin, die mit einem kleinen Mühlstein Gerste drischt, nach dem Weg. Ihr Mann entzündet seine Pfeife am Feuer des Herdes, der in den Fußboden des Hauses eingelassen ist; davor, unter der Dachkante ganz links im Bild, hängen Tabakblätter zum Trocknen. Auf einen Baum zufliegende Schwalben machen die Idylle perfekt.

Die Station Okegawa ist nirgends zu sehen. Ihr Name wird erstmals in einem Edikt von 1352 erwähnt, das von Ashikaga Takauji (1305–1358) erlassen wurde, dem ersten Shogun der Ashikaga-Familie. Okegawa war das Zentrum des Färberdistelanbaus. Der Farbstoff der Blüten wurde in ganz Japan als „Okegawa enji" (Okegawa-Dunkelrot) vermarktet.

L'illustration d'Eisen pour la station située à Okegawa est assez neutre et pourrait représenter quasiment n'importe quel lieu de la plaine japonaise. Le sous-titre indique que le sujet principal est la plaine de Kantō, visible à l'arrière-plan. Avec 17 000 kilomètres carrés, c'est la plus vaste plaine du Japon. À l'extrême droite, Eisen a placé un cheval de louage monté par son propriétaire, lequel s'est trouvé incapable de trouver un voyageur à transporter en rentrant chez lui. Au premier plan, un voyageur demande sa route à une fermière qui continue de moudre de l'orge avec une petite meule. Son mari allume sa pipe en la portant près du feu qui brûle dans l'âtre encastré dans le plancher de la maison. Un vol d'hirondelles se dirigeant vers un arbre accentue le caractère idyllique de la scène.

La station d'Okegawa proprement dite est invisible. On trouve une première mention de son nom dans un décret de 1352 proclamé par Ashikaga Takauji (1305–1358), premier shogun de la famille Ashikaga. Okegawa était le centre de la production du carthame des teinturiers, commercialisé dans tout le pays sous l'appellation « Okegawa enji » (rouge sombre d'Okegawa).

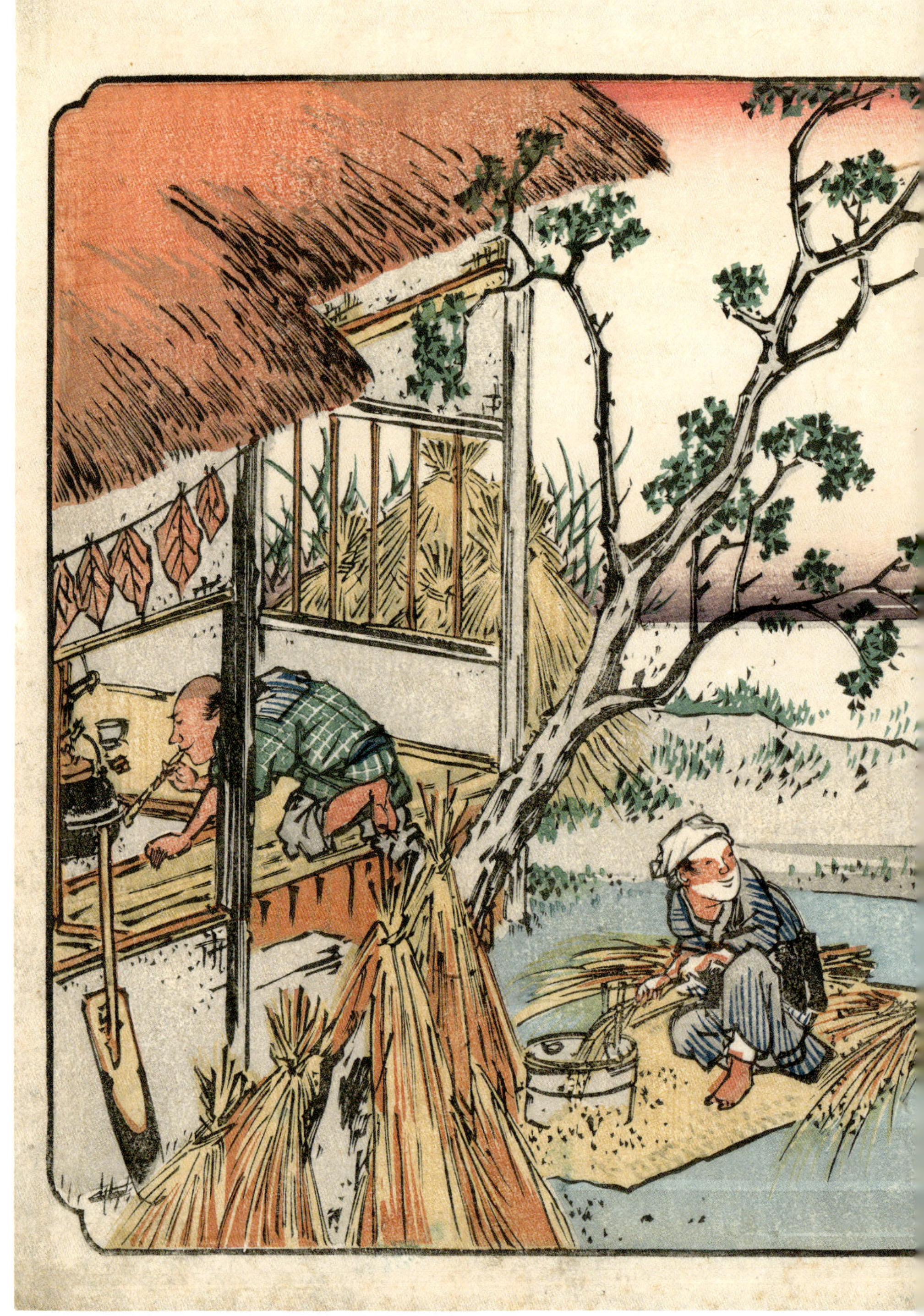

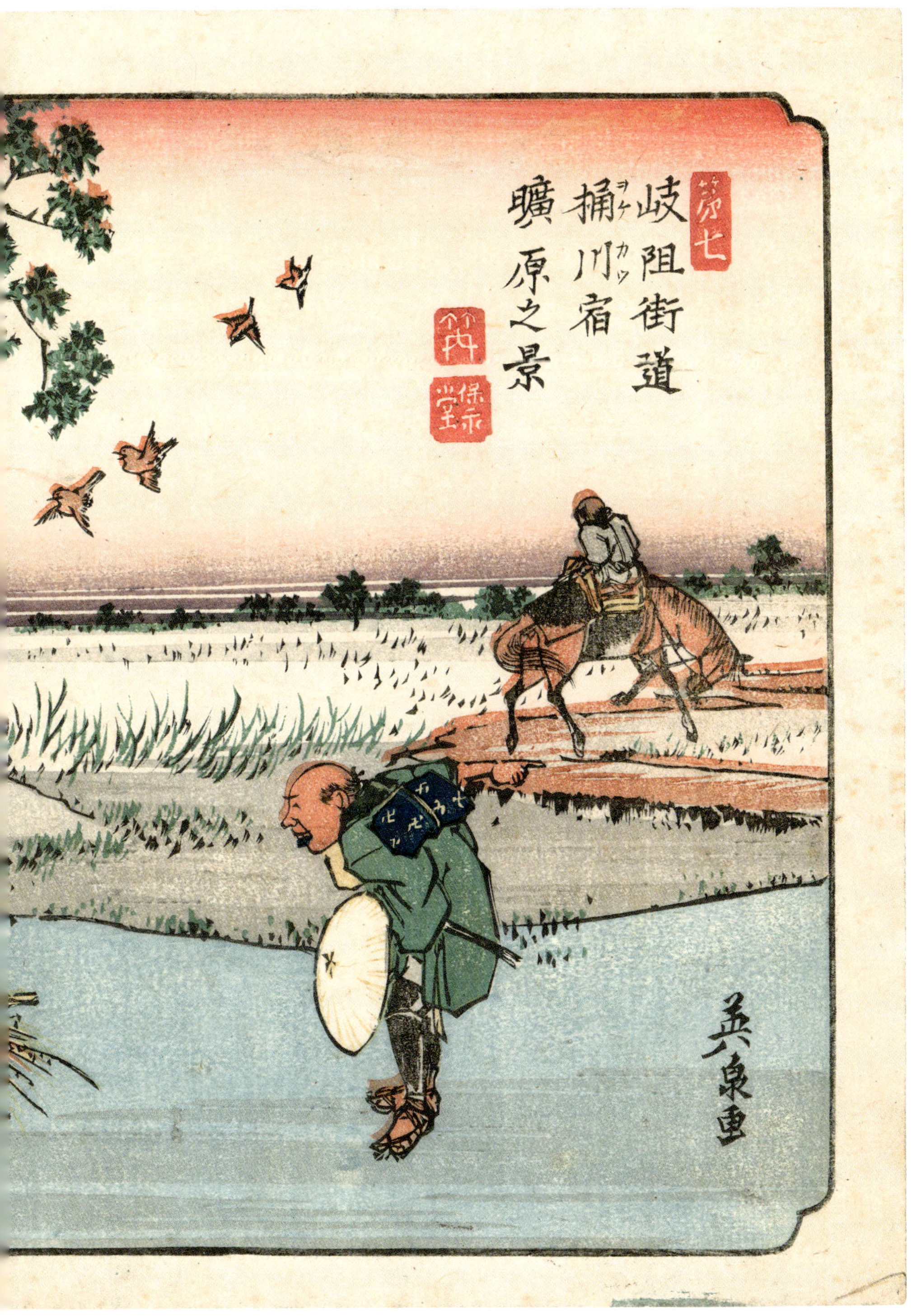
第七
岐阻街道
桶川宿
曠原之景

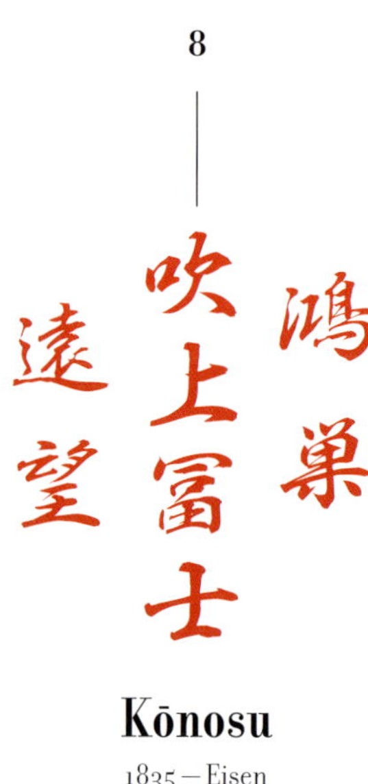

8

Kōnosu

1835 – Eisen

After Ōmiya, this is the second of three designs in this series that feature Mount Fuji (the third is Shiojiri). The 3,776-metre (12,388 feet) peak of Japan's holy mountain, located 115 kilometres (72 miles) from the station, appears as a white cone rising above horizontal bands representing stylised clouds, and other mountains and hills. According to the sub-title, this is the view from Fukiage, a village between Kōnosu and the next station, Kumagaya. Neither village is depicted here; as with the previous station, Eisen presents a road zigzagging across the Kantō Plain. This time, however, there are no houses and instead he increased the number of travellers walking towards the west in order to fill out the composition.

One of the travellers, shown on the left, is a mendicant monk (*komusō*) who wears a *tengai* – a typical, conical straw hat that was meant to obscure the wearer's identity and symbolised detachment from a worldly life and an absence of ego. *Komusō* were practitioners of the Fuke School of Zen Buddhism, a belief system that was brought over from China in 1254 by returning monks. Instead of meditating by sitting quietly, *komusō* played a bamboo flute which each of these priests carried with them. The flute could also be used to request alms.

The samurai in the centre, who is walking in the direction of Edo, has hung his pipe case and tobacco pouch on one of the bundles of his belongings he carries on a pole on his shoulder. He has taken the pipe out and seems to be about to have a smoke.

Nach Ōmiya ist dies das zweite von drei Blättern in dieser Serie, die den Fuji zeigen (das dritte ist Shiojiri). Japans heiliger Berg, 3776 Meter hoch und 115 Kilometer von der Station entfernt, erscheint als weißer Kegel über stilisierten Wolken, die als horizontale Streifen dargestellt sind, und über den kleineren Bergen und Hügeln im Mittelgrund. Dem Untertitel zufolge zeigt der Druck den Blick von Fukiage aus, einem Dorf zwischen Kōnosu und der nächsten Station, Kumagaya. Keine dieser Ortschaften ist hier abgebildet. Wie bei der vorherigen Station präsentiert Eisen eine Straße, die sich über die Kantō-Ebene schlängelt, wobei er diesmal jedoch keine Häuser hinzufügte, sondern die Komposition durch eine größere Anzahl Fußreisender auf dem Weg nach Westen ausfüllte.

Der Reisende ganz links im Bild ist ein Bettelmönch *(komusō)*, der einen *tengai* trägt. Dieser typische bienenkorbähnliche Strohhut sollte die Identität seines Trägers verbergen und symbolisierte die Loslösung vom weltlichen Leben und die Abwesenheit des Ichs. Die *komusō* waren Anhänger der Fuke-Schule des Zen-Buddhismus, eines Glaubenssystems, das Mönche mitbrachten, als sie 1254 aus China zurückkehrten. Statt still sitzend zu meditieren, spielten die *komusō* auf einer Bambusflöte, die jeder dieser Geistlichen bei sich trug. Die Flöte konnte auch eingesetzt werden, um Almosen zu erbitten.

Der Samurai in der Bildmitte, der in Richtung Edo unterwegs ist, trägt seine Habseligkeiten an einem Stab auf der Schulter mit sich; Pfeifenetui und Tabaksbeutel hängen an einem seiner Bündel herab. Er hat die Pfeife herausgeholt und scheint sie gerade rauchen zu wollen.

Après Ōmiya, c'est le deuxième des trois dessins de cette série représentant le mont Fuji (le troisième est Shiojiri). La montagne sacrée du Japon, qui culmine à 3776 mètres et se trouve à 115 kilomètres de cette station, prend la forme d'un cône blanc s'élevant au-dessus de rayures horizontales, figurant des nuages stylisés, et d'autres montagnes et collines. Selon le sous-titre, il s'agit de la vue depuis Fukiage, village situé entre Kōnosu et Kumagaya, la station suivante. Aucun des deux villages n'est représenté ici ; comme avec la station précédente, Eisen a dessiné une route zigzaguant à travers la plaine de Kantō. Mais, cette fois, il n'y a pas de maison, et l'artiste a préféré ajouter des voyageurs se dirigeant vers l'ouest afin de remplir la composition.

L'un des voyageurs visibles à gauche est un moine mendiant *(komusō)* portant un *tengai*, chapeau de paille conique caractéristique, destiné à dissimuler l'identité de son propriétaire et symbolisant le détachement à l'égard de la vie terrestre et l'absence d'ego. Les *komusō* étaient des adeptes de l'école *fuke* du bouddhisme zen, croyance rapportée de Chine par des moines en 1254. Au lieu de méditer paisiblement en position assise, les *komusō* jouaient de la flûte de bambou dont chacun de ces prêtres était muni. Ils pouvaient aussi se servir de leur flûte pour demander l'aumône.

Le samouraï situé au centre, et qui se dirige vers Edo, a accroché l'étui de sa pipe et sa blague à tabac à l'un des ballots contenant ses affaires, qu'il porte sur l'épaule à l'aide d'une palanche. Il a sorti sa pipe et semble s'apprêter à fumer.

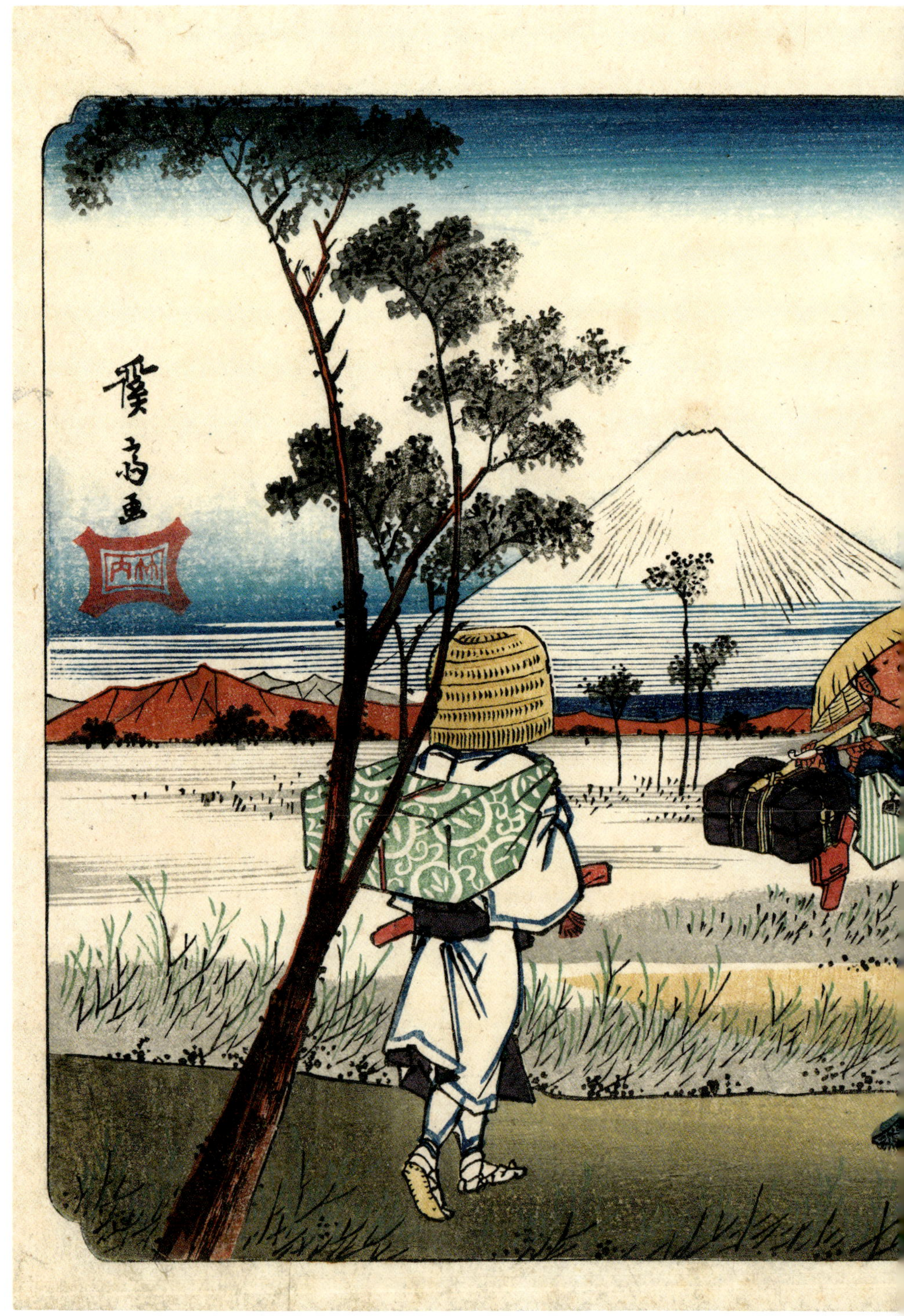

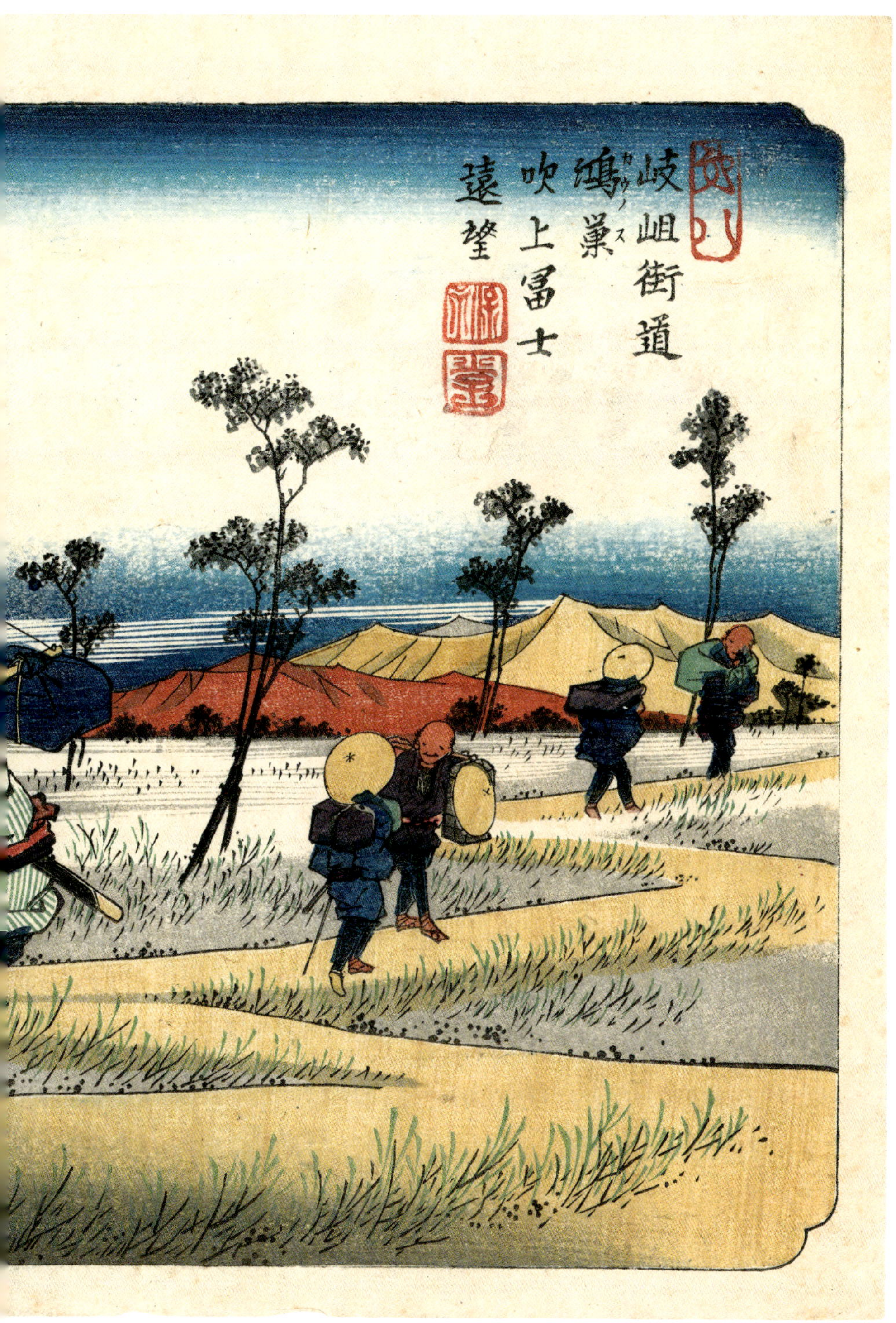
岐岨街道
鴻巣
吹上冨士
遠望

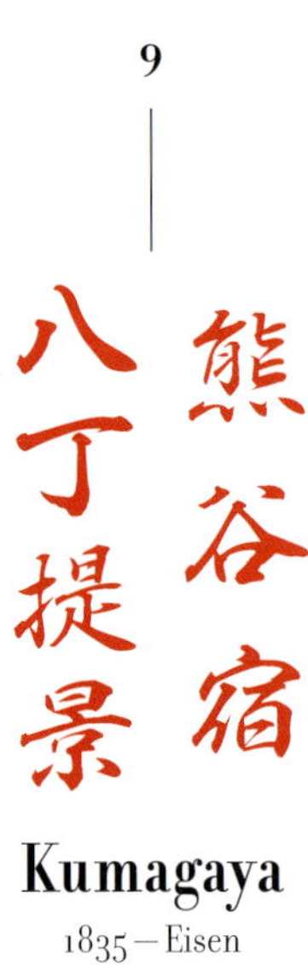

9

Kumagaya

1835 — Eisen

The Kumagaya station is named after its most famous son, the warrior hero Kumagai Jirō Naozane (1141–1208), who fought for the Minamoto/Genji clan in the battle at Ichinotani against the Taira/Heike in 1184. In the aftermath of victory, Kumagai took the tonsure and became a disciple of the priest Hōnen (1133–1212). The Yūkokuji temple, which still exists today, was built here and named after Kumagai.

In the background, two travellers are walking towards the next station, Fukaya, following the uphill road on the Hatchō embankment alongside the Ara River. The stone marker on the right is inscribed with directions: "Left, Fukaya, two *ri* 20 *chō*", "Right, road to Oshi, Gyōda". The town of Gyōda, in the Oshi Domain, is not on the Kisokaidō road.

On the right and behind the stone marker is a stone sculpture of the bodhisattva Jizō with a red cloth on its head which is protected by a wooden roof. Worshippers have lit incense at the base of the sculpture which offers protection to travellers, women and children. A wealthy merchant who is being carried in a sedan chair by two porters, is chatting with one of the locals. The restaurant on the left serves *udon*, thick noodles, and *ankoro*, small rice cakes wrapped in red bean paste. Even though the name of the restaurant is not inscribed, it is believed to be the famous Mikariya.

The composition somewhat resembles Hiroshige's design of Totsuka in his first Tōkaidō series, issued a few years before, which also shows the front of a restaurant on the left, together with a serving waitress and travellers with horses.

Die Station Kumagaya ist nach ihrem berühmtesten Sohn benannt, dem Heldenkrieger Kumagai Jirō Naozane (1141–1208), der 1184 in der Schlacht von Ichinotani für den Minamoto- oder Genji-Clan gegen die auch Heike genannten Taira kämpfte. Nach der siegreichen Schlacht ließ Kumagai sich tonsurieren und schloss sich dem Priestermönch Hōnen (1133–1212) an. Der Yūkokuji-Tempel, der bis heute existiert, wurde hier erbaut und nach Kumagai benannt.

Im Hintergrund entfernen sich zwei Fußreisende in Richtung der nächsten Station, Fukaya. Sie folgen der ansteigenden Straße, die auf dem Hatchō-Deich am Fluss Ara entlangführt. Der Meilenstein rechts ist mit Richtungsangaben versehen: „Links, Fukaya, zwei *ri* 20 *chō*", „Rechts, Straße nach Oshi, Gyōda". Die Ortschaft Gyōda im damaligen Lehen Oshi liegt nicht am Kisokaidō.

Rechts hinter dem Stein steht unter einem schützenden Holzdach eine Statue des Bodhisattva Jizō mit einem roten Tuch auf dem Kopf. Gläubige haben am Fuß der Statue, die Reisenden, Frauen und Kindern Schutz verspricht, Weihrauch entzündet. Ein reicher Kaufmann, der von zwei Trägern in einer Sänfte transportiert wird, unterhält sich mit einem Ortsansässigen. Das Rasthaus links im Bild serviert *udon*, dicke Nudeln, und *ankoro*, kleine Reiskuchen in einer Hülle aus Rote-Bohnen-Paste. Wenngleich der Name des Rasthauses nicht genannt wird, nimmt man an, dass es sich um das berühmte Mikariya handelt.

Die Komposition ähnelt ein wenig Hiroshiges Entwurf für Totsuka in seiner ersten, einige Jahre zuvor erschienenen Tōkaidō-Serie. Auch er zeigt vor einem Rasthaus zur Linken eine Serviererin bei der Arbeit und Reisende mit Pferden.

La station de Kumagaya tire son nom de son fils le plus célèbre, le héros guerrier Kumagai Jirō Naozane (1141–1208) qui se battit pour le clan Minamoto/Genji à la bataille d'Ichinotani contre les Taira/Heike en 1184. Après la victoire, Kumagai décida de porter la tonsure et se fit disciple du prêtre Hōnen (1133–1212). C'est là qu'a été construit le temple de Yūkokuji, qui existe toujours aujourd'hui et porte le nom de Kumagai.

Au fond, deux voyageurs marchent en direction de Fukaya, la station suivante, en suivant la route qui gravit le talus longeant la rivière Ara. La borne située à droite indique les directions : « À gauche, Fukaya, deux *ri* vingt *chō* », « À droite, route d'Oshi, Gyōda ». La ville de Gyōda, dans le domaine d'Oshi, ne se trouve pas sur la Kisokaidō.

À droite, derrière la borne, se dresse une sculpture en pierre du bodhisattva Jizō, coiffé d'un linge rouge et protégé d'un toit de bois. Les fidèles ont allumé de l'encens au pied de la sculpture qui veille sur les voyageurs, les femmes et les enfants. Un riche marchand voyageant dans une chaise à porteurs bavarde avec un habitant. Dans le restaurant situé à gauche, on sert des *udon*, des nouilles épaisses, et des *ankoro*, de petits gâteaux de riz enrobés d'une pâte aux haricots rouges. Bien qu'aucune enseigne ne soit visible, il s'agit probablement du célèbre restaurant Mikariya.

Cette composition ressemble un peu au dessin d'Hiroshige représentant Totsuka qui figure dans sa première série de la Tōkaidō, publiée quelques années auparavant, où l'on voit également la façade d'un restaurant à gauche, ainsi qu'une serveuse et des voyageurs accompagnés de chevaux.

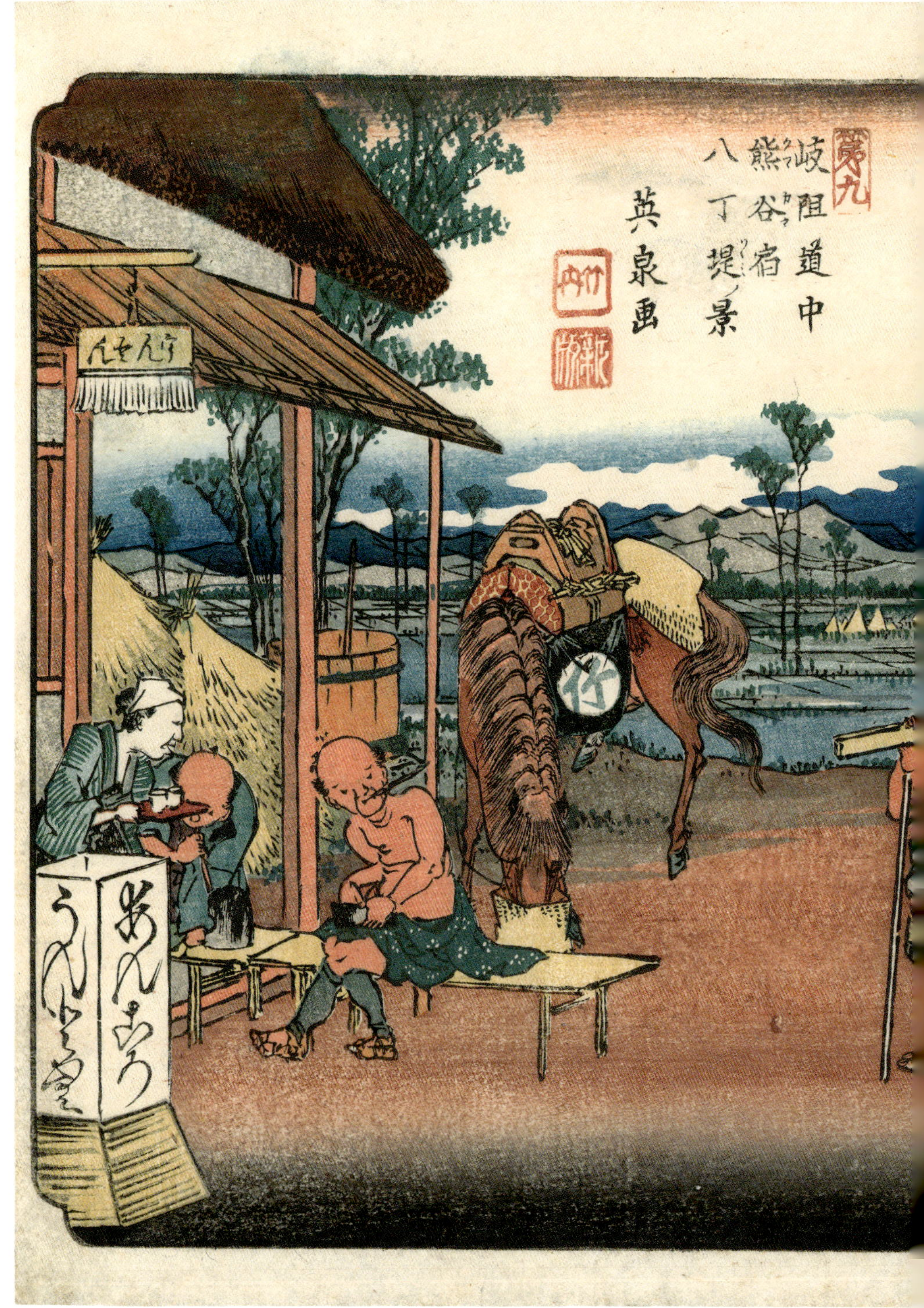
第九
岐阻道中
熊谷宿
八丁堤ノ景
英泉画

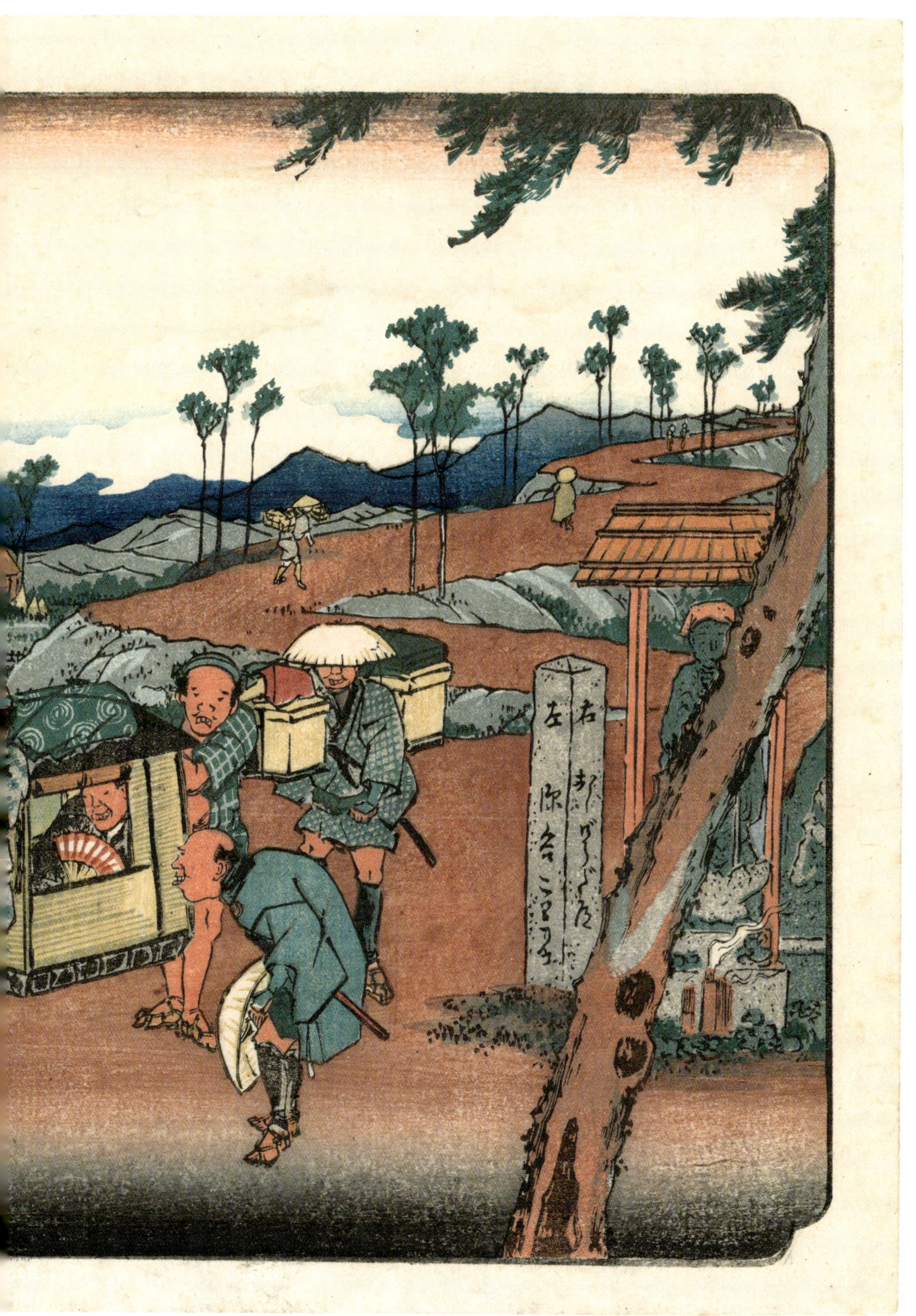

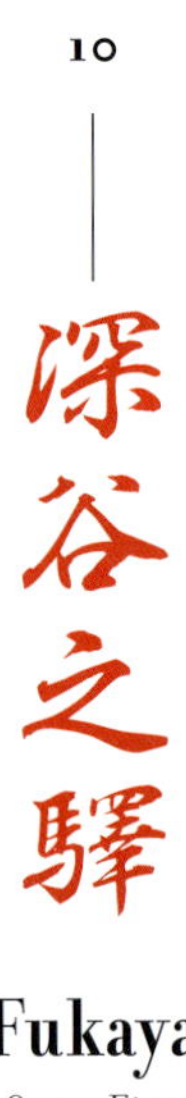

Fukaya

1835 — Eisen

Fukaya had 80 inns for regular travellers and was therefore by far the post town with the largest number of lodgings, as compared to the average of 28 inns for one of these towns. Fukaya established itself as a popular resting-place for the night and was known for its many brothels that offered services by lower-ranking and therefore more affordable prostitutes. This was indeed what the town became famous for, and Eisen focused on exactly this aspect for his design. In his night scene, five women are shown in the street outside a house.

On the left of the house is the typical architecture of an Edo-period (1603–1868) brothel with a display window facing the street that is protected by a lattice. Behind this the women would sit so that passers-by could easily see them and feel tempted to visit the establishment. Women also more actively worked the streets in order to lure customers inside. The women behind the lattice were higher ranking than those in the street and their price was therefore about double.

Eisen specialised in beautiful women rather than landscapes and was therefore very familiar with how to draw bodies and the way the folds of a kimono and obi fell. In the background on the right some potential clients are depicted but only as silhouettes, in stark contrast to the women in their colourful robes.

Mit 80 Herbergen allein für gewöhnliche Reisende hatte Fukaya im Vergleich zu den durchschnittlich 28 Gasthöfen je Station die bei Weitem größte Anzahl an Unterkünften zu bieten. Die Stadt etablierte sich als beliebter Rastplatz für die Nacht und war bekannt für die vielen Bordelle, in denen weniger hochrangige und daher nicht so teure Prostituierte ihre Dienste anboten. Tatsächlich machten sie Fukaya berühmt, und Eisen stellte genau diesen Aspekt in den Mittelpunkt seines Entwurfs. In seiner nächtlichen Straßenszene stehen fünf Frauen wie aufgereiht vor einem Haus.

Der linke Flügel des Gebäudes weist die für ein Freudenhaus der Edo-Zeit (1603–1868) typische Architektur auf: Das zur Straße gerichtete Schaufenster ist durch ein Gitter geschützt. Dahinter saßen die Frauen, sodass Passanten sie leicht sehen konnten und versucht waren, das Etablissement zu betreten. Andere Frauen boten sich vor dem Haus an, um Kunden hereinzulocken. Die Frauen hinter dem Gitter waren nicht nur höheren Ranges als die auf der Straße, sondern auch etwa doppelt so teuer.

Eisen war eher auf schöne Frauen als auf Landschaften spezialisiert und wusste daher sehr genau, wie man Körper zeichnete und wie die Falten von Kimonos und Obi fielen. Im Hintergrund rechts sind einige potenzielle Kunden abgebildet, jedoch lediglich als dunkle Silhouetten, ganz anders als die Frauen in ihren farbenprächtigen Gewändern.

Avec quatre-vingts auberges destinées aux voyageurs ordinaires, Fukaya était de loin le relais de poste où l'on trouvait le plus de gîtes, par rapport aux vingt-huit auberges que ce genre de ville possédait en moyenne. Fukaya s'était fait une bonne réputation de ville étape, connue pour ses nombreux bordels proposant les services de prostituées de rang inférieur, par conséquent plus abordables. C'est bien à cela que la ville devait sa notoriété, et c'est précisément cet aspect qu'Eisen a choisi de dépeindre. Dans sa scène de nuit, on voit cinq femmes dans la rue devant une maison.

Sur la gauche de cette maison s'élève l'architecture typique d'une maison close de l'ère Edo (1603–1868), avec sa devanture donnant sur la rue, protégé par une claire-voie derrière laquelle les femmes s'asseyaient afin que les passants puissent bien les voir et être tentés d'entrer dans l'établissement. D'autres femmes arpentaient activement les rues pour attirer les clients. Les femmes assises derrière la claire-voie étaient de rang supérieur et demandaient un prix environ deux fois plus élevé.

Davantage spécialiste des belles femmes que des paysages, Eisen savait parfaitement comment dessiner les corps et la manière dont tombaient les plis d'un kimono et d'un obi. À l'arrière-plan à droite, des clients potentiels, seulement représentés sous forme de silhouettes, contrastent nettement avec les femmes aux vêtements colorés.

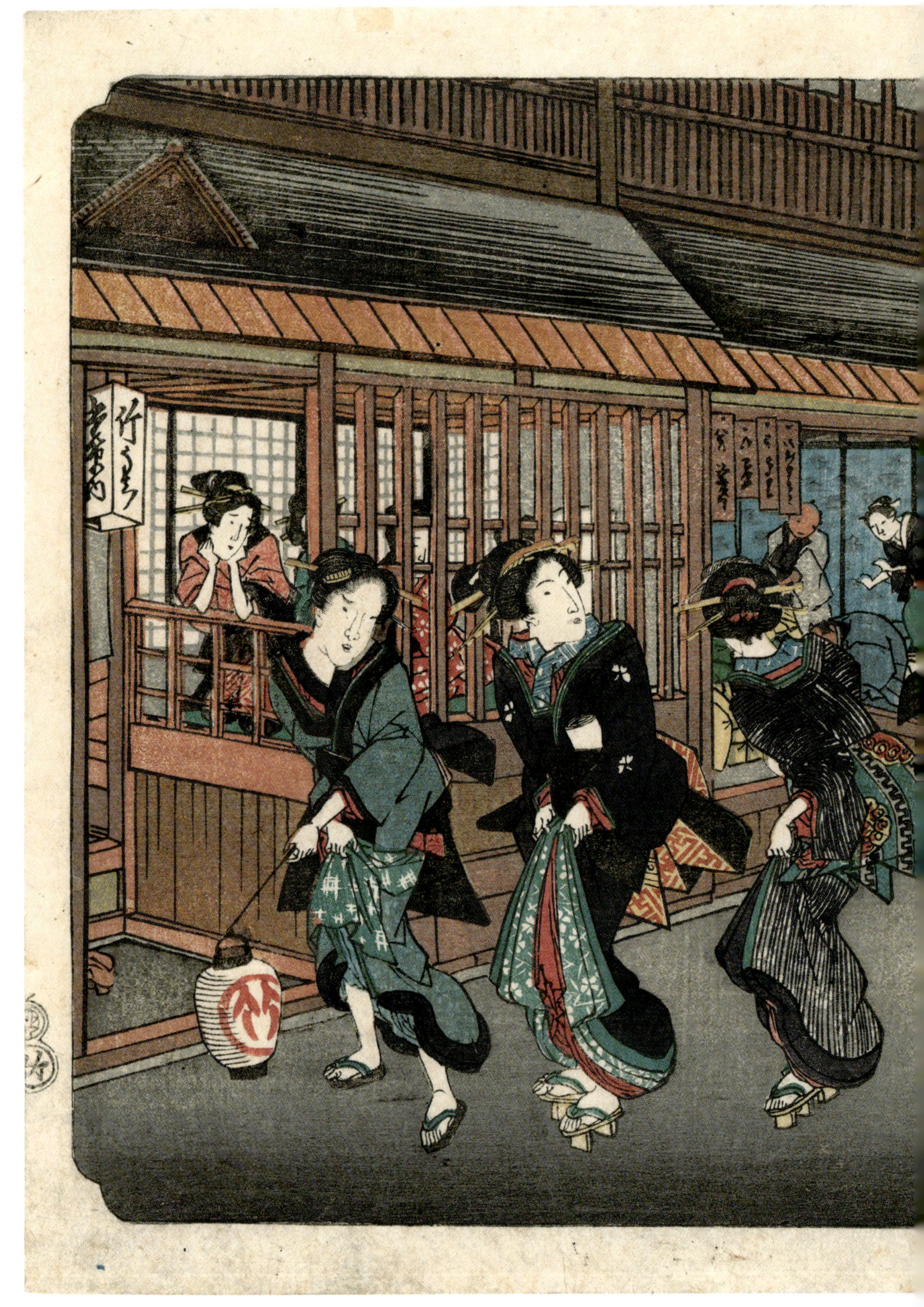

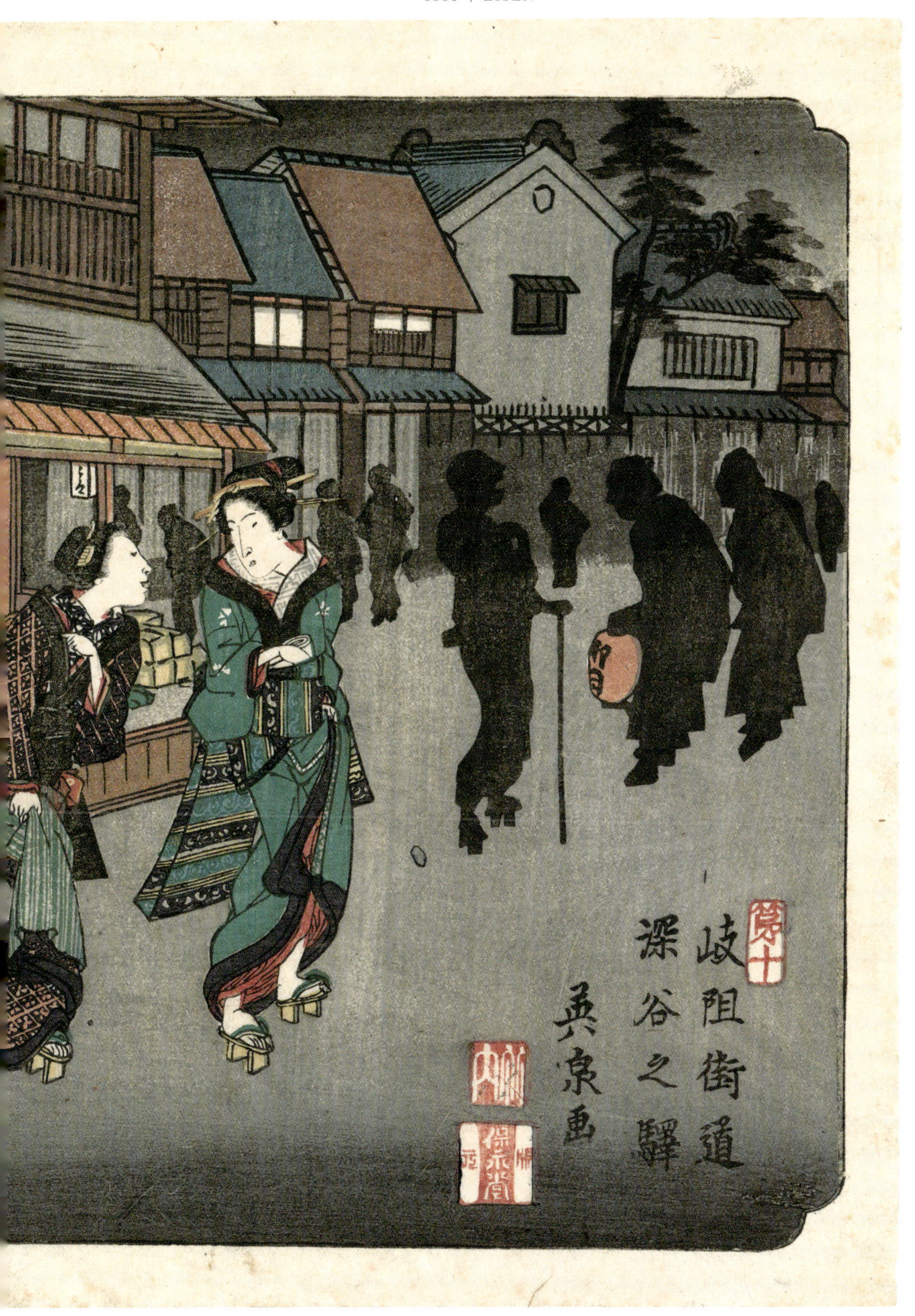

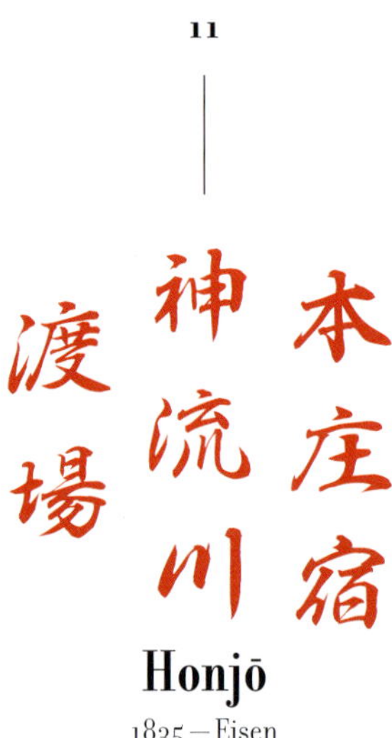

11

Honjō

1835 — Eisen

The Kanna River is a tributary of the Tone River, which at 322 kilometres (200 miles) is the second longest in Japan. In Eisen's design, a feudal procession is crossing the Kanna first by marching over a trestle bridge to a sandbank and then by boarding ferries. On the other side of the river in the left background are the houses of the next station, Shinmachi. This was the first station in Kōzuke Province and the river marks the border with Musashi Province and its last station, Honjō; in today's terms, the road leaves Saitama Prefecture and enters Gunma. With a population of over 4,500 in 1843, Honjō was the second largest station town after Ōtsu (the last station before Kyoto).

In the middle of the procession is the lord, travelling comfortably and guarded in a large, red palanquin which is carried by several men in front and back. While a few prints from this series feature the vanguard or rearguard of a procession, this is the only one that depicts a procession almost in its entirety.

On either side of the river crossing is a large stone lantern to guide travellers. According to records, they were built in 1815 with the financial support of the famous *haiku* poet Kobayashi Issa (1763–1828), who had spent a night in Shinmachi in 1810.

The three mountains in the background are presumably (from right to left) Akagi, Haruna and Myōgi, also known as the Jōmō-sanzan, the "Three Mountains of Jōmō", as this area was called. Mount Akagi is, at 1,828 metres (5,997 feet), the highest of the three, followed by Haruna (1,449 metres / 4,754 feet) and Myōgi (1,104 metres / 3,622 feet), which is not a stratovolcano like the other two.

Der Kanna ist ein Zufluss des Tone, des mit 322 Kilometern zweitlängsten Flusses in Japan. In Eisens Entwurf überquert eine *daimyō*-Prozession den Kanna zuerst über eine Blockbrücke zu Fuß bis zu einer Sandbank und von dort weiter mit Fährbooten. Am anderen Flussufer liegen links im Hintergrund die Häuser von Shinmachi, der nächsten Station und zugleich ersten in der Provinz Kōzuke. Der Fluss bildet die Grenze zur Provinz Musashi und ihrer letzten Station, Honjō. Aus heutiger Sicht übertritt die Route hier die Grenze zwischen den Präfekturen Saitama und Gunma. Mit mehr als 4500 Einwohnern war Honjō im Jahr 1843 der zweitgrößte Stationsort nach Ōtsu (der letzten Station vor Kyoto).

In der Mitte des Zuges reist bequem und gut bewacht der Fürst in einer großen roten Sänfte, die vorn und hinten von mehreren Männern getragen wird. Während etliche Blätter aus diesem Zyklus die Vor- oder Nachhut eines *daimyō*-Zuges zeigen, ist dies das einzige Blatt, das eine solche Prozession nahezu vollständig abbildet.

Auf beiden Seiten des Flussübergangs weist eine große Steinlaterne Reisenden den Weg. Den Aufzeichnungen zufolge wurden die Laternen 1815 mit finanzieller Unterstützung des berühmten Haiku-Dichters Kobayashi Issa (1763–1828) errichtet, der 1810 eine Nacht in Shinmachi verbracht hatte.

Im Hintergrund sind vermutlich (von rechts nach links) der Akagi, der Haruna und der Myōgi dargestellt, auch bekannt als die Jōmō-sanzan, die „Drei Berge von Jōmō", wie diese Gegend genannt wurde. Der Akagi als der höchste unter ihnen bringt es auf 1828 Meter, gefolgt vom Haruna mit 1449 Metern und vom Myōgi, der anders als die beiden anderen kein Schichtvulkan ist, mit 1104 Metern.

La rivière Kanna est un affluent du fleuve Tone, le deuxième du Japon avec ses 322 kilomètres. Dans le dessin d'Eisen, une procession d'un seigneur féodal est en train de traverser la Kanna, en empruntant d'abord un pont sur chevalets qui les conduit à un banc de sable, puis en montant à bord de barques de passeurs. Sur l'autre rive, à l'arrière-plan à gauche, se trouvent les maisons de la station suivante, Shinmachi. Il s'agissait de la première station de la province de Kōzuke, la rivière marquant la limite entre celle-ci et la province de Musashi et sa dernière station, Honjō ; aujourd'hui, la route quitte ici la préfecture de Saitama pour entrer dans celle de Gunma. Avec plus de 4500 âmes en 1843, Honjō était la deuxième station en nombre d'habitants après Ōtsu (dernière étape avant Kyoto).

Au milieu de la procession, le seigneur voyage confortablement dans un grand palanquin rouge, gardé et porté par plusieurs hommes à l'avant et à l'arrière. Plusieurs estampes de cette série représentent l'avant-garde ou l'arrière-garde de cette procession, mais celle-ci est la seule à montrer presque toute la procession.

De part et d'autre de la rivière se dressent des lanternes en pierre servant de repères aux voyageurs. D'après les archives, elles furent érigées en 1815 grâce au soutien financier de Kobayashi Issa (1763–1828), célèbre auteur de haïkus, qui passa une nuit à Shinmachi en 1810.

Les trois montagnes visibles au fond sont vraisemblablement (de droite à gauche) l'Akagi, l'Haruna et le Myōgi, aussi connues sous l'appellation de Jōmō-sanzan, les « trois montagnes de Jōmō », nom donné à la région. Le plus haut sommet est celui du mont Akagi (1828 mètres), suivi de l'Haruna (1449 mètres) et du Myōgi (1104 mètres) qui, contrairement aux deux premiers, n'est pas un stratovolcan.

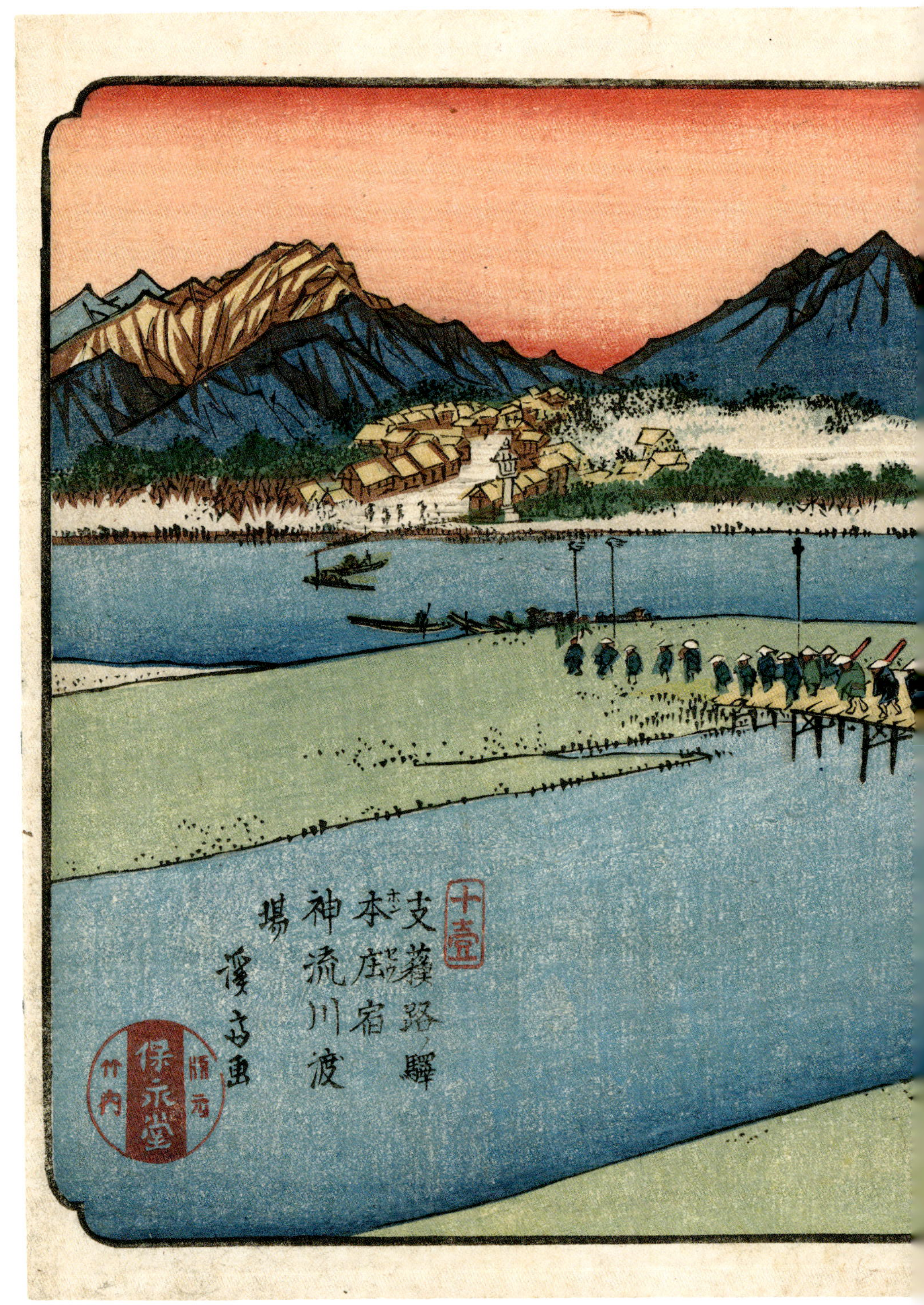
十一
支蘿路ノ驛
本庄宿
神流川渡
場
溪斎画
保永堂
竹内　勝元

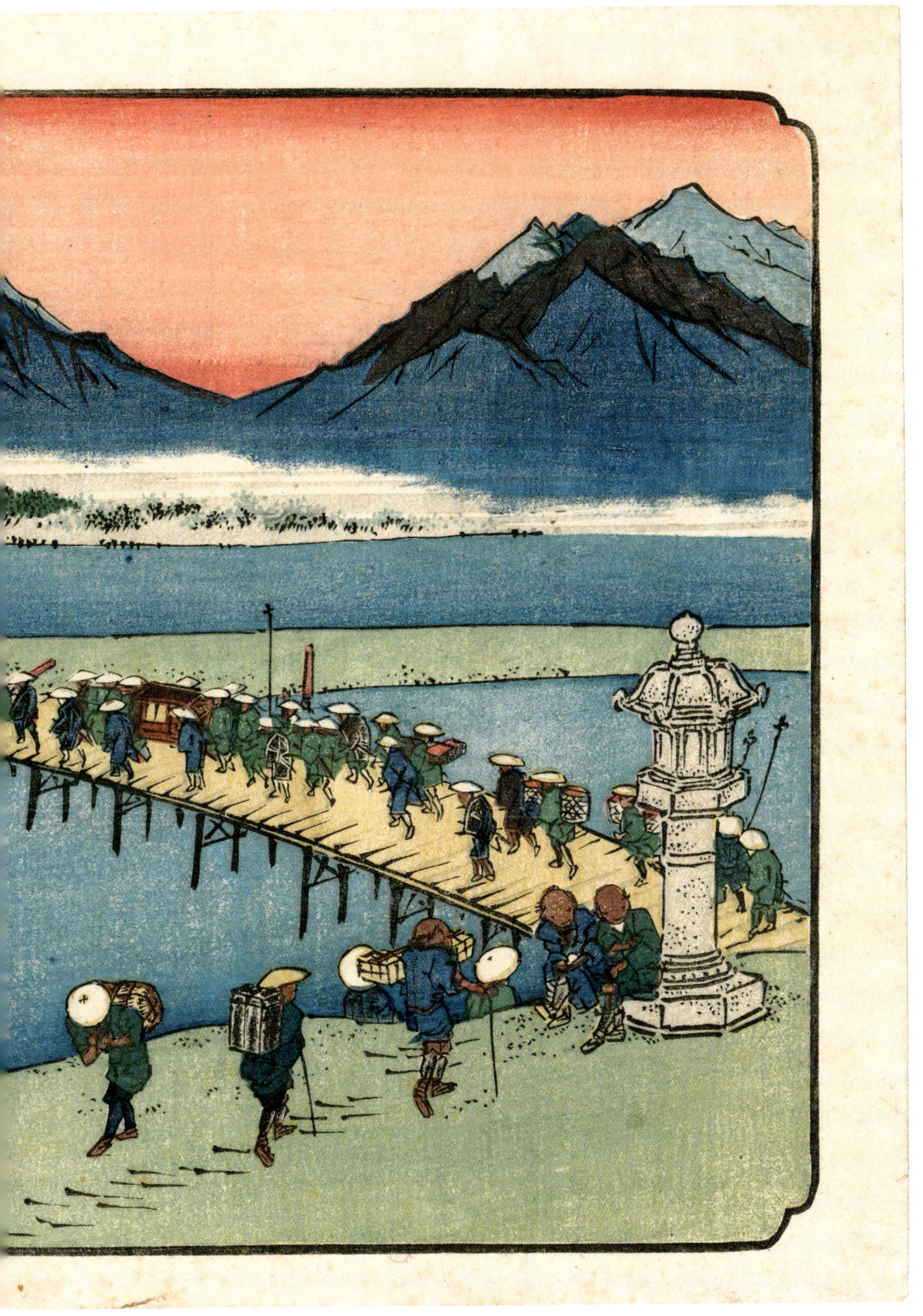

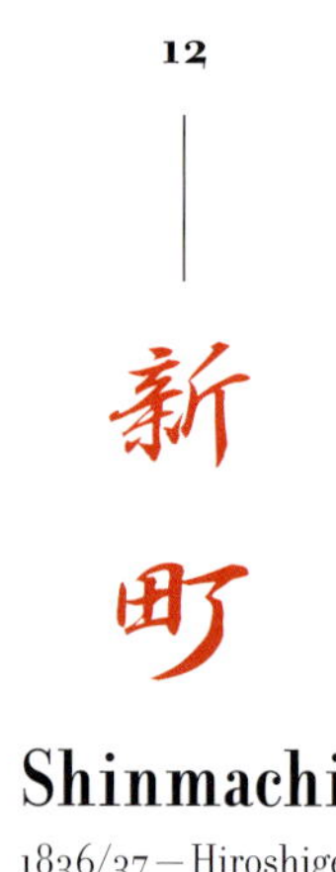

12

Shinmachi
1836/37 — Hiroshige

Shinmachi is the first print by Hiroshige that appears in the series, but because artists tended to design prints in the order of their own preference rather than in numerical order, it cannot be determined today if Shinmachi was actually the first design he contributed. The image shows the view west from Shinmachi towards Kuragano along the banks of the Nukui River. The blue peak in the distance is Mount Akagi, which is thought to have last erupted in 1254. When devising this composition, Hiroshige may have had in mind a description in Akisato Ritō's entry on Shinmachi in his pictorial travel-guide on the Kisokaidō from 1805, *Views of Famous Sights along the Kiso Road* (*Kisoji meisho zue*), "to the left, you can see Mount Akagi. It looks like the peak of Mount Fuji" (vol. 4); it is certainly unlikely that Hiroshige travelled here before designing the print. In the distance on the right is the Benten Bridge, named after a nearby shrine to the goddess Benzaiten. The two porters crossing the bridge are probably carrying raw silk and cocoons to sell in the neighbouring town of Kuragano, where sericulture was an important source of supplementary income for farmers. The rectangular packages shouldered by the man on the left riverbank likely contain *kōji*, or fermented rice.

Shinmachi, located on the south bank of the Karasu River, was the first station travellers came to upon entering Kōzuke Province, and was almost 8 kilometres (5 miles) from the previous station, Honjō. In 1843, the town had a population of 1,437 along with 407 houses, 43 inns, 2 *honjin* (luxurious inns to accommodate travelling lords) and one *waki-honjin* for his close subordinates. Originally, the road between Honjō and Kuragano followed the north bank via Tamamura. It was later diverted along the south bank through Ochiai-Shinmachi and Fueki-Shinmachi, and in 1724 these two stations were amalgamated, making Shinmachi the last station of the Kisokaidō road to be established.

Shinmachi taucht als erstes Blatt von Hiroshige in dieser Serie auf. Da Künstler jedoch dazu neigten, ihre Entwürfe nicht den Nummern der Blätter folgend, sondern nach ihren eigenen Vorlieben anzufertigen, lässt sich heute nicht mehr feststellen, ob Shinmachi tatsächlich auch sein erster Beitrag zu der Serie war. Das Bild zeigt den Blick am Ufer des Nukui entlang von Shinmachi Richtung Westen nach Kuragano. Der blaue Gipfel in der Ferne ist der Akagi, der zuletzt im Jahr 1254 ausgebrochen sein soll. Als Hiroshige diese Komposition ersann, könnte ihm der Eintrag zu Shinmachi in Akisato Ritōs bebildertem Reiseführer des Kisokaidō von 1805, *Ansichten berühmter Stätten an der Kiso-Straße (Kisoji meisho zue)*, vor Augen gehabt haben: „Zur Linken können Sie den Akagi sehen. Er sieht aus wie der Gipfel des Fuji" (Bd. 4); jedenfalls ist es höchst unwahrscheinlich, dass Hiroshige den Ort besuchte, bevor er den Druck entwarf. Die Brücke im Mittelgrund rechts ist die Bentenbashi, die nach einem in der Nähe gelegenen Schrein für die Göttin Benzaiten benannt wurde. Die beiden Lastenträger, die die Brücke überqueren, transportieren vermutlich Rohseide und Kokons, um sie im Nachbarort Kuragano zu verkaufen, wo der Seidenbau eine wichtige zusätzliche Einnahmequelle für die Bauern darstellte. Die kartonförmigen Pakete, die der Mann am linken Flussufer geschultert hat, enthalten wahrscheinlich *kōji*, fermentierten Reis.

Shinmachi lag am Südufer des Karasu, knapp acht Kilometer von der vorherigen Station, Honjō, entfernt und war die erste Station für Reisende in der Provinz Kōzuke. 1843 zählte der Ort 1437 Einwohner, 407 Häuser, 43 Gasthäuser, zwei *honjin*, Luxusherbergen für durchreisende Fürsten, und ein *waki-honjin* für ihre nächsten Untergebenen. Ursprünglich folgte die Straße zwischen Honjō und Kuragano dem Nordufer über Tamamura. Später wurde sie ans Südufer verlegt und verlief durch Ochiai-Shinmachi und Fueki-Shinmachi. Als diese beiden Stationen im Jahr 1724 fusionierten, entstand mit Shinmachi die letzte neu gegründete Poststation am Kisokaidō.

Shinmachi est la première estampe d'Hiroshige figurant dans cette série. Toutefois, étant donné que les artistes créaient les gravures selon leur préférence plutôt qu'en suivant un ordre numérique, il est aujourd'hui impossible de dire si Shinmachi est effectivement la première estampe qu'Hiroshige ait réalisée. Cette image représente Shinmachi vue de l'ouest, en direction de Kuragano, sur la rive de la Nukui. Le sommet bleu visible au loin est le mont Akagi, dont on pense que la dernière éruption a eu lieu en 1254. Pour réaliser cette composition, Hiroshige a peut-être eu à l'esprit une description d'Akisato Ritō figurant dans l'article consacré à Shinmachi de son guide de voyage illustré de la Kisokaidō, *Collection de vues de paysages célèbres sur la route Kiso (Kisoji meisho zue)*, publié en 1805 : « À gauche, on peut voir le mont Akagi. Il ressemble au sommet du mont Fuji » (vol. 4) ; il est fort peu probable qu'Hiroshige se soit rendu sur les lieux avant de dessiner cette estampe. À droite, au loin, se trouve le pont Benten qui tire son nom d'un sanctuaire des environs, dédié à la déesse Benzaiten. Les deux porteurs qui franchissent le pont transportent probablement de la soie grège et des cocons afin de les vendre dans la ville voisine de Kuragano où la sériciculture constituait une importante source de revenus complémentaires pour les fermiers. Les paquets rectangulaires que porte sur ses épaules l'homme marchant sur la rive de gauche contiennent sans doute du *kōji*, ou riz fermenté.

Située sur la rive sud de la Karasu, Shinmachi était la première station à laquelle parvenaient les voyageurs dans la province de Kōzuke ; elle se trouvait à près de huit kilomètres de la précédente, Honjō. En 1843, cette ville avait 1437 habitants, 407 maisons, quarante-trois auberges, deux *honjin*, auberges de luxe destinées aux seigneurs, et une *waki-honjin* pour ses proches subordonnés. Initialement, entre Honjō et Kuragano, la route suivait la rive nord via Tamamura. Elle fut détournée par la suite le long de la rive sud et traversait Ochiai-Shinmachi et Fueki-Shinmachi ; en 1724, ces deux stations furent réunies en une seule et firent ainsi de Shinmachi la dernière station créée sur la Kisokaidō.

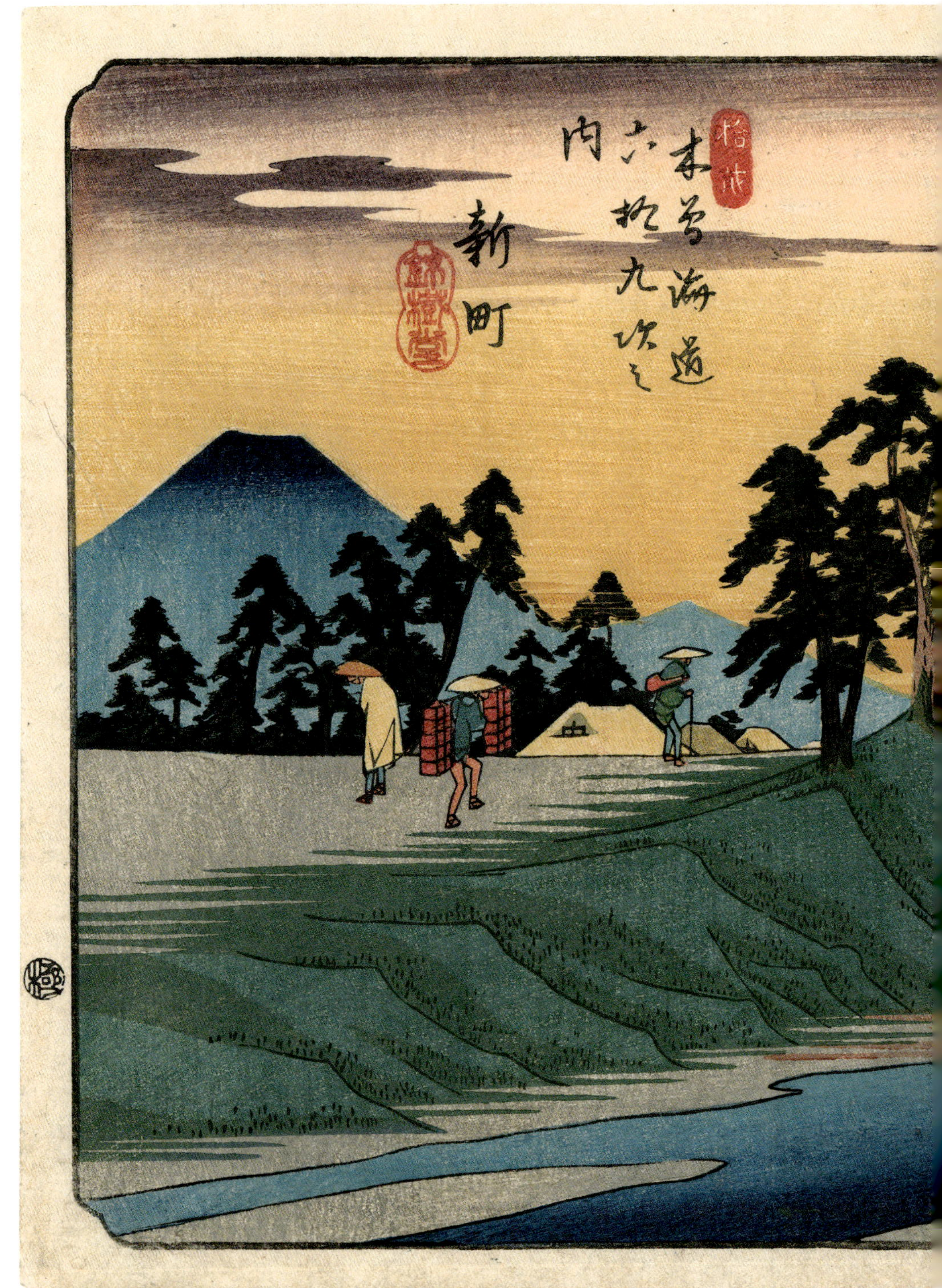
木曾街道六拾九次之内
新町

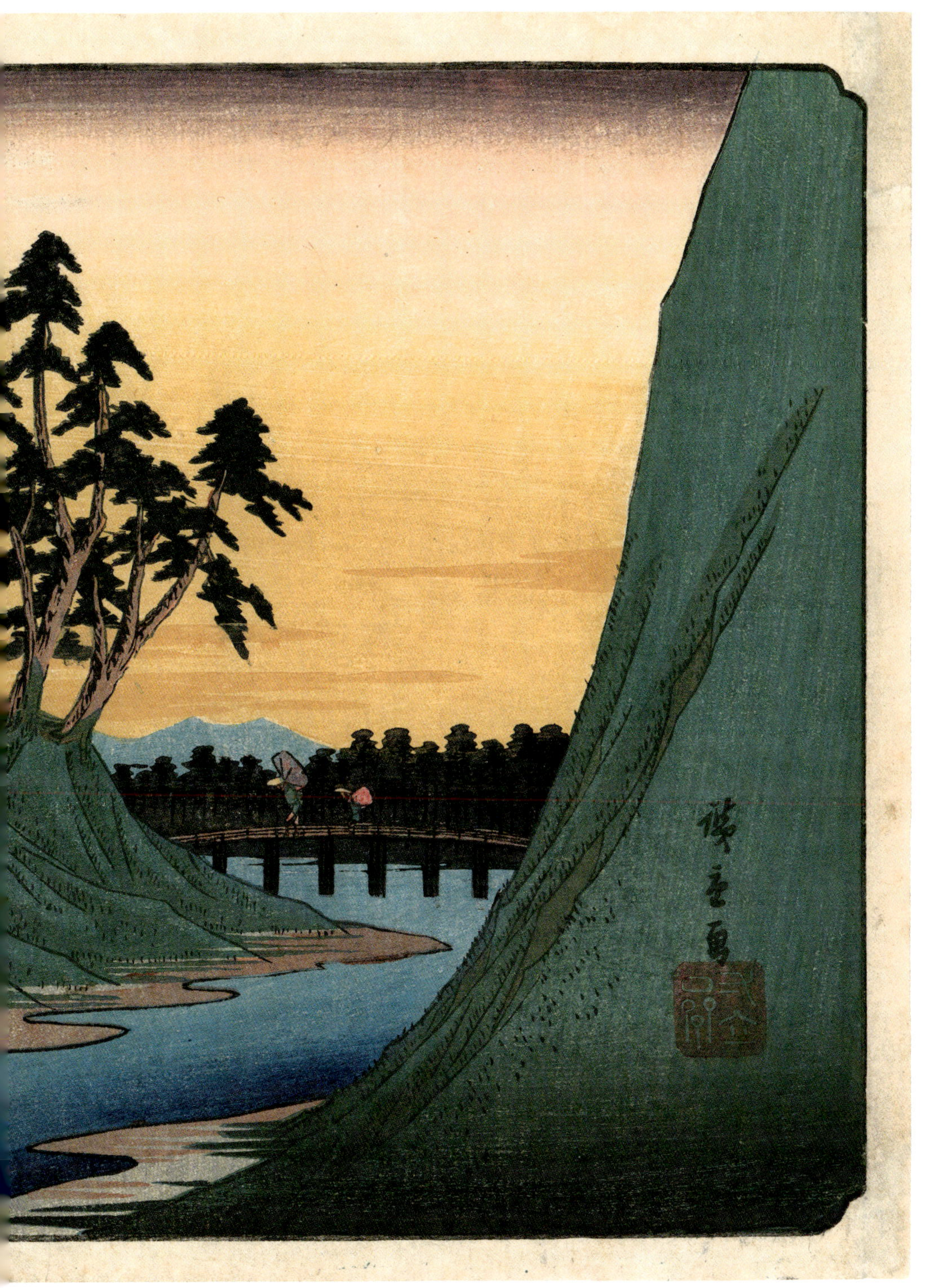

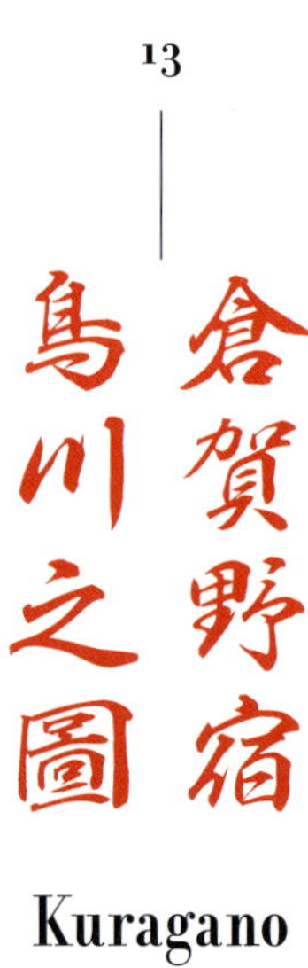

13

Kuragano

1835/36 — Eisen

Another of the five main roads that started at Edo's Nihonbashi was the Nikkō Kaidō, which connected Edo with the Tōshōgū shrine in Nikkō, dedicated to Ieyasu (1543–1616), the first shogun of the ruling Tokugawa family. The Kuragano station was the start of a branch of the Nikkō Kaidō, called Nikkō Reiheishi Kaidō, which was built in 1814 to connect the Kisokaidō with the town of Nikkō by skirting Edo.

The Karasu River, depicted here, is an almost 62-kilometre-long tributary (38 miles) of the Tone River that lies south of Kuragano. Even further south is the Kabura River, and both of these join at Kuragano but then soon flow into the Tone River which runs north of Kuragano. Kuragano was therefore an important crossing point, and its houses are visible in the background here, as are goods being transported on the Karasu. Using the current of the Tone moving eastwards, goods could reach Edo in three to four days by boat, while the return journey took 17 to 18 days.

Eisen depicted four children in the foreground playing in an irrigation channel while a maid with a towel wrapped around her head is washing an iron kettle. A female traveller observes the scene from the right, whilst having a cup of tea at a rest-stop.

Eine der fünf Hauptstraßen, die von der Nihonbashi in Edo ausgingen, war der Nikkō Kaidō. Er verband Edo mit dem Tōshōgū-Schrein in Nikkō, der dem ersten Shogun der Tokugawa-Dynastie, Ieyasu (1543–1616), gewidmet war. An der Station Kuragano begann der Nikkō Reiheishi Kaidō, der 1814 als Abzweig des Nikkō Kaidō gebaut wurde, um den Kisokaidō ohne den Umweg über Edo mit Nikko zu verbinden.

Der hier abgebildete Karasu, ein fast 62 Kilometer langer Nebenfluss des Tone, verläuft südlich von Kuragano. Noch weiter südlich fließt der Kabura, und beide vereinigen sich in Kuragano mit dem Karasu, bevor dieser kurz darauf in den Tone mündet, dessen Flusslauf wiederum nördlich des Ortes liegt. Kuragano war somit ein wichtiger Querungspunkt auf dem Kisokaidō. Vor den im Hintergrund zu erkennenden Häusern der Station werden Waren auf dem Karasu transportiert. Frachten, die die Strömung des Tone nach Osten ausnutzten, erreichten Edo in drei bis vier Tagen. Die Rückfahrt flussaufwärts dagegen dauerte 17 bis 18 Tage.

Eisen zeigt im Vordergrund vier in einem Bewässerungskanal spielende Kinder und ein Dienstmädchen, das mit einem Handtuch um den Kopf einen Eisenkessel auswäscht. Von rechts beobachtet eine Reisende, die an einer Raststätte eine Tasse Tee trinkt, die Szene.

L'une des cinq autres grandes routes partant du Nihonbashi à Edo était la Nikkō Kaidō, qui reliait Edo au sanctuaire de Tōshōgū à Nikkō, lieu consacré à Ieyasu (1543–1616), premier shogun de la famille des souverains Tokugawa. La station de Kuragano était le point de départ de la Nikkō Reiheishi Kaidō, subdivision de la Nikkō Kaidō, construite en 1814 afin de relier la Kisokaidō et la ville de Nikkō en évitant Edo.

La Karasu, représentée ici, est un affluent du fleuve Tone, d'une longueur de près de soixante-deux kilomètres, au sud de Kuragano. Encore plus au sud se trouve la Kabura ; ces deux rivières se rejoignent à Kuragano avant de se jeter bientôt dans le Tone qui passe au nord de Kuragano, ville qui constituait donc un important carrefour. On en voit les maisons à l'arrière-plan, de même que des marchandises transportées sur la Karasu. Grâce au courant du Tone qui coule vers l'est, les marchandises pouvaient atteindre Edo en trois ou quatre jours, tandis qu'il fallait dix-sept à dix-huit jours pour le voyage de retour.

Au premier plan, Eisen a représenté quatre enfants jouant dans un canal d'irrigation, alors qu'une servante, coiffée d'une serviette, lave une bouilloire en fer blanc. À droite, une voyageuse observe la scène en buvant une tasse de thé à une halte.

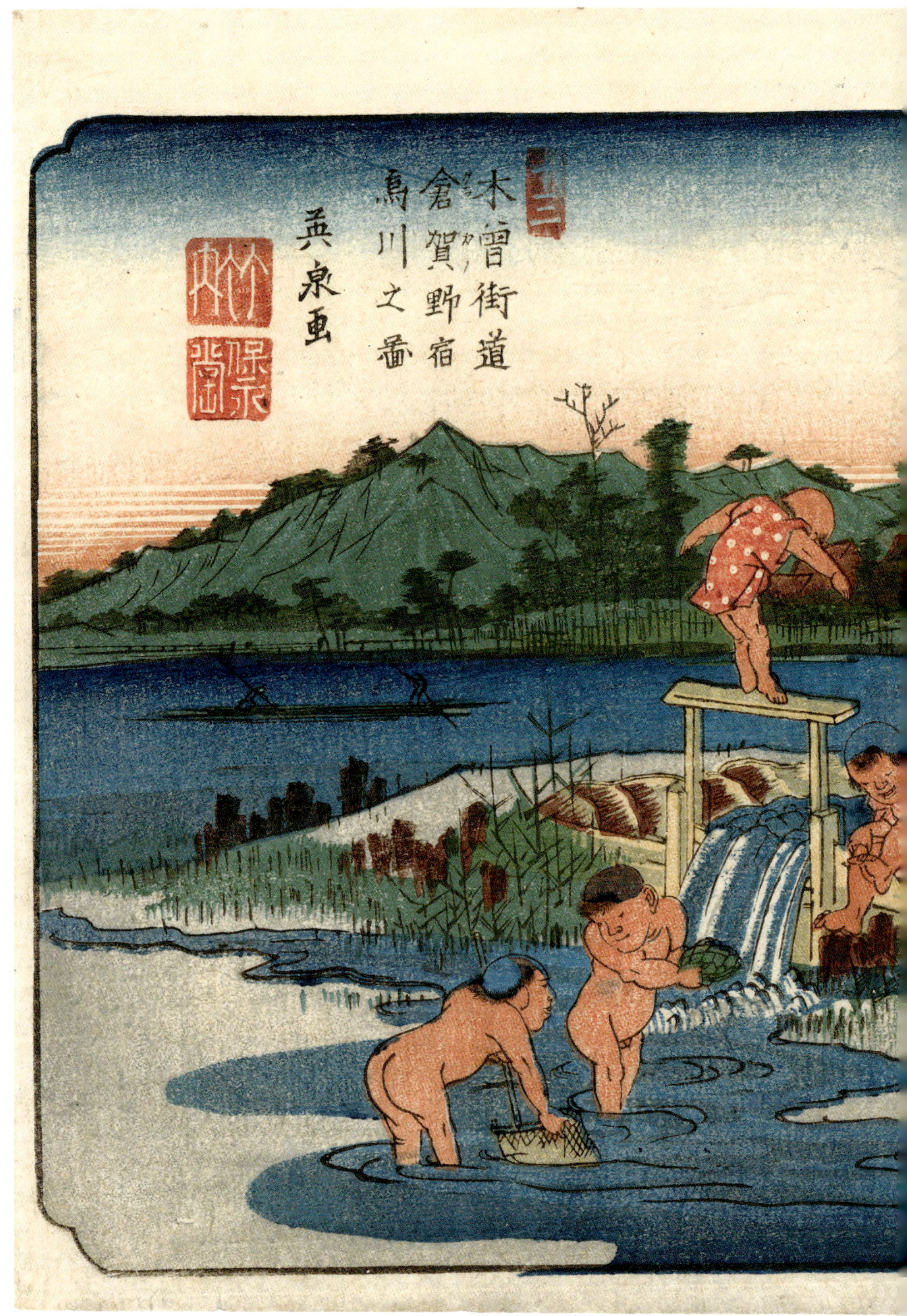
木曾街道
倉賀野宿
烏川之圖
英泉画

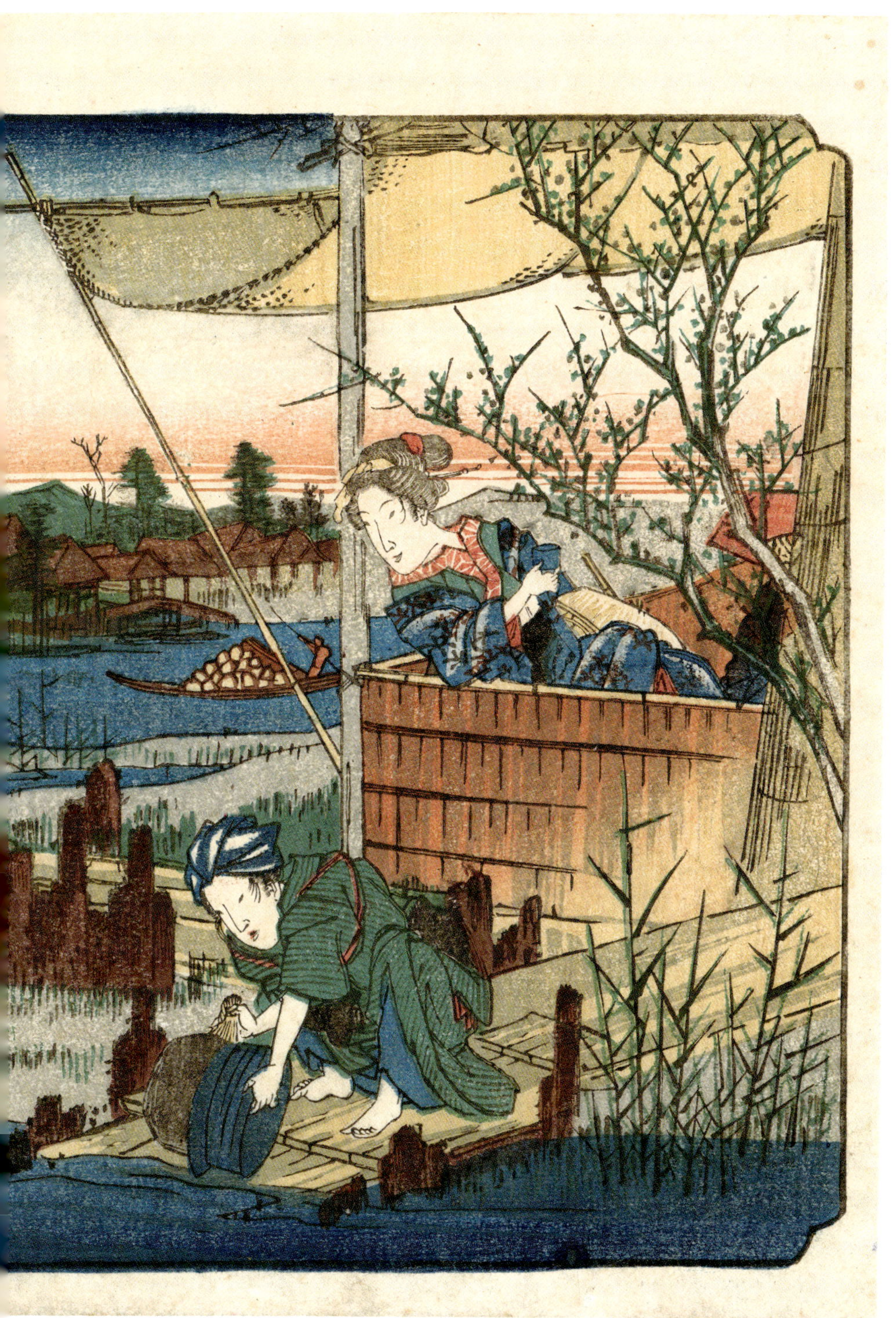

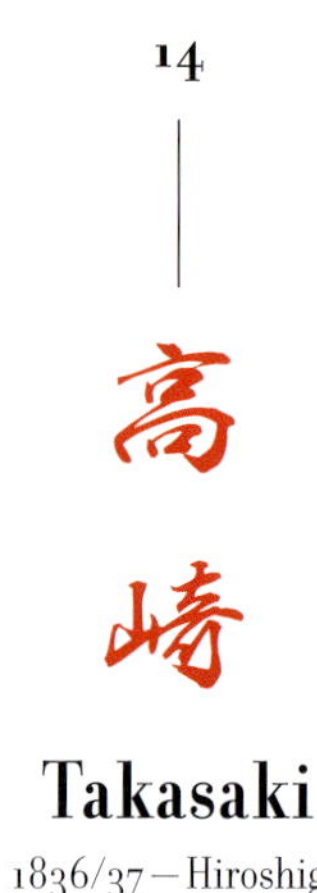

14

Takasaki

1836/37 — Hiroshige

Takasaki was among the first four prints by Hiroshige that were produced when the publisher Iseya Rihei took over the series from Takenouchi Magohachi. The print imagines the view north-east towards the road which crosses the Karasu River just downstream from its confluence with the Usui River, over the Kimigayo Bridge in the distance.

In the foreground, a beggar is accosting a young couple, and as they hesitate, another one rushes towards them, with his palm open. On the veranda of a teahouse, a man is smoking his pipe while enjoying the evening view. Beyond the embankment and our line of sight on the right is Takasaki Castle, constructed in 1598 on the orders of Tokugawa Ieyasu and subsequently controlled by several generations of the Matsudaira family. Most of the castle complex was demolished at the end of the 19th century and the only two original structures have since been relocated. Mount Haruna, silhouetted against the softly fading light, provides a theatrical backdrop.

In 1843, the town's population stood at 3,235, with 837 houses and 15 inns. The German geographer Johannes Justus Rein (1835–1918) travelled along the Kisokaidō in 1874 and 1875 and noted that it then took between 12 and 13 hours by horse and carriage to travel from Takasaki to Tokyo. During this journey, the horses were changed seven times.

Takasaki gehörte zu den ersten vier Drucken von Hiroshige, die produziert wurden, als der Verleger Iseya
Rihei die Serie von Takenouchi Magohachi übernahm. Das Blatt richtet den Blick nach Nordosten auf die
in der Ferne sichtbare Kimigayohashi, eine an der Route gelegene Brücke, die kurz hinter der Einmün-
dung des Usui den Karasu quert.

Im Vordergrund behelligt ein Bettler ein junges Paar. Während die beiden noch zögern, läuft ein
zweiter Bettler mit offener Hand auf sie zu. Auf der Veranda eines Teehauses genießt ein Pfeifenraucher
den abendlichen Ausblick. Hinter der Uferböschung rechts liegt außerhalb des Blickfeldes die Burg
Takasaki, die 1598 auf Befehl von Tokugawa Ieyasu erbaut und anschließend über mehrere Generationen
von der Matsudaira-Familie kontrolliert wurde. Weite Teile der Burganlage wurden Ende des 19. Jahrhunderts abgerissen, die beiden einzig verbliebenen Originalgebäude nachher umgesetzt. Die Silhouette des Berges Haruna gibt gegen das sanfte Licht der Dämmerung eine dramatische Kulisse ab.

1843 gab es in der 3235 Einwohner zählenden Stadt 837 Häuser und 15 Herbergen. Der deutsche
Geograf Johannes Justus Rein (1835–1918) bereiste 1874 und 1875 den Kisokaidō und notierte, dass man
für die Fahrt mit der Pferdekutsche von Takasaki nach Tokio zwischen 12 und 13 Stunden benötige.
Währenddessen wurden siebenmal die Pferde gewechselt.

Takasaki est l'une des quatre premières estampes réalisées par Hiroshige et publiées par l'éditeur Iseya
Rihei quand ce dernier reprit la série à la suite de Takenouchi Magohachi. Cette estampe imagine un
point de vue vers le nord-est, en direction de la route qui franchit la Karasu en aval de son confluent avec
l'Usui en empruntant le pont Kimigayohashi, visible au loin.

Au premier plan, un mendiant aborde un jeune couple ; voyant qu'ils hésitent, un autre mendiant
se précipite vers eux en ouvrant la paume. À la terrasse d'une maison de thé, un homme fumant la pipe
contemple le paysage du soir. À droite, au-delà de la colline qui descend vers la rivière, mais caché à
notre vue, s'élève le château de Takasaki, bâti en 1598 sur ordre de Tokugawa Ieyasu, puis occupé par
plusieurs générations de membres de la famille Matsudaira. La majeure partie du domaine de ce château a été détruite au XIXe siècle, et seules subsistent les deux structures originelles, transférées depuis
dans un autre lieu. Se détachant dans la lumière qui s'atténue doucement, la silhouette du mont Haruna
offre un décor spectaculaire.

En 1843, la ville comptait 3235 habitants, 837 maisons et quinze auberges. Johannes Justus Rein
(1835–1918), géographe allemand ayant voyagé sur la Kisokaidō en 1874 et 1875, avait noté qu'il fallait de
douze à treize heures pour se rendre à cheval et en carriole de Takasaki à Tokyo. Au cours de ce déplacement, les chevaux devaient être changés sept fois.

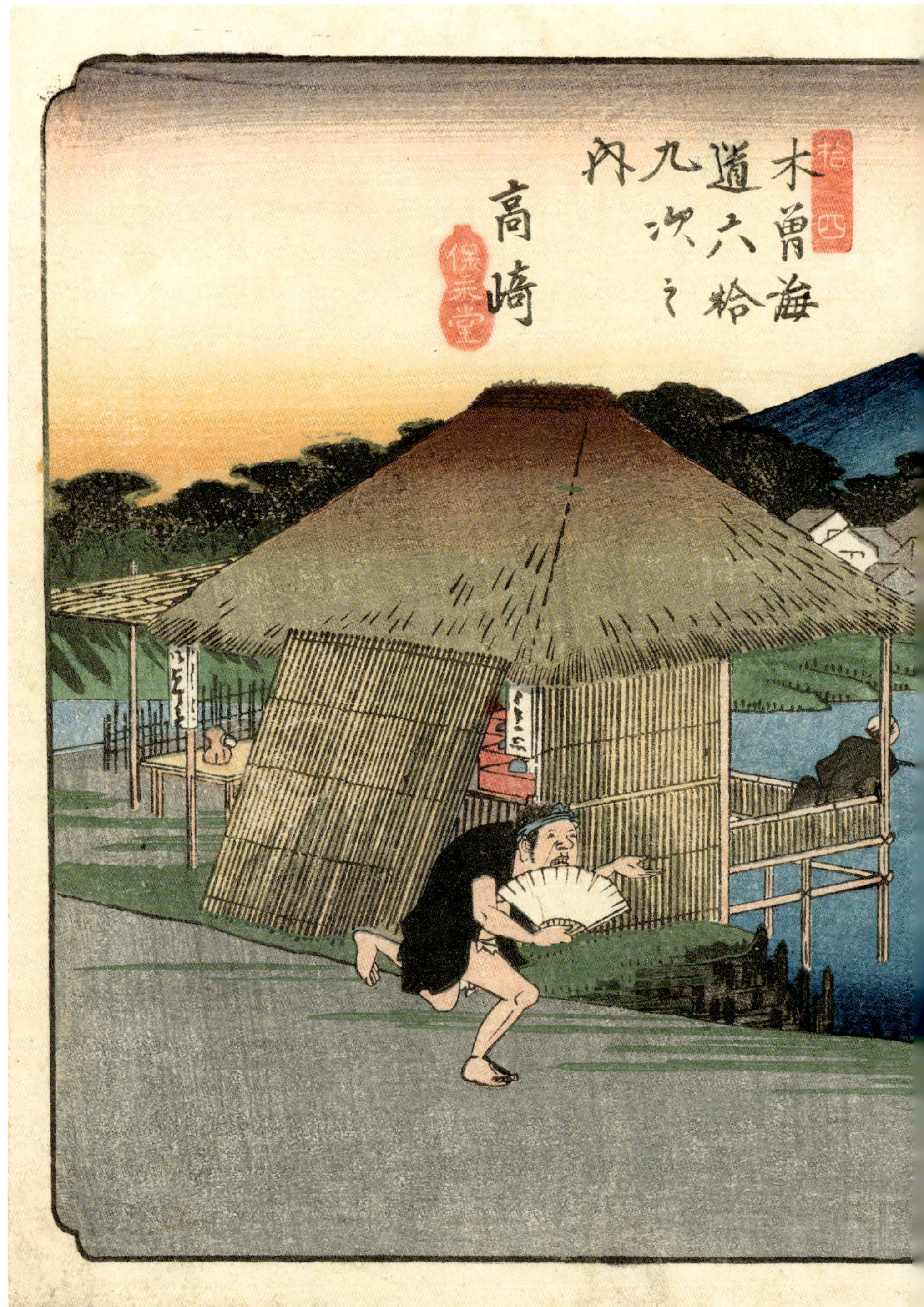

拾
四
木曽海
道六拾
九次之
内
高崎
保永堂

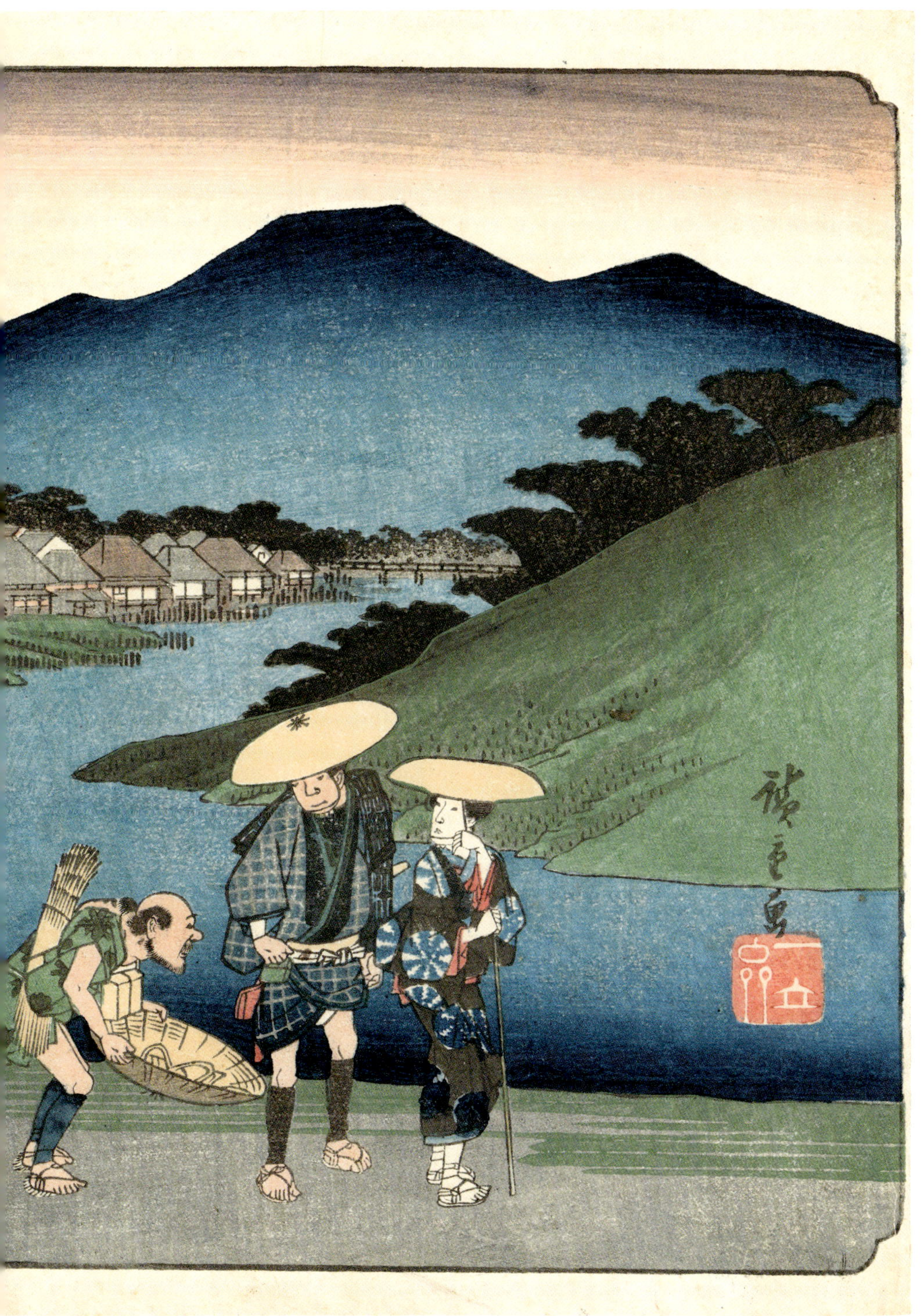

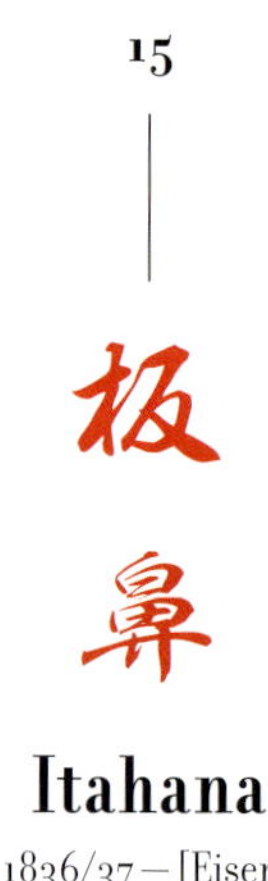

15

Itahana

1836/37 — [Eisen]

The road continues west from Takasaki along the Usui River, into which the Tsukumo River flows shortly after Itahana. The landscape in this design is covered in deep snow which also rests on the shoulders and hats of the travellers making their way through the cold. The stretch of road in the foreground provides a view of the pine trees that were planted as road markers along either side. The travellers are crossing a small bridge before reaching Itahana on the left.

Another stretch of this road and its remarkably large trees further to the east was mentioned by Johannes Justus Rein: "In the centre of the road between the Itahana and Takasaki stations lies a temple opposite a teahouse on the outskirts of the village Toyoōka that is remarkable because of the magnificent trees in front of this temple. These are *keaki* (*Zelkova acuminata*, Planch.) of unusual dimensions as none like them can be found anywhere else along the Nakasendō." (Rein 1880, p. 33)

Princess Kazu (1846–1877), half-sister of the reigning Emperor Kōmei (1831–1867), who was forced in early 1862 to marry the shogun Tokugawa Iemochi (1846–1866), reportedly stayed for one night at the *honjin* of Itahana during her relocation from Kyoto to Edo in late 1861. Her procession along the Kisokaidō took almost one month because of her enormous entourage of approximately 30,000 people, which formed a column 50 kilometres (30 miles) in length.

This design is unsigned but is believed to have been created by Eisen for the publisher Takenouchi, who then decided not to issue it until later on when he published it jointly with Iseya Rihei.

Von Takasaki führt die Straße weiter nach Westen, am Usui entlang, in den sich kurz hinter Itahana der Tsukumo ergießt. Die Landschaft auf diesem Blatt ist tief verschneit. Auch auf den Schultern und Hüten der Reisenden, die sich gegen die Kälte stemmen, liegt Schnee. Der Streckenabschnitt im Vordergrund bietet einen Blick auf die Kiefern, die rechts und links der Straße als Wegmarkierungen gepflanzt wurden. Die Reisenden überqueren eine kleine Brücke, bevor sie die Station Itahana links im Bild erreichen.

Ein anderer, weiter östlich gelegener Streckenabschnitt mit bemerkenswert großen Bäumen wurde von Johannes Justus Rein erwähnt: „Mitte Wegs zwischen der Station Itahana und Takasaki ist am Eingang zum Dorfe Toyoōka einem Theehause gegenüber ein Tempel, besonders wegen der prächtigen Bäume vor demselben bemerkenswerth. Es sind Keaki *(Zelkova acuminata,* Planch.*)* von ungewöhnlichen Dimensionen, wie man sie am ganzen Nakasendō nicht findet." (Rein 1880, S. 33)

Die Prinzessin Kazu (1846–1877), Halbschwester des regierenden Kaisers Kōmei (1831–1867), die Anfang 1862 zur Ehe mit dem Shogun Tokugawa Iemochi (1846–1866) gezwungen wurde, soll während ihres Umzugs von Kyoto nach Edo Ende 1861 eine Nacht im *honjin* von Itahana verbracht haben. Ihre Prozession auf dem Kisokaidō dauerte wegen des gewaltigen Gefolges, das mit etwa 30 000 Personen eine 50 Kilometer lange Schlange bildete, fast einen Monat.

Dieser Entwurf ist nicht signiert. Man nimmt jedoch an, dass er von Eisen für den Verleger Takenouchi geschaffen wurde, der zunächst beschloss, ihn nicht zu veröffentlichen, bis er den Druck dann später doch gemeinsam mit Iseya Rihei herausgab.

À partir de Takasaki, la route continue vers l'ouest le long de l'Usui, rivière dans laquelle se jette la Tsukumo, peu après Itahana. Dans ce dessin, une épaisse couche de neige recouvre le paysage, ainsi que les épaules et les chapeaux des voyageurs qui marchent dans le froid. La partie de la route visible au premier plan permet d'observer les pins qui avaient été plantés pour borner la route de part et d'autre. Les voyageurs franchissent un petit pont avant d'entrer dans Itahana, à gauche.

Johannes Justus Rein a décrit une autre partie de cette route, située plus à l'est, ainsi que ses arbres extrêmement hauts : « À mi-chemin entre les stations d'Itahana et de Takasaki se trouve un temple situé en face d'une maison de thé, à la périphérie du village de Toyoōka, remarquable pour les arbres magnifiques qui se dressent devant ce temple. Ce sont des *keaki* (*Zelkova acuminata,* Planch.) de dimensions inhabituelles que l'on ne trouve nulle part ailleurs le long de la Nakasendō. » (Rein 1880, p. 33)

La princesse Kazu (1846–1877), demi-sœur de l'empereur régnant Komei (1831–1867), fut contrainte, au début de 1862, d'épouser le shogun Tukugawa Iemochi (1846–1866) ; elle aurait passé une nuit à la *honjin* d'Itahana au cours de son déménagement de Kyoto à Edo à la fin de 1861. Il lui fallut près d'un mois pour parcourir la Kisokaidō, en raison de son gigantesque entourage composé d'environ 30 000 personnes, qui formait une procession longue de cinquante kilomètres.

Bien que non signé, ce dessin a probablement été réalisé par Eisen pour l'éditeur Takenouchi qui décida ensuite de ne le publier que plus tard, en collaboration avec Iseya Rihei.

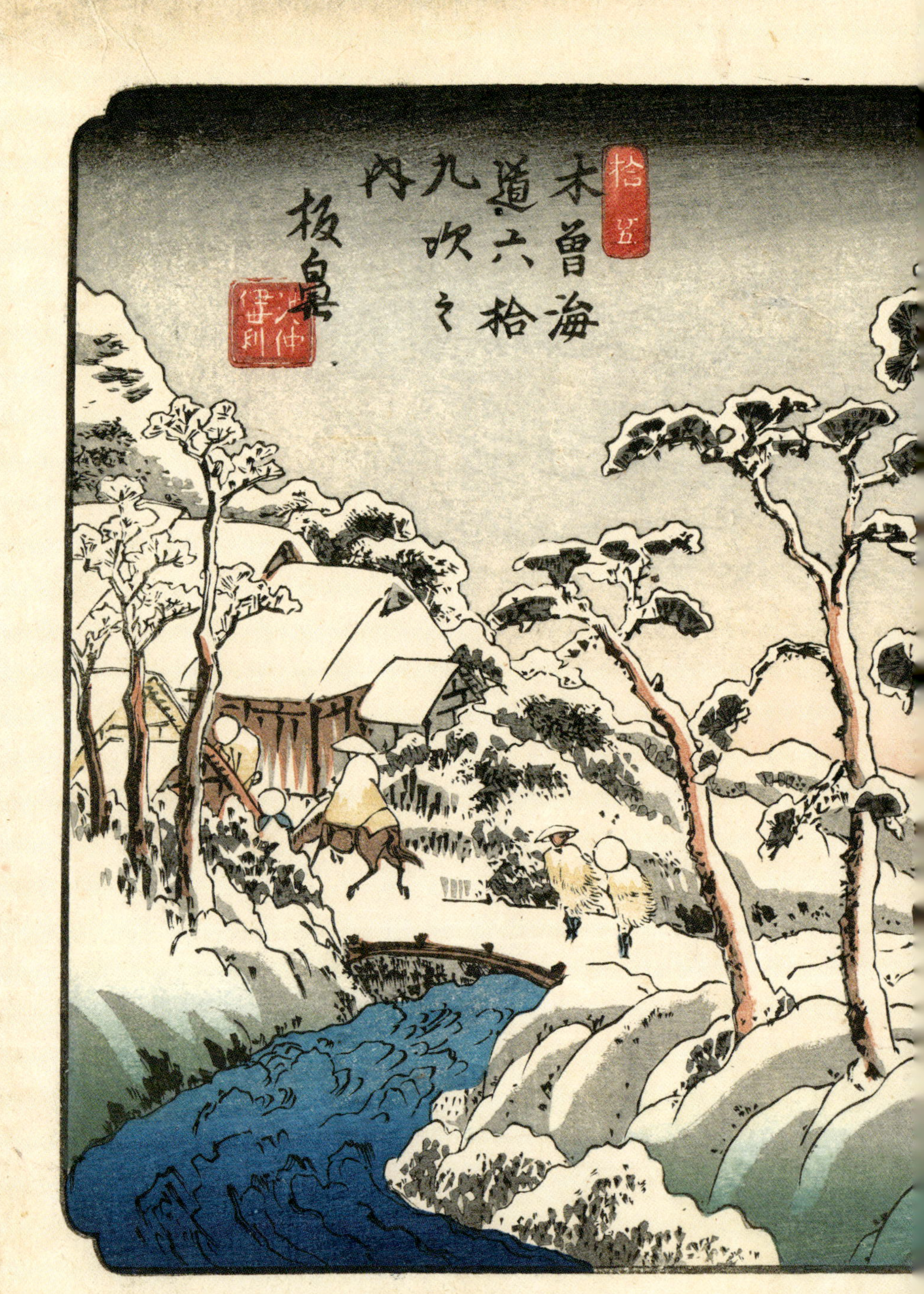
木曽海道六拾九次之内
板鼻

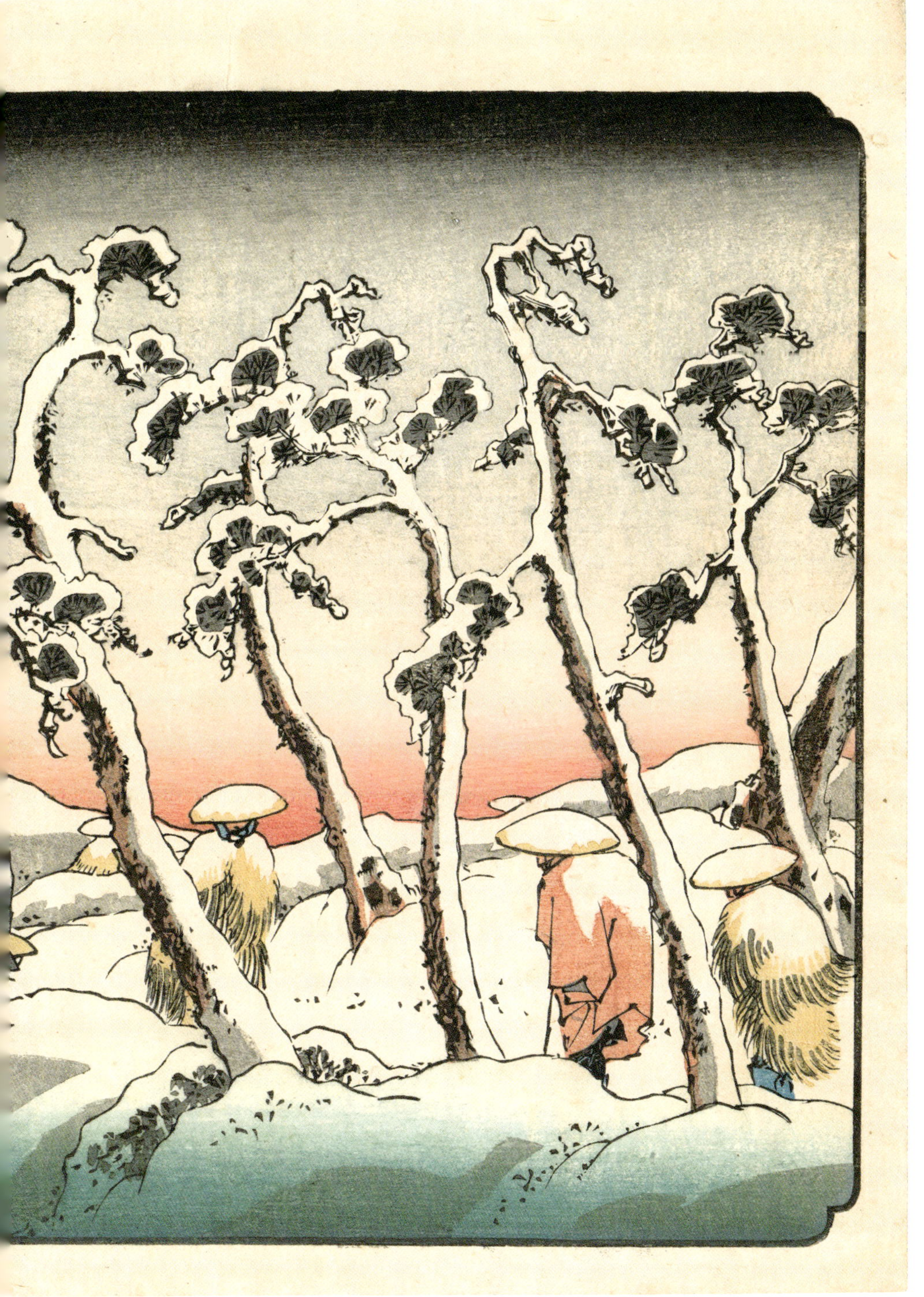

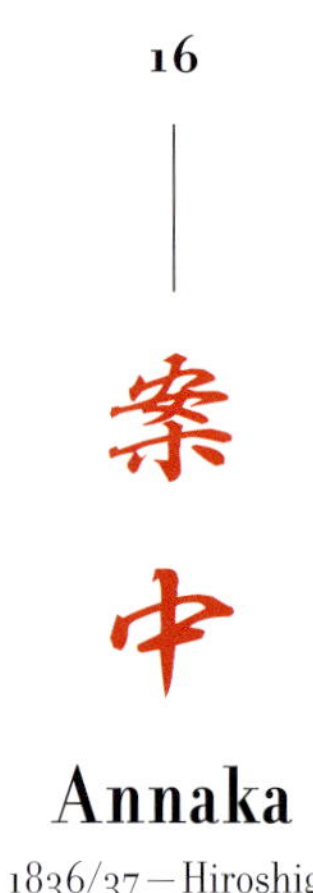

16

Annaka

1836/37 — Hiroshige

From Takasaki to Annaka, the Kisokaidō followed the passage of the Usui River along the valley floor, but after leaving Annaka the road began to wind up into the foothills of the Japanese Central Alps. The print shows the head of a lord's procession and his retinue on the western outskirts of the town, making the long journey from Edo back to their domain. Further along the path are several travellers with walking-sticks and bundles slung over their shoulders. From the silhouettes of the plum trees we can gather that it is early spring.

Annaka Castle, built in 1559, was more a walled compound than an actual castle. After a few years it was destroyed by the powerful warlord Takeda Shingen (1521–1573) during the civil war. It was rebuilt in 1615 by the lord Ii Naokatsu (1590–1662) after the Tokugawa clan claimed victory. In the 1870s, Annaka prospered as a centre for silk production; early Western travellers to Japan admired the town's fine houses and handsome cryptomeria trees (Lawrence 1873, p. 63). Annaka Church, established in 1878 by local converts, was the centre of Protestantism in the region (Shinpo 1968, p. 54).

Von Takasaki bis Annaka folgte der Kisokaidō in der Talsohle dem Verlauf des Usui, bevor er sich hinter Annaka ins Vorgebirge der japanischen Zentralalpen hinaufzuwinden begann. Der Druck zeigt die Spitze der fürstlichen Entourage einer *daimyō*-Prozession am Westrand der Station auf dem langen Marsch von Edo ins heimische Lehen. Die Straße hinauf sind ein paar Reisende mit Wanderstäben und über die Schulter geworfenen Bündeln zu erkennen. Die Silhouetten der Pflaumenbäume künden vom Vorfrühling.

Annaka war eher ein von Mauern umgebenes Anwesen als eine Burg. Wenige Jahre nach ihrem Bau 1559 wurde sie von dem mächtigen Kriegsherrn Takeda Shingen (1521–1573) im Bürgerkrieg zerstört und 1615, nachdem der Tokugawa-Clan den Sieg für sich reklamiert hatte, vom *daimyō* Ii Naokatsu (1590–1662) wieder aufgebaut. In den 1870er Jahren prosperierte Annaka als Zentrum der Seiden-herstellung; frühe Japanreisende aus dem Westen bewunderten die schönen Häuser und stattlichen Sicheltannen des Ortes (Lawrence 1873, S. 63). Die Kirche von Annaka, 1878 von örtlichen Konvertiten gegründet, war das Zentrum des Protestantismus in der Region (Shinpo 1968, S. 54).

De Takasaki à Annaka, la Kisokaidō suivait le cours de l'Usui au fond de la vallée, mais après Annaka, la route commençait à monter en lacets sur les contreforts des Alpes japonaises centrales. Cette estampe représente la tête de la procession d'un seigneur et de son escorte à la périphérie occidentale de la ville, dans leur long voyage de retour d'Edo à leur domaine. Un peu plus loin sur la route se trouvent plusieurs voyageurs munis de bâtons de marche et portant des ballots sur les épaules. La silhouette des pruniers indique que nous sommes au début du printemps.

Construit en 1559, le château d'Annaka était plutôt une place forte. Quelques années plus tard, il fut détruit par le puissant seigneur de guerre Takeda Shingen (1521–1573) au cours de la guerre civile. Il fut reconstruit par le seigneur Ii Naokatsu (1590–1662) en 1615, après la victoire du clan Tokugawa. Au cours des années 1870, Annaka dut sa prospérité à la production de soie ; les premiers visiteurs occidentaux du Japon admirèrent les belles demeures et les magnifiques cryptomérias (ou cèdres du Japon) de la ville (Lawrence 1873, p. 63). Créée en 1878 par des habitants convertis, l'église d'Annaka fut le centre du protestantisme dans la région (Shinpo 1968, p. 54).

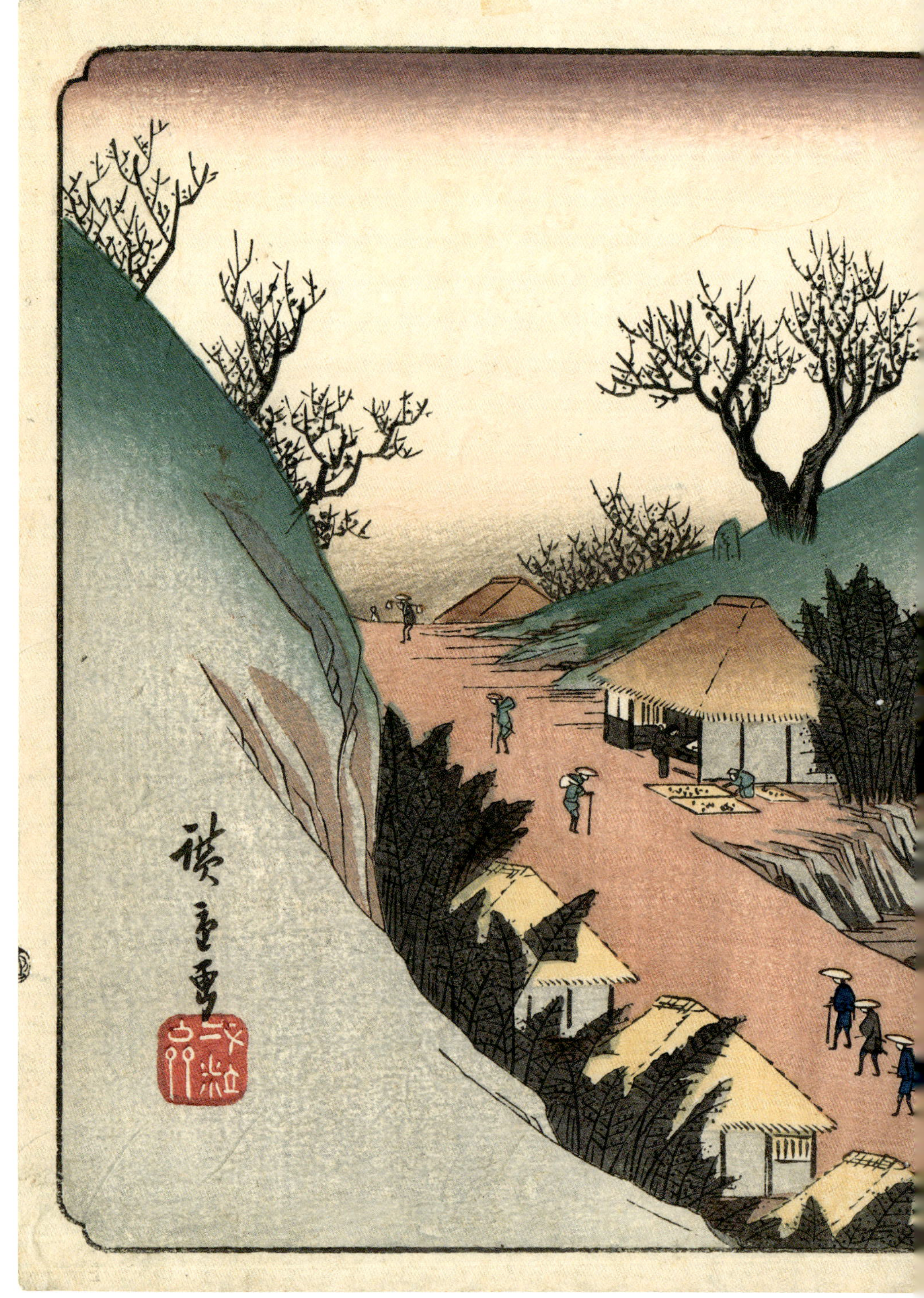

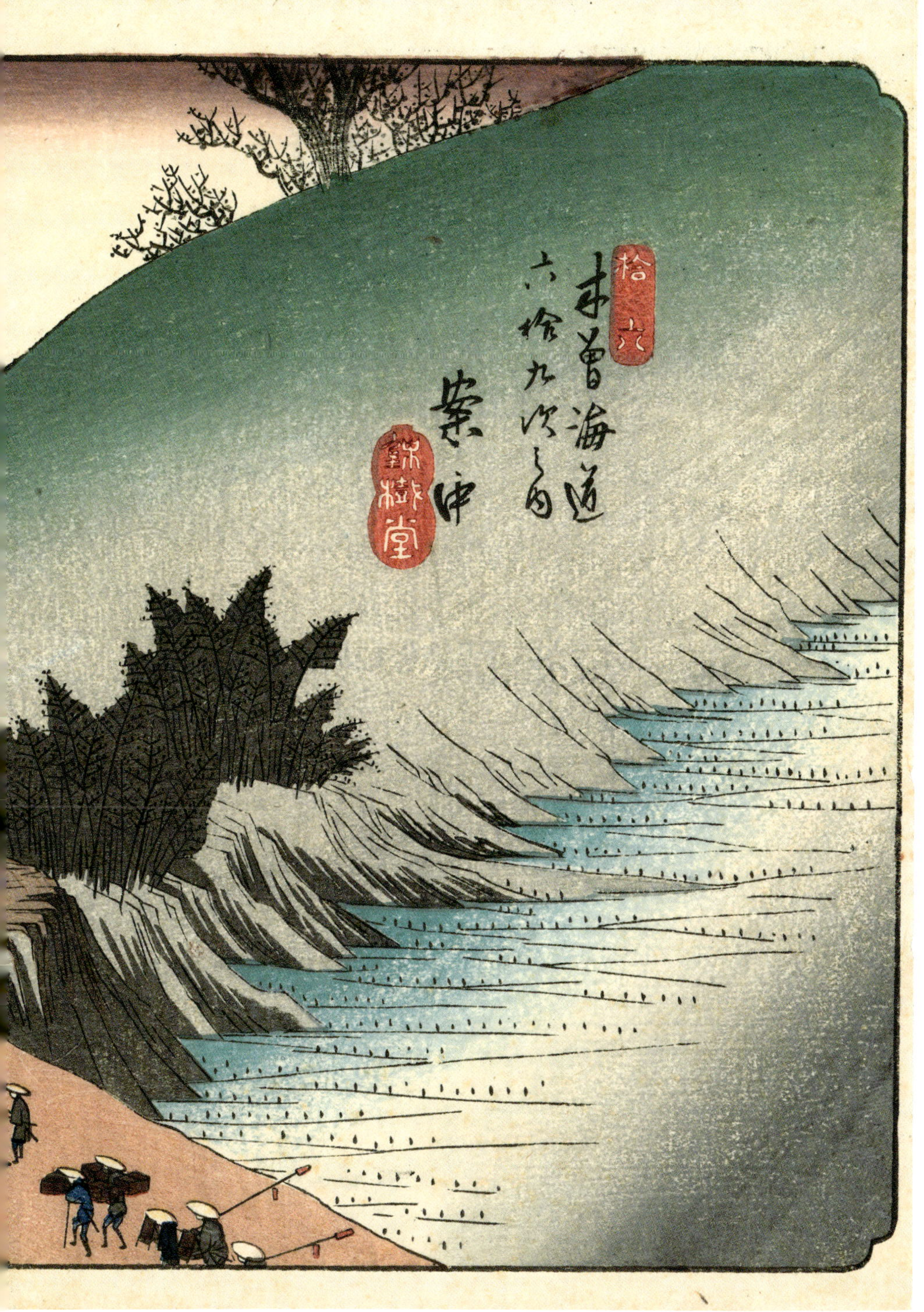

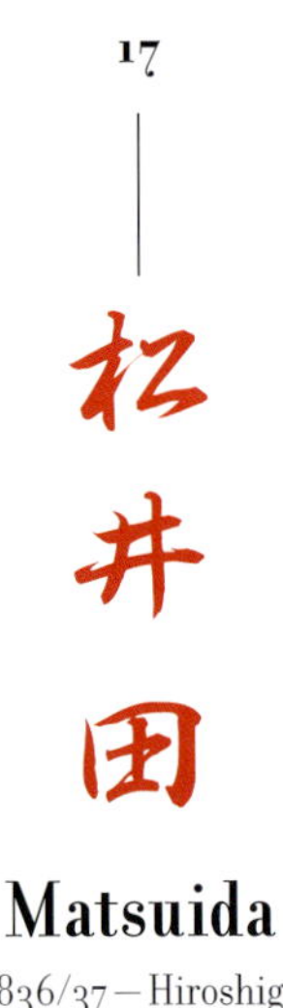

17

Matsuida

1836/37 — Hiroshige

According to the travel guidebook *Illustrated Guide to the Kiso Road* (*Kisoji anken ezu*), as the town of Matsuida was approached from Annaka, the Kisokaidō passed by a place called Biwa Basin (Biwagakubo) before climbing steeply up a tree-lined slope called Ōsaka. Between Edo and this point, the Kisokaidō was relatively flat, but from here it began the ascent towards the Usui Pass (Usuitōge). It is likely that Hiroshige consulted this guidebook in order to create this design.

Flanking the large tree in the centre are two boundary-marker posts, and beyond the tree a signboard and a wayside shrine to a tutelary deity or *dōsojin*. Such shrines were placed at the edges of villages for the safety of travellers and to ward off epidemics and evil spirits. Fluttering banners may announce an event associated with the Kōshin cult, a folk religion related to Daoism, or connected to a local agricultural god. Two pack horses trudge unsteadily in opposite directions under their burdens of rice bales and rice products.

Walking a little further, travellers would have been able to gaze upon one of the famous "Three Mountains of Jōmō", Mount Myōgi, which stood four kilometres (2½ miles) south-west of the town. At only 1,104 metres (3,622 feet) it was not Myōgi's height that attracted travellers, but its fantastically weathered rocks, for which it was widely known. After Japan opened its doors to the West, the mountain became a popular destination for Western tourists and mountaineers from the 1870s. Hiroshige was certainly aware of Mount Myōgi; its rugged outline appears in Hokusai's bird's-eye-view map from 1819, *Famous Sights along the Kiso Road at a Glance* (*Kisoji meisho ichiran*). In his design for Matsuida, however, Hiroshige rendered Mount Myōgi as a pair of rather diminutive hills in the distance.

Situated 9.6 kilometres (6 miles) from Annaka, Matsuida was a town of 1,009 people, with 252 houses, 2 *honjin*, 2 *waki-honjin* and 14 inns in 1843. It prospered as a centre for the trade of rice collected as tax from the various districts of Shinshū Province. A portion of the harvest would be sold to

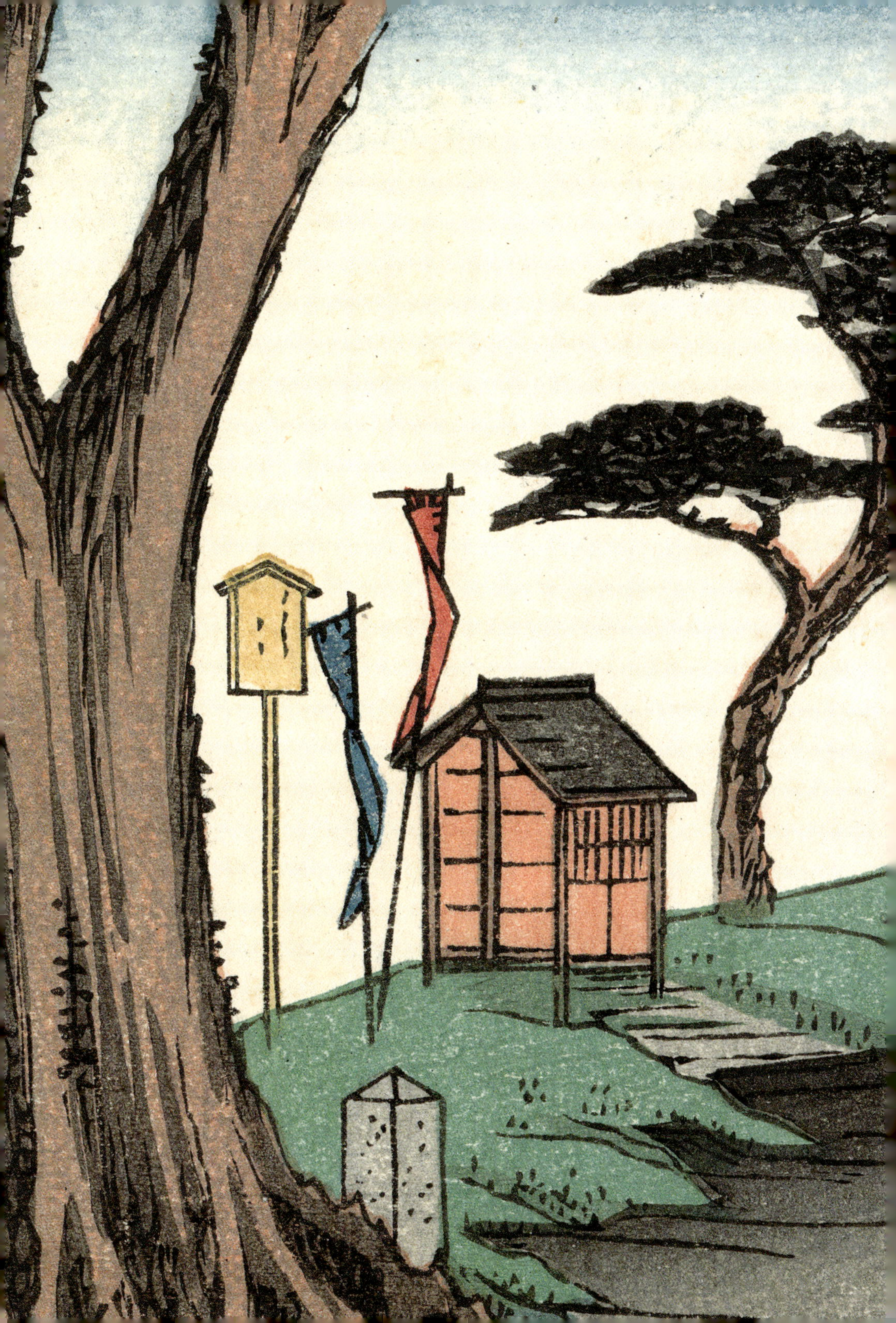

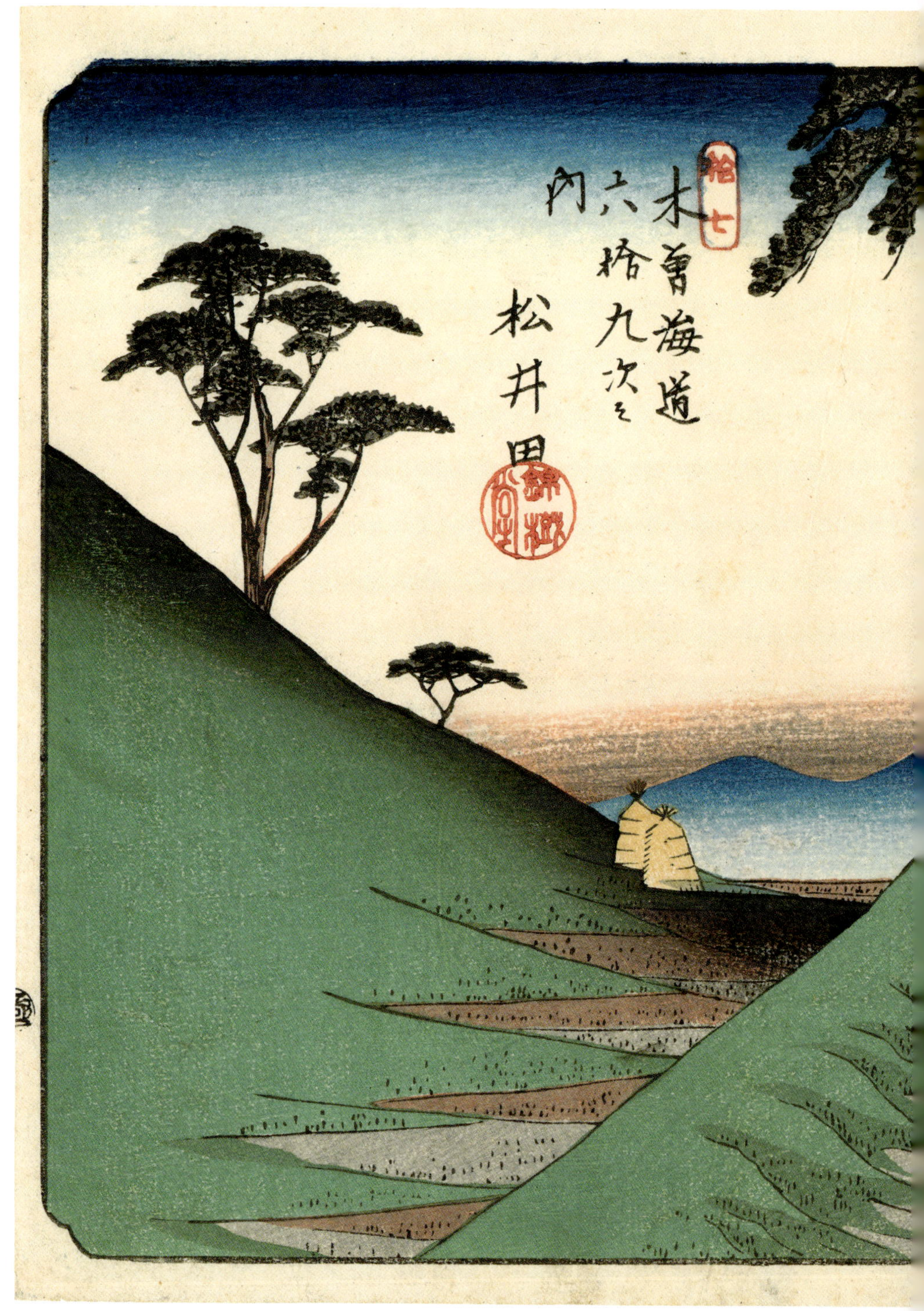

拾七
木曽海道
六拾九次之
内
松井田

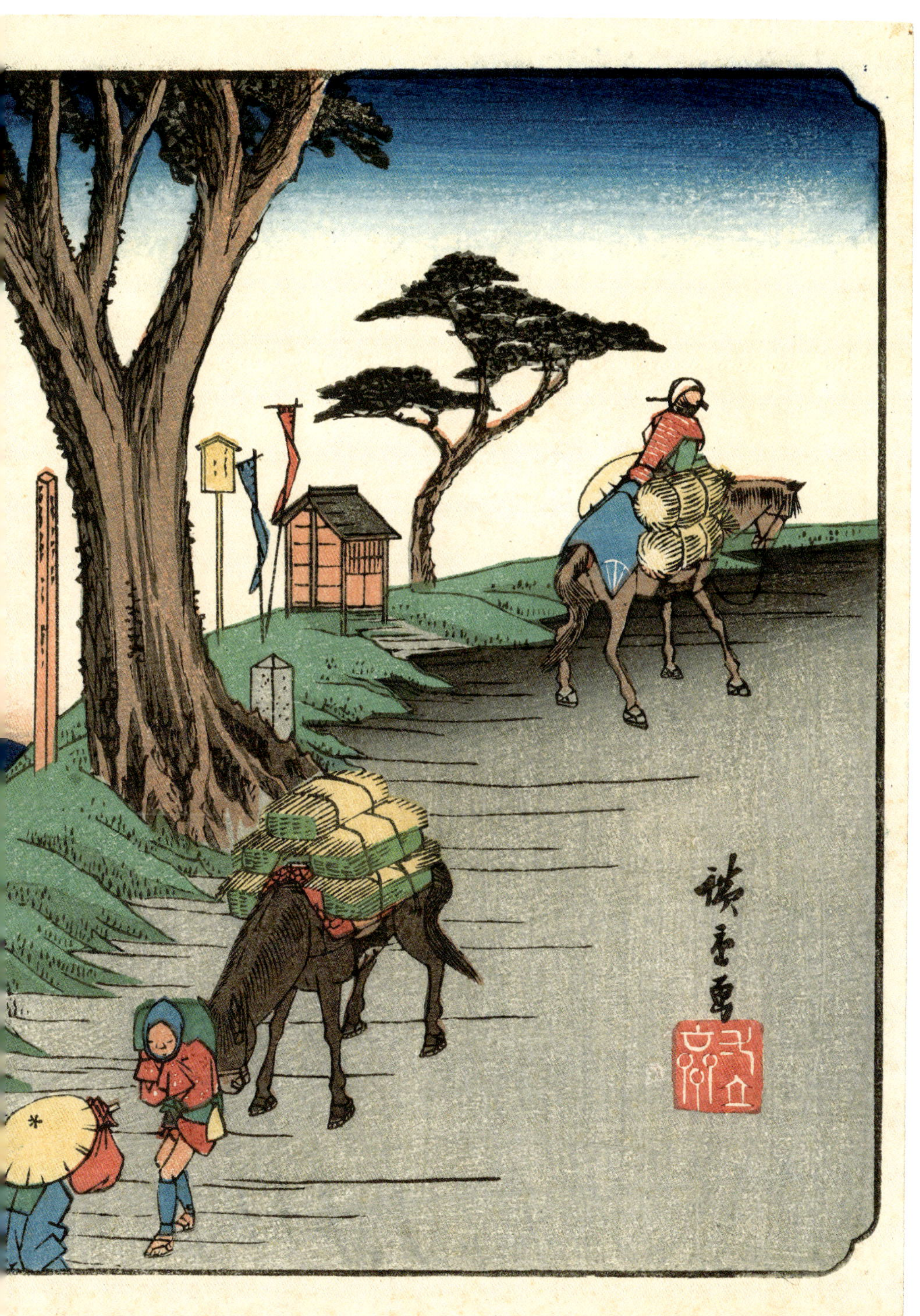

merchants in Matsuida, and the remainder carried to Kugano by horse to be transported to Edo by boat. Prior to becoming a trade hub, Matsuida briefly served a short-lived hilltop fortification, Matsuida Castle, located to the north of the town. Constructed in the mid-16th century, it was abandoned after the Siege of Odawara in 1590.

Between Matsuida and the next station to the west, Sakamoto, was the gated Usui checkpoint, where inspections of all travellers and their documents were carried out daily between the hours of 6 am and 6 pm. The checkpoint was reputed to be the strictest barrier along the Kisokaidō. Of particular concern to the authorities were female family members of *daimyō* absconding from Edo, where they served as virtual hostages of the shogunate, as well as guns being smuggled into the capital.

Dem Reiseführer *Illustrierter Wegweiser für die Kiso-Straße (Kisoji anken ezu)* zufolge streifte der Kisokaidō auf dem Weg von Annaka nach Matsuida eine Stätte namens Biwa-Becken (Biwagakubo), bevor er einen steilen, baumbestandenen Hang mit Namen Ōsaka hinaufführte. Von Edo bis hierher war die Straße relativ flach, doch jetzt begann der Aufstieg zum Usui-Pass (Usuitōge). Wahrscheinlich zog Hiroshige den Reiseführer zurate, als er dieses Blatt entwarf.

Der große Baum in der Bildmitte wird von zwei Grenzmarkierungen flankiert. Dahinter stehen ein Hinweisschild und ein Wegschrein für einen Schutzgott oder *dōsojin*. Derartige Schreine wurden am Rand von Siedlungen aufgestellt, um Reisenden Sicherheit zu bieten und um Seuchen und böse Geister abzuwehren. Die flatternden Fahnen könnten ein Ereignis im Zusammenhang mit einer örtlichen Agrargottheit oder mit dem Kōshin-Kult ankündigen, einer mit dem Taoismus verwandten Volksreligion. Zwei Packpferde trotten, unter der Last von Reisballen und Reiserzeugnissen schwankend, in entgegengesetzte Richtungen.

Ein Stück weiter auf der Route konnten Reisende mit dem Myōgi, der vier Kilometer südwestlich des Ortes aufragte, einen der berühmten „Drei Berge von Jōmō" bestaunen. Der Myōgi beeindruckte nicht mit seiner Höhe, die lediglich 1104 Meter betrug, sondern mit seinen fantastisch verwitterten Zinnen, für die er weithin bekannt war. Nachdem Japan sich dem Westen geöffnet hatte, wurde der Berg ab den 1870er Jahren zum beliebten Reiseziel für westliche Touristen und Bergsteiger. Mit Sicherheit wusste auch Hiroshige um den Myōgi, dessen zerklüftete Gipfel schon 1819 in Hokusais vogelperspektivischer Karte *Berühmte Stätten der Kiso-Straße im Überblick (Kisoji meisho ichiran)* aufgetaucht waren. In seinem Entwurf für Matsuida jedoch stellte Hiroshige ihn als ein Paar kleiner Hügel in der Ferne dar.

Die 9,6 Kilometer von Annaka entfernte Ortschaft Matsuida zählte 1009 Einwohner, mit 252 Häusern, zwei *honjin*, zwei *waki-honjin* und 14 Herbergen im Jahr 1843. Sie florierte als Zentrum für den Handel mit Reis, der von den verschiedenen Kreisen der Provinz Shinshū als Steuer erhoben wurde. Ein Teil der Ernte wurde an Händler in Matsuida verkauft, der Rest mit Pferden nach Kugano transportiert, um von dort nach Edo verschifft zu werden. Vor seiner Zeit als Handelszentrum diente Matsuida für begrenzte Zeit der Burg Matsuida, einer kurzlebigen Bergfestung im Norden der Stadt. Mitte des 16. Jahrhunderts erbaut, wurde sie nach der Belagerung von Odawara schon 1590 wieder aufgegeben.

Zwischen Matsuida und Sakamoto, der nächsten Station in westlicher Richtung, lag die beschrankte Kontrollstelle Usui, an der täglich zwischen sechs Uhr morgens und sechs Uhr abends alle Reisenden und ihre Dokumente überprüft wurden. Die Kontrollstelle galt als strengste Sperranlage auf dem Kisokaidō. Das besondere Augenmerk der Behörden galt den weiblichen Familienmitgliedern der *daimyō*, die sich heimlich aus Edo davonstahlen, wo sie praktisch als Geiseln des Shogunats leben mussten, und dem Waffenschmuggel in die Hauptstadt.

Selon le *Guide illustré de la route Kiso (Kisoji anken ezu)*, à l'approche de la ville de Matsuida en venant d'Annaka, la Kisokaidō passait par un lieu nommé « bassin de Biwa » (Biwagakubo) avant une montée abrupte le long d'un versant boisé appelé Ōsaka. D'Edo à ce lieu, la Kisokaidō était relativement plate, mais la montée vers le col d'Usui (Usuitōge) commençait ici. Il est probable qu'Hiroshige ait consulté ce guide pour réaliser cette estampe.

Deux bornes de démarcation flanquent le grand arbre situé au centre ; au-delà de l'arbre se trouvent un panneau et un petit sanctuaire de bord de route, dédié à une divinité tutélaire ou *dōsojin*. Des sanctuaires de ce genre étaient érigés à l'orée des villages pour protéger les voyageurs et conjurer épidémies et esprits malins. Des bannières flottent au vent et annoncent peut-être un événement lié au culte *kōshin*, religion populaire apparentée au taoïsme, ou bien en rapport avec une divinité agricole locale. Deux chevaux de bât avancent d'un pas mal assuré dans des directions opposées, sous de lourdes balles de riz et de produits dérivés du riz.

En allant un peu plus loin, les voyageurs auraient découvert la vue donnant sur l'une des fameuses « trois montagnes de Jōmō », le mont Myōgi s'élevant à quatre kilomètres au sud-ouest de la ville. Ce n'était pas son altitude modeste de 1104 mètres qui attirait les voyageurs, mais ses pics spectaculaires, battus par les éléments, qui ont fait sa réputation. À la suite de l'ouverture du Japon à l'Occident, cette montagne devint une destination prisée des touristes et des alpinistes occidentaux à partir des années 1870. Hiroshige avait certainement connaissance du mont Myōgi ; ses pics déchiquetés sont visibles dans la carte aérienne dessinée par Hokusai en 1819, *Collection de vues de paysages célèbres sur la route Kiso en un clin d'œil (Kisoji meisho ichiran)*. En revanche, dans son dessin de Matsuida, Hiroshige a représenté cette montagne sous la forme de collines modestes dans le lointain.

Située à 9,6 kilomètres d'Annaka, Matsuida était une bourgade de 1009 habitants, dotée de 252 maisons, deux *honjin*, deux *waki-honjin* et quatorze auberges en 1843. Elle connut sa fortune grâce au commerce du riz collecté pour les impôts dans les différentes circonscriptions de la province de Shinshū. Une partie de la récolte était vendue aux négociants de Matsuida, et le reste était transporté à cheval à Kugano, puis par bateau jusqu'à Edo. Avant de devenir une ville marchande, Matsuida avait brièvement servi de place forte au sommet d'une colline, avec le château de Matsuida situé au nord de la ville. Bâti au milieu du XVIe siècle, celui-ci fut abandonné après le siège d'Odawara en 1590.

Entre Matsuida et Sakamato, la station suivante en allant vers l'ouest, se trouvait le poste de contrôle avec barrière d'Usui, où tous les voyageurs et leurs documents étaient inspectés chaque jour de six heures du matin à six heures du soir. Ce poste de contrôle était connu comme l'obstacle le plus difficile à franchir sur la Kisokaidō. Les autorités surveillaient particulièrement les femmes des familles de *daïmio* s'étant échappées d'Edo, où elles servaient d'otages virtuelles du shogunat, ainsi que les armes que l'on cherchait à faire passer en contrebande dans la capitale.

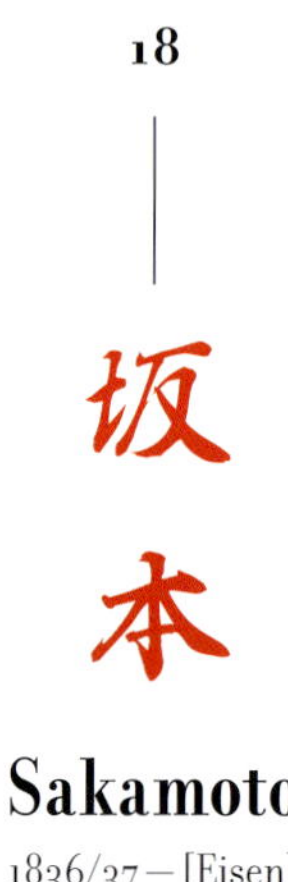

18

Sakamoto

1836/37 – [Eisen]

This is the second unsigned print in this series which is assumed to have been designed by Eisen for the publisher Takenouchi, who did not issue it but instead passed it on to Iseya Rihei when he took over the Kisokaidō series. It shows the Sakamoto station that was built in 1625 on an elevation some 480 metres (1,575 feet) in height. Sakamoto is situated at the foot of the 810-metre-high (2,660 feet) Mount Haneishi, which towers up in the background shrouded in brown autumn foliage. The road climbs higher and circles around Mount Haneishi, bypassing Lake Usui, invisible here on the left. While the road continued to climb west to the next station at Karuizawa, it eventually reached the Usui Pass, 960 metres (3,150 feet) above sea level, and one of the highest and most exhausting elevations along the Kisokaidō.

Coming from the east, and before reaching Sakamoto, travellers had to pass the Usui checkpoint at Yokogawa, one of the two checkpoints along the Kisokaidō where travel permits were inspected. Sakamoto had 40 regular inns and was a popular overnight stop for travellers because it was located between the checkpoint and the pass.

Dieses Blatt ist der zweite unsignierte Druck der Serie, der mutmaßlich von Eisen für den Verleger Takenouchi entworfen, von ihm aber nicht veröffentlicht, sondern an Iseya Rihei weitergereicht wurde, als dieser den Kisokaidō-Zyklus übernahm. Er zeigt die Station Sakamoto, die im Jahr 1625 auf rund 480 Metern Meereshöhe errichtet wurde. Die Ortschaft liegt am Fuß des 810 Meter hohen Haneishi, der, in herbstlich braunes Laubwerk gehüllt, im Hintergrund emporragt. Die Straße steigt von der Station aus weiter an, führt am links des Bildausschnitts gelegenen Usui-See vorbei und umkreist den Haneishi. Auf ihrem stetigen Anstieg nach Westen zur nächsten Station, Karuizawa, erreicht sie schließlich den Usui-Pass, der 960 Metern über dem Meeresspiegel liegt und zu den höchsten und besonders kraftraubenden Erhebungen des Kisokaidō zählt.

Bevor sie nach Sakamoto kamen, mussten alle Reisenden aus östlicher Richtung die Kontrollstelle Usui in Yokogawa passieren, eine der beiden Schranken am Kisokaidō, an denen die Reisegenehmigungen überprüft wurden. Sakamoto hatte 40 reguläre Herbergen und war als Nachtquartier bei Reisenden beliebt, weil es zwischen der Kontrollstelle und dem Gebirgspass lag.

Il s'agit de la deuxième estampe non signée de cette série, qui aurait été réalisée par Eisen pour l'éditeur Takenouchi ; ne l'ayant pas publiée, celui-ci l'avait remise à Iseya Rihei lorsqu'il reprit l'édition de la série de la Kisokaidō. Elle représente la station de Sakamoto, construite sur une élévation en 1625, à une altitude d'environ 480 mètres. Sakamoto se trouve au pied du mont Haneishi, qui s'élève à 810 mètres, visible ici à l'arrière-plan, enveloppé d'un feuillage roux automnal. La route gravit les versants de la montagne en cercles successifs, en contournant le lac Usui, situé à gauche mais invisible. La route continuait de monter vers l'ouest jusqu'à la station suivante de Karuizawa et finissait par atteindre le col d'Usui, situé à 960 mètres au-dessus du niveau de la mer, l'un des points les plus élevés et les plus épuisants du parcours.

En venant de l'est et avant de parvenir à Sakamoto, les voyageurs devaient passer par le poste de contrôle d'Usui à Yokogawa, l'un des deux lieux d'inspection des permis de voyage sur la Kisokaidō. Avec quarante auberges ordinaires, Sakamoto était une étape très appréciée des voyageurs en raison de sa situation entre le poste de contrôle et le col.

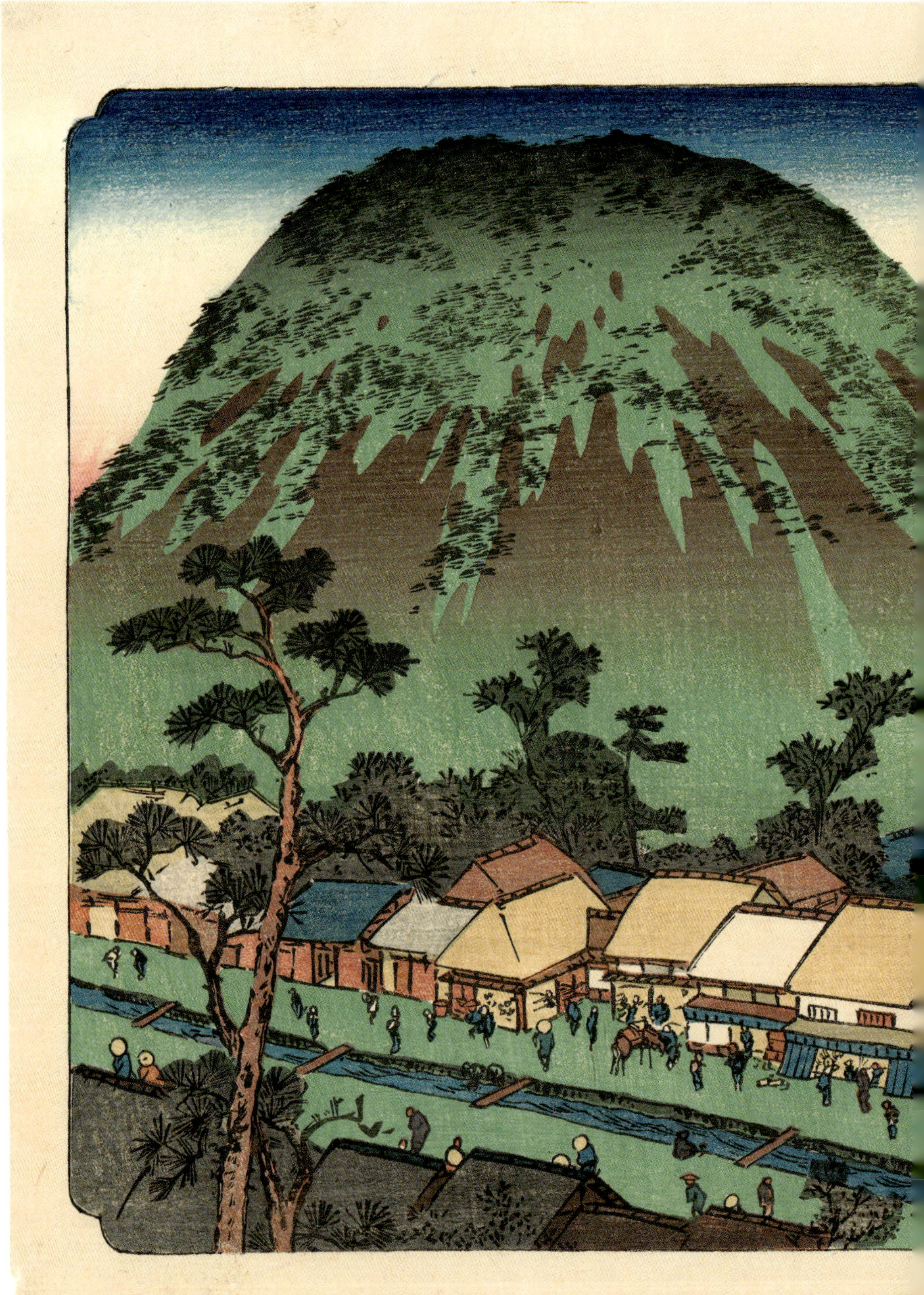

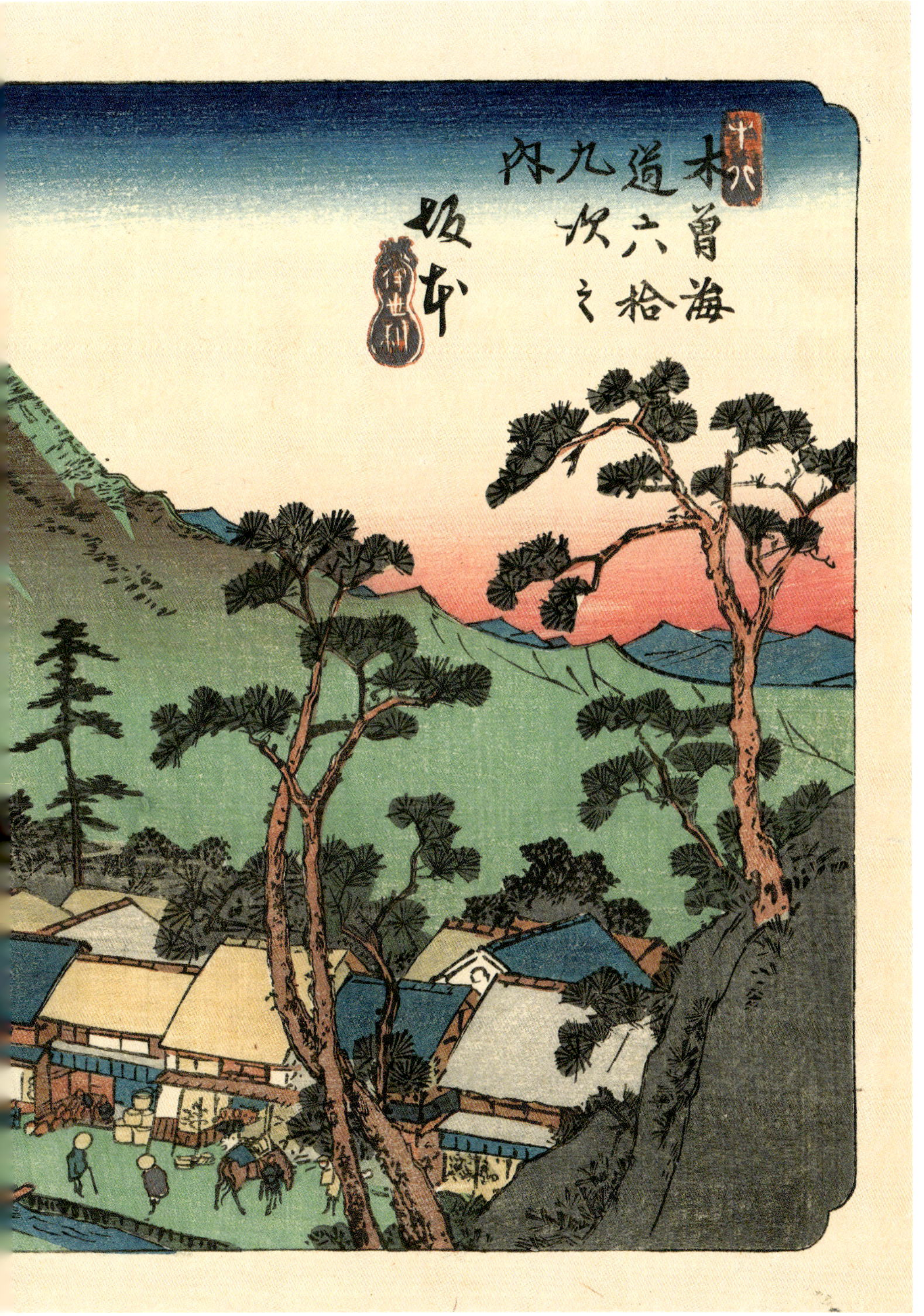
十八
木曽海
道六拾
九次之
内
坂本

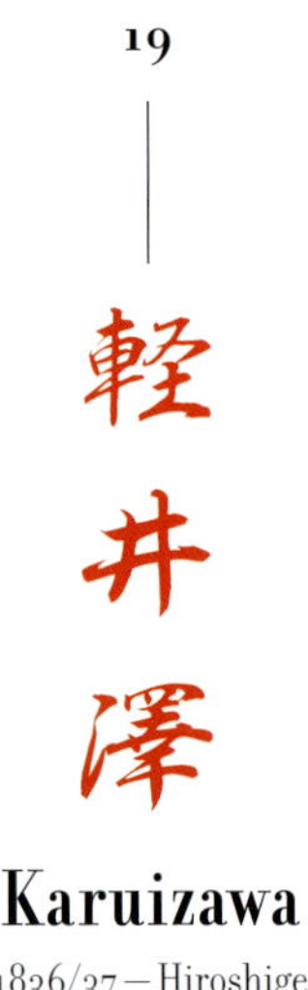

Karuizawa

1836/37 — Hiroshige

The stillness of night has descended except for two travellers and their horse driver who have paused to light their pipes in an open field on the western outskirts of Karuizawa. Two columns of smoke produced by the burning piles of straw and rice husks break the darkness. The bright glow of the fire in the foreground brings a stately cedar out of the monochrome and into colour. Ploughed into the soil, the ashes from these fires would fertilise the next planting of crops. The silhouette of Mount Asama, an active volcano, closes in the scene from the north-west.

The horse driver solicitously raises his pipe to provide a light for his client, who hunches under a *kasuri* blanket against the chilly night air. Their steed is fitted with woven straw sandals, vital equipment for protecting the hooves and providing traction on the precipitous mountain paths at a time when metal was scarce. A paper lantern suspended on the near side of the horse bears the name "Iseri", referring to one of the publishers, Iseya Rihei.

The grassy highlands of Karuizawa are bound by the Usui Pass to the east and Mount Asama to the north-west. In 1843, the town was a small village of only 451 inhabitants who were critically dependent on the traffic of the Kisokaidō. Karuizawa suffered economically when the obligation to maintain two residences for lords was abolished with the fall of the Tokugawa shogunate in 1868. Its fortunes changed in the 1880s and 1890s, however, when Western missionaries seeking respite from the heat and humidity of Tokyo began travelling here via the growing railway networks. The village was reborn as a summer resort town catering to Western tastes and comforts.

Nächtliche Stille liegt über der Szenerie. Nur zwei Reisende und ihr Pferdeführer sind zu sehen, die eine Pause einlegen, um sich auf einem offenen Feld am westlichen Ortsrand von Karuizawa eine Pfeife anzustecken. Zwei Rauchsäulen, die von brennenden Haufen aus Stroh und Reisspelzen aufsteigen, durchbrechen die Dunkelheit. Der helle Schein des Feuers im Vordergrund verleiht einer prächtigen, ins Grau der Nacht getauchten Zeder ein wenig Farbe. Die an den Feuerstellen zurückbleibende Asche wird, untergepflügt, im nächsten Erntezyklus als Dünger dienen. Die Silhouette des Asama, eines aktiven Vulkans, beschließt die Szene im Nordwesten.

Der Pferdeführer hebt eifrig seine Pfeife an, um seinem Kunden, der zum Schutz gegen die kühle Nachtluft unter einer *kasuri*-Decke kauert, Feuer zu geben. Die gewebten Strohsandalen des Pferdes gehörten in einer Zeit, da Metall knapp war, unbedingt zur Ausrüstung, um die Hufe zu schützen und auf den abschüssigen Bergpfaden Trittsicherheit zu geben. Der an der rechten Flanke des Pferdes auf einer Papierlaterne zu lesende Name „Iseri" verweist auf einen der Verleger, Iseya Rihei.

Das grasbewachsene Hochland von Karuizawa wird im Osten vom Usui-Pass und im Nordwesten vom Asama begrenzt. 1843 war der Ort ein kleines Dorf mit nur 451 Einwohnern, die entschieden auf den Kisokaidō-Verkehr angewiesen waren. Karuizawa litt wirtschaftliche Not, als die Pflicht der Lehensfürsten, zwei Residenzen zu unterhalten, mit dem Sturz des Tokugawa-Shogunats 1868 aufgehoben wurde. In den 1880er und 1890er Jahren aber wendete sich das Blatt: Mit dem zunehmenden Ausbau des Eisenbahnnetzes begannen westliche Missionare, die Erholung von der schwülen Hitze in Tokio suchten, die Gegend zu bereisen. Auf westliche Geschmäcker und Annehmlichkeiten ausgerichtet, wurde das Dorf zu einem beliebten Sommerausflugsziel.

La nuit a déployé son manteau de tranquillité, mais deux voyageurs et le conducteur de leur cheval font une pause pour allumer leur pipe dans une prairie, à la périphérie ouest de Karuizawa. L'obscurité est brisée par deux colonnes de fumée qui s'élèvent des brasiers de paille et d'enveloppes de riz. Au premier plan, la vive lueur du feu donne de la couleur à un cèdre majestueux et le fait ressortir sur les teintes monochromes. Mélangées à la terre au moment des labours, les cendres de ces feux fertiliseront les prochaines semences. Au nord-ouest, la silhouette du volcan actif du mont Asama clôt le décor.

Le conducteur du cheval lève sa pipe avec sollicitude pour allumer celle de son client recroquevillé sous un *kasuri*, couverture qui le protège du froid nocturne. Leur monture porte des chaussons de paille tressée, équipement vital pour préserver les sabots et assurer une traction suffisante sur les chemins escarpés de montagne, à une époque où le métal se faisait rare. Une lanterne en papier suspendue au flanc du cheval porte l'inscription « Iseri », référence à Iseya Rihei, l'un des éditeurs.

Ces régions de montagnes herbeuses sont encadrées à l'est par le col d'Usui et, au nord-ouest, par le mont Asama. En 1843, Karuizawa n'était qu'un petit village de 451 habitants qui dépendaient fortement de la fréquentation de la Kisokaidō. Avec la chute du shogunat des Tokugawa en 1868, l'obligation pour les seigneurs d'entretenir deux résidences fut abolie, ce qui eut de graves conséquences économiques pour le village. Toutefois, son sort changea dans les années 1880 et 1890, lorsque les missionnaires occidentaux cherchant à se protéger de la chaleur et de l'humidité de Tokyo commencèrent à venir dans la région grâce au réseau ferroviaire en expansion. Le village connut un nouvel essor sous la forme d'une station estivale satisfaisant au goût et au confort des Occidentaux.

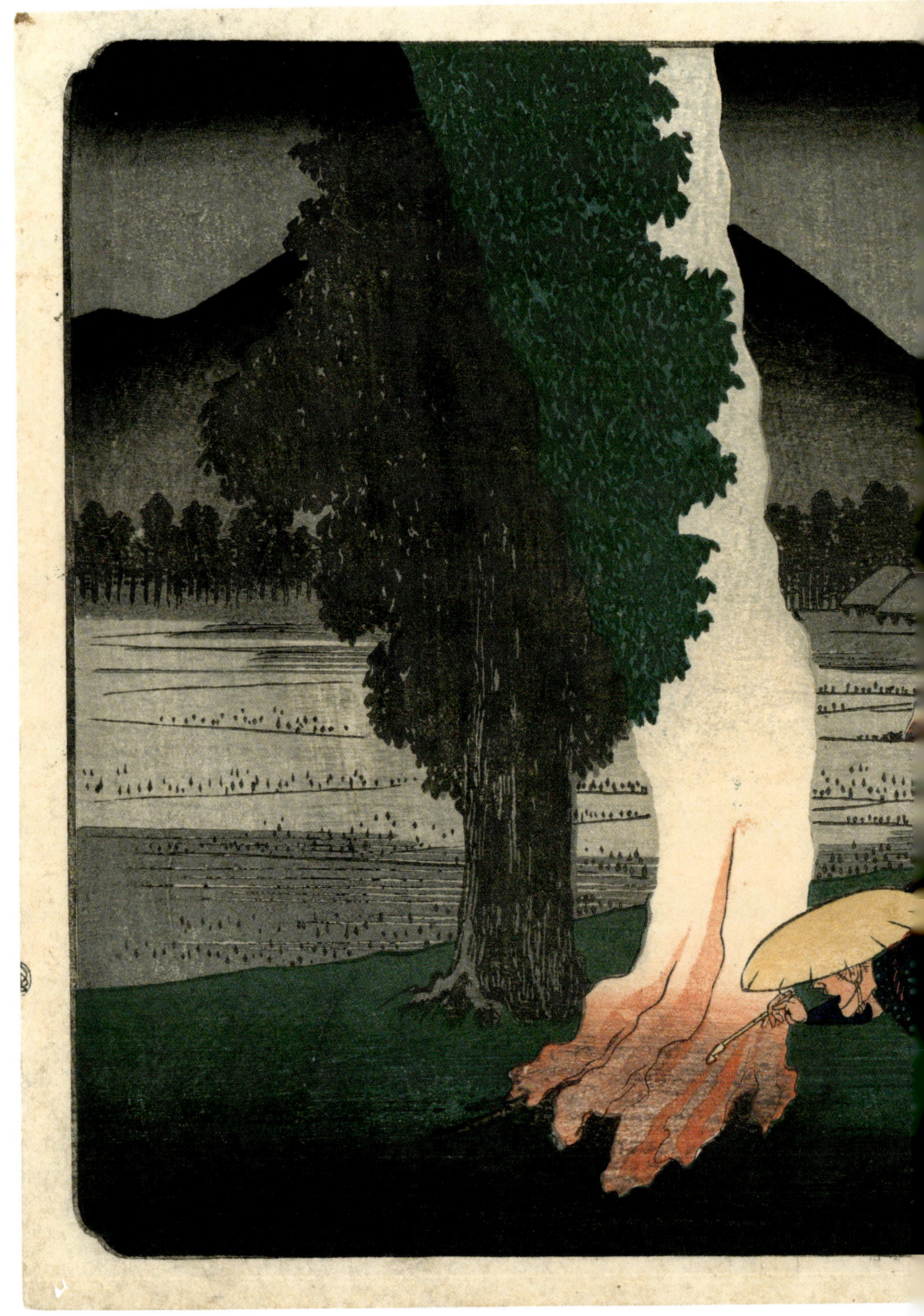

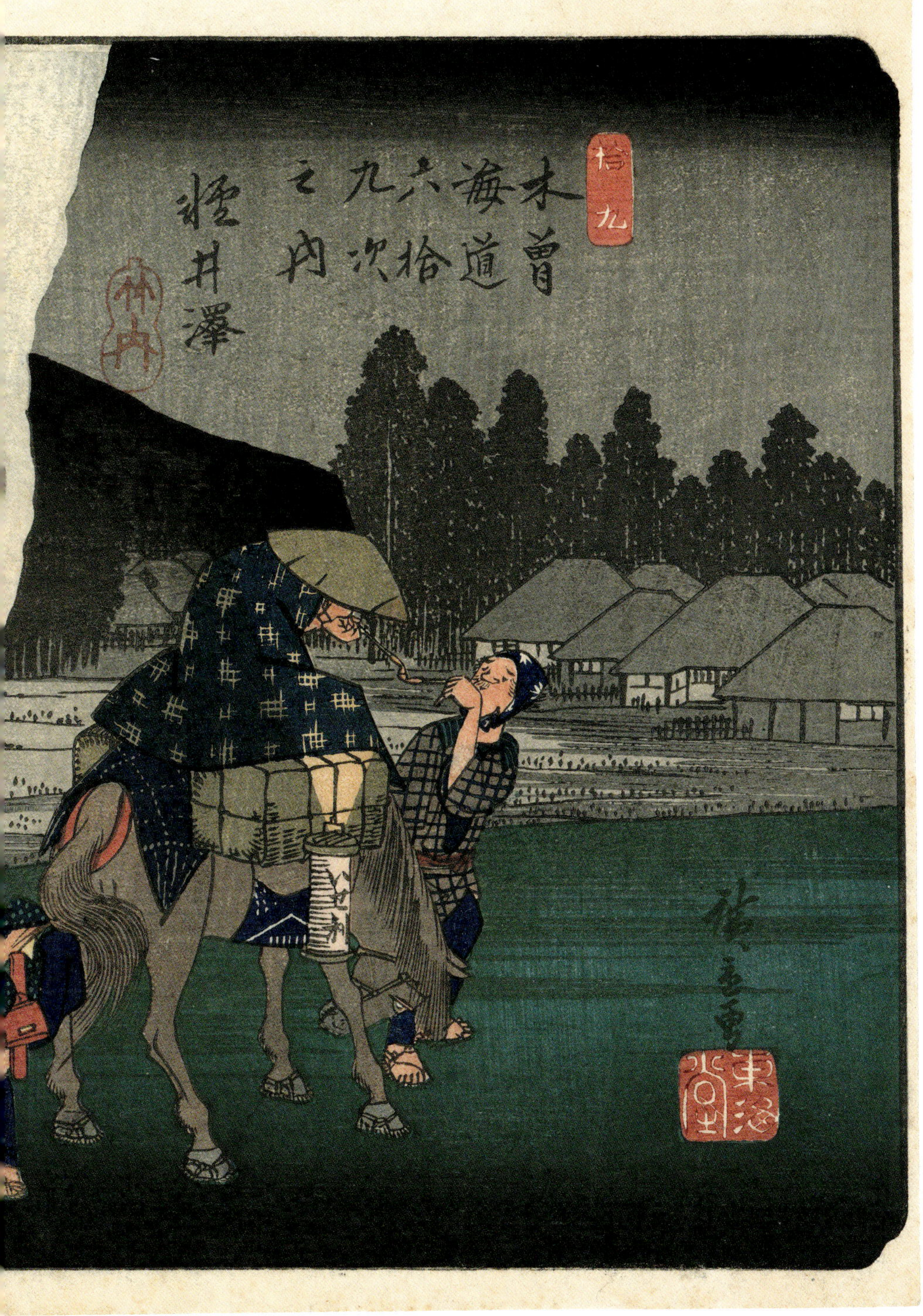

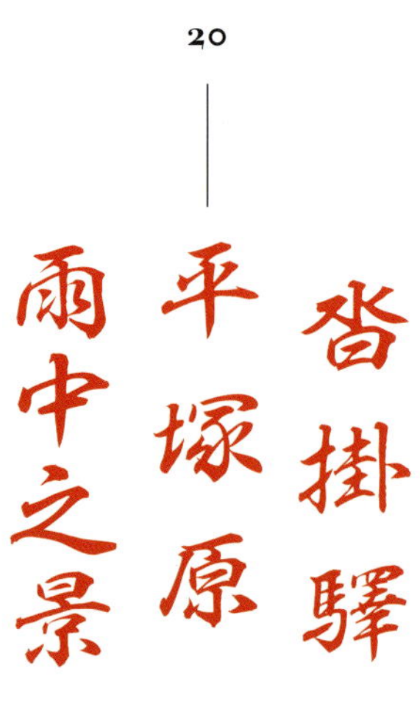

Kutsukake

1835/36 — Eisen

A heavy autumn storm with diagonal streaks of rain makes walking along the road more tiring for these travellers who are trying to protect their faces while struggling on. In their midst are two heavily loaded pack oxen that are also fighting against the weather. In the background on the right is a long row of roofs belonging to the houses of a village that could be Hanare. According to the title, this is a view of the Hiratsuka Plain, shown in the left background, which was situated between the two villages of Hanare and Maesawa near the southern slope of Mount Asama. The stream winding its way over the plain is the Yukawa, a tributary of the Shinano River, the longest and widest river in Japan.

Basil Stewart in 1922 and Edward Strange in 1925 considered this design to be one of Eisen's best contributions to the Kisokaidō series (Stewart 1922, p. 101; Strange [1925] 1983, p. 58).

Ein schwerer Herbststurm mit schräg peitschendem Regen macht das Fortkommen für diese Reisenden besonders anstrengend: Sie versuchen ihre Gesichter zu schützen, während sie sich vorwärts mühen. Mitten unter ihnen kämpfen zwei schwer beladene Packochsen ebenfalls gegen das Wetter. Die lange Häuserzeile im Hintergrund rechts, von der nur die Dächer zu sehen sind, könnte zum Dorf Hanare gehören. Dem Titel zufolge zeigt das Bild links im Hintergrund die Hiratsuka-Ebene, die zwischen den Dörfern Hanare und Maesawa an der Südflanke des Vulkans Asama lag. Der kleine Fluss, der sich durch die Ebene schlängelt, heißt Yukawa und mündet in den Shinano, den längsten und breitesten Fluss Japans.

1922 hielt Basil Stewart und 1925 Edward Strange das Blatt für einen der besten Beiträge Eisens zur Kisokaidō-Serie (Stewart 1922, S. 101; Strange [1925] 1983, S. 58).

Une violente tempête d'automne, avec sa pluie qui barre le paysage en diagonales, rend épuisante la progression de ces voyageurs qui tentent de se protéger le visage en avançant péniblement. Entre eux, deux bœufs lourdement chargés luttent aussi contre les éléments. À droite, à l'arrière-plan, on voit une succession de toits d'un village qui pourrait être Hanare. D'après son titre, cette estampe est une vue de la plaine d'Hiratsuka, visible à gauche, située entre les villages d'Hanare et de Maesawa, non loin du versant sud du mont Asama. La rivière qui serpente dans la plaine est la Yukawa, un affluent du Shinano, le fleuve le plus long et le plus large du Japon.

Basil Stewart, en 1922, et par la suite Edward Strange, en 1925, considéraient cette estampe comme l'une des meilleures contributions d'Eisen à la série du Kisokaidō (Stewart, 1922, p. 101 ; Strange [1925] 1983, p. 58).

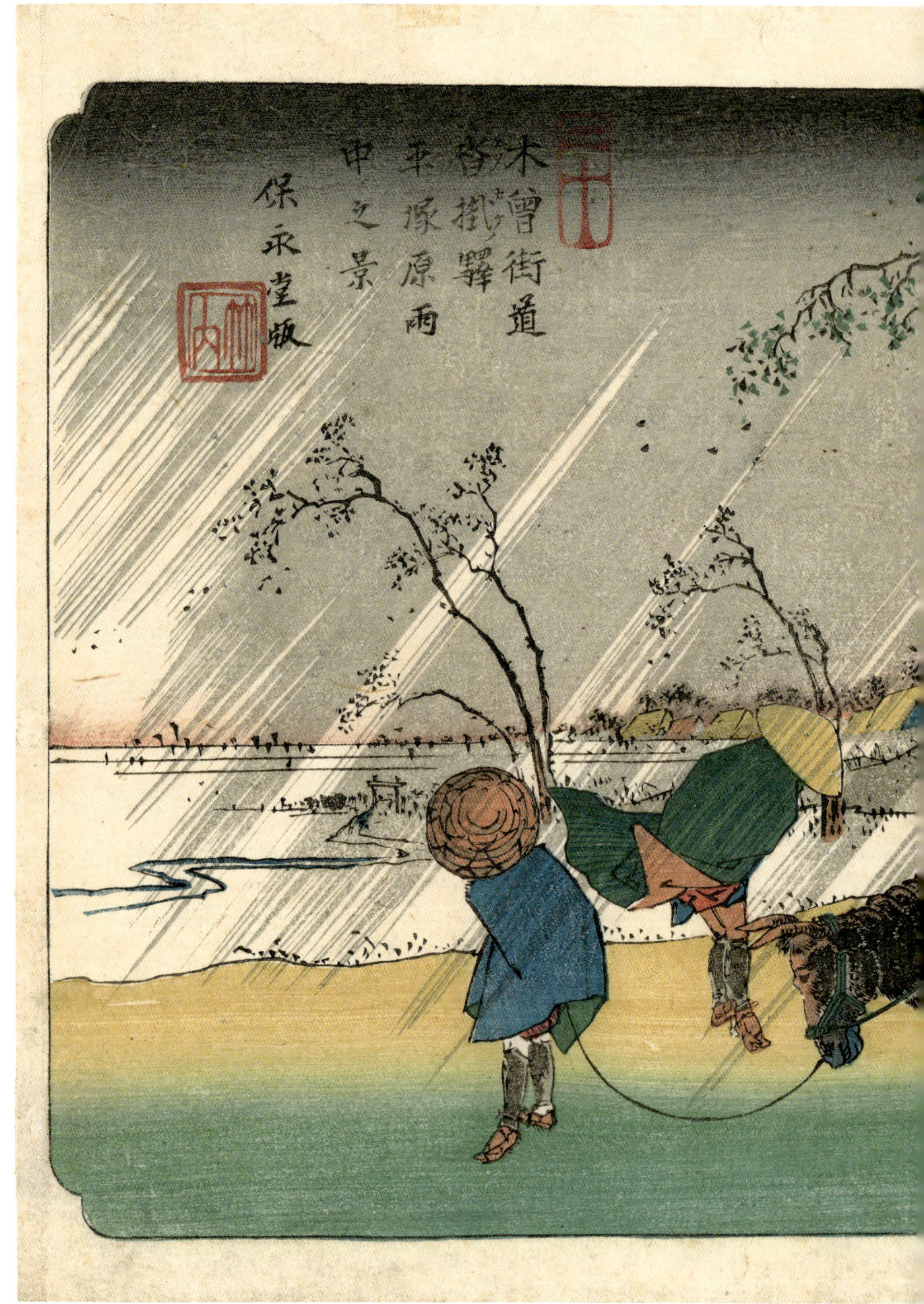
木曽街道
督䑓驛
平塚原雨
中之景
保永堂板

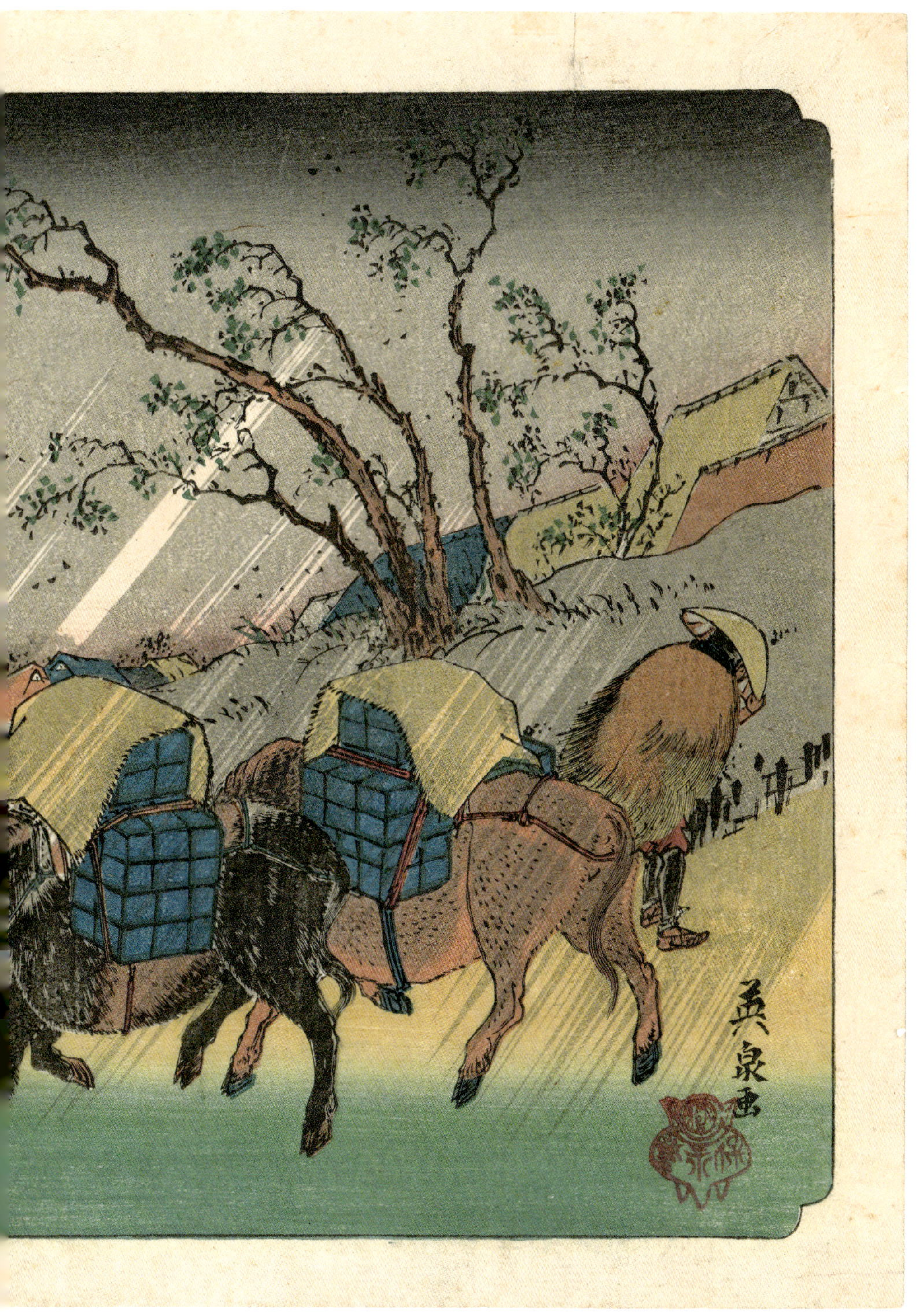

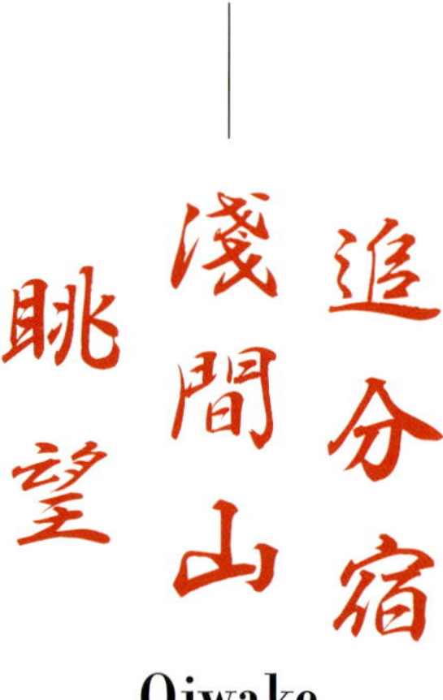

Oiwake

1835/36 – Eisen

A procession of travellers and porters is filing along the Kisokaidō as it continues in a south-westerly direction over the grassy plains of Oiwake. The station's name, literally "forked road", was derived from its position at the point of junction of the Kisokaidō and Hokkoku Kaidō, the "North Country Road" leading to Jōetsu on the Japan Sea coast.

It is the distinctive cone of Mount Asama, however, that dominates the landscape; this is the highest mountain in the vicinity and one of Japan's most active volcanoes. In the half-century before the time this print was published, it had erupted on four occasions: in 1783, twice in 1803 and in 1815. The catastrophic eruption in 1783, known as the Tenmei eruption, is estimated to have killed 1,400 people and destroyed 1,800 houses, choking the waterways and causing widespread damage to crops and farmland. Further stricken by adverse weather conditions, much of the Kantō region then suffered a famine which resulted in 20,000 more deaths. The metropolis of Edo, 150 kilometres (93 miles) away, was covered in a blanket of ash 2.5 centimetres (1 inch) deep (on the Tenmei eruption and its aftermath, see Totman 1993, pp. 238–240).

Eisen is unlikely to have visited Oiwake, but the fame of Mount Asama was such that there were many images of it in circulation. A possible source for the composition of this design is a depiction of the smoking volcano towering over Karuizawa, Kutsukake, Oiwake and the road between them, in the second volume of Fuchigami Kyokkō's (1753–1816) *Gleanings of Marvellous Landscapes* (*Sansui kikan shūi*, 1802). The travel guidebooks *Illustrated Guide to the Kiso Road* (*Kisoji anken ezu*) and *Views of Famous Sights along the Kiso Road* (*Kisoji meisho zue*) also include depictions of the mountain with smoke coiling upwards from its caldera.

The red seal to the right of the title contains the number 22 – a misprint, as 21 is correct according to the numbering system of the series. Below the left elbow of the pack-horse driver in the foreground a white gap usually appears in the image, another fault, which was corrected on some impressions by in-painting this gap by hand.

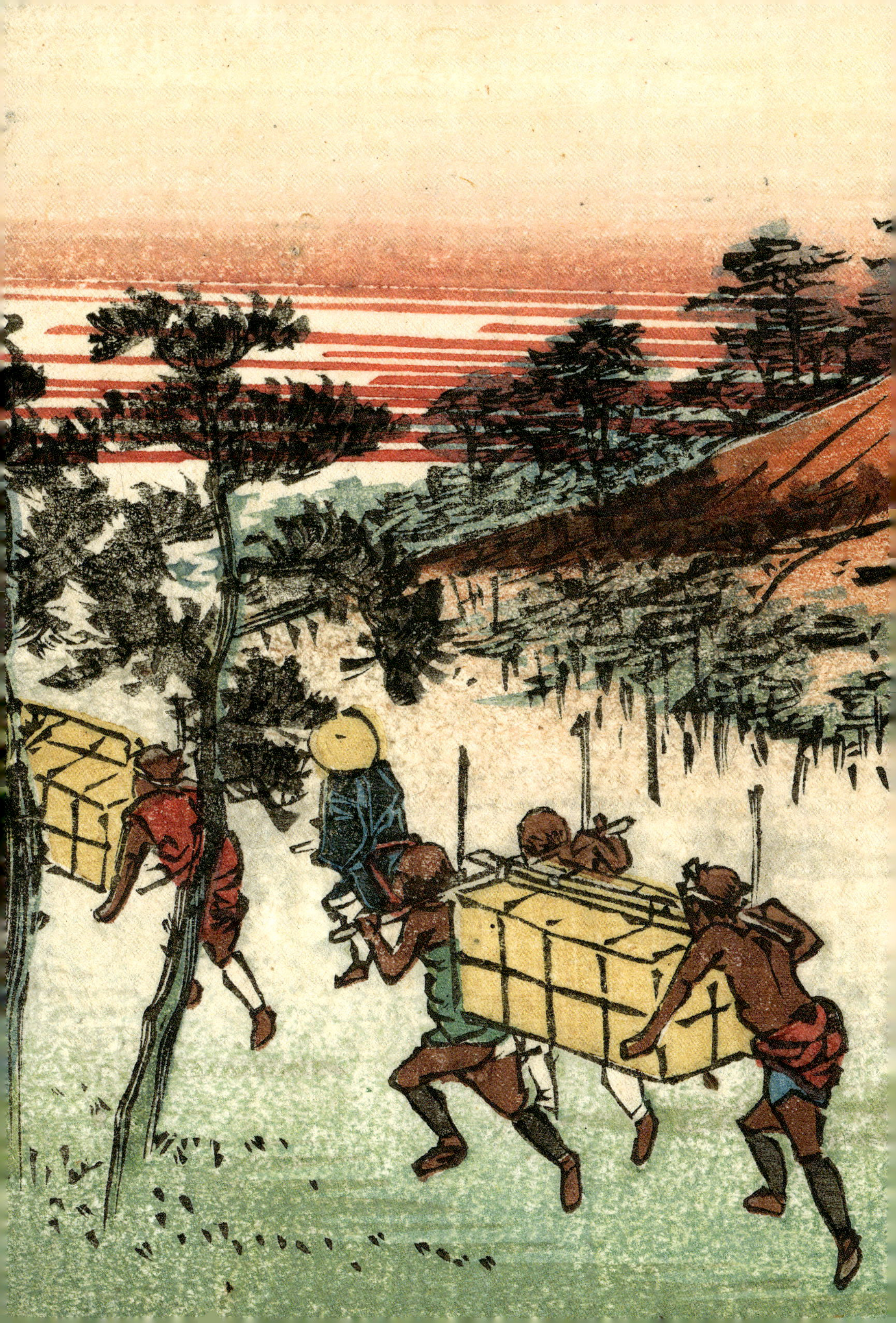

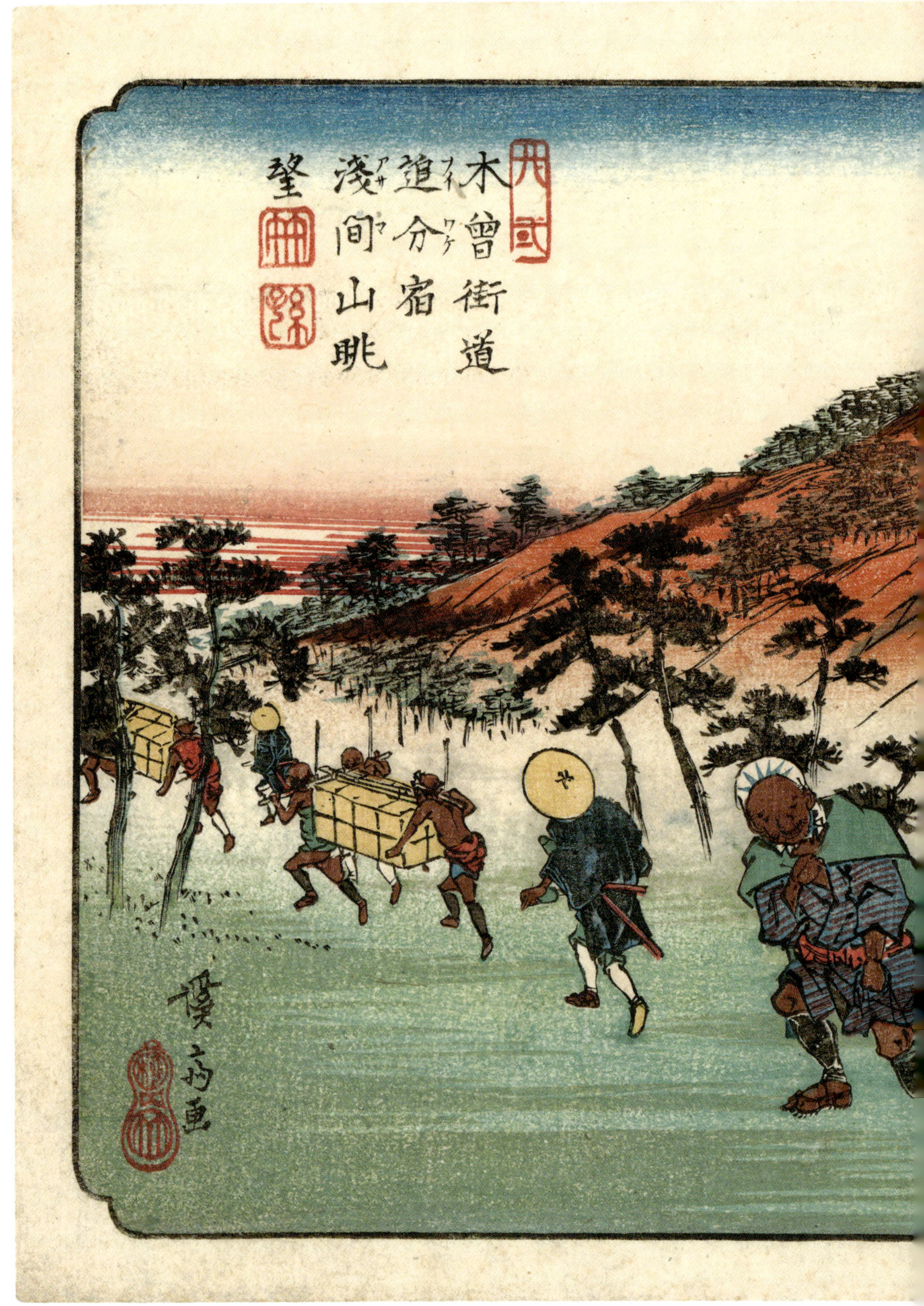

木曽街道
追分宿
浅間山眺望

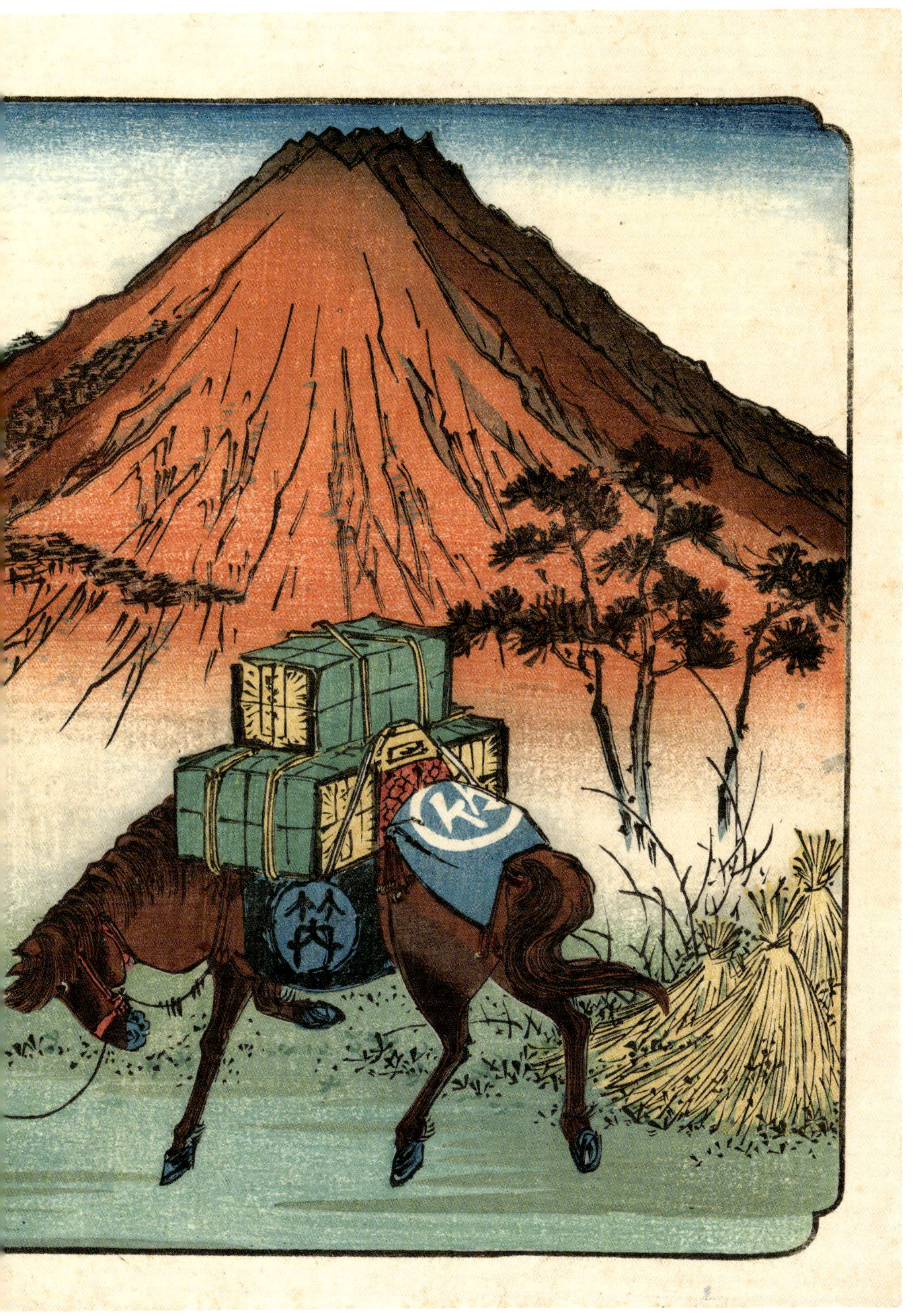

Eine Prozession von Reisenden und Lastenträgern zieht im Gänsemarsch auf dem Kisokaidō dahin, der über die grasbewachsenen Ebenen von Oiwake nach Südwesten führt. Der Stationsname bedeutet wörtlich „Straßengabelung" und leitete sich von der Lage der Station an der Kreuzung zwischen Kisokaidō und Hokkoku Kaidō ab, der „Nordlandstraße", die nach Jōetsu am Japanischen Meer führte.

Dominiert jedoch wird die Landschaft vom markanten Kegel des Asama, der nicht nur der höchste Berg der Gegend ist, sondern auch einer der aktivsten Vulkane Japans. In dem halben Jahrhundert, das der Veröffentlichung dieses Drucks vorausging, brach er viermal aus: 1783, zweimal 1803 und zuletzt 1815. Dem katastrophalen Ausbruch von 1783, auch als Tenmei-Eruption bekannt, fielen schätzungsweise 1400 Menschen und 1800 Häuser zum Opfer, Wasserwege wurden verschüttet, Ackerland und Ernten großflächig vernichtet. Zusätzlich von widrigen Wetterverhältnissen geplagt, litten weite Teile der Kantō-Region unter einer Hungersnot, die weitere 20 000 Menschenleben kostete. Die Hauptstadt Edo, immerhin 150 Kilometer entfernt, versank nach der Tenmei-Eruption unter einer 2,5 Zentimeter dicken Aschedecke (zur Tenmei-Eruption und ihren Folgen siehe Totman 1993, S. 238–240).

Eisen hat Oiwake wahrscheinlich nie besucht, doch der Asama war so berühmt, dass zahlreiche Bilder von dem Berg kursierten. Als Quelle für die Komposition dieses Entwurfs diente möglicherweise eine Abbildung in Band zwei der 1802 erschienenen *Sammlung wundervoller Landschaften (Sansui kikan shūi)* von Fuchigami Kyokkō (1753–1816). Sie zeigt den rauchenden Vulkan, wie er hoch über Karuizawa, Kutsukake, Oiwake und der sie verbindenden Straße thront. In den Reisehandbüchern *Illustrierter Wegweiser für die Kiso-Straße (Kisoji anken ezu)* und *Ansichten berühmter Stätten an der Kiso-Straße (Kisoji meisho zue)* ist der Berg ebenfalls abgebildet, und auch hier steigt aus seinem Krater Rauch auf.

Bei der Nummernangabe „22" im roten Stempel rechts neben dem Titel handelt es sich um einen Druckfehler; der Zählweise der Serie entsprechend müsste es „21" heißen. Unter dem linken Ellenbogen des Packpferdtreibers im Vordergrund klafft üblicherweise ein weißer Fleck im Bild, ein weiterer Mangel, der auf einigen Abzügen von Hand übermalt wurde.

Voyageurs et porteurs se succèdent en file indienne le long de la Kisokaidō, dont le parcours se poursuit vers le sud-ouest à travers les plaines herbeuses d'Oiwake. Le nom de cette station, littéralement « la bifurcation », vient de sa situation au point de jonction de la Kisokaidō et de l'Hokkoku Kaidō, la « route rurale du nord » menant à Jōetsu, sur le littoral de la mer du Japon.

Mais c'est le cône caractéristique du mont Asama qui domine ce paysage ; cette montagne est le plus haut sommet de la région et l'un des volcans les plus actifs du Japon. Au cours du demi-siècle ayant précédé la publication de cette estampe, il est entré en éruption à quatre reprises : en 1783, deux fois en 1803, puis en 1815. La catastrophe de 1783, connue sous le nom d'éruption de l'ère Tenmei, aurait fait 1400 victimes, détruit 1800 maisons, engorgé les voies navigables et causé des dommages considérables aux cultures et aux terres arables. De surcroît accablée par de très mauvaises conditions météorologiques, une grande partie de la région de Kantō subit une famine qui provoqua la mort de 20 000 personnes. À 150 kilomètres de là, la métropole d'Edo fut recouverte d'une couche de cendres de deux centimètres et demi (à propos de l'éruption de l'ère Tenmei et de ses conséquences, voir Totman 1993, pp. 238–240).

Il est peu probable qu'Eisen ait visité Oiwake, mais la célébrité du mont Asama était telle que de nombreuses illustrations du volcan étaient diffusées. L'une des sources possibles de la composition de ce dessin est une description du volcan fumant qui domine Karuizawa, Kutsukake, Oiwake et la route qui relie ces localités, figurant dans le deuxième volume de la *Collection de paysages merveilleux* (*Sansui kikan shūi*, 1802) de Fuchigami Kyokkō (1753–1816). On trouve aussi des descriptions de cette montagne, avec des volutes de fumée s'échappant de sa caldeira, dans les guides de voyage, *Guide illustré de la route Kiso* (*Kisoji anken ezu*) et *Collection de vues de paysages célèbres sur la route Kiso* (*Kisoji meisho zue*).

Le sceau rouge situé à droite du titre contient le numéro vingt-deux : il s'agit d'une faute d'impression, car le numéro correct est vingt et un, selon la numérotation de cette série. Sous le coude gauche du conducteur du cheval de bât visible au premier plan, un espace blanc apparaît généralement dans l'image : c'est aussi un défaut d'impression, corrigée par une retouche de peinture à la main sur certaines épreuves.

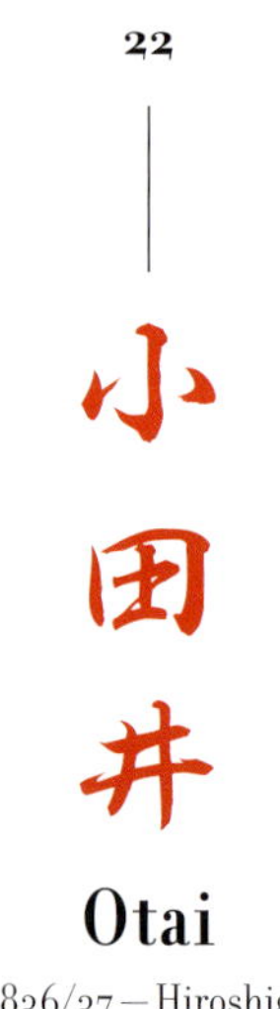

小田井

Otai

1836/37 — Hiroshige

At Otai, the Kisokaidō continues west, traversing the pampas grass moors that fan out from the foot of Mount Asama. In Hiroshige's design for this station, two parties of pilgrims travelling in opposite directions cross paths at a meandering stream. A ditch flowing through the centre of the village with clean water for irrigation is mentioned in the travel guidebook *Views of Famous Sights along the Kiso Road* (*Kisoji meisho zue*), and it is possible that Hiroshige had this description in mind when designing his print. The ditch provides the setting for a simple narrative of a group of wayfarers passing each other, and also relieves the otherwise monotonous landscape at this point in the journey.

The pilgrims wear white surplices and are carrying on their backs box-like packs made from wicker or wood called *oi*. The group on the left appears to be a family. The phrase "dōgyō sannin", meaning "three travelling together", can be read on the sedge hats of the adults. There are in fact four people here, as the mother leading her family has a baby bound to her chest. The figure approaching from the right is carrying a banner marked with the phrase "hondō zōritsu", announcing that the purpose of his pilgrimage is to raise funds for the construction of a *hondō* or main hall of a temple.

In 1843, Otai was a tiny village of just 319 people that offered few options for lodging, so ordinary travellers would be more conveniently accommodated at the neighbouring stations of Oiwake or Iwamurata. There were, however, lodgings specifically reserved for female members of the imperial and *daimyō* families, thus earning the station the nickname "Hime no yado" (lodging for princesses).

Durch die Pampasgrasmoore, die sich am Fuß des Asama ausbreiten, führt der Kisokaidō in Otai weiter nach Westen. In Hiroshiges Entwurf zu dieser Station kommt einer Pilgergruppe an einem mäandernden Wasserlauf ein einzelner Pilger entgegen. Ein von klarem Wasser gespeister Bewässerungsbach, der durch die Dorfmitte fließt, wird in dem Reiseführer *Ansichten berühmter Stätten an der Kiso-Straße (Kisoji meisho zue)* erwähnt, und möglicherweise hatte Hiroshige diese Beschreibung im Sinn, als er das Blatt entwarf. Der Bach bildet die Kulisse für eine schlichte Szene, in der sich die Wege einer Gruppe Fußreisender kreuzen, und lockert zudem die ansonsten monotone Landschaft an diesem Punkt der Reise auf.

Die Pilger tragen weiße Gewänder und auf dem Rücken kistenförmige Bündel aus Korb oder Holz namens *oi*. Bei der Gruppe links scheint es sich um eine Familie zu handeln. Auf den Grashüten der Eltern ist die Wendung „dōgyō sannin" zu lesen, was so viel heißt wie „drei, die gemeinsam reisen". Tatsächlich aber ist die Familie zu viert: Die Mutter, die die Gruppe anführt, hat sich ihr Baby vor die Brust gebunden. Der sich von rechts nähernde Wanderer trägt ein Banner in der Hand, dessen Aufschrift „hondō zōritsu" den Zweck seiner Pilgerreise verkündet: Er sammelt Geld für den Bau eines *hondō*, der Haupthalle eines Tempels.

1843 war Otai ein winziges Dorf mit 319 Einwohnern, das nur wenige Übernachtungsmöglichkeiten bot, sodass gewöhnliche Reisende bequemer in den Nachbarstationen Oiwake und Iwamurata unterkamen. Es gab jedoch Herbergen, die speziell für weibliche Mitglieder der kaiserlichen Familie und der *daimyō*-Clans reserviert waren, was der Station den Spitznamen „Hime no yado" (Prinzessinnenunterkunft) einbrachte.

À Otai, la Kisokaidō continue vers l'ouest à travers les landes d'herbe des pampas qui s'évasent au pied du mont Asama. Dans l'estampe réalisée par Hiroshige pour cette station, deux groupes de pèlerins allant dans des directions opposées se croisent à un cours d'eau sinueux. La *Collection de vues de paysages célèbres sur la route Kiso (Kisoji meisho zue)* fait mention d'un fossé traversant le centre du village, dans lequel coule une eau propre pour l'irrigation ; il est possible qu'Hiroshige ait pensé à cette description en réalisant cette illustration. Ce fossé est le cadre d'une histoire simple mettant en scène un groupe de voyageurs qui se croisent ; il permet aussi d'animer le paysage, monotone à ce stade du périple.

Les pèlerins sont vêtus de surplis blancs et portent sur le dos des ballots en forme de boîtes, faits en osier ou dans un bois appelé *oi*. Le groupe de gauche semble être une famille. Sur les chapeaux en carex des adultes on peut lire l'inscription « dōgyō sannin » qui signifie « trois personnes voyagent ensemble ». En réalité, ils sont quatre, car la mère qui conduit la famille porte un bébé tout contre sa poitrine. Le personnage arrivant de la droite porte une bannière sur laquelle sont inscrits les mots « hondō zōritsu » : ils annoncent le but de son pèlerinage qui consiste à récolter de l'argent pour la construction d'un *hondō*, ou salle principale d'un temple.

En 1843, Otai était un tout petit village de 319 habitants seulement, qui ne proposait guère d'hébergements, de sorte que les voyageurs ordinaires trouvaient plus facilement le gîte dans les stations voisines d'Oiwake et d'Iwamurata. Toutefois, des logements spécialement réservés aux femmes des familles de l'empereur et des *daïmio* étaient disponibles, ce qui valut à la station le surnom de « Hime no yado » (logements pour les princesses).

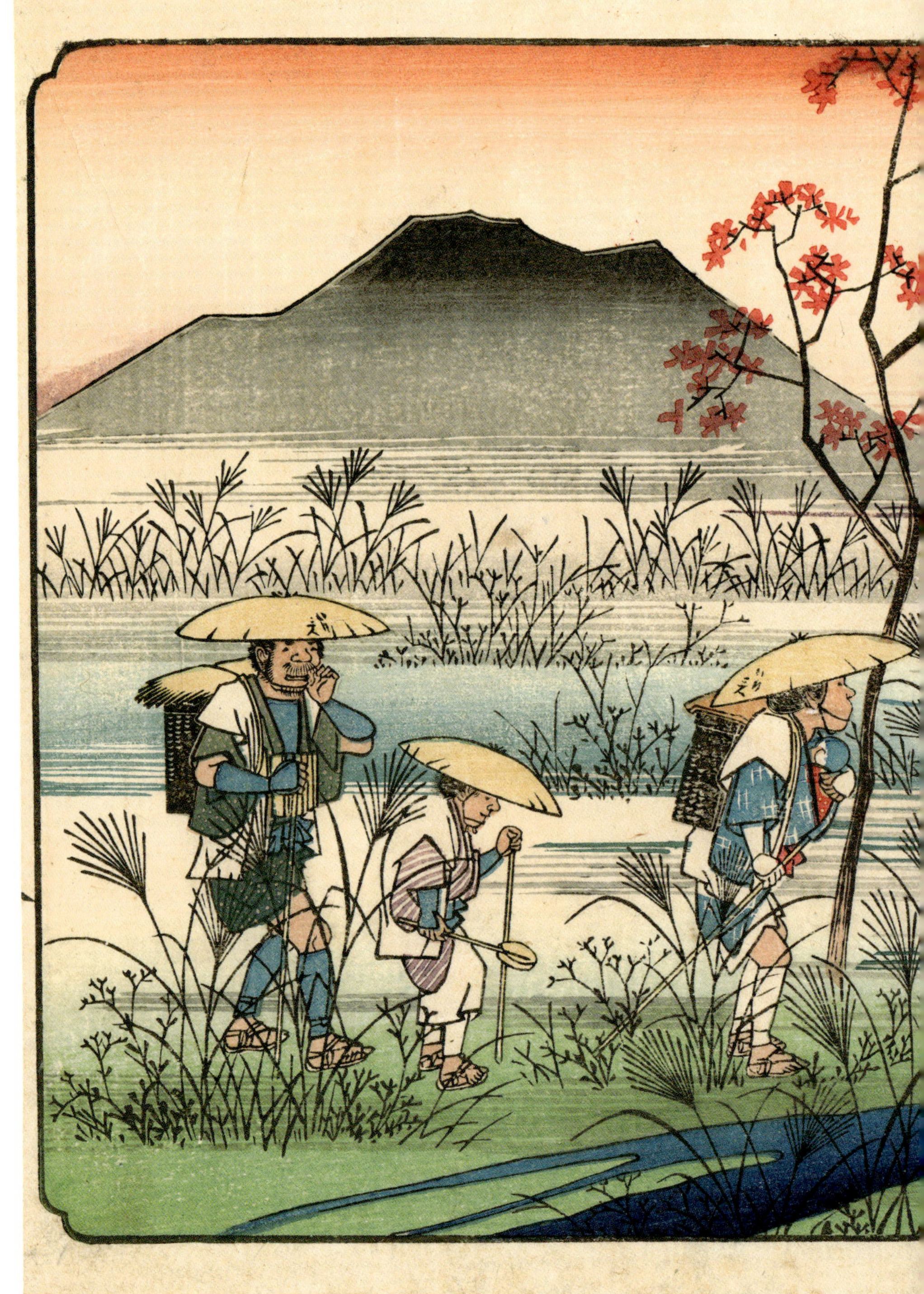
えちこ
いちこ
え

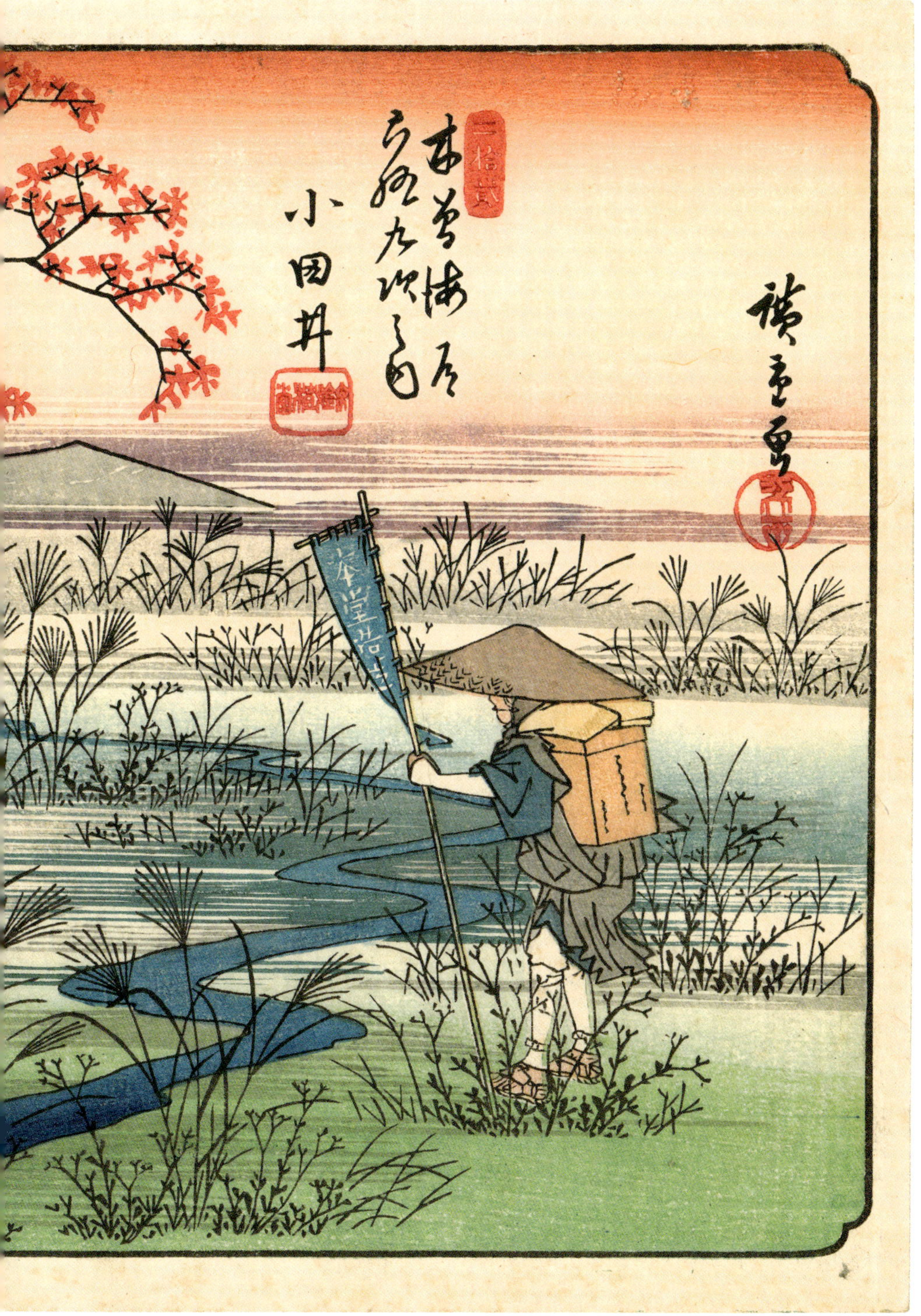

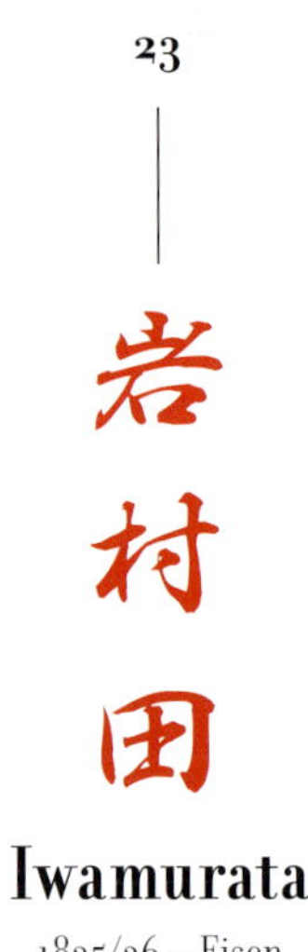

23

Iwamurata

1835/36 – Eisen

Eisen's design for Iwamurata shows seven blind men in the midst of a wayside brawl. Purses have been dropped and coins scattered, suggesting that the scuffle has broken out over money; perhaps the men are beggars vying for rights over this stretch of the road. To the right, a dog is barking excitedly at the spectacle. Further into the distance is a cluster of farmhouses with thatched roofs, and beyond these, Mount Asama. On the left, scarecrows made from string and strips of paper or rags protect an embankment planted with new crops. If we consult the travel guidebook *Illustrated Guide to the Kiso Road* (*Kisoji anken ezu*), Eisen's composition seems to locate the viewer in the south-west outskirts of the town, looking north-west over the plains of Imaigahara.

The crude humour of this design is something of an anomaly among the picturesque landscapes and bucolic scenery that dominate the rest of the series. The theory that the fracas may allude to an altercation between the publisher Takenouchi Magohachi and the two artists, Eisen and Hiroshige, is unfounded as this print was published long before Hiroshige joined the series. Eisen was actually inspired by a scene in the book *An Album of Pictures by Itchō* (*Itchō gafu*, 1770), a collection of compositions by Hanabusa Itchō (1652–1724) compiled in 1770 by Suzuki Rinshō (1732–1803). The scene is entitled *Quarrel of Blind Men* (*Zatō no kenka*) and shows three blind men fighting in a similar way. Eisen increased the number of men to seven and swapped the position of the barking dog, from left to right, with that of the wooden fence.

In 1703 Iwamurata was transferred from Akanuma Domain, in Musashino Province, to Shinano Province, thus becoming the seat of the Naitō clan. Located 4.7 kilometres (3 miles) from Otai, at the intersection of the Kōshūkaidō, Shimonitaidō and Zenkōji Kaidō roads, Iwamurata flourished as a trade hub. The town had a population of 1,637 in 1843 and, according to the travel guidebook *Views of Famous Sights along the Kiso Road* (*Kisoji meisho zue*), many merchants resided here. Construction work on a castle began in the early 1860s under Naitō Masanobu (1845–1880), but the project was abandoned shortly thereafter with the collapse of the Tokugawa shogunate and the abolition of feudal domains.

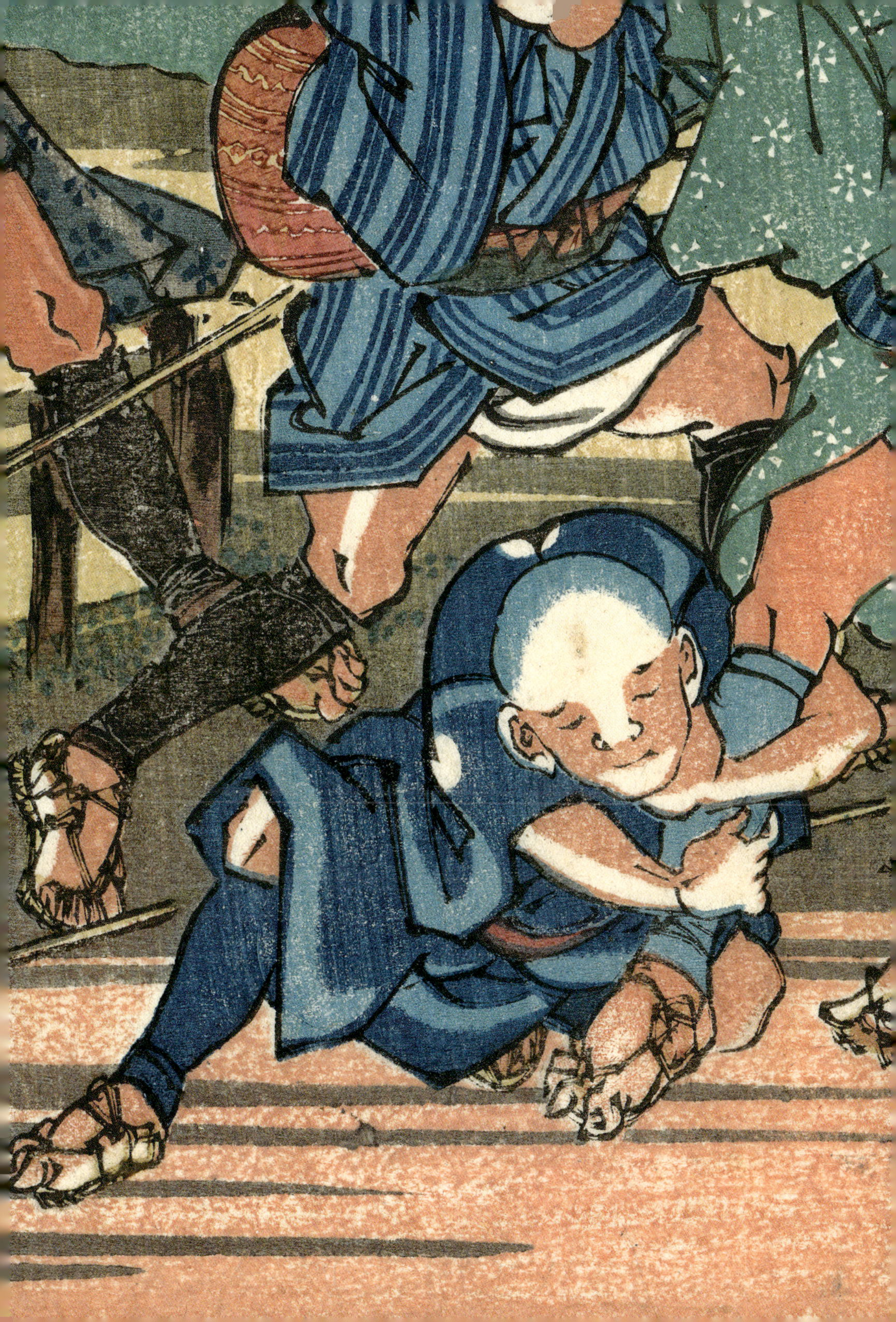

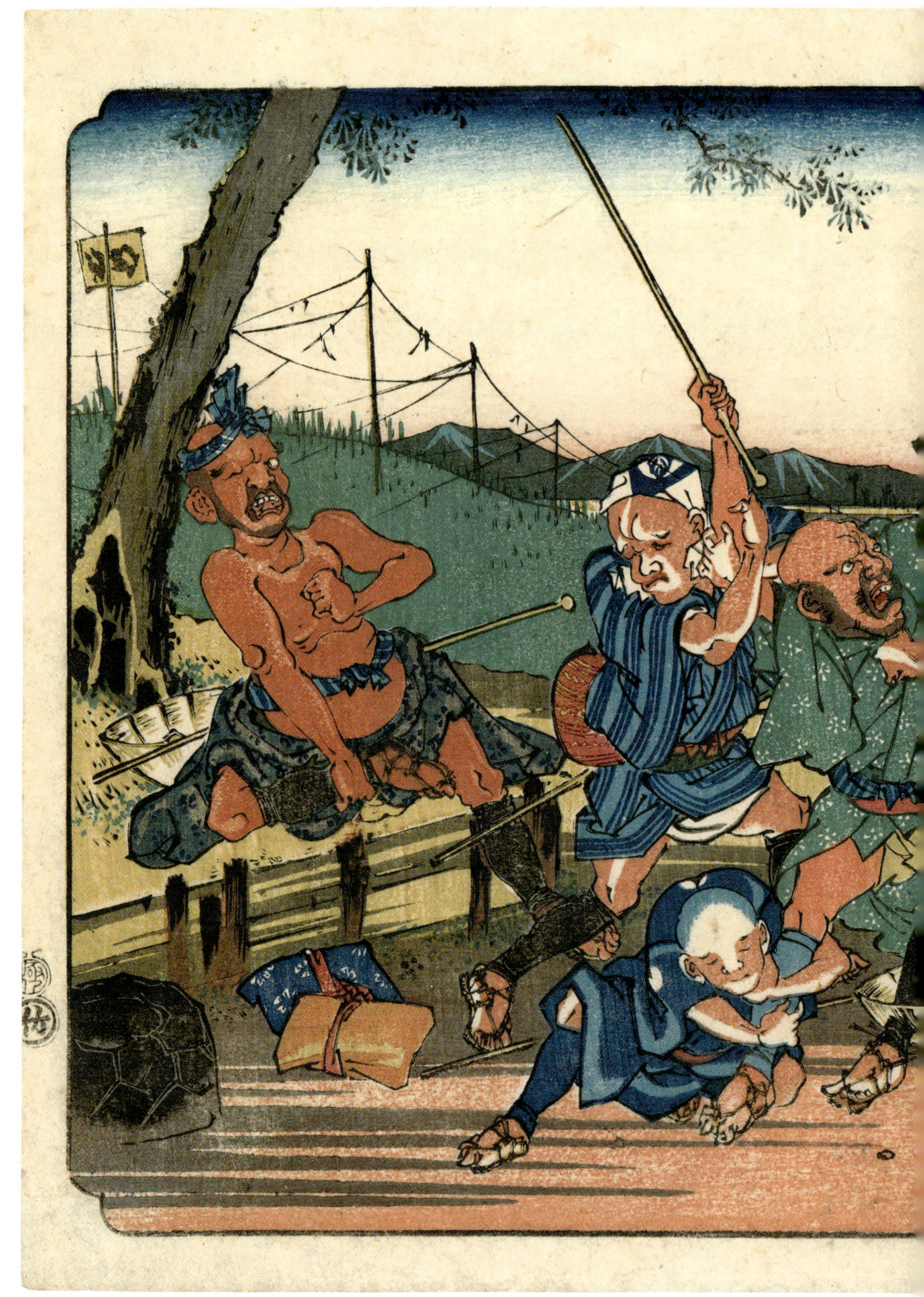

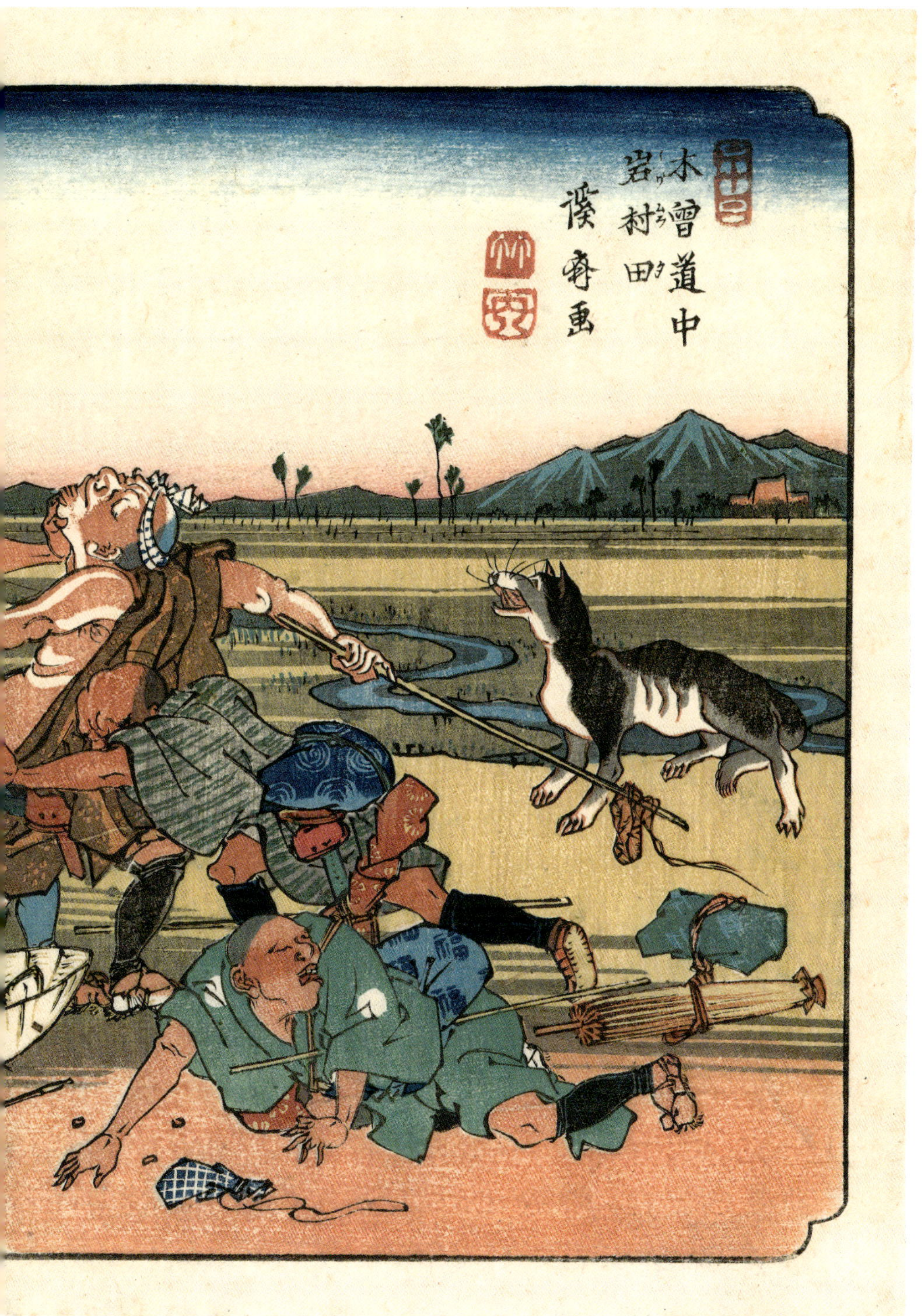
二十二
木曾道中
岩村田
溪斎画

Eisens Entwurf für Iwamurata zeigt sieben blinde Männer bei einer Prügelei am Wegesrand. Am Boden liegende Geldbeutel und verstreute Münzen deuten darauf hin, dass Geldstreitigkeiten hinter dem Handgemenge stecken. Vielleicht sind die Männer Bettler und kämpfen um ihre Vorrechte auf diesem Straßenabschnitt. Rechts im Bild verbellt ein Hund aufgeregt das Spektakel. In der Ferne ragt hinter einer Gruppe strohgedeckter Bauernhäuser der Vulkan Asama auf. Auf einer Böschung zur Linken sichern Vogelscheuchen aus Schnüren und Papierstreifen ein frisch bestelltes Feld. Zieht man den Reiseführer *Illustrierter Wegweiser für die Kiso-Straße (Kisoji anken ezu)* hinzu, scheint der Betrachter in Eisens Komposition den Blick vom südwestlichen Ortsrand über die Ebene von Imaigahara nach Nordwesten zu richten.

Zwischen den malerischen Landschaften und idyllischen Kulissen, die den übrigen Zyklus beherrschen, fällt das Blatt mit seinem derben Humor ein wenig aus dem Rahmen. Die Theorie, dass der Tumult auf eine Auseinandersetzung zwischen dem Verleger Takenouchi Magohachi und den beiden Künstlern Eisen und Hiroshige anspielen könnte, entbehrt der Grundlage, da dieser Druck veröffentlicht wurde, lange bevor Hiroshige zu dem Projekt stieß. Tatsächlich ließ sich Eisen von einer Szene in dem Band *Ein Itchō-Bilderalbum (Itchō gafu, 1770)* inspirieren, einer Sammlung von Werken Hanabusa Itchōs (1652–1724), die Suzuki Rinshō (1732–1803) im Jahr 1770 zusammengestellt hatte. Die Szene mit dem Titel *Streit unter Blinden (Zatō no kenka)* zeigt drei blinde Männer, die auf ähnliche Weise miteinander kämpfen. Eisen erhöhte die Personenzahl auf sieben und tauschte die Position des bellenden Hundes ebenso wie die des Holzzauns von links nach rechts.

Iwamurata wurde 1703 vom in der Provinz Musashino gelegenen Lehen Akanuma in die Provinz Shinano verlegt und zum Sitz des Naitō-Clans erklärt. 4,7 Kilometer von Otai entfernt am Schnittpunkt der Straßen Kōshūkaidō, Shimonitaidō und Zenkōji Kaidō gelegen, war der Ort 1843 ein florierendes Handelszentrum mit 1637 Einwohnern, unter denen sich laut Reiseführer *Ansichten berühmter Stätten an der Kiso-Straße (Kisoji meisho zue)* zahlreiche Kaufleute befanden. Unter Naitō Masanobu (1845–1880) begannen Anfang der 1860er Jahre Bauarbeiten für eine Burg, die mit dem Zusammenbruch des Tokugawa-Shogunats und der Abschaffung des Feudalsystems schon kurze Zeit später wieder aufgegeben wurden.

Dans l'illustration d'Eisen pour Iwamurata, on voit sept hommes aveugles en pleine bagarre sur le bord de la route. Des bourses sont à terre et des pièces de monnaie sont éparpillées, signes que l'argent doit être la cause de la rixe ; ces hommes sont peut-être des mendiants qui se disputent pour avoir le droit de demander l'aumône sur cette partie de la route. À droite, un chien aboie avec excitation devant ce spectacle. On devine au loin un groupe de maisons aux toits de chaume et, au-delà, le mont Asama. À gauche, des épouvantails faits de ficelle et de bandes de papier ou de vieux tissus protègent un talus où poussent de nouvelles cultures. La consultation du *Guide illustré de la route Kiso* (*Kisoji anken ezu*) semble indiquer que la composition d'Eisen situe le spectateur à la périphérie sud-ouest de la ville et lui offre le point de vue nord-ouest sur les plaines d'Imaigahara.

L'humour rudimentaire de cette estampe relève un peu de l'anomalie parmi les paysages pittoresques et les cadres bucoliques qui dominent le reste de cette série. La théorie selon laquelle cette bagarre ferait allusion à une altercation entre l'éditeur Takenouchi Magohachi et les deux artistes, Eisen et Hiroshige, paraît sans fondement, car cette gravure a été publiée bien avant qu'Hiroshige ne participe à la série. En réalité, Eisen a été inspiré par une scène figurant dans l'*Album d'images d'Itchō* (*Itchō gafu*, 1770), recueil de compositions signées Hanabusa Itchō (1652–1724) et réunies par Suzuki Rinshō (1732–1803) en 1770. Dans cette scène intitulée *Querelle entre aveugles* (*Zatō no kenka*), trois hommes aveugles se battent de manière semblable. Eisen y a ajouté quatre hommes et inversé la position du chien qui aboie, passé de gauche à droite, avec celle de la clôture en bois.

Iwamurata est née à l'occasion de son transfert du domaine d'Akanuma, situé dans la province de Musashino-kuni, vers celle de Shinano-kuni en 1703, devenant ainsi le siège du clan Naitō. Localisée à 4,7 kilomètres d'Otai, au carrefour des routes Kōshūkaidō, Shimonitaidō et Zenkōji Kaidō, Iwamurata dut sa prospérité au commerce. La ville comptait 1637 habitants en 1843 et, selon la *Collection de vues de paysages célèbres sur la route Kiso* (*Kisoji meisho zue*), de nombreux marchands y résidaient. Au début des années 1860 fut entamée la construction d'un château sous le régime de Naitō Masanobu (1845–1880), mais le projet fut abandonné peu de temps après, en raison de la chute du shogunat de Tokugawa et de l'abolition des domaines féodaux.

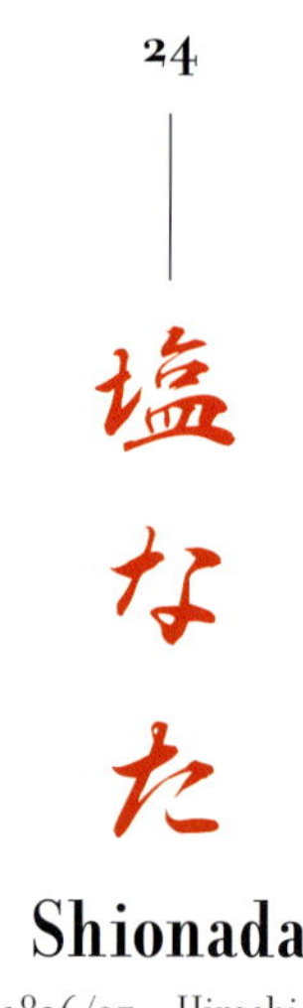

24

Shionada

1836/37 – Hiroshige

Shionada was located on the eastern bank of the Chikuma River. Fed by melting snow from the eastern slopes of the Shinano and Hida mountains, the Chikuma is the longest river in Japan. After winding through present-day north-eastern Nagano Prefecture, it converges with the Sai River near Nagano city before crossing into Niigata Prefecture, where its name changes to the Shinano River, finally emptying into the Japan Sea near Niigata city.

To reach the village from Iwamurata, 5.1 kilometres (3.2 miles) to the east, the 80-metre (263 feet) expanse of the Chikuma had to be crossed by ferry, porter, or simply walking across, depending on the depth and current of the river. Hiroshige's design depicts three porters, wincing from the cold, returning from a crossing to a riverside ferry station to join their comrades warming themselves by the hearth. One has wrapped himself in a straw mat to cover up against the chill. The mountains in the background, printed in two different colours to enhance the illusion of depth, suggest that the near bank is the Shionada side of the river.

Frequent and sometimes catastrophic floods washed away the bridges constructed over the river and made the crossing hazardous or even unfeasible at certain times of the year. It was for this reason that in 1602 villagers from three surrounding villages were relocated and Shionada established here, just 2.9 kilometres (1.8 miles) from the next station, Yawata.

Shionada lag am Ostufer des Chikuma. Von der Schneeschmelze an den Osthängen der Berge Shinano und Hida gespeist, ist der Chikuma der längste Fluss Japans. Nachdem er sich durch den Nordosten der heutigen Präfektur Nagano gewunden hat, fließt er nahe der Stadt Nagano mit dem Sai zusammen, bevor er die Präfektur Niigata erreicht, wo er den Namen Shinano annimmt und schließlich in der Nähe der Stadt Niigata ins Japanische Meer mündet.

Um das Dorf vom 5,1 Kilometer weiter östlich gelegenen Iwamurata aus zu erreichen, musste der 80 Meter breite Chikuma je nach Tiefe und Strömung per Fähre, mit Trägern oder schlicht zu Fuß überwunden werden. In Hiroshiges Entwurf kehren drei fröstelnde Träger nach einer Flussdurchquerung zu ihren Kameraden zurück, die sich an der Feuerstelle einer am Ufer gelegenen Fährstation aufwärmen. Einer der drei hat sich zum Schutz gegen die Kälte in eine Strohmatte gehüllt. Die Berge im Hintergrund, die in zwei Farben gedruckt wurden, um die Illusion von Tiefe zu erzeugen, deuten darauf hin, dass das im Vordergrund gezeigte Ufer dasjenige ist, an dem auch Shionada liegt.

Häufige und mitunter verheerende Überschwemmungen rissen die über den Fluss gebauten Brücken mit sich fort und machten die Querung zu bestimmten Jahreszeiten gefährlich oder sogar unmöglich. Aus diesem Grund wurden 1602 die Bewohner dreier umliegender Dörfer umgesiedelt, um hier, nur 2,9 Kilometer von der nächsten Station Yawata entfernt, die Station Shionada zu gründen.

Shionada se trouvait sur la rive orientale du Chikuma. Alimenté par la fonte des neiges provenant des versants est des chaînes de montagnes Shinano et Hida, le Chikuma est le plus long fleuve du Japon. Après avoir serpenté à travers le nord-est de l'actuelle préfecture de Nagano, il se mélange à la rivière Sai, près de la ville de Nagano, avant de traverser la préfecture de Niigata, où il prend le nom de Shinano, et de se jeter enfin dans la mer du Japon, près de Niigata.

Pour atteindre ce village depuis Iwamurata, situé à 5,1 kilomètres à l'est, il fallait franchir les quatre-vingts mètres qui séparent les rives du Chikuma par bateau ou porteur, ou tout simplement à gué si la profondeur et le courant le permettaient. L'estampe d'Hiroshige représente trois porteurs, grelottant de froid, alors qu'ils reviennent d'une traversée et se dirigent vers un embarcadère où ils vont se joindre à leurs collègues qui se réchauffent auprès d'un âtre. L'un d'eux s'est emmitouflé dans une natte de paille pour se protéger du froid. Les montagnes visibles au loin, imprimées avec deux teintes différentes afin d'accentuer l'illusion de profondeur, semblent indiquer que la rive la plus proche est celle de Shionada.

Des inondations fréquentes, et parfois catastrophiques, emportaient les ponts construits sur le fleuve et rendaient sa traversée dangereuse, voire impossible, à certaines périodes de l'année. C'est pour cette raison qu'en 1602 les habitants de trois villages voisins furent déplacés et que naquit Shionada, à 2,9 kilomètres seulement de la station suivante, Yawata.

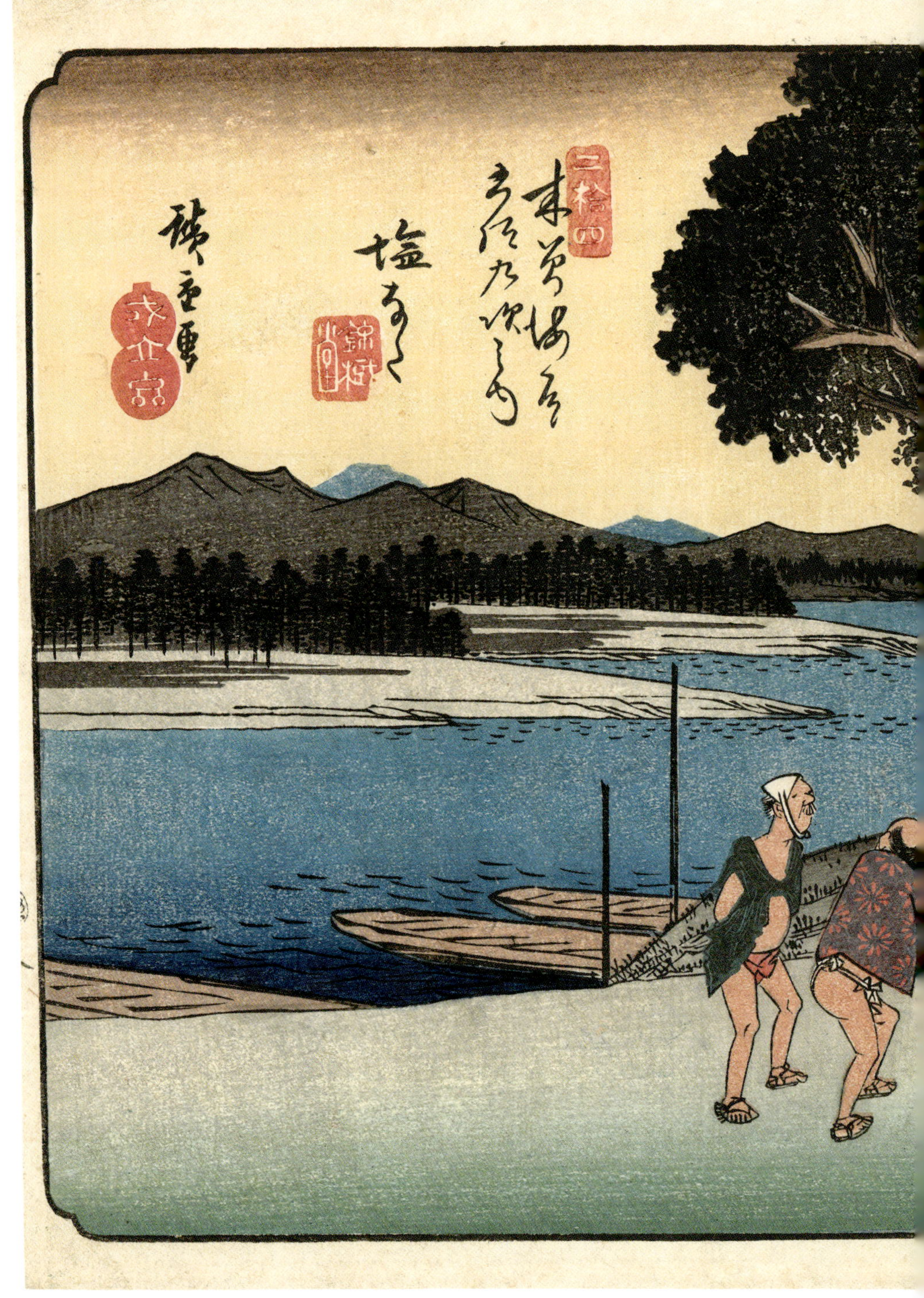

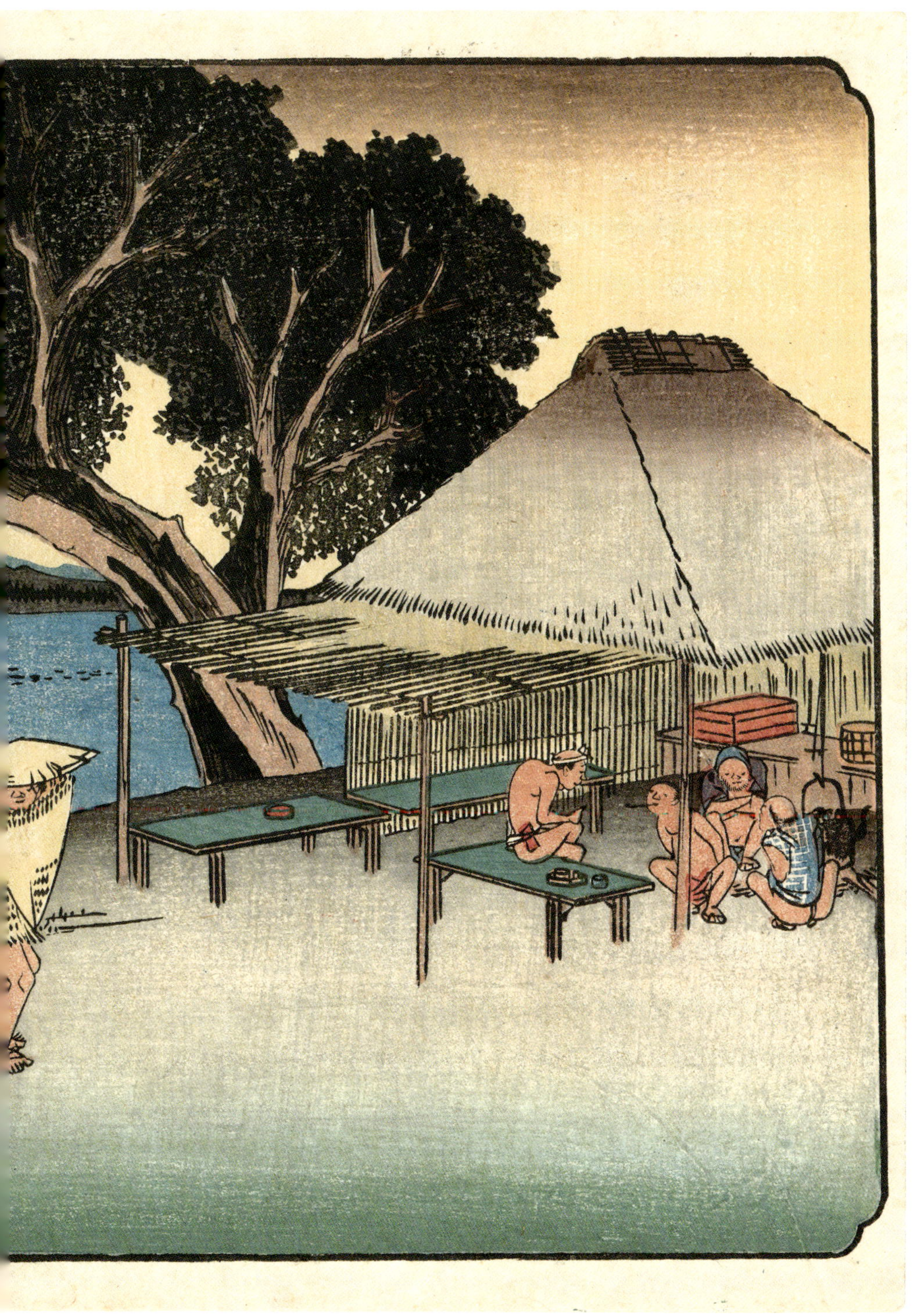

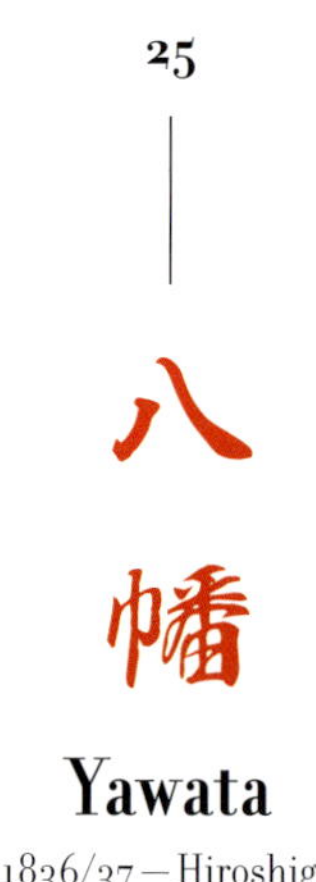

Yawata

1836/37 — Hiroshige

Hiroshige's design for Yawata focuses on the comings and goings over a rickety wooden bridge under the shadow of Mount Asama. Approaching the near bank, an elderly wayfarer is carrying a straw mat; behind him, a peasant has a carrying pole on his shoulder. Further into the distance, a woman is just emerging over the rise with a bundle under one arm and a baby tucked into the back of her kimono. Heading in the opposite direction, a small child stoops under the weight of a basket heavily laden with cut grass or branches. Ahead of him, a farm worker carrying a hoe is enjoying his pipe on his way home. A tobacco pouch and pipe case can be seen dangling from his left hand. The fading light of late afternoon is conveyed masterfully by the depiction of the mountains in the background without outlining, by the grey bamboo bowing with the evening breeze and the black *bokashi* at the upper limit of the sky.

To protect the soft banks of the river from eroding, wooden posts have been driven into the muddy flats in the foreground and gabions made from bamboo and rocks placed at the river bend. The river crossing is likely to be on the Nakazawa River on the east side of Yawata, and the flimsy bridge in Hiroshige's design would have been rather unsuitable for the traffic that must have gone over it. Shortly after crossing the river, travellers coming from the direction of Shionada would see the *torii* gateway of the Hachiman shrine on the right, from which the station received its name, "Yawata" being the old reading of the characters used to write "Hachiman". The oldest extant building at the shrine is a hall called Kōrasha, situated at the rear of the shrine grounds. Constructed in 1491 by the lord of Mochizuki Castle, Shigeno Tōtōmi-no-kami Mitsushige (dates unknown), the Kōrasha was designated an Important Cultural Property in 1950. Because the name "Kōra" was originally written with the same Chinese characters used to write "Goryeo", as in the Korean kingdom Goryeo (918–1392), the hall is reputed to have been dedicated to Korean migrants to Japan. Alternatively, Hiroshige may have had in mind a waterway that flowed through the village of Momozawa to the west of the town.

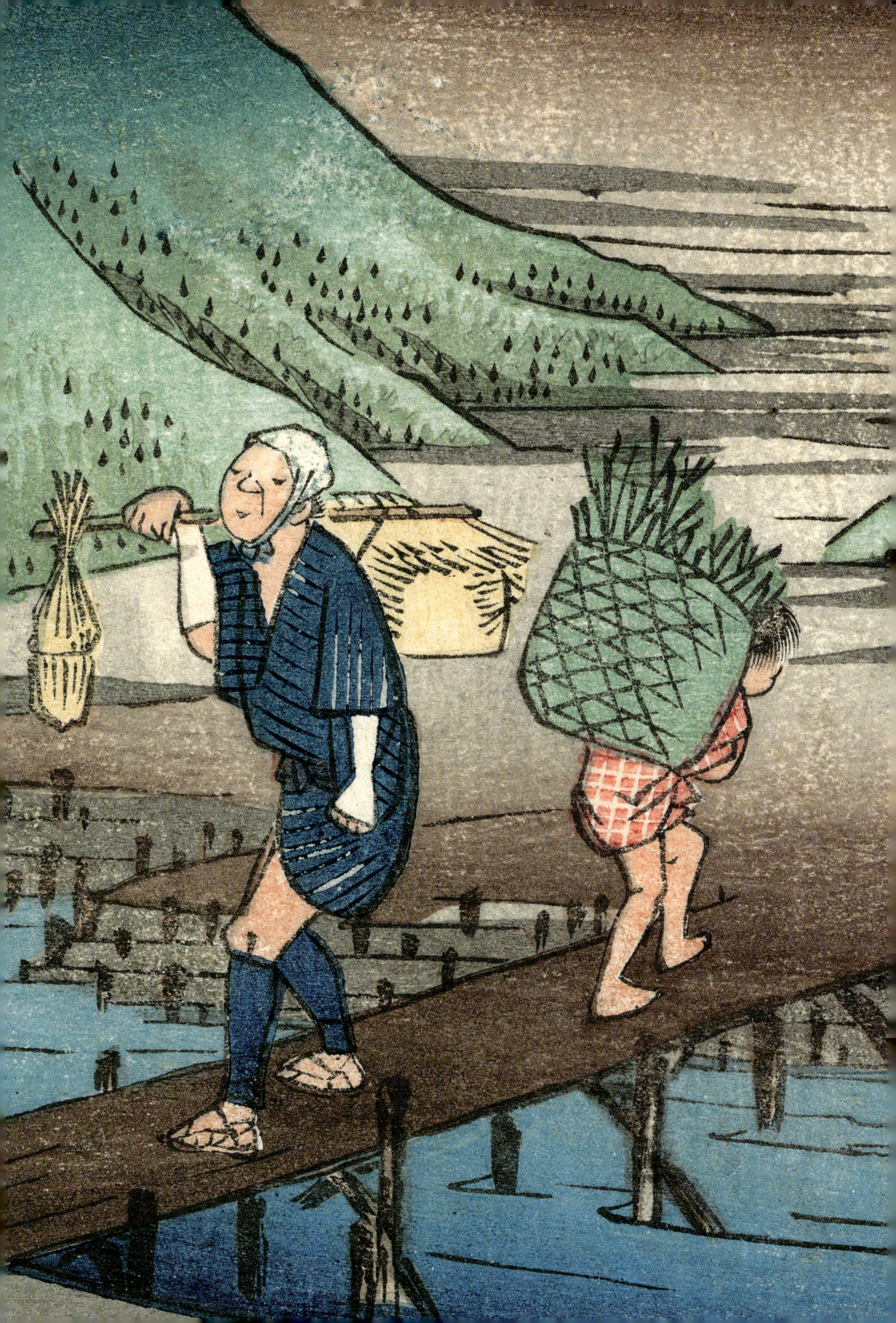

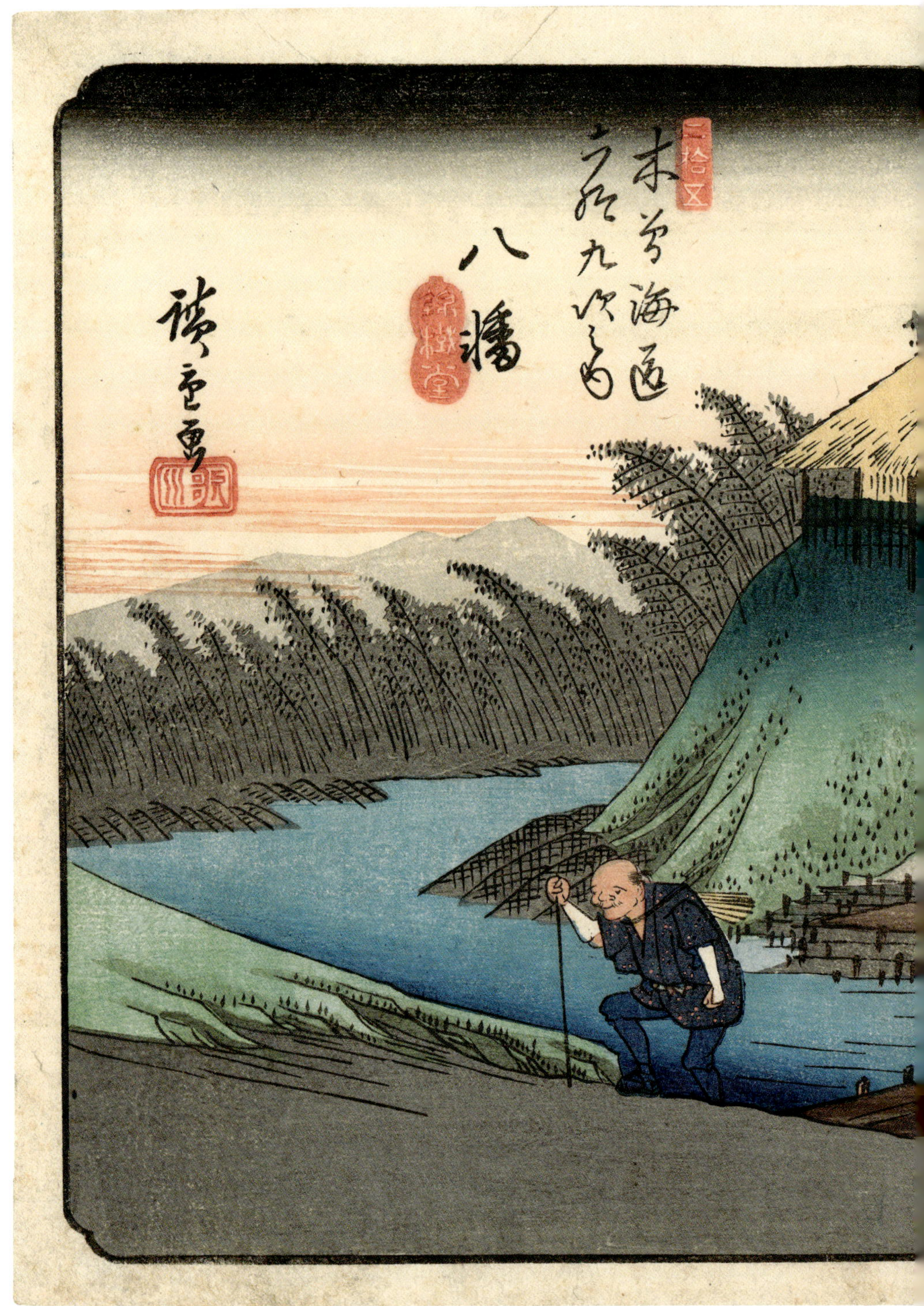

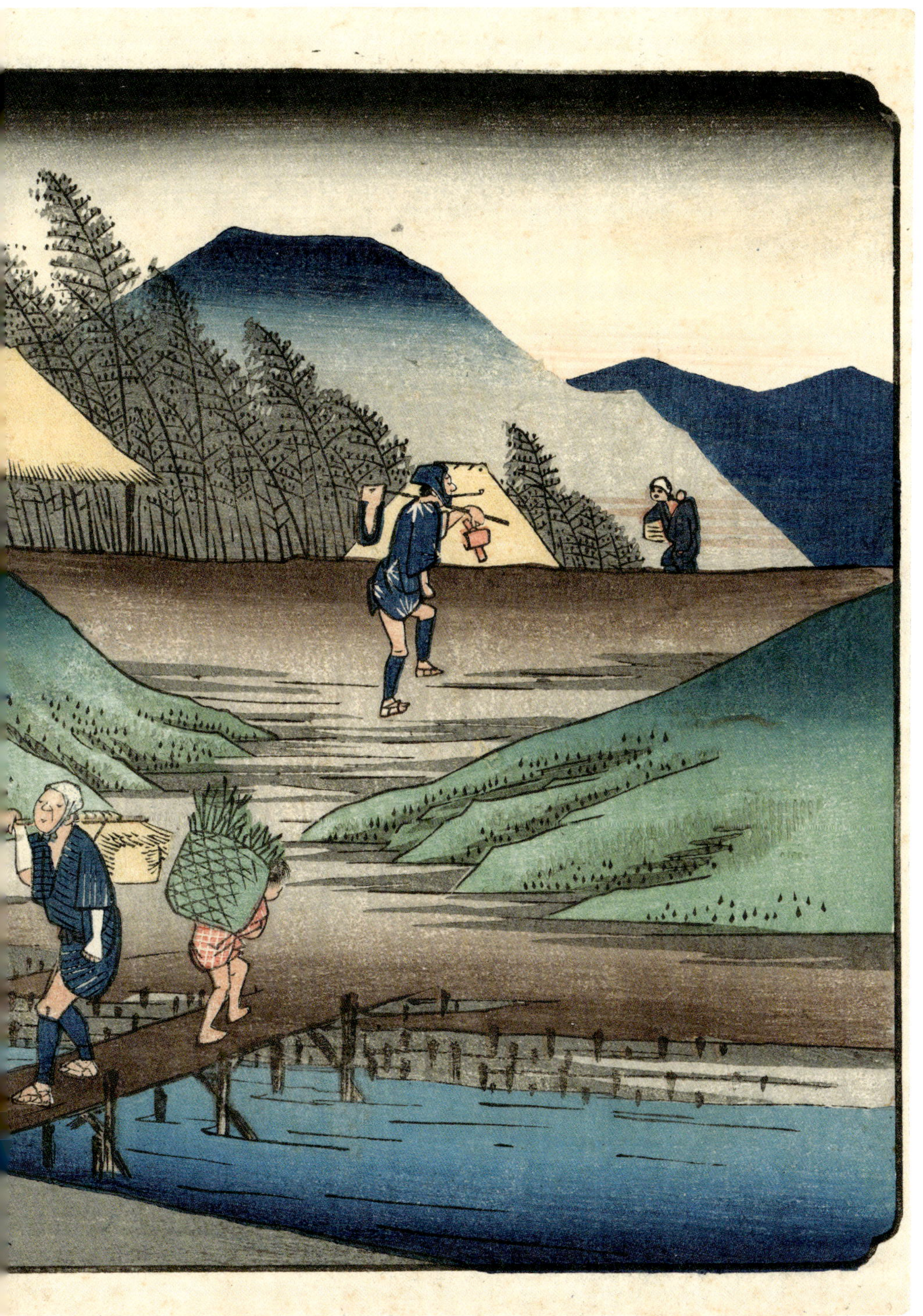

The station was established to facilitate passage between Mochizuki and Shionada, as poor weather and difficult terrain made this leg of the route challenging at certain times of the year. Between the late 16th and early 17th centuries, villagers were relocated from surrounding villages to serve the new station. However, in 1843, Yawata still had only three inns for regular travellers, the smallest number of any post station on this route.

Hiroshiges Entwurf für Yawata stellt im Schatten des Vulkans Asama das Kommen und Gehen auf einer wackeligen Holzbrücke in den Mittelpunkt. Ein älterer Wanderer mit Strohmatte nähert sich dem diesseitigen Uferdamm. Ihm folgt ein Bauer mit einer Tragestange über der Schulter. Weiter hinten taucht gerade eine Frau hinter der Anhöhe auf, die ein Bündel unter dem Arm und ein Baby unter ihrem Kimono auf dem Rücken trägt. In entgegengesetzter Richtung schleppt sich ein kleines Kind unter dem Gewicht einer mit Gras oder Zweigen schwer beladenen Kiepe in gebeugter Haltung vorwärts. Vor ihm genießt ein Landarbeiter auf dem Heimweg, die Hacke geschultert, seine Pfeife. Tabaksbeutel und Pfeifenetui baumeln lose in seiner linken Hand. Die ohne Umrisslinien angelegten Berge im Hintergrund, der graue Bambus, der sich in der Abendbrise wiegt, und das schwarze *bokashi* am oberen Himmelsrand geben das nachlassende Licht des späten Nachmittags meisterhaft wieder.

Wie im Vordergrund des Bildes zu sehen, wurden Holzpfähle in den Schlick getrieben, um ein Auswaschen der weichen Uferböschungen zu verhindern. Aus demselben Grund sind mit Steinen gefüllte Schotterkästen aus Bambus, sog. Gabionen, in der Biegung des Flusses platziert. Der Flussübergang führt vermutlich im Osten Yawatas über den Nakazawa, und der schmale Steg in Hiroshiges Blatt wäre für das tatsächliche Verkehrsaufkommen an dieser Stelle eher untauglich gewesen. Kurz nach der Flussquerung erblickten Reisende aus Richtung Shionada auf der rechten Seite das *torii* (Tor) zum Hachiman-Schrein, dem die Station ihren Namen verdankt: „Yawata" war die alte Lesart der Zeichen für „Hachiman". Das älteste erhaltene Gebäude des Schreins ist eine Halle namens Kōrasha im hinteren Teil des Geländes. Sie wurde 1491 von Shigeno Tōtōmi-no-kami Mitsushige (Lebensdaten unbekannt), dem Fürsten der Burg Mochizuki, erbaut und 1950 zum „bedeutenden Kulturgut" erklärt. Weil für den Namen „Kōra" ursprünglich dieselben chinesischen Schriftzeichen verwendet wurden wie für das koreanische Königreich „Goryeo" (918–1392), soll die Halle angeblich koreanischen Einwanderern gewidmet gewesen sein. Alternativ könnte Hiroshige einen Wasserweg im Sinn gehabt haben, der durch das Dorf Momozawa im Westen Yawatas verlief.

Die Station wurde gegründet, um die Reise zwischen Mochizuki und Shionada zu erleichtern, da dieser Streckenabschnitt wegen schlechten Wetters und des schwierigen Terrains den Reisenden zu bestimmten Jahreszeiten einiges abverlangte. Obwohl zwischen dem späten 16. und frühen 17. Jahrhundert Bewohner aus umliegenden Dörfern umgesiedelt worden waren, um der neuen Station zu dienen, gab es in Yawata 1843 nur drei Herbergen für gewöhnliche Reisende, die wenigsten unter allen Poststationen auf dem Kisokaidō.

L'illustration d'Hiroshige pour la station de Yawata met en scène des allées et venues sur une passerelle en bois branlante, à l'ombre du mont Asama. Abordant la rive la plus proche, un vieil homme marche en portant une natte de paille ; un paysan le suit, une palanche sur l'épaule. Au loin, une femme apparaît au sommet de la montée, portant un ballot sous le bras et, sur le dos, un bébé enveloppé dans son kimono. Venant de l'autre direction, un petit enfant peine sous le poids d'un panier lourdement chargé d'herbe coupée ou de branchages. Devant lui, un ouvrier agricole portant une houe fume la pipe en rentrant chez lui. De sa main gauche pendent une blague à tabac et un étui pour sa pipe. La lumière de fin de journée est rendue à la perfection par les montagnes représentées sans contour à l'arrière-plan, par le gris des bambous qui ploient dans le vent du soir et par le *bokashi* noir qui délimite la partie supérieure du ciel.

Afin d'empêcher l'érosion des rives meubles de la rivière, des pieux en bois ont été plantés dans le lit vaseux, au premier plan, et des gabions de bambous et de pierres déposés dans la courbe de la rivière. Il s'agit probablement du franchissement de la Nakazawa, à l'est de Yawata ; la passerelle fragile dessinée par Hiroshige n'aurait guère convenu au trafic qui l'aurait empruntée. Peu après avoir traversé la rivière, les voyageurs venant de Shionada découvraient la porte *torii* du sanctuaire d'Hachiman, à droite, qui a donné à la station son nom de « Yawata », ancienne lecture des caractères employés pour écrire « Hachiman ». Le bâtiment le plus ancien du sanctuaire encore existant est une salle appelée Kōrasha, située au fond de l'enceinte du sanctuaire. Édifiée en 1491 par Shigeno Tōtōmi-no-kami Mitsushige (dates inconnues), seigneur du château de Mochizuki, la Kōrasha a été inscrite sur la liste du « patrimoine culturel important » en 1950. Étant donné que le nom « Kōra » s'écrivait initialement avec les caractères chinois employés pour écrire « Goryeo », comme dans le « royaume coréen » Goryeo (918–1392), cette salle est censée avoir été consacrée aux Coréens ayant immigré au Japon. Autre explication, c'est peut-être à un cours d'eau qui traversait le village de Momozawa, à l'ouest de la ville, qu'Hiroshige a pensé.

Cette station avait été créée afin de faciliter le passage entre Mochizuki et Shionada, car le mauvais temps et le terrain accidenté rendaient cette section du parcours très difficile à certaines époques de l'année. Au tournant des XVIe et XVIIe siècles, les habitants des villages voisins furent déplacés pour faire vivre la nouvelle station. Pourtant, en 1843, Yawata ne comptait toujours que trois auberges pour les voyageurs ordinaires ; c'était le plus petit nombre d'auberges qu'on pouvait trouver dans une station de cette route.

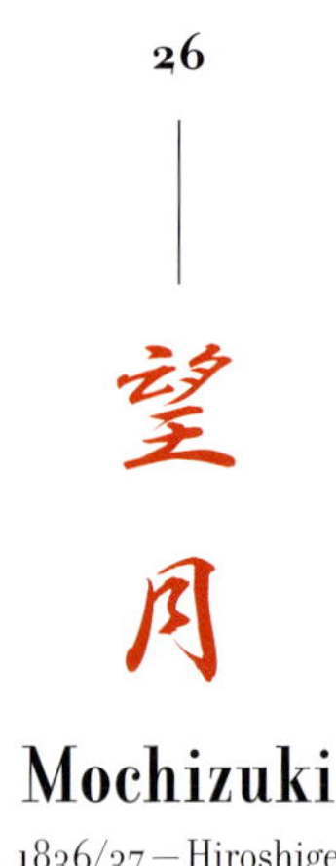

Mochizuki

1836/37 — Hiroshige

Hiroshige's design for Mochizuki is one of the most striking and most reprinted of the Kisokaidō series. The composition shows a stream of travellers, porters and pack horses climbing a steep, tree-lined slope. The moon seen gleaming through the trees is a visual pun on the name of the station, which means "full moon"; the region was renowned for its excellent horses, and received this name for its annual gift of horses to the imperial court and shogunate on the full moon in the eighth month of the traditional Japanese lunar calendar.

The station of Mochizuki is located to the west of the Kanayamazaka and Uriuzaka hills, which therefore seem likely candidates for the setting of this design. According to the travel guidebook *Illustrated Guide to the Kiso Road (Kisoji anken ezu)*, however, there were no trees like those depicted in Hiroshige's design on either of these hills, although the book does indicate a substantial stand of trees several kilometres away, where the road climbs up to the Kasatori Pass to the west of Ashida station. As Hiroshige had not yet travelled the Kisokaidō at the time he created this design, it is not plausible that the trees originated from any specific locale on the road, nor does it seem likely that the magnificent examples in this design were inspired by the schematic representation of them in the guidebook. If there was a particular source for this image, we must look elsewhere for it.

Travellers heading west would then cross a bridge over the Kakuma River and turn sharply right before entering the village, which was planned on a grid with its axis running south-east to north-west. Inns for lords and their entourage were located near the centre. A handful of Edo-period buildings survive today, including Sanayamake, an inn and *ton'ya* (wholesaler's warehouse) dating from 1765 which has been designated an Important Cultural Property. Continuing north-west, the road climbed a terraced slope towards Motai village and Ashida station.

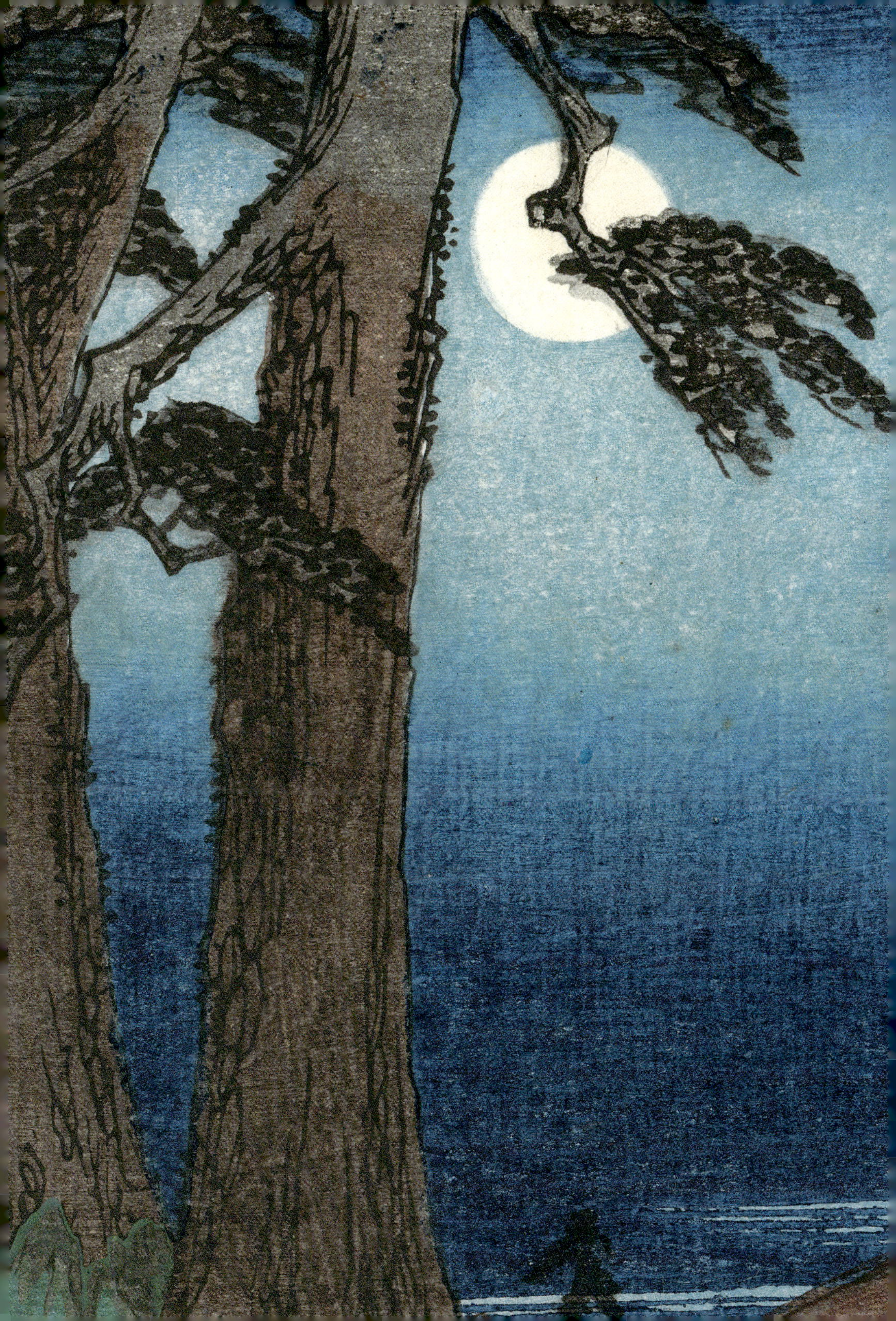

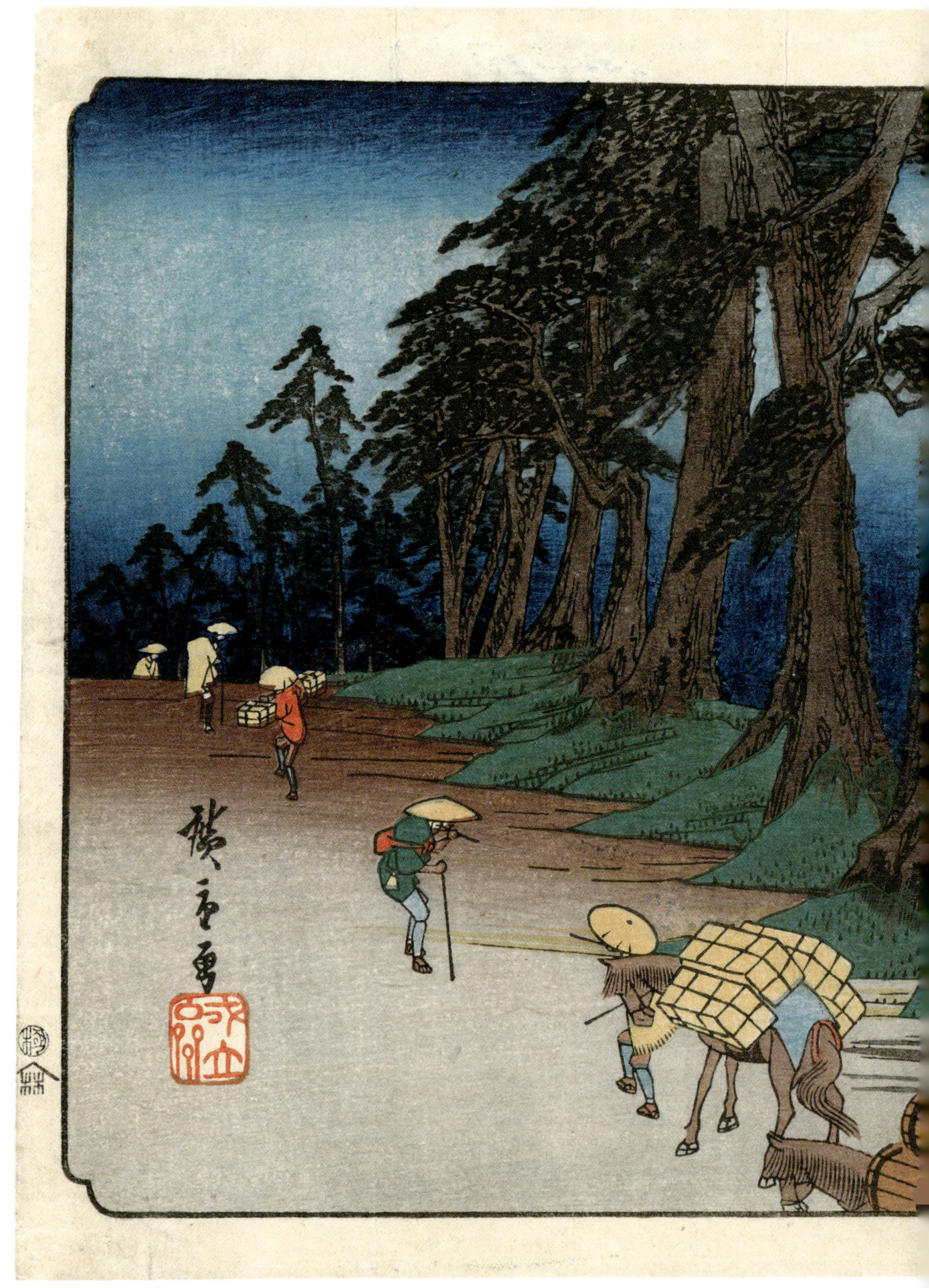

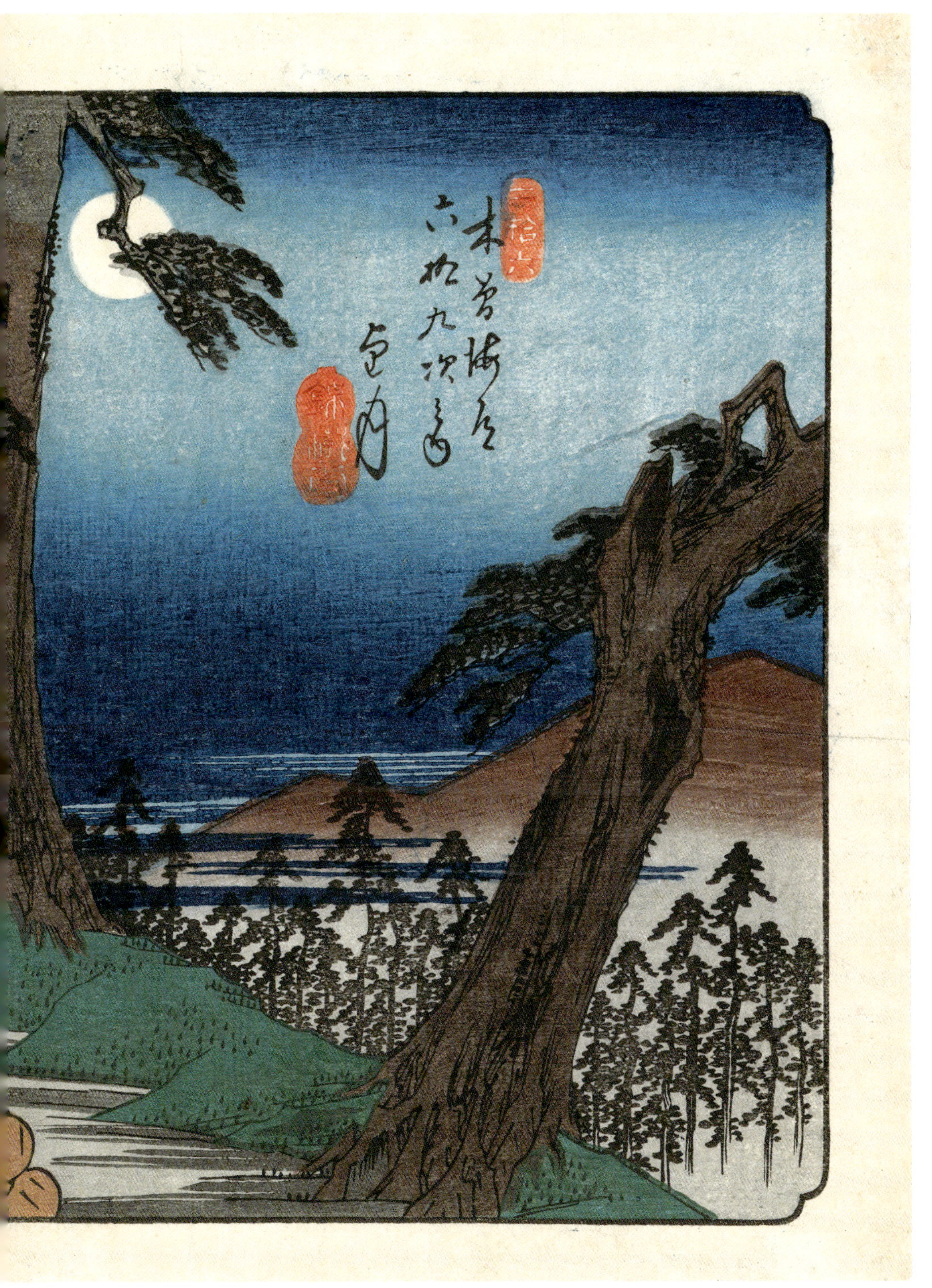

Inhabitants from the neighbouring settlements of Komiya, Kani and Hara were relocated when Mochizuki was first built, and while it lacked a castle proper there was a *yamashiro* or fortified hill at the north-eastern extremity of the village, on the opposite bank of the Kakuma River. A Sōtō Zen temple, Jōkōin, was established at the foot of the hill in 1475. On the west side of the river was the Ōtomo shrine, which is mentioned in the ninth-century text *The True History of Emperor Montoku of Japan* (*Nihon Montoku Tennō Jitsuroku*).

Hiroshiges Entwurf für Mochizuki gehört zu den eindrucksvollsten und am häufigsten nachgedruckten Blättern der Kisokaidō-Serie. Die Komposition zeigt einen Strom von Reisenden, Lastenträgern und Packpferden, die einen steilen, von Kiefern gesäumten Abhang hinaufsteigen. Der durch die Zweige schimmernde Mond spielt auf den Stationsnamen an; er bedeutet „Vollmond" und wurde der Region, die für ihre Spitzenpferde berühmt war, für ihre jährliche Pferdegabe an den Kaiserhof und das Shogunat verliehen. Diese fand nach dem traditionellen japanischen Mondkalender immer am Vollmond des achten Monats statt.

Die Station Mochizuki liegt westlich der Anhöhen Kanayamazaka und Uriuzaka, die folglich eine für dieses Blatt geeignete Kulisse abgegeben hätten. Dem Reisehandbuch *Illustrierter Wegweiser für die Kiso-Straße (Kisoji anken ezu)* zufolge kamen Bäume wie die von Hiroshige gezeigten jedoch auf keinem der beiden Hügel vor, während in dem Buch ein beträchtlicher Baumbestand einige Kilometer weiter verzeichnet ist, dort, wo die Straße westlich der Station Ashida zum Kasatori-Pass ansteigt. Da Hiroshige, als er den Entwurf anfertigte, den Kisokaidō noch nicht bereist hatte, ist es weder plausibel, dass seine Bäume auf einen konkreten Schauplatz an der Straße zurückgehen, noch scheint es naheliegend, dass die prächtigen Exemplare in diesem Entwurf von der schematischen Darstellung im Reiseführer inspiriert waren. Sofern für dieses Bild eine spezifische Quelle existierte, ist sie anderswo zu suchen.

Reisende in Richtung Westen mussten im Folgenden eine Brücke über den Kakuma überqueren und scharf nach rechts abbiegen, um in den Ort zu gelangen, dessen rechtwinkliges Straßennetz entlang einer von Südosten nach Nordwesten verlaufenden Achse angelegt war. Die Herbergen für Fürsten und ihre Gefolge lagen in der Nähe des Zentrums. Eine Handvoll Gebäude aus der Edo-Zeit ist bis heute erhalten, darunter auch das Sanayamake, ein Gasthaus und *ton'ya* (Großhandelslager) aus dem Jahr 1765, das zum „bedeutenden Kulturgut" erklärt wurde. Die Straße setzte sich in nordwestlicher Richtung fort und führte über einen stufig ansteigenden Hang ins Dorf Motai und zur Station Ashida.

Zur Gründung Mochizukis wurden Bewohner aus den benachbarten Siedlungen Komiya, Kani und Hara an einen gemeinsamen Ort umgesiedelt, und während ihm eine echte Burg fehlte, besaß er im äußersten Nordosten, am gegenüberliegenden Ufer des Kakuma, einen *yamashiro* oder befestigten Hügel. 1475 wurde am Fuß des Hügels der Jōkōin errichtet, ein Zen-Tempel der Sōtō-Schule. Westlich des Flusses lag der Ōtomo-Schrein, der im 9. Jahrhundert in dem Schriftwerk *Die wahre Geschichte des Kaisers Montoku von Japan (Nihon Montoku Tennō Jitsuroku)* erwähnt wird.

L'illustration d'Hiroshige pour la station de Mochizuki est l'une des estampes les plus saisissantes et les plus reproduites de la série de la Kisokaidō. Dans cette composition, voyageurs, porteurs et chevaux de bât se succèdent pour gravir une pente raide, bordée d'arbres. La lune qui luit à travers les arbres est une allusion visuelle au nom de la station qui signifie « pleine lune » ; réputée pour ses excellentes montures, la région devait son nom au don annuel de chevaux à la cour impériale et au shogunat, effectué le jour de la pleine lune du huitième mois du calendrier lunaire traditionnel japonais.

Mochizuki se situe à l'ouest des collines de Kanayamazaka et d'Uriuzaka ; ces collines constituent probablement le décor de cette estampe. Toutefois, selon le *Guide illustré de la route Kiso (Kisoji anken ezu)*, on ne trouvait dans ces collines aucun arbre ressemblant à ceux du dessin d'Hiroshige, bien que cet ouvrage mentionne un important bosquet à plusieurs kilomètres de là, à l'endroit où la route monte vers le col de Kasatori, à l'ouest de la station d'Ashida. Hiroshige n'ayant pas encore emprunté la Kisokaidō lorsqu'il réalisa cette estampe, il n'est pas plausible que ces arbres soient ceux d'un lieu particulier de la route, et les magnifiques spécimens de ce dessin n'ont sans doute pas plus été inspirés par les représentations schématiques qu'on en trouve dans le guide de voyage. Si cette image est associée à une source précise, c'est ailleurs qu'il faut la chercher.

Les voyageurs se dirigeant vers l'ouest allaient ensuite franchir un pont enjambant la Kakuma et suivre un virage serré sur la droite avant d'entrer dans le village, conçu sur un plan quadrillé suivant un axe sud-est/nord-ouest. Près du centre se trouvaient des auberges destinées aux seigneurs et à leur entourage. Aujourd'hui, il reste quelques bâtiments de l'ère Edo, dont Sanayamake, auberge et *ton'ya* (entrepôt de grossiste) datant de 1765, inscrit sur la liste du « patrimoine culturel important ». La route continue vers le nord-ouest et monte le long d'un versant en terrasses vers le village de Motai et la station d'Ashida.

Les habitants des petits villages voisins de Komiya, Kani et Hara avaient été déplacés à Mochizuki lors de la construction du nouveau village ; si celui-ci était dépourvu d'un véritable château, il possédait un *yamashiro*, colline fortifiée située à son extrémité nord-est, sur l'autre rive de la Kakuma. Le temple zen Sōtō de Jōkōin fut édifié au pied de cette colline en 1475. Sur la rive occidentale de la rivière se trouvait le sanctuaire d'Ōtomo, cité dans un texte du IXe siècle, *La véritable histoire de l'empereur Montoku du Japon (Nihon Montoku Tennō Jitsuroku)*.

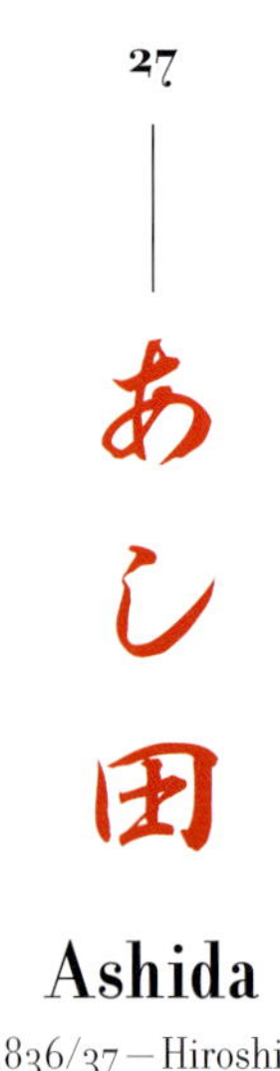

Ashida

1836/37 – Hiroshige

On leaving Ashida, the westbound traveller would begin to climb the Kasatori Pass, the second-most challenging ascent of the Kisokaidō. The name of the pass implies that the wind was so fierce here it could take the hat off a person's head. Hiroshige gave full play to his imagination in the creation of this design, exaggerating the treacherous incline for which the locale was known into a parabolic curve. Curiously formed cedar trees, famous along this stretch of the road, are scattered at intervals over the slopes. The road is busy with travellers and porters heading in both directions. At the bottom of the dip, two figures – an adult and a child – are resting at a wayside shelter before embarking on the climb. Another such shelter for travellers who have reached the top is visible at the peak.

The town of Ashida was relatively small and dates from the final years of the 16th century. It was designated a station in 1601. In 1861, Princess Kazu, half-sister of the Emperor Kōmei, rested at the *honjin* on her way from Kyoto to Edo to marry the 14th shogun, Tokugawa Iemochi. With a vast retinue of attendants, porters and security personnel, as well as thousands of people mobilised to assist on-site, the princess's procession was an enormous logistical feat. The *honjin,* now designated a Nagano Prefectural Treasure, is one of several structures surviving from the Edo period, including a *ton'ya* or wholesaler's warehouse, a sake brewery and various signposts.

Beim Verlassen der Station Ashida begann für westwärts Reisende der zweitschwierigste Anstieg des Kisokaidō, hinauf zum Kasatori-Pass. Der Name der Passhöhe besagt, dass der Wind an dieser Stelle so heftig war, dass er einem Menschen den Hut vom Kopf fegen konnte. Bei der Anfertigung dieses Entwurfs ließ Hiroshige seiner Fantasie freien Lauf und übersteigerte den heimtückischen Hang, für den der Ort bekannt war, zu einer parabolischen Kurve. Berühmt für diesen Streckenabschnitt waren auch die eigentümlich gewachsenen, in Abständen über die Steigung verteilten Zedern. Reisende und Träger ziehen in beide Richtungen die belebte Straße entlang. Am Fuß der Senke ruhen zwei Figuren – ein Erwachsener und ein Kind – an einem Unterstand am Wegesrand aus, bevor sie den Hügel hinaufsteigen. Auf der Hügelkuppe ist ein weiterer Unterstand für Reisende zu erkennen, die den Anstieg bereits gemeistert haben.

Die im späten 16. Jahrhundert gegründete Ortschaft Ashida war relativ klein. 1601 wurde sie zur Station bestimmt. Prinzessin Kazu, eine Halbschwester des Kaisers Kōmei, machte 1861 auf ihrem Weg von Kyoto nach Edo, wo sie den 14. Shogun, Tokugawa Iemochi, heiraten sollte, im *honjin* von Ashida Rast. Mit einem riesigen Gefolge von mitreisenden Bediensteten, Trägern und Sicherheitskräften sowie Tausenden von Menschen, die vor Ort assistierten, war die Prozession der Prinzessin ein enormer logistischer Kraftakt. Der *honjin*, heute auf der Liste der Kulturschätze der Präfektur Nagano, gehört wie ein *ton'ya* (Großhandelslager), eine Sakebrauerei und verschiedene Wegweiser zu den bis heute erhaltenen Anlagen aus der Edo-Zeit.

En quittant Ashida, le voyageur se dirigeant vers l'ouest entamait la montée qui mène au col de Kasatori, deuxième des plus difficiles ascensions de la Kisokaidō. Le nom de ce col signale que le vent y est si violent qu'il peut faire tomber les chapeaux. Hiroshige a donné libre cours à son imagination pour réaliser cette estampe, en transformant exagérément en une courbe parabolique la pente périlleuse qui a rendu ce lieu célèbre. Des cèdres aux formes étranges, qui ont fait la réputation de cette partie de la route, sont répartis à intervalles réguliers sur les versants. La route est très empruntée dans les deux sens par des voyageurs et des porteurs. Tout en bas, deux personnages – un adulte et un enfant – se reposent sous un abri de bord de route avant de gravir la pente. Un autre abri du même genre, pour les voyageurs parvenus en haut de la colline, est visible à son sommet.

De taille relativement petite, la fondation de la ville d'Ashida remonte aux dernières années du XVIᵉ siècle. C'est en 1601 qu'elle est devenue une station. En 1861, la princesse Kazu, demi-sœur de l'empereur Kōmei, avait fait étape à la *honjin*, alors qu'elle se rendait de Kyoto à Edo pour épouser le quatorzième shogun, Tokugawa Iemochi. La princesse voyagea avec une importante escorte de domestiques, porteurs et gardes et mobilisa des milliers de personnes pour la servir lors de ses étapes ; sa procession constitua un exploit en matière de logistique. Classée parmi les trésors de la préfecture de Nagano, la *honjin* est l'une des quelques constructions encore existantes de l'ère Edo, avec un *ton'ya*, entrepôt de grossiste, une brasserie de sake et divers poteaux indicateurs.

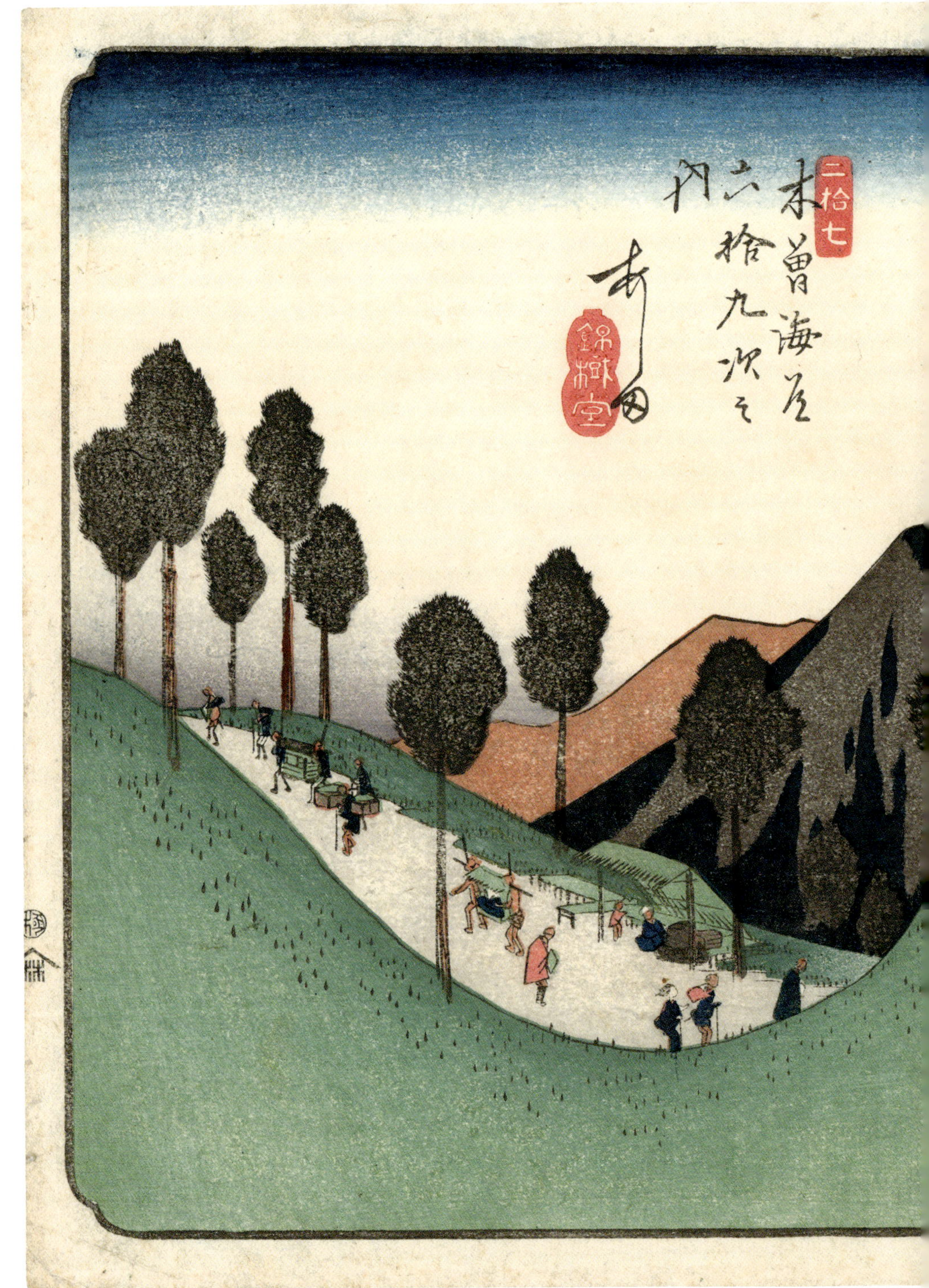

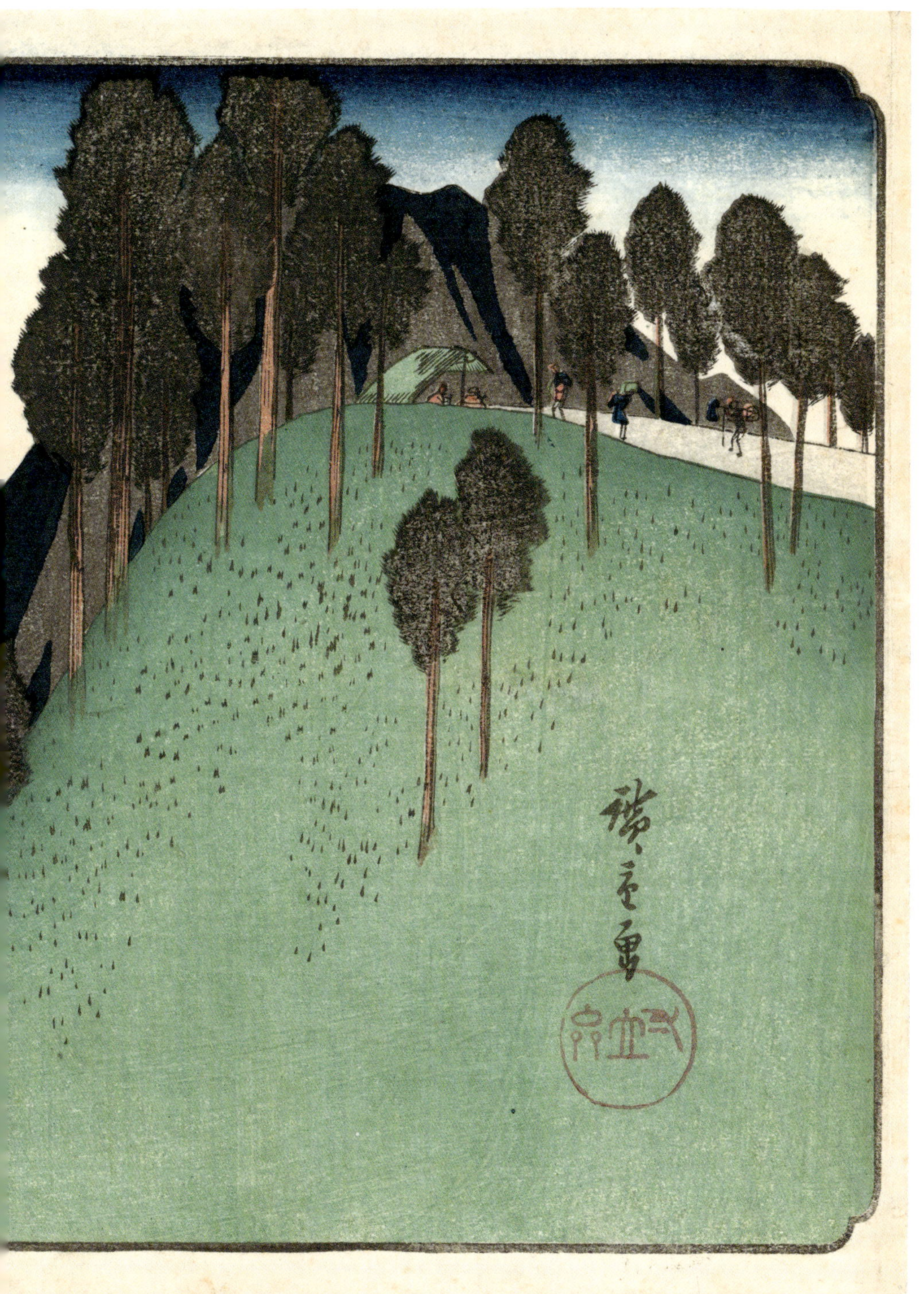

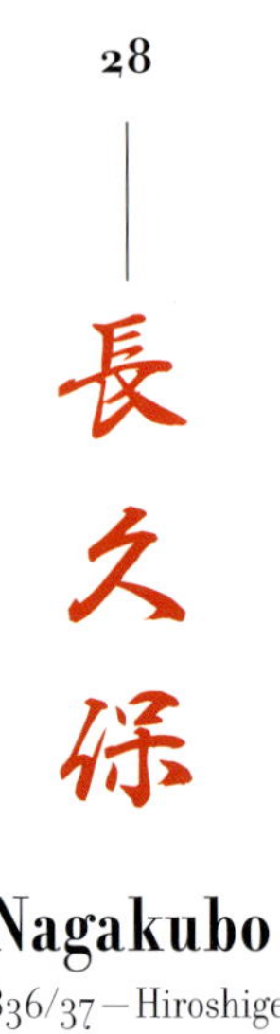

Nagakubo

1836/37 – Hiroshige

A full moon hangs heavily above the meandering Yoda River, guiding four travellers and a horse as they cross over a wooden bridge. The head of the traveller on horseback has fallen forward on his chest in sleep. The printer has layered two intensities of black in the rendering of the pine tree and bamboo on the riverbank and the gently arching bridge to suggest moonlight reflecting off their surfaces. The gentle humour in the depiction of the children and dogs playing on the riverbank in the foreground offers a distraction from the lyrical quality of the rest of the scene. Behind them, a guide is returning with his horse, which is wearing a blanket marked with the emblem of the publisher, Iseya Rihei.

Moving west from Ashida, travellers would ascend a tree-lined slope called Ishiwarizaka, which, according to the guidebook *Views of Famous Sights along the Kiso Road (Kisoji meisho zue)*, afforded a distant view of Mount Myōgi. After journeying through the Kasatori Pass and crossing a river, travellers would next arrive in the village of Nagakubo. The town was L-shaped, with a "horizontal district" running north-south in which most of the town's inns were located, and a "vertical district" running from east to west, where the *honjin*, *waki-honjin* and administrative buildings could be found. Between the late 18th and early 19th centuries, numbers of *meshimori onna*, serving women who also worked as prostitutes, increased dramatically; such was one of the particular pleasures of the Kisokaidō.

Continuing west, travellers would cross the Ochiai Bridge over the Yoda River, a tributary of the Chikuma. This locale appears to provide the setting for Hiroshige's design. The town was originally located closer to these waterways, but was relocated in 1630 after a flood washed the original settlement away.

Das Licht des Vollmonds, der schwer über dem mäandernden Yoda hängt, geleitet vicr Reisende und ein Pferd über eine hölzerne Brücke. Dem Reisenden zu Pferd ist der Kopf im Schlaf auf die Brust gefallen. Um anzudeuten, wie sich das Mondlicht in der Kiefer, im Bambus am Flussufer und in der leicht gewölbten Brücke spiegelt, hat der Drucker in den entsprechenden Partien zwei unterschiedlich intensive Schwarztöne übereinandergelegt. Der leise Humor in der Wiedergabe der Kinder und Hunde, die im Vordergrund am Ufer spielen, lenkt von der lyrischen Qualität der übrigen Szene ab. Hinter den Spielenden kehrt ein Führer mit seinem Pferd zur Station zurück; auf der Satteldecke prangt das Zeichen des Verlegers, Iseya Rihei.

Von Ashida in Richtung Westen stiegen Reisende einen baumgesäumten Hang namens Ishiwarizaka hinauf, der dem Handbuch *Ansichten berühmter Stätten an der Kiso-Straße (Kisoji meisho zue)* zufolge einen Fernblick auf den Myōgi gewährte. Nachdem sie den Kasatori-Pass bewältigt und einen Fluss überquert hatten, erreichten sie als Nächstes das Dorf Nagakubo. Die L-förmig angelegte Ortschaft bestand aus einem „horizontalen Viertel", das sich von Nord nach Süd erstreckte und in dem sich die meisten Herbergen befanden, und einem „vertikalen Viertel" in Ost-West-Richtung, in dem die *honjin*, *waki-honjin* und Verwaltungsgebäude zu finden waren. Zwischen dem späten 18. und frühen 19. Jahrhundert stieg die Zahl der *meshimori onna*, dramatisch an; diese Serviererinnen, die auch als Prostituierte arbeiteten, bildeten eine der speziellen Vergnügungen am Kisokaidō.

Die Weiterreise nach Westen führte auf der Ochiai-Brücke über den Yoda, einen Nebenfluss des Chikuma. Hier scheint Hiroshige seinen Entwurf angesiedelt zu haben. Nagakubo selbst lag anfangs näher an diesen Wasserläufen, wurde jedoch 1630 verlegt, nachdem ein Hochwasser die ursprüngliche Siedlung weggeschwemmt hatte.

Bien visible au-dessus des méandres de la Yoda, la pleine lune guide de sa lumière quatre voyageurs et un cheval tandis qu'ils traversent un pont de bois. Celui ou celle qui voyage à cheval a la tête affaissée sur la poitrine. L'imprimeur a appliqué à l'estampe deux nuances de noir pour reproduire le pin et les bambous qui poussent sur la rive, ainsi que la courbe légère du pont, afin de suggérer les reflets de l'éclat de la lune sur leur surface. La petite scène comique qui, au premier plan, réunit les enfants et les chiens au bord de la rivière constitue un divertissement par rapport à l'aspect lyrique du reste de l'illustration. Derrière eux, un guide rentre chez lui avec son cheval protégé par une couverture sur laquelle est inscrit l'emblème de l'éditeur, Iseya Rihei.

En se dirigeant vers l'ouest après avoir quitté Ashida, les voyageurs gravissaient une pente bordée d'arbres appelée Ishiwarizaka, laquelle, selon le guide de voyage *Collection de vues de paysages célèbres sur la route Kiso (Kisoji meisho zue)*, permettait d'admirer au loin le mont Myōgi. Une fois passé le col de Kasatori et une rivière, les voyageurs atteignaient le village de Nagakubo. Cette petite ville en forme de « L » était composée d'un « quartier horizontal » suivant un axe nord-sud, où se trouvaient la plupart des auberges, et d'un « quartier vertical », orienté est-ouest, comprenant les *honjin* et *waki-honjin* ainsi que les bâtiments administratifs. Au tournant des XVIIIe et XIXe siècles, le nombre de *meshimori onna* – serveuses qui jouaient aussi le rôle de prostituées – augmenta de façon spectaculaire ; tel était l'un des plaisirs particuliers de la Kisokaidō.

Poursuivant leur route vers l'ouest, les voyageurs franchissaient ensuite le pont Ochiai sur la Yoda, affluent du Chikuma. C'est cet endroit qui semble servir de cadre à l'estampe d'Hiroshige. À l'origine, la ville était située plus près de ces cours d'eau, mais fut déplacée en 1630 à la suite d'une inondation qui avait emporté les habitations initiales.

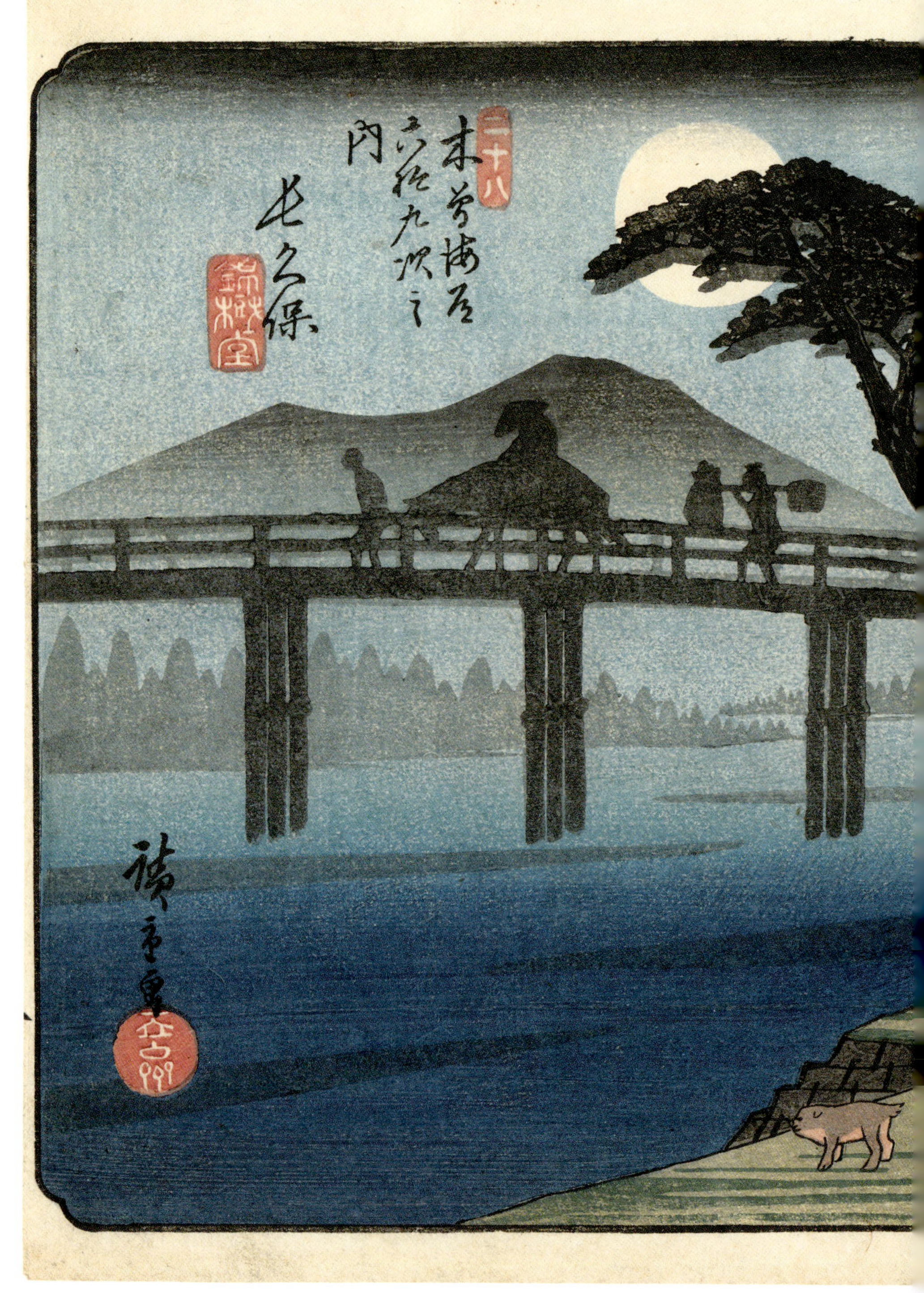

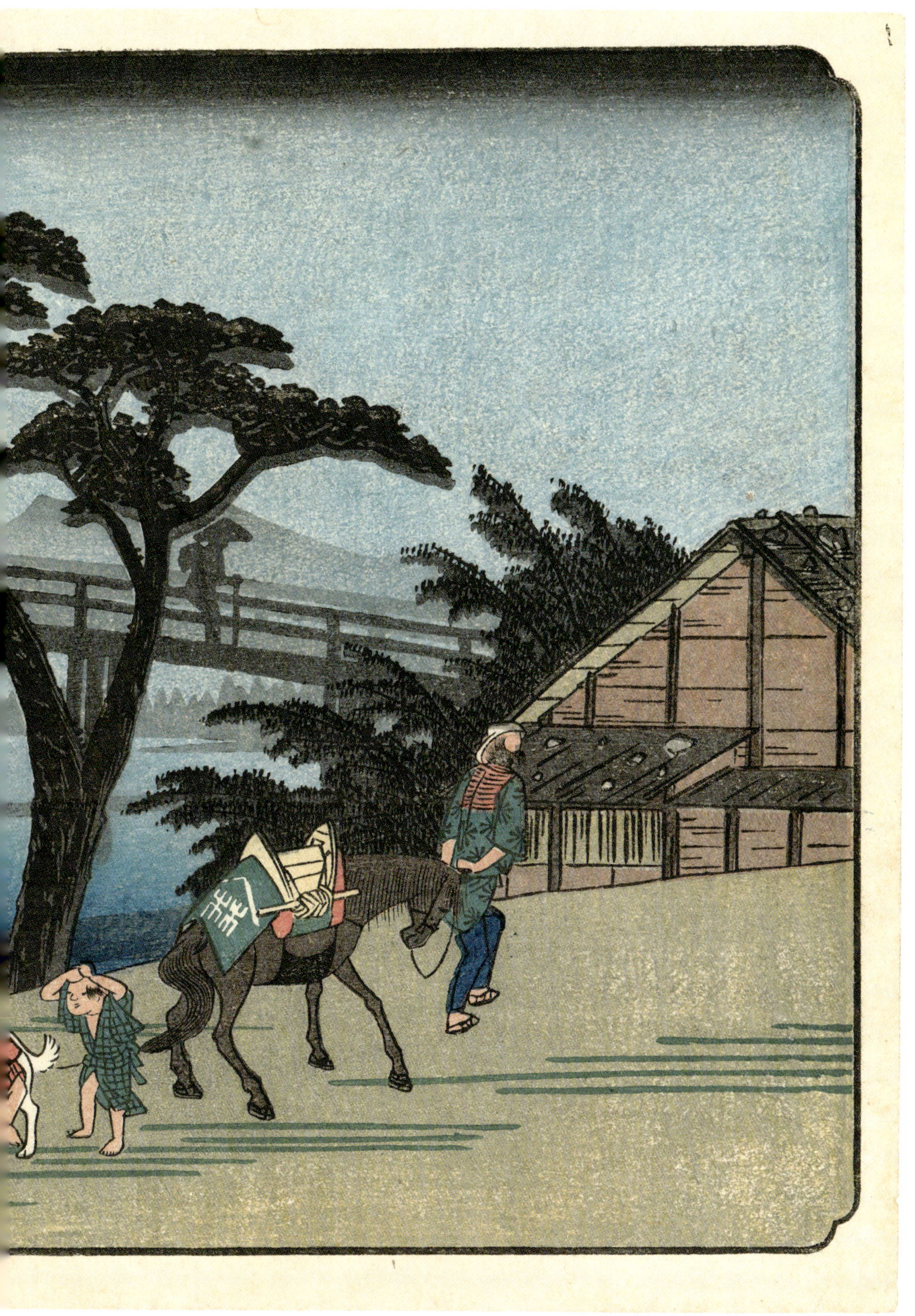

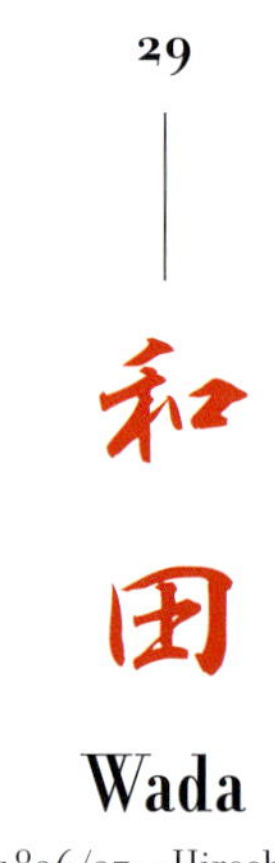

Wada

1836/37 — Hiroshige

After leaving Wada, the road went through a valley before climbing over the precipitous Wada Pass, which at 1,646 metres (5,400 feet) above sea level is the highest point on the Kisokaidō. In their 1884 guidebook, *A Handbook for Travellers in Central & Northern Japan,* authors Sir Ernest Mason Satow and Lieutenant A. G. S. Hawes described the magnificent view that could be seen from the top of the pass: "N. E. rises Asama yama; S. E. Tateshina, and Yatsu-ga-take; S. W. the eye rests upon the basin of the Suwa lake; further to its W. stand Koma- ga-take and Ontake, while to the N. W. a great portion of the Hida-Shin-shiū [*sic*] range is visible." (Satow/Hawes 1884, p. 234)

Wada also experienced heavy snowfalls and fog, and was the most isolated station, located more than 20 kilometres from Shimosuwa and 8.9 kilometres from Nagakubo (12.5 and 5.5 miles respectively). For those who needed more than the promise of a splendid view to get them over the pass, the Tokugawa administration authorised the operation of five establishments along the pass selling tea, refreshments, accommodation and general assistance to travellers. Of these, the Higashimochiya, founded in 1660 on the eastern slope of the pass, comprised five teahouses that were particularly known for their energy-rich *mochi* (rice cakes). The business remains in operation today.

Hiroshige's design for Wada focuses on the eastern approach to the pass. A porter with a carrying pole on his shoulder and three travellers with smaller bundles are making their way along the road as it winds steeply upwards. At the top, the figure in the blue cloak has stopped and is looking back, perhaps urging on the traveller in green, who is lagging behind. Far in the distance is the conical peak of the volcano Mount Ontake, which was long thought to have been inactive until an eruption in 2014 killed 54 people. A legacy of the region's volatile past is the deposits of obsidian, a naturally occurring volcanic glass which has been collected since prehistoric times.

Before the official construction of the Kisokaidō began, Wada station was established on the existing road in 1602, with villagers being relocated from surrounding areas to form the town. The town was quite small, but with 28 inns was relatively well equipped to cater for weary travellers. A second *honjin* was added in 1820.

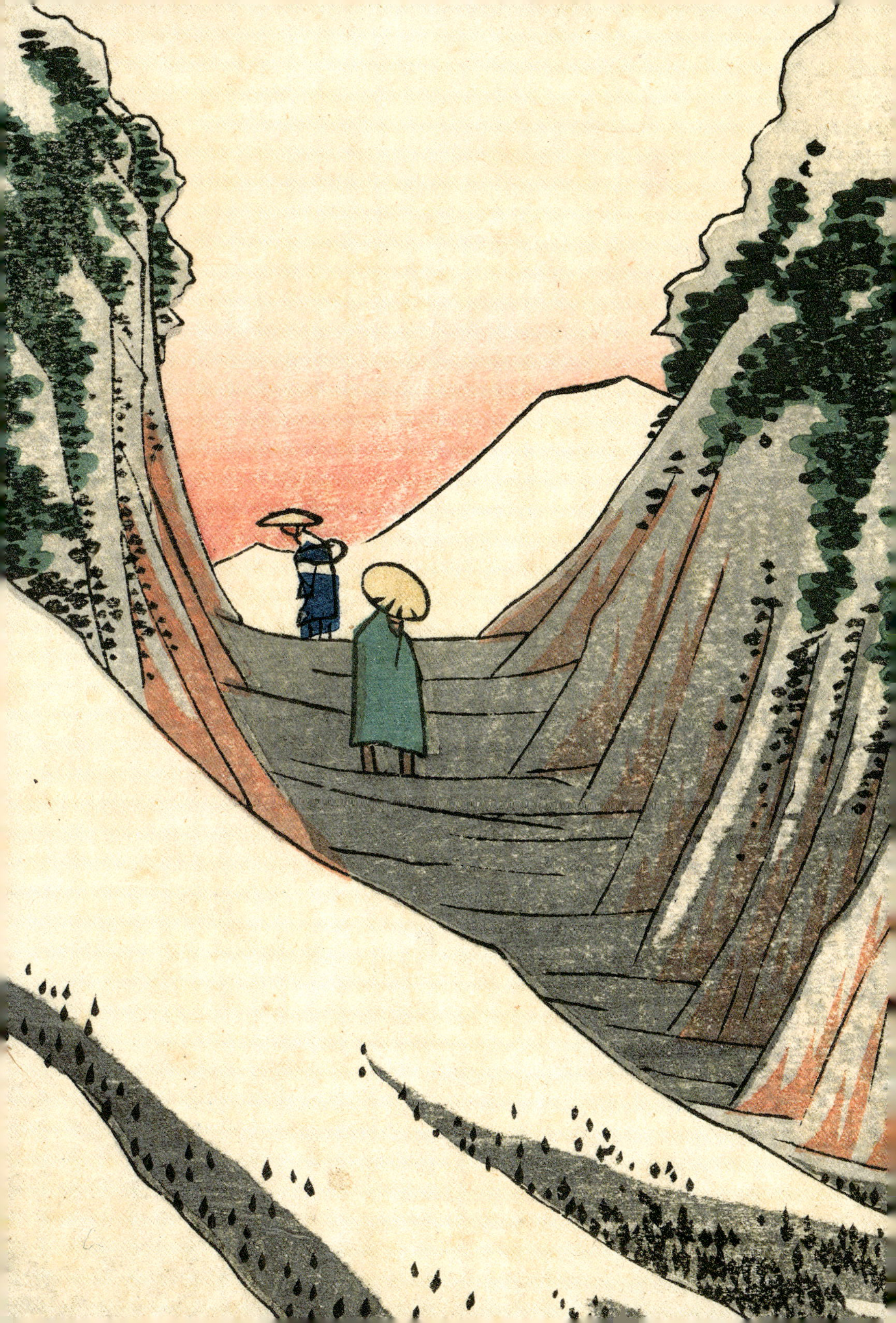

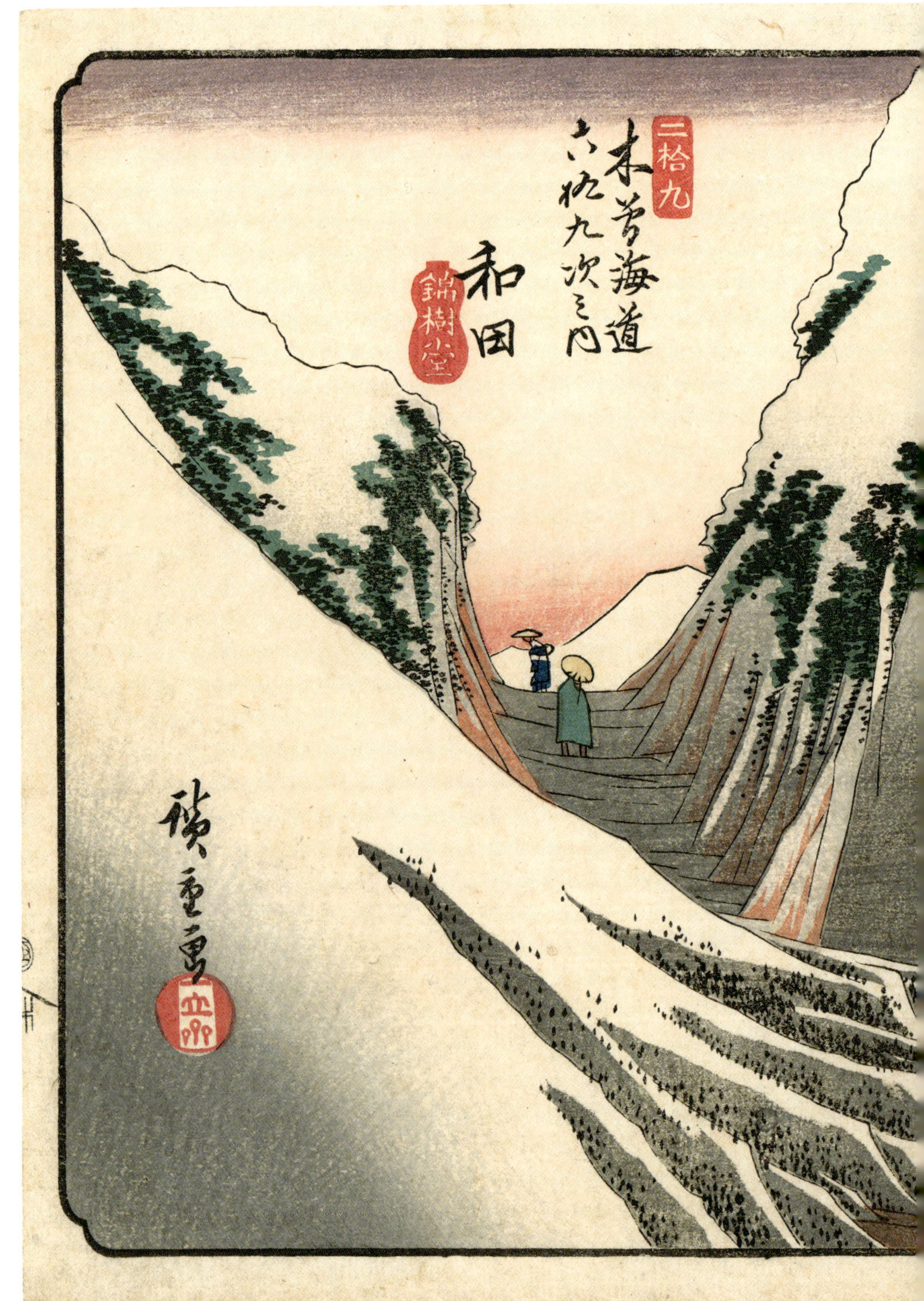

二拾九
木曽海道六拾九次之内
和田
錦樹堂
廣重画

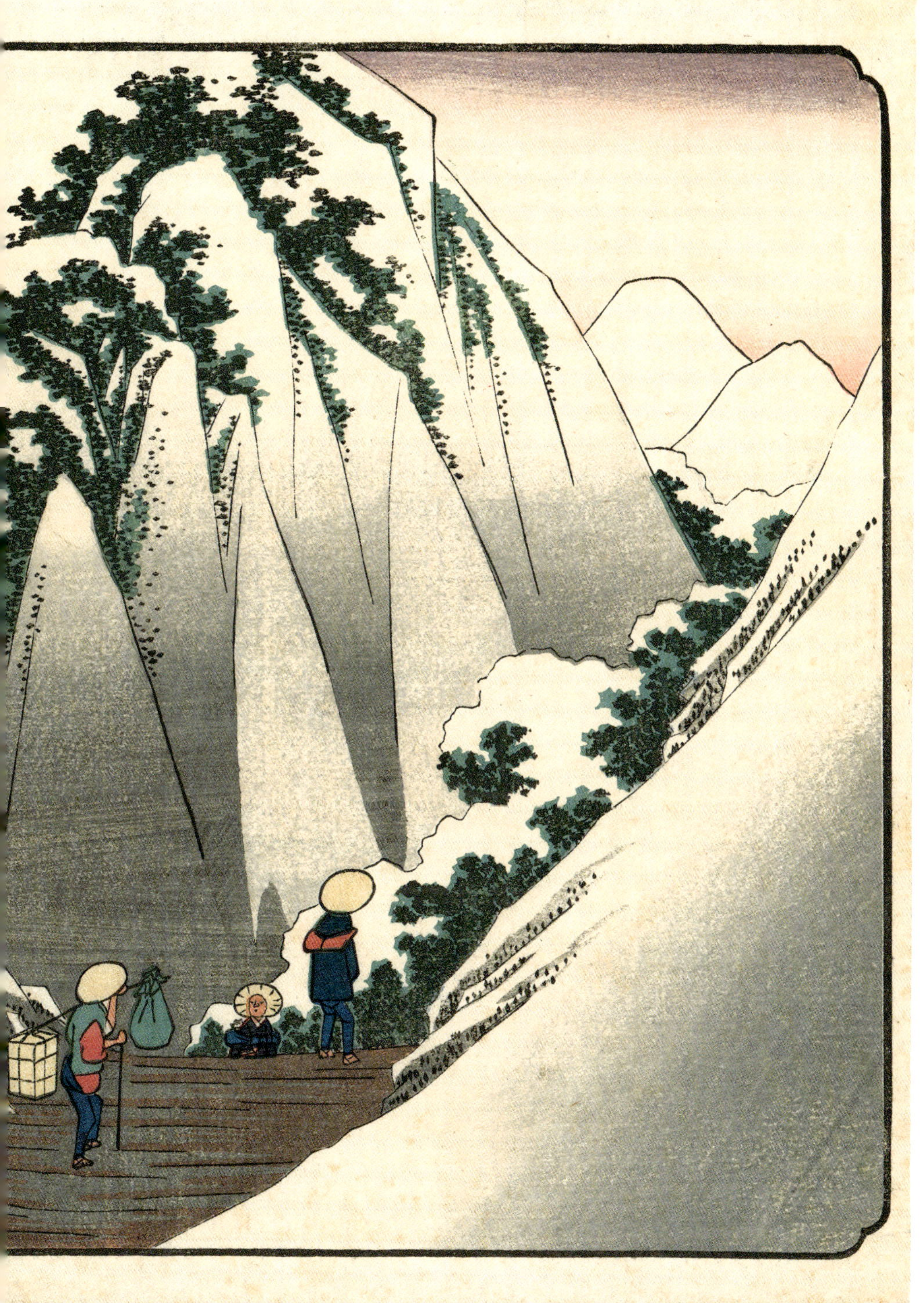

Hinter Wada verlief die Straße durch ein Tal, bevor sie den steil ansteigenden Wada-Pass erklomm, der auf 1646 Metern Meereshöhe den höchsten Punkt des Kisokaidō bildete. In ihrem Reiseführer *A Handbook for Travellers in Central & Northern Japan* aus dem Jahr 1884 beschrieben Sir Ernest Mason Satow und Leutnant A. G. S. Hawes den überwältigenden Ausblick vom Scheitel des Passes: „Im NO ragt der Asama empor, im SO [die Gipfel von] Tateshina und Yatsu-ga-take; im SW ruht das Auge auf dem Becken des Suwa-Sees; weiter im W des Sees liegen Koma-ga-take und Ontake, während im NW ein großer Teil der Bergkette Hida-Shin-shiū [sic] zu sehen ist." (Satow/Hawes 1884, S. 234)

Heftige Schneefälle und Nebel waren in Wada keine Seltenheit. Zudem lag der Ort 20 Kilometer von Shimosuwa und 8,9 Kilometer von Nagabuko entfernt und war damit die einsamste Station auf dem Kisokaidō. Für diejenigen, denen die Verheißung eines großartigen Ausblicks allein nicht genügte, um den Pass zu bewältigen, hatte die Tokugawa-Regierung fünf Geschäften entlang der Passstraße erlaubt, Tee, Erfrischungen, Unterkünfte und allgemeine Hilfsdienste für Reisende anzubieten. Eines dieser Unternehmen, das Higashimochiya, wurde 1660 auf der Ostseite des Passes gegründet und bestand aus fünf Teehäusern, die besonders für ihre Kraft spendenden *mochi* (Reiskuchen) bekannt waren. Es ist bis heute in Betrieb.

Hiroshiges Entwurf für Wada konzentriert sich auf den östlichen Passanstieg. Ein Lastenträger mit Tragestab auf den Schultern und drei Reisende mit leichterem Gepäck folgen den steilen Aufwärtswindungen der Straße. Ganz oben steht eine Figur im blauen Mantel und blickt sich um, womöglich, um den zurückgebliebenen Reisenden in Grün anzutreiben. In weiter Ferne erhebt sich der Kegel des Vulkans Ontake, der lange für inaktiv gehalten wurde, bevor ein Ausbruch im Jahr 2014 insgesamt 54 Menschen das Leben kostete. Ein Erbe der explosiven Vergangenheit dieser Region sind ihre Obsidianvorkommen. Das natürlich auftretende vulkanische Gesteinsglas wird hier seit prähistorischer Zeit abgebaut.

Bevor der Bau des Kisokaidō offiziell in Angriff genommen wurde, entstand 1602 an der damals bereits bestehenden Straße die Station Wada, deren Bewohner aus der Umgebung dorthin umgesiedelt wurden. Trotz seiner geringen Größe war die Ortschaft mit 28 Herbergen vergleichsweise gut gerüstet, um erschöpfte Reisende zu versorgen. 1820 kam sogar ein zweites *honjin* hinzu.

Au sortir de Wada, la route traversait une vallée avant de monter vers le col escarpé de Wada qui, à 1646 mètres au-dessus du niveau de la mer, est le point culminant de la Kisokaidō. Dans leur ouvrage de 1884, *A Handbook for Travellers in Central & Northern Japan* [Manuel de voyage pour le Japon du centre et du nord], Sir Ernest Mason Satow et le lieutenant A. G. S. Hawes décrivent le magnifique panorama visible depuis le col : « Au N.-E. s'élève Asama yama ; au S.-E. Tateshina et Yatsu-ga-take ; au S.-O. le regard s'attarde sur le bassin du lac Suwa ; plus à l'O. se trouvent Koma-ga-take et Ontake, tandis qu'au N.-O. une grande partie de la chaîne des Hida-Shin-shiū [*sic*] est visible. » (Satow/Hawes 1884, p. 234)

Souvent affectée par de fortes chutes de neige et par le brouillard, Wada était la station la plus isolée du parcours, située à plus de vingt kilomètres de Shimosuwa et à 8,9 kilomètres de Nagakubo. À l'intention de ceux qui espéraient davantage que la promesse d'une superbe vue pour franchir ce col, l'administration des Tokugawa avait autorisé l'activité de cinq établissements tout au long du col : on y trouvait du thé, des rafraîchissements, des hébergements et, plus généralement, de l'aide. Parmi ceux-ci, l'Higashimochiya, fondé en 1660 sur le versant est du col, comprenait cinq maisons de thé réputées pour leurs *mochi* (gâteaux de riz) riches en énergie. Cet établissement fonctionne toujours aujourd'hui.

L'estampe réalisée par Hiroshige pour la station de Wada représente le col en venant de l'est. Un porteur muni d'une palanche et trois voyageurs portant des ballots plus petits progressent sur la route qui monte abruptement en lacets. Au sommet, la figure vêtue de bleu s'est arrêtée et regarde derrière elle, incitant peut-être le voyageur en vert à la traîne à marcher plus vite. Tout au fond apparaît le sommet conique du volcan Ontake, dont on crut longtemps qu'il était inactif jusqu'à une éruption qui causa en 2014 la mort de cinquante-quatre personnes. Des gisements d'obsidienne, verre volcanique naturel récolté depuis les temps préhistoriques, constituent un héritage du passé instable de la région.

Avant la construction officielle de la Kisokaidō, la station de Wada fut créée sur la route déjà existante en 1602, par le déplacement des habitants de villages environnants. C'était une petite ville, mais ses vingt-huit auberges étaient relativement bien équipées pour accueillir les voyageurs épuisés. On ouvrit une seconde *honjin* en 1820.

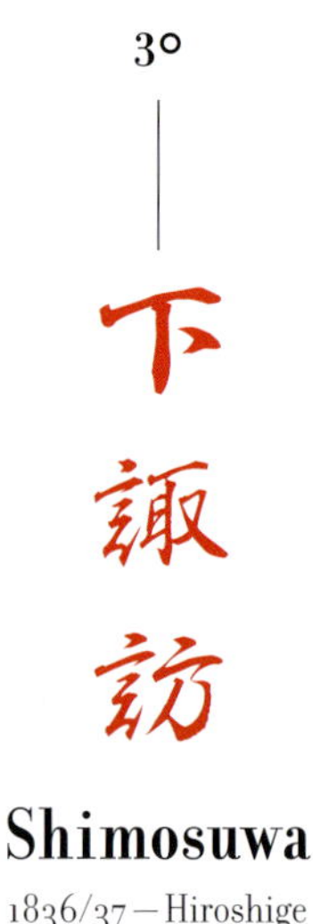

Shimosuwa

1836/37 — Hiroshige

Located between Shiojiri and Wada stations, Shimosuwa prospered because of its proximity to the Wada Pass, the highest point along the Kisokaidō, and as the terminus of the Kōshūkaidō, the highway connecting Edo with Kai and Shinano Provinces. It also attracted pilgrims visiting the Suwa Grand Shrine (Suwa Taisha), which comprises four complexes and is over 1,200 years old.

Shimosuwa was considered to be the source of the finest silk in Japan. Perhaps even more compelling, however, were Shimosuwa's natural hot springs, which made the town an enticing place for travellers to break their journey since at least the 13th century. According to a census conducted in 1843, Shimosuwa had 45 inns; the town's *honjin*, Iwanamiya, and two *waki-honjin*, Maruya and Kikyōya, are still extant today. The subject of Hiroshige's design for Shimosuwa is the rear view of an inn. Through an opening between the wings of the two buildings, we spy a guest soaking on his own in a wooden tub, scrubbing his ears with a blue towel. His kimono is lying in a khaki bundle on the floor nearby.

In the room to the right, six travellers seated at *zen*, or low dining tables, are tucking into their meal, while an attentive serving woman refills their rice bowls. Towels hanging from the wall above their heads suggest that some of the men have already visited the bath. In anticipation of an after-dinner smoke, a wooden tray of smoking utensils and a pipe has been laid out at the front left of the room, while the man in the blue robe on the opposite side has already taken out a red tobacco pouch. The *fusuma* or sliding doors at the back of the room are decorated with the crest of the publisher, Iseya Rihei.

In the print we can find two kinds of roofing customarily used in the Shinano region. The roof of the building on the right, where the travellers are taking their meal, is thatched densely with straw, while on the left, the roof there is clad in thin shingles secured with rocks against the fierce gales. The heavy wooden doors that would be fitted between the eaves and the *engawa* or veranda during the colder months of the year have been removed to allow air to circulate.

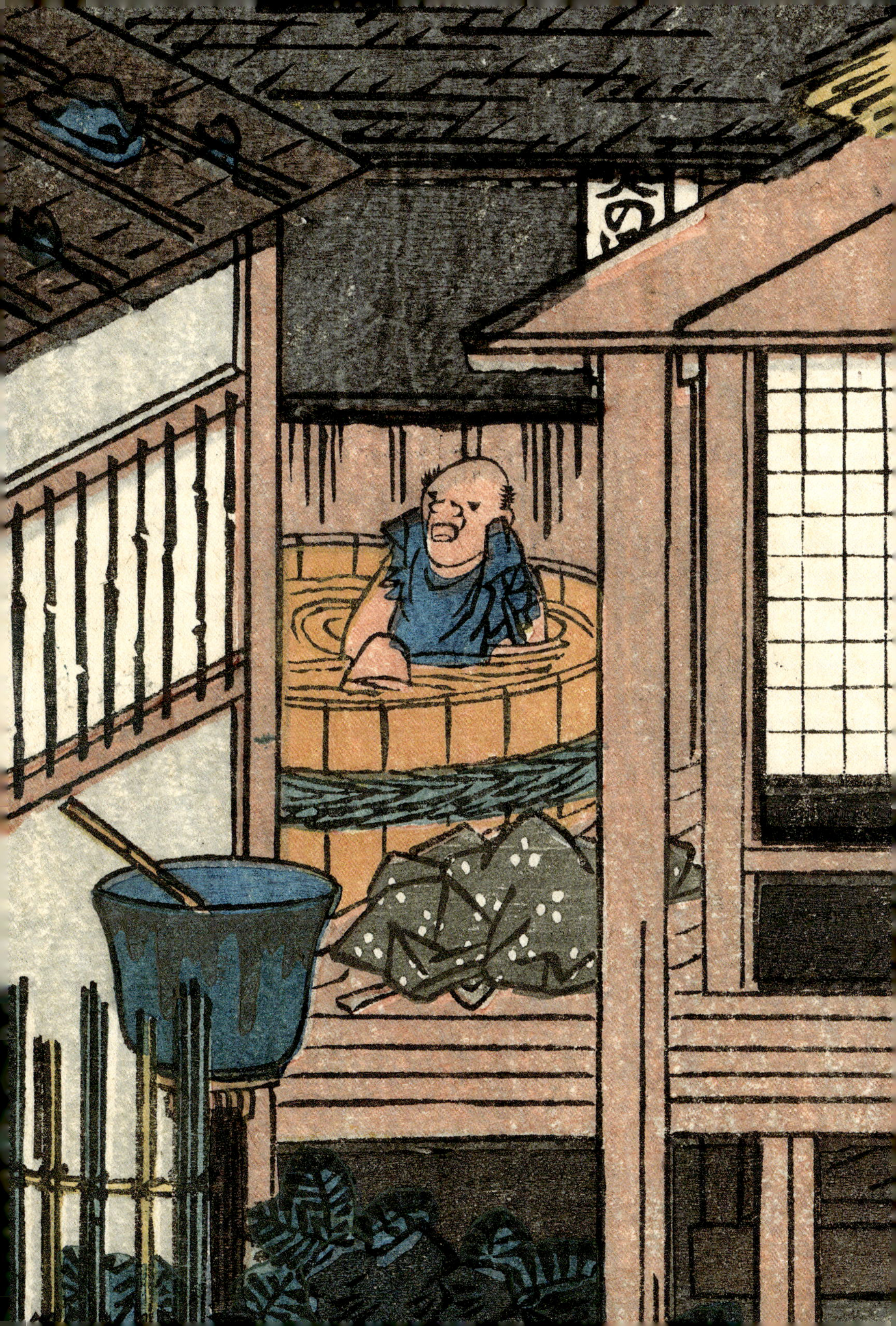

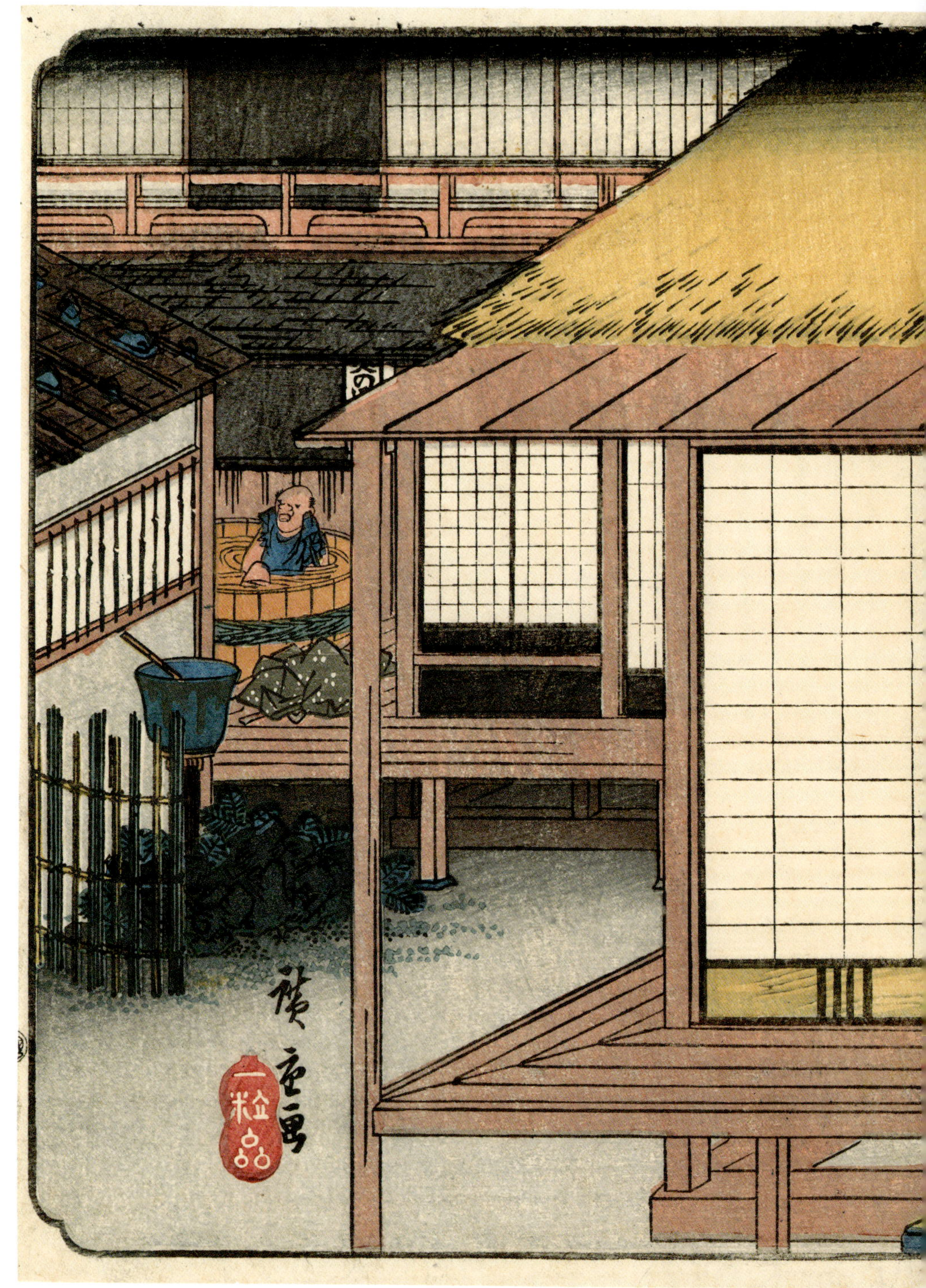

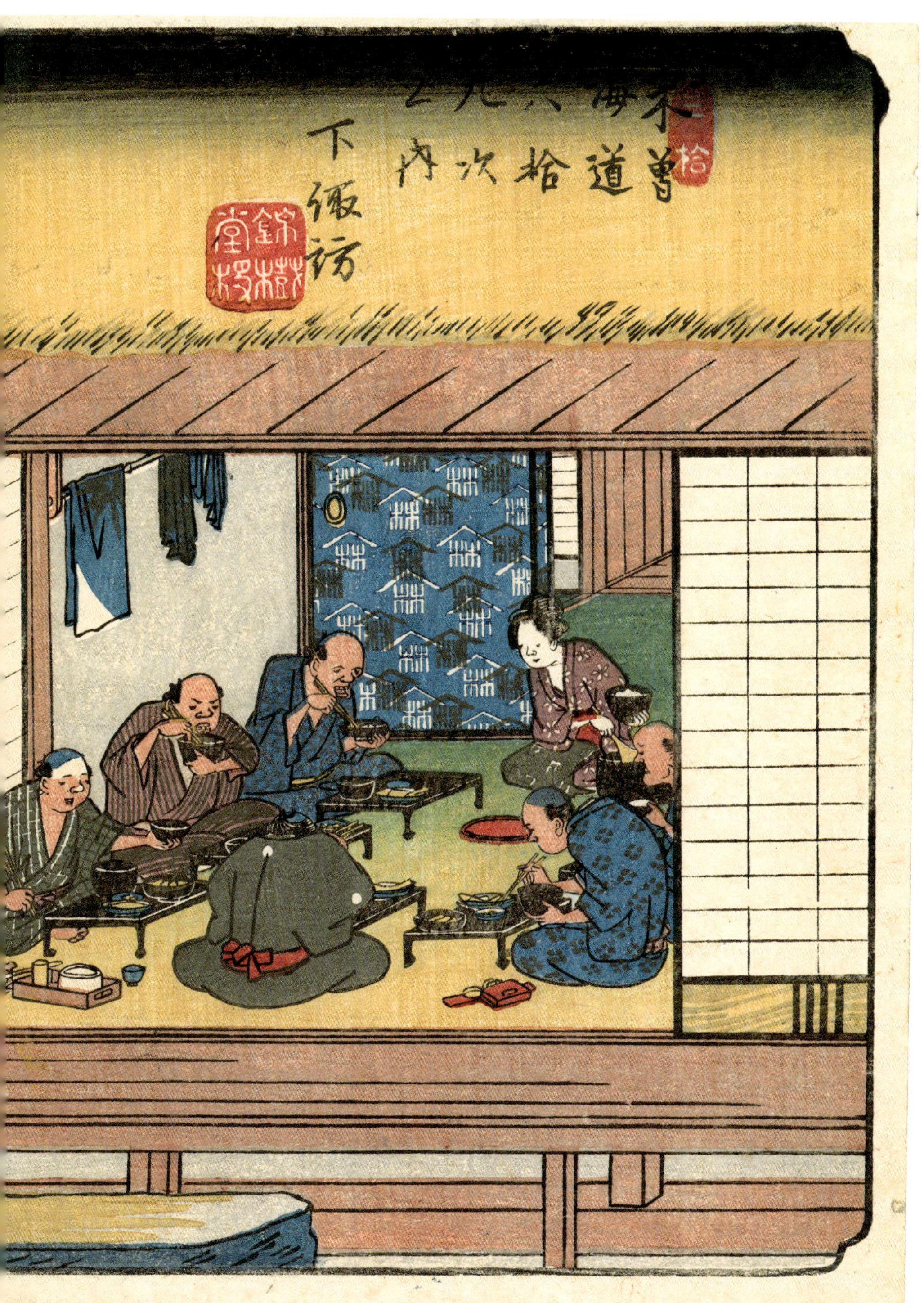

Die zwischen Wada und Shiojiri gelegene Station Shimosuwa profitierte von ihrer Nähe zum Wada-Pass, dem höchsten Punkt des Kisokaidō, und von ihrer Funktion als Endstation des Kōshūkaidō, der als Überlandstraße die Hauptstadt Edo mit den Provinzen Kai und Shinano verband. Außerdem zog sie Pilger an, die den Großschrein von Suwa (Suwa Taisha) besuchen wollten. Er besteht aus vier Gebäudekomplexen und ist mehr als 1200 Jahre alt.

Shimosuwa galt als Ursprungsort der feinsten Seide Japans. Vermutlich noch verlockender waren jedoch seine heißen Quellen, die dafür sorgten, dass sich spätestens seit dem 13. Jahrhundert Reisende gern zu einer Rast in dem Städtchen verführen ließen. Einer 1843 durchgeführten Erhebung zufolge besaß Shimosuwa 45 Herbergen; das *honjin* der Stadt, Iwanamiya, und zwei *waki-honjin*, Maruya und Kikyōya, existieren noch heute. Hiroshiges Entwurf für Shimosuwa zeigt die Rückansicht einer Herberge. Durch eine Öffnung zwischen den Flügeln der beiden Gebäude erblicken wir einen einzelnen Gast, der sich in einem Badezuber durchweichen lässt und mit einem blauen Handtuch seine Ohren abreibt. Sein Kimono liegt als khakifarbenes Bündel davor auf dem Boden.

Im Gastraum rechts sitzen sechs Reisende an niedrigen Tischen oder *zen* und lassen sich das Essen schmecken, während eine aufmerksame Serviererin ihre Reisschalen auffüllt. An der Wand über ihren Köpfen herabhängende Handtücher deuten darauf hin, dass einige der Männer bereits gebadet haben. Für den Rauchgenuss nach dem Essen stehen vorn links im Raum ein Tablett mit Rauchutensilien und eine Pfeife bereit, direkt gegenüber hat der Mann im blauen Gewand seinen roten Tabaksbeutel hervorgeholt. Das Markenzeichen des Verlegers, Iseya Rihei, ziert in Form eines Musters die *fusuma* (Schiebetüren) im hinteren Teil des Raums.

Der Druck zeigt zwei verschiedene Bedachungsarten, die in der Region Shinano üblich waren. Das Dach des Gebäudes rechts, in dem die Reisenden ihr Mahl einnehmen, ist dicht mit Stroh gedeckt, während das Dach zur Linken mit dünnen Schindeln belegt wurde, die mit Steinen gegen heftige Stürme gesichert sind. Die schweren Holztüren, die in kälteren Monaten zwischen dem Dachvorsprung und dem *engawa*, der Veranda, angebracht waren, sind entfernt worden, damit die Luft zirkulieren kann.

Située entre les stations de Shiojiri et de Wada, Shimosuwa dut sa prospérité à sa proximité avec le col de Wada, point le plus élevé de la Kisokaidō, et parce qu'elle était le terminus de la Kōshūkaidō, la grande route reliant Edo à Kai et à la province de Shinano. Elle attirait aussi les pèlerins qui se rendaient au grand sanctuaire de Suwa (Suwa Taisha), composé de quatre complexes et datant de plus de 1200 ans.

Shimosuwa était considéré comme le lieu de production de la plus belle soie du Japon. Toutefois, ce sont ses sources chaudes naturelles qui rendaient peut-être la station encore plus attrayante pour les voyageurs souhaitant faire une halte, et ce, depuis le XIIIe siècle au moins. D'après un recensement effectué en 1843, Shimosuwa possédait quarante-cinq auberges ; Iwanamiya, la *honjin* de la ville, existe encore aujourd'hui, de même que deux *waki-honjin*, Maruya et Kikyōya. Le sujet de l'estampe d'Hiroshige est ici une vue de la façade arrière d'une auberge. À travers une ouverture séparant les ailes des deux bâtiments, nous pouvons observer un client prenant un bain, seul dans une baignoire en bois, et se frottant les oreilles avec une serviette bleue. Son kimono vert kaki est posé tout près, en tas sur le sol.

Dans la pièce visible à droite, six voyageurs sont assis devant des *zen*, tables basses où l'on prend les repas, et mangent avec assiduité, tandis qu'une servante attentive remplit leur bol de riz. Des serviettes accrochées au mur indiquent que certains d'entre eux ont déjà pris leur bain. En prévision de l'après-dîner, un plateau de bois, sur lequel se trouvent des ustensiles de fumeur et une pipe, a été déposé à gauche près de l'ouverture de la pièce, alors que l'homme vêtu de bleu, assis de l'autre côté, a déjà sorti une blague à tabac rouge. Au fond de la pièce, les *fusuma*, ou portes coulissantes, sont ornées du blason de l'éditeur, Iseya Rihei.

Cette estampe montre deux modes de couverture des toits, typiques de la région de Shinano. Le toit de la maison de droite, où les voyageurs se restaurent, est recouvert d'un épais chaume, tandis que, sur celui de gauche, de minces bardeaux sont maintenus par des pierres qui les protègent des vents violents. Les lourdes portes de bois installées durant les mois d'hiver les plus froids entre les avant-toits et l'*engawa*, la terrasse, ont été retirées pour permettre la ventilation de la maison.

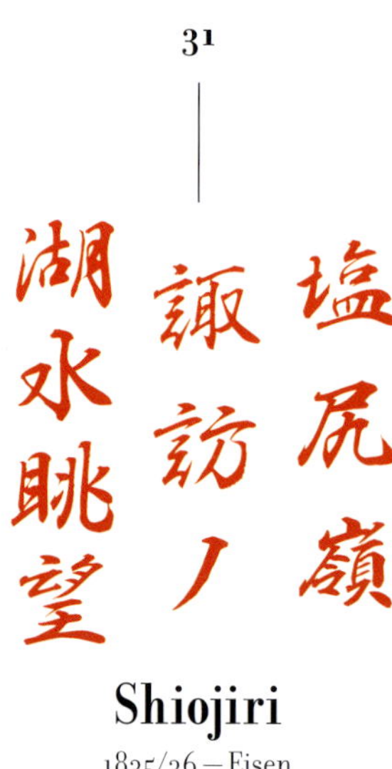

Shiojiri

1835/36 — Eisen

Eisen's design for Shiojiri represents the commanding southward view from a point along the 1,012-metre-high (3,320 feet) Shiojiri Pass, where the Kisokaidō climbs after leaving Shimosuwa station. Below lies Lake Suwa, with a present-day surface elevation of 759 metres (2,490 feet), and from left to right can be seen Mount Yatsudake, Takashima Castle and Mount Fuji in the distance. The latter is depicted only twice elsewhere in this series. Takashima Castle was built in 1598 by Hineno Takayoshi (1539–1600) a retainer of the military commander Hideyoshi Toyotomi (1536/37–1598). During the Edo period, the castle became the administrative seat of Suwa Domain. It was originally constructed on a small promontory extending into the lake, but the shoreline has shifted over the centuries, leaving it stranded today some distance from the water's edge.

When winters are particularly cold, a natural phenomenon known as *omiwatari*, "the pathway of the gods", sometimes occurs at Lake Suwa. The pressure created from the daily cycle of expansion and contraction can cause the surface of the frozen lake to crack, and forces up a ridge of ice shards as high as 180 centimetres (71 inches). As local folklore has it, this icy rampart appears when Takeminakata-no-kami, the god of the Upper Shrine of Suwa Grand Shrine (Suwa Taisha) located on the south-east side of the lake, crosses over to visit his lover, the goddess Yasakatome-no-kami, at the Lower Shrine on the northern side.

According to custom, priests in the Suwa Shrine watch for signs of *omiwatari* and make predictions for the quality of the harvest from the appearance of the cracks. Records of *omiwatari* events have been kept since 1443, and are used today in the study of climate change. In Eisen's design, the lake has frozen solidly enough to support the weight of a train of travellers and a horse, but there is no sign of the god's footsteps.

The four complexes of the Suwa Grand Shrine attracted many travellers to Shiojiri; only Fukaya, which had 80 inns, offered more accommodation options than Shiojiri, which had 75.

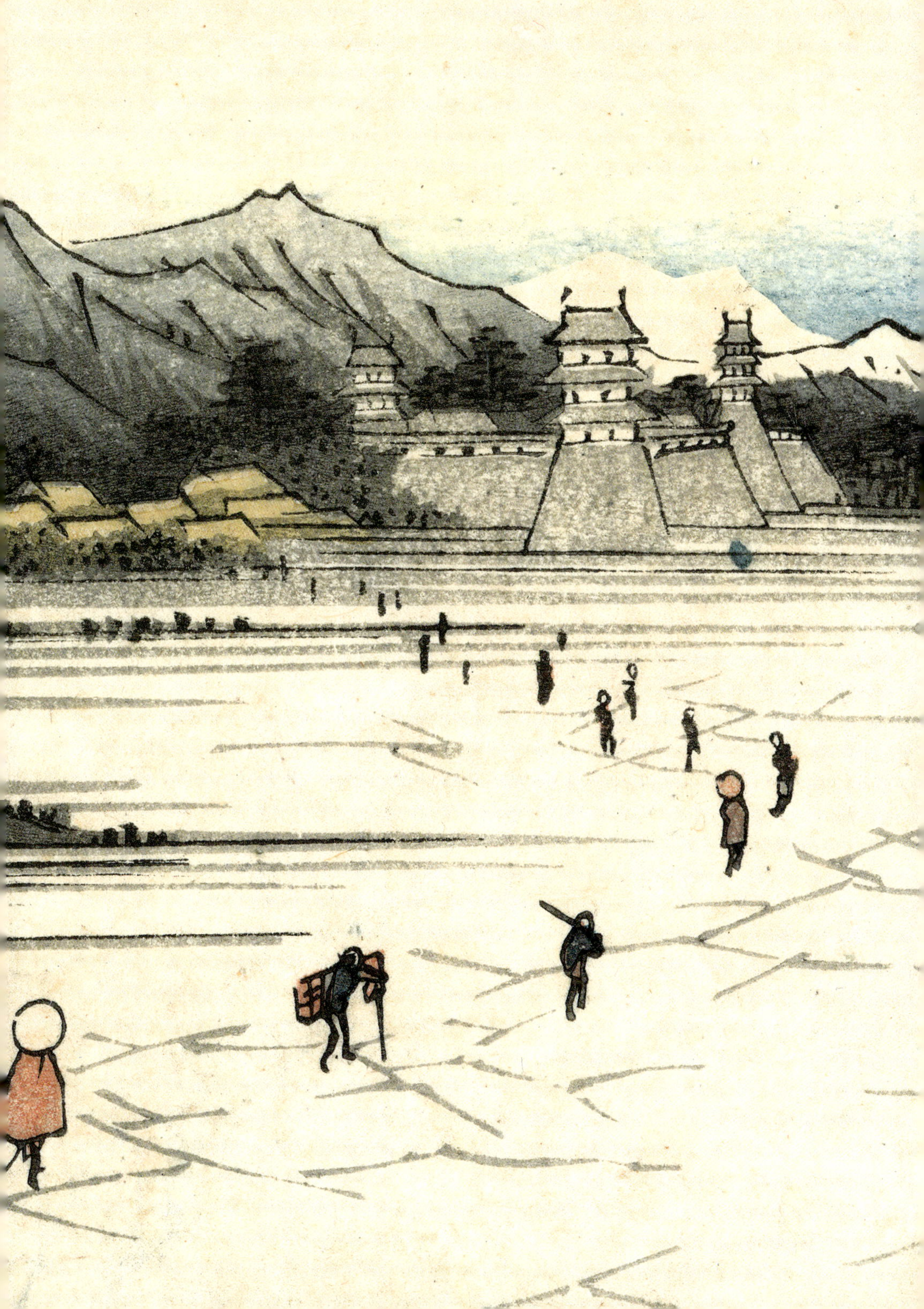

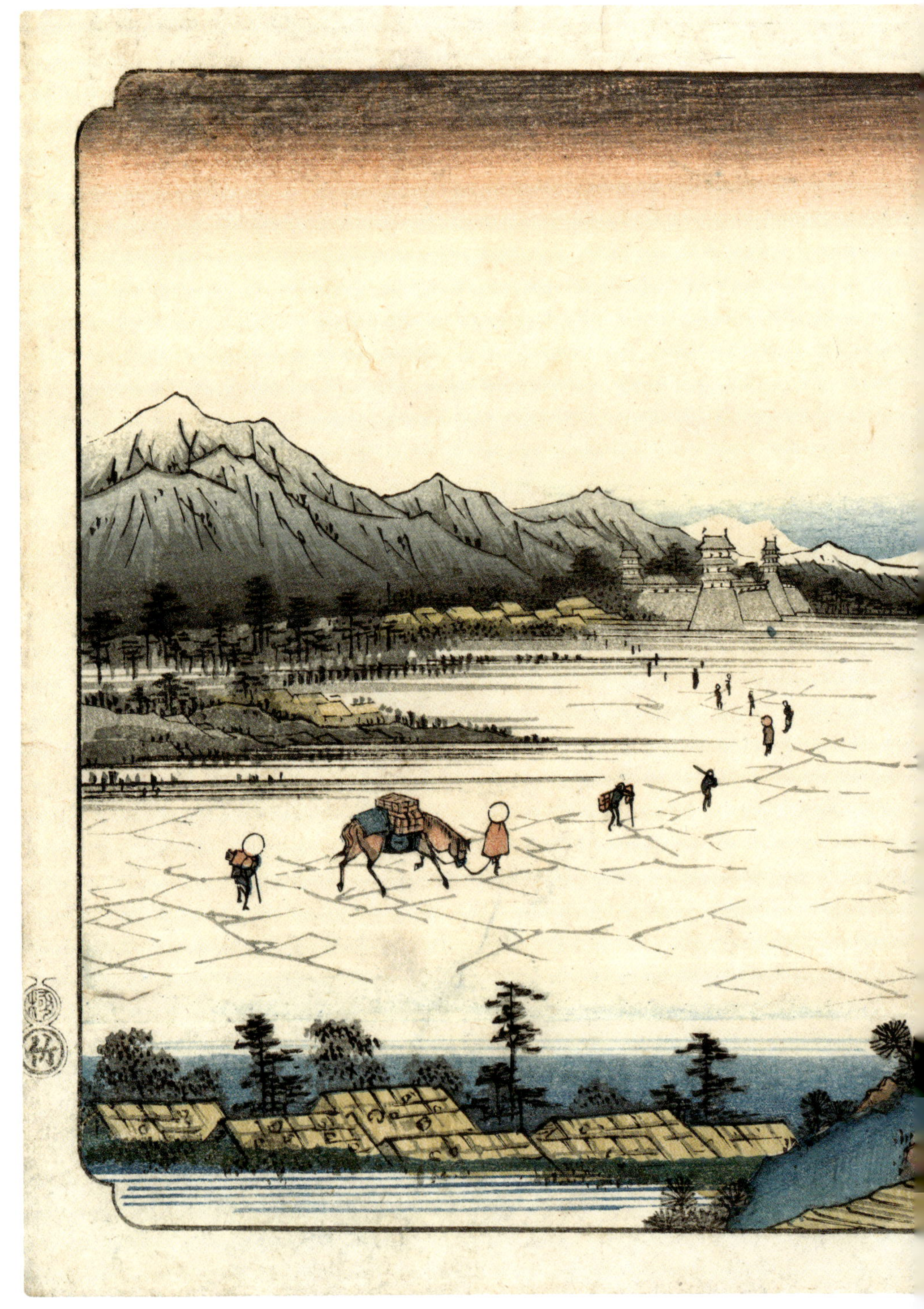

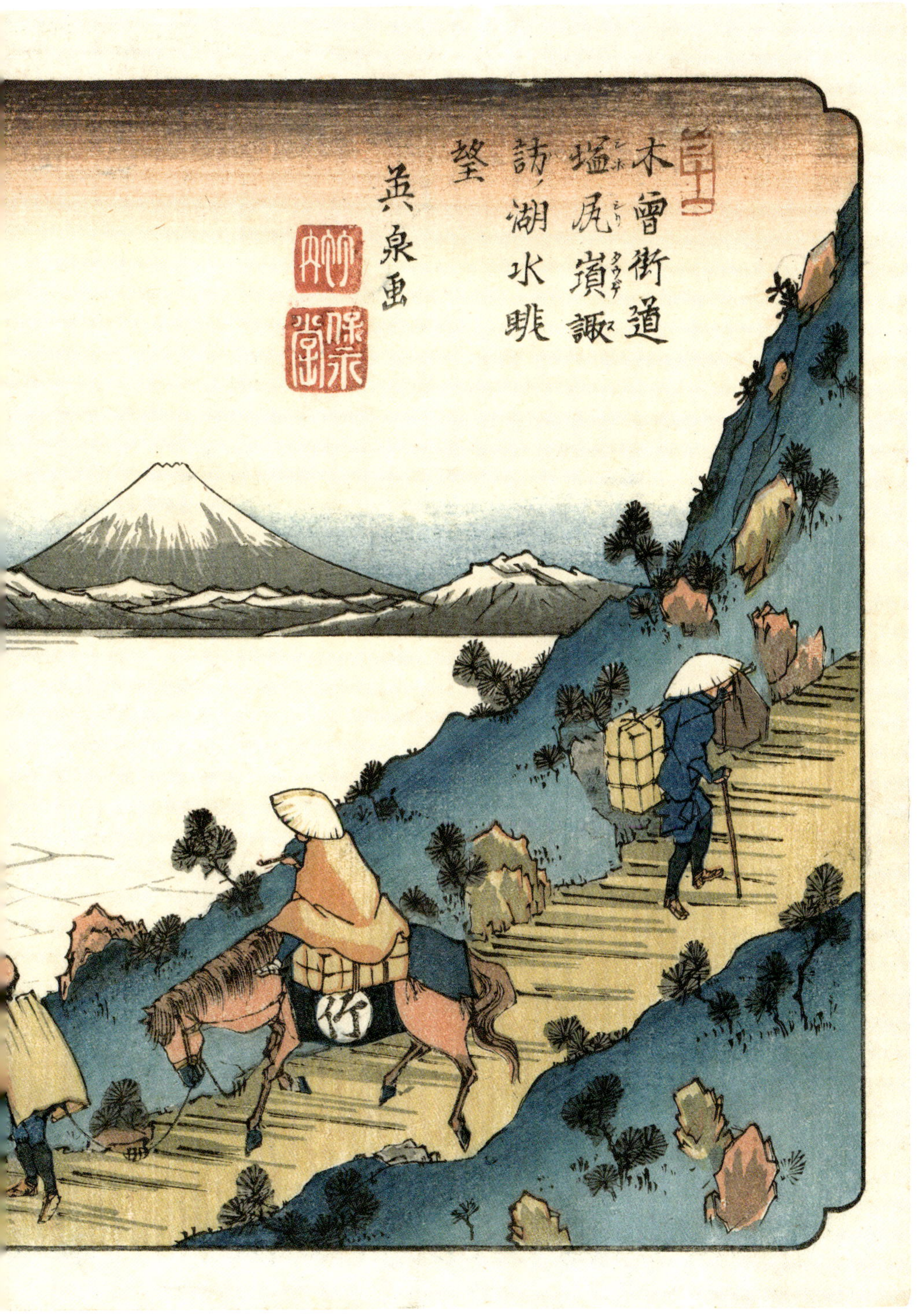
木曾街道
塩尻嶺諏
訪ノ湖水眺
望
英泉画

Hinter der Station Shimosuwa wand sich der Kisokaidō zum 1012 Meter hohen Shiojiri-Pass hinauf. Den atemberaubenden Blick von der Passstraße in Richtung Süden hielt Eisen in seinem Entwurf für Shiojiri fest. Die Straße führt hinab zum Suwa-See, dessen Wasserspiegel heute 759 Meter über dem Meer liegt. Vom Gebirgszug des Yatsudake links im Bild wandert der Blick über die Burg Takashima zum in der Ferne aufragenden Fuji, der im gesamten Kisokaidō-Zyklus nur zwei weitere Male auftaucht. Die Burg Takashima wurde 1598 von Hineno Takayoshi (1539–1600) erbaut, einem Gefolgsmann des Militärbefehlshabers Hideyoshi Toyotomi (1536/37–1598). Während der Edo-Zeit wurde sie zum Verwaltungssitz des Lehens Suwa. Ursprünglich stand die Burg auf einer kleinen Landzunge, die in den See hineinragte, doch da sich die Uferlinie über die Jahrhunderte verschoben hat, liegt sie heute in einiger Entfernung zum Wasser auf dem Trockenen.

In besonders kalten Wintern ist der Suwa-See gelegentlich Schauplatz einer als *omiwatari* oder „Pfad der Götter" bekannten Naturerscheinung. Der Druck, der erzeugt wird, wenn das Eis sich tagsüber ausdehnt und nachts wieder zusammenzieht, kann Risse in der Eisdecke erzeugen und einen bis zu 1,80 Meter hohen Rücken aus Eisschollen aufwerfen. Wie der örtliche Volksglaube sagt, erscheint dieser eisige Wall, wenn Takeminakata-no-kami, der Gott des am südöstlichen Seeufers gelegenen Oberen Schreins des Großschreins von Suwa (Suwa Taisha), den See überquert, um seine Geliebte, die Göttin Yasakatome-no-kami, im Unteren Schrein am Nordufer zu besuchen.

Dem Brauch entsprechend halten die Priester des Suwa-Schreins nach Zeichen des *omiwatari* Ausschau und treffen anhand des Aussehens der Risse und Brüche im Eis Vorhersagen über die Qualität der nächsten Ernte. Heute werden die seit 1443 archivierten Aufzeichnungen von *omiwatari*-Ereignissen zur Erforschung des Klimawandels herangezogen. In Eisens Entwurf ist die Eisdecke des Sees dick genug, um einen Zug von Reisenden und ein Pferd zu tragen. Anzeichen für göttliche Fußabdrücke sind jedoch nicht auszumachen.

Die vier Gebäudekomplexe des Großschreins von Suwa lockten zahlreiche Reisende nach Shiojiri; nur die Station Fukaya hatte mit 80 Herbergen mehr Übernachtungsoptionen anzubieten als Shiojiri mit 75.

L'estampe réalisée par Eisen pour la station de Shiojiri représente l'impressionnant panorama qu'offre un point de vue orienté vers le sud, au col de Shiojiri (à une altitude de 1012 mètres), auquel conduit la Kisokaidō après avoir quitté Shimosuwa. L'endroit domine le lac Suwa dont la surface est aujourd'hui à une altitude de 759 mètres ; on voit, de gauche à droite, le mont Yatsudake, le château de Takashima et le mont Fuji. Ce dernier n'est figuré que dans deux autres estampes de cette série. Le château de Takashima fut construit en 1598 par Hineno Takayoshi (1539–1600), vassal du commandant militaire Hideyoshi Toyotomi (1536/37–1598). Durant l'ère Edo, le château devint le siège administratif du domaine de Suwa. Il avait été bâti sur un petit promontoire s'enfonçant dans le lac mais la rive s'étant déplacée au fil des siècles, le château s'en trouve à présent éloigné.

Au cours des hivers particulièrement rudes, un phénomène naturel, appelé *omiwatari*, « le chemin des dieux », se produit parfois sur le lac Suwa. La pression causée par le cycle quotidien de dilatation et de compression peut entraîner des fissures à la surface du lac et faire naître une crête de fragments de glace pointus, pouvant atteindre une hauteur de 1,80 mètre. Selon la légende populaire, ce rempart de glace apparaît lorsque Takeminakata-no-kami, le dieu du sanctuaire supérieur du grand sanctuaire de Suwa (Suwa Taisha), situé au sud-est du lac, traverse celui-ci pour rendre visite à celle qui l'aime, la déesse Yasakatome-no-kami, qui se trouve au sanctuaire inférieur, sur la rive nord.

Selon la coutume, les prêtres du sanctuaire de Suwa guettent les signes d'un *omiwatari* et font des prédictions sur la qualité des récoltes en fonction de l'aspect des fissures. L'apparition des *omiwatari* est consignée depuis 1443, et les archives servent aujourd'hui à l'étude du changement climatique. Dans le dessin d'Eisen, le lac est suffisamment gelé pour soutenir le poids d'une procession de voyageurs et d'un cheval, mais on ne distingue aucune empreinte de pas du dieu.

Les quatre complexes du grand sanctuaire de Suwa attiraient de nombreux voyageurs à Shiojiri ; seule Fukaya, avec ses quatre-vingts auberges, proposait davantage d'hébergements que Shiojiri, qui en comptait soixante-quinze.

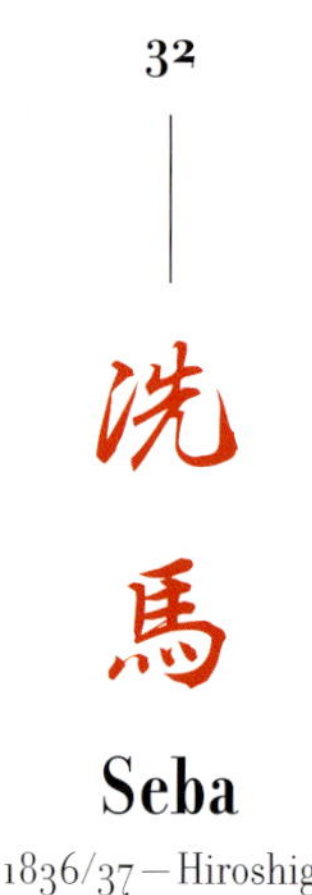

32

Seba

1836/37 — Hiroshige

Hiroshige's design for Seba is one of the most lyrical of the series. The print depicts two boatmen, one with a cargo of firewood, poling their vessels along under a fading sky. The combination of the full moon, sitting low and heavy on the horizon, the tall rushes on the riverbank and the willow trees and grasses bending in the wind evoke the melancholy of late summer or early autumn. In the distance, thatch-roofed farmhouses nestled into the earth are a bitter-sweet reminder of the displacement felt by wayfarers.

The river is thought to represent the Narai, which runs in a north-easterly direction between its source on the northern face of Mount Chausu and its confluence with the Azusa River at Matsumoto, where its name changes to the Sai. Between these points, it flows past the north-west outskirts of Seba.

The Seba station and its neighbours Motoyama and Shiojiri are thought to have been established around 1615 when the route of the Kisokaidō was altered. In 1712, the town was equipped with a weighing station so that couriers could verify the weight of their cargo. To the east of Seba, the Hokkoku Nishi Kaidō (North-Western Road) branches off from the Kisokaidō and heads north-east through Matsumoto as far as the seventh-century Zenkōji Temple in northern Nagano Prefecture, and is thus also known as Zenkōji Kaidō.

Hiroshiges Entwurf für die Station Seba zählt zu den lyrischsten des gesamten Zyklus. Der Druck zeigt zwei Bootsführer, die ihre Fahrzeuge, ein Boot mit einer Ladung Brennholz und ein Floß, im Licht der Dämmerung vorwärtsstaken. Der Vollmond, der tief und schwer über dem Horizont hängt, dazu die langen Binsen am Flussufer und die Weiden und Gräser, die sich im Wind biegen, beschwören die Melancholie des Spätsommers oder Frühherbstes. Die im Hintergrund in die Landschaft geschmiegten strohgedeckten Bauernhäuser evozieren bittersüß das Heimweh der Wanderer.

Man nimmt an, dass der Fluss Narai dargestellt ist, der von seiner Quelle an der Nordseite des Chausu in Richtung Nordosten verläuft und nach seiner Vereinigung mit dem Azusa in Matsumoto den Namen Sai annimmt. Zwischen diesen beiden Punkten fließt er am nordwestlichen Ortsrand von Seba vorbei.

Die Station Seba und ihre Nachbarstationen Motoyama und Shiojiri sollen um 1615 gegründet worden sein, als der Verlauf des Kisokaidō verändert wurde. 1712 erhielt der Ort eine Wiegestation, sodass Kuriere das Gewicht ihrer Fracht überprüfen konnten. Östlich von Seba zweigt der Hokkoku Nishi Kaidō (Nordweststraße) vom Kisokaidō ab und führt über Matsumoto nach Nordosten bis zum Zenkōji-Tempel, der im 7. Jahrhundert im Norden der heutigen Präfektur Nagano erbaut wurde; dieser Abzweig ist daher auch als Zenkōji Kaidō bekannt.

L'estampe réalisée par Hiroshige pour la station de Seba est l'une des plus lyriques de la série. On y voit deux bateliers, dont l'un transporte un chargement de bois de chauffage, poussant leur embarcation à l'aide d'une perche sous un ciel de crépuscule. La pleine lune, basse et grosse sur l'horizon, les grands roseaux bordant la rive, les herbes et les saules ployés par le vent concourent à l'évocation mélancolique d'une fin d'été ou d'un début d'automne. Dans le lointain, des fermes au toit de chaume blotties dans la terre rappellent avec nostalgie aux voyageurs qu'ils sont loin de leur foyer.

On estime que la rivière illustrée est la Narai, dont le cours suit une direction nord-est entre sa source, sur le versant nord du mont Chausu, et sa confluence avec l'Azusa à Matsumoto, à partir de laquelle la Narai prend le nom de Sai. Entre ces deux points, elle passe à la périphérie nord-ouest de Seba.

Comme ses voisines de Motoyama et de Shiojiri, la station de Seba aurait été créée vers 1615, avec la modification du tracé de la Kisokaidō. En 1712, la petite ville fut équipée d'une station de pesage afin que les portefaix puissent vérifier le poids de leur chargement. À l'est de Seba, l'Hokkoku Nishi Kaidō (route du nord-ouest) se sépare de la Kisokaidō vers le nord-est et traverse Matsumoto pour atteindre le temple de Zenkōji, datant du VIIe siècle, dans le nord de la préfecture de Nagano, et est donc également appelée Zenkōji Kaidō.

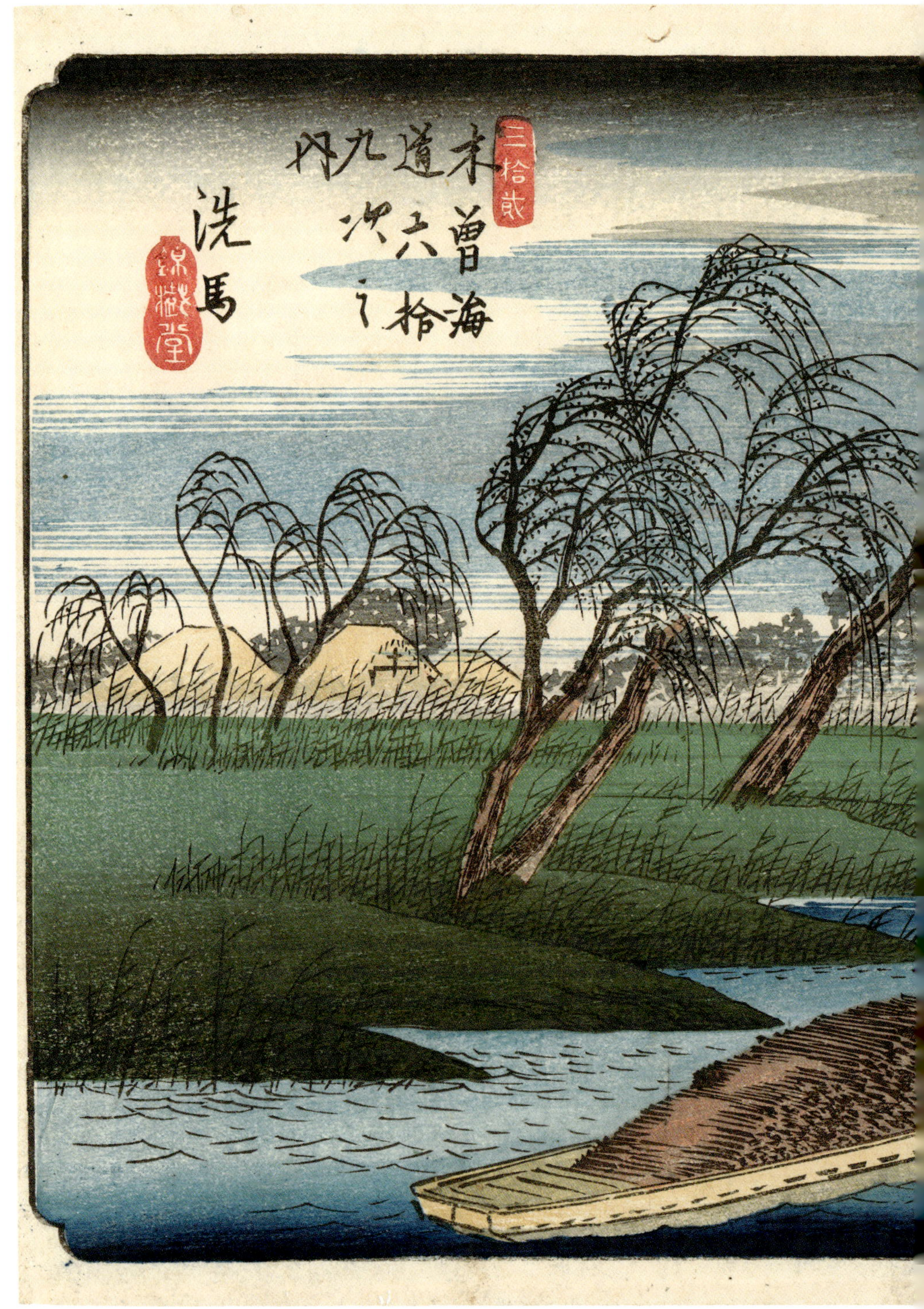

三拾貳
木曽海道六拾九次之内
洗馬

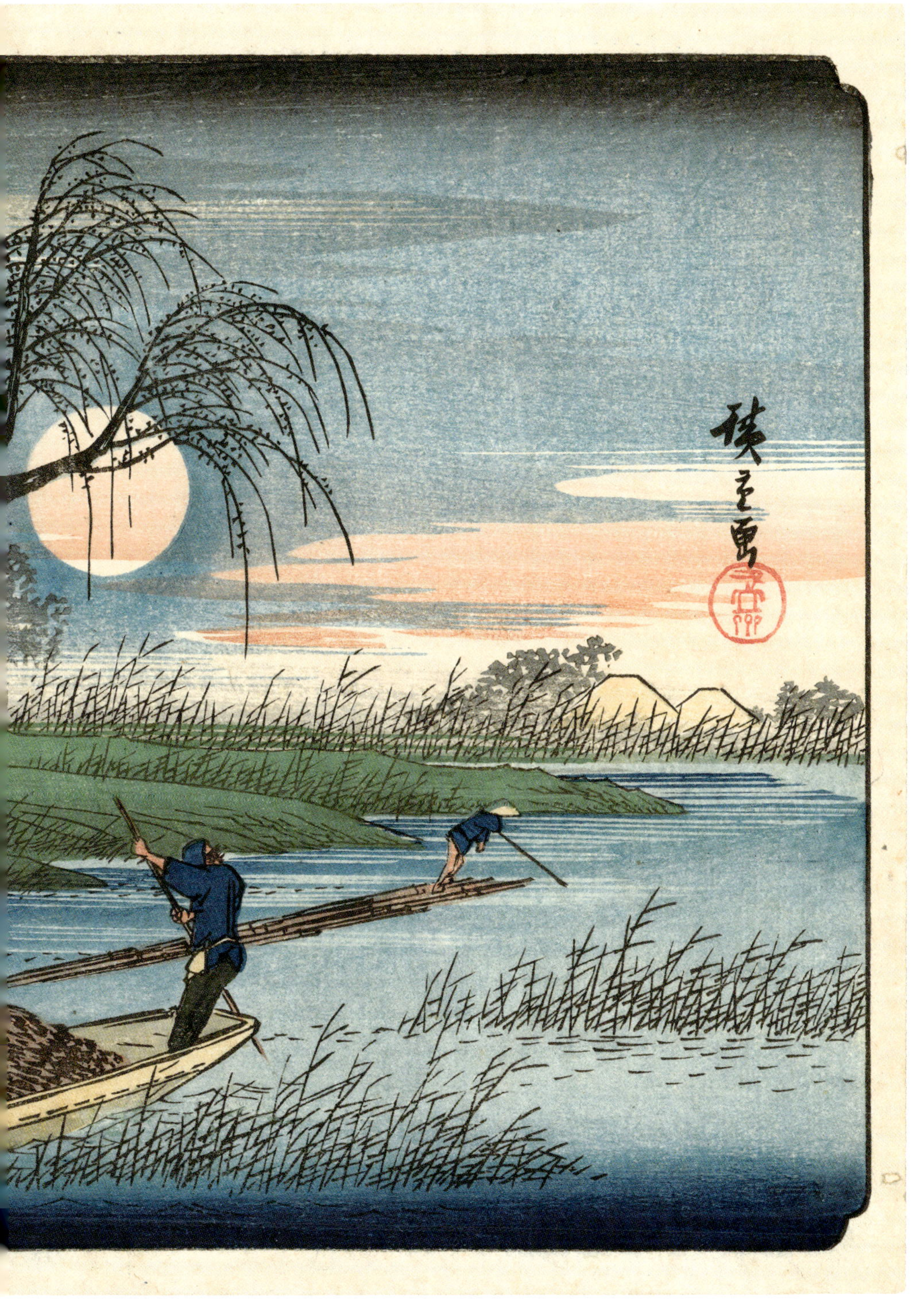

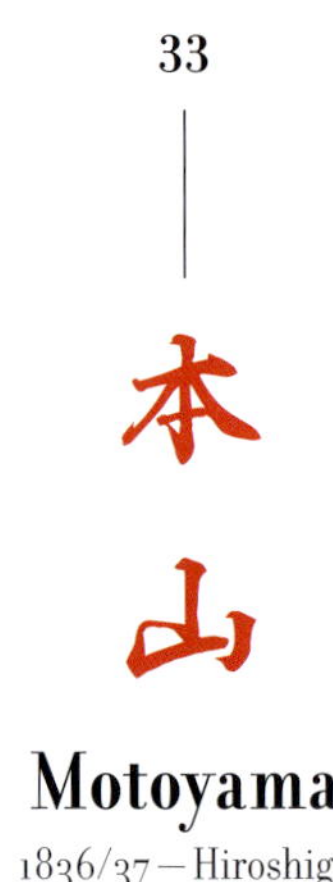

33

Motoyama

1836/37 – Hiroshige

Motoyama station was positioned on the north-east side of an incline. Assuming Hiroshige had studied maps of the area prior to designing this print, it is probable that this was the site he chose for his design for Motoyama.

In Hiroshige's print, the road passes under a magnificent cedar tree that has been knocked over by strong winds. The undisturbed earth at its base suggests that this was not a recent occurrence. Below, two lumberjacks are resting beside a campfire, sitting on a tree they have just felled – or perhaps another victim of inclement weather. Propped up against the fallen tree beside the worker on the right is his hatchet, secure in its woven sheath. Pine needles and cones are scattered on the ground as a result of their labour.

A traveller wearing a broad woven hat and with his belongings tied in a wrapping cloth or *furoshiki* knotted around his shoulders is climbing up the pass. Two small boys are gathering kindling in baskets as big as they are.

Motoyama station was established in around 1615 at a distance of only 3.3 kilometres (2.1 miles) from Seba. The road through here is believed to date from the eighth century. According to the text *Popular Literary Selections* (*Fūzoku monzen*, 1706) by Morikawa Kyoroku (1656–1715), the farmland around Motoyama is the birthplace of buckwheat cultivation in Japan. Like many areas, the village was periodically ravaged by fire; the most recent at the time of this print's creation was in 1825.

Die Station Motoyama lag an der Nordostseite eines Abhangs. Gesetzt den Fall, dass Hiroshige Landkarten der Gegend studiert hatte, bevor er dieses Blatt anfertigte, dürfte dies vermutlich der Schauplatz gewesen sein, den er für die Darstellung der Station Motoyama auswählte.

In Hiroshiges Druck führt die Straße unter eine mächtigen Zeder hindurch, die vom Sturm umgeworfen wurde. Der unversehrte Untergrund an der Wurzel deutet darauf hin, dass der Vorfall länger zurückliegt. Unter dem abgestützten Baum machen zwei Holzfäller am Lagerfeuer Pause. Sie sitzen auf dem Stamm eines Baumes, den sie gerade gefällt haben – sofern er nicht ebenfalls dem schlechten Wetter zum Opfer gefallen ist. Gegen den Stamm hat der Arbeiter rechts sein mit einer Schutzhülle aus Strohgeflecht gesichertes Beil gelehnt. Als Ergebnis ihrer Arbeit liegen Kiefernnadeln und -zapfen auf dem Boden verstreut.

Ein Reisender, der einen breiten Flechthut trägt und seine Habseligkeiten in einem Umschlagtuch oder *furoshiki* um die Schultern geknotet hat, steigt den Pass hinauf. Zwei kleine Jungen sammeln Kleinholz in Kiepen, die so groß sind wie sie selbst.

Die Station Motoyama wurde um 1615 in nur 3,3 Kilometern Entfernung von Seba gegründet. Die durch den Ort verlaufende Straße soll aus dem 8. Jahrhundert stammen. Der Anthologie *Auswahl beliebter literarischer Texte* (*Fūzoku monzen*, 1706) von Morikawa Kyoroku (1656–1715) zufolge war das Ackerland rund um Motoyama die Wiege des japanischen Buchweizenanbaus. Wie viele Landstriche wurde der Ort regelmäßig von verheerenden Bränden heimgesucht – vor der Entstehung dieses Drucks zuletzt 1825.

La station de Motoyama se trouvait au nord-est d'une déclivité. Si l'on suppose qu'Hiroshige avait étudié les cartes de la région avant de réaliser cette estampe, il est probable qu'il s'agisse bien du site qu'il avait retenu pour représenter Motoyama.

Son dessin montre une route qui passe sous un magnifique cèdre abattu par des vents violents. L'événement n'est sans doute pas récent car, au pied de l'arbre, l'herbe en a recouvert les traces. Sous cet arbre se reposent près d'un feu deux bûcherons assis sur un arbre qu'ils viennent d'abattre ou qui, lui aussi, a été victime d'une tempête. Près du bûcheron de droite, une hachette est appuyée contre l'arbre abattu, bien rangée dans son étui. Le sol est jonché d'aiguilles et de pommes de pin, résultat de leur labeur.

Un voyageur coiffé d'un large chapeau tressé porte ses affaires dans une étoffe, appelée *furoshiki*, nouée autour des épaules, et escalade le col. Deux petits garçons ramassent du petit bois dans des paniers qui sont aussi grands qu'eux.

C'est vers 1615 que la station de Motoyama fut établie, à 3,3 kilomètres seulement de Seba. La route qui la traverse daterait du VIIIe siècle. Selon le texte de Morikawa Kyoroku (1656–1715), *Choix de célèbres écrits littéraires* (*Fūzoku monzen*, 1706), c'est sur les terres agricoles des environs de Motoyama qu'est née la culture du sarrasin au Japon. Comme bien d'autres endroits, ce village fut régulièrement ravagé par des incendies ; au moment de la réalisation de cette estampe, le plus récent avait eu lieu en 1825.

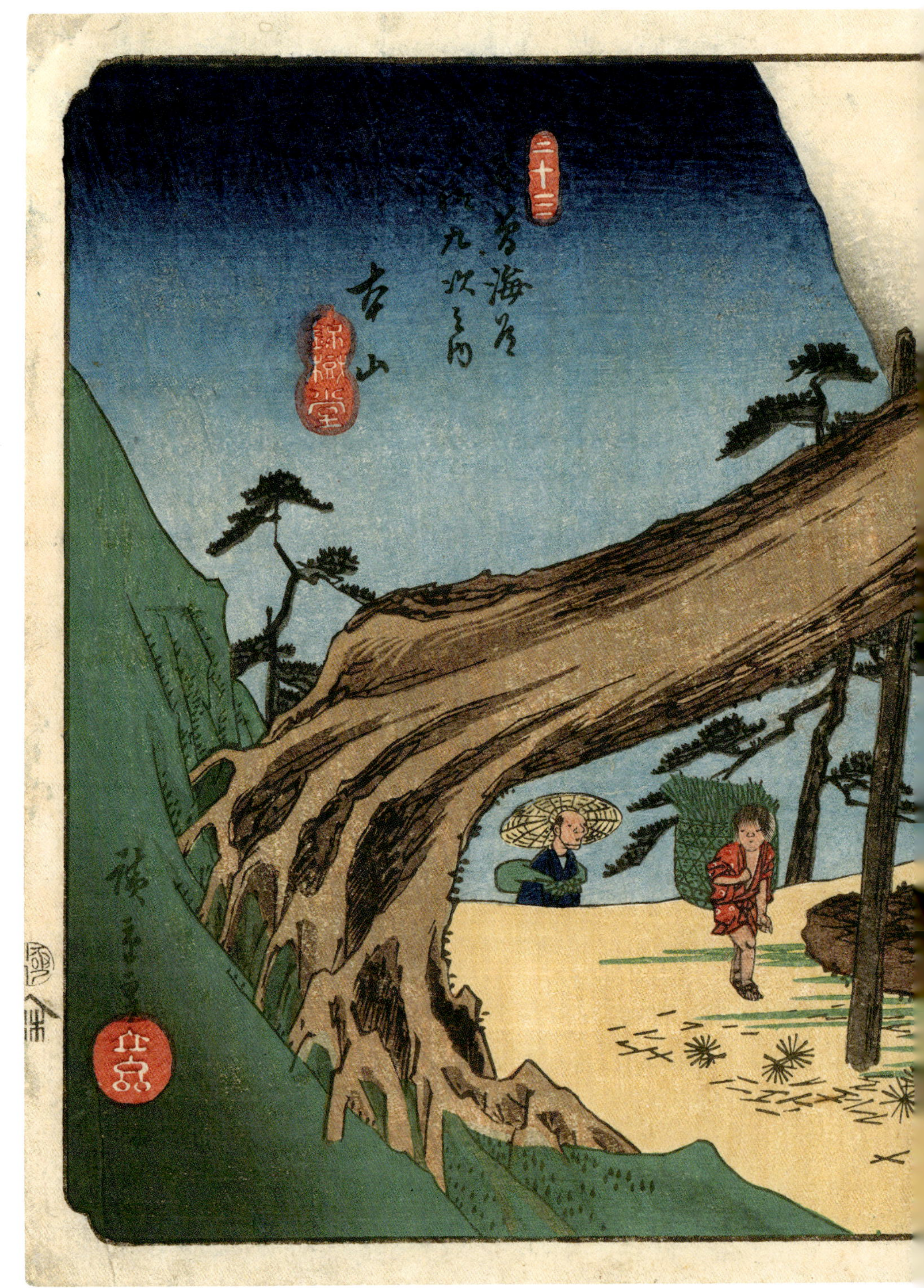

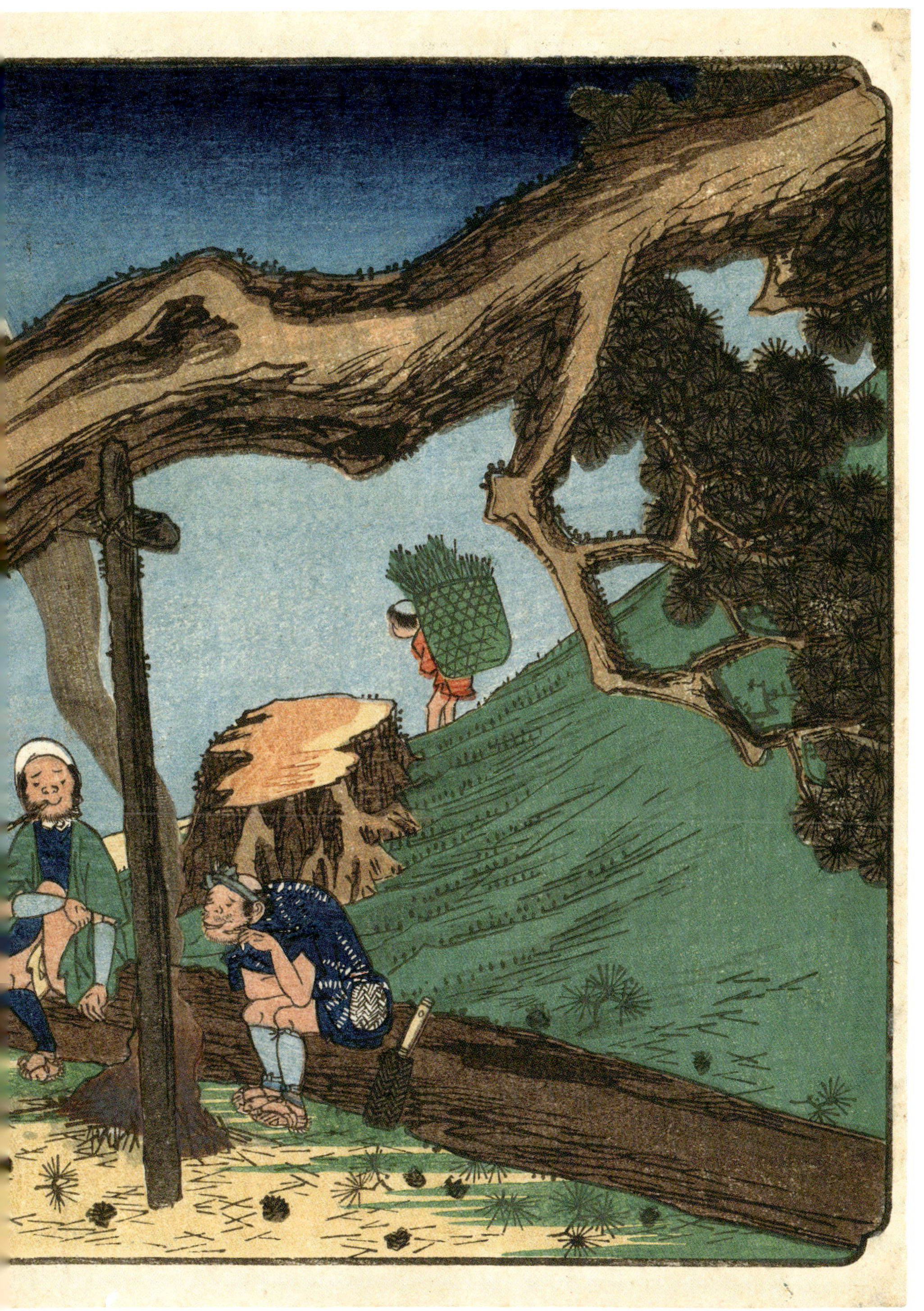

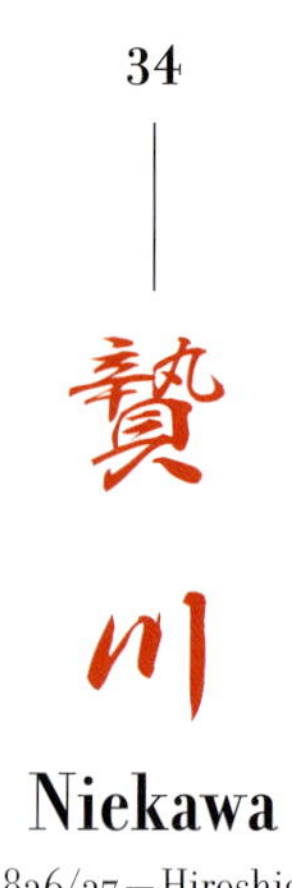

34

Niekawa

1836/37 — Hiroshige

Niekawa is one of the original stations on the Kisokaidō road, established between 1532 and 1555. According to the 1805 guidebook *Views of Famous Sights along the Kiso Road* (*Kisoji meisho zue*), the name Niekawa, which can be written with Chinese characters meaning "hot river", originally referred to its volcanic springs, which have long since run dry.

At the northern entrance there was a border station in the 1590s to regulate movement through the Kiso valley. During the Edo period, this was superseded by a subsidiary border-post overseen by officials from the nearby town of Kiso-Fukushima, the site of one of two strict checkpoints along the road (the other being at Usui). The existing building was reconstructed in the 1970s based on historical records. Another landmark in the village is the compound of the Fukasawa merchant family. The oldest part of this structure, the northern warehouse, dates to 1821; other parts were built in the 1850s and 1860s, and in 2005 the complex was designated an Important Cultural Property.

The design presents the front of a well-appointed inn as two guests arrive. Their hostess brings tea on a tray as they remove their *waraji* sandals and wash the dust of the journey from their feet. The master of the establishment bows from the corridor to the side. Trays of crockery are stacked neatly behind him, ready for use. Towards the back of the inn, a second woman is struggling with two packages, and another figure is carrying a tray of smoking utensils up to two guests on the second level. In front of the building, a palanquin-bearer is resting his legs while a pack-horse driver adjusts the horse's load. Both man and beast wear *waraji* to protect their feet and hooves on the hard surfaces and to provide traction on steep paths.

The cloth over the horse's rump displays the number 34, indicating the number of this design in the series. The name-board of the inn, affixed to the post on the left of the entrance, actually announces the name of the publisher of the print. The names of the block-cutter Matsushima Fusajirō, the printers Matsumura Yasugorō and Kita Ichitarō also appear, on the panels hanging on the left. One of these signs is an advertisement for a brand of skin-whitening face powder, Bien Senjokō, sold at the store of Mr. Sakamoto of Kyōbashi in Edo.

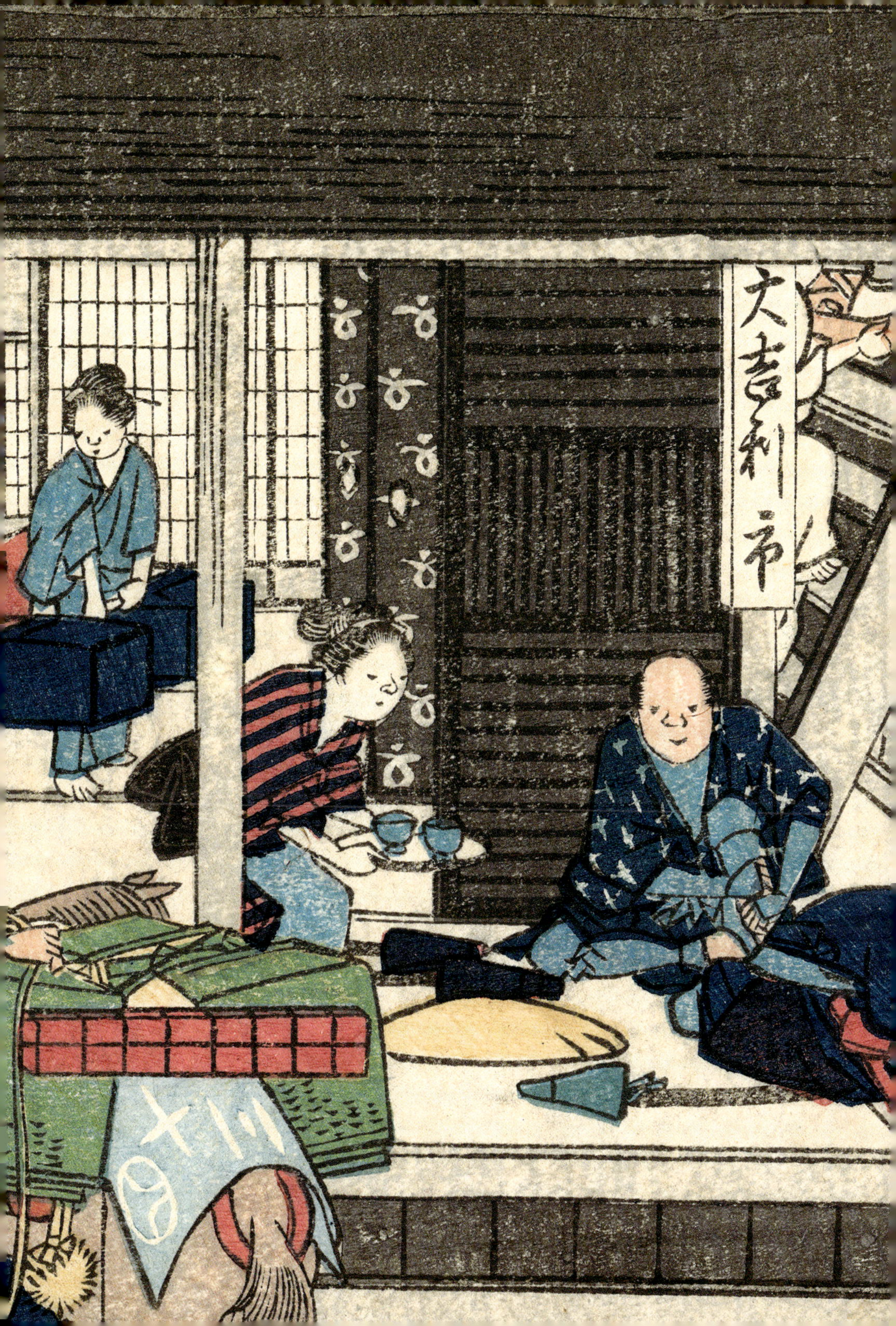

大吉利市

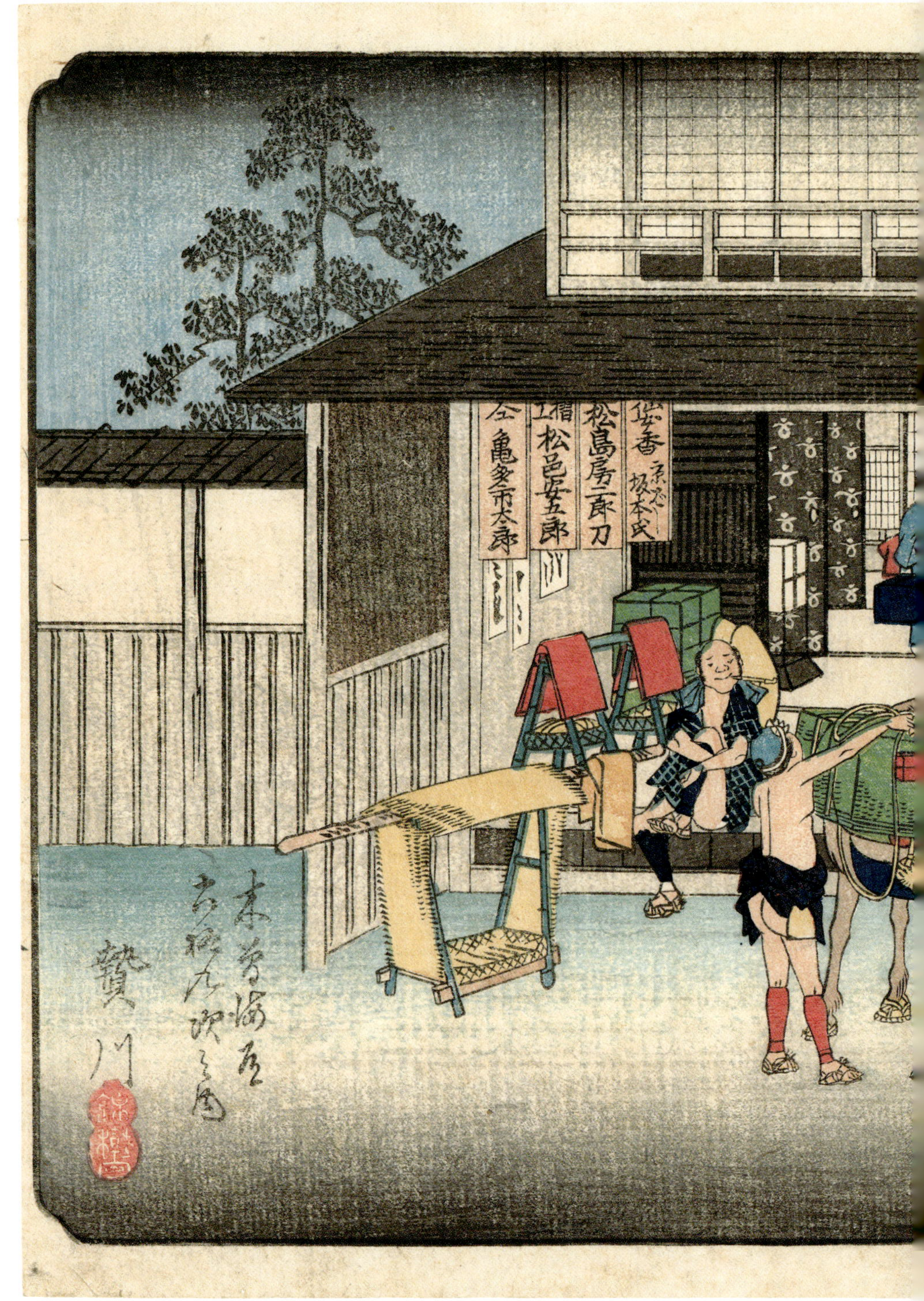

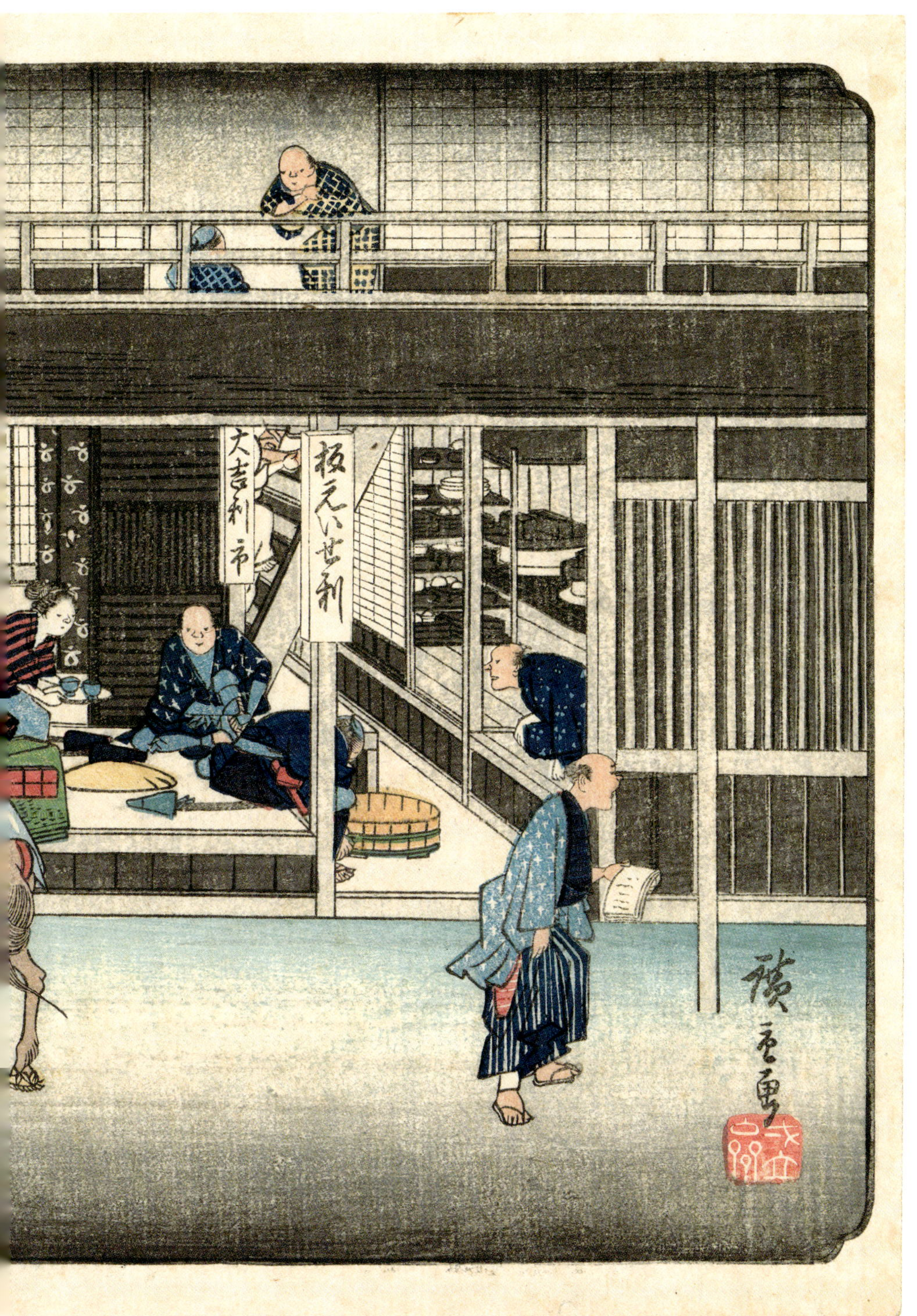

Niekawa gehört zu den Originalstationen des Kisokaidō und wurde zwischen 1532 und 1555 gegründet. Dem 1805 erschienenen Reisehandbuch *Ansichten berühmter Stätten an der Kiso-Straße (Kisoji meisho zue)* zufolge bezog sich der Name Niekawa, der in chinesischer Schreibweise „heißer Fluss" bedeutet, ursprünglich auf die vulkanischen Quellen des Ortes, die in der Zwischenzeit längst versiegt sind.

Am nördlichen Zugang zum Kiso-Tal regulierte in den 1590er Jahren eine Grenzstation den Verkehr durch das Tal. Während der Edo-Zeit (1603–1868) wurde sie durch einen untergeordneten Grenzposten ersetzt, den Beamte aus dem Nachbarort Kiso-Fukushima beaufsichtigten, wo sich eine der beiden strengen Kontrollstellen am Kisokaidō befand (die zweite stand in Usui). Das Gebäude, das sich heute dort erhebt, wurde in den 1970er Jahren anhand von historischen Aufzeichnungen rekonstruiert. Ein weiteres Wahrzeichen des Ortes ist das Anwesen der Kaufmannsfamilie Fukasawa. Der älteste Teil der Anlage, das nördliche Lagerhaus, stammt aus dem Jahr 1821, andere Teile aus den 1850er und 1860er Jahren. 2005 wurde der Komplex zum „bedeutenden Kulturgut" erklärt.

Das Blatt zeigt die Fassade einer gut ausgestatteten Herberge und die Ankunft zweier Gäste. Während sie ihre *waraji* (Sandalen aus Pflanzenfasern) ausziehen und sich den Staub der Reise von den Füßen waschen, serviert ihnen die Wirtin Tee auf einem Tablett. Der Hausherr grüßt vom seitlich gelegenen Flur mit einer Verbeugung. Hinter ihm stehen fein säuberlich gestapelt gebrauchsfertige Tabletts mit Geschirr. Im Rückraum der Herberge kämpft eine zweite Frau mit zwei Paketen, eine weitere Person trägt ein Tablett mit Rauchutensilien zu zwei Gästen in den ersten Stock hinauf. Vor dem Haus ruht ein Sänftenträger seine Beine aus, während ein Packpferdtreiber die Ladung seines Tieres justiert. Mann und Pferd tragen *waraji*, die auf den harten Untergründen Füße und Hufe schützen und auf steilen Wegen für die nötige Bodenhaftung sorgen sollten.

Die Zahl 34 auf der Satteldecke des Pferdes zeigt die laufende Nummer des Drucks in der Serie an. Die am Pfosten links des Eingangs befestigte Namenstafel der Herberge verkündet in Wirklichkeit den Namen des Verlegers. Der Holzschneider Matsushima Fusajirō und die Drucker Matsumura Yasugorō und Kita Ichitarō werden auf den Hängetafeln links im Bild ebenfalls namentlich erwähnt. Die vierte dieser Tafeln wirbt für einen weißen Gesichtspuder, Bien Senjokō, erhältlich bei einem Herrn Sakamoto aus Kyōbashi in seinem Geschäft in Edo.

Créée entre 1532 et 1555, la station de Niekawa est l'une des toutes premières de la Kisokaidō. D'après le guide de voyage, *Collection de vues de paysages célèbres sur la route Kiso (Kisoji meisho zue)* publié en 1805, le nom de Niekawa, qui peut s'écrire avec les caractères chinois signifiant « rivière chaude », faisait initialement allusion à ses sources volcaniques, aujourd'hui taries depuis longtemps.

À l'entrée nord de la station, il y avait, dans les années 1590, un poste à la limite du territoire qui régulait la circulation dans la vallée de Kiso. À l'ère Edo (1603–1868), celui-ci fut remplacé par un poste de contrôle secondaire surveillé par des fonctionnaires de la ville voisine de Kiso-Fukushima, où se trouvait l'un des deux postes de contrôle les plus stricts de la route (l'autre étant à Usui). Le bâtiment existant a été reconstruit dans les années 1970 à partir de documents historiques. Un autre haut lieu du village est le complexe des Fukasawa, une famille de marchands. L'entrepôt nord, la plus ancienne partie de cette structure, date de 1821 ; les autres bâtiments ont été édifiés dans les années 1850 et 1860. En 2005, ce complexe a été inscrit sur la liste du « patrimoine culturel important ».

Cette estampe représente la façade d'une auberge confortable, au moment où arrivent deux clients. Tandis qu'ils retirent leurs *wajari* (sandales) et qu'ils nettoient la poussière accumulée sur leurs pieds au cours du voyage, leur hôtesse apporte du thé sur un plateau. Dans le couloir visible sur le côté, le maître de l'établissement s'incline. Derrière lui, la vaisselle est soigneusement rangée sur des plateaux, prête à l'emploi. Au fond de l'auberge, une autre femme peine à porter deux paquets, tandis qu'un autre personnage monte l'escalier en portant un plateau d'ustensiles de fumeur, destiné aux deux clients visibles à l'étage. À l'extérieur de l'auberge, un porteur de palanquin se détend les jambes, tandis qu'un conducteur de cheval de bât ajuste sa charge sur la monture. L'homme et l'animal portent tous deux des *waraji* afin de protéger pieds et sabots de la chaussée rude et d'avoir une meilleure traction sur les chemins escarpés.

Le morceau de tissu qui recouvre la croupe du cheval porte le chiffre « 34 », indiquant le numéro d'ordre de cette estampe dans la série. L'enseigne de l'auberge, accrochée au poteau à gauche de l'entrée, porte le nom de l'éditeur de l'estampe. Sur les panneaux suspendus à gauche sont inscrits ceux de Matsushima Fusajirō, le graveur, de Matsumura Yasugorō et de Kita Ichitarō, les imprimeurs. L'un de ces panneaux est une publicité pour une marque de poudre à blanchir le visage, Bien Senjokō, en vente dans la boutique de M. Sakamoto, située dans le quartier de Kyōbashi, à Edo.

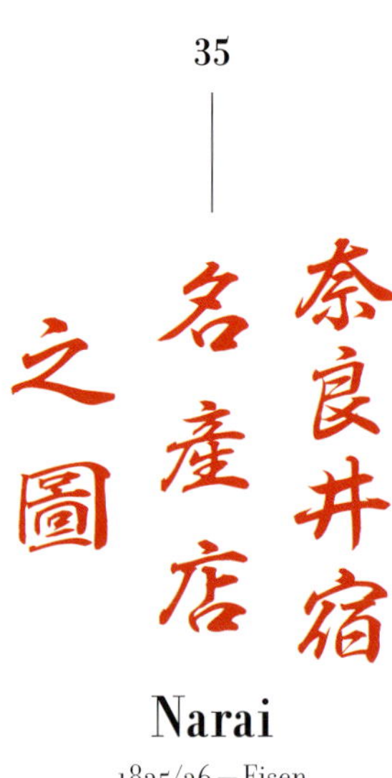

Narai

1835/36 – Eisen

The station of Narai is situated at the foot of the Torii Pass, one of the most challenging obstacles along the Kisokaidō. Eisen has chosen for the subject of his print a shop perched on a steep section of the pass selling fine-toothed combs called *Oroku-gushi*, a renowned product associated with the neighbouring station of Yabuhara but found elsewhere in this region as well. The combs are made by hand from dense cherry-birch wood, a slow-growing tree once abundant on the pass, and treated with camellia oil. *Oroku-gushi* are still produced today and are designated an official craft product by the prefectural governor of Nagano.

According to local lore, the popularity of these combs dates from the late 17th or early 18th century, when a young woman named Oroku made a pilgrimage to Mount Ontake in the hope of finding a cure for her brain disease. After praying there, she received a divine message to comb her hair with a comb made from the wood of a cherry birch, and after using it morning and night, her illness disappeared. Narai prospered from the demand for *Oroku-gushi* and other craft products such as lacquerware.

The scene created by Eisen is busy with activity. Two samurai seated at the front of the shop are choosing, perhaps for female family members or for lovers, from an array of combs in shallow trays a saleswoman is showing them. Seated with his back to us is a craftsman, and stacked in the background are stores of wood from which the combs are made. A courier, unburdened of his panniers, is wiping the sweat from his armpits while a man in a dark jacket inspects his wares before handing over payment. Two samurai, heading towards Edo, glance back before embarking on the steep descent.

High above, a peasant carrying brush is negotiating a narrow path which leads directly down the slope. The shingles of the roofs are weighted with rocks and branches to hold them in place during strong winds. The mountains in the background show the peaks of Mount Kiso Komagatake.

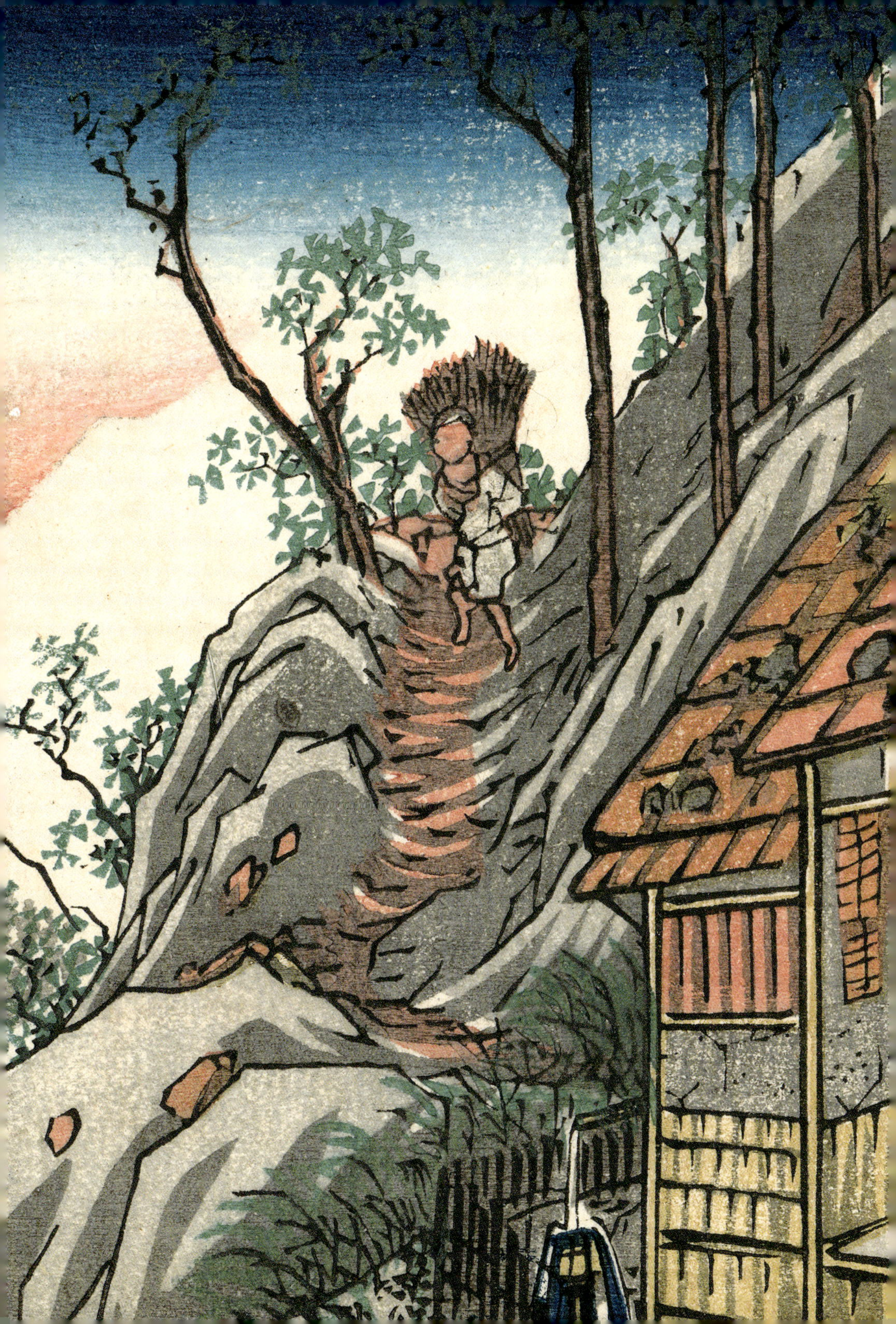

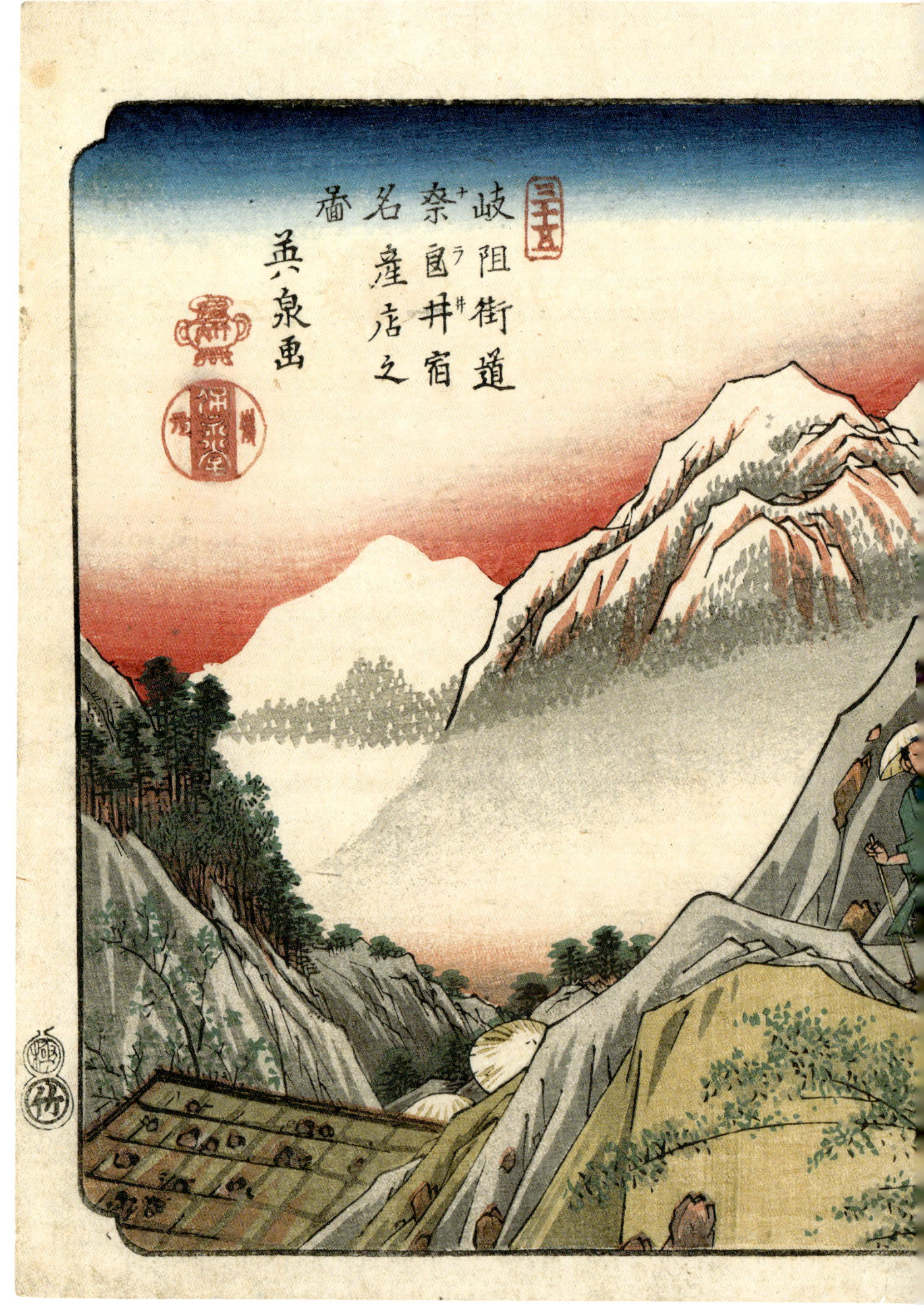
岐阻街道
奈良井宿
名産店之
番
英泉画

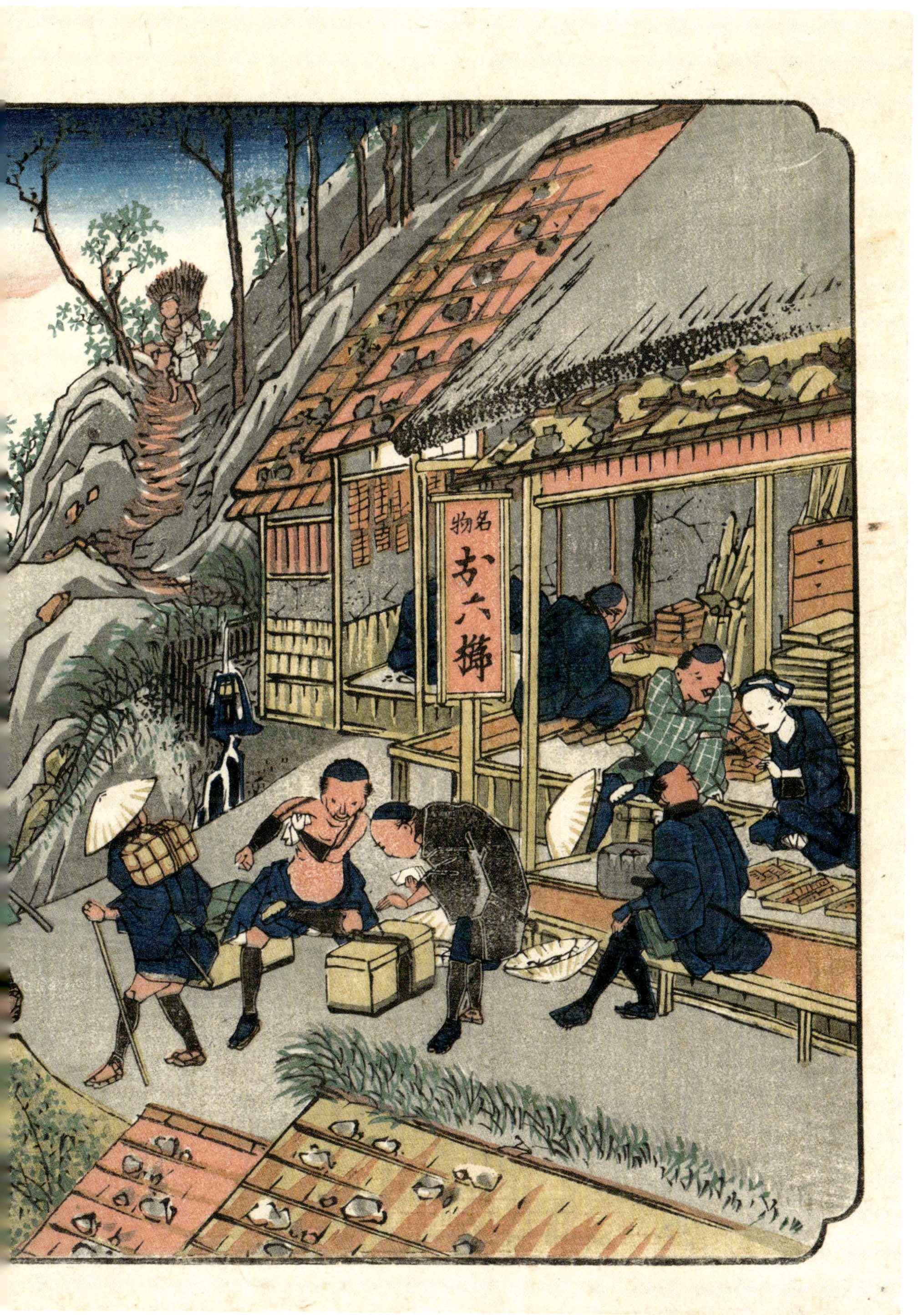

名物
古久壽

Die Station Narai liegt am Fuß des Torii-Passes, eines der anspruchsvollsten Hindernisse auf dem Kisokaidō. Als Motiv für seinen Druck wählte Eisen ein Geschäft an einem steilen Abschnitt des Passes, das mit feinzahnigen Kämmen handelt. Diese berühmten *Oroku-gushi* wurden eigentlich mit der Nachbarstation Yabuhara assoziiert, waren aber auch in anderen Teilen der Region zu finden. Sie werden aus dem Hartholz der Eisenbirke, eines langsam wachsenden und am Torii-Pass einst weit verbreiteten Laubbaums, gefertigt und mit Kamelienöl behandelt. *Oroku-gushi* werden bis heute hergestellt und tragen das Siegel „offizielles kunsthandwerkliches Erzeugnis", verliehen vom Gouverneur der Präfektur Nagano.

Örtlichen Überlieferungen zufolge geht die Popularität der Kämme bis ins späte 17. oder frühe 18. Jahrhundert zurück, als eine junge Frau namens Oroku in der Hoffnung, von ihrer Hirnerkrankung geheilt zu werden, eine Pilgerreise zum Vulkan Ontake unternahm. Nachdem sie dort gebetet hatte, empfing sie die göttliche Weisung, ihr Haar mit einem Kamm aus dem Holz der Eisenbirke zu kämmen, und nachdem sie diesen jeden Morgen und Abend verwendet hatte, verschwand ihre Krankheit. Die Nachfrage nach *Oroku-gushi*, Lackgegenständen und anderen kunsthandwerklichen Erzeugnissen ließ die Stadt Narai aufblühen.

Die von Eisen gestaltete Szene strotzt vor Betriebsamkeit. Im vorderen Teil des Ladens sitzen zwei Samurai und lassen sich von einer Verkäuferin eine Auswahl an Kämmen in flachen Schaukästen zeigen, vielleicht, weil sie eine weibliche Angehörige oder Geliebte damit bedenken wollen. Ein Handwerker kehrt uns sitzend den Rücken zu, und im Hintergrund lagert aufgestapelt das Holz, aus dem die Kämme geschnitten werden. Ein Kurier hat seine Packtaschen abgestellt und wischt sich den Schweiß aus den Achseln, während ein Mann in dunkler Jacke erst die Ware begutachtet, bevor er dafür bezahlt. Zwei Samurai auf dem Weg nach Edo werfen noch einen Blick zurück, ehe sie sich auf den steilen Abstieg begeben.

Weit oben im Bild bezwingt ein mit Reisig beladener Bauer einen schmalen Pfad, der direkt den Hang hinunterführt. Die Schindeln auf den Dächern sind mit Steinen und Ästen beschwert, um sie bei Sturm am Platz zu halten. Im Hintergrund ragen die Gipfel des Kiso Komagatake auf.

La station de Narai se trouve au pied du col de Torii, l'un des obstacles les plus difficiles à franchir sur la Kisokaidō. Comme sujet de cette estampe, Eisen a choisi une échoppe perchée au sommet d'une côte escarpée du col, où l'on vend des peignes aux dents fines, appelés *Oroku-gushi*, article ayant fait la réputation de la station voisine de Yabuhara, mais que l'on trouve également dans ses environs. Ces peignes sont faits à la main avec du bois dense de bouleau flexible, arbre à croissance lente jadis abondant sur le col, et traité à l'huile de théier. Toujours fabriqués de nos jours, les *Oroku-gushi* ont reçu le label de « produit artisanal officiel », attribué par le gouverneur de la préfecture de Nagano.

Selon la légende locale, la popularité de ces peignes date de la fin du XVIIe siècle ou du début du XVIIIe siècle, lorsqu'une jeune femme nommée Oroku fit un pèlerinage au mont Ontake dans l'espoir de trouver un remède contre la maladie du cerveau dont elle souffrait. Après qu'elle y eut prié, un message divin lui dit de se coiffer avec un peigne fait en bois de théier ; elle se servit du peigne matin et soir, et sa maladie finit par disparaître. Narai dut sa prospérité à la demande d'*Oroku-gushi* et d'autres objets artisanaux, comme des laques.

La scène dépeinte par Eisen déborde d'activités. Deux samouraïs assis à l'entrée de l'échoppe sont en train de choisir, peut-être pour des femmes de leur famille ou pour celles qu'ils aiment, des peignes parmi ceux que leur présente une vendeuse sur des plateaux peu profonds. Un artisan assis nous tourne le dos, tandis qu'à l'arrière-plan sont visibles des réserves de bois destiné à la fabrication des peignes. Un portefaix s'étant déchargé de ses paniers s'essuie les aisselles, pendant qu'un homme vêtu de noir examine la marchandise avant de la payer. Deux autres samouraïs se dirigeant vers Edo se retournent avant de s'engager dans la descente abrupte.

Tout en haut, un paysan portant des broussailles taillées descend sur un sentier étroit menant en ligne droite au bas de la pente. Des pierres et des branches empêchent les bardeaux des toits d'être soulevés par les vents forts. À l'arrière-plan se détachent les sommets du mont Kiso Komagatake.

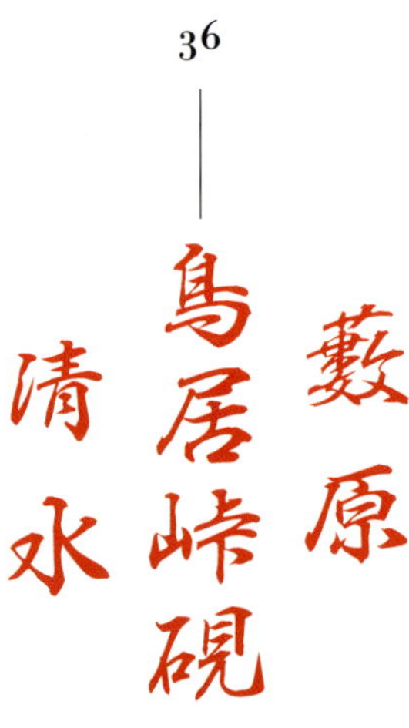

Yabuhara

1835/36 – Eisen

Eisen's design for Yabuhara (also called Yagohara) depicts a scene on the Torii Pass which, at an elevation of 1,197 metres (3,927 feet), was one of the highest points along the Kisokaidō and one of the steepest ascents. Two male travellers have paused by the side of the path to smoke their pipes and contemplate the view of Mount Ontake (also pronounced Mitake), although the gentleman on the right seems to have been distracted by the appearance of two peasant women carrying bundles of firewood on their heads.

Situated at the border of Shinano and Mino Provinces, the pass had for centuries served as a critical point of defence for the protection of the Kiso region. According to legend, it takes its name from a Shinto gate or *torii* erected in honour of Mount Ontake by Kiso Yoshimoto (1475–1504) to mark a prayer for victory over the rival Ogasawara clan.

Earlier still, the Lord of Kiso, Minamoto Yoshinaka (1154–1184), constructed a fortress to defend his territory from the enemy Taira clan at nearby Minokoshi. In an incident mentioned briefly in the classic text *Tales of the Heike* (*Heike monogatari*, 13th century), Yoshinaka paused by a spring to dictate to his scribe a petition for victory to the Shinto deity Hachiman. The place was subsequently known as Suzuri-no-Mizu, "water for an ink stone", or as Eisen has rendered it in the sub-title of this print, "spring water for an ink stone". Behind the spring is a stone engraved with a haiku by the wandering poet Matsuo Bashō (1644–1694), who passed along the Kisokaidō.

Eisen seems to have consulted the guidebook *Views of Famous Sights along the Kiso Road* (*Kisoji meisho zue*), which similarly depicts a pair of travellers resting by the side of the road before a splendid view of the sacred mountain. Further up the road is a right-leaning pine tree with the spring at its foot and the stone carved with Bashō's poem.

Eisens Entwurf für Yabuhara (auch Yagohara genannt) zeigt eine Szene auf dem Torii-Pass, der mit 1197 Metern über dem Meer zu den höchsten Punkten des Kisokaidō und zu seinen steilsten Anstiegen zählte. Am Wegesrand pausieren zwei männliche Reisende, um ihre Pfeifen zu rauchen und die Aussicht auf den Ontake (auch Mitake ausgesprochen) zu genießen – wenngleich der Herr rechts vom Auftauchen zweier Bäuerinnen abgelenkt scheint, die gebündeltes Feuerholz auf dem Kopf tragen.

Der Grenzpass zwischen den Provinzen Shinano und Mino hatte jahrhundertelang als strategischer Verteidigungspunkt für den Schutz der Kiso-Region gedient. Der Legende nach ist er nach dem Shinto-Tor oder *torii* benannt, das von Kiso Yoshimoto (1475–1504) zu Ehren des Ontake errichtet wurde, um ein Gebet für den Sieg über den gegnerischen Ogasawara-Clan zu markieren.

In noch fernerer Vergangenheit baute der Fürst von Kiso, Minamoto Yoshinaka (1154–1184), hier eine Festung, um sein Hoheitsgebiet gegen den feindlichen Taira-Clan im benachbarten Minokoshi zu verteidigen. Einer Begebenheit zufolge, die kurz in dem klassischen Epos *Die Erzählungen des Hauses Heike* (*Heike monogatari*, 13. Jahrhundert) erwähnt wird, rastete Yoshinaka an einer Quelle, um seinem Schreiber ein Siegesgesuch an die Shinto-Gottheit Hachiman zu diktieren. Der Ort wurde daraufhin unter dem Namen Suzuri-no-Mizu, „Wasser für einen Tuschestein“, bekannt, den Eisen im Untertitel seines Entwurfs zu „Quellwasser für einen Tuschestein“ abwandelte. In einen Stein hinter der Quelle ist ein Haiku des Wanderdichters Matsuo Bashō (1644–1694) eingraviert, der den Kisokaidō bereiste.

Eisen scheint den Reiseführer *Ansichten berühmter Stätten an der Kiso-Straße* (*Kisoji meisho zue*) konsultiert zu haben, in dem ebenfalls zwei Reisende abgebildet sind, die vor der prächtigen Kulisse des heiligen Berges am Straßenrand eine Pause einlegen. Ein Stück weiter die Straße hinauf ist gleich neben der Quelle und dem Stein mit dem eingemeißelten Bashō-Gedicht eine nach rechts geneigte Kiefer zu sehen.

L'estampe réalisée par Eisen pour la station de Yabuhara (aussi appelée Yagohara) représente une scène située au col de Torii qui, à une altitude de 1197 mètres, est l'un des points culminants de la Kisokaidō et l'une de ses ascensions les plus difficiles. Deux hommes font une pause sur le bord de la route afin de fumer la pipe et de contempler la vue sur le mont Ontake (que l'on prononce aussi Mitake), bien que celui de droite semble distrait par l'apparition de deux paysannes portant sur la tête des fagots de petit bois.

Aux confins des provinces de Shinano et de Mino, le col servait d'important poste de defense de la région de Kiso depuis des siècles. La légende veut qu'il tienne son nom d'une porte shinto, ou *torii*, érigée en l'honneur du mont Ontake par Kiso Yoshimoto (1475–1504) pour marquer la victoire sur le clan rival des Ogasawara. Bien avant, Minamoto Yoshinaka (1154–1184), seigneur de Kiso, avait bâti une forteresse pour défendre son territoire contre le clan ennemi des Taira, dans la localité voisine de Minokoshi. L'ouvrage classique *Contes de l'Heike* (*Heike monogatari;* XIIIe siècle) relate que Yoshinaka avait fait halte près d'une source afin de dicter à son scribe une requête pour que la divinité shinto Hachiman lui accorde la victoire. Par la suite, l'endroit fut ainsi nommé Suzuri-no-Mizu, « de l'eau pour une pierre à encre » ou, comme Eisen l'a écrit dans le sous-titre de cette estampe, « de l'eau de source pour une pierre à encre ». Derrière la source se dresse une pierre sur laquelle est gravé un haïku du poète itinérant Matsuo Bashō (1644–1694), qui emprunta la Kisokaidō.

Eisen semble avoir consulté la *Collection de vues de paysages célèbres sur la route Kiso* (*Kisoji meisho zue*) qui représente elle aussi deux voyageurs se reposant sur le bord de la route, face au superbe panorama de la montagne sacrée. Un peu plus loin sur la route se trouve un pin incliné vers la droite, au pied duquel apparaissent une source et une pierre sur laquelle est gravé le poème de Bashō.

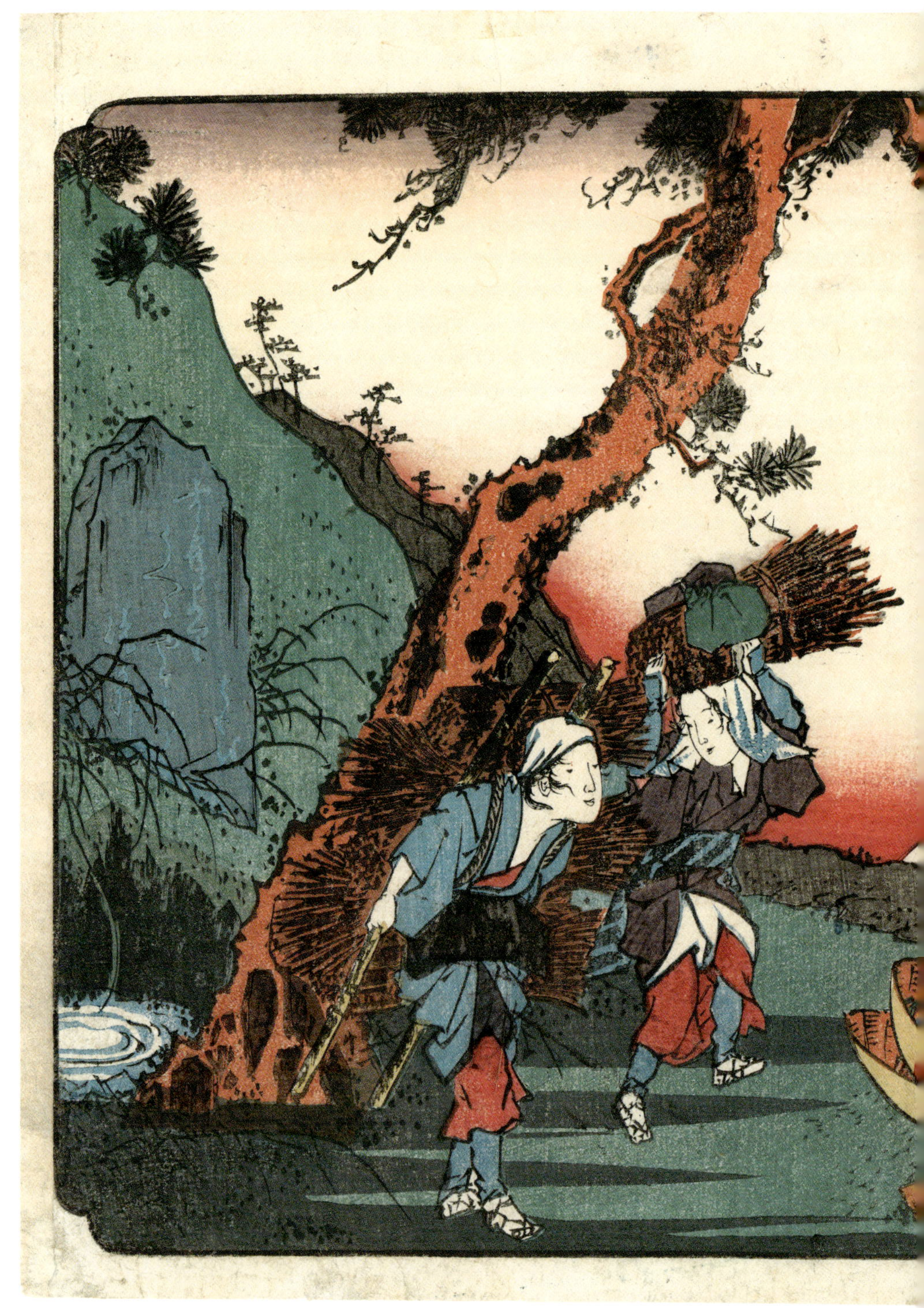

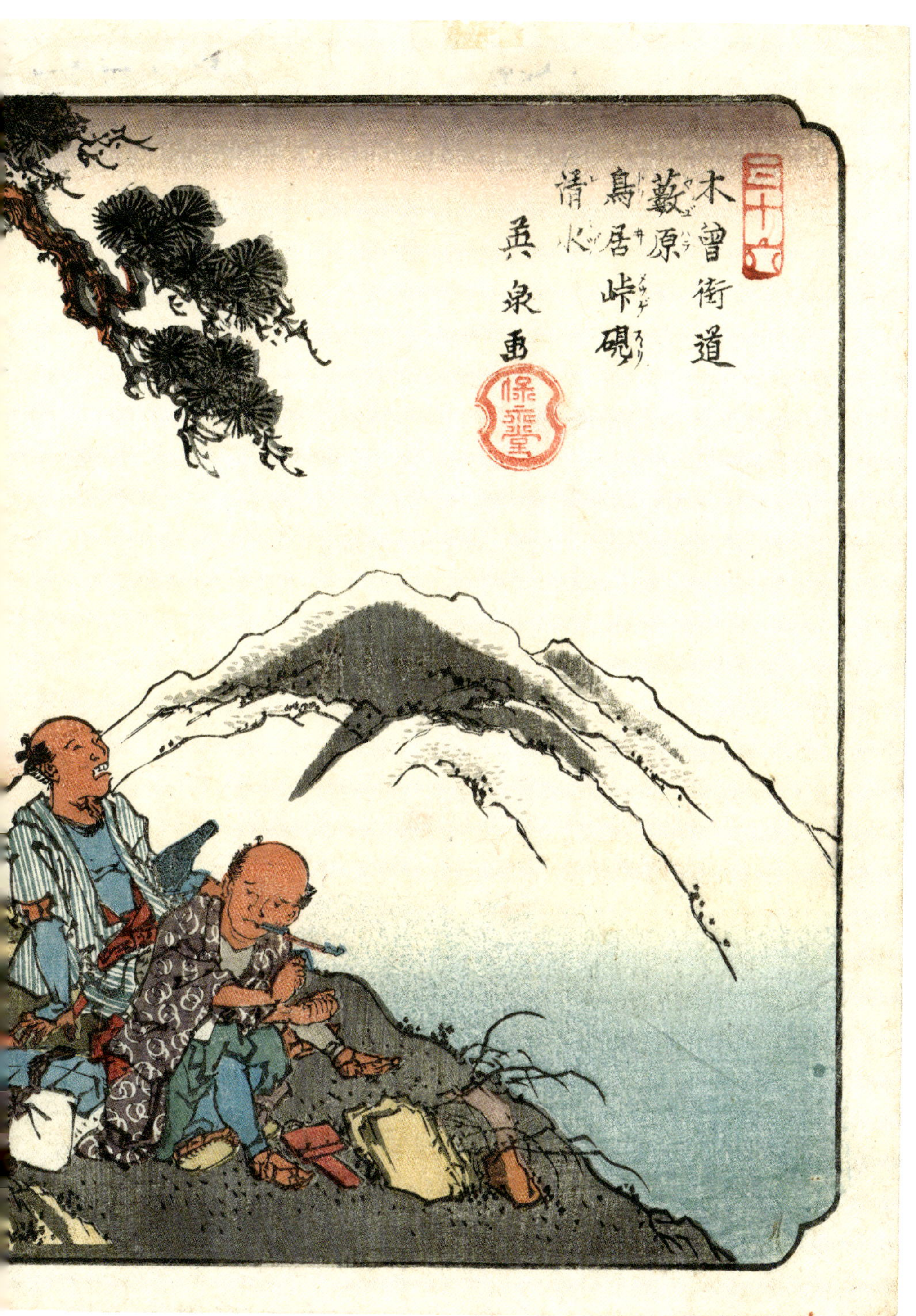
木曾街道
藪原
鳥居峠硯
清水
英泉画

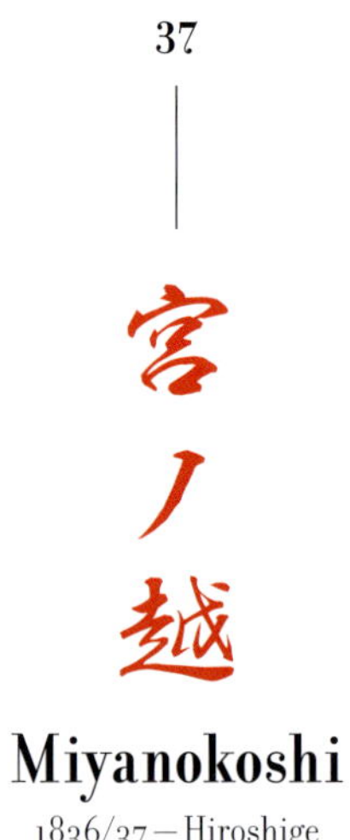

Miyanokoshi

1836/37 — Hiroshige

After Mochizuki, Nagakubo and Seba, Hiroshige's design for Miyanokoshi is the fourth and final moonlit view of the series. The print depicts a family of five wayfarers crossing the Aoki Bridge over the Kiso River under the full moon, perhaps returning home from a festival. The middle child, exhausted from the excitement, has fallen heavily asleep on her father's shoulders. The elder girl turns back, as if reluctant to leave the festivities. It could also be speculated that the family is fleeing their debts under the cover of darkness. The rounded forms, lack of outlining and extensive use of *bokashi* all evoke the foggy evening air.

The lyrical design gives little intimation of the locale's fraught history. It was here in 1180 that Minamoto Yoshinaka, who changed his name to Kiso Yoshinaka, raised an army against the rival Taira clan while also fielding threats from his cousin, Minamoto Yoritomo (1147–1199). Yoshinaka triumphed against the Taira in 1183, but was killed in battle against his cousins the following year at Awazu. Yoshinaka's remains were interred at Gichūji Temple in Ōtsu, but his mausoleum and the graves of several family members together with his comrade, the female warrior Tomoe Gozen (1157?–1247), are located at Tokuonji Temple in Miyanokoshi.

Nach Mochizuki, Nagakubo und Seba ist Hiroshiges Entwurf für Miyanokoshi die vierte und letzte mondbeschienene Szene der Serie. Der Druck zeigt eine fünfköpfige Familie, die bei Vollmond, möglicherweise auf dem Heimweg von einem Fest, zu Fuß die Aoki-Brücke über den Kiso überquert. Erschöpft von der Aufregung, ist das mittlere Kind auf den Schultern des Vaters eingeschlafen. Die ältere Schwester wendet sich zurück, als wollte sie noch nicht gehen. Alternativ könnte man mutmaßen, die Familie wolle im Schutz der Dunkelheit vor ihren Schulden fliehen. Die gerundeten Formen, die fehlenden Umrisslinien und der großflächige Einsatz von *bokashi* erzeugen den Eindruck nebliger Abendluft.

Der lyrische Entwurf vermittelt kaum eine Ahnung von der belasteten Geschichte des Ortes. Im Jahr 1180 mobilisierte Minamoto Yoshinaka, der seinen Namen in Kiso Yoshinaka änderte, an dieser Stelle eine Armee gegen den rivalisierenden Taira-Clan, während er gleichzeitig Bedrohungen durch seinen Cousin Minamoto Yoritomo (1147–1199) abwehrte. Nach dem Sieg gegen die Taira 1183 fiel er im Jahr darauf in der Schlacht gegen seine Cousins bei Awazu. Yoshinakas sterbliche Überreste wurden am Gichūji-Tempel in Ōtsu begraben, sein Mausoleum aber befindet sich zusammen mit den Gräbern mehrerer Familienangehöriger und der Grabstätte seiner Kameradin, der Kriegerin Tomoe Gozen (1157?–1247), am Tokuonji-Tempel in Miyanokoshi.

Après Mochizuki, Nagakubo et Seba, l'estampe d'Hiroshige pour Miyanokoshi est le quatrième et dernier clair de lune de la série. Cette image représente une famille de cinq voyageurs franchissant le pont d'Aoki sur la Kiso éclairé par la pleine lune ; ils reviennent peut-être d'une fête. Épuisée par l'excitation, la deuxième de leurs enfants s'est lourdement endormie sur les épaules de son père. Leur fille aînée se retourne, comme si elle ne voulait pas quitter les festivités. On pourrait aussi imaginer que cette famille s'enfuit à la faveur de la nuit pour échapper à des dettes. Les formes arrondies, l'absence de contour et le recours important au *bokashi* évoquent l'atmosphère d'une soirée brumeuse.

Cette illustration lyrique ne témoigne guère de l'histoire tumultueuse du lieu. C'est ici qu'en 1180 Minamoto Yoshinaka, qui prit le nom de Kiso Yoshinaka, leva une armée contre le clan rival des Taira, tout en répondant aux menaces de son cousin, Minamoto Yoritomo (1147–1199). En 1183, Yoshinaka vainquit les Taira, mais fut tué dans une bataille contre ses cousins l'année suivante à Awazu. Les restes de Yoshinaka furent inhumés au temple de Gichūji à Ōtsu. Toutefois, son mausolée et les tombes de plusieurs membres de sa famille, ainsi que celle de sa sœur d'armes, la guerrière Tomoe Gozen (1157 ?–1247), se trouvent au temple de Tokuonji à Miyanokoshi.

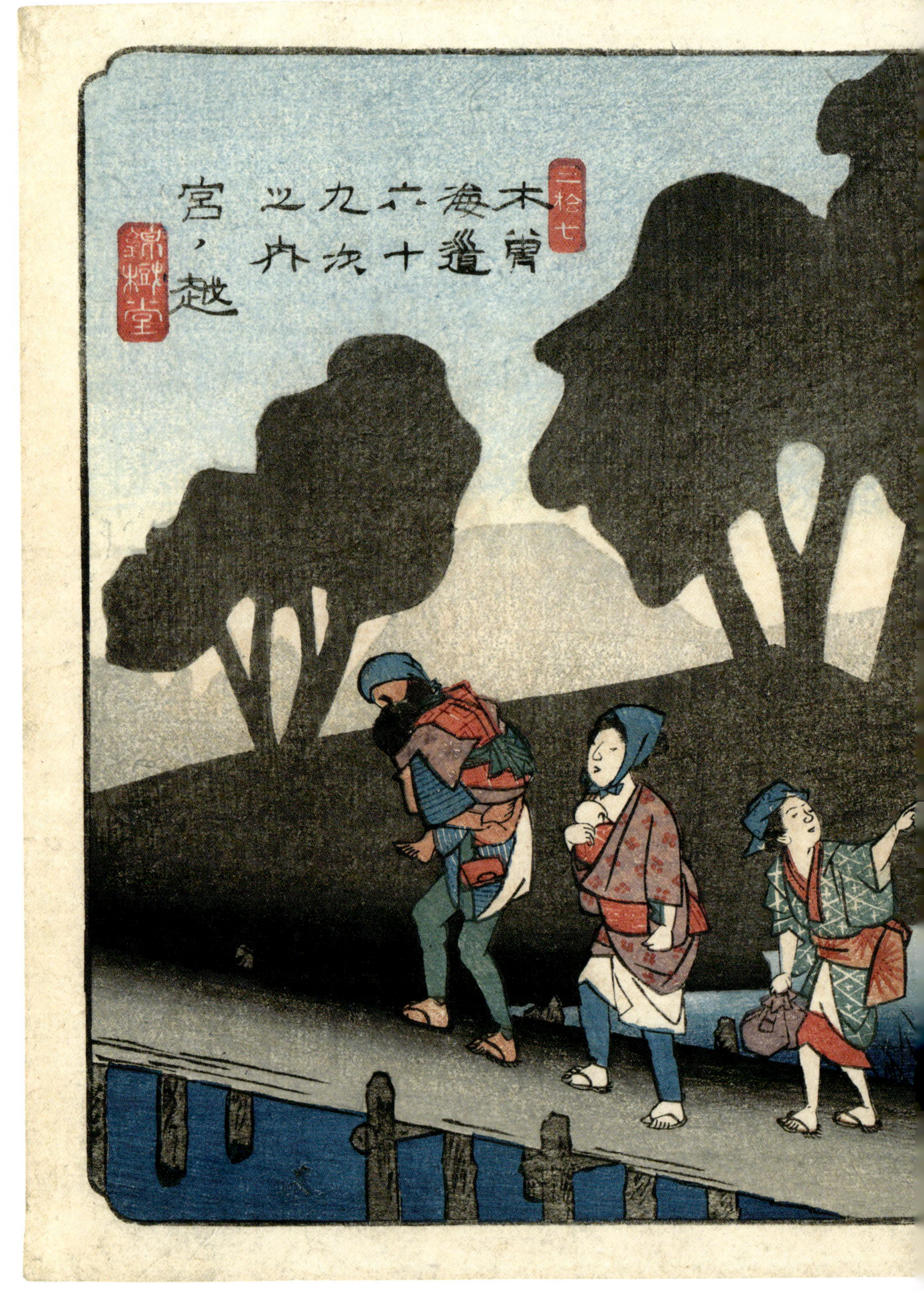

木曾街道六十九次之内
宮ノ越
二拾七

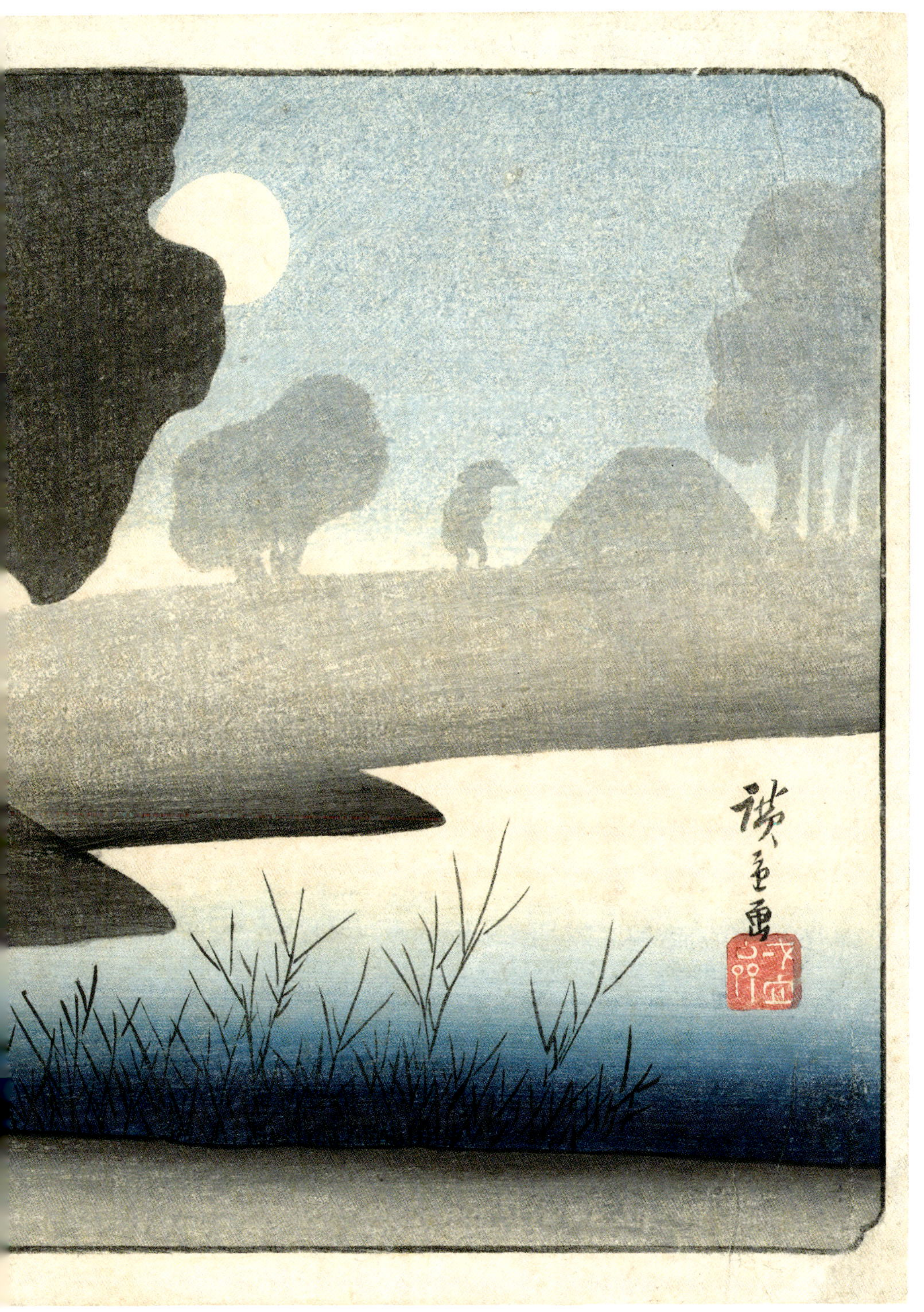

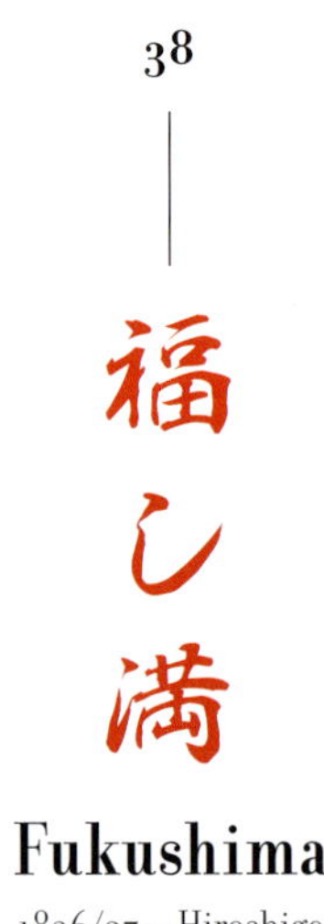

Fukushima

1836/37 — Hiroshige

Fukushima was the site of one of the two checkpoints along the Kisokaidō. Hiroshige's design depicts travellers and couriers coming and going through the gates of the checkpoint, enclosed by a picket fence. Through the open gateway we glimpse the administrative building, from which an official is questioning two travellers who are kneeling on the ground before him.

Like the Usui checkpoint between Matsuida and Sakamoto stations, the Fukushima checkpoint collected a road tax from traders and travellers. Its principal concerns, however, were the unauthorised movements of guns into the capital, and female relatives of regional lords leaving Edo, where they were generally required to reside as a kind of insurance policy against insubordination. The Chief Administrator of the checkpoint was a hereditary position held by the Yamamura family, whose house is still extant today. The checkpoint structure was reconstructed as a museum.

A post station was established at Fukushima in the third quarter of the 16th century. Marking the midpoint between Edo and Kyoto, it prospered as both an economic and administrative centre. In the 19th century, Fukushima was the most prosperous village in the Kiso Valley and one of only a handful that boasted more than a single main street.

In Fukushima stand eine der beiden Kontrollstellen des Kisokaidō. Hiroshiges Entwurf zeigt, wie Reisende und Kuriere durch die Sperren des rundherum mit Palisaden eingezäunten Kontrollpostens kommen und gehen. Durch das geöffnete Tor erkennen wir das Verwaltungsgebäude, aus dem heraus ein Beamter zwei Reisende befragt, die vor ihm am Boden knien.

Wie auch die Kontrollstelle Usui zwischen den Stationen Matsuida und Sakamoto erhob die Kontrollstelle Fukushima von Händlern und Reisenden einen Wegzoll. Hauptsächlich aber hatte sie es auf ungenehmigte Waffentransporte in die Hauptstadt und auf weibliche Angehörige von Lehensfürsten abgesehen, die Edo verließen, obwohl sie sich dort als eine Art Versicherung gegen aufständische Umtriebe grundsätzlich aufzuhalten hatten. Die Stelle des Verwaltungschefs, der den Kontrollposten leitete, war erblich und wurde von der Familie Yamamura gehalten, deren Geschlecht bis heute fortbesteht. Die Anlage selbst wurde als Museum rekonstruiert.

Eine Poststation wurde in Fukushima zwischen 1550 und 1575 eingerichtet. Auf halber Strecke zwischen Edo und Kyoto florierte der Ort als Wirtschafts- und Verwaltungszentrum. Im 19. Jahrhundert war Fukushima das reichste Dorf im Kiso-Tal und eines von nur einer Handvoll, die mehr als eine Hauptstraße vorzuweisen hatten.

À Fukushima se trouvait l'un des deux postes de contrôle de la Kisokaidō. Dans l'estampe d'Hiroshige, voyageurs et portefaix vont et viennent à travers la porte du poste, entouré d'une palissade. La porte ouverte laisse deviner le bâtiment administratif dans lequel un fonctionnaire interroge deux voyageurs agenouillés devant lui à l'extérieur.

De même que le poste de contrôle d'Usui, situé entre les stations de Matsuida et de Sakamoto, celui de Fukushima percevait une taxe de circulation auprès des marchands et des voyageurs. Mais il servait avant tout à surveiller les mouvements interdits d'armes vers la capitale et ceux des femmes membres des familles de seigneurs régionaux quittant Edo où elles étaient généralement tenues de résider, en guise de garantie contre l'insubordination. La fonction d'administrateur en chef du poste de contrôle était une charge héréditaire, détenue par la famille Yamamura, dont la demeure existe toujours. Le bâtiment du poste de contrôle a été reconstruit sous forme de musée.

C'est dans le troisième quart du XVIe siècle qu'un relais de poste fut établi à Fukushima. À mi-chemin entre Edo et Kyoto, Fukushima prospéra à la fois comme centre économique et administratif. Au XIXe siècle, c'était le village le plus florissant de la vallée de la Kiso et l'un des rares à s'enorgueillir de posséder plus de voies qu'une unique grand-rue.

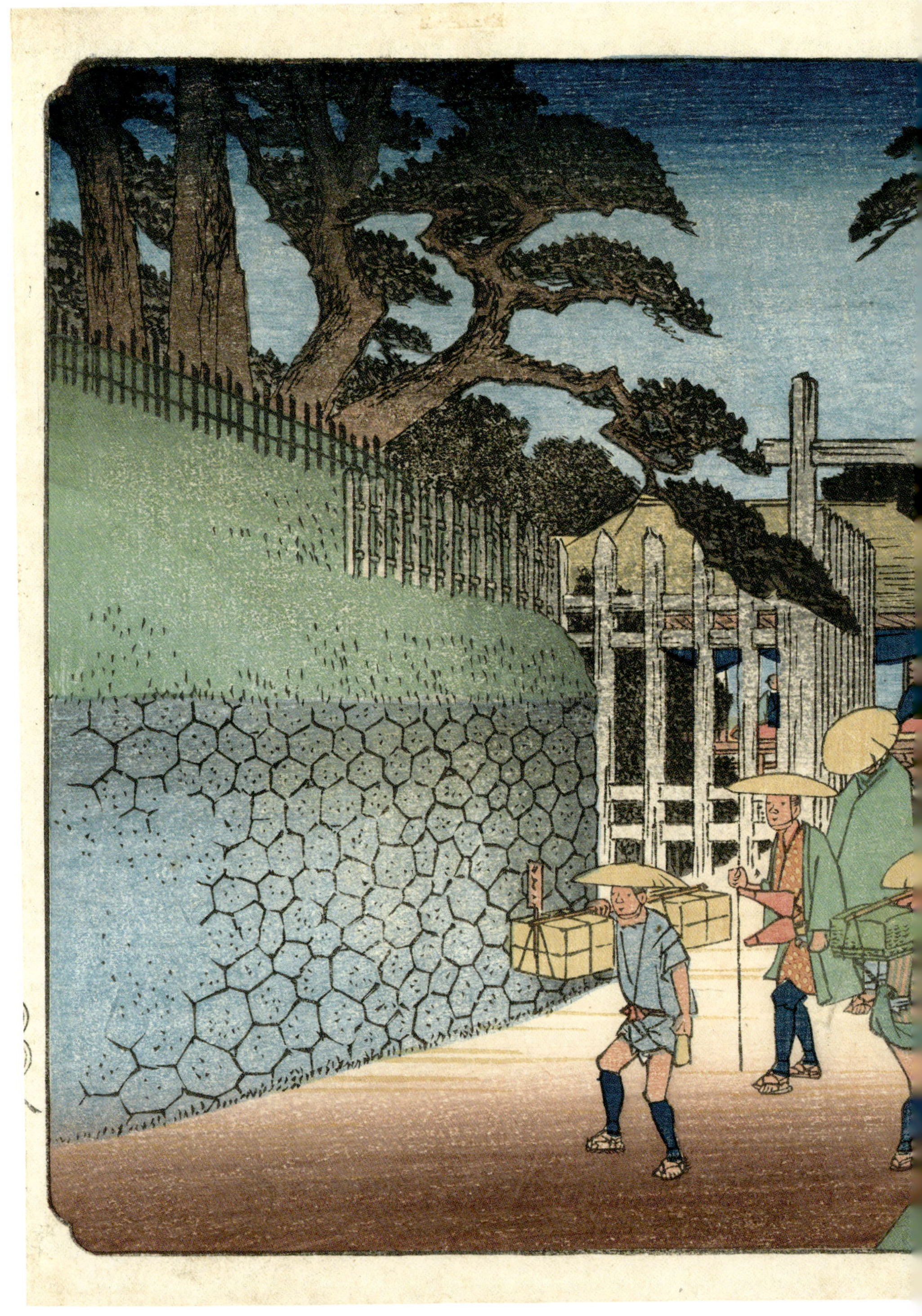

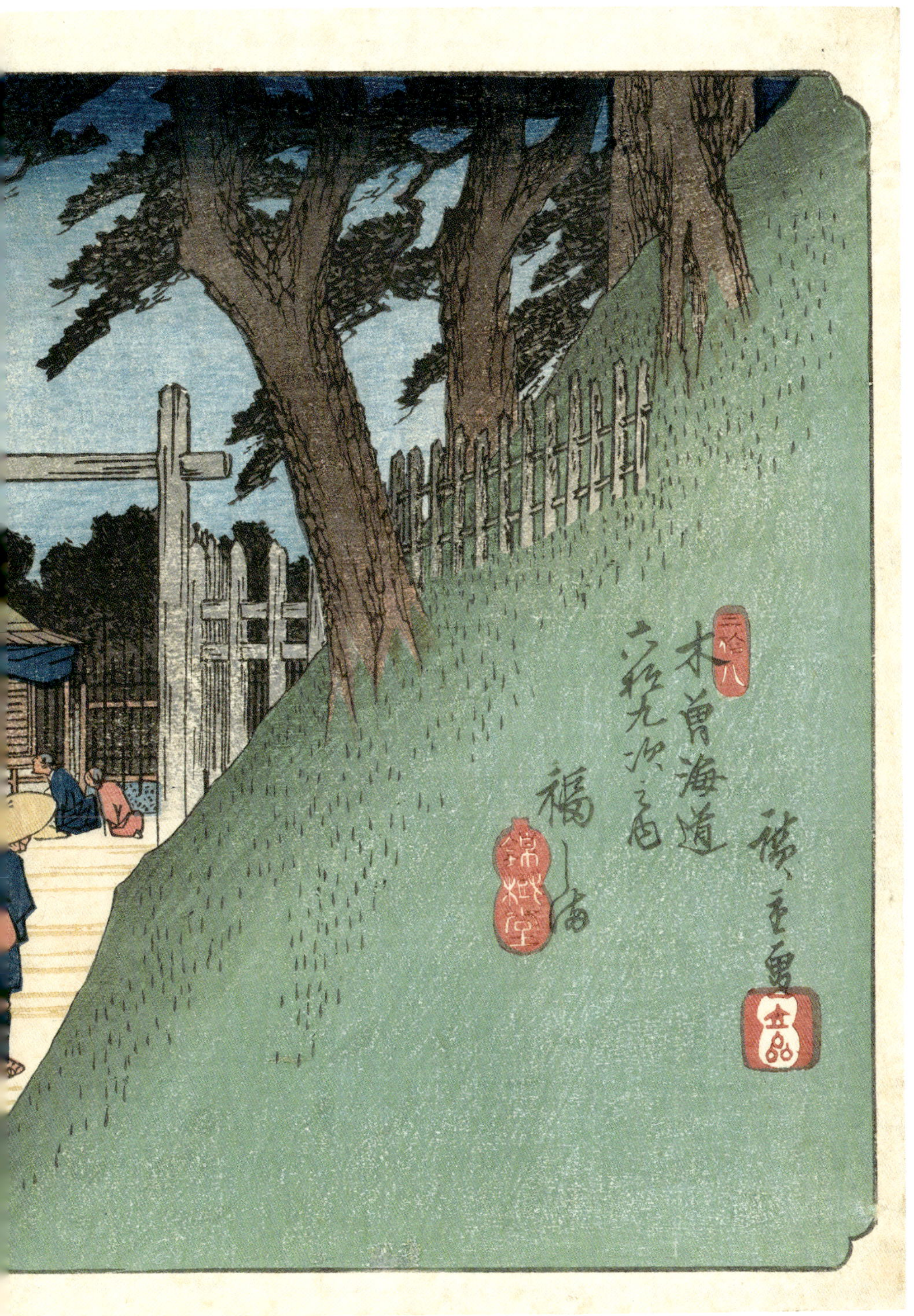

39

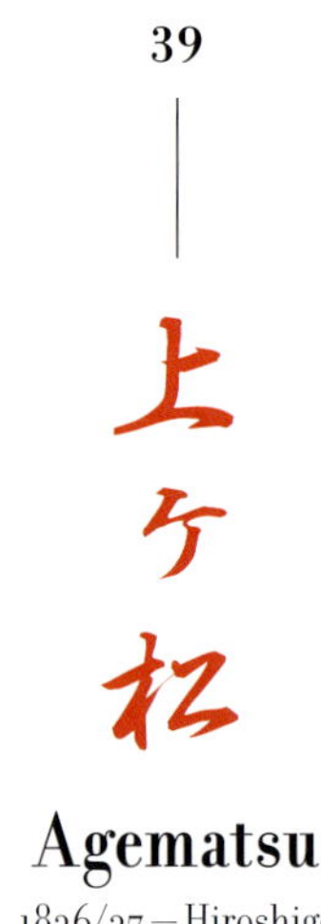

Agematsu

1836/37 – Hiroshige

The Ono Waterfall near Agematsu was one of the "Eight Views of Kiso". The guidebook *Views of Famous Sights along the Kiso Road* (*Kisoji meisho zue*) described the falls thus: "The height is 3 *jō* (9.1 metres/30 feet), and the water falls directly from the mountain valley over the rocks like linen."

In homage to Katsushika Hokusai, Hiroshige reworked his elder colleague's design of the falls from Hokusai's series *A Tour of Waterfalls in Various Provinces* (*Shokoku taki meguri*, c. 1832) for Agematsu station. In Hokusai's version, the fantastic shapes and colours of the rocky outcrops and the water falling almost the entire height of the vertical composition dominate the design; the small figures on the bridge serve primarily to convey the scale of this natural spectacle. Hiroshige simplified the composition and converted it into a horizontal format. He reduced the figures to two travellers and a woodcutter carrying firewood, but increased their relative size in the design. The landscape elements are simultaneously diminished in size and importance; the grotesque forms of the crags are smoothed out, mist and spray are gone, the rapids below stylised.

The station itself was established between the 1530s and 1550s and was designated a station around 1601. The waterfall was in fact of lesser interest than the magnificent formations at Nezame-no-toko Gorge, worn into the granite by the Kiso River. The name of the gorge means "bed of awakening"; local legend claims that Urashima Tarō "awoke" from his dreamlike, 300-year journey to the undersea Palace of the Dragon King at this place.

During the late 19th century, Agematsu became popular among Western hikers for its picturesque scenery and as an access point to Mount Komagatake. The scenic value of the area was much diminished from the Meiji period, with the construction of an iron railway bridge almost directly over the waterfall in 1909 and upstream dams that reduced the once-powerful river to a thin and shallow stream.

270

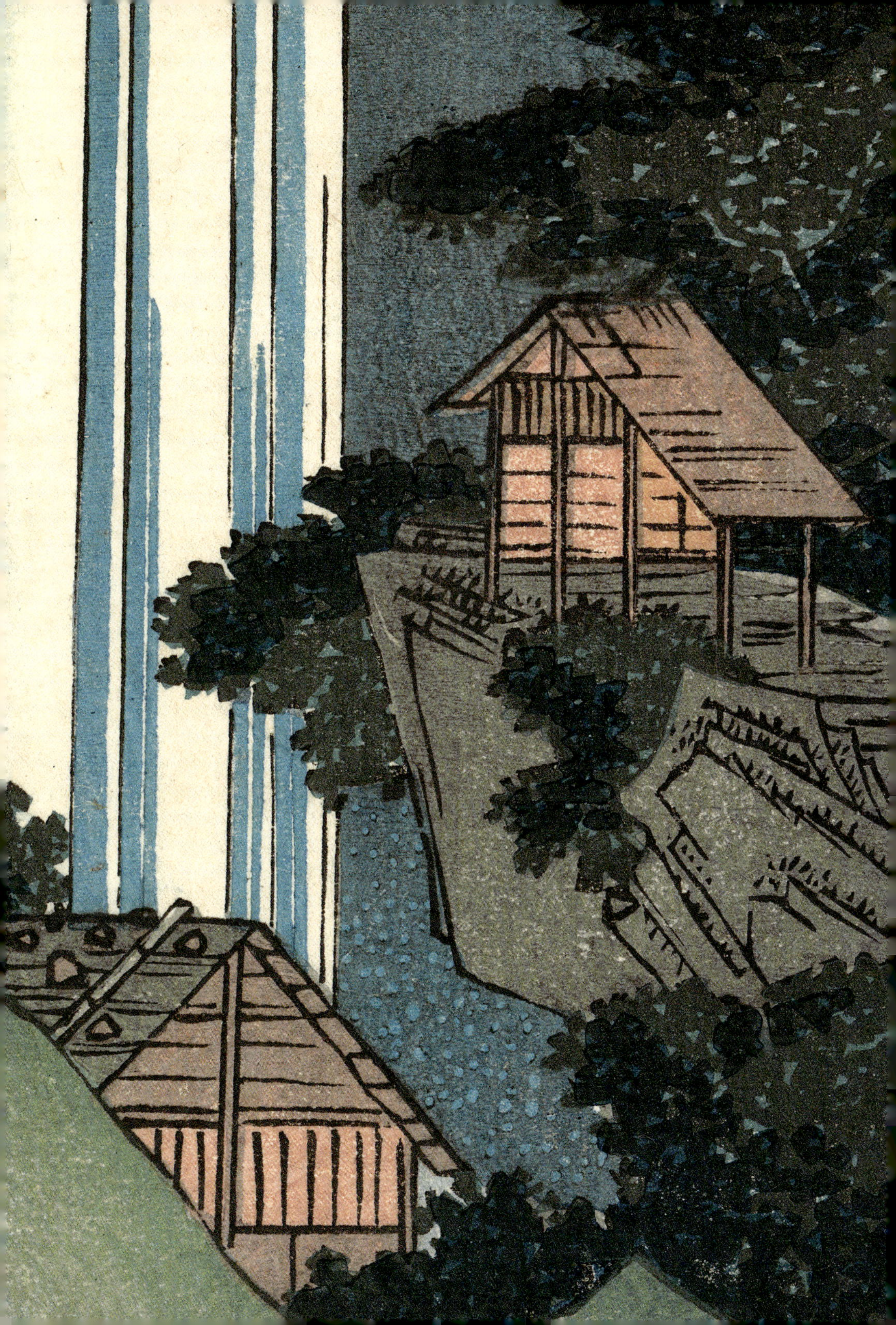

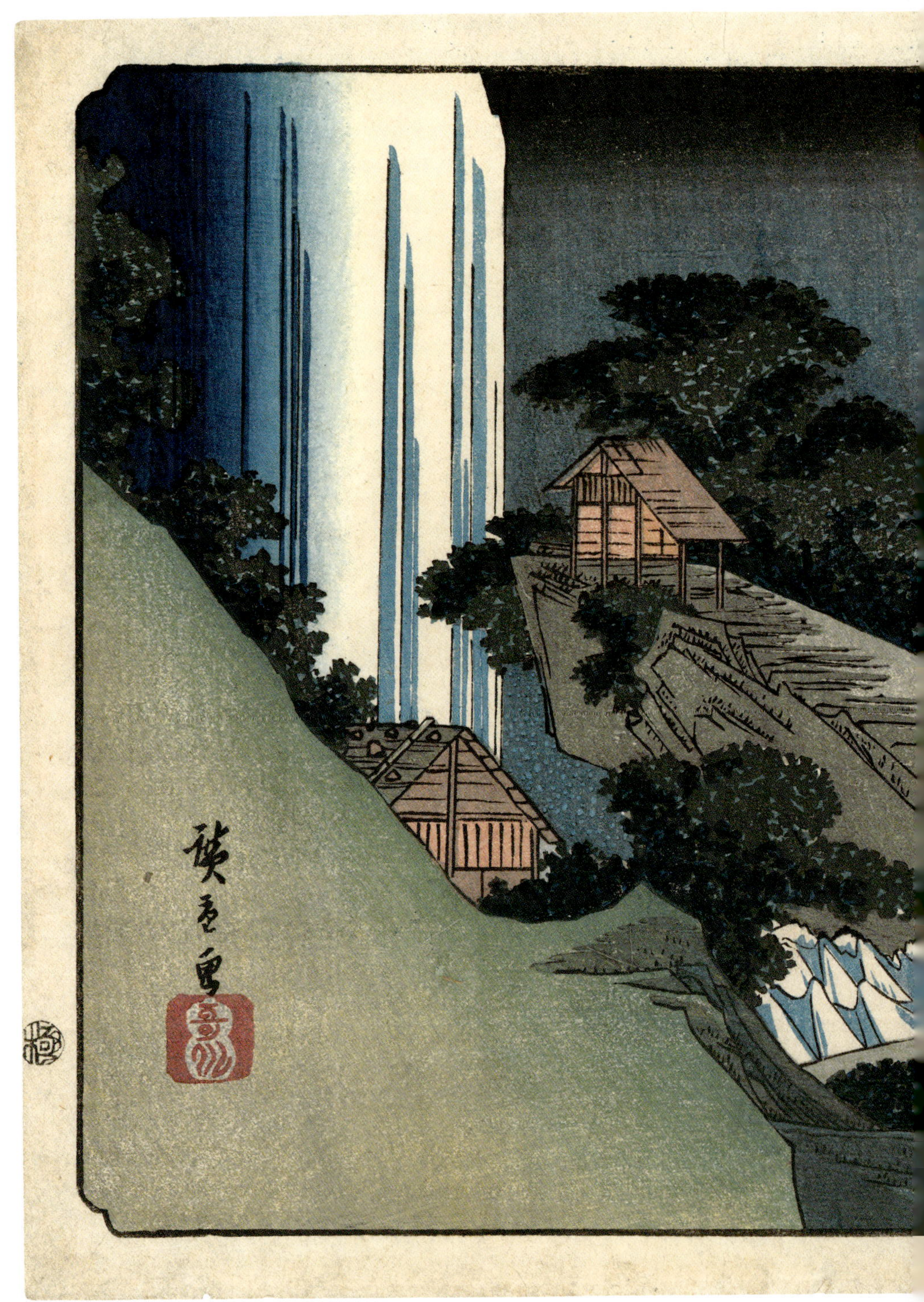

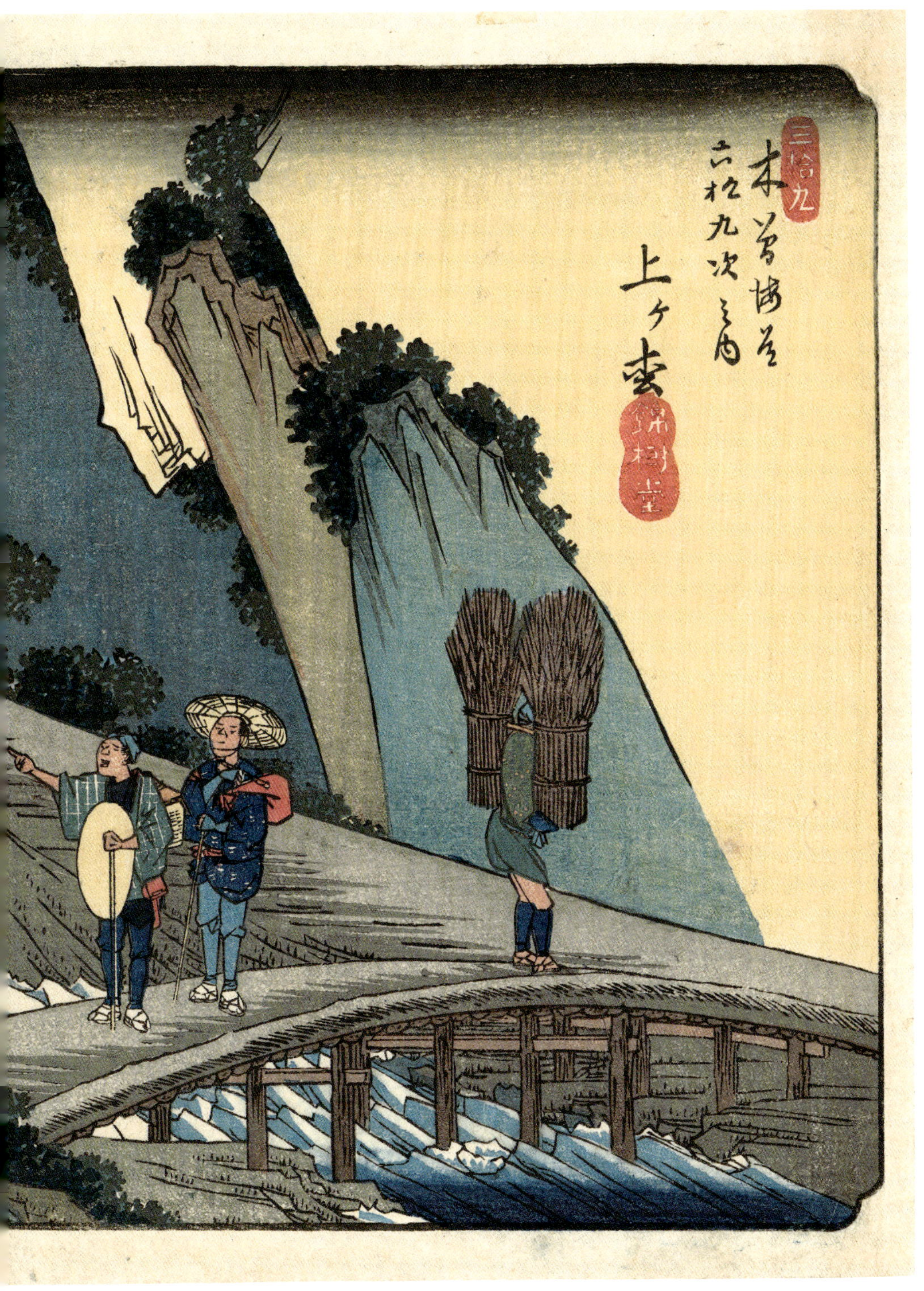
三拾九
木曽街道
六拾九次之内
上ヶ松

Der Ono-Wasserfall bei Agematsu gehörte zu den „Acht Ansichten des Kiso". Der Reiseführer *Ansichten berühmter Stätten an der Kiso-Straße (Kisoji meisho zue)* beschrieb ihn folgendermaßen: „Er ist 3 *jō* (9,10 Meter) hoch, und das Wasser fällt wie Leinen direkt vom Gebirgstal über die Felsen."

Als Hommage an seinen älteren Kollegen Katsushika Hokusai überarbeitete Hiroshige für die Station Agematsu das Motiv, das Hokusai für seine Serie *Eine Reise zu den Wasserfällen in verschiedenen Provinzen (Shokoku taki meguri,* um 1832) von dem Wasserfall entworfen hatte. In Hokusais Version dominieren die fantastischen Formen und Farben der Felssporne und das Wasser, das beinahe über die gesamte Höhe der hochformatigen Komposition hinabstürzt. Die kleinen Figuren auf der Brücke dienen hauptsächlich dazu, die Dimension dieses Naturschauspiels zu vermitteln. Hiroshige vereinfachte die Komposition und veränderte sie zu einem Querformat. Er reduzierte die Figuren auf zwei Reisende und einen mit Brennholz beladenen Holzfäller, die er im Verhältnis größer darstellte. Im Gegenzug wurden die Größe und Bedeutung der Landschaftselemente verringert, die bizarren Felsformen geglättet, Dunst und Gischt entfernt und die Stromschnellen unten im Bild stilisiert.

Die Station selbst wurde zwischen den 1530er und 1550er Jahren gegründet und um 1601 zur Station erklärt. Der Wasserfall war in Wirklichkeit weniger interessant als die großartigen Formationen der Nezame-no-toko-Schlucht, die der Kiso in den Granit gegraben hatte. Der Name der Schlucht bedeutet „Bett des Erwachens"; die örtliche Legende besagt, dass der Fischer Urashima Tarō an diesem Ort aus seiner traumähnlichen, 300 Jahre währenden Reise zum unterseeischen Palast des Drachenkönigs „erwachte".

Im späten 19. Jahrhundert begannen Wanderer aus dem Westen Agematsu für seine pittoreske Landschaft und als Zugang zum Komagatake-Massiv zu schätzen. In der Meiji-Zeit wurde die Gegend in ihrer malerischen Wirkung stark beeinträchtigt, als eine eiserne Bahnbrücke 1909 fast direkt über den Wasserfall geführt wurde und Talsperren flussaufwärts den einst mächtigen Fluss in ein schmales und flaches Rinnsal verwandelten.

La chute d'Ono, près d'Agematsu, est l'une des « huit vues de la Kiso ». Le guide de voyage *Collection de vues de paysages célèbres sur la route Kiso* (*Kisoji meisho zue*) la décrit ainsi : « D'une hauteur de 3 *jō* (9,10 mètres), l'eau descend directement de la montagne sur les rochers comme un drap. »

En hommage à Katsushika Hokusai, Hiroshige a repris l'illustration réalisée par son aîné pour la station d'Agematsu, dans sa série *Visite des chutes d'eau de diverses provinces* (*Shokoku taki meguri*, vers 1832). La version d'Hokusai est dominée par les formes et les couleurs fantasmagoriques des roches qui affleurent, et par la chute d'eau qui occupe presque toute la hauteur de la composition verticale ; les petites figures situées sur le pont servent avant tout à donner une idée de l'échelle de ce spectacle naturel. Hiroshige a simplifié la composition et lui a donné un format horizontal. Il a réduit le nombre des personnages à deux voyageurs et un bûcheron portant des fagots, mais en augmentant leur taille relative. Simultanément, les éléments du paysage ont perdu en dimension et en importance ; les formes grotesques des rochers escarpés ont été atténuées, la brume et les nuages de gouttelettes supprimés, les rapides situés en contrebas stylisés.

La station proprement dite fut fondée entre les années 1530 et 1550, et désignée ville étape vers 1601. La chute d'eau était, en réalité, moins attrayante que les splendides formations rocheuses de la gorge de Nezame-no-toko, creusées dans le granit par l'eau de la Kiso. Le nom de cette gorge signifie « lit de l'éveil » ; selon la légende locale, c'est ici que s'était « éveillé » Urashima Tarō, après un voyage onirique de trois siècles jusqu'au palais sous-marin du Roi-Dragon.

Au cours du XIXe siècle, Agematsu est devenue très prisée des randonneurs occidentaux pour ses paysages pittoresques et comme point d'accès au mont Komagatake. Cette région a grandement perdu de son intérêt à partir de l'ère Meiji, avec la construction, en 1909, d'un pont de chemin de fer quasiment au-dessus de la chute d'eau et de barrages en amont qui ont rabaissé la rivière puissante d'autrefois au rang de petit cours d'eau peu profond.

40

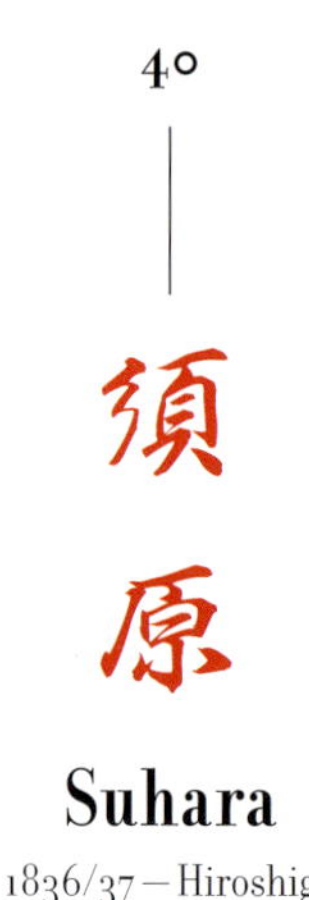

Suhara

1836/37 – Hiroshige

Hiroshige's design for Suhara station focuses on a disparate assortment of travellers taking refuge from a summer downpour within a roadside shrine. To the far right, a *komusō* monk is smoking a pipe underneath his deep, basket-like hat. A second itinerant monk, wearing a shallow, banded hat, is offering a prayer to the resident deity. Further to the left, a traveller takes advantage of the delay to mark his presence on one of the posts of the structure. Two palanquin-bearers are dashing towards the shrine, with their transport disassembled into a jumble of parts. In the distance, two travellers, one mounted on a horse, are forging stoically onwards through the rain.

The print is one of several memorable depictions of landscapes in rain by Hiroshige. Prior to creating this design for Suhara station, he portrayed travellers, peasants and townspeople caught in sudden downpours in his other landscape series from the 1830s, and he would revisit the theme again around 20 years later in *One Hundred Famous Views of Edo* (*Meisho Edo hyakkei*). However, the inspiration for this particular design comes from *An Album of Pictures by Itchō* (*Itchō gafu*), a collection of compositions by Hanabusa Itchō compiled by Suzuki Rinshō. The illustration, "Taking Shelter from Rain" (*Amayadori*), depicts a fantastical assortment of gods and mortals sheltering together from the pouring rain under a thatched roof.

The station of Suhara was founded during the 16th century, but was rebuilt further upstream after the village was almost entirely washed away when the Kiso River flooded in 1715. The town flourished as a centre for silk production, and in the 19th century visitors including the English mountaineer Walter Weston (1860–1940) noted that the village and its surrounds were planted with groves of mulberry trees. In 1874, when Suhara was merged with several other nearby villages, the locale was renamed Ōkuwamura, "Village of the Great Mulberry Tree".

Notwithstanding repeated flooding and a fire in 1888, a number of historic buildings remain standing today, including the Rinzai sect temple Jōshōji. The temple was founded in the 1380s, and the present structure, an Important Cultural Property, dates from 1598.

276

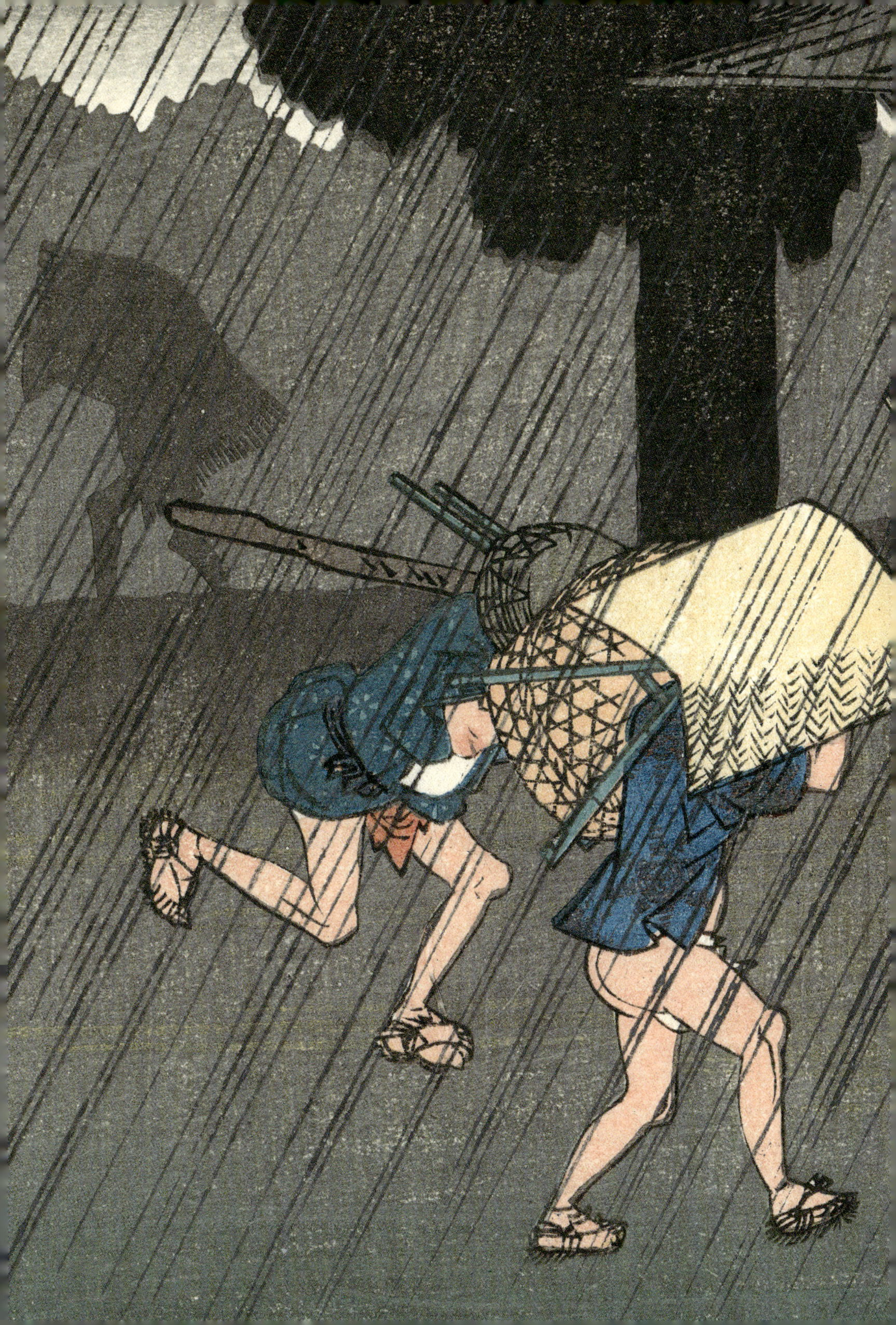

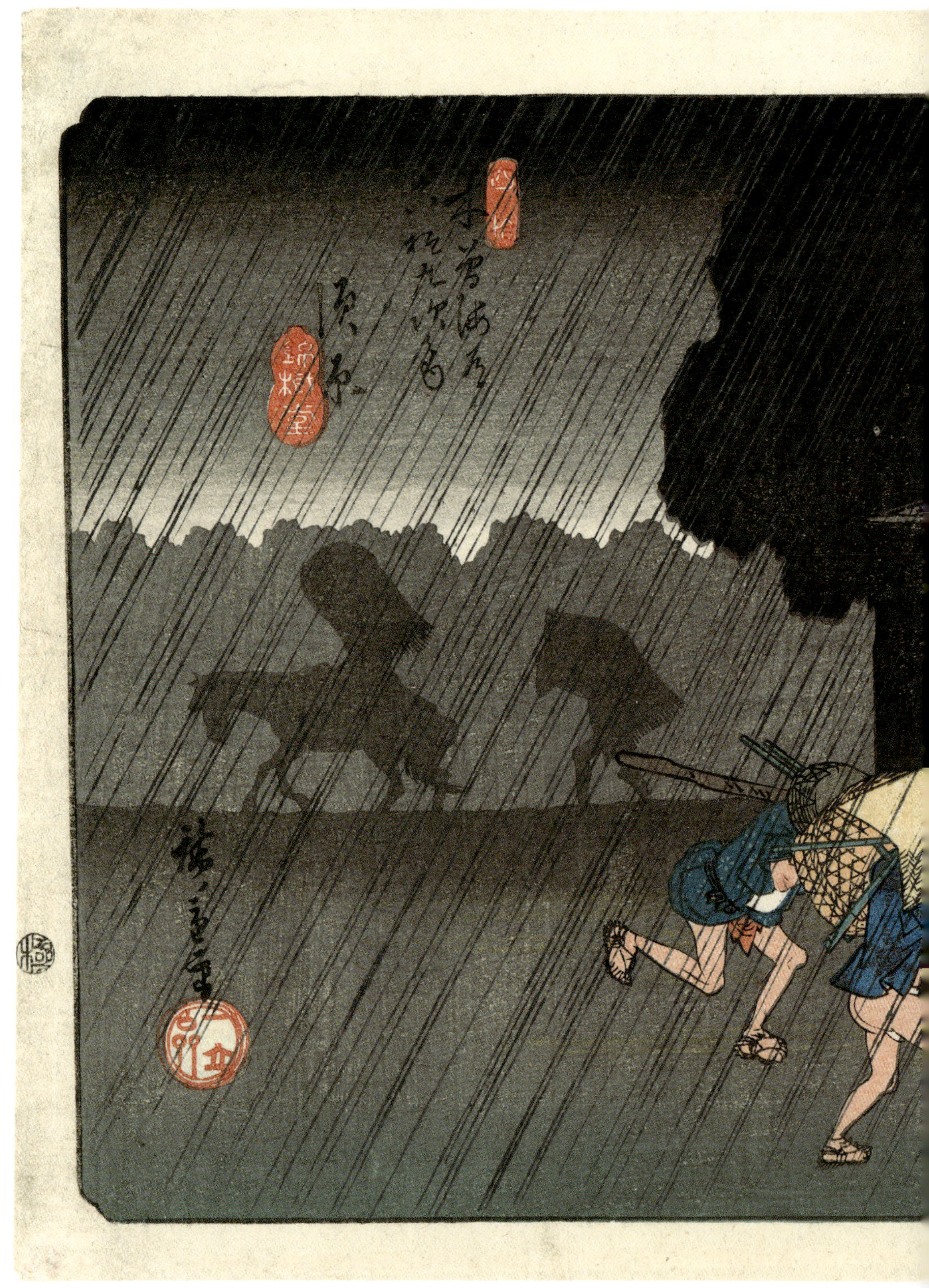

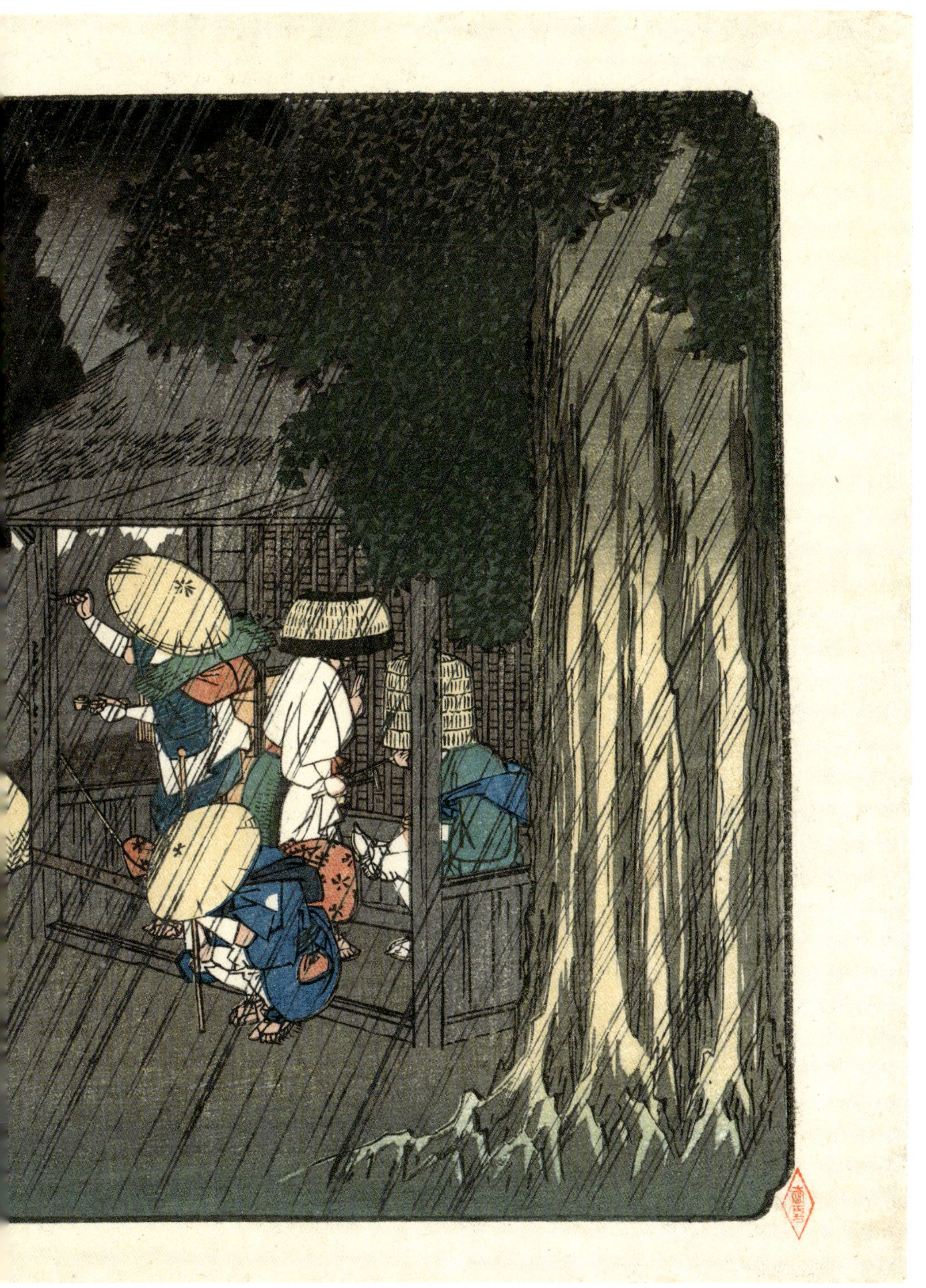

In den Mittelpunkt seines Entwurfs für die Station Suhara stellte Hiroshige eine bunte Mischung von Reisenden, die in einem Wegschrein Zuflucht vor einem sommerlichen Wolkenbruch suchen. Ganz rechts raucht ein Mönch *(komusō)* unter seinem weit heruntergezogenen, bienenkorbartigen Hut eine Pfeife. Ein zweiter Wandermönch mit flachem, gestreiftem Hut bringt der Schreingottheit ein Gebet dar. Links daneben nutzt ein Reisender die Verzögerung, um seine Anwesenheit auf einem der Stützpfeiler des Bauwerks zu dokumentieren. Zwei Sänftenträger laufen mit ihrem Transportmittel, das in ein Gewirr von Einzelteilen zerlegt ist, auf den Schrein zu. In der Ferne kämpfen sich zwei Reisende – der eine zu Pferd, der andere zu Fuß – stoisch durch den Regen voran.

Der Druck gehört zu den denkwürdigen Landschaftsdarstellungen im Regen, von denen Hiroshige etliche geschaffen hat. Schon vor diesem Entwurf für Suhara porträtierte er in anderen Landschaftsserien der 1830er Jahre Reisende, Bauern und Stadtbewohner, die von Regengüssen überrascht werden. Rund 20 Jahre später griff er das Thema in der Reihe *Einhundert berühmte Ansichten von Edo (Meisho Edo hyakkei)* erneut auf. Doch die Inspiration für dieses Motiv lieferte das *Itchō-Bilderalbum (Itchō gafu)*, eine von Suzuki Rinshō zusammengestellte Sammlung von Werken Hanabusa Itchōs. Dessen Illustration *Suche nach Schutz vor dem Regen (Amayadori)* zeigt eine fantastische Mischung aus Göttern und Sterblichen, die gemeinsam unter einem Strohdach Schutz vor dem strömenden Regen suchen.

Die Station Suhara wurde im 16. Jahrhundert gegründet, jedoch nach einem Kiso-Hochwasser, das 1715 weite Teile des Dorfes vernichtete, weiter flussaufwärts neu aufgebaut. Die Ortschaft gedieh als Zentrum der Seidenzucht, und im 19. Jahrhundert notierten Besucher wie der englische Bergsteiger Walter Weston (1860–1940), dass Maulbeerhaine den Ort und seine Umgebung prägten. Als Suhara 1874 mit mehreren Nachbardörfern zusammengelegt wurde, erhielt die neue Gemeinde den Namen Ōkuwamura, „Dorf des großen Maulbeerbaums".

Trotz wiederholter Überschwemmungen und eines Brandes im Jahr 1888 blieben mehrere historische Gebäude erhalten, darunter der Jōshōji-Tempel der Rinzai-Schule, dessen Anfänge in die 1380er Jahre zurückreichen. Der heutige Bau, ein „bedeutendes Kulturgut", stammt aus dem Jahr 1598.

L'estampe réalisée par Hiroshige pour la station de Suhara réunit toutes sortes de voyageurs qui s'abritent d'une averse estivale torrentielle dans un petit sanctuaire de bord de route. Tout à droite, un moine *komusō* fume la pipe, coiffé d'un chapeau en forme de panier qui descend très bas. Un second moine itinérant, portant un chapeau de faible hauteur entouré de rubans, prie la divinité du sanctuaire. À sa gauche, un voyageur profite du retard causé par la pluie pour laisser sa trace sur l'un des piliers de la structure. Deux porteurs de palanquin se précipitent pour s'abriter ; leur chargement est tout disloqué. Au loin, deux voyageurs, dont l'un à cheval, avancent stoïquement dans la pluie.

Cette estampe constitue l'une des représentations mémorables de paysages sous la pluie qu'a signées Hiroshige. Avant de réaliser l'estampe de Suhara, l'artiste avait fait le portrait de voyageurs, de paysans et de citadins surpris par des averses soudaines, dans son autre série d'images de paysages des années 1830, et il allait reprendre ce thème une vingtaine d'années plus tard avec *Cent Vues célèbres d'Edo* (*Meisho Edo hyakkei*). Toutefois, pour ce dessin, il tient son inspiration de l'*Album d'images d'Itchō* (*Itchō gafu*), recueil de compositions d'Hanabusa Itchō), réunies par Suzuki Rinshō. L'illustration en question, *S'abriter de la pluie* (*Amayadori*), dépeint une foule de dieux et de mortels s'abritant ensemble, sous un toit de chaume, de la pluie qui tombe à verse.

Fondée au XVIe siècle, la station de Suhara fut reconstruite en amont après que le village avait été emporté par la crue de la Kiso en 1715. La production de soie apporta la prospérité à la petite ville et, au XIXe siècle, des visiteurs comme l'alpiniste anglais Walter Weston (1860–1940) remarquèrent que la localité et ses environs étaient plantés de bosquets de mûriers. Avec la fusion de Suhara et de plusieurs villages voisins en 1874, le lieu fut rebaptisé Ōkuwamura, « village du grand mûrier ».

En dépit d'inondations répétées et d'un incendie en 1888, plusieurs bâtiments historiques ont subsisté jusqu'à nos jours, parmi lesquels le temple Jōshōji de la secte Rinzai. La structure actuelle de ce temple, fondé dans les années 1380, date de 1598 et appartient aujourd'hui au « patrimoine culturel important » du Japon.

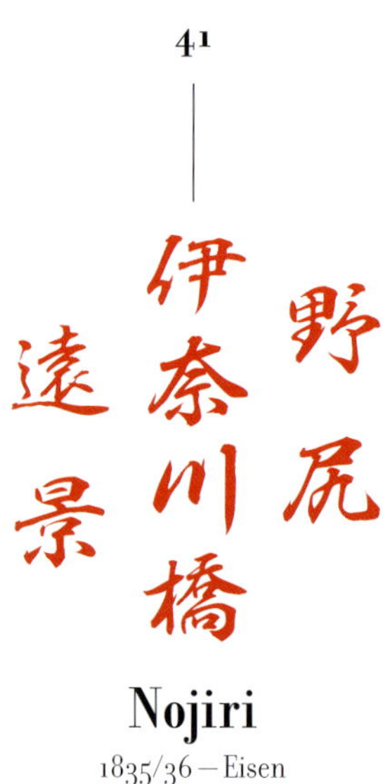

41

Nojiri

1835/36 – Eisen

The Nojiri station is situated in the Kiso River valley although Eisen did not depict that river in his design but envisioned instead a distant view of the bridge over the Ina River, a tributary of the Kiso, which was very close to the previous station, Suhara. Eisen found the idea for his design in the guidebook *Views of Famous Sights along the Kiso Road* (*Kisoji meisho zue*), which featured this scenery from an even greater distance and from higher up while also including more of the landscape to the right of this image.

The wooden bridge is constructed on stone piers and arches upwards at a steep angle. The accounts of Western travellers from the 1870s make no mention of this locale, which is somewhat surprising, given Eisen's dramatic rendering. However, little resemblance can be found between Eisen's design and his source image, or the geography as it is today. While topography can change over time according to natural processes and human intervention, it seems that Eisen has exaggerated the narrowness of the river, the steepness, height and form of its banks, and the incline of the watercourse, which in the print appears as a cascade but in reality flows evenly into the Kiso River.

Batō Kannon, the Horse-Headed Bodhisattva of Compassion, is worshipped at the Jōshōji temple depicted top left. High up on the mountain amidst the trees, Jōshōji can only be reached by way of a very long flight of steps, which Eisen has included. However, what is not shown is the remarkable architecture of Jōshōji which is comparable with Kyoto's famous Kiyomizu Temple, since both buildings stand on very tall wooden pillars. Jōshōji was probably built in the 18th century and was then destroyed by fire. It was reconstructed in 1813 and the construction made solid in 1983 with cement. Today's bridge over the Ina River is a horizontal steel construction.

Die Station Nojiri liegt im Kiso-Tal, das Eisen allerdings in seinem Entwurf nicht zeigt. Er stellte sich stattdessen einen Fernblick auf die Brücke über den Ina vor, einen Nebenfluss des Kiso, der sehr nah an der vorherigen Station Suhara vorbeifloss. Eisen fand die Idee zu diesem Druck in dem Reiseführer *Ansichten berühmter Stätten an der Kiso-Straße (Kisoji meisho zue)*, der die Szenerie aus noch größerer Entfernung und Höhe zeigte und mehr von der Landschaft rechts des hier gewählten Ausschnitts einbezog.

Die Holzbrücke steht auf steinernen Stützpfeilern und wölbt sich steil nach oben. In Berichten westlicher Reisender aus den 1870er Jahren wird dieser Ort nicht erwähnt, was angesichts der dramatischen Darstellung Eisens einigermaßen überrascht. Allerdings besitzt Eisens Entwurf auch wenig Ähnlichkeit mit seinem Vorbild oder den heutigen geografischen Gegebenheiten. Während sich die Topografie durch natürliche Prozesse und menschliche Eingriffe mit der Zeit verändern kann, scheint Eisen die Enge des Flusses, die Steilheit, Höhe und Form seiner Ufer und das Gefälle des Wasserlaufs, der im Druck als Kaskade erscheint, in Wirklichkeit aber gleichmäßig in den Kiso fließt, übertrieben zu haben.

Batō Kannon, der pferdeköpfige Bodhisattva der Barmherzigkeit, wird im Jōshōji-Tempel ganz oben links im Bild verehrt. Weit oben in den Bergen zwischen Bäumen gelegen, ist der Tempel nur über eine sehr lange Treppe zu erreichen, die Eisen ebenfalls abbildet. Was jedoch nicht gezeigt wird, ist die bemerkenswerte Architektur des Jōshōji, die mit der des berühmten Kiyomizu-Tempels in Kyoto vergleichbar ist, da beide Gebäude auf sehr langen Holzpfeilern stehen. Der Jōshōji wurde vermutlich im 18. Jahrhundert erbaut und dann durch ein Feuer zerstört. 1813 wurde er wieder aufgebaut, 1983 wurde die Konstruktion durch Zement verstärkt. Anstelle der Holzbrücke überspannt heute eine waagerechte Stahlkonstruktion den Ina.

La station de Nojiri se trouve dans la vallée de la Kiso, mais Eisen ne l'a pas représentée dans son estampe, lui préférant plutôt une vue lointaine du pont qui enjambe l'Ina, affluent de la Kiso, situé tout près de la station précédente de Suhara. Eisen s'est inspiré d'une illustration de ce lieu figurant dans le guide de voyage *Collection de vues de paysages célèbres sur la route Kiso (Kisoji meisho zue)*, qui montre ce paysage depuis un point encore plus éloigné et plus élevé, et donne à voir une plus grande partie du paysage se trouvant à droite.

Le pont de bois est bâti sur des piles de pierres, et son arche dessine un angle aigu. Les récits des voyageurs occidentaux datant des années 1870 ne mentionnent pas ce lieu, ce qui est quelque peu surprenant étant donné la représentation spectaculaire qu'en a proposée Eisen. Même si la topographie peut changer avec le temps sous l'effet des processus naturels et des interventions humaines, il semble qu'Eisen ait exagéré l'étroitesse de la rivière, la pente, la hauteur et la forme de ses rives, ainsi que l'inclinaison du cours d'eau qui, dans l'estampe, a l'allure d'une cascade, alors qu'en réalité celui-ci coule de façon uniforme.

Batō Kannon, le bodhisattva de la compassion à tête de cheval, est l'objet du culte du temple de Jōshōji, visible en haut à gauche. On ne peut atteindre ce temple perché au sommet d'une montagne parmi les arbres que par un très long escalier qu'Eisen a représenté. En revanche, l'artiste n'a rien rendu de son architecture remarquable, comparable à celle du célèbre temple de Kiyomizu à Kyoto, les deux édifices étant construits sur de très hauts pilotis de bois. Probablement bâti au XVIIIe siècle, le temple de Jōshōji a, par la suite, été détruit par un incendie. Reconstruit en 1813, il a été consolidé avec du ciment en 1983. Aujourd'hui, le pont qui enjambe l'Ina est un ouvrage d'art horizontal en acier.

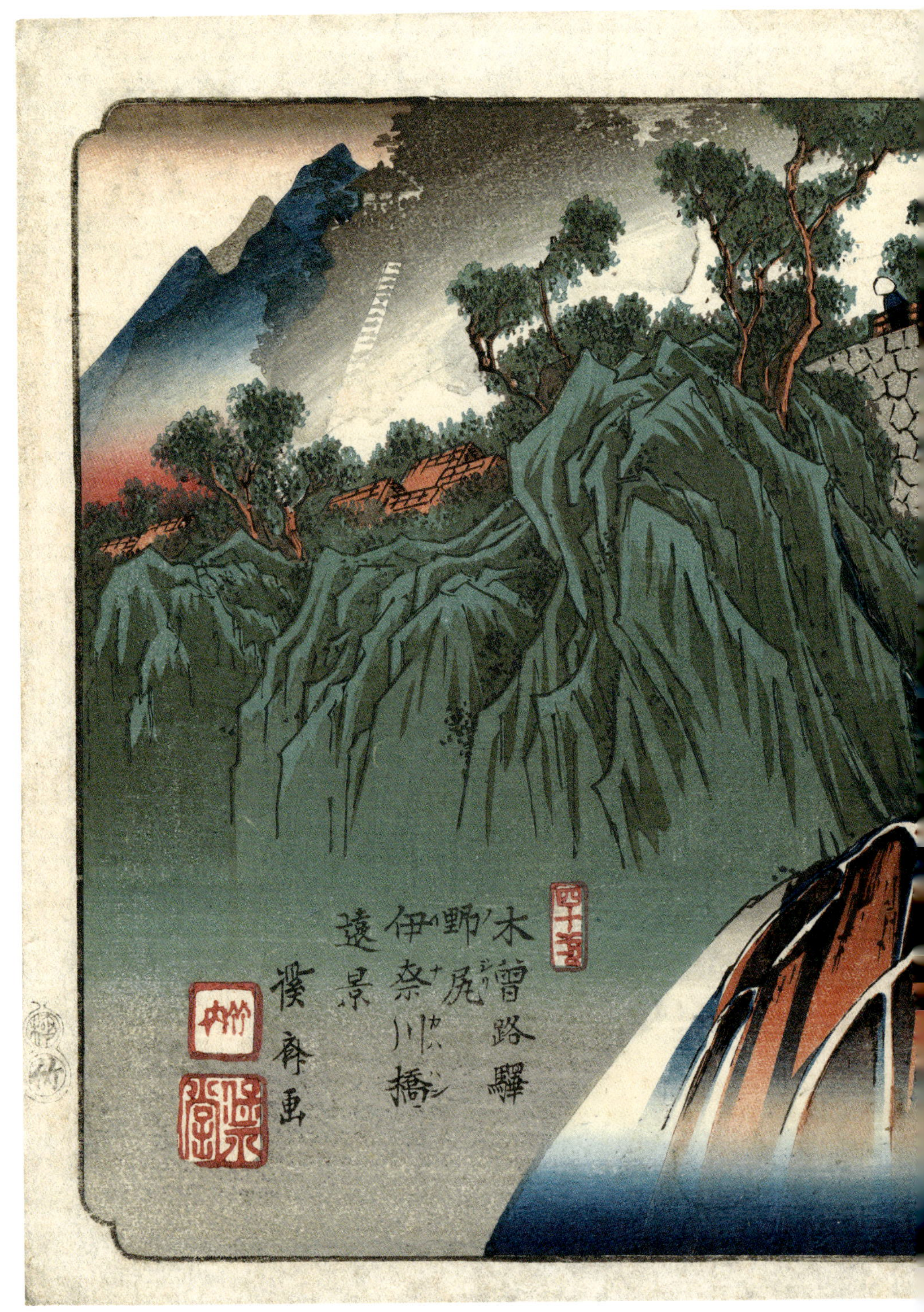
木曽路駅
野尻
伊奈川橋
遠景
渓斎画

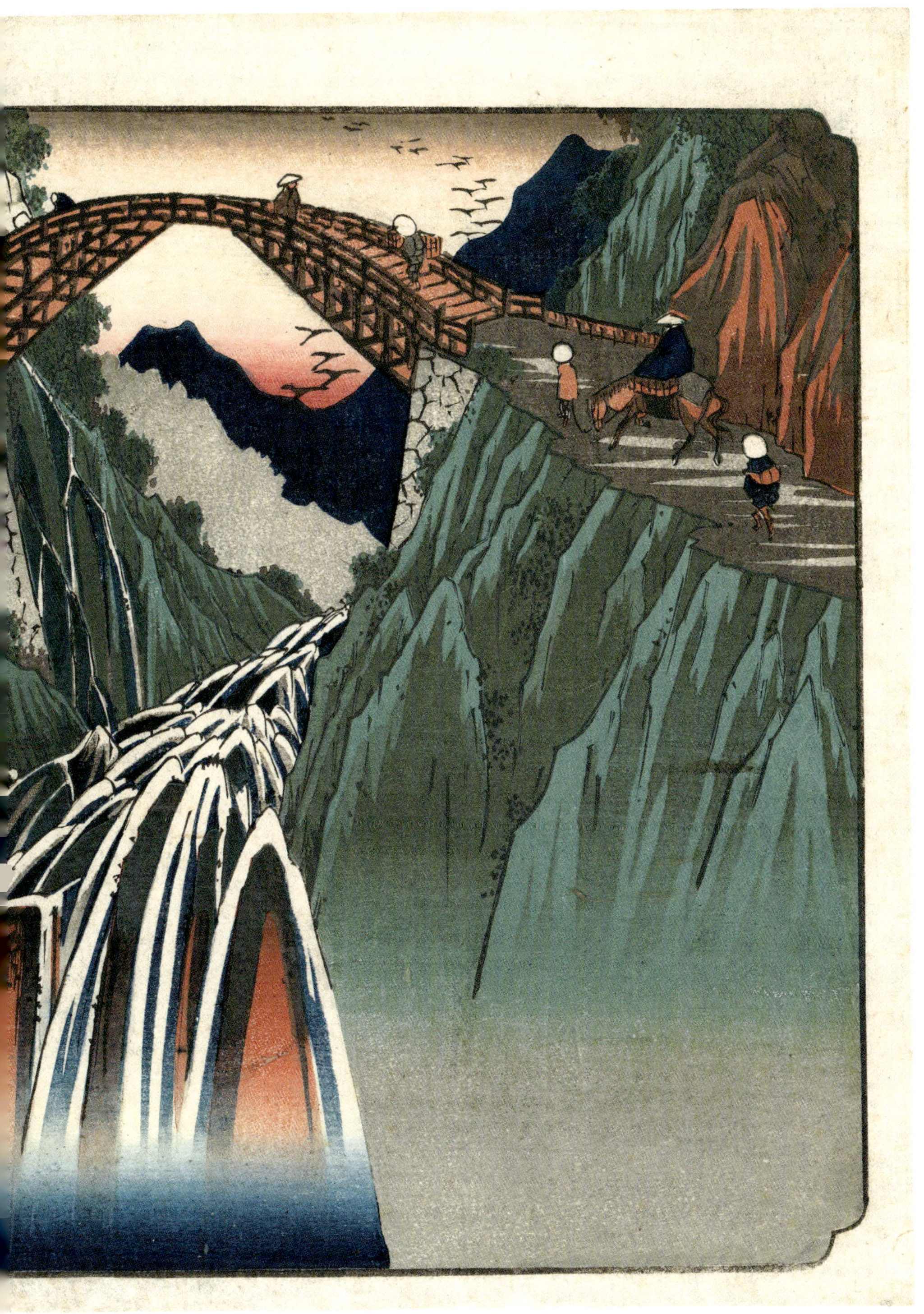

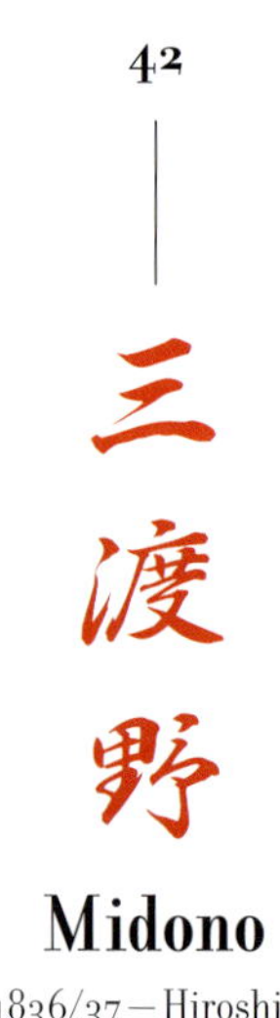

Midono

1836/37 — Hiroshige

Some of the most splendid scenery of the Kisokaidō was between Nojiri and Midono stations. An illustration in the guidebook *Views of Famous Sights along the Kiso Road* (*Kisoji meisho zue*) shows the Kiso Valley narrowing into a gorge, the road a shallow ledge cut into its steep walls, and the Kiso River treacherous with rapids below. Several bridge crossings, including a particularly hair-raising suspension bridge, made it also one of the more dangerous legs of the road.

Instead, Hiroshige created a picturesque pastoral scene for Midono. A farmer with a pipe protruding from the corner of his mouth is bending over in a golden field of barley that sways gently in the breeze. A traveller is ambling along the path to the left, his hands clasping a tobacco pouch behind his back. Heading briskly in the opposite direction is a woman dragging a small child by one hand and supporting a tray laden with a kettle and other articles balanced on her head with the other – a delivery of lunch for her husband, perhaps. A row of sturdily thatched rooftops can be seen in the background.

The green hill is surmounted by a pair of Shinto gates or *torii* strung with boundary ropes. The gates have straight rather than curved lintels and tie beams, the simplest and oldest type of construction. Beyond the crest of the hill can be seen flowering plum trees, indicating that the season is early spring.

The name of the town, which is not illustrated, was originally written with Chinese characters meaning "palace", after a mansion of the ruling Kiso clan that was located here. The town was largely destroyed in a fire during the Meiji period; amongst the little that remained was a pink blossoming plum tree in the ruins of the *honjin*. The village is also distinguished by a wooden sculpture of the bodhisattva Skanda (Japanese: Idaten) set up by the wandering priest Enkū (1632–1695). As he travelled throughout eastern and northern Japan, Enkū left approximately 5,300 roughly hewn wooden sculptures, which he created in exchange for food and lodging.

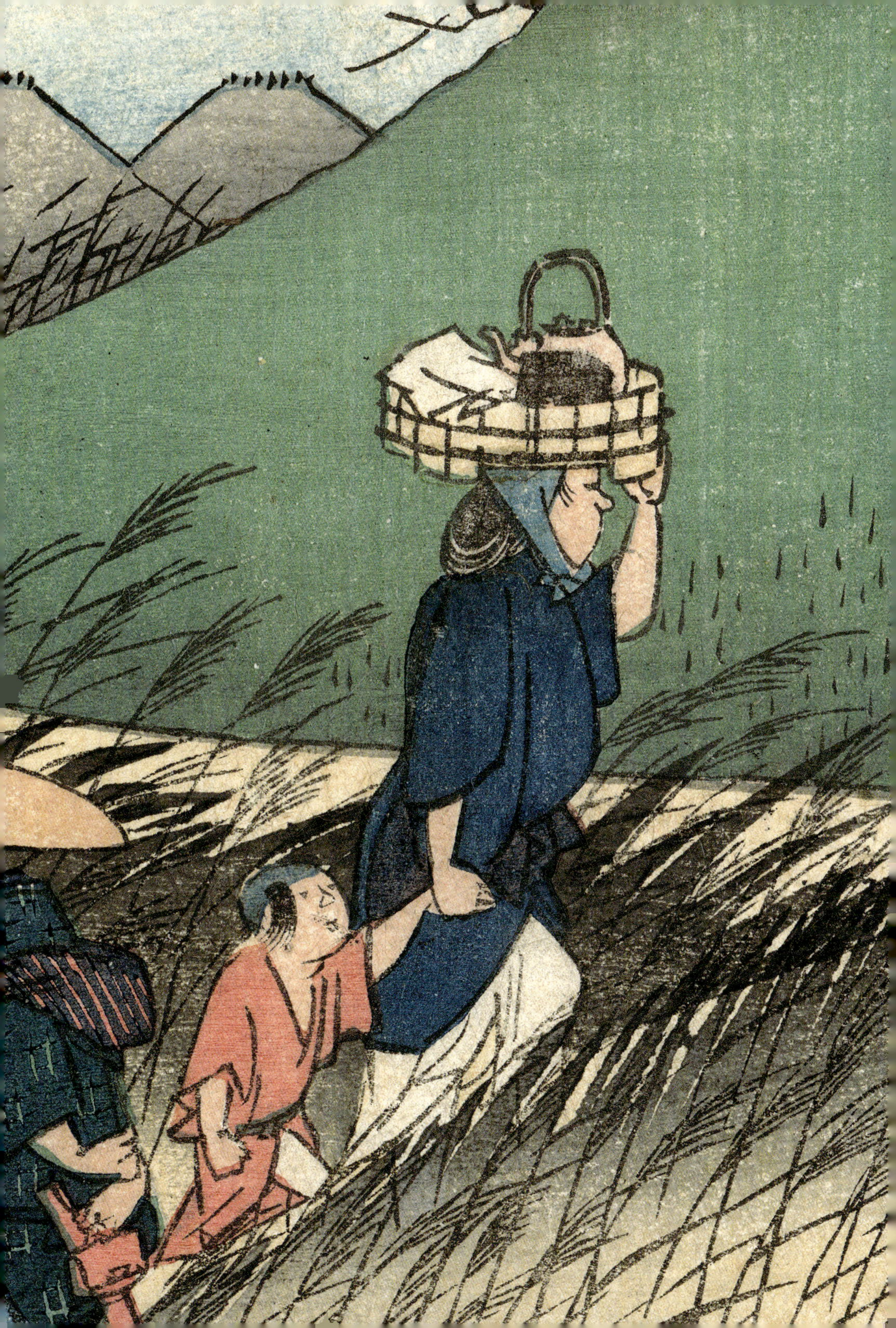

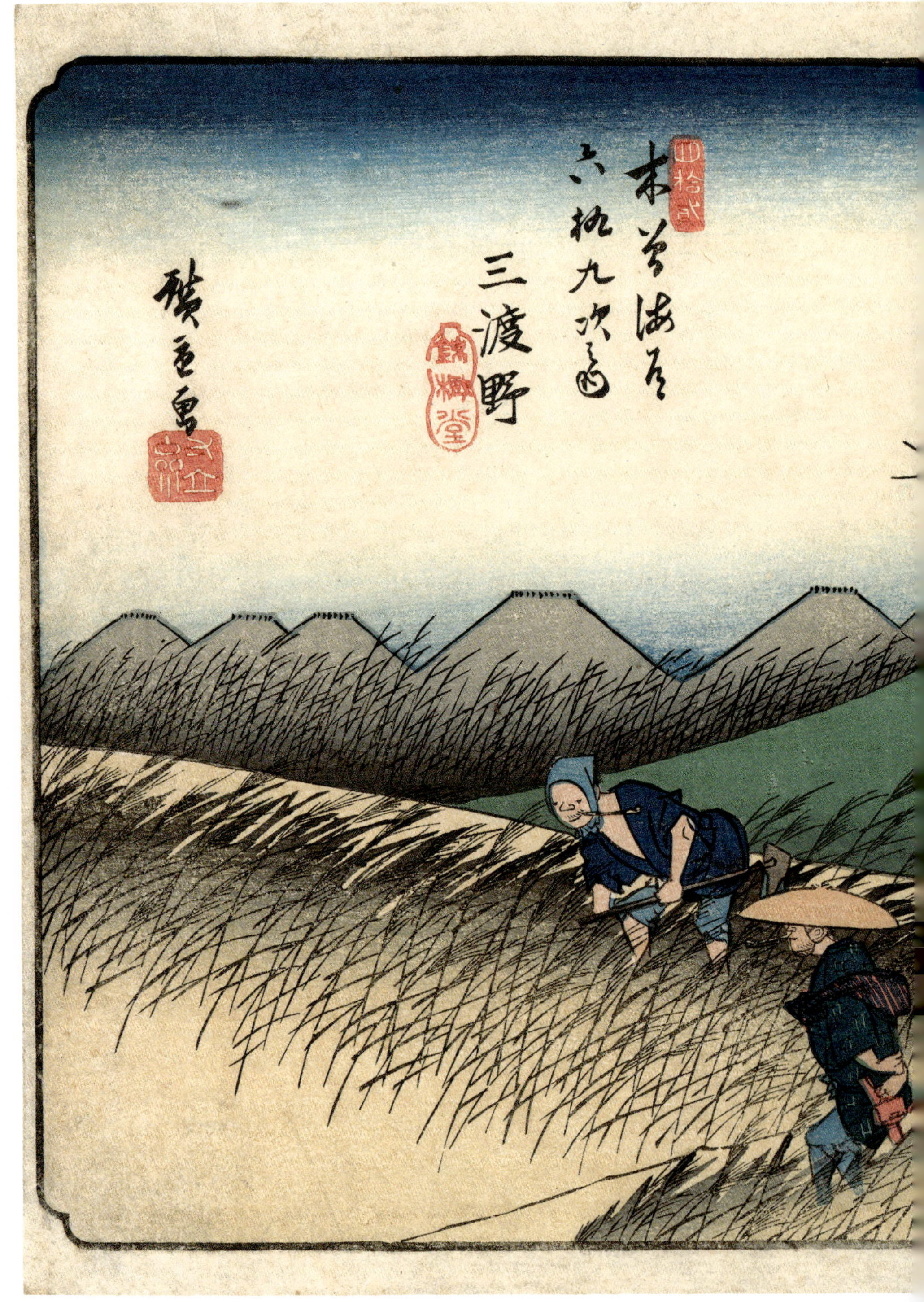

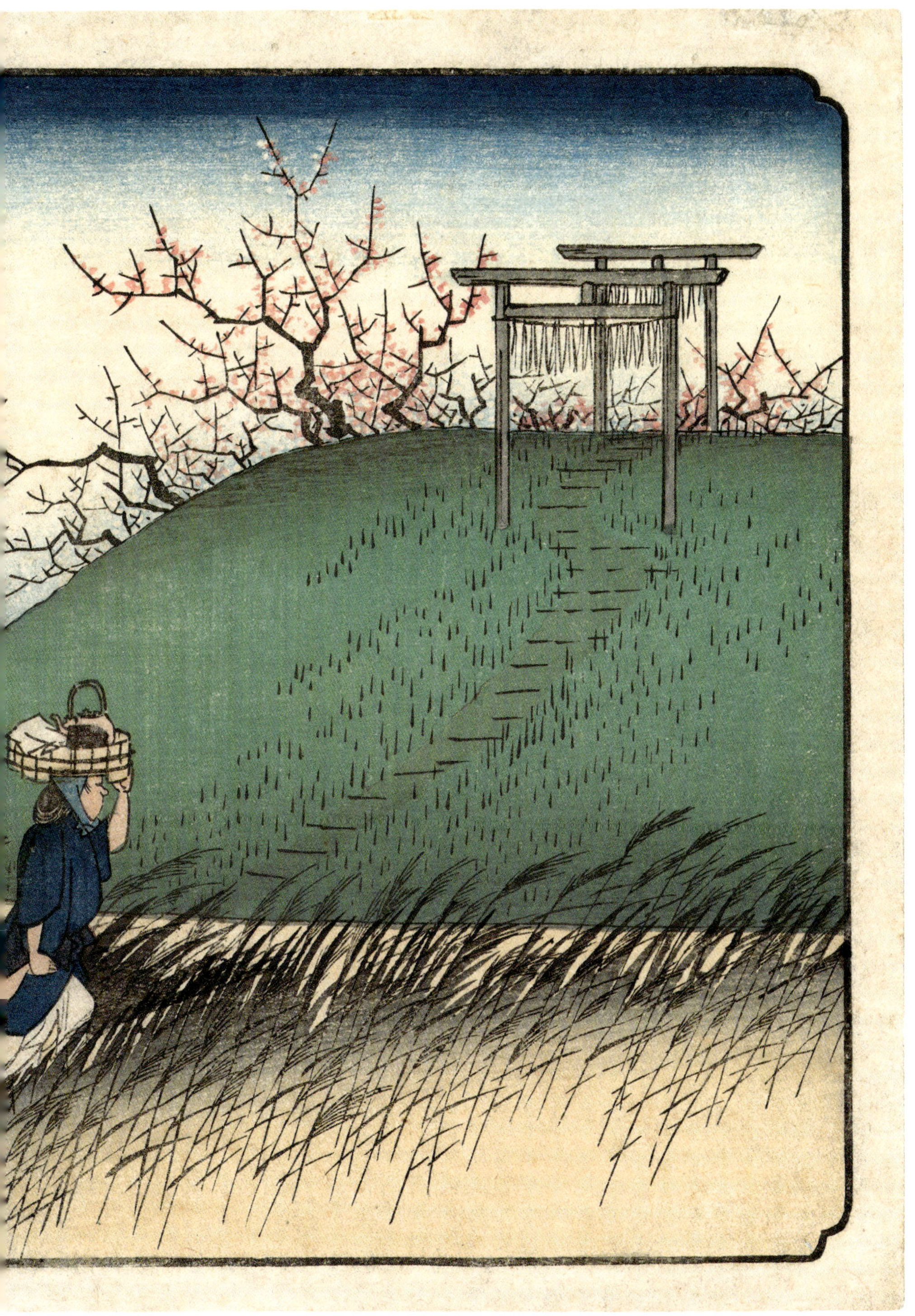

Eine der prächtigsten Landschaften am Kisokaidō lag zwischen den Stationen Nojiri und Midono. Eine Abbildung im Reisehandbuch *Ansichten berühmter Stätten an der Kiso-Straße (Kisoji meisho zue)* zeigt, wie sich das Kiso-Tal zu einer Schlucht verengt und die Straße zu einem in die steilen Felswände gehauenen flachen Vorsprung wird, der hoch über den tückischen Stromschnellen des Kiso verläuft. Mehrere Brückenübergänge, darunter eine besonders haarsträubende Hängebrücke, machten den Abschnitt zusätzlich zu einer der gefährlicheren Etappen des Kisokaidō.

Hiroshige aber schuf für Midono ein pittoreskes ländliches Idyll. Ein Bauer mit Pfeife im Mundwinkel beugt sich in einem goldenen, sanft im Wind wogenden Gerstenfeld vornüber. Ein Reisender, der mit den Händen auf dem Rücken seinen Tabaksbeutel umklammert, schlendert den Weg entlang nach links. In die entgegengesetzte Richtung strebt schnellen Schrittes eine Frau. An der einen Hand zieht sie ein Kind hinter sich her, mit der anderen stützt sie ein mit einem Kessel und anderen Gegenständen beladenes Tablett ab, das sie auf dem Kopf balanciert – ein Mittagessen für ihren Mann vielleicht. Im Hintergrund ist eine Reihe dicht gedeckter Strohdächer zu erkennen.

Zwei mit Begrenzungsschnüren geschmückte *torii* (Tore von Shinto-Schreinen) überragen den grasgrünen Hügel. Die Stürze und Querbalken der *torii* sind, wie es dem einfachsten und ältesten Bautyp entspricht, eher gerade als geschwungen. Hinter der Hügelkuppe ragen als Zeichen des Vorfrühlings blühende Pflaumenbäume hervor.

Der Name der Ortschaft, die nicht abgebildet ist, wurde ursprünglich mit den chinesischen Zeichen für „Palast" geschrieben – nach einem Anwesen des herrschenden Kiso-Clans, der hier ansässig war. In der Meiji-Zeit wurde der Ort durch ein Feuer weitgehend zerstört; unter den wenigen unversehrten Überresten fand sich ein rosa blühender Pflaumenbaum in den Ruinen des *honjin*. Midono ist auch für seine hölzerne Statue des Bodhisattva Skanda (japanisch: Idaten) bekannt, die vom Wanderprediger Enkū (1632–1695) errichtet wurde. Auf seinen Reisen durch den Osten und Norden Japans hinterließ Enkū etwa 5300 grob behauene Skulpturen, die er im Tausch gegen Kost und Logis angefertigt hatte.

Les paysages situés entre les stations de Nojiri et de Midono comptent parmi les plus beaux de la Kisokaidō. Une illustration du guide de voyage *Collection de vues de paysages célèbres sur la route Kiso (Kisoji meisho zue)* représente la vallée de la Kiso réduite à une gorge, dans laquelle la route devient une mince corniche taillée dans ses parois escarpées, surplombant les rapides de la périlleuse rivière. Le franchissement de plusieurs ponts, dont un pont suspendu particulièrement terrifiant, faisait aussi de cette section l'une des plus dangereuses du parcours.

Pourtant, Hiroshige a préféré pour Midono une pittoresque scène pastorale. Sa pipe fichée dans un coin de la bouche, un fermier se penche sur un champ d'orge dorée qui se balance lentement dans le vent. Un voyageur suit sans se presser un chemin vers la gauche, tenant fermement dans ses mains une blague à tabac derrière son dos. Dans l'autre direction, une femme avance d'un pas vif, en traînant un petit enfant d'une main et en maintenant de l'autre, sur sa tête, un plateau chargé d'une bouilloire et d'autres articles, peut-être le déjeuner de son mari. À l'arrière-plan se dessine une rangée de robustes toits de chaume.

Sur la colline verte se dressent deux *torii*, ou portes shinto, d'où pendent des cordes marquant une démarcation. Les poutres de liaison et linteaux droits, et non courbés, répondent au mode de construction le plus simple et le plus ancien. Derrière la crête s'élèvent des pruniers en fleur, signe que la scène se passe au début du printemps.

Le nom de la petite ville, qui n'est pas représenté, s'écrivait initialement avec les caractères chinois signifiant « palais », en raison d'un manoir du clan des Kiso qui régnait alors, situé sur place. La plus grande partie de Midono fut ravagée par un incendie au cours de l'ère Meiji ; parmi les rares choses ayant échappé au feu, un prunier en fleur était resté intact au milieu des ruines de la *honjin*. La localité se distingue aussi par une sculpture en bois du bodhisattva Skanda (Idaten, en japonais), installée par le prêtre itinérant Enkū (1632–1695). Au cours de ses pérégrinations dans l'est et le nord du Japon, Enkū a laissé derrière lui environ 5300 sculptures grossièrement taillées dans le bois, qu'il réalisait en échange du gîte et du couvert.

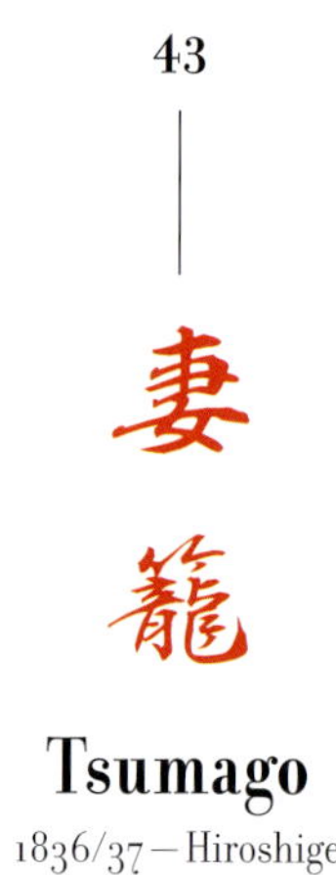

Tsumago

1836/37 – Hiroshige

Travellers approaching Tsumago from Midono pass the remnants of a hilltop fortification, which affords a commanding view over the surrounding countryside. The fort was built in 1584 and decommissioned in 1616 as part of the incoming shogun's policy of "one castle per province" (*ikkoku ichijō*) implemented to ensure that rebellious samurai were in no position to stage an uprising.

A little further on is a boulder thought to resemble a leaping carp and the ruins of a checkpoint, which until the early 17th century regulated traffic along the Kisokaidō and the roads to Mino and Ina that intersected at Tsumago. This area has been identified as a possible locale for the scene Hiroshige depicted for Tsumago, although it is unlikely that he travelled the Kisokaidō before creating this design.

Hiroshige populated his composition with a familiar cast of wayfarers. A pilgrim, dressed in white and carrying a portable shrine, is making his way along the path while a traveller is heading in the opposite direction. Strapped to the latter's back is a bundle of straw, possibly containing fermented soya beans. Straw is host to a strain of bacteria that transforms boiled soya beans into a pungent source of protein enjoyed in eastern Japan for thousands of years. Further ahead are a courier with panniers, and two travellers approaching over the crest of the hill.

Like many post towns, Tsumago fell into decline after the abolition of the alternating attendance system (*sankin kōtai*). However, in 1968, before too much of the local heritage was lost, local citizens campaigned to create a preservation district, which is currently the largest in the country. Within the district, the buildings, mostly dating from the late 19th and early 20th centuries – well after Tsumago's days as a post town – were restored and surrounding hillsides protected, thus maintaining an old village atmosphere which attracts close to a million tourists a year.

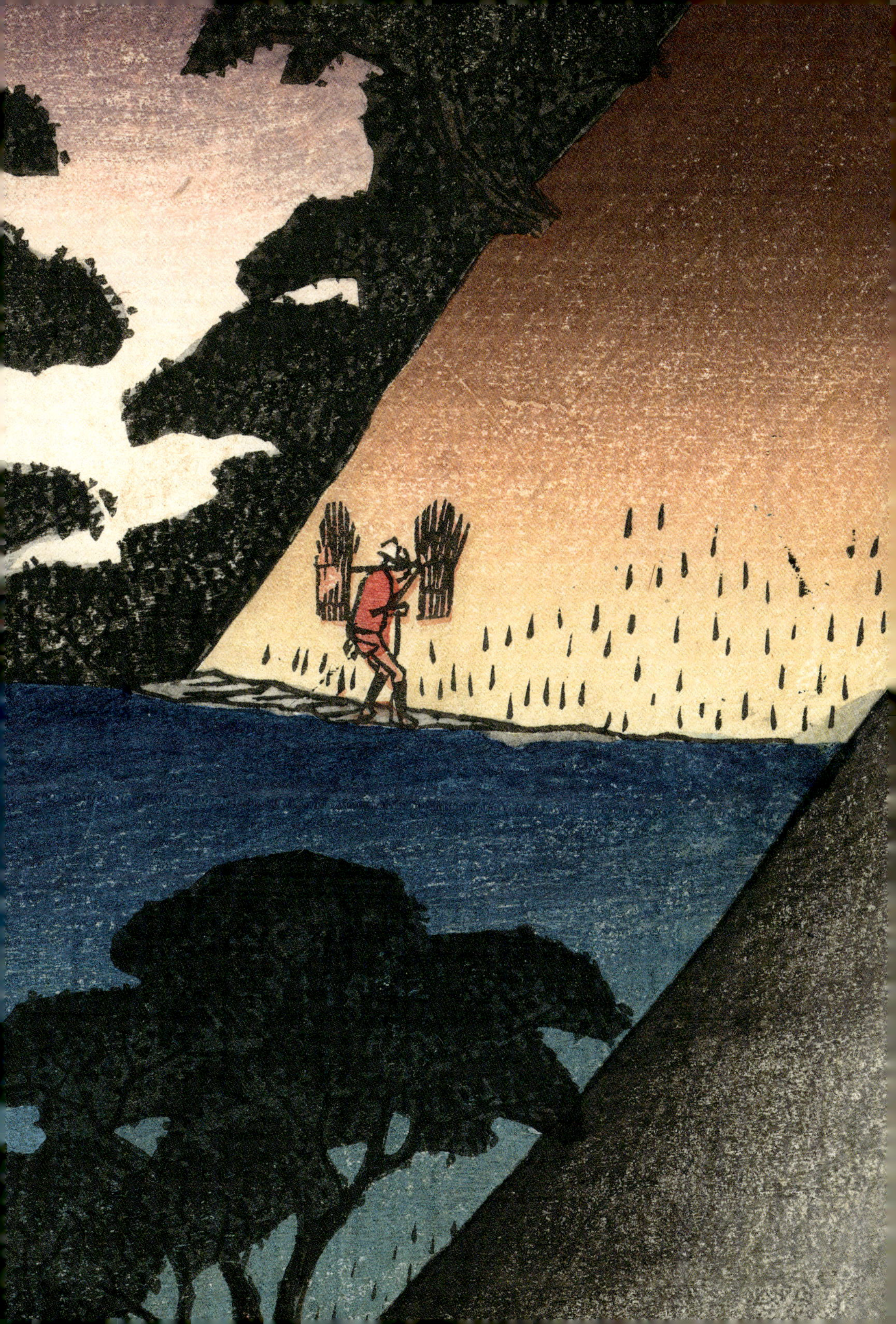

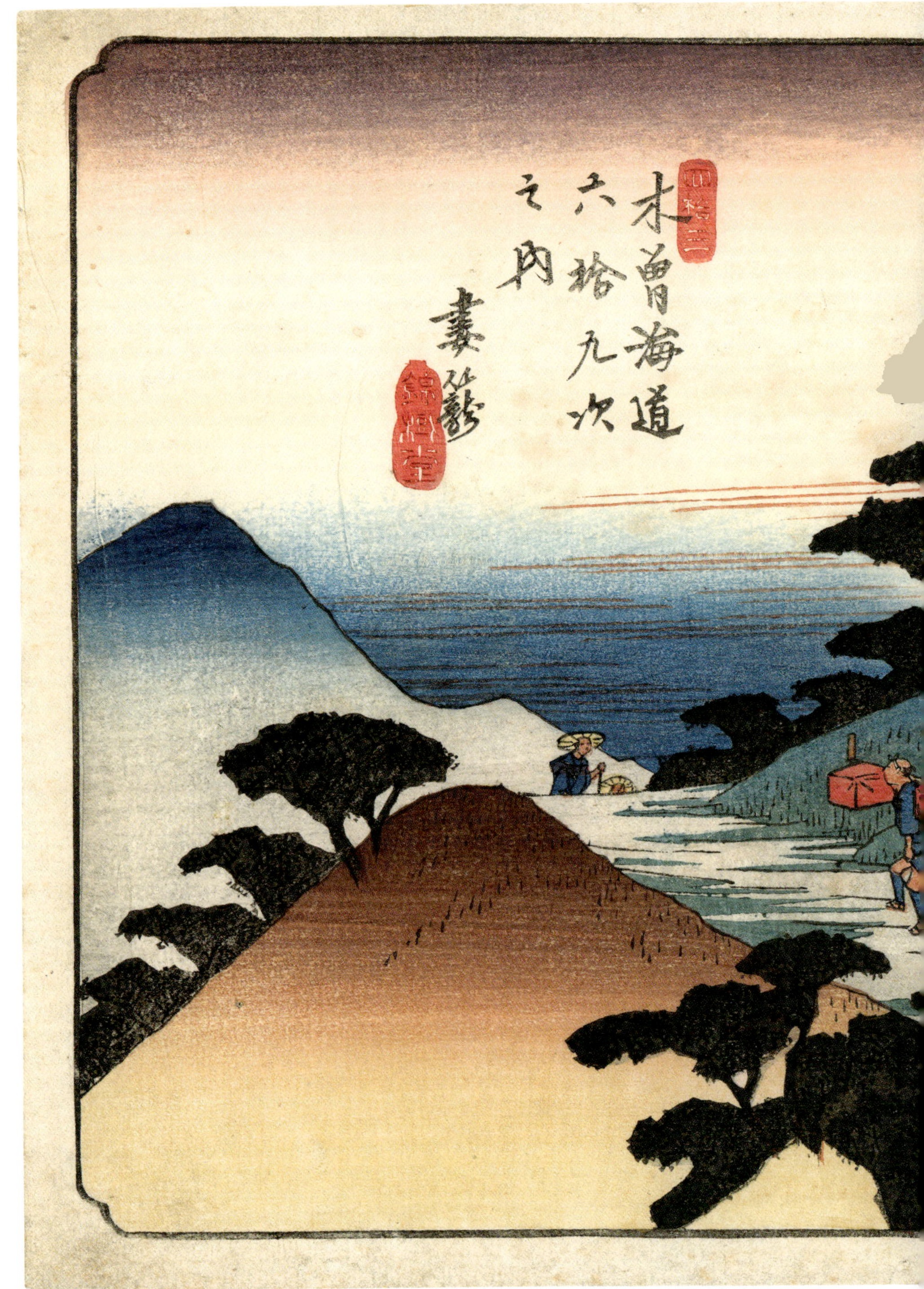

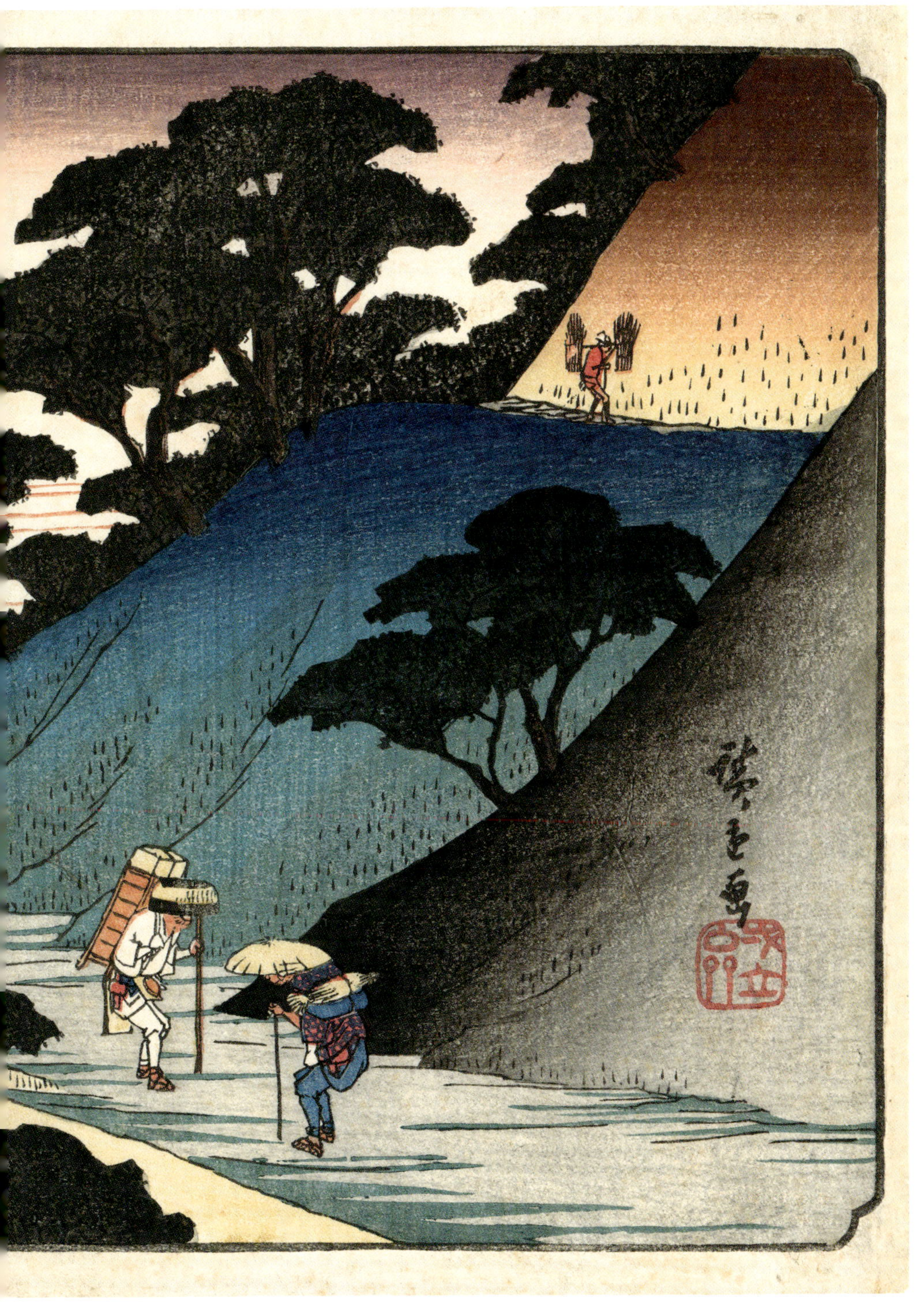

Reisende, die sich Tsumago über den Midono-Pass nähern, passieren die Überreste einer Höhenfestung mit einem imposanten Ausblick über die umliegende Landschaft. Die Festung wurde 1584 erbaut und bereits 1616 stillgelegt. Dies geschah im Zuge der Politik „Eine Burg pro Provinz" *(ikkoku ichijō)*, die der neue Shogun einführte, um sicherzustellen, dass widerspenstige Samurai nicht dazu in der Lage waren, einen Aufstand anzuzetteln.

Ein Stück weiter liegen ein Felsblock, der einem springenden Karpfen ähneln soll, und die Ruinen einer Kontrollstelle, die bis ins frühe 17. Jahrhundert den Verkehr auf dem Kisokaidō und auf den Straßen nach Mino und Ina regulierte, die sich in Tsumago kreuzten. Diese Gegend wurde als möglicher Schauplatz der Szene identifiziert, die Hiroshige hier abbildete, obwohl es unwahrscheinlich ist, dass er den Kisokaidō bereiste, bevor er diesen Entwurf schuf.

Hiroshige bevölkerte seine Komposition mit einer vertrauten Besetzung von Fußreisenden. Ein in Weiß gekleideter Pilger, der einen tragbaren Schrein mit sich führt, geht die Straße hinunter. Ihm kommt ein Reisender mit einem Strohbündel auf dem Rücken entgegen, das möglicherweise mit fermentierten Sojabohnen gefüllt ist. Die im Stroh enthaltene Bakterienart verwandelt gekochte Sojabohnen in eine streng schmeckende Eiweißquelle, die im Osten Japans seit Jahrtausenden als Delikatesse gilt. Weiter vorn geht ein Kurier mit geschulterten Packtaschen, und ganz links tauchen zwei Reisende hinter der Hügelkuppe auf.

Wie viele Post-Ortschaften erlebte auch Tsumago nach der Abschaffung des Systems der „wechselnden Anwesenheit" *(sankin kōtai)* einen Niedergang. Doch bevor allzu große Teile des heimischen Erbes verschwunden waren, setzten sich 1968 Bürger vor Ort für die Schaffung eines Denkmalschutzbezirks ein, der heute der größte des Landes ist. Innerhalb dieses Bezirks wurden die Gebäude, die größtenteils aus dem späten 19. und frühen 20. Jahrhundert stammen – als Tsumagos Tage als Poststation lange vorüber waren –, restauriert und die umliegenden Hänge unter Schutz gestellt. Auf diese Weise bewahrte man die Atmosphäre eines alten Dorfes, die jedes Jahr fast eine Million Touristen anzieht.

En venant de Midono, les voyageurs sur le point d'arriver à Tsumago passent devant les ruines d'une fortification édifiée au sommet d'une colline d'où l'on jouit d'un splendide panorama sur la campagne environnante. Construit en 1584, ce fort fut désaffecté en 1616, conformément à la politique du nouveau shogun qui voulait « un château par province » (*ikkoku ichijō*), afin d'empêcher les samouraïs rebelles de fomenter une insurrection.

Un peu plus loin se trouvent un rocher, dont on dit qu'il a la forme d'une carpe bondissante, et les ruines d'un poste de contrôle qui, jusqu'au début du XVIIe siècle, régulait la circulation de la Kisokaidō et des routes menant à Mino et à Ina, dont Tsumago était le carrefour. Il est possible qu'Hiroshige ait choisi ce lieu pour illustrer Tsumago, mais il est peu probable que l'artiste ait voyagé sur la Kisokaidō avant de réaliser cette estampe.

Les personnages dont Hiroshige a peuplé sa composition sont un ensemble habituel de voyageurs. Vêtu de blanc et chargé d'un autel portatif, un pèlerin progresse sur la route, tandis qu'un voyageur avance dans la direction opposée. Ce dernier porte, attachée sur son dos, une petite balle de paille qui contient peut-être des graines de soja fermentées. La paille renferme un type de bactéries qui transforment les graines de soja bouillies en une substance âcre contenant des protéines, appréciée depuis des millénaires dans le Japon oriental. Un peu plus loin se trouve un portefaix chargé de paniers, alors que deux voyageurs sont visibles en haut de la côte.

Comme nombre de villes étapes, Tsumago connut le déclin après l'abolition du système de résidence alternée (*sankin kōtai*). Toutefois, en 1968, avant la disparition d'une partie trop importante du patrimoine, les habitants de la région ont fait campagne pour la création d'une zone de sauvegarde, actuellement la plus grande du pays. Au sein de cette zone, les édifices, datant pour la plupart du tournant des XIXe et XXe siècles – bien après la prospérité de Tsumago comme relais de poste –, ont été restaurés, et les collines environnantes protégées. Grâce au maintien d'une ambiance de village d'autrefois, un million de touristes visitent Tsumago chaque année.

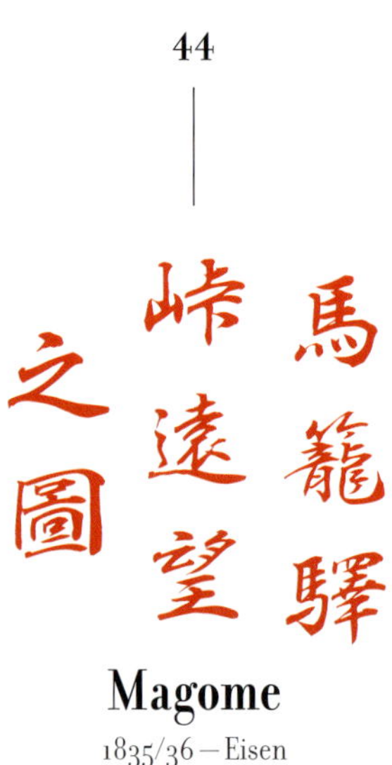

44

Magome

1835/36 — Eisen

Eisen's design for Magome imagines the view of the town from Magome Pass, an obstacle with an elevation of just over 800 metres (2,625 feet) that separates the station from the neighbouring village of Tsumago. The path is busy: a team of palanquin-bearers pauses while one adjusts his sandal, a traveller with a wrapping cloth containing his luggage knotted around his shoulders approaches a dip in the road, while further on the conical hat of another traveller can be noticed. An oxherd perched on his gentle beast is passing along the high road ahead. To the left, a small waterfall runs down the face of the hillside; this is perhaps a reference to the Otaki or male waterfall, a counterpart to the female waterfall Metaki. Towering above the village is Mount Ena, whose peak reaches 2,191 metres (7,188 feet). The scene inverts the illustration in the guidebook *Views of Famous Sights along the Kiso Road (Kisoji meisho zue)*, which shows the view towards Tsumago from the pass.

Perched on the side of a steep incline, Magome is the last of the 11 stations of the Kisoji, an ancient trade route through Mino and Shinano Provinces, which later became part of the Kisokaidō. Like Tsumago, it fell into decline after the abolition of the alternating attendance system, but from the 1960s and '70s, and following the initiative of Tsumago, locals set to work preserving and restoring its heritage of buildings and today Magome is a popular tourist destination, although few of the buildings date from the village's days as a post station. Magome is also known as the birthplace and childhood home of the writer Shimazaki Tōson (1872–1943), and provided the setting for his novel *Before the Dawn (Yoake mae*, 1929). A memorial museum to the writer was constructed on the site of the *honjin*, which had burnt down in 1895.

Eisens Entwurf für Magome folgt dem Blick vom Magome-Pass, einem Hindernis auf etwas über 800 Metern Meereshöhe, hinunter auf den Ort. Auf dem Pass, der die Station vom Nachbardorf Tsumago trennt, herrscht Hochbetrieb: Zwei Sänftenträger halten kurz an, während einer von ihnen seine Sandale richtet, und ein Reisender mit einem um die Schultern geknoteten Umschlagtuch, das sein Gepäck enthält, nähert sich dem Scheitelpunkt des Weges, hinter dem der Kegelhut eines weiteren Reisenden auftaucht. Auf der oberen ansteigenden Straße bewegt sich ein Ochsenhirte auf dem Rücken seines sanftmütigen Tieres voran. Links neben ihm stürzt ein kleiner Wasserfall den Hang hinab, der womöglich auf den Otaki oder „männlichen Wasserfall" anspielt, das Gegenstück zum „weiblichen Wasserfall" Metaki. Über dem Dorf ragt der 2191 Meter hohe Ena empor. Die Szene kehrt die Abbildung in dem Reiseführer *Ansichten berühmter Stätten an der Kiso-Straße (Kisoji meisho zue)* um, die den Blick vom Pass in Richtung Tsumago zeigt.

Am Fuß eines steilen Abhangs gelegen, ist Magome die letzte der elf Stationen des Kisoji, einer alten Handelsroute durch die Provinzen Mino und Shinano, die später Teil des Kisokaidō wurde. Wie in Tsumago führte die Abschaffung des Systems der „wechselnden Anwesenheit" auch hier zum Verfall, bevor in den 1960er und 1970er Jahren einige Einheimische nach dem Vorbild Tsumagos darangingen, ihr Architekturerbe zu bewahren und zu restaurieren. Heute ist Magome eine beliebte Touristenattraktion, auch wenn nur noch wenige Gebäude aus der Poststationszeit des Dorfes stammen. Bekannt wurde es auch als Geburtsort des Schriftstellers Shimazaki Tōson (1872–1943), der seine Kindheit hier verbrachte, und als Schauplatz für dessen 1929 erschienenen Roman *Vor der Dämmerung (Yoake mae)*. Am Standort des *honjin*, das 1895 niederbrannte, wurde ein Gedenkmuseum für den Autor errichtet.

Pour la station de Magome, Eisen a imaginé la vue de la petite ville depuis le col de Magome, obstacle situé à une altitude de 800 mètres, qui sépare la station du village voisin de Tsumago. Le col est très fréquenté : deux porteurs de palanquin font une pause pendant que l'un d'eux ajuste sa sandale ; un voyageur portant ses bagages dans une bande de tissu nouée autour des épaules aborde la crête de la colline, au-delà de laquelle on devine le chapeau conique d'un autre voyageur. Plus loin, un bouvier assis sur le dos de sa bête placide progresse sur la route. À gauche, une petite cascade tombe le long de la colline ; il s'agit peut-être d'une allusion à l'Otaki, cascade masculine, homologue de la Metaki, cascade féminine. Dominant le village, le mont Ena culmine à 2191 mètres. Cette scène est le point de vue exactement inverse de celui décrit dans le guide de voyage *Collection de vues de paysages célèbres sur la route Kiso (Kisoji meisho zue)*, qui présente la vue de Tsumago depuis le col.

Perchée sur le flanc d'un coteau escarpé, Magome est la dernière des onze stations de la Kisoji, ancienne route commerciale qui traversait les provinces de Mini et de Shinano et, plus tard, devint une section de la Kisokaidō. Comme Tsumago, elle connut le déclin après l'abolition de la résidence alternée. Cependant, à partir des années 1960 et 1970, les habitants de la région, suivant en cela l'initiative de Tsumago, se sont chargés de préserver et de restaurer le patrimoine construit. Aujourd'hui, Magome est une destination prisée des touristes, même si très peu de bâtiments datent de l'époque où le village était un relais de poste. Magome est aussi le lieu de naissance de l'écrivain Shimazaki Tōson (1872–1943), qui y a aussi grandi, ainsi que le cadre de son roman *Avant l'aube (Yoake mae*, 1929). Un musée commémoratif qui lui est consacré a été bâti à l'emplacement de la *honjin*, détruite par un incendie en 1895.

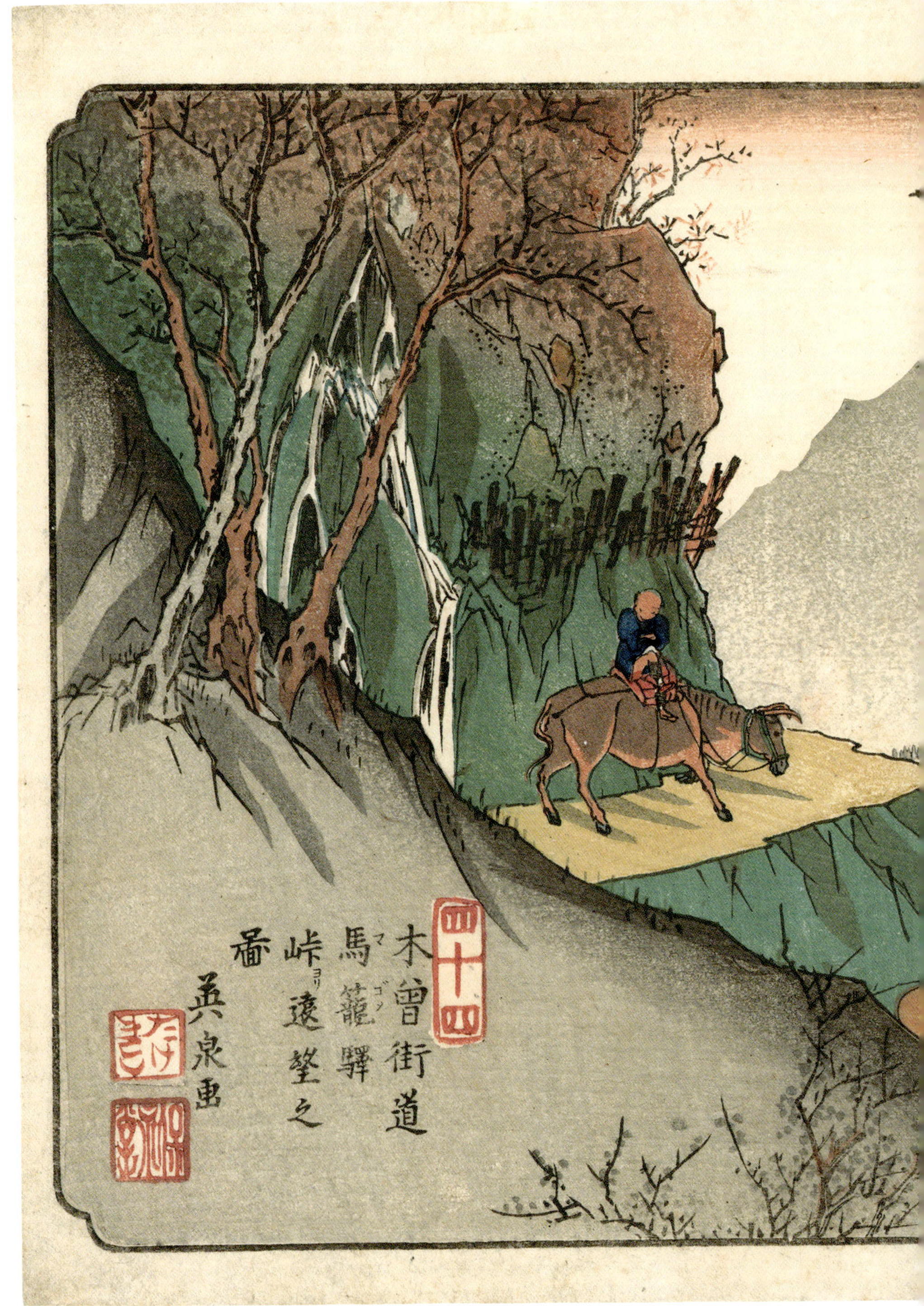
四十四
木曾街道
馬籠驛
峠遠墾之
番
英泉畫

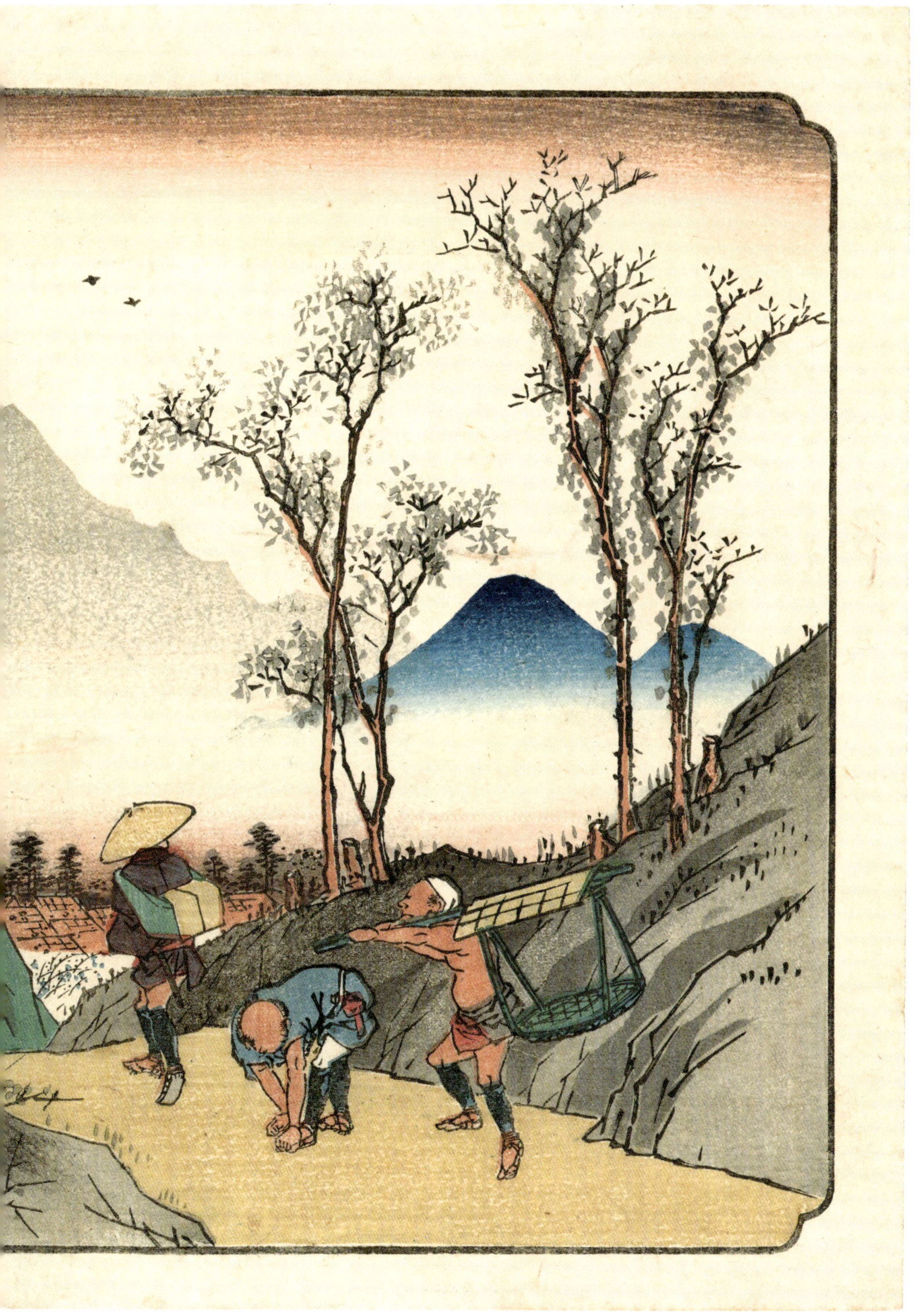

45

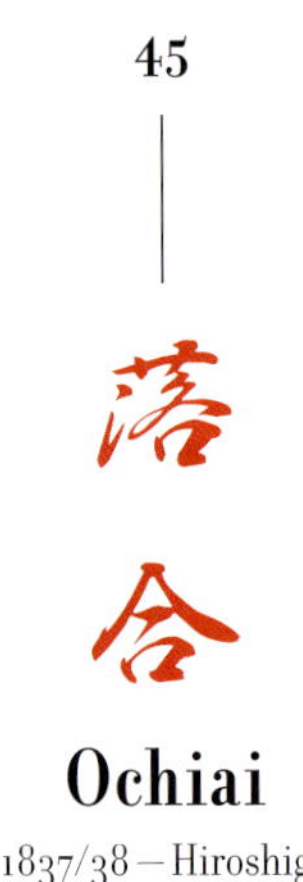

Ochiai

1837/38 — Hiroshige

Coming from Shinano Province, travellers climb over the Jikkoku Pass and then reach the next province, Mino. Shortly thereafter comes Ochiai, the first station in Mino, present-day Gifu Prefecture.

Ochiai is the first image in this series based on a sketch created by Hiroshige during his journey along the Kisokaidō. The representation of the geography in this print, from the houses uphill to the zigzag path that moves down to the bridge over the Yubunezawa River, is extremely close to his sketch. The river, a tributary of the Kiso, flooded on a regular basis and in 1789 washed away the bridge. It was later renamed the Ochiai River. Hiroshige's sketch also includes a mountain range in the background that features Mount Ena, which was depicted with ridged lines in the sketch that become much rounder in the final print.

Hiroshige did not include any travellers in his sketch, and it therefore lacks the procession that is seen in the corresponding print. There are no annotations either that would suggest such a procession passed through while Hiroshige was there, but while he could have remembered it when he drew the design for this print, he could also have just freely added it to enliven the scene.

Aus der Provinz Shinano führt der Kisokaidō über den Jikkoku-Pass in die Provinz Mino. Kurz hinter dem Pass liegt Ochiai, die erste Station in Mino, der heutigen Präfektur Gifu.

Als erstes Blatt dieser Serie beruht Ochiai auf einer Skizze, die Hiroshige während seiner Reise auf dem Kisokaidō anfertigte. Die Wiedergabe der Topografie in diesem Druck kommt seiner Skizze sehr nahe, von den hügelaufwärts gelegenen Häusern bis zum Zickzack des Weges, der zur Brücke über den Yubunezawa hinabführt. Der Fluss, ein Zufluss des Kiso, trat regelmäßig über die Ufer und schwemmte die Brücke 1789 davon. Später wurde er in Ochiai umbenannt. Hiroshiges Skizze enthält im Hintergrund auch eine Bergkette, die den Ena zeigt; die in der Skizze gezackten Linien des Gebirgszugs fallen im endgültigen Druck deutlich runder aus.

Da Hiroshige in seiner Skizze auf Figuren gänzlich verzichtete, taucht die Prozession, die im zugehörigen Druck zu sehen ist, darin nicht auf. Auch gibt es keine Aufzeichnungen, die darauf hindeuten, dass während der Anwesenheit des Künstlers ein solcher Zug den Ort durchquerte. Dennoch könnte Hiroshige sich an ein solches Ereignis erinnert haben, als er dieses Blatt entwarf, oder aber er hat die Prozession freihändig hinzugefügt, um die Szene zu beleben.

Les voyageurs arrivant de la province de Shinano passent par le col de Jikkoku pour entrer dans la province suivante de Mino. Ils parviennent peu après à Ochiai, première station de cette province, l'actuelle préfecture de Gifu.

L'estampe d'Ochiai est la première illustration de cette série inspirée d'une esquisse réalisée par Hiroshige pendant son voyage sur la Kisokaidō. Dans cette estampe, la représentation de la géographie – les maisons perchées sur la colline, la route descendant en zigzag vers le pont qui enjambe la Yubunezawa – est très fidèle à l'esquisse. Affluent de la Kiso, cette rivière connaissait des crues fréquentes qui, en 1789, emportèrent le pont. Elle fut ensuite rebaptisée Ochiai. L'esquisse d'Hiroshige comprend aussi à l'arrière-plan une chaîne de montagnes, dont le mont Ena ; la crête accidentée des montagnes de l'esquisse est devenue une ligne plus arrondie dans l'estampe définitive.

Hiroshige n'avait dessiné aucun voyageur dans son esquisse d'où, par conséquent, est absente la procession visible dans l'estampe. Aucune annotation n'indique qu'Hiroshige a été témoin du passage d'une telle procession ; toutefois, il a pu s'en souvenir au moment de dessiner l'estampe, à moins qu'il ne l'ait librement ajoutée pour animer cette scène.

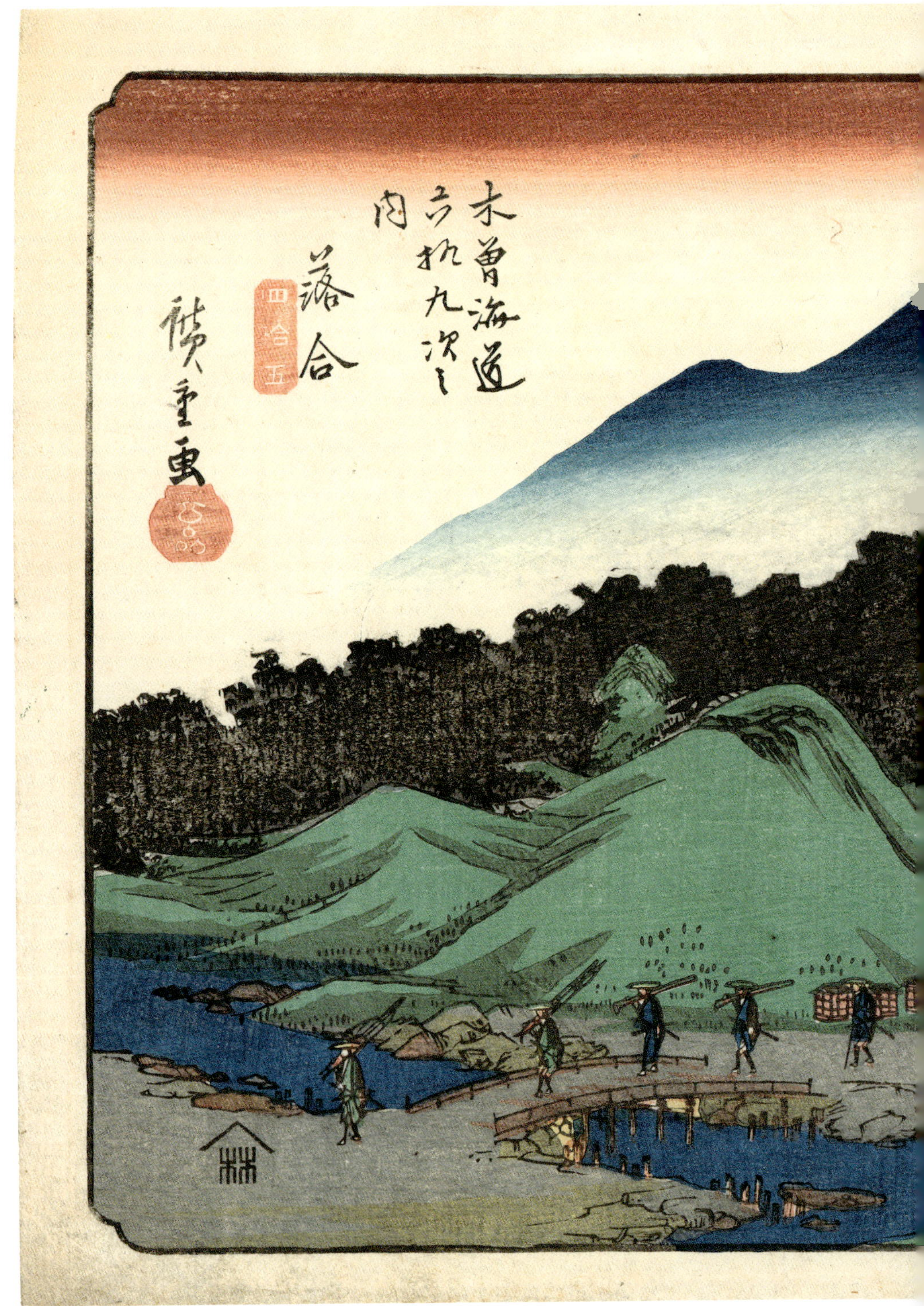

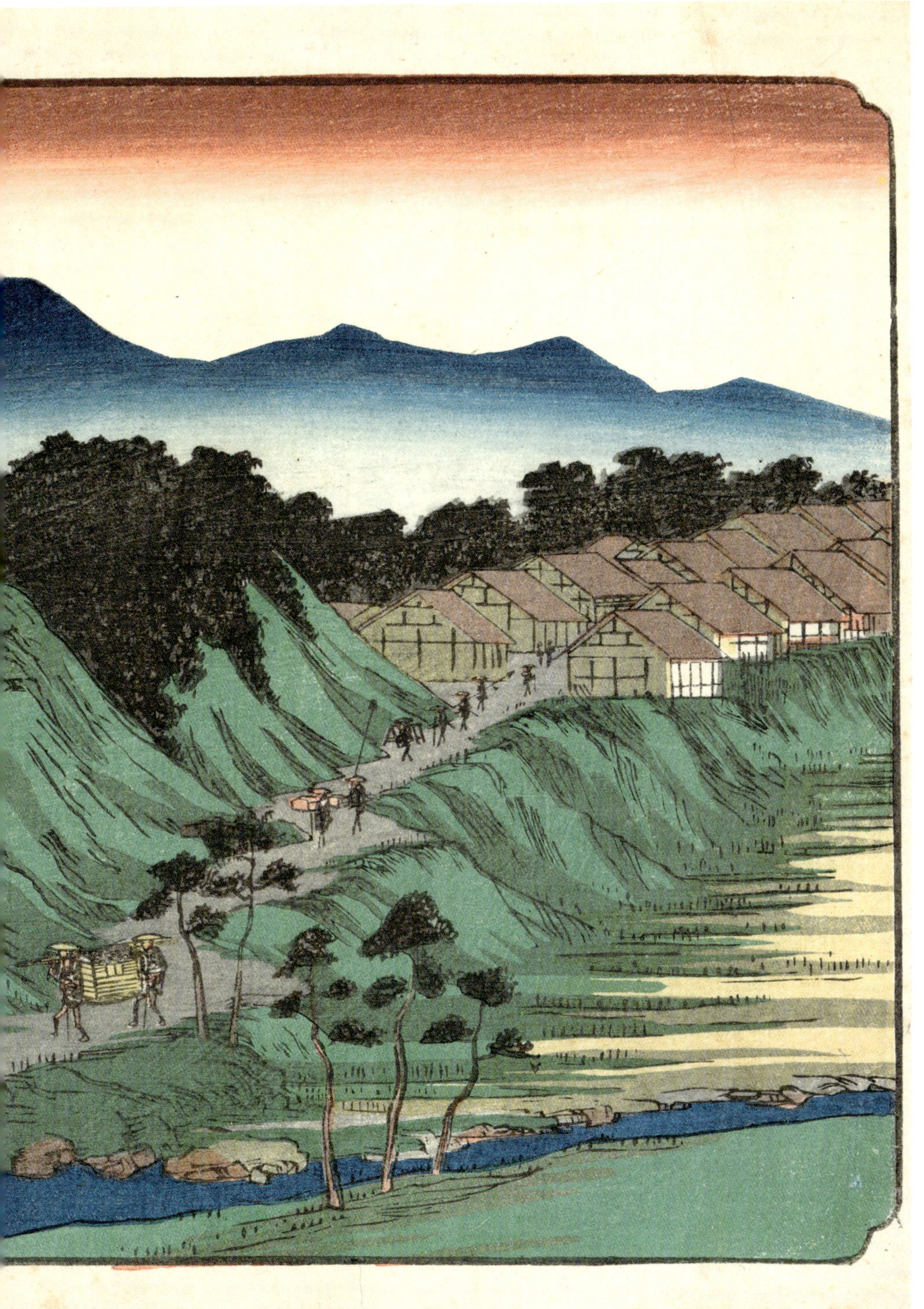

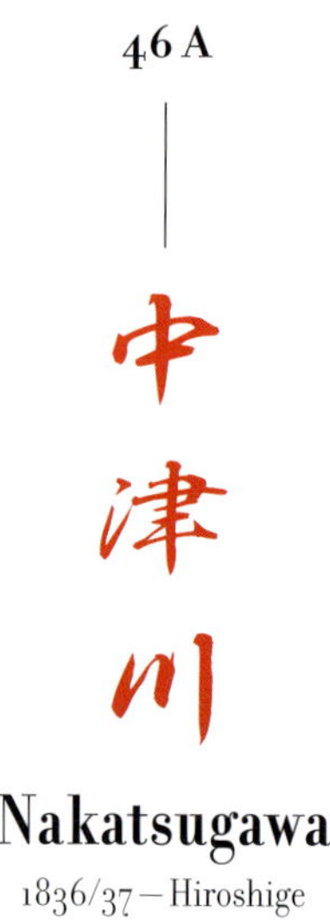

Nakatsugawa

1836/37 – Hiroshige

This is the first of two designs for the Nakatsugawa station created by Hiroshige for this Kisokaidō series. Of the very few impressions of this first design that are extant, all follow the same colour scheme, suggesting that after the first batch of prints was completed the blocks were irreparably damaged. As demand for this series continued, the publisher Iseya Rihei recognised the advantage of being able to offer a complete set of all the stations and so sought to fill this void. One option would have been to have a carver create new blocks based on the existing version of Nakatsugawa. However, Iseya decided instead to commission Hiroshige to design a completely new scene. One possible reason for this is that the first version of Nakatsugawa was very costly to produce with its five areas of *bokashi* plus the vertical lines of rain that were printed with a white pigment to intensify the illusion. The second version of Nakatsugawa, on the other hand, featured only two areas of *bokashi* and was therefore simpler and more economical to print.

The evening scene depicts three samurai, clad in raincoats and straw hats, slowly making their way through the pounding rain. More travellers are shown in the background, walking along the main road through the station of Nakatsugawa. The body of water could be the Nakatsu River or its tributary, the Yotsume, which flow into the Kiso River further north. As with the previous station, Ochiai, Hiroshige placed Mount Ena in the background.

Dieser Entwurf für Nakatsugawa ist das erste von zwei Blättern zu dieser Station, die Hiroshige für den Kisokaidō-Zyklus anfertigte. Die sehr wenigen erhaltenen Abzüge dieses Drucks folgen alle demselben Farbschema, was darauf hindeutet, dass nach der Fertigstellung der ersten Auflage die Druckstöcke irreparabel beschädigt wurden. Da der Verleger Iseya Rihei angesichts der anhaltenden Beliebtheit der Blattfolge erkannte, dass es vorteilhaft war, einen vollständigen Satz mit allen Stationen anzubieten, bemühte er sich, die Lücke zu füllen. Bei einem Holzschneider auf der Grundlage der bestehenden Version von Nakatsugawa neue Druckstöcke zu bestellen, wäre eine Möglichkeit gewesen. Stattdessen beschloss Iseya jedoch, Hiroshige mit einem vollkommen neuen Entwurf zu beauftragen – möglicherweise, weil die erste Version mit ihren fünf *bokashi*-Bereichen und den senkrechten Linien, die mit einem weißen Pigment gedruckt wurden, um den Eindruck von Regen zu verstärken, sehr teuer in der Herstellung war. Die zweite Nakatsugawa-Version dagegen wies nur noch zwei *bokashi*-Bereiche auf und war daher einfacher und wirtschaftlicher zu drucken.

Die Abendszene der ersten Version zeigt drei in Regenmäntel gehüllte Samurai mit Strohhüten, die sich langsam durch den prasselnden Regen kämpfen. Im Hintergrund sind auf der Hauptstraße der Station weitere Reisende und ein Pferd zu sehen. Das Gewässer könnte den Nakatsu oder seinen Nebenfluss, den Yotsume, darstellen, die weiter nördlich in den Kiso münden. Wie bei der vorherigen Station Ochiai fügte Hiroshige den Ena als bergigen Abschluss ein.

Cette estampe est la première des deux illustrations consacrées à la station de Nakatsugawa par Hiroshige dans cette série de la Kisokaidō. Les très rares épreuves parvenues jusqu'à nous ont toutes les mêmes couleurs, ce qui indique qu'à la suite du premier tirage les matrices furent irrémédiablement endommagées. Comme la demande d'estampes de cette série ne tarissait pas, l'éditeur Iseya Rihei comprit l'avantage qu'il y avait à proposer un ensemble complet des stations et souhaita combler ce vide. Il aurait été possible de demander à un graveur de réaliser de nouvelles matrices à partir de l'estampe existante de Nakatsugawa. Toutefois, Iseya préféra passer commande d'une scène entièrement nouvelle à Hiroshige. L'une des explications a peut-être à voir avec le fait que l'impression de la première version de Nakatsugawa était très coûteuse, avec ses cinq zones de *bokashi* et les lignes verticales figurant la pluie, imprimées avec un pigment blanc pour accentuer l'illusion. En revanche, la seconde version, ne comprenant que deux zones de *bokashi*, fut plus simple et plus économique à imprimer.

Dans cette scène vespérale, trois samouraïs vêtus de manteaux imperméables et de chapeaux de paille avancent lentement dans la pluie battante. À l'arrière-plan, d'autres voyageurs traversent la station de Nakatsugawa via la route principale. L'étendue d'eau pourrait être la Nakatsu ou son affluent, la Yotsume, qui se jettent toutes deux dans la Kiso, plus au nord. Comme dans l'estampe de la station précédente, Ochiai, Hiroshige a placé le mont Ena à l'arrière-plan.

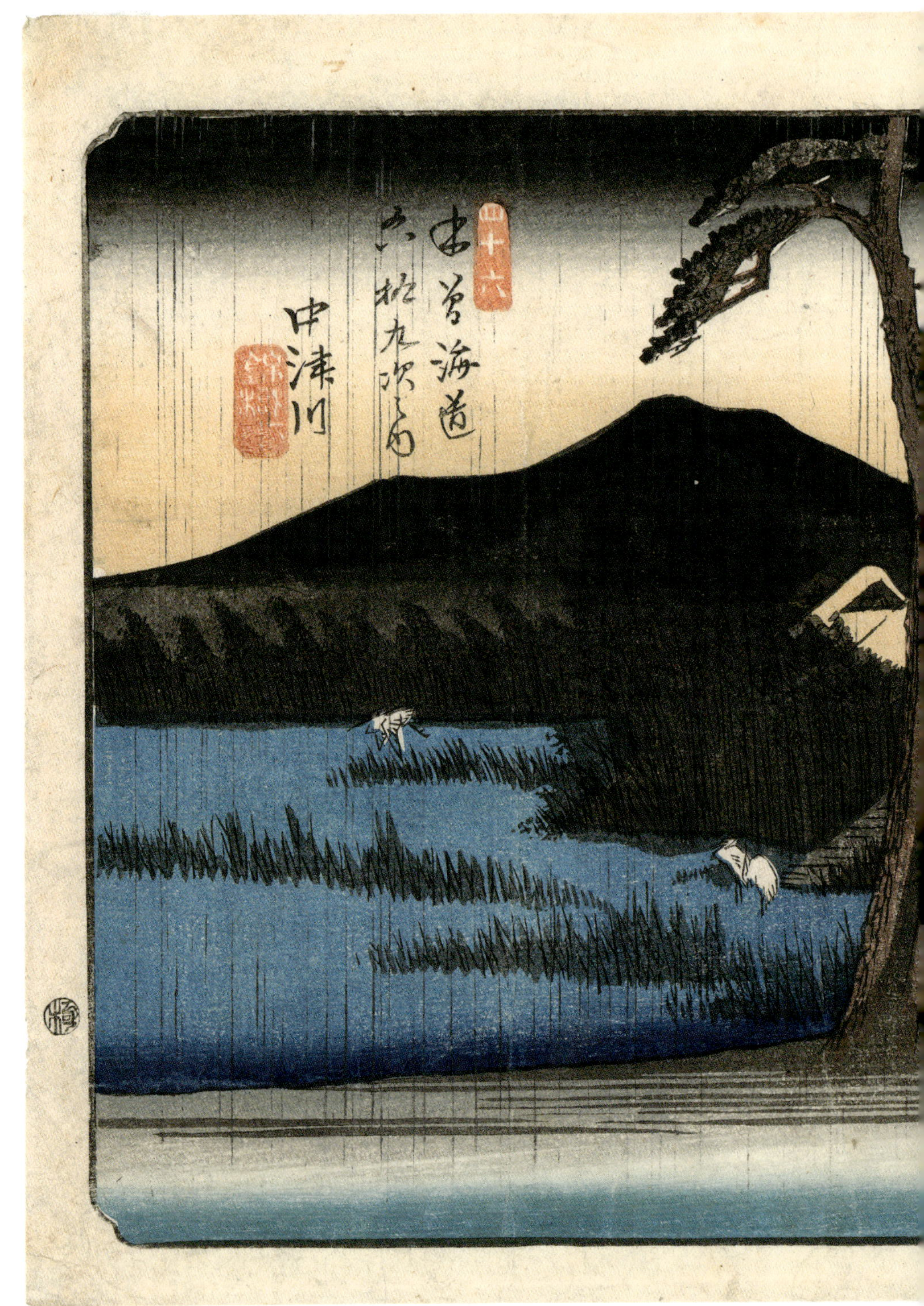

四十六
木曽海道
六拾九次之内
中津川

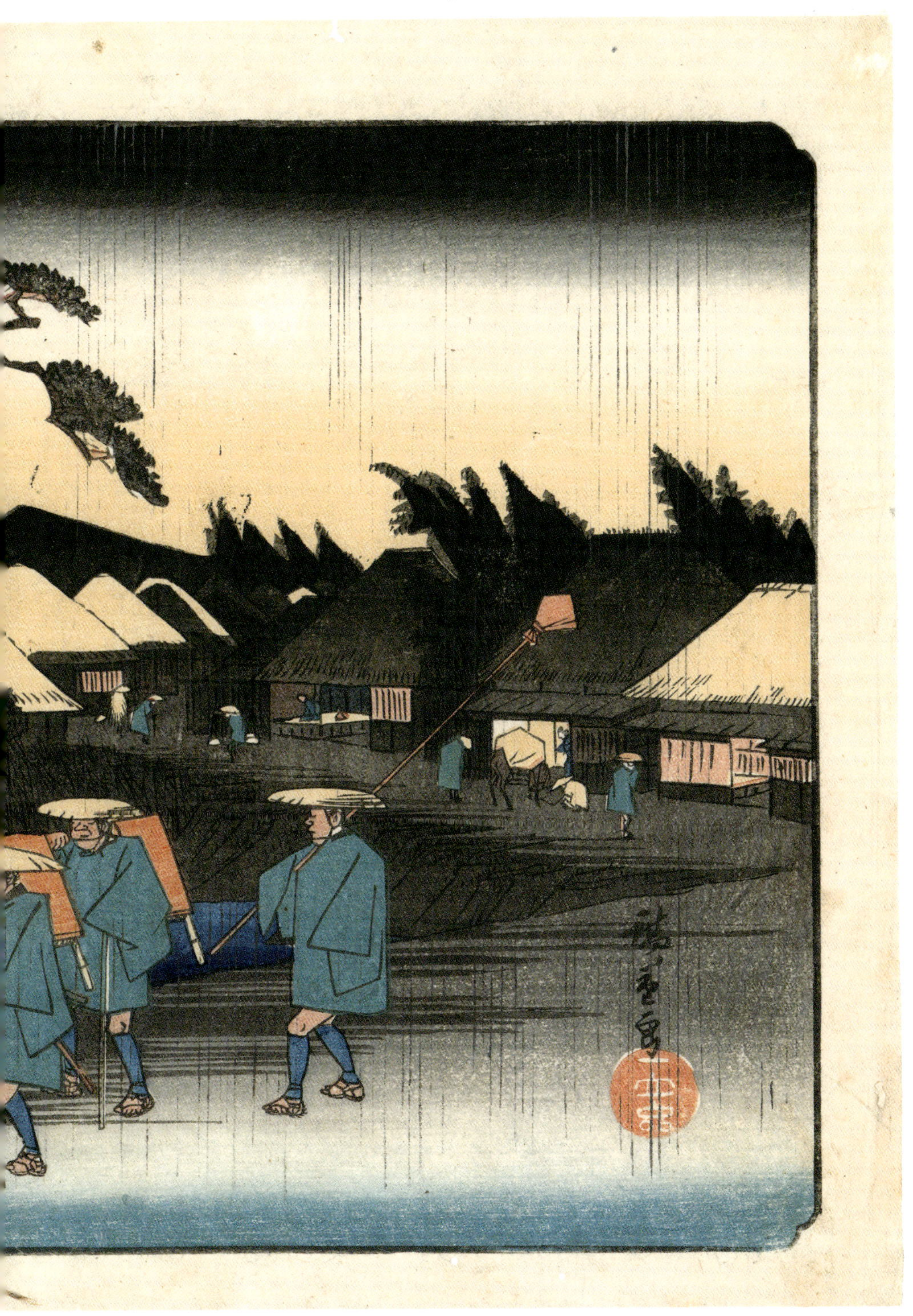

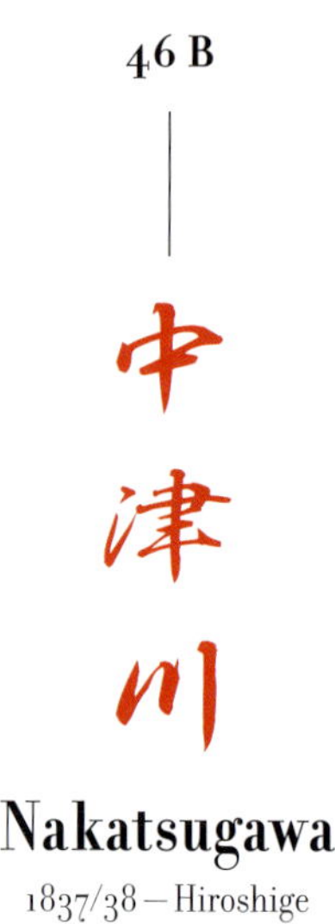

Nakatsugawa

1837/38 – Hiroshige

As the first version of the Nakatsugawa station design could not be reprinted, Hiroshige provided the publisher Iseya Rihei with a second version that presents a very different view of the locale. The first version was designed by Hiroshige before he had actually been to Nakatsugawa and is therefore a product of his imagining the landscape and human activity there. The second version was created after his own journey along the Kisokaidō and is based on a similar scene in one of his sketchbooks. It is produced with considerably fewer special printing effects than the first version, presumably to keep costs down, as the publisher's investment now included not only the first design and its production but also this second version.

In the foreground is the embankment and bridge over the 14-kilometre (8.7 miles) Nakatsu River, a tributary of the Kiso. The road then continues in a zigzag through the fields towards the station in the background, with Mount Ena behind. Hiroshige slightly deviated from his sketch by reducing the number of trees on the left of the bridge to only two and omitting the trees on the right side entirely, thus providing a more open view of the plain.

Nachdem die erste Version der Station Nakatsugawa nicht nachgedruckt werden konnte, lieferte Hiroshige dem Verleger Iseya Rihei eine zweite Version, die eine ganz andere Ansicht der Örtlichkeit präsentierte. Die erste Version hatte der Künstler entworfen, bevor er tatsächlich in Nakatsugawa gewesen war; sie war daher ein Produkt seiner Vorstellung von der dortigen Landschaft und dem menschlichen Treiben vor Ort. Die zweite Version entstand, nachdem Hiroshige den Kisokaidō bereist hatte, und basiert auf einer ähnlichen Szene in einem seiner Skizzenbücher. Sie ließ sich mit deutlich weniger Spezialtechniken drucken als die erste Version. Dahinter stand wohl das Bestreben, die Kosten zu senken – schließlich hatte der Verleger nun nicht nur in den ersten Entwurf und seine Herstellung investiert, sondern auch noch in diese zweite Version.

Im Vordergrund sind das Ufer des Nakatsu und eine Brücke über diesen 14 Kilometer langen Nebenfluss des Kiso abgebildet. Von hier aus führt die Straße im Zickzack durch die Felder zu der Station, die vor der bergigen Kulisse des Ena im Hintergrund liegt. Hiroshige wich geringfügig von seiner Skizze ab, indem er die Anzahl der Bäume links der Brücke auf zwei reduzierte und die Bäume auf der rechten Seite ganz wegließ; so gewährte er einen freieren Blick auf die Ebene.

Puisqu'il était impossible de réimprimer la première version de la station de Nakatsugawa, Hiroshige remit à l'éditeur Iseya Rihei une seconde version qui présente un point de vue très différent de la localité. L'artiste avait conçu la première version avant de se rendre sur les lieux ; le paysage et l'activité humaine de son dessin ne sont donc qu'une vue de l'esprit. Réalisée après son voyage sur la Kisokaidō, cette seconde version s'inspire d'une scène semblable figurant dans l'un de ses carnets à croquis. Elle a nécessité beaucoup moins d'effets d'impression particuliers que la première version, vraisemblablement pour éviter des dépenses trop importantes, car l'investissement de l'éditeur devait désormais couvrir à la fois la réalisation de la première estampe et celle de la seconde.

Au premier plan apparaissent le remblai et le pont qui enjambe la Nakatsu, affluent de la Kiso, dont le cours est de quatorze kilomètres. La route traverse les champs en zigzag jusqu'à la station visible à l'arrière-plan, derrière laquelle s'élève le mont Ena. Hiroshige s'est légèrement éloigné de son esquisse en réduisant à deux le nombre d'arbres situés à gauche du pont et en supprimant ceux qui se trouvaient à droite, offrant ainsi une meilleure vue de la plaine.

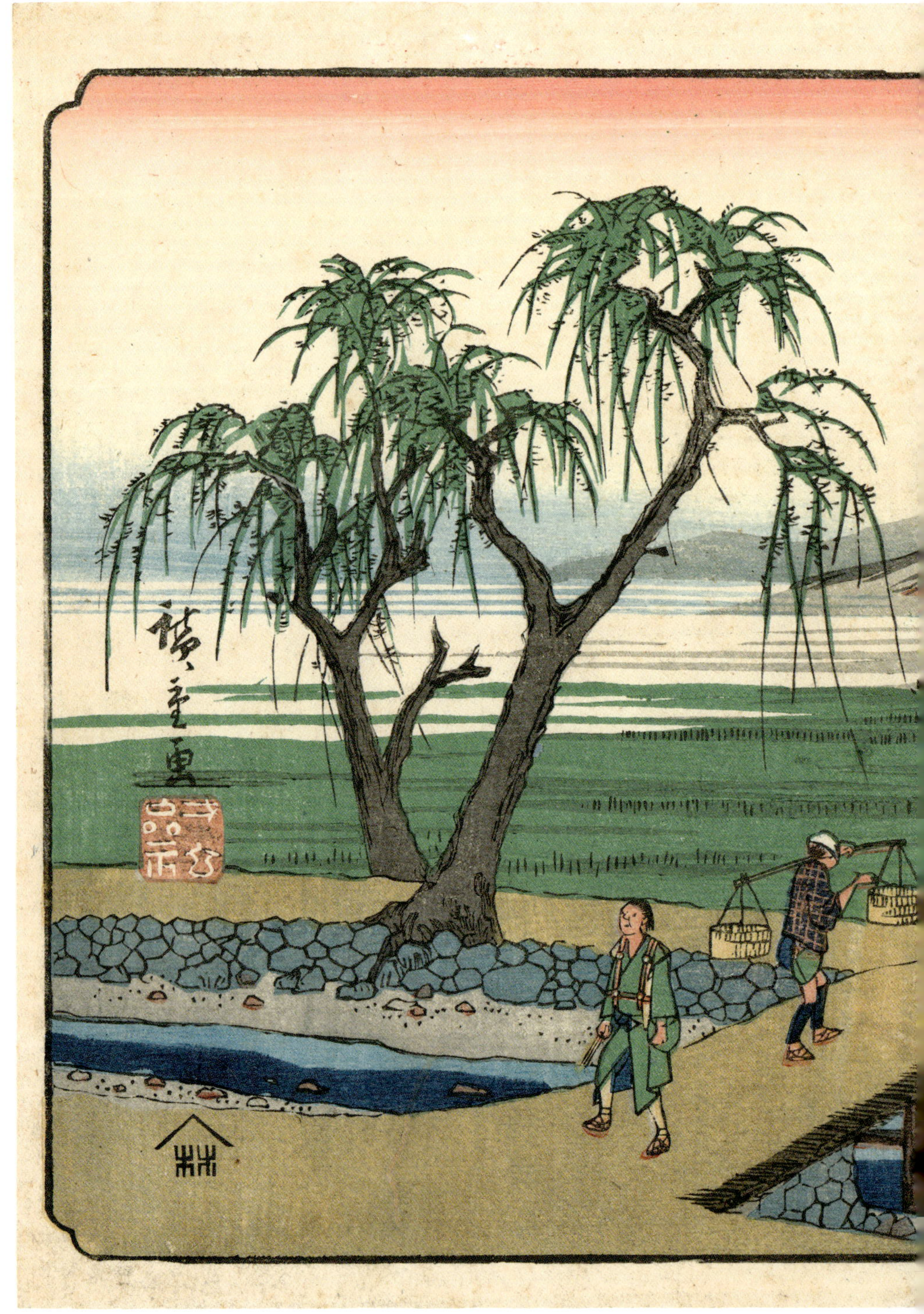

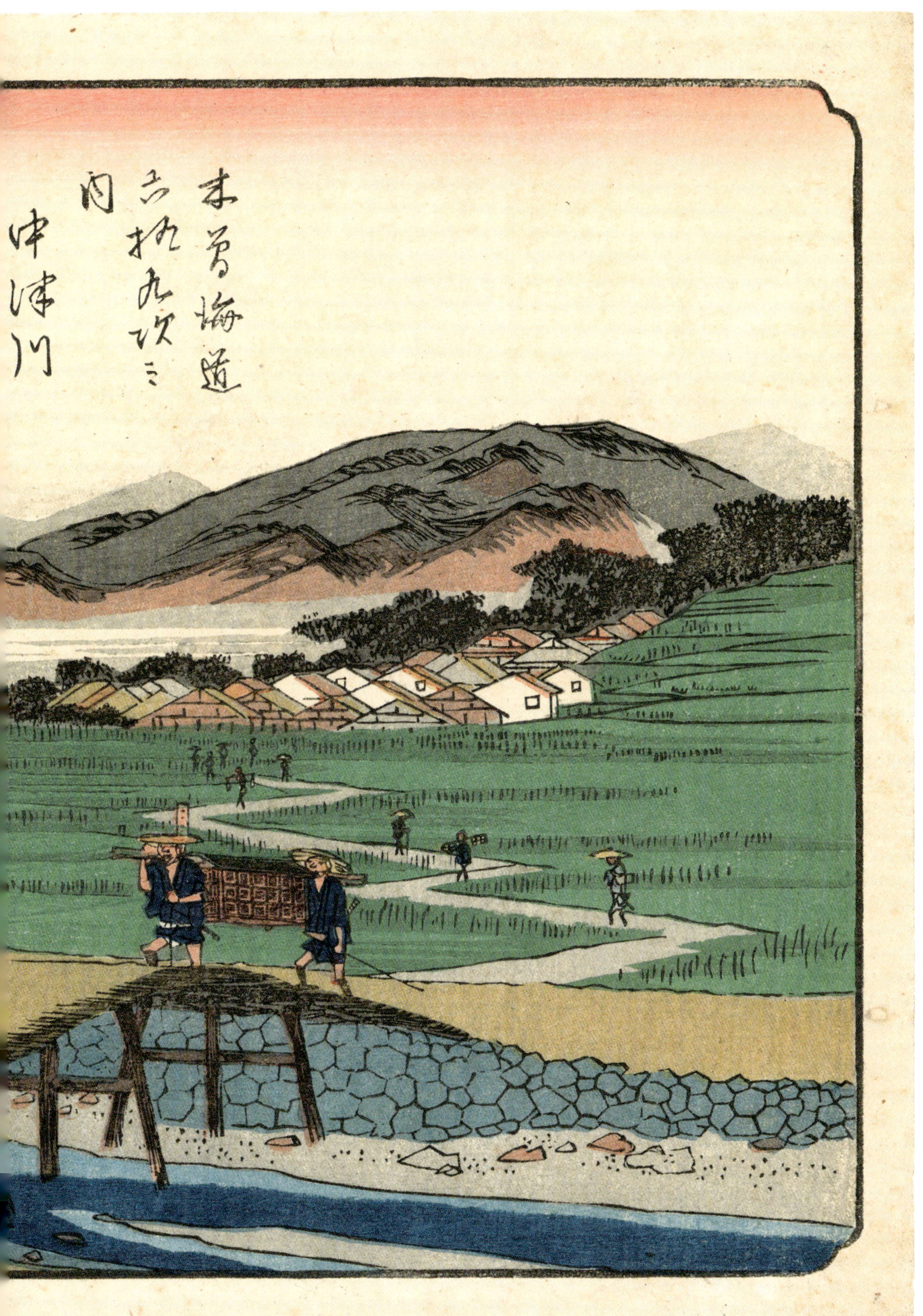

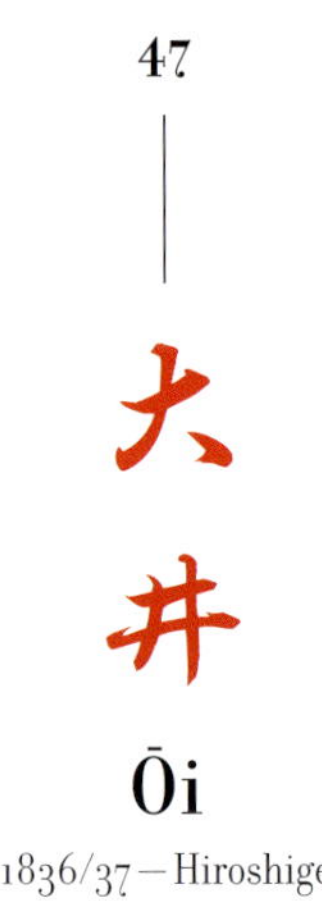

47

Ōi

1836/37 — Hiroshige

Two travellers on horseback are being led by their grooms between a pair of stately pine trees in a land-scape deeply blanketed in white. Judging by the large packages loaded on either side of their shaggy-haired steeds, the mounted figures are merchants. A mantle of snow over their heavy clothing makes the figures and horses alike seem almost part of the terrain. The horizon is ominously gloomy, and bands of dark *bokashi* closing in the composition along the upper and lower edges enhance its sombre aspect.

Ōi was not a major hub, but travellers headed for Nagoya could take the Shitakaidō or "low road" that branched off the Kisokaidō after Ōi and from there the journey was around 53 kilometres (33 miles). On account of its hilly terrain, as depicted in this design, the 14-kilometre (8.7 miles) road between Ōi and its neighbouring station Ōkute was known as the Jūsan Pass. One of the highest points along this route was named "Shichibon Matsu Zaka" or "Seven Pine Hill", which commanded a view of the mountains to the north and east. The larger of the peaks depicted on the right in Hiroshige's print is perhaps intended to represent Mount Ena. Both the pass and the hill are illustrated in *Views of Famous Sights along the Kiso Road (Kisoji meisho zue)*; it is possible that Hiroshige had this locale in mind when designing his print.

Eingerahmt von zwei stattlichen Kiefern werden zwei berittene Reisende von ihren Pferdeführern durch eine tief verschneite Landschaft geleitet. Nach den großen Paketen zu urteilen, mit denen ihre struppigen Rösser beidseitig beladen sind, handelt es sich bei den Reitern um Kaufleute. Ein Umhang aus Schnee über ihren schweren Textilien lässt Menschen und Pferde gleichermaßen mit dem Gelände verschmelzen. Der Horizont ist unheilverheißend trüb, und dunkle *bokashi*-Streifen am oberen und unteren Rand der Komposition verstärken den düsteren Anblick.

Ōi war kein bedeutender Knotenpunkt, doch Reisende mit dem Ziel Nagoya konnten hier den Shitakaidō nehmen. Die „tiefe Straße" zweigte hinter Ōi vom Kisokaidō ab; von dort aus waren es etwa 53 Kilometer bis Nagoya. Wegen ihres hügeligen Terrains, das der Druck deutlich zeigt, war die 14 Kilometer lange Strecke zwischen Ōi und der Nachbarstation Ōkute als Jūsan-Pass bekannt. Einer der höchsten Punkte an dieser Route wurde „Shichibon Matsu Zaka" genannt, „Hügel der sieben Kiefern", und bot eine Aussicht auf die nördlich und östlich gelegenen Berge. Der höhere der beiden rechten Gipfel in Hiroshiges Druck soll möglicherweise den Ena darstellen. Sowohl der Pass als auch der Hügel sind in den *Ansichten berühmter Stätten an der Kiso-Straße (Kisoji meisho zue)* abgebildet; möglicherweise hatte Hiroshige diesen Ort im Sinn, als er das Blatt entwarf.

Deux voyageurs à cheval sont guidés par leurs palefreniers entre deux pins imposants, dans un paysage recouvert d'un épais manteau blanc. D'après les gros chargements attachés de part et d'autre de chevaux à la crinière hirsute, les personnages qui les montent sont des marchands. La couche de neige qui dissimule leurs vêtements lourds transforme presque personnages et animaux en éléments du paysage. L'horizon particulièrement sombre est accentué par les bandes noires de *bokashi* qui encadrent la composition le long des bords supérieur et inférieur.

Ōi n'avait rien d'un centre important, mais les voyageurs se rendant à Nagoya pouvaient emprunter la Shitakaidō, ou « route basse », qui formait après Ōi une bifurcation avec la Kisokaidō. À partir de ce point, il fallait parcourir environ cinquante-trois kilomètres. En raison des nombreuses collines qu'elle traversait, comme on le voit dans cette estampe, la section de quatorze kilomètres séparant Ōi de la station voisine d'Ōkute était connue sous le nom de « col de Jūsan ». L'un des points culminants de cette section était appelé « Shichibon Matsu Zaka », ou « colline des sept pins », d'où l'on jouissait d'un panorama sur les montagnes situées au nord et à l'est. Le sommet le plus important qu'Hiroshige a dessiné à droite de son estampe représente peut-être le mont Ena. Le col et la colline sont illustrés l'un et l'autre dans la *Collection de vues de paysages célèbres sur la route Kiso (Kisoji meisho zue)* ; il est possible que l'artiste ait pensé à ce lieu pour réaliser son estampe.

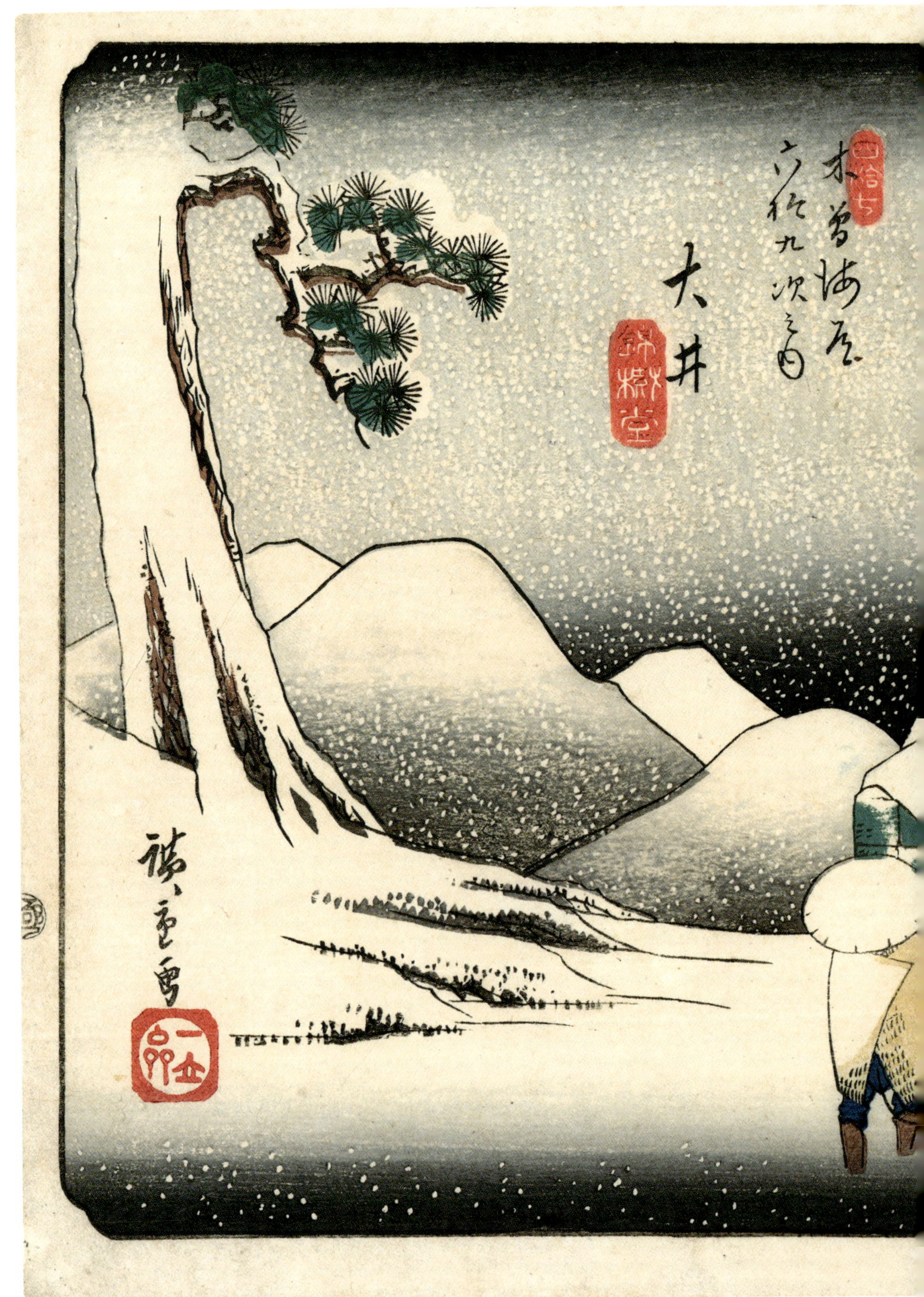

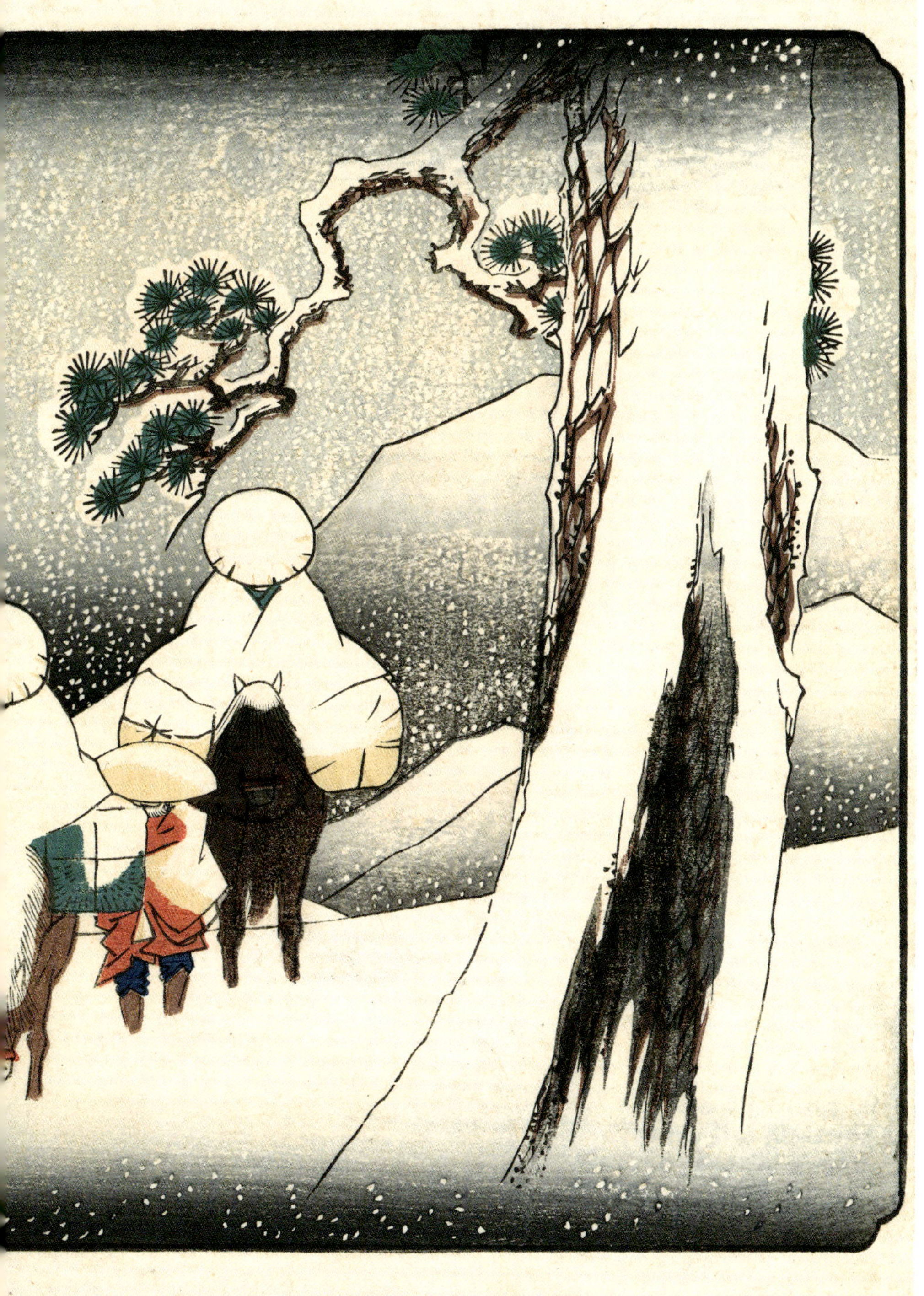

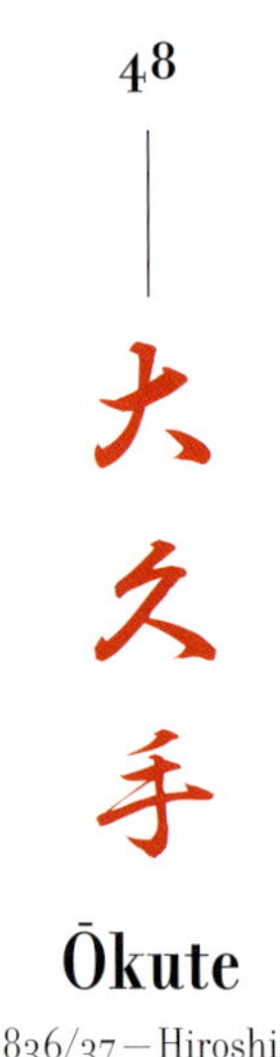

48

Ōkute

1836/37 – Hiroshige

The curious rock formations jutting out from the cliff on the left-hand side of this composition are thought to represent two famous landmarks on the western side of Ōkute called Horo-iwa and Eboshi-iwa. The first name refers to a balloon-like cape worn by samurai over their armour to protect their backs from enemy arrows, and the second to the tall hat worn by courtiers in pre-modern Japan. The writer Ōta Nanpo (1749–1823) admired the boulders on his journey north-east along the Kisokaidō in 1802 and described them in his travelogue:

"To the left of the road are two large rocks. One is called Eboshi Rock. It is about six metres in height and over nine metres wide [20/30 feet]. The other is called Horo Rock, which is of similar height but is twice as wide. The form of each resembles its name. Between the rocks, pines and grasses grow. They are truly an astonishing sight." (Ōta Nanpo, p. 743)

The strange protuberances in Hiroshige's print little resemble how the boulders appear today, nor even how they are depicted in the guidebooks *Illustrated Guide to the Kiso Road* (*Kisoji anken ezu*) or *Views of Famous Sights along the Kiso Road* (*Kisoji meisho zue*).

Ōkute, the first station in the domain of the Owari clan as travellers headed west, has the distinction of having hosted Princess Kazu, half-sister of the reigning Emperor Kōmei, on the 28th day of the 10th month of 1861, on her journey from Kyoto to Edo to marry, against her inclinations, the shogun Tokugawa Iemochi. As travellers continued towards the next station, Hosokute, the grasslands shown here gave way to a succession of hills called the Biwa Pass. Mount Ontake in the north-east, as well as Mount Haku to the north, Mount Ibuki to the west and Ise Bay to the south, could be glimpsed at various points along the path.

Die merkwürdigen Felsformationen an der Steilwand links im Bild sollen wohl zwei berühmte Landmarken westlich von Ōkute mit Namen Horo-iwa und Eboshi-iwa darstellen. Die erste Bezeichnung bezieht sich auf einen ballonähnlichen Umhang, den Samurai über der Rüstung tragen, um ihren Rücken vor feindlichen Pfeilen zu schützen, die zweite auf den hohen Hut, der für Höflinge im vormodernen Japan typisch war. Der Schriftsteller Ōta Nanpo (1749–1823) bewunderte die Felsbrocken am Kisokaidō auf seiner 1802 unternommenen Reise nach Nordosten und beschrieb sie in seinem Reisebericht:

„Links der Straße befinden sich zwei große Felsen. Einer wird Eboshi-Felsen genannt. Er ist etwa sechs Meter hoch und über neun Meter breit. Der andere heißt Horo-Felsen, ist genauso hoch, aber doppelt so breit. Ihre Formen entsprechen ihren Namen. Zwischen den Felsen wachsen Kiefern und Gräser. Sie bieten einen wahrhaft erstaunlichen Anblick." (Ōta Nanpo, S. 743)

Die seltsamen Vorsprünge in Hiroshiges Druck haben weder große Ähnlichkeit mit dem heutigen Aussehen der Felsblöcke noch mit ihren Abbildungen in den Reiseführern *Illustrierter Wegweiser für die Kiso-Straße (Kisoji anken ezu)* und *Ansichten berühmter Stätten an der Kiso-Straße (Kisoji meisho zue)*.

Ōkute, für westwärts Reisende die erste Station im Lehen des Owari-Clans, zeichnete sich dadurch aus, dass am 28. Tag des 10. Monats im Jahr 1861 Prinzessin Kazu, eine Halbschwester des damaligen Kaisers Kōmei, dort übernachtete. Sie befand sich auf ihrer Reise von Kyoto nach Edo, wo sie gegen ihren Willen den Shogun Tokugawa Iemochi heiraten sollte. Auf dem Weg zur nächsten Station, Hosokute, wich das hier gezeigte Grasland einer Abfolge von Hügeln namens Biwa-Pass. An verschiedenen Stellen entlang des Weges waren im Nordosten der Ontake, im Norden der Haku, im Westen der Ibuki und im Süden die Ise-Bucht zu sehen.

Les curieuses formations rocheuses faisant saillie avec la falaise à la gauche de cette composition représenteraient deux sites célèbres situés à l'ouest d'Ōkute, nommés Horo-iwa et Eboshi-iwa. La première appellation fait référence à la cape en forme de ballon portée par les samouraïs par-dessus leur armure afin de se protéger le dos des flèches de l'ennemi, la seconde au chapeau haut-de-forme dont étaient coiffés les messagers japonais avant l'ère moderne. L'écrivain Ōta Nanpo (1749–1823) avait admiré ces rochers en empruntant la Kisokaidō lors de son itinéraire vers le nord-est en 1802 et les a décrits dans son journal de voyage :

« À gauche de la route se trouvent deux gros rochers. L'un s'appelle le rocher Eboshi. Il mesure environ six mètres de haut et plus de neuf mètres de large. L'autre, le rocher Horo, est d'une hauteur identique, mais deux fois plus large. Par sa forme, chacun ressemble à son nom. Entre les rochers poussent des pins et de l'herbe. C'est un spectacle proprement étonnant. » (Ōta Nanpo, p. 743)

Les étranges protubérances de l'estampe d'Hiroshige ne ressemblent guère à l'aspect qu'ont aujourd'hui les rochers, ni même à la manière dont ils sont illustrés dans le *Guide illustré de la route Kiso (Kisoji anken ezu)* ou la *Collection de vues de paysages célèbres sur la route Kiso (Kisoji meisho zue)*.

Première station du domaine du clan des Owari rencontrée par les voyageurs allant vers l'ouest, Ōkute se distingue pour avoir accueilli la princesse Kazu demi-sœur de l'empereur régnant Kōmei, le 28e jour du 10e mois de 1861, alors qu'elle se rendait de Kyoto à Edo pour épouser, contre son gré, le shogun Tokugawa Iemochi. À mesure qu'ils progressaient vers la station suivante d'Hosokute, les voyageurs traversaient les plaines herbeuses visibles ici, avant de parvenir à une enfilade de collines, appelée « col de Biwa ». À différents stades du chemin, ils pouvaient apercevoir le mont Ontake au nord-est, le mont Haku au nord, le mont Ibuki à l'ouest et la baie d'Ise au sud.

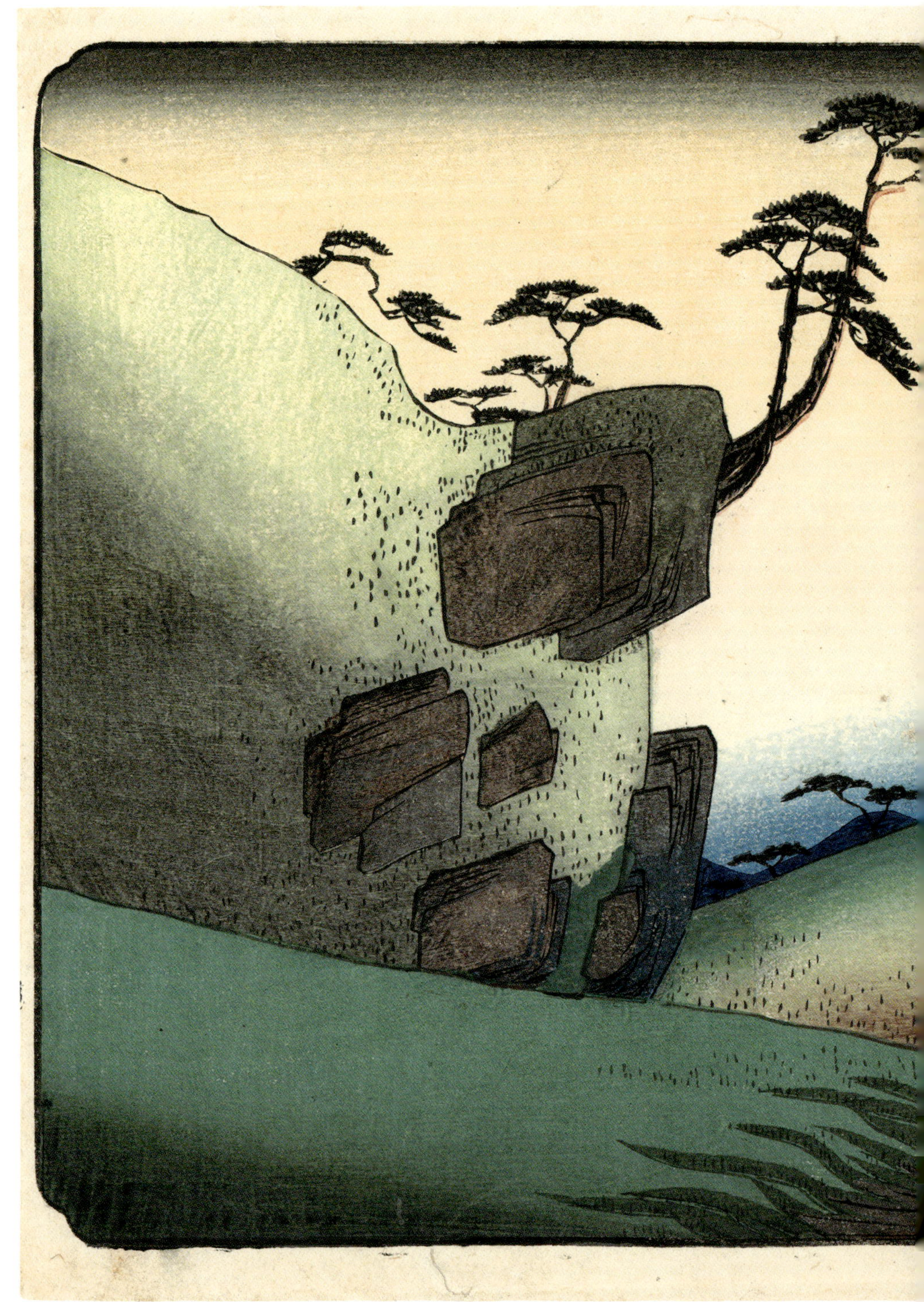

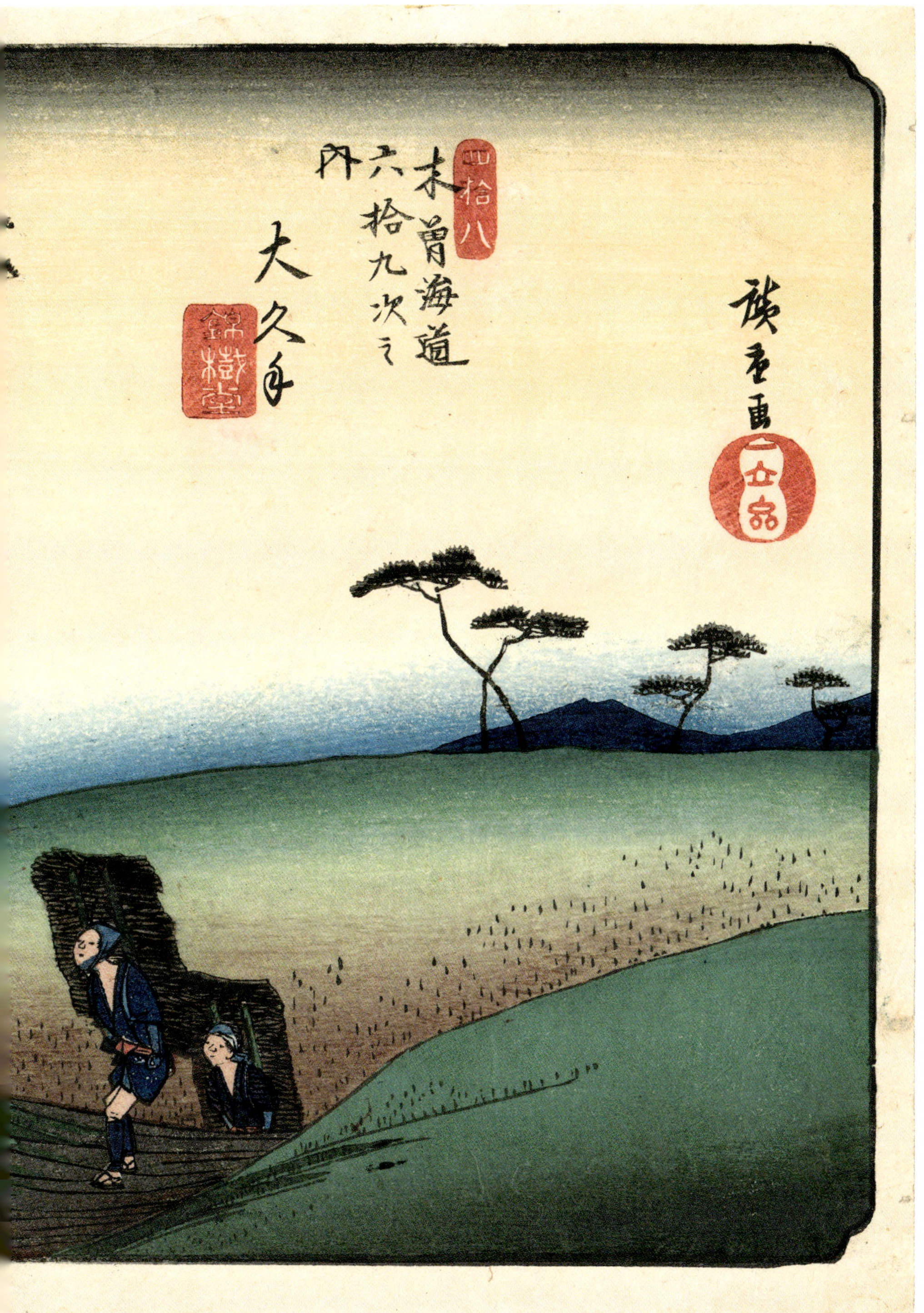

四拾八
木曽海道
六拾九次之
内
大久手
廣重画

49

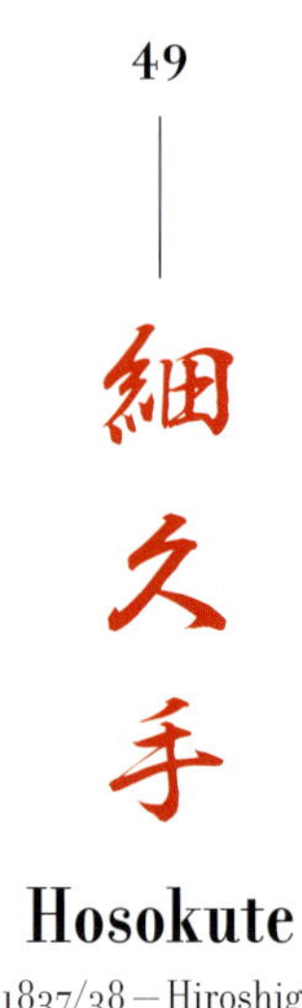

Hosokute

1837/38 – Hiroshige

Upon examining the pictures in the guidebook *Illustrated Guide to the Kiso Road* (*Kisoji anken ezu*) it would seem that in Hiroshige's design for this station, based loosely on an untitled sketch made during his travels along the Kisokaidō, the view may represent the western outskirts of Hosokute as the road descends towards the settlements between it and the neighbouring station of Mitake. The guidebook also maps out, albeit in an abbreviated and schematic manner, the slope of the road, the clusters of houses and the pine trees planted in clumps on either side of the road, much like those presented here.

Hiroshige embellished this sketch with a cast of characters. Approaching the crest of the hill is a traveller, while a samurai carrying a halberd, with a bamboo flask dangling from its end, is heading in the opposite direction. To the right of the path are two peasants with sickles, for harvesting mulberry leaves to feed the silkworms. Heading off to the right is a man wearing a *shōiko* or carrying-frame on his back, for use in transporting firewood or fodder. Hiroshige replaced the solitary pine in his original study with four steeply leaning trees, and clarified the forms and position of the mountains in the distance. The combination of the mountains diminishing on the horizon and the large trees in the foreground creates a compelling sense of depth.

Travellers visiting Hosokute left few remarks of note to distinguish this locale; however, in their 1884 guidebook, *A Handbook for Travellers in Central & Northern Japan*, authors Sir Ernest Mason Satow and Lieutenant A. G. S. Hawes urged their readers to sample the local fare: "At Hosokute (Inn, Matsu-ya) the traveller should be careful to ask for a *tsugumi* (a sort of thrush) preserved in yeast (*kōjidsuke* [sic]), which when slightly roasted is delicious, and forms a welcome addition to the ordinary fare in a region where fresh fish is scarce." (Satow/Hawes 1884, pp. 245–246)

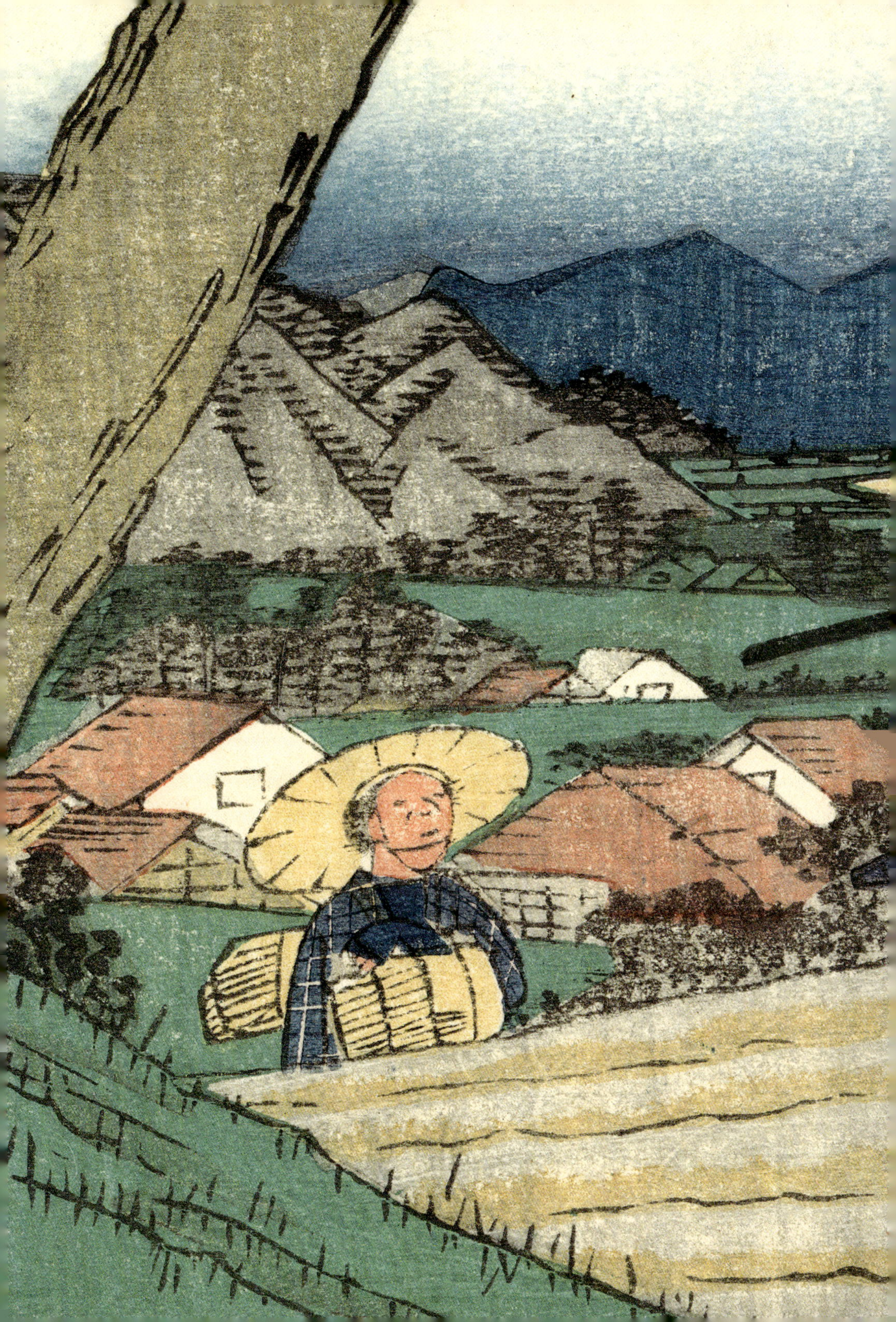

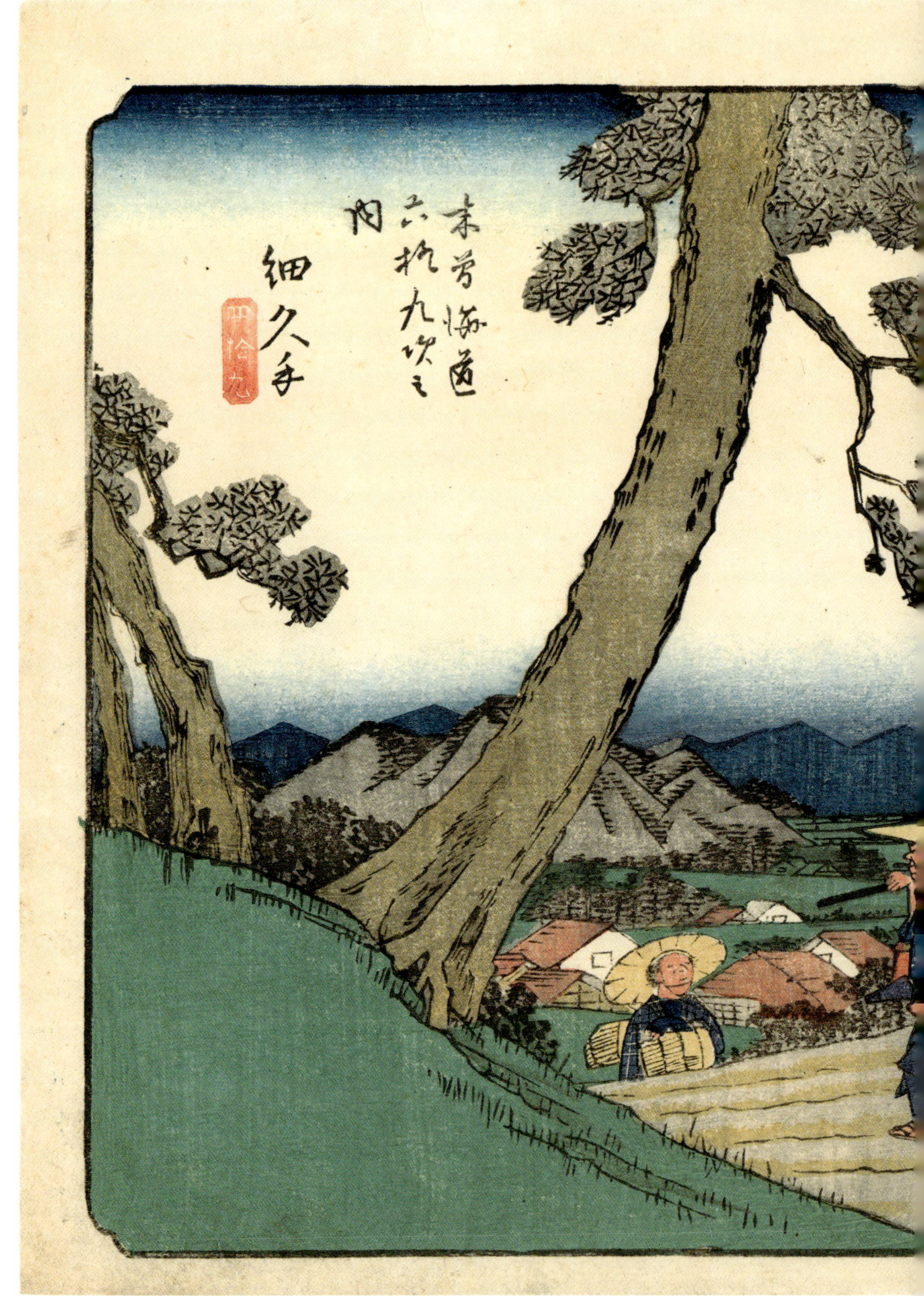
木曽海道
六拾九次之
内
細久手

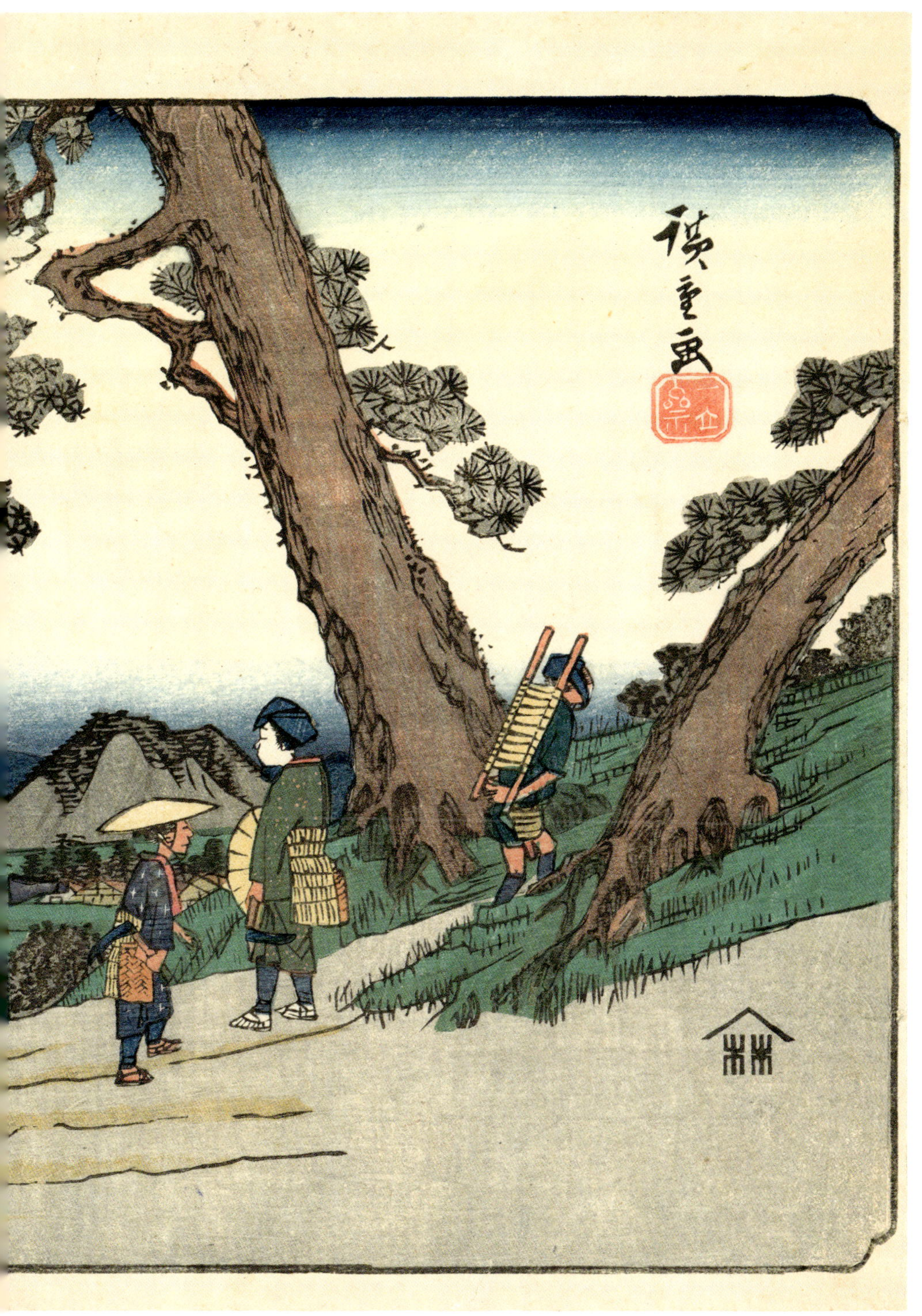

Hiroshiges Entwurf für diese Station ist die freie Umsetzung einer unbetitelten Skizze, die er während seiner Kisokaidō-Reise anfertigte. Betrachtet man den bebilderten Reiseführer *Illustrierter Wegweiser für die Kiso-Straße (Kisoji anken ezu)*, so hat es den Anschein, als fiele in dem Druck der Blick auf den westlichen Ortsrand von Hosokute, da zwischen dieser Station und dem benachbarten Mitake die Straße zur Siedlung hin abfällt. Zudem verzeichnet der Reiseführer auf einer Karte, wenn auch nur verkürzt und schematisch, das Gefälle der Straße, die Häusertrauben und die in Gruppen gepflanzten Kiefern auf beiden Seiten des Weges, ganz wie hier gezeigt.

Hiroshige garnierte das Blatt mit einer Reihe von Figuren. Hinter dem Scheitelpunkt des Hügels nähert sich ein Reisender, während ein Samurai mit einer Hellebarde, an deren Spitze eine Bambusflasche baumelt, in entgegengesetzter Richtung unterwegs ist. Am rechten Straßenrand gehen zwei Bauern mit Sicheln für die Ernte der Maulbeerblätter, mit denen die Seidenraupen gefüttert werden. Nach rechts entfernt sich ein Bauer mit einer *shōiko* genannten Rückentrage, die zum Transport von Feuerholz oder Viehfutter diente. Hiroshige ersetzte die einzelne Kiefer in seiner Originalstudie durch vier stark geneigte Bäume und konkretisierte die Lage und Form der Gebirgszüge in der Ferne. Die Kombination der zum Horizont hin kleiner werdenden Berge mit den großen Bäumen im Vordergrund erzeugt eine faszinierende Tiefe.

Reisende, die Hosokute besuchten, hinterließen nur wenige Ausführungen, die diesen Ort besonders hervorgehoben hätten. In ihrem Reiseführer *A Handbook for Travellers in Central & Northern Japan* aus dem Jahr 1884 jedoch drängten die Autoren Sir Ernest Mason Satow und Leutnant A. G. S. Hawes ihre Leser, eine örtliche Delikatesse zu probieren:

„In Hosokute (Gasthaus Matsu-ya) sollte der Reisende unbedingt darauf bedacht sein, nach einer in Hefe (*kōjidsuke*[sic]) eingelegten *tsugumi* (einer Drosselart) zu fragen, die leicht geröstet köstlich schmeckt und in einer Region, in der frischer Fisch selten ist, eine willkommene Ergänzung zur Alltagskost darstellt." (Satow/Hawes 1884, S. 245–246)

L'examen du guide de voyage illustré *Guide illustré de la route Kiso* (*Kisoji anken ezu*) semble révéler que, dans l'estampe réalisée par Hiroshige pour cette station, vaguement inspirée d'une esquisse sans titre dessinée lors de ses voyages sur la Kisokaidō, cette vue pourrait représenter les abords occidentaux d'Hosokute, à l'endroit où la route descend vers les habitations, entre ce village et la station voisine de Mitake. Ce guide rend aussi compte, bien que de manière succincte et schématique, de la pente de la route, des groupes de maisons et des pins plantés en bosquets de part et d'autre de la route, sous une forme très proche de celle qui est présentée ici.

Hiroshige a enrichi son esquisse de plusieurs personnages. Un voyageur s'approche de la crête de la colline, tandis qu'un samouraï portant une hallebarde, à laquelle est suspendue une bouteille en bambou, se déplace dans la direction opposée. Sur la partie droite du chemin se trouvent deux paysans munis de faucilles qui vont récolter des feuilles de mûrier dont ils nourriront les vers à soie. À l'extrême droite, un homme porte sur le dos un *shōiko*, cadre de portage destiné au transport de fagots ou de fourrage. Hiroshige a remplacé le pin solitaire de son étude initiale par quatre pins fortement inclinés et clarifié les formes et la position des montagnes visibles au loin. L'association des montagnes diminuant successivement à l'horizon et des grands arbres du premier plan crée une forte impression de profondeur.

Les voyageurs ayant visité Hosokute ont laissé peu de témoignages marquants à propos de cette localité ; toutefois, dans *A Handbook for Travellers in Central & Northern Japan* [Manuel de voyage pour le Japon du centre et du nord], le guide qu'ils cosignèrent en 1884, Sir Ernest Mason Satow et le lieutenant A. G. S. Hawes incitèrent leurs lecteurs, à goûter un mets local :

« À Hosokute (Auberge, Matsu-ya), le voyageur veillera à demander un *tsugumi* (sorte de grive) conservé dans la levure (*kōjidsuke* [*sic*]) qui, légèrement rôti, est délicieux et améliore avantageusement l'ordinaire dans une région où le poisson frais est rare. » (Satow/Hawes 1884, pp. 245–246)

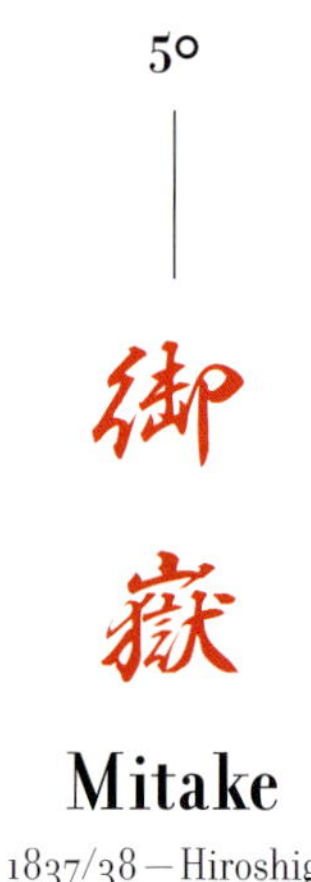

50

Mitake

1837/38 – Hiroshige

Hiroshige's sketchbooks from his journey along the Kisokaidō include a number of studies of the appearance and habits of the local people he encountered on the way. Among these is a sketch of a woman carrying a pair of buckets in a pose very similar to the woman to the right of this composition, the existence of which suggests that Hiroshige created this design after undertaking the journey.

Mitake station is situated on a plain, but Hiroshige has conceived a hillside inn as his setting. The lettering on the paper screen at the front announces the establishment to be a *kichin'yado* or "firewood-fee inn", that is to say, a very low-end lodging-house where guests had to supply and prepare their own meals in the facilities provided. Inside, an assortment of travellers, including a female pilgrim, are warming themselves around the hearth. By the entrance hangs a votive lantern offered to the sacred Mount Ontake, seen in the distance to the north-east.

Outside, a second pilgrim holding a weather-beaten conical hat in front of him is carrying a woven mat and a deep ladle for collecting alms. His gaze is directed at a man washing rice in a wooden tub beside the irrigation channel. Just beyond the corner of the building, a rooster with its magnificent tail feathers erect is hovering behind a hen, whose attention is absorbed elsewhere.

Mitake's principal attraction was the temple of Gankōji, which was reputedly established by the priest Saichō (767–822) during a missionary tour of Japan following his return from China. The building was repeatedly burnt down and rebuilt, and the current structure of the main hall dates from 1582. The temple is dedicated to the Medicine Buddha, Yakushi Nyōrai.

Hiroshiges Skizzenbücher von seiner Reise auf dem Kisokaidō enthalten eine Reihe von Studien zum äußeren Erscheinungsbild und zu den Gewohnheiten der Einheimischen, denen er unterwegs begegnete.

Darunter ist auch die Skizze einer zwei Eimer tragenden Frau in einer Haltung, die dem Gestus der Frauenfigur am rechten Rand dieser Komposition sehr ähnlich ist. Die Existenz einer solchen Skizze deutet darauf hin, dass Hiroshige das Blatt entwarf, nachdem er die Reise unternommen hatte.

Obwohl die Station Mitake in einer Ebene liegt, wählte Hiroshige eine Herberge in Hanglage als Kulisse. Der Schriftzug auf der Papierwand an der Fassade kennzeichnet das Etablissement als *kichin'yado* oder „Holzgebühr-Herberge", also als eine sehr billige Unterkunft, in der Gäste ihr eigenes Essen mitbringen und in den vorgehaltenen Räumlichkeiten zubereiten mussten. Im Inneren wärmen sich unterschiedlichste Reisende, darunter eine Pilgerin, rund um den Herd auf. Eine Votivlaterne neben dem Eingang ist dem heiligen Berg Ontake gewidmet, der weit entfernt im Nordosten zu erkennen ist.

Vor dem Haus steht ein zweiter Pilger mit einer Strohmatte und einem tiefen Schöpflöffel zum Almosensammeln im Gepäck und einem wettergegerbten Kegelhut in der Hand. Sein Blick geht zu einem Mann, der in einem Holzbottich am Bewässerungskanal Reis wäscht. Direkt hinter der Hausecke versucht ein Hahn mit der Pracht seiner aufgestellten Schwanzfedern eine Henne zu beeindrucken, deren Aufmerksamkeit jedoch anderweitig beansprucht wird.

Mitakes Hauptattraktion war der Gankōji-Tempel, den der Priester Saichō (767–822) während einer Missionsreise durch Japan gegründet haben soll, nachdem er aus China zurückgekehrt war. Das Gebäude brannte wiederholt nieder und wurde stets neu aufgebaut; die heutige Konstruktion der Haupthalle geht auf das Jahr 1582 zurück. Der Tempel ist dem Medizin-Buddha Yakushi Nyōrai geweiht.

Dans les carnets de croquis réalisés par Hiroshige au cours de son voyage sur la Kisokaidō, on trouve plusieurs études rendant compte de l'aspect et des coutumes des habitants qu'il avait rencontrés en chemin. L'un de ces croquis montre une femme portant deux seaux, dans une pose très semblable à celle de la femme visible à droite dans cette composition ; l'existence de ce croquis semble attester qu'Hiroshige a réalisé cette estampe au retour de ce voyage.

La station de Mitake se trouve dans une plaine, mais l'artiste lui a donné pour cadre une auberge au sommet d'une colline. D'après l'inscription figurant sur la cloison en papier, l'établissement est un *kichin'yado*, ou « auberge où l'on paie le bois », autrement dit une pension très modeste où les clients doivent apporter et préparer leurs repas avec l'équipement fourni. À l'intérieur, divers voyageurs, dont une pèlerine, se réchauffent autour du foyer. À l'entrée, une lanterne votive est suspendue en guise d'offrande au mont Ontake, montagne sacrée visible au loin, vers le nord-est.

À l'extérieur, un autre pèlerin, tenant devant lui un chapeau conique abîmé par les intempéries, porte une natte tissée et une sorte de louche profonde lui servant à demander l'aumône. Il observe un homme en train de rincer du riz dans un baquet en bois, au bord du canal d'irrigation. Tout près de l'angle du bâtiment, un coq, dont les magnifiques plumes de la queue sont dressées, domine une poule qui ne lui prête pas attention.

L'attraction principale de Mitake était le temple de Gankōji, qui aurait été fondé par le prêtre Saichō (767–822) au cours d'une mission dans tout le Japon, après son retour de Chine. L'édifice fut régulièrement détruit par des incendies, puis reconstruit ; la structure actuelle de la salle principale date de 1582. Ce temple est consacré au bouddha médecin, Yakushi Nyōrai.

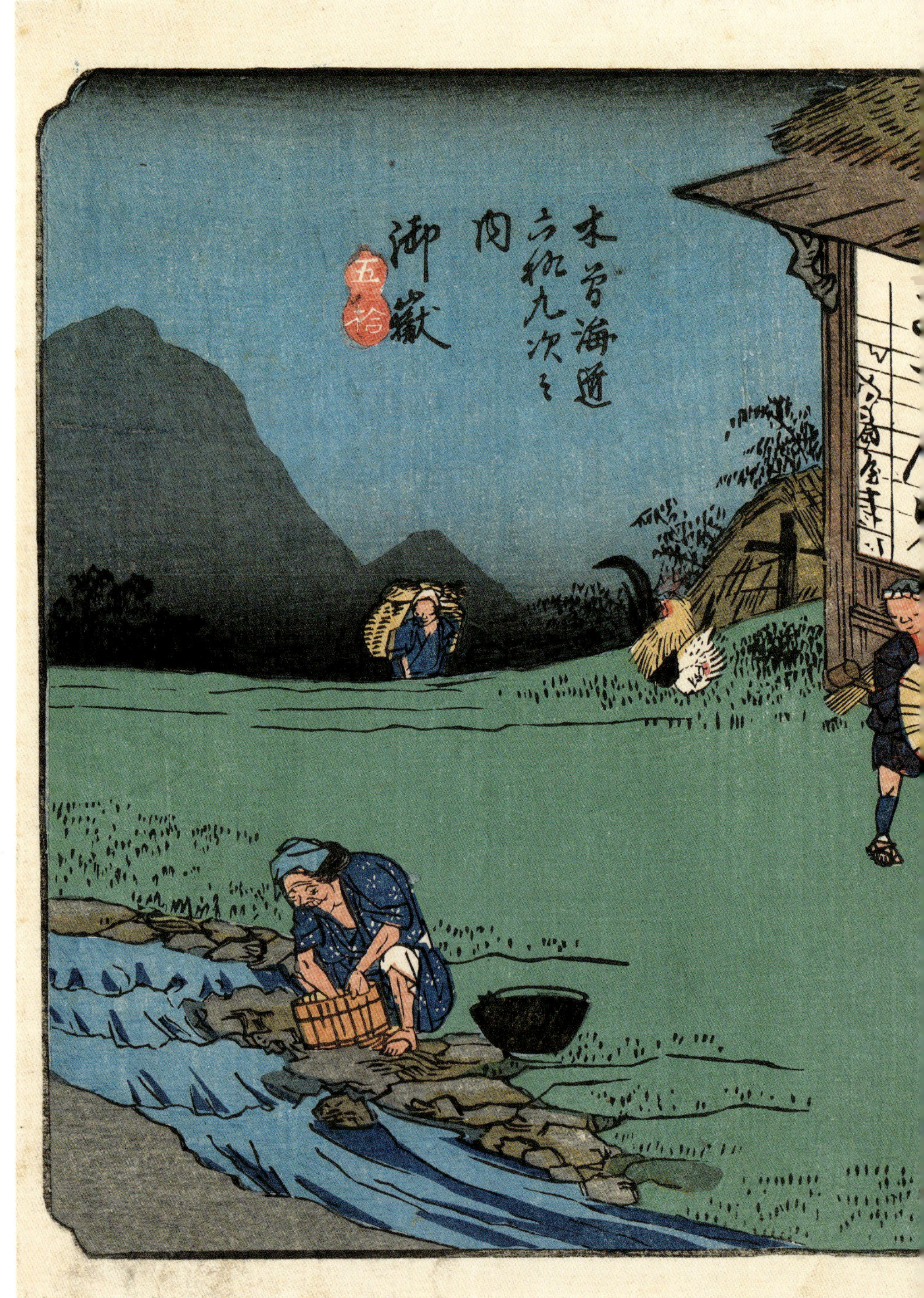
御嶽
五拾
木曽海道
六拾九次之
内

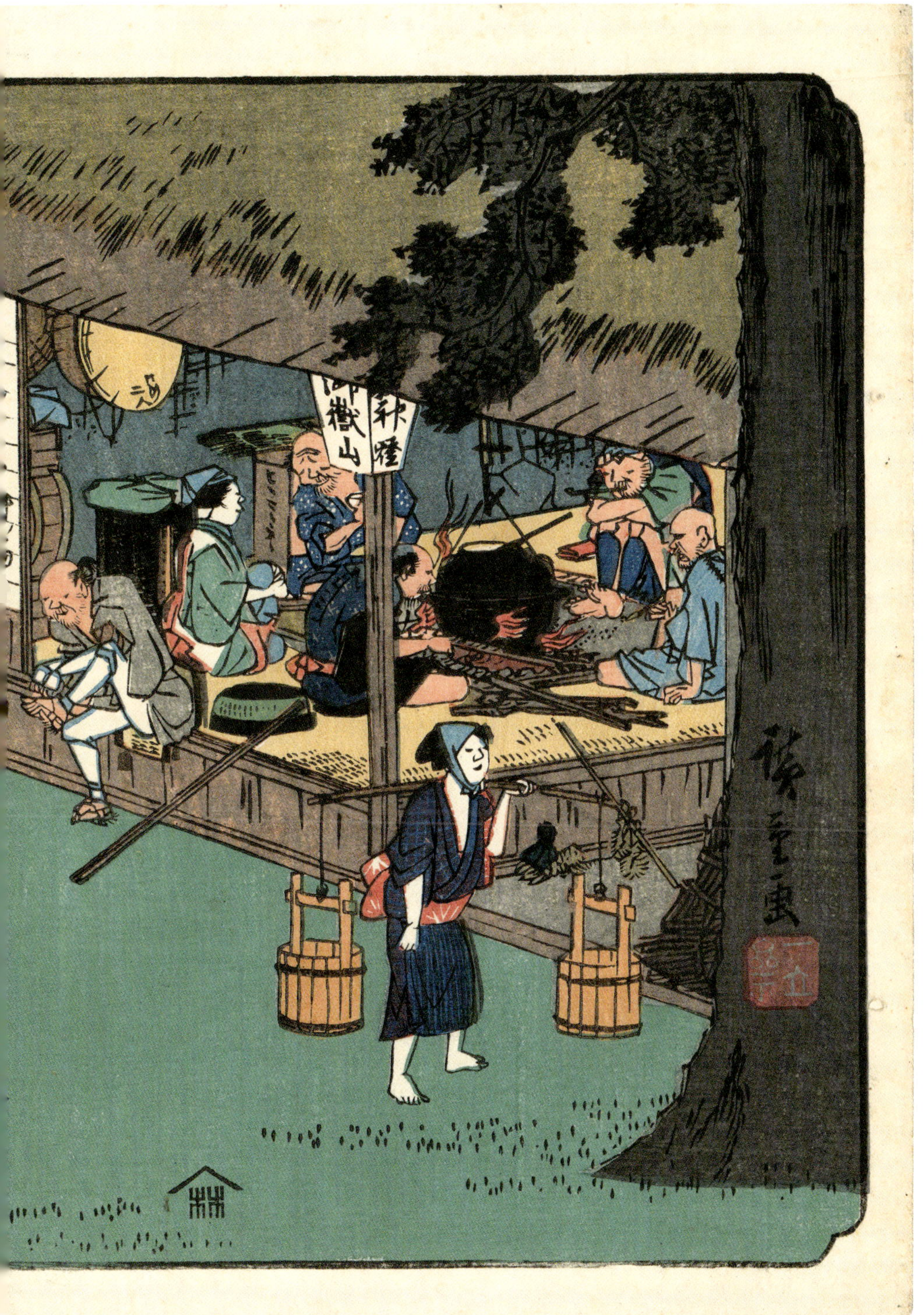

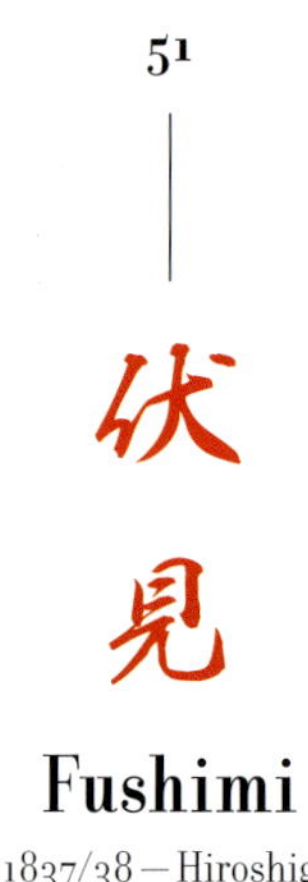

Fushimi

1837/38 — Hiroshige

The shade of a magnificent cedar provides an inviting place on a warm summer's day for a couple, on the right, to break for lunch, and a solo pilgrim, on the left, to enjoy an afternoon snooze, using his hat for a pillow. The tree was perhaps inspired by a famous local landmark, the Fushimi Ōsugi, also known as the Nakaedo Ōsugi, which Hiroshige may have known about. This great cedar grew along the Inuyama Road (Inuyama Kaidō), which branched off on the left of the Kisokaidō to the west of Fushimi station and towards Nagoya.

In the foreground of Hiroshige's design are two samurai with their umbrellas, essential equipage for the pageantry that was a *daimyō* procession. While one of them stoops to adjust his sandal, the other avails himself of the moment to take a puff on his pipe. The three women approaching from behind are blind musicians, and the two on the right are carrying their *shamisens*. Blind female musicians, often organised into professional guilds, were a familiar sight in certain parts during the Edo period, including Mino Province where Fushimi was located. Approaching from the left is a prosperous-looking village doctor wearing a sword at his waist and carrying a paper parasol in one hand and a fan in the other. His medical kit is tied in a wrapping cloth, which is knotted around his shoulders.

An einem heißen Sommertag lädt der Schatten einer mächtigen Zeder ein junges Paar (rechts) zur Mittagspause und einen einzelnen Pilger, der seinen Hut als Kissen benutzt (links), zu einem erholsamen Schläfchen ein. Zur Darstellung des Baumes könnte Hiroshige eine berühmte örtliche Landmarke namens Fushimi Ōsugi, auch bekannt als Nakaedo Ōsugi, inspiriert haben, von der er womöglich wusste. Die gigantische Zeder stand am Inuyama Kaidō, an der Inuyama-Straße, die westlich der Station Fushimi vom Kisokaidō links nach Nagoya abzweigte.

Die Schirme der beiden Samurai im Vordergrund gehörten zur unerlässlichen Ausrüstung im Gepränge einer *daimyō*-Prozession. Während einer der Männer stehen bleibt, um seine Sandale zu richten, nutzt der andere den Moment, um einen Zug aus seiner Pfeife zu rauchen. Die drei Frauen, die sich hinter ihm nähern, sind blinde Musikerinnen, von denen die beiden rechten jeweils eine *shamisen* bei sich tragen. Die blinden Frauen waren oft in Berufsgilden organisiert und gehörten während der Edo-Zeit in bestimmten Regionen zum Straßenbild, so auch in der Provinz Mino, in der Fushimi lag. Von links nähert sich ein wohlhabend wirkender Dorfarzt mit einem Schwert an der Hüfte, einem Papiersonnenschirm in der einen und einem Fächer in der anderen Hand. Seinen Arztkoffer hat er in ein Tuch gewickelt, das um seine Schultern geknotet ist.

Par une chaude journée d'été, l'ombre d'un magnifique cèdre est propice au déjeuner d'un couple, à droite, et à la sieste d'un pèlerin solitaire qui, à gauche, se sert de son chapeau comme d'un oreiller. Pour dessiner cet arbre, Hiroshige a peut-être été inspiré par un site remarquable, le Fushimi Ōsugi, aussi appelé Nakaedo Ōsugi, dont l'artiste a pu avoir connaissance. Ce grand cèdre s'élevait le long de la route Inuyama (Inuyama Kaidō) qui, à l'ouest de la station de Fushimi, bifurquait de la Kisokaidō vers la gauche en direction de Nagoya.

Au premier plan de cette estampe se trouvent deux samouraïs munis d'ombrelles, matériel essentiel à l'apparat d'une procession de *daïmio*. Tandis que l'un se penche pour ajuster sa sandale, l'autre profite de l'occasion pour tirer quelques bouffées de sa pipe. Les trois femmes qui arrivent derrière eux sont des musiciennes aveugles, les deux de droite portant leur *shamisen*. Souvent organisées en guildes professionnelles, les musiciennes aveugles étaient courantes dans certaines régions au cours de l'ère Edo, notamment dans la province de Mino où se trouvait Fushimi. À gauche, c'est un médecin de village prospère qui approche, portant une épée à la taille, une ombrelle en papier dans une main et un éventail dans l'autre. Son matériel médical est enveloppé dans un morceau de tissu noué autour de ses épaules.

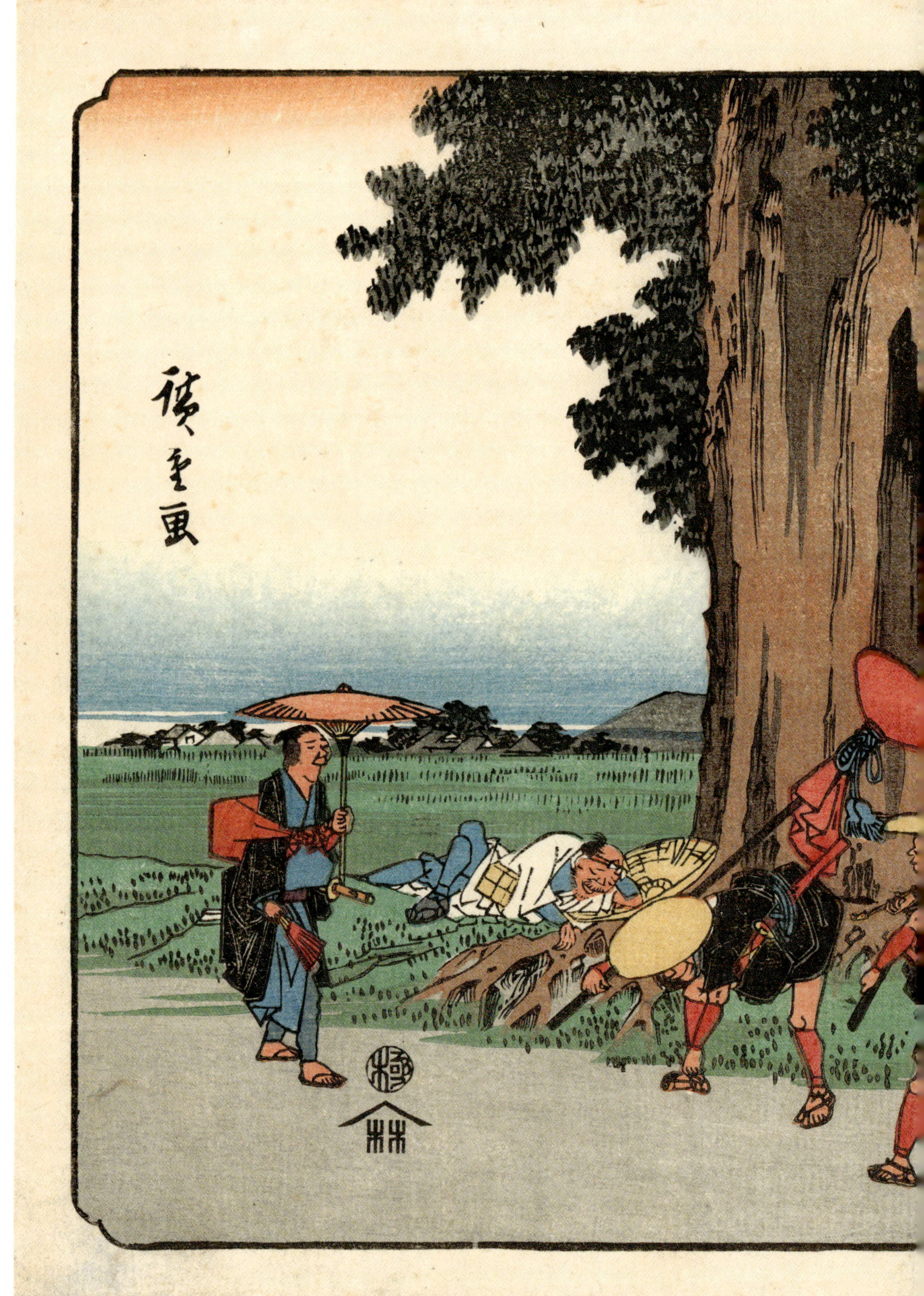

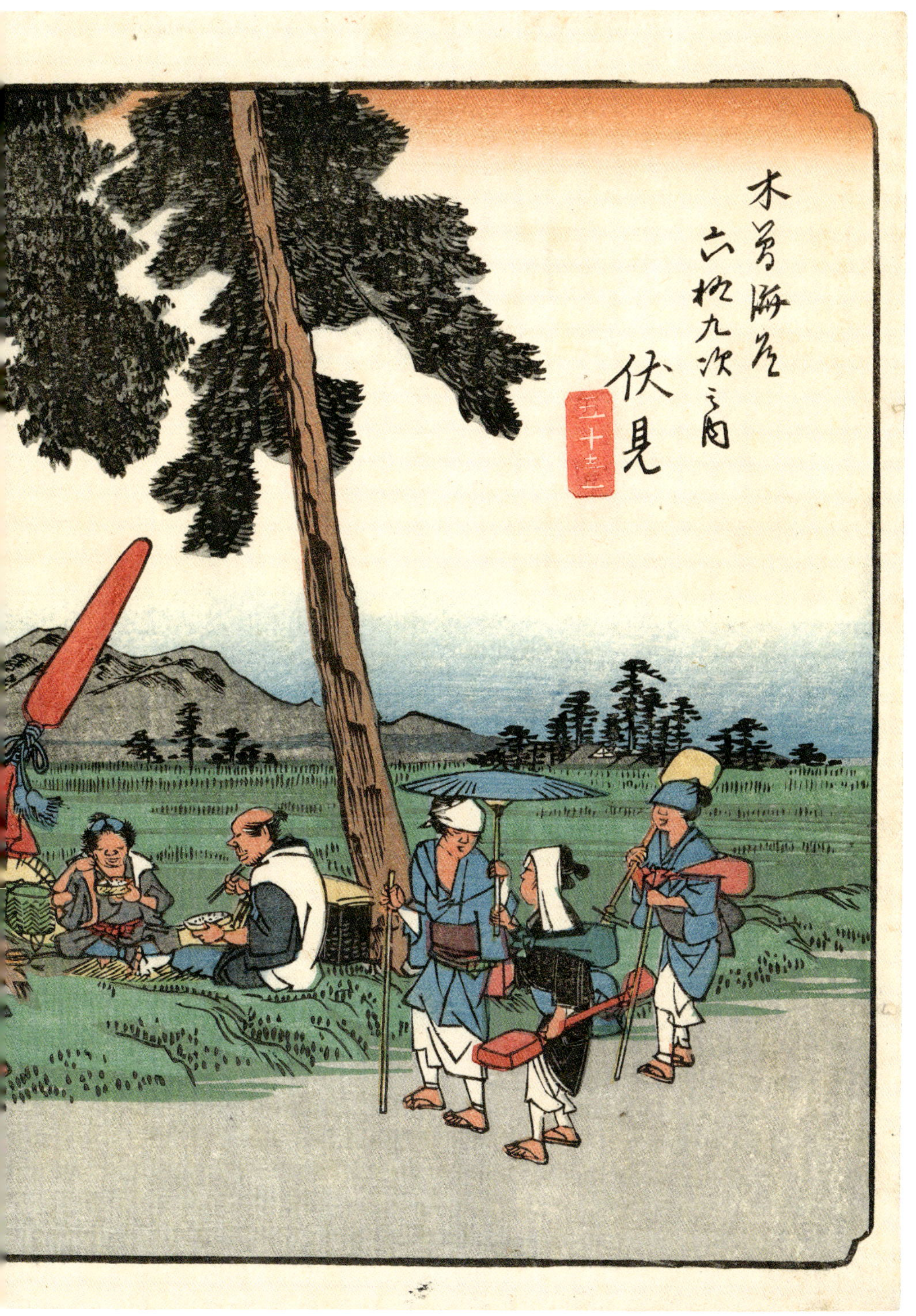

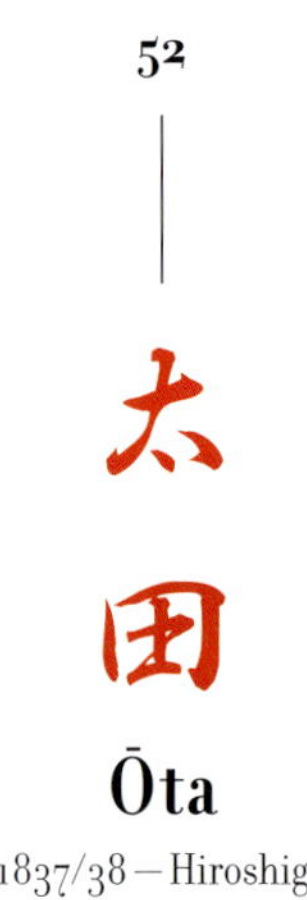

Ōta

1837/38 — Hiroshige

Travellers leaving the Ōta station heading southwards to Kyoto soon arrived at the Kiso River, which had to be crossed by ferry. It is this ferry landing Hiroshige chose to depict as the motif for this station. Downstream from where it was joined by the Hida River, the Kiso was around 50 metres (165 feet) wide here, and this part of the road was considered one of the more difficult sections of the route. In modern times the Kiso River, at 229 kilometres (142 miles) in length, has been dubbed the "Japanese Rhine" on account of its swift current and many rapids.

Hiroshige's design is based on the sketch *Ōta River Crossing* (*Ōta no watashi*) which he presumably completed when reaching this crossing during his journey along the Kisokaidō to Kyoto. The scenery itself is very close to his sketch: the three trees on the left, the boulders on the right and the background of trees lined up along the riverbank with Mount Hatobuki (313 metres/1,027 feet) rising in the distance, are all included in the original study. The ferry on the left waiting at the riverbank for customers, the boat in the centre, with its ferryman on the left and three seated passengers, as well as the raft heading east all featured in the drawing as well. The three groups of travellers waiting on the near bank for the next ferry, however, are additions not found in Hiroshige's sketch.

Reisende, die die Station Ōta nach Süden in Richtung Kyoto verließen, erreichten bald den Kiso, der per Fähre zu überqueren war. Hiroshige wählte den Fähranleger als Motiv für diese Station. Unterhalb der Stelle, an der der Hida in den Kiso mündete, war der Fluss etwa 50 Meter breit, weshalb dieser Streckenabschnitt als einer der schwierigeren Teile der Route galt. Heute nennt man den 229 Kilometer langen Kiso wegen seiner starken Strömung und der zahlreichen Stromschnellen auch den „japanischen Rhein".

Hiroshiges Entwurf basiert auf der Skizze *Ōta no watashi* oder *Flussquerung bei Ōta*, die er vermutlich vollendete, als er auf seiner Kisokaidō-Reise nach Kyoto an diese Querung kam. Die Szenerie selbst ist seiner Skizze sehr ähnlich: Die drei Bäume links, die Felsbrocken rechts und die am jenseitigen Flussufer aufgereihten Bäume vor dem 313 Meter hohen Hatokubi, der sich in der Ferne erhebt, tauchen allesamt bereits in der Originalstudie auf. Das Fährboot, das links im Bild auf Kunden wartet, das Boot in der Mitte mit dem Fährmann links und drei sitzenden Passagieren sowie das ostwärts fahrende Floß sind in der Zeichnung ebenfalls enthalten. Die drei Gruppen von Reisenden dagegen, die am diesseitigen Ufer auf die nächste Fähre warten, sind Hinzufügungen und kommen in Hiroshiges Skizze nicht vor.

Après avoir quitté la station d'Ōta en allant vers le sud en direction de Kyoto, les voyageurs arrivaient bientôt à la Kiso, rivière qu'il fallait traverser en bateau. C'est l'embarcadère qu'Hiroshige a choisi pour représenter cette station. En aval de sa confluence avec l'Hida, la Kiso mesurait une cinquantaine de mètres de large ; cette partie de la route était considérée comme l'une des plus difficiles du parcours. À l'époque moderne, la Kiso, dont le cours est de 229 kilomètres, a été surnommée le « Rhin japonais » en raison de son fort courant et de ses nombreux rapides.

Pour cette estampe, Hiroshige s'est inspiré de son esquisse intitulée *Traversée de l'Ōta (Ōta no watashi)*, qu'il a vraisemblablement achevée en parvenant à cet embarcadère, durant le voyage qui le mena à Kyoto par la Kisokaidō. Le paysage est très proche de celui de l'esquisse : les trois arbres situés à gauche, les rochers de droite et, à l'arrière-plan, l'alignement d'arbres sur la rive, ainsi qu'au loin le mont Hatobuki (313 mètres), tous ces éléments figurent dans l'esquisse initiale. Il en va de même du passeur qui, à gauche, attend les clients sur la rive, de la barque visible au centre, avec son batelier à gauche et ses trois passagers assis, et du radeau qui se dirige vers l'est. En revanche, les trois groupes de voyageurs qui, non loin du bord, attendent le bateau suivant sont des ajouts ne figurant pas dans l'esquisse d'Hiroshige.

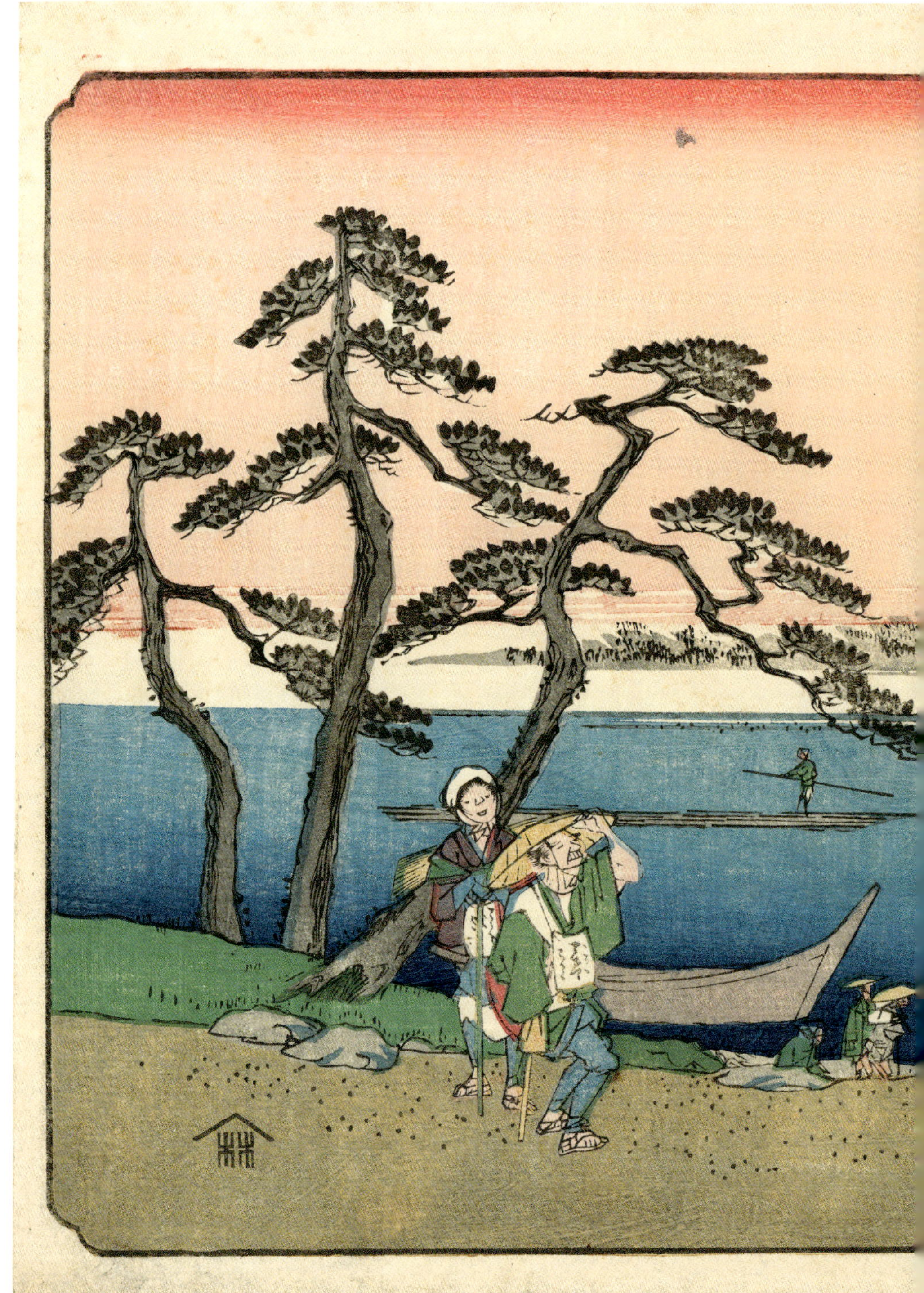

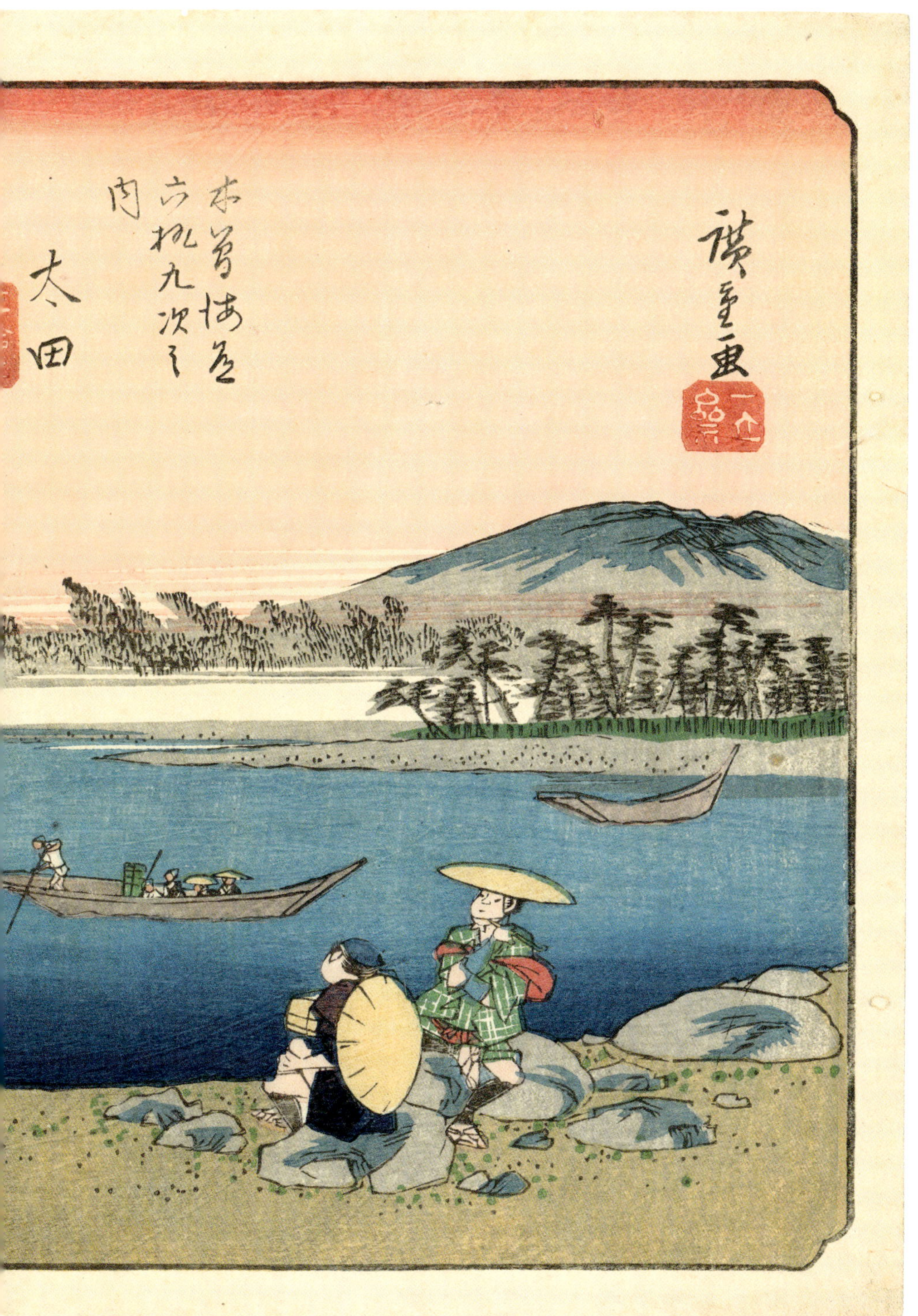
木曾街道
六拾九次之
内
太田

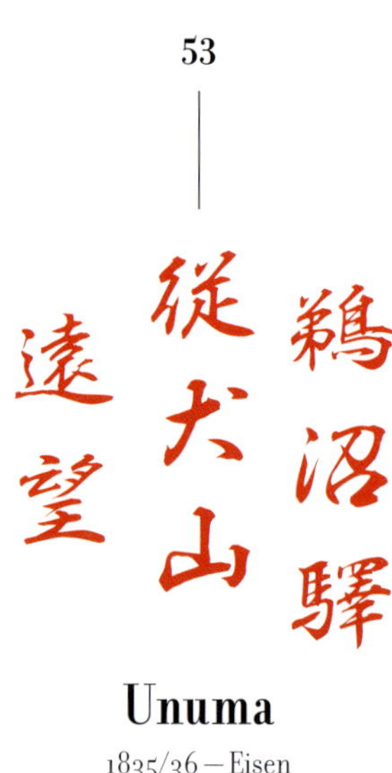

53

Unuma

1835/36 — Eisen

Eisen depicts the Unuma station, scarcely visible in the far distance, from a remote and high vantage point near Inuyama Castle. His composition is likely to have been inspired by a bird's-eye view of Inuyama's Haritsuna Shrine and the surrounding topography in the guidebook *Views of Famous Sights along the Kiso Road (Kisoji meisho zue)*. The upper-left corner of this illustration, entitled "Inuyama, Haritsuna Shrine", features almost the same scene depicted in the print. Eisen apparently extracted the section that includes Unuma and Inuyama Castle on opposite sides of the Kiso River, but greatly exaggerated the distance between them, which is in fact less than one kilometre (0.6 miles).

Inuyama Castle stands on a hill around 88 metres (289 feet) in height above the Kiso River. The imposing structure dates back to the 15th century, but its current form was completed in 1537 with the central, three-storey tower 19 metres (62 feet) in height being built between 1601 and 1620. The castle is one of only 12 built before the Edo period that still exist today, and is registered as a National Treasure. Unuma station, on the other hand, was, with only 246 inhabitants in 1843, the smallest station along the Kisokaidō.

Eisen stellt die Station Unuma, in weiter Ferne kaum sichtbar, aus der Perspektive einer hohen, entlegenen Warte nahe der Burg Inuyama dar. Wahrscheinlich ist die Komposition von einer vogelperspektivischen Ansicht des Haritsuna-Schreins von Inuyama und des umliegenden Geländes im Reiseführer *Ansichten berühmter Stätten an der Kiso-Straße (Kisoji meisho zue)* inspiriert. Die Szene in der linken oberen Ecke dieser als *Inuyama, Haritsuna-Schrein* betitelten Abbildung ist mit der des Drucks nahezu identisch. Offenbar verwendete Eisen den Bildausschnitt von Unuma und der Burg Inuyama, die sich an den Ufern des Kiso gegenüberlagen, als Vorlage, übertrieb aber die Entfernung zwischen ihnen gewaltig; in Wirklichkeit beträgt sie weniger als einen Kilometer.

Die Burg Inuyama thront auf einem Hügel etwa 88 Meter über dem Kiso. Das imposante Bauwerk reicht bis ins 15. Jahrhundert zurück und wurde in seiner heutigen Form 1537 fertiggestellt, jedoch erst zwischen 1601 und 1620 um den 19 Meter hohen dreistöckigen Turm im Zentrum ergänzt. Inuyama gehört zu einem Dutzend noch existierender Burgen, die bereits vor der Edo-Zeit errichtet wurden, und ist als Nationalschatz registriert. Unuma dagegen war 1843 mit nur 246 Einwohnern die kleinste Station am Kisokaidō.

Eisen a représenté la station d'Unuma, à peine visible dans le lointain, depuis un point de vue éloigné et surélevé, près du château d'Inuyama. Sa composition s'inspire probablement d'une vue aérienne du sanctuaire Haritsuna d'Inuyama et de la topographie environnante figurant dans le guide de voyage *Collection de vues de paysages célèbres sur la route Kiso (Kisoji meisho zue)*. L'angle supérieur gauche de cette illustration, intitulée *Inuyama, sanctuaire Haritsuna*, présente quasiment la même scène que celle de cette estampe. Eisen semble en avoir extrait la partie comprenant Unuma et le château d'Inuyama, chacun situé sur une rive de la Kiso, mais il a grandement exagéré la distance qui les sépare, laquelle est, en réalité, inférieure à un kilomètre.

Le château d'Inuyama surplombe la Kiso à une altitude d'environ 88 mètres, au sommet d'une colline. Cet imposant édifice date du XVe siècle, mais sa forme actuelle a été achevée en 1537, avec la tour centrale de 19 mètres de haut, comprenant trois étages et construite entre 1601 et 1620. Faisant partie des douze châteaux antérieurs à l'ère Edo qui existent encore aujourd'hui, cette forteresse est inscrite sur la liste des « trésors nationaux ». Unuma, quant à elle, ne comptait que 246 habitants en 1843, ce qui en faisait la plus petite station de la Kisokaidō.

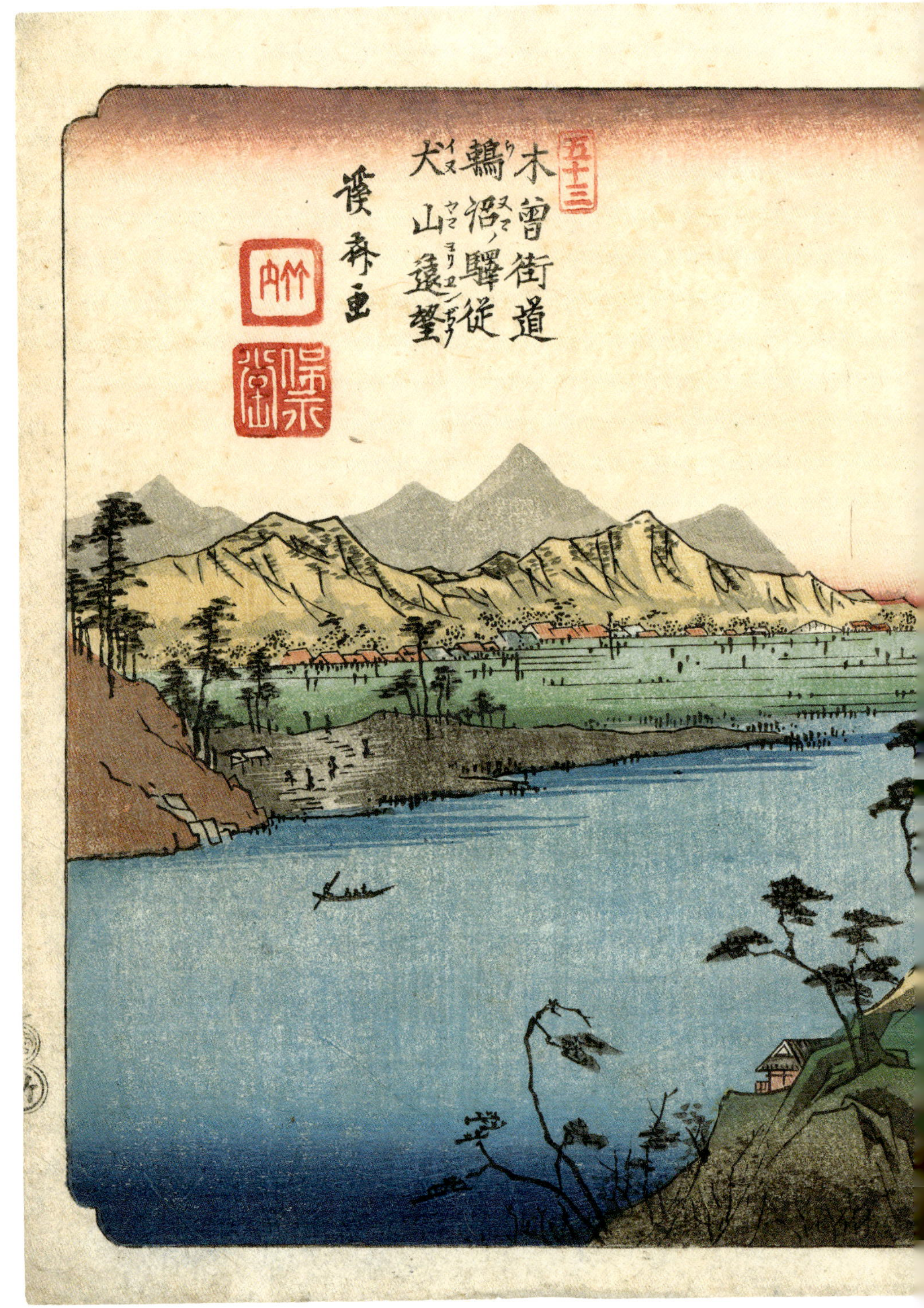

木曾街道
鵜沼ノ驛従
犬山遠望
渓斎画

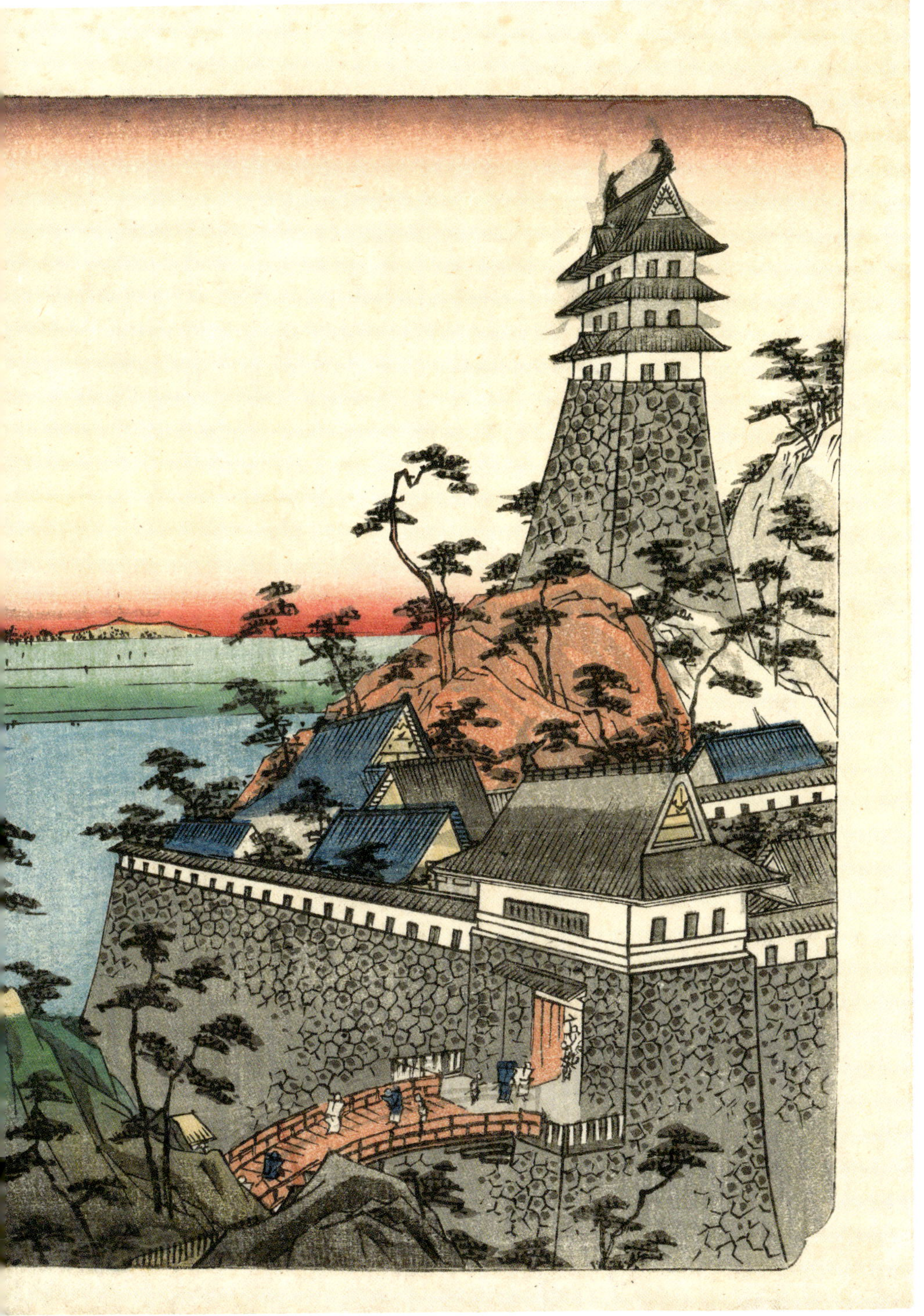

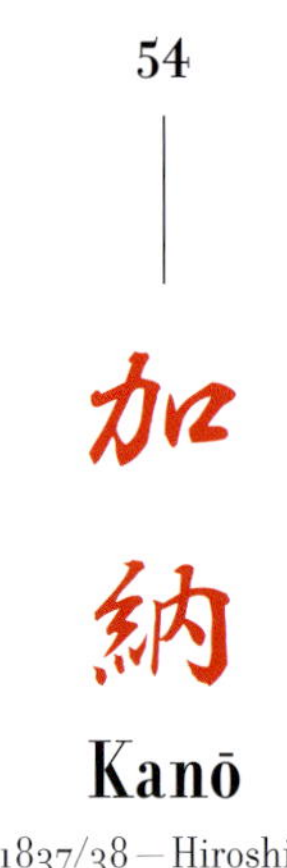

54

Kanō

1837/38 — Hiroshige

After Honjō, Annaka and Ochiai, but ahead of Tarui, the design for Kanō is the fourth of five prints in the series to depict a *daimyō* procession. Under the alternating attendance system implemented in 1635, provincial lords were required to spend every other year or several months every year in Edo before returning to their respective provinces. The processions of *daimyō* travelling to and from the capital evolved into elaborate, parade-like spectacles involving hundreds, even thousands of uniformed retainers on foot and horseback, as well as various props, such as the decorative lances topped with fur or horsehair held aloft by the pair second from the front. These exercises of pomp and logistics were designed to impress upon the populace the power and splendour of the *daimyō* and the shogun, even as the military function of samurai diminished over the course of the 17th to 19th centuries.

As demanded by law, the two travellers on the left have removed their hats and are kneeling at the side of the road to express deference to the lord's authority and allow the procession to pass unhindered. The *daimyō* is being conveyed in the large palanquin on the far right of composition.

In the background is Kanō Castle, which started out as a modest fortification but became the principal castle in the region after Gifu Castle was demolished as a result of the battle of the same name of 1600. During his journey along the Kisokaidō, Hiroshige made an abbreviated sketch of the castle from the roadside. The vantage point presented in the finished design follows this drawing, but Hiroshige augmented this original design by replacing the row of cottages in the foreground with a single, larger roadside stall, enhancing the forms of the pine trees, and adding the procession.

Nach Honjō, Annaka und Ochiai, aber vor Tarui zeigt der Entwurf für Kanō als viertes von fünf Blättern der Serie eine *daimyō*-Prozession. Das 1635 eingeführte System der „wechselnden Anwesenheit" verpflichtete die Provinzfürsten, jedes zweite Jahr oder mehrere Monate eines Jahres in Edo zu verbringen, bevor sie in ihre jeweiligen Lehen zurückkehren durften. Die *daimyō*-Prozessionen, die in die Hauptstadt zogen oder sie verließen, entwickelten sich zu aufwendigen, paradeähnlichen Spektakeln mit Hunderten oder gar Tausenden von uniformierten Gefolgsleuten zu Fuß oder zu Pferd und verschiedensten Requisiten wie den mit Fell oder Pferdehaar gekrönten Zierlanzen, die vom zweiten Glied hinter der Spitze des Zuges präsentiert wurden. Diese Übungen in Prunk und Logistik sollten der Bevölkerung die Macht und Herrlichkeit des jeweiligen Lehensfürsten und des Shoguns einschärfen, auch wenn die militärische Funktion der Samurai im Verlauf des 17., 18. und 19. Jahrhunderts an Bedeutung verlor.

Wie vom Gesetz verlangt, haben die beiden Reisenden links ihre Hüte abgenommen und knien am Straßenrand, um ihre Hochachtung vor der Autorität des Fürsten auszudrücken und die Prozession ungehindert passieren zu lassen. Der *daimyō* wird in der großen Sänfte am rechten Bildrand befördert.

Die im Hintergrund gelegene Burg Kanō begann als bescheidene Festung, avancierte jedoch zur ersten Burg der Region, nachdem die Burg Gifu infolge der nach ihr benannten Schlacht im Jahr 1600 zerstört worden war. Während seiner Reise auf dem Kisokaidō fertigte Hiroshige eine einfache Skizze der Burg an, gesehen von der Straße aus. Der Blickwinkel des fertigen Entwurfs entspricht dem der Zeichnung, doch Hiroshige vervollkommnete seine Originalskizze, indem er die Hüttenreihe im Vordergrund durch einen einzelnen größeren Verkaufsstand am Wegesrand ersetzte, die Formen der Kiefern weiterentwickelte und die Prozession hinzufügte.

Après Honjō, Annaka et Ochiai, et avant Tarui, cette illustration de Kanō est la quatrième des cinq estampes de la série représentant une procession de *daïmio*. Selon le système de la résidence alternée mis en place en 1635, les seigneurs provinciaux étaient tenus de passer une année sur deux, ou plusieurs mois par an, à Edo avant de regagner leurs provinces respectives. Les processions de *daïmio* qui se rendaient à la capitale ou la quittaient devinrent des spectacles élaborés, semblables à des parades auxquelles participaient des centaines, voire des milliers, de serviteurs en livrée, à pied et à cheval, munis de divers accessoires comme les lances décoratives surmontées de fourrure ou de crin de cheval, tenues bien haut par la deuxième paire d'hommes à l'avant de cette procession. Ces opérations d'apparat et de logistique étaient des démonstrations de la puissance et de la splendeur des *daïmio* et du shogun, destinées à impressionner le peuple, même si la fonction militaire des samouraïs s'est atténuée du XVIIe au XIXe siècle.

Comme l'exige la loi, les deux voyageurs visibles à gauche ont ôté leur chapeau et se sont agenouillés sur le bord de la route en signe de déférence à l'égard de l'autorité du seigneur et pour céder le passage à la procession. Le *daïmio* est transporté dans le grand palanquin situé à l'extrême droite de la composition.

On aperçoit à l'arrière-plan le château de Kanō qui, d'abord modeste fortification, devint le principal château de la région après la démolition de celui de Gifu, à la suite de la bataille éponyme en 1600. Au cours de son voyage sur la Kisokaidō, Hiroshige avait fait un croquis rapide du château vu du bord de la route. Le point de vue de l'illustration définitive reprend celui du croquis, mais l'artiste en a remplacé l'alignement de maisons du premier plan par une unique échoppe de belle taille le long de la route ; il a aussi accentué les formes des pins et ajouté la procession.

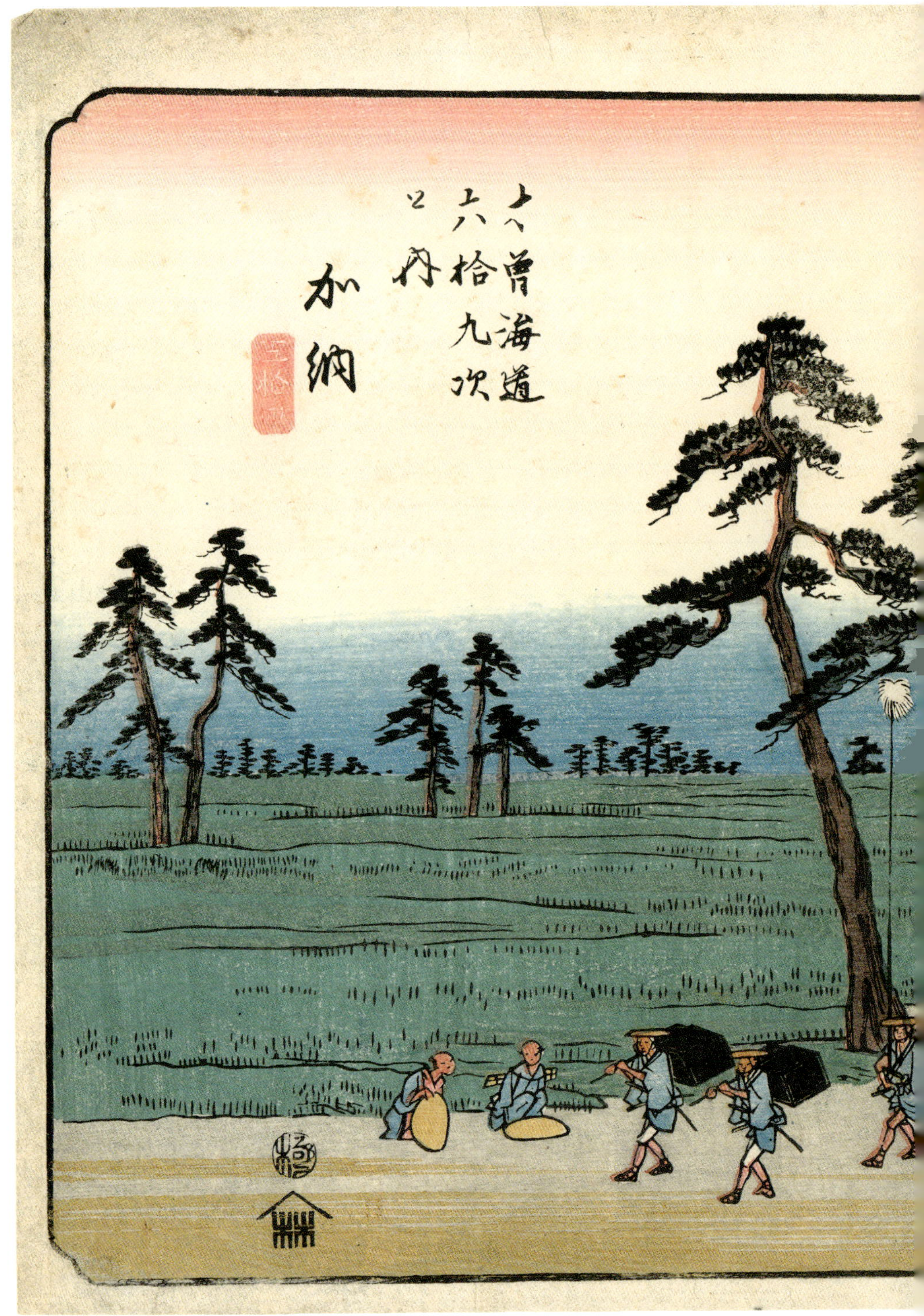
木曾海道
六拾九次
之内
加納

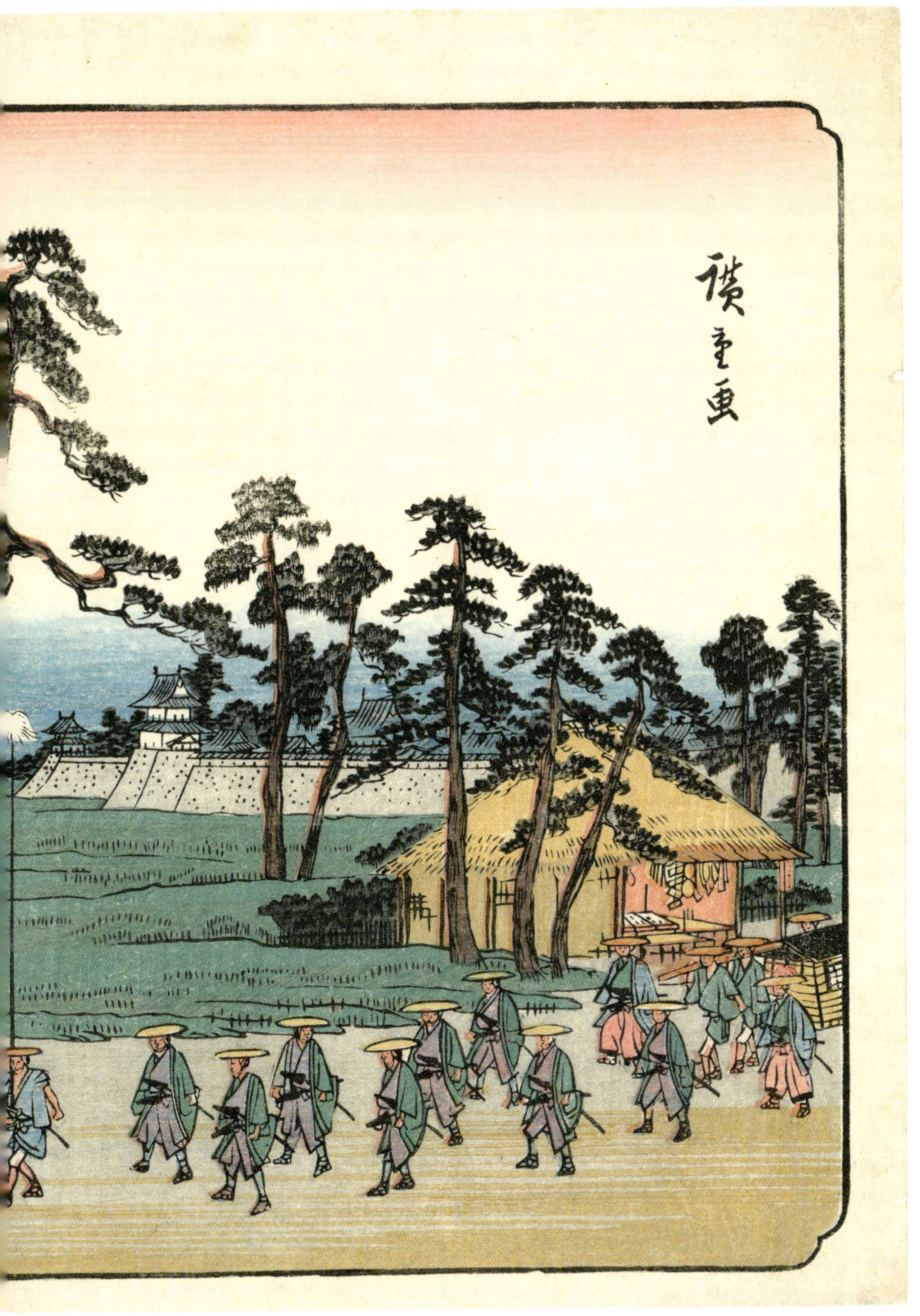

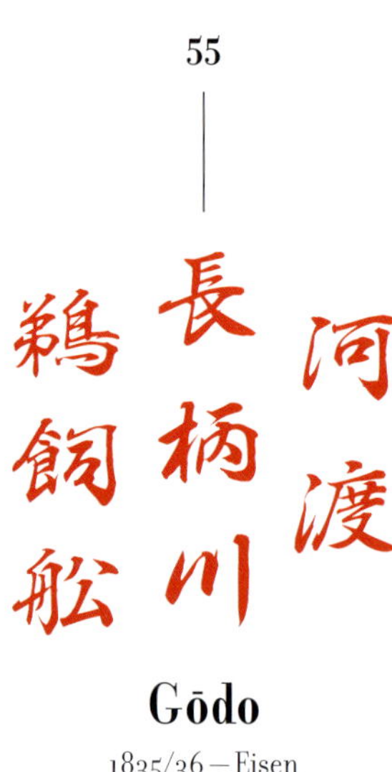

Gōdo

1835/36 – Eisen

Fishing for *ayu* (sweetfish) with the help of cormorants has been a tradition on the Nagara River since the Heian Period (794–1185); its purpose, however, has shifted from providing a livelihood for local inhabitants to becoming a tourist attraction today. Every year between May and October, the boats head out in the evenings and use a flaming light source attached to the boat to attract the fish in the dark. The cormorants, with narrow rings fitted around their necks to prevent them from swallowing the fish whole, are then released to catch them. The birds are pulled back into the boats by a rope attached to them and the fish they have cought are removed and put in the boat. The spectacle can be watched today on the river itself from organised tour-boats.

Eisen based this design, one of his most famous in the Kisokaidō series, on a corresponding illustration in the guidebook *Views of Famous Sights along the Kiso Road* (*Kisoji meisho zue*) with the identical title, "Cormorant Fishing Boats on the Nagara River" (*Nagaragawa ukaibune*). In contrast to the cluttered composition of that illustration, which has six boats in the foreground, each with three fishermen, he concentrated on one boat with two fishermen and no pilot. All the other boats are in the background and rendered only in black silhouettes, as is Mount Kinka (329 metres /1,080 feet) as it rises in the distance along the Nagara River. The characters for the word Nagara are usually read "Nagae", but not in this case; however, this false pronunciation is here erroneously suggested in the small script next to the title.

Die Jagd auf den stintartigen Wanderfisch *ayu* mit abgerichteten Kormoranen hat auf dem Nagara seit der Heian-Zeit (794–1185) Tradition, doch was einst der örtlichen Bevölkerung als Lebensgrundlage diente, ist heute zur Touristenattraktion geworden. Jedes Jahr zwischen Mai und Oktober fahren die Fischer abends auf den Fluss hinaus, um mit Fackeln, die sie als Lichtquellen an ihren Booten anbringen, die Fische aus der Dunkelheit anzulocken. Dann werden die Kormorane losgelassen, um sie zu fangen. Ein enger Ring um ihren Hals verhindert, dass sie ihre Beute gänzlich verschlucken. Die an Leinen geführten Vögel werden anschließend in die Boote zurückgezogen, und ihr Fang wird gesichert. Heutzutage kann man das Schauspiel auf organisierten Bootstouren direkt vom Fluss aus beobachten.

Eisen legte diesem Blatt, das zu seinen berühmtesten Entwürfen im Kisokaidō-Zyklus gehört, eine entsprechende Abbildung in dem Reisehandbuch *Ansichten berühmter Stätten an der Kiso-Straße (Kisoji meisho zue)* zugrunde, die denselben Titel trägt, *Kormoran-Fischerboote auf dem Nagara (Nagaragawa ukaibune)*. Im Gegensatz zu der überladenen Illustration, die im Vordergrund sechs Boote mit je drei Fischern zeigt, konzentrierte er sich auf nur ein Boot mit zwei Fischern ohne Steuermann. Alle anderen Boote sind als schwarze Silhouetten in den Hintergrund gerückt, wo sich am Ufer des Nagara in der Ferne auch der 329 Meter hohe Kinka erhebt. Anders als üblich werden die Zeichen für Nagara in diesem Fall nicht wie „Nagae" ausgesprochen; dennoch legt die kleine Aufschrift neben dem Titel diese inkorrekte Aussprache hier fälschlicherweise nahe.

La pêche à l'*ayu* (ou poisson doux) avec des cormorans se pratique traditionnellement sur la Nagara depuis l'ère Heian (794–1185) ; initialement destinée à nourrir les habitants de la région, elle est aujourd'hui devenue une attraction touristique. Chaque année, de mai à octobre, les bateaux sortent le soir et, à l'aide d'un éclairage à la flamme fixé à l'embarcation, on attire le poisson dans l'obscurité. On lâche alors les cormorans qui portent autour du cou un anneau étroit qui les empêchent d'avaler le poisson entier. Les oiseaux sont ensuite ramenés à bord par la corde à laquelle ils sont attachés : leur proie leur est retirée du bec et déposée dans le bateau. De nos jours, on peut assister à ce spectacle sur la rivière à bord de bateaux de voyages organisés.

Pour cette estampe, l'une des plus célèbres qu'il ait réalisées dans la série de la Kisokaidō, Eisen s'est inspiré d'une illustration de la *Collection de vues de paysages célèbres sur la route Kiso (Kisoji meisho zue)*. Mais, contrairement à cette image qui compte, au premier plan, six barques transportant chacune trois pêcheurs, l'artiste n'a représenté qu'une seule barque, sans pilote, à bord de laquelle se trouvent deux pêcheurs. Toutes les autres barques se détachent à l'arrière-plan, uniquement sous la forme de silhouettes noires, de même que le mont Kinka (329 mètres) qui s'élève au loin le long de la Nagara. Les caractères du mot Nagara se lisent généralement « Nagae », mais pas dans ce cas ; pourtant, cette prononciation incorrecte est ici suggérée par erreur dans les petits caractères figurant près du titre.

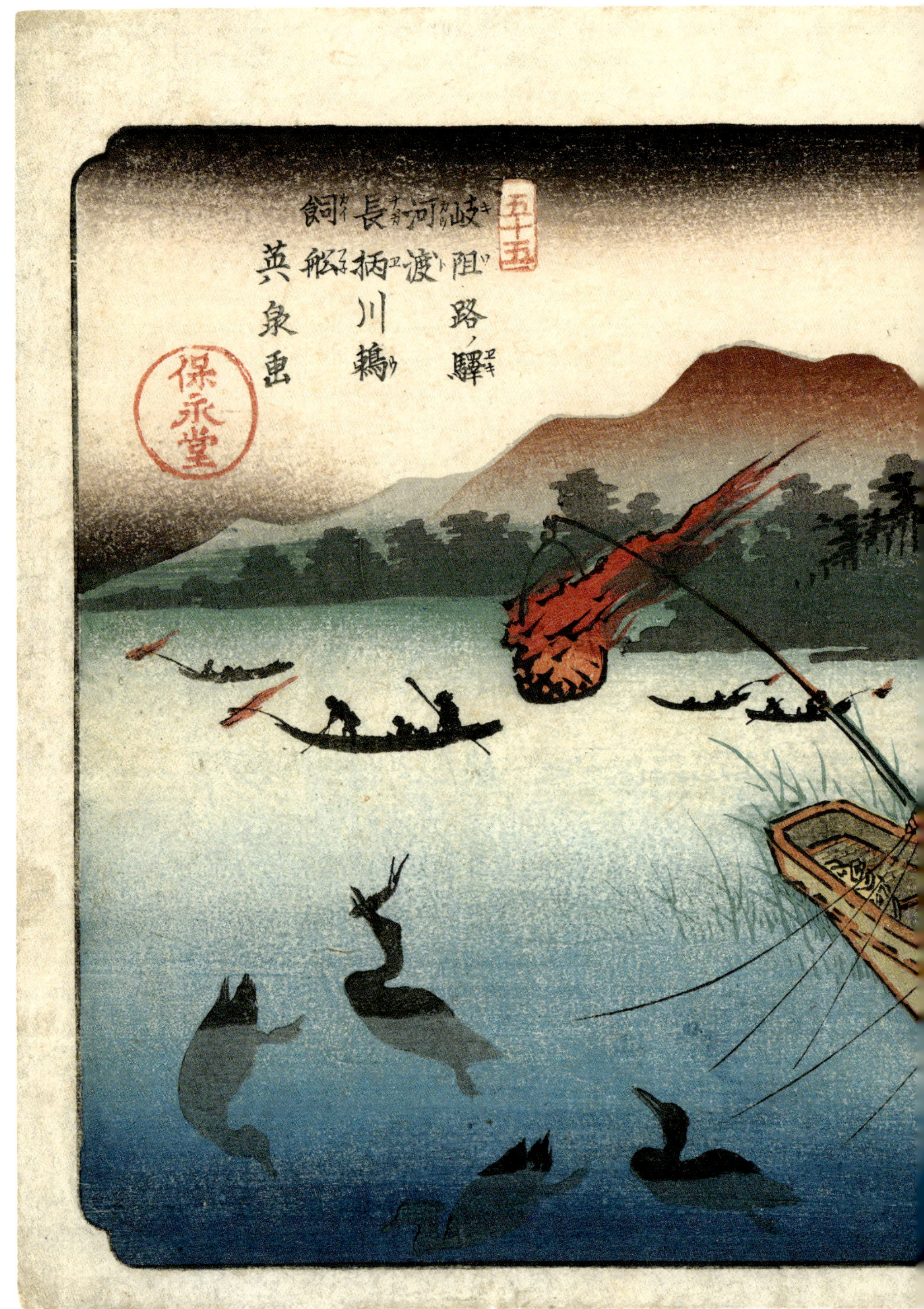
岐阻路ノ駅
河渡ト
長柄川
飼船
英泉画

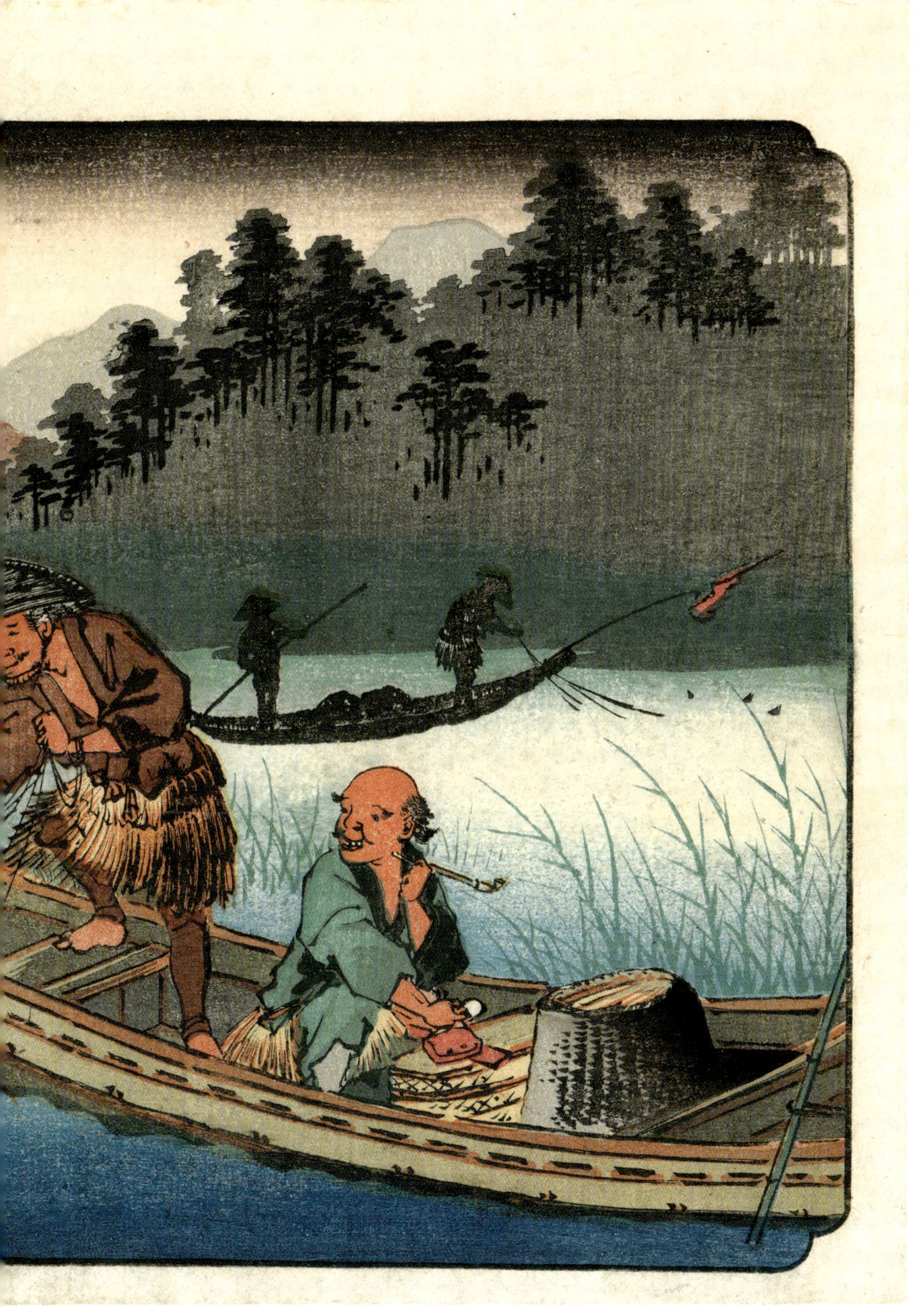

56

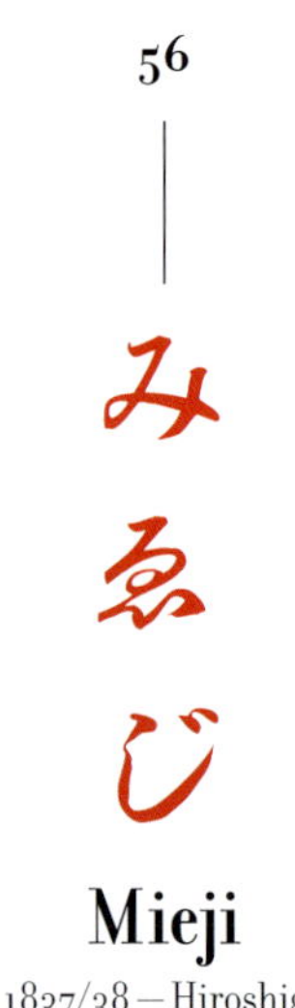

Mieji

1837/38 – Hiroshige

An old monk is asking a farmer carrying a long-bladed hoe over his shoulder for directions in this idyllic scene representing the Mieji station. On their right are two flowering camellia trees while behind them tall bamboo is swaying with the wind and a flock of sparrows is flying towards a river.

The name Mieji comes from a temple that dates back to 717, but was relocated from the village in 1549 by Saitō Dōsan (1494–1556), the magistrate of Mino Province who lived in Inabayama Castle and later became the father-in-law of the famous *daimyō* Oda Nobunaga (1534–1582). In 1637, Mieji was designated a post station and its *honjin* was built in 1669.

The river in the picture might be either the Goroku to the east or the Sai to the west, two tributaries of the Nagara River that passed alongside Mieji station. As Hiroshige's design is after a sketch he drew during his journey west to Kyoto, it seems likely that the houses in the background represent Mieji and this is the road towards the village, which would mean it was the Goroku River. The swaying bamboo is featured in the sketch as well, but in his print Hiroshige replaced the grove growing on the right of the ascending road with the red flowering camellia trees, presumably for their greater visual impact.

Diese idyllische Szene repräsentiert die Station Mieji. Ein alter Mönch fragt einen Bauern, der eine Hacke mit langem Blatt geschultert hat, nach dem Weg. Rechts von ihnen stehen zwei blühende Kamelienbäume, während sich hinter ihnen lange Bambusruten im Wind wiegen und ein Schwarm Sperlinge auf den Fluss zufliegt.

Der Name Mieji rührt von einem Tempel her, der auf das Jahr 717 zurückgeht, aber 1549 von Saitō Dōsan (1494–1556) an einen Standort außerhalb des Dorfes versetzt wurde. Dōsan, der Magistrat der Provinz Mino, lebte auf der Burg Inabayama und wurde später Schwiegervater des berühmten *daimyō* Oda Nobunaga (1534–1582). Mieji wurde 1637 als Poststation ausgewiesen und erhielt 1669 ein *honjin*.

Es könnte hier entweder der Goroku oder der Sai abgebildet sein, zwei Nebenflüsse des Nagara, die Mieji in östlicher bzw. westlicher Richtung passierten. Da Hiroshiges Entwurf auf einer Skizze beruht, die er während seiner Reise westwärts nach Kyoto ausführte, stellen die Häuser im Hintergrund wahrscheinlich Mieji dar. Somit dürfte dies die Straße sein, die auf das Dorf zuführt, und der Fluss der Goroku. Der sich wiegende Bambus taucht in der Skizze ebenfalls auf, jedoch versetzte Hiroshige für seinen Druck den Hain, der eigentlich rechts neben der ansteigenden Straße wuchs. Dies geschah vermutlich, um die rot blühenden Kamelien besser in Szene setzen zu können.

Un vieux moine demande son chemin à un paysan qui porte sur l'épaule une houe à longue lame, dans cette scène idyllique représentant la station de Mieji. À leur droite se trouvent deux camélias en fleurs, tandis que, derrière eux, de grands bambous se balancent dans le vent et que des oiseaux volent vers une rivière.

Le nom de Mieji vient d'un temple datant de 717, mais qui fut retiré au village et déplacé en 1549 par Saitō Dōsan (1494–1556), le magistrat de la province de Mino qui vivait au château d'Inabayama et devint par la suite le beau-père du célèbre *daïmio* Oda Nobunaga (1534–1582). Mieji fut désigné comme relais de poste en 1637 et l'on y construisit une *honjin* en 1669.

La rivière de cette estampe pourrait être la Goroku à l'est ou bien la Sai à l'ouest, deux affluents de la Nagara qui coulaient dans les environs de la station de Mieji. Ce dessin d'Hiroshige s'inspirant d'un croquis qu'il avait réalisé lors de son périple vers l'ouest pour aller à Kyoto, il est probable que les maisons visibles à l'arrière-plan représentent Mieji et que cette route soit celle qui mène au village : la rivière serait alors la Goroku. Les bambous qui se balancent figurent aussi dans le croquis, mais, dans son estampe, Hiroshige a remplacé le bosquet d'arbres, situé à droite du chemin qui monte, par des camélias rouges en fleurs, vraisemblablement pour leur effet visuel plus frappant.

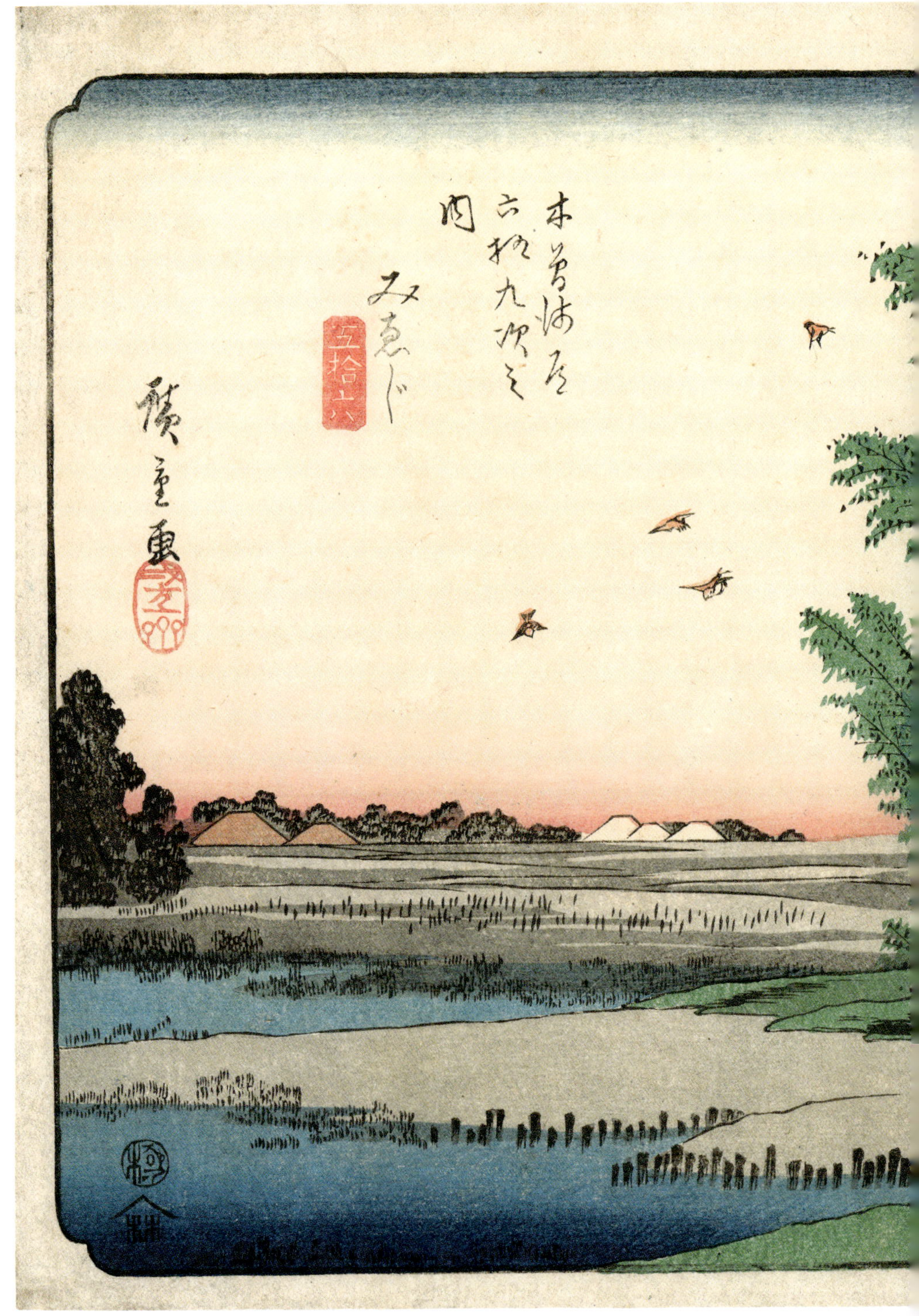

木曽街道六拾九次之内
みゑじ
五拾八
廣重画

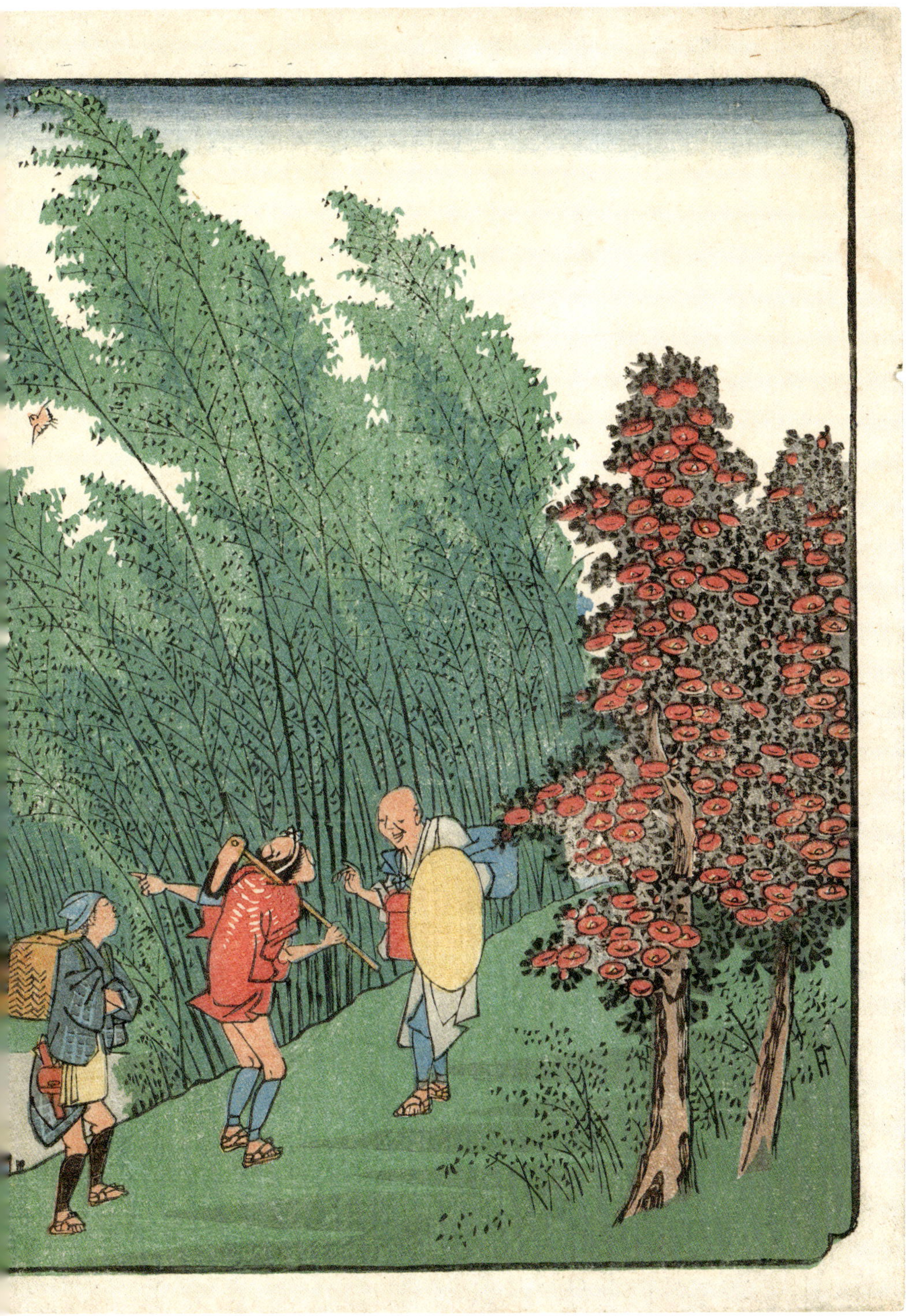

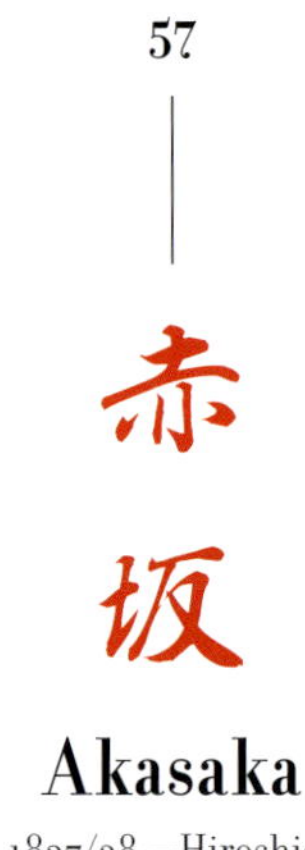

57

Akasaka

1837/38 — Hiroshige

A few travellers are making their way across the bridge over the Kuise River away from the Akasaka station, represented by the cluster of low-set cottages in the background with their steeply peaked, thatched roofs. A signpost on the far side of the bridge marks the entry to the village. The source of the Kuise River, 24 kilometres (15 miles) in length, is Mount Ikeda. The Kuise flows into the Makita River, which is itself a tributary of the Ibi that ultimately empties into Ise Bay.

Akasaka was on the pilgrimage route to the Kegonji temple on Mount Tanigumi, located around 20 kilometres (12.5 miles) to the north. Kegonji was built in 798 and remains today a popular destination for the faithful, as well as for those seeking beautiful scenery. In Akasaka itself there are still a number of older buildings while a replica of an Edo-period fire watchtower has been built as an extra attraction.

The design of this print is based on a sketch called *Entrance to Akasaka* (*Akasaka iriguchi*) which Hiroshige created from the far side of the bridge during his journey to Kyoto. However, he shifted the vantage point from the right of the bridge, as implied in the sketch, to the left side. He further augmented the original sketch by adding a wooden supporting pillar to the centre of the bridge, making it seem longer and giving it a more robust visual presence.

Ein paar Reisende entfernen sich auf der Brücke über den Kuise von der Station Akasaka, die im Hintergrund als Ansammlung in die Landschaft eingebetteter Hütten mit steil zulaufenden Strohdächern dargestellt ist. Ein Wegweiser am hinteren Brückenende markiert den Eingang zum Dorf. Der 24 Kilometer lange Kuise entspringt am Berg Ikeda und fließt in den Makita, der seinerseits ein Zufluss des schließlich in die Ise-Bucht mündenden Ibi ist.

Akasaka lag an der Pilgerroute zum Kegonji-Tempel, der rund 20 Kilometer weiter nördlich auf dem Berg Tanigumi stand. Der Kegonji wurde 798 erbaut und ist bis heute ein beliebtes Reiseziel für Gläubige und Liebhaber schöner Landschaften. In Akasaka selbst sind zahlreiche ältere Gebäude erhalten; als zusätzliche Attraktion wurde ein Feuerwachturm aus der Edo-Zeit rekonstruiert.

Der Entwurf für diesen Druck basiert auf einer Skizze mit dem Titel *Akasaka iriguchi* oder *Eingang nach Akasaka*, die Hiroshige auf seiner Reise nach Kyoto diesseits der Brücke, aber von der anderen Wegseite aus anfertigte. Doch dann verlegte er den Blickwinkel von der rechten Seite der Brücke, wie in der Skizze gegeben, auf die linke. Außerdem erweiterte er die Originalstudie, indem er unter der Mitte der Brücke ein hölzernes Joch einfügte und sie so länger und optisch robuster erscheinen ließ.

Quelques voyageurs traversent le pont qui enjambe la rivière Kuise en s'éloignant de la station d'Akasaka, figurée, à l'arrière-plan, par un groupe de maisons basses aux toits de chaume à forte pente. À l'extrémité la plus éloignée du pont, un poteau indicateur marque l'entrée du village. La Kuise, dont le cours est de 24 kilomètres, prend sa source au mont Ikeda. Elle se jette dans la Makita, elle-même affluent de l'Ibi dont l'embouchure se trouve dans la baie d'Ise.

Akasaka se situait sur la route des pèlerins se rendant au temple de Kegonji, sur le mont Tanigumi, à une vingtaine de kilomètres au nord. Édifié en 798, ce temple demeure aujourd'hui une destination prisée des fidèles et des amateurs de beaux paysages. Akasaka compte encore un certain nombre de bâtiments anciens, tandis qu'une réplique d'une tour à signaux de l'ère Edo a été construite comme attraction supplémentaire.

La composition de cette estampe s'inspire d'une esquisse intitulée *Entrée d'Akasaka* (*Akasaka iriguchi*), qu'Hiroshige avait réalisée depuis l'extrémité la plus éloignée du pont pendant le périple qui le mena jusqu'à Kyoto. Toutefois, il a déplacé vers la gauche le point de vue initial qui, d'après l'esquisse, se situait à droite du pont. Il a enrichi le dessin d'origine en ajoutant une pile de bois au centre du pont, qui semble allonger celui-ci et lui donner une présence visuelle plus robuste.

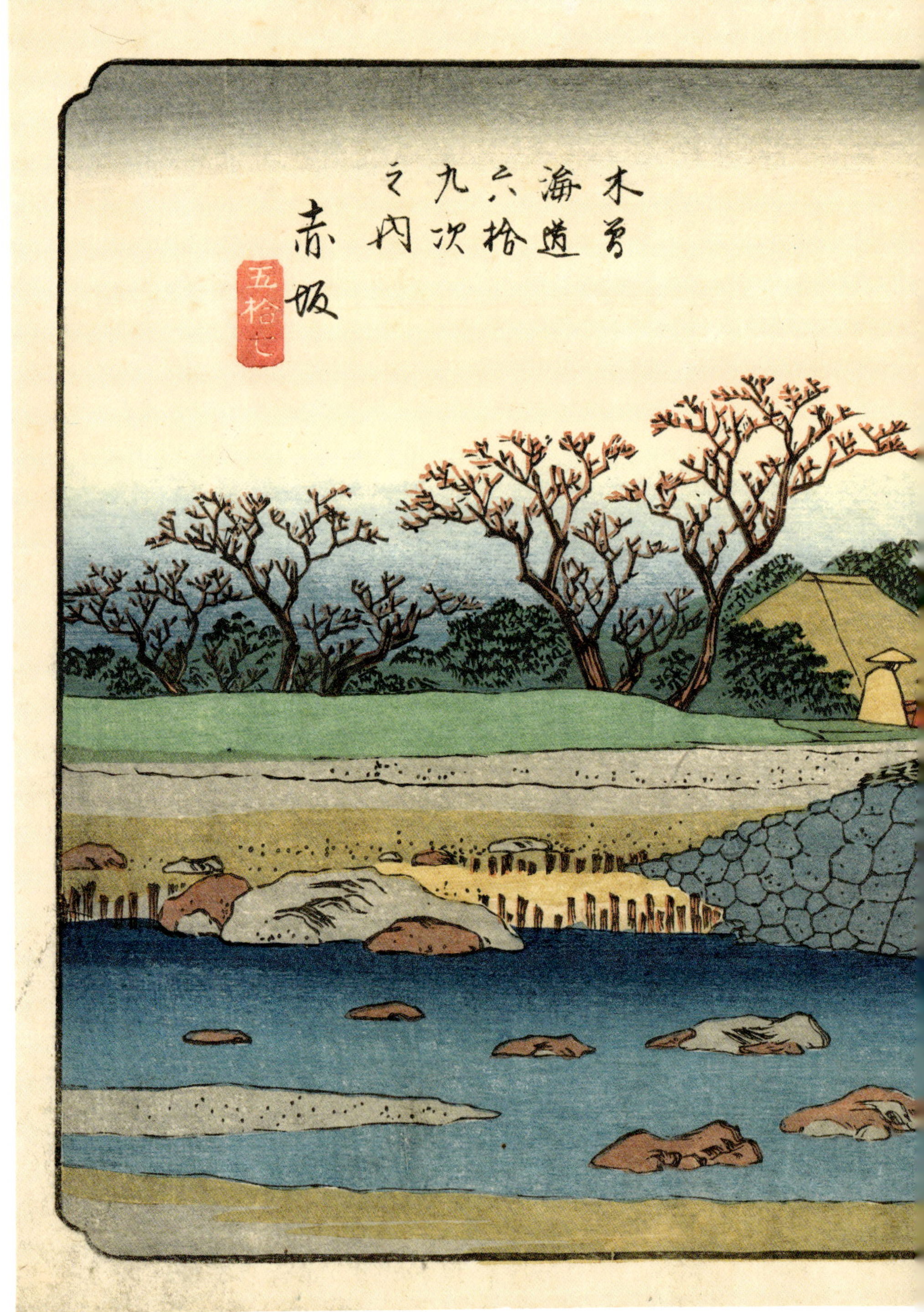

木曽
海道
六拾
九次
之内
赤阪
五拾七

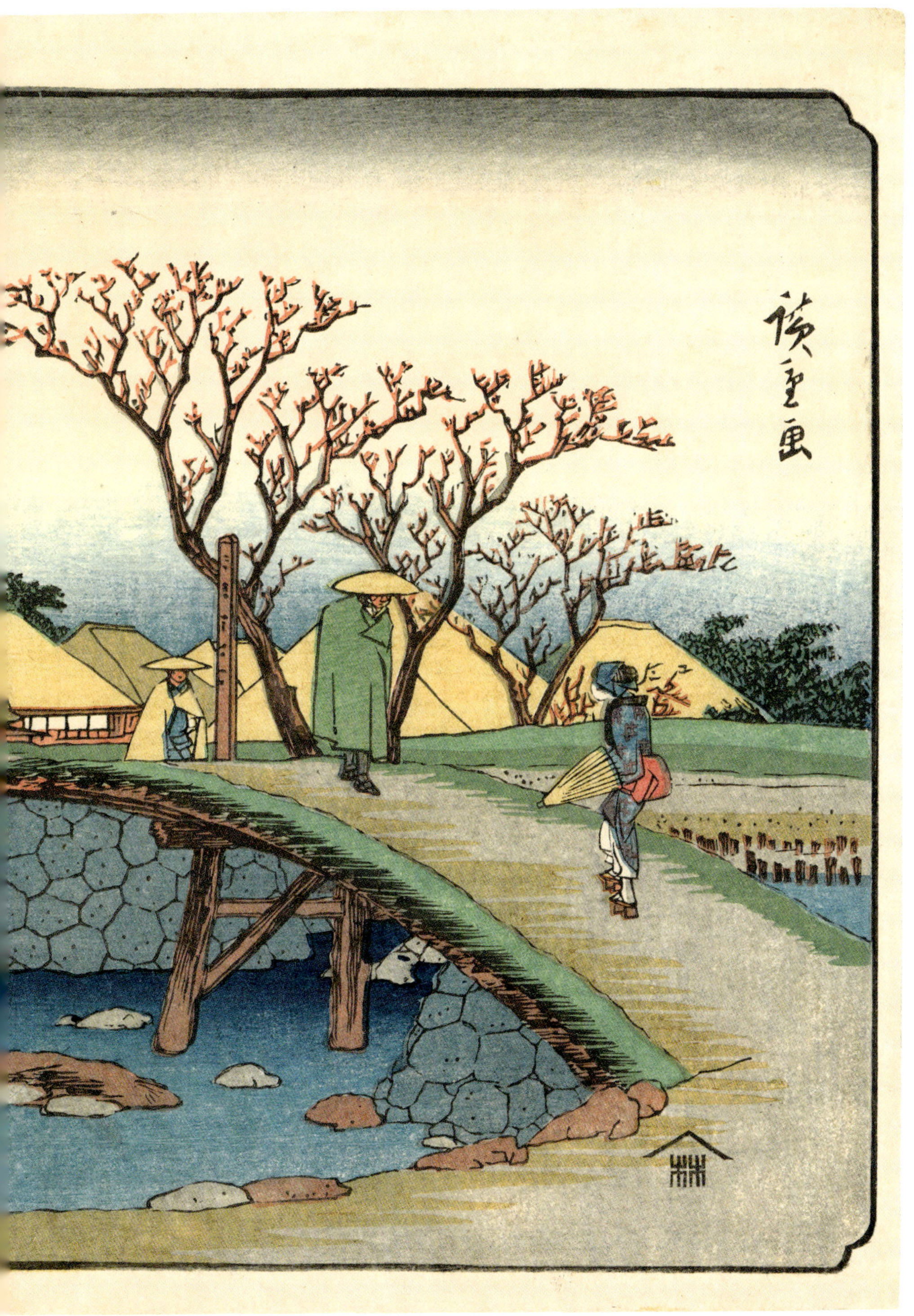

58

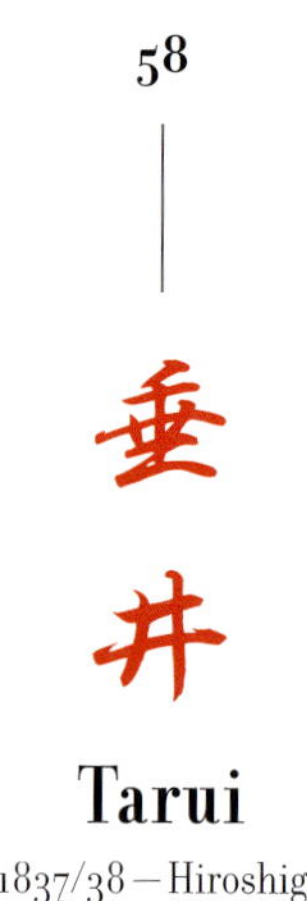

Tarui

1837/38 — Hiroshige

Between Tarui and the next station, Sekigahara, lies the Ai River, a tributary of the Kuise that flows out into Ise Bay. Tarui was not only a post station on the Kisokaidō, but also a terminal point of the Minoji (i.e. Mino Road), which connected the Kisokaidō with the Tōkaidō, the coastal route between Edo and Kyoto. At 60 kilometres (37 miles) in length, the Minoji was equipped with nine stations between Tarui on the Kisokaidō and the Tōkaidō station Miya.

The avenue of pine trees along the road in the background, the stone-fortified entrance to the town and the stores on either side of the road follow, albeit in greater detail, Hiroshige's sketch of this station made during his journey to Kyoto. To animate the scene, he added in the arrival of a lord's procession during a shower of rain. The village alderman is rushing up to greet the procession with an umbrella in his hand. The lord is being conveyed in the green sedan chair that appears in the background. Other travellers and store-owners are kneeling along both sides of the road to pay their respects.

Hiroshige did not indicate in his sketch what kind of businesses operated in the houses at the end of the road. The one on the left is advertising *ochazuke*, a simple dish of hot tea, broth or hot water poured over boiled rice and topped with savouries. In a humorous twist, both the stores in the print also appear to be selling woodblock designs; the one on the left even carries the emblem of Iseya Rihei, the publisher of this print, suggesting that it would be his store. Examples of the prints of beautiful women and landscapes for sale are pasted on the walls. The three horizontal landscape prints in the right-hand store may represent the stations at Kakegawa, Hara and Kawasaki from Hiroshige's earlier *Hōeidō Tōkaidō* series.

Zwischen Tarui und der nächsten Station Sekigahara liegt der Ai, ein Nebenfluss des Kuise, der sich seinerseits über Umwege in die Ise-Bucht ergießt. Tarui war nicht nur Poststation am Kisokaidō, sondern

360

auch Endpunkt des Minoji, der den Kisokaidō mit dem Tōkaidō, der Küstenroute zwischen Edo und Kyoto, verband. Auf ihren 60 Kilometern Länge verlief diese Mino-Straße zwischen Tarui auf dem Kisokaidō und der Tōkaidō-Station Miya durch neun Poststationen.

Die Kiefernallee im Hintergrund, der mit Steinmauern befestigte Ortseingang und die Geschäfte auf beiden Seiten der Straße entsprechen, abgesehen vom größeren Detailreichtum, der Skizze, die Hiroshige auf seiner Reise nach Kyoto anfertigte. Zur Belebung der Szene fügte er die Ankunft einer *daimyō*-Prozession während eines Regenschauers hinzu. Der Dorfälteste eilt mit einem Regenschirm in der Hand herbei, um den Zug zu begrüßen. Die Anwesenheit des Fürsten wird durch die grüne Sänfte angedeutet, die im Hintergrund auftaucht. Andere Reisende und die Geschäftsinhaber knien auf beiden Seiten der Straße, um ihm Respekt zu zollen.

In Hiroshiges Skizze fehlt jeglicher Hinweis auf die Art der Geschäfte in den Häusern am Ende der Straße. Auf der linken Seite wird für *ochazuke* geworben, eine einfache Speise, für die heißer Tee, Brühe oder heißes Wasser über gekochten Reis gegossen und das Ganze mit Appetithappen garniert wird. Es zeugt von einem gewissen Humor, dass beide Geschäfte anscheinend auch Holzschnitte verkaufen; vor dem linken prangt sogar das Firmenlogo von Iseya Rihei, dem Verleger dieses Drucks, so als würde ihm der Laden gehören. An den Wänden kleben Beispiele der zum Verkauf angebotenen Darstellungen schöner Frauen und Landschaften. Die drei querformatigen Landschaftsdrucke im Geschäft rechts könnten die Stationen Kakegawa, Hara und Kawasaki aus dem *Hōeidō-Tōkaidō* darstellen, Hiroshiges erster Tōkaidō-Serie.

Entre Tarui et la station suivante de Sekigahara coule l'Ai, affluent de la Kuise qui se jette dans la baie d'Ise. Tarui était non seulement un relais de poste sur la Kisokaidō, mais aussi le terminus de la Minoji (littéralement, route Mino) qui reliait la Kisokaidō et la Tōkaidō, la route du littoral entre Edo et Kyoto. Longue de 60 kilomètres, la Minoji comptait neuf stations entre Tarui, sur la Kisokaidō, et Miya, la station de la Tōkaidō.

L'alignement de pins qui bordent la route à l'arrière-plan, l'entrée fortifiée en pierres et les échoppes situées de part et d'autre de la route imitent, de manière plus détaillée, le croquis réalisé par Hiroshige pour cette station alors qu'il se rendait à Kyoto. Pour donner plus de vie à la scène, l'artiste a ajouté l'arrivée de la procession d'un seigneur sous une averse. Un parapluie à la main, l'échevin du village se précipite pour accueillir la procession. Le seigneur est transporté dans la chaise à porteurs verte que l'on aperçoit à l'arrière-plan. D'autres voyageurs, ainsi que les propriétaires des échoppes, sont agenouillés de chaque côté de la route en signe d'hommage.

Dans son croquis, Hiroshige n'a pas indiqué la nature des boutiques installées au bout de la route. Celle de gauche propose de l'*ochazuke*, mets ordinaire composé de thé chaud, de bouillon ou d'eau chaude, que l'on verse sur du riz bouilli et pimente d'ingrédients salés. Clin d'œil humoristique, les deux boutiques semblent aussi vendre des xylogravures ; celle de gauche porte même l'emblème d'Iseya Rihei, l'éditeur de cette estampe, indice qu'il pourrait s'agir de son échoppe. Des échantillons d'estampes de belles femmes et de paysages à vendre sont affichés sur les murs. Les trois estampes horizontales de paysages visibles dans la boutique de droite pourraient représenter les stations de Kakegawa, Hara et Kawasaki, figurant dans la série antérieure d'Hiroshige, *Hōeidō Tōkaidō*.

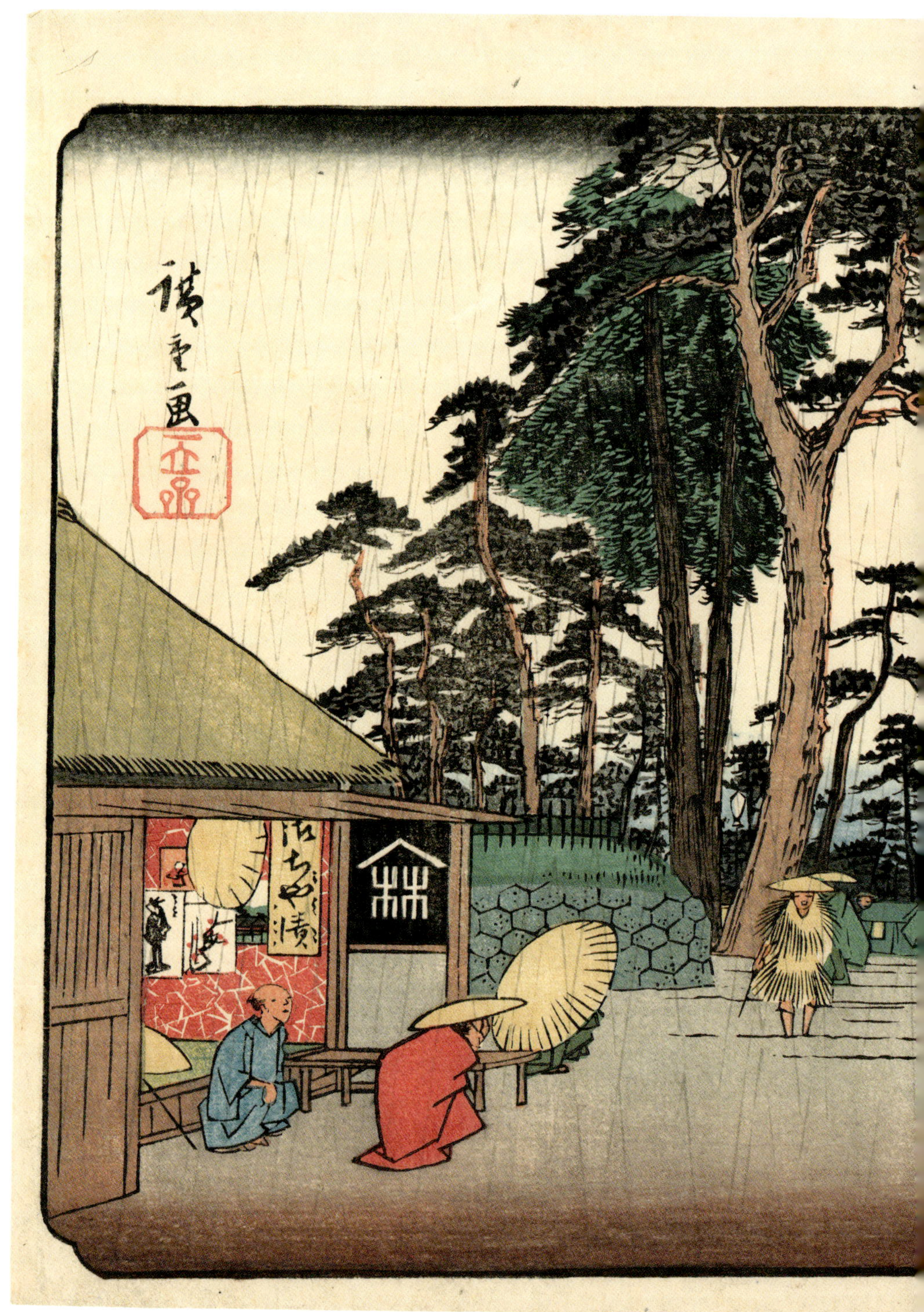

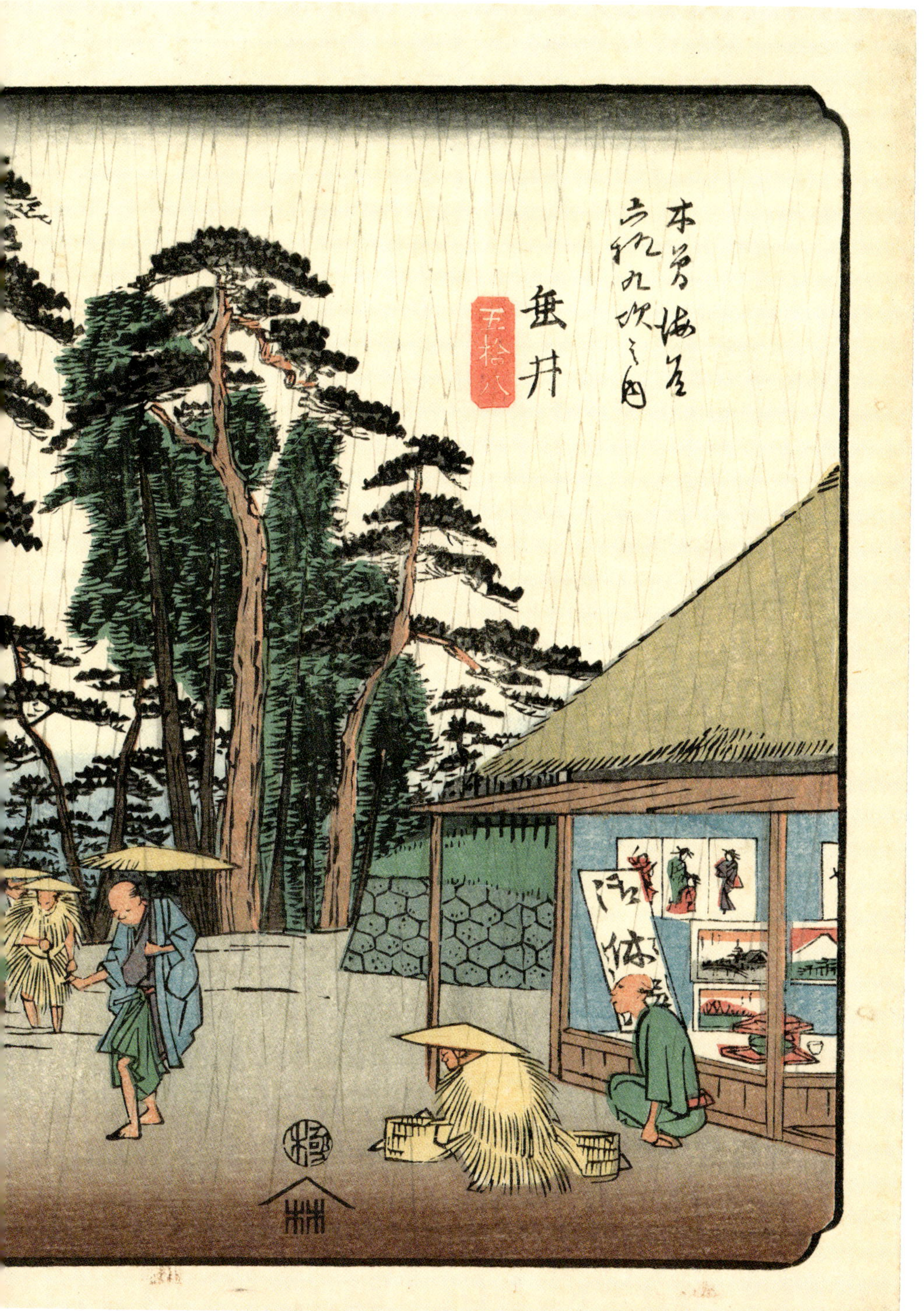

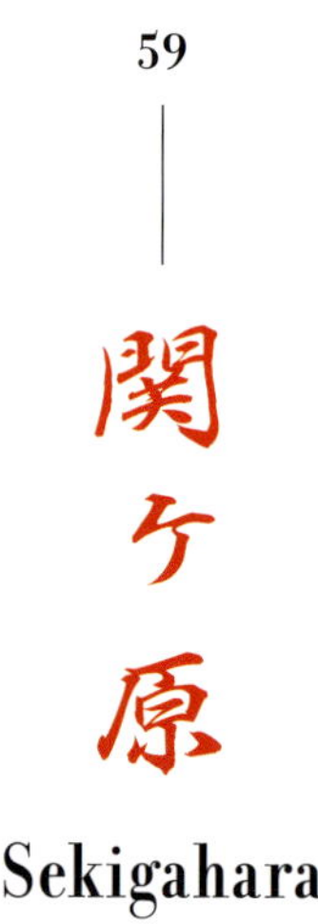

59

Sekigahara

1837/38 — Hiroshige

Sekigahara, meaning "checkpoint in the field", is a name synonymous with the blood-soaked struggles for power in Japanese history. In 672, the Jinshin War broke out near here in a dispute over the imperial succession. The ascension to the throne of Prince Ōtomo (Emperor Kōbun, 648–672), the son of the deceased Emperor Tenji (626–671), was challenged by the late emperor's brother, Prince Ōama, with the backing of a substantial military force. The latter was victorious and proceeded to claim the throne, being posthumously known as Emperor Tenmu (631–686). In 1600, almost a millennium later, the cataclysmic Battle of Sekigahara broke out when the forces of general Tokugawa Ieyasu defeated those of Ishida Mitsunari (1560–1600). The outcome of the conflict was the Tokugawa shogunate, which would rule Japan until the middle of the 19th century.

The rise of Ieyasu in the early 17th century heralded the beginning of a period of relative peace that would last two and a half centuries. As civil war faded from popular memory, the village prospered as a result of its situation at the junction of the Kisokaidō, Hokkoku Kaidō (North Country Road) and Isekaidō (Ise Road) roads. Hiroshige's design gives no indication of the district's wartime history, and instead depicts a scene showing a tea stall with a thatched roof catering to travellers along a wooded section of the road at Sekigahara that speaks of its mercantile character and scenic charm.

The season is spring, as indicated by a red blossoming plum tree. The round red-and-white lantern announces the shop's speciality: sweet rice cakes. To the left, a rectangular menu advertises two other dishes available: buckwheat noodles (*soba kiri*) and wheat noodles (*undon*, more generally known as *udon* today). An elderly waitress is welcoming a guest in a green jacket with a cup of tea. Seated opposite him, another traveller is beginning to tuck into what appears to be a serving of the aforementioned rice cakes. Nearby, a pack-horse driver is hovering, hoping to pick up a customer. Other than refreshments, the stall offers a range of items essential for travellers, including paper fans, umbrellas and plaited straw sandals.

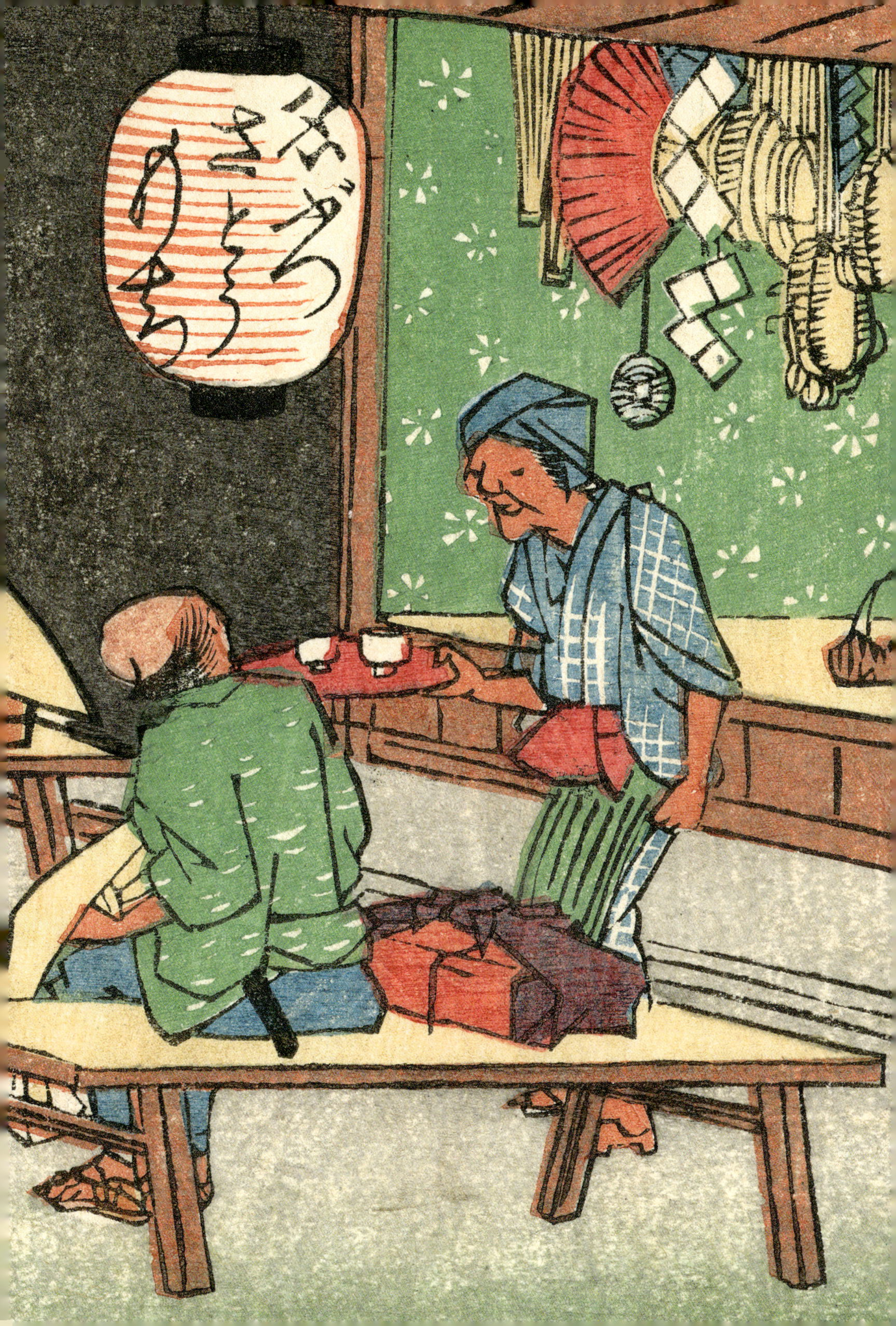

はし本
うどん
そば

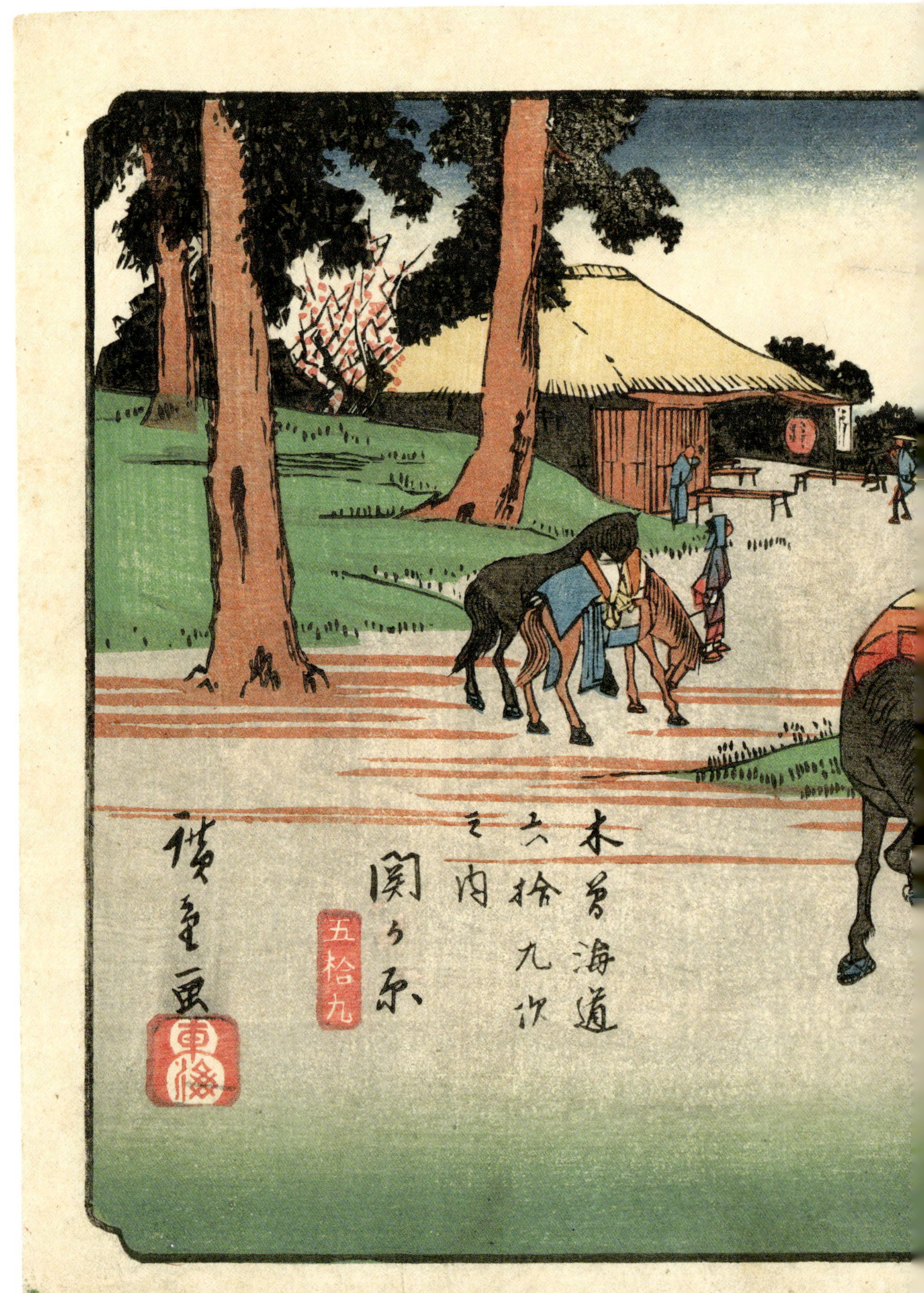

木曽海道
六拾九次
之内
関ヶ原
五拾九
廣重画

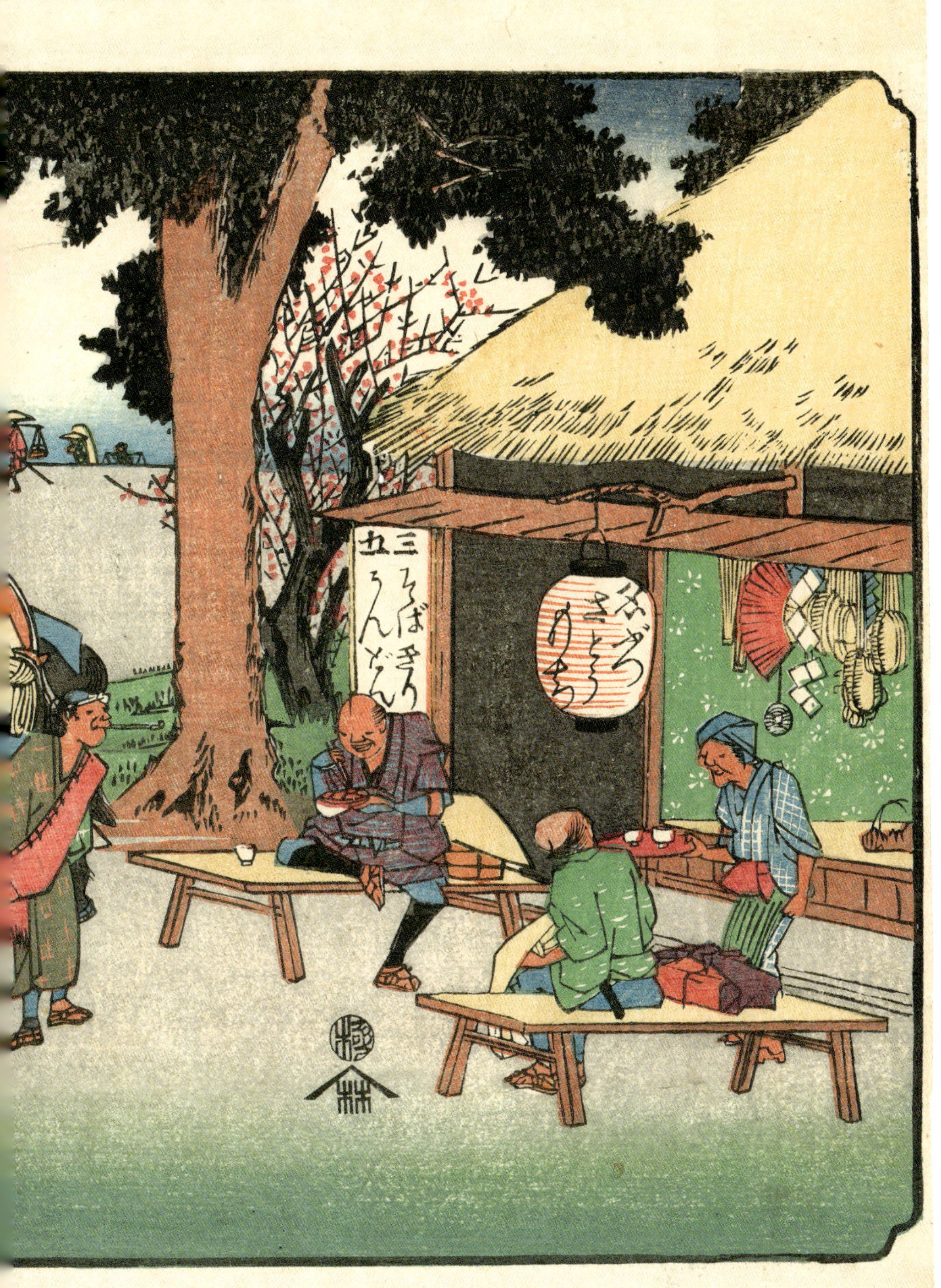

Der Name Sekigahara oder „Kontrollpunkt im Felde" steht für zwei blutgetränkte Machtkämpfe in der japanischen Geschichte. 672 brach hier in der Nähe über einen kaiserlichen Erbfolgestreit der Jinshin-Krieg aus. Die Thronbesteigung des Prinzen Ōtomo (648–672), der als Kaiser Kōbun seinem verstorbenen Vater, Kaiser Tenji (626–671), nachfolgte, wurde von Tenjis Bruder, dem Prinzen Ōama, mit Unterstützung einer schlagkräftigen Militärmacht angefochten. Der siegreiche Ōama bestieg schließlich den Thron und wurde posthum als Kaiser Tenmu (631–686) bekannt. Im Jahr 1600, fast ein Jahrtausend später, besiegte die von General Tokugawa Ieyasu angeführte Armee in der verheerenden Schlacht von Sekigahara die Truppen des Heerführers Ishida Mitsunari (1560–1600). Aus dem Konflikt ging das Tokugawa-Shogunat hervor, das Japan bis in die zweite Hälfte des 19. Jahrhunderts regierte.

Ieyasus Aufstieg Anfang des 17. Jahrhunderts läutete den Beginn einer Phase relativen Friedens ein, die zweieinhalb Jahrhunderte andauern sollte. Während der Bürgerkrieg allmählich aus der Erinnerung der Menschen verschwand, blühte das Dorf an der Kreuzung von Kisokaidō, Hokkoku Kaidō (Nordland-straße) und Isekaidō (Ise-Straße) auf. Hiroshiges Entwurf enthält keinen Hinweis auf die kriegerische Geschichte der Gegend, sondern zeugt eher von der kaufmännischen Prägung und vom landschaftlichen Charme des Ortes. Die Szene zeigt einen Verkaufsstand mit strohgedecktem Dach, der an einem baumreichen Abschnitt der Straße bei Sekigahara Reisende mit Tee versorgt.

Ein rot blühender Pflaumenbaum kündet vom Frühling. Der runde rot-weiße Lampion wirbt für die Spezialität des Hauses, süße Reiskuchen. Links daneben preist eine rechteckige Speisekarte zwei weitere Gerichte an, *soba kiri* und *undon* (heute bekannter unter der Bezeichnung *udon*), Buchweizen- und Weizennudeln. Eine ältere Serviererin begrüßt einen Gast in grüner Jacke mit einer Tasse Tee. Ihm gegenüber sitzt ein weiterer Reisender und macht sich wohl über eine Portion der zuvor erwähnten Reiskuchen her. Nicht weit davon entfernt steht ein Packpferdtreiber in der Hoffnung auf Kunden. Neben Erfrischungen bietet der Verkaufsstand eine Reihe wichtiger Reiseutensilien an, darunter Papierfächer, Schirme und geflochtene Strohsandalen.

Sekigahara, c'est-à-dire « poste de contrôle dans le champ », est synonyme des combats sanglants pour le pouvoir qui ont marqué l'histoire du Japon. En 672 éclate dans les environs la guerre de Jinshin, en raison d'un conflit à propos de la succession impériale. L'accession au trône du prince Ōtomo (l'empereur Kōbun, 648–672), fils de l'empereur défunt Tenji (626–671), est remise en cause par le prince Ōama, frère du souverain décédé, qui dispose du soutien d'une force militaire considérable. Après sa victoire, ce dernier revendique le trône et sera connu, à titre posthume, sous le nom d'empereur Tenmu (631–686). En 1600, près d'un millénaire plus tard, la bataille cataclysmique de Sekigahara voit les forces du général Tokugawa Ieyasu écraser celles d'Ishida Mitsunari (1560–1600). Ce conflit donnera naissance au shogunat des Tokugawa, qui règnera sur le Japon jusqu'au milieu du XIXe siècle.

L'ascension d'Ieyasu au début du XVIIe siècle correspond à l'avènement d'une période de paix relative qui allait durer deux siècles et demi. À mesure que la guerre civile disparaissait de la mémoire collective, le village prospéra grâce à sa situation au carrefour de la Kisokaidō, de l'Hokkoku Kaidō (route rurale du nord) et de l'Isekaidō (route d'Ise). L'estampe d'Hiroshige ne laisse rien deviner de l'histoire guerrière de la région ; l'artiste a préféré dépeindre une scène composée d'une échoppe de thé au toit de chaume, accueillant les voyageurs dans une partie boisée de la route à Sekigahara, évoquant le caractère marchand et le paysage séduisant du lieu.

Nous sommes au printemps, comme l'indique un prunier rouge en fleurs. La lanterne ronde, rouge et blanche proclame la spécialité de l'échoppe : des gâteaux à la farine de riz. À gauche de la lanterne, un menu rectangulaire annonce deux autres plats : nouilles de sarrasin (*soba kiri*) et nouilles de blé (*undon*, aujourd'hui plus couramment connues sous le nom d'*udon*). Une serveuse âgée accueille avec une tasse de thé un hôte vêtu d'une veste verte. En face de lui se trouve un autre voyageur qui s'apprête à entamer un gâteau à la farine de riz. Un conducteur de cheval de bât tourne autour d'eux dans l'espoir de trouver un client. Outre des rafraîchissements, l'échoppe propose des articles indispensables aux voyageurs, comme des éventails en papier, des ombrelles et des sandales en paille tressée.

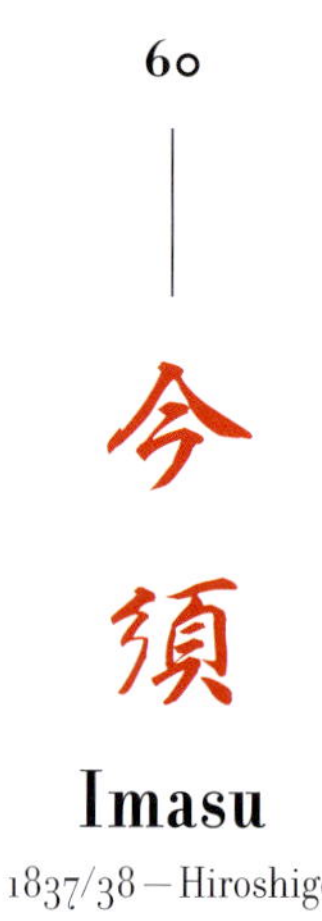

60

今須

Imasu

1837/38 – Hiroshige

The Imasu station was right on the border between the provinces of Mino in the east and Ōmi in the west. This border was marked by a stone signpost in the centre of the town reading "Kōnō Ryōkokukyō" (Ōmi-Mino Two-Country Border), which Hiroshige incorporated into his design. Because of its unusual location, Imasu was dubbed the "Sleep-Talk Village" (Nemonogatari no sato), suggesting that people from different provinces could talk to each other from their beds. A hint of this was included by Hiroshige in the signboard to the left of the post that reads "origins of sleep talk" (Nemonogatari yurai).

The guidebook Views of Famous Sights along the Kiso Road (Kisoji meisho zue) from 1805 features an image of the road through the town with signposts set up in front of the spaces between the houses on either side. These gaps are absent from Hiroshige's sketch, which he drew during his journey to Kyoto. The sketch does, however, include annotations about the nature of this locale that are not usually found in his sketches. One such note reads "Fuwa no sekiya" which Hiroshige added to the signboard on the far left, indicating that this was the location for the Fuwa Barrier Post, a guardhouse dating from the late 7th century and which was located on the ancient Tōsandō road.

The signboard above the two men lighting their pipes on the left is not derived from the sketch but is instead an example of product placement – an advertisement for the face powder Bien Senjokō, which was sold in Edo.

Die Station Imasu lag direkt auf der Grenze zwischen den Provinzen Mino im Osten und Ōmi im Westen. Der Grenzverlauf wurde in der Ortsmitte durch einen Markstein mit der Inschrift „Kōnō Ryōkokukyō“ (Zweiländergrenze Ōmi-Mino) gekennzeichnet, den Hiroshige in seinen Entwurf aufnahm. Wegen seiner ungewöhnlichen Lage nannte man Imasu auch das „Dorf des Bettgeflüsters“ (*Nemonogatari no sato*): Hier konnten sich Menschen aus verschiedenen Provinzen von ihren Betten aus miteinander unterhalten. Hiroshige griff diese Besonderheit in dem Schriftzug „Ursprung des Bettgeflüsters“ (*Nemonogatari yurai*) auf, den er auf dem Ausleger links der Stele platzierte.

Ein Bild des Ortsdurchgangs im Reiseführer *Ansichten berühmter Stätten an der Kiso-Straße* (*Kisoji meisho zue*) von 1805 zeigt zwischen den Häusern auf beiden Seiten der Straße Lücken, vor denen Hinweisschilder aufgestellt waren. Diese Lücken fehlen in der Skizze, die Hiroshige während seiner Reise nach Kyoto zeichnete. Dafür enthält sie Anmerkungen zu den Besonderheiten dieser Örtlichkeit, wie sie in seinen Skizzen normalerweise nicht vorkommen. Eine dieser Anmerkungen lautet „Fuwa no sekiya“ und wurde vom Künstler in das Ladenschild ganz links eingefügt, um damit den Standort der Wegsperre Fuwa kenntlich zu machen, einer Wache aus dem späten 7. Jahrhundert, die an der alten Tōsandō-Straße stand.

Die Tafel über den beiden Männern, die ihre Pfeifen anzünden, war nicht Bestandteil der Skizze. Mit ihrer Werbung für den Gesichtspuder Bien Senjokō, der in Edo verkauft wurde, ist sie ein frühes Beispiel für Product Placement.

La station d'Imasu se trouvait exactement sur la frontière séparant les provinces de Mino à l'est et d'Ōmi à l'ouest. Cette frontière était matérialisée par un poteau indicateur en pierre, situé au centre du village et sur lequel on pouvait lire « Kōnō Ryōkokukyō » (frontière entre les deux pays Ōmi et Mino), qu'Hiroshige a intégré dans son dessin. En raison de sa situation insolite, Imasu était surnommé le « village où l'on parle en dormant » (*Nemonogatari no sato*), évoquant la manière dont les habitants des deux provinces pouvaient se parler depuis leur lit respectif. L'artiste y fait allusion dans l'enseigne située à gauche du poteau indicateur, sur laquelle on peut lire « origines du parler en dormant » (*Nemonogatari yurai*).

Dans le guide de voyage *Collection de vues de paysages célèbres sur la route Kiso* (*Kisoji meisho zue*) de 1805 se trouve une image de la route traversant la petite ville, bordée de poteaux indicateurs placés devant les espaces qui séparent les maisons de part et d'autre. Ces espaces n'apparaissent pas dans le croquis réalisé par Hiroshige pendant son voyage vers Kyoto. En revanche, ce croquis comprend des annotations sur la nature du lieu que l'on ne trouve généralement pas dans ses esquisses. L'artiste a ajouté l'une d'elles, « Fuwa no sekiya » sur l'enseigne située à l'extrême gauche, indiquant qu'il s'agit du site du poste-frontière de Fuwa, maison des gardes datant du VIIe siècle qui se trouvait sur l'ancienne route Tōsandō.

L'enseigne située au-dessus des deux hommes qui allument leur pipe ne vient pas du croquis, mais constitue un exemple de « placement de produit » : c'est une publicité pour la poudre de riz Bien Senjokō, que l'on vendait à Edo.

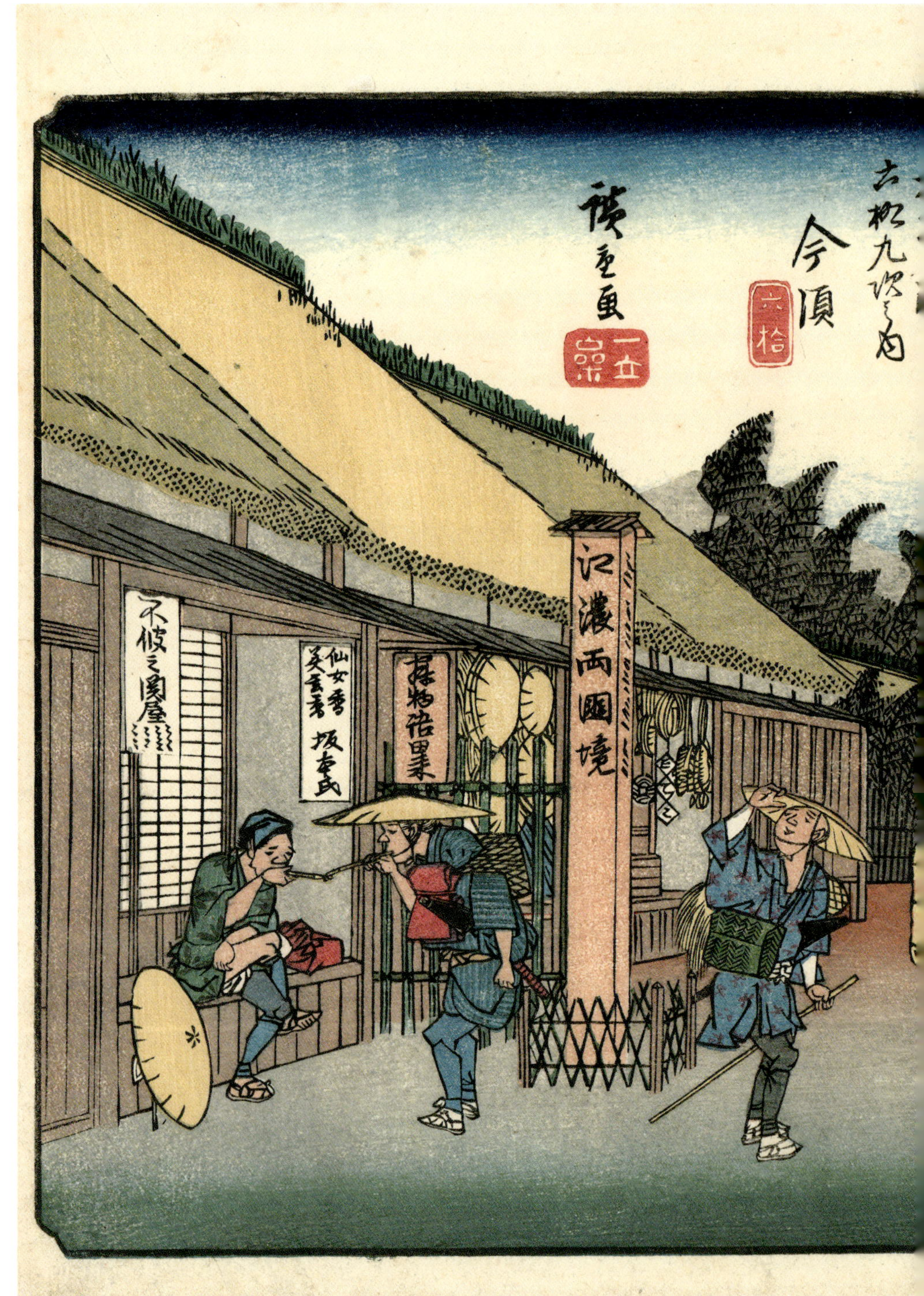
六拾九次之内
今須
廣重画
六拾
一立齋
江濃両國境
不彼ゝ關屋
仙女香
美玉署
坂本氏
名物諸果

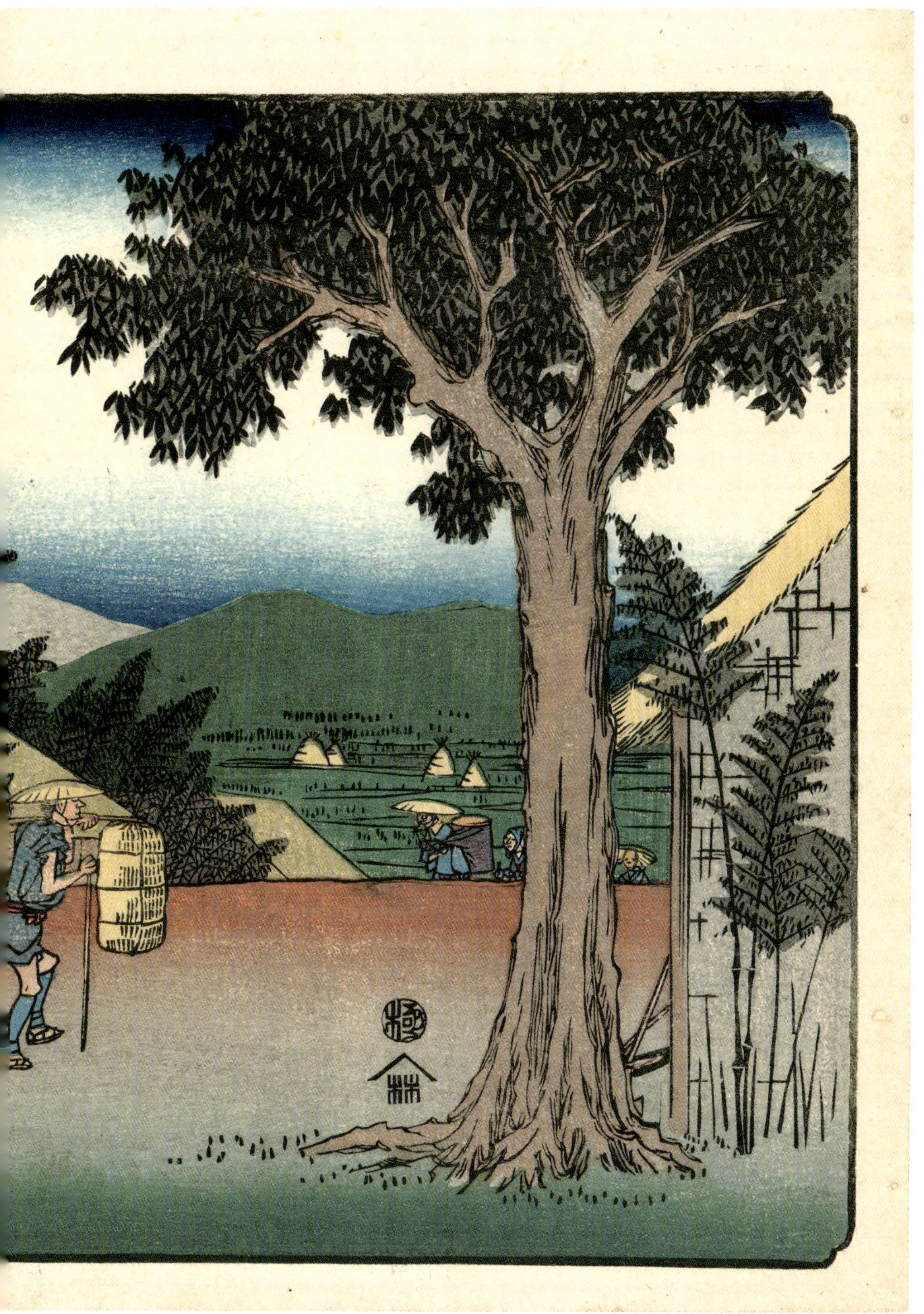

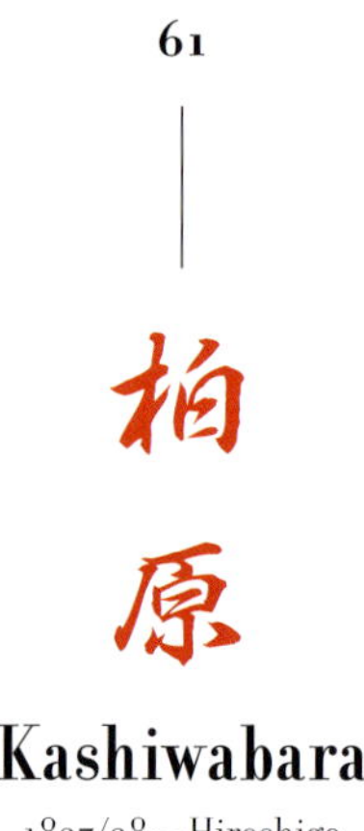

Kashiwabara

1837/38 — Hiroshige

Kashiwabara, the first station along the Kisokaidō in Ōmi Province, was established as a post station as early as 646. The village appears in the late 14th-century epic *Chronicle of Great Peace (Taiheiki)*, a fictionalised historical record that retells the intrigues and battles which occured between 1318 and 1367. By 1724, the village had 475 houses and a population of 1,654, but was devastated by a large fire in 1767 that destroyed 75 of the houses, and again four years later, with the loss of 47 more.

Hiroshige concentrates here on a single store, the Kameya. During his journey to Kyoto he drew a sketch of the Kameya to which he added details and annotations that are found only rarely in his sketches.

The Kameya Sakyō began operating in 1661 and still exists today, selling *Ibuki mogusa*, dried mugwort from Ibuki which is used for moxibustion (in which the plant is burned in various ways for medicinal purposes). The mugwort is depicted in the middle of the store as a large green pile of fluff that is in the process of being packaged into small envelopes, which are arranged around the pile as well as on the far right of the store. A *fukusuke* doll with a very large head is standing on a platform in the right corner to bring good luck. The left side of the building is a teahouse where travellers could have a meal of fish, *sake* or *Kintoki mochi*, a small sort of confectionery made of sticky rice. Travellers could enjoy the view of the garden with its stone lanterns and pond. In the left corner is a statue of Kintarō, a legendary child folk hero who is identified with the warrior Sakata Kintoki, after whom the type of *mochi* sold here is named.

Kashiwabara, die erste Station des Kisokaidō in der Provinz Ōmi, wurde bereits 646 als Poststation gegründet. Das Dorf taucht in dem Epos *Chronik des großen Friedens (Taiheiki)* aus dem späten

14. Jahrhundert auf, das ein historisches Dokument fingiert und Intrigen und Schlachten zwischen 1318 und 1367 nacherzählt. Der Ort war im Jahr 1724 auf 475 Häuser und 1654 Einwohner angewachsen, wurde jedoch 1767 von einem Großbrand heimgesucht, der 75 Häuser vernichtete, und vier Jahre später von einem weiteren Feuer, dem wiederum 47 Häuser zum Opfer fielen.

Hiroshige konzentriert sich hier auf ein einzelnes Geschäft, das Kameya. Auf seiner Reise nach Kyoto fertigte er davon eine Skizze und fügte ihr Detailangaben und Anmerkungen hinzu, wie man sie in seinen Skizzen nur selten findet.

Das Kameya Sakyō nahm 1661 seinen Betrieb auf und existiert noch heute. Es handelt mit *Ibuki mogusa*, getrocknetem Beifuß aus Ibuki, der für die Moxibustion oder Moxa-Therapie verwendet wird, bei der die Pflanzenfasern zu medizinischen Zwecken auf verschiedene Weise verbrannt werden. Der Beifuß, im Zentrum des Ladenlokals als flaumiger grüner Berg dargestellt, wird gerade in kleine Kuverts abgepackt, die dann rund um den Haufen und ganz rechts im Bild zum Verkauf dekoriert werden. Eine *fukusuke*-Puppe mit übergroßem Kopf steht als Glücksbringer rechts in der Ecke auf einem Podest. Im Teehaus in der linken Hälfte des Gebäudes konnten Reisende Fisch, Sake und *Kintoki mochi*, kleine Süßwaren aus klebrigem Reis, bestellen und die Aussicht auf den Garten mit seinen Steinlaternen und einem Teich genießen. In der linken Ecke steht eine Statue des legendären Volkshelden Kintarō. Der Junge mit den übermenschlichen Kräften wird mit dem Krieger Sakata Kintoki gleichgesetzt, nach dem die hier verkaufte *mochi*-Sorte benannt ist.

Première station de la Kisokaidō située dans la province d'Ōmi, Kashiwabara est devenue un relais de poste dès 646. Ce village est mentionné dans la *Chronique de la grande paix (Taiheiki)*, épopée de la fin du XIVe siècle et récit historique romancé qui relate les intrigues et les batailles ayant eu lieu de 1318 à 1367. En 1724, le village comptait 475 maisons et 1654 habitants, mais il fut ravagé par un grand incendie en 1767, qui détruisit 75 maisons, puis par un autre incendie quatre ans plus tard, dans lequel 47 maisons disparurent.

Hiroshige s'est intéressé à un seul magasin, le Kameya. Au cours de son périple jusqu'à Kyoto, il avait dessiné un croquis du Kameya, auquel il ajouta des détails et des annotations assez rares dans ses autres esquisses.

C'est en 1661 qu'a débuté l'activité du Kameya Sakyō, magasin qui existe toujours aujourd'hui. On y vend de l'*Ibuki mogusa*, armoise commune d'Ibuki employée pour la moxibustion (technique dans laquelle la plante est brûlée de différentes manières à des fins médicinales). Dans cette estampe, l'armoise est représentée au milieu du magasin sous la forme d'un grand tas vert pelucheux que l'on est en train d'emballer dans de petites enveloppes disposées autour du tas, ainsi qu'à l'extrême droite du magasin. Une poupée *fukusuke* à grosse tête est juchée sur un piédestal dans l'angle de droite, en guise de porte-bonheur. La partie gauche du bâtiment est une maison de thé où les voyageurs pouvaient se restaurer avec un plat de poisson, du saké ou un *Kintoki mochi*, petite sucrerie faite avec du riz gluant. Les clients pouvaient profiter de la vue sur le jardin, avec ses lanternes de pierre et son étang. Dans l'angle de gauche, on peut voir une statue de Kintarō, enfant-héros populaire et légendaire considéré comme le guerrier Sakata Kintoki, qui a donné son nom au type de *mochi* vendu dans ce magasin.

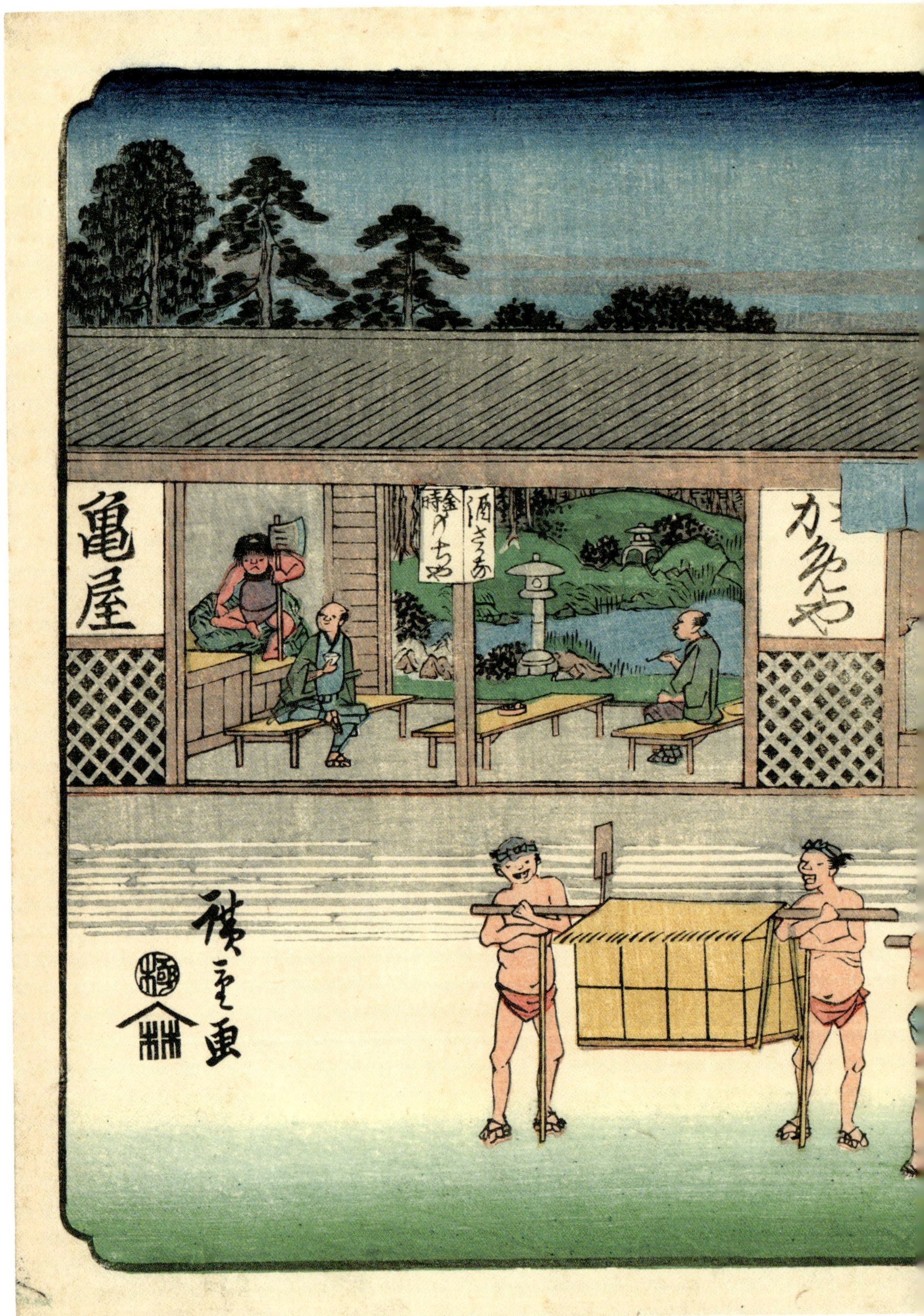
亀屋
かめや
酒さゝゑ
時ゝあり
金ゑあ
つうちや

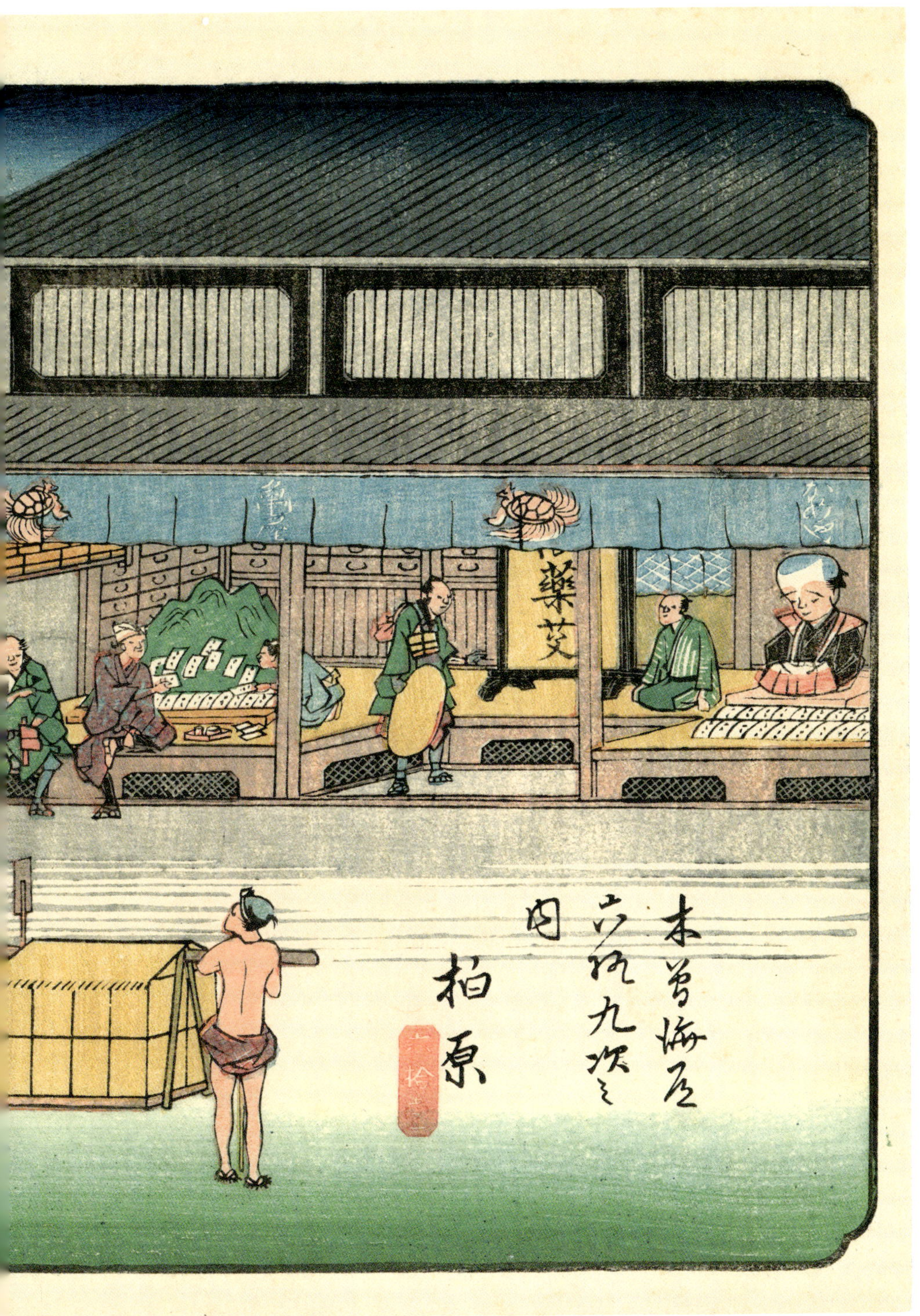

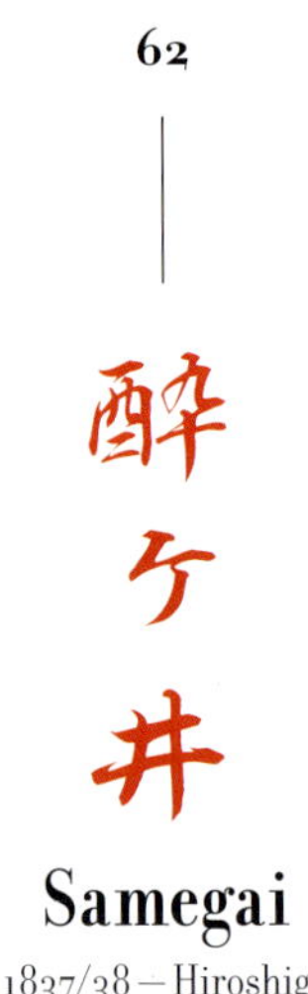

Samegai

1837/38 — Hiroshige

Samegai is mentioned in the *Chronicles of Japan* (*Nihon shoki*), a collection of historical records that was completed in 720. This station was known for its clear springs of water and remarkable rocks, of which it had quite a few, to be precise: Three Waters and Four Rocks (*Sansui shiseki*). The three springs, Isame no shimizu, Jūōsui and Saigyōsui are sources of the Jizō River. The four rocks are Yamato Takeru no mikoto no koshikake-ishi (lit. rock on which Prince Yamato Takeru sat), Kurakake-ishi (lit. saddle-seat rock), Kani-ishi (lit. crab rock) and Egō-seki (lit. shadow-defying rock).

Neither the Three Waters nor the Four Rocks are, however, motifs used in Hiroshige's design, which is based on a sketch he made when he reached Samegai on his journey to Kyoto. Hiroshige created a view of the houses on the east side of the village as travellers approached. At the end of the west side of the village, again not depicted here, was a line of six inns in succession called the Rokken Chaya, literally six teahouses. Further downhill, not depicted here either, is Lake Biwa. The earliest edition of this print includes a mountain peak faintly visible in the distance that could be Mount Hira on the other side of the lake. This mountain is an addition to the print design that doesn't appear in Hiroshige's sketch.

Samegai wird in den *Chroniken Japans (Nihon shoki)* erwähnt, einer im Jahr 720 abgeschlossenen Sammlung mit Schilderungen historischer Begebenheiten. Die Station war für ihre klaren Wasserquellen und auffälligen Felsen bekannt, von denen es jeweils mehrere gab, genauer: „Drei Wasser und vier Felsen" *(Sansui shiseki)*, wie die Bezeichnung lautete. Die drei Quellen Isame no shimizu, Jūōsui und Saigyōsui bilden den Ursprung des Jizō, die vier Felsen heißen Yamato Takeru no mikoto no koshikake-ishi (wörtlich: der Felsen, auf dem Prinz Yamato Takeru saß), Kurakake-ishi (wörtlich: Sattelsitzfelsen), Kani-ishi (wörtlich: Krabbenfelsen) und Egō-seki (wörtlich: dem Schatten trotzender Felsen).

Hiroshige aber verwendete weder die „drei Wasser" noch die „vier Felsen" als Motive für seinen Entwurf. Er basiert auf einer Skizze, die der Künstler auf seiner Reise nach Kyoto bei der Ankunft in Samegai anfertigte, und die gewählte Ansicht zeigt die aus der Sicht des Reisenden am östlichen Dorfeingang gelegenen Häuser. Am anderen, westlichen Ende des Dorfes stand, hier nicht abgebildet, eine zusammenhängende Reihe von sechs Herbergen, die man die Rokken Chaya nannte, die „sechs Teehäuser". Weiter hügelabwärts und wiederum jenseits der hier gezeigten Szene liegt der Biwa-See. Die erste Auflage dieses Drucks zeigt einen in der Ferne kaum sichtbaren Berggipfel, möglicherweise der Hira am anderen Seeufer. Der Berg fehlt in Hiroshiges Skizze und wurde für die Druckvorlage hinzugefügt.

Samegai est mentionné dans les *Chroniques du Japon (Nihon shoki)*, recueil de comptes rendus historiques, achevé en 720. Cette station était connue pour ses sources d'eau limpide et ses rochers remarquables dont elle comptait plusieurs exemplaires, les Trois Eaux et les Quatre Rochers *(Sansui shiseki)* pour être précis. Les trois sources, Isame no shimizu, Jūōsui et Saigyōsui, sont aussi la source de la rivière Jizō. Les quatre rochers ont été baptisés Yamato Takeru no mikoto no koshikake-ishi (« le rocher où s'assit le prince Yamato Takeru »), Kurakake-ishi (« le rocher en forme de selle »), Kani-ishi (« le rocher en forme de crabe ») et Egō-seki (« le rocher qui défie l'ombre »).

Pourtant, ni les Trois Eaux ni les Quatre Rochers ne sont des motifs de l'estampe d'Hiroshige ; celle-ci s'inspire d'un croquis réalisé par l'artiste en arrivant à Samegai, durant son voyage vers Kyoto. Il a représenté une vue des maisons du village quand on vient de l'est. À l'extrémité ouest de Samegai, invisible sur ce dessin, six auberges se succédaient, appelées Rokken Chaya, les six maisons de thé. En contrebas de la colline se trouve le lac Biwa qui, lui non plus, n'est pas illustré ici. La toute première édition de cette estampe comprend un sommet à peine visible au loin, qui pourrait être le mont Hira situé de l'autre côté du lac. Ajoutée à l'estampe, cette montagne ne figure pas dans le croquis d'Hiroshige.

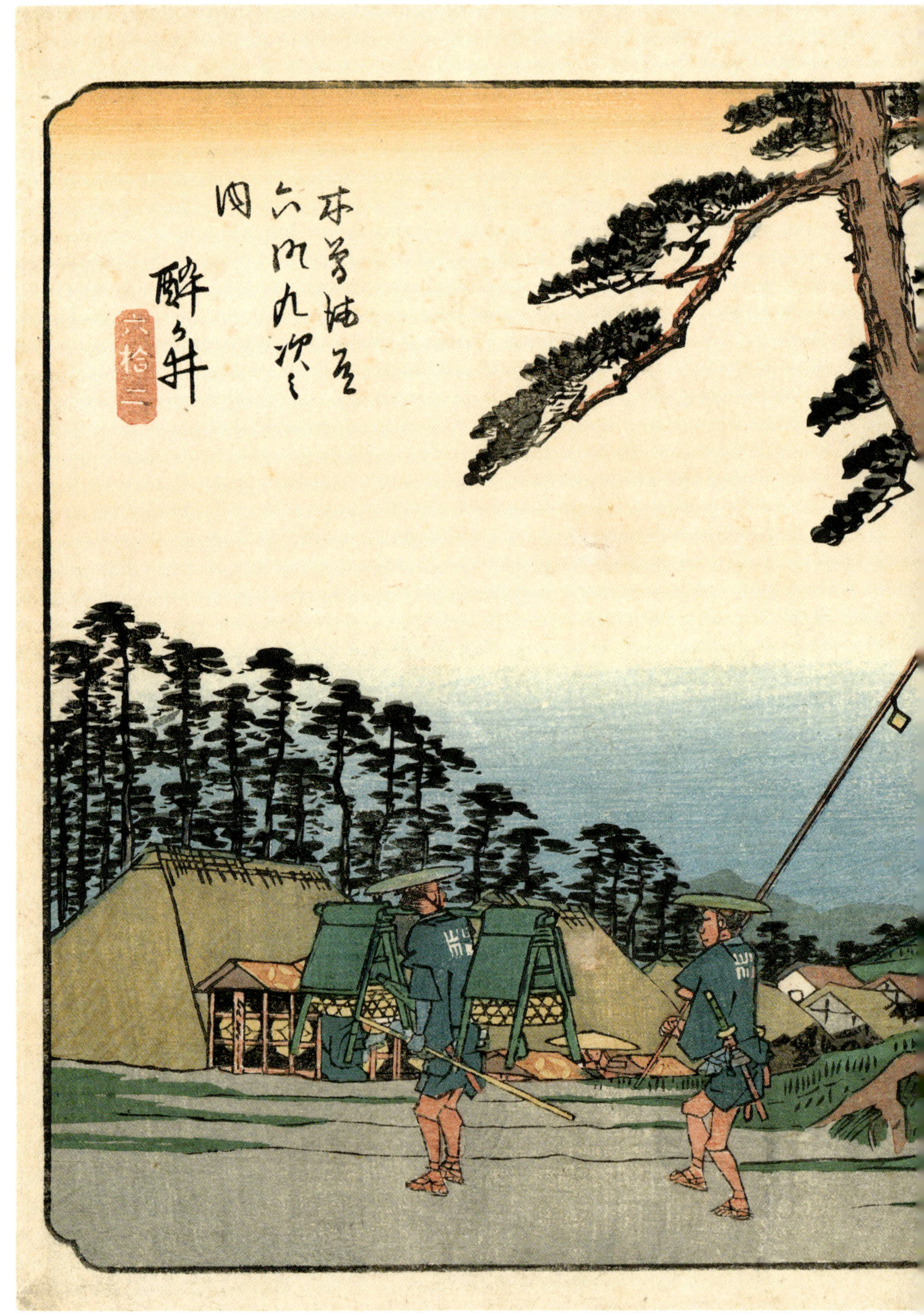
木曽海道
六拾九次之
内
醒ヶ井
六拾二

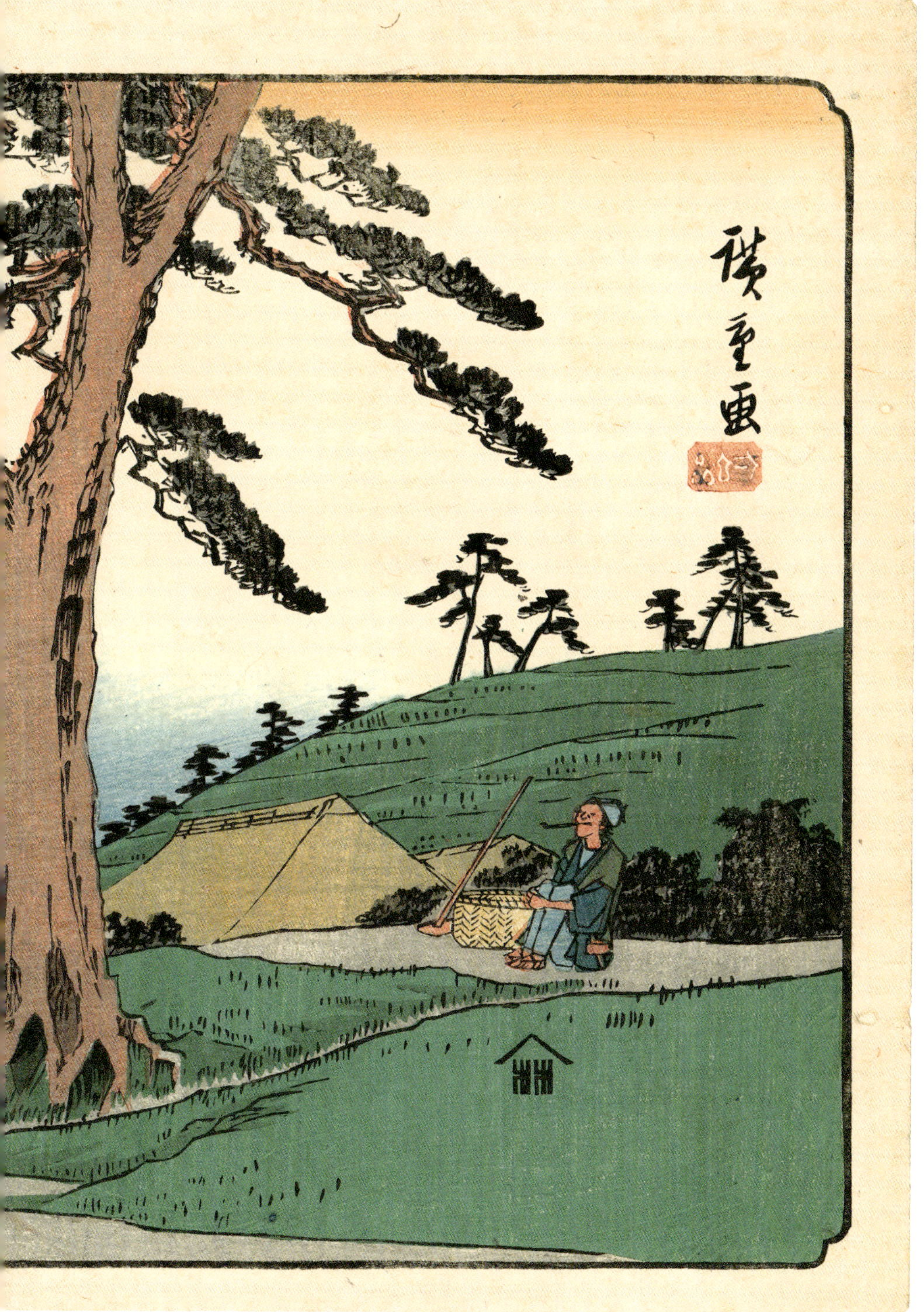

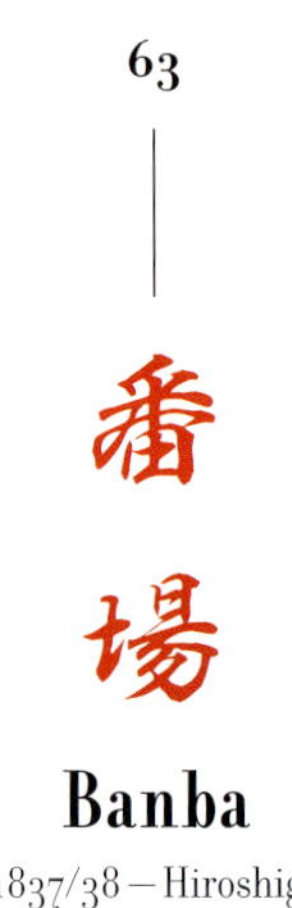

Banba

1837/38 – Hiroshige

Banba was a post station on the ancient Tōsandō road centuries before the Kisokaidō was established. In 1246, the retired shogun Fujiwara Yoritsune (1218–1256) stayed overnight here on his way from Kamakura to Kyoto. Banba's importance increased noticeably when the port of Maibara was opened on the north-east shore of Lake Biwa in 1611, which offered a significant shortcut for water transport between here and Ōtsu, the last station before Kyoto.

Hiroshige captured the east entrance to Banba as he saw it and sketched it on his journey to Kyoto. On the left is a stone-fortified structure resembling those built at a castle entrance; Hiroshige's sketch reveals that an identical rampart existed on the opposite side of the road but he chose not to integrate it into his print design.

The white lantern hanging from the restaurant on the right evidently caught Hiroshige's interest as he made a second sketch of it in greater detail, including the inscription, which announces, "Ichizen-meshi, sake, sakana", that is, "quick lunch, *sake*, fish". The lantern of the restaurant on the left is advertising *soba* noodles, while the rectangular signboard above the horses is marked with Hiroshige's seal at the top followed by his artistic family name, "Utagawa". The rectangular signboard on the left of the near lantern bears the seal and name of the publisher, "Iseya".

Jahrhunderte bevor der Kisokaidō geschaffen wurde, war Banba bereits Poststation an der alten Tōsandō-Straße. 1246 verbrachte der zurückgetretene Shogun Fujiwara Yoritsune (1218–1256) auf seinem Weg von Kamakura nach Kyoto hier die Nacht. Banba gewann spürbar an Bedeutung, als 1611 am Nordostufer des Biwa-Sees der Hafen von Maibara eröffnet wurde. Von dort aus war Ōtsu, die letzte Station vor Kyoto, per Schiff erheblich schneller zu erreichen.

Hiroshige fing den östlichen Ortseingang Banbas so ein, wie er ihn auf seiner Reise nach Kyoto gesehen und skizziert hatte. Die mit Steinen befestigte Erhebung am linken Bildrand ähnelt dem Eingang einer Burg; Hiroshiges Skizze verrät, dass ein identischer Schutzwall auch auf der anderen Straßenseite existierte, den er in die Druckvorlage jedoch nicht aufnehmen wollte.

Der weiße Lampion vor dem Restaurant rechts weckte offensichtlich das Interesse des Künstlers. Eine zweite, ausführlichere Studie, die er von diesem Detail anfertigte, enthält auch die Aufschrift, die für „Ichizenmeshi, sake, sakana" wirbt, „Mittagstisch, Sake, Fisch". Der Lampion des Restaurants links im Bild bietet *soba*-Nudeln an, auf dem Ladenschild rechts daneben sind Hiroshiges Künstlersiegel und darunter sein Künstlernachname „Utagawa" zu erkennen. Der rechteckige Ausleger links neben dem vorderen Lampion trägt das Siegel und den Namen des Verlegers, „Iseya".

Sur l'ancienne route Tōsandō, le relais de poste de Banba avait été fondé plusieurs siècles avant la construction de la Kisokaidō. En 1246, le shogun Fujiwara Yoritsune (1218–1256), qui avait quitté ses fonctions, y passa une nuit en se rendant de Kamakura à Kyoto. L'importance de Banba fut considérablement renforcée avec l'ouverture, en 1611, du port de Maibara, sur la rive nord-est du lac Biwa, offrant désormais un raccourci notable pour le transport sur le lac entre ici et Ōtsu, dernière station avant Kyoto.

C'est l'entrée orientale de Banba qu'Hiroshige a représentée telle qu'il l'avait vue et dessinée pendant son voyage vers Kyoto. À gauche se trouve une structure fortifiée en pierres, ressemblant à celles que l'on voit à l'entrée d'un château ; le croquis de l'artiste révèle l'existence d'une fortification identique de l'autre côté de la route, mais Hiroshige a choisi de ne pas la conserver dans son estampe.

La lanterne blanche suspendue dans le restaurant de droite a manifestement suscité l'intérêt de l'artiste, car il en avait fait un second croquis plus détaillé, comprenant l'inscription « Ichizenmeshi, sake, sakana », c'est-à-dire « déjeuner rapide, saké, poisson ». Sur la lanterne du restaurant de gauche, on peut lire « nouilles *soba* », tandis que l'enseigne rectangulaire visible au-dessus des chevaux porte, en haut, le sceau d'Hiroshige, suivi de son nom de famille d'artiste, « Utagawa ». L'enseigne rectangulaire qui se trouve à gauche de la lanterne la plus proche porte, elle, le sceau et le nom de l'éditeur, « Iseya ».

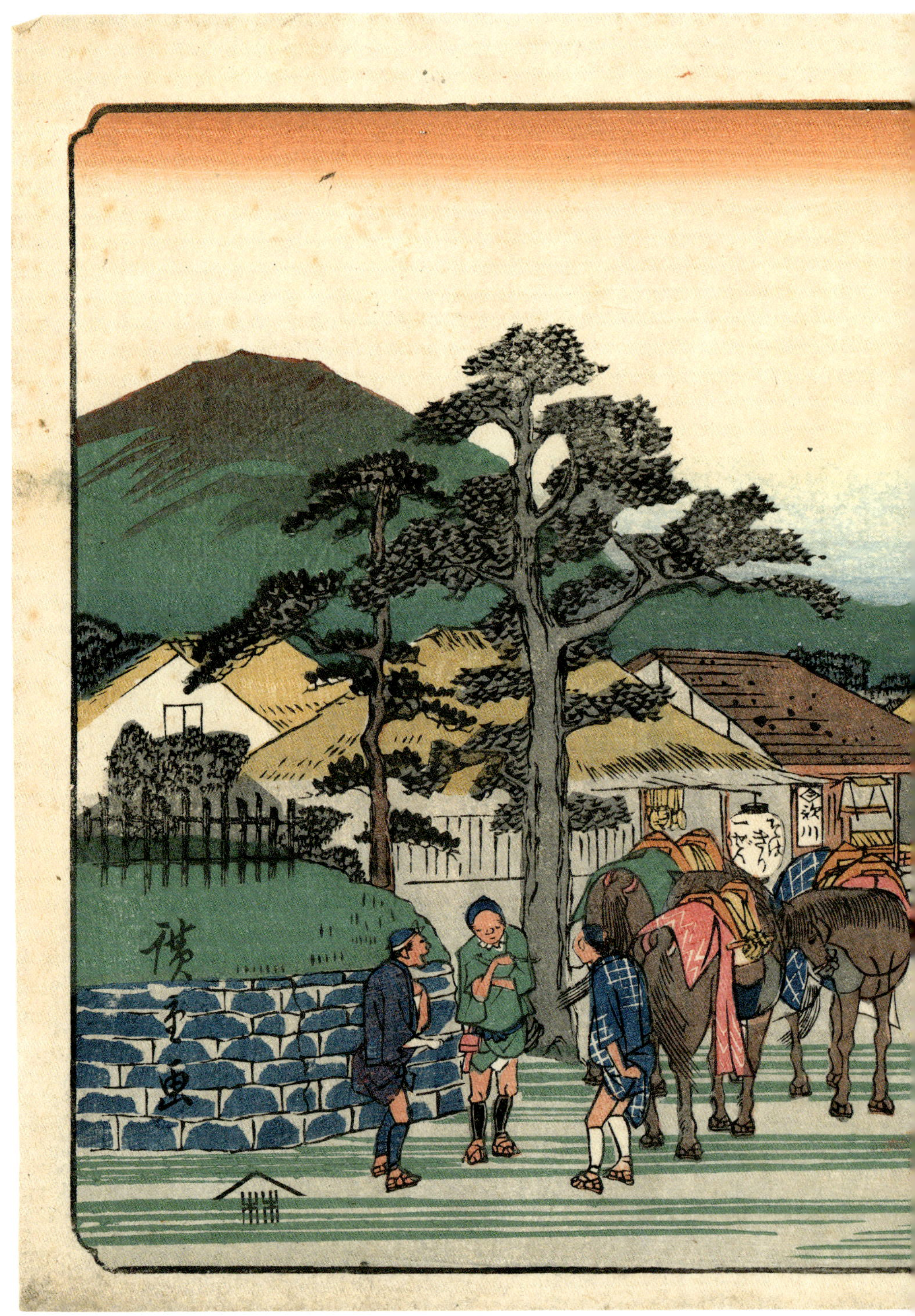

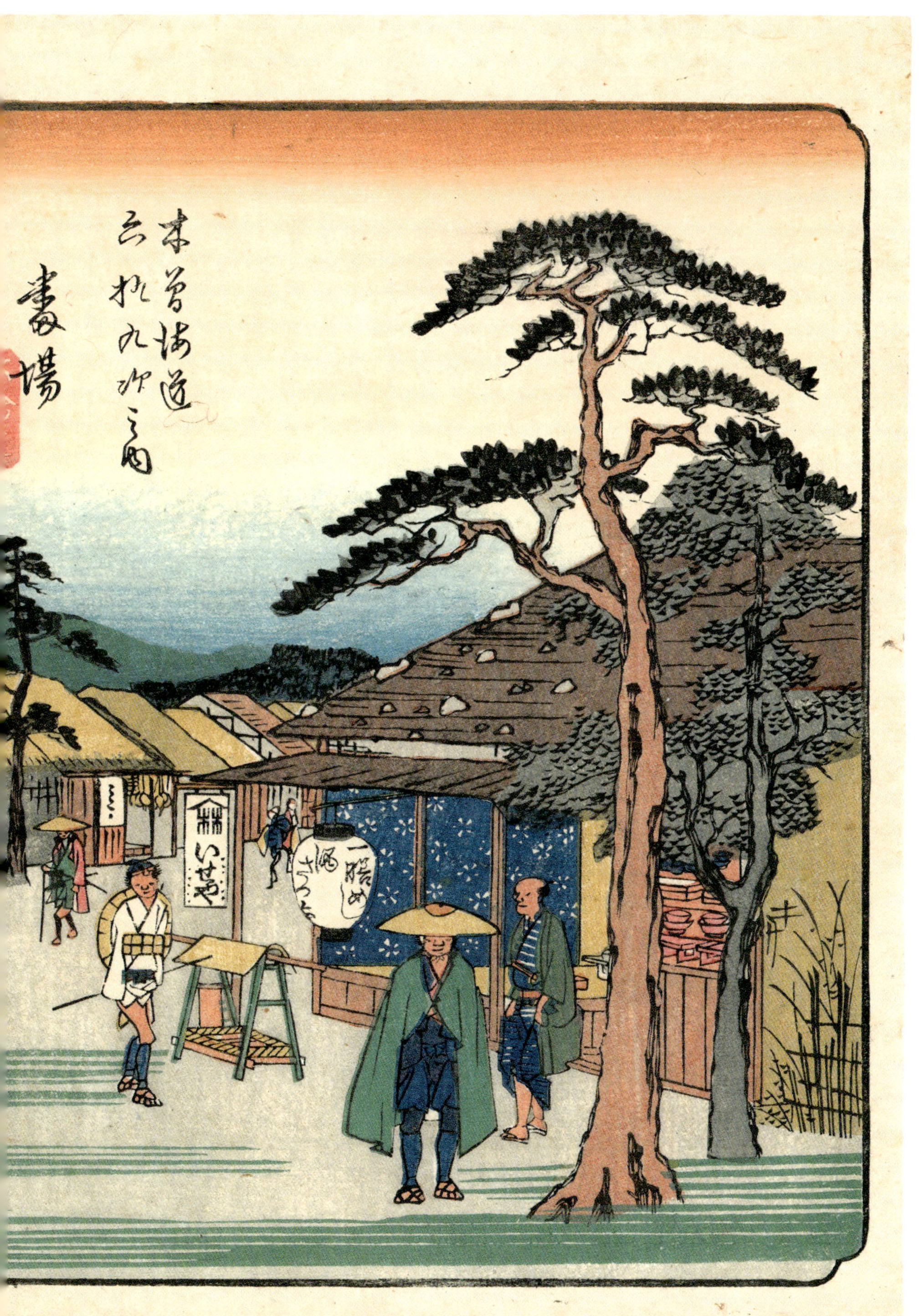

64

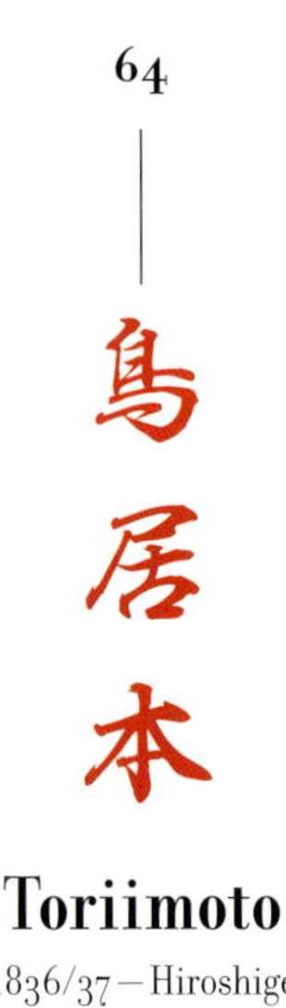

Toriimoto

1836/37 — Hiroshige

Between Banba and Toriimoto the road inclined again as it crossed over the Surihari Pass. From an elevation of 187 metres (614 feet), the road then descended steeply to Toriimoto, 99 metres (325 feet) above sea level. Toriimoto, literally "at the gate [of a shrine]", took its name from the large *torii* gate that once marked the entrance to a shrine at this point on the road.

Before his journey along the Kisokaidō, Hiroshige created the design for this print based on an illustration in the guidebook *Views of Famous Sights along the Kiso Road* (*Kisoji meisho zue*) entitled *Surihari Pass*. On the left is the Bōkodō teahouse, which was constructed on a stone foundation at the top of the pass and afforded guests a commanding view over the surrounding countryside from its terrace. It burnt down in 1991. On the right is the roof of another teahouse, the Rinkodō. Hiroshige moved the pine tree leaning over the cliff in the direction of the lake from the corner of the Bōkodō teahouse away to a more prominent position in the middle of the print.

In the background is Lake Biwa with Mount Hira on the far right and Chikubu Island towards the front. The view depicted in the guidebook is verified by Hiroshige's sketch, which he drew later on when he travelled this stretch of the road to Kyoto.

A mistake was made in the numbering of this design, writing 63 instead of 64.

386

Hinter Banba stieg die Straße zum Surihari-Pass erneut an, fiel dann aus 187 Metern Meereshöhe steil ab und führte ins 99 Meter über dem Meer gelegene Toriimoto. Die Station, die wörtlich „am Tor [eines Schreins]" heißt, wurde nach dem großen *torii* benannt, das an diesem Punkt der Straße einst den Zugang zu einem Schrein markierte.

Hiroshige schuf dieses Blatt bereits vor seiner Reise zum Kisokaidō. Es basiert auf einer Abbildung im Reiseführer *Ansichten berühmter Stätten an der Kiso-Straße (Kisoji meisho zue)*, die den Titel *Surihari-Pass* trägt. Zur Linken steht das Teehaus Bōkodō, das am höchsten Punkt des Passes auf einem Steinfundament errichtet wurde und den Gästen von der Terrasse einen atemberaubenden Ausblick auf die umliegende Landschaft bot. Es brannte 1991 nieder. Das Dach rechts gehört zu einem weiteren Teehaus, dem Rinkodō. Die über die Klippe emporragende Kiefer versetzte Hiroshige von der Ecke des Bōkodō in Richtung See, um sie in der Bildmitte stärker zur Geltung zu bringen.

Vor dem Berg Hira, der im Hintergrund rechts über dem Biwa-See aufragt, liegt die Insel Chikubu. Die Abbildung im Reiseführer wird von der Skizze bestätigt, die Hiroshige anfertigte, als er später auf diesem Abschnitt der Straße nach Kyoto unterwegs war.

Ein Fehler trat bei der Nummerierung des Blattes auf, das eine 63 anstelle der 64 trägt.

De Banba à Toriimoto, la route s'élevait à nouveau et passait par le col de Surihari. Depuis une altitude de 187 mètres, la route redescendait ensuite en pente raide jusqu'à Toriimoto, village situé à 99 mètres au-dessus du niveau de la mer. Le nom de ce village, qui signifie littéralement « à la porte [d'un sanctuaire] » vient de la grande porte *torii* qui, jadis, marquait l'entrée d'un sanctuaire à cet endroit de la route.

Avant d'entreprendre son périple sur la Kisokaidō, Hiroshige avait réalisé le dessin de cette estampe d'après une illustration du guide de voyage *Collection de vues de paysages célèbres sur la route Kiso (Kisoji meisho zue)*, intitulée *Col de Surihari*. On voit à gauche la maison de thé Bōkodō, construite sur une fondation de pierres au sommet du col et qui offrait, depuis sa terrasse, un vaste panorama sur la campagne environnante. Cet établissement fut détruit par un incendie en 1991. À droite se trouve le toit d'une autre maison de thé, la Rinkodō. Le pin incliné vers le lac au-dessus de la falaise a été déplacé par Hiroshige depuis l'angle de la Bōkodō jusqu'à une position plus avantageuse, au milieu de l'estampe.

Le lac Biwa est à l'arrière-plan, avec le mont Hira à l'extrême droite et l'île de Chikubu en avant de la montagne. La vue illustrée dans le guide de voyage est confirmée par le croquis dessiné plus tard par Hiroshige, lorsque l'artiste emprunta cette partie de la route en se rendant à Kyoto.

Une erreur de numérotation attribue à cette estampe le numéro 63 au lieu du 64.

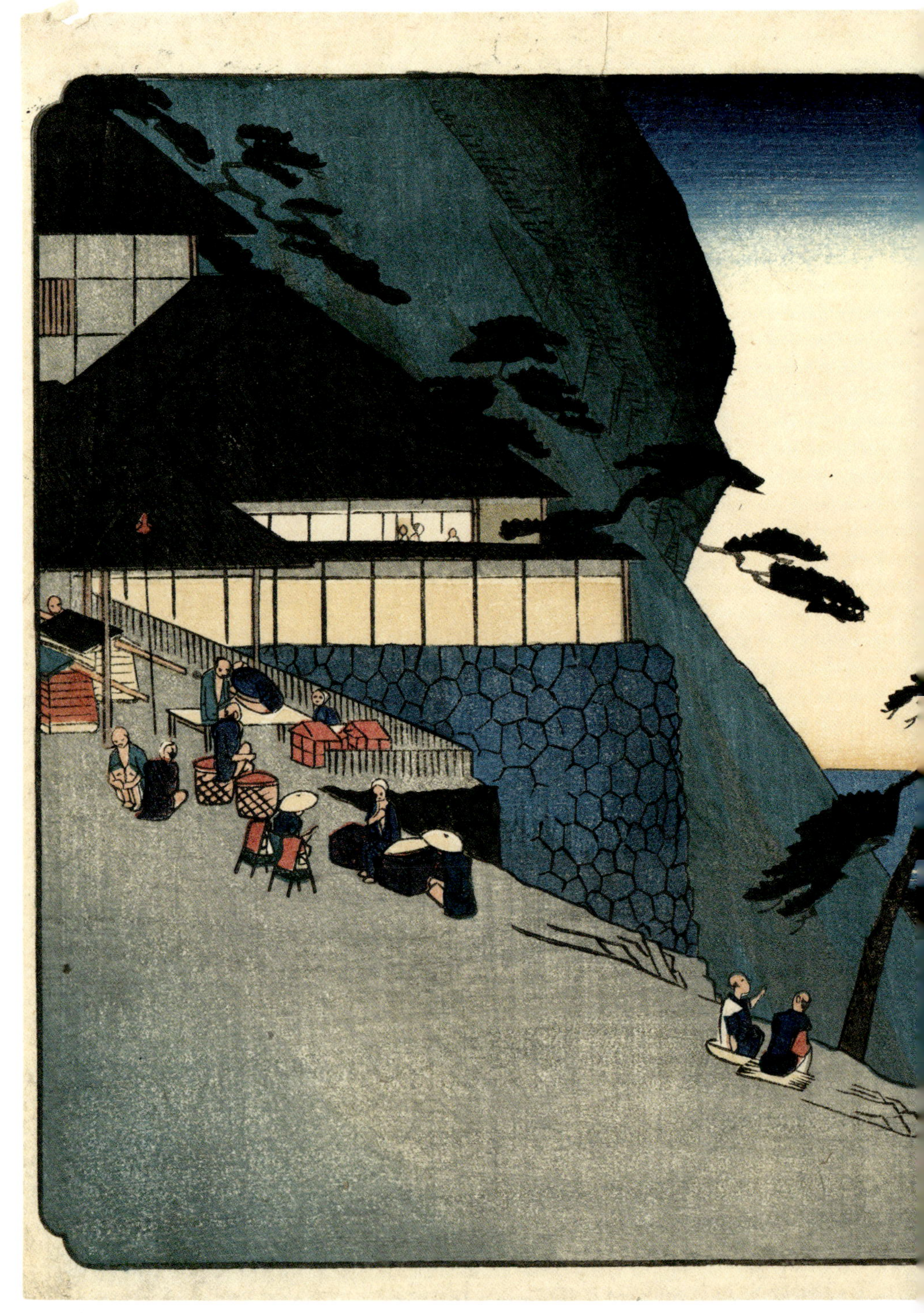

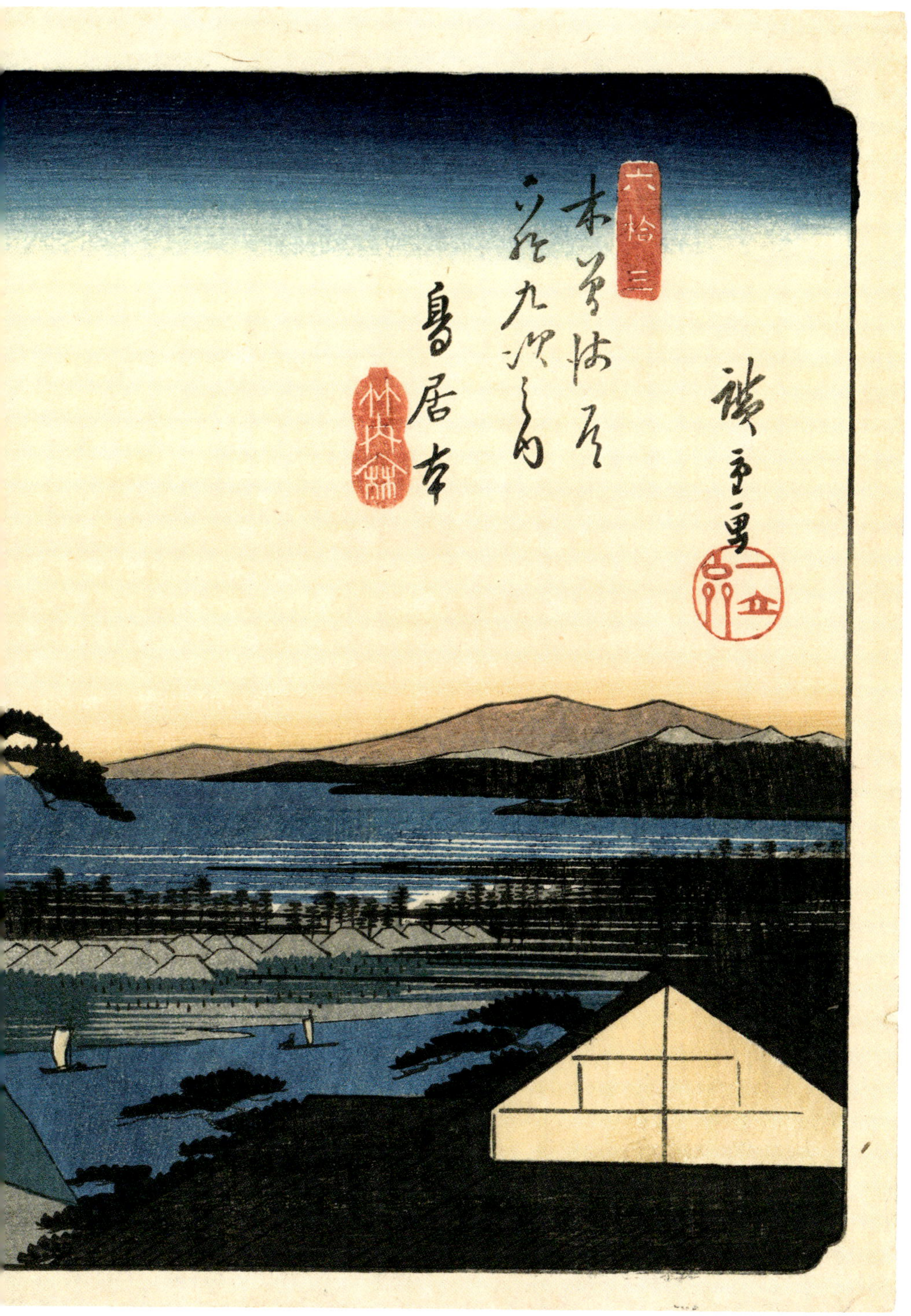

65

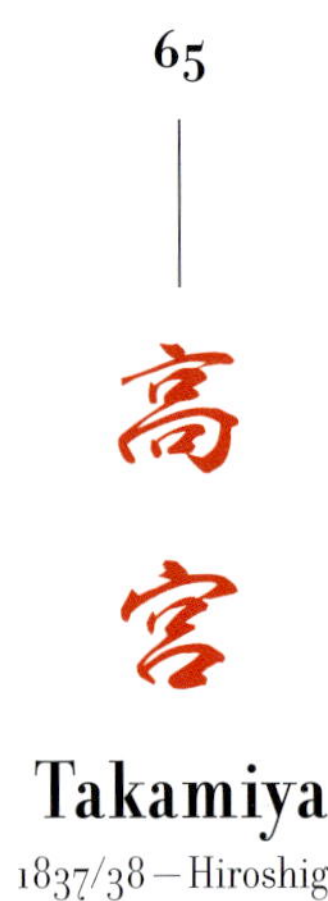

Takamiya

1837/38 — Hiroshige

Depicted here is the view to the north after passing through Takamiya and crossing the low waters of the Inugami River south of the station. The scene is based on a sketch created by Hiroshige during his journey to Kyoto, apparently looking back at the village and the mountains in the far distance from whence he has come.

Two large pine trees marking the sides of the road frame the image, while supports lined up across the river, precisely as was shown in the sketch, suggest that a bridge was about to be constructed here. The sketch also includes the stone lantern to the left of the south entrance of Takamiya.

From Takamiya, a road marked by a *torii* gate led east to the Taga Taisha, a shrine built in the 7th century and dedicated to Izanagi and Izanami, the mythical founders of Japan. Takamiya was famous for its hemp fabric that was produced here and named after the area, *Takamiya-nuno*. The two farmer women in the centre are carrying bales of hemp reed on their backs, the raw material from which the yarn was made. That Hiroshige saw such a farmer woman somewhere during his road trip is clear from a matching figure in a group of drawings he titled "People on the Ōmi Road" included in one of his sketchbooks.

Wendet man sich um, nachdem man Takamiya passiert und das nahezu ausgetrocknete Flussbett des Inugami südlich der Station durchquert hat, dann eröffnet sich der hier gezeigte Blick in Richtung Norden. Die Szene basiert auf einer Skizze, die Hiroshige auf seiner Reise nach Kyoto schuf, während er allem Anschein nach auf den Ort und die weit entfernten Berge zurückblickte, aus denen er gekommen war.

Zwei große Kiefern markieren die Straßenränder und rahmen das Bild ein. Im Flussbett aufgereihte Stützen deuten genau wie in Hiroshiges Skizze darauf hin, dass hier demnächst eine Brücke entstehen soll. Die Skizze enthält auch die Steinlaterne auf der linken Seite des südlichen Ortseingangs.

Von Takamiya führte eine Straße, die durch ein *torii* (Tor) gekennzeichnet war, ostwärts zum Großschrein von Taga (Taga Taisha), der im 7. Jahrhundert erbaut wurde und den mythischen Gründern Japans, Izanagi und Izanami, gewidmet ist. Takamiya war berühmt für das Hanfgewebe, das hier produziert wurde und als *Takamiya-nuno* auch nach der Region benannt war. Die beiden Bäuerinnen in der Bildmitte tragen Ballen von Hanfstängeln auf dem Rücken, die als Rohstoff für die Garnherstellung dienten. Dass Hiroshige irgendwo auf seiner Kisokaidō-Reise eine solche Bäuerin sah, belegt eine entsprechende Figur in einem seiner Skizzenbücher mit einer Gruppe von Zeichnungen, die er „Menschen auf der Straße von Ōmi" nannte.

Cette illustration présente la vue vers le nord qu'avaient les voyageurs après avoir traversé Takamiya et franchi les eaux peu profondes de l'Inugami, au sud de la station. Cette scène reprend celle d'une esquisse réalisée par Hiroshige pendant son voyage vers Kyoto : l'artiste semble regarder le village et, au loin, les montagnes, par lesquels il vient de passer.

Deux grands pins marquant les deux côtés de la route encadrent l'image, tandis que des supports alignés en travers de la rivière, exactement comme dans l'esquisse, indiquent qu'un pont est en cours de construction. La lanterne de pierre, visible à gauche de l'entrée sud de Takamiya, figure aussi dans le croquis.

À partir de Takamiya, une route marquée par une porte *torii* menait vers l'est au Taga Taisha, sanctuaire édifié au VIIe siècle et dédié à Izanagi et Izanami, les fondateurs mythiques du Japon. Takamiya était connu pour son tissu de chanvre, confectionné sur place et baptisé du nom de la région, *Takamiya-nuno*. Les deux paysannes visibles au centre de l'image portent sur le dos des balles de tiges de chanvre, matière première à partir de laquelle est fabriqué le fil de chanvre. On sait qu'Hiroshige a vu l'une de ces paysannes au cours de son voyage sur la Kisokaidō grâce à un personnage semblable qui se trouve dans un ensemble de dessins intitulés « Gens sur la route d'Ōmi », figurant dans l'un de ses carnets à croquis.

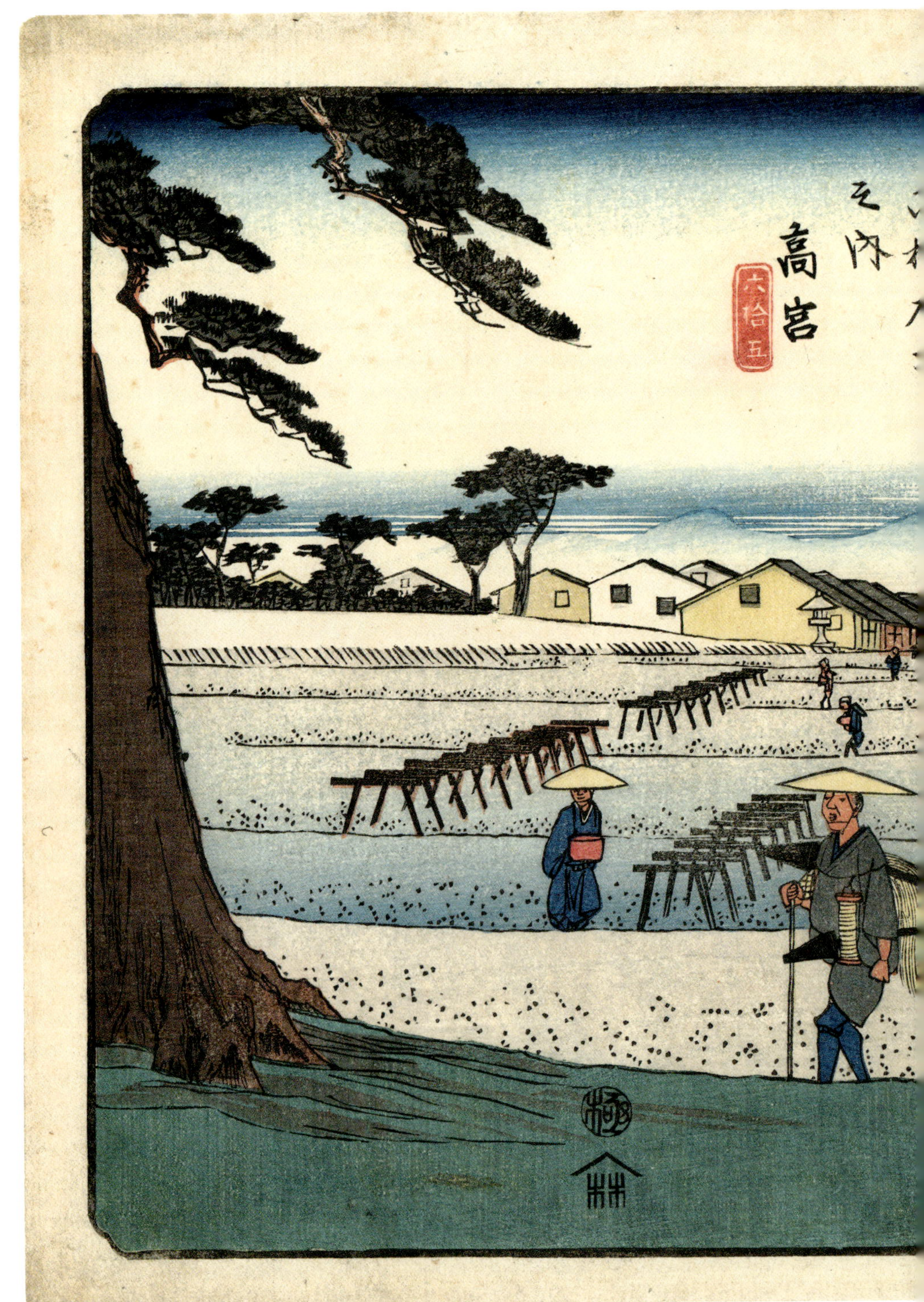
高宮

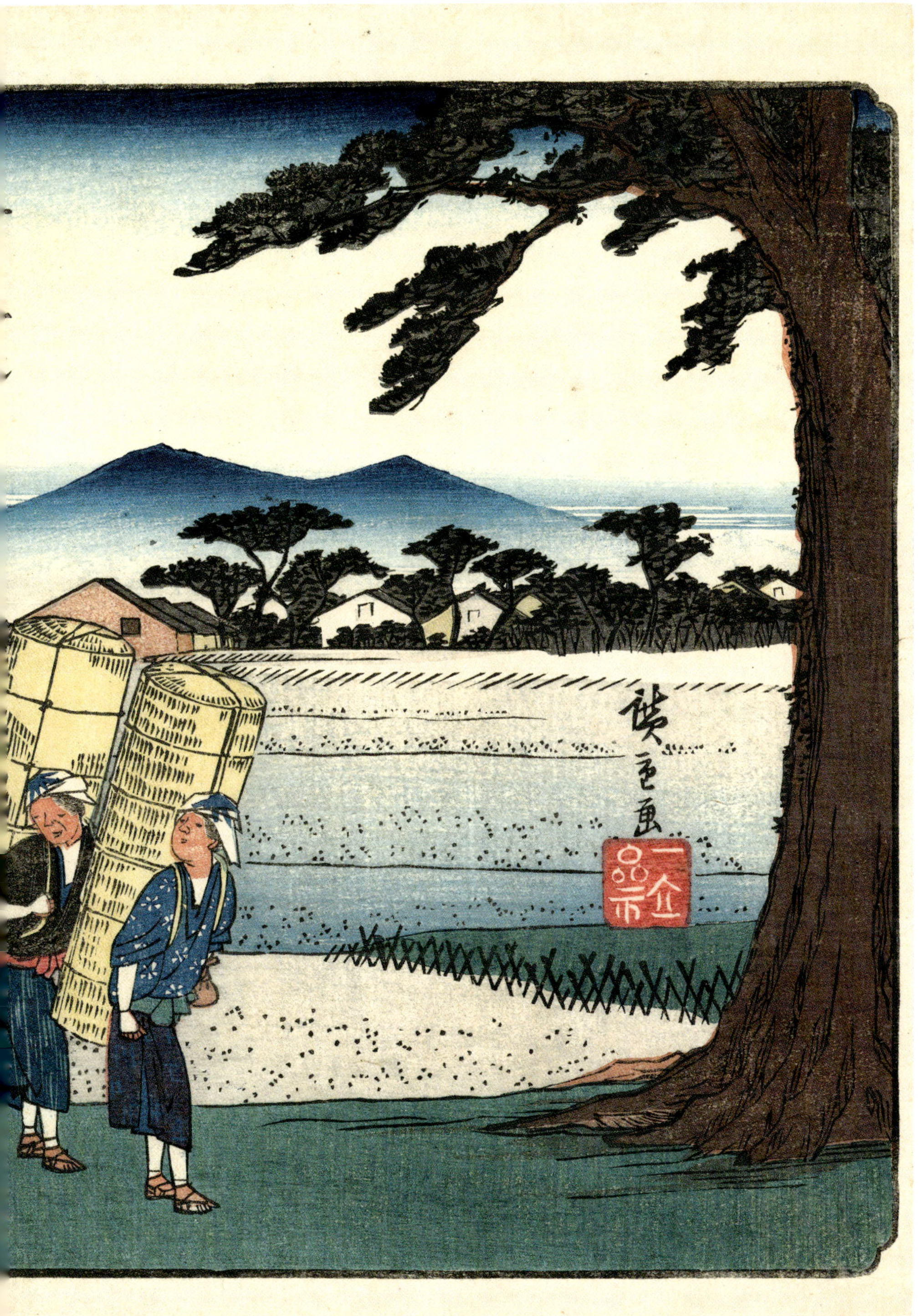

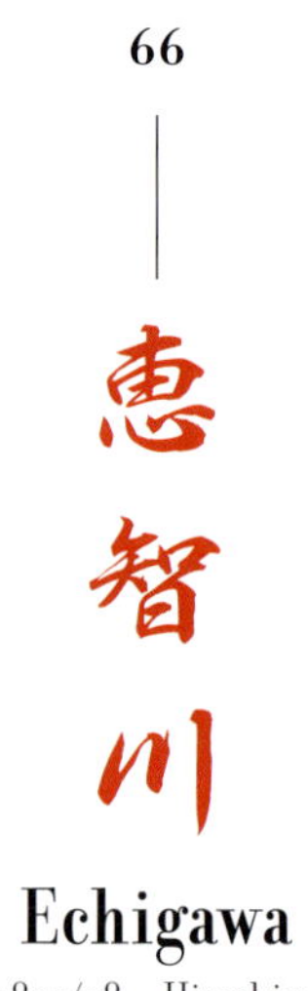

66

Echigawa

1837/38 — Hiroshige

Echigawa was originally a post station on the old Tōsandō road and because the court noble Kitabatake Akiie (1318–1338) stayed here in 1336 it is mentioned in the *Chronicle of Great Peace (Taiheiki)*, a late 14th-century epic.

After passing through the Echigawa station heading southwards, travellers came to the Echi River after which this station was named. The river begins in the Suzuka Mountains at an altitude of 1,200 metres (3,937 feet) and has a length of 48 kilometres (30 miles), before flowing into Lake Biwa, around 10 kilometres (6 miles) from the point depicted here. In the background on the right behind the trees is Mount Wada; on the left is Mount Kinugasa, famous for its Kannonshōji temple, which was struck by lightning in 1993.

Hiroshige's design is once again based on the sketch he made during his journey to Kyoto. The sign-post on the right seems to have piqued his interest, as he has meticulously noted what was written on it: "muchinbashi, hashi sen irazu", or "toll-free bridge, no payment required for bridge". It was common practice to have to pay a toll when crossing a bridge, but this particular one, constructed by the merchant Narumiya Yajiemon (1781–1855) along with four other bridges between 1829 and 1831 to make the river crossing safer, was famously left toll-free.

The peasant woman in the centre leading an ox appears to have been taken from a drawing on another, untitled page in Hiroshige's sketchbook.

Echigawa war ursprünglich eine Poststation an der alten Tōsandō-Straße, und weil der Hofadlige Kitabatake Akiie (1318–1338) hier im Jahr 1336 übernachtete, wird sie in der *Chronik des großen Friedens
(Taiheiki)* erwähnt, einem historischen Epos aus dem späten 14. Jahrhundert.

Nachdem sie Echigawa in Richtung Süden durchquert hatten, erreichten die Reisenden den
Echi, nach dem die Station benannt ist. Der Fluss entspringt auf 1200 Metern Meereshöhe in den Bergen von Suzuka und mündet nach 48 Kilometern, etwa zehn Kilometer von der hier gezeigten Stelle
entfernt, in den Biwa-See. Im Hintergrund rechts hinter den Bäumen erhebt sich der Wada, während
links der Kinugasa emporragt. Der Kannonshōji-Tempel, für den der Berg berühmt ist, wurde 1993 vom
Blitz getroffen.

Hiroshiges Entwurf basiert wiederum auf einer Skizze, die er während seiner Reise nach Kyoto anfertigte. Der Wegweiser rechts im Bild scheint ihn interessiert zu haben, denn er notierte peinlich genau,
was darauf geschrieben stand: „muchinbashi, hashi sen irazu" oder „gebührenfreie Brücke, Entgelt für
die Brücke nicht erforderlich". Es war übliche Praxis, dass für das Überqueren von Brücken ein Wegzoll
fällig wurde, doch diese spezielle Brücke, die der Kaufmann Narumiya Yajiemon (1781–1855) zusammen
mit vier weiteren Brücken zwischen 1829 und 1831 errichten ließ, war bekanntermaßen gebührenfrei.

Die Bäuerin in der Bildmitte, die einen Ochsen an der Leine führt, scheint Hiroshige aus einer Zeichnung übernommen zu haben, die sich auf einer anderen, unbetitelten Seite seines Skizzenbuchs findet.

Echigawa fut d'abord un relais de poste sur la vieille route Tōsandō, mais, à la suite du séjour en 1336 de
Kitabatake Akiie (1318–1338), noble de la cour, le village fut mentionné dans la *Chronique de la grande
paix (Taiheiki)*, épopée de la fin du XIVe siècle.

Après avoir traversé la station d'Echigawa en direction du sud, les voyageurs arrivaient à la rivière
Echi qui a donné son nom à la station. L'Echi prend sa source dans les monts Suzuka, à une altitude de
1200 mètres ; son cours de 48 kilomètres se termine dans le lac Biwa, à une dizaine de kilomètres du lieu
illustré dans cette estampe. On devine le mont Wada, à l'arrière-plan à droite, derrière les arbres ; à
gauche s'élève le mont Kinugasa, célèbre pour son temple de Kannonshōji, frappé par la foudre en 1993.

Là encore, l'estampe d'Hiroshige s'inspire d'un croquis réalisé par l'artiste pendant son voyage vers
Kyoto. Le poteau indicateur situé à droite a dû susciter son intérêt, car il en a minutieusement recopié
les inscriptions : « muchinbashi, hashi sen irazu », c'est-à-dire « pont gratuit, aucun tribut n'est requis ».
Il était alors courant de payer un tribut pour franchir un pont, mais celui-ci, construit par le marchand
Narumiya Yajiemon (1781–1855), comme quatre autres ponts bâtis de 1829 à 1831 pour traverser la rivière
en toute sécurité, était connu pour sa gratuité.

La paysanne qui conduit un bœuf, visible au centre, semble provenir d'un dessin figurant sur une
autre page sans titre du carnet de croquis d'Hiroshige.

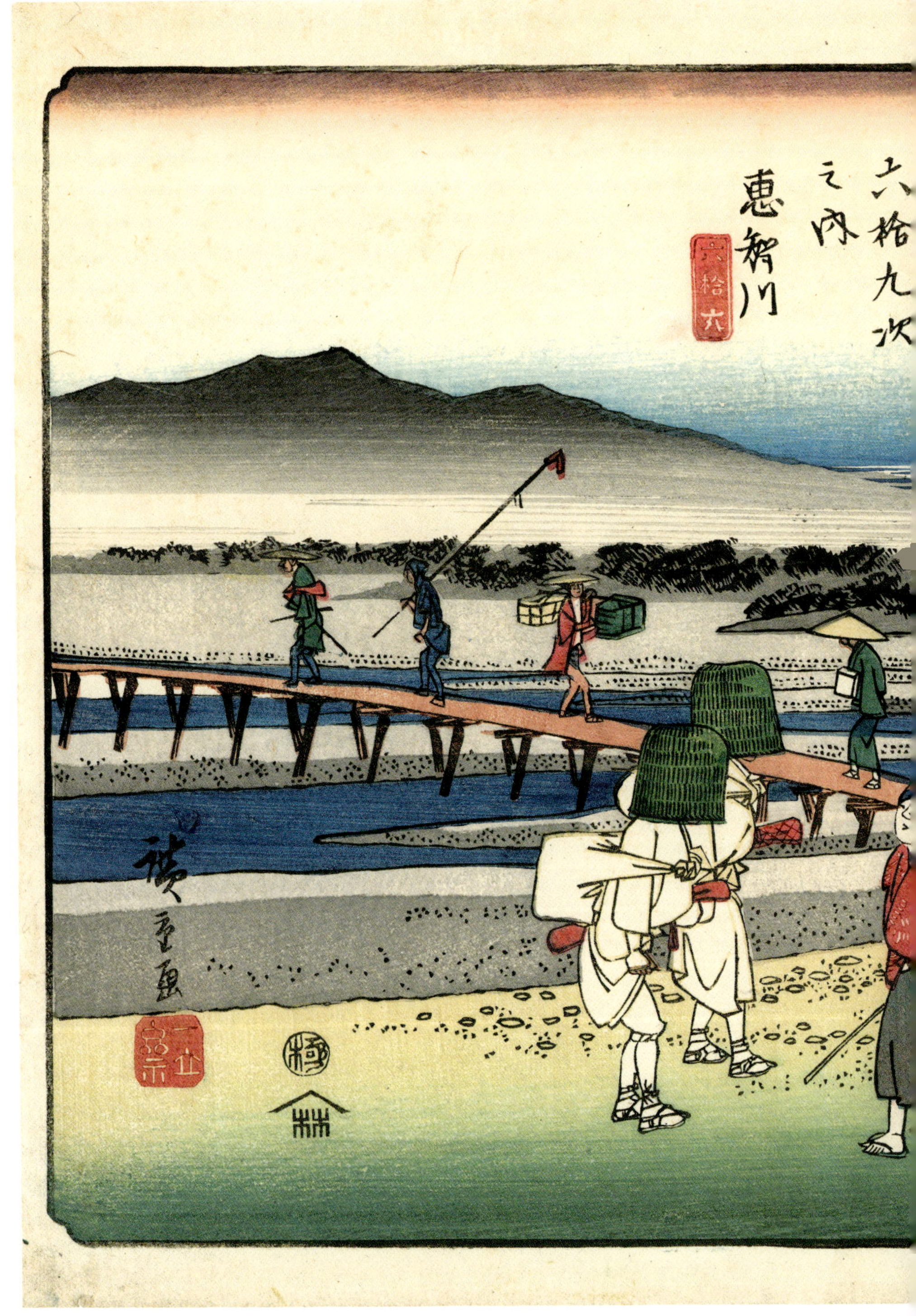

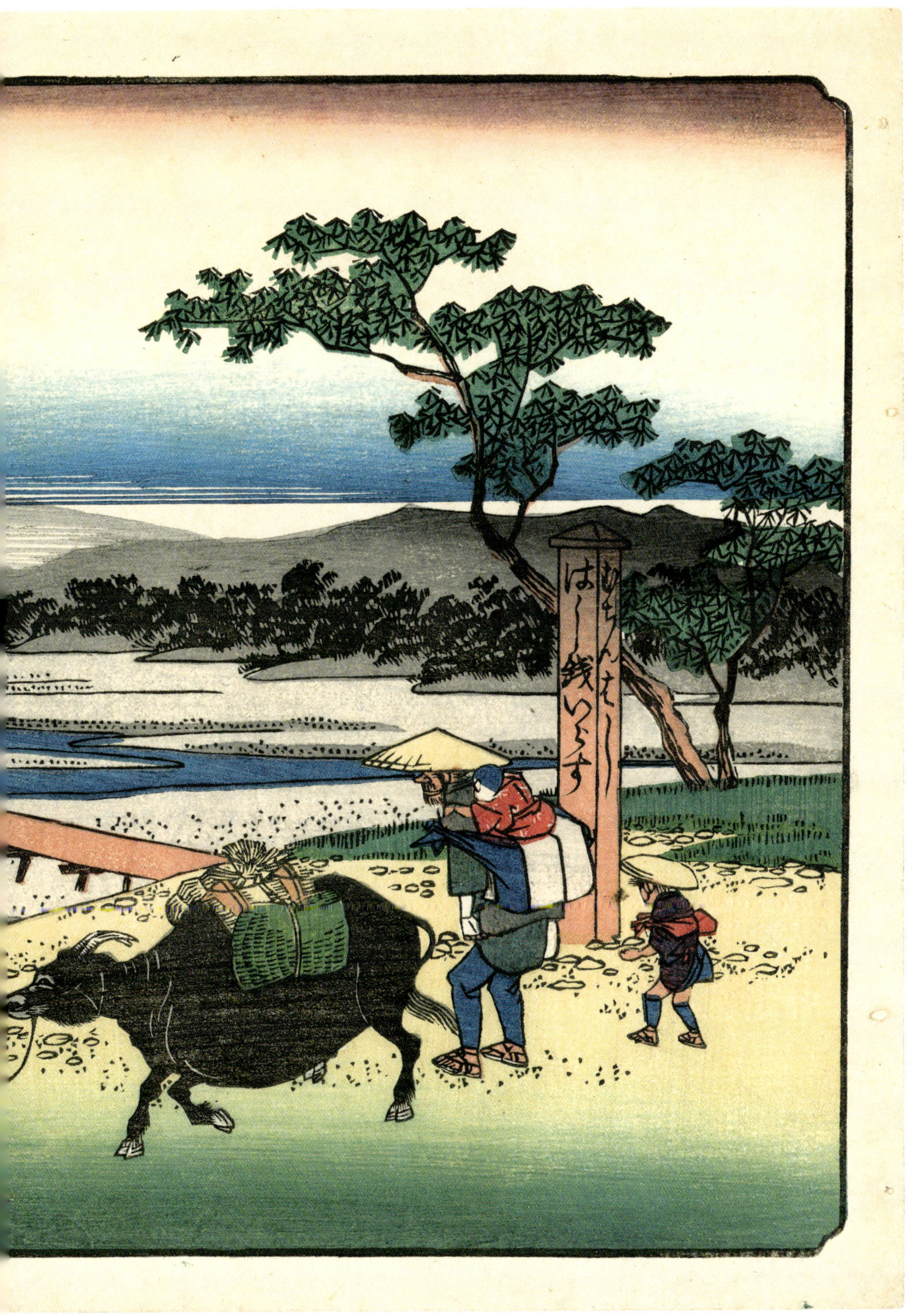
はし一錢いくらす

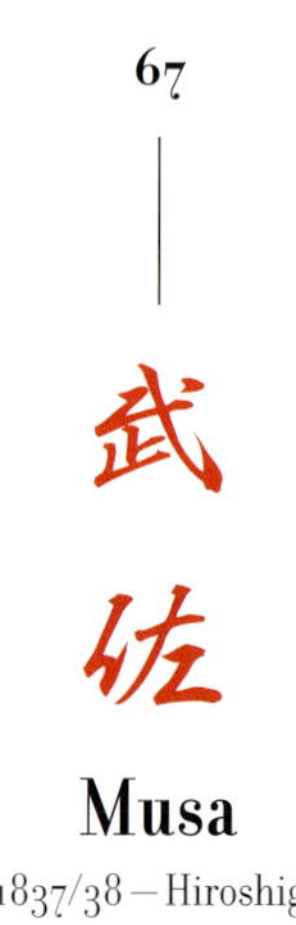

67

Musa

1837/38 – Hiroshige

After passing through the Musa station, travellers arrived at the Yokozeki River (today's Hino River), which could be crossed using a pontoon bridge. When the water level was low, as seen here, just two boats were sufficient, secured with stakes on either side. This detail was recorded in the *Panorama Map of the Nakasendō* (*Nakasendō bunken nobe ezu*), a set of hand-scrolls that were created for official purposes in 1806. In his travel diary from 1802, the poet and writer Ōta Nanpo also mentioned a pontoon bridge at this location. A solid bridge was built in 1875.

Hiroshige's design is based as elsewhere on a sketch he drew during his journey to Kyoto. This sketch also features the rest stop in the left background and the swaying reeds, but there is no line of trees in the background nor the large tree in the centre. On the right of this tree Hiroshige shows an old man slowly crossing the bridge, bent double with the weight of the luggage he is carrying on his back. Hiroshige seems to have seen just such a man since one features in a drawing elsewhere in his sketch-books on a page showing various people he encountered during his journey.

This design should be numbered 67 but was erroneously given the number 66.

Hinter Musa führte die Straße ans Ufer des Yokozeki (des heutigen Hino), der auf einer Pontonbrücke zu überqueren war. Wenn er wenig Wasser führte, wie hier zu sehen, reichten zwei Boote, die beidseitig mit Pfählen gesichert wurden, als Pontons aus. Dokumentiert wurde dieses Detail in der *Panoramakarte des Nakasendō (Nakasendō bunken nobe ezu)*, einer Abfolge von Bildrollen, die 1806 zu amtlichen Zwecken erstellt wurde. In seinem Reisetagebuch von 1802 erwähnte auch der Dichter und Schriftsteller Ōta Nanpo eine Pontonbrücke an dieser Stelle. Eine feste Brücke wurde 1875 errichtet.

Wie in anderen Fällen lag auch hier Hiroshiges Entwurf eine Skizze zugrunde, die während seiner Reise nach Kyoto entstanden war. Sie zeigt das Rasthaus hinten links und das wogende Schilf, nicht aber die Baumreihe im Hintergrund und den großen Baum im Zentrum. Rechts von diesem Baum überquert ein alter Mann die Brücke, langsam und gebeugt unter der Last des Gepäcks, das er auf dem Rücken trägt. Hiroshige scheint genau so einen Mann gesehen zu haben, denn an anderer Stelle in seinen Skizzenbüchern taucht dieser in einer Zeichnung auf. Die entsprechende Seite zeigt verschiedene Menschen, denen Hiroshige auf seiner Reise begegnete.

Das Blatt sollte eigentlich mit 67 nummeriert sein, erhielt aber versehentlich die Nummer 66.

Ayant quitté la station de Musa, les voyageurs atteignaient ensuite la rivière Yokozeki (aujourd'hui l'Hino) que l'on traversait par un pont flottant. Lorsque le niveau de l'eau était bas, comme ici, deux barques suffisaient, maintenues par des pieux sur chaque bord. Ce détail figure dans la *Carte panoramique de la Nakasendō (Nakasendō bunken nobe ezu)*, ensemble de rouleaux réalisés à la main à des fins officielles en 1806. Dans son journal de voyage de 1802, le poète et écrivain Ōta Nanpo cite également l'existence d'un pont flottant à cet endroit. Un pont en dur y fut construit en 1875.

Comme d'autres estampes d'Hiroshige, celle-ci s'inspire d'un croquis réalisé par l'artiste lors de son voyage vers Kyoto. Ce croquis comprend également la halte visible à l'arrière-plan à gauche, ainsi que les roseaux qui se balancent, mais on n'y trouve ni l'alignement d'arbres de l'estampe, ni le grand arbre placé au centre. À droite de cet arbre, Hiroshige a dessiné un vieil homme qui traverse lentement le pont, courbé sous le poids du bagage qu'il porte sur le dos. L'artiste a probablement vu un homme semblable, comme en témoigne un dessin figurant sur une page de son carnet de croquis décrivant différentes personnes rencontrées en chemin.

Alors qu'elle devrait porter le numéro 67, cette estampe a été numérotée 66 par erreur.

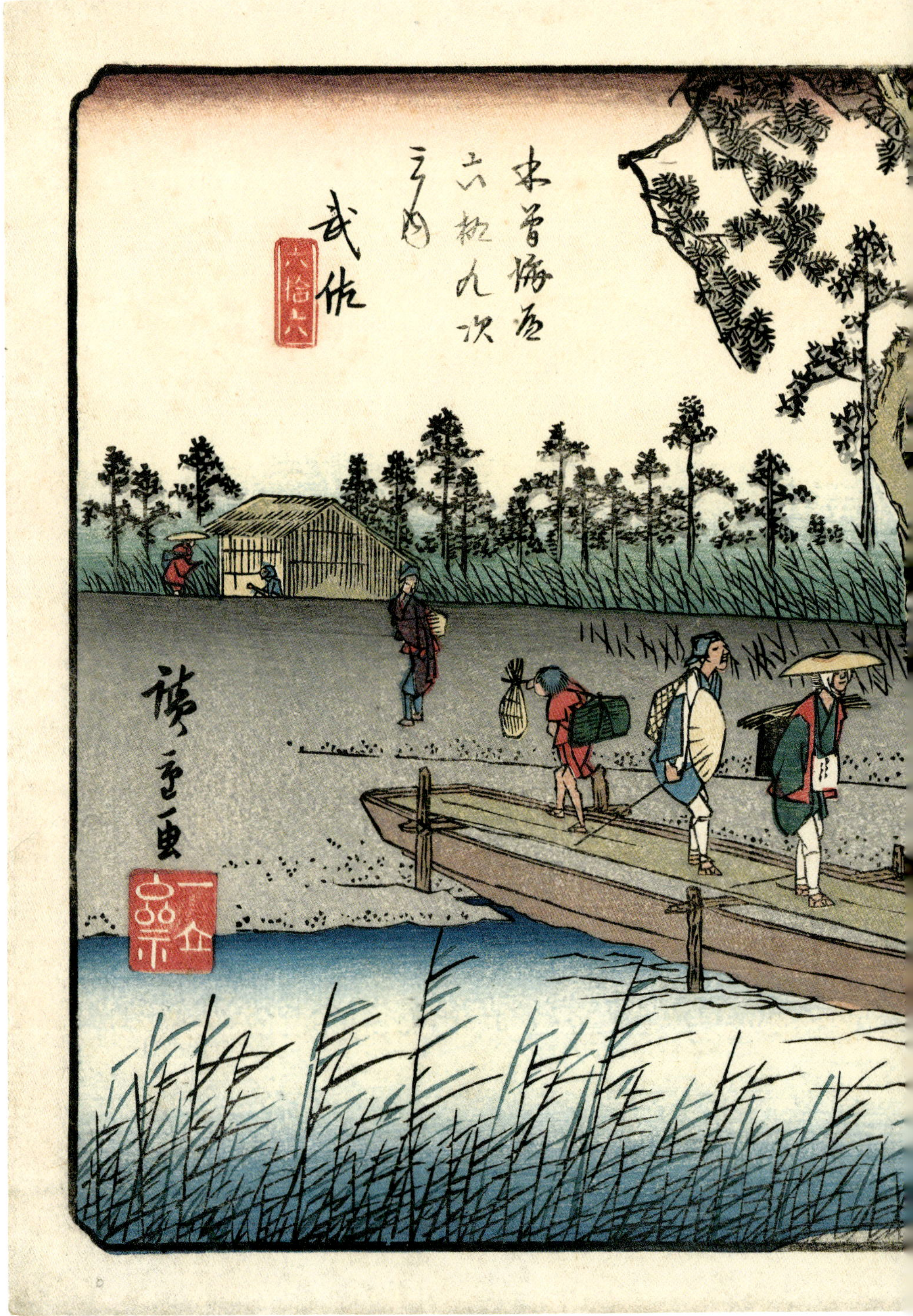

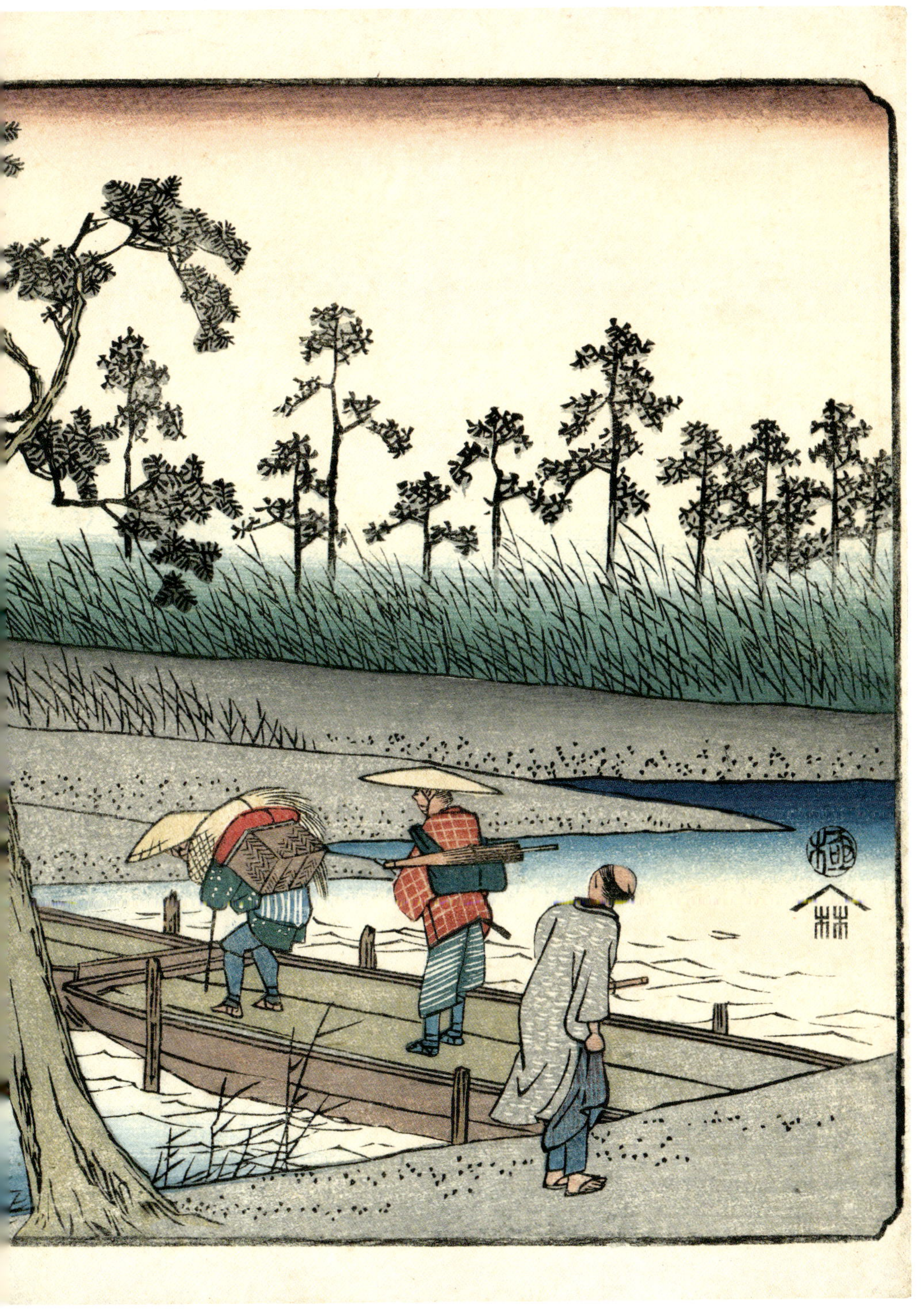

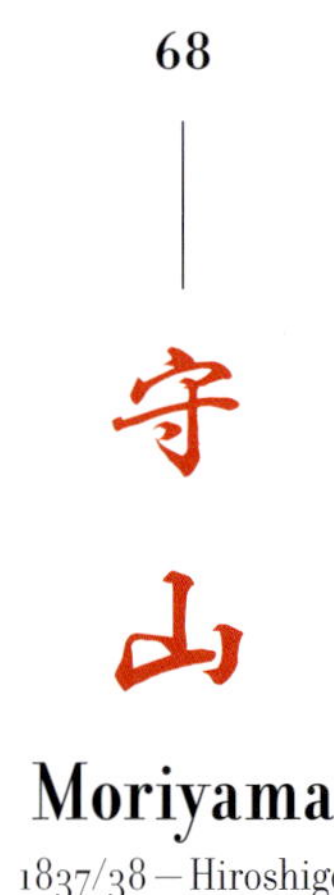

守山

Moriyama
1837/38 – Hiroshige

For travellers leaving Kyoto, Moriyama was ideally situated for the first night of lodging after a full day of walking. Hiroshige has imagined the village well furnished with an orderly row of inviting places to rest, with cherry blossom blooming alongside the river and into the hills rising in the mid-ground. The mountain in the background may be intended to represent Mount Mikami, a hill of just over 400 metres (1,315 feet) elevation. Its conical form rising from the relatively flat terrain led to the nickname "Ōmi Fuji". In the foreground is perhaps the Yasu River, although this ran perpendicular to the main street of the town, not parallel to it as depicted here. Based on Hiroshige's signature, it can be surmised that this design was created after his journey. However, no sketch from this locale survives; it may be that he created the design as best he could from memory, "borrowed" scenery from elsewhere, drew from his own imagination, or a combination of these elements.

The publisher Iseya Rihei has left his mark in two places in the design. A yellow banner emblazoned with his crest hangs from the eaves of the third shopfront from the right, just above the horse's rump. Next door, the name "Iseri" appears on a similar banner. The numbering in the cartouche of the impression illustrated here has been mistakenly "corrected" by hand from 68 to 67, although the printed number is correct. The cause of this misunderstanding is probably that the design for Musa, the previous station, was incorrectly printed with the number 66 instead of 67.

Für Reisende, die aus Kyoto kamen, war Moriyama nach einer ganztägigen Wanderung der ideale Ort für die erste Übernachtung. Hiroshige zeigt ein gut ausgestattetes Dorf mit einer geordneten Reihe von einladenden Gasthäusern und mit Kirschbäumen, die entlang des Flussufers und auf dem Hügel im Mittelgrund in voller Blüte stehen. Der Berg im Hintergrund soll möglicherweise den nur gut 400 Meter hohen Mikami darstellen. Wegen seiner Kegelform, die aus relativ flachem Terrain aufsteigt, erhielt er den Spitznamen „Fuji von Ōmi". Der Fluss im Vordergrund könnte der Yasu sein, obwohl er eigentlich quer und nicht, wie hier abgebildet, parallel zur Hauptstraße des Dorfes verlief. Hiroshiges Signatur gibt Anlass zu der Vermutung, dass der Entwurf nach seiner Kisokaidō-Reise entstand. Da von dieser Örtlichkeit jedoch keine Skizze existiert, könnte es sein, dass der Künstler die Szene, so gut er konnte, nach der Erinnerung entwarf, Landschaftselemente anderswo „ausborgte" oder seine Fantasie einsetzte – oder aber alle drei Herangehensweisen miteinander kombinierte

Der Verleger Iseya Rihei hat an zwei Stellen des Entwurfs seine Spuren hinterlassen. Auf einem gelben Banner, das an der dritten Ladenfassade von rechts vom Dachvorsprung herabhängt, prangt sein Logo knapp über dem Hinterteil des Pferdes, und nebenan steht auf einem ähnlichen Banner der Name „Iseri". Die Nummerierung in der Kartusche dieses Abzugs wurde per Hand irrigerweise von 68 auf 67 abgeändert, obwohl die eingedruckte Nummer stimmte. Das Missverständnis ist vermutlich darauf zurückzuführen, dass der Entwurf für die vorherige Station Musa mit der falschen Nummer 66 anstelle der 67 gedruckt wurde.

Pour les voyageurs en provenance de Kyoto, la situation de Moriyama était idéale pour une première nuit après une longue journée de marche. Hiroshige a imaginé un village bien doté en lieux d'hébergement soigneusement alignés, entourés de cerisiers en fleurs qui bordent la rivière et ornent les collines s'élevant entre le premier plan et l'arrière-plan. La montagne visible au fond pourrait représenter le mont Mikami, dont l'altitude dépasse à peine 400 mètres. Sa forme conique surplombant un territoire relativement plat lui a valu le surnom d'« Ōmi Fuji ». La rivière visible au premier plan est peut-être la Yasu ; toutefois, celle-ci traversait perpendiculairement la grand-rue de la ville, au lieu de lui être parallèle comme dans cette estampe. D'après la signature d'Hiroshige, on peut supposer que l'artiste a réalisé ce dessin après son voyage. Toutefois, il n'existe aujourd'hui plus aucun croquis de ce lieu ; il est possible qu'Hiroshige ait dessiné cette estampe de mémoire du mieux qu'il a pu, qu'il ait « emprunté » le paysage à un autre lieu ou inventé ce décor de toutes pièces, ou encore que l'illustration soit le fruit d'un mélange de tous ces éléments.

L'éditeur Iseya Rihei a laissé sa marque en deux endroits de cette estampe. Une bannière jaune portant ses armoiries est accrochée sous l'avant-toit de la troisième devanture à partir de la droite, juste au-dessus de la croupe du cheval. Dans la boutique voisine, le nom « Iseri » est inscrit sur une bannière semblable. Le numéro 68 visible dans le cartouche de cette épreuve a été corrigé à la main et remplace le numéro 67, bien que le numéro imprimé soit correct. Cette méprise vient probablement du fait que l'estampe de Musa, la station précédente, a été imprimée par erreur avec le numéro 66, au lieu du 67.

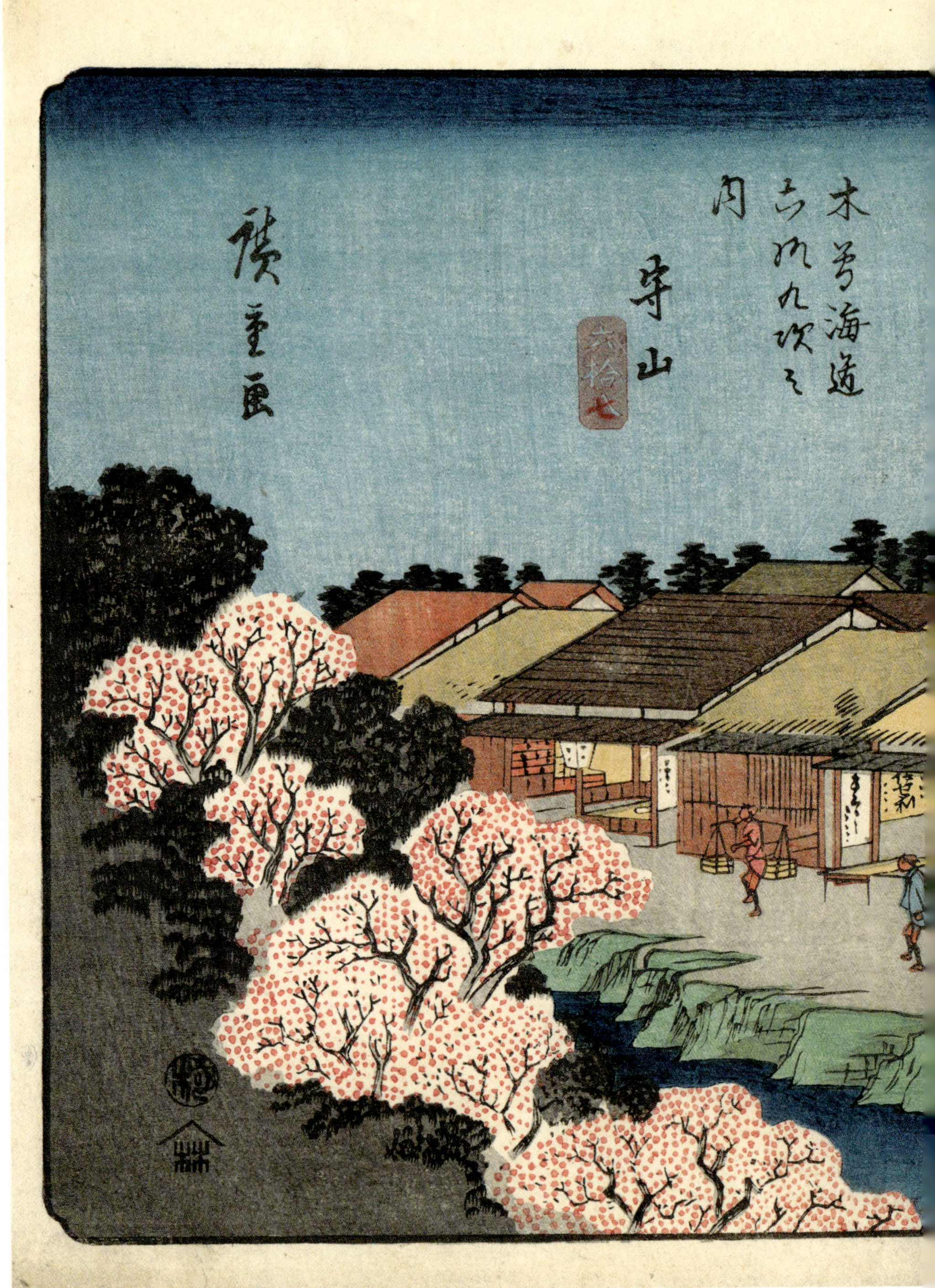

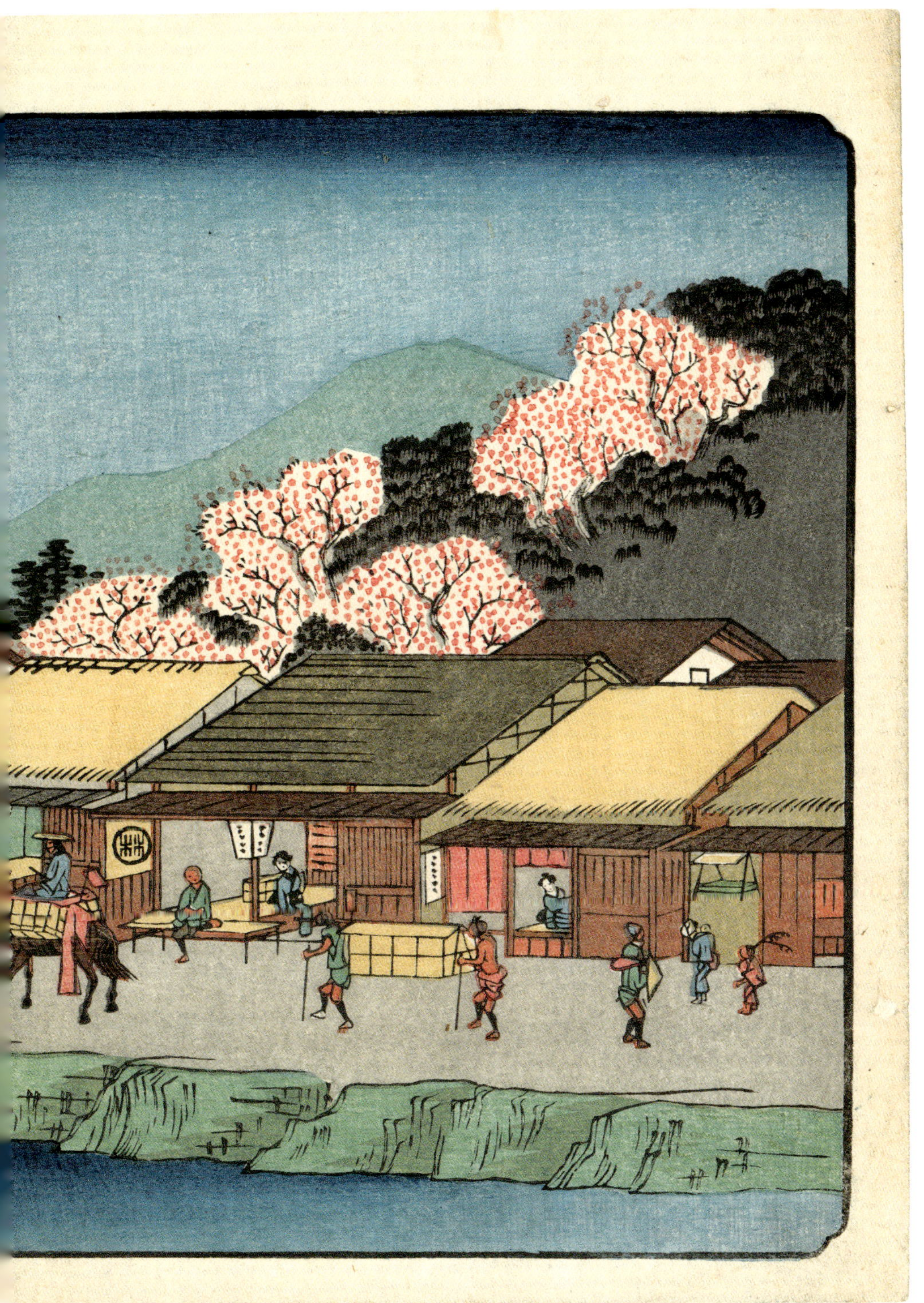

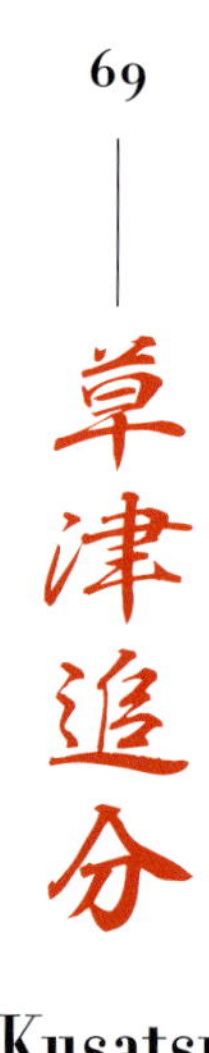

69

Kusatsu

1837/38 – Hiroshige

Kusatsu, around 23 kilometres (14 miles) from Kyoto, is a crossing point where the Kisokaidō and the Tōkaidō, the coastal route between Edo and Kyoto, unite. It is therefore not only a station of the Kisokaidō but also a station of the Tōkaidō. One of the two *honjin* in Kusatsu was built in 1635 but closed in 1870 as a result of the abolition of compulsory *daimyō* processions; since 1996 it has been a museum, operated by the City of Kusatsu.

Before entering the town from the north, travellers had to cross the Kusatsu River that flows west into Lake Biwa. A wooden lantern structure was installed on the left of the entrance to the town, shown here, following a sketch Hiroshige made during his journey to Kyoto. The vantage point of the sketch and the print are the same, suggesting that he saw the wide road with hills and trees on either side, and the roofs of the houses in the background, exactly like this. The stream in the foreground, the oddly small bridge and the mountain range in the far distance, are all absent, however, from his sketch. The mountain profile looks something like Mount Hiei; however, the view here is facing south towards the station whereas Mount Hiei is to the west opposite the lake, which means these peaks should be Mount Iwama (443 metres/1,454 feet) and Mount Otowa (593 metres/1,946 feet).

The figures in the centre of the print also derive from drawings Hiroshige made during the journey, but ones found elsewhere in his sketchbooks. On the left is a firewood-seller, in the centre a young girl holding an umbrella as she crosses the bridge, and on the right a group that may be a young woman with her elderly parents.

This design is mistakenly numbered 68 but should be 69.

Am Kreuzungspunkt Kusatsu rund 23 Kilometer vor Kyoto vereinigt sich der Kisokaidō mit dem Tōkaidō, der Küstenstraße zwischen Edo und Kyoto. Kusatsu ist daher nicht nur eine Station des Kisokaidō, sondern auch des Tōkaidō. Eines der beiden *honjin* von Kusatsu wurde 1635 erbaut, aber 1870 geschlossen, nachdem man die obligatorischen *daimyō*-Prozessionen abgeschafft hatte. Seit 1996 unterhält die Stadt Kusatsu in dem Gebäude ein Museum.

Bevor sie die Ortschaft von Norden her betraten, mussten Reisende den Kusatsu überqueren, der nach Westen in den Biwa-See fließt. Nach einer Skizze, die Hiroshige auf seiner Reise nach Kyoto anfertigte, ist hier der Ortseingang wiedergegeben, mit einer Holzlaterne links davon. Die Blickwinkel von Skizze und Druck sind identisch, was darauf hindeutet, dass der Künstler die breite, beidseitig von Hügeln und Bäumen gesäumte Straße und die Dächer der Häuser im Hintergrund genau so sah. Der Bach im Vordergrund, der merkwürdig kleine Steg und die Bergkette am Horizont fehlen jedoch in der Skizze. Das Bergprofil könnte auf den Hiei passen; da der Blick hier aber nach Süden auf die Station geht, während der Hiei gegenüber dem See im Westen liegt, dürften diese Gipfel den 443 Meter hohen Iwama und den 593 Meter hohen Otowa darstellen.

Die Figuren im Zentrum des Drucks sind Zeichnungen entlehnt, die Hiroshige ebenfalls während seiner Reise anfertigte, die aber an anderer Stelle in seinen Skizzenbüchern zu finden sind. Links geht ein Brennholzverkäufer, in der Mitte überquert ein junges Mädchen mit Schirm die Brücke, und bei der Gruppe rechts könnte es sich um eine junge Frau mit ihren betagten Eltern handeln.

Das Blatt ist fälschlicherweise mit 68 nummeriert, sollte aber Nummer 69 sein.

Située à environ 23 kilomètres de Kyoto, Kusatsu est le carrefour où se rejoignent la Kisokaidō et la Tōkaidō, route littorale reliant Edo à Kyoto. Il s'agit donc non seulement de la station de la Kisokaidō, mais aussi de la station de la Tōkaidō. Construite en 1635, l'une des deux *honjin* de Kusatsu a fermé ses portes en 1870 après l'abolition des processions obligatoires de *daïmio* ; en 1996, elle a été transformée en un musée géré par la Ville de Kusatsu.

Avant d'entrer dans la ville par le nord, les voyageurs devaient franchir la rivière Kusatsu qui se jette dans le lac Biwa à l'ouest. Une structure en bois abritant une lanterne a été édifiée à gauche de l'entrée de la ville, visible ici, selon un croquis réalisé par Hiroshige durant son voyage vers Kyoto. Les points de vue identiques du croquis et de l'estampe laissent penser que c'est exactement ainsi que l'artiste a vu la large route bordée, de part et d'autre, de collines et d'arbres, et les toits des maisons à l'arrière-plan. Toutefois, le cours d'eau du premier plan, le pont curieusement petit et la chaîne de montagnes visible dans le lointain sont tous absents du croquis. La silhouette de la montagne rappelle un peu le mont Hiei ; cependant, la vue de l'estampe est orientée au sud, vers la station, tandis que le mont Hiei se trouve à l'ouest, de l'autre côté du lac : il devrait alors s'agir des monts Iwama (443 mètres) et Otowa (593 mètres).

Les personnages placés au centre de l'estampe proviennent également de dessins réalisés par Hiroshige pendant son voyage, mais présents dans d'autres pages de ses carnets de croquis. On voit à gauche un vendeur de bois de chauffage, au centre une jeune fille qui traverse le pont, une ombrelle à la main, et, à droite, un groupe qui pourrait être composé d'une jeune femme et de ses vieux parents.

Cette estampe porte par erreur le numéro 68, au lieu du 69.

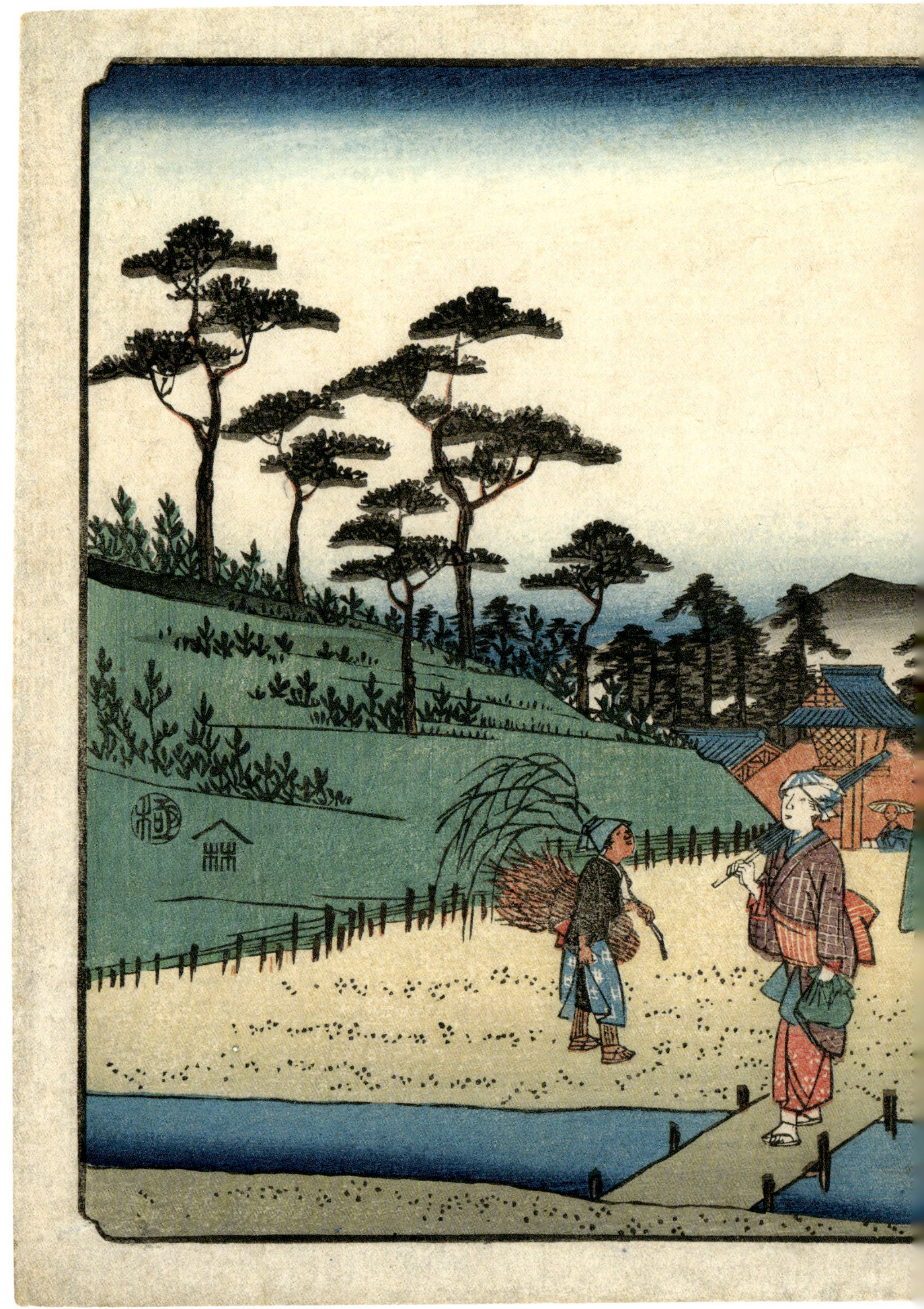

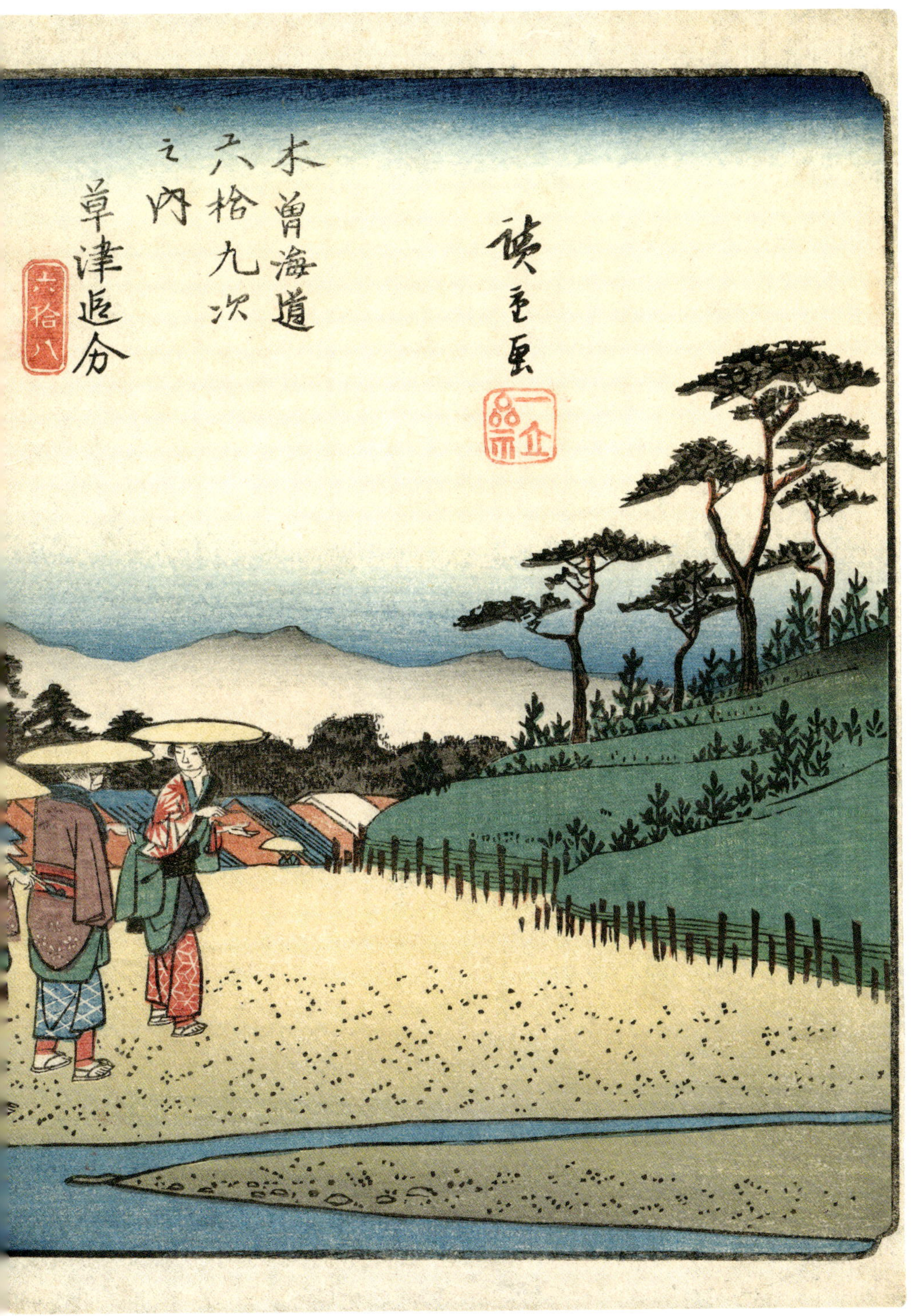

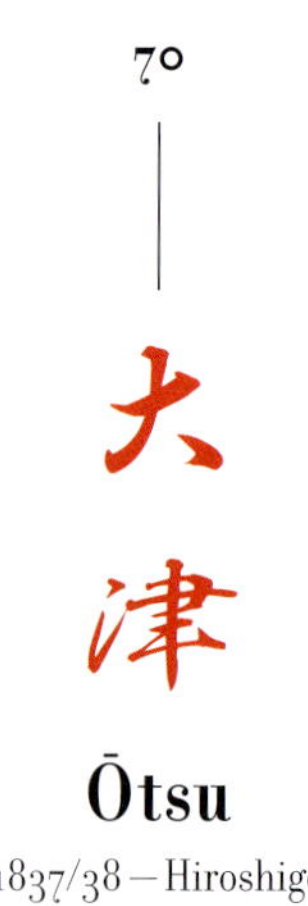

70

Ōtsu

1837/38 – Hiroshige

Featuring the view along the main street of Ōtsu looking out over Lake Biwa, Hiroshige's design for the final station of the Kisokaidō, and the concluding design of the series, is a celebratory finale to the physical and imaginative journey represented by *The Sixty-Nine Stations along the Kisokaidō*.

Banners and signs in assorted colours and shapes scattered throughout the design enhance the festive aspect of the scene and proclaim the names of those involved in the print's production. "Kin", the first character of the name of the publishing house of Iseya Rihei, Kinjudō, is displayed in a circle suspended from the upper storey of the first building on the right-hand side of the street, as well as on the paper lantern affixed to the entrance below. The square and round signs displayed on the neighbouring buildings spell out "Hiro" and "shige", i.e. the name of the artist. The large grey banner below is emblazoned with a Chinese character meaning "complete".

Midway along the row of buildings on the left, a yellow octagonal sign announces "New Publication". The crest of the publisher, Iseya Rihei, is suspended from the upper storey of the first inn on the left, and "Iseri" and "Ri", referring to his name, are inscribed on the near side of the white lantern beneath and on the yellow sign further down the hill. The words "great success", written on the offside of the lantern facing on to the street, and "excellent luck", on the gourd-shaped lantern further along, confidently proclaim the artist's and publisher's hopes for this venture.

As well as the Kisokaidō, Ōtsu was also a station on the coastal Tōkaidō route to Edo. The oxen lumbering up the slope with heavily loaded carts allude to the busy port located on the shore of Lake Biwa, Japan's largest body of fresh water. In addition to being a transit hub, Ōtsu was also a site of great cultural significance. According to legend, it was at the Ishiyama Temple here that Murasaki Shikibu (c. 973–1014) was moved by the reflection of the full moon in Lake Biwa to begin writing the world's first novel, *The Tale of Genji*.

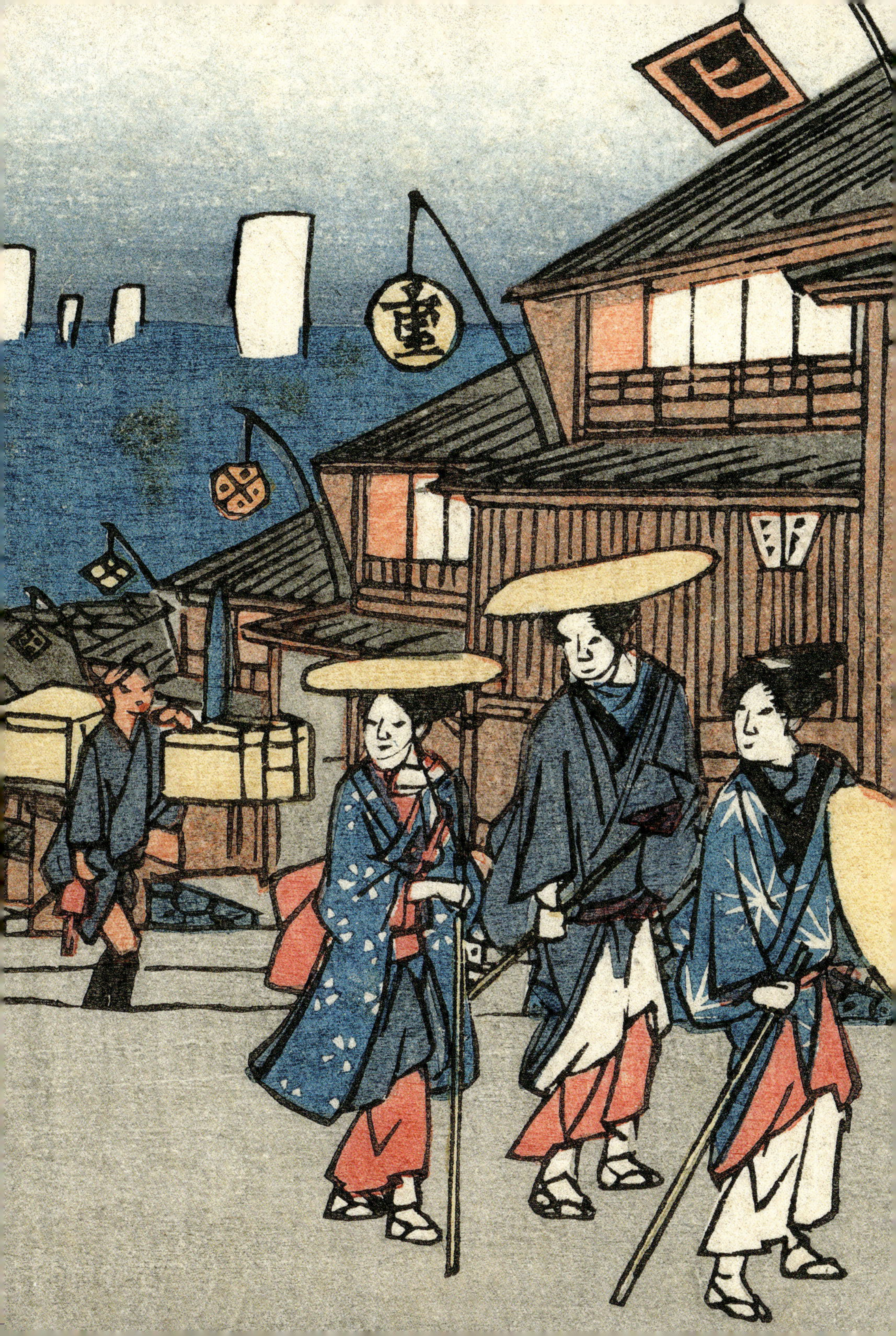

重
ヒ

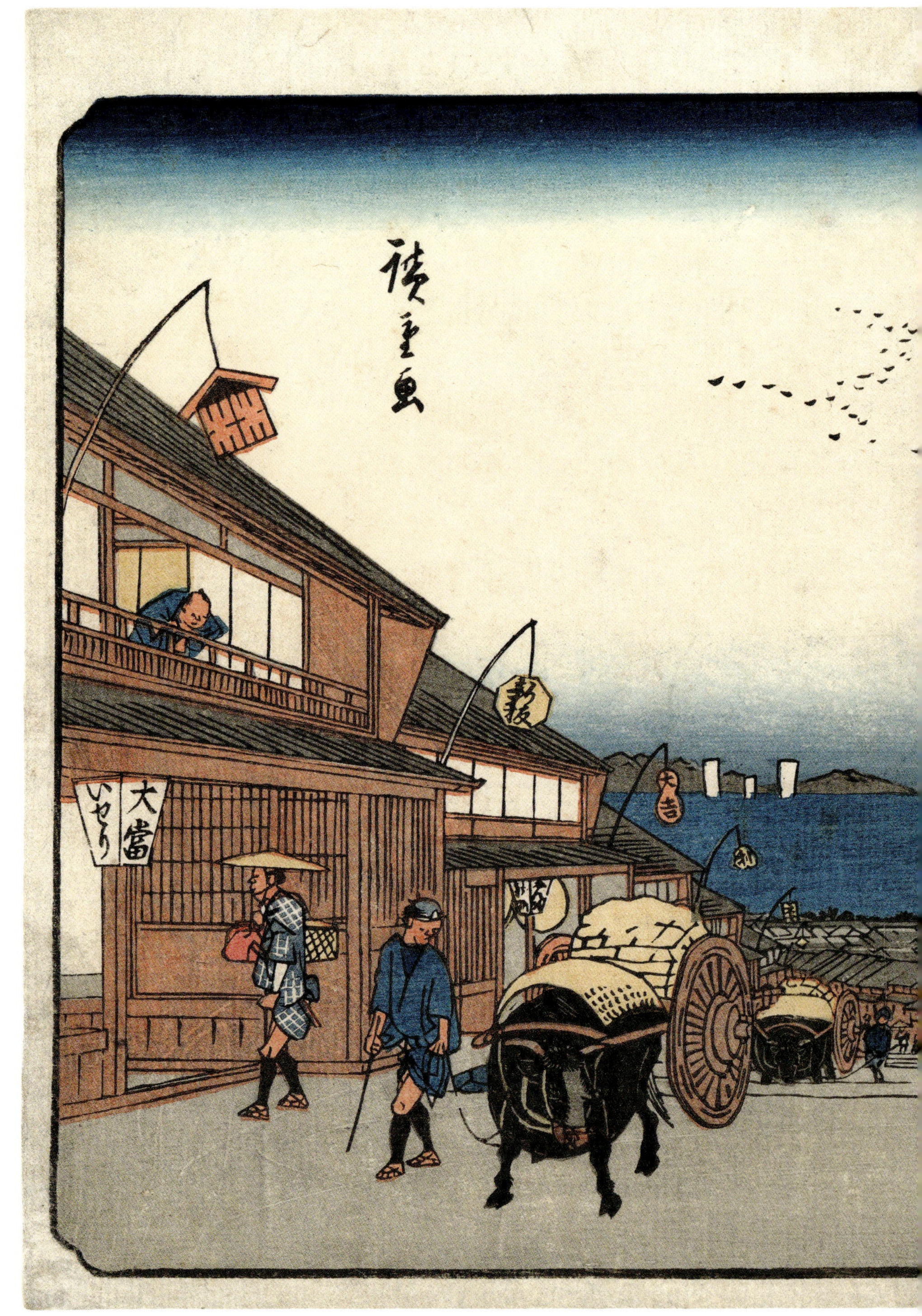

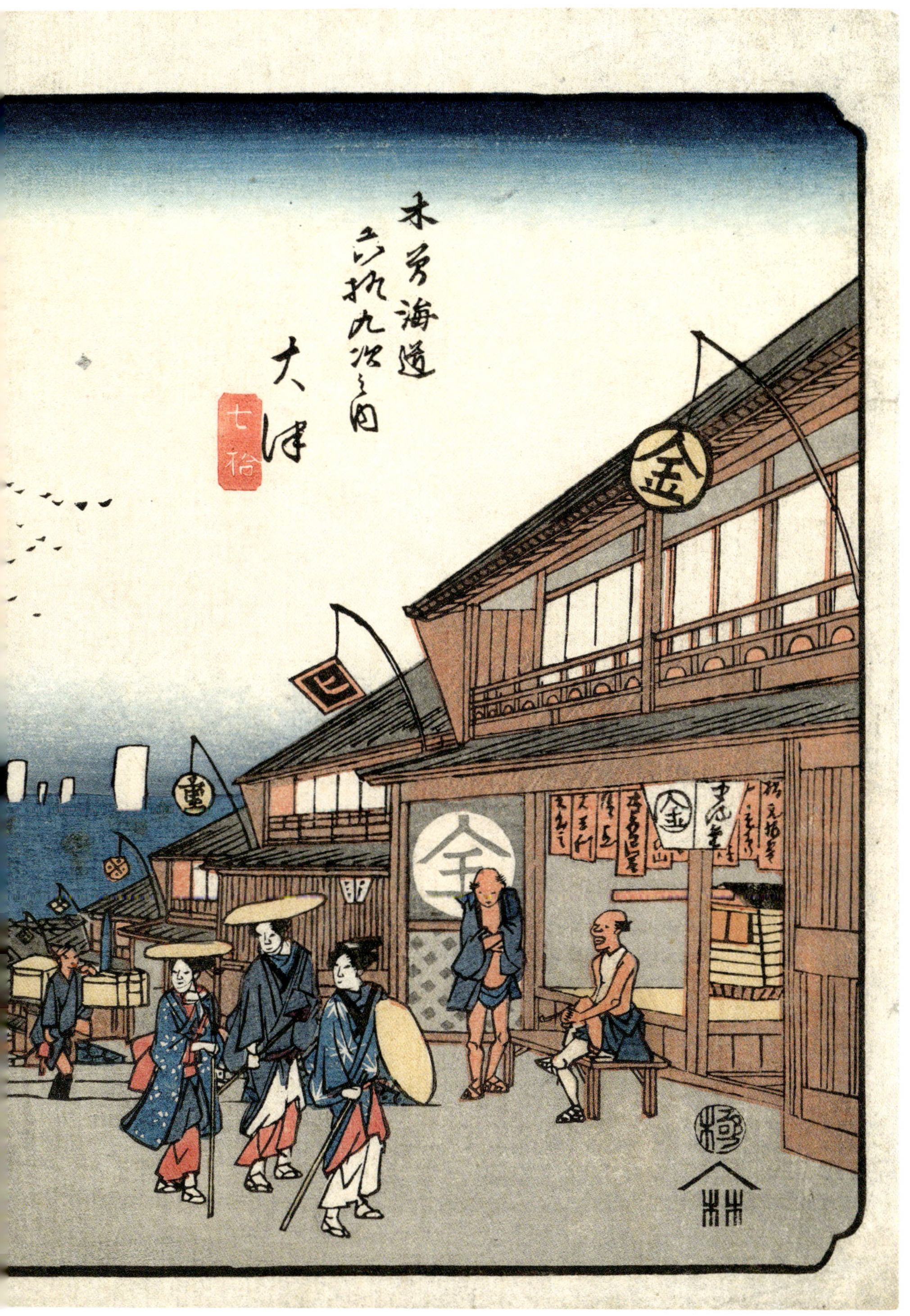

木曽海道
六拾九次之内
大津
七柁
金
金
金

Mit seinem Blick durch die Hauptstraße von Ōtsu hinaus über den Biwa-See bildet Hiroshiges Entwurf für die letzte Station des Kisokaidō – und das abschließende Blatt der Serie – einen feierlichen Schlussakkord der physischen und imaginären Reise durch *Die neunundsechzig Stationen des Kisokaidō*.

Über das ganze Blatt verstreute Banner und Schilder in allerlei Farben und Formen verstärken den festlichen Aspekt der Szene und verkünden die Namen all derer, die an der Entstehung des Druckwerks beteiligt waren. „Kin", das erste Zeichen im Namen des Verlages von Iseya Rihei, Kinjudō, schmückt sowohl das runde Schild, das vom Obergeschoss des ersten Gebäudes auf der rechten Straßenseite herabhängt, als auch die Papierlaterne im Eingang darunter. Die eckigen und runden Schilder an den Nachbargebäuden buchstabieren mit „Hiro" und „shige" den Namen des Künstlers. Auf dem großen grauen Banner darunter prangt ein chinesisches Schriftzeichen mit der Bedeutung „vollendet".

In der Mitte der Häuserreihe links kündigt ein achteckiges Schild eine „Neuerscheinung" an. Das Firmenlogo des Verlegers Iseya Rihei weht im Obergeschoss der ersten Herberge links im Wind, die Schriftzüge „Iseri" und „Ri", die sich auf seinen Namen beziehen, sind diesseits auf der weißen Laterne darunter und auf einem gelben Schild hügelabwärts zu lesen. Die Worte „großer Erfolg" auf der straßenabgewandten Seite der Laterne und „vortreffliches Glück" auf dem kalebassenförmigen Lampion weiter die Straße hinunter verlautbaren selbstbewusst die Hoffnungen, die der Künstler und der Verleger für ihr Projekt hegten.

Ōtsu war eine gemeinsame Station des Kisokaidō und des Tōkaidō, der an der Küste entlang nach Edo führte. Die Ochsen, die mit schwer beladenen Wagen nur mühsam den Anstieg bewältigen, sind ein Hinweis auf den betriebsamen Hafen am Ufer des Biwa-Sees, Japans größtem Süßgewässer. Neben seiner Funktion als Drehscheibe des Durchgangsverkehrs spielte Ōtsu auch kulturell eine bedeutende Rolle. Der Legende nach wurde die kaiserliche Hofdame und Schriftstellerin Murasaki Shikibu (um 973–1014) am hiesigen Ishiyama-Tempel von der Spiegelung des Vollmonds im Biwa-See angeregt, den ersten Roman der Welt zu beginnen, *Die Geschichte vom Prinzen Genji*.

La vue de la grand-rue d'Ōtsu donnant sur le lac Biwa, sujet de l'estampe d'Hiroshige pour la dernière station de la Kisokaidō et ultime illustration de cette série, constitue une apothéose exaltant le voyage physique et imaginaire que représentent *Les soixante-neuf stations de la Kisokaidō*.

Réparties dans l'ensemble de l'image, des bannières et des enseignes aux couleurs et aux formes assorties soulignent l'ambiance de festivité de la scène et proclament les noms de ceux qui ont participé à la réalisation de l'estampe. « Kin », le premier caractère de Kinjudō, nom de la maison d'édition d'Iseya Rihei, est inscrit dans un cercle accroché au premier étage du premier bâtiment situé à droite de la rue, ainsi que sur la lanterne de papier fixée au-dessous, à l'entrée. Les enseignes, carrée et ronde, qui ornent les bâtiments voisins portent les inscriptions « Hiro » et « shige », nom de l'artiste. La grande bannière visible au-dessous arbore un caractère chinois signifiant « terminé ».

À mi-chemin de la rangée de constructions située à gauche, une enseigne octogonale jaune indique « Nouvelle publication ». Les armoiries de l'éditeur, Iseya Rihei, sont suspendues à l'étage de la première auberge à gauche, tandis qu'on lit « Iseri » et « Ri », allusion à son nom, sur la face la plus proche de la lanterne blanche accrochée sous l'étage et sur l'enseigne jaune qui se trouve tout en bas de la colline. Les mots « grand succès », inscrits sur la face de la lanterne donnant sur la rue, et « excellente chance », visibles sur la lanterne en forme de gourde un peu plus loin, annoncent avec confiance les espoirs qu'ont placés l'artiste et l'éditeur dans leur entreprise.

Ōtsu était une station située à la fois sur la Kisokaidō et sur la route littorale de la Tōkaidō qui menait à Edo. Les bœufs qui gravissent pesamment la pente en tractant des charrettes lourdement chargées font allusion au port très fréquenté des bords du lac Biwa, la plus grande réserve d'eau douce du Japon. En plus d'être un important lieu de transit, Ōtsu était un haut lieu culturel. Selon la légende, c'est au temple d'Ishiyama, situé dans la ville, que Murasaki Shikibu (vers 973–1014), émue par le reflet de la pleine lune sur le lac Biwa, entama la rédaction du tout premier roman au monde, *Le Dit du Genji*.

Facts on the Stations and Colour Variations
Angaben zu den Stationen und Farbvarianten
Indications sur les stations et variantes chromatiques

Note: The distances between the stations are taken from the 1805 guidebook *Views of Famous Sights along the Kiso Road (Kisoji meisho zue)*. Information on the populations of stations, houses and inns is taken from the 1843 census *General Register of the Station Villages along the Nakasendō (Nakasendō shukuson daigaichū)*. The reference number after the station name indicates the variation illustrated in the respective plates on pp. 100–413. Some examples are illustrated on pp. 434–441. Capital letters after the number of a print indicate the publisher, as follows: A = Takenouchi Magohachi; AB = Takenouchi Magohachi and Iseya Rihei; B = Iseya Rihei; C = Yamadaya Shjirō. Numbers after these capitals refer to a new state within a publisher's edition for which changes were made to the block or blocks. Lower-case letters at the end indicate colour variations.

1 – NIHONBASHI | 1.A1b

Post station details

distance to next station: 2 *ri*
(7.85 km/4.88 miles)

Publishing details

1.A1, 1835, No. 1, First of the Kisokaidō Series: *Snowy Morning on Nihonbashi*
ARTIST: Eisen
SIGNED: Eisen ga 英泉画
PUBLISHER: Takenouchi Magohachi,
PUBLISHER SEAL(S): Takenouchi 竹内, Hōeidō han 保永堂版

1.B1a–c, No. 1, First of the Kisokaidō Series: *Snowy Morning on Nihonbashi*
ARTIST: Eisen. SIGNED: removed
PUBLISHER: Iseya Rihei
PUBLISHER SEAL(S): Takenouchi 竹内, Hōeidō han 保永堂版

1.C1a–b, No. 1, First of the Kisokaidō Series: *Snowy Morning on Nihonbashi*
ARTIST: Eisen. SIGNED: removed
PUBLISHER: Yamadaya Shōbei
PUBLISHER SEAL(S): Takenouchi 竹内, Hōeidō han 保永堂版

2 – ITABASHI | 2.A1a

Post station details

573 houses, 1 *honjin*, 3 *waki-honjin*, 54 *hatagoya*, population: 2,448, distance to next station: 2 *ri* 8 *chō* (8.72 km/5.42 miles)

Publishing details

2.A1a–b, 1835, No. 2, *Kisokaidō: Itabashi Station*
ARTIST: Eisen
SIGNED: Eisen ga 英泉画
PUBLISHER: Takenouchi Magohachi
PUBLISHER SEAL(S): Takenouchi 竹内, Hōeidō 保永堂

2.B1a–b, No. 2, *Kisokaidō: Itabashi Station*
ARTIST: Eisen. SIGNED: removed
PUBLISHER: Iseya Rihei
PUBLISHER SEAL(S): Takenouchi 竹内 (removed), Hōeidō 保永堂

2.B2, No. 2, *Kisokaidō: Itabashi Station*
ARTIST: Eisen. SIGNED: removed
PUBLISHER: Iseya Rihei
PUBLISHER SEAL(S): both removed

2.C1, No. 2, *Kisokaidō: Itabashi Station*
ARTIST: Eisen. SIGNED: removed
PUBLISHER: Yamadaya Shōbei
PUBLISHER SEAL(S): both removed

3 – WARABI | 3.A1a

Post station details

430 houses, 2 *honjin*, 1 *waki-honjin*, 23 *hatagoya*, population: 2,223, distance to next station: 1 *ri han* (5.89 km/3.66 miles)

Publishing details

3.A1a–b, 1835, No. 3, *Kisokaidō: Warabi Station, Toda River Crossing*
ARTIST: Eisen
SIGNED: Keisai ga 渓斎画
PUBLISHER: Takenouchi Magohachi
PUBLISHER SEAL(S): Hōei 保永, Takenouchi 竹内

3.B1a–c, No. 3, *Kisokaidō: Warabi Station, Toda River Crossing*
ARTIST: Eisen. SIGNED: removed
PUBLISHER: Iseya Rihei
PUBLISHER SEAL(S): Hōei 保永, Takenouchi 竹内 (removed)

3.C1, No. 3, *Kisokaidō: Warabi Station, Toda River Crossing*
ARTIST: Eisen. SIGNED: removed
PUBLISHER: Yamadaya Shōbei
PUBLISHER SEAL(S): Hōei 保永, Takenouchi 竹内 (removed)

4 – URAWA | 4.A1

Post station details

273 houses, 1 *honjin*, 3 *waki-honjin*, 15 *hatagoya*, population: 1,230, distance to next station: 1 *ri* 10 *chō* (5.02 km/3.12 miles)

Publishing details

4.A1, 1835, No. 4, *Stations on the Kiso Road: Urawa Post Town, Distant View of Mount Asama*
ARTIST: Eisen
SIGNED: Eisen ga 英泉画
PUBLISHER: Takenouchi Magohachi
PUBLISHER SEAL(S): Takenouchi 竹内, Hōeidō hanten 保永堂板店

4.B1a–b, No. 4, *Stations on the Kiso Road: Urawa Post Town, Distant View of Mount Asama*
ARTIST: Eisen. SIGNED: removed
PUBLISHER: Iseya Rihei
PUBLISHER SEAL(S): Takenouchi 竹内 (removed), Hōeidō hanten 保永堂板店

4.C1a–b, No. 4, *Stations on the Kiso Road: Urawa Post Town, Distant View of Mount Asama*
ARTIST: Eisen. SIGNED: removed
PUBLISHER: Yamadaya Shōbei
PUBLISHER SEAL(S): both removed

5 – ŌMIYA | 5.A1

Post station details

319 houses, 1 *honjin*, 9 *waki-honjin*, 25 *hatagoya*, population: 1,508, distance to next station: 2 *ri* 8 *chō* (8.72 km/5.42 miles)

Publishing details

5.A1, 1835, No. 5, *Kisokaidō: Ōmiya Post Town, Distant Scenery of Mount Fuji*
ARTIST: Eisen
SIGNED: Keisai ga 渓斎画
PUBLISHER: Takenouchi Magohachi
PUBLISHER SEAL(S): Hōeidō han 保永堂版, Takenouchi 竹内

5.B1, No. 5, *Kisokaidō: Ōmiya Post Town, Distant Scenery of Mount Fuji*
ARTIST: Eisen. SIGNED: removed
PUBLISHER: Iseya Rihei
PUBLISHER SEAL(S): Hōeidō han 保永堂版, Takenouchi 竹内

5.C1a–c, No. 5, *Kisokaidō: Ōmiya Post Town, Distant Scenery of Mount Fuji*
ARTIST: Eisen. SIGNED: removed
PUBLISHER: Yamadaya Shōbei
PUBLISHER SEAL(S): Hōeidō han 保永堂版, Takenouchi 竹内 (removed)

6 – AGEO | 6.A1

Post station details

182 houses, 1 *honjin*, 3 *waki-honjin*, 41 *hatagoya*, population: 793, distance to next station: 30 *chō* (3.27 km/2.03 miles)

Publishing details

6.A1, 1835, No. 6, *Kisokaidō: Ageo Post Town, Kamo Shrine*
ARTIST: Eisen
SIGNED: Keisai ga 渓斎画
PUBLISHER: Takenouchi Magohachi
PUBLISHER SEAL(S): Takenouchi han 竹内板

6.B1, No. 6, *Kisokaidō: Ageo Post Town, Kamo Shrine*
ARTIST: Eisen. SIGNED: removed
PUBLISHER: Iseya Rihei
PUBLISHER SEAL(S): Takenouchi han 竹内板

6.C1, No. 6, *Kisokaidō: Ageo Post Town, Kamo Shrine*
ARTIST: Eisen. SIGNED: removed
PUBLISHER: Yamadaya Shōbei
PUBLISHER SEAL(S): Takenouchi han 竹内板

7 – OKEGAWA | 7.A1

Post station details

347 houses, 1 *honjin*, 2 *waki-honjin*, 36 *hatagoya*, population: 1,444, distance to next station: 1 *ri* 30 *chō* (7.2 km/4.47 miles)

Publishing details

7.A1, 1835, No. 7, *Kisokaidō: Okegawa Post Town, View of the Plain*
ARTIST: Eisen
SIGNED: Eisen ga 英泉画
PUBLISHER: Takenouchi Magohachi
PUBLISHER SEAL(S): Takenouchi 竹内, Hōeidō 保永堂

7.B1a–b, No. 7, *Kisokaidō: Okegawa Post Town, View of the Plain*
ARTIST: Eisen. SIGNED: removed
PUBLISHER: Iseya Rihei
PUBLISHER SEAL(S): Takenouchi 竹内 (removed), Hōeidō 保永堂

7.C1, No. 7, *Kisokaidō: Okegawa Post Town, View of the Plain*
ARTIST: Eisen. SIGNED: removed
PUBLISHER: Yamadaya Shōbei
PUBLISHER SEAL(S): Takenouchi 竹内 (removed), Hōeidō 保永堂

8 – KŌNOSU | 8.A1

Post station details

566 houses, 1 *honjin*, 1 *waki-honjin*, 58 *hatagoya*, population: 2,274, distance to next station: 4 *ri* 8 *chō* (16.58 km/10.30 miles)

Publishing details

8.A1, 1835, No. 8, *Kisokaidō: Kōnosu, Distant View of Fuji at Fukiage*
ARTIST: Eisen
SIGNED: Keisai ga 渓斎画
PUBLISHER: Takenouchi Magohachi
PUBLISHER SEAL(S): Hōei 保永, Dō 堂, Takenouchi 竹内

8.B1a–b, No. 8, *Kisokaidō: Kōnosu, Distant View of Fuji at Fukiage*
ARTIST: Eisen. SIGNED: removed
PUBLISHER: Iseya Rihei
PUBLISHER SEAL(S): Hōei 保永, Dō 堂, Takenouchi 竹内

8.C1a–b, No. 8, *Kisokaidō: Kōnosu, Distant View of Fuji at Fukiage*
ARTIST: Eisen. SIGNED: removed
PUBLISHER: Yamadaya Shōbei
PUBLISHER SEAL(S): Hōei 保永, Dō 堂, Takenouchi 竹内 (removed)

9 – KUMAGAYA | 9.A1

Post station details

1,075 houses, 2 *honjin*, 1 *waki-honjin*, 19 *hatagoya*, population: 3,263, distance to next station: 2 *ri* 30 *chō* (11.12 km/6.91 miles)

Publishing details

9.A1, 1835, No. 9, *Along the Kiso: Kumagaya Post Town, View of Hatchōzutsumi*
ARTIST: Eisen
SIGNED: Eisen ga 英泉画
PUBLISHER: Takenouchi Magohachi
PUBLISHER SEAL(S): Takenouchi 竹内, Shinpan 新版

9.B1, No. 9, *Along the Kiso: Kumagaya Post Town, View of Hatchōzutsumi*
ARTIST: Eisen. SIGNED: removed
PUBLISHER: Iseya Rihei
PUBLISHER SEAL(S): Takenouchi 竹内 (removed), Shinpan 新版

9.C1, No. 9, *Along the Kiso: Kumagaya Post Town, View of Hatchōzutsumi*
ARTIST: Eisen. SIGNED: removed
PUBLISHER: Yamadaya Shōbei
PUBLISHER SEAL(S): Takenouchi 竹内 (removed), Shinpan 新版

10 – FUKAYA | 10.A1a

Post station details

525 houses, 1 *honjin*, 4 *waki-honjin*, 80 *hatagoya*, population: 1,928, distance to next station: 2 *ri* 29 *chō*, (11.01 km/6.84 miles)

Publishing details

10.A1a–b, 1835, No. 10, *Kisokaidō: Fukaya Station*
ARTIST: Eisen
SIGNED: Eisen ga 英泉画
PUBLISHER: Takenouchi Magohachi
PUBLISHER SEAL(S): Takenouchi 竹内, Hōeidō hanmoto 保永堂　版元

10.B1a–c, No. 10, *Kisokaidō: Fukaya Station*
ARTIST: Eisen. SIGNED: removed
PUBLISHER: Iseya Rihei
PUBLISHER SEAL(S): Takenouchi 竹内 (removed), Hōeidō hanmoto 保永堂　版元

10.C1, No. 10, *Kisokaidō: Fukaya Station*
ARTIST: Eisen. SIGNED: removed
PUBLISHER: Yamadaya Shōbei
PUBLISHER SEAL(S): Takenouchi 竹内 (removed), Hōeidō hanmoto 保永堂　版元

11 – HONJŌ | 11.A1

Post station details

1,212 houses, 2 *honjin*, 2 *waki-honjin*, 70 *hatagoya*, population: 4,554, distance to next station: 2 *ri* (7.85 km/4.88 miles)

Publishing details

11.A1, 1835, No. 11, *Stations on the Kiso Road: Honjō Post Town, Crossing the Kanna River*
ARTIST: Eisen
SIGNED: Keisai ga 渓斎画
PUBLISHER: Takenouchi Magohachi
PUBLISHER SEAL(S): Hanmoto Takenouchi Hōeidō 版元　竹内　保永堂

11.B1, No. 11, *Stations on the Kiso Road: Honjō Post Town, Crossing the Kanna River*
ARTIST: Eisen. SIGNED: removed
PUBLISHER: Iseya Rihei
PUBLISHER SEAL(S): Hanmoto Takenouchi Hōeidō 版元　竹内　保永堂 (removed)

11.C1, No. 11, *Stations on the Kiso Road: Honjō Post Town, Crossing the Kanna River*
ARTIST: Eisen. SIGNED: removed
PUBLISHER: Yamadaya Shōbei
PUBLISHER SEAL(S): Hanmoto Takenouchi Hōeidō 版元　竹内　保永堂 (removed)

12 – SHINMACHI | 12.B1b

Post station details

407 houses, 2 *honjin*, 1 *waki-honjin*, 43 *hatagoya*, population: 1,437, distance to next station: 1 *ri han* (5.89 km/3.66 miles)

Publishing details

12.B1a–b, 1836/37, No. 12, *The Sixty-Nine Stations along the Kisokaidō: Shinmachi*
ARTIST: Utagawa Hiroshige
SIGNED: Hiroshige ga 広重画
ARTIST SEAL: Ichiryūsai 一立斎
PUBLISHER: Iseya Rihei
PUBLISHER SEAL(S): Kinjudō 錦樹堂

12.B2a–c, No. 12, *The Sixty-Nine Stations along the Kisokaidō: Shinmachi*
ARTIST: Utagawa Hiroshige
SIGNED: Hiroshige ga 広重画
ARTIST SEAL: removed
PUBLISHER: Iseya Rihei
PUBLISHER SEAL(S): Kinjudō 錦樹堂

12.C1, No. 12, *The Sixty-Nine Stations along the Kisokaidō: Shinmachi*
ARTIST: Utagawa Hiroshige
SIGNED: Hiroshige ga 広重画
ARTIST SEAL: Ichiryūsai 一立斎
PUBLISHER: Yamadaya Shōbei
PUBLISHER SEAL(S): Kinjudō 錦樹堂

13 – KURAGANO | 13.A1c

Post station details

297 houses, 1 *honjin*, 2 *waki-honjin*, 32 *hatagoya*, population: 2,032, distance to next station: 1 *ri* 19 *chō*, (6 km/3.73 miles)

Publishing details

13.A1a–c, 1835/36, No. 13, *Kisokaidō: Kuragano Post Town, Picture of the Karasu River*
ARTIST: Eisen
SIGNED: Eisen ga 英泉画
PUBLISHER: Takenouchi Magohachi
PUBLISHER SEAL(S): Takenouchi 竹内, Hōeidō 保永堂

13.B1a–b, No. 13, *Kisokaidō: Kuragano Post Town, Picture of the Karasu River*
ARTIST: Eisen. SIGNED: removed
PUBLISHER: Iseya Rihei
PUBLISHER SEAL(S): Takenouchi 竹内, Hōeidō 保永堂

13.C1, No. 13, *Kisokaidō: Kuragano Post Town, Picture of the Karasu River*
ARTIST: Eisen. SIGNED: removed
PUBLISHER: Yamadaya Shōbei
PUBLISHER SEAL(S): Takenouchi 竹内, Hōeidō 保永堂

14 – TAKASAKI | 14.AB1a

Post station details

837 houses, 15 *hatagoya*, population: 3,235, distance to next station: 1 *ri* 30 *chō* (7.2 km/4.47 miles)

Publishing details

14.AB1a–b, 1836/37, No. 14, *The Sixty-Nine Stations along the Kisokaidō: Takasaki*
ARTIST: Utagawa Hiroshige
SIGNED: Hiroshige ga 広重画
ARTIST SEAL: Ichiryūsai 一立斎

PUBLISHER: Takenouchi Magohachi &
Iseya Rihei
PUBLISHER SEAL(S): Hōeidō 保永堂

14.B1, No. 14, *The Sixty-Nine Stations
along the Kisokaidō: Takasaki*
ARTIST: Utagawa Hiroshige
SIGNED: Hiroshige ga 広重画
ARTIST SEAL: Ichiryūsai 一立斎
PUBLISHER: Iseya Rihei
PUBLISHER SEAL(S): Hōeidō 保永堂

14.C1, No. 14, *The Sixty-Nine Stations
along the Kisokaidō: Takasaki*
ARTIST: Utagawa Hiroshige
SIGNED: Hiroshige ga 広重画
ARTIST SEAL: Ichiryūsai 一立斎
PUBLISHER: Yamadaya Shōbei
PUBLISHER SEAL(S): Hōeidō 保永堂

15 – ITAHANA | 15.B1a

Post station details
312 houses, 1 *honjin*, 1 *waki-honjin*,
54 *hatagoya*, population: 1,422,
distance to next station: 30 *chō*
(3.27 km/2.03 miles)

Publishing details
15.AB1, 1836/37, No. 15,
*The Sixty-Nine Stations along
the Kisokaidō: Itahana*
ARTIST: [Eisen]. SIGNED: unsigned
PUBLISHER: Takenouchi Magohachi
& Iseya Rihei
PUBLISHER SEAL(S): Ike Naka Iseri
池仲伊世利

15.B1, No. 15, *The Sixty-Nine Stations
along the Kisokaidō: Itahana*
ARTIST: [Eisen]. SIGNED: unsigned
PUBLISHER: Iseya Rihei
PUBLISHER SEAL(S): Ike Naka Iseri
池仲伊世利

15.B2a–b, No. 15, *The Sixty-Nine
Stations along the Kisokaidō: Itahana*
ARTIST: Eisen. SIGNED: unsigned
PUBLISHER: Iseya Rihei
PUBLISHER SEAL(S): Iseri 伊世利

15.C1, No. 15, *The Sixty-Nine Stations
along the Kisokaidō: Itahana*
ARTIST: [Eisen]. SIGNED: unsigned
PUBLISHER: Yamadaya Shōbei
PUBLISHER SEAL(S): Iseri 伊世利

16 – ANNAKA | 16.B1a

Post station details
64 houses, 1 *honjin*, 2 *waki-honjin*,
17 *hatagoya*, population: 348,
distance to next station: 1 *ri* 30 *chō*
(7.2 km/4.47 miles)

Publishing details
16.B1a–b, 1836/37, No. 16,
*The Sixty-Nine Stations along
the Kisokaidō: Annaka*
ARTIST: Utagawa Hiroshige
SIGNED: Hiroshige ga 広重画
ARTIST SEAL: Ichiryūsai 弐粒斎
PUBLISHER: Iseya Rihei
PUBLISHER SEAL(S): Kinjudō 錦樹堂

16.C1, No. 16, *The Sixty-Nine
Stations along the Kisokaidō: Annaka*
ARTIST: Utagawa Hiroshige
SIGNED: Hiroshige ga 広重画
ARTIST SEAL: Ichiryūsai 弐粒斎
PUBLISHER: Yamadaya Shōbei
PUBLISHER SEAL(S): Kinjudō 錦樹堂

17 – MATSUIDA | 17.B1b

Post station details
252 houses, 2 *honjin*, 2 *waki-honjin*,
14 *hatagoya*, population: 1,009,
distance to next station: 2 *ri han*
(9.82 km/6.10 miles)

Publishing details
17.B1a–c, 1836/37, No. 17,
*The Sixty-Nine Stations along
the Kisokaidō: Matsuida*
ARTIST: Utagawa Hiroshige
SIGNED: Hiroshige ga 広重画
ARTIST SEAL: Ichiryūsai 弐立斎
PUBLISHER: Iseya Rihei
PUBLISHER SEAL(S): Kinjudō 錦樹堂

17.C1, No. 17, *The Sixty-Nine Stations
along the Kisokaidō: Matsuida*
ARTIST: Utagawa Hiroshige
SIGNED: Hiroshige ga 広重画
ARTIST SEAL: Ichiryūsai 弐立斎
PUBLISHER: Yamadaya Shōbei
PUBLISHER SEAL(S): Kinjudō 錦樹堂

18 – SAKAMOTO | 18.B1

Post station details
162 houses, 2 *honjin*, 2 *waki-honjin*,

40 *hatagoya*, population: 732,
distance to next station: 2 *ri* 8 *chō*
(8.72 km/5.42 miles)

Publishing details
18.B1, 1836/37, No. 18, *The Sixty-Nine
Stations along the Kisokaidō:
Sakamoto*
ARTIST: [Eisen]. SIGNED: unsigned
PUBLISHER: Iseya Rihei
PUBLISHER SEAL(S): Iseri 伊世利

18.C1, No. 18, *The Sixty-Nine Stations
along the Kisokaidō: Sakamoto*
ARTIST: [Eisen]. SIGNED: unsigned
PUBLISHER: Yamadaya Shōbei
PUBLISHER SEAL(S): Iseri 伊世利

19 – KARUIZAWA | 19.AB1a

Post station details
119 houses, 1 *honjin*, 4 *waki-honjin*,
21 *hatagoya*, population: 451,
distance to next station: 1 *ri* 5 *chō*
(4.48 km/2.78 miles)

Publishing details
19.AB1a–b, 1836/37, No. 19,
*The Sixty-Nine Stations along
the Kisokaidō: Karuizawa*
ARTIST: Utagawa Hiroshige
SIGNED: Hiroshige ga 広重画
ARTIST SEAL: Tōkaidō 東海道
PUBLISHER: Takenouchi Magohachi
& Iseya Rihei
PUBLISHER SEAL(S): Takenouchi 竹内

19.B1, No. 19, *The Sixty-Nine Stations
along the Kisokaidō: Karuizawa*
ARTIST: Utagawa Hiroshige
SIGNED: Hiroshige ga 広重画
ARTIST SEAL: Tōkaidō 東海道
PUBLISHER: Iseya Rihei
PUBLISHER SEAL(S): Takenouchi
竹内 (removed)

19.C1, No. 19, *The Sixty-Nine Stations
along the Kisokaidō: Karuizawa*
ARTIST: Utagawa Hiroshige
SIGNED: Hiroshige ga 広重画
ARTIST SEAL: Tōkaidō 東海道
PUBLISHER: Yamadaya Shōbei
PUBLISHER SEAL(S): Takenouchi
竹内 (removed)

20 – KUTSUKAKE | 20.A1a

Post station details

166 houses, 1 *honjin*, 3 *waki-honjin*, 17 *hatagoya*, population: 502, distance to next station: 1 *ri* 3 *chō* (4.26 km/2.65 miles)

Publishing details

20.A1a–b, 1835/36, No. 20, *Kisokaidō: Kutsukake Station, View of Rain on the Plain of Hiratsuka*
ARTIST: Eisen
SIGNED: Eisen ga 英泉画
PUBLISHER: Takenouchi Magohachi
PUBLISHER SEAL(S): Hōeidō han 保永堂版 (in black), Takenouchi 竹内

20.B1, No. 20, *Kisokaidō: Kutsukake Station, View of Rain on the Plain of Hiratsuka*
ARTIST: Eisen. SIGNED: removed
PUBLISHER: Iseya Rihei
PUBLISHER SEAL(S): Takenouchi 竹内 Hōeidō han 保永堂版 (removed)

20.C1, No. 20, *Kisokaidō: Kutsukake Station, View of Rain on the Plain of Hiratsuka*
ARTIST: Eisen. SIGNED: removed
PUBLISHER: Yamadaya Shōbei
PUBLISHER SEAL(S): Takenouchi 竹内, Hōeidō han 保永堂版 (removed)

21 – OIWAKE | 21.A1a

Post station details

103 houses, 1 *honjin*, 2 *waki-honjin*, 35 *hatagoya*, population: 712, distance to next station: 1 *ri* 10 *chō* (5.02 km/3.12 miles)

Publishing details

21.A1a–b, 1835/36, No. 22 [*sic*; actually 21], *Kisokaidō: Oiwake Post Town, Outlook on Mount Asama*
ARTIST: Eisen
SIGNED: Keisai ga 渓斎画
PUBLISHER: Takenouchi Magohachi
PUBLISHER SEAL(S): Take 竹, Mago 孫

21.B1a–c, No. 22 [*sic*; actually 21], *Kisokaidō: Oiwake Post Town, Outlook on Mount Asama*
ARTIST: Eisen. SIGNED: removed

PUBLISHER: Iseya Rihei
PUBLISHER SEAL(S): Take 竹, Mago 孫

21.C1, No. 22 [*sic*; actually 21], *Kisokaidō: Oiwake Post Town, Outlook on Mount Asama*
ARTIST: Eisen. SIGNED: removed
PUBLISHER: Yamadaya Shōbei
PUBLISHER SEAL(S): Take 竹, Mago 孫

22 – OTAI | 22.B1a

Post station details

107 houses, 1 *honjin*, 1 *waki-honjin*, 5 *hatagoya*, population: 319, distance to next station: 1 *ri* 7 *chō* (4.69 km/2.91 miles)

Publishing details

22.B1a–b, 1836/37, No. 22, *The Sixty-Nine Stations along the Kisokaidō: Otai*
ARTIST: Utagawa Hiroshige
SIGNED: Hiroshige ga 広重画
ARTIST SEAL: Ichiryūsai 一立斎
PUBLISHER: Iseya Rihei
PUBLISHER SEAL(S): Kinjudō 錦樹堂, Rin 林 (in margin in black)

22.C1, No. 22, *The Sixty-Nine Stations along the Kisokaidō: Otai*
ARTIST: Utagawa Hiroshige
SIGNED: Hiroshige ga 広重画
ARTIST SEAL: Ichiryūsai 一立斎
PUBLISHER: Yamadaya Shōbei
PUBLISHER SEAL(S): Kinjudō 錦樹堂, Rin 林 (in margin in black)

23 – IWAMURATA | 23.A1a

Post station details

350 houses, 8 *hatagoya*, population: 1,637, distance to next station: 1 *ri han* (5.10 km/3.17 miles)

Publishing details

23.A1a–b, 1835/36, No. 23, *Along the Kiso: Iwamurata*
ARTIST: Eisen
SIGNED: Keisai ga 渓斎画
PUBLISHER: Takenouchi Magohachi
PUBLISHER SEAL(S): Take 竹, Uchi 内

23.B1, No. 23, *Along the Kiso: Iwamurata*
ARTIST: Eisen. SIGNED: removed
PUBLISHER: Iseya Rihei
PUBLISHER SEAL(S): Take 竹, Uchi 内

23.C1, No. 23, *Along the Kiso: Iwamurata*
ARTIST: Eisen. SIGNED: removed
PUBLISHER: Yamadaya Shōbei
PUBLISHER SEAL(S): Take 竹, Uchi 内

24 – SHIONADA | 24.B1b

Post station details

116 houses, 2 *honjin*, 1 *waki-honjin*, 7 *hatagoya*, population: 574, distance to next station: 27 *chō* (2.95 km/1.83 miles)

Publishing details

24.B1a–c, 1836/37, No. 24, *The Sixty-Nine Stations along the Kisokaidō: Shionada*
ARTIST: Utagawa Hiroshige
SIGNED: Hiroshige ga 広重画
ARTIST SEAL: Ichiryūsai 弌立斎
PUBLISHER: Iseya Rihei
PUBLISHER SEAL(S): Kinjudō 錦樹堂, Rin 林 (in margin in black)

24.C1, No. 24, *The Sixty-Nine Stations along the Kisokaidō: Shionada*
ARTIST: Utagawa Hiroshige
SIGNED: Hiroshige ga 広重画
ARTIST SEAL: Ichiryūsai 弌立斎
PUBLISHER: Yamadaya Shōbei
PUBLISHER SEAL(S): Kinjudō 錦樹堂, Rin 林 (in margin in black)

25 – YAWATA | 25.B1b

Post station details

143 houses, 1 *honjin*, 4 *waki-honjin*, 3 *hatagoya*, population: 719, distance to next station: 32 *chō* (3.49 km/2.17 miles)

Publishing details

25.B1a–b, 1836/37, No. 25, *The Sixty-Nine Stations along the Kisokaidō: Yawata*
ARTIST: Utagawa Hiroshige
SIGNED: Hiroshige ga 広重画
ARTIST SEAL: Utagawa 歌川

PUBLISHER: Iseya Rihei
PUBLISHER SEAL(S): Kinjudō 錦樹堂

25.C1, No. 25, *The Sixty-Nine
Stations along the Kisokaidō: Yawata*
ARTIST: Utagawa Hiroshige
SIGNED: Hiroshige ga 広重画
ARTIST SEAL: Utagawa 歌川
PUBLISHER: Yamadaya Shōbei
PUBLISHER SEAL(S): Kinjudō 錦樹堂

26 – MOCHIZUKI | 26.B1c

Post station details

82 houses, 1 *honjin*, 1 *waki-honjin*,
9 *hatagoya*, population: 360,
distance to next station: 1 *ri* 8 *chō*
(4.8 km/2.98 miles)

Publishing details

26.B1a–d, 1836/37, No. 26,
*The Sixty-Nine Stations along
the Kisokaidō: Mochizuki*
ARTIST: Utagawa Hiroshige
SIGNED: Hiroshige ga 広重画
ARTIST SEAL: Ichiryūsai 弌立斎
PUBLISHER: Iseya Rihei
PUBLISHER SEAL(S): Kinjudō 錦樹堂,
Rin 林 (in margin in black)

26.C1, No. 26, *The Sixty-Nine Stations
along the Kisokaidō: Mochizuki*
ARTIST: Utagawa Hiroshige
SIGNED: Hiroshige ga 広重画
ARTIST SEAL: Ichiryūsai 弌立斎
PUBLISHER: Yamadaya Shōbei
PUBLISHER SEAL(S): Kinjudō 錦樹堂,
Rin 林 (in margin in black)

27 – ASHIDA | 27.B1a

Post station details

80 houses, 1 *honjin*, 2 *waki-honjin*,
6 *hatagoya*, population: 326,
distance to next station: 1 *ri han*
(5.89 km/3.66 miles)

Publishing details

27.B1a–b, 1836/37, No. 27,
*The Sixty-Nine Stations along
the Kisokaidō: Ashida*
ARTIST: Utagawa Hiroshige
SIGNED: Hiroshige ga 広重画
ARTIST SEAL: Ichiryūsai 弌立斎
PUBLISHER: Iseya Rihei

PUBLISHER SEAL(S): Kinjudō 錦樹堂,
Rin 林 (in margin in black)

27.C1, No. 27, *The Sixty-Nine
Stations along the Kisokaidō: Ashida*
ARTIST: Utagawa Hiroshige
SIGNED: Hiroshige ga 広重画
ARTIST SEAL: Ichiryūsai 弌立斎
PUBLISHER: Yamadaya Shōbei
PUBLISHER SEAL(S): Kinjudō 錦樹堂,
Rin 林 (in margin in black)

28 – NAGAKUBO | 28.B1a

Post station details

187 houses, 1 *honjin*, 1 *waki-honjin*,
43 *hatagoya*, population: 721,
distance to next station: 2 *ri*
(7.85 km/5.53 miles)

Publishing details

28.B1a–c, 1836/37, No. 28,
*The Sixty-Nine Stations along
the Kisokaidō: Nagakubo*
ARTIST: Utagawa Hiroshige
SIGNED: Hiroshige ga 広重画
ARTIST SEAL: Ichiryūsai 一立斎
PUBLISHER: Iseya Rihei
PUBLISHER SEAL(S): Kinjudō 錦樹堂,
Rin 林 (in margin in black)

28.C1a–b, No. 28, *The Sixty-Nine
Stations along the Kisokaidō: Nagakubo*
ARTIST: Utagawa Hiroshige
SIGNED: Hiroshige ga 広重画
ARTIST SEAL: Ichiryūsai 一立斎
PUBLISHER: Yamadaya Shōbei
PUBLISHER SEAL(S): Kinjudō 錦樹堂,
Rin 林 (in margin in black)

29 – WADA | 29.B1a

Post station details

126 houses, 1 *honjin*, 2 *waki-honjin*,
28 *hatagoya*, population: 522,
distance to next station: 5 *ri* 8 *chō*
(20.51 km/12.74 miles)

Publishing details

29.B1a–b, 1836/37, No. 29,
*The Sixty-Nine Stations along
the Kisokaidō: Wada*
ARTIST: Utagawa Hiroshige
SIGNED: Hiroshige ga 広重画
ARTIST SEAL: Ichiryūsai 一立斎

PUBLISHER: Iseya Rihei
PUBLISHER SEAL(S): Kinjudō 錦樹堂,
Rin 林 (in margin in black)

29.C1, No. 29, *The Sixty-Nine
Stations along the Kisokaidō: Wada*
ARTIST: Utagawa Hiroshige
SIGNED: Hiroshige ga 広重画
ARTIST SEAL: Ichiryūsai 一立斎
PUBLISHER: Yamadaya Shōbei
PUBLISHER SEAL(S): Kinjudō 錦樹堂,
Rin 林 (in margin in black)

30 – SHIMOSUWA | 30.B1a

Post station details

315 houses, 1 *honjin*, 1 *waki-honjin*,
40 *hatagoya*, population: 1,345,
distance to next station: 3 *ri*
(11.78 km/7.32 miles)

Publishing details

30.B1a–d, 1836/37, No. 30,
*The Sixty-Nine Stations along
the Kisokaidō: Shimosuwa*
ARTIST: Utagawa Hiroshige
SIGNED: Hiroshige ga 広重画
ARTIST SEAL: Ichiryūsai 一粒斎
PUBLISHER: Iseya Rihei
PUBLISHER SEAL(S): Kinjudō han
錦樹堂版

30.C1, No. 30, *The Sixty-Nine Stations
along the Kisokaidō: Shimosuwa*
ARTIST: Utagawa Hiroshige
SIGNED: Hiroshige ga 広重画
ARTIST SEAL: Ichiryūsai 一粒斎
PUBLISHER: Yamadaya Shōbei
PUBLISHER SEAL(S): Kinjudō han
錦樹堂版

31 – SHIOJIRI | 31.A1b

Post station details

166 houses, 1 *honjin*, 1 *waki-honjin*,
75 *hatagoya*, population: 794,
distance to next station: 1 *ri* 30 *chō*
(7.2 km/4.47 miles)

Publishing details

31.A1a–b, 1835/36, No. 31,
*Kisokaidō: Outlook on Lake Suwa
from Shiojiri Pass*
ARTIST: Eisen
SIGNED: Eisen ga 英泉画

PUBLISHER: Takenouchi Magohachi
PUBLISHER SEAL(S): Takenouchi 竹内,
Hōeidō 保永堂

31.B1a–b, No. 31, *Kisokaidō: Outlook
on Lake Suwa from Shiojiri Pass*
ARTIST: Eisen. SIGNED: removed
PUBLISHER: Iseya Rihei
PUBLISHER SEAL(S): Hōeidō 保永堂
Takenouchi 竹内 (removed)

31.C1, No. 31, *Kisokaidō: Outlook
on Lake Suwa from Shiojiri Pass*
ARTIST: Eisen. SIGNED: removed
PUBLISHER: Yamadaya Shōbei
PUBLISHER SEAL(S): Hōeidō 保永堂
Takenouchi 竹内 (removed)

32 – SEBA | 32.B1a

Post station details

163 houses, 1 *honjin*, 1 *waki-honjin*,
29 *hatagoya*, population: 661,
distance to next station: 30 *chō*
(3.27 km/2.03 miles)

Publishing details

32.B1a–d, 1836/37, No. 32, *The Sixty-
Nine Stations along the Kisokaidō: Seba*
ARTIST: Utagawa Hiroshige
SIGNED: Hiroshige ga 広重画
ARTIST SEAL: Ichiryūsai 弌立斎
PUBLISHER: Iseya Rihei
PUBLISHER SEAL(S): Kinjudō 錦樹堂

32.C1a–b, No. 32, *The Sixty-Nine
Stations along the Kisokaidō: Seba*
ARTIST: Utagawa Hiroshige
SIGNED: Hiroshige ga 広重画
ARTIST SEAL: Ichiryūsai 弌立斎
PUBLISHER: Yamadaya Shōbei
PUBLISHER SEAL(S): Kinjudō 錦樹堂

33 – MOTOYAMA | 33.B1a

Post station details

117 houses, 1 *honjin*, 1 *waki-honjin*,
34 *hatagoya*, population: 592,
distance to next station: 2 *ri*
(7.85 km/4.88 miles)

Publishing details

33.B1a–b, 1836/37, No. 33,
*The Sixty-Nine Stations along
the Kisokaidō: Motoyama*
ARTIST: Utagawa Hiroshige

SIGNED: Hiroshige ga 広重画
ARTIST SEAL: Ichiryūsai 一立斎
PUBLISHER: Iseya Rihei
PUBLISHER SEAL(S): Kinjudō 錦樹堂,
Rin 林 (in margin in black)

33.C1, No. 33, *The Sixty-Nine Stations
along the Kisokaidō: Motoyama*
ARTIST: Utagawa Hiroshige
SIGNED: Hiroshige ga 広重画
ARTIST SEAL: Ichiryūsai 一立斎
PUBLISHER: Yamadaya Shōbei
PUBLISHER SEAL(S): Kinjudō 錦樹堂,
Rin 林 (in margin in black)

34 – NIEKAWA | 34.B1b

Post station details

124 houses, 1 *honjin*, 1 *waki-honjin*,
25 *hatagoya*, population: 545,
distance to next station: 1 *ri han*
(5.89 km/3.66 miles)

Publishing details

34.B1a–b, 1836/37, No. 34,
*The Sixty-Nine Stations along
the Kisokaidō: Niekawa*
ARTIST: Utagawa Hiroshige
SIGNED: Hiroshige ga 広重画
ARTIST SEAL: Ichiryūsai 弌立斎
PUBLISHER: Iseya Rihei
PUBLISHER SEAL(S): Kinjudō 錦樹堂,
Rin 林 (in margin in black)

34.C1, No. 34, *The Sixty-Nine Stations
along the Kisokaidō: Niekawa*
ARTIST: Utagawa Hiroshige
SIGNED: Hiroshige ga 広重画
ARTIST SEAL: Ichiryūsai 弌立斎
PUBLISHER: Yamadaya Shōbei
PUBLISHER SEAL(S): Kinjudō 錦樹堂,
Rin 林 (in margin in black)

35 – NARAI | 35.A1a

Post station details

409 houses, 1 *honjin*, 1 *waki-honjin*,
5 *hatagoya*, population: 2,155,
distance to next station: 1 *ri han*
(5.89 km/3.66 miles)

Publishing details

35.A1a–b, 1835/36, No. 35,
*Kisokaidō: Narai Station,
Picture of the Souvenir Shop*

ARTIST: Eisen
SIGNED: Eisen ga 英泉画
PUBLISHER: Takenouchi Magohachi
PUBLISHER SEAL(S): Takenouchi 竹内,
Hanmoto Hōeidō 版元保永堂

35.B1, No. 35, *Kisokaidō: Narai
Station, Picture of the Souvenir Shop*
ARTIST: Eisen. SIGNED: removed
PUBLISHER: Iseya Rihei
PUBLISHER SEAL(S): Takenouchi 竹内,
Hanmoto Hōeidō 版元保永堂

35.C1, No. 35, *Kisokaidō: Narai
Station, Picture of the Souvenir Shop*
ARTIST: Eisen. SIGNED: removed
PUBLISHER: Yamadaya Shōbei
PUBLISHER SEAL(S): Takenouchi 竹内,
Hanmoto Hōeidō 版元保永堂

36 – YABUHARA | 36.A1a

Post station details

266 houses, 1 *honjin*, 1 *waki-honjin*,
10 *hatagoya*, population: 1,493,
distance to next station: 2 *ri*
(7.85 km/4.88 miles)

Publishing details

36.A1a–b, 1835/36, No. 36,
*Kisokaidō: Yabuhara, The Ink-stone
Spring at Torii Pass*
ARTIST: Eisen
SIGNED: Eisen ga 英泉画
PUBLISHER: Takenouchi Magohachi
PUBLISHER SEAL(S): Hōeidō 保永堂

36.B1a–b, No. 36, *Kisokaidō: Yabuhara,
The Ink-stone Spring at Torii Pass*
ARTIST: Eisen. SIGNED: removed
PUBLISHER: Iseya Rihei
PUBLISHER SEAL(S): Hōeidō 保永堂

36.C1, No. 36, *Kisokaidō: Yabuhara,
The Ink-stone Spring at Torii Pass*
ARTIST: Eisen. SIGNED: removed
PUBLISHER: Yamadaya Shōbei
PUBLISHER SEAL(S): Hōeidō 保永堂

37 – MIYANOKOSHI | 37.B1a

Post station details

137 houses, 1 *honjin*, 1 *waki-honjin*,
21 *hatagoya*, population: 585,
distance to next station: 1 *ri han*
(5.89 km/3.66 miles)

Publishing details

37.B1a–e, 1836/37, No. 37, *The Sixty-Nine Stations along the Kisokaidō: Miyanokoshi*
ARTIST: Utagawa Hiroshige
SIGNED: Hiroshige ga 広重画
ARTIST SEAL: Ichiryūsai 弌立斎
PUBLISHER: Iseya Rihei
PUBLISHER SEAL(S): Kinjudō 錦樹堂

37.C1, No. 37, *The Sixty-Nine Stations along the Kisokaidō: Miyanokoshi*
ARTIST: Utagawa Hiroshige
SIGNED: Hiroshige ga 広重画
ARTIST SEAL: Ichiryūsai 弌立斎
PUBLISHER: Yamadaya Shōbei
PUBLISHER SEAL(S): Kinjudō 錦樹堂

38 – FUKUSHIMA | 38.AB1b

Post station details

158 houses, 1 *honjin*, 1 *waki-honjin*, 14 *hatagoya*, population: 972, distance to next station: 2 *ri han* (9.82 km/6.10 miles)

Publishing details

38.AB1a–b, 1836/37, No. 38, *The Sixty-Nine Stations along the Kisokaidō: Fukushima*
ARTIST: Utagawa Hiroshige
SIGNED: Hiroshige ga 広重画
ARTIST SEAL: Ichiryūsai 一立斎
PUBLISHER: Takenouchi Magohachi & Iseya Rihei
PUBLISHER SEAL(S): Kinjudō 錦樹堂, Rin 林 (in margin in black)

38.B1, No. 38, *The Sixty-Nine Stations along the Kisokaidō: Fukushima*
ARTIST: Utagawa Hiroshige
SIGNED: Hiroshige ga 広重画
ARTIST SEAL: Ichiryūsai 一立斎
PUBLISHER: Iseya Rihei
PUBLISHER SEAL(S): Kinjudō 錦樹堂, Rin 林 (in margin in black)

38.C1, No. 38, *The Sixty-Nine Stations along the Kisokaidō: Fukushima*
ARTIST: Utagawa Hiroshige
SIGNED: Hiroshige ga 広重画
ARTIST SEAL: Ichiryūsai 一立斎
PUBLISHER: Yamadaya Shōbei
PUBLISHER SEAL(S): Kinjudō 錦樹堂, Rin 林 (in margin in black) removed

39 – AGEMATSU | 39.B1a

Post station details

362 houses, 1 *honjin*, 1 *waki-honjin*, 35 *hatagoya*, population: 2,482, distance to next station: 3 *ri* 9 *chō* (12.76 km/7.93 miles)

Publishing details

39.B1a–c, 1836/37, No. 39, *The Sixty-Nine Stations along the Kisokaidō: Agematsu*
ARTIST: Utagawa Hiroshige
SIGNED: Hiroshige ga 広重画
ARTIST SEAL: Utagawa 歌川
PUBLISHER: Iseya Rihei
PUBLISHER SEAL(S): Kinjudō 錦樹堂

39.C1, No. 39, *The Sixty-Nine Stations along the Kisokaidō: Agematsu*
ARTIST: Utagawa Hiroshige
SIGNED: Hiroshige ga 広重画
ARTIST SEAL: Utagawa 歌川
PUBLISHER: Yamadaya Shōbei
PUBLISHER SEAL(S): Kinjudō 錦樹堂

40 – SUHARA | 40.B1a

Post station details

104 houses, 1 *honjin*, 1 *waki-honjin*, 24 *hatagoya*, population: 748, distance to next station: 1 *ri* 30 *chō* (7.2 km/4.47 miles)

Publishing details

40.B1a–c, 1836/37, No. 40, *The Sixty-Nine Stations along the Kisokaidō: Suhara*
ARTIST: Utagawa Hiroshige
SIGNED: Hiroshige ga 広重画
ARTIST SEAL: Ichiryūsai 一立斎
PUBLISHER: Iseya Rihei
PUBLISHER SEAL(S): Kinjudō 錦樹堂

40.C1, No. 40, *The Sixty-Nine Stations along the Kisokaidō: Suhara*
ARTIST: Utagawa Hiroshige
SIGNED: Hiroshige ga 広重画
ARTIST SEAL: Ichiryūsai 一立斎
PUBLISHER: Yamadaya Shōbei
PUBLISHER SEAL(S): Kinjudō 錦樹堂

41 – NOJIRI | 41.A1a

Post station details

108 houses, 1 *honjin*, 1 *waki-honjin*, 19 *hatagoya*, population: 986, distance to next station: 2 *ri han* (9.82 km/6.10 miles)

Publishing details

41.A1a–b, 1835/36, No. 41, *Stations on the Kiso Road: Nojiri, Distant Scenery of the Ina River Bridge*
ARTIST: Eisen
SIGNED: Keisai ga 渓斎画
PUBLISHER: Takenouchi Magohachi
PUBLISHER SEAL(S): Takenouchi 竹内, Hōeidō 保永堂

41.B1a–c, No. 41, *Stations on the Kiso Road: Nojiri, Distant Scenery of the Ina River Bridge*
ARTIST: Eisen. SIGNED: removed
PUBLISHER: Iseya Rihei
PUBLISHER SEAL(S): Takenouchi 竹内, Hōeidō 保永堂

41.C1, No. 41, *Stations on the Kiso Road: Nojiri, Distant Scenery of the Ina River Bridge*
ARTIST: Eisen. SIGNED: removed
PUBLISHER: Yamadaya Shōbei
PUBLISHER SEAL(S): Takenouchi 竹内, Hōeidō 保永堂

42 – MIDONO | 42.B1a

Post station details

77 houses, 1 *honjin*, 1 *waki-honjin*, 32 *hatagoya*, population: 594, distance to next station: 1 *ri han* (5.89 km/3.66 miles)

Publishing details

42.B1a–d, 1836/37, No. 42, *The Sixty-Nine Stations along the Kisokaidō: Midono*
ARTIST: Utagawa Hiroshige
SIGNED: Hiroshige ga 広重画
ARTIST SEAL: Ichiryūsai 弌立斎
PUBLISHER: Iseya Rihei
PUBLISHER SEAL(S): Kinjudō 錦樹堂

42.C1, No. 42, *The Sixty-Nine Stations along the Kisokaidō: Midono*
ARTIST: Utagawa Hiroshige
SIGNED: Hiroshige ga 広重画

ARTIST SEAL: Ichiryūsai 弌立斎
PUBLISHER: Yamadaya Shōbei
PUBLISHER SEAL(S): Kinjudō 錦樹堂

43 – TSUMAGO | 43.B1a

Post station details

83 houses, 1 *honjin*, 1 *waki-honjin*,
31 *hatagoya*, population: 418,
distance to next station: 2 *ri*
(7.85 km/4.88 miles)

Publishing details

43.B1a–b, 1836/37, No. 43,
*The Sixty-Nine Stations along
the Kisokaidō: Tsumago*
ARTIST: Utagawa Hiroshige
SIGNED: Hiroshige ga 広重画
ARTIST SEAL: Ichiryūsai 弌立斎
PUBLISHER: Iseya Rihei
PUBLISHER SEAL(S): Kinjudō 錦樹堂

43.C1, No. 43, *The Sixty-Nine Stations
along the Kisokaidō: Tsumago*
ARTIST: Utagawa Hiroshige
SIGNED: Hiroshige ga 広重画
ARTIST SEAL: Ichiryūsai 弌立斎
PUBLISHER: Yamadaya Shōbei
PUBLISHER SEAL(S): Kinjudō 錦樹堂

44 – MAGOME | 44.A1b

Post station details

69 houses, 1 *honjin*, 1 *waki-honjin*,
18 *hatagoya*, population: 717,
distance to next station: 1 *ri* 5 *chō*
(4.48 km/2.78 miles)

Publishing details

44.A1a–b, 1835/36, No. 44, *Kisokaidō:
Magome Station, Picture of the Distant
View from the Pass*
ARTIST: Eisen
SIGNED: Eisen ga 英泉画
PUBLISHER: Takenouchi Magohachi
PUBLISHER SEAL(S): Takemago
たけまこ, Hōeidō 保永堂

44.B1a–b, No. 44, *Kisokaidō: Magome
Station, Picture of the Distant View
from the Pass*
ARTIST: Eisen. SIGNED: removed
PUBLISHER: Iseya Rihei
PUBLISHER SEAL(S): Takemago
たけまこ, Hōeidō 保永堂

44.C1, No. 44, *Kisokaidō: Magome
Station, Picture of the Distant View
from the Pass*
ARTIST: Eisen. SIGNED: removed
PUBLISHER: Yamadaya Shōbei
PUBLISHER SEAL(S): Takemago たけま
こ, Hōeidō 保永堂

45 – OCHIAI | 45.B1b

Post station details

75 houses, 1 *honjin*, 1 *waki-honjin*,
14 *hatagoya*, population: 370,
distance to next station: 1 *ri* 5 *chō*
(4.48 km/2.78 miles)

Publishing details

45.B1a–b, 1837/38, No. 45,
*The Sixty-Nine Stations along
the Kisokaidō: Ochiai*
ARTIST: Utagawa Hiroshige
SIGNED: Hiroshige ga 広重画
ARTIST SEAL: Ichiryūsai 一立斎
PUBLISHER: Iseya Rihei
PUBLISHER SEAL(S): Rin 林

45.C1, No. 45, *The Sixty-Nine Stations
along the Kisokaidō: Ochiai*
ARTIST: Utagawa Hiroshige
SIGNED: Hiroshige ga 広重画
ARTIST SEAL: Ichiryūsai 一立斎
PUBLISHER: Yamadaya Shōbei
PUBLISHER SEAL(S): Rin 林 (removed)

46A&B – NAKATSUGAWA
46a.B1 | 46b.B1

Post station details

228 houses, 1 *honjin*, 1 *waki-honjin*,
29 *hatagoya*, population: 928,
distance to next station: 2 *ri han*
(9.82 km/6.10 miles)

Publishing details

46a.B1, 1836/37, No. 46, *The Sixty-
Nine Stations along the Kisokaidō:
Nakatsugawa* [first design]
ARTIST: Utagawa Hiroshige
SIGNED: Hiroshige ga 広重画
ARTIST SEAL: Ichiryūsai 一立斎
PUBLISHER: Iseya Rihei
PUBLISHER SEAL(S): Kinjudō 錦樹堂

46b.B1, No. 46, *The Sixty-Nine
Stations along the Kisokaidō:
Nakatsugawa* [second design]
ARTIST: Utagawa Hiroshige
SIGNED: Hiroshige ga 広重画
ARTIST SEAL: Ichiryūsai 弌立斎
PUBLISHER: Iseya Rihei
PUBLISHER SEAL(S): Rin 林

46b.C1, No. 46, *The Sixty-Nine
Stations along the Kisokaidō:
Nakatsugawa* [second design]
ARTIST: Utagawa Hiroshige
SIGNED: Hiroshige ga 広重画
ARTIST SEAL: Ichiryūsai 弌立斎
PUBLISHER: Yamadaya Shōbei
PUBLISHER SEAL(S): Rin 林
(sometimes removed)

47 – ŌI | 47.B1

Post station details

110 houses, 1 *honjin*, 1 *waki-honjin*,
41 *hatagoya*, population: 466,
distance to next station: 3 *ri han*
(13.75 km/8.54 miles)

Publishing details

47.B1, 1836/37, No. 47,
*The Sixty-Nine Stations along
the Kisokaidō: Ōi*
ARTIST: Utagawa Hiroshige
SIGNED: Hiroshige ga 広重画
ARTIST SEAL: Ichiryūsai 一立斎
PUBLISHER: Iseya Rihei
PUBLISHER SEAL(S): Kinjudō 錦樹堂

47.C1, No. 47, *The Sixty-Nine
Stations along the Kisokaidō: ōi*
ARTIST: Utagawa Hiroshige
SIGNED: Hiroshige ga 広重画
ARTIST SEAL: Ichiryūsai 一立斎
PUBLISHER: Yamadaya Shōbei
PUBLISHER SEAL(S): Kinjudō 錦樹堂

48 – ŌKUTE | 48.B1a

Post station details

66 houses, 1 *honjin*, 1 *waki-honjin*,
30 *hatagoya*, population: 338,
distance to next station: 1 *ri* 30 *chō*
(7.2 km/4.47 miles)

Publishing details

48.B1a–c, 1836/37, No. 48,
*The Sixty-Nine Stations along
the Kisokaidō: Ōkute*
ARTIST: Utagawa Hiroshige
SIGNED: Hiroshige ga 広重画
ARTIST SEAL: Ichiryūsai 一立斎
PUBLISHER: Iseya Rihei
PUBLISHER SEAL(S): Kinjudō 錦樹堂

48.C1, No. 48, *The Sixty-Nine
Stations along the Kisokaidō: Ōkute*
ARTIST: Utagawa Hiroshige
SIGNED: Hiroshige ga 広重画
ARTIST SEAL: Ichiryūsai 一立斎
PUBLISHER: Yamadaya Shōbei
PUBLISHER SEAL(S): Kinjudō 錦樹堂

49 – HOSOKUTE | 49.B1a

Post station details

65 houses, 1 *honjin*, 1 *waki-honjin*,
24 *hatagoya*, population: 256,
distance to next station: 3 *ri*
(11.78 km/7.32 miles)

Publishing details

49.B1a–b, 1837/38, No. 49,
*The Sixty-Nine Stations along
the Kisokaidō: Hosokute*
ARTIST: Utagawa Hiroshige
SIGNED: Hiroshige ga 広重画
ARTIST SEAL: Ichiryūsai 一立斎
PUBLISHER: Iseya Rihei
PUBLISHER SEAL(S): Rin 林

49.C1a–b, No. 49, *The Sixty-Nine
Stations along the Kisokaidō: Hosokute*
ARTIST: Utagawa Hiroshige
SIGNED: Hiroshige ga 広重画
ARTIST SEAL: Ichiryūsai 一立斎
PUBLISHER: Yamadaya Shōbei
PUBLISHER SEAL(S): Rin 林 (removed)

50 – MITAKE | 50.B1

Post station details

66 houses, 1 *honjin*, 1 *waki-honjin*,
28 *hatagoya*, population: 600,
distance to next station: 1 *ri* 5 *chō*
(4.48 km/2.78 miles)

Publishing details

50.B1, 1837/38, No. 50, *The Sixty-Nine
Stations along the Kisokaidō: Mitake*

ARTIST: Utagawa Hiroshige
SIGNED: Hiroshige ga 広重画
ARTIST SEAL: Ichiryūsai 一立斎
PUBLISHER: Iseya Rihei
PUBLISHER SEAL(S): Rin 林

50.C1, No. 50, *The Sixty-Nine
Stations along the Kisokaidō: Mitake*
ARTIST: Utagawa Hiroshige
SIGNED: Hiroshige ga 広重画
ARTIST SEAL: Ichiryūsai 一立斎
PUBLISHER: Yamadaya Shōbei
PUBLISHER SEAL(S): Rin 林 (removed)

51 – FUSHIMI | 51.B1a

Post station details

82 houses, 1 *honjin*, 1 *waki-honjin*,
29 *hatagoya*, population: 485,
distance to next station: 2 *ri*
(7.85 km/4.88 miles)

Publishing details

51.B1a–b, 1837/38, No. 51,
*The Sixty-Nine Stations along
the Kisokaidō: Fushimi*
ARTIST: Utagawa Hiroshige
SIGNED: Hiroshige ga 広重画
PUBLISHER: Iseya Rihei
PUBLISHER SEAL(S): Rin 林

51.C1, No. 51, *The Sixty-Nine Stations
along the Kisokaidō: Fushimi*
ARTIST: Utagawa Hiroshige
SIGNED: Hiroshige ga 広重画
PUBLISHER: Yamadaya Shōbei
PUBLISHER SEAL(S): Rin 林
(sometimes removed)

52 – ŌTA | 52.B1a

Post station details

118 houses, 1 *honjin*, 1 *waki-honjin*,
20 *hatagoya*, population: 505,
distance to next station: 2 *ri*
(7.85 km/4.88 miles)

Publishing details

52.B1a–b, 1837/38, No. 52, *The Sixty-
Nine Stations along the Kisokaidō: Ōta*
ARTIST: Utagawa Hiroshige
SIGNED: Hiroshige ga 広重画
ARTIST SEAL: Ichiryūsai 一立斎
PUBLISHER: Iseya Rihei
PUBLISHER SEAL(S): Rin 林

52.C1, No. 52, *The Sixty-Nine Stations
along the Kisokaidō: Ōta*
ARTIST: Utagawa Hiroshige
SIGNED: Hiroshige ga 広重画
ARTIST SEAL: Ichiryūsai 一立斎
PUBLISHER: Yamadaya Shōbei
PUBLISHER SEAL(S): Shō 庄

53 – UNUMA | 53.A1a

Post station details

68 houses, 1 *honjin*, 1 *waki-honjin*,
25 *hatagoya*, population: 246,
distance to next station: 4 *ri* 8 *chō*
(16.58 km/10.30 miles)

Publishing details

53.A1, 1835/36, No. 53, *Kisokaidō:
Unuma Station, Distant View from
Inuyama*
ARTIST: Eisen
SIGNED: Keisai ga 渓斎画
PUBLISHER: Takenouchi Magohachi
PUBLISHER SEAL(S): Takenouchi 竹内,
Hōeidō 保永堂

53.B1a–b, No. 53, *Kisokaidō: Unuma
Station, Distant View from Inuyama*
ARTIST: Eisen. SIGNED: removed
PUBLISHER: Iseya Rihei
PUBLISHER SEAL(S): Hōeidō 保永堂
Takenouchi 竹内 (removed)

53.C1, No. 53, *Kisokaidō: Unuma
Station, Distant View from Inuyama*
ARTIST: Eisen. SIGNED: removed
PUBLISHER: Yamadaya Shōbei
PUBLISHER SEAL(S): Hōeidō 保永堂
Takenouchi 竹内 removed

54 – KANŌ | 54.B1a

Post station details

805 houses, 1 *honjin*, 1 *waki-honjin*,
35 *hatagoya*, population: 2,728,
distance to next station: 1 *ri han*
(5.89 km/3.66 miles)

Publishing details

54.B1a–b, 1837/38, No. 54, *The Sixty-
Nine Stations along the Kisokaidō: Kanō*
ARTIST: Utagawa Hiroshige
SIGNED: Hiroshige ga 広重画
PUBLISHER: Iseya Rihei
PUBLISHER SEAL(S): Rin 林

54.C1, No. 54, *The Sixty-Nine Stations along the Kisokaidō: Kanō*
ARTIST: Utagawa Hiroshige
SIGNED: Hiroshige ga 広重画
PUBLISHER: Iseya Rihei
PUBLISHER SEAL(S): Rin 林 (removed)

55 – GŌDO | 55.A1a

Post station details
64 houses, 1 *honjin*, 1 *waki-honjin*,
24 *hatagoya*, population: 272,
distance to next station: 1 *ri* 6 *chō*
(4.58 km/2.85 miles)

Publishing details
55.A1a–b, 1835/36, No. 55,
*Stations on the Kiso Road:
Gōdo, Cormorant Fishing Boats
on the Nagara River*
ARTIST: Eisen
SIGNED: Eisen ga 英泉画
PUBLISHER: Takenouchi Magohachi
PUBLISHER SEAL(S): Hōeidō 保永堂

55.B1a–c, No. 55, *Stations on the Kiso
Road: Gōdo, Cormorant Fishing Boats
on the Nagara River*
ARTIST: Eisen. SIGNED: removed
PUBLISHER: Iseya Rihei
PUBLISHER SEAL(S): Hōeidō 保永堂
(removed)

55.C1, No. 55, *Stations on the Kiso
Road: Gōdo, Cormorant Fishing Boats
on the Nagara River*
ARTIST: Eisen. SIGNED: removed
PUBLISHER: Yamadaya Shōbei
PUBLISHER SEAL(S): Hōeidō 保永堂
(removed)

56 – MIEJI | 56.B1

Post station details
136 houses, 1 *honjin*, 1 *waki-honjin*,
11 *hatagoya*, population: 582,
distance to next station: 2 *ri* 8 *chō*
(8.72 km/5.42 miles)

Publishing details
56.B1, 1837/38, No. 56, *The Sixty-Nine
Stations along the Kisokaidō: Mieji*
ARTIST: Utagawa Hiroshige
SIGNED: Hiroshige ga 広重画
ARTIST SEAL: Ichiryūsai 弌立斎

PUBLISHER: Iseya Rihei
PUBLISHER SEAL(S): Rin 林

56.C1, No. 56, *The Sixty-Nine
Stations along the Kisokaidō: Mieji*
ARTIST: Utagawa Hiroshige
SIGNED: Hiroshige ga 広重画
ARTIST SEAL: Ichiryūsai 弌立斎
PUBLISHER: Yamadaya Shōbei
PUBLISHER SEAL(S): Rin 林 (removed)

57 – AKASAKA | 57.B1

Post station details
292 houses, 1 *honjin*, 1 *waki-honjin*,
17 *hatagoya*, population: 1,129,
distance to next station: 1 *ri* 12 *chō*
(5.24 km/3.26 miles)

Publishing details
57.B1, 1837/38, No. 57, *The Sixty-Nine
Stations along the Kisokaidō: Akasaka*
ARTIST: Utagawa Hiroshige
SIGNED: Hiroshige ga 広重画
PUBLISHER: Iseya Rihei
PUBLISHER SEAL(S): Rin 林

57.C1, No. 57, *The Sixty-Nine
Stations along the Kisokaidō: Akasaka*
ARTIST: Utagawa Hiroshige
SIGNED: Hiroshige ga 広重画
PUBLISHER: Yamadaya Shōbei
PUBLISHER SEAL(S): Rin 林 (removed)

58 – TARUI | 58.B1a

Post station details
315 houses, 1 *honjin*, 1 *waki-honjin*,
27 *hatagoya*, population: 1,179,
distance to next station: 1 *ri*
(3.93 km/2.44 miles)

Publishing details
58.B1a–b, 1837/38, No. 58,
*The Sixty-Nine Stations along
the Kisokaidō: Tarui*
ARTIST: Utagawa Hiroshige
SIGNED: Hiroshige ga 広重画
ARTIST SEAL: Ichiryūsai 一立斎
PUBLISHER: Iseya Rihei
PUBLISHER SEAL(S): Rin 林

58.C1, No. 58, *The Sixty-Nine Stations
along the Kisokaidō: Tarui*
ARTIST: Utagawa Hiroshige
SIGNED: Hiroshige ga 広重画

ARTIST SEAL: Ichiryūsai 一立斎
PUBLISHER: Yamadaya Shōbei
PUBLISHER SEAL(S): Rin 林 (removed)

59 – SEKIGAHARA | 59.B1

Post station details
269 houses, 1 *honjin*, 1 *waki-honjin*,
33 *hatagoya*, population: 1,389,
distance to next station: 1 *ri*
(3.93 km/2.44 miles)

Publishing details
59.B1, 1837/38, No. 59,
*The Sixty-Nine Stations along
the Kisokaidō: Sekigahara*
ARTIST: Utagawa Hiroshige
SIGNED: Hiroshige ga 広重画
ARTIST SEAL: Tōkai 東海
PUBLISHER: Iseya Rihei
PUBLISHER SEAL(S): Rin 林

59.C1, No. 59, *The Sixty-Nine Stations
along the Kisokaidō: Sekigahara*
ARTIST: Utagawa Hiroshige
SIGNED: Hiroshige ga 広重画
ARTIST SEAL: Tōkai 東海
PUBLISHER: Yamadaya Shōbei
PUBLISHER SEAL(S): Rin 林 (removed)

60 – IMASU | 60.B1

Post station details
464 houses, 1 *honjin*, 2 *waki-honjin*,
13 *hatagoya*, population: 1,784,
distance to next station: 1 *ri*
(3.93 km/2.44 miles)

Publishing details
60.B1, 1837/38, No. 60, *The Sixty-Nine
Stations along the Kisokaidō: Imasu*
ARTIST: Utagawa Hiroshige
SIGNED: Hiroshige ga 広重画
ARTIST SEAL: Ichiryūsai 一立斎
PUBLISHER: Iseya Rihei
PUBLISHER SEAL(S): Rin 林

60.C1, No. 60, *The Sixty-Nine Stations
along the Kisokaidō: Imasu*
ARTIST: Utagawa Hiroshige
SIGNED: Hiroshige ga 広重画
ARTIST SEAL: Ichiryūsai 一立斎
PUBLISHER: Yamadaya Shōbei
PUBLISHER SEAL(S): Rin 林

61 – KASHIWABARA | 61.B1

Post station details

344 houses, 1 *honjin*, 1 *waki-honjin*, 22 *hatagoya*, population: 1,468, distance to next station: 1 *ri han* (5.89 km/3.66 miles)

Publishing details

61.B1, 1837/38, No. 61, *The Sixty-Nine Stations along the Kisokaidō: Kashiwabara*
ARTIST: Utagawa Hiroshige
SIGNED: Hiroshige ga 広重画
PUBLISHER: Iseya Rihei
PUBLISHER SEAL(S): Rin 林

61.C1, No. 61, *The Sixty-Nine Stations along the Kisokaidō: Kashiwabara*
ARTIST: Utagawa Hiroshige
SIGNED: Hiroshige ga 広重画
PUBLISHER: Yamadaya Shōbei
PUBLISHER SEAL(S): Rin 林 (removed)

62 – SAMEGAI | 62.B1a

Post station details

138 houses, 1 *honjin*, 1 *waki-honjin*, 11 *hatagoya*, population: 539, distance to next station: 30 *chō* (3.27 km/2.03 miles)

Publishing details

62.B1a–c, 1837/38, No. 62, *The Sixty-Nine Stations along the Kisokaidō: Samegai*
ARTIST: Utagawa Hiroshige
SIGNED: Hiroshige ga 広重画
ARTIST SEAL: Ichiryūsai 一立斎
PUBLISHER: Iseya Rihei
PUBLISHER SEAL(S): Rin 林

62.C1, No. 62, *The Sixty-Nine Stations along the Kisokaidō: Samegai*
ARTIST: Utagawa Hiroshige
SIGNED: Hiroshige ga 広重画
ARTIST SEAL: removed
PUBLISHER: Yamadaya Shōbei
PUBLISHER SEAL(S): Rin 林 (removed)

63 – BANBA | 63.B1a

Post station details

178 houses, 1 *honjin*, 1 *waki-honjin*, 10 *hatagoya*, population: 808, distance to next station: 1 *ri* 6 *chō* (4.58 km/2.85 miles)

Publishing details

63.B1a–b, 1837/38, No. 63, *The Sixty-Nine Stations along the Kisokaidō: Banba*
ARTIST: Utagawa Hiroshige
SIGNED: Hiroshige ga 広重画
PUBLISHER: Iseya Rihei
PUBLISHER SEAL(S): Rin 林

63.C1, No. 63, *The Sixty-Nine Stations along the Kisokaidō: Banba*
ARTIST: Utagawa Hiroshige
SIGNED: Hiroshige ga 広重画
PUBLISHER: Yamadaya Shōbei
PUBLISHER SEAL(S): Rin 林 (removed)

64 – TORIIMOTO | 64.B1

Post station details

293 houses, 1 *honjin*, 2 *waki-honjin*, 35 *hatagoya*, population: 1,448, distance to next station: 1 *ri han* (5.89 km/3.66 miles)

Publishing details

64.AB1, 1836/37, No. 63 [*sic*; actually 64], *The Sixty-Nine Stations along the Kisokaidō: Toriimoto*
ARTIST: Utagawa Hiroshige
SIGNED: Hiroshige ga 広重画
ARTIST SEAL: Ichiryūsai 一立斎
PUBLISHER: Takenouchi Magohachi & Iseya Rihei
PUBLISHER SEAL(S): Takenouchi Rin 竹内林

64.B1, No. 63 [*sic*; actually 64], *The Sixty-Nine Stations along the Kisokaidō: Toriimoto*
ARTIST: Utagawa Hiroshige
SIGNED: Hiroshige ga 広重画
ARTIST SEAL: Ichiryūsai 一立斎
PUBLISHER: Iseya Rihei
PUBLISHER SEAL(S): Takenouchi Rin 竹内林

64.C1, No. 63 [*sic*; actually 64], *The Sixty-Nine Stations along the Kisokaidō: Toriimoto*
ARTIST: Utagawa Hiroshige
SIGNED: Hiroshige ga 広重画

ARTIST SEAL: Ichiryūsai 一立斎
PUBLISHER: Yamadaya Shōbei
PUBLISHER SEAL(S): Takenouchi Rin 竹内林

65 – TAKAMIYA | 65.B1a

Post station details

835 houses, 1 *honjin*, 2 *waki-honjin*, 23 *hatagoya*, population: 3,560, distance to next station: 2 *ri* 8 *chō* (8.72 km/5.42 miles)

Publishing details

65.B1a–b, 1837/38, No. 65, *The Sixty-Nine Stations along the Kisokaidō: Takamiya*
ARTIST: Utagawa Hiroshige
SIGNED: Hiroshige ga 広重画
ARTIST SEAL: Ichiryūsai 一立斎
PUBLISHER: Iseya Rihei
PUBLISHER SEAL(S): Rin 林

65.C1, No. 65, *The Sixty-Nine Stations along the Kisokaidō: Takamiya*
ARTIST: Utagawa Hiroshige
SIGNED: Hiroshige ga 広重画
ARTIST SEAL: Ichiryūsai 一立斎
PUBLISHER: Yamadaya Shōbei
PUBLISHER SEAL(S): Rin 林 (removed)

66 – ECHIGAWA | 66.B1

Post station details

199 houses, 1 *honjin*, 1 *waki-honjin*, 28 *hatagoya*, population: 929, distance to next station: 2 *ri han* (9.82 km/6.10 miles)

Publishing details

66.B1, 1837/38, No. 66, *The Sixty-Nine Stations along the Kisokaidō: Echigawa*
ARTIST: Utagawa Hiroshige
SIGNED: Hiroshige ga 広重画
ARTIST SEAL: Ichiryūsai 一立斎
PUBLISHER: Iseya Rihei
PUBLISHER SEAL(S): Rin 林

66.C1, No. 66, *The Sixty-Nine Stations along the Kisokaidō: Echigawa*
ARTIST: Utagawa Hiroshige
SIGNED: Hiroshige ga 広重画
ARTIST SEAL: Ichiryūsai 一立斎

PUBLISHER: Yamadaya Shōbei
PUBLISHER SEAL(S): Rin 林

67 – MUSA | 67.B1a

Post station details

183 houses, 1 *honjin*, 1 *waki-honjin*,
23 *hatagoya*, population: 537,
distance to next station: 3 *ri han*,
(13.75 km/8.54 miles)

Publishing details

67.B1a–c, 1837/38, No. 66
[*sic*; actually 67],
*The Sixty-Nine Stations along the
Kisokaidō: Musa*
ARTIST: Utagawa Hiroshige
SIGNED: Hiroshige ga 広重画
ARTIST SEAL: Ichiryūsai 一立斎
PUBLISHER: Iseya Rihei
PUBLISHER SEAL(S): Rin 林

67.C1, No. 66 [*sic*; actually 67],
*The Sixty-Nine Stations along the
Kisokaidō: Musa*
ARTIST: Utagawa Hiroshige
SIGNED: Hiroshige ga 広重画
ARTIST SEAL: Ichiryūsai 一立斎
PUBLISHER: Yamadaya Shōbei
PUBLISHER SEAL(S): Rin 林

68 – MORIYAMA | 68.B1a

Post station details

415 houses, 2 *honjin*, 1 *waki-honjin*,
30 *hatagoya*, population: 1,700,
distance to next station: 1 *ri han*
(5.89 km/3.66 miles)

Publishing details

68.B1a–b, 1837/38, No. 68,
*The Sixty-Nine Stations along
the Kisokaidō: Moriyama*
ARTIST: Utagawa Hiroshige
SIGNED: Hiroshige ga 広重画
PUBLISHER: Iseya Rihei
PUBLISHER SEAL(S): Rin 林

68.C1, No. 68, *The Sixty-Nine Stations
along the Kisokaidō: Moriyama*
ARTIST: Utagawa Hiroshige
SIGNED: Hiroshige ga 広重画
PUBLISHER: Yamadaya Shōbei
PUBLISHER SEAL(S): Rin 林 (removed)

69 – KUSATSU | 69.B1

Post station details

586 houses, 2 *honjin*, 2 *waki-honjin*,
72 *hatagoya*, population: 2,351,
distance to next station: 3 *ri han* 6 *chō*,
14.4 km/8.95 miles)

Publishing details

69.B1, 1837/38, No. 68
[*sic*; actually 69], *The Sixty-Nine
Stations along the Kisokaidō:
Crossroad at Kusatsu*
ARTIST: Utagawa Hiroshige
SIGNED: Hiroshige ga 広重画
ARTIST SEAL: Ichiryūsai 一立斎
PUBLISHER: Iseya Rihei
PUBLISHER SEAL(S): Rin 林

69.C1, No. 68 [*sic*; actually 69],
*The Sixty-Nine Stations along the
Kisokaidō: Crossroad at Kusatsu*
ARTIST: Utagawa Hiroshige
SIGNED: Hiroshige ga 広重画
ARTIST SEAL: Ichiryūsai 一立斎
PUBLISHER: Yamadaya Shōbei
PUBLISHER SEAL(S): Rin 林

70 – ŌTSU | 70.B1

Post station details

3,650 houses, 2 *honjin*, 1 *waki-honjin*,
71 *hatagoya*, population: 14,892,
distance to next station: 3 *ri*
(11.78 km/7.32 miles)

Publishing details

70.B1, 1837/38, No. 70, *The Sixty-Nine
Stations along the Kisokaidō: Ōtsu*
ARTIST: Utagawa Hiroshige
SIGNED: Hiroshige ga 広重画
PUBLISHER: Iseya Rihei
PUBLISHER SEAL(S): Rin 林

70.C1, No. 70, *The Sixty-Nine Stations
along the Kisokaidō: Ōtsu*
ARTIST: Utagawa Hiroshige
SIGNED: Hiroshige ga 広重画,
PUBLISHER: Yamadaya Shōbei
PUBLISHER SEAL(S): Rin 林 (removed)

Banba (detail from plate 63)

P. 432
Karuizawa (detail from plate 19)

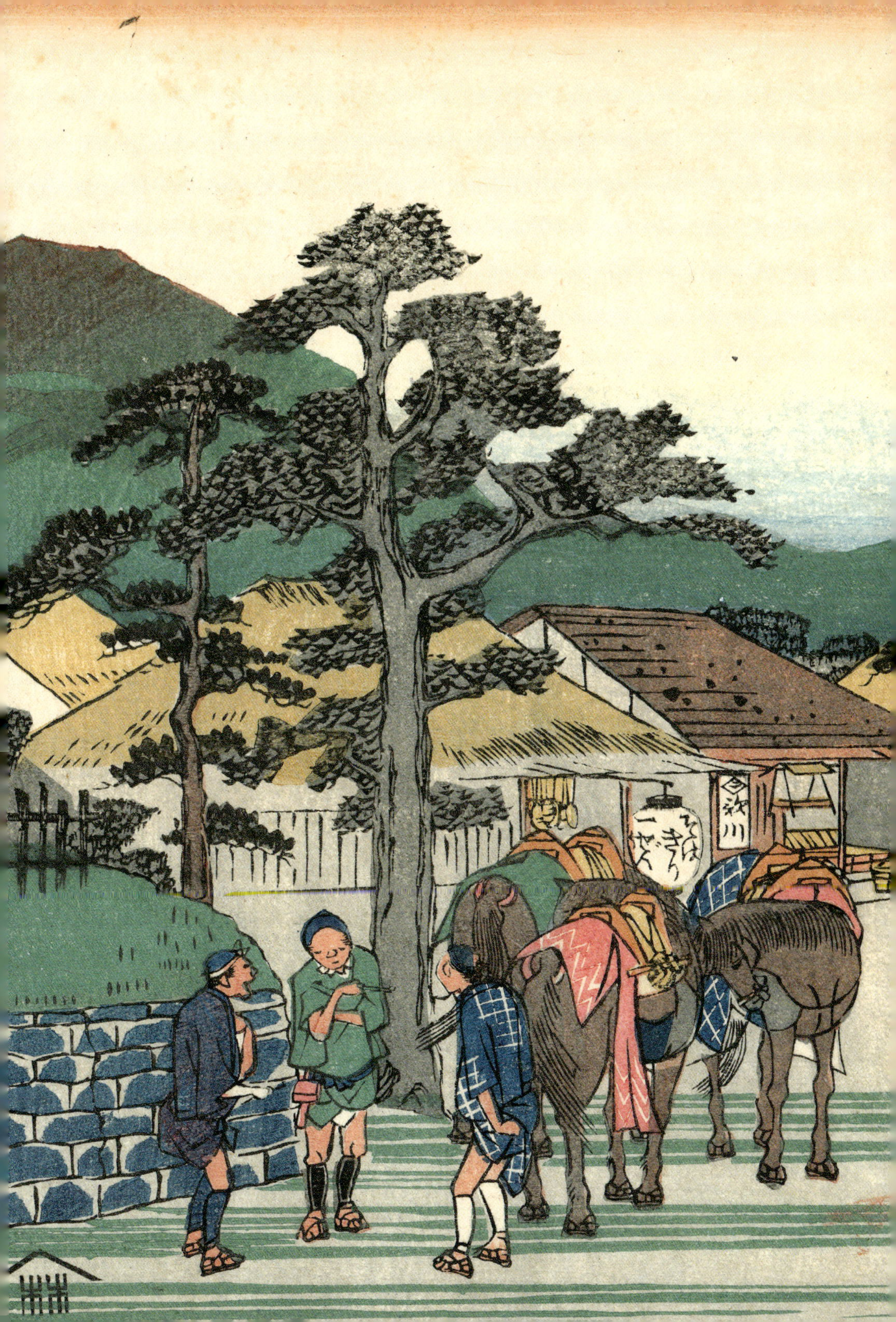
そばきりうどん
一ぜん
祇川

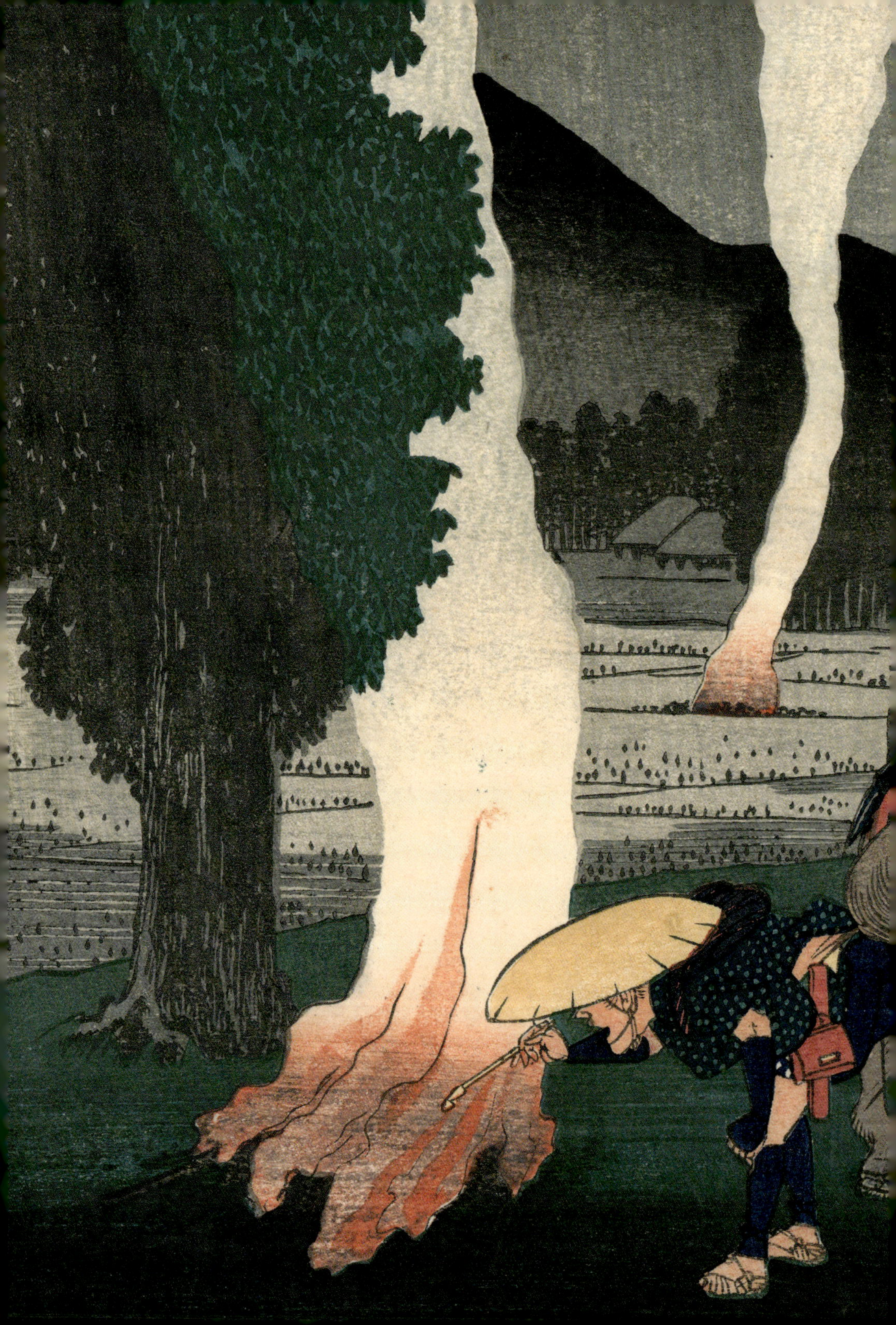

Colour Variations
Farbvarianten
Variantes chromatiques

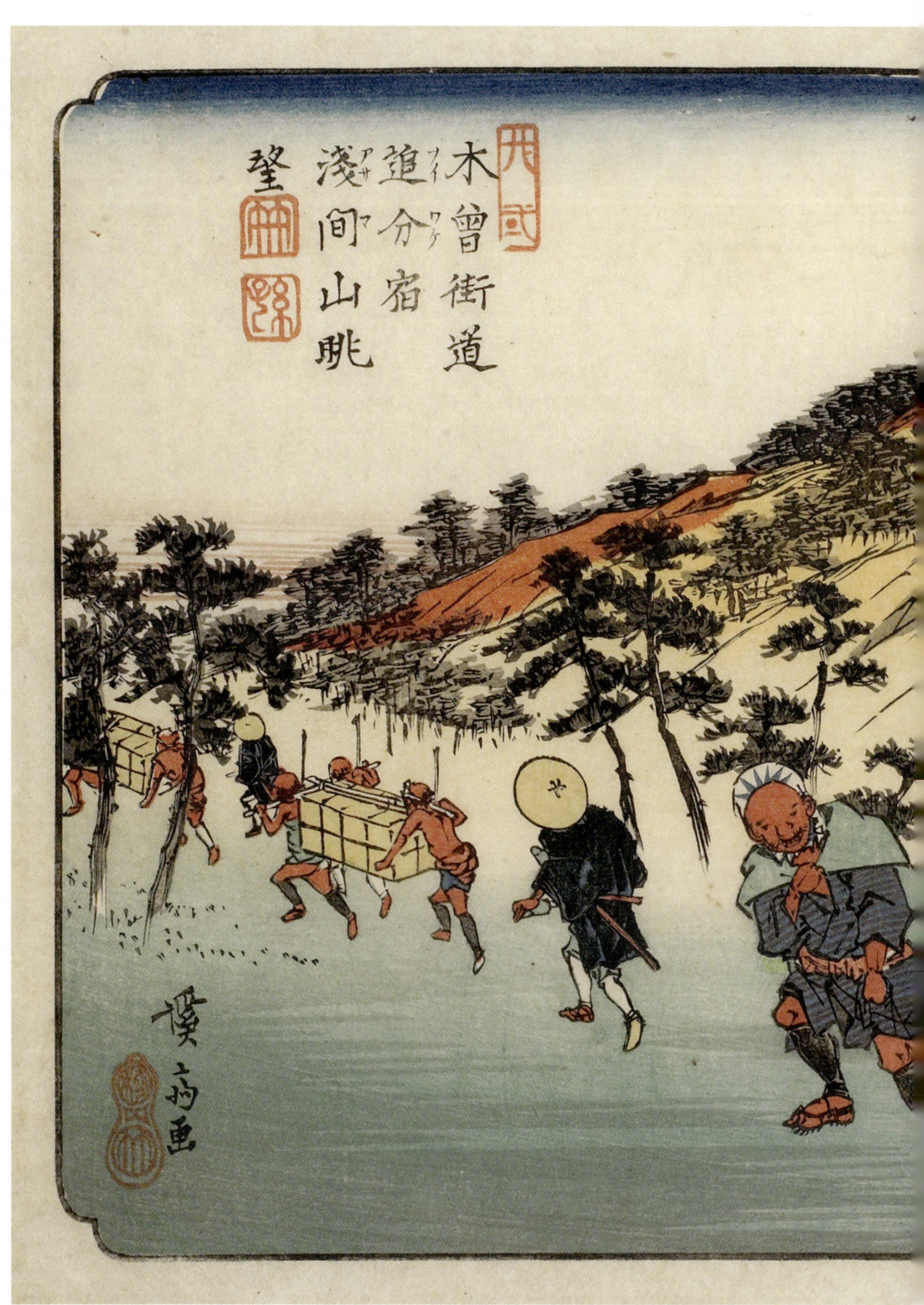

21.A1b

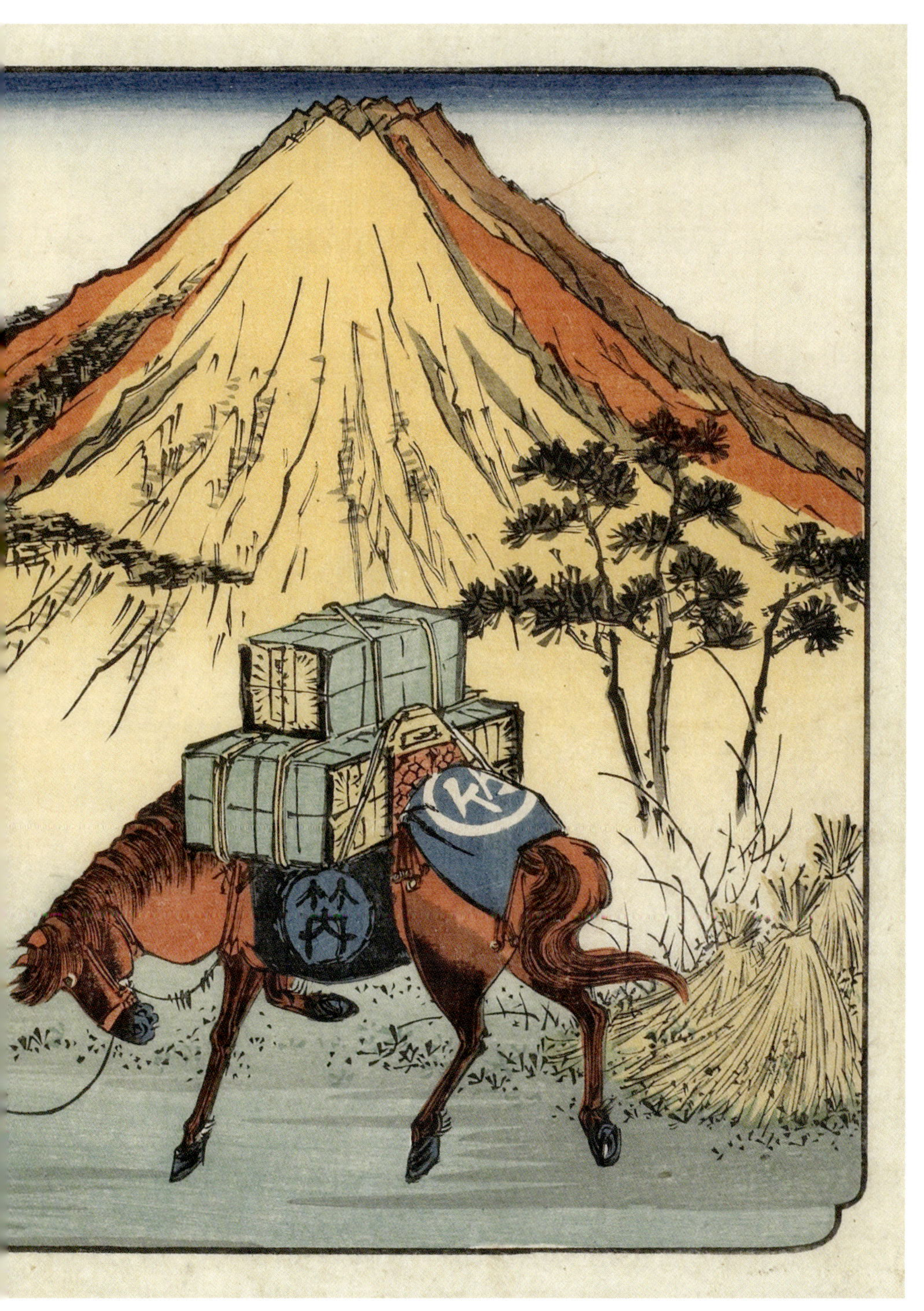
竹内

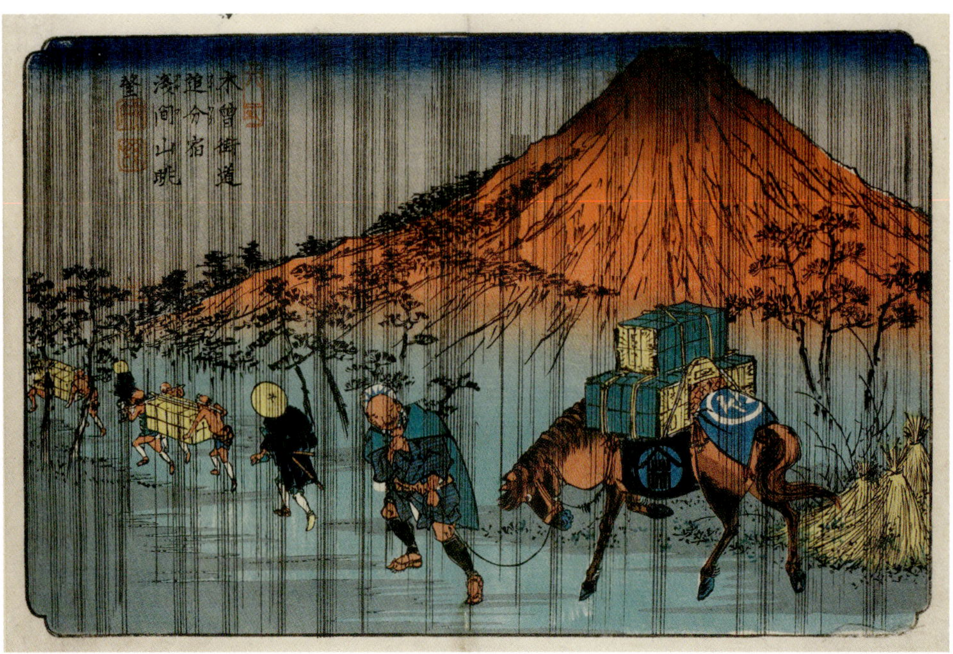

21.B1a

21 – OIWAKE

The cloth panels hanging over the belly and rump of the pack horse in the foreground bear crests reading "Takenouchi" and "Take", referring to the publisher Takenouchi. In the second edition (21.B1), the writing on the cloth over the horse's belly was changed to "Rin", representing the publisher Iseya. This edition usually lacks Eisen's signature and the censor and publisher combination seal in a red gourd, but there are a few exceptions, possibly early impressions by Iseya, in which the seal was retained. Illustrated on pages 182–183 is what appears to be a unique trial proof of the first edition (21.A1) in which a dark brown was used for the block of the figures' skin, the horse and the left and right ridges of the mountain, which are usually printed in a light reddish-brown. The same light reddish-brown colour was in this impression used only for the front of the mountain, which is usually in yellow-ochre. Also, the placement of the red seals in the top left is lower than on any other known impression. The second edition (21.B1) exists in several colour variations, for example, with the peak of the mountain in black

bokashi or with the whole sheet overprinted with vertical lines representing rain. A very late edition (21.C1) strips the mountain and the foreground of all colour, rendering them instead just in grey.

Die Tücher am Bauch und Rumpf des Packpferdes im Vordergrund tragen Wappen mit den Schriftzügen „Takenouchi" und „Take", die auf den Verleger Takenouchi verweisen. In der zweiten Auflage (21.B1) repräsentiert die geänderte Aufschrift „Rin" auf dem Satteltuch den Verleger Iseya. In dieser Auflage fehlen in der Regel Eisens Signatur und das kombinierte Zensur- und Verlegersiegel in roter Kalebasse – mit wenigen Ausnahmen, möglicherweise frühen Abzügen von Iseya, auf denen das Siegel erhalten blieb. Bei dem auf S. 182–183 abgebildeten Druck scheint es sich um einen einmaligen Probeabzug für die erste Auflage (21.A1) zu handeln, bei dem die Druckplatte für die Haut der Figuren, das Pferd und die linke und rechte Flanke des Berges, die für gewöhnlich ein helles Rotbraun aufweisen, dunkelbraun eingefärbt wurde. Das helle Rotbraun

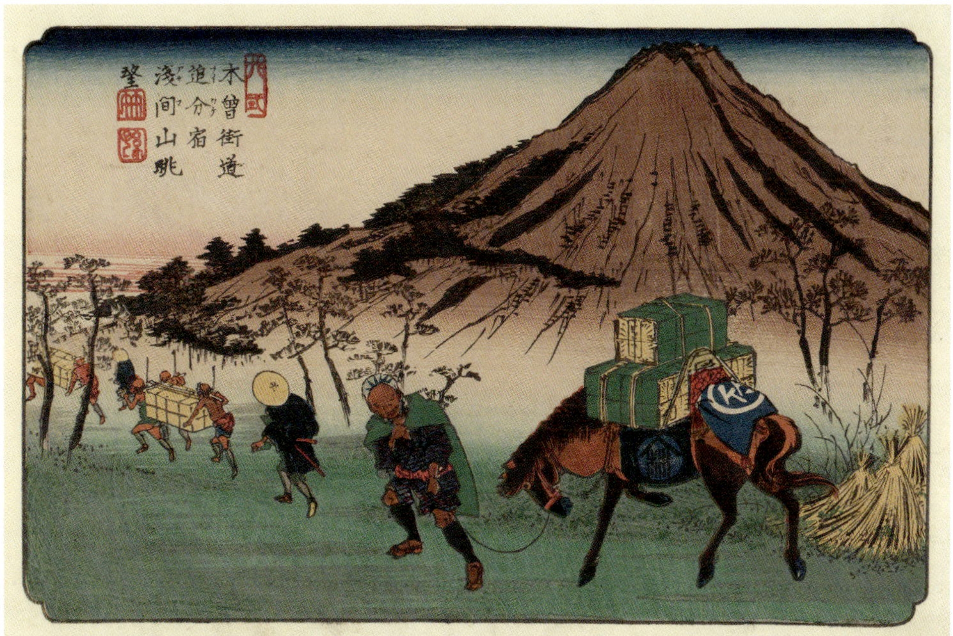

21.B1c

wurde in diesem Abzug nur für die Stirnseite des Berges verwendet, die in der Regel ockergelb ist. Außerdem sind die roten Siegel oben links tiefer platziert als in allen anderen bekannten Abzügen. Die zweite Auflage (21.B1) existiert in mehreren Farbvarianten, für die z. B. der Berggipfel in schwarzes *bokashi* getaucht oder das gesamte Blatt mit senkrechten Linien überdruckt wurde, die Regen darstellen. Eine sehr späte Auflage (21.C1) beraubt den Berg und den Vordergrund sämtlicher Farbe und gibt sie stattdessen in Grau wieder.

Les morceaux d'étoffe qui recouvrent le ventre et la croupe du cheval de bât, au premier plan, portent les armoiries « Takenouchi » et « Take », en référence à l'éditeur Takenouchi. Dans la deuxième édition (21.B1), l'inscription figurant sur l'étoffe recouvrant le ventre du cheval a été remplacée par « Rin », signe de l'éditeur Iseya. Cette édition est généralement dépourvue de la signature d'Eisen et du sceau réunissant le censeur et l'éditeur dans une gourde rouge, mais, dans quelques exceptions, peut-être les premières épreuves d'Iseya, le sceau a été conservé. L'illustration aux pages 182–183 semble être une unique épreuve d'essai de la première édition (21.A1), dans laquelle on a employé un brun foncé pour la peau des figures, le cheval et les arêtes situées de part et d'autre de la montagne, éléments habituellement imprimés dans un brun rougeâtre clair. Dans cette épreuve, ce même brun rougeâtre clair a été utilisé, mais seulement pour la face de la montagne, habituellement imprimée en ocre jaune. En outre, le placement des sceaux rouges dans la partie supérieure gauche est plus bas que dans toute autre épreuve connue. Il existe plusieurs variantes chromatiques de la deuxième édition (21.B1) : par exemple, le sommet de la montagne comporte un *bokashi* noir, ou bien l'épreuve est entièrement recouverte de lignes verticales représentant la pluie. Dans une édition très tardive (21.C1), la montagne et le premier plan n'ont plus aucune couleur et sont uniformément grises.

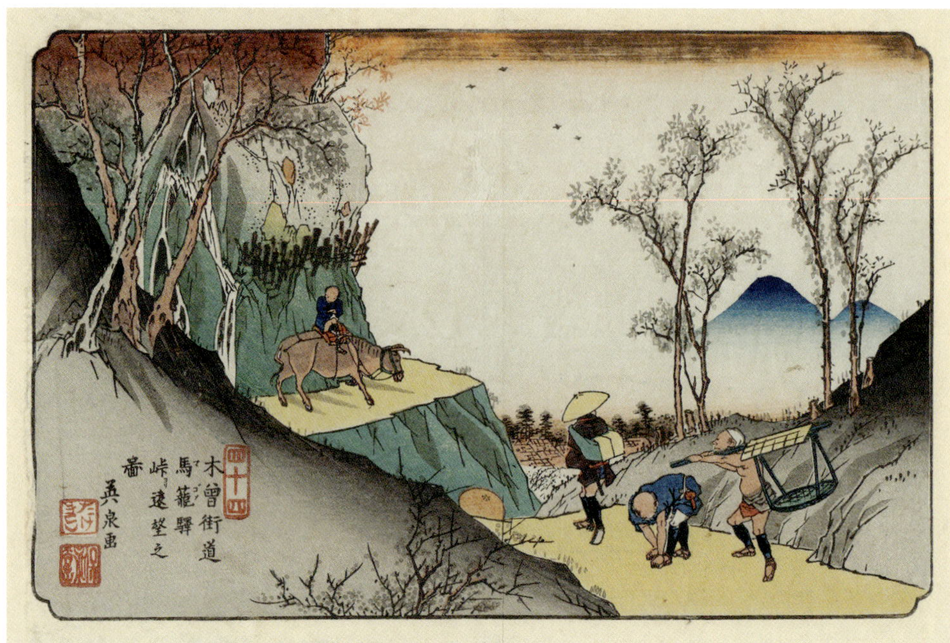

44.A1a

44 - MAGOME

The first version of Magome's first edition (44.A1) lacks the large mountain in the centre of the image. That mountain appears for the first time in the second, finest variation of this design, as does the darker rendering of the grey mountain on the right of the travellers in the centre (see pp. 300–301). These changes are apparent in the earliest variation of the second edition (44.B1), which lacks Eisen's signature. The second variation of this edition is without red *bokashi* in the top-left corner. The last edition (44.C1) has a red band at the top and shows only the peak of the central mountain in a deep black; the lower mountains in the background are an even blue, and the rocks above and below the farmer with the ox are green.

In der ersten Version der ersten Auflage (44.A1) von Magome fehlt der große Berg in der Bildmitte. Er taucht zuerst in der zweiten und schönsten Variante des Entwurfs auf, ebenso wie die dunklere Wiedergabe des grauen Berghangs, der rechts neben den Reisenden im Vordergrund ansteigt (vgl. S. 300–301). Sichtbar werden diese Änderungen auch in der frühesten Variante der zweiten Auflage (44.B1), aus der Eisens Signatur getilgt wurde. In der zweiten Variante dieser Auflage ist das rote *bokashi* aus der oberen linken Ecke verschwunden. Die letzte Auflage (44.C1) zeigt einen roten Streifen am oberen Bildrand und nur die Spitze des zentralen Berges in Tiefschwarz. Die weniger hohen Berge im Hintergrund sind gleichmäßig blau, die Felsen ober- und unterhalb des Bauern mit dem Ochsen grün.

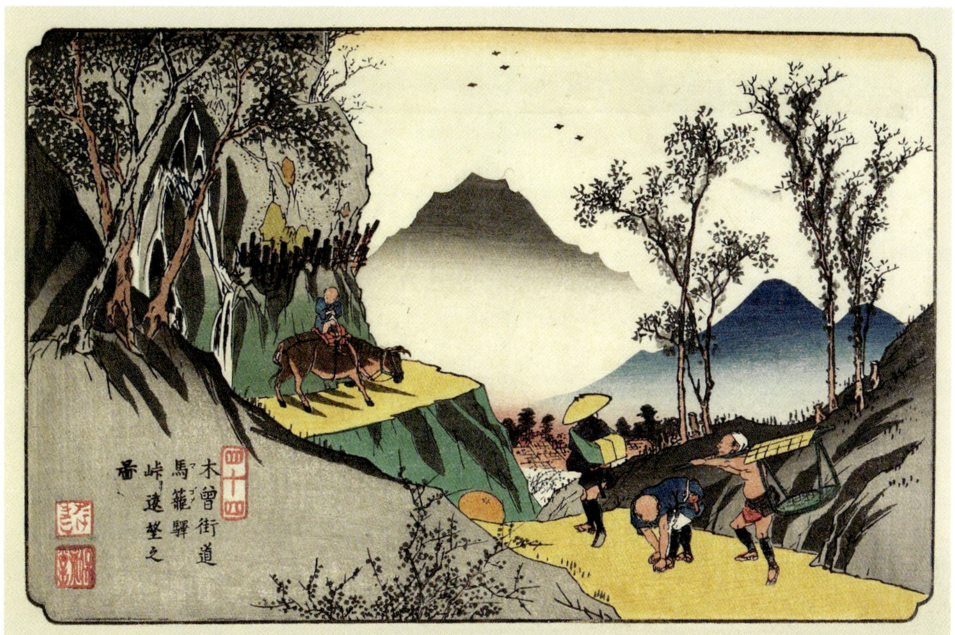

44.B1b

La grande montagne visible au centre de l'image est
absente de la première version de la première édition
(44.A1) de Magome. C'est dans la deuxième variante, la
plus belle (voir pp. 300–301), de cette estampe qu'elle
apparaît pour la première fois, de même que le rendu
plus sombre de la montagne grise qui se trouve à droite
des voyageurs situés au centre. Ces changements sont
visibles dans la première variante de la deuxième édition (44.B1) qui ne porte pas la signature d'Eisen. Dans
la deuxième variante de cette édition, il n'y a pas de
bokashi rouge dans l'angle supérieur gauche. Dans la
dernière édition (44.C1), on peut voir une bande rouge
dans la partie supérieure, et seul le sommet de la montagne centrale est d'un noir profond ; les montagnes
moins élevées de l'arrière-plan sont d'un bleu uniforme,
et les rochers situés au-dessus et au-dessous du fermier
montant le bœuf sont verts.

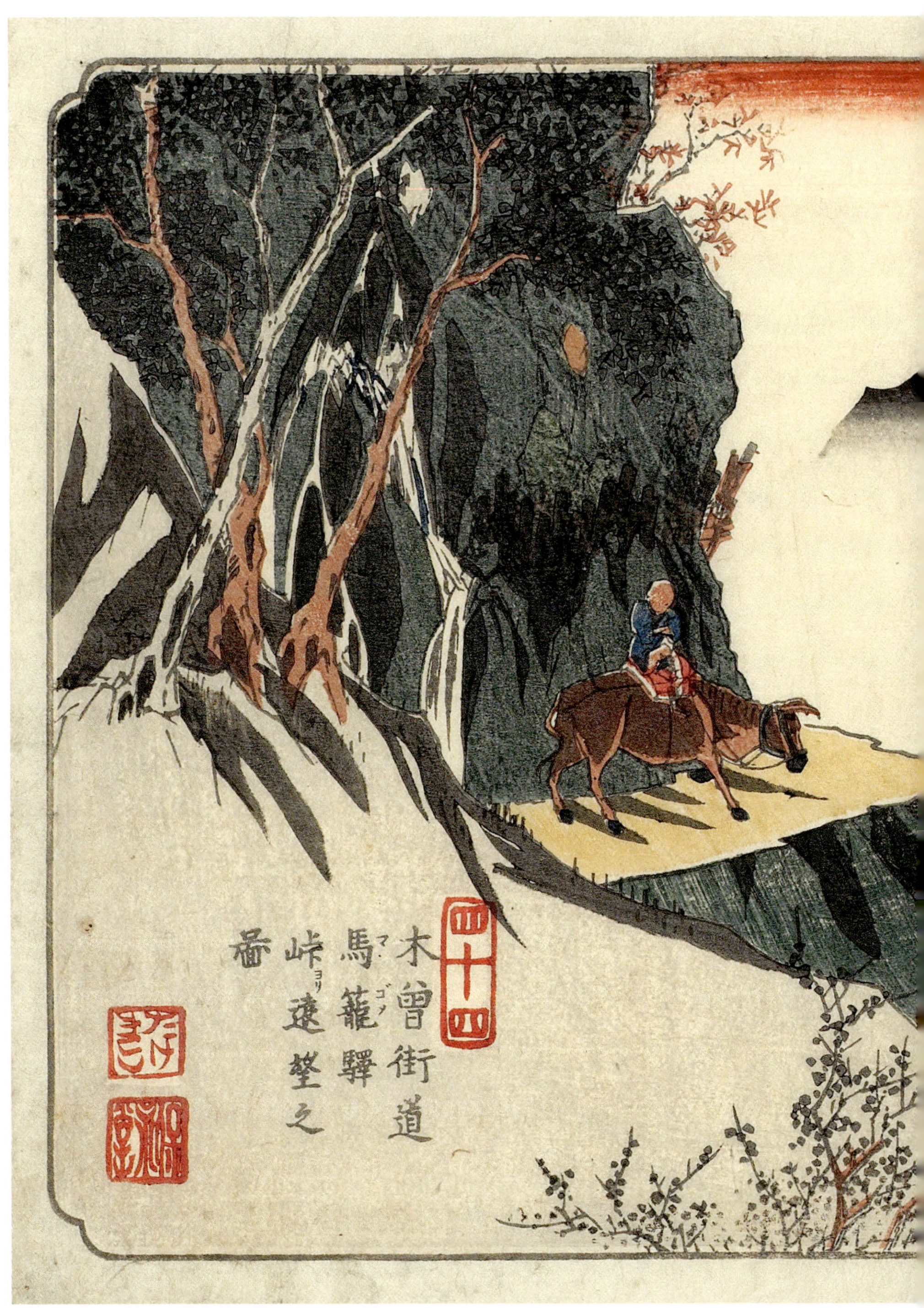

44.C1

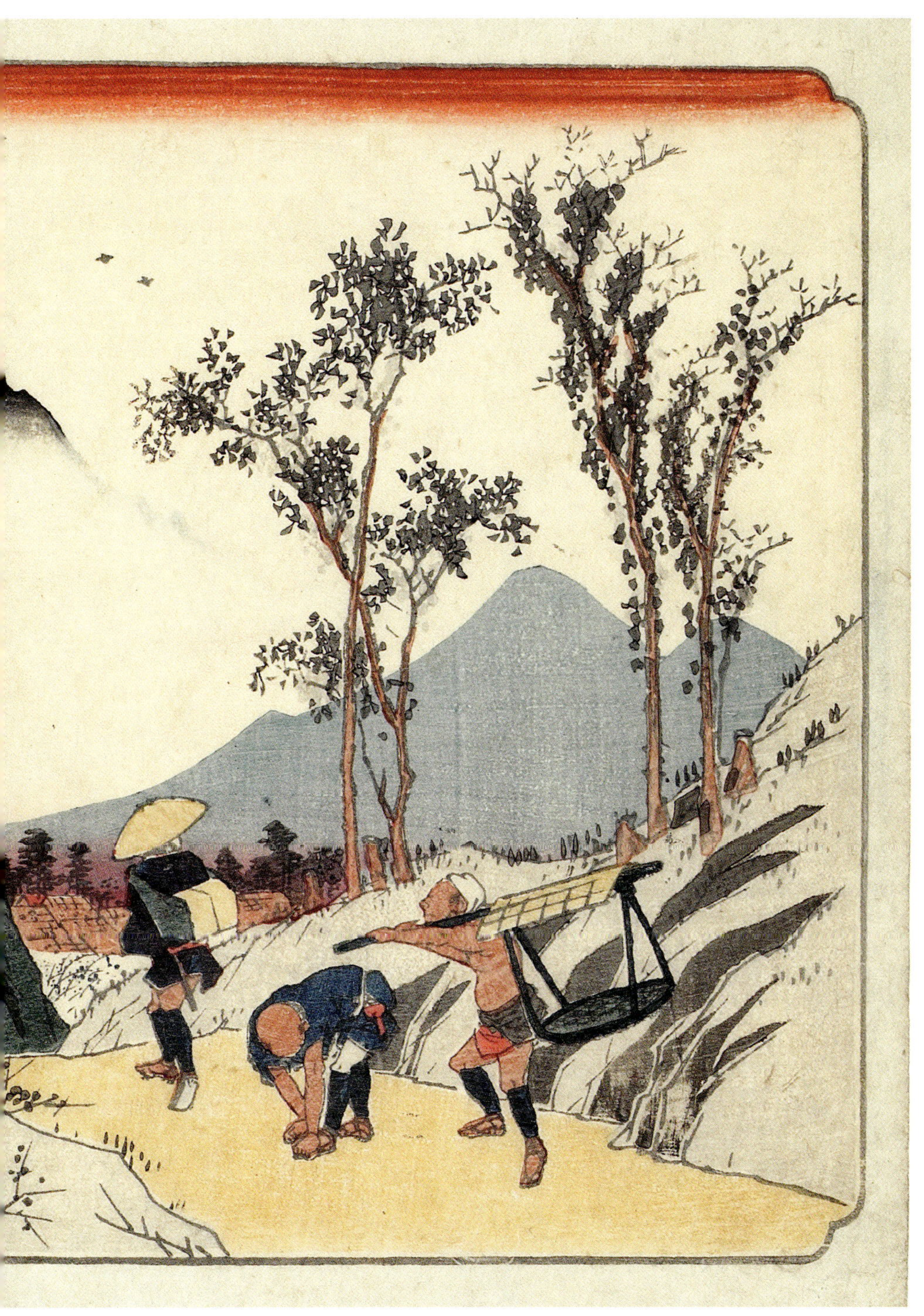

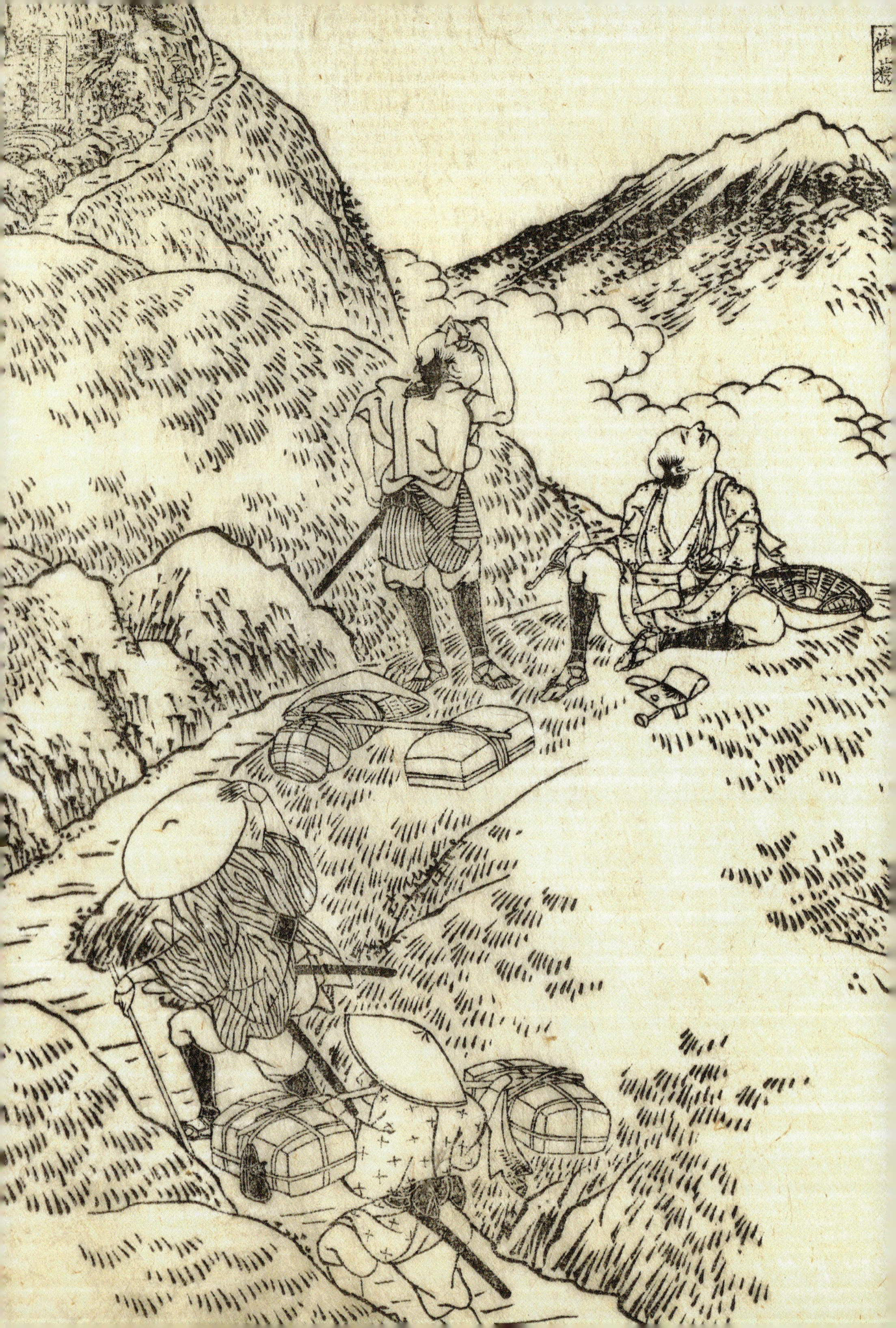

Sources and Preparatory Sketches for the Plates
Quellen und Vorzeichnungen zu den Tafeln
Sources et esquisses préparatoires pour les planches

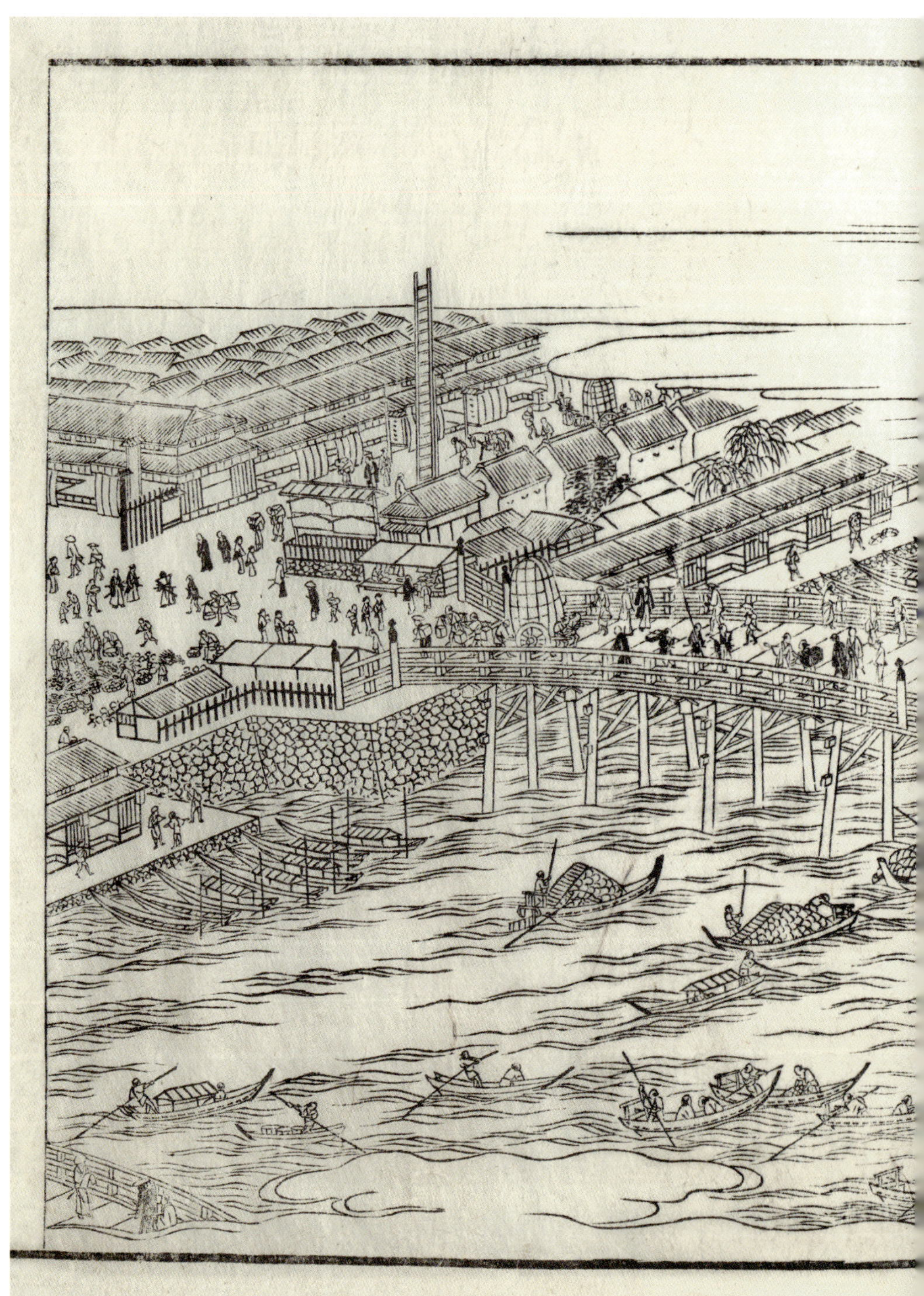

1 – **Nihonbashi**   *Akisato Ritō: Kisoji meisho zue, vol. 5, 1805*

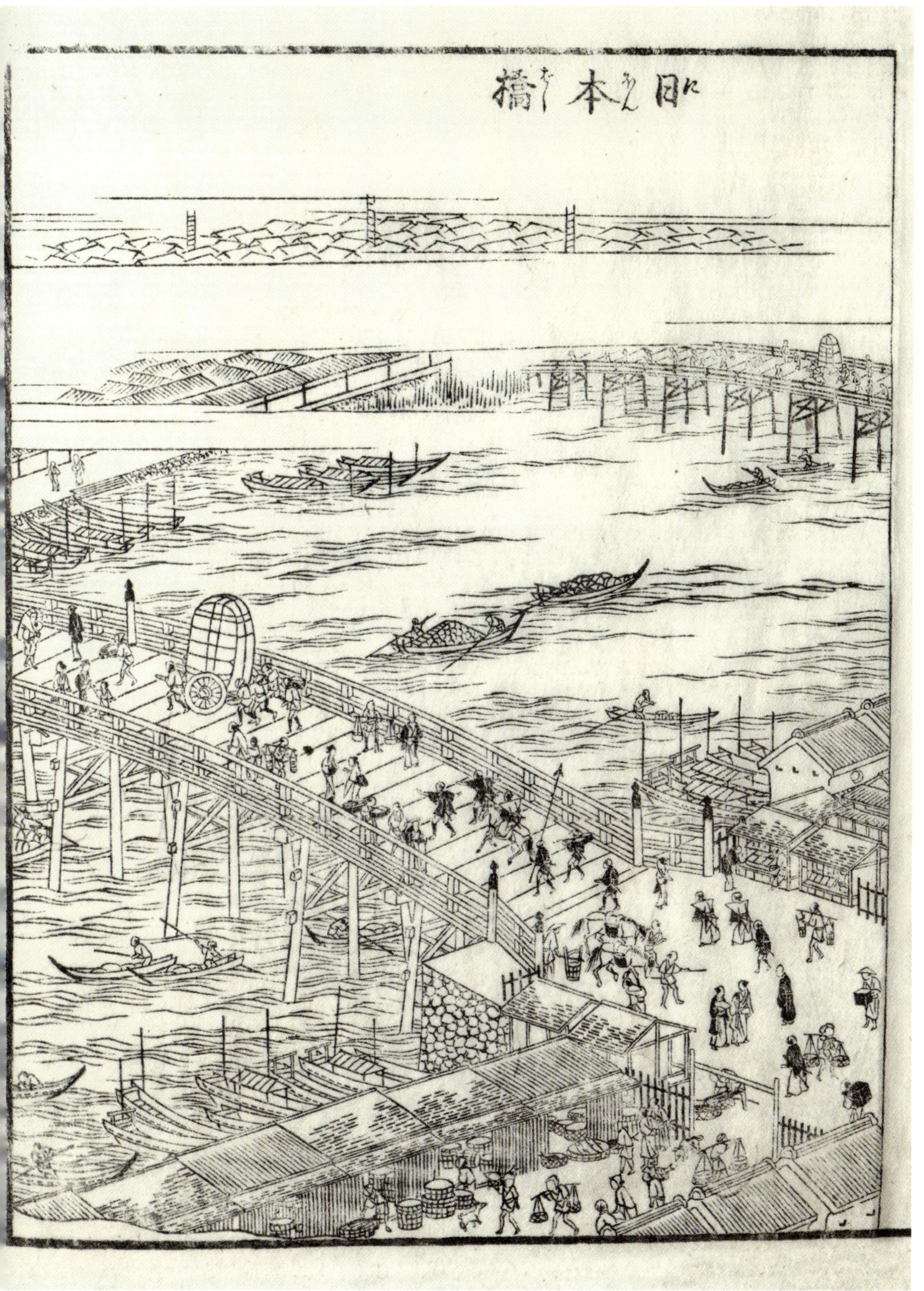
日本橋

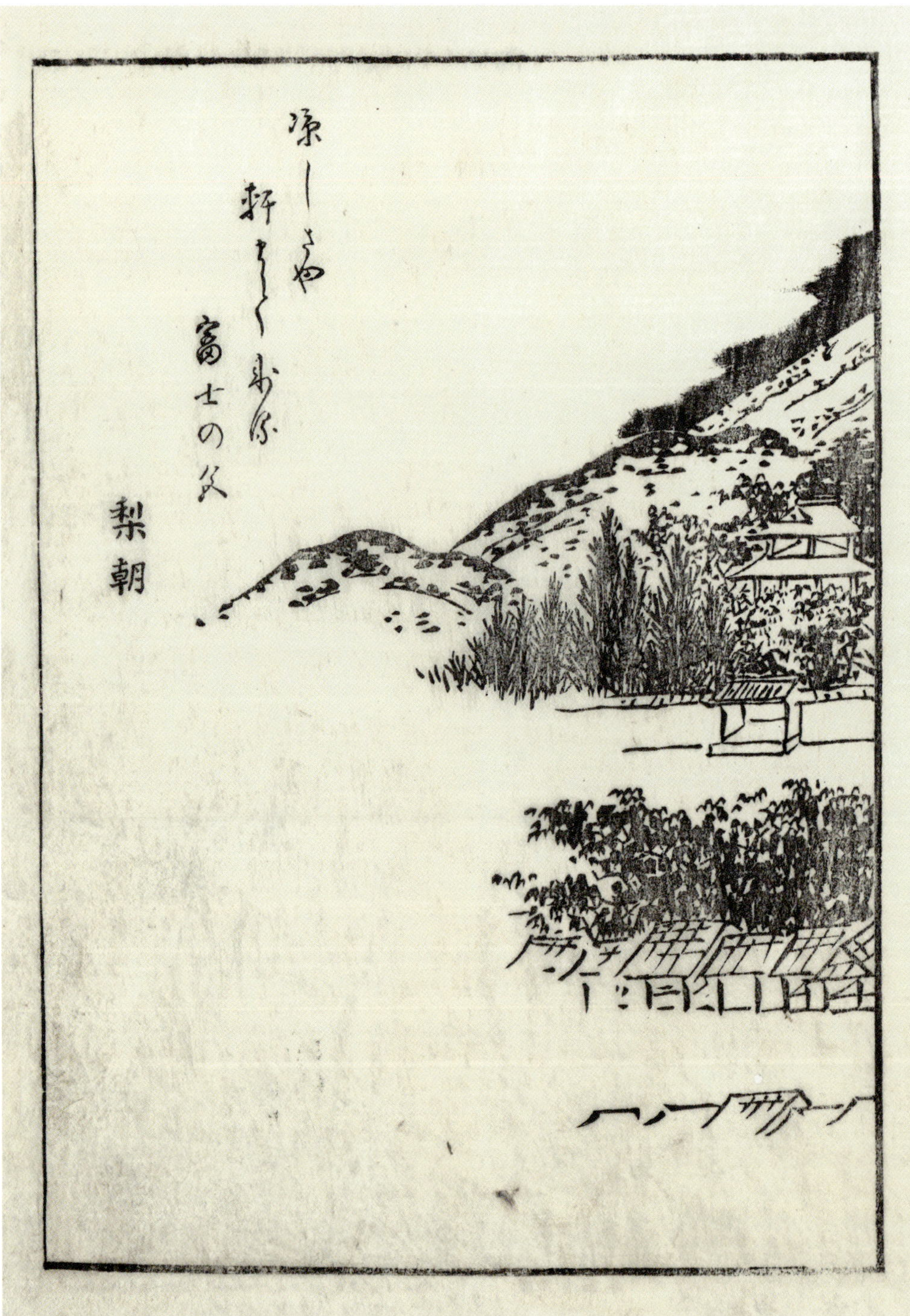

5 – **Ōmiya**   *Akisato Ritō: Kisoji meisho zue, vol. 5, 1805*

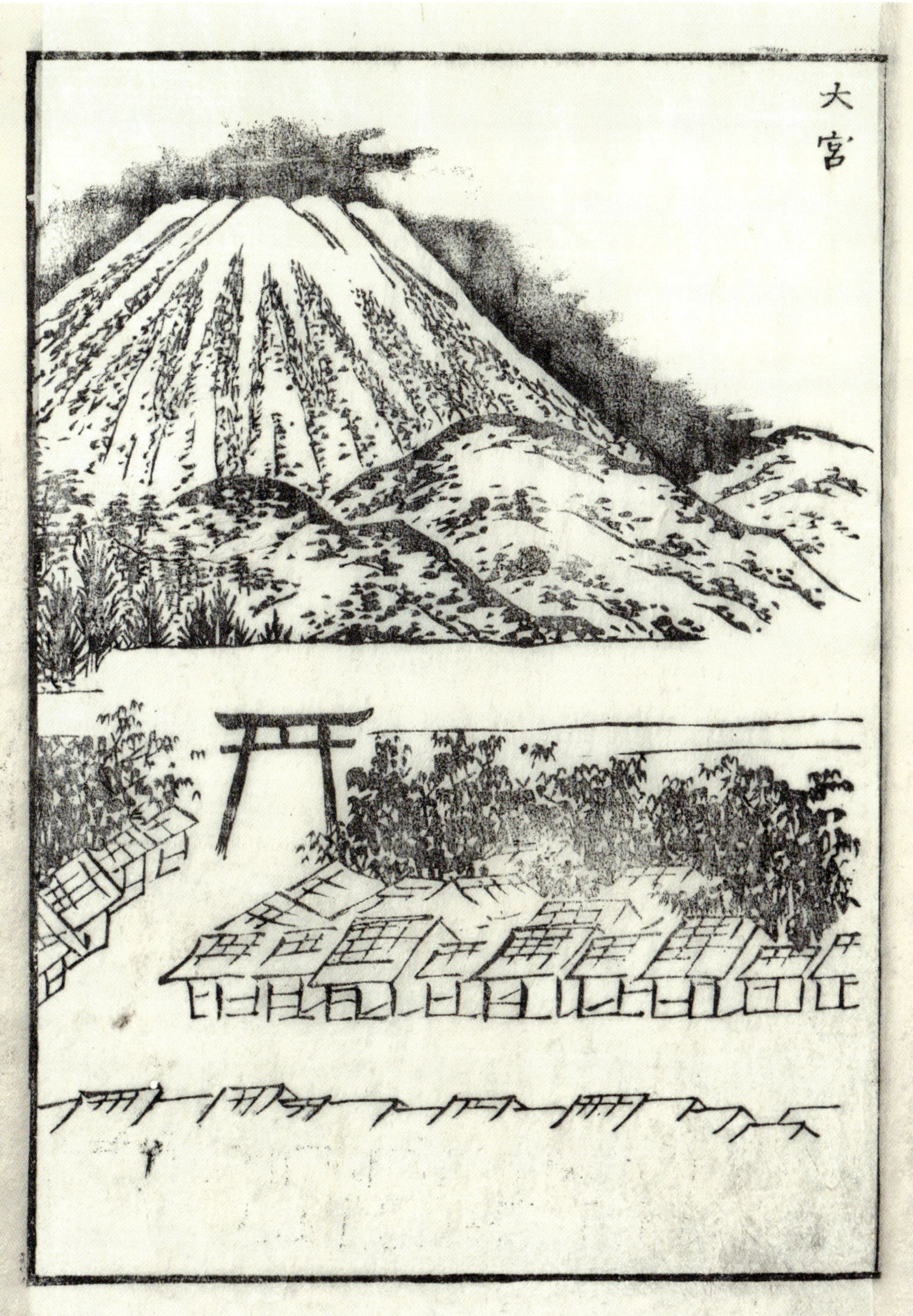

大宮

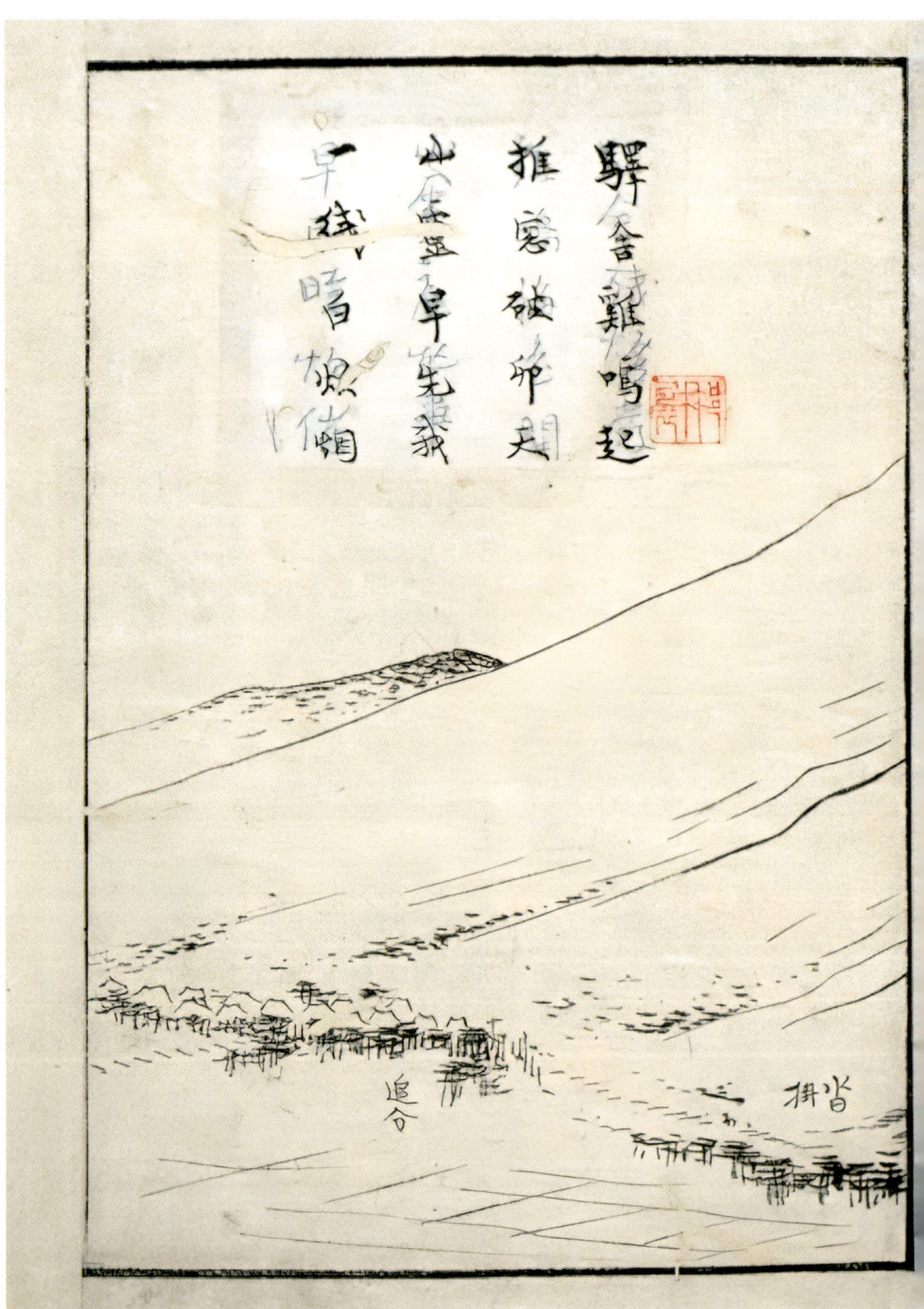

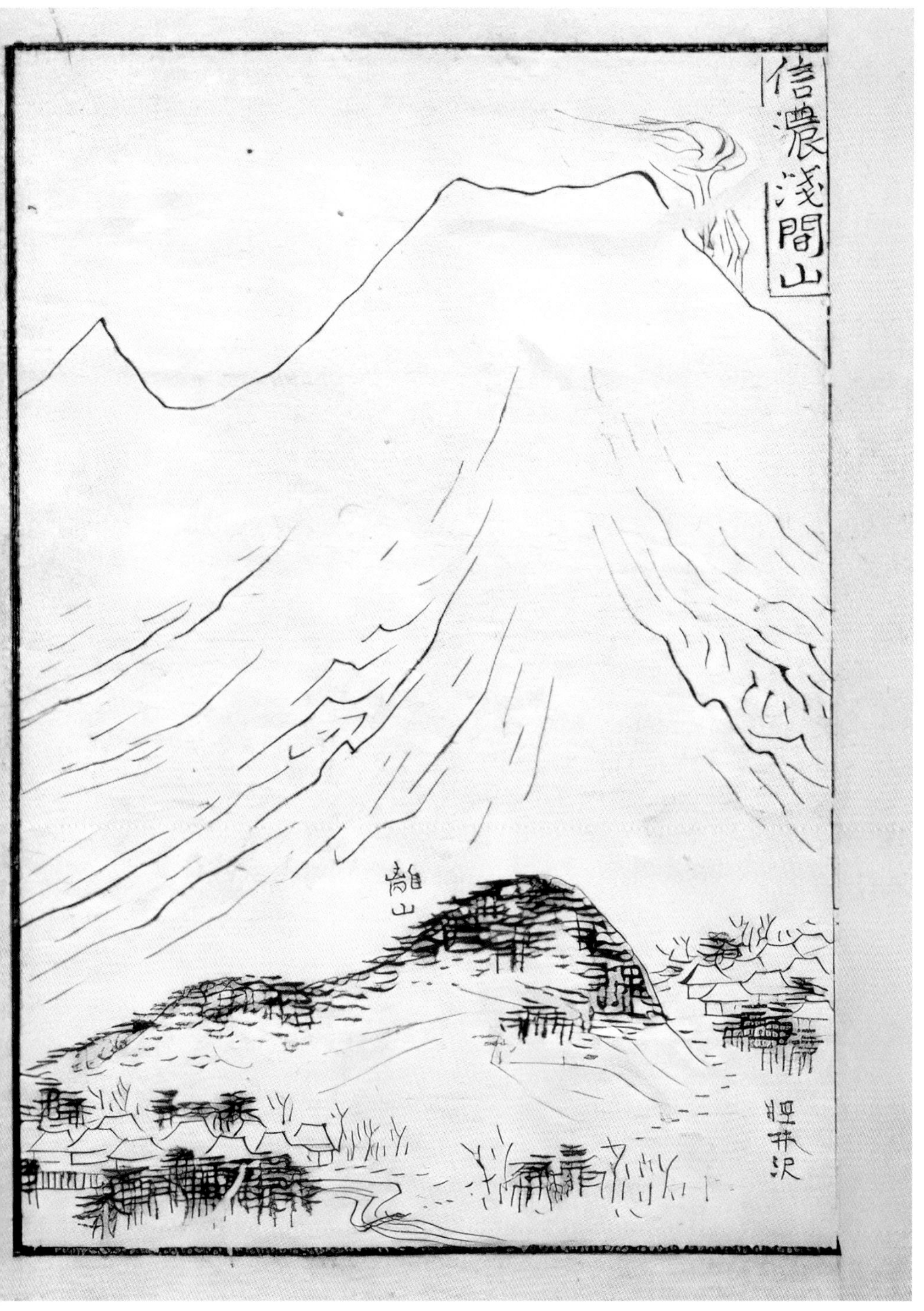

信濃浅間山
離山
輕井沢

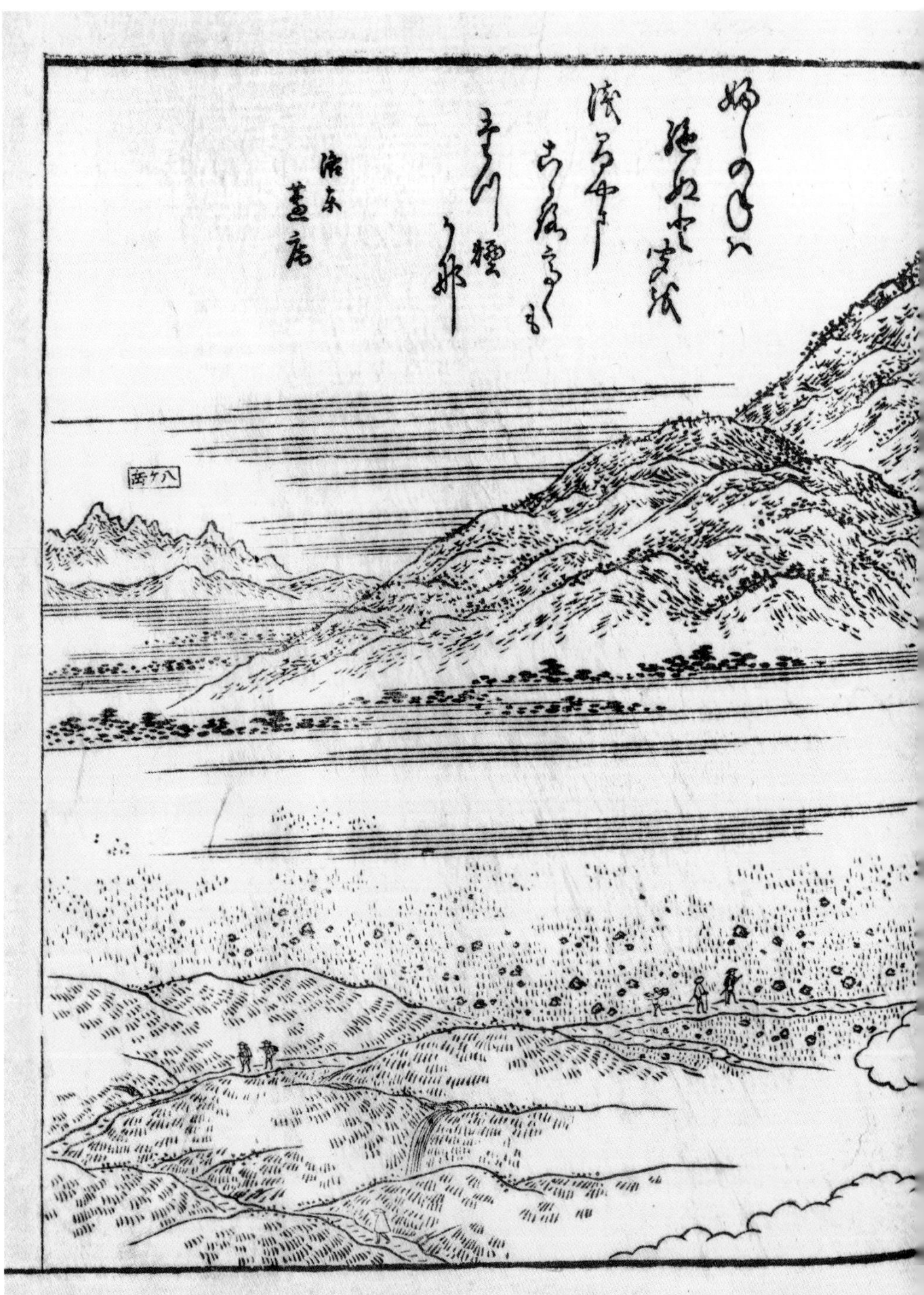

21 – Oiwake   *Akisato Ritō: Kisoji meisho zue, vol. 5, 1805*

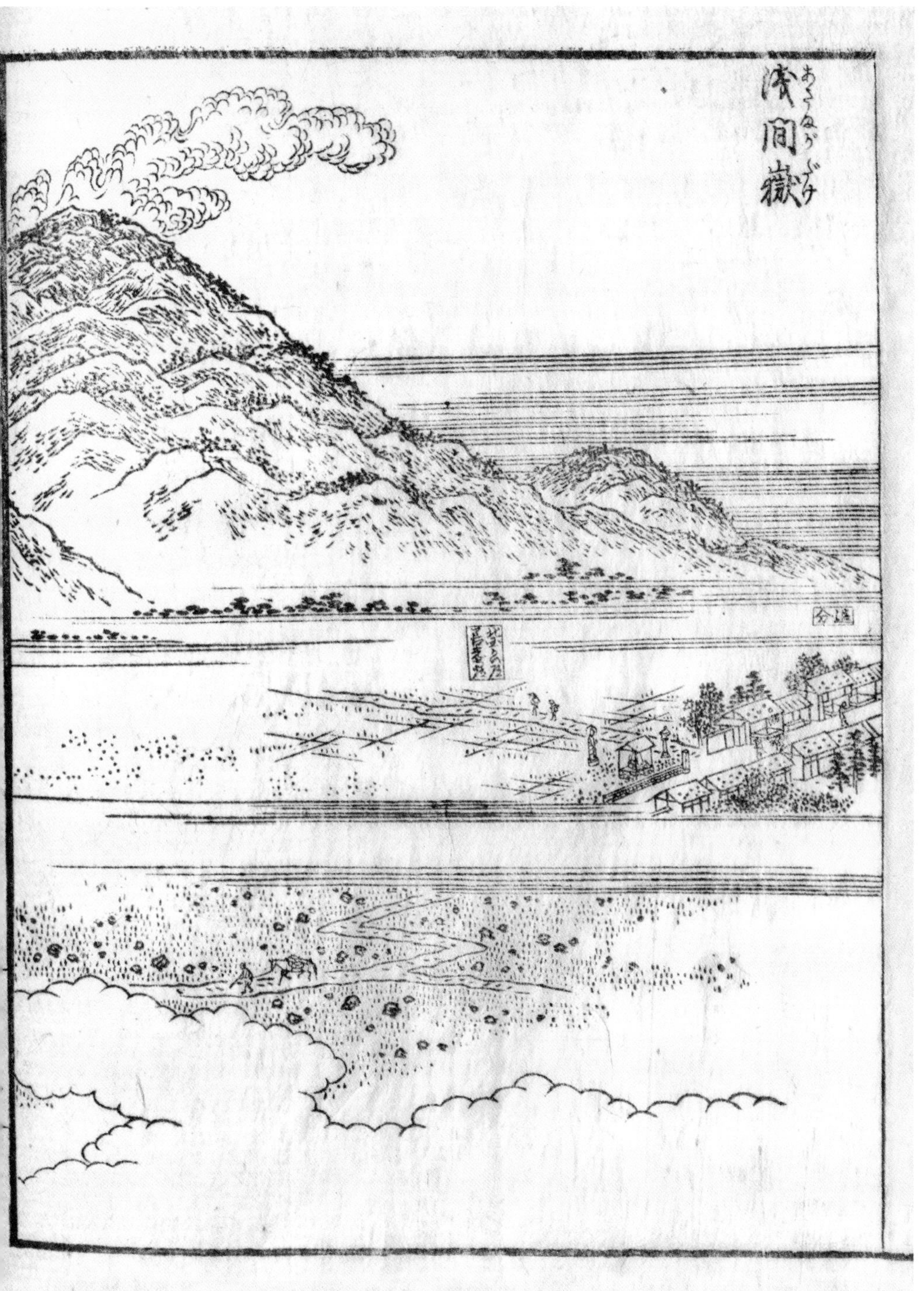
あさまがだけ
淺間嶽
分遣

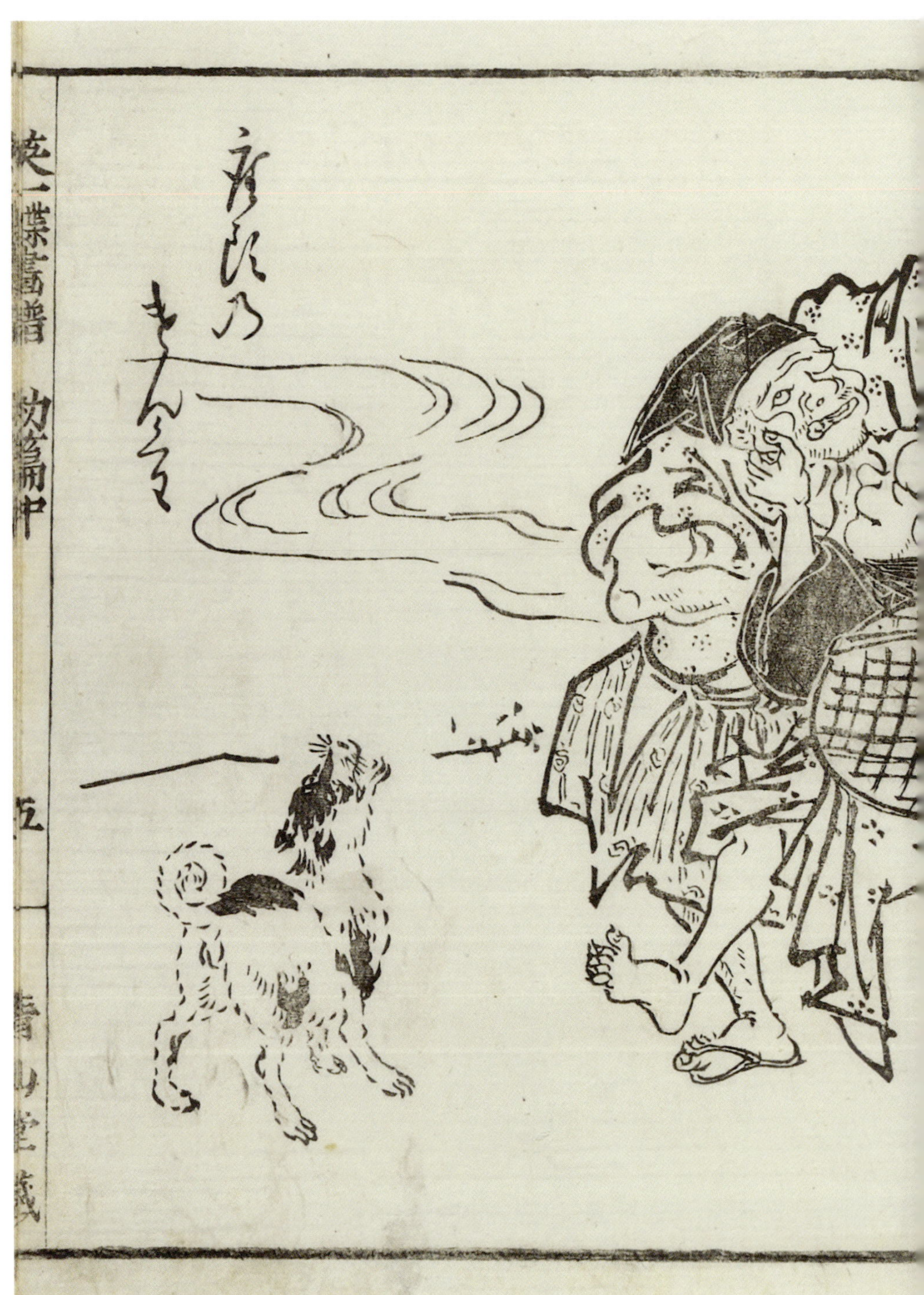

23 – Iwamurata   *Suzuki Rinshō: Itchō gafu, 1770*

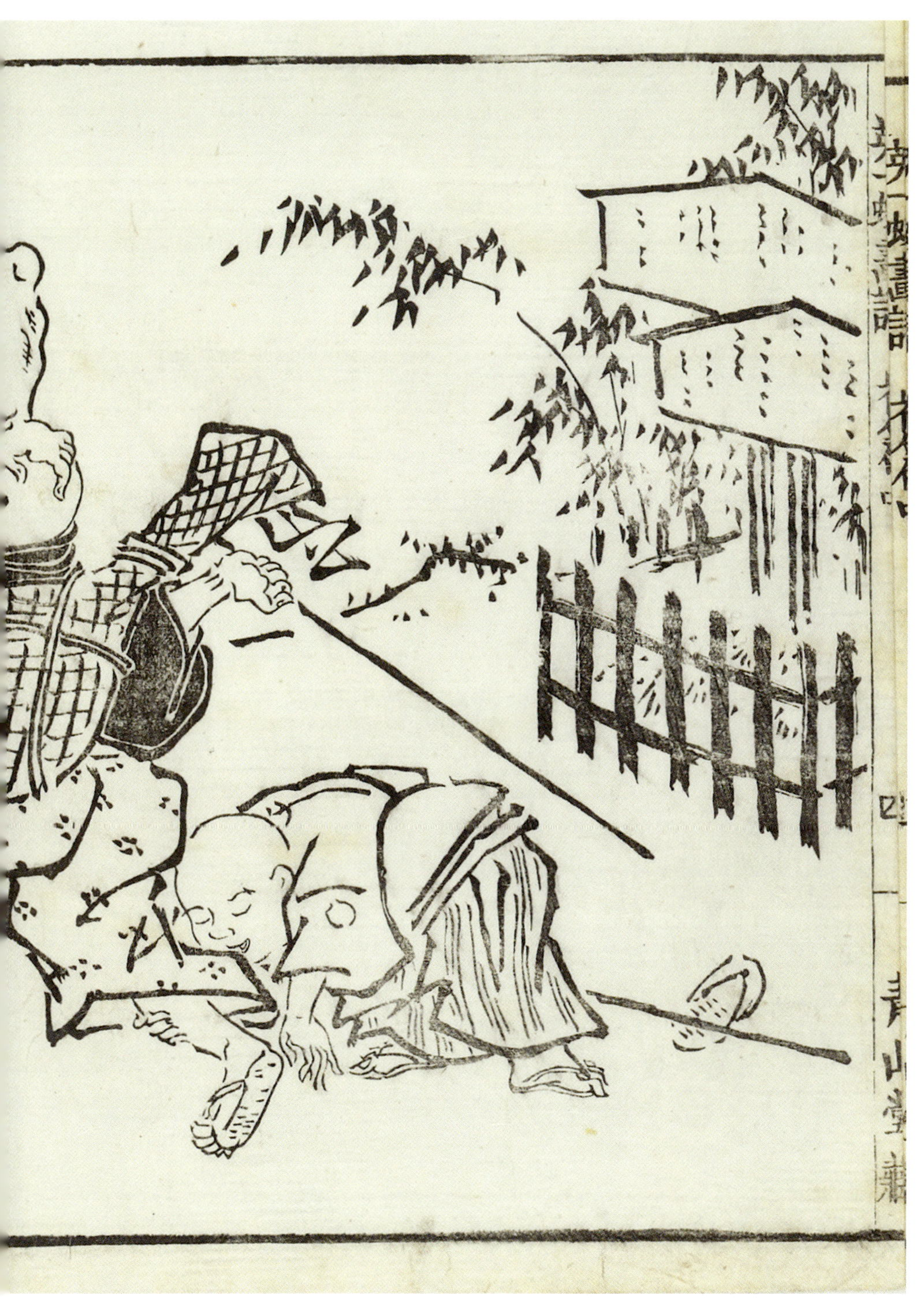

第一奇書畫諸才秘
青山堂藏

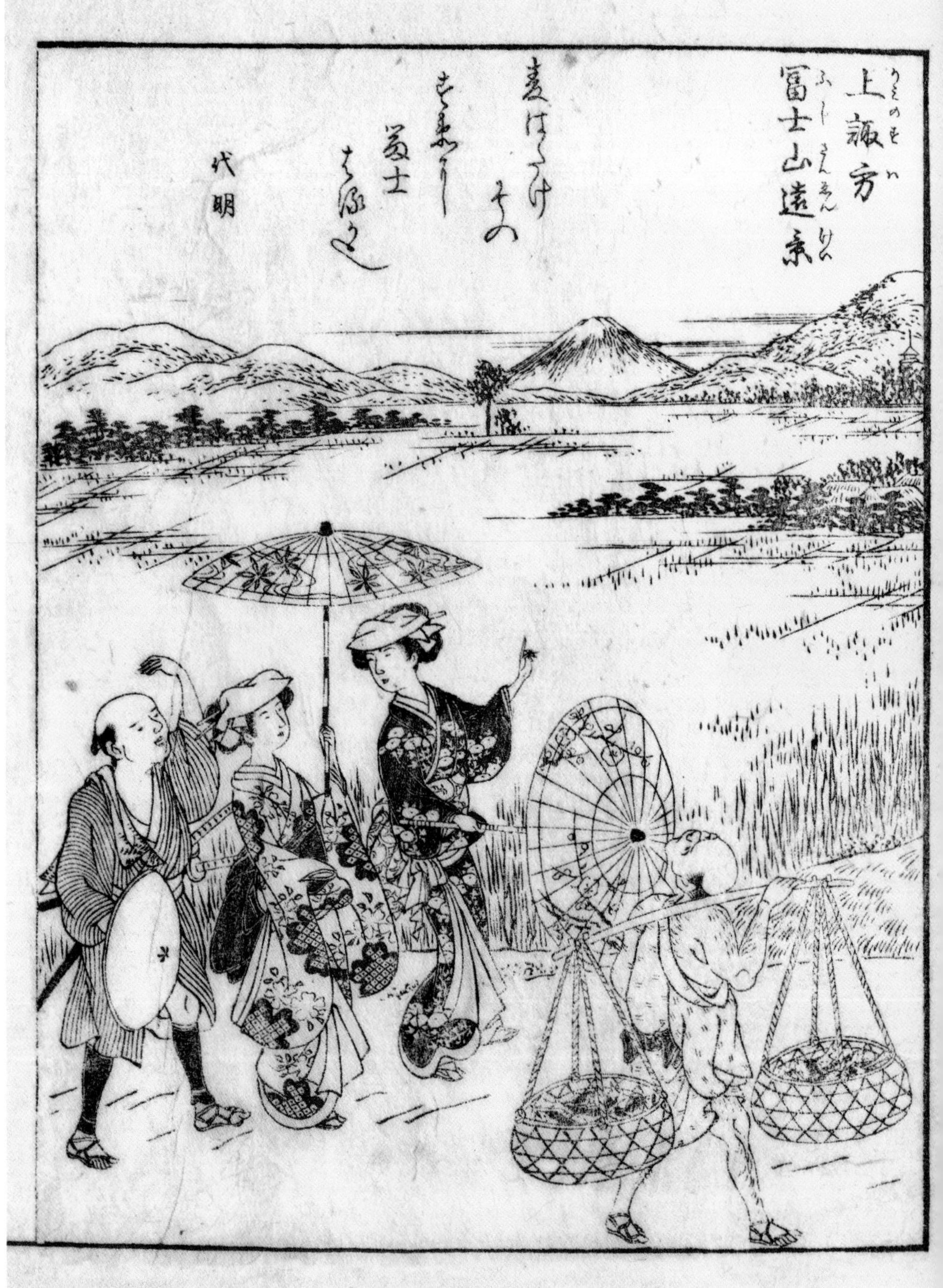

上諏方
冨士山遠景
麦けつけ
その
富士
代明

木曽路名所圖會卷之四目録　終

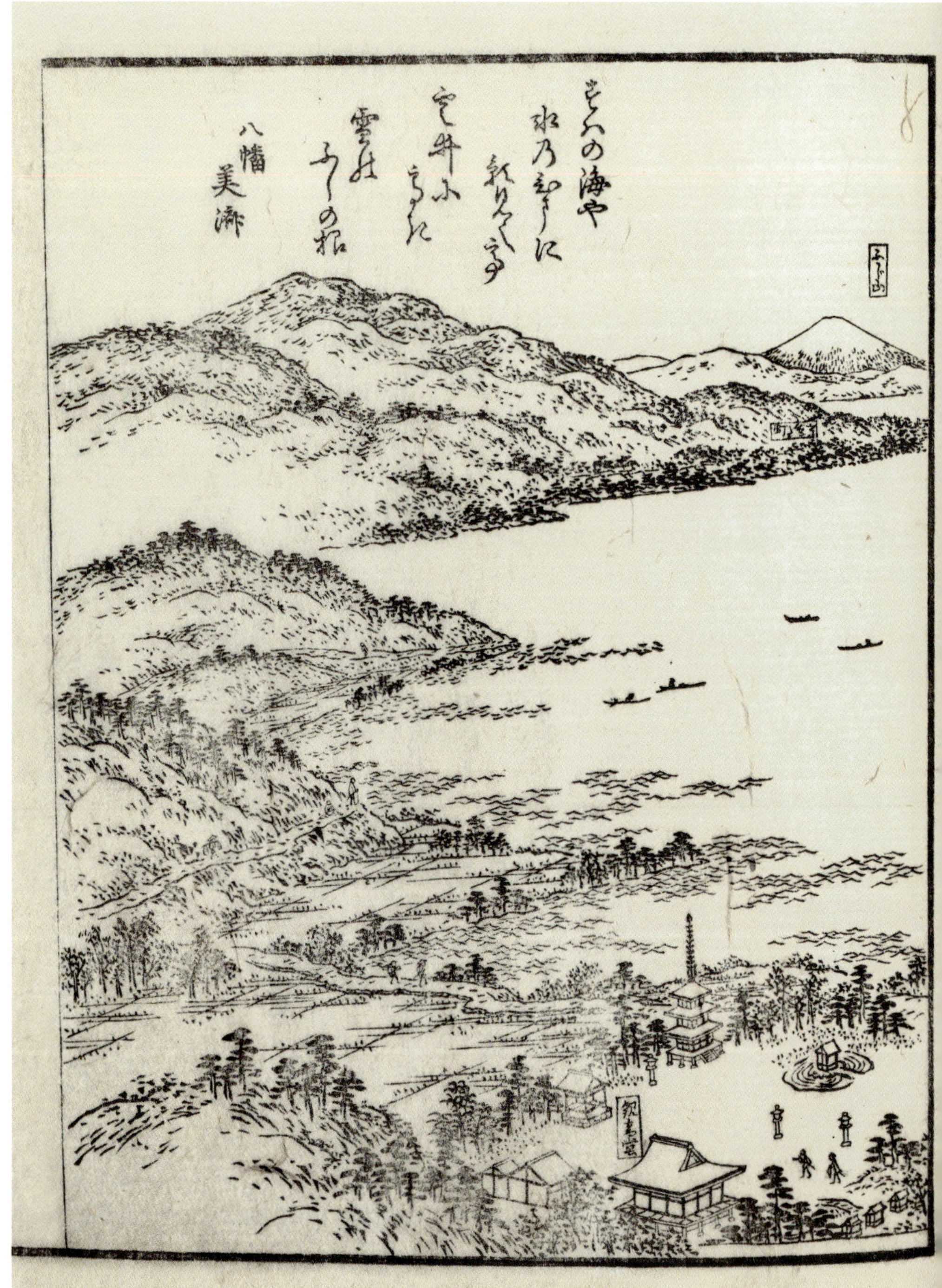

31 – Shiojiri *Akisato Ritō: Kisoji meisho zue, vol. 5, 1805*

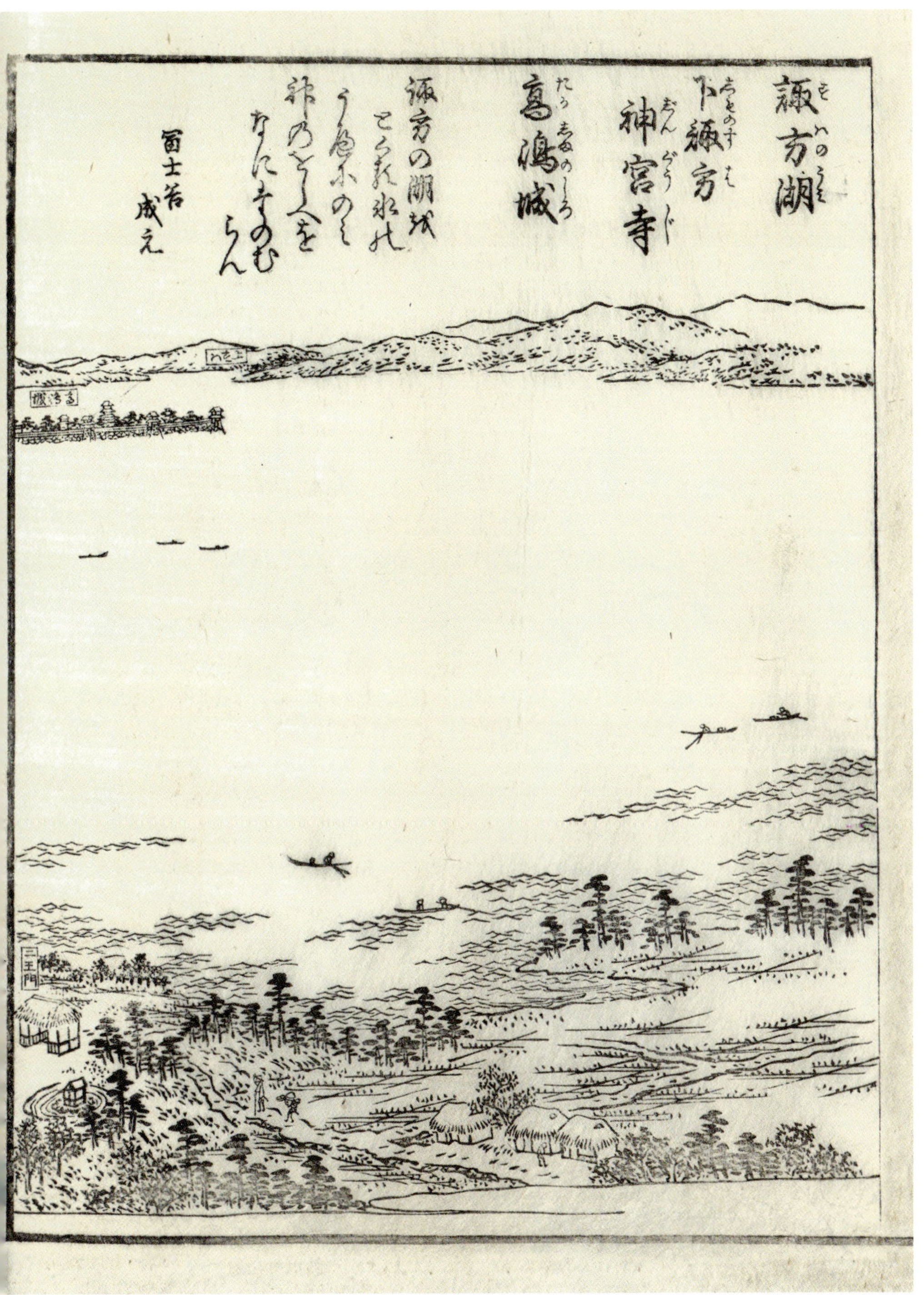

諏方湖（すはのうみ）
下諏方（しものすは）神宮寺（ぎんぐうじ）
高鴻城（たかしまのしろ）

諏方の湖城
こほり氷れ
うを水の
神の戸と人を
なにそのむ
らん

冨士若
成え

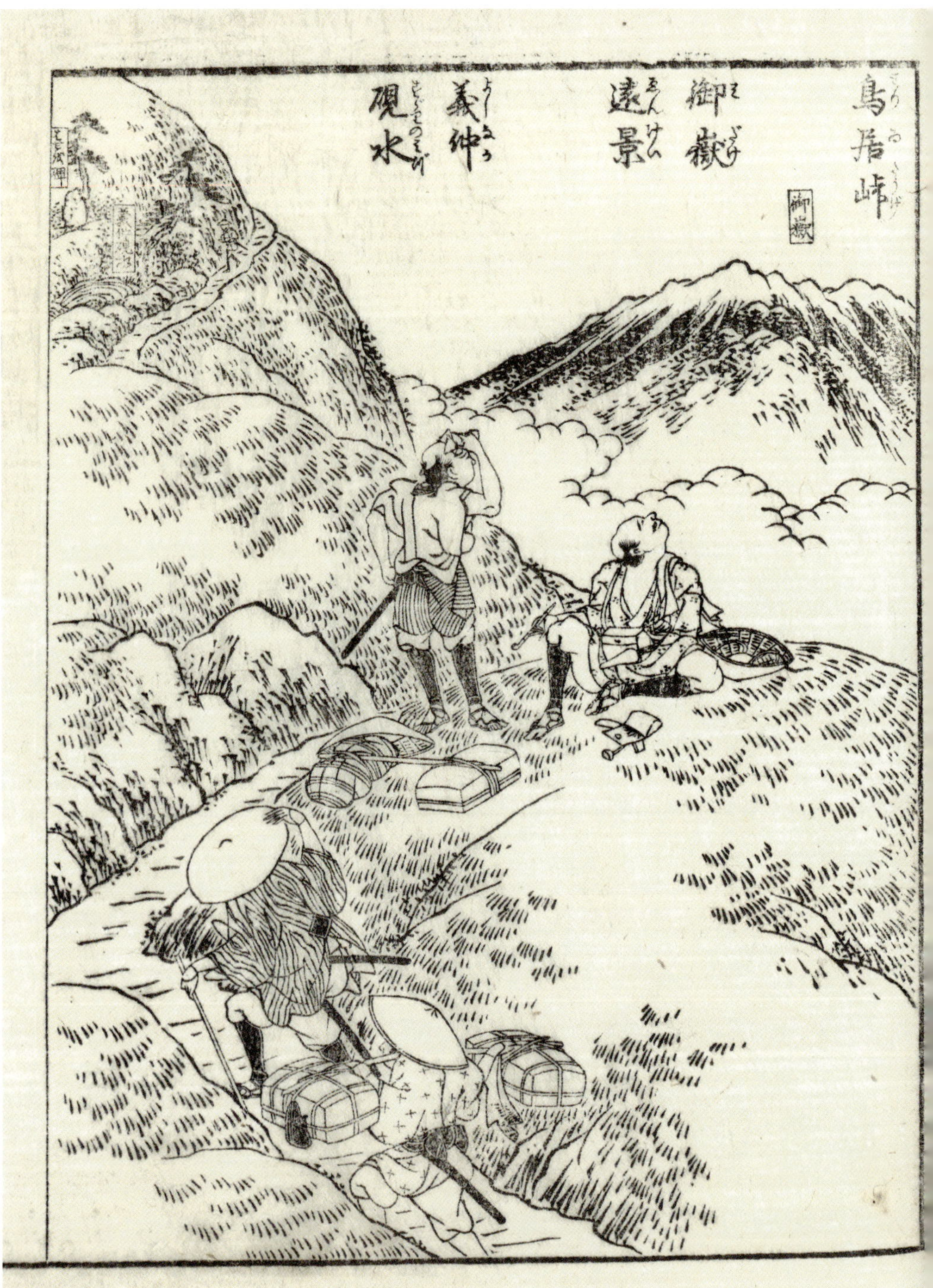

鳥居峠
御嶽
遠景
義仲
硯水
御嶽

鳥居嶺

明神と祭り社を立神と祭る其恩惠報をべし

駒嶺坂嶮しく馬も上がらぬ難所なり御嶽の宮據てふありしより

信玄雲本る義康とてに合戦あり其後天正十年武田勝頼

今福筑前守宮残大将として人数八千余此軍勢四郎へ法

馬頭義昌信長公の御方として七千余人馬頭義昌其外数萬

頼ひけるが本る勝利を得く甲州勢を討る支配書ふ之へり

武田民部私欲月ごとに小童を率く小揆くる本る義昌其外数軍

謀反と企ける中略十二月信忠卿破軍して御出陣ありくその

夜も土田小御宿あり十三日高遠十四日岩村小御着あり瀧河左の道

将監毛利河内守水聖監物同宗意清尉る十二月の未明小岩村より

信州伊奈口へ発途也八月十四日小信州松尾の城主小笠原掃部助縁方

小泰を忠節と致屋さとや紙み付く圍平八森勝蔵差をさる前

早手合をして小笠原掃部助左之前く綱を揚うるを飯田城小

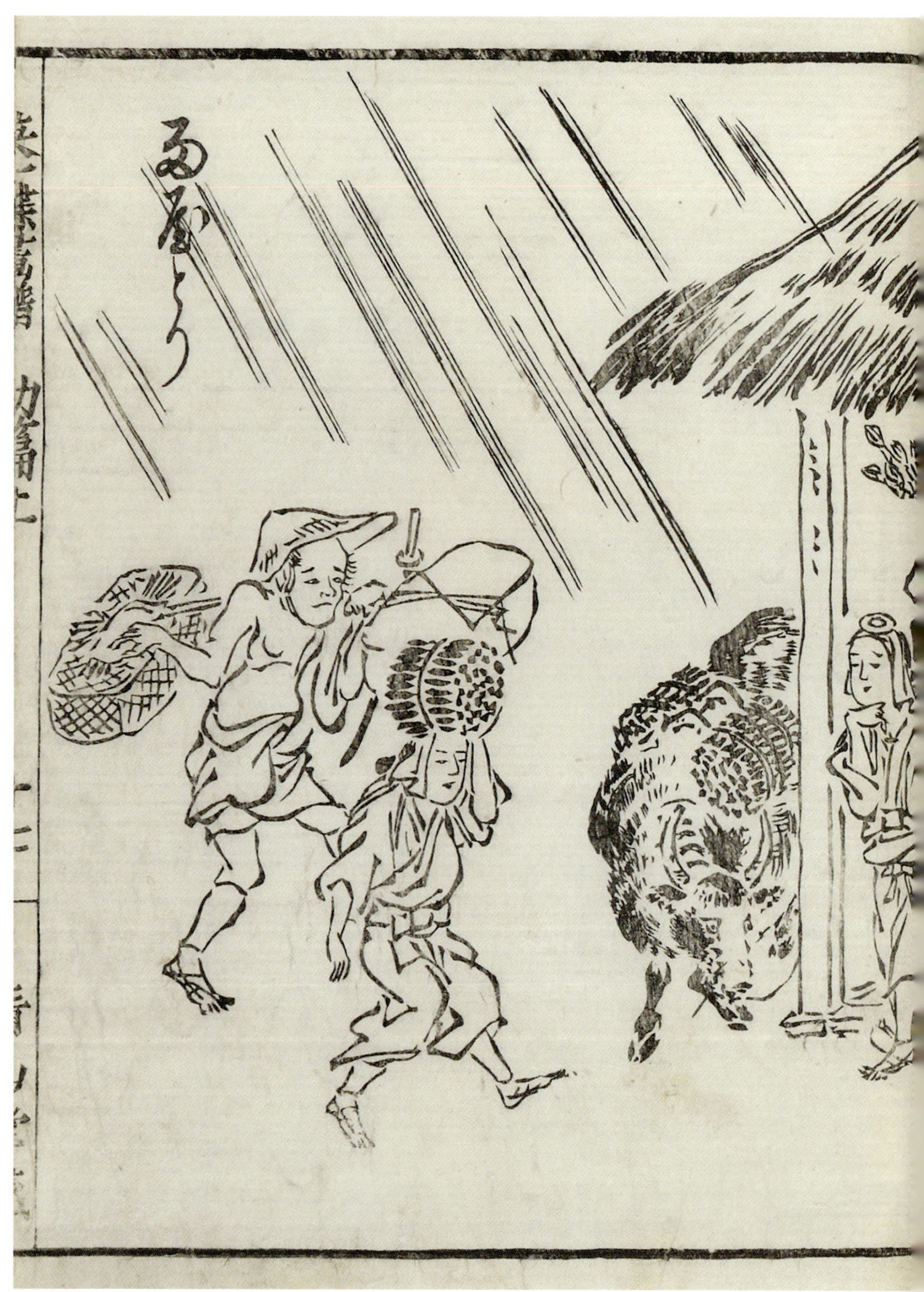

40 – **Suhara**   *Suzuki Rinshō: Itchō gafu, 1770*

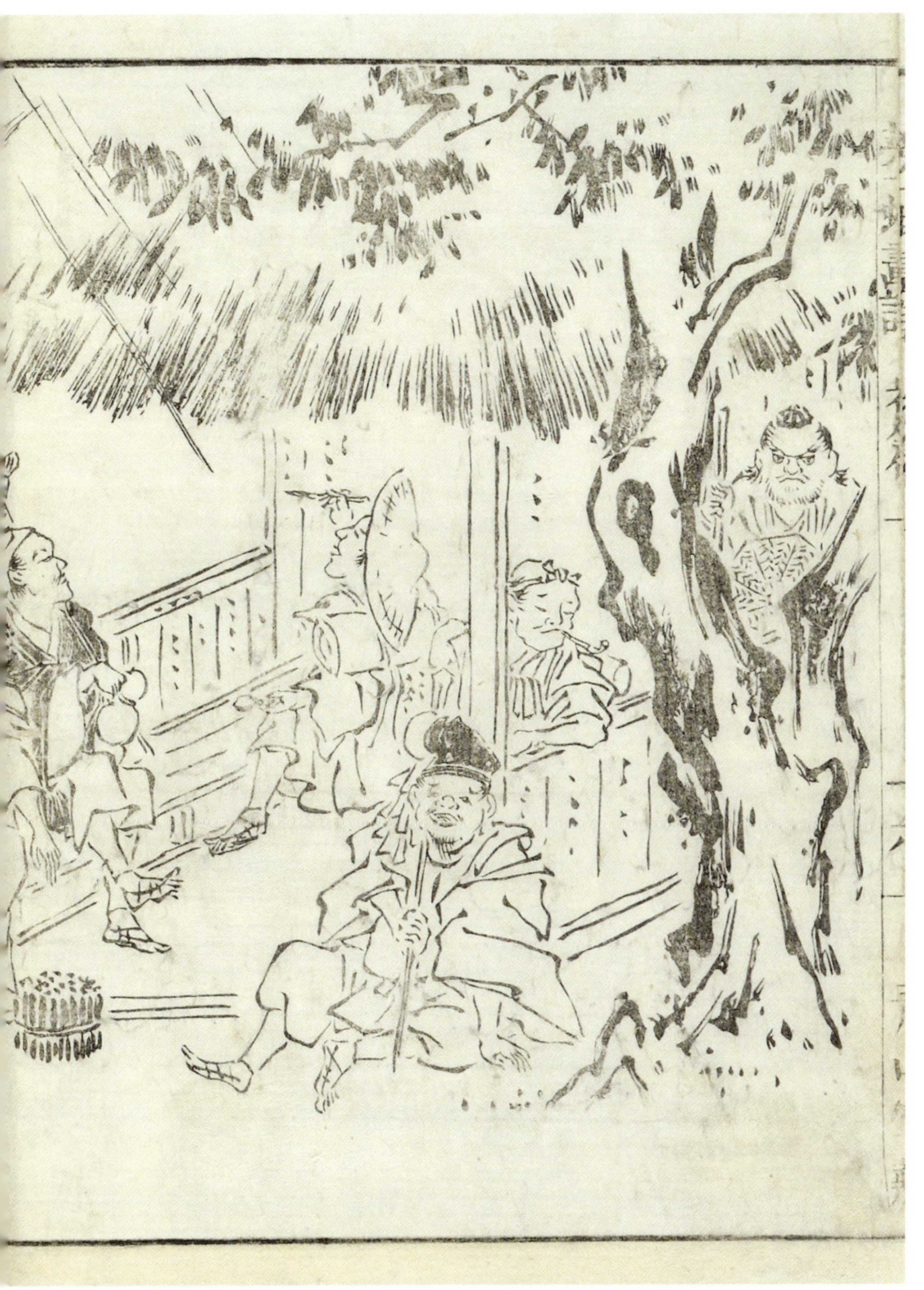

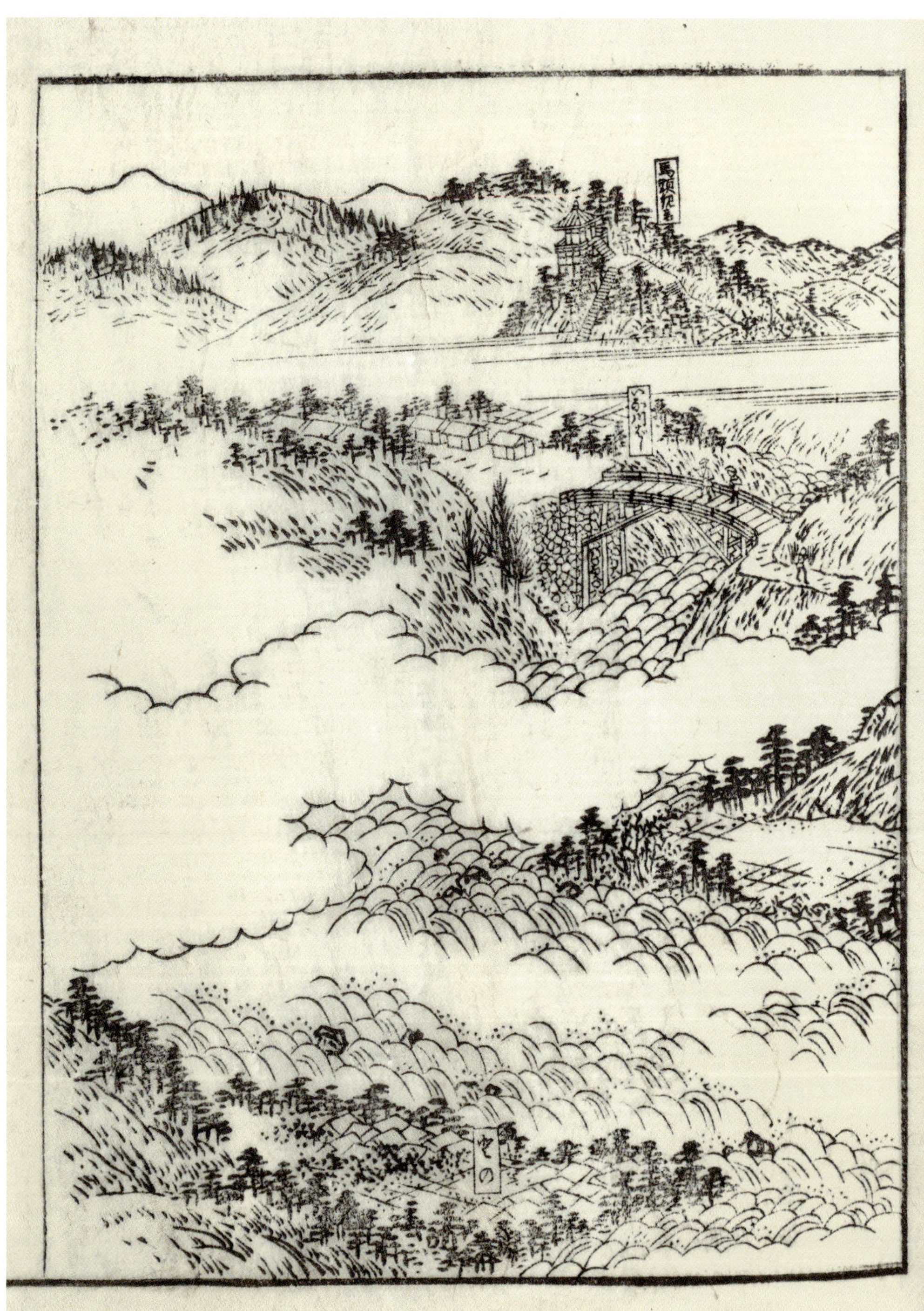

41 – Nojiri   *Akisato Ritō: Kisoji meisho zue, vol. 4, 1805*

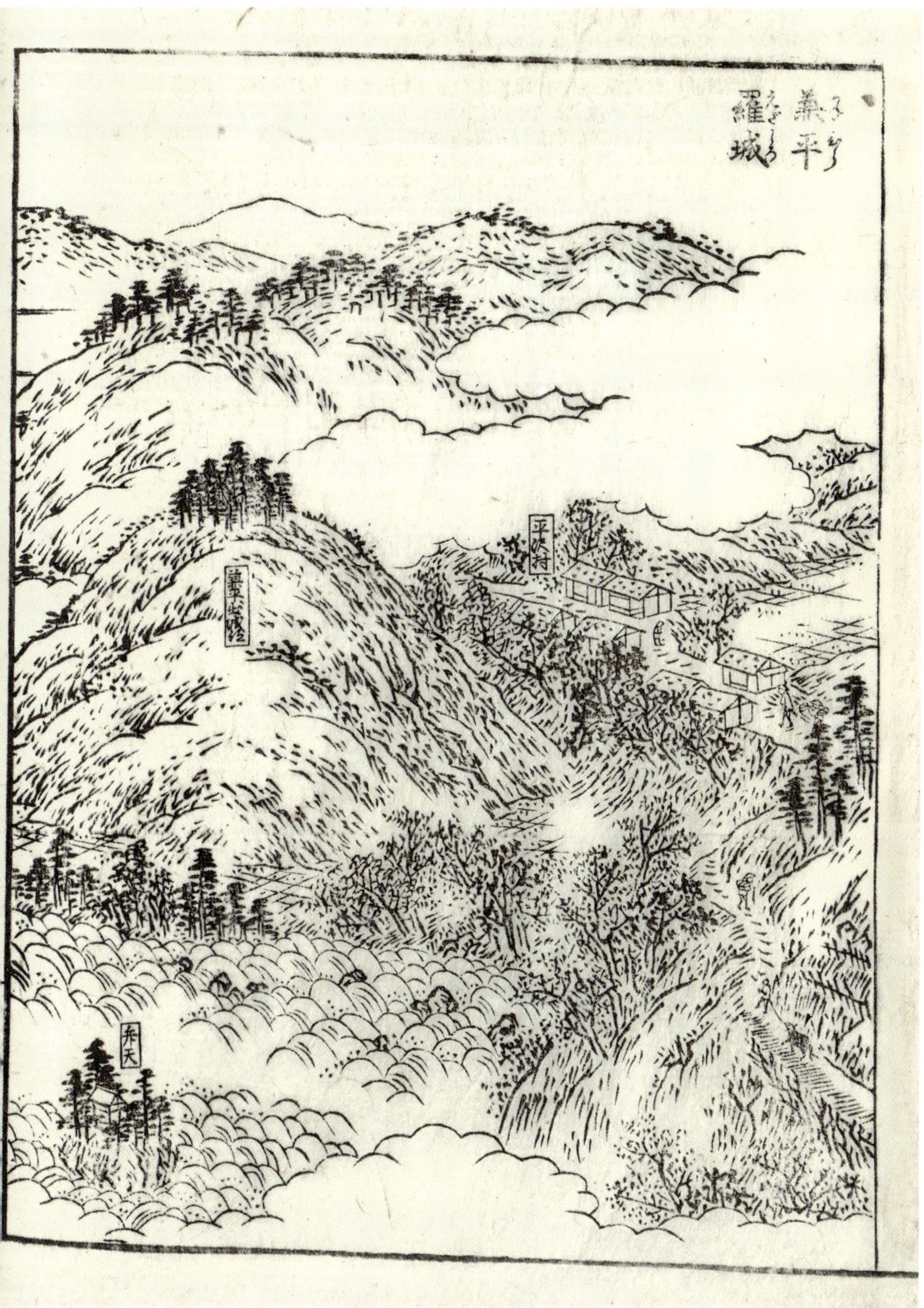

よしつね
義平
えぎろ
羅城
平次村
蓬平城（　）
弁天

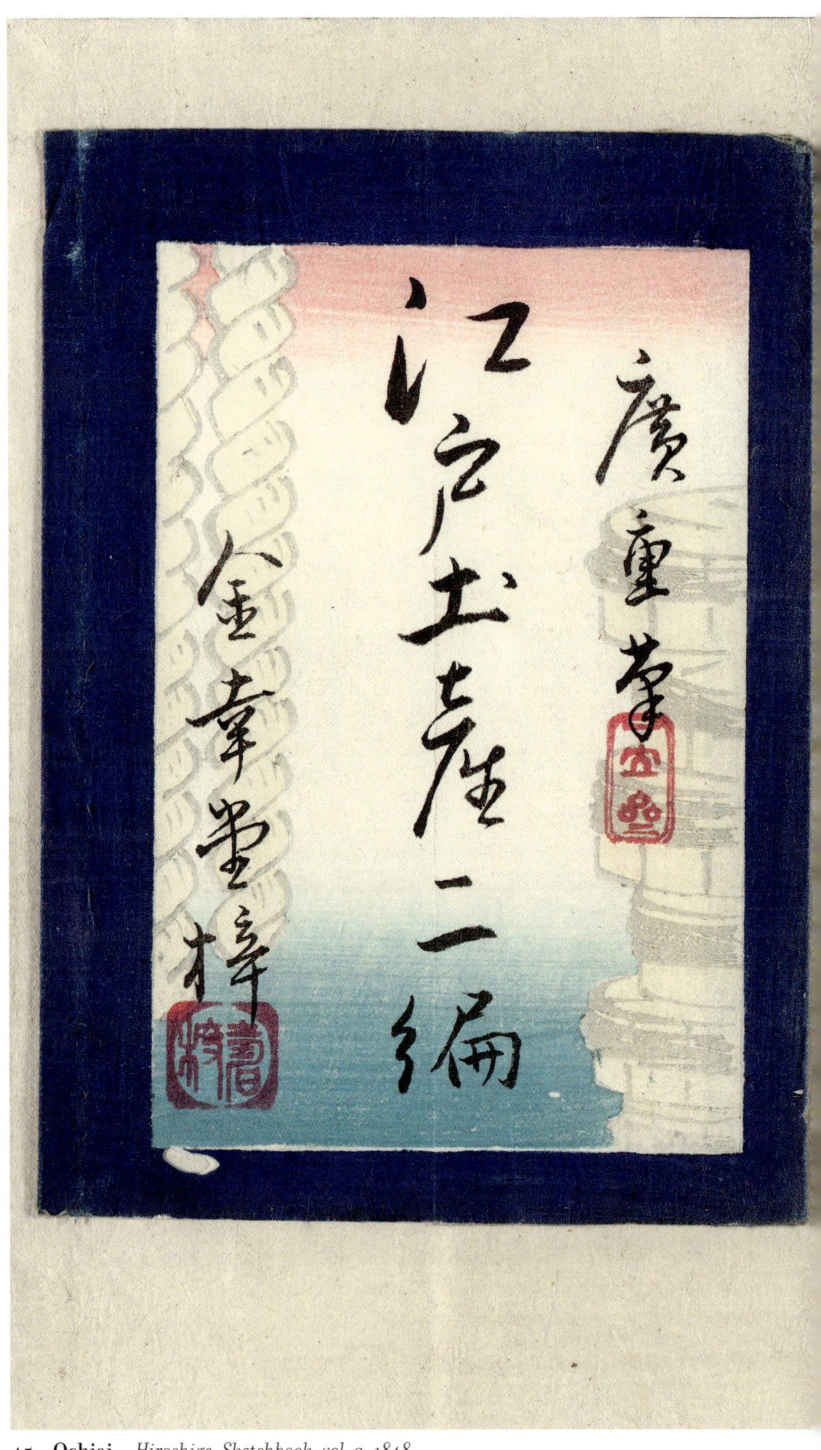

45 – Ochiai   *Hiroshige, Sketchbook, vol. 2, 1848*

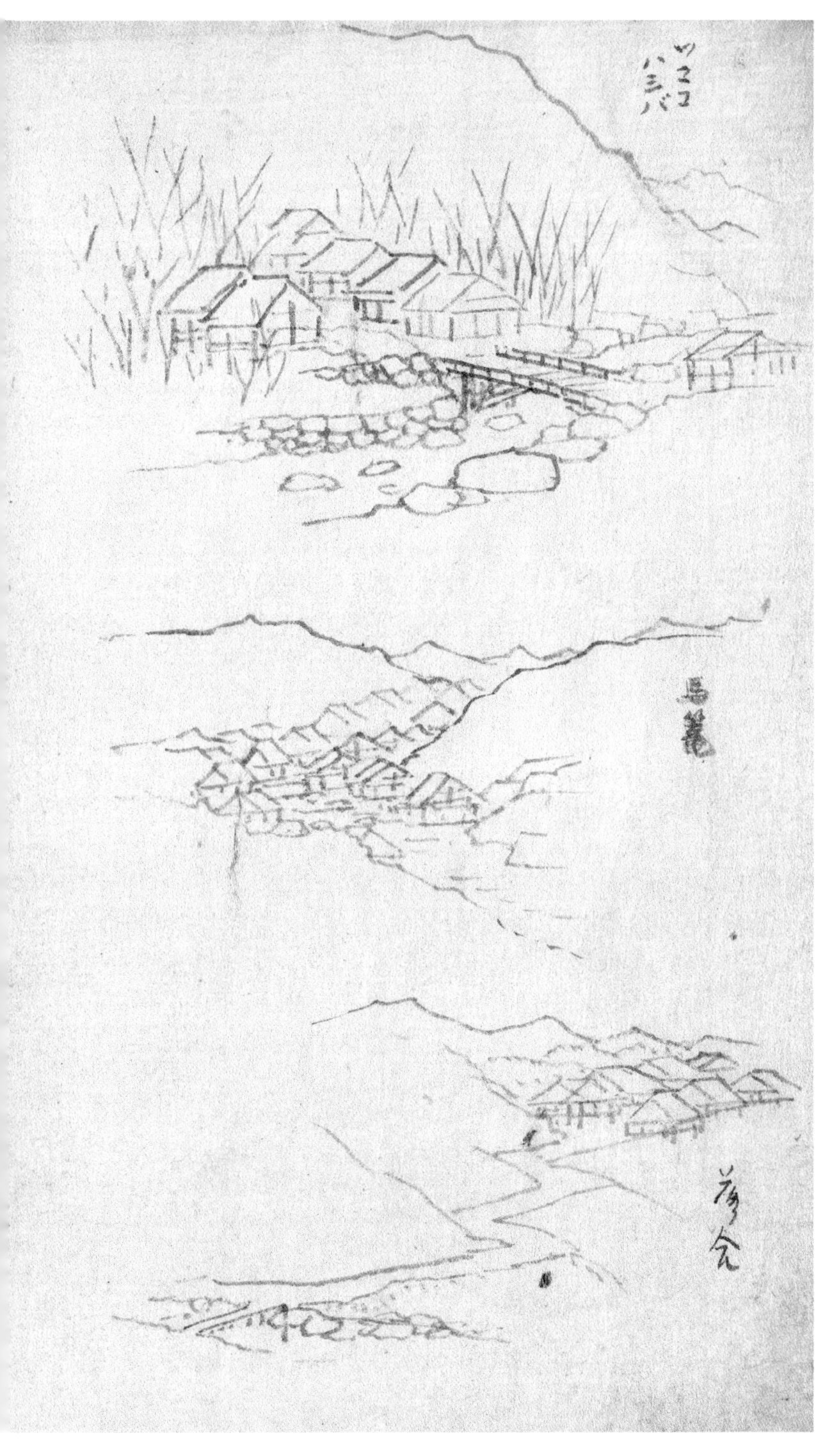

つまご
はしば
馬籠
落合

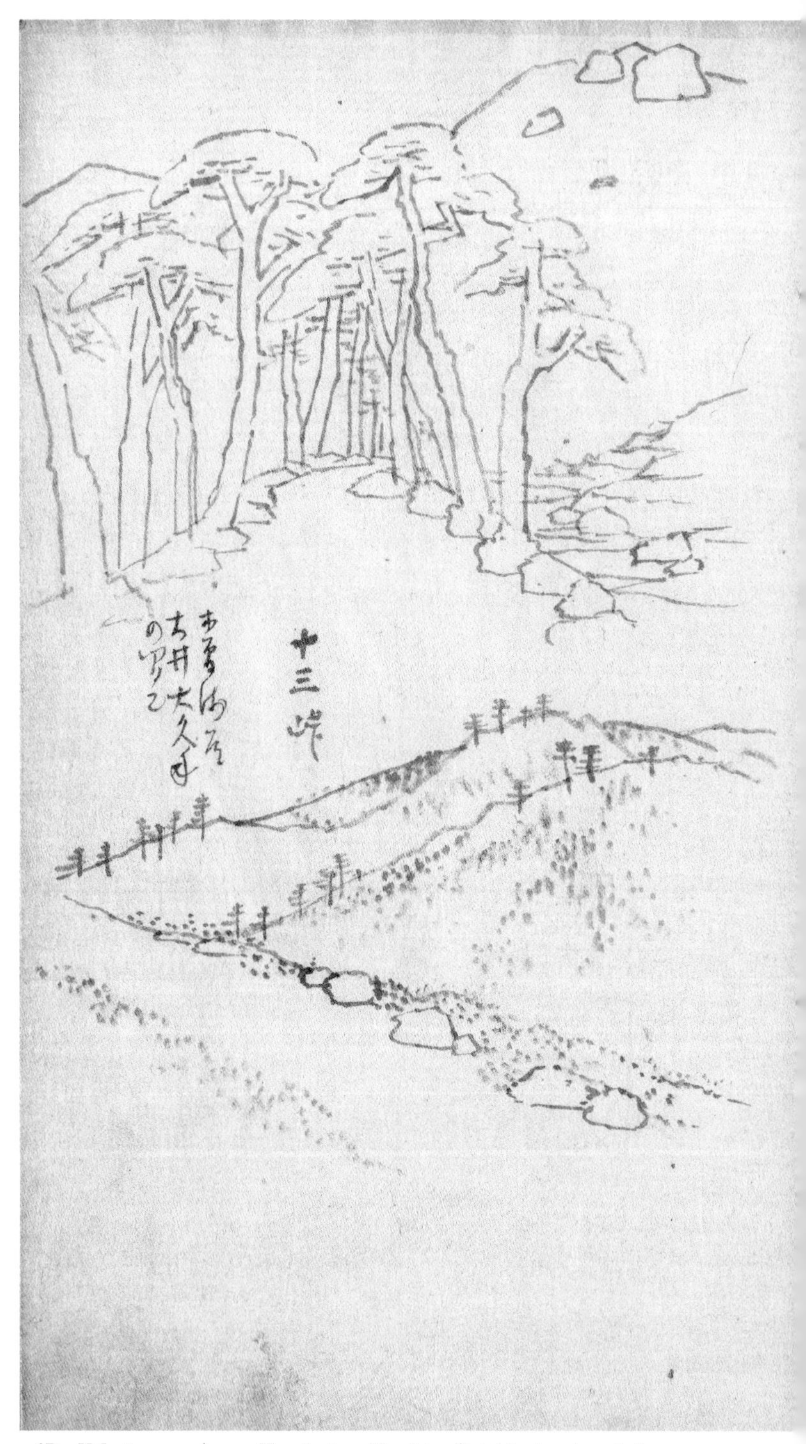

46B – Nakatsugawa ǀ **49 – Hosokute**   *Hiroshige, Sketchbook, vol. 2, 1848*

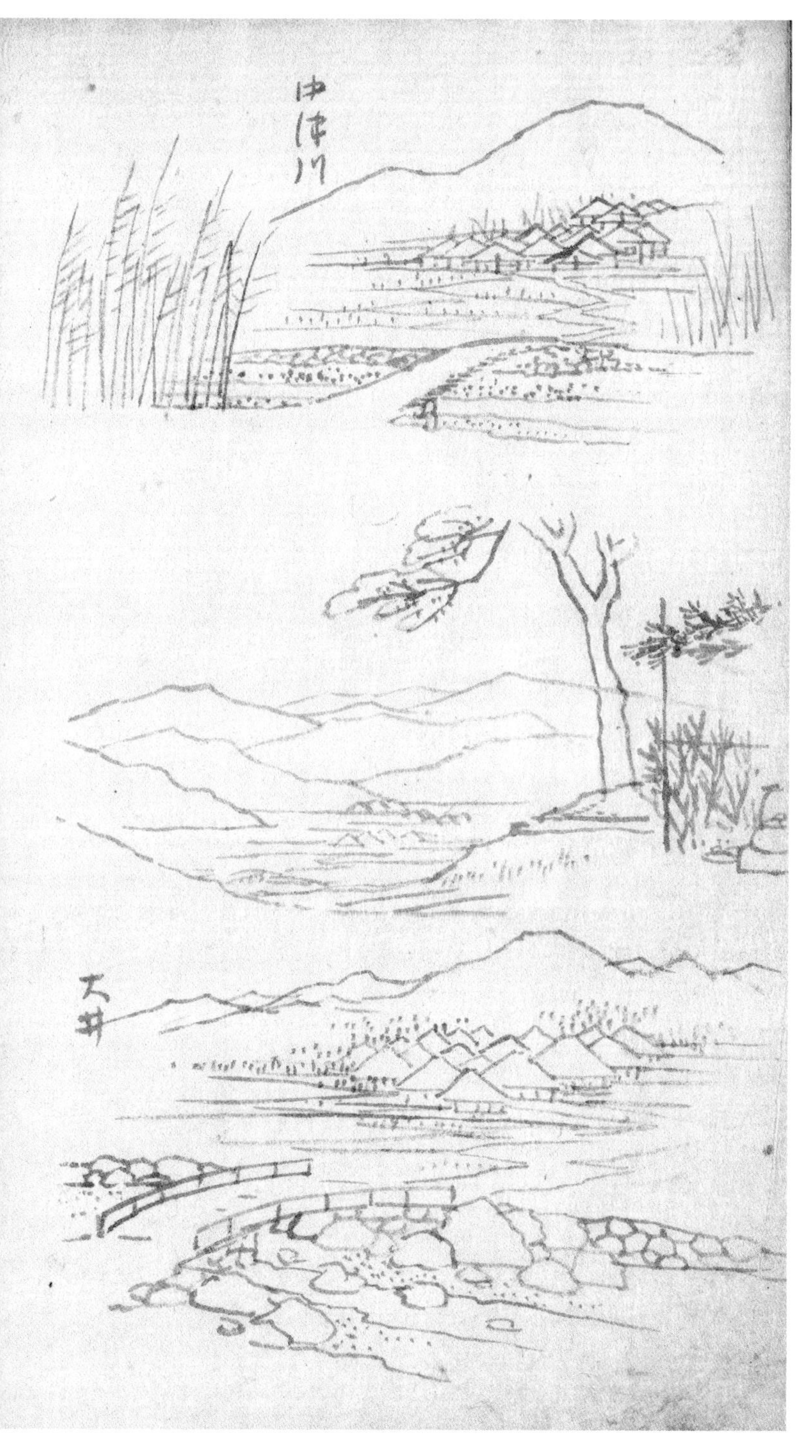
中津川
大井

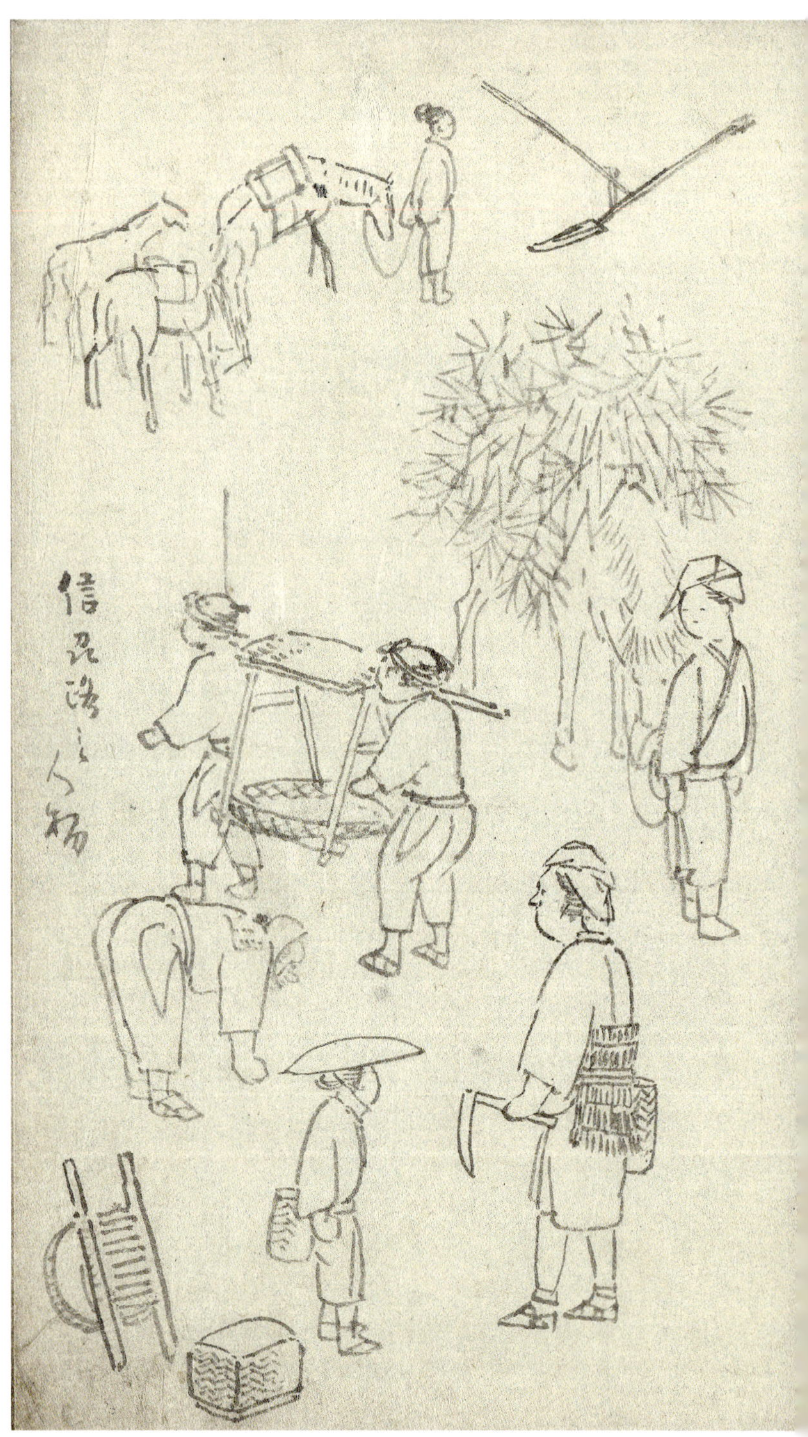

50 – Mitake   *Hiroshige, Sketchbook, vol. 2, 1848*

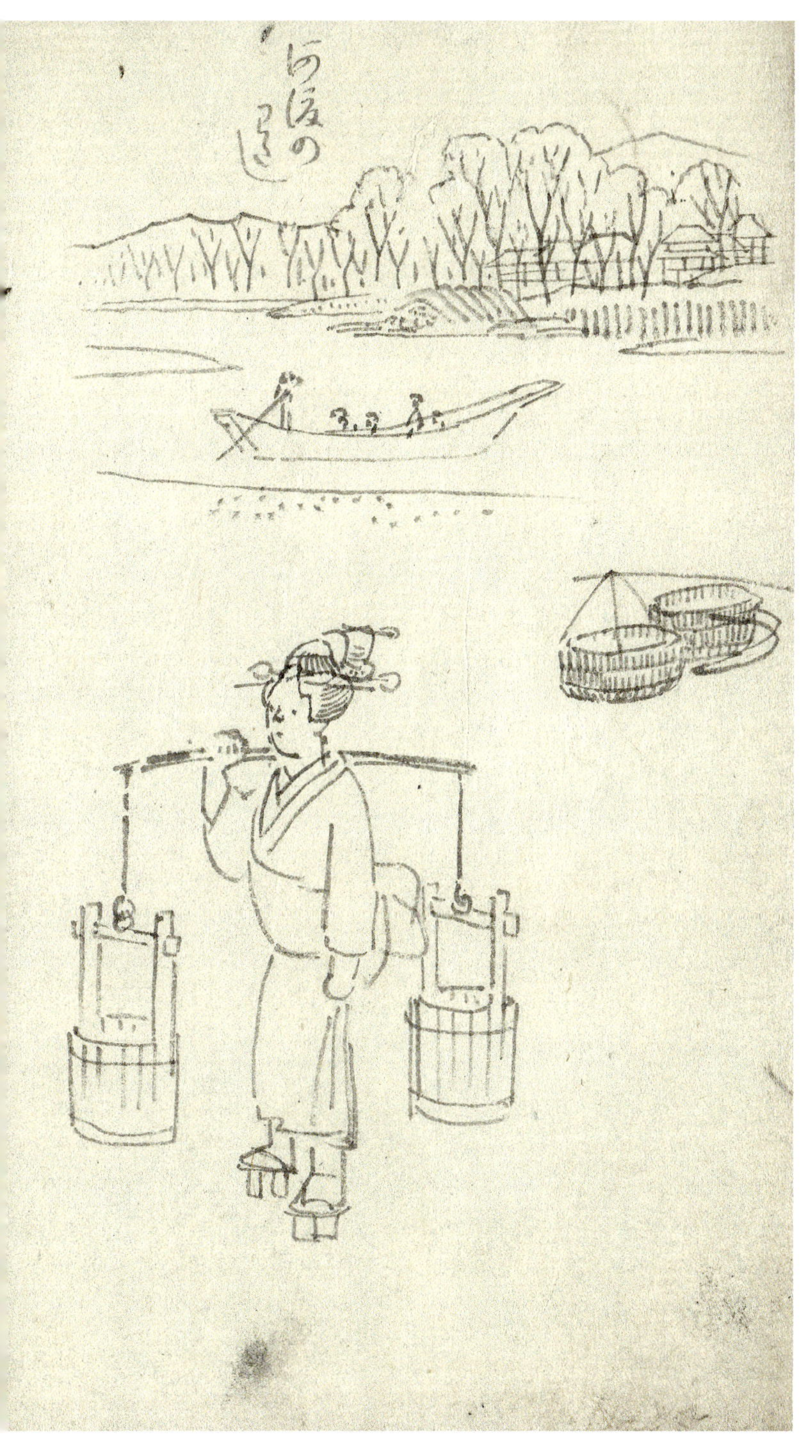
河原の
づく

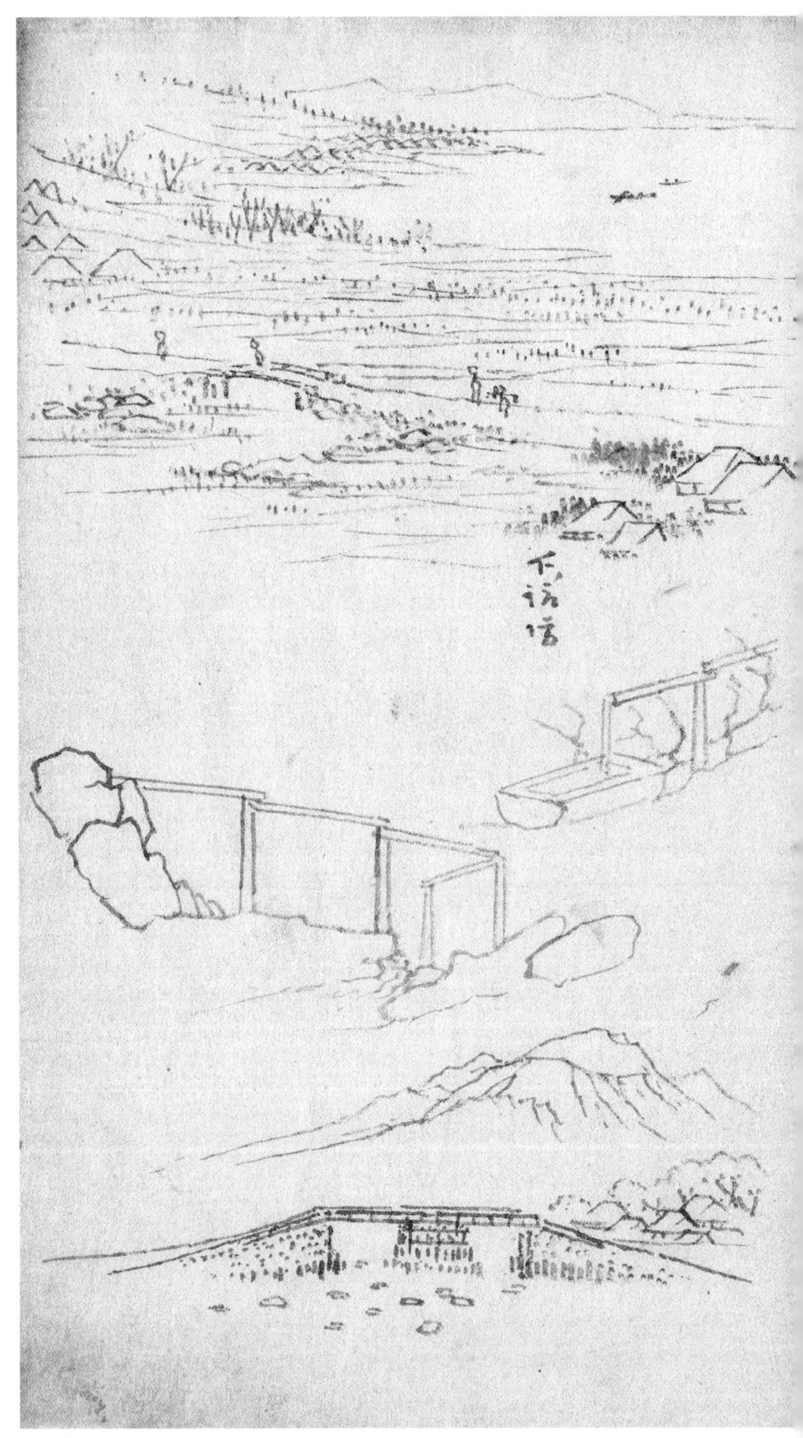

52 – Ōta   *Hiroshige, Sketchbook, vol. 2, 1848*

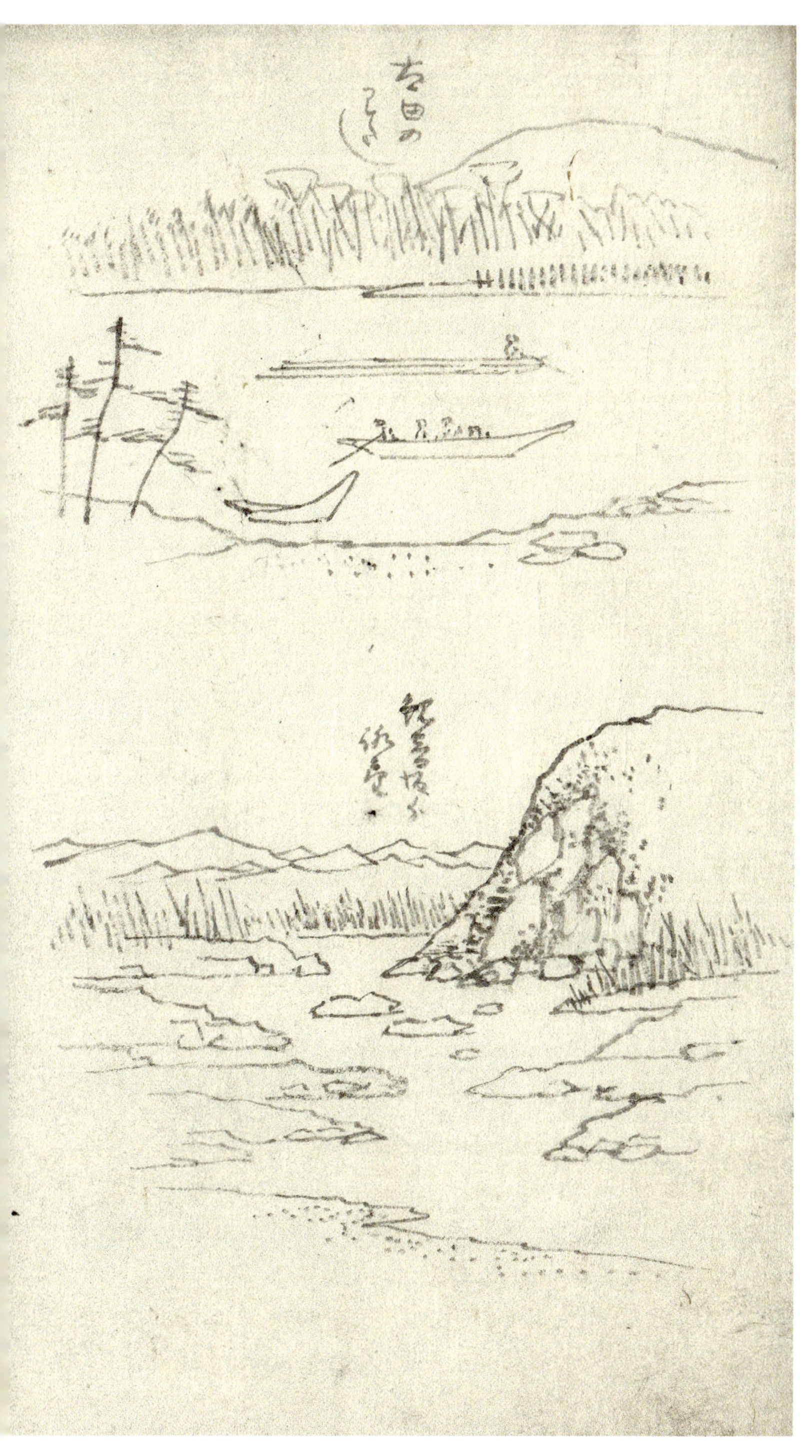

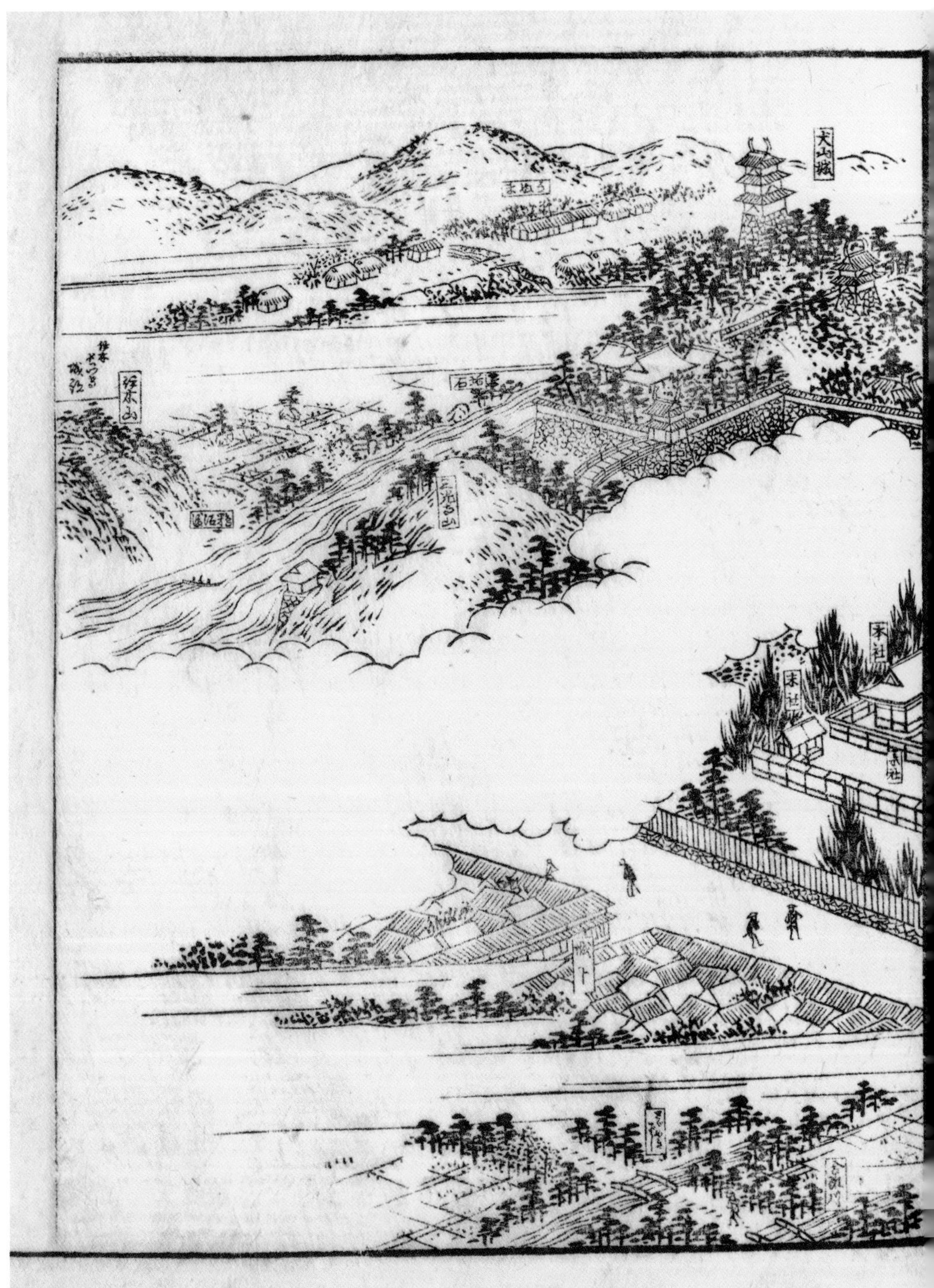

53 – **Unuma**   *Akisato Ritō: Kisoji meisho zue, vol. 3, 1805*

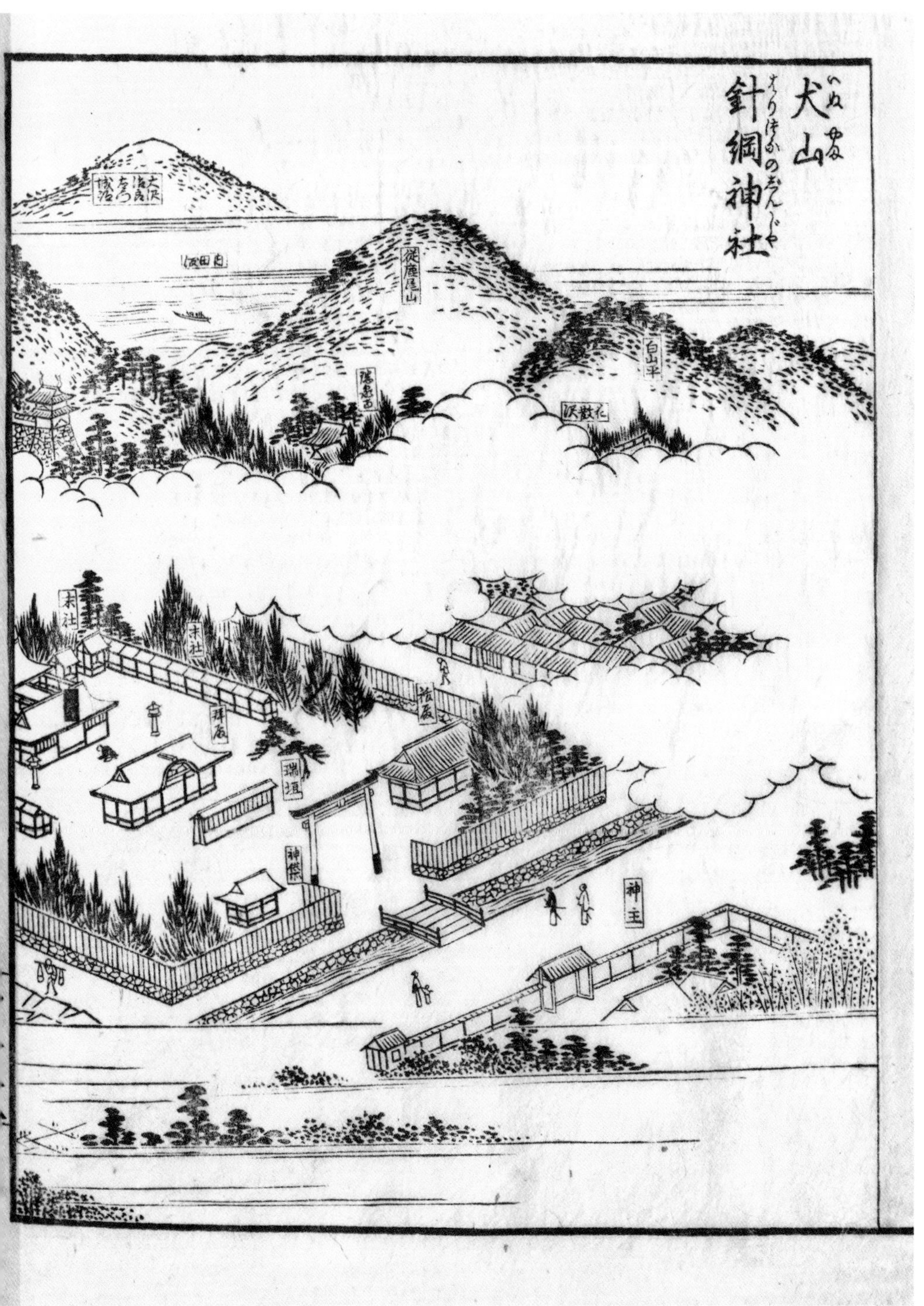
犬山
針綱神社
大沢海
塚宮
嶋田城
従鹿尾山
尾張富
白山平
花敷沢
末社
末社
拝殿
瑞垣
神供
神主
神社

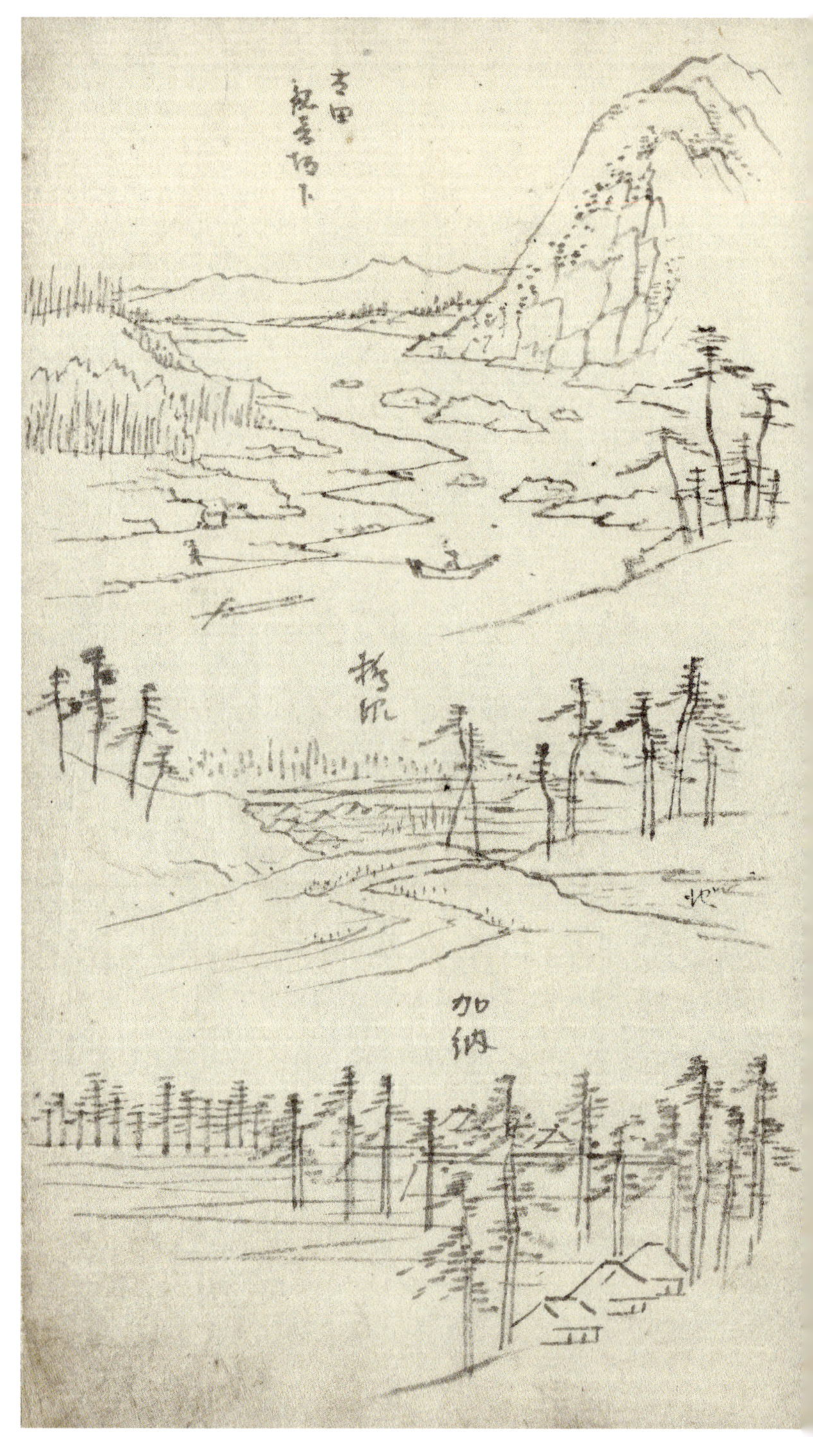

54 – **Kanō**   *Hiroshige, Sketchbook, vol. 2, 1848*

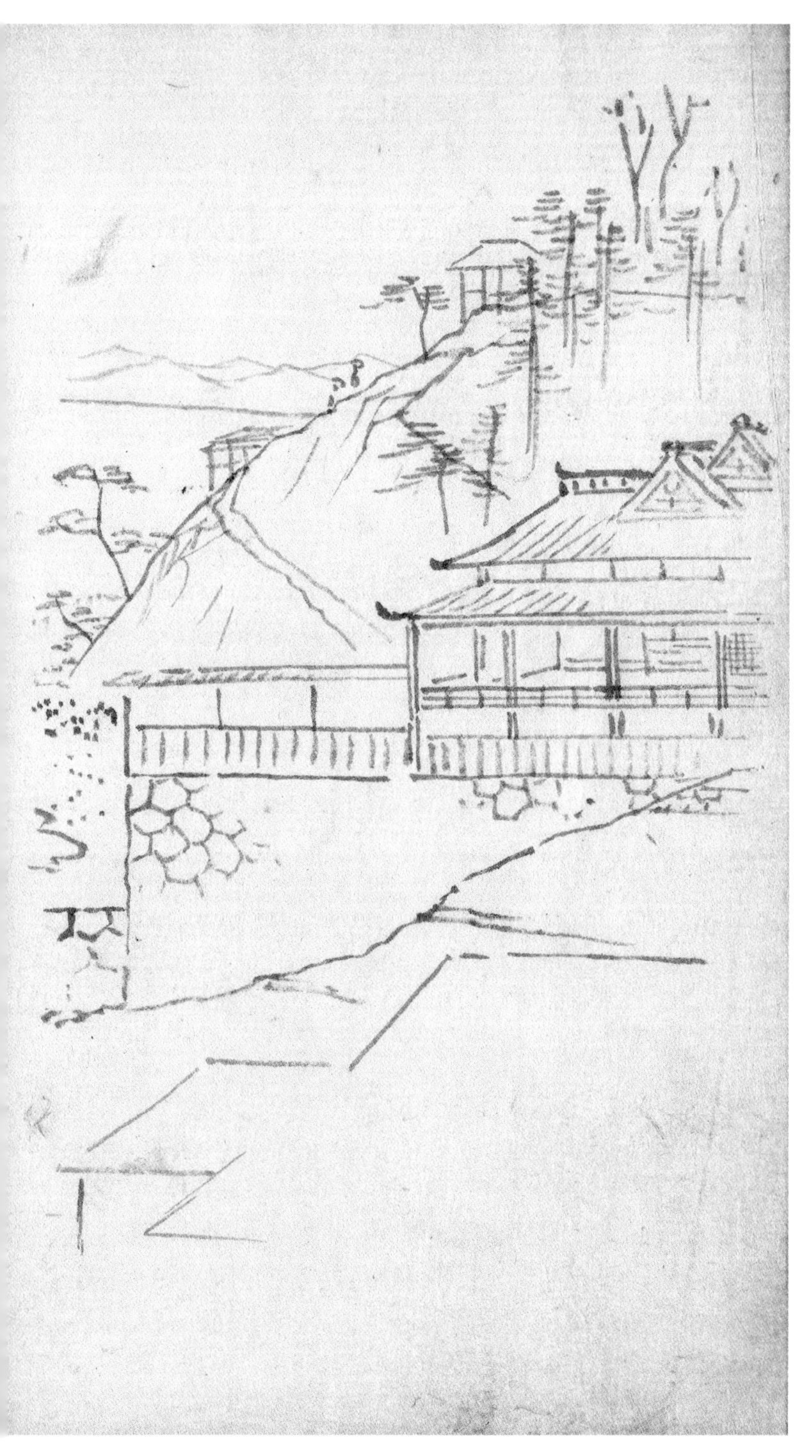

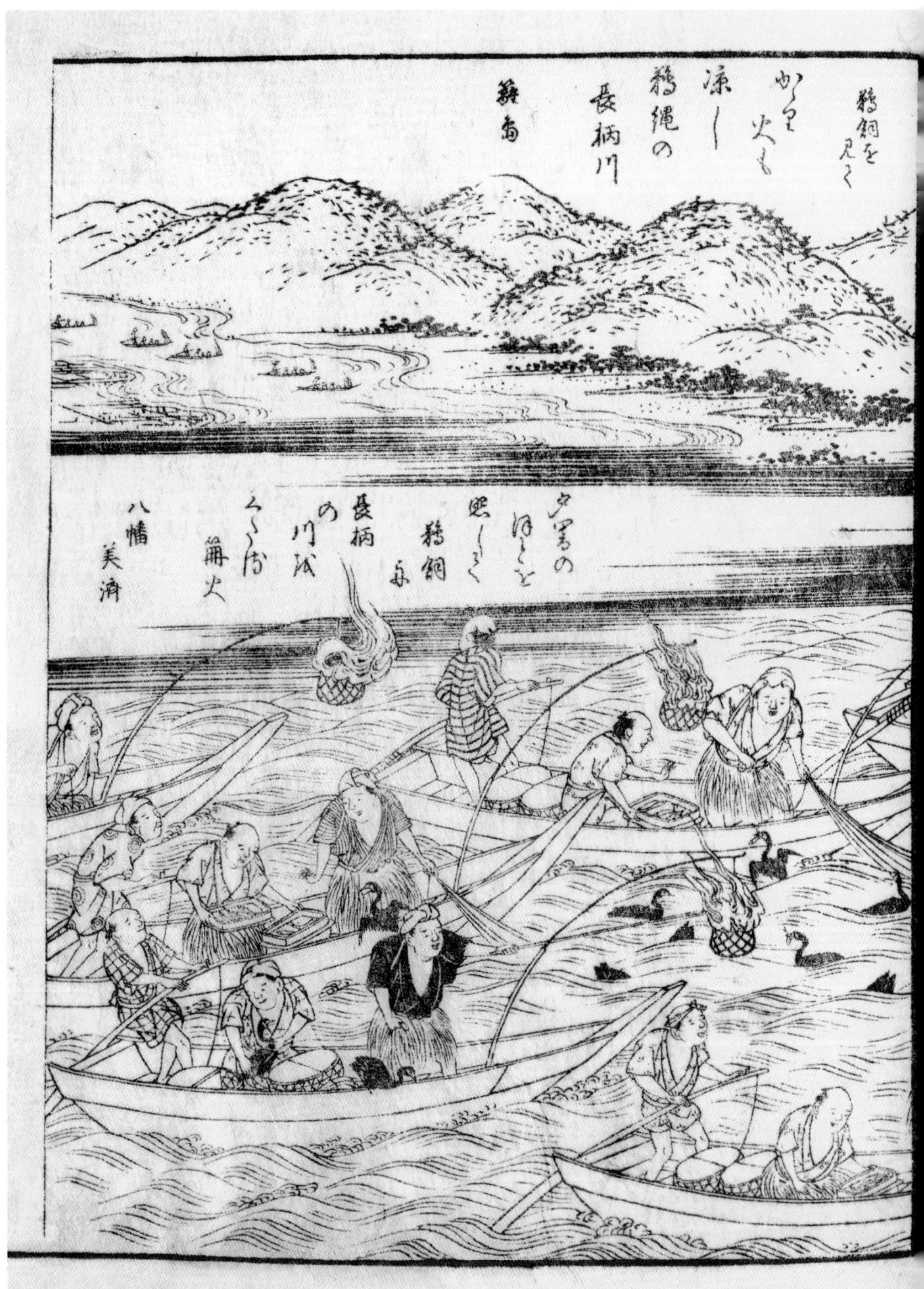

55 – Gōdo   *Akisato Ritō: Kisoji meisho zue, vol. 4, 1805*

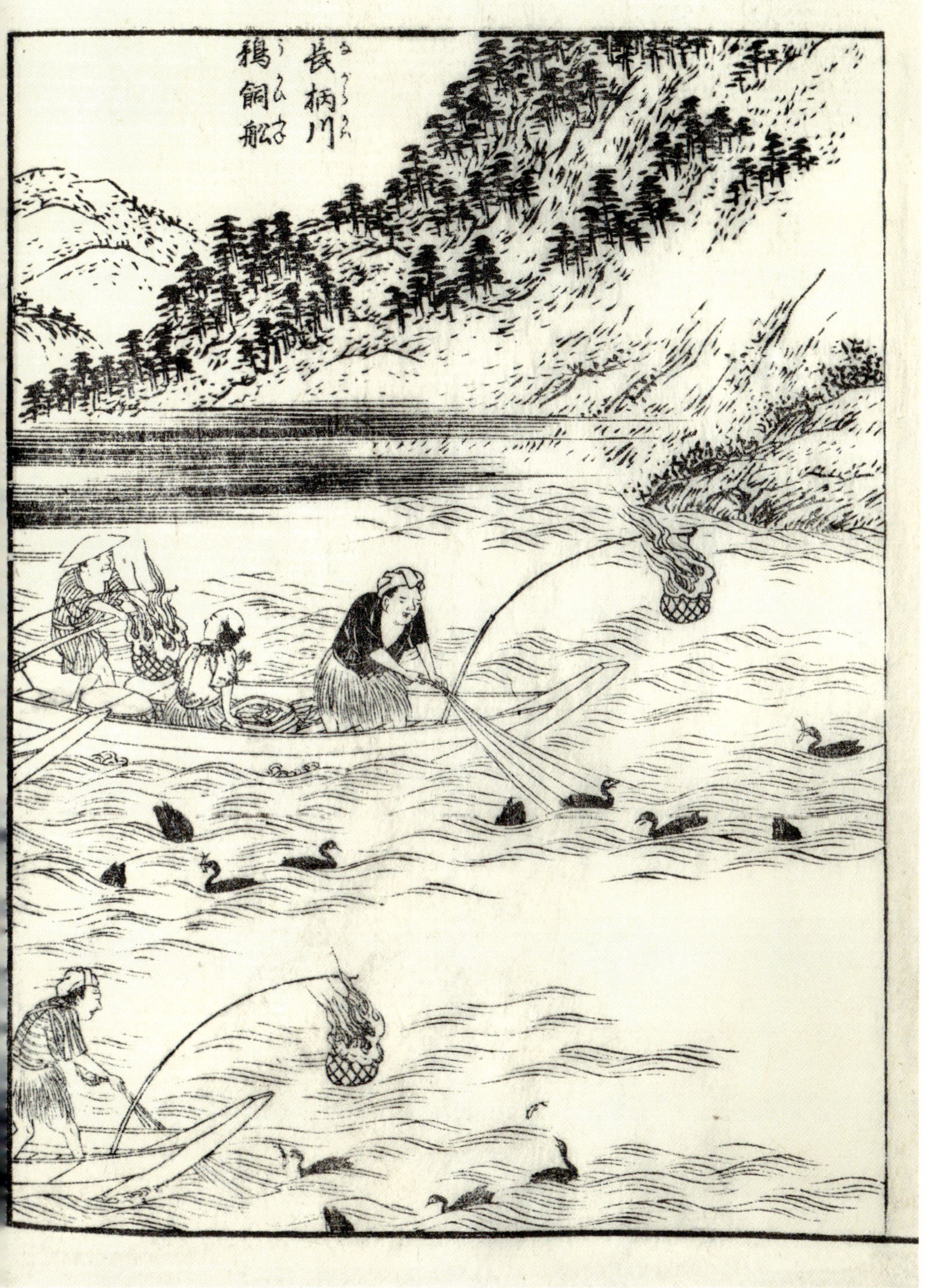

長柄川　鵜飼舩

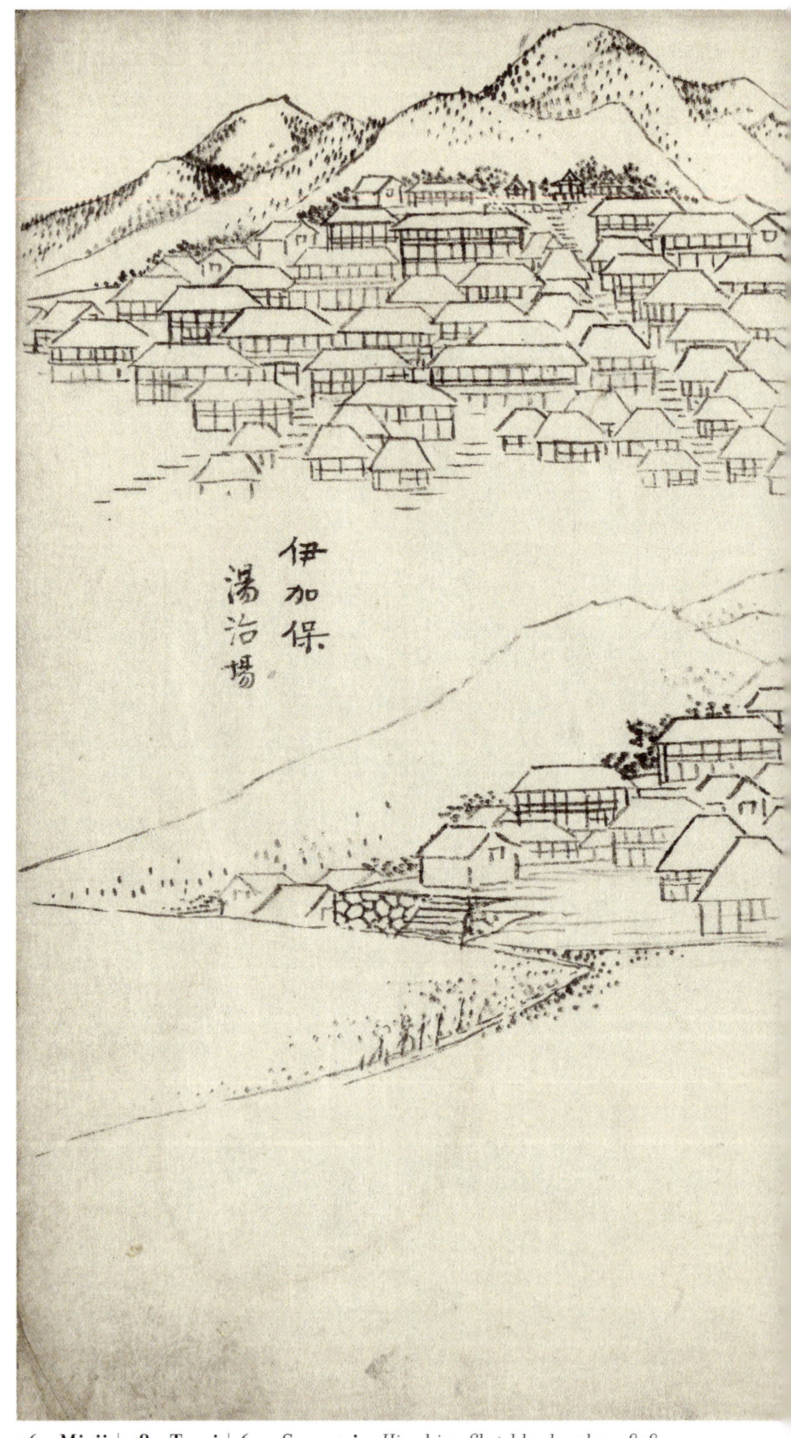

56 – Mieji | 58 – Tarui | 62 – Samegai   *Hiroshige, Sketchbook, vol. 2, 1848*

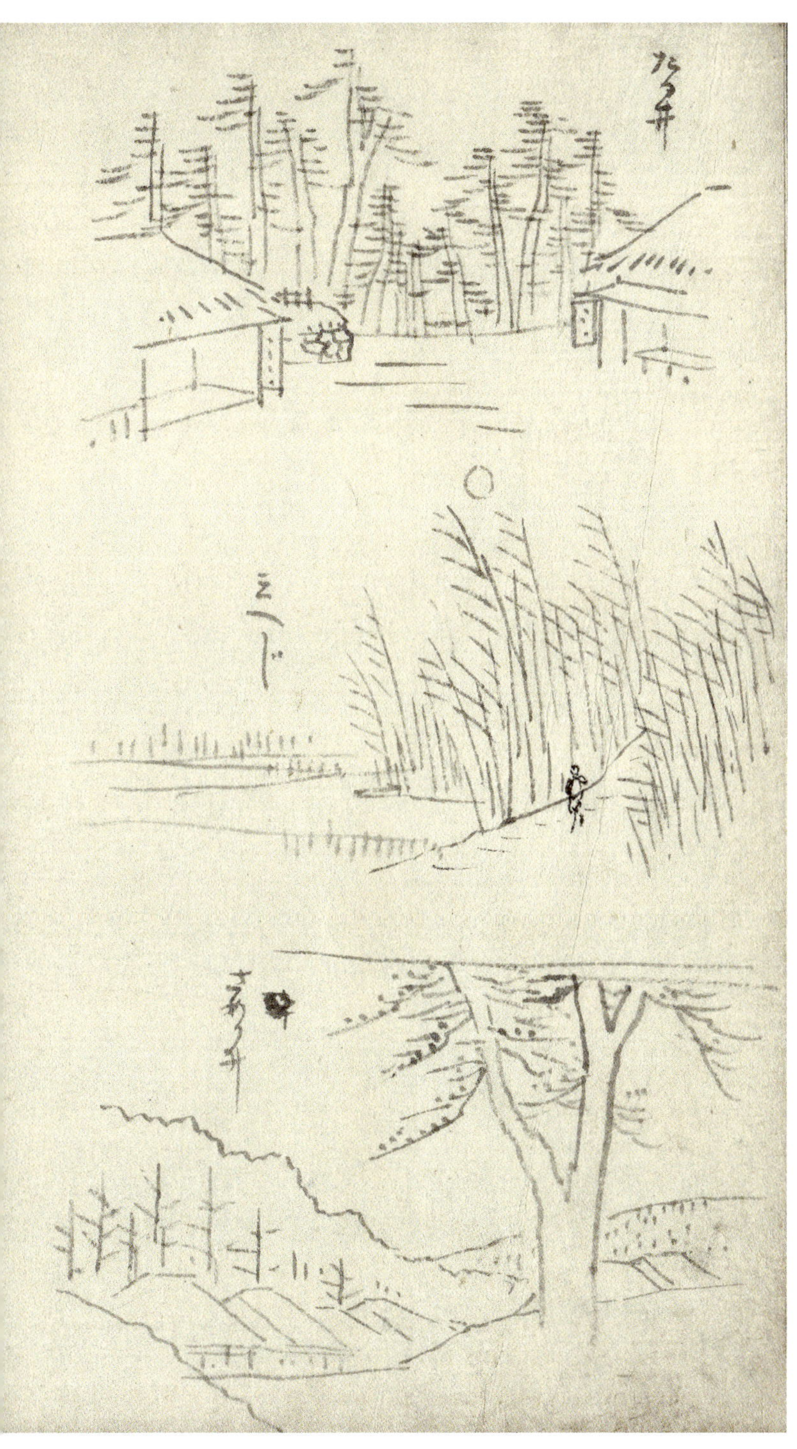

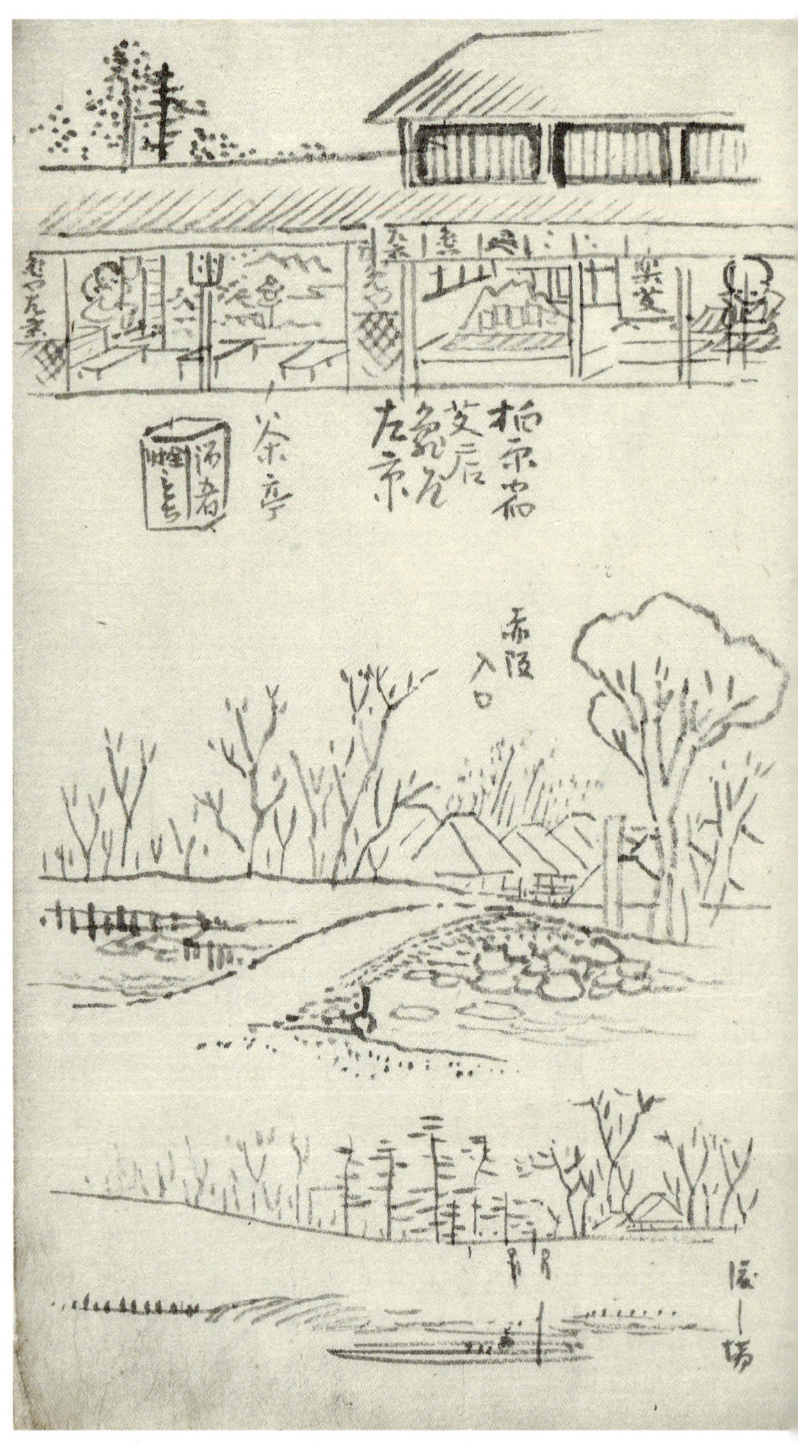

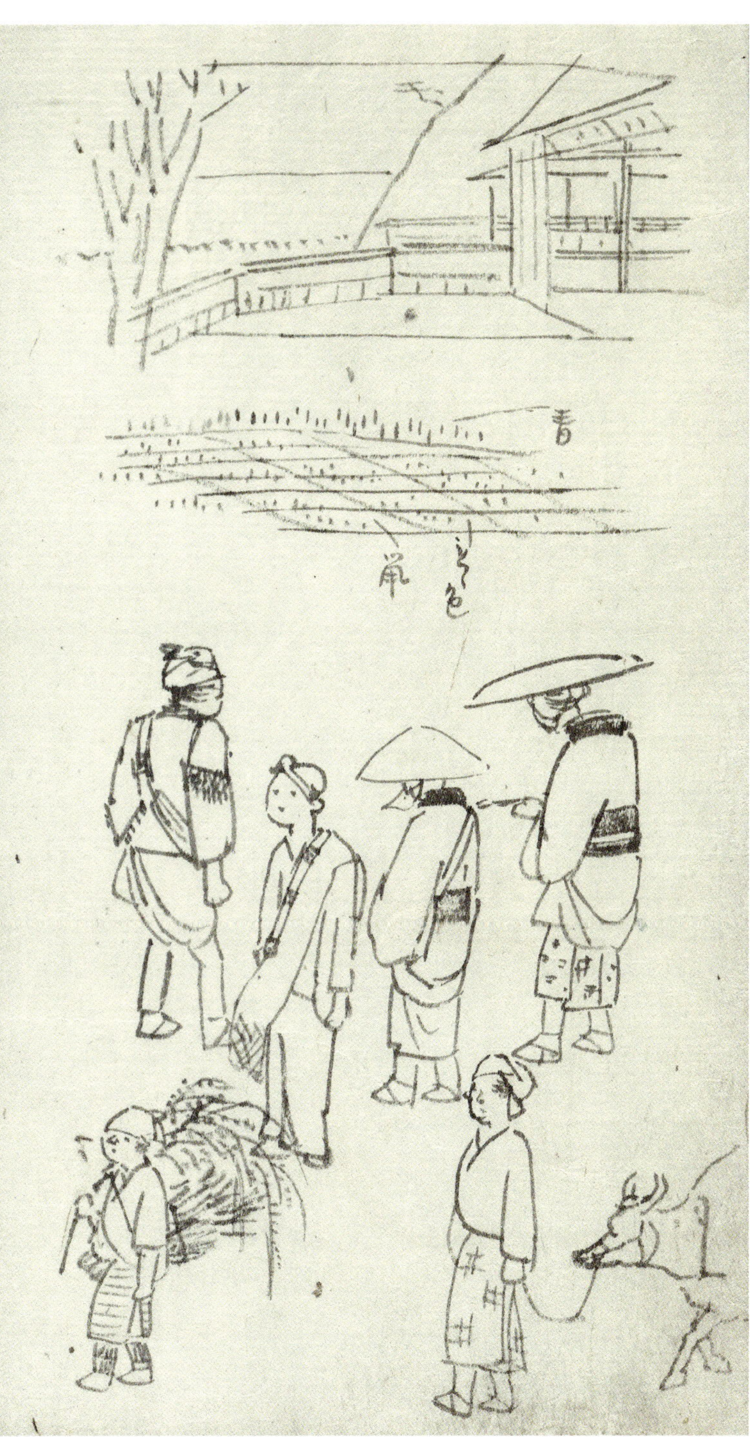

Hiroshige, Sketchbook, vol. 2, 1848

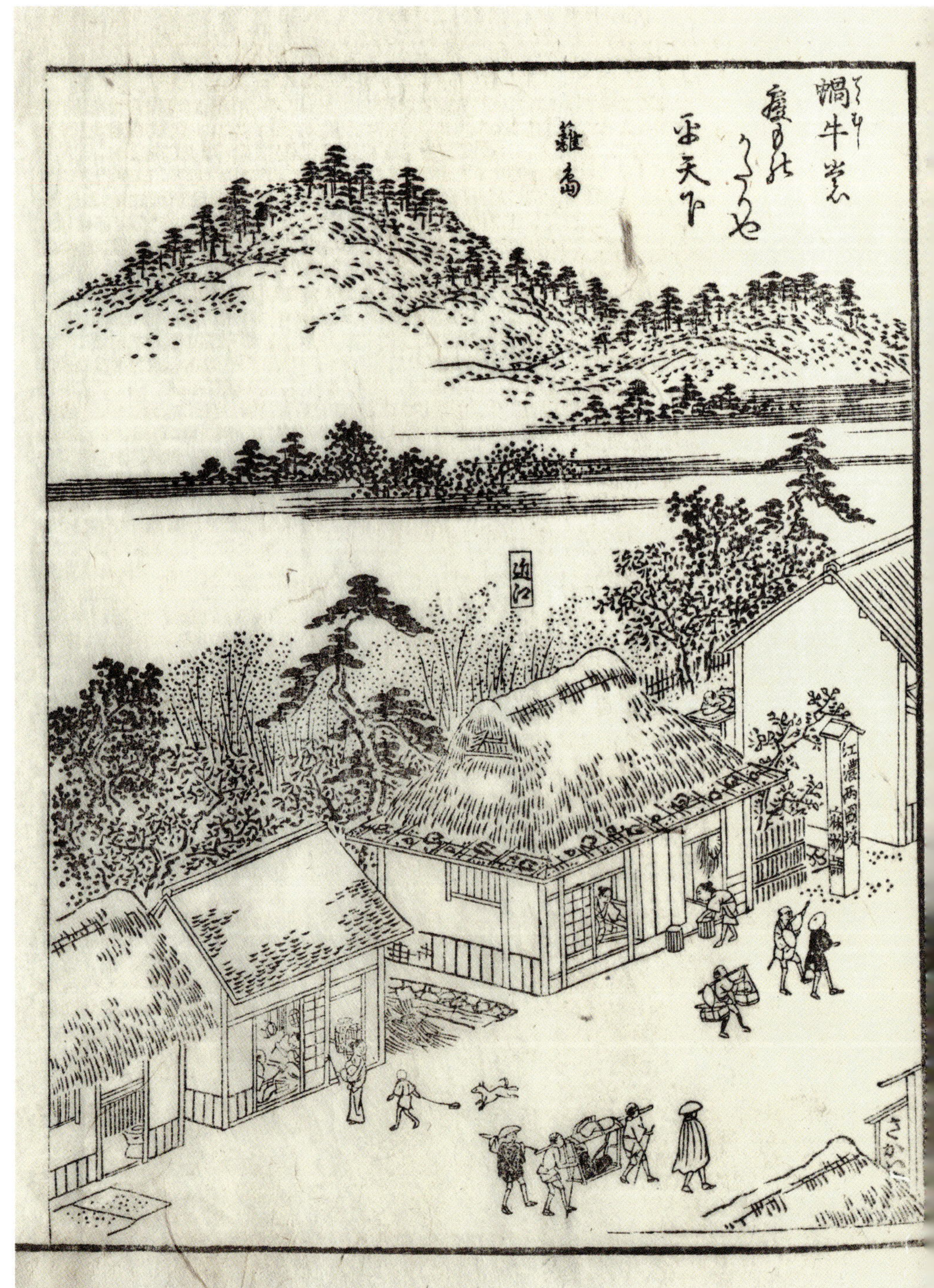

60 – Imasu   *Akisato Ritō: Kisoji meisho zue, vol. 3, 1805*

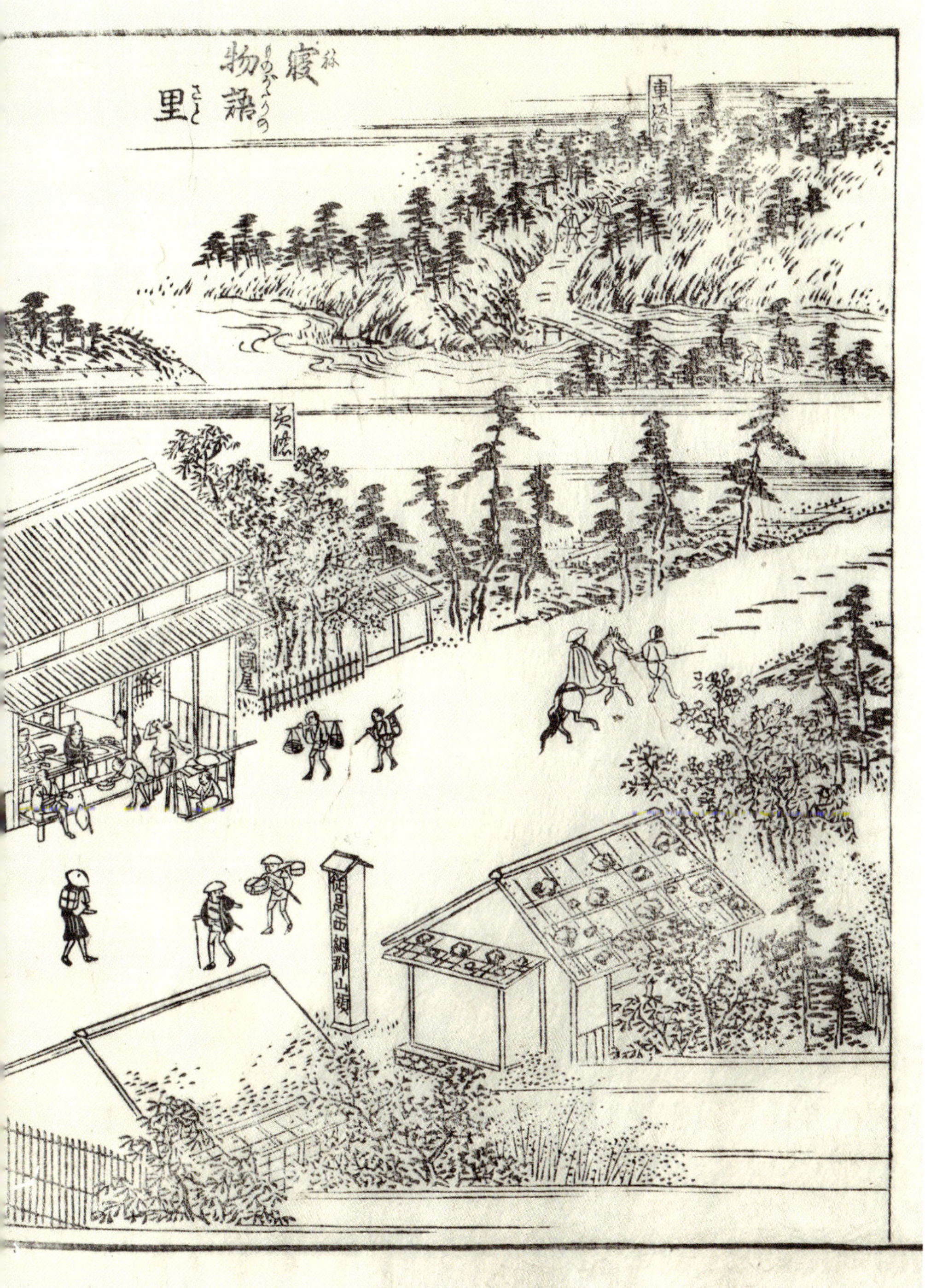
寝
物語
里

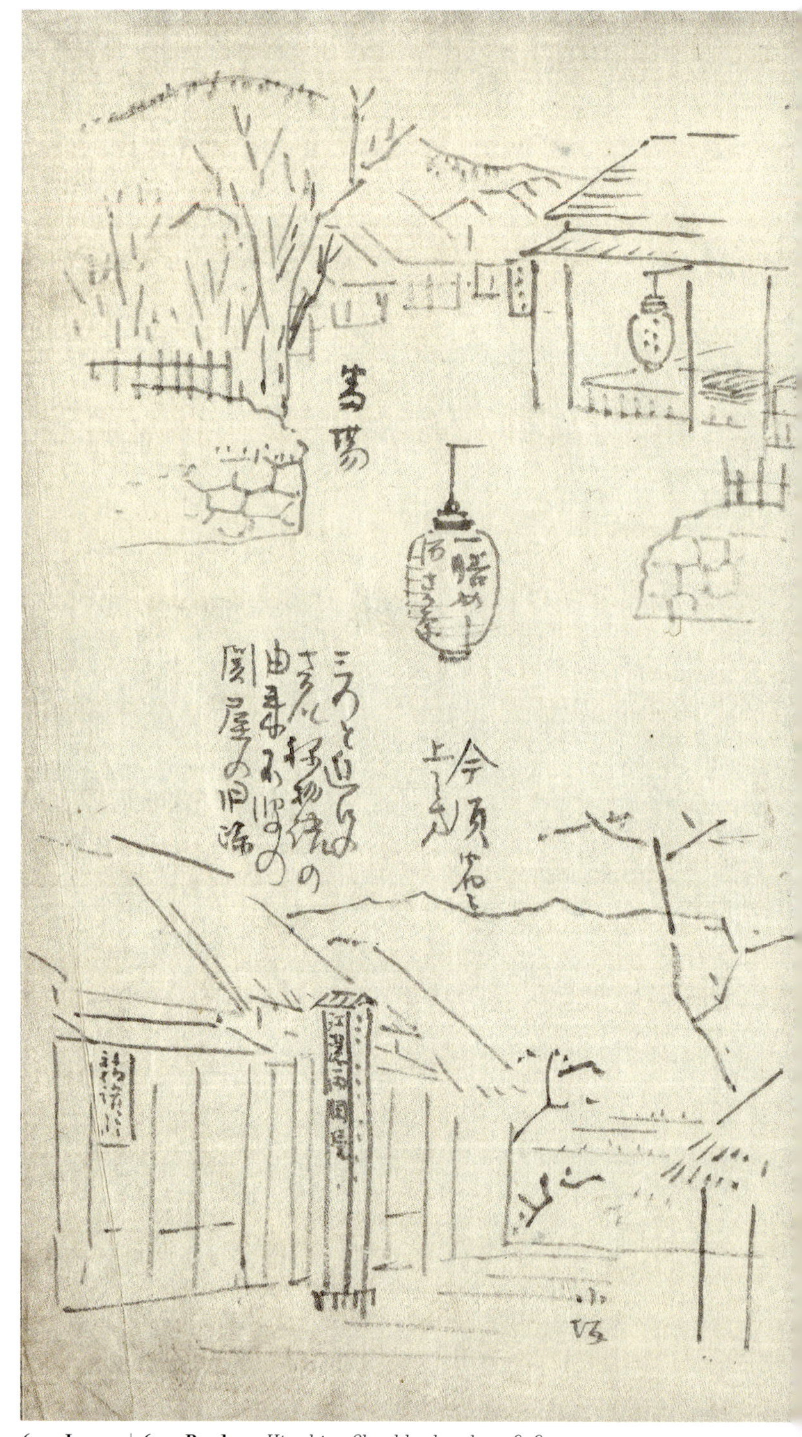

60 – Imasu | 63 – Banba   *Hiroshige, Sketchbook, vol. 2, 1848*

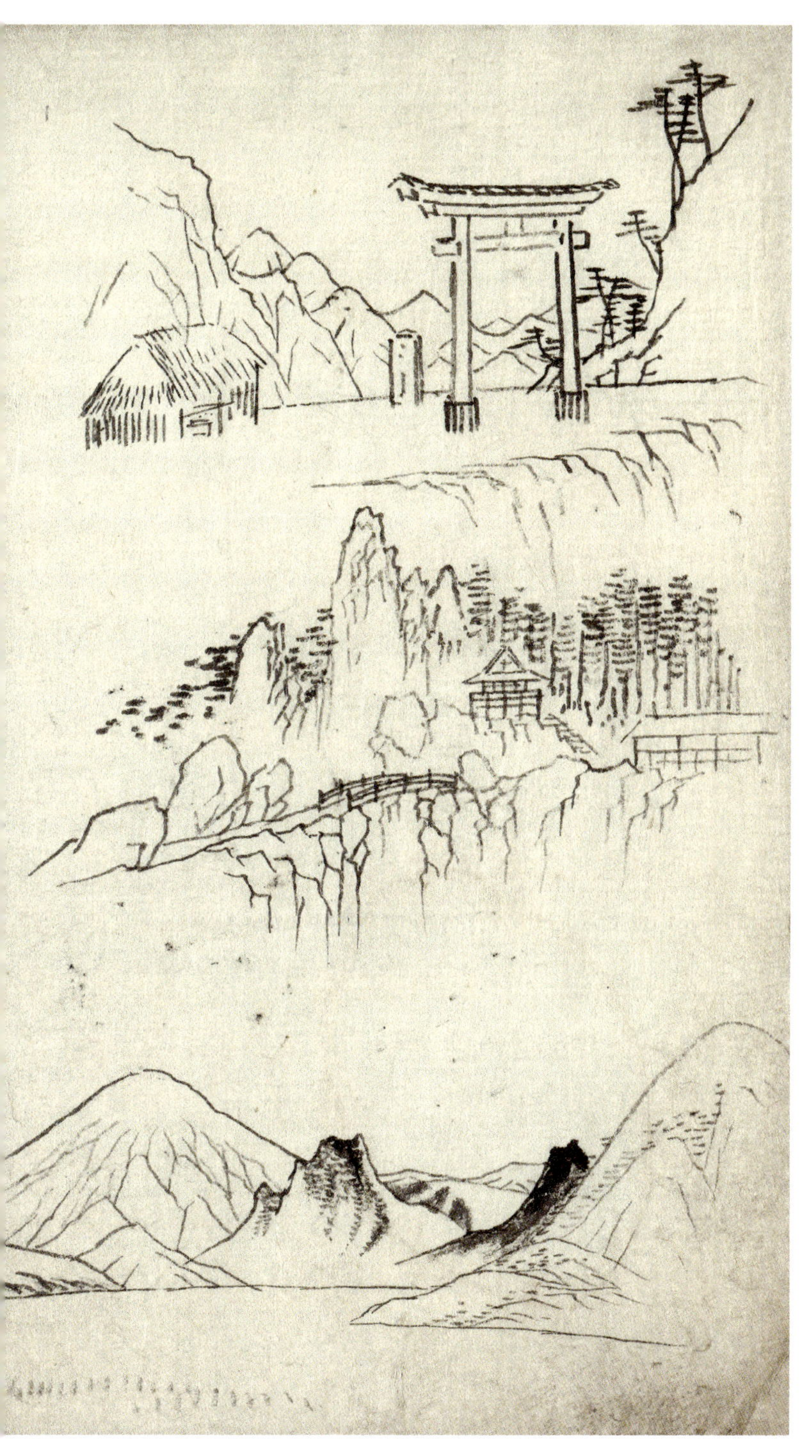

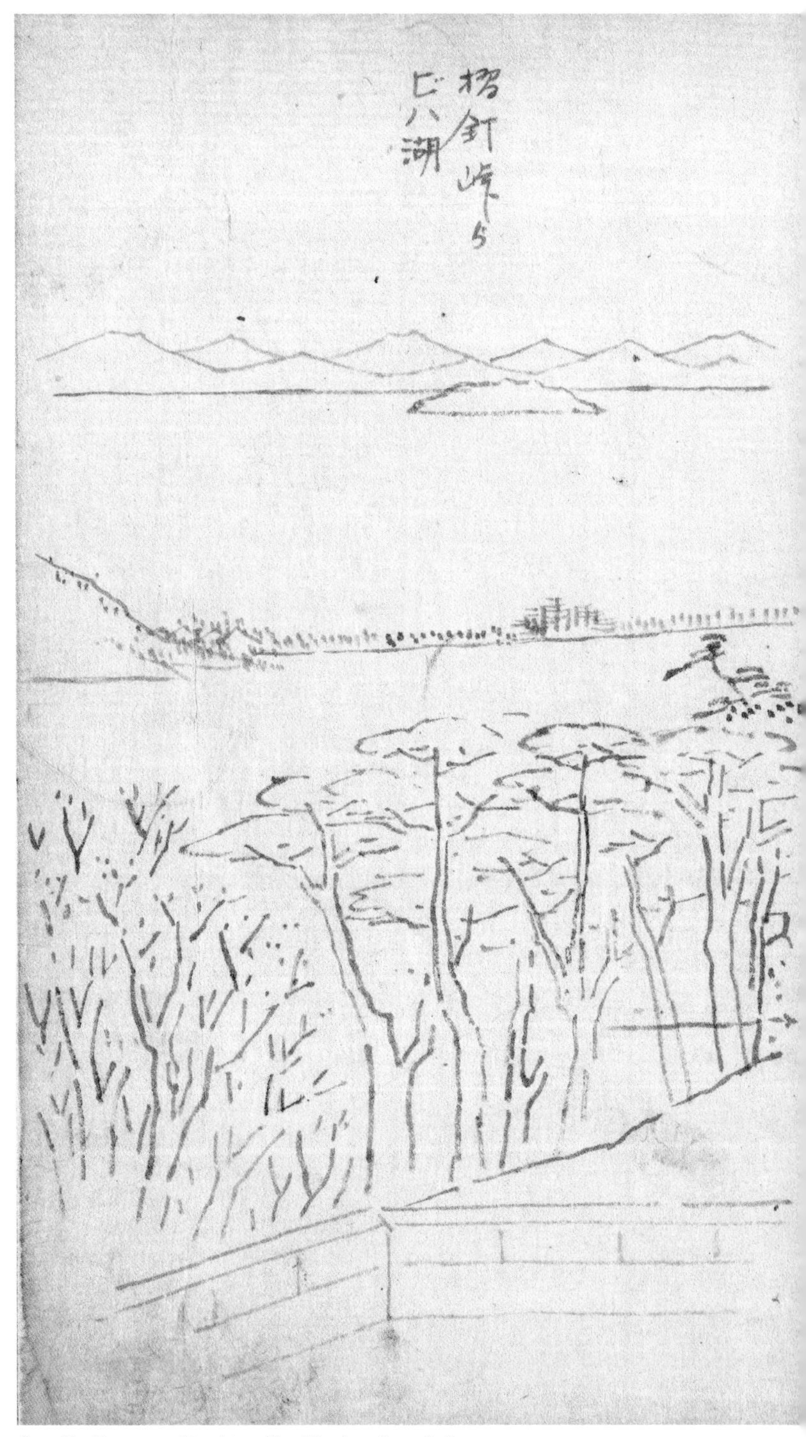

64 – Toriimoto *Hiroshige, Sketchbook, vol. 2, 1848*

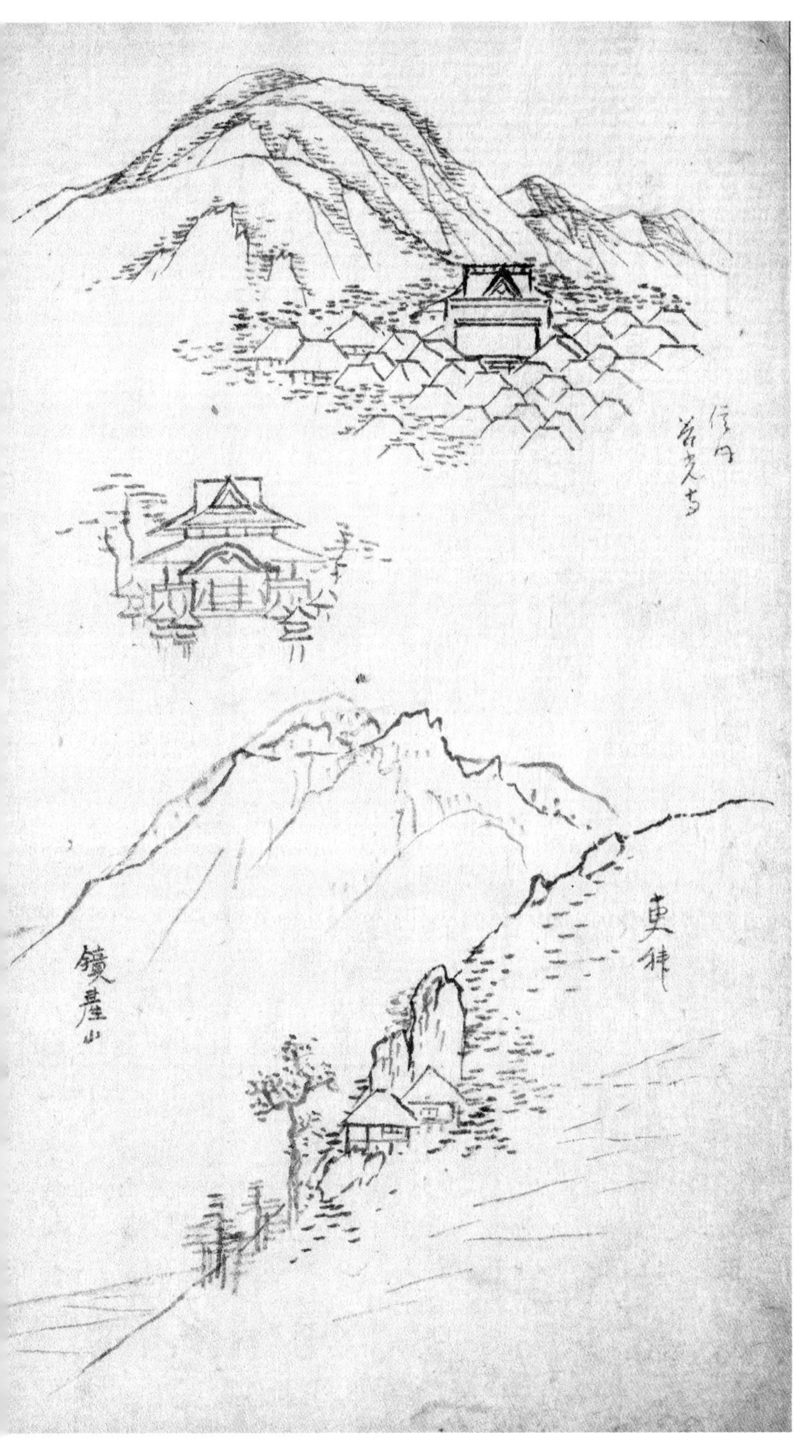

信州
善光寺
更科
鏡臺山

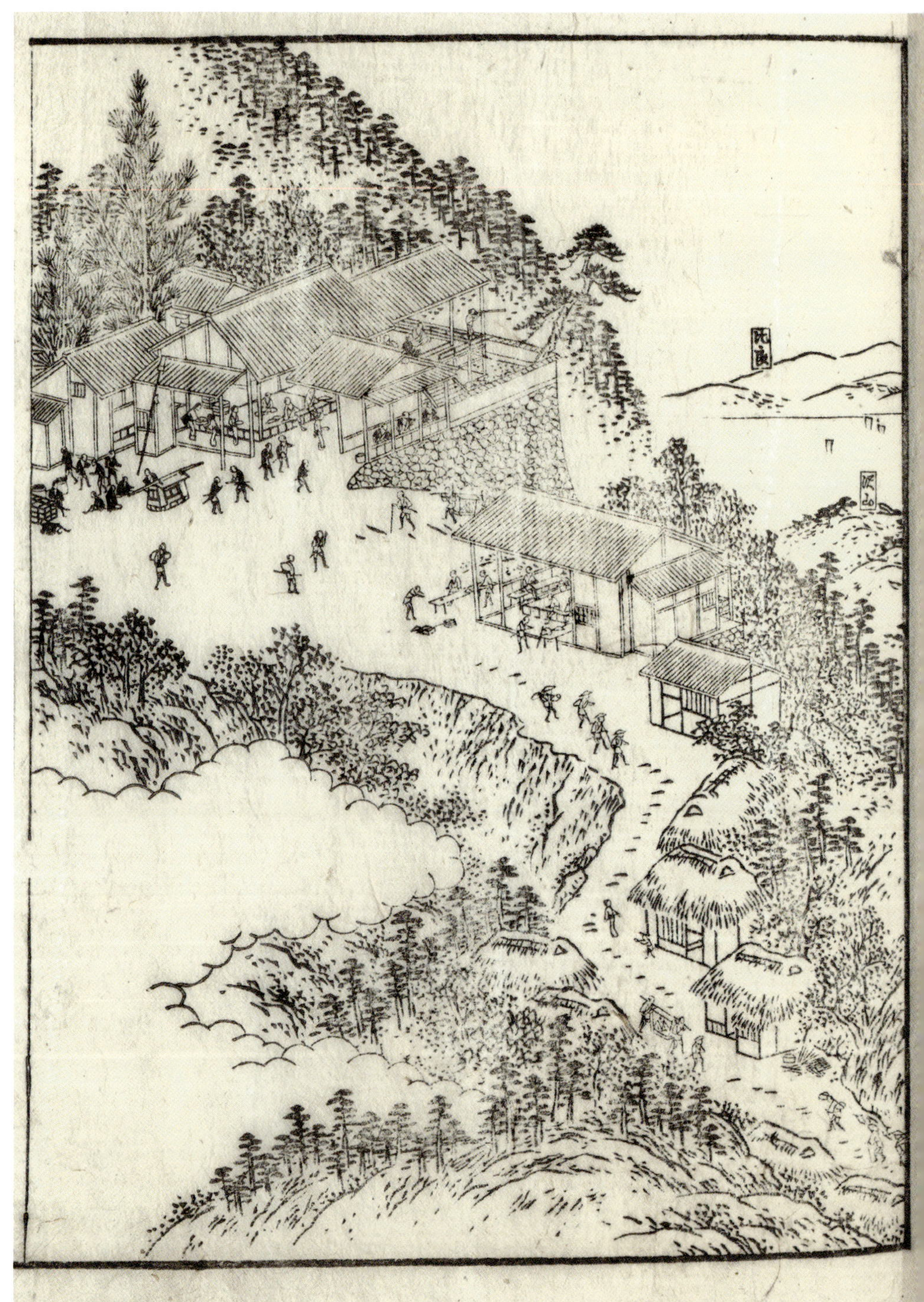

64 – Toriimoto   *Akisato Ritō: Kisoji meisho zue, vol. 2, 1805*

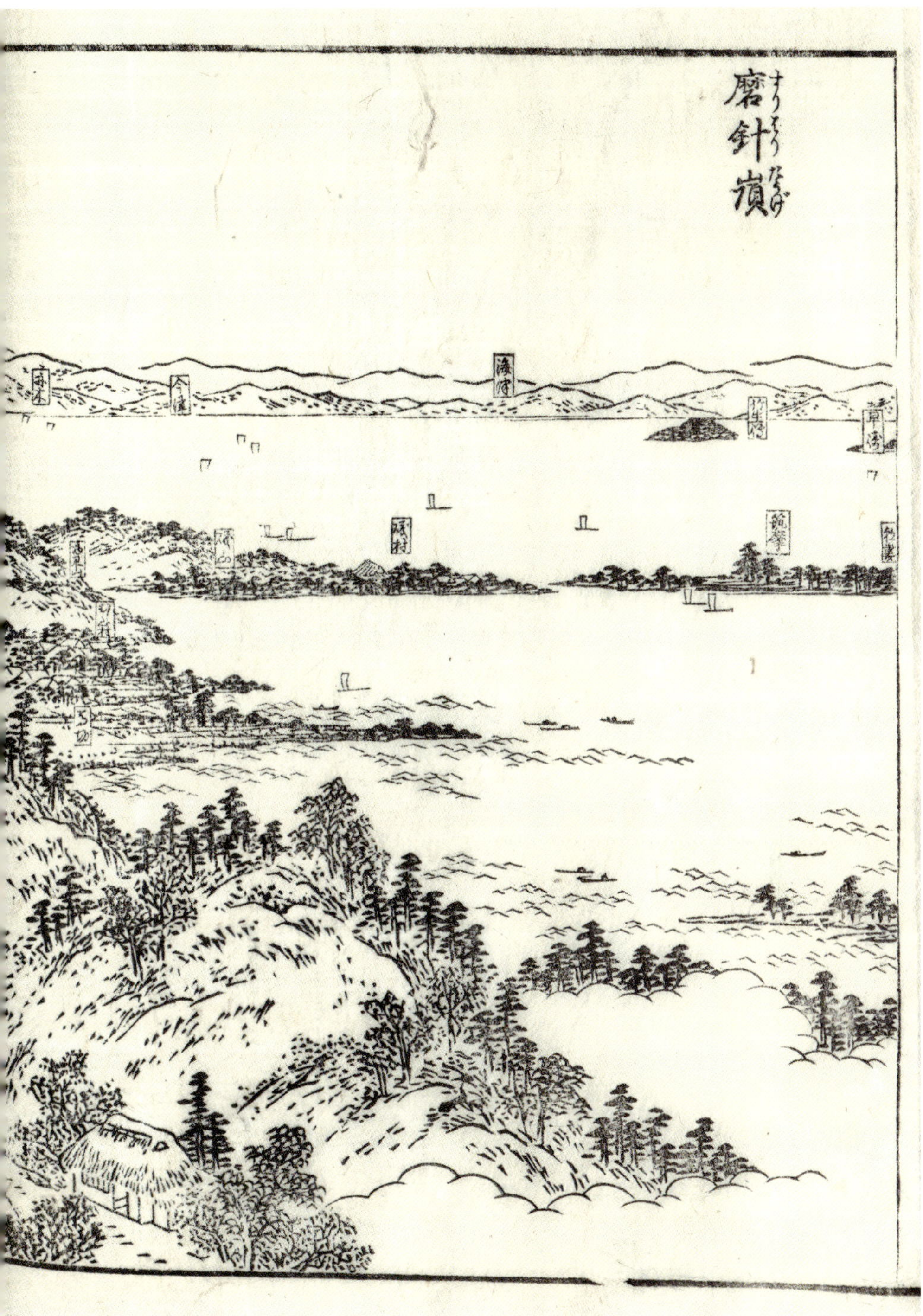

磨針嶺
すりはり たうげ

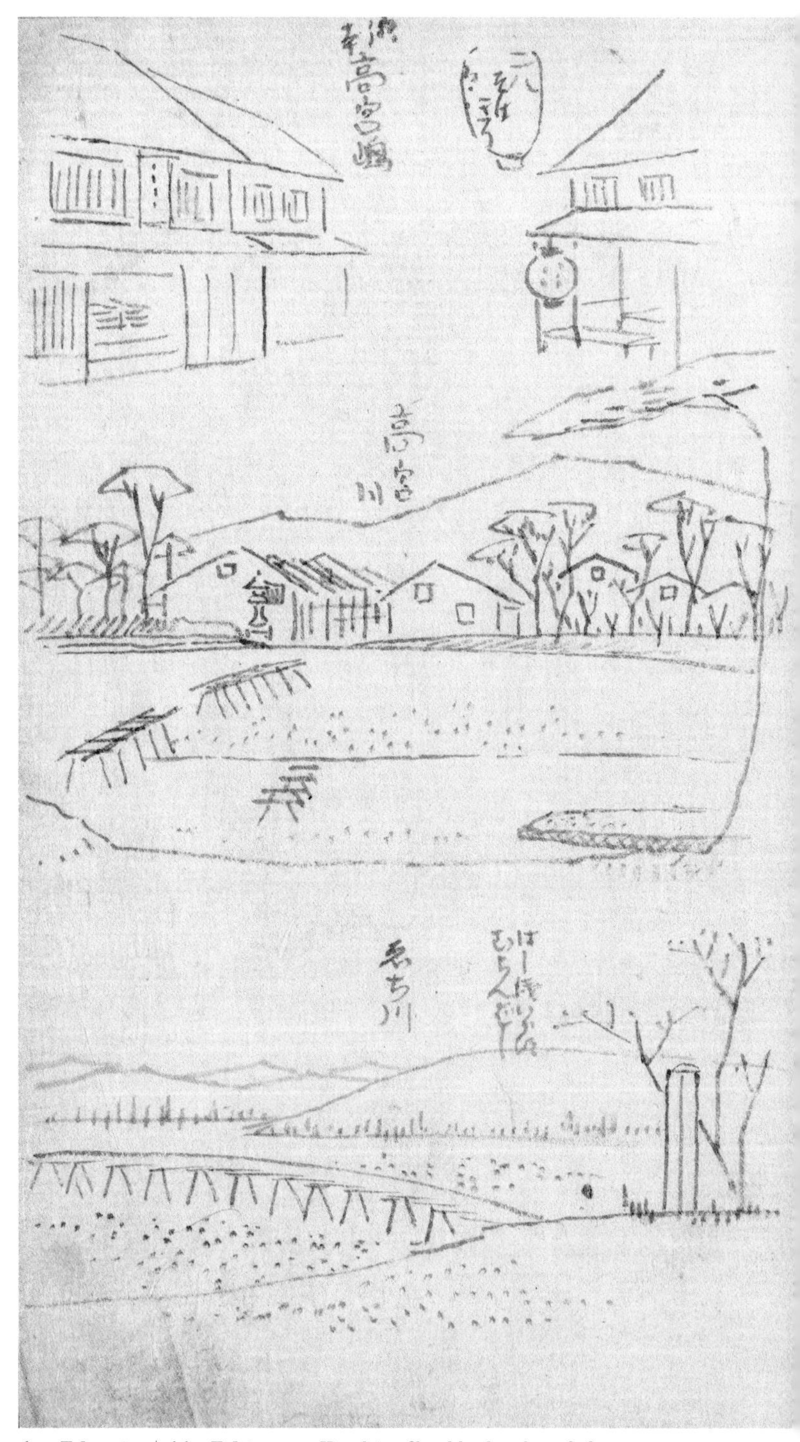

65 – Takamiya | 66 – Echigawa   *Hiroshige, Sketchbook, vol. 5, 1848*

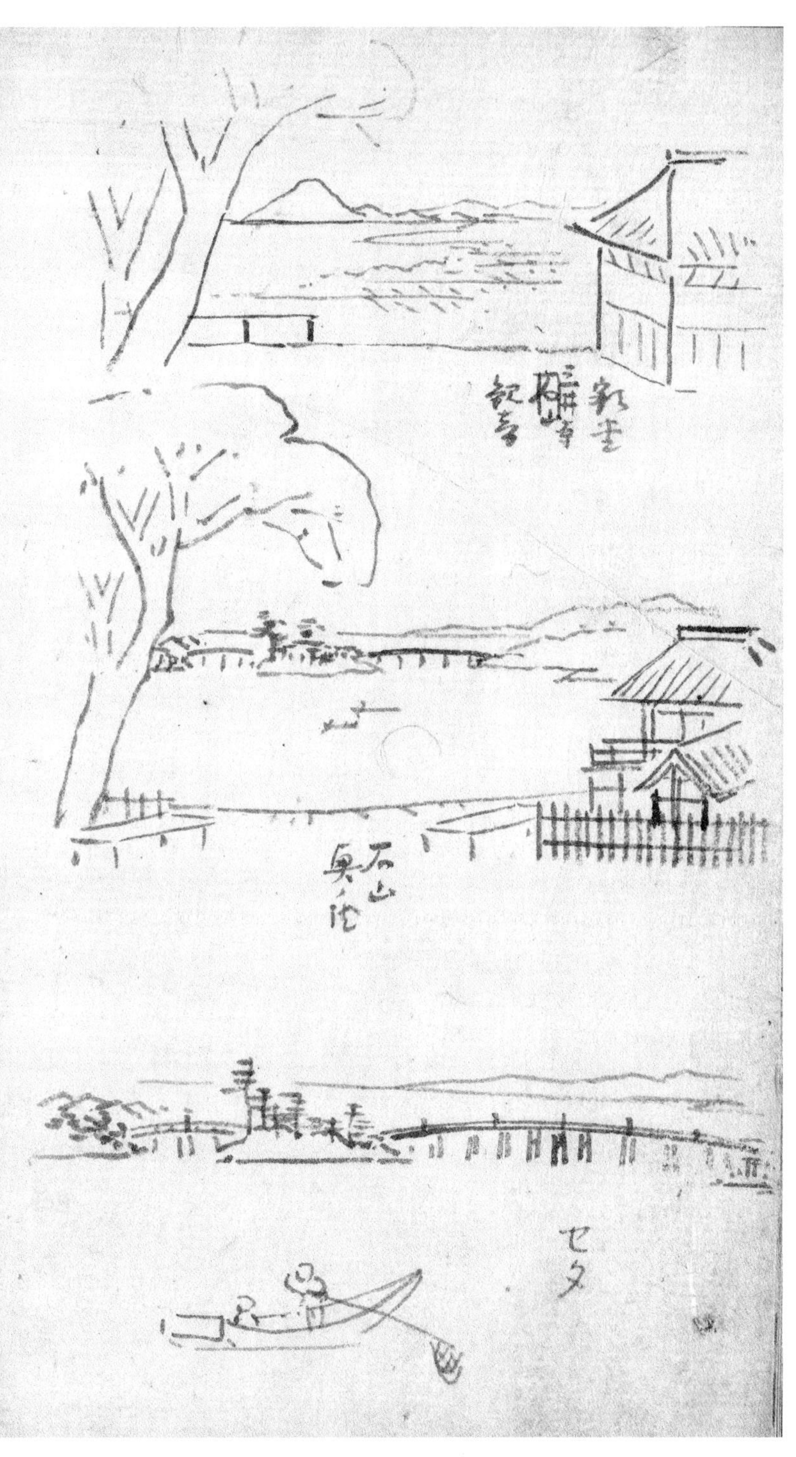
三井寺
記事
石山
セタ

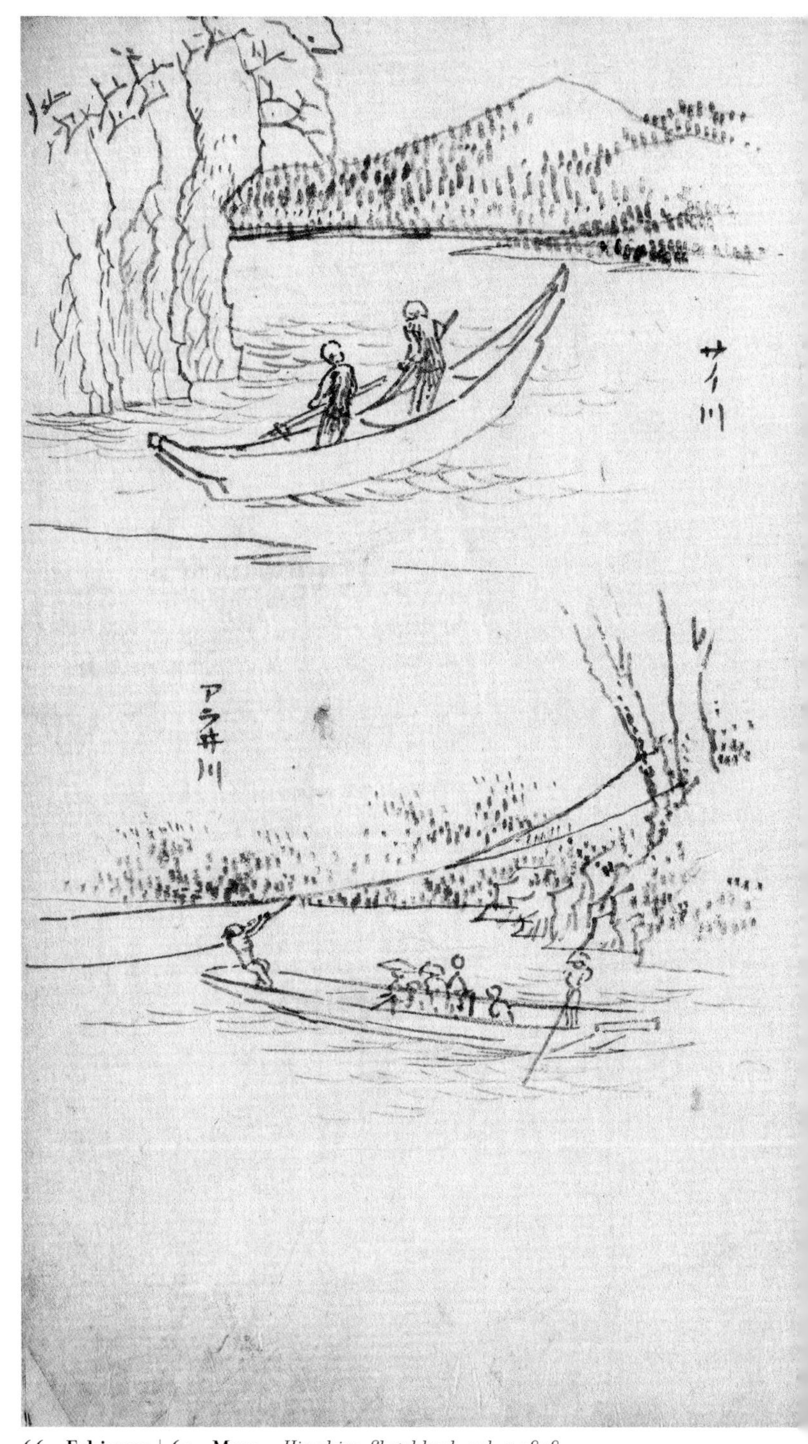

66 – Echigawa | 67 – Musa *Hiroshige, Sketchbook, vol. 5, 1848*

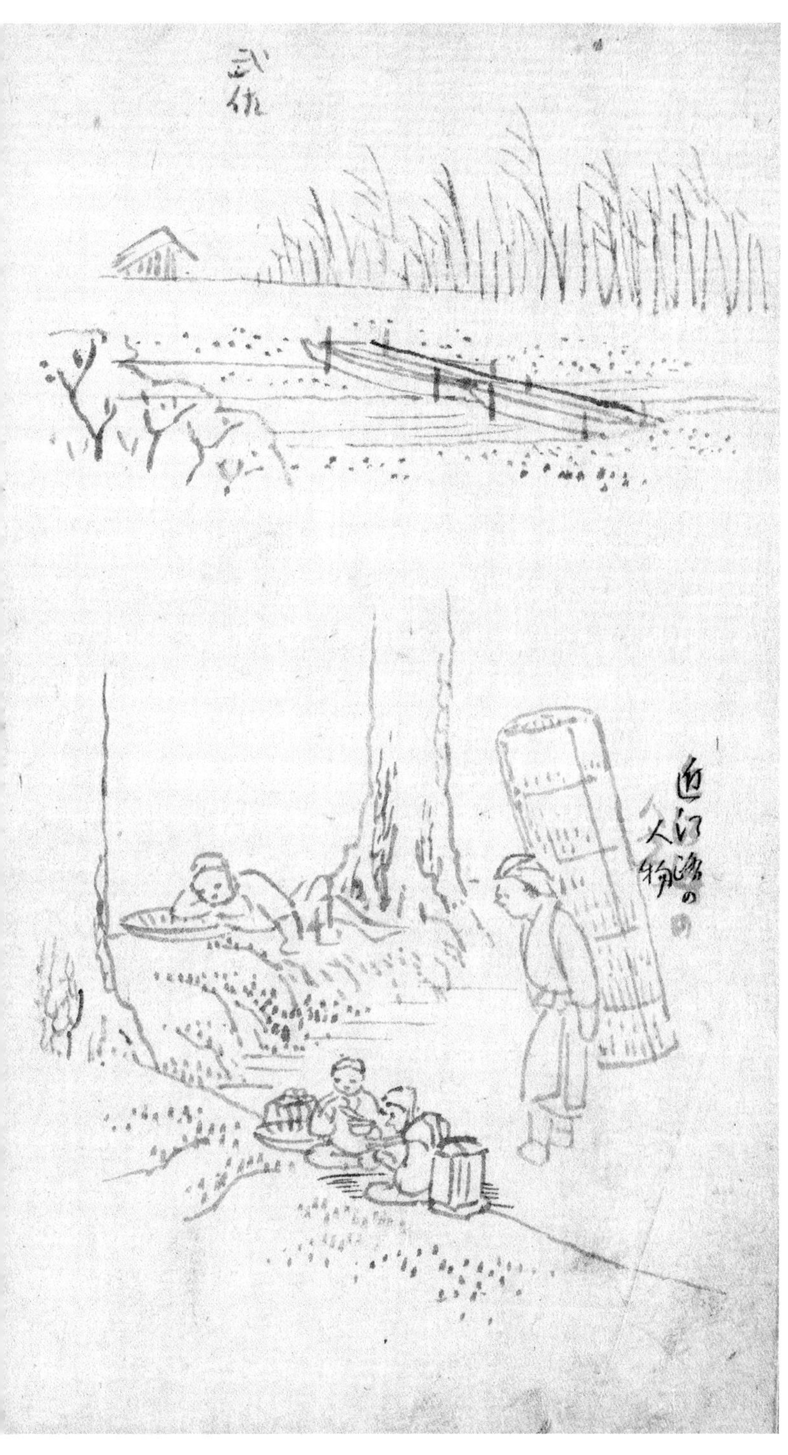

武佐
近江路の人物

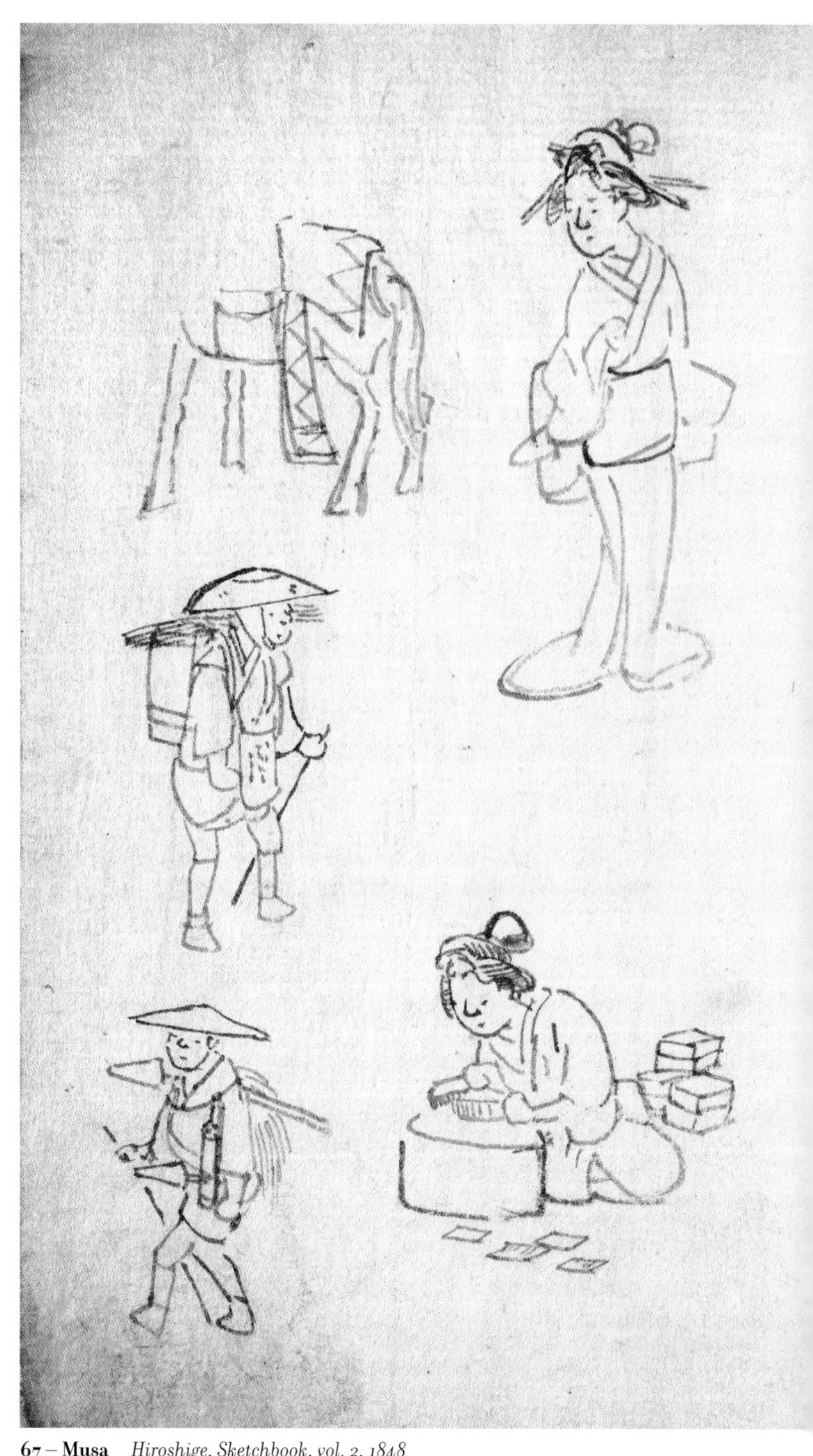

67 – Musa   *Hiroshige, Sketchbook, vol. 2, 1848*

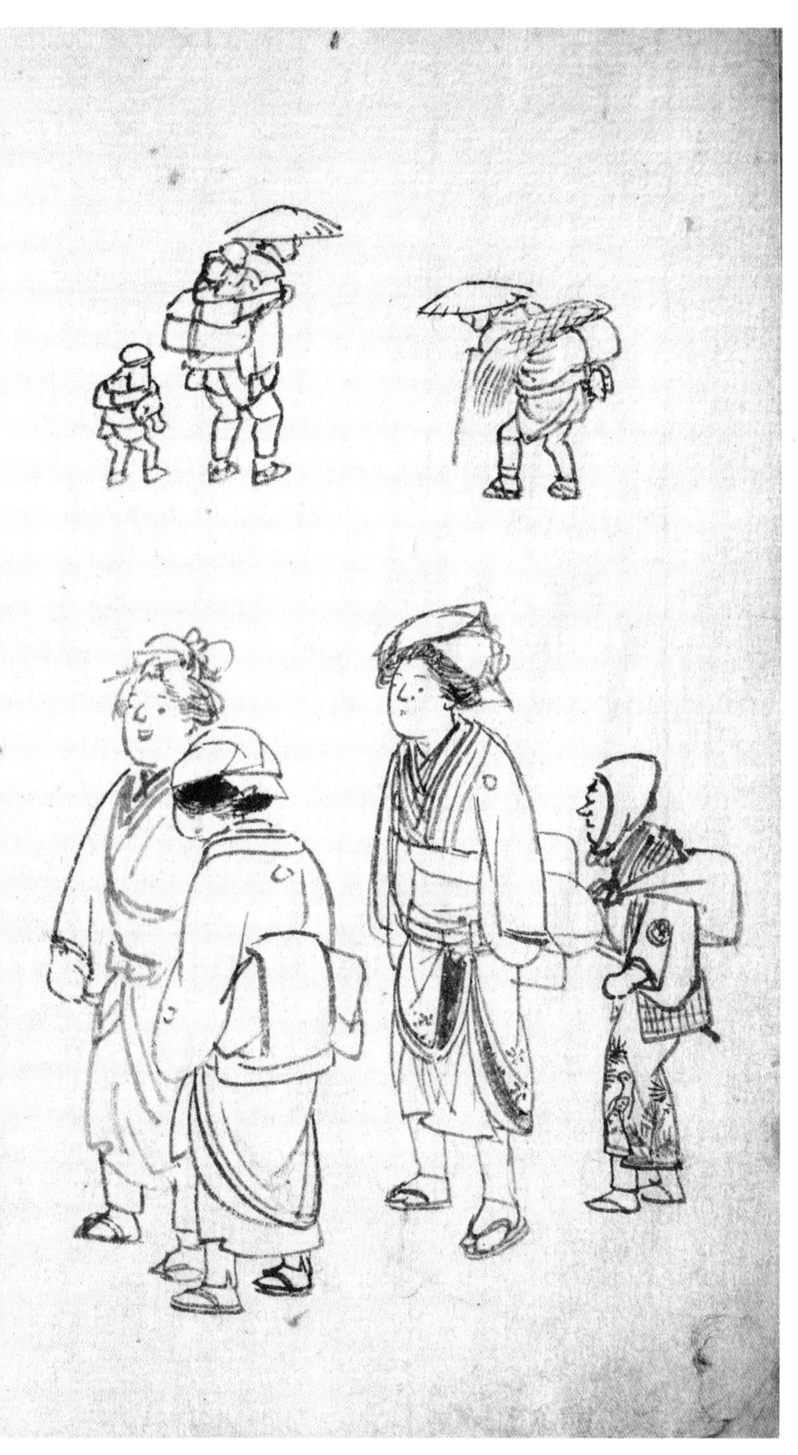

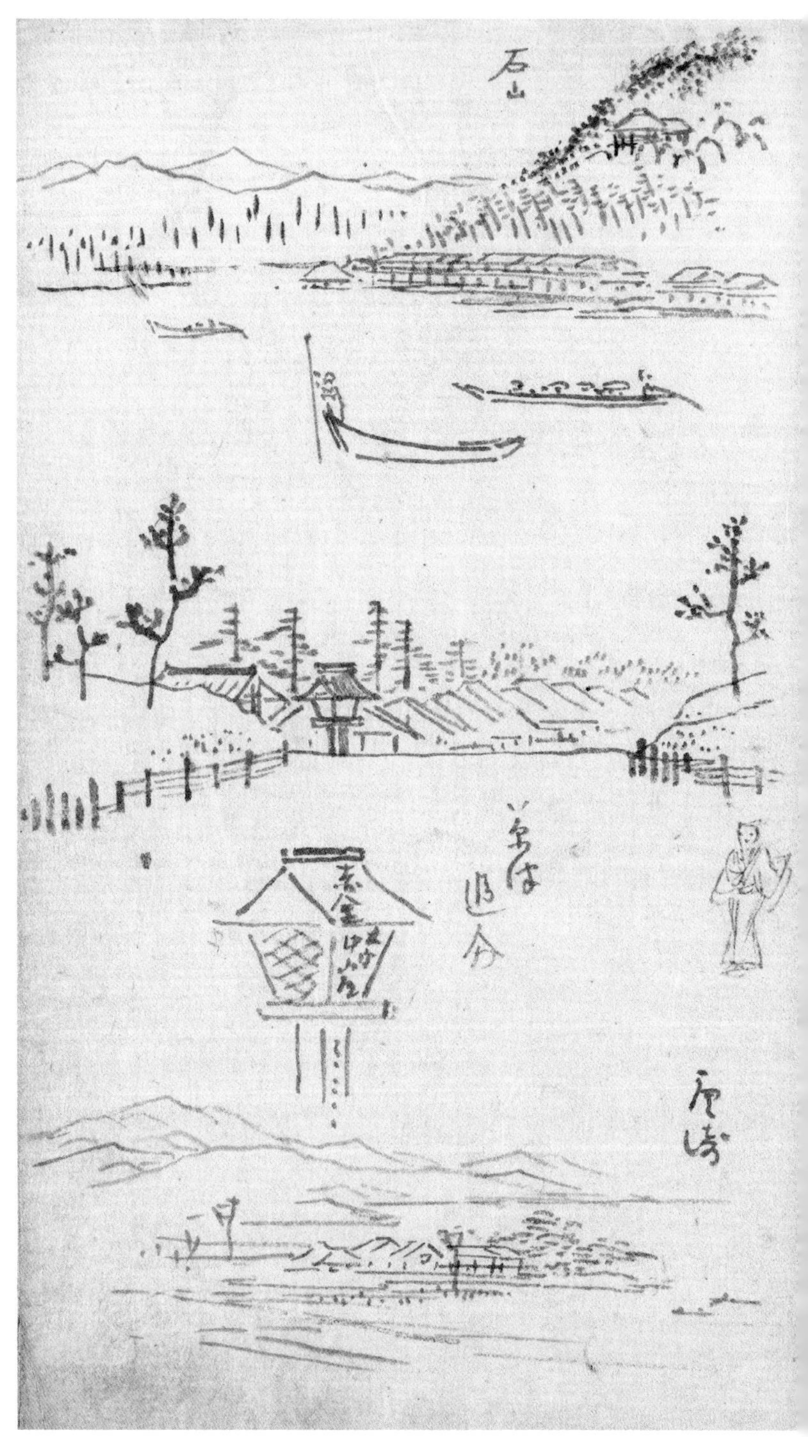

69 – Kusatsu   *Hiroshige, Sketchbook, vol. 2, 1848*

496

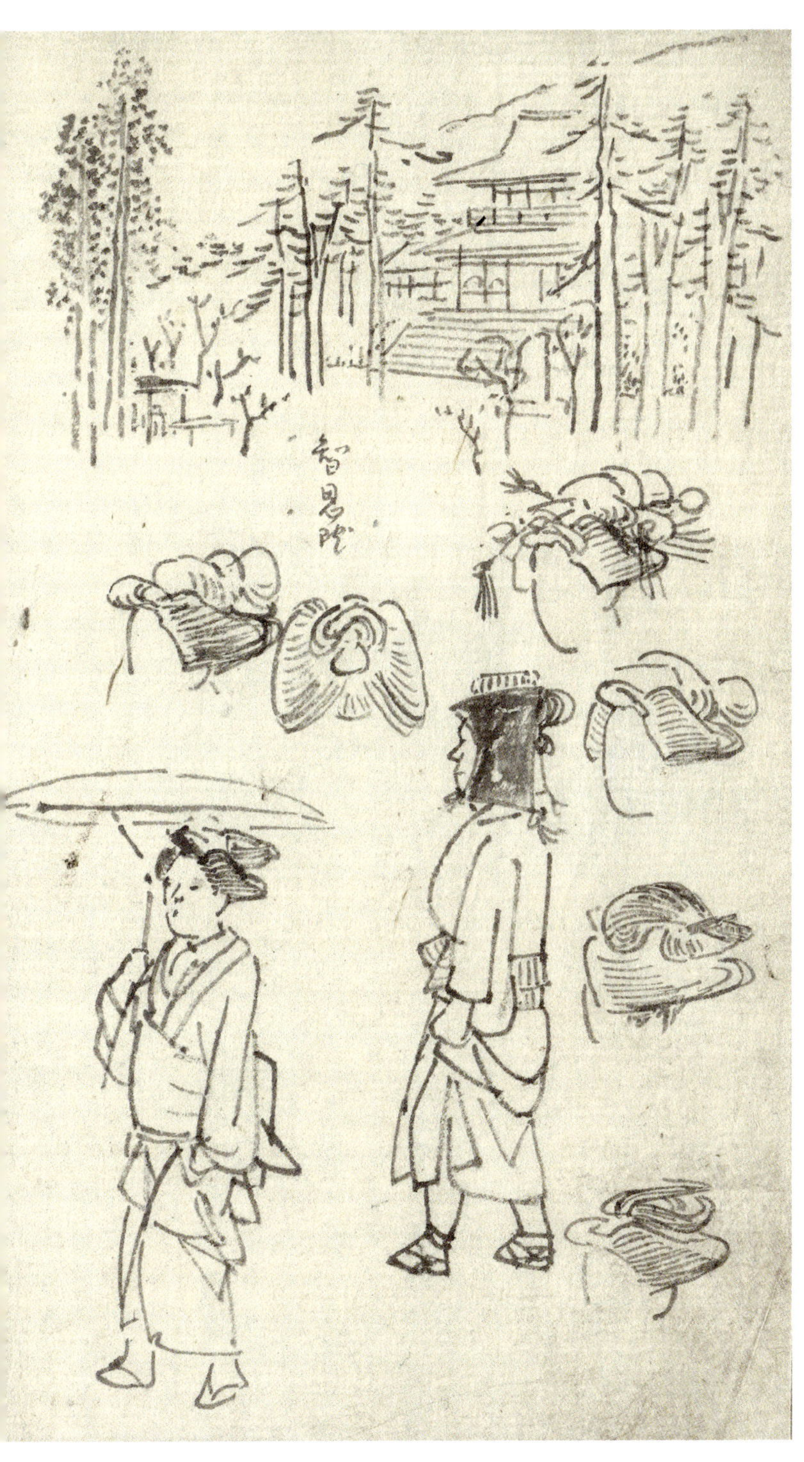
智恩院

Asano Shūgō

Eisen and Hiroshige's
The Sixty-Nine Stations along the Kisokaidō
from the Georges Leskowicz Collection

The Sixty-Nine Stations along the Kisokaidō, jointly created by Eisen and Hiroshige, is renowned as one of the major *meisho-e* (pictures of famous sights) series of Japanese woodblock prints. The works by Hiroshige in this series have received widespread acclaim for their richly emotive images that equate human endeavour with natural scenery. Conversely, while the Eisen prints have not always been highly valued, in fact many of Eisen's images in the series turn a warmly compassionate eye on the actions of the people depicted, while his sharply angled lines reveal the stern face of nature.

Takenouchi Magohachi (Hōeidō), the publisher of Hiroshige's *The Fifty-Three Stations along the Tōkaidō*, commissioned Eisen to work on the *Kisokaidō* series and publication began around the spring of 1835. While originally the commission was supposed to go to Hiroshige, for some reason in the end it went to Eisen. One plausible reason for Eisen taking Hiroshige's place could be that at this time Hiroshige's work on the *Tōkaidō* series had not yet been completed. Even so, because of difficulties in the working situation with Takenouchi, Iseya Rihei (Kinjudō) soon joined the project as publisher. Then Hiroshige replaced Eisen. While it is not clear why this change occurred, there are two possible reasons, namely that originally the commission was intended for Hiroshige, or that Eisen's prints were not that well received. As a result, Takenouchi withdrew from his participation in the series and Iseya completed it with Hiroshige. Today 24 prints by Eisen and 47 by Hiroshige (there are two images for Nakatsugawa) remain extant.

In recent years more light has been shed on the close connection between Hiroshige's works in this series and his *Kiso Road Sketchbook* (*Kisoji shaseichō*), in the collection of the British Museum, which Hiroshige created in the course of the important journey he made during the spring and summer of 1837. The 47 prints by Hiroshige show differences in style and signature, and can thus be divided into two groups, the first consisting of 26 prints and the second 21. The division is based on the way in which the last stroke of his signature, "Hiroshige ga", was drawn: prints in which the stroke goes from upper right to lower left are in the first group, while those in which the stroke goes from upper left to lower right are in the second group. These differences in signature are also linked to stylistic differences, with the standard interpretation being that many works in the first group are characterised by bold compositions, whereas the second group tends to be marked by a clearer, simpler approach. A comparison of these works with the *Sketchbook* reveals certain resemblances with 15 out of the 21 works in the second group. On the other hand, there is not a single print in the first group that shows any resemblance with images in the *Sketchbook*. As a result, the conclusion can be drawn that the preparatory drawings for the first group were completed by spring 1837, while those for the second group were completed that summer or later after Hiroshige returned from his journey. It is not certain when the full series of prints was completed, but it was likely around 1838.

Given the vicissitudes of the production process described above, there are today very few public or private collections that have a complete set of the *Kisokaidō* series. Indeed, this set in the collection of Georges Leskowicz is the only one that has a full run of first editions and first printings for the whole series.

Of particular note in the Leskowicz series are the prints of Okegawa (plate 7) and Honjō (plate 11) by Eisen, because they include Eisen's signature. At the time of writing no other impressions of these two prints bearing Eisen's signature have been located. Okegawa not only features the signature "Eisen ga", in the lower right, but also a "Takenouchi" publisher seal above the "Hōeidō" publisher seal, while red (*beni*) has been added to some sections of the print such as the woman's face. Honjō bears the "Keisai ga" signature but also has the round "Hōeidō" seal to the left of it, and the slopes of the mountains in the distance are rendered in a more simple manner. The red gradation above the mountains is particularly beautiful.

Many of the works by Eisen apart from Okegawa and Honjō are also marked by details not found in other extant impressions. Narai (plate 35) features red gradation on its distant mountains, while a grey gradation is used halfway up the central mountain. Yabuhara (plate 36) has vivid red gradation in the sky behind the people. While impressions of Magome (plate 44) bearing the "Eisen ga" signature do not usually include Mount Ena, the version of Magome here with its "Eisen ga" signature does represent Mount Ena, using downward grey shading. Similarly, Nojiri (plate 41) differs from the typical first-edition version in that it has no blank space along the bottom but instead the block for the two cliffs continues right to the lower edge and was executed in grey. The bottom edge of the rushing stream has indigo gradation, as if to halt the great flow of water. The contrast between the red and green of the waterfall and the indigo and white is an almost surreal expression.

This set in the collection of Georges Leskowicz includes not only fine images by Hiroshige, but also particularly superior impressions by Eisen that show almost no fading, and indeed, the feeling of the original state of this series can still be enjoyed across the entire set.

Asano Shūgō

Die neunundsechzig Stationen des Kisokaidō
von Eisen und Hiroshige
aus der Sammlung Georges Leskowicz

Der von Eisen und Hiroshige geschaffene Bilderzyklus *Die neunundsechzig Stationen des Kisokaidō* zählt im japanischen Holzschnitt zu den großen *meisho-e*-Serien mit Bildern berühmter Stätten. Hiroshiges Beiträge zu dieser Serie wurden weithin für ihre hochemotionale Bildsprache, die menschliches Tun und landschaftliche Szenerie verbindet, gelobt. Obwohl Eisens Holzschnitte nicht immer große Anerkennung fanden, werfen viele seiner Kisokaidō-Motive umgekehrt einen Blick voller Wärme und Mitgefühl auf das Handeln der dargestellten Personen, während sich in seinen kantigen Linien das strenge Gesicht der Natur offenbart.

Takenouchi Magohachi (Hōeidō), der bereits Hiroshiges Holzschnittserie *Die dreiundfünfzig Stationen des Tōkaidō* verlegt hatte, gab die *Kisokaidō*-Serie bei Eisen in Auftrag und begann etwa im Frühjahr 1835 die ersten Blätter zu veröffentlichen. Ursprünglich sollte Hiroshige die Aufgabe übernehmen, doch dann erhielt aus irgendeinem Grund Eisen den Zuschlag. Dass er Hiroshiges Platz einnahm, könnte u. a. daran gelegen haben, dass Hiroshige die Arbeiten an seiner *Tōkaidō*-Serie noch nicht abgeschlossen hatte. Da die Arbeitsumstände bei Takenouchi jedoch schwierig waren, schloss sich schon bald Iseya Rihei (Kinjudō) als Verleger dem Projekt an. Dann wurde Eisen durch Hiroshige ersetzt. Wenngleich ungeklärt ist, warum es zu dem Wechsel kam, gibt es nur zwei Möglichkeiten: Es lag entweder daran, dass der Auftrag ursprünglich für Hiroshige bestimmt war, oder daran, dass Eisens Drucke beim Publikum nicht gut ankamen. Im Ergebnis zog sich Takenouchi aus der Serie zurück, die anschließend von Iseya und Hiroshige vollendet wurde. Unter den heute erhaltenen 71 Blättern (für die Station Nakatsugawa existieren zwei Entwürfe) stammen 24 von Eisen und 47 von Hiroshige.

In den letzten Jahren gewann man neue Erkenntnisse über die enge Verbindung zwischen Hiroshiges Werken in dieser Serie und seinem im British Museum verwahrten *Skizzenbuch der Kiso-Straße (Kisoji shaseichō)*, das er während seiner maßgeblichen Reise im Frühjahr und Sommer 1837 schuf. Die 47 Blätter aus seiner Hand weisen Unterschiede in Stil und Signatur auf und lassen sich in zwei Gruppen einteilen, von denen die erste 26 und die zweite 21 Blätter umfasst. Die Einteilung basiert darauf, wie Hiroshige den letzten Pinselstrich seiner Signatur, „Hiroshige ga", setzte: Verläuft der Strich von rechts oben nach links unten, gehört das Blatt in die erste Gruppe, verläuft er von links oben nach rechts unten, ist es der zweiten zuzuordnen. Die verschiedenen Signaturen sind mit stilistischen Unterschieden verknüpft, die oft so beschrieben werden, dass viele Arbeiten der ersten Gruppe durch kühne Kompositionen gekennzeichnet sind, während die Entwürfe der zweiten Gruppe ein klarerer und schlichterer Ansatz prägt. Ein Vergleich dieser Arbeiten mit dem Skizzenbuch offenbart bei 15 der 21 Blätter aus der zweiten Gruppe gewisse Ähnlichkeiten. Andererseits weist in der ersten Gruppe kein einziges Blatt eine Ähnlichkeit mit den Darstellungen im Skizzenbuch auf. Das lässt den Schluss zu, dass die vorbereitenden Zeichnungen für die erste Gruppe im Frühjahr 1837 abgeschlossen waren, während die Vorzeichnungen für die zweite Gruppe im folgenden Sommer oder später ausgeführt wurden, nachdem Hiroshige seine Reise beendet hatte. Dass die letzten Blätter um 1838 in den Druck gingen, ist nicht sicher, gilt aber als wahrscheinlich.

Angesichts der bedauerlichen Umstände, die die Fertigstellung des *Kisokaidō*-Zyklus begleiteten, sind heute nur sehr wenige öffentliche oder private Sammlungen im Besitz eines vollständigen Satzes dieser Serie. Genau genommen ist der hier abgedruckte Satz aus der Sammlung Georges Leskowicz der einzige, der ausnahmslos aus Erstauflagen und Erstdrucken besteht.

Die Entwürfe von Eisen für Okegawa (Tafel 7) und Honjō (Tafel 11) in der Leskowicz-Serie sind von besonderem Interesse, weil sie die Signatur des Künstlers enthalten. Bis heute sind keine weiteren von Eisen signierten Abzüge dieser beiden Blätter bekannt. Das Blatt Okegawa trägt nicht nur die Signatur „Eisen ga" in der rechten unteren Ecke, sondern übereinander auch die Verlegersiegel „Takenouchi" und „Hōeidō". In einigen Bereichen des Drucks, wie im Gesicht der Frau, wurde Rot (*beni*) ergänzt. Das Blatt Honjō weist nicht nur die Signatur „Keisai ga" auf, sondern links daneben auch das runde „Hōeidō"-Siegel. So schlicht die Berghänge in der Ferne ausgeführt sind, so außergewöhnlich schön ist die rote Farbabstufung darüber gelungen.

Neben den Blättern Okegawa und Honjō zeichnen sich viele weitere Arbeiten Eisens durch Details aus, die in anderen erhaltenen Abzügen nicht zu finden sind.

Narai (Tafel 35) zeigt rote Abstufungen über den Bergen im Hintergrund, denen in der unteren Hälfte des zentralen Bergmassivs ein abgestuftes Grau gegenübersteht. In Yabuhara (Tafel 36) fällt die kräftige Rotabstufung des Himmels hinter den Figuren auf. Auf jenen Abzügen von Magome (Tafel 44), die Eisens Signatur „Eisen ga" enthalten, fehlt in der Regel der Berg Ena, der in die hier gezeigte und mit „Eisen ga" signierte Version jedoch aufgenommen und in aufsteigenden Graustufen dargestellt ist. Ganz ähnlich unterscheidet sich Nojiri (Tafel 41) vom Standardabzug der Erstauflage, weil es am unteren Rand keinen unbedruckten Raum aufweist, sondern der Druckstock für die beiden Felswände bis an den Bildrand reichte und grau eingefärbt wurde. Die indigoblaue Abstufung am unteren Ende des Flusses erweckt den Eindruck, als sollte sie die herabstürzenden Wassermassen aufhalten. Der Kontrast zwischen dem Rot und Grün des Wasserfalls und dem Indigo und Weiß wirkt geradezu surrealistisch.

Der *Kisokaidō*-Satz aus der Sammlung Georges Leskowicz umfasst nicht nur ausgezeichnete Drucke von Hiroshige, sondern auch besonders herausragende Abzüge von Eisen, die so gut wie gar nicht verblasst sind. Und tatsächlich lässt sich der Originalzustand des *Kisokaidō*-Zyklus durchgängig an jedem einzelnen der hier präsentierten Abzüge nachempfinden und genießen.

Asano Shūgō

Les soixante-neuf stations de la route Kisokaidō
d'Eisen et Hiroshige,
dans la collection de Georges Leskowicz

Réalisées conjointement par Eisen et Hiroshige, *Les soixante-neuf stations de la route Kisokaidō* ont la réputation d'être l'une des plus belles séries de gravures sur bois japonaises, dans le genre des *meisho-e* (images de vues célèbres). Les estampes signées par Hiroshige pour cette série ont été très largement saluées pour la puissance de leurs sentiments, car elles mettent sur un pied d'égalité les activités des hommes et les paysages naturels. En revanche, les estampes d'Eisen n'ont pas toujours été bien considérées. Pourtant, un grand nombre des illustrations qu'Eisen a réalisées pour cette série posent un regard chaleureux et compatissant sur les actes des personnages représentés, tandis que son trait aux angles aigus exprime le visage austère de la nature.

C'est Takenouchi Magohachi (Hōeidō), éditeur des *Cinquante-trois stations de la route Tōkaidō*, qui commandita Eisen pour la réalisation de la série de la *Kisokaidō*, dont la publication débuta vers le printemps 1835. Alors que cette commande aurait dû être attribuée à Hiroshige, c'est Eisen qui l'obtint pour une raison que nous ignorons. Si Eisen remplaça Hiroshige, c'est peut-être parce qu'à cette époque le travail de ce dernier pour la *Tōkaidō* n'était pas encore achevé. Quoi qu'il en soit, à la suite de complications professionnelles avec Takenouchi, un second éditeur rejoignit bientôt le projet, Iseya Rihei (Kinjudō). Puis c'est Hiroshige qui prit la place d'Eisen. On ignore pourquoi ce remplacement eut lieu, mais deux explications sont possibles : la commande était peut-être destinée initialement à Hiroshige,

et les estampes d'Eisen n'auraient pas été bien accueillies. Takenouchi se serait alors retiré de ce projet de série, et Iseya l'aurait mené à son terme avec Hiroshige. Subsistent aujourd'hui 24 estampes d'Eisen et 47 d'Hiroshige (il existe deux illustrations de Nakatsugawa).

Depuis quelques années, nous en savons davantage sur les liens étroits entre les œuvres d'Hiroshige pour cette série et son *Carnet de croquis de la route Kiso* (*Kisoji shaseichō*), conservé au British Museum et que l'artiste a réalisé au cours de l'important voyage qu'il effectua pendant le printemps et l'été 1837. Les 47 estampes d'Hiroshige révèlent des différences de style et de signature, ce qui permet de les classer en deux groupes distincts, le premier comprenant 26 estampes et le second 21. Cette distinction s'appuie sur la manière dont est dessiné le dernier trait de la signature « Hiroshige ga » : le premier groupe est constitué des estampes dans lesquelles ce trait est incliné à gauche vers le bas ; dans le second groupe, le trait est incliné à droite vers le bas. À ces différences de signature correspondent des différences stylistiques. Selon l'interprétation courante, de nombreuses œuvres du premier groupe se caractérisent par des compositions aux traits épais, tandis que celles du second groupe sont marquées par un traitement plus clair et plus simple. La comparaison de ces œuvres avec le *Carnet de croquis* met en évidence certaines ressemblances avec 15 des 21 œuvres du second groupe. Toutefois, aucune estampe du premier groupe ne trahit la moindre ressemblance avec les illustrations du *Carnet de croquis*. On peut donc en conclure que les dessins préparatoires du premier groupe furent achevés au printemps 1837, tandis que l'artiste termina ceux du second groupe durant l'été ou plus tard, une fois revenu de son voyage. La date de l'achèvement de la série n'est pas connue précisément, mais elle se situe probablement vers 1838.

Étant donné les complications décrites plus haut à propos de la réalisation de cette série, il existe aujourd'hui très peu de collections publiques ou privées possédant la totalité des estampes de la série de la *Kisokaidō*. L'ensemble figurant dans la collection de Georges Leskowicz est même le seul qui comporte un tirage complet de premières éditions et de premières épreuves pour la totalité de la série.

Dans cet ensemble, les estampes d'Okegawa (planche 7) et de Honjō (planche 11), dues à Eisen, sont particulièrement remarquables, car elles arborent la signature de l'artiste. Au moment de la rédaction de ce texte, aucun autre tirage de ces deux estampes portant la signature d'Eisen n'a été localisé. Okegawa comporte la signature « Eisen ga », en bas à droite, mais aussi le sceau d'éditeur « Takenouchi » au-dessus du sceau « Hōeidō », tandis que du rouge (*beni*) a été ajouté dans certaines parties de l'estampe, comme par exemple le visage de la femme. L'estampe d'Honjō porte la signature « Keisai ga », à laquelle s'y juxtapose le sceau circulaire « Hōeidō », à gauche, et les versants des montagnes visibles au loin sont rendus avec plus de simplicité. Au-dessus des montagnes, le dégradé de rouge s'avère particulièrement resplendissant.

Mises à part Okegawa et Honjō, un grand nombre d'œuvres d'Eisen se distinguent également par des détails invisibles dans d'autres épreuves existantes. Un dégradé de rouge orne les montagnes de l'arrière-plan dans Narai (planche 35), tandis qu'un dégradé de gris recouvre la moitié inférieure de la montagne centrale. Dans Yabuhara (planche 36), c'est un dégradé de rouge vif que l'on trouve dans le ciel, derrière les personnages. Alors que le mont Ena est habituellement absent des épreuves de Magome (planche 44) portant la signature « Eisen ga », cette montagne est figurée par un dégradé de gris vers le bas dans la version de cette estampe représentée ici, qui comporte également la signature « Eisen ga ». De même, Nojiri (planche 41) se distingue de la première édition courante en ce qu'elle est dépourvue d'espace sans couleur au bas de l'image, l'ensemble formé par les deux falaises, exécuté en gris, se poursuivant jusqu'au bord inférieur. La partie inférieure du torrent est illustrée par un dégradé d'indigo, comme pour stopper la cascade. Le contraste entre le rouge et le vert de la chute d'eau et l'indigo et le blanc relève presque de l'onirique.

Cet ensemble de la collection de Georges Leskowicz comprend de très belles images d'Hiroshige, mais aussi des épreuves d'excellente qualité des estampes d'Eisen qui ne présentent quasiment aucune trace de décoloration. Cet ensemble complet permet aujourd'hui de ressentir l'émoi suscité par l'état initial de cette série.

Notes

Editorial Notes

Romanisation: Japanese words are given in the standard revised Hepburn romanisation.

Names: Japanese personal names are given with the surname preceding the given name or artist name.

Order of characters: Japanese script is traditionally read from top to bottom, and the columns from right to left.

Pronunciation: The vowels in the Hepburn romanisation system have approximately the values they have in Italian. They are pronounced short unless they have a macron. An exception is "ei", as in the name Eisen, which is pronounced as a long "e".

The macron has been omitted in words that have been anglicised (e.g. Tokyo, shogun). Two vowels in succession are sometimes pronounced separately (e.g. *ukiyo-e*), sometimes as diphthongs. Consonants are pronounced much as in English; double consonants are pronounced double, as in Italian. The consonant "g" is always pronounced as in "get"; the Japanese "r" is pronounced with a single flap of the tongue.

Titles: To reduce repetition in the plate captions, the series title *The Sixty-Nine Stations along the Kisokaidō* is omitted. The titles have also been standardised and give only the name of the respective station. Complete titles can be found in the Notes under *Facts on the Stations and Colour Variations*.

Print sizes: *Ōban* (c. 39 × 27 cm / 15 ⅜ × 10 ⅝ in.), *aiban* (c. 33 × 23 cm / 13 × 9 in.), *yotsugiriban* (c. 19 × 13 cm / 7 ½ × 5 ⅛ in.).

From Edo to Kyoto

1 "Wer sich an schönen japanischen Gebirgslandschaften erfreuen will, der mag den Nakasendô wählen, denn kaum findet er in ganz Japan eine Strasse, welche ihm ein so reiches Maass [sic] der verschiedensten Natur-schönheiten bietet;" Rein 1880, p. 3.

2 Eisen's titles are not identical but those on all other prints are and this is the title generally used for this series. His titles appear as *Kisokaidō*, written in two different ways (木曾街道 and 岐阻街道), as well as *Stations on the Kiso Road* (*Kisoji no eki*), written in three different ways (支蘇路ノ驛, 岐阻路ノ驛, and 木曾路驛), and *Along the Kiso* (*Kiso dōchū*), written in two different ways (木曾道中 and 岐阻道中).

3 Vaporis 1994, p. 280.

4 Vaporis 1994, p. 42.

5 Vaporis 1994, p. 27.

6 Vaporis 1994, pp. 265–266; Hori 2001, pp. 71, 93.

7 With 248 *hatagoya*, Miya had the largest number of inns of the Tōkaidō post stations.

8 In Japanese this scroll is titled *Edo yori Fushimi made Kisoji Nakasendō Tōkaidō ezu* 従江戸伏見迄木曽路中山道東海道絵図.

9 For a detailed description of Tōkaidō prints, see Marks 2013, pp. 45–54.

10 Kadomaruya had issued six volumes of *Hokusai's Sketchbook* (*Hokusai manga*) since 1815; volume one was published by Eirakuya Tōshirō in 1814.

11 The designs were so popular that the new firm of Takenouchi could not keep up with production and so recruited the well-established firm Senkakudō of Tsuruya Kiemon as a partner. By the end of 1833 they had produced 55 different designs.

12 A practice that was not unusual and which did not prevent Hiroshige's prints from becoming extremely successful; Marks 2013, pp. 76–79.

13 The book is titled *Eitai dango* 永代談語, and written by Shinrotei. Eisen signed himself as *Keisai Shōsen* 渓斎小泉.

14 Advertising lists in volumes *jō* and *ge* of *Mikuni Tarō sairai den* 三国太郎再来伝, written by Jippensha Ikku and illustrated by Kuniyoshi, Bizan (i.e. Takenouchi Magohachi) and Kuninao. These lists also advertise Takenouchi's Tōkaidō series as *Series of Horizontal Pictures of the Fifty-Three Stations along the Tōkaidō* (*Tōkaidō gojūsan tsugi yoko-e tsuzuki* 東海道五十三次横画続).

15 Chiba City Museum of Art 2012, nos. 83–91.

16 Chiba City Museum of Art 2012, nos. 217–271; Marks 2013, p. 287, no. T18.

17 The year Tenpō six corresponds to 29 January, 1835 until 16 February, 1836 in the Gregorian calendar. To the left of the character *hitsuji* are three characters that look like the number 5,001 (*gosenichi* 五千一), however, the meaning remains unclear. A recent interpretation in Friese 2010, pp. 11–12, that this number should be read as 53 (*gojūsan* 五十三) and was intended to relate to Takenouchi's earlier Tōkaidō series, is wishful thinking as the reading of the second character as 10 (*jū*) is rather imaginative and

the third character certainly does not resemble three (*san*).

18 In the book *Yamato nishiki mamoribukuro* 大和錦守袋, illustrated by Utagawa Sadahide.

19 In the book *Harugasumi* 春がすみ, illustrated by Eisen; see Suzuki, Kimura and Ōkubo 2004, p. 197.

20 This untitled series was published by Tsutaya Kichizō, see Chiba City Museum of Art 2012, nos. 325, 327–333; Marks 2013, p. 287, no. T19.

21 Kuniyoshi's series *Kisokaidō rokujūkyū tsugi no uchi* 木曾街道六十九次之内 was published from the fifth month of 1852 to the second month of 1853. Kunisada's series *Kiso rokujūkyū tsugi* 木曽六十九驛 was published from the tenth to the twelfth months of 1852.

22 See plates 21, 36, 41, 53 and 55.

23 Hiroshige used some of these sketches again for the illustrations in the three-volume work *Kiso meisho zue* 岐蘇名所圖會 which follow the sketches even more closely. Volumes one and two are dated to 1851 and volume three is from 1852. For more information on the sketchbooks, see Asano 2010a.

24 On the prints designed before the journey, the last stroke of the third character of Hiroshige's signature, "Hiroshige ga", in the bottom right corner looks like a hook that goes from the top right to the bottom left. In the prints designed after the journey, this last stroke is a diagonal line from the top left to the bottom right.

25 Strange (1925) 1983, pp. 55–56.

26 This impression is in the collection of Chiba City Museum of Art, in Japan; see Sugawara 2009, p. 52; Asano 2010b, p. 229.

27 Marks 2011, p. 25.

28 Prints started to appear again from the second half of the 1860s on into the late 1870s. See Marks 2010 and 2011.

29 This idea was first published by Edward F. Strange in 1925 who suggested that the omission of Eisen's "name was conceived in order to put forward at least an implication that the whole work was by Hiroshige". Strange [1925] 1983, p. 57.

30 All illustrations in Mochizuki 2011, apart from 46B, are Yamadaya edition prints.

31 In recent years, watercolours of 11 prints surfaced for Eisen's designs of Warabi, Kōnosu, Kuragano, Kutsukake, Yabuhara and Kōdo as well as Hiroshige's designs for Annaka, Mochizuki, Motoyama, Toriimoto and Echigawa; however, they all seem to be by the same hand, created after the prints and not preparatory works for creating prints. Ten were in the collection of Huguette Berès (Sotheby's 2003, no. 173), and are now in the collection of Harlow Higinbotham; Mochizuki was in the collection of Richard P. Gale (Hillier 1970, vol. 2, no. 273), and is now in the Minneapolis Institute of Art.

32 Stewart 1922, p. 101; Strange (1925) 1983, p. 58.

33 Stewart 1922, p. 102; Strange (1925) 1983, p. 58.

34 Stewart 1922, p. 105; Strange (1925) 1983, p. 59.

The Creation of the Series

Date	Prints	Numbers in Series	Artist	Publisher(s)
Mid-/late 1835	11	1–11	Eisen	Takenouchi Magohachi
Late 1835–mid-1836	11	13, 20–21, 23, 31, 35–36, 41, 44, 53, 55	Eisen	Takenouchi Magohachi
Late 1836–early 1837	4	14, 19, 38, 64	Hiroshige	Takenouchi Magohachi & Iseya Rihei
	1	15	Eisen	Takenouchi Magohachi & Iseya Rihei
1837	1	18	Eisen	Iseya Rihei
	22	12, 16–17, 22, 24–30, 32–34, 37, 39–40, 42–43, 46a, 47–48	Hiroshige	Iseya Rihei
Late 1837–early 1838	21	45, 46b, 49–52, 54, 56–63, 65–70	Hiroshige	Iseya Rihei

Anmerkungen

Editorische Anmerkungen

Umschrift: Japanische Wörter wurden in der üblichen revidierten Hepburn-Umschrift transkribiert.

Namen: Bei der Nennung japanischer Namen wird der Nachname dem Vor- bzw. Künstlernamen vorangestellt.

Leserichtung: Die japanische Schrift wird traditionell von rechts nach links und von oben nach unten gelesen.

Aussprache: Die Vokale werden wie im Deutschen kurz ausgesprochen, wenn sie nicht durch ein Längungszeichen gekennzeichnet sind. Eine Ausnahme bildet „ei", wie es auch im Namen Eisen vorkommt, welches wie ein langes „e" ausgesprochen wird. Bei japanischen Namen, die im Deutschen geläufig sind (z. B. Tokio, Shogun), wird auf das Längungszeichen verzichtet, außer bei Eigennamen. Doppelvokale werden zum Teil als Diphthonge ausgesprochen (z. B. *ukiyoe*), Konsonanten annähernd wie im Englischen, Doppelkonsonanten ähnlich wie im Italienischen. Ausnahmen stellen die Konsonanten „g" (Aussprache wie im Deutschen) und „r" dar (zwischen Zungen-r und l).

Titel: Bei der Widergabe der Tafeltitel wurde auf die Wiederholung des Seriennames *Die neunundsechzig Stationen des Kisokaidō* verzichtet. Zudem wurden die Überschriften im Tafelteil vereinheitlicht, indem stets nur der Stationsname genannt werden. Vollständige Tafeltitel sind in den Anmerkungen unter *Angaben zu den Stationen und Farbvarianten* zu finden.

Druckformate: *Ōban* (ca. 39 × 27 cm), *aiban* (ca. 33 × 23 cm), *yotsugiriban* (ca. 19 × 13 cm)

Von Edo nach Kyoto

1 Rein 1880, S. 3.

2 Außer bei Eisen taucht der Titel auf allen Blättern auf und wird im Allgemeinen für diese Serie verwendet. Die von Eisen verwendeten Titel lauten, in jeweils zwei, drei und wieder zwei verschiedenen Schreibweisen: *Kisokaidō* (木曾街道 und 岐阻街道), *Stationen der Kiso-Straße* (*Kisoji no eki*; 支蘇路ノ驛, 岐阻路ノ驛 und 木曾路驛) und *Am Kiso* (*Kiso dōchū*; 木曾道中 und 岐阻道中).

3 Vaporis 1994, S. 280.

4 Vaporis 1994, S. 42.

5 Vaporis 1994, S. 27.

6 Vaporis 1994, S. 265–266; Hori 2001, S. 71, 93.

7 Mit 248 *hatagoya* besaß Miya von allen Poststationen am Tōkaidō die meisten Gasthäuser.

8 Auf Japanisch heißt diese Rolle *Edo yori Fushimi made Kisoji Nakasendō Tōkaidō ezu* 従江戸伏見迄木曽路中山道東海道絵図.

9 Für eine detaillierte Beschreibung der Tōkaidō-Drucke siehe Marks 2013, S. 45–54.

10 Bei Kadomaruya waren seit 1815 sechs Bände von *Hokusais Skizzenbuch (Hokusai manga)* erschienen; den ersten Band hatte 1814 Eirakuya Tōshirō herausgegeben.

11 Die Motive waren so beliebt, dass Takenouchis neues Verlagshaus mit der Produktion nicht nachkam und daher Tsuruya Kiemons etablierten Verlag Senkakudō als Partner anwarb. Bis Ende 1833 hatten sie 55 verschiedene Motive produziert.

12 Eine nicht unübliche Praxis, die dem außergewöhnlichen Erfolg der Holzschnitte Hiroshiges keinen Abbruch tat; Marks 2013, S. 76–79.

13 Das Buch trägt den Titel *Eitai dango* 永代談語, der Autor heißt Shinrotei. Eisen selbst signierte als Keisai Shōsen 渓斎小泉.

14 Werbelisten in den Bänden *jō* und *ge* von *Mikuni Tarō sairai den* 三国太郎再来伝, verfasst von Jippensha Ikku und illustriert von Kuniyoshi, Bizan (d. i. Takenouchi Magohachi) und Kuninao. Diese Listen machen auch Werbung für Takenouchis Tōkaidō-Zyklus als *Folge von Bildern der dreiundfünfzig Stationen des Tōkaidō im Querformat* (*Tōkaidō gojūsan tsugi yoko-e tsuzuki* 東海道五十三次横画続).

15 Chiba City Museum of Art 2012, Nr. 83–91.

16 Chiba City Museum of Art 2012, Nr. 217–271; Marks 2013, S. 287, Nr. T18.

17 Das Jahr Tenpō 6 entspricht im Gregorianischen Kalender dem Zeitraum 29. Januar 1835 bis 16. Februar 1836. Links vom Schriftzeichen *hitsuji* stehen drei Zeichen, die aussehen wie die Zahl 5001 (*gosenichi* 五千一); ihre Bedeutung ist jedoch bis heute ungeklärt. Eine neuere Interpretation in Friese 2010, S. 11–12, dass diese Zahl als 53 (*gojūsan* 五十三) zu lesen sei und einen Bezug zu Takenouchis älterer Tōkaidō-Serie herstellen sollte, ist Wunschdenken, da die Deutung des zweiten Zeichens als Zehn (*jū*) recht fantasiereich erscheint und das dritte Zeichen ganz gewiss keine Ähnlichkeit mit einer Drei (*san*) hat.

18 In dem Buch *Yamato nishiki mamoribukuro* 大和錦守袋, illustriert von Utagawa Sadahide.

19 In dem Buch *Harugasumi* 春がすみ, illustriert von Eisen, siehe Suzuki, Kimura und Ôkubo 2004, S. 197.

20 Diese unbezeichnete Serie wurde von Tsutaya Kichizô verlegt, siehe Chiba City Museum of Art 2012, Nr. 325, 327–333; Marks 2013, S. 287, Nr. T19.

21 Kuniyoshis Serie *Kisokaidō rokujūkyū tsugi no uchi* 木曾街道六十九次之内 wurde in der Zeit vom 5. Monat des Jahres 1852 bis zum 2. Monat des Jahres 1853 veröffentlicht, Kunisadas Serie *Kiso rokujūkyū tsugi* 木曽六十九驛 erschien zwischen dem 10. und 12. Monat des Jahres 1852.

22 Siehe die Tafeln 21, 36, 41, 53 und 55.

23 Hiroshige nutzte einige dieser Skizzen erneut für seine Illustrationen in dem dreibändigen Werk *Kiso meisho zue* 岐蘇名所圖會, die sich sogar noch genauer an den Skizzen orientieren. Die Bände eins und zwei datieren von 1851, Band drei erschien 1852. Für weitere Informationen zu den Skizzenbüchern siehe Asano 2010a.

24 Auf den vor Reiseantritt entworfenen Drucken sieht der letzte Pinselstrich des dritten Schriftzeichens von Hiroshiges Signatur, „Hiroshige ga", in der rechten unteren Ecke wie ein Haken aus, der von rechts oben nach links unten verläuft. Auf den nach der Reise entstandenen Entwürfen bildet dieser letzte Strich eine diagonale Linie von links oben nach rechts unten.

25 Strange (1925) 1983, S. 55–56.

26 Dieser Abzug befindet sich in der Sammlung des Chiba City Museum of Art in Japan, siehe Sugawara 2009, S. 52; Asano 2010b, S. 229.

27 Marks 2011, S. 25.

28 Ab der zweiten Hälfte der 1860er Jahre erschienen bis in die späten 1870er Jahre wieder neue Drucke; vgl. Marks 2010 und 2011.

29 Diesen Gedanken äußerte zuerst Edward F. Strange, der 1925 nahelegte, dass der Plan, Eisens Namen wegzulassen, „gefasst wurde, um zumindest anzudeuten, das gesamte Werk stamme von Hiroshige", Strange (1925) 1983, S. 57.

30 Alle Illustrationen in Mochizuki 2011, ausgenommen 46 B, zeigen Drucke der Yamadaya-Ausgabe.

31 In den letzten Jahren sind Aquarelle von elf Motiven aufgetaucht, die Eisens Entwürfen für Warabi, Kōnosu, Kuragano, Kutsukake, Yabuhara und Kōdo sowie Hiroshiges Entwürfen für Annaka, Mochizuki, Motoyama, Toriimoto und Echigawa zugeordnet werden können; allerdings scheinen sie alle von derselben Hand nach den Holzschnitten angefertigt worden zu sein, nicht zu ihrer Vorbereitung. Zehn der Aquarelle kamen aus der Sammlung Huguette Berès (Sotheby's 2003, Nr. 173) und befinden sich heute in der Sammlung Harlow Higinbotham; das elfte, Mochizuki, gehörte zur Sammlung Richard S. Gale (Hillier 1970, Bd. 2, Nr. 273) und befindet sich heute im Minneapolis Institute of Art.

32 Stewart 1922, S. 101; Strange (1925) 1983, S. 58.

33 Stewart 1922, S. 102; Strange (1925) 1983, S. 58.

34 Stewart 1922, S. 105; Strange (1925) 1983, S. 59.

Die Entstehung der Serie

Datum	Drucke	Blattnummern in der Serie	Künstler	Verleger
Mitte/Ende 1835	11	1–11	Eisen	Takenouchi Magohachi
Ende 1835 bis Mitte 1836	11	13, 20–21, 23, 31, 35–36, 41, 44, 53, 55	Eisen	Takenouchi Magohachi
Ende 1836 bis Anfang 1837	4	14, 19, 38, 64	Hiroshige	Takenouchi Magohachi & Iseya Rihei
	1	15	Eisen	Takenouchi Magohachi & Iseya Rihei
1837	1	18	Eisen	Iseya Rihei
	22	12, 16–17, 22, 24–30, 32–34, 37, 39–40, 42–43, 46a, 47–48	Hiroshige	Iseya Rihei
Ende 1837 bis Anfang 1838	21	45, 46b, 49–52, 54, 56–63, 65–70	Hiroshige	Iseya Rihei

Notes

Remarques de l'éditeur

Transcription : Les termes japonais sont donnés dans l'habituelle transcription Hepburn modifiée.

Noms de personnes : Pour les noms de personnes japonais, le nom de famille est cité avant le prénom ou le nom d'artiste.

Sens de lecture : L'écriture japonaise se lit traditionnellement de droite à gauche et de haut en bas.

Prononciation : La prononciation des voyelles est brève, sauf lorsqu'elles portent des macrons (accents d'allongement). « ei » tel qu'il apparaît dans le nom Eisen, est une exception, il se prononce comme un « e » allongé. Pour les noms japonais couramment utilisés en français (Tokyo, shogun etc.), on a renoncé aux macrons, hormis dans les noms propres. Certaines doubles voyelles sont prononcées en faisant la diérèse, la prononciation des consonnes suit à peu près celle de l'anglais, les doubles consonnes celle de l'italien. Deux exceptions à cette règle : la consonne « g », qui se prononce « gu » comme dans « guépard », la consonne « r », qui se prononce entre « r » lingual et « l ».

Titre : Le nom de série *Les soixante-neuf Stations du Kisokaidō* n'a pas été répété pour chaque titre de planche. On a en outre uniformisé les titres dans la partie réservée aux planches, en ne nommant plus que le nom de la station. Les titres complets des planches peuvent être consultés dans les *Indications sur les stations et des variantes chromatiques*.

Les formats : *Ōban* (ca. 39 × 27 cm), *aiban* (ca. 33 × 23 cm), *yotsugiriban* (ca. 19 × 13 cm)

D'Edo à Kyoto

1 Rein 1880, p. 3.

2 Les titres d'Eisen ne sont pas tous identiques, contrairement à ceux de toutes les autres estampes ; c'est là le titre généralement employé pour cette série. Ces titres sont : *Kisokaidō*, écrit de deux façons (木曾街道 et 岐阻街道), *Stations sur la route Kiso* (*Kisoji no eki*), écrit de trois manières différentes (支蘓路ノ驛, 岐阻路ノ驛 et 木曾路驛) et *Sur la Kiso* (*Kiso dōchū*), écrit de deux façons différentes (木曾道中 et 岐阻道中).

3 Vaporis 1994, p. 280.

4 Vaporis 1994, p. 42.

5 Vaporis 1994, p. 27.

6 Vaporis 1994, pp. 265-266 ; Hori 2001, pp. 71, 93.

7 Avec ses 248 *hatayoga*, Miya était le relais de poste de la Tōkaidō qui comptait le plus grand nombre d'auberges.

8 Le titre japonais de ce rouleau est *Edo yori Fushimi made Kisoji Nakasendō Tōkaidō ezu* 従江戸伏見迄木曾路中山道東海道絵図.

9 Pour une description détaillée des estampes de la Tōkaidō, voir Marks 2013, pp. 45-54.

10 Kadomaruya avait publié six volumes du *Carnet de dessins d'Hokusai* (*Hokusai manga*) depuis 1815 ; le volume 1 avait été publié par Eirakuya Tōshirō en 1814.

11 Ces dessins sont tellement appréciés que la nouvelle entreprise de Takenouchi n'arrive pas à satisfaire la demande et s'associe à Senkakudō, la maison de Tsuruya Kiemon ayant pignon sur rue. À la fin de 1833, cinquante-cinq motifs différents sont réalisés.

12 Cette pratique n'était pas rare et n'a pas empêché les estampes d'Hiroshige de connaître un succès considérable ; Marks 2013, pp. 76-79.

13 Répertoires publicitaires figurant dans les volumes *jō* et *ge* de *Mikuni Tarō sairai den* 三国太郎再来伝, rédigés par Jippensha Ikku et illustrés par Kuniyoshi, Bizan (c'est-à-dire Takenouchi Magohachi) et Kuninao. Ces répertoires font aussi la publicité de la série de la Tōkaidō publiée par Takenouchi, sous le titre *Série d'images horizontales des cinquante-trois stations sur la route Tōkaidō* (*Tōkaidō gojūsan tsugi yoko-e tsuzuki* 東海道五十三次横画続).

14 Musée des beaux-arts de la Ville de Chiba 2012, n° 83-91.

15 Musée des beaux-arts de la Ville de Chiba 2012, n° 217-271 ; Marks 2013, p. 287, n° T18.

16 L'an six de l'ère Tenpō correspond à la période allant du 29 janvier 1835 au 16 février 1836 du calendrier grégorien. À gauche du caractère *hitsuji* se trouvent trois autres caractères qui ressemblent au chiffre 5001 (*gosenichi* 五千一*), mais le sens en reste obscur. Selon une récente interprétation de Friese (2010, pp. 11-12), ce chiffre serait plutôt 53 (*gojūsan* 五十三) et ferait référence à la première série de la Tōkaidō de Takenouchi. Ceci n'est qu'une vue de l'esprit, car il faut avoir de l'imagination pour décrypter dans le deuxième caractère le chiffre 10 (*jū*) ; quant au troisième, il ne ressemble en rien à un 3 (*san*).

17 Dans l'ouvrage *Yamato nishiki mamoribukuro* 大和錦守袋, illustré par Utagawa Sadahide.

18 Dans l'ouvrage *Harugasumi* 春がすみ, illustré par Eisen ; voir Suzuki, Kimura et Ōkubo 2004, p. 197.

19 Cette série sans titre a été publiée par Tsutaya Kichizō, voir Musée des beaux-arts de la Ville de Chiba 2012, n° 325, 327–333 ; Marks 2013, p. 287, n° T19.

20 La série de Kuniyoshi, *Kisokaidō rokujūkyū tsugi no uchi* 木曾街道六十九次之内, a paru du cinquième mois de 1852 au deuxième mois de 1853. Celle de Kunisada, *Kiso rokujūkyū tsugi* 木曽六十九驛, a été publiée du dixième au douzième mois de 1852.

21 Voir les planches 21, 36, 41, 53 et 55.

22 Hiroshige s'est à nouveau servi de ces croquis pour les illustrations de l'ouvrage en trois volumes *Kiso meisho zue* 岐蘇名所圖會, qui suivent d'encore plus près les croquis. Les volumes 1 et 2 sont datés de 1851, le volume 3 de 1852. Pour en savoir plus sur les carnets de croquis, voir Asano 2010a.

23 Sur les estampes réalisées avant le voyage, le dernier trait du troisième caractère de la signature d'Hiroshige, « Hiroshige ga », dans l'angle inférieur droit, ressemble à un crochet dirigé du haut à droite vers le bas à gauche. Dans les estampes effectuées après le voyage, ce dernier signe est un trait diagonal allant du haut à gauche vers le bas à droite.

24 Strange (1925) 1983, pp. 55–56.

25 Cette épreuve est conservée dans la collection du Musée des beaux-arts de la Ville de Chiba ; voir Sugawara 2009, p. 52 ; Asano 2010b, p. 229.

26 Marks 2011, p. 25.

27 La publication d'estampes reprend à partir de la seconde moitié des années 1860 et jusqu'à la fin des années 1870, voir Marks 2010 et 2011.

28 C'est Edward F. Strange qui, en 1925, avance le premier cette idée en affirmant que l'omission « du nom [d'Eisen] avait pour but d'indiquer, à tout le moins implicitement, que toute l'œuvre était due à Hiroshige », Strange (1925) 1983, p. 57.

29 Toutes les illustrations figurant dans Mochizuki 2011, sauf 46 B, montrent des estampes de l'édition Yamadaya.

30 Au cours de ces dernières années sont apparues des aquarelles de onze estampes reproduisant les dessins réalisés par Eisen des stations Warabi, Kōnosu, Kuragano, Kutsukake, Yabuhara et Kōdo, ainsi que ceux d'Hiroshige pour les stations Annaka, Mochizuki, Motoyama, Toriimoto et Echigawa ; toutefois, elles semblent toutes de la même main, réalisées à partir des épreuves et non de dessins préparatoires à ces épreuves. Dix d'entre elles, qui figuraient dans la collection d'Huguette Berès (Sotheby's 2003, n° 173), figurent actuellement dans la collection de Harlow Higinbotham ; Mochizuki, qui se trouvait dans la collection de Richard P. Gale (Hillier 1970, vol. 2, n° 273), est maintenant conservée au Minneapolis Institute of Art.

31 Stewart 1922, p. 101 ; Strange (1925) 1983, p. 58.

32 Stewart 1922, p. 102 ; Strange (1925) 1983, p. 58.

33 Stewart 1922, p. 105 ; Strange (1925) 1983, p. 59.

La création de la série

Date	Estampes	Numéros dans la série	Artiste	Éditeur(s)
Milieu/fin 1835	11	1–11	Eisen	Takenouchi Magohachi
Fin 1835–milieu 1836	11	13, 20–21, 23, 31, 35–36, 41, 44, 53, 55	Eisen	Takenouchi Magohachi
Fin 1836–début 1837	4	14, 19, 38, 64	Hiroshige	Takenouchi Magohachi & Iseya Rihei
	1	15	Eisen	Takenouchi Magohachi & Iseya Rihei
1837	1	18	Eisen	Iseya Rihei
	22	12, 16–17, 22, 24–30, 32–34, 37, 39–40, 42–43, 46a, 47–48	Hiroshige	Iseya Rihei
Fin 1837–début 1838	21	45, 46b, 49–52, 54, 56–63, 65–70	Hiroshige	Iseya Rihei

Bibliography

Asano, Shūgō. 2010a. "Daieihakubutsukan shozō, Hiroshige hitsu 'Kisoji shaseichō' o megutte"; in: *Yamato Bunko* (122): pp. 9–34.

———. 2010b. *Ukiyoe wa kataru*. Tokyo: Kōdansha.

Chiba City Museum of Art, ed. 2012. *Keisai Eisen*. Chiba: Chiba City Museum of Art.

Forrer, Matthi, Jūzō Suzuki and Henry D. Smith, II. 1997. *Hiroshige: Prints and Drawings*. Munich, New York: Prestel.

Friese, Gordon. 2010. *Keisai Eisen, Utagawa Hiroshige, Die 69 Stationen des Kisokaidō: Eine vollständige Serie japanischer Farbholzschnitte und ihre Druckvarianten*. 2nd ed. Unna: Verlag im Bücherzentrum.

Hillier, Jack R. 1970. *Catalogue of the Japanese Paintings and Prints in the Collection of Mr. & Mrs. Richard P. Gale*. London: Routledge & Kegan Paul.

Hori, Teruaki. 2001. *Tenpō kuniezu de tadoru: Hiroshige, Eisen no Kisokaidō rokujūkyū tsugi tabigeshiki*. Kochizu raiburari 8. Tokyo: Jinbunsha.

Inagaki, Shin'ichi. 1978. "Kisokaidō rokujūkyū tsugi jitchi tōsa 1"; in: *Ukiyoe geijutsu* (60): pp. 13–20, 12.

———. 1981. "Kisokaidō rokujūkyū tsugi jitchi tōsa 2"; in: *Ukiyoe geijutsu* (69): pp. 20–29.

———. 1983. "Kisokaidō rokujūkyū tsugi jitchi tōsa 3"; in: *Ukiyoe geijutsu* (77): pp. 25–37.

———. 1986. "Korekushon haikenki: Tanaka korekushon Kisokaidō rokujūkyū tsugi"; in: *Ukiyoe geijutsu* (86): pp. 26–28.

Izzard, Sebastian. 2008. *Hiroshige, Eisen: The Sixty-Nine Stations of the Kisokaido*. New York: George Braziller.

Kikuchi, Sadao. 1976. *Kisokaidō rokujūkyū tsugi*. Ukiyoe taikei 15. Tokyo: Shūeisha.

Koike, Makiko, ed. 2006. *Hiroshige nidai kaidō ukiyoe ten: Tōkaidō, Kiso Kaidō*. Tokyo: NHK Puromōshon.

Lawrence, C. W. 1873. "Journey from Kiōto to Yedo by the Nakasendō Road"; in: *The Journal of the Royal Geographical Society of London*, vol. 43.

Marks, Andreas. 2010. *Japanese Woodblock Prints: Artists, Publishers, and Masterworks, 1680-1900*. North Clarendon, VT: Tuttle.

———. 2011. *Publishers of Japanese Woodblock Prints: A Compendium*. Leiden, Boston: Hotei.

———. 2013. *Kunisada's Tōkaidō: Riddles in Japanese Woodblock Prints*. Leiden: Hotei.

Mochizuki, Yoshinari, ed. 2011. *Hiroshige, Eisen Kisokaidō rokujūkyū tsugi*. Mochizuki Yoshinari Collection 2. Tokyo: Gōdō.

Nakasendō Hiroshige Bijutsukan, ed. 2013. *Utagawa Hiroshige, Keisai Eisen Kisokaidō rokujūkyū tsugi no uchi: Zōhoban*. Ena: Nakasendō Hiroshige Bijutsukan.

Ōta, Nanpo. 1930. "Jinjutsu kikō"; in: Yanagita Kunio (ed.), *Kikō Bunshū*. Tokyo: Hakubunkan.

Rein, Johannes J. 1880. *Der Nakasendō in Japan: Nach eigenen Beobachtungen und Studien im Anschluss an die Itinerar-Aufnahme von E. Knipping und mit Benutzung von dessen Notizen*. Ergänzungsheft zu A. Petermanns Mitteilungen aus Justus Perthes' Geographischer Anstalt 59. Gotha: Perthes.

Satow, Sir Ernest Mason and A.G.S. Hawes. 1884. *A Handbook for Travellers in Central & Northern Japan*, 2nd ed., London: Murray/Yokohama: Kelly.

Shinpo, Mitsuru. 1968. "Impact, Congruence, and New Equilibrium: A Case Study of Annaka Church, Gumma Prefecture"; in: Kiyomi Morika (ed.), *The Sociology of Japanese Religion*. Leiden: Brill Archive.

Sotheby's. 2003. *Collection Huguette Berès: Estampes, dessins et livres illustrés japonais (seconde vente)*. Paris: Sotheby's.

Stewart, Basil. 1922. *Subjects Portrayed in Japanese Colour-Prints: A Collector's Guide to All the Subjects Illustrated* ... London: Kegan Paul, Trench, Trubner.

Strange, Edward F. (1925) 1983. *Hiroshige's Woodblock Prints: A Guide*. New York: Dover.

Sugawara, Mayumi. 2002. "Bijutsukan shōkai Nakasendō Hiroshige Bijutsukan shozō 'Kisokaidō rokujūkyū tsugi no uchi' ni tsuite"; in: *Ukiyoe geijutsu* (142): pp. 24–31.

———. 2009. *Ukiyoe hanga no jūkyūseiki: Fūkei no jikan, rekishi no kūkan*. Tokyo: Buryukke; Hatsubaimoto Seiunsha.

Suzuki, Jūzō, Yaeko Kimura and Jun'ichi Ōkubo, eds. 2004. *Hiroshige Tōkaidō gojūsan tsugi: Hōeidō ban*. Tokyo: Iwanami Shoten.

Suzuki, Michio. 1995. "Hiroshige ga Kisokaidō rokujūkyū tsugi 'Miyanokoshi' no sakuga hensen nitsuite"; in: *Ukiyoe geijutsu* (116): pp. 3–4.

Totman, Conrad D. 1993. *Early Modern Japan*. Berkeley: University of California Press.

Uhlenbeck, Chris and Marije Jansen, eds. 2008. *Hiroshige: Shaping the Image of Japan*. Leiden: Hotei.

Vaporis, Constantine N. 1994. *Breaking Barriers: Travel and State in Early Modern Japan*. Cambridge, MA: Harvard University Press.

Photo Credits

The publisher wishes to thank the museums, libraries, archives and other institutions mentioned in the captions and in the credits for their kind assistance.

All plates from the series *The Sixty-Nine Stations along the Kisokaidō*: Collection of Georges Leskowicz, Paris.

Photographs: © Karol Baginski/FOTO-GRAFIKA.

Bayerische Staatsbibliothek, Munich, 4 L.jap. D 47, 1–6 / 4 L.jap. K 269–1/4: pp. 23, 30, 49, 86, 442, 444–445, 446–447, 450–451, 454–455, 456–457, 458–459, 462–463, 472–473, 476–477, 482–483, 488–489.

Freer and Sackler Galleries, Freer Study Collection, Washington: p. 90.

Gifu University Library, Gifu: pp. 10, 11.

Honolulu Museum of Art: Gift of James A. Michener, 1970: pp. 434–435 (21.A1b: 15609); Gift of James A. Michener, 1991: pp. 440–441 (44.C1: 24875).

Kjeld Duits Collection/MeijiShowa.com: pp. 31, 80.

Library of Congress, Washington: p. 64.

Marc Walter Collection, courtesy of Marc Walter, Paris: pp. 16, 17, 22, 37, 53, 56, 59, 87, 91.

Minneapolis Institute of Art, Minneapolis: pp. 9, 13, 44, 45, 69, 70, 71, 74, 81, 83, 438 (44.A1a: P.78.64.44).

National Diet Library, Tokyo: pp. 43, 77, 448–449.

Niedersächsische Staats- und Universitätsbibliothek Göttingen: p. 68.

Photograph © 2017 Museum of Fine Arts, Boston: William Sturgis Bigelow Collection: p. 438 (44.A1a: 11.25657); William S. and John T. Spaulding Collection: p. 437 (21.B1c: 21.4812).

Pump Park Collection/MeijiShowa.com: pp. 19, 82, 89.

San Diego Museum of Art, USA/Bridgeman Images, San Diego: pp. 50–51.

Tokyo National Museum/TNM Image Archives, Tokyo: p. 39.

© Trustees of the British Museum, London: pp. 24–25, 436, 452–453, 460–461, 464–465, 466–467, 468–469, 470–471, 474–475, 478–479, 480–481, 484–485, 486–487, 490–491, 492–493, 494–495, 496–497.

Waseda University Library, Tokyo: pp. 28, 42.

Acknowledgements / The Authors

This reprint is based on the unique Kisokaidō series owned by Georges Leskowicz and has been made possible through his generous permission. We are grateful to Georges Leskowicz for his unstinting support for this project from the outset. Special thanks are due to Lydie Decline for her kind assistance during all stages of this undertaking.

The originals were digitally reproduced by Karol Baginski (FOTOGRAFIKA, Warsaw).

We wish to thank him for the good collaboration.

Andreas Marks studied East Asian art history at the University of Bonn and obtained his PhD in Japanese studies from Leiden University with a thesis on 19th-century actor prints. From 2008 to 2013, he was director and chief curator of the Clark Center for Japanese Art & Culture in Hanford, California, and since 2013, has been the Mary Griggs Burke curator of Japanese and Korean Art, head of the Department of Japanese and Korean Art, and director of the Clark Center for Japanese Art and Culture at the Minneapolis Institute of Art. He is the author of TASCHEN's *Japanese Woodblock Prints (1680–1938)* and *Hokusai. Thirty-six Views of Mount Fuji.*

Rhiannon Paget studied at Tokyo University of the Arts and received her doctorate in Japanese art history from the University of Sydney, Australia. The curator of Asian art at the John & Mable Ringling Museum of Art in Sarasota, Florida, she has published research on Japanese woodblock prints, textiles, board games and *nihonga*.

**EACH AND EVERY TASCHEN BOOK
PLANTS A SEED!**
TASCHEN is a carbon neutral publisher. Each
year, we offset our annual carbon emissions
with carbon credits at the Instituto Terra, a
reforestation program in Minas Gerais, Brazil,
founded by Lélia and Sebastião Salgado. To find
out more about this ecological partnership,
please check: www.taschen.com/zerocarbon
Inspiration: unlimited. Carbon footprint: zero.

To stay informed about TASCHEN and our
upcoming titles, please subscribe to our free
magazine at www.taschen.com/magazine,
follow us on Instagram and Facebook, or e-mail
your questions to contact@taschen.com.

French translation: Jean-François Cornu, France
German translation: Kurt Rehkopf, Hamburg

© 2024 TASCHEN GmbH
Hohenzollernring 53, D–50672 Köln
www.taschen.com

Printed in Bosnia-Herzegovina
ISBN 978-3-8365-9487-5

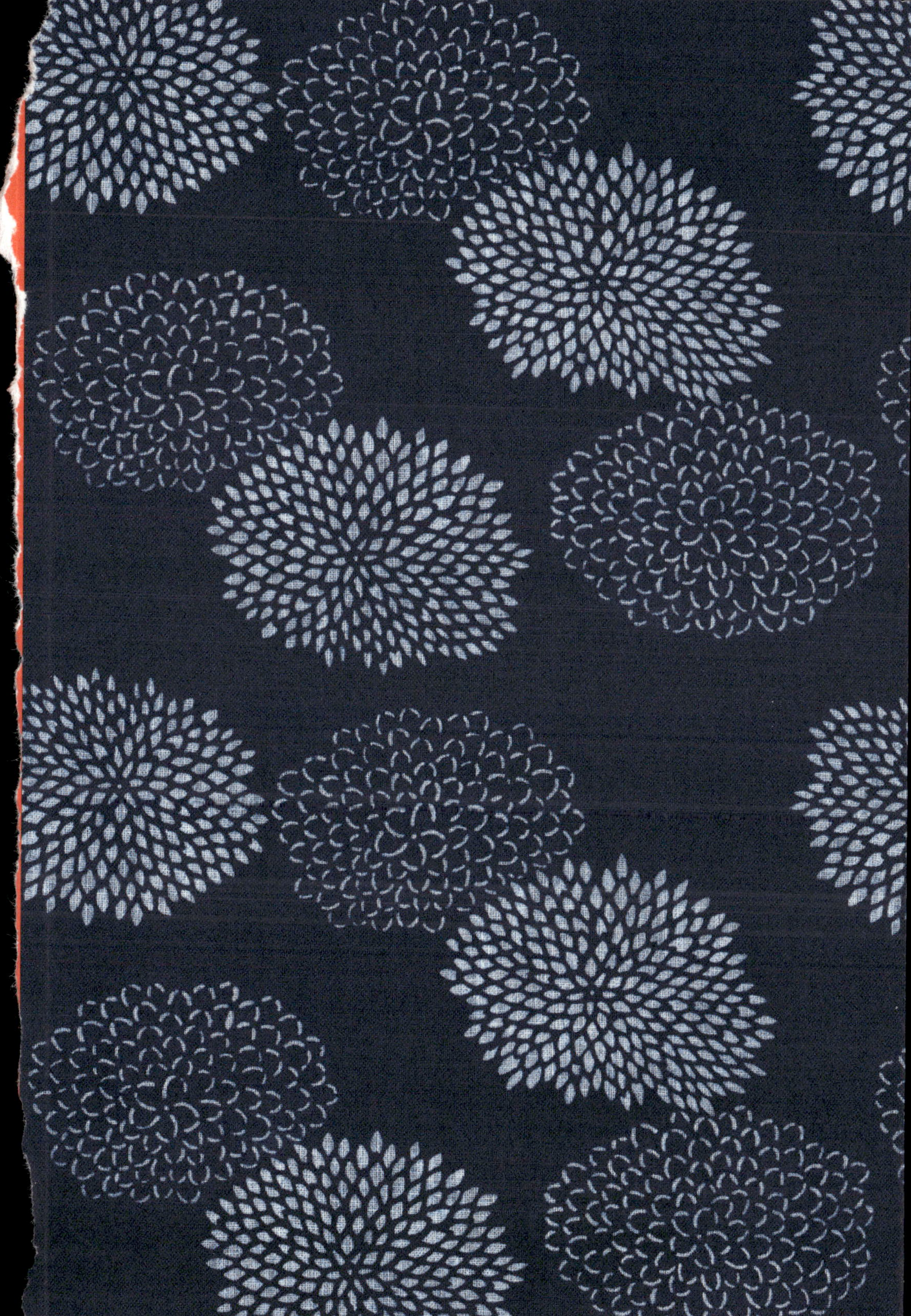

TASCHEN is 40! Since we started our work as cultural archaeologists in 1980, TASCHEN has become synonymous with accessible publishing, helping bookworms around the world curate their own library of art, anthropology and aphrodisia at an unbeatable price. Today we celebrate 40 years of incredible books by staying true to our company credo. The *40* series presents new editions of some of the stars of our program – now more compact, friendly in price and still realized with the same commitment to impeccable production.

The editor and author: **Andreas Marks** studied East Asian art history at the University of Bonn and obtained his PhD in Japanese studies from Leiden University with a thesis on 19th-century actor prints. From 2008 to 2013, he was director and chief curator of the Clark Center for Japanese Art in Hanford, California, and since 2013, has been the Mary Griggs Burke Curator of Japanese and Korean Art, head of the Department of Japanese and Korean Art, and director of the Clark Center for Japanese Art at the Minneapolis Institute of Art. He is the author of TASCHEN's *Japanese Woodblock Prints* and *Hokusai. Thirty-six Views of Mount Fuji*.

The author: **Rhiannon Paget** studied at Tokyo University of the Arts and received her doctorate in Japanese art history from the University of Sydney, Australia. The curator of Asian art at the John & Mable Ringling Museum of Art in Sarasota, Florida, she has published research on Japanese woodblock prints, textiles, board games and *nihonga*.

Case
Tsumago (detail from plate 43), 1836/37. Hiroshige

Station to Station
*A historic trail through the heart of Japan,
as told by two legendary woodblock artists*

This edition reprints Keisai Eisen and Utagawa Hiroshige's
legendary series *The Sixty-Nine Stations along the Kisokaidō*,
a stunning representation of the historic route between Edo
and Kyoto. This vivid tapestry of 19th-century Japan is in equal
parts a major artifact of its imperial past and a masterwork of
woodblock practice.

Wanderer im Mondlicht
*Eine historische Reise durch das Herz Japans,
erzählt von zwei legendären Holzschnittkünstlern*

Gebirge im Mondschein, friedlich plätschernde Flüsse, ent-
legene Poststationen und geschäftige Ortschaften: Mit ihrer
legendären Serie *Die neunundsechzig Stationen des
Kisokaidō* schufen Keisai Eisen und Utagawa Hiroshige eine
atemberaubende Darstellung der historischen Route zwischen
Edo und Kyoto – zu gleichen Teilen ein bedeutendes Zeugnis
der Kaiserzeit und ein Meisterwerk des Holzschnitts.

De station en station
*Une traversée historique au cœur du Japon,
par deux estampistes légendaires*

Cette réédition redonne vie à la légendaire série d'estampes
de Keisai Eisen et Utagawa Hiroshige. *Les soixante-neuf
stations de la route Kisokaidō*, évocation éblouissante de la
route historique entre Edo et Kyoto. Présentant des esquisses
originales, cette fresque envoûtante du Japon au XIXᵉ siècle
est un témoignage majeur de l'ère impériale.

*"An
incredible
ticket
to travel."*
L'EXPRESS

*"A masterpiece of Japanese
woodblock prints – an exquisitely
designed illustrated book."*
KULTURZEIT

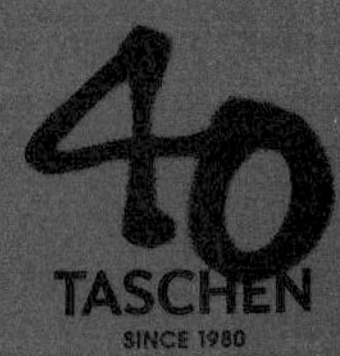

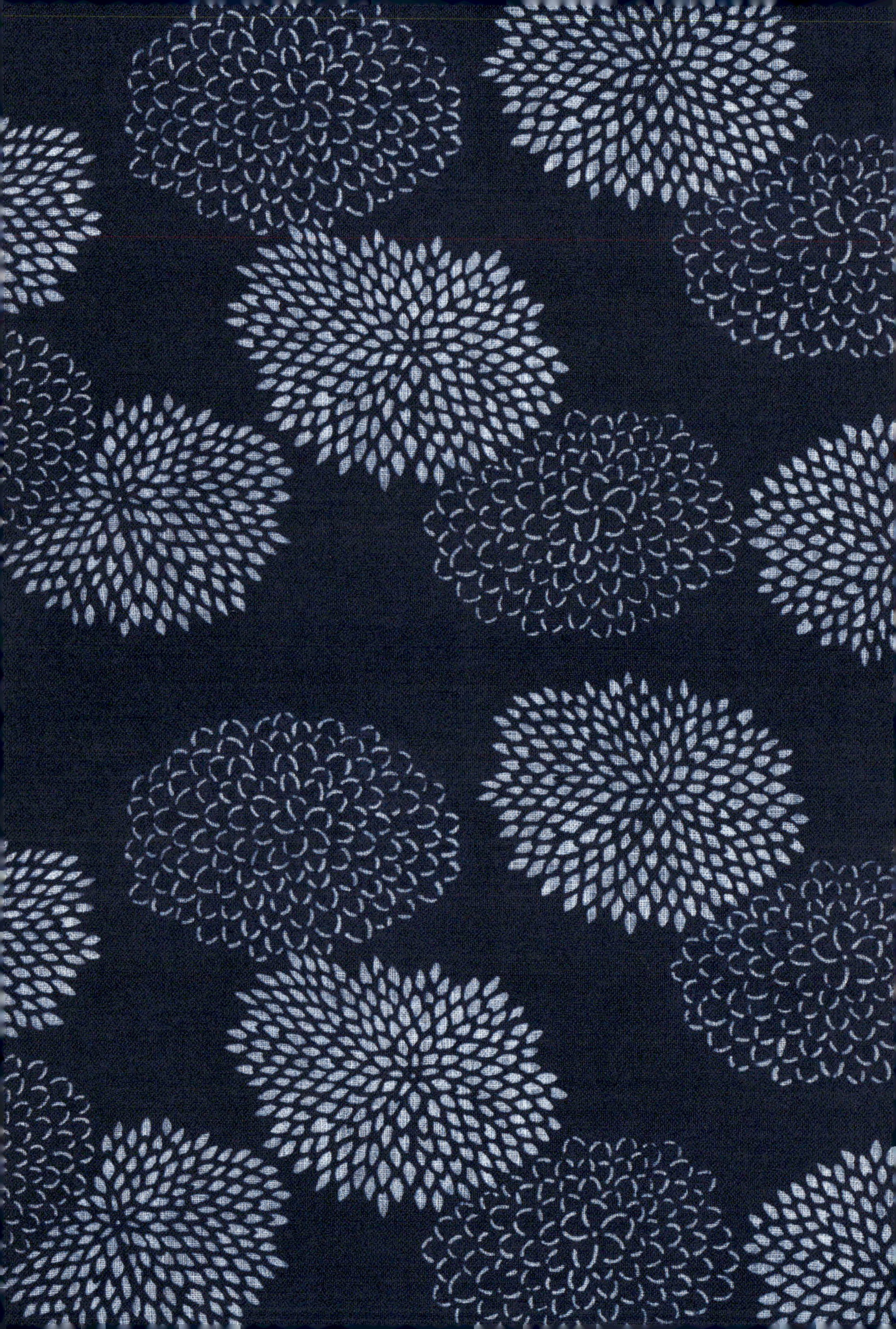